LUTHERAN BOOK OF WORSHIP

LUTHERAN BOOK OF WORSHIP

Prepared by the churches
participating in the
Inter-Lutheran Commission on Worship
Lutheran Church in America
The American Lutheran Church
The Evangelical Lutheran Church of Canada
The Lutheran Church—Missouri Synod

Published by
Augsburg Publishing House, Minneapolis
Board of Publication, Lutheran Church in America, Philadelphia

Third Printing, December 1978

Manufactured in the United States of America

Library of Congress Catalog Card No. 77-92160

CONTENTS

Introduction..6
Calendar..9
Prayers of the Day, Psalms, and Lessons..13
Petitions, Intercessions, and Thanksgivings..42
Athanasian Creed..54
Brief Order for Confession and Forgiveness..56
Holy Communion, Setting One..57
Brief Order for Confession and Forgiveness..77
Holy Communion, Setting Two..78
Brief Order for Confession and Forgiveness..98
Holy Communion, Setting Three..99
Chorale Service of Holy Communion..120
Holy Baptism..121
Service of the Word..126
Morning Prayer (Matins)..131
Evening Prayer (Vespers)..142
Prayer at the Close of the Day (Compline)..154
Responsive Prayer 1..161
Responsive Prayer 2..164
The Litany..168
Propers for Daily Prayer..174
Psalms for Daily Prayer..178
Daily Lectionary..179
Corporate Confession and Forgiveness..193
Individual Confession and Forgiveness..196
Affirmation of Baptism..198
Marriage..202
Burial of the Dead..206
The Psalms..215
Singing the Psalms..290
Canticles..293
Hymns..317
National Songs..918
Indexes..922

INTRODUCTION

Corporate worship expresses the unity of the people of God and their continuity with Christians across the ages. In the liturgical tradition are the gestures, songs, and words by which Christians have identified themselves and each other. The Lutheran Confessions set our liturgical life within that mainstream of Christian worship: "We do not abolish the Mass but religiously keep and defend it. . . . We keep traditional liturgical forms" (*Apology to the Augsburg Confession,* 24).

All that is edifying and authentic in the life of the Church of every time and every place is affirmed. Only that which is contrary to the Gospel is rejected. Empowered by the Holy Spirit, the reformers led the people of God across the barrier between Latin and the vernaculars of the West, just as the barrier between Greek and Latin had been crossed centuries earlier. The transition in language contributed to a new outpouring in the arts of worship, notably in hymns and other music.

The flowering of popular hymnody is the greatest of the artistic contributions of the Lutheran churches. Not since the early years of the Latin Church had there been such an outpouring by hymnists and composers. The Reformation hymn provided, once again, an open channel through which the people's thanks and praise for the Gospel could flow. And, all the while, it sang that Gospel into their hearts. The elemental merging of tune and text resulted in a rugged, vital song which, still today, inspires an ever-growing choral and instrumental literature. The key to the particularity of Lutheran worship is the Lutheran love of hymns.

Europeans carried out the task of reforming the liturgy and returning it to the language of the people by territories. A large number of Lutheran church liturgies in the languages of Germany, Scandinavia, central Europe, and the Baltic countries was the result. Lutherans who emigrated to North America took with them their hymnals and service books; the traditions were transplanted, but almost immediately the emigrants began to respond to the new situation and the new land.

The worship life of Lutherans in North America has been enriched by this variegated heritage and by the transition to the English language. Worshiping in English led to the use of English hymns and the majestic language of the Authorized Version of the Bible and the *Book of Common Prayer.*

Common use of English also stimulated the quest for liturgical uniformity. The foundation was laid in 1748 by the German liturgy of Henry Melchior Muhlenberg. It exhibited clearly the fundamental elements of the classic church orders. After a period of decline from that standard, the next milestone was reached with the publication of the *Church Book* (1868) by the General Council. Building on that English-language work, the General Synod and the United Synod in the South joined with the General Council to produce the Common Service (1888), forming it on the principle of "the common consent of the pure Lutheran liturgies of the sixteenth century." Further joint efforts resulted in the *Common Service Book* (1917), the appearance of which coincided with the formation of The United Lutheran Church in America, the merger of the three church bodies.

Meanwhile Lutheran immigrants continued to arrive. They formed new groupings of congregations. Swedes formed The Augustana Evangelical Lutheran Church. German groups centered in Buffalo, Iowa, Ohio, and Texas combined to form the American Lutheran Church. The Lutheran Church—Missouri Synod and other churches of the Evangelical Lutheran Synodical Conference of North America represented other segments of the northern European heritage. The Evangelical Lutheran Church and the Lutheran Free Church exemplified the Norwegian tradition. The American Evangelical Lutheran Church and the United Evangelical Lutheran Church were groupings of Danish congregations. The Finnish Evangelical-Lutheran Church of America (Suomi Synod), one of the several Finnish Lutheran synods, and the Icelandic Evangelical Lutheran Synod of America completed the Scandinavian circle. As these churches began to worship in English, most of them eventually included the Common Service in their hymnals. The liturgical tradition was becoming uniform, but the hymn traditions remained diverse.

Eight churches began work in 1945 on a service book and hymnal through the Joint Commission on the Liturgy and Hymnal. The endeavor grew out of their desire for a common worship in a common tongue as a sign of a common Lutheran heritage. The desire to express more clearly the breadth of the ecumenical heritage in worship, part of the Lutheran birthright, also motivated their work. The step could be contemplated because of increased knowledge of liturgical origins and development, and also because of the dawning of a keener ecumenical awareness.

The *Service Book and Hymnal* (1958) was published jointly by the churches soon to form The American Lutheran Church (1960) and the Lutheran Church in America (1962). Liturgically, it marked both the culmination of the Common Service tradition and the first step into the larger ecumenical heritage. Musically, the liturgies continued the style of the *Common Service Book,* but added the northern European type of unison chant derived from plainsong and the chorale. The hymnal was conceived as a collection for Lutherans who had become Americans in speech and culture. It combined translations of Lutheran hymns from Germany and Scandinavia with English versions of Greek and Latin hymns, while giving preeminence to the Anglo-American tradition.

The Lutheran Church—Missouri Synod together with other churches of the Synodical Conference had published *The Lutheran Hymnal* in 1941 and was understandably reluctant to join a new project in 1945. The liturgy of *The Lutheran Hymnal* is similar to that in the *Common Service Book,* though with different musical settings in the style of Anglican chant. The hymns are predominantly Germanic in origin, preserving in translation not only the classic body of chorales but also many pietistic hymns of the eighteenth and nineteenth centuries.

At the beginning of the 1960s, most Lutherans in North America used either the *Service Book and Hymnal* or *The Lutheran Hymnal.* The liturgical traditions were similar in form and musical style; the hymnals were markedly different.

In 1965, after abandoning work on a project of its own begun in 1953, The Lutheran Church—Missouri Synod issued an invitation to other Lutheran churches in North America to join it in work toward a common hymnal and service book. Groundwork for such a venture had been laid in joint work on *Culto Cristiano* (1964), a book for Spanish-speaking Lutherans. The invitation was accepted by the Lutheran Church in America, the Synod of Evangelical Lutheran Churches (Slovak), and The American Lutheran Church, and in 1966 the Inter-Lutheran Commission on Worship was formed. Soon thereafter the Slovak church merged with The Lutheran Church—Missouri Synod, and was replaced as a partner in the ILCW by The Evangelical Lutheran Church of Canada, formerly the Canadian district of The American Lutheran Church.

The Inter-Lutheran Commission on Worship entered into dialog with congregations, pastors, musicians, and theologians on the basis of a series of trial-use booklets, *Contemporary Worship.* These were supplemented with testing programs, conferences, and questionnaires. Congregations for whom the revised services and hymns are intended have been able to participate in shaping the project. The result is this *Lutheran Book of Worship.*

An examination of the contents will reveal the several goals toward which the Commission worked in liturgy: to restore to Holy Baptism the liturgical rank and dignity implied by Lutheran theology, and to draw out the baptismal motifs in such acts as the confession of sin and the burial of the dead; to continue to move into the larger ecumenical heritage of liturgy while, at the same time, enhancing Lutheran convictions about the Gospel; to involve lay persons as assisting ministers who share the leadership of corporate worship; to bring the language of prayer and praise into conformity with the best current usage; to offer a variety of musical styles.

Compilers of the hymnal have worked for an equitable balance among hymns of the various Lutheran language traditions, while acting on the premise that most North American Lutherans no longer regard themselves as transplanted Europeans. The Anglo-American hymn tradition is given, therefore, a rightful and large place. More early American tunes are included than in previous hymnals; fewer late nineteenth-century English tunes are included.

Through participation in groups such as the Consultation on Common Texts, the Consultation on Ecumenical Hymnody, and the International Consultation on English Texts, the Inter-Lutheran Commission on Worship has done its work in concert with other English-speaking churches. Through the Lutheran World Federation, contact has been maintained with other Lutheran churches of the world.

The services of the *Lutheran Book of Worship* embody the tradition of worship which received its characteristic shape during the early centuries of the Church's existence and was reaffirmed during the Reformation era. As such, they are an emblem of continuity with the whole Church and of particular unity with Lutherans throughout the world. At the same time, the services are adaptable to various circumstances and situations. Freedom and flexibility in worship is a Lutheran inheritance, and there is room for ample variety in ceremony, music, and liturgical form.

Having considered their resources and their customs, congregations will find their own balance between fully using the ritual and musical possibilities of the liturgy, and a more modest practice. A full service should not allow secondary ceremonies to eclipse central elements of the liturgy, nor should a simple service omit essential or important parts. Every service, whether elaborate or spare, sung or said, should be within the framework of the common rite of the Church, so that the integrity of the rite is always respected and maintained.

With informed and imaginative use, this book can open to congregations the riches of the Church's heritage of liturgy and song, and thus become a worthy instrument in the praise and thanksgiving of the people of God.

This edition is intended for use by the congregation. The Accompaniment Edition—Liturgy includes keyboard settings for the music of the liturgy which are needed to support congregational singing. The Ministers Edition is designed to assist the leaders of worship and to provide supplementary resources. All three editions are needed if use of the *Lutheran Book of Worship* is to achieve its full potential.

CALENDAR

SUNDAYS AND PRINCIPAL FESTIVALS

The Christmas Cycle

Advent Season

First Sunday in Advent B/P*
Second Sunday in Advent B/P
Third Sunday in Advent B/P
Fourth Sunday in Advent B/P

Christmas Season

The Nativity of Our Lord W
Christmas Eve
Christmas Day
First Sunday after Christmas W
Second Sunday after Christmas W

Epiphany Season

The Epiphany of Our Lord W
The Baptism of Our Lord W
First Sunday after the Epiphany
Second Sunday after the Epiphany G
Third Sunday after the Epiphany G
Fourth Sunday after the Epiphany G
Fifth Sunday after the Epiphany G
Sixth Sunday after the Epiphany G
Seventh Sunday after the Epiphany G
Eighth Sunday after the Epiphany G
The Transfiguration of Our Lord W
Last Sunday after the Epiphany

The Easter Cycle

Lenten Season

Ash Wednesday BK/P
First Sunday in Lent P
Second Sunday in Lent P
Third Sunday in Lent P
Fourth Sunday in Lent P
Fifth Sunday in Lent P

Holy Week

Sunday of the Passion S/P
Palm Sunday
Monday in Holy Week S/P
Tuesday in Holy Week S/P
Wednesday in Holy Week S/P
Maundy Thursday S/W
Good Friday
Saturday in Holy Week

Easter Season

The Resurrection of Our Lord
Vigil of Easter W
Easter Day W/GO
Easter Evening W/GO
Second Sunday of Easter W
Third Sunday of Easter W
Fourth Sunday of Easter W
Fifth Sunday of Easter W
Sixth Sunday of Easter W
The Ascension of Our Lord W
Seventh Sunday of Easter W
Pentecost R
Vigil of Pentecost
The Day of Pentecost

The Time of the Church

The Season after Pentecost

The Holy Trinity W
First Sunday after Pentecost

Second through
Twenty-seventh Sunday after Pentecost G

Christ the King W
Last Sunday after Pentecost

* *The letters indicate the suggested colors: B = blue, P = purple, W = white, G = green, BK = black, S = scarlet, GO = gold, R = red*

LESSER FESTIVALS AND COMMEMORATIONS

January

1 The Name of Jesus* W
2 Johann Konrad Wilhelm Loehe, pastor, 1872 W
5 Kaj Munk, martyr, 1944 R
13 George Fox, renewer of society, 1691 W
14 Eivind Josef Berggrav, Bishop of Oslo, 1959 W
15 Martin Luther King Jr., renewer of society, martyr, 1968 R
18 The Confession of St. Peter W
Week of Prayer for Christian Unity begins
19 Henry, Bishop of Uppsala, missionary to Finland, martyr, 1156 R
25 The Conversion of St. Paul W
Week of Prayer for Christian Unity ends
26 Timothy, Titus, and Silas W
27 Lydia, Dorcas, and Phoebe W

February

2 The Presentation of Our Lord W
3 Ansgar, Archbishop of Hamburg, missionary to Denmark and Sweden, 865 W
5 The Martyrs of Japan, 1597 R
14 Cyril, monk, 869; Methodius, bishop, 885; missionaries to the Slavs W
18 Martin Luther, renewer of the Church, 1546 W
20 Rasmus Jensen, the first Lutheran pastor in North America, 1620 W
23 Polycarp, Bishop of Smyrna, martyr, 156 R
Bartholomaeus Ziegenbalg, missionary to India, 1719 W
24 St. Matthias, Apostle R
25 Elizabeth Fedde, deaconess, 1921 W

**The Lesser Festivals are listed in small capital letters; the other listings are Commemorations.*

March

1 George Herbert, priest, 1633 W
2 John Wesley, 1791; Charles Wesley, 1788; renewers of the Church W
7 Perpetua and her companions, martyrs at Carthage, 202 R
Thomas Aquinas, teacher, 1274 W
12 Gregory the Great, Bishop of Rome, 604 W
17 Patrick, bishop, missionary to Ireland, 461 W
19 Joseph, guardian of our Lord W
22 Jonathan Edwards, teacher, missionary to the American Indians, 1758 W
25 The Annunciation of Our Lord W
29 Hans Nielsen Hauge, renewer of the Church, 1824 W
31 John Donne, priest, 1631 W

April

6 Albrecht Dürer, painter, 1528; Michelangelo Buonarroti, artist, 1564 W
9 Dietrich Bonhoeffer, teacher, 1945 R
10 Mikael Agricola, Bishop of Turku, 1557 W
19 Olavus Petri, priest, 1552; Laurentius Petri, Archbishop of Uppsala, 1573; renewers of the Church W
21 Anselm, Archbishop of Canterbury, 1109 W
23 Toyohiko Kagawa, renewer of society, 1960 W
25 St. Mark, Evangelist R
29 Catherine of Siena, teacher, 1380 W

May

1 St. Philip and St. James, Apostles R
2 Athanasius, Bishop of Alexandria, 373 W
4 Monica, mother of Augustine, 387 W
18 Erik, King of Sweden, martyr, 1160 R
19 Dunstan, Archbishop of Canterbury, 988 W
21 John Eliot, missionary to the American Indians, 1690 W

23 Ludwig Nommensen, missionary to Sumatra, 1918 W
24 Nicolaus Copernicus, 1543; Leonhard Euler, 1783; teachers W
27 John Calvin, renewer of the Church, 1564 W
29 Jiři Tranovský, hymnwriter, 1637 W
31 THE VISITATION W

June

1 Justin, martyr at Rome, c. 165 R
3 John XXIII, Bishop of Rome, 1963 W
5 Boniface, Archbishop of Mainz, missionary to Germany, martyr, 754 R
7 Seattle, chief of the Duwamish Confederacy, 1866 W
9 Columba, 597; Aidan, 651; Bede, 735; confessors W
11 ST. BARNABAS, APOSTLE R
14 Basil the Great, Bishop of Caesarea, 379 W
Gregory of Nazianzus, Bishop of Constantinople, c. 389 W
Gregory, Bishop of Nyssa, c. 385 W
21 Onesimos Nesib, translator, evangelist, 1931 W
24 THE NATIVITY OF ST. JOHN THE BAPTIST W
25 Presentation of the Augsburg Confession, 1530 W
Philipp Melanchthon, renewer of the Church, 1560 W
28 Irenaeus, Bishop of Lyons, c. 202 W
29 ST. PETER AND ST. PAUL, APOSTLES R
30 Johan Olof Wallin, Archbishop of Uppsala, hymnwriter, 1839 W

July

1 Catherine Winkworth, 1878; John Mason Neale, 1866; hymnwriters W
6 Jan Hus, martyr, 1415 R
11 Benedict of Nursia, Abbot of Monte Cassino, c. 540 W
12 Nathan Söderblom, Archbishop of Uppsala, 1931 W
15 Vladimir, first Christian ruler of Russia, 1015 W
Olga, confessor, 969 W
17 Bartolomé de Las Casas, missionary to the Indies, 1566 W
22 ST. MARY MAGDALENE W
23 Birgitta of Sweden, 1373 W
25 ST. JAMES THE ELDER, APOSTLE R
28 Johann Sebastian Bach, 1750; Heinrich Schütz, 1672; George Frederick Handel, 1759; musicians W
29 Mary, Martha, and Lazarus of Bethany W
Olaf, King of Norway, martyr, 1030 R

August

10 Lawrence, deacon, martyr, 258 R
13 Florence Nightingale, 1910; Clara Maass, 1901; renewers of society W
15 MARY, MOTHER OF OUR LORD W
20 Bernard, Abbot of Clairvaux, 1153 W
24 ST. BARTHOLOMEW, APOSTLE R
28 Augustine, Bishop of Hippo, 430 W
31 John Bunyan, teacher, 1688 W

September

2 Nikolai Frederik Severin Grundtvig, bishop, renewer of the Church, 1872 W
4 Albert Schweitzer, missionary to Africa, 1965 W
13 John Chrysostom, Bishop of Constantinople, 407 W
14 HOLY CROSS DAY R
18 Dag Hammarskjöld, peacemaker, 1961 W
21 ST. MATTHEW, APOSTLE AND EVANGELIST R
25 Sergius of Radonezh, Abbot of Holy Trinity, Moscow, 1392 W
29 ST. MICHAEL AND ALL ANGELS W
30 Jerome, translator, teacher, 420 W

October

4 Francis of Assisi,
renewer of the Church, 1226 W
Theodor Fliedner,
renewer of society, 1864 W
6 William Tyndale, translator, martyr, 1536 R
7 Henry Melchior Muhlenberg,
missionary to America, 1787 W
17 Ignatius, Bishop of Antioch,
martyr, c. 115 R
18 St. Luke, Evangelist R
23 James of Jerusalem, martyr R
26 Philipp Nicolai, 1608;
Johann Heermann, 1647;
Paul Gerhardt, 1676; hymnwriters W
28 St. Simon and St. Jude,
Apostles R
31 Reformation Day R

November

1 All Saints' Day W
7 John Christian Frederick Heyer,
missionary to India, 1873 W
11 Martin, Bishop of Tours, 397 W
Søren Aabye Kierkegaard, teacher, 1855 W
17 Elizabeth of Thuringia,
Princess of Hungary, 1231 W
23 Clement, Bishop of Rome, c. 100 W
25 Isaac Watts, hymnwriter, 1748 W
30 St. Andrew, Apostle R

December

3 Francis Xavier, missionary to Asia, 1552 W
6 Nicholas, Bishop of Myra, c. 342 W
7 Ambrose, Bishop of Milan, 397 W
11 Lars Olsen Skrefsrud,
missionary to India, 1910 W
14 John of the Cross,
renewer of the Church, 1591 W
Teresa of Avila,
renewer of the Church, 1582 W
21 St. Thomas, Apostle R
26 St. Stephen, Deacon and
Martyr R
27 St. John, Apostle and
Evangelist W
28 The Holy Innocents, Martyrs R

PRAYERS OF THE DAY, PSALMS, AND LESSONS

SUNDAYS AND PRINCIPAL FESTIVALS

FIRST SUNDAY IN ADVENT

Stir up your power, O Lord, and come. Protect us by your strength and save us from the threatening dangers of our sins, for you live and reign with the Father and the Holy Spirit, one God, now and forever. (1)

A. Psalm 122
Isaiah 2:1–5
Romans 13:11–14
Matthew 24:37–44
or Matthew 21:1–11

B. Psalm 80:1–7*
Isaiah 63:16b–17; 64:1–8
1 Corinthians 1:3–9
Mark 13:33–37
or Mark 11:1–10

C. Psalm 25:1–9
Jeremiah 33:14–16
1 Thessalonians 3:9–13
Luke 21:25–36
or Luke 19:28–40

SECOND SUNDAY IN ADVENT

Stir up our hearts, O Lord, to prepare the way for your only Son. By his coming give us strength in our conflicts and shed light on our path through the darkness of this world; through your Son, Jesus Christ our Lord, who lives and reigns with you and the Holy Spirit, one God, now and forever. (2)

A. Psalm 72:1–14 (15–19)
Isaiah 11:1–10
Romans 15:4–13
Matthew 3:1–12

B. Psalm 85
Isaiah 40:1–11
2 Peter 3:8–14
Mark 1:1–8

C. Psalm 126
Malachi 3:1–4
Philippians 1:3–11
Luke 3:1–6

THIRD SUNDAY IN ADVENT

Almighty God, you once called John the Baptist to give witness to the coming of your Son and to prepare his way. Grant us, your people, the wisdom to see your purpose today and the openness to hear your will, that we may witness to Christ's coming and so prepare his way; through Jesus Christ our Lord, who lives and reigns with you and the Holy Spirit, one God, now and forever. (3)

OR

* *The Psalm references indicate the versification of the translation in this book.*

Lord, hear our prayers and come to us, bringing light into the darkness of our hearts; for you live and reign with the Father and the Holy Spirit, one God, now and forever. (4)

A. Psalm 146
Isaiah 35:1–10
James 5:7–10
Matthew 11:2–11

B. Luke 1:46b–55
Isaiah 61:1–3, 10–11
1 Thessalonians 5:16–24
John 1:6–8, 19–28

C. Isaiah 12:2–6
Zephaniah 3:14–18a
(. . . day of festival)
Philippians 4:4–7 (8–9)
Luke 3:7–18

FOURTH SUNDAY IN ADVENT

Stir up your power, O Lord, and come. Take away the hindrance of our sins and make us ready for the celebration of your birth, that we may receive you in joy and serve you always; for you live and reign with the Father and the Holy Spirit, now and forever. (5)

A. Psalm 24
Isaiah 7:10–14 (15–17)
Romans 1:1–7
Matthew 1:18–25

B. Psalm 89:1–4, 14–18
2 Samuel 7:(1–7)
8–11, 16
Romans 16:25–27
Luke 1:26–38

C. Psalm 80:1–7
Micah 5:2–4
Hebrews 10:5–10
Luke 1:39–45 (46–55)

THE NATIVITY OF OUR LORD
Christmas Day

Almighty God, you made this holy night shine with the brightness of the true Light. Grant that here on earth we may walk in the light of Jesus' presence and in the last day wake to the brightness of his glory; through your only Son, Jesus Christ our Lord, who lives and reigns with you and the Holy Spirit, one God, now and forever. (6)

OR

Almighty God, you have made yourself known in your Son, Jesus, redeemer of the world. We pray that his birth as a human child will set us free from the old slavery of our sin; through Jesus Christ our Lord, who lives and reigns with you and the Holy Spirit, one God, now and forever. (7)

A, B, C.

1. Psalm 96
Isaiah 9:2–7
Titus 2:11–14
Luke 2:1–20

2. Psalm 97
Isaiah 52:7–10
Hebrews 1:1–9
John 1:1–14

3. Psalm 98
Isaiah 62:10–12
Titus 3:4–7
Luke 2:1–20

FIRST SUNDAY AFTER CHRISTMAS

Almighty God, you wonderfully created and yet more wonderfully restored the dignity of human nature. In your mercy, let us share the divine life of Jesus Christ who came to share our humanity, and who now lives and reigns with you and the Holy Spirit, one God, now and forever. (8)

A. Psalm 111
Isaiah 63:7–9
Galatians 4:4–7
Matthew 2:13–15, 19–23

B. Psalm 111
Isaiah 45:22–25
Colossians 3:12–17
Luke 2:25–40

C. Psalm 111
Jeremiah 31:10–13
Hebrews 2:10–18
Luke 2:41–52

SECOND SUNDAY AFTER CHRISTMAS

Almighty God, you have filled us with the new light of the Word who became flesh and lived among us. Let the light of our faith shine in all that we do; through your Son, Jesus Christ our Lord, who lives and reigns with you and the Holy Spirit, one God, now and forever. (9)

A, B, C. Psalm 147:12–20
Isaiah 61:10—62:3
Ephesians 1:3–6, 15–18
John 1:1–18

THE EPIPHANY OF OUR LORD

January 6

Lord God, on this day you revealed your Son to the nations by the leading of a star. Lead us now by faith to know your presence in our lives, and bring us at last to the full vision of your glory, through your Son, Jesus Christ our Lord, who lives and reigns with you and the Holy Spirit, one God, now and forever. (10)

A, B, C. Psalm 72
Isaiah 60:1–6
Ephesians 3:2–12 (You have heard . . .)
Matthew 2:1–12

THE BAPTISM OF OUR LORD

First Sunday after the Epiphany

Father in heaven, at the baptism of Jesus in the River Jordan you proclaimed him your beloved Son and anointed him with the Holy Spirit. Make all who are baptized into Christ faithful in their calling to be your children and inheritors with him of everlasting life; through your Son, Jesus Christ our Lord, who lives and reigns with you and the Holy Spirit, one God, now and forever. (11)

A. Psalm 45:7–9
Isaiah 42:1–7
Acts 10:34–38
Matthew 3:13–17

B. Psalm 45:7–9
Isaiah 42:1–7
Acts 10:34–38
Mark 1:4–11

C. Psalm 45:7–9
Isaiah 42:1–7
Acts 10:34–38
Luke 3:15–17, 21–22

SECOND SUNDAY AFTER THE EPIPHANY

Lord God, you showed your glory and led many to faith by the works of your Son. As he brought gladness and healing to his people, grant us these same gifts and lead us also to perfect faith in him, Jesus Christ our Lord. (12)

A. Psalm 40:1–12
Isaiah 49:1–6
1 Corinthians 1:1–9
John 1:29–41

B. Psalm 67
1 Samuel 3:1–10
1 Corinthians 6:12–20
John 1:43–51

C. Psalm 36:5–10
Isaiah 62:1–5
1 Corinthians 12:1–11
John 2:1–11

THIRD SUNDAY AFTER THE EPIPHANY

Almighty God, you sent your Son to proclaim your kingdom and to teach with authority. Anoint us with the power of your Spirit, that we, too, may bring good news to the afflicted, bind up the brokenhearted, and proclaim liberty to the captive; through your Son, Jesus Christ our Lord. (13)

A. Psalm 27:1-9
Isaiah 9:1b-4
(In the former time. . .)
or Amos 3:1-8
1 Corinthians 1:10-17
Matthew 4:12-23

B. Psalm 62:6-14
Jonah 3:1-5, 10
1 Corinthians 7:29-31
Mark 1:14-20

C. Psalm 113
Isaiah 61:1-6
1 Corinthians 12:12-21, 26-27
Luke 4:14-21

FOURTH SUNDAY AFTER THE EPIPHANY

O God, you know that we cannot withstand the dangers which surround us. Strengthen us in body and spirit so that, with your help, we may be able to overcome the weakness that our sin has brought upon us; through Jesus Christ, your Son our Lord. (14)

A. Psalm 1
Micah 6:1-8
1 Corinthians 1:26-31
Matthew 5:1-12

B. Psalm 1
Deuteronomy 18:15-20
1 Corinthians 8:1-13
Mark 1:21-28

C. Psalm 71:1-6, 15-17
Jeremiah 1:4-10
1 Corinthians 12:27—13:13
Luke 4:21-32

FIFTH SUNDAY AFTER THE EPIPHANY

Almighty God, you sent your only Son as the Word of life for our eyes to see and our ears to hear. Help us to believe with joy what the Scriptures proclaim, through Jesus Christ our Lord. (15)

A. Psalm 112
Isaiah 58:5-9a
1 Corinthians 2:1-5
Matthew 5:13-20

B. Psalm 147:1-13
Job 7:1-7
1 Corinthians 9:16-23
Mark 1:29-39

C. Psalm 85:8-13
Isaiah 6:1-8 (9-13)
1 Corinthians 14:12b-20
(Since you are eager . . .)
Luke 5:1-11

SIXTH SUNDAY AFTER THE EPIPHANY

Lord God, mercifully receive the prayers of your people. Help us to see and understand the things we ought to do, and give us grace and power to do them; through your Son, Jesus Christ our Lord. (16)

A. Psalm 119:1-16
Deuteronomy 30:15-20
1 Corinthians 2:6-13
Matthew 5:20-37

B. Psalm 32
2 Kings 5:1-14
1 Corinthians 9:24-27
Mark 1:40-45

C. Psalm 1
Jeremiah 17:5-8
1 Corinthians 15:12, 16-20
Luke 6:17-26

SEVENTH SUNDAY AFTER THE EPIPHANY

Lord God, we ask you to keep your family, the Church, always faithful to you, that all who lean on the hope of your promises may gain strength from the power of your love; through your Son, Jesus Christ our Lord. (17)

OR

God of compassion, keep before us the love you have revealed in your Son, who prayed even for his enemies; in our words and deeds help us to be like him through whom we pray, Jesus Christ our Lord. (18)

A. Psalm 103:1-13
Leviticus 19:1-2, 17-18
1 Corinthians 3:10-11, 16-23
Matthew 5:38-48

B. Psalm 41
Isaiah 43:18-25
2 Corinthians 1:18-22
Mark 2:1-12

C. Psalm 103:1-13
Genesis 45:3-8a (. . . but God), 15
1 Corinthians 15:35-38a, 42-50
Luke 6:27-38

EIGHTH SUNDAY AFTER THE EPIPHANY

Almighty and everlasting God, ruler of heaven and earth: Hear our prayer and give us your peace now and forever; through your Son, Jesus Christ our Lord. (19)

A. Psalm 62
Isaiah 49:13–18
1 Corinthians 4:1–13
Matthew 6:24–34

B. Psalm 103:1–13
Hosea 2:14–16 (17–18) 19–20
2 Corinthians 3:1b–6
(Do we need . . .)
Mark 2:18–22

C. Psalm 92
Jeremiah 7:1–7 (8–15)
1 Corinthians 15:51–58
Luke 6:39–49

THE TRANSFIGURATION OF OUR LORD

Last Sunday after the Epiphany

Almighty God, on the mountain you showed your glory in the transfiguration of your Son. Give us the vision to see beyond the turmoil of our world and to behold the king in all his glory; through your Son, Jesus Christ our Lord, who lives and reigns with you and the Holy Spirit, one God, now and forever. (20)

OR

O God, in the transfiguration of your Son you confirmed the mysteries of the faith by the witness of Moses and Elijah, and in the voice from the bright cloud you foreshadowed our adoption as your children. Make us with the king heirs of your glory, and bring us to enjoy its fullness, through Jesus Christ our Lord, who lives and reigns with you and the Holy Spirit, one God, now and forever. (21)

A. Psalm 2:6–13
Exodus 24:12, 15–18
2 Peter 1:16–19
(20–21)
Matthew 17:1–9

B. Psalm 50:1–6
2 Kings 2:1–12a
(. . . saw him no more)
2 Corinthians 3:12—
4:2
Mark 9:2–9

C. Psalm 99:1–5
Deuteronomy 34:1–12
2 Corinthians 4:3–6
Luke 9:28–36

ASH WEDNESDAY

Almighty and ever-living God, you hate nothing you have made and you forgive the sins of all who are penitent. Create in us new and honest hearts, so that, truly repenting of our sins, we may obtain from you, the God of all mercy, full pardon and forgiveness; through your Son, Jesus Christ our Lord, who lives and reigns with you and the Holy Spirit, one God, now and forever. (22)

A, B, C. Psalm 51:1–13
Joel 2:12–19
2 Corinthians 5:20b—6:2
(We beseech you . . .)
Matthew 6:1–6, 16–21

FIRST SUNDAY IN LENT

O Lord God, you led your ancient people through the wilderness and brought them to the promised land. Guide now the people of your Church, that, following our Savior, we may walk through the wilderness of this world toward the glory of the world to come; through your Son, Jesus Christ our Lord, who lives and reigns with you and the Holy Spirit, one God, now and forever. (24)

OR

Lord God, our strength, the battle of good and evil rages within and around us, and our ancient foe tempts us with his deceits and empty promises. Keep us steadfast in your Word and, when we fall, raise us again and restore us through your Son, Jesus Christ our Lord, who lives and reigns with you and the Holy Spirit, one God, now and forever. (25)

A. Psalm 130
Genesis 2:7–9, 15–17; 3:1–7
Romans 5:12 (13–16) 17–19
Matthew 4:1–11

B. Psalm 6
Genesis 22:1–18
Romans 8:31–39
Mark 1:12–15

C. Psalm 91
Deuteronomy 26:5–10
Romans 10:8b–13 (The word is near . . .)
Luke 4:1–13

SECOND SUNDAY IN LENT

Heavenly Father, it is your glory always to have mercy. Bring back all who have erred and strayed from your ways; lead them again to embrace in faith the truth of your Word and to hold it fast; through Jesus Christ your Son our Lord, who lives and reigns with you and the Holy Spirit, one God, now and forever. (26)

OR

God our Father, your Son once welcomed an outcast woman because of her faith. Give us faith like hers, that we also may trust only in your love for us and may accept one another as we have been accepted by you; through your Son, Jesus Christ our Lord, who lives and reigns with you and the Holy Spirit, one God, now and forever. (27)

A. Psalm 105:4–11
Genesis 12:1–8
Romans 4:1–5, 13–17
John 4:5–26 (27–30, 39–42)

B. Psalm 115:1, 9–18
Genesis 28:10–17 (18–22)
Romans 5:1–11
Mark 8:31–38

C. Psalm 42:1–7, 11–15
Jeremiah 26:8–15
Philippians 3:17—4:1
Luke 13:31–35

THIRD SUNDAY IN LENT

Eternal Lord, your kingdom has broken into our troubled world through the life, death, and resurrection of your Son. Help us to hear your Word and obey it, so that we become instruments of your redeeming love; through your Son, Jesus Christ our Lord, who lives and reigns with you and the Holy Spirit, one God, now and forever. (28)

A. Psalm 142
Isaiah 42:14–21
Ephesians 5:8–14
John 9:1–41
or John 9:13–17, 34–39

B. Psalm 19:7–14
Exodus 20:1–17
1 Corinthians 1:22–25
John 2:13–22

C. Psalm 126
Exodus 3:1–8b (. . . milk and honey), 10–15
1 Corinthians 10:1–13
Luke 13:1–9

FOURTH SUNDAY IN LENT

God of all mercy, by your power to heal and to forgive, graciously cleanse us from all sin and make us strong; through your Son, Jesus Christ our Lord, who lives and reigns with you and the Holy Spirit, one God, now and forever. (29)

A. Psalm 43
Hosea 5:15—6:2
Romans 8:1–10
Matthew 20:17–28

B. Psalm 27:1–9 (10–18)
Numbers 21:4–9
Ephesians 2:4–10
John 3:14–21

C. Psalm 32
Isaiah 12:1–6
1 Corinthians 1:18–31
or 1 Corinthians 1:18, 22–25
Luke 15:1–3, 11–32

FIFTH SUNDAY IN LENT

Almighty God, our redeemer, in our weakness we have failed to be your messengers of forgiveness and hope in the world. Renew us by your Holy Spirit, that we may follow your commands and proclaim your reign of love; through your Son, Jesus Christ our Lord, who lives and reigns with you and the Holy Spirit, one God, now and forever. (30)

A. Psalm 116:1–8
Ezekiel 37:1–3 (4–10) 11–14
Romans 8:11–19
John 11:1–53
or John 11:47–53

B. Psalm 51:11–16
Jeremiah 31:31–34
Hebrews 5:7–9
John 12:20–33

C. Psalm 28:1–3, 7–11
Isaiah 43:16–21
Philippians 3:8–14
Luke 20:9–19

SUNDAY OF THE PASSION
Palm Sunday

Almighty God, you sent your Son, our Savior Jesus Christ, to take our flesh upon him and to suffer death on the cross. Grant that we may share in his obedience to your will and in the glorious victory of his resurrection; through your Son, Jesus Christ our Lord, who lives and reigns with you and the Holy Spirit, one God, now and forever. (31)

A. Psalm 31:1–5, 9–16
Isaiah 50:4–9a (. . . declare me guilty?)
Philippians 2:5–11
Matthew 26:1—27:66
or Matthew 27:11–54

B. Psalm 31:1–5, 9–16
Zechariah 9:9–10
Philippians 2:5–11
Mark 14:1—15:47
or Mark 15:1–39

C. Psalm 31:1–5, 9–16
Deuteronomy 32:36–39
Philippians 2:5–11
Luke 22:1—23:56
or Luke 23:1–49

MONDAY IN HOLY WEEK

O God, your Son chose the path which led to pain before joy and the cross before glory. Plant his cross in our hearts, so that in its power and love we may come at last to joy and glory; through your Son, Jesus Christ our Lord. (34)

A, B, C. Psalm 36:5–10
Isaiah 42:1–9
Hebrews 9:11–15
John 12:1–11

TUESDAY IN HOLY WEEK

Lord Jesus, you have called us to follow you. Grant that our love may not grow cold in your service, and that we may not fail or deny you in the hour of trial. (35)

A, B, C. Psalm 71:1–12
Isaiah 49:1–6
1 Corinthians 1:18–25
John 12:20–36

WEDNESDAY IN HOLY WEEK

Almighty God, your Son our Savior suffered at the hands of men and endured the shame of the cross. Grant that we may walk in the way of his cross and find it the way of life and peace; through your Son, Jesus Christ our Lord. (36)

A, B, C. Psalm 70:1–2, 4–6
Isaiah 50:4–9a
(. . . declare me guilty?)
Romans 5:6–11
Matthew 26:14–25

MAUNDY THURSDAY

Holy God, source of all love, on the night of his betrayal, Jesus gave his disciples a new commandment: To love one another as he had loved them. By your Holy Spirit write this commandment in our hearts; through your Son, Jesus Christ our Lord, who lives and reigns with you and the Holy Spirit, one God, now and forever. (37)

OR

Lord God, in a wonderful Sacrament you have left us a memorial of your suffering and death. May this Sacrament of your body and blood so work in us that the way we live will proclaim the redemption you have brought; for you live and reign with the Father and the Holy Spirit, one God, now and forever. (38)

A. Psalm 116:10–17
Exodus 12:1–14
1 Corinthians 11:17–32
or 1 Corinthians 11:
23–26
John 13:1–17, 34

B. Psalm 116:10–17
Exodus 24:3–11
1 Corinthians 10:
16–17 (18–21)
Mark 14:12–26

C. Psalm 116:10–17
Jeremiah 31:31–34
Hebrews 10:15–39
Luke 22:7–20

GOOD FRIDAY

Almighty God, we ask you to look with mercy on your family, for whom our Lord Jesus Christ was willing to be betrayed and to be given over to the hands of sinners and to suffer death on the cross; who now lives and reigns with you and the Holy Spirit, one God, forever and ever. (39)

OR

Lord Jesus, you carried our sins in your own body on the tree so that we might have life. May we and all who remember this day find new life in you now and in the world to come, where you live and reign with the Father and the Holy Spirit, now and forever. (40)

A, B, C. Psalm 22:1–23
Isaiah 52:13—53:12 *or* Hosea 6:1–6
Hebrews 4:14–16; 5:7–9
John 18:1—19:42 *or* John 19:17–30

THE RESURRECTION OF OUR LORD
Easter Day

O God, you gave your only Son to suffer death on the cross for our redemption, and by his glorious resurrection you delivered us from the power of death. Make us die every day to sin, so that we may live with him forever in the joy of the resurrection;

through Jesus Christ our Lord, who lives and reigns with you and the Holy Spirit, one God, now and forever. (62)

OR

Almighty God, through your only Son you overcame death and opened for us the gate of everlasting life. Give us your continual help; put good desires into our minds and bring them to full effect; through Jesus Christ our Lord, who lives and reigns with you and the Holy Spirit, one God, now and forever. (63)

A. Psalm 118:1–2, 15–24
Acts 10:34–43
Colossians 3:1–4
John 20:1–9 (10–18)
or Matthew 28:1–10

B. Psalm 118:1–2, 15–24
Isaiah 25:6–9
1 Corinthians 15:19–28
Mark 16:1–8
or John 20:1–9 (10–18)

C. Psalm 118:1–2, 15–24
Exodus 15:1–11
or Psalm 118:14–24
1 Corinthians 15:1–11
Luke 24:1–11
or John 20:1–9 (10–18)

THE RESURRECTION OF OUR LORD

Easter Evening

Almighty God, you give us the joy of celebrating our Lord's resurrection. Give us also the joys of life in your service, and bring us at last to the full joy of life eternal; through your Son, Jesus Christ our Lord, who lives and reigns with you and the Holy Spirit, one God, now and forever. (64)

A, B, C. Psalm 150
Daniel 12:1c–3
(But at that time . . .)
or Jonah 2:2–9 (I called . . .)
1 Corinthians 5:6–8
Luke 24:13–49

SECOND SUNDAY OF EASTER

Almighty God, we have celebrated with joy the festival of our Lord's resurrection. Graciously help us to show the power of the resurrection in all that we say and do; through your Son, Jesus Christ our Lord, who lives and reigns with you and the Holy Spirit, one God, now and forever. (65)

A. Psalm 105:1–7
Acts 2:14a (. . . and addressed them), 22–32
1 Peter 1:3–9
John 20:19–31

B. Psalm 148
Acts 3:13–15, 17–26
1 John 5:1–6
John 20:19–31

C. Psalm 149
Acts 5:12, 17–32
Revelation 1:4–18
John 20:19–31

THIRD SUNDAY OF EASTER

O God, by the humiliation of your Son you lifted up this fallen world, rescuing us from the hopelessness of death. Grant your faithful people a share in the joys that are eternal; through your Son, Jesus Christ our Lord, who lives and reigns with you and the Holy Spirit, one God, now and forever. (66)

A. Psalm 16
Acts 2:14a, 36–47
1 Peter 1:17–21
Luke 24:13–35

B. Psalm 139:1–11
Acts 4:8–12
1 John 1:1—2:2
Luke 24:36–49

C. Psalm 30
Acts 9:1–20
Revelation 5:11–14
John 21:1–14

FOURTH SUNDAY OF EASTER

God of all power, you called from death our Lord Jesus, the great shepherd of the sheep. Send us as shepherds to rescue the lost, to heal the injured, and to feed one another with knowledge and understanding; through your Son, Jesus Christ our Lord, who lives and reigns with you and the Holy Spirit, one God, now and forever. (67)

OR

Almighty God, you show the light of your truth to those in darkness, to lead them into the way of righteousness. Give strength to all who are joined in the family of the Church, so that they will resolutely reject what erodes their faith and firmly follow what faith requires; through your Son, Jesus Christ our Lord, who lives and reigns with you and the Holy Spirit, one God, now and forever. (68)

A. Psalm 23
Acts 6:1–9; 7:2a, 51–60
1 Peter 2:19–25
John 10:1–10

B. Psalm 23
Acts 4:23–33
1 John 3:1–2
John 10:11–18

C. Psalm 23
Acts 13:15–16a (. . . his hand said), 26–33
Revelation 7:9–17
John 10:22–30

FIFTH SUNDAY OF EASTER

O God, form the minds of your faithful people into a single will. Make us love what you command and desire what you promise, that, amid all the changes of this world, our hearts may be fixed where true joy is found; through your Son, Jesus Christ our Lord, who lives and reigns with you and the Holy Spirit, one God, now and forever. (69)

A. Psalm 33:1–11
Acts 17:1–15
1 Peter 2:4–10
John 14:1–12

B. Psalm 22:24–30
Acts 8:26–40
1 John 3:18–24
John 15:1–8

C. Psalm 145:1–13
Acts 13:44–52
Revelation 21:1–5
John 13:31–35

SIXTH SUNDAY OF EASTER

O God, from whom all good things come: Lead us by the inspiration of your Spirit to think those things which are right, and by your goodness help us to do them; through your Son, Jesus Christ our Lord, who lives and reigns with you and the Holy Spirit, one God, now and forever. (70)

A. Psalm 66:1–6, 14–18
Acts 17:22–31
1 Peter 3:15–22 (In your hearts . . .)
John 14:15–21

B. Psalm 98
Acts 11:19–30
1 John 4:1–11
John 15:9–17

C. Psalm 67
Acts 14:8–18
Revelation 21:10–14, 22–23
John 14:23–29

THE ASCENSION OF OUR LORD

Almighty God, your only Son was taken up into heaven and in power intercedes for us. May we also come into your presence and live forever in your glory; through your Son, Jesus Christ our Lord, who lives and reigns with you and the Holy Spirit, one God, now and forever. (71)

A, B, C. Psalm 110
Acts 1:1–11
Ephesians 1:16–23
Luke 24:44–53

SEVENTH SUNDAY OF EASTER

Almighty and eternal God, your Son our Savior is with you in eternal glory. Give us faith to see that, true to his promise, he is among us still, and will be with us to the end of time; who lives and reigns with you and the Holy Spirit, one God, now and forever. (72)

OR

God, our creator and redeemer, your Son Jesus prayed that his followers might be one. Make all Christians one with him as he is one with you, so that in peace and concord we may carry to the world the message of your love; through Jesus Christ our Lord, who lives and reigns with you and the Holy Spirit, one God, now and forever. (73)

A. Psalm 47
Acts 1:(1–7) 8–14
1 Peter 4:12–17; 5:6–11
John 17:1–11

B. Psalm 47
Acts 1:15–26
1 John 4:13–21
John 17:11b–19

C. Psalm 47
Acts 16:6–10
Revelation 22:12–17, 20
John 17:20–26

VIGIL OF PENTECOST

Almighty and ever-living God, you fulfilled the promise of Easter by sending your Holy Spirit to unite the races and nations on earth and thus to proclaim your glory. Look upon your people gathered in prayer, open to receive the Spirit's flame. May it come to rest in our hearts and heal the divisions of word and tongue, that with one voice and one song we may praise your name in joy and thanksgiving; through your Son, Jesus Christ our Lord, who lives and reigns with you and the Holy Spirit, one God, now and forever. (74)

A, B, C. Psalm 33:12–22 *or* Psalm 130
Exodus 19:1–9
or Acts 2:1–11
Romans 8:14–17, 22–27
John 7:37–39a
(. . . were to receive)

THE DAY OF PENTECOST

God, the Father of our Lord Jesus Christ, as you sent upon the disciples the promised gift of the Holy Spirit, look upon your Church and open our hearts to the power of the Spirit. Kindle in us the fire of your love, and strengthen our lives for service in your kingdom; through your Son, Jesus Christ our Lord, who lives and reigns with you in the unity of the Holy Spirit, one God, now and forever. (75)

OR

God our creator, earth has many languages, but your Gospel announces your love to all nations in one heavenly speech. Make us messengers of the good news that, through the power of your Spirit, everyone everywhere may unite in one song of praise; through your Son, Jesus Christ our Lord, who lives and reigns with you in the unity of the Holy Spirit, one God, now and forever. (76)

A. Psalm 104:25–34
or Veni, Creator Spiritus
Joel 2:28–29
Acts 2:1–21
John 20:19–23

B. Psalm 104:25–34
or Veni, Creator Spiritus
Ezekiel 37:1–14
Acts 2:1–21
John 7:37–39a
(. . . were to receive)

C. Psalm 104:25–34
or Veni, Creator Spiritus
Genesis 11:1–9
Acts 2:1–21
John 15:26–27;
16:4b–11

THE HOLY TRINITY
First Sunday after Pentecost

Almighty God our Father, dwelling in majesty and mystery, renewing and fulfilling creation by your eternal Spirit, and revealing your glory through our Lord, Jesus Christ: Cleanse us from doubt and fear, and enable us to worship you, with your Son and the Holy Spirit, one God, living and reigning, now and forever. (77)

OR

Almighty and ever-living God, you have given us grace, by the confession of the true faith, to acknowledge the glory of the eternal Trinity and, in the power of your divine majesty, to worship the unity. Keep us steadfast in this faith and worship, and bring us at last to see you in your eternal glory, one God, now and forever. (78)

A. Psalm 29
- Genesis 1:1—2:3 *or* Deuteronomy 4:32–34, 39–40
- 2 Corinthians 13:11–14
- Matthew 28:16–20

B. Psalm 149
- Deuteronomy 6:4–9
- Romans 8:14–17
- John 3:1–17

C. Psalm 8
- Proverbs 8:22–31
- Romans 5:1–5
- John 16:12–15

SECOND SUNDAY AFTER PENTECOST

Lord God of all nations, you have revealed your will to your people and promised your help to us all. Help us to hear and to do what you command, that the darkness may be overcome by the power of your light; through your Son, Jesus Christ our Lord. (79)

A. Psalm 31:1–5 (6–18) 19–24
- Deuteronomy 11:18–21, 26–28
- Romans 3:21–25a (. . . received by faith), 27–28
- Matthew 7:(15–20) 21–29

B. Psalm 81:1–10
- Deuteronomy 5:12–15
- 2 Corinthians 4:5–12
- Mark 2:23–28

C. Psalm 117
- 1 Kings 8:(22–23, 27–30) 41–43
- Galatians 1:1–10
- Luke 7:1–10

THIRD SUNDAY AFTER PENTECOST

O God, the strength of those who hope in you: Be present and hear our prayers; and, because in the weakness of our mortal nature we can do nothing good without you, give us the help of your grace, so that in keeping your commandments we may please you in will and deed; through your Son, Jesus Christ our Lord. (80)

A. Psalm 50:1–15
- Hosea 5:15—6:6
- Romans 4:18–25
- Matthew 9:9–13

B. Psalm 61:1–5, 8
- Genesis 3:9–15
- 2 Corinthians 4:13–18
- Mark 3:20–35

C. Psalm 30
- 1 Kings 17:17–24
- Galatians 1:11–24
- Luke 7:11–17

FOURTH SUNDAY AFTER PENTECOST

God, our maker and redeemer, you have made us a new company of priests to bear witness to the Gospel. Enable us to be faithful to our calling to make known your promises to all the world; through your Son, Jesus Christ our Lord. (81)

A. Psalm 100
- Exodus 19:2–8a (. . . we will do)
- Romans 5:6–11
- Matthew 9:35—10:8

B. Psalm 92:1–5 (6–10) 11–14
- Ezekiel 17:22–24
- 2 Corinthians 5:1–10
- Mark 4:26–34

C. Psalm 32
- 2 Samuel 11:26—12:10, 13–15
- Galatians 2:11–21
- Luke 7:36–50

FIFTH SUNDAY AFTER PENTECOST

O God our defender, storms rage about us and cause us to be afraid. Rescue your people from despair, deliver your sons and daughters from fear, and preserve us all from unbelief; through your Son, Jesus Christ our Lord. (82)

A. Psalm 69:1–20
Jeremiah 20:7–13
Romans 5:12–15
Matthew 10:24–33

B. Psalm 107:1–3, 23–32
Job 38:1–11
2 Corinthians 5:14–21
Mark 4:35–41

C. Psalm 63:1–8
Zechariah 12:7–10
Galatians 3:23–29
Luke 9:18–24

SIXTH SUNDAY AFTER PENTECOST

O God, you have prepared for those who love you joys beyond understanding. Pour into our hearts such love for you that, loving you above all things, we may obtain your promises, which exceed all that we can desire; through your Son, Jesus Christ our Lord. (83)

A. Psalm 89:1–4, 15–18
Jeremiah 28:5–9
Romans 6:1b–11
(Are we to . . .)
Matthew 10:34–42

B. Psalm 30
Lamentations 3:22–33
2 Corinthians 8:1–9, 13–14
Mark 5:21–24a, 35–43
or Mark 5:24b–34

C. Psalm 16
1 Kings 19:14–21
Galatians 5:1, 13–25
Luke 9:51–62

SEVENTH SUNDAY AFTER PENTECOST

God of glory, Father of love, peace comes from you alone. Send us as peacemakers and witnesses to your kingdom, and fill our hearts with joy in your promises of salvation; through your Son, Jesus Christ our Lord. (84)

A. Psalm 145:1–2 (3–13) 14–22
Zechariah 9:9–12
Romans 7:15–25a
Matthew 11:25–30

B. Psalm 143:1–2, 5–8
Ezekiel 2:1–5
2 Corinthians 12:7–10
Mark 6:1–6

C. Psalm 66:1–11, 14–18
Isaiah 66:10–14
Galatians 6:1–10, 14–16
Luke 10:1–12, 16 (17–20)

EIGHTH SUNDAY AFTER PENTECOST

Almighty God, we thank you for planting in us the seed of your word. By your Holy Spirit help us to receive it with joy, live according to it, and grow in faith and hope and love; through your Son, Jesus Christ our Lord. (85)

OR

Lord God, use our lives to touch the world with your love. Stir us, by your Spirit, to be neighbor to those in need, serving them with willing hearts; through your Son, Jesus Christ our Lord. (86)

A. Psalm 65
Isaiah 55:10–11
Romans 8:18–25
Matthew 13:1–9 (18–23)

B. Psalm 85:8–13
Amos 7:10–15
Ephesians 1:3–14
Mark 6:7–13

C. Psalm 25:1–9
Deuteronomy 30:9–14
Colossians 1:1–14
Luke 10:25–37

NINTH SUNDAY AFTER PENTECOST

Pour out upon us, O Lord, the spirit to think and do what is right, that we, who cannot even exist without you, may have the strength to live according to your will; through your Son, Jesus Christ our Lord. (87)

OR

O God, you see how busy we are with many things. Turn us to listen to your teachings and lead us to choose the one thing which will not be taken from us, Jesus Christ our Lord. (88)

A. Psalm 86:11–17
Isaiah 44:6–8
Romans 8:26–27
Matthew 13:24–30 (36–43)

B. Psalm 23
Jeremiah 23:1–6
Ephesians 2:13–22
Mark 6:30–34

C. Psalm 15
Genesis 18:1–10a (10b–14)
Colossians 1:21–28
Luke 10:38–42

TENTH SUNDAY AFTER PENTECOST

O God, your ears are open always to the prayers of your servants. Open our hearts and minds to you, that we may live in harmony with your will and receive the gifts of your Spirit; through your Son, Jesus Christ our Lord. (89)

A. Psalm 119:129–136
1 Kings 3:5–12
Romans 8:28–30
Matthew 13:44–52

B. Psalm 145
Exodus 24:3–11
Ephesians 4:1–7, 11–16
John 6:1–15

C. Psalm 138
Genesis 18:20–32
Colossians 2:6–15
Luke 11:1–13

ELEVENTH SUNDAY AFTER PENTECOST

Gracious Father, your blessed Son came down from heaven to be the true bread which gives life to the world. Give us this bread, that he may live in us and we in him, Jesus Christ our Lord. (90)

OR

Almighty God, judge of us all, you have placed in our hands the wealth we call our own. Give us such wisdom by your Spirit that our possessions may not be a curse in our lives, but an instrument for blessing; through your Son, Jesus Christ our Lord. (91)

A. Psalm 104:25–31
Isaiah 55:1–5
Romans 8:35–39
Matthew 14:13–21

B. Psalm 78:23–29
Exodus 16:2–15
Ephesians 4:17–24
John 6:24–35

C. Psalm 49:1–11
Ecclesiastes 1:2; 2:18–26
Colossians 3:1–11
Luke 12:13–21

TWELFTH SUNDAY AFTER PENTECOST

Almighty and everlasting God, you are always more ready to hear than we are to pray, and to give more than we either desire or deserve. Pour upon us the abundance of your mercy, forgiving us those things of which our conscience is afraid, and giving us those good things for which we are not worthy to ask, except through the merit of your Son, Jesus Christ our Lord. (92)

A. Psalm 85:8–13
1 Kings 19:9–18
Romans 9:1–5
Matthew 14:22–33

B. Psalm 34:1–8
1 Kings 19:4–8
Ephesians 4:30—5:2
John 6:41–51

C. Psalm 33
Genesis 15:1–6
Hebrews 11:1–3, 8–16
Luke 12:32–40

THIRTEENTH SUNDAY AFTER PENTECOST

Almighty and ever-living God, you have given great and precious promises to those who believe. Grant us the perfect faith which overcomes all doubts, through your Son, Jesus Christ our Lord. (93)

A. Psalm 67
Isaiah 56:1, 6–8
Romans 11:13–15, 29–32
Matthew 15:21–28

B. Psalm 34:9–14
Proverbs 9:1–6
Ephesians 5:15–20
John 6:51–58

C. Psalm 82
Jeremiah 23:23–29
Hebrews 12:1–13
Luke 12:49–53

FOURTEENTH SUNDAY AFTER PENTECOST

God of all creation, you reach out to call people of all nations to your kingdom. As you gather disciples from near and far, count us also among those who boldly confess your Son Jesus Christ as Lord. (94)

A. Psalm 138
Exodus 6:2–8
Romans 11:33–36
Matthew 16:13–20

B. Psalm 34:15–22
Joshua 24:1–2a (. . . all the people), 14–18
Ephesians 5:21–31
John 6:60–69

C. Psalm 117
Isaiah 66:18–23
Hebrews 12:18–24
Luke 13:22–30

FIFTEENTH SUNDAY AFTER PENTECOST

O God, we thank you for your Son who chose the path of suffering for the sake of the world. Humble us by his example, point us to the path of obedience, and give us strength to follow his commands; through your Son, Jesus Christ our Lord. (95)

A. Psalm 26
Jeremiah 15:15–21
Romans 12:1–8
Matthew 16:21–26

B. Psalm 15
Deuteronomy 4:1–2, 6–8
Ephesians 6:10–20
Mark 7:1–8, 14–15, 21–23

C. Psalm 112
Proverbs 25:6–7
Hebrews 13:1–8
Luke 14:1, 7–14

SIXTEENTH SUNDAY AFTER PENTECOST

Almighty and eternal God, you know our problems and our weaknesses better than we ourselves. In your love and by your power help us in our confusion and, in spite of our weakness, make us firm in faith; through your Son, Jesus Christ our Lord. (96)

A. Psalm 119:33–40
Ezekiel 33:7–9
Romans 13:1–10
Matthew 18:15–20

B. Psalm 146
Isaiah 35:4–7a (. . . springs of water)
James 1:17–22 (23–25) 26–27
Mark 7:31–37

C. Psalm 10:12–15, 17–19
Proverbs 9:8–12
Philemon 1 (2–9) 10–21
Luke 14:25–33

SEVENTEENTH SUNDAY AFTER PENTECOST

O God, you declare your almighty power chiefly in showing mercy and pity. Grant us the fullness of your grace, that, pursuing what you have promised, we may share your heavenly glory; through your Son, Jesus Christ our Lord. (97)

A. Psalm 103:1–13
Genesis 50:15–21
Romans 14:5–9
Matthew 18:21–35

B. Psalm 116:1–8
Isaiah 50:4–10
James 2:1–5, 8–10, 14–18
Mark 8:27–35

C. Psalm 51:1–18
Exodus 32:7–14
1 Timothy 1:12–17
Luke 15:1–10

EIGHTEENTH SUNDAY AFTER PENTECOST

Lord God, you call us to work in your vineyard and leave no one standing idle. Set us to our tasks in the work of your kingdom, and help us to order our lives by your wisdom; through your Son, Jesus Christ our Lord. (98)

A. Psalm 27:1–13
Isaiah 55:6–9
Philippians 1:1–5 (6–11), 19–27
Matthew 20:1–16

B. Psalm 54:1–4, 6–7a
Jeremiah 11:18–20
James 3:16—4:6
Mark 9:30–37

C. Psalm 113
Amos 8:4–7
1 Timothy 2:1–8
Luke 16:1–13

NINETEENTH SUNDAY AFTER PENTECOST

God of love, you know our frailties and failings. Give us your grace to overcome them; keep us from those things that harm us; and guide us in the way of salvation; through your Son, Jesus Christ our Lord. (99)

A. Psalm 25:1–9
Ezekiel 18:1–4, 25–32
Philippians 2:1–5 (6–11)
Matthew 21:28–32

B. Psalm 135:1–7, 13–14
Numbers 11:4–6, 10–16, 24–29
James 4:7–12 (13—5:6)
Mark 9:38–50

C. Psalm 146
Amos 6:1–7
1 Timothy 6:6–16
Luke 16:19–31

TWENTIETH SUNDAY AFTER PENTECOST

Our Lord Jesus, you have endured the doubts and foolish questions of every generation. Forgive us for trying to be judge over you, and grant us the confident faith to acknowledge you as Lord. (100)

A. Psalm 80:7–14
Isaiah 5:1–7
Philippians 3:12–21
Matthew 21:33–43

B. Psalm 128
Genesis 2:18–24
Hebrews 2:9–11 (12–18)
Mark 10:2–16

C. Psalm 95:6–11
Habakkuk 1:1–3; 2:1–4
2 Timothy 1:3–14
Luke 17:1–10

TWENTY-FIRST SUNDAY AFTER PENTECOST

Almighty God, source of every blessing, your generous goodness comes to us anew every day. By the work of your Spirit lead us to acknowledge your goodness, give thanks for your benefits, and serve you in willing obedience; through your Son, Jesus Christ our Lord. (101)

A. Psalm 23
Isaiah 25:6–9
Philippians 4:4–13
Matthew 22:1–10 (11–14)

B. Psalm 90:12–17
Amos 5:6–7, 10–15
Hebrews 3:1–6
Mark 10:17–27 (28–30)

C. Psalm 111
Ruth 1:1–19a (. . . until they came to Bethlehem)
2 Timothy 2:8–13
Luke 17:11–19

TWENTY-SECOND SUNDAY AFTER PENTECOST

Almighty and everlasting God, in Christ you have revealed your glory among the nations. Preserve the works of your mercy, that your Church throughout the world may persevere with steadfast faith in the confession of your name; through your Son, Jesus Christ our Lord. (102)

A. Psalm 96
Isaiah 45:1–7
1 Thessalonians 1:1–5a
(. . . conviction)
Matthew 22:15–21

B. Psalm 91:9–16
Isaiah 53:10–12
Hebrews 4:9–16
Mark 10:35–45

C. Psalm 121
Genesis 32:22–30
2 Timothy 3:14—4:5
Luke 18:1–8a
(. . . vindicate them speedily)

TWENTY-THIRD SUNDAY AFTER PENTECOST

Almighty and everlasting God, increase in us the gifts of faith, hope, and charity; and, that we may obtain what you promise, make us love what you command; through your Son, Jesus Christ our Lord. (103)

A. Psalm 1
Leviticus 19:1–2, 15–18
1 Thessalonians 1:5b–10 (You know . . .)
Matthew 22:34–40 (41–46)

B. Psalm 126
Jeremiah 31:7–9
Hebrews 5:1–10
Mark 10:46–52

C. Psalm 34
Deuteronomy 10:12–22
2 Timothy 4:6–8, 16–18
Luke 18:9–14

TWENTY-FOURTH SUNDAY AFTER PENTECOST

Lord, when the day of wrath comes we have no hope except in your grace. Make us so to watch for the last days that the consummation of our hope may be the joy of the marriage feast of your Son, Jesus Christ our Lord. (104)

A. Psalm 63:1–8
Amos 5:18–24
1 Thessalonians 4:13–14 (15–18)
Matthew 25:1–13

B. Psalm 119:1–16
Deuteronomy 6:1–9
Hebrews 7:23–28
Mark 12:28–34 (35–37)

C. Psalm 145
Exodus 34:5–9
2 Thessalonians 1:1–5, 11–12
Luke 19:1–10

TWENTY-FIFTH SUNDAY AFTER PENTECOST

Stir up, O Lord, the wills of your faithful people to seek more eagerly the help you offer, that, at the last, they may enjoy the fruit of salvation; through our Lord Jesus Christ. (105)

A. Psalm 90:12–17
Hosea 11:1–4, 8–9
1 Thessalonians 5:1–11
Matthew 25:14–30

B. Psalm 107:1–3, 33–43
1 Kings 17:8–16
Hebrews 9:24–28
Mark 12:41–44

C. Psalm 148
1 Chronicles 29:10–13
2 Thessalonians 2:13—3:5
Luke 20:27–38

TWENTY-SIXTH SUNDAY AFTER PENTECOST

Lord God, so rule and govern our hearts and minds by your Holy Spirit that, always keeping in mind the end of all things and the day of judgment, we may be stirred up to holiness of life here and may live with you forever in the world to come, through your Son, Jesus Christ our Lord. (106)

A. Psalm 131
Malachi 2:1–2, 4–10
1 Thessalonians 2:8–13
Matthew 23:1–12

B. Psalm 16
Daniel 12:1–3
Hebrews 10:11–18
Mark 13:1–13

C. Psalm 98
Malachi 4:1–2a
(. . . in its wings)
2 Thessalonians 3:6–13
Luke 21:5–19

TWENTY-SEVENTH SUNDAY AFTER PENTECOST

Almighty and ever-living God, before the earth was formed and even after it ceases to be, you are God. Break into our short span of life and let us see the signs of your final will and purpose, through your Son, Jesus Christ our Lord. (107)

A. Psalm 105:1–7
Jeremiah 26:1–6
1 Thessalonians 3:7–13
Matthew 24:1–14

B. Psalm 111
Daniel 7:9–10
Hebrews 13:20–21
Mark 13:24–31

C. Psalm 68:1–4
Isaiah 52:1–6
1 Corinthians 15:54–58
Luke 19:11–27

CHRIST THE KING
Last Sunday after Pentecost

Almighty and everlasting God, whose will it is to restore all things to your beloved Son, whom you anointed priest forever and king of all creation: Grant that all the people of the earth, now divided by the power of sin, may be united under the glorious and gentle rule of your Son, our Lord Jesus Christ, who lives and reigns with you and the Holy Spirit, one God, now and forever. (108)

A. Psalm 95:1–7a
Ezekiel 34:11–16, 23–24
1 Corinthians 15:20–28
Matthew 25:31–46

B. Psalm 93
Daniel 7:13–14
Revelation 1:4b–8
(Grace to you . . .)
John 18:33–37

C. Psalm 95:1–7a
Jeremiah 23:2–6
Colossians 1:13–20
Luke 23:35–43

LESSER FESTIVALS

ST. ANDREW, APOSTLE
November 30

Almighty God, as the apostle Andrew readily obeyed the call of Christ and followed him without delay, grant that we, called by your holy Word, may in glad obedience offer ourselves to your service; through your Son, Jesus Christ our Lord, who lives and reigns with you and the Holy Spirit, one God, now and forever. (109)

A, B, C. Psalm 19:1–6
Ezekiel 3:16–21
Romans 10:10–18
John 1:35–42

ST. THOMAS, APOSTLE
December 21

Almighty and ever-living God, you have given great and precious promises to those who believe. Grant us that perfect faith which overcomes all doubts; through your Son, Jesus Christ our Lord, who lives and reigns with you and the Holy Spirit, one God, now and forever. (110)

A, B, C. Psalm 136:1–4, 23–26
Judges 6:36–40
Ephesians 4:11–16
John 14:1–7

ST. STEPHEN, DEACON AND MARTYR
December 26

Grant us grace, O Lord, that like Stephen we may learn to love even our enemies and seek forgiveness for those who desire our hurt; through your Son, Jesus Christ our

Lord, who lives and reigns with you and the Holy Spirit, one God, now and forever. (111)

A, B, C. Psalm 17:1–9, 16
2 Chronicles 24:17–22
Acts 6:8—7:2a (. . . Stephen said), 51–60
Matthew 23:34–39

ST. JOHN, APOSTLE AND EVANGELIST
December 27

Merciful Lord, let the brightness of your light shine on your Church, so that all of us, instructed by the teachings of John, your apostle and evangelist, may walk in the light of your truth and attain eternal life; through your Son, Jesus Christ our Lord, who lives and reigns with you and the Holy Spirit, one God, now and forever. (112)

A, B, C. Psalm 116:10–17
Genesis 1:1–5, 26–31
1 John 1:1—2:2
John 21:20–25

THE HOLY INNOCENTS, MARTYRS
December 28

We remember today, O God, the slaughter of the holy innocents of Bethlehem by order of King Herod. Receive, we pray, into the arms of your mercy all innocent victims, and by your great might frustrate the designs of evil tyrants and establish your rule of justice, love, and peace; through Jesus Christ our Lord, who lives and reigns with you and the Holy Spirit, one God, now and forever. (113)

A, B, C. Psalm 124
Jeremiah 31:15–17
1 Peter 4:12–19
Matthew 2:13–18

THE NAME OF JESUS
January 1

Eternal Father, you gave your Son the name of Jesus to be a sign of our salvation. Plant in every heart the love of the Savior of the world, Jesus Christ our Lord, who lives and reigns with you and the Holy Spirit, one God, now and forever. (114)

A, B, C. Psalm 8
Numbers 6:22–27
Romans 1:1–7 *or* Philippians 2:9–13
Luke 2:21

THE CONFESSION OF ST. PETER
January 18

Almighty God, you inspired Simon Peter to confess Jesus as the Messiah and Son of the living God. Keep your Church firm on the rock of this faith, that in unity and peace it may proclaim one truth and follow one Lord, your Son, our Savior Jesus Christ, who lives and reigns with you and the Holy Spirit, one God, now and forever. (115)

A, B, C. Psalm 18:1–7, 17–20
Acts 4:8–13
1 Corinthians 10:1–5
Matthew 16:13–19

THE CONVERSION OF ST. PAUL
January 25

Lord God, through the preaching of your apostle Paul, you established one Church from among the nations. As we celebrate his conversion, we pray that we may follow his example and be witnesses to the truth in your Son, Jesus Christ our Lord, who lives and reigns with you and the Holy Spirit, one God, now and forever. (116)

A, B, C. Psalm 67
Acts 9:1–22
Galatians 1:11–24
Luke 21:10–19

THE PRESENTATION OF OUR LORD
February 2

Blessed are you, O Lord our God, for you have sent us your salvation. Inspire us by your Holy Spirit to see with our own eyes him who is the glory of Israel and the light for all nations, your Son, Jesus Christ our Lord. (117)

A, B, C. Psalm 84
1 Samuel 1:21–28
Hebrews 2:14–18
Luke 2:22–40

ST. MATTHIAS, APOSTLE
February 24

Almighty God, you chose your faithful servant Matthias to be numbered among the Twelve. Grant that your Church, being delivered from false apostles, may always be taught and guided by faithful and true pastors; through your Son, Jesus Christ our Lord, who lives and reigns with you and the Holy Spirit, one God, now and forever. (118)

A, B, C. Psalm 56
Isaiah 66:1–2
Acts 1:15–26
Luke 6:12–16

THE ANNUNCIATION OF OUR LORD
March 25

Pour your grace into our hearts, O Lord, that we, who have known the incarnation of your Son, Jesus Christ, announced by an angel, may by his cross and Passion be brought to the glory of his resurrection; who lives and reigns with you and the Holy Spirit, one God, now and forever. (119)

A, B, C. Psalm 45
Isaiah 7:10–14
(add: for God is with us [8:10c])
1 Timothy 3:16
Luke 1:26–38

ST. MARK, EVANGELIST
April 25

Almighty God, you have enriched your Church with Mark's proclamation of the Gospel. Give us grace to believe firmly in the good news of salvation and to walk daily in accord with it; through your Son, Jesus Christ our Lord, who lives and reigns with you and the Holy Spirit, one God, now and forever. (120)

A, B, C. Psalm 57
Isaiah 52:7–10
2 Timothy 4:6–11, 18
Mark: 1:1–15

ST. PHILIP AND ST. JAMES, APOSTLES
May 1

Almighty God, to know you is to have eternal life. Grant us to know your Son as the way, the truth, and the life; and guide our footsteps along the way of Jesus Christ our Lord, who lives and reigns with you and the Holy Spirit, one God, now and forever. (121)

A, B, C. Psalm 44:1–3, 20–26
Isaiah 30:18–21
2 Corinthians 4:1–6
John 14:8–14

THE VISITATION
May 31

Almighty God, in choosing the virgin Mary to be the mother of your Son, you made known your gracious regard for the poor and the lowly and the despised. Grant us grace to receive your Word in humility, and so to be made one with your Son, Jesus Christ our Lord, who lives and reigns with you and the Holy Spirit, one God, now and forever. (122)

A, B, C. Psalm 113
Isaiah 11:1–5
Romans 12:9–16
Luke 1:39–47

ST. BARNABAS, APOSTLE
June 11

Grant, almighty God, that we may follow the example of your faithful servant Barnabas, who, seeking not his own renown but the well-being of your Church, gave generously of his life and substance for the relief of the poor and the spread of the Gospel; through Jesus Christ our Lord, who lives and reigns with you and the Holy Spirit, one God, now and forever. (123)

A, B, C. Psalm 112
Isaiah 42:5–12
Acts 11:19–30; 13:1–3
Matthew 10:7–16

THE NATIVITY OF ST. JOHN THE BAPTIST
June 24

Almighty God, you called John the Baptist to give witness to the coming of your Son and to prepare his way. Grant to your people the wisdom to see your purpose and the openness to hear your will, that we too may witness to Christ's coming and so prepare his way; through your Son, Jesus Christ our Lord, who lives and reigns with you and the Holy Spirit, one God, now and forever. (124)

A, B, C. Psalm 141
Malachi 3:1–4
Acts 13:13–26
Luke 1:57–67 (68–80)

ST. PETER AND ST. PAUL, APOSTLES
June 29

Almighty God, whose blessed apostles Peter and Paul glorified you by their martyrdom: Grant that your Church, instructed by their teaching and example, and knit together in unity by your Spirit, may ever stand firm upon the one foundation, which is Jesus Christ our Lord, who lives and reigns with you and the Holy Spirit, one God, now and forever. (125)

A, B, C. Psalm 87:1–2, 4–6
Ezekiel 34:11–16
1 Corinthians 3:16–23
Mark 8:27–35

ST. MARY MAGDALENE
July 22

Almighty God, your Son Jesus Christ restored Mary Magdalene to health of body and mind, and called her to be a witness of his resurrection. Heal us now in body and mind, and call us to serve you in the power of the resurrection of Jesus Christ, who lives and reigns with you and the Holy Spirit, one God, now and forever. (126)

A, B, C. Psalm 73:23–29
Ruth 1:6–18
or Exodus 2:1–10
Acts 13:26–33a
John 20:1–2, 11–18

ST. JAMES THE ELDER, APOSTLE
July 25

O gracious God, we remember before you today your servant and apostle James, first among the Twelve to suffer martyrdom for the name of Jesus Christ. Pour out upon the leaders of your Church that spirit of self-denying service which is the true mark of authority among your people; through Jesus Christ our Lord, who lives and reigns with you and the Holy Spirit, one God, now and forever. (127)

A, B, C. Psalm 7:1–11
1 Kings 19:9–18
Acts 11:27—12:3a
Mark 10:35–45

MARY, MOTHER OF OUR LORD
August 15

Almighty God, you chose the virgin Mary to be the mother of your only Son. Grant that we, who have been redeemed by his blood, may share with her in the glory of your eternal kingdom; through your Son, Jesus Christ our Lord, who lives and reigns with you and the Holy Spirit, one God, now and forever. (128)

A, B, C. Psalm 45:11–16
Isaiah 61:7–11
Galatians 4:4–7
Luke 1:46–55

ST. BARTHOLOMEW, APOSTLE
August 24

Almighty and everlasting God, who gave to your apostle Bartholomew grace truly to believe and to preach your Word: Grant that your Church may love what he believed and preach what he taught; through your Son, Jesus Christ our Lord, who lives and reigns with you and the Holy Spirit, one God, now and forever. (129)

A, B, C. Psalm 12
Exodus 19:1–6
1 Corinthians 12:27–31a
John 1:43–51

HOLY CROSS DAY

September 14

Almighty God, your Son Jesus Christ was lifted high upon the cross so that he might draw the whole world to himself. Grant that we who glory in his death for our salvation may also glory in his call to take up our cross and follow him; through your Son, Jesus Christ our Lord, who lives and reigns with you and the Holy Spirit, one God, now and forever. (130)

A, B, C. Psalm 98:1–5
Isaiah 45:21–25
1 Corinthians 1:18–24
John 12:20–33

ST. MATTHEW, APOSTLE AND EVANGELIST

September 21

Almighty God, your Son our Savior called a despised collector of taxes to become one of his apostles. Help us, like Matthew, to respond to the transforming call of your Son, Jesus Christ our Lord, who lives and reigns with you and the Holy Spirit, one God, now and forever. (131)

A, B, C. Psalm 119:33–40
Ezekiel 2:8—3:11
Ephesians 2:4–10
Matthew 9:9–13

ST. MICHAEL AND ALL ANGELS

September 29

Everlasting God, you have ordained and constituted in a wonderful order the ministries of angels and mortals. Mercifully grant that, as your holy angels always serve and worship you in heaven, so by your appointment they may help and defend us here on earth; through your Son, Jesus Christ our Lord, who lives and reigns with you and the Holy Spirit, one God, now and forever. (132)

A, B, C. Psalm 103:1–5, 20–22
Daniel 10:10–14; 12:1–3
Revelation 12:7–12
Luke 10:17–20

ST. LUKE, EVANGELIST

October 18

Almighty God, you inspired your servant Luke the physician to reveal in his Gospel the love and healing power of your Son. Give your Church the same love and power to heal, to the glory of your name; through your Son, Jesus Christ our Lord, who lives and reigns with you and the Holy Spirit, one God, now and forever. (133)

A, B, C. Psalm 124
Isaiah 43:8–13 *or* Isaiah 35:5–8
2 Timothy 4:5–11
Luke 1:1–4; 24:44 (Then *Jesus* said. . .)–53*

---

* *Because the two parts of the reading are not sequential, the reader should pause between them.*

ST. SIMON AND ST. JUDE, APOSTLES

October 28

O God, we thank you for the glorious company of the apostles and, especially on this day, for Simon and Jude. We pray that, as they were faithful and zealous in their mission, so we may with ardent devotion make known the love and mercy of our Lord and Savior Jesus Christ, who lives and reigns with you and the Holy Spirit, one God, now and forever. (134)

A, B, C. Psalm 11
Jeremiah 26:(1–6) 7–16
1 John 4:1–6
John 14:21–27

REFORMATION DAY

October 31

Almighty God, gracious Lord, pour out your Holy Spirit upon your faithful people. Keep them steadfast in your Word, protect and comfort them in all temptations, defend them against all their enemies, and bestow on the Church your saving peace; through your Son, Jesus Christ our Lord, who lives and reigns with you and the Holy Spirit, one God, now and forever. (135)

A, B, C. Psalm 46
Jeremiah 31:31–34
Romans 3:19–28
John 8:31–36

ALL SAINTS' DAY

November 1

Almighty God, whose people are knit together in one holy Church, the body of Christ our Lord: Grant us grace to follow your blessed saints in lives of faith and commitment, and to know the inexpressible joys you have prepared for those who love you; through your Son, Jesus Christ our Lord, who lives and reigns with you and the Holy Spirit, one God, now and forever. (136)

A, B, C. Psalm 34:1–10
Isaiah 26:1–4, 8–9, 12–13, 19–21
Revelation 21:9–11, 22–27 (22:1–5)
Matthew 5:1–12

COMMEMORATIONS

SAINTS

Lord God, you have surrounded us with so great a cloud of witnesses. Grant that we [encouraged by the example of your *servant/servants* ______name______] may persevere in the course that is set before us, to be living signs of the Gospel and at last, with all the saints, to share in your eternal joy; through your Son, Jesus Christ our Lord. (137)

A, B, C. Psalm 9:1–10
Micah 6:6–8
1 Corinthians 1:26–31
Luke 6:20–23

MARTYRS

Gracious Lord, in every age you have sent men and women who have given their lives for the message of your love. Inspire us with the memory of those martyrs for the Gospel [like your *servant/servants* _____name_____] whose faithfulness led them in the way of the cross, and give us courage to bear full witness with our lives to your Son's victory over sin and death; through Jesus Christ our Lord. (138)

A, B, C. Psalm 5
Ezekiel 20:40–42
Revelation 6:9–11
Mark 8:34–38

MISSIONARIES

God of grace and might, we praise you for your *servant/servants* _____name_____, to whom you gave gifts to make the good news known. Raise up, we pray, in every country, heralds and evangelists of your kingdom, so that the world may know the immeasurable riches of our Savior, Jesus Christ our Lord. (139)

A, B, C. Psalm 48
Isaiah 62:1–7
Romans 10:11–17
Luke 24:44–53

RENEWERS OF THE CHURCH

Almighty God, we praise you for the men and women you have sent to call the Church to its tasks and renew its life [such as your *servant/servants* _____name_____]. Raise up in our own day teachers and prophets inspired by your Spirit, whose voices will give strength to your Church and proclaim the reality of your kingdom; through your Son, Jesus Christ our Lord. (140)

A, B, C. Psalm 46
Jeremiah 1:4–10
1 Corinthians 3:11–23
Mark 10:35–45

RENEWERS OF SOCIETY

Lord God, your Son came among us to serve and not to be served, and to give his life for the world. Lead us by his love to serve all those to whom the world offers no comfort and little help. Through us give hope to the hopeless, love to the unloved, peace to the troubled, and rest to the weary; through your Son, Jesus Christ our Lord. (141)

OR

Holy and righteous God, you created us in your image. Grant us grace to contend fearlessly against evil and to make no peace with oppression. Help us [like your *servant/servants* _____name_____] to use our freedom to bring justice among people and nations, to the glory of your name; through your Son, Jesus Christ our Lord. (142)

A, B, C. Psalm 94:1–14
Hosea 2:18–23
Romans 12:9–21
Luke 6:20–36

PASTORS AND BISHOPS

Heavenly Father, shepherd of your people, we thank you for your *servant/servants* _____name_____, who *was/were* faithful in the care and nurture of your flock; and we pray that, following *his/her* example and the teaching of *his/her* holy life, we may by your grace grow into the full stature of our Lord and Savior Jesus Christ. (143)

OR

Almighty God, you have raised up faithful bishops and leaders of your Church. May the memory of their lives be a source of joy for us and a bulwark of our faith, so that we may serve you and confess your name before the world; through your Son, Jesus Christ our Lord. (144)

A, B, C. Psalm 84
Ezekiel 34:11–16
or Acts 20:17–35
1 Peter 5:1–4
or Ephesians 3:14–21
John 21:15–17
or Matthew 24:42–47

THEOLOGIANS

Almighty God, your Holy Spirit gives to one the word of wisdom, and to another the word of knowledge, and to another the word of faith. We praise you for the gifts of grace imparted to your *servant/servants* _____name_____, and we pray that by *his/her* teaching we may be led to a fuller knowledge of the truth which we have seen in your Son Jesus Christ our Lord. (145)

A, B, C. Psalm 119:89–104
Proverbs 3:1–7
or Wisdom 7:7–14
1 Corinthians 2:6–10, 13–16
or 1 Corinthians 3:5–11
John 17:18–23
or Matthew 13:47–52

ARTISTS AND SCIENTISTS

Almighty God, beautiful in majesty, majestic in holiness: You have shown us the splendor of creation in the work of your *servant/servants* _____name_____. Teach us to drive from the world the ugliness of chaos and disorder, that our eyes may not be blind to your glory, and that at length everyone may know the inexhaustible richness of your new creation in Jesus Christ our Lord. (146)

A, B, C. Psalm 96
Isaiah 28:5–6
or Hosea 14:5–8
or 2 Chronicles 20:20–21
Philippians 4:8–9
or Ephesians 5:18b–20
Matthew 13:44–52

OCCASIONS

UNITY

God our Father, your Son Jesus prayed that his followers might be one. Make all Christians one with him as he is one with you, so that in peace and concord we may carry to the world the message of your love; through your Son, Jesus Christ our Lord, who lives and reigns with you and the Holy Spirit, one God, now and forever. (147)

A, B, C. Psalm 133
Isaiah 2:2–4
Ephesians 4:1–6
John 17:15–23

DEDICATION AND ANNIVERSARY

Most High God, whom the heavens cannot contain, we give you thanks for the gifts of those who have built this house of prayer to your glory; we praise you for the fellowship of those who by their use *will make it/have made it* holy; and we pray that all who seek you here may find you and be filled with your joy and peace; through your Son, Jesus Christ our Lord. (148)

OR

O God, you have promised through your Son to be with your Church forever. We give you thanks for those who founded this community of believers and for the signs of your presence in our congregation. Increase in us the spirit of faith and love, and make us worthy of our heritage. Knit us together in the communion of saints, and make our fellowship an example to all believers and to all nations. We pray through your Son, Jesus Christ our Lord. (149)

A, B, C. Psalm 84
1 Kings 8:22–30
1 Peter 2:1–9
John 10:22–30

HARVEST

O Lord, maker of all things, you open your hand and satisfy the desire of every living creature. We praise you for crowning the fields with your blessings and enabling us once more to gather in the fruits of the earth. Teach us to use your gifts carefully, that our land may continue to yield her increase; through your Son, Jesus Christ our Lord. (150)

A, B, C. Psalm 65
Deuteronomy 26:1–11
2 Corinthians 9:6–15
Matthew 13:24–30 (36–43)

DAY OF PENITENCE

Lord God, accept our humble confession of the wrongs we have done, the injustice to which we have been party, and the countless denials of your mercy we have expressed. Turn us toward the love offered in your Son, and cleanse us by your grace; through Jesus Christ our Lord. (151)

These Propers may be used in observing a Day of Penitence for the slaying by Christians of others because of their faith or race or nation. The occasion may coincide with a local remembrance of the Holocaust. The following Prayer of the Day may be used:

Almighty God, in penitence we come before you, acknowledging the sin that is within us. We share the guilt of all those who, bearing the name Christian, slay their fellow human beings because of race or faith or nation. Whether killing or standing silent while others kill, we crucify our Lord anew. Forgive us and change us by your love, that your Word of hope may be heard clearly throughout the world; through your Son, Jesus Christ our Lord. (152)

A, B, C. Psalm 6
Nehemiah 1:4–11a
1 John 1:5—2:2
Luke 15:11–32

NATIONAL HOLIDAY

Lord of the nations, guide our people by your Spirit to go forward in justice and freedom. Give us what outward prosperity may be your will, but above all things give us faith in you, that our nation may bring glory to your name and blessings to all peoples; through your Son, Jesus Christ our Lord. (153)

A, B, C. Psalm 20
Jeremiah 29:4–14
Romans 13:1–10
Mark 12:13–17

PEACE

Almighty God, all thoughts of truth and peace come from you. Kindle in the hearts of all your children the love of peace, and guide with your wisdom the leaders of the nations, so that your kingdom will go forward in peace and the earth will be filled with the knowledge of your love; through your Son, Jesus Christ our Lord. (154)

A, B, C. Psalm 85
Micah 4:1–5
Ephesians 2:13–18
John 15:9–12

DAY OF THANKSGIVING

Almighty God our Father, your generous goodness comes to us new every day. By the work of your Spirit lead us to acknowledge your goodness, give thanks for your benefits, and serve you in willing obedience; through your Son, Jesus Christ our Lord. (155)

A, B, C. Psalm 65
Deuteronomy 8:1–10
Philippians 4:6–20
or 1 Timothy 2:1–4
Luke 17:11–19

STEWARDSHIP OF CREATION

Almighty God, Lord of heaven and earth, we humbly pray that your gracious providence may give and preserve to our use the fruitfulness of the land and of the seas, and may prosper all who labor therein, that we, who are constantly receiving good things from your hand, may always give you thanks; through your Son, Jesus Christ our Lord. (156)

OR

O merciful Creator, your hand is open wide to satisfy the needs of every living creature. Make us always thankful for your loving providence; and grant that we, remembering the account that we must one day give, may be faithful stewards of your good gifts; through your Son, Jesus Christ our Lord. (157)

OR

Almighty God, whose Son Jesus Christ in his earthly life shared our toil and hallowed our labor: Be present with our people where they work; make those who carry on the industry and commerce of this land responsive to your will; and give to us all a pride in what we do, and a just return for our labor; through your Son, Jesus Christ our Lord. (158)

A, B, C. Psalm 104:1, 13–24
or Psalm 104:25–37
Job 39:1–11, 16–18
1 Timothy 6:7–10, 17–19
Luke 12:13–21

NEW YEAR'S EVE

Eternal Father, you have placed us in a world of space and time, and through the events of our lives you bless us with your love. Grant that in this new year we may know your presence, see your love at work, and live in the light of the event which gives us joy forever—the coming of your Son, Jesus Christ our Lord. (159)

A, B, C. Psalm 102:24–28
Jeremiah 24:1–7
1 Peter 1:22–25
Luke 13:6–9

PETITIONS, INTERCESSIONS, AND THANKSGIVINGS

PEACE AMONG THE NATIONS

Almighty God, heavenly Father, guide the nations of the world into ways of justice and truth, and establish among them that peace which is the fruit of righteousness, that they may become the kingdom of our Lord and Savior Jesus Christ. (165)

PEACE

O God, it is your will to hold both heaven and earth in a single peace. Let the design of your great love shine on the waste of our wraths and sorrows, and give peace to your Church, peace among nations, peace in our homes, and peace in our hearts; through your Son, Jesus Christ our Lord. (166)

SOCIAL JUSTICE

Grant, O God, that your holy and life-giving Spirit may move every human heart, that the barriers which divide us may crumble, suspicions disappear, and hatreds cease, and that, with our divisions healed, we might live in justice and peace; through your Son, Jesus Christ our Lord. (167)

THE VARIETY OF RACES AND CULTURES

O God, you created all people in your image. We thank you for the astonishing variety of races and cultures in this world. Enrich our lives by ever-widening circles of fellowship, and show us your presence in those who differ most from us, until our knowledge of your love is made perfect in our love for all your children; through your Son, Jesus Christ our Lord. (168)

OUR COUNTRY

Almighty God, you have given us this good land as our heritage. Make us always remember your generosity and constantly do your will. Bless our land with honest industry, truthful education, and an honorable way of life. Save us from violence, discord, and confusion; from pride and arrogance, and from every evil course of action. Make us who came from many nations with many different languages a united people. Defend our liberties and give those whom we have entrusted with the authority of government the spirit of wisdom, that there might be justice and peace in our land. When times are prosperous, let our hearts be thankful; and, in troubled times, do not let our trust in you fail. We ask all this through Jesus Christ our Lord. (169)

STATE/PROVINCIAL AND LOCAL GOVERNMENTS

Almighty God, our heavenly Father, bless those who hold office in the government [of this *state/province/city/town/*______________], that they may do their work in a spirit of wisdom, kindness, and justice. Help them use their authority to serve faithfully and to promote the general welfare, through your Son, Jesus Christ our Lord. (170)

RESPONSIBLE CITIZENSHIP

Lord, keep this nation under your care. Bless the leaders of our land, that we may be a people at peace among ourselves and a blessing to other nations of the earth. Help us elect trustworthy leaders, contribute to wise decisions for the general welfare, and thus serve you faithfully in our generation to the honor of your holy name, through Jesus Christ our Lord. (171)

THOSE IN CIVIL AUTHORITY

O Lord our governor, your glory shines throughout the world. We commend our nation to your merciful care, that we may live securely in peace and may be guided by your providence. Give all in authority the wisdom and strength to know your will and to do it. Help them remember that they are called to serve the people as lovers of truth and justice; through Jesus Christ our Lord. (172)

COURTS OF JUSTICE

Almighty God, you sit in judgment to declare what is just and right. Bless the courts and the magistrates in our land. Give them the spirit of wisdom and understanding, that they may perceive the truth and administer the law impartially as instruments of your divine will. We pray in the name of him who will come to be our judge, your Son, Jesus Christ our Lord. (173)

CITIES

Heavenly Father, in your Word you have given us a vision of that holy city to which the nations of the world bring their glory. Look upon and visit the cities of the earth. Renew the ties of mutual regard which form our civic life. Send us honest and able leaders. Help us to eliminate poverty, prejudice, and oppression, that peace may prevail with righteousness, and justice with order, and that men and women from various cultures and with differing talents may find with one another the fulfillment of their humanity; through Jesus Christ our Lord. (174)

TOWNS AND RURAL AREAS

God, our creator, you have ordered seedtime and harvest, sunshine and rain. Grant that all the people of our nation may give thanks to you for food, drink, and all that sustains life; may honor the land and water from which these good things come; and may respect those who labor to produce them; through your Son, Jesus Christ our Lord. (175)

THE NEIGHBORHOOD

O Lord, our creator, by your holy prophet you taught your ancient people to seek the welfare of the cities in which they lived. We commend our neighborhood to your care, that it might be kept free from social strife and decay. Give us strength of purpose and concern for others, that we may create here a community of justice and peace where your will may be done; through your Son, Jesus Christ our Lord. (176)

THE HUMAN FAMILY

O God, you made us in your own image and redeemed us through Jesus your Son. Look with compassion on the whole human family; take away the arrogance and hatred which infect our hearts; break down the walls that separate us; unite us in bonds of love; and, through our struggle and confusion, work to accomplish your purposes on earth; that, in your good time, all nations and races may serve you in harmony around your heavenly throne; through Jesus Christ our Lord. (177)

COMMERCE AND INDUSTRY

Almighty God, your Son Jesus Christ dignified our labor by sharing our toil. Be with your people where they work; make those who carry on the industries and commerce of this land responsive to your will; and to all of us, give pride in what we do and a just return for our labor; through your Son, Jesus Christ our Lord. (178)

THE UNEMPLOYED

Heavenly Father, we remember before you those who suffer want and anxiety from lack of work. Guide the people of this land so to use our wealth and resources that all persons may find suitable and fulfilling employment and receive just payment for their labor; through your Son, Jesus Christ our Lord. (179)

OUR ENEMIES

O God, the Lord of all, your Son commanded us to love our enemies and to pray for them. Lead us from prejudice to truth; deliver us from hatred, cruelty, and revenge; and enable us to stand before you, reconciled through your Son, Jesus Christ our Lord. (180)

THE POOR AND THE NEGLECTED

Almighty and most merciful God, we call to mind before you all those whom it would be easy to forget: the homeless, the destitute, the sick, the aged, and all who have none to care for them. Help us to heal those who are broken in body or spirit, and to turn their sorrow into joy. Grant this, Father, for the love of your Son, who for our sake became poor, Jesus Christ our Lord. (181)

THE OPPRESSED

Look with pity, O heavenly Father, upon the people in this land who live with injustice, terror, disease, and death as their constant companions. Have mercy upon us. Help us to eliminate cruelty to these our neighbors. Strengthen those who spend their lives establishing equal protection of the law and equal opportunities for all. And grant that every one of us may enjoy a fair portion of the abundance of this land; through your Son, Jesus Christ our Lord. (182)

THE PROPER USE OF WEALTH

Almighty God, all that we possess is from your loving hand. Give us grace that we may honor you with all we own, always remembering the account we must one day give to Jesus Christ our Lord. (183)

SCHOOLS

O Eternal God, bless all schools, colleges, and universities [and especially ____________], that they may be lively places for sound learning, new discovery, and the pursuit of wisdom; and grant that those who teach and those who learn may find you to be the source of all truth; through Jesus Christ our Lord. (184)

AGRICULTURE

Almighty God, we thank you for making the fruitful earth produce what is needed for life. Bless those who work in the fields; give us favorable weather; and grant that we may all share the fruits of the earth, rejoicing in your goodness; through your Son, Jesus Christ our Lord. (185)

PRISONS AND CORRECTIONAL INSTITUTIONS

Lord Jesus, for our sake you were condemned as a criminal. Visit our jails and prisons with your pity and judgment. Remember all prisoners and bring the guilty to repentance and amendment of life according to your will, and give them hope for their future. When any are held unjustly, bring them release; forgive us and teach us to improve our justice. Remember those who work in these institutions; keep them humane and compassionate; and save them from becoming brutal or callous. And since what we do for those in prison, O Lord, we do for you, lead us to improve their lot. All this we ask for your mercy's sake. (186)

THOSE WHO SUFFER FOR THE SAKE OF CONSCIENCE

God of love and strength, your Son forgave his enemies while he was suffering shame and death. Strengthen those who suffer for the sake of conscience. When they are accused, save them from speaking in hate; when they are rejected, save them from bitterness; when they are imprisoned, save them from despair. To us, your servants, give grace to respect their witness and to discern the truth, that our society may be cleansed and strengthened. This we ask for the sake of our merciful and righteous judge, Jesus Christ our Lord. (187)

USE OF LEISURE

O God, give us times of refreshment and peace in the course of this busy life. Grant that we may so use our leisure to rebuild our bodies and renew our minds that our spirits may be opened to the goodness of your creation; through Jesus Christ our Lord. (188)

THE CHURCH

Gracious Father, we pray for your holy catholic Church. Fill it with all truth and peace. Where it is corrupt, purify it; where it is in error, direct it; where in anything it is amiss, reform it; where it is right, strengthen it; where it is in need, provide for it; where it is divided, reunite it; for the sake of Jesus Christ, your Son our Savior. (189)

SPREAD OF THE GOSPEL

O God, increase the faith and energy of your Church to desire and work for the salvation of all people, that they might be freed from sin and that hope be renewed in many hearts, to the increase of the kingdom of your Son, Jesus Christ our Lord. (190)

MISSIONS

Merciful Father, your kindness caused the light of the Gospel to shine among us. Extend your mercy now, we pray, to all the people of the world who do not have hope in Jesus Christ, that your salvation may be made known to them also and that all hearts would turn to you; through the same Jesus Christ, your Son our Lord. (191)

THE MISSION OF THE CHURCH

Lord God of our salvation, it is your will that all people might come to you through your Son Jesus Christ. Inspire our witness to him, that all may know the power of his forgiveness and the hope of his resurrection. We pray in his name. (192)

THE SAINTS

We give thanks to you, O Lord our God, for all your servants and witnesses of time past: for Abraham, the father of believers, and for Sarah, his wife; for Moses, the lawgiver, and Aaron, the priest; for Miriam and Joshua, Deborah and Gideon, Samuel and Hannah, his mother; for Isaiah and all the prophets; for Mary, the mother of our Lord; for Peter and Paul and all the apostles; for Mary, Martha, and Mary Magdalene; for Stephen, the first martyr, and all the saints and martyrs in every time and in every land. In your mercy, give us, as you gave them, the hope of salvation and the promise of eternal life; through the first-born from the dead, Jesus Christ our Lord. (193)

MINISTERS OF THE WORD

Almighty God, through your Son Jesus Christ you gave the holy apostles many gifts and commanded them to feed your flock. Inspire all pastors to preach your Word diligently and your people to receive it willingly, that finally we may receive the crown of eternal glory; through Jesus Christ our Lord. (194)

THE ELECTION OF A PRESIDENT OR PASTOR

Almighty God, giver of all good gifts: Look on your Church with grace and guide the minds of those who shall choose a *pastor/president* for this ____________, that we may receive a faithful servant who will care for your people and equip us for our ministries; through Jesus Christ our Lord. (195)

DEACONESSES AND DEACONS

O God, through the ages you have called *women/men* to the diaconate in your Church. Let your blessing rest now on all who answer that call. Grant them understanding of the Gospel, sincerity of purpose, diligence in ministry, and the beauty of life in Christ, that many people will be served and your name be glorified; through your Son, Jesus Christ our Lord. (196)

CHURCH MUSICIANS AND ARTISTS

God of majesty, whom saints and angels delight to worship in heaven: Be with your servants who make art and music for your people, that with joy we on earth may glimpse your beauty, and bring us to the fulfillment of that hope of perfection which will be ours as we stand before your unveiled glory. We pray in the name of Jesus Christ our Lord. (197)

TEACHERS

O God of wisdom, in your goodness you provide faithful teachers for your Church. By your Holy Spirit give all teachers insight into your Word, holy lives as examples to us all, and the courage to know and do the truth; through your Son, Jesus Christ our Lord. (198)

RENEWAL

Almighty God, by our baptism into the death and resurrection of your Son Jesus Christ, you turn us from the old life of sin. Grant that we who are reborn to new life in him may live in righteousness and holiness all our days, through your Son, Jesus Christ our Lord. (199)

RENEWAL

Almighty God, grant that we, who have been redeemed from the old life of sin by our baptism into the death and resurrection of your Son Jesus Christ, may be renewed in your Holy Spirit to live in righteousness and true holiness; through Jesus Christ our Lord. (200)

GRACE TO RECEIVE THE WORD

Blessed Lord, you speak to us through the Holy Scriptures. Grant that we may hear, read, respect, learn, and make them our own in such a way that the enduring benefit and comfort of the Word will help us grasp and hold the blessed hope of everlasting life, given us through our Savior Jesus Christ. (201)

ENLIGHTENMENT OF THE HOLY SPIRIT

Lord God, you taught the hearts of your faithful people by sending them the light of your Holy Spirit. Grant that we, by your Spirit, may have a right judgment in all things and evermore rejoice in his holy counsel; through your Son, Jesus Christ our Lord. (202)

SELF-DEDICATION

Almighty God, draw our hearts to you, guide our minds, fill our imaginations, control our wills, so that we may be wholly yours. Use us as you will, always to your glory and the welfare of your people; through our Lord and Savior Jesus Christ. (203)

TRUSTFULNESS

O most loving Father, you want us to give thanks for all things, to fear nothing except losing you, and to lay all our cares on you, knowing that you care for us. Protect us from faithless fears and worldly anxieties, and grant that no clouds in this mortal life may hide from us the light of your immortal love shown to us in your Son, Jesus Christ our Lord. (204)

BEFORE WORSHIP

Almighty God, you pour out on all who desire it the spirit of grace and supplication. Deliver us, as we come into your presence, from cold hearts and wandering thoughts, that with steady minds and burning zeal we may worship you in spirit and in truth; through your Son, Jesus Christ our Lord. (205)

BEFORE WORSHIP

Bless us, O God, with a reverent sense of your presence, that we may be at peace and may worship you with all our mind and spirit; through Jesus Christ our Lord. (206)

BEFORE HOLY COMMUNION

O Jesus, our great high priest, be present with us as you were present with your disciples and make yourself known to us in the breaking of bread. (207)

BEFORE HOLY COMMUNION

We do not presume to come to your table, O merciful Lord, trusting in our own righteousness, but in your manifold and great mercies. We are not worthy to gather up the crumbs under your table. But you are the same Lord whose property is always to have mercy. Grant us, therefore, gracious Lord, so to eat the flesh of your dear Son Jesus Christ, and so to drink his blood, that we may evermore dwell in him and he in us. (208)

AFTER HOLY COMMUNION

Almighty God, you provide the true bread from heaven, your Son, Jesus Christ our Lord. Grant that we who have received the Sacrament of his body and blood may abide in him and he in us, that we may be filled with the power of his endless life, now and forever. (209)

AFTER WORSHIP

Almighty God, grant that the words we have heard this day with our ears may be grafted onto our hearts through your grace, that they may produce in us the fruit of a good life, to the praise and honor of your name, through Jesus Christ, your Son our Lord. (210)

ANSWER TO PRAYER

Almighty God, to whom our needs are known before we ask: Help us to ask only what accords with your will; and those good things which we dare not or, in our blindness, cannot ask, grant us for the sake of your Son, Jesus Christ our Lord. (211)

ANSWER TO PRAYER

Almighty God, you have given us grace at this time with one accord to make our common supplication to you, and you have promised through your well-beloved Son that when two or three are gathered together in his name, you will be in the midst of them. Fulfill now, O Lord, our desires and petitions as may be best for us, granting us, in this world, knowledge of your truth and, in the age to come, life everlasting. (212)

A PRAYER ATTRIBUTED TO ST. FRANCIS

Lord, make us instruments of your peace.
  Where there is hatred, let us sow love;
  where there is injury, pardon;
  where there is discord, union;
  where there is doubt, faith;
  where there is despair, hope;
  where there is darkness, light;
  where there is sadness, joy.
Grant that we may not so much seek
  to be consoled as to console;
  to be understood as to understand;
  to be loved as to love.
For it is in giving that we receive;
  it is in pardoning that we are pardoned; and
  it is in dying that we are born to eternal life. (213)

GENERAL THANKSGIVING

Almighty God, Father of all mercies, we your unworthy servants give you humble thanks for all your goodness and loving-kindness to us and to all whom you have made. We bless you for our creation, preservation, and all the blessings of this life; but above all for your immeasurable love in the redemption of the world by our Lord Jesus Christ, for the means of grace, and for the hope of glory. And, we pray, give us such an awareness of your mercies that with truly thankful hearts we may show forth your praise, not only with our lips, but also in our lives, by giving up ourselves to your service, and by walking before you in holiness and righteousness all our days; through Jesus Christ our Lord, to whom, with you and the Holy Spirit, be honor and glory throughout all ages. (214)

HARVEST OF LANDS AND WATERS

O gracious Father, when you open your hand you satisfy the desire of every living thing. Bless the land and waters, and give the world a plentiful harvest; let your Spirit go forth to renew the face of the earth. As you show us your love and kindness in the bounty of the land and sea, save us from selfish use of your gifts, so that men and women everywhere may give you thanks; through Jesus our Lord. (215)

CONSERVATION OF NATURAL RESOURCES

Almighty God, in giving us dominion over things on earth, you made us fellow workers in your creation. Give us wisdom and reverence to use the resources of nature, so that no one may suffer from our abuse of them, and that generations yet to come may continue to praise you for your bounty; through your Son, Jesus Christ our Lord. (216)

THANKS FOR THE HARVEST

Most gracious God, according to your wisdom the deep waters are opened up and clouds drop gentle moisture. We praise you for the return of planting and harvest seasons, for the fertility of the soil, for the harvesting of the crops, and for all other blessings which you in your generosity pour on this nation and people. Give us a full understanding of your mercy, and lives which will be respectful, holy, and obedient to you throughout all our days; through Jesus Christ our Lord. (217)

IN TIME OF SCARCE RAINFALL

O God, giver and sustainer of life, in this time of need send us the gentle rain, so that we may receive the fruits of the earth for our benefit and for your praise; through Jesus Christ our Lord. (218)

DANGERS OF ABUNDANCE

O God, in your love you have given us gifts which our forebears neither knew nor dreamed of. Mercifully grant that we may not be so occupied with material things that we forget the things which are spiritual and thus, even though we have gained the whole world, lose our souls; through Jesus Christ our Lord. (219)

GUIDANCE

Direct us, O Lord, in all our doings with your most gracious favor and further us with your continual help, that in all our works, begun, continued, and ended in you, we may glorify your holy name and finally, by your mercy, obtain everlasting life; through Jesus Christ our Lord. (220)

GENERAL INTERCESSION

Watch, dear Lord, with those who wake or watch or weep, and give your angels charge over those who sleep. Tend the sick, rest the weary, bless the dying, soothe the suffering, pity the afflicted, shield the joyous. In your love, give us all this, through Jesus Christ our Lord. (221)

PROTECTION THROUGH LIFE

O Lord, mercifully assist us in our supplications and prayers. Direct the lives of your servants toward the goal of everlasting salvation, that, surrounded by all the changes and uncertainties of life, we may be defended by your gracious and ready help in Jesus Christ our Lord. (222)

THOSE IN AFFLICTION

Almighty and everlasting God, comfort of the sad and strength to those who suffer: Let the prayers of your children who are in any trouble rise to you. To everyone in distress grant mercy, grant relief, grant refreshment; through Jesus Christ our Lord. (223)

THOSE IN MENTAL DISTRESS

Heavenly Father, have mercy on all your children who live in mental distress. Restore them to strength of mind and cheerfulness of spirit, and give them health and peace; through Jesus Christ our Lord. (224)

THOSE IN TROUBLE OR BEREAVEMENT

O merciful Father, you teach us in your holy Word that you do not willingly afflict or grieve your children. Look with pity on the sorrows of ____name____, your servant, for whom we pray. Remember *him/her,* O Lord, in mercy. Strengthen *him/her* in patience, comfort *him/her* with the memory of your goodness, let your presence shine on *him/her,* and give *him/her* peace through Jesus Christ our Lord. (225)

RECOVERY FROM SICKNESS

O God, the strength of the weak and the comfort of sufferers: Mercifully hear our prayers and grant to your servant, ____name____, the help of your power, that *his/her* sickness may be turned into health and our sorrow into joy; through Jesus Christ. (226)

THOSE SUFFERING FROM ADDICTION

O blessed Jesus, you ministered to all who came to you. Look with compassion upon all who through addiction have lost their health and freedom. Restore to them the assurance of your unfailing mercy; remove the fears that attack them; strengthen them in the work of their recovery; and to those who care for them, give patient understanding and persevering love; for your mercy's sake. (227)

RESTORATION OF HEALTH

Almighty and gracious God, we give thanks that you have restored the health of your servant, ____name____, on whose behalf we bless and praise your name. Grant that *he/she* may continue the mission you have given *him/her* in this world and also share in eternal glory at the appearing of your Son, Jesus Christ our Lord. (228)

THE AGED

O Lord God, look with mercy on all whose increasing years bring them isolation, distress, or weakness. Provide for them homes of dignity and peace; give them understanding helpers and the willingness to accept help; and, as their strength diminishes, increase their faith and their assurance of your love. We pray in the name of Jesus Christ our Lord. (229)

FAMILIES

Almighty God, our heavenly Father, you set the solitary in families. We commend to your care all the homes where your people live. Keep them, we pray, free from bitterness, from the thirst for personal victory, and from pride in self. Fill them with faith, virtue, knowledge, moderation, patience, and godliness. Knit together in enduring affection those who have become one in marriage. Let children and parents have full respect for one another; and light the fire of kindliness among us all, that we may show affection for each other; through Jesus Christ our Lord. (230)

BIRTH OF A CHILD

Heavenly Father, you sent your own Son into this world as the child of Mary and Joseph. We thank you for the life of this child, ______name______, entrusted to our care. Help us to remember that we are all your children, and so to love and nurture *him/her* that *he/she* may attain to that full stature intended for *him/her* in your eternal kingdom; for the sake of Jesus Christ, your Son and our Lord. (231)

THE CARE OF CHILDREN

Almighty God, heavenly Father, you have blessed us with the joy and care of children. As we bring them up, give us calm strength and patient wisdom, that we may teach them to love whatever is just and true and good, following the example of our Savior Jesus Christ. (232)

YOUNG PERSONS

God our Father, you see your children growing up in an uncertain and confusing world. Show them that your ways give more life than the ways of the world, and that following you is better than chasing after selfish goals. Help them to take failure, not as a measure of their worth, but as an opportunity for a new start. Give them strength to hold their faith in you and to keep alive their joy in your creation, through Jesus Christ our Lord. (233)

THOSE WHO LIVE ALONE

Almighty God, grant that those who live alone may not be lonely in their solitude, but may find fulfillment in loving you and their neighbors as they follow in the footsteps of Jesus Christ our Lord. (234)

REMEMBRANCE OF THE FAITHFUL DEPARTED

With reverence and affection we remember before you, O everlasting God, all our departed friends and relatives. Keep us in union with them here through faith and love toward you, that hereafter we may enter into your presence and be numbered with those who serve you and look upon your face in glory everlasting, through your Son, Jesus Christ our Lord. (235)

PRAYER OF THE CHURCH

Almighty God, giver of all things, with gladness we give thanks for all your goodness. We bless you for the love which has created and which sustains us from day to day. We praise you for the gift of your Son our Savior, through whom you have made known your will and grace. We thank you for the Holy Spirit, the comforter; for your holy Church; for the means of grace; for the lives of all faithful and good people; and for the hope of the life to come. Help us to treasure in our hearts all that our Lord has done for us, and enable us to show our thankfulness by lives that are wholly given to your service.

C **Hear us, good Lord.**

Save and defend your whole Church, purchased with the precious blood of Christ. Give it pastors and ministers filled with your Spirit, and strengthen it through the Word and the holy sacraments. Make it perfect in love and in all good works, and establish it in the faith delivered to the saints. Sanctify and unite your people in all the world, that one holy Church may bear witness to you, the creator and redeemer of all.

C **Hear us, good Lord.**

Give your wisdom and heavenly grace to all pastors and to those who hold office in your Church, that, by their faithful service, faith may abound and your kingdom increase.

C **Hear us, good Lord.**

Send the light of your truth into all the earth. Raise up faithful servants of Christ to labor in the Gospel both at home and in distant lands.

C **Hear us, good Lord.**

In your mercy strengthen the younger churches and support them in times of trial. Make them steadfast, abounding in the work of the Lord, and let their faith and zeal for the Gospel refresh and renew the witness of your people everywhere.

C **Hear us, good Lord.**

Preserve our nation in justice and honor, that we may lead a peaceable life of integrity. Grant health and favor to all who bear office in our land

(Canada) *especially to Her Gracious Majesty, the Queen; the Governor General; the Prime Minister and the Parliament; the Government of this Province and all who have authority over us*

(USA) *especially to the President of the United States, the Governor of this State, and all those who make, administer, and judge our laws*

and help them to serve this people according to your holy will.

C **Hear us, good Lord.**

Take from us all hatred and prejudice, give us the spirit of love, and dispose our days in your peace. Prosper the labors of those who take counsel for the nations of the world, that mutual understanding and common endeavor may be increased among all peoples.

C **Hear us, good Lord.**

Bless the schools of the Church and all colleges, universities, and centers of research and those who teach in them. Bestow your wisdom in such measure that people may serve you in Church and state and that our common life may be conformed to the rule of your truth and justice.

C Hear us, good Lord.

Sanctify our homes with your presence and joy. Keep our children in the covenant of their baptism and enable their parents to rear them in a life of faith and devotion. By the spirit of affection and service unite the members of all families, that they may show your praise in our land and in all the world.

C Hear us, good Lord.

Let your blessing rest upon the seedtime and harvest, the commerce and industry, the leisure and rest, the arts and culture of our people. Take under your special protection those whose work is difficult or dangerous, and be with all who lay their hands to any useful task. Give them just rewards for their labor and the knowledge that their work is good in your sight.

C Hear us, good Lord.

Special supplications, intercessions, and thanksgivings may be made.

Comfort with the grace of your Holy Spirit all who are in sorrow or need, sickness or adversity. Remember those who suffer persecution for the faith. Have mercy on those to whom death draws near. Bring consolation to those in sorrow or mourning. And to all grant a measure of your love, taking them into your tender care.

C Hear us, good Lord.

We remember with thanksgiving those who have loved and served you in your Church on earth, who now rest from their labors [especially those most dear to us, whom we name in our hearts before you]. Keep us in fellowship with all your saints, and bring us at last to the joy of your heavenly kingdom.

C Hear us, good Lord.

All these things and whatever else you see that we need, grant us, Father, for the sake of him who died and rose again, and now lives and reigns with you in the unity of the Holy Spirit, one God forever.

C Amen

ATHANASIAN CREED

Quicunque Vult

Whoever wants to be saved
 should above all cling
 to the catholic faith.
Whoever does not guard it
 whole and inviolable
 will doubtless perish eternally.
Now this is the catholic faith:
 We worship one God in trinity
 and the Trinity in unity,
 neither confusing the persons
 nor dividing the divine being.
For the Father is one person,
 the Son is another,
 and the Spirit is still another.
But the deity of the Father, Son,
 and Holy Spirit
 is one, equal in glory,
 coeternal in majesty.
What the Father is,
 the Son is,
 and so is the Holy Spirit.
Uncreated is the Father;
 uncreated is the Son;
 uncreated is the Spirit.
The Father is infinite;
 the Son is infinite;
 the Holy Spirit is infinite.
Eternal is the Father;
 eternal is the Son;
 eternal is the Spirit:
And yet there are not
 three eternal beings,
 but one who is eternal;
as there are not
 three uncreated and unlimited beings,
 but one who is uncreated
 and unlimited.
Almighty is the Father;
 almighty is the Son;
 almighty is the Spirit:
And yet there are not
 three almighty beings,
 but one who is almighty.
Thus the Father is God;
 the Son is God;
 the Holy Spirit is God:
And yet there are not three gods,
 but one God.
Thus the Father is Lord;
 the Son is Lord;
 the Holy Spirit is Lord:
And yet there are not three lords,
 but one Lord.
As Christian truth compels us
 to acknowledge each distinct person
 as God and Lord,
 so catholic religion forbids us
 to say that there are
 three gods or lords.
The Father was neither made
 nor created nor begotten;
the Son was neither made nor created,
 but was alone begotten of the Father;
the Spirit was neither made nor created,
 but is proceeding
 from the Father and the Son.
Thus there is one Father,
 not three fathers;
 one Son, not three sons;
 one Holy Spirit, not three spirits.
And in this Trinity,
 no one is before or after,
 greater or less than the other;
but all three persons are in themselves,
 coeternal and coequal;
 and so we must worship
 the Trinity in unity
 and the one God in three persons.
Whoever wants to be saved should
 think thus about the Trinity.
It is necessary for eternal salvation
 that one also faithfully believe that
 our Lord Jesus Christ became flesh.
For this is the true faith
 that we believe and confess:
 That our Lord Jesus Christ,
 God's Son, is both God and man.
He is God, begotten before all worlds
 from the being of the Father,
and he is man, born in the world

from the being of his mother—
existing fully as God,
and fully as man
with a rational soul
and a human body;
equal to the Father in divinity,
subordinate to the Father in humanity.
Although he is God and man,
he is not divided,
but is one Christ.
He is united because God has taken
humanity into himself;
he does not transform deity
into humanity.
He is completely one
in the unity of his person,
without confusing his natures.
For as the rational soul and body
are one person,
so the one Christ is God and man.
He suffered death for our salvation.
He descended into hell
and rose again from the dead.
He ascended into heaven
and is seated at the right hand
of the Father.
He will come again
to judge the living and the dead.
At his coming
all people shall rise bodily
to give an account of their own deeds.
Those who have done good
will enter eternal life,
those who have done evil
will enter eternal fire.
This is the catholic faith.
One cannot be saved
without believing this
firmly and faithfully.

BRIEF ORDER FOR CONFESSION AND FORGIVENESS

Stand

1. The minister leads the congregation in the invocation. The sign of the cross may be made by all in remembrance of their Baptism.

P In the name of the Father, and of the ☩ Son, and of the Holy Spirit.

C Amen

P Almighty God, to whom all hearts are open, all desires known, and from whom no secrets are hid: Cleanse the thoughts of our hearts by the inspiration of your Holy Spirit, that we may perfectly love you and worthily magnify your holy name, through Jesus Christ our Lord. (236)

C Amen

P If we say we have no sin, we deceive ourselves, and the truth is not in us. But if we confess our sins, God who is faithful and just will forgive our sins and cleanse us from all unrighteousness.

Kneel/Stand

2. Silence for reflection and self-examination.

P Most merciful God,

C we confess that we are in bondage to sin and cannot free ourselves. We have sinned against you in thought, word, and deed, by what we have done and by what we have left undone. We have not loved you with our whole heart; we have not loved our neighbors as ourselves. For the sake of your Son, Jesus Christ, have mercy on us. Forgive us, renew us, and lead us, so that we may delight in your will and walk in your ways, to the glory of your holy name. Amen

3. The minister stands and addresses the congregation.

P Almighty God, in his mercy, has given his Son to die for us and, for his sake, forgives us all our sins. As a called and ordained minister of the Church of Christ, and by his authority, I therefore declare to you the entire forgiveness of all your sins, in the name of the Father, and of the ☩ Son, and of the Holy Spirit.

OR

P In the mercy of almighty God, Jesus Christ was given to die for you, and for his sake God forgives you all your sins. To those who believe in Jesus Christ he gives the power to become the children of God and bestows on them the Holy Spirit.

C Amen

HOLY COMMUNION

Setting One

1. The Brief Order for Confession and Forgiveness, page 56, may be used before this service.

2. The minister may announce the day and its significance before the Entrance Hymn, before the lessons, or at another appropriate time.

3. When there is no Communion, the service is concluded after the Creed as indicated.

Stand

4. The ENTRANCE HYMN or Psalm is sung.

5. The minister greets the congregation.

P The grace of our Lord Jesus Christ, the love of God, and the communion of the Holy Spirit be with you all.

C **And also with you.**

6. The KYRIE may follow.

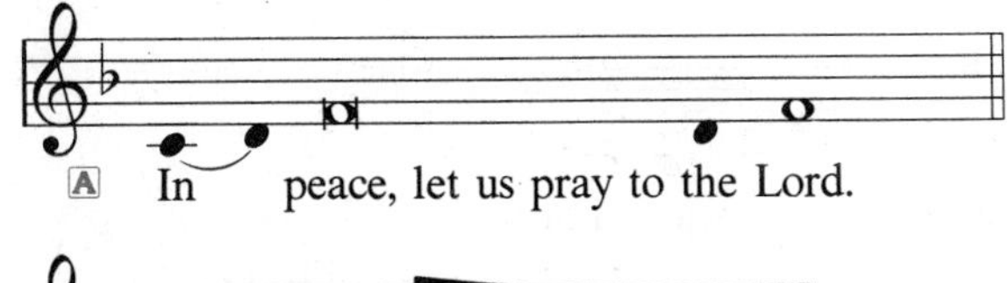

A In peace, let us pray to the Lord.

C **Lord, have mer - cy.**

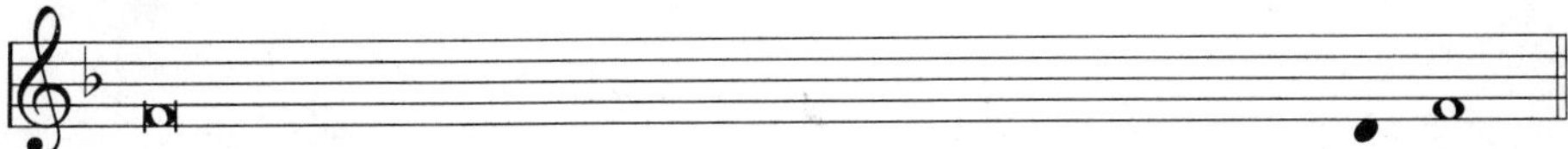

A For the peace from above, and for our salvation, let us pray to the Lord.

C **Lord, have mer - cy.**

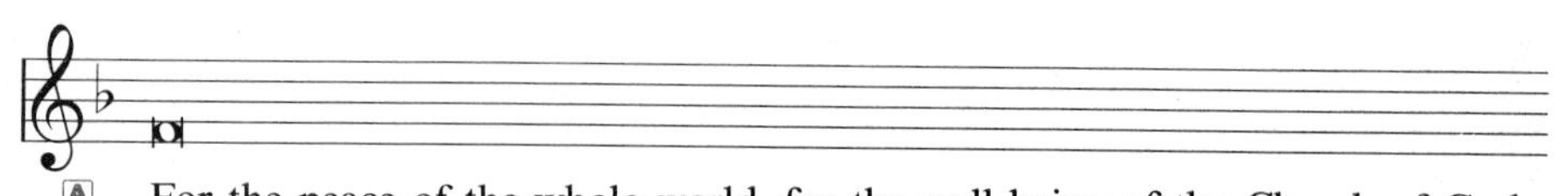
A For the peace of the whole world, for the well-being of the Church of God,

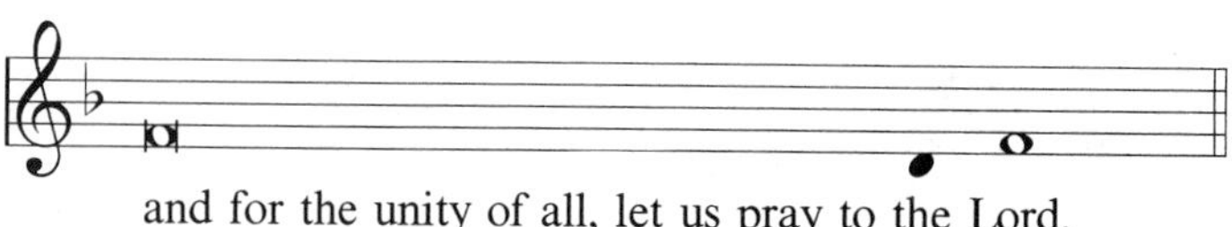
and for the unity of all, let us pray to the Lord.

C **Lord, have mer - cy.**

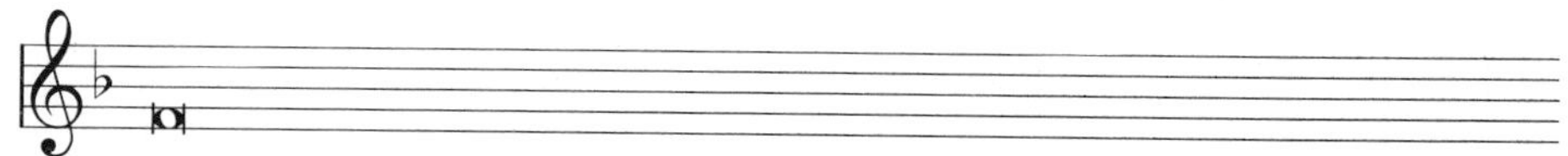
A For this holy house, and for all who offer here their worship and praise,

let us pray to the Lord.

C **Lord, have mer - cy.**

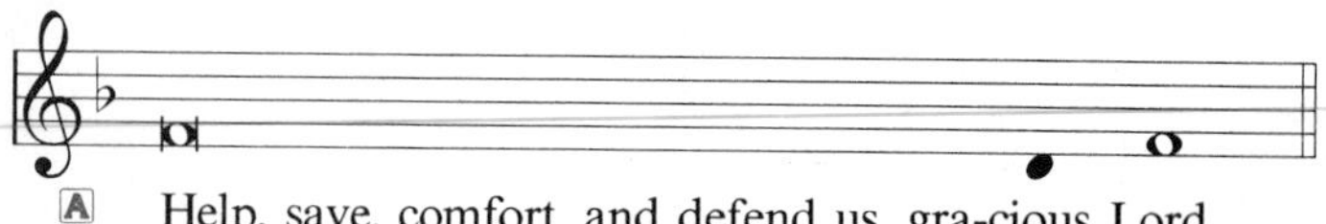
A Help, save, comfort, and defend us, gra-cious Lord.

C **A - men**

7. The HYMN OF PRAISE or another appropriate hymn may be sung.

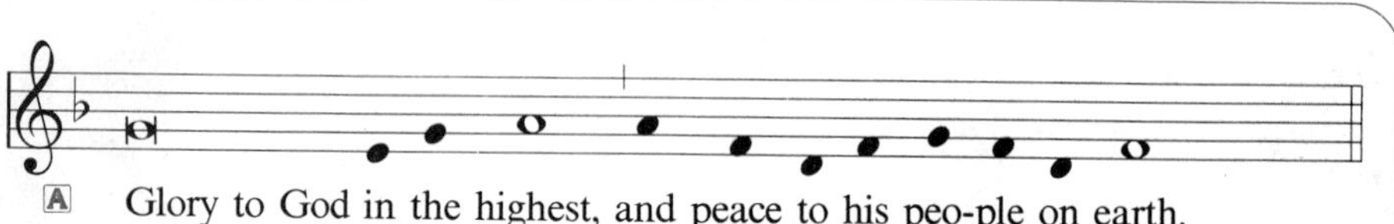
A Glory to God in the highest, and peace to his peo-ple on earth.

C
Lord God, heav-en-ly king, al-might-y God and Fa - ther:
We wor-ship you, we give you thanks, we praise you for your
glo - ry. Lord Je - sus Christ, on-ly Son of the Fa-ther,
Lord God, Lamb of God: You take a-way the sin of the world;
have mer-cy on us. You are seat-ed at the right hand of the
Fa - ther; re-ceive our prayer. For you a -
lone are the Ho - ly One, you a-lone are the Lord,
you a-lone are the Most High, Je-sus Christ, with the Ho-ly Spir - it,
in the glo - ry of God the Fa-ther. A - men

OR

C This is the feast of vic-to-ry for our God.
Al-le-lu - ia, al-le-lu-ia, al - le - lu - ia.
I Wor-thy is Christ, the Lamb who was slain, whose
blood set us free to be peo - ple of God.
C This is the feast of vic-to-ry for our God.
Al-le-lu - ia, al-le-lu-ia, al - le - lu - ia.
II Pow - er, rich - es, wis - dom, and strength, and
hon - or, bless - ing, and glo - ry are his.
C This is the feast of vic-to-ry for our God.
Al-le-lu - ia, al-le-lu-ia, al - le - lu - ia.

I Sing with all the peo - ple of God, and
join in the hymn of all cre - a - tion:
Bless - ing, hon - or, glo - ry, and might be to
God and the Lamb for - ev - er. A - men.
C This is the feast of vic - to - ry for our God.
Al - le - lu - ia, al - le - lu - ia, al - le - lu - ia.
II For the Lamb who was slain has be -
gun his reign. Al - le - lu - ia.
C This is the feast of vic - to - ry for our God.
Al - le - lu - ia, al - le - lu - ia, al - le - lu - ia.

8. The PRAYER OF THE DAY is said; the salutation may precede it.

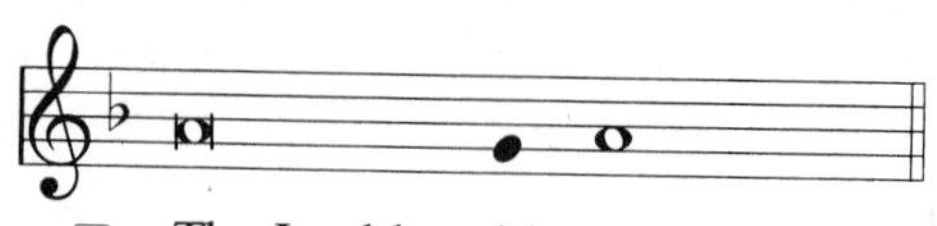

P The Lord be with you.

C **And al - so with you.**

P Let us pray. . . .

C **Amen**

Sit

9. The FIRST LESSON is announced and read.

A The First Lesson is from the ______________ chapter of ______________.

10. After the lesson the reader may say: "Here ends the reading."

11. The appointed PSALM is sung or said.

12. The SECOND LESSON is announced and read.

A The Second Lesson is from the ______________ chapter of ______________.

13. After the lesson the reader may say: "Here ends the reading."

14. The appointed VERSE is sung by the choir, or the congregation may sing the appropriate Verse below.

Stand

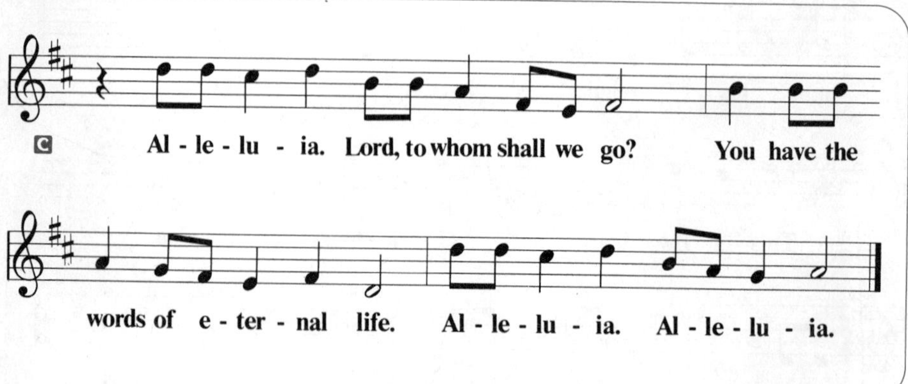
C **Al - le - lu - ia. Lord, to whom shall we go? You have the**
words of e - ter - nal life. Al - le - lu - ia. Al - le - lu - ia.

OR

LENT

C Re - turn to the Lord, your God, for he is gra - cious and
mer - ci - ful, slow to an - ger, and a - bound - ing in
stead - fast love, and a - bound - ing in stead - fast love.

15. The GOSPEL is announced.

P The Holy Gospel according to St. ______________, the ______________ chapter.

C
Glo - ry to you, O Lord.

16. After the reading the minister may say: "The Gospel of the Lord."

C
Praise to you, O Christ.

17. The Hymn of the Day may be sung before the Sermon.

Sit

18. The SERMON. Silence for reflection may follow.

Stand

19. The HYMN OF THE DAY is sung.

20. The CREED may be said. The Nicene Creed is said on all festivals and on Sundays in the seasons of Advent, Christmas, Lent, and Easter. The Apostles' Creed is said at other times. The Creed is omitted here if the service of Holy Baptism or another rite with a creed is used.

NICENE CREED

C We believe in one God,
the Father, the Almighty,
maker of heaven and earth,
of all that is, seen and unseen.

We believe in one Lord, Jesus Christ,
the only Son of God,
eternally begotten of the Father,
God from God, Light from Light,
true God from true God,
begotten, not made,
of one Being with the Father.
Through him all things were made.
For us and for our salvation
he came down from heaven;
by the power of the Holy Spirit
he became incarnate from the virgin Mary, and was made man.
For our sake he was crucified under Pontius Pilate;
he suffered death and was buried.
On the third day he rose again
in accordance with the Scriptures;
he ascended into heaven
and is seated at the right hand of the Father.
He will come again in glory to judge the living and the dead,
and his kingdom will have no end.

We believe in the Holy Spirit, the Lord, the giver of life,
who proceeds from the Father and the Son.
With the Father and the Son he is worshiped and glorified.
He has spoken through the prophets.
We believe in one holy catholic and apostolic Church.
We acknowledge one Baptism for the forgiveness of sins.
We look for the resurrection of the dead,
and the life of the world to come. Amen

OR

APOSTLES' CREED

C I believe in God, the Father almighty,
creator of heaven and earth.

I believe in Jesus Christ, his only Son, our Lord.
He was conceived by the power of the Holy Spirit
and born of the virgin Mary.
He suffered under Pontius Pilate,
was crucified, died, and was buried.
He descended into hell.*
On the third day he rose again.
He ascended into heaven,
and is seated at the right hand of the Father.
He will come again to judge the living and the dead.

I believe in the Holy Spirit,
the holy catholic Church,
the communion of saints,
the forgiveness of sins,
the resurrection of the body,
and the life everlasting. Amen

**Or,* He descended to the dead.

21. When there is no Communion, the service continues on page 75. ▶

22. THE PRAYERS are said.

A Let us pray for the whole people of God in Christ Jesus, and for all people according to their needs.

Prayers are included for the whole Church, the nations, those in need, the parish, special concerns.

The congregation may be invited to offer petitions and thanksgivings.

Prayers of confession may be included if the Brief Order for Confession and Forgiveness has not been used earlier.

The minister gives thanks for the faithful departed, especially for those who recently have died.

After each portion of the prayers:

A Lord, in your mercy,

C **hear our prayer.**

OR

A Let us pray to the Lord.

C **Lord, have mercy.**

The prayers conclude:

P Into your hands, O Lord, we commend all for whom we pray, trusting in your mercy; through your Son, Jesus Christ our Lord.

C **Amen**

23. The PEACE is shared at this time or after the Lord's Prayer, prior to the distribution.

P The peace of the Lord be with you always.

C **And also with you.**

The ministers and congregation may greet one another in the name of the Lord.

Peace be with you. ℟ Peace be with you.

Sit

24. The OFFERING is received as the Lord's table is prepared.

25. The appointed OFFERTORY may be sung by the choir as the gifts are presented, or the congregation may sing one of the following offertories, or an appropriate hymn or psalm may be sung.

Stand

C Let the vine - yards be fruit - ful, Lord, and fill to the brim our
cup of bless - ing. Gath - er a har - vest from the seeds that were
sown, that we may be fed with the bread of life. Gath - er the
hopes and the dreams of all; u - nite them with the prayers we
of - fer now. Grace our ta - ble with your pres - ence, and
give us a fore - taste of the feast to come.

OR

C What shall I ren-der to the Lord for all his ben-e-fits to
me? I will of - fer the sac-ri-fice of thanks-giv-ing and will
call on the name of the Lord. I will take the cup of sal-
va - tion and will call on the name of the Lord. I will pay my
vows to the Lord now in the pres-ence of all his peo-ple, in the
courts of the Lord's house, in the midst of you, O Je-ru - sa - lem.

26. *After the gifts have been presented, one of these prayers is said.*

A Let us pray.

A Merciful Father,

C **we offer with joy and thanksgiving what you have first given us—our selves, our time, and our possessions, signs of your gracious love. Receive them for the sake of him who offered himself for us, Jesus Christ our Lord. Amen** (239)

OR

A Blessed are you,

C O Lord our God, maker of all things. Through your goodness you have blessed us with these gifts. With them we offer ourselves to your service and dedicate our lives to the care and redemption of all that you have made, for the sake of him who gave himself for us, Jesus Christ our Lord. Amen (240)

27. The ministers make ready the bread and wine.

28. The GREAT THANKSGIVING is begun by the minister standing at the altar.

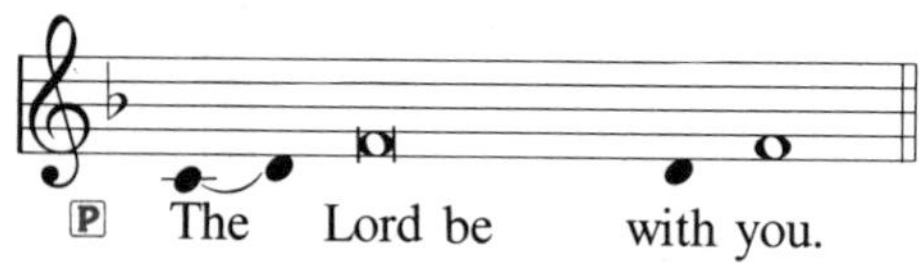
P The Lord be with you.

C And al - so with you.

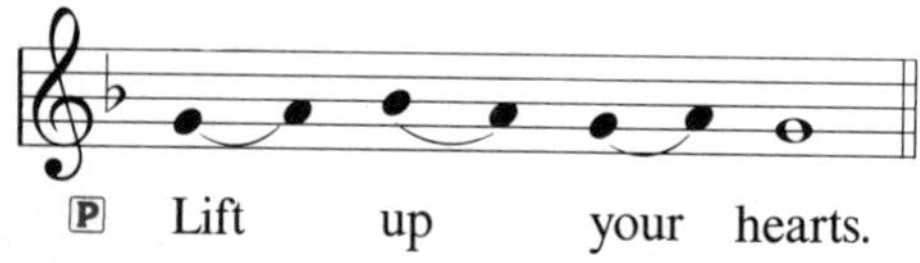
P Lift up your hearts.

C We lift them to the Lord.

P Let us give thanks to the Lord our God.

C It is right to give him thanks and praise.

29. The preface appropriate to the day or season is sung or said.

P It is indeed right and salutary . . . we praise your name and join their unending hymn:

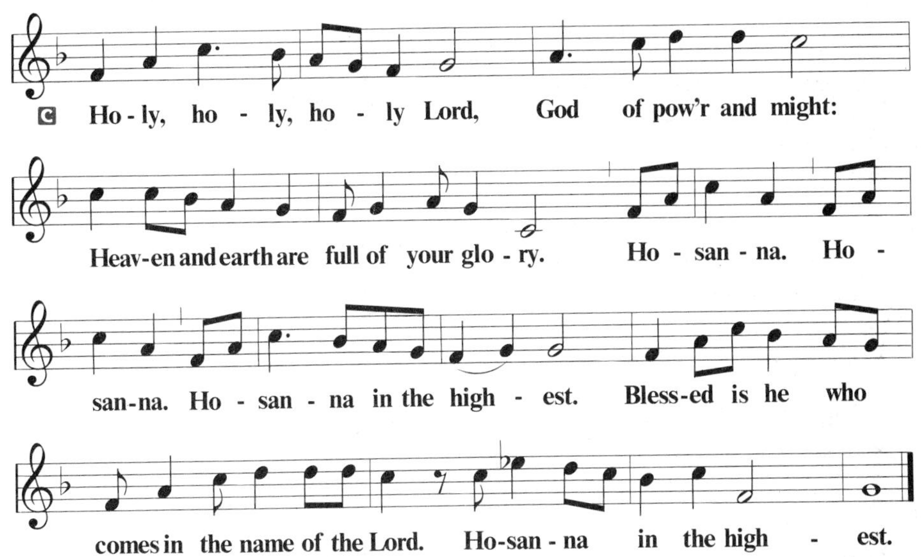
C Ho - ly, ho - ly, ho - ly Lord, God of pow'r and might:
Heav-en and earth are full of your glo - ry. Ho - san - na. Ho -
san-na. Ho - san - na in the high - est. Bless-ed is he who
comes in the name of the Lord. Ho-san - na in the high - est.

30. The minister continues, using one of the sections below.

31. The minister may say:

P Holy God, mighty Lord,
gracious Father:
Endless is your mercy
and eternal your reign.

You have filled all creation
with light and life;
heaven and earth
are full of your glory.

Through Abraham you promised
to bless all nations.
You rescued Israel,
your chosen people.

Through the prophets
you renewed your promise;
and, at this end of all the ages,
you sent your Son,
who in words and deeds
proclaimed your kingdom
and was obedient to your will,
even to giving his life.

In the night
in which he was betrayed,
our Lord Jesus took bread,
and gave thanks; broke it,

OR

32. The minister may say:

P In the night
in which he was betrayed,
our Lord Jesus took bread,
and gave thanks; broke it,
and gave it to his disciples,
saying: Take and eat;
this is my body, given for you.

Do this for the remembrance of me.

Again, after supper,
he took the cup, gave thanks,
and gave it for all to drink,
saying: This cup is
the new covenant in my blood,
shed for you and for all people
for the forgiveness of sin.

Do this for the remembrance of me.

OR

and gave it to his disciples,
saying: Take and eat;
this is my body, given for you.
Do this for the remembrance of me.

Again, after supper,
he took the cup, gave thanks,
and gave it for all to drink,
saying: This cup is
the new covenant in my blood,
shed for you and for all people
for the forgiveness of sin.
Do this for the remembrance of me.

For as often as we eat
of this bread
and drink from this cup,
we proclaim the Lord's death,
until he comes.

C **Christ has died. Christ is risen. Christ will come again.**

P Therefore, gracious Father,
with this bread and cup
we remember the life
our Lord offered for us.

And, believing the witness
of his resurrection,
we await his coming in power
to share with us
the great and promised feast.

C **Amen. Come, Lord Jesus.**

P Send now, we pray,
your Holy Spirit,
the spirit of our Lord
and of his resurrection,
that we who receive
the Lord's body and blood
may live to the praise
of your glory
and receive our inheritance
with all your saints in light.

C **Amen. Come, Holy Spirit.**

P Join our prayers
with those of your servants
of every time and every place,
and unite them
with the ceaseless petitions

33. The minister may say:

P Blessed are you,
Lord of heaven and earth.

In mercy for our fallen world
you gave your only Son,
that all those who believe in him
should not perish,
but have eternal life.

We give thanks to you
for the salvation
you have prepared
for us through Jesus Christ.

Send now your Holy Spirit
into our hearts,
that we may receive our Lord
with a living faith
as he comes to us
in his holy supper.

C **Amen. Come, Lord Jesus.**

P In the night
in which he was betrayed
our Lord Jesus took bread,
and gave thanks; broke it,
and gave it to his disciples,
saying: Take and eat;
this is my body, given for you.
Do this for the remembrance of me.

Again, after supper,
he took the cup, gave thanks,
and gave it for all to drink,
saying: This cup is
the new covenant in my blood,
shed for you and for all people
for the forgiveness of sin.
Do this for the remembrance of me.

of our great high priest
until he comes
as victorious Lord of all.

C Through him, with him, in him, in the u - ni-ty of the
Ho - ly Spir - it, all hon - or and glo - ry is yours, al -
might-y Fa - ther, now and for-ev - er. A - men

C Our Father in heaven,
hallowed be your name,
your kingdom come,
your will be done,
on earth as in heaven.
Give us today our daily bread.
Forgive us our sins
as we forgive those
who sin against us.
Save us from the time of trial
and deliver us from evil.
For the kingdom, the power,
and the glory are yours,
now and forever. Amen

OR

C Our Father, who art in heaven,
hallowed be thy name,
thy kingdom come,
thy will be done,
on earth as it is in heaven.
Give us this day our daily bread;
and forgive us our trespasses,
as we forgive those
who trespass against us;
and lead us not into temptation,
but deliver us from evil.
For thine is the kingdom,
and the power, and the glory,
forever and ever. Amen

Sit

34. The COMMUNION follows. The bread may be broken for distribution.

35. The presiding minister and the assisting ministers receive the bread and wine and then give them to those who come to receive. As the ministers give the bread and wine, they say these words to each communicant:

The body of Christ, given for you.

The blood of Christ, shed for you.

36. The communicant may say: "Amen."

37. Hymns and other music may be used during the ministration of Communion. One of the hymns may be the following.

C Lamb of God, you take a - way the sin of the world; have
mer-cy on us. Lamb of God, you take a - way the sin of the
world; have mer-cy on us. Lamb of God, you take a - way the
sin of the world; grant us peace.

Stand

38. After all have returned to their places, the minister may say these or similar words.

P The body and blood of our Lord Jesus Christ strengthen you and keep you in his grace.

C Amen

39. The POST-COMMUNION canticle or an appropriate hymn is sung as the table is cleared.

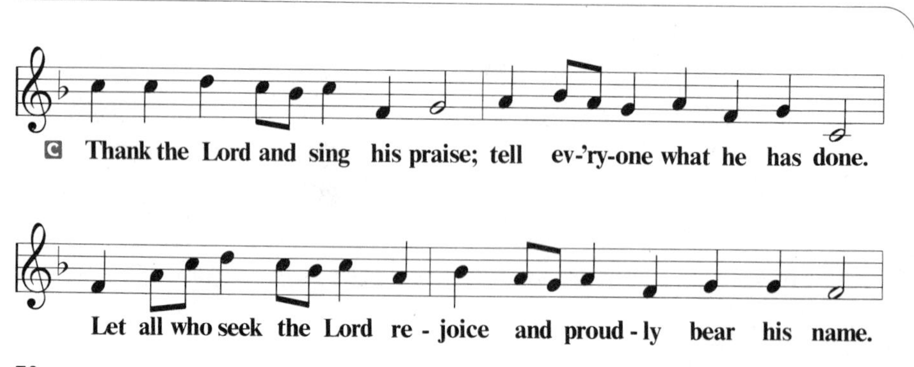
C Thank the Lord and sing his praise; tell ev-'ry-one what he has done.
Let all who seek the Lord re - joice and proud - ly bear his name.

He re-calls his prom-is - es and leads his peo-ple forth in joy with
shouts of thanks-giv - ing. Al - le - lu - ia. Al - le - lu - ia.
OR
C
Lord, now you let your ser-vant go in peace; your word has been ful -
filled. My own eyes have seen the sal - va - tion which you have pre -
pared in the sight of ev - 'ry peo - ple: A light to re -
veal you to the na - tions and the glo - ry of your peo-ple Is - ra - el.
Glo - ry to the Fa - ther, and to the Son, and to the Ho - ly Spir - it,
as it was in the be-gin - ning, is now, and will be for-ev - er. A - men

40. One of these prayers is said.

A Let us pray.

A We give you thanks, almighty God, that you have refreshed us through the healing power of this gift of life; and we pray that in your mercy you would strengthen us, through this gift, in faith toward you and in fervent love toward one another; for the sake of Jesus Christ our Lord. (241)

OR

A Pour out upon us the spirit of your love, O Lord, and unite the wills of those whom you have fed with one heavenly food; through Jesus Christ our Lord. (242)

OR

A Almighty God, you gave your Son both as a sacrifice for sin and a model of the godly life. Enable us to receive him always with thanksgiving, and to conform our lives to his; through the same Jesus Christ our Lord. (243)

C **Amen**

41. Silence for reflection.

42. The minister blesses the congregation.

P Almighty God, Father, ✠ Son,
and Holy Spirit, bless you now . . . . . and for-ever.

OR

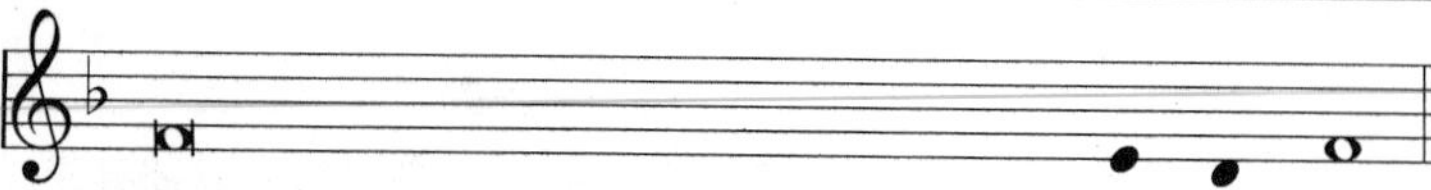

P The Lord bless you and keep you.
The Lord make his face shine on you
and be gracious to you.
The Lord look upon you with favor and ✠ give you peace.

C **A - men**

43. The minister may dismiss the congregation.

A Go in peace. Serve the Lord.

C **Thanks be to God.**

44. ▶ *When there is no Communion, the service concludes as follows.*

45. *The OFFERING is received and may be presented at the altar.*

46. *The following Psalm or an appropriate hymn may be sung when the gifts are presented.*

Stand

C Cre - ate in me a clean heart, O God, and re - new a
right spir - it with - in me. Cast me not a - way from your
pres - ence, and take not your Ho - ly Spir - it from
me. Re - store to me the joy of your sal - va - tion,
and up - hold me with your free Spir - it.

47. *THE PRAYERS are said. One of the following or another form of prayer may be used.*

A Let us pray.

A O Lord our God, you have commanded the light to shine out of darkness, and you have again brought us to your house of prayer to praise your goodness and ask for your gifts. Accept now in your endless mercy the sacrifice of our worship and thanksgiving, and grant us those requests which will be wholesome for us. Make us to be children of the light and of the day and heirs of your everlasting inheritance. Remember, O Lord, according to the multitude of your mercies, your whole Church, all who join with us in prayer, all our sisters and brothers wherever they may be in your vast kingdom who stand in need of your help and comfort. Pour out upon them the riches of your mercy, so that we, redeemed in soul and body and steadfast in faith, may ever praise your wonderful and holy name; through Jesus Christ our Lord, who lives and reigns with you in the unity of the Holy Spirit, one God, now and always through all ages of ages. (244)

C Amen

OR

A Let us pray for the whole people of God in Christ Jesus, and for all people according to their needs.

Prayers are included for the whole Church, the nations, those in need, the parish, special concerns.

The congregation may be invited to offer petitions and thanksgivings.

Prayers of confession may be included if the Brief Order for Confession and Forgiveness has not been used earlier.

The minister gives thanks for the faithful departed, especially for those who recently have died.

After each portion of the prayers:

A Lord, in your mercy,

C **hear our prayer.**

OR

A Let us pray to the Lord.

C **Lord, have mercy.**

The prayers conclude:

P Into your hands, O Lord, we commend all for whom we pray, trusting in your mercy; through your Son, Jesus Christ our Lord.

C **Amen**

C **Our Father in heaven,**
hallowed be your name,
your kingdom come,
your will be done,
on earth as in heaven.
Give us today our daily bread.
Forgive us our sins
as we forgive those
who sin against us.
Save us from the time of trial
and deliver us from evil.
For the kingdom, the power,
and the glory are yours,
now and forever. Amen

OR

C **Our Father, who art in heaven,**
hallowed be thy name,
thy kingdom come,
thy will be done,
on earth as it is in heaven.
Give us this day our daily bread;
and forgive us our trespasses,
as we forgive those
who trespass against us;
and lead us not into temptation,
but deliver us from evil.
For thine is the kingdom,
and the power, and the glory,
forever and ever. Amen

48. *The minister blesses the congregation.*

P The Lord bless you and keep you.
The Lord make his face shine on you
and be gracious to you.
The Lord look upon you with favor
and ✠ give you peace.

C **Amen**

BRIEF ORDER FOR CONFESSION AND FORGIVENESS

Stand

1. The minister leads the congregation in the invocation. The sign of the cross may be made by all in remembrance of their Baptism.

P In the name of the Father, and of the ✠ Son, and of the Holy Spirit.

C Amen

P Almighty God, to whom all hearts are open, all desires known, and from whom no secrets are hid: Cleanse the thoughts of our hearts by the inspiration of your Holy Spirit, that we may perfectly love you and worthily magnify your holy name, through Jesus Christ our Lord. (236)

C Amen

P If we say we have no sin, we deceive ourselves, and the truth is not in us. But if we confess our sins, God who is faithful and just will forgive our sins and cleanse us from all unrighteousness.

Kneel/Stand

2. Silence for reflection and self-examination.

P Most merciful God,

C we confess that we are in bondage to sin and cannot free ourselves. We have sinned against you in thought, word, and deed, by what we have done and by what we have left undone. We have not loved you with our whole heart; we have not loved our neighbors as ourselves. For the sake of your Son, Jesus Christ, have mercy on us. Forgive us, renew us, and lead us, so that we may delight in your will and walk in your ways, to the glory of your holy name. Amen

3. The minister stands and addresses the congregation.

P Almighty God, in his mercy, has given his Son to die for us and, for his sake, forgives us all our sins. As a called and ordained minister of the Church of Christ, and by his authority, I therefore declare to you the entire forgiveness of all your sins, in the name of the Father, and of the ✠ Son, and of the Holy Spirit.

OR

P In the mercy of almighty God, Jesus Christ was given to die for you, and for his sake God forgives you all your sins. To those who believe in Jesus Christ he gives the power to become the children of God and bestows on them the Holy Spirit.

C Amen

HOLY COMMUNION

Setting Two

1. The Brief Order for Confession and Forgiveness, page 77, may be used before this service.

2. The minister may announce the day and its significance before the Entrance Hymn, before the lessons, or at another appropriate time.

3. When there is no Communion, the service is concluded after the Creed as indicated.

Stand

4. The ENTRANCE HYMN or Psalm is sung.

5. The minister greets the congregation.

P The grace of our Lord Jesus Christ, the love of God, and the communion of the Holy Spirit be with you all.

C **And also with you.**

6. The KYRIE may follow.

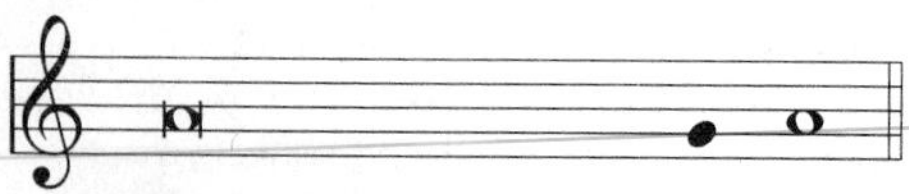

A In peace, let us pray to the Lord.

C **Lord, have mer - cy.**

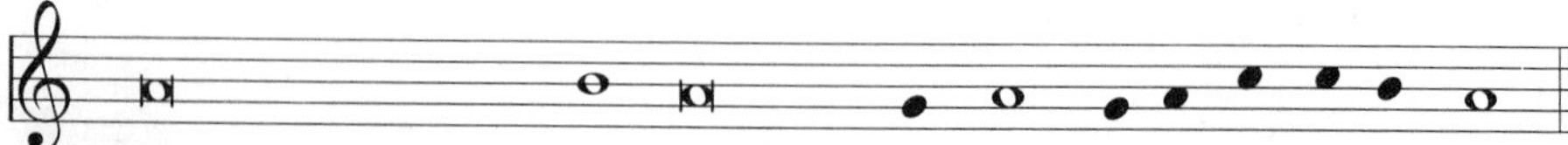

A For the peace from a-bove, and for our sal-vation, let us pray to the Lord.

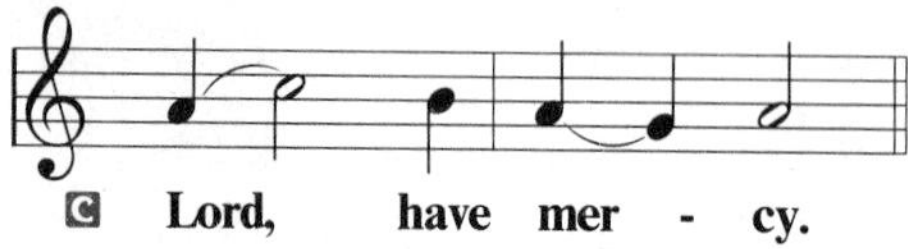

C **Lord, have mer - cy.**

A For the peace of the whole world, for the well-being of the Church of God,

and for the uni-ty of all, let us pray to the Lord.

C **Lord, have mer - cy.**

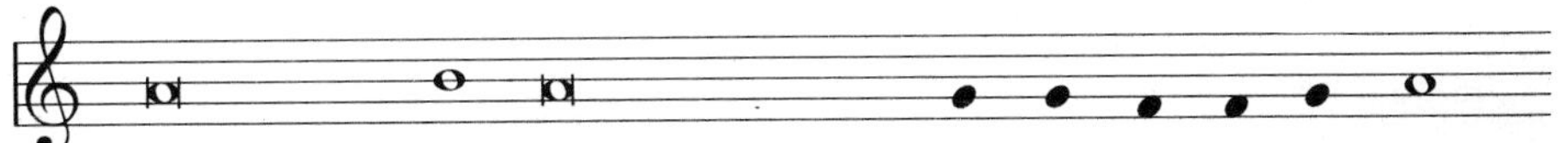

A For this holy house, and for all who offer here their wor-ship and praise,

let us pray to the Lord.

C **Lord, have mer - cy.**

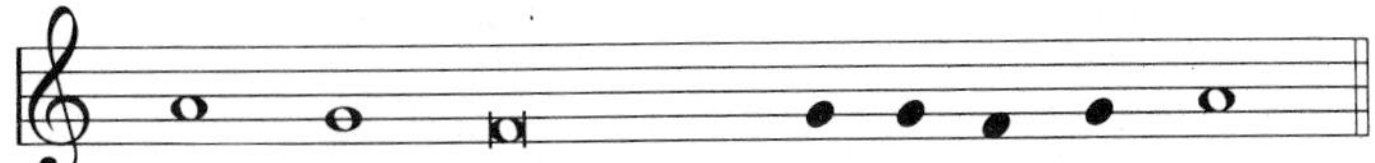

A Help, save, comfort, and de-fend us, gra-cious Lord.

C **A - men**

7. The HYMN OF PRAISE or another appropriate hymn may be sung.

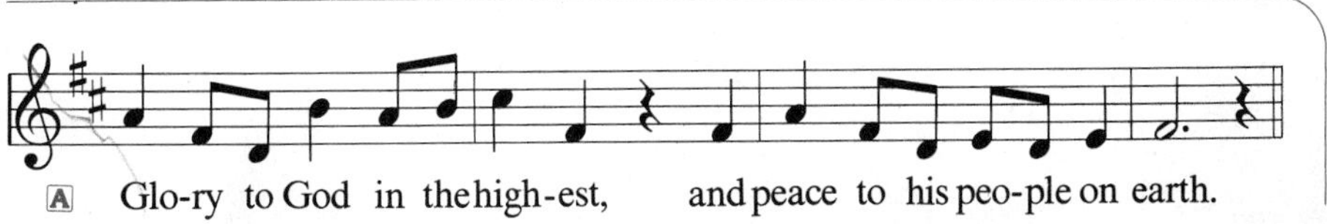
A Glo-ry to God in the high-est, and peace to his peo-ple on earth.

C
Lord God, heav - en - ly king, al-might - y God and
Fa - ther: We wor - ship you, we give you thanks, we
praise you for your glo - ry. Lord Je - sus Christ, on - ly
Son of the Fa - ther, Lord God, Lamb of God: You
take a - way the sin of the world; have mer - cy on
us. You are seat - ed at the right hand of the
Fa-ther; re-ceive our prayer. For you a-lone are the
Ho-ly One, you a-lone are the Lord, you a-
lone are the Most High, Je - sus Christ, with the Ho - ly Spir - it,
in the glo - ry of God the Fa-ther. A - men

OR

A This is the feast of vic-to-ry for our God. Al - le - lu - ia.
C Wor - thy is Christ, the Lamb who was slain, whose
blood set us free to be peo - ple of God.
Pow - er and rich - es and wis - dom and strength, and
hon - or and bless - ing and glo - ry are his.
This is the feast of vic - to - ry for our God. Al - le -
lu - ia. Sing with all the peo - ple of
God and join in the hymn of all cre - a - tion:
Bless - ing and hon - or and glo - ry and might be to
God and the Lamb for - ev - er. A - men.

This is the feast of vic-to-ry for our God, for the
Lamb who was slain has be-gun his reign. Al-
-le-lu-ia. Al-le-lu-ia.

8. The PRAYER OF THE DAY is said; the salutation may precede it.

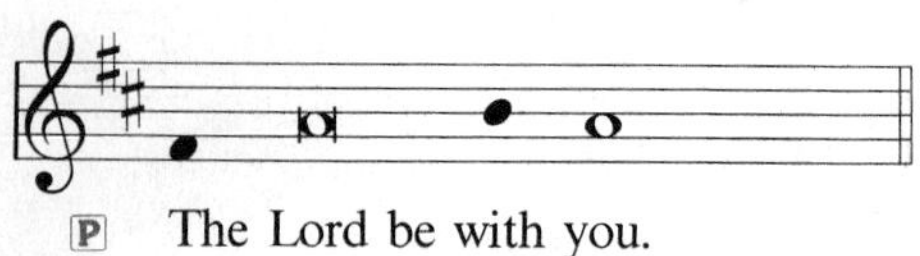
P The Lord be with you.

C And al-so with you.

P Let us pray. . . .

C Amen

Sit

9. The FIRST LESSON is announced and read.

A The First Lesson is from the ________________ chapter of ________________.

10. After the lesson the reader may say: "Here ends the reading."

11. The appointed PSALM is sung or said.

12. The SECOND LESSON is announced and read.

A The Second Lesson is from the ________________ chapter of ________________.

13. After the lesson the reader may say: "Here ends the reading."

14. The appointed VERSE is sung by the choir, or the congregation may sing the appropriate Verse below.

Stand

C
Al - le - lu - ia. Lord, to whom shall we go?
You have the words of e - ter - nal life. Al - le - lu - ia.

OR

LENT

C
Re-turn to the Lord, your God, for he is gra-cious and mer-ci-ful,
slow to an - ger, and a-bound - ing in stead - fast love.

15. The GOSPEL is announced.

P The Holy Gospel according to St. _______________, the _______________ chapter.

C
Glo - ry to you, O Lord.

16. After the reading the minister may say: "The Gospel of the Lord."

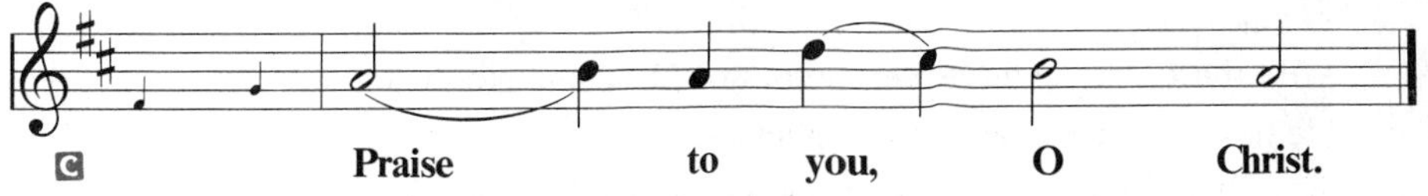
C
Praise to you, O Christ.

17. The Hymn of the Day may be sung before the Sermon.

Sit

18. The SERMON. Silence for reflection may follow.

Stand

19. The HYMN OF THE DAY is sung.

20. The CREED may be said. The Nicene Creed is said on all festivals and on Sundays in the seasons of Advent, Christmas, Lent, and Easter. The Apostles' Creed is said at other times. The Creed is omitted here if the service of Holy Baptism or another rite with a creed is used.

NICENE CREED

C We believe in one God,
the Father, the Almighty,
maker of heaven and earth,
of all that is, seen and unseen.

We believe in one Lord, Jesus Christ,
the only Son of God,
eternally begotten of the Father,
God from God, Light from Light,
true God from true God,
begotten, not made,
of one Being with the Father.
Through him all things were made.
For us and for our salvation
he came down from heaven;
by the power of the Holy Spirit
he became incarnate from the virgin Mary, and was made man.
For our sake he was crucified under Pontius Pilate;
he suffered death and was buried.
On the third day he rose again
in accordance with the Scriptures;
he ascended into heaven
and is seated at the right hand of the Father.
He will come again in glory to judge the living and the dead,
and his kingdom will have no end.

We believe in the Holy Spirit, the Lord, the giver of life,
who proceeds from the Father and the Son.
With the Father and the Son he is worshiped and glorified.
He has spoken through the prophets.
We believe in one holy catholic and apostolic Church.
We acknowledge one Baptism for the forgiveness of sins.
We look for the resurrection of the dead,
and the life of the world to come. Amen

OR

APOSTLES' CREED

C **I believe in God, the Father almighty,**
creator of heaven and earth.

I believe in Jesus Christ, his only Son, our Lord.
He was conceived by the power of the Holy Spirit
and born of the virgin Mary.
He suffered under Pontius Pilate,
was crucified, died, and was buried.
He descended into hell.*
On the third day he rose again.
He ascended into heaven,
and is seated at the right hand of the Father.
He will come again to judge the living and the dead.

I believe in the Holy Spirit,
the holy catholic Church,
the communion of saints,
the forgiveness of sins,
the resurrection of the body,
and the life everlasting. Amen

* *Or,* He descended to the dead.

21. When there is no Communion, the service continues on page 96. ▶

22. THE PRAYERS are said.

A Let us pray for the whole people of God in Christ Jesus, and for all people according to their needs.

Prayers are included for the whole Church, the nations, those in need, the parish, special concerns.

The congregation may be invited to offer petitions and thanksgivings.

Prayers of confession may be included if the Brief Order for Confession and Forgiveness has not been used earlier.

The minister gives thanks for the faithful departed, especially for those who recently have died.

After each portion of the prayers:

A Lord, in your mercy,

C **hear our prayer.**

OR

A Let us pray to the Lord.

C **Lord, have mercy.**

The prayers conclude:

P Into your hands, O Lord, we commend all for whom we pray, trusting in your mercy; through your Son, Jesus Christ our Lord.

C **Amen**

23. The PEACE is shared at this time or after the Lord's Prayer, prior to the distribution.

P The peace of the Lord be with you always.

C And also with you.

The ministers and congregation may greet one another in the name of the Lord.

Peace be with you. R Peace be with you.

Sit

24. The OFFERING is received as the Lord's table is prepared.

25. The appointed OFFERTORY may be sung by the choir as the gifts are presented, or the congregation may sing one of the following offertories, or an appropriate hymn or psalm may be sung.

Stand

C Let the vine - yards be fruit - ful, Lord, and fill to the brim our
cup of bless - ing. Gath - er a har - vest from the seeds that were sown, that
we may be fed with the bread of life. Gath - er the hopes and
dreams of all; u - nite them with the prayers we of - fer. Grace our ta - ble
with your pres - ence, and give us a fore - taste of the feast to come.

OR

C What shall I ren - der to the Lord for all his ben - e-fits to
me? I will of - fer the sac - ri - fice of thanks - giv - ing and will
call on the name of the Lord. I will take the cup of sal -
va-tion and will call on the name of the Lord. I will pay my vows to the
Lord now in the pres-ence of all his peo - ple, in the courts of the Lord's
house, in the midst of you, O Je-ru - sa - lem.

26. *After the gifts have been presented, one of these prayers is said.*

A Let us pray.

A Merciful Father,

C we offer with joy and thanksgiving what you have first given us—our selves, our time, and our possessions, signs of your gracious love. Receive them for the sake of him who offered himself for us, Jesus Christ our Lord. Amen (239)

OR

A Blessed are you,

C **O Lord our God, maker of all things. Through your goodness you have blessed us with these gifts. With them we offer ourselves to your service and dedicate our lives to the care and redemption of all that you have made, for the sake of him who gave himself for us, Jesus Christ our Lord. Amen** (240)

27. The ministers make ready the bread and wine.

28. The GREAT THANKSGIVING is begun by the minister standing at the altar.

P The Lord be with you.

C And al - so with you.

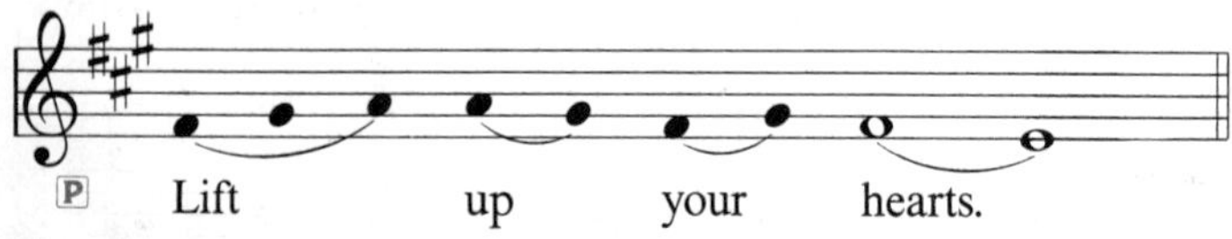
P Lift up your hearts.

C We lift them to the Lord.

P Let us give thanks to the Lord our God.

C It is right to give him thanks and praise.

29. The preface appropriate to the day or season is sung or said.

P It is indeed right and salutary . . . we praise your name and join their unending hymn:

C Ho - ly, ho - ly, ho - ly Lord, Lord God of
pow'r and might: Heav'n and earth are full of your
glo - ry. Ho - san - na in the high - est.
Bless - ed is he who comes in the name
of the Lord. Ho - san - na in the high - est.

30. The minister continues, using one of the sections below.

31. The minister may say:

P Holy God, mighty Lord,
gracious Father:
Endless is your mercy
and eternal your reign.

You have filled all creation
with light and life;
heaven and earth
are full of your glory.

Through Abraham you promised
to bless all nations.
You rescued Israel,
your chosen people.

Through the prophets
you renewed your promise;
and, at this end of all the ages,
you sent your Son,
who in words and deeds
proclaimed your kingdom
and was obedient to your will,
even to giving his life.

OR

32. The minister may say:

P In the night
in which he was betrayed,
our Lord Jesus took bread,
and gave thanks; broke it,
and gave it to his disciples,
saying: Take and eat;
this is my body, given for you.

Do this for the remembrance of me.

Again, after supper,
he took the cup, gave thanks,
and gave it for all to drink,
saying: This cup is
the new covenant in my blood,
shed for you and for all people
for the forgiveness of sin.

Do this for the remembrance of me.

OR

In the night
in which he was betrayed,
our Lord Jesus took bread,
and gave thanks; broke it,
and gave it to his disciples,
saying: Take and eat;
this is my body, given for you.
Do this for the remembrance of me.

Again, after supper,
he took the cup, gave thanks,
and gave it for all to drink,
saying: This cup is
the new covenant in my blood,
shed for you and for all people
for the forgiveness of sin.
Do this for the remembrance of me.

For as often as we eat
of this bread
and drink from this cup,
we proclaim the Lord's death,
until he comes.

C **Christ has died. Christ is risen. Christ will come again.**

P Therefore, gracious Father,
with this bread and cup
we remember the life
our Lord offered for us.

And, believing the witness
of his resurrection,
we await his coming in power
to share with us
the great and promised feast.

C **Amen. Come, Lord Jesus.**

P Send now, we pray,
your Holy Spirit,
the spirit of our Lord
and of his resurrection,
that we who receive
the Lord's body and blood
may live to the praise
of your glory
and receive our inheritance
with all your saints in light.

C **Amen. Come, Holy Spirit.**

P Join our prayers

33. The minister may say:

P Blessed are you,
Lord of heaven and earth.

In mercy for our fallen world
you gave your only Son,
that all those who believe in him
should not perish,
but have eternal life.

We give thanks to you
for the salvation
you have prepared
for us through Jesus Christ.

Send now your Holy Spirit
into our hearts,
that we may receive our Lord
with a living faith
as he comes to us
in his holy supper.

C **Amen. Come, Lord Jesus.**

P In the night
in which he was betrayed
our Lord Jesus took bread,
and gave thanks; broke it,
and gave it to his disciples,
saying: Take and eat;
this is my body, given for you.
Do this for the remembrance of me.

Again, after supper,
he took the cup, gave thanks,
and gave it for all to drink,
saying: This cup is
the new covenant in my blood,
shed for you and for all people
for the forgiveness of sin.
Do this for the remembrance of me.

with those of your servants
of every time and every place,
and unite them
with the ceaseless petitions
of our great high priest
until he comes
as victorious Lord of all.

C Through him, with him, in him, in the u-ni-ty
of the Ho-ly Spir-it, all hon-or and glo-ry is
yours, al-might-y Fa-ther, now and for-ev-er. A-men

C Our Father in heaven,
hallowed be your name,
your kingdom come,
your will be done,
on earth as in heaven.
Give us today our daily bread.
Forgive us our sins
as we forgive those
who sin against us.
Save us from the time of trial
and deliver us from evil.
For the kingdom, the power,
and the glory are yours,
now and forever. Amen

OR

C Our Father, who art in heaven,
hallowed be thy name,
thy kingdom come,
thy will be done,
on earth as it is in heaven.
Give us this day our daily bread;
and forgive us our trespasses,
as we forgive those
who trespass against us;
and lead us not into temptation,
but deliver us from evil.
For thine is the kingdom,
and the power, and the glory,
forever and ever. Amen

Sit

34. The COMMUNION follows. The bread may be broken for distribution.

35. The presiding minister and the assisting ministers receive the bread and wine and then give them to those who come to receive. As the ministers give the bread and wine, they say these words to each communicant:

The body of Christ, given for you.

The blood of Christ, shed for you.

36. The communicant may say: "Amen."

37. Hymns and other music may be used during the ministration of Communion. One of the hymns may be the following.

C Lamb of God, you take a-way the sin of the world; have
mer-cy on us. Lamb of God, you take a-way the
sin of the world; have mer-cy on us. Lamb of
God, you take a-way the sin of the world;
grant us peace, grant us peace.

Stand

38. After all have returned to their places, the minister may say these or similar words.

P The body and blood of our Lord Jesus Christ strengthen you and keep you in his grace.

C **Amen**

39. The POST-COMMUNION canticle or an appropriate hymn is sung as the table is cleared.

C Thank the Lord and sing his praise; tell ev-'ry-one what

he has done. Let ev - 'ry - one who seeks the Lord re -
joice and proud - ly bear his name. He re - calls his prom - is -
es and leads his peo - ple forth in joy with shouts of thanks -
giv - ing. Al - le - lu - ia. Al - le - lu - ia.
OR
C Lord, now you let your ser - vant go in peace; your
word has been ful - filled. My own eyes have seen the sal -
va - tion which you have pre - pared in the sight of ev - 'ry
peo - ple: A light to re - veal you to the na -
tions and the glo - ry of your peo - ple Is - ra - el.

Glo-ry to the Fa - ther, and to the Son, and to the Ho - ly
Spir - it, as it was in the be - gin - ning, is
now, and will be for - ev - er. A - men

40. One of these prayers is said.

A We give you thanks, almighty God, that you have refreshed us through the healing power of this gift of life; and we pray that in your mercy you would strengthen us, through this gift, in faith toward you and in fervent love toward one another; for the sake of Jesus Christ our Lord. (241)

OR

A Pour out upon us the spirit of your love, O Lord, and unite the wills of those whom you have fed with one heavenly food; through Jesus Christ our Lord. (242)

OR

A Almighty God, you gave your Son both as a sacrifice for sin and a model of the godly life. Enable us to receive him always with thanksgiving, and to conform our lives to his; through the same Jesus Christ our Lord. (243)

C Amen

41. Silence for reflection.

42. The minister blesses the congregation.

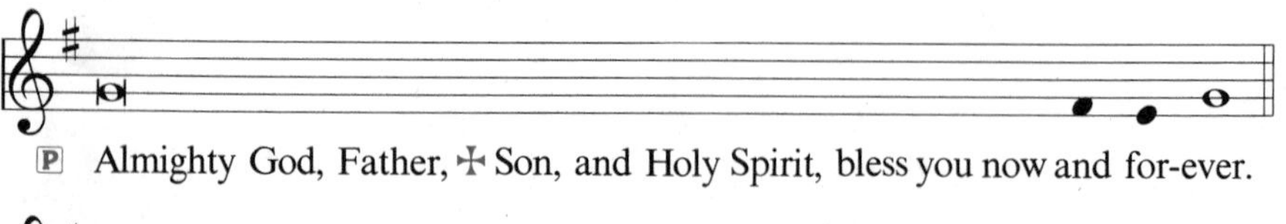

P Almighty God, Father, ✠ Son, and Holy Spirit, bless you now and for-ever.

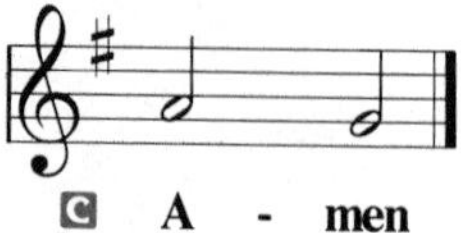

C A - men

OR

P
The Lord bless you and keep you.
The Lord make his face shine on you
and be gracious to you.
The Lord look upon you with favor and .... ☩ give you peace.
C
A - men

43. The minister may dismiss the congregation.

A Go in peace. Serve the Lord.

C **Thanks be to God.**

44. ▶ When there is no Communion, the service concludes as follows.

45. The OFFERING is received and may be presented at the altar.

46. The following Psalm or an appropriate hymn may be sung when the gifts are presented.

Stand

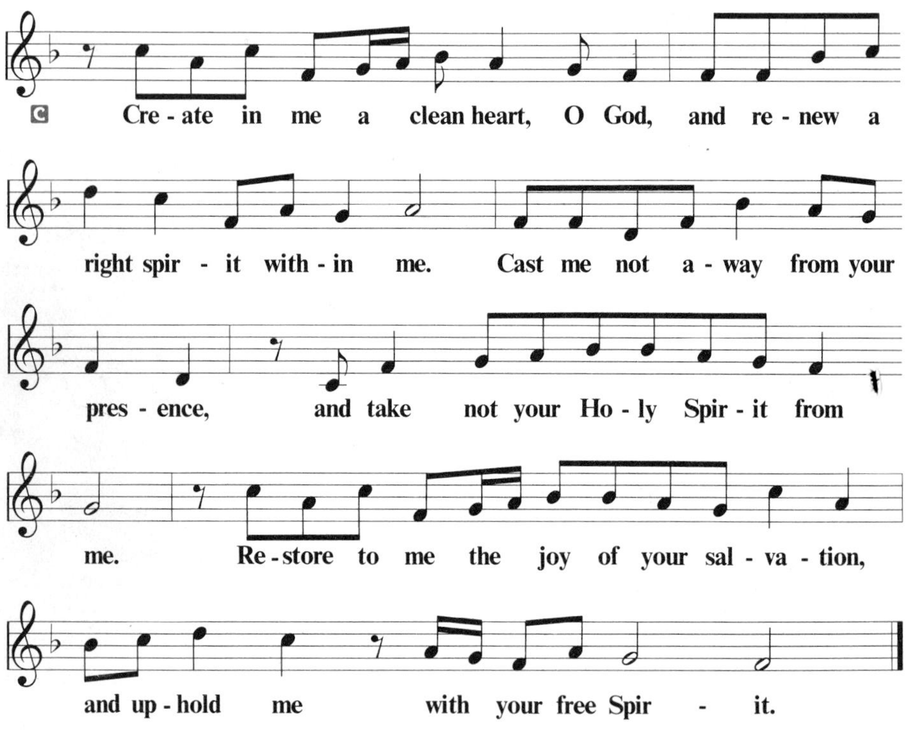

C Cre - ate in me a clean heart, O God, and re - new a
right spir - it with - in me. Cast me not a - way from your
pres - ence, and take not your Ho - ly Spir - it from
me. Re - store to me the joy of your sal - va - tion,
and up - hold me with your free Spir - it.

47. THE PRAYERS are said. One of the following or another form of prayer may be used.

A Let us pray.

A O Lord our God, you have commanded the light to shine out of darkness, and you have again brought us to your house of prayer to praise your goodness and ask for your gifts. Accept now in your endless mercy the sacrifice of our worship and thanksgiving, and grant us those requests which will be wholesome for us. Make us to be children of the light and of the day and heirs of your everlasting inheritance. Remember, O Lord, according to the multitude of your mercies, your whole Church, all who join with us in prayer, all our sisters and brothers wherever they may be in your vast kingdom who stand in need of your help and comfort. Pour out upon them the riches of your mercy, so that we, redeemed in soul and body and steadfast in faith, may ever praise your wonderful and holy name; through Jesus Christ our Lord, who lives and reigns with you in the unity of the Holy Spirit, one God, now and always through all ages of ages. (244)

C Amen

OR

Ⓐ Let us pray for the whole people of God in Christ Jesus, and for all people according to their needs.

Prayers are included for the whole Church, the nations, those in need, the parish, special concerns.

The congregation may be invited to offer petitions and thanksgivings.

Prayers of confession may be included if the Brief Order for Confession and Forgiveness has not been used earlier.

The minister gives thanks for the faithful departed, especially for those who recently have died.

After each portion of the prayers:

Ⓐ Lord, in your mercy,

Ⓒ **hear our prayer.**

OR

Ⓐ Let us pray to the Lord.

Ⓒ **Lord, have mercy.**

The prayers conclude:

Ⓟ Into your hands, O Lord, we commend all for whom we pray, trusting in your mercy; through your Son, Jesus Christ our Lord.

Ⓒ **Amen**

Ⓒ **Our Father in heaven,**
hallowed be your name,
your kingdom come,
your will be done,
on earth as in heaven.
Give us today our daily bread.
Forgive us our sins
as we forgive those
who sin against us.
Save us from the time of trial
and deliver us from evil.
For the kingdom, the power,
and the glory are yours,
now and forever. Amen

OR

Ⓒ **Our Father, who art in heaven,**
hallowed be thy name,
thy kingdom come,
thy will be done,
on earth as it is in heaven.
Give us this day our daily bread;
and forgive us our trespasses,
as we forgive those
who trespass against us;
and lead us not into temptation,
but deliver us from evil.
For thine is the kingdom,
and the power, and the glory,
forever and ever. Amen

48. *The minister blesses the congregation.*

Ⓟ The Lord bless you and keep you.
The Lord make his face shine on you
and be gracious to you.
The Lord look upon you with favor
and ☩ give you peace.

Ⓒ **Amen**

BRIEF ORDER FOR CONFESSION AND FORGIVENESS

Stand

1. The minister leads the congregation in the invocation. The sign of the cross may be made by all in remembrance of their Baptism.

P In the name of the Father, and of the ☩ Son, and of the Holy Spirit.

C **Amen**

P Almighty God, to whom all hearts are open, all desires known, and from whom no secrets are hid: Cleanse the thoughts of our hearts by the inspiration of your Holy Spirit, that we may perfectly love you and worthily magnify your holy name, through Jesus Christ our Lord. (236)

C **Amen**

P If we say we have no sin, we deceive ourselves, and the truth is not in us. But if we confess our sins, God who is faithful and just will forgive our sins and cleanse us from all unrighteousness.

Kneel/Stand

2. Silence for reflection and self-examination.

P Most merciful God,

C **we confess that we are in bondage to sin and cannot free ourselves. We have sinned against you in thought, word, and deed, by what we have done and by what we have left undone. We have not loved you with our whole heart; we have not loved our neighbors as ourselves. For the sake of your Son, Jesus Christ, have mercy on us. Forgive us, renew us, and lead us, so that we may delight in your will and walk in your ways, to the glory of your holy name. Amen**

3. The minister stands and addresses the congregation.

P Almighty God, in his mercy, has given his Son to die for us and, for his sake, forgives us all our sins. As a called and ordained minister of the Church of Christ, and by his authority, I therefore declare to you the entire forgiveness of all your sins, in the name of the Father, and of the ☩ Son, and of the Holy Spirit.

OR

P In the mercy of almighty God, Jesus Christ was given to die for you, and for his sake God forgives you all your sins. To those who believe in Jesus Christ he gives the power to become the children of God and bestows on them the Holy Spirit.

C **Amen**

HOLY COMMUNION

Setting Three

1. The Brief Order for Confession and Forgiveness, page 98, may be used before this service.

2. The minister may announce the day and its significance before the Entrance Hymn, before the lessons, or at another appropriate time.

3. When there is no Communion, the service is concluded after the Creed as indicated.

Stand

4. The ENTRANCE HYMN or Psalm is sung.

5. The minister greets the congregation.

P The grace of our Lord Jesus Christ, the love of God, and the communion of the Holy Spirit be with you all.

C And also with you.

6. The KYRIE may follow.

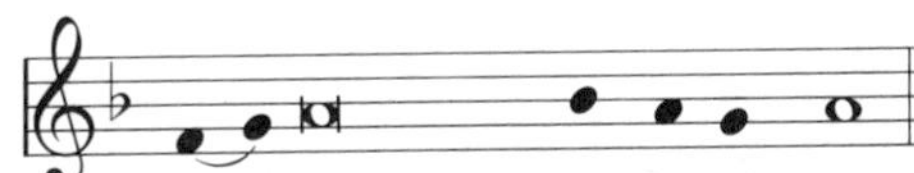

A In peace, let us pray to the Lord.

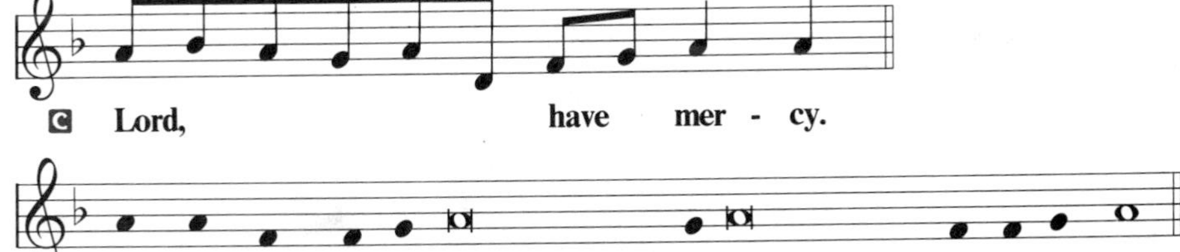

C Lord, have mer - cy.

A For the peace from a-bove, and for our sal-va-tion, let us pray to the Lord.

C Lord, have mer - cy.

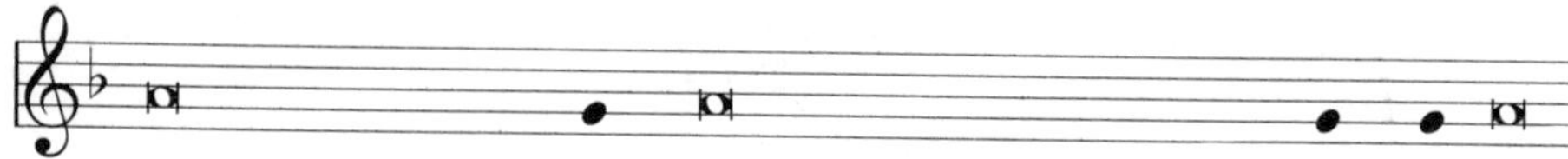

A For the peace of the whole world, for the well-being of the Church of God,

and for the uni-ty of all, let us pray to the Lord.

C **Lord, have mer - cy.**

A For this ho-ly house, and for all who of-fer here their wor-ship and praise,

let us pray to the Lord.

C **Lord, have mer - cy.**

A Help, save, com-fort, and de-fend us, gra-cious Lord.

C **A - men**

7. The HYMN OF PRAISE or another appropriate hymn may be sung.

A Glo - ry to God in the high - est, and peace to his peo-ple on earth.

C
Lord God, heav'n-ly king, al-might-y God and Fa - ther:
We wor - ship you, we give you thanks, we
praise you for your glo - ry. Lord Je-sus Christ, on-ly
Son of the Fa - ther, O Lord God, Lamb of
God: You take a-way the sin of the world; have
mer-cy on us. You are seat-ed at the right hand of the
Fa - ther; re-ceive our prayer. For you a-lone
are the Ho - ly One, you a-lone are the
Lord, you a-lone are the Most High, Je-sus Christ,
with the Ho - ly Spir-it, in the glo - ry of

God the Fa - ther. A - men
OR
A Al - le - lu - ia. This is the feast of vic - to - ry for our God.
C Al - le - lu - ia. Wor - thy is Christ, the Lamb who was slain, whose
blood set us free to be peo - ple of God. Pow - er, rich - es,
wis-dom, and strength, hon-or, and bless-ing, and glo - ry are his.
A This is the feast of vic - to - ry for our God. C Sing with all the
peo-ple of God, and join in the hymn of all cre - a -
tion: Bless-ing, hon - or, glo - ry, and might be to God and the Lamb for-
ev - er. A - men. This is the feast of vic - to - ry for our God, for the
Lamb who was slain has be - gun his reign. Al - le - lu - ia.

8. The PRAYER OF THE DAY is said; the salutation may precede it.

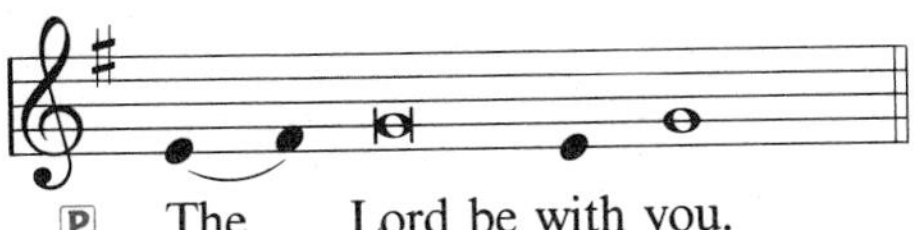
P The Lord be with you.

C **And al - so with you.**

P Let us pray. . . .

C **Amen**

Sit

9. The FIRST LESSON is announced and read.

A The First Lesson is from the ______________ chapter of ______________.

10. After the lesson the reader may say: "Here ends the reading."

11. The appointed PSALM is sung or said.

12. The SECOND LESSON is announced and read.

A The Second Lesson is from the ______________ chapter of ______________.

13. After the lesson the reader may say: "Here ends the reading."

14. The appointed VERSE is sung by the choir, or the congregation may sing the appropriate Verse below.

Stand

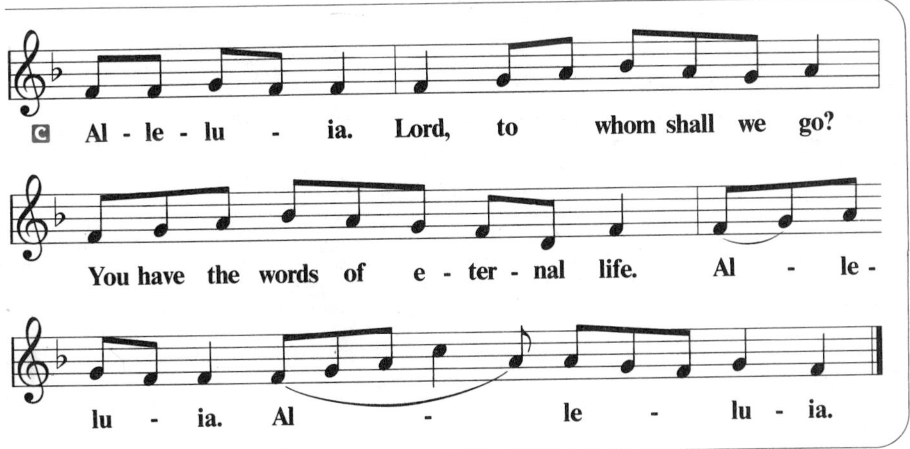
C **Al - le - lu - ia. Lord, to whom shall we go?**
You have the words of e - ter - nal life. Al - le -
lu - ia. Al - le - lu - ia.

OR

LENT

C Re - turn to the Lord, your God, for he is
gra - cious and mer - ci - ful, slow to an - ger,
and a - bound - ing in stead - fast love.

15. The GOSPEL is announced.

P The Holy Gospel according to St. ______________, the ______________ chapter.

C
Glo - ry to you, O Lord.

16. After the reading the minister may say: "The Gospel of the Lord."

C
Praise to you, O Christ.

17. The Hymn of the Day may be sung before the Sermon.

Sit

18. The SERMON. Silence for reflection may follow.

Stand

19. The HYMN OF THE DAY is sung.

20. The CREED may be said. The Nicene Creed is said on all festivals and on Sundays in the seasons of Advent, Christmas, Lent, and Easter. The Apostles' Creed is said at other times. The Creed is omitted here if the service of Holy Baptism or another rite with a creed is used.

NICENE CREED

C **We believe in one God,**
the Father, the Almighty,
maker of heaven and earth,
of all that is, seen and unseen.

We believe in one Lord, Jesus Christ,
the only Son of God,
eternally begotten of the Father,
God from God, Light from Light,
true God from true God,
begotten, not made,
of one Being with the Father.
Through him all things were made.
For us and for our salvation
he came down from heaven;
by the power of the Holy Spirit
he became incarnate from the virgin Mary, and was made man.
For our sake he was crucified under Pontius Pilate;
he suffered death and was buried.
On the third day he rose again
in accordance with the Scriptures;
he ascended into heaven
and is seated at the right hand of the Father.
He will come again in glory to judge the living and the dead,
and his kingdom will have no end.

We believe in the Holy Spirit, the Lord, the giver of life,
who proceeds from the Father and the Son.
With the Father and the Son he is worshiped and glorified.
He has spoken through the prophets.
We believe in one holy catholic and apostolic Church.
We acknowledge one Baptism for the forgiveness of sins.
We look for the resurrection of the dead,
and the life of the world to come. Amen

OR

APOSTLES' CREED

C **I believe in God, the Father almighty,**
creator of heaven and earth.

I believe in Jesus Christ, his only Son, our Lord.
He was conceived by the power of the Holy Spirit
and born of the virgin Mary.
He suffered under Pontius Pilate,
was crucified, died, and was buried.
He descended into hell.*
On the third day he rose again.
He ascended into heaven,
and is seated at the right hand of the Father.
He will come again to judge the living and the dead.

I believe in the Holy Spirit,
the holy catholic Church,
the communion of saints,
the forgiveness of sins,
the resurrection of the body,
and the life everlasting. Amen

* *Or,* He descended to the dead.

21. *When there is no Communion, the service continues on page 118.* ▶

22. *THE PRAYERS are said.*

A Let us pray for the whole people of God in Christ Jesus, and for all people according to their needs.

Prayers are included for the whole Church, the nations, those in need, the parish, special concerns.

The congregation may be invited to offer petitions and thanksgivings.

Prayers of confession may be included if the Brief Order for Confession and Forgiveness has not been used earlier.

The minister gives thanks for the faithful departed, especially for those who recently have died.

After each portion of the prayers:

A Lord, in your mercy,

C **hear our prayer.**

OR

A Let us pray to the Lord.

C **Lord, have mercy.**

The prayers conclude:

P Into your hands, O Lord, we commend all for whom we pray, trusting in your mercy; through your Son, Jesus Christ our Lord.

C **Amen**

23. The PEACE is shared at this time or after the Lord's Prayer, prior to the distribution.

P The peace of the Lord be with you always.

C **And also with you.**

The ministers and congregation may greet one another in the name of the Lord.

Peace be with you. ℟ Peace be with you.

Sit

24. The OFFERING is received as the Lord's table is prepared.

25. The appointed OFFERTORY may be sung by the choir as the gifts are presented, or the congregation may sing one of the following offertories, or an appropriate hymn or psalm may be sung.

Stand

C
Let the vine-yards be fruit - ful, Lord, and fill to the brim our
cup of bless-ing. Ga - ther a har - vest from the seeds that were
sown, that we may be fed with the bread of life.
Gath-er the hopes and dreams of all; u - nite them with the
prayers we of - fer. Grace our ta - ble with your pres - ence, and
give us a fore - taste of the feast to come.

OR

C What shall I ren - der to the Lord for all his
ben - e - fits to me? I will of - fer the sac - ri - fice
of thanks-giv - ing and will call on the name of the
Lord. I will take the cup of sal - va - tion and will
call on the name of the Lord. I will pay my
vows to the Lord now in the pres - ence of
all his peo - ple, in the courts of the Lord's house,
in the midst of you, O Je - ru - sa - lem.

26. After the gifts have been presented, one of these prayers is said.

A Let us pray.

A Merciful Father,

C we offer with joy and thanksgiving what you have first given us—our selves, our time, and our possessions, signs of your gracious love. Receive them for the sake of him who offered himself for us, Jesus Christ our Lord. Amen (239)

OR

A Blessed are you,

C O Lord our God, maker of all things. Through your goodness you have blessed us with these gifts. With them we offer ourselves to your service and dedicate our lives to the care and redemption of all that you have made, for the sake of him who gave himself for us, Jesus Christ our Lord. Amen (240)

27. The ministers make ready the bread and wine.

28. The GREAT THANKSGIVING is begun by the minister standing at the altar.

P The Lord be with you.

C And al - so with you.

P Lift up your hearts.

C We lift them to the Lord.

P Let us give thanks to the Lord our God.

C It is right to give him thanks and praise.

29. The preface appropriate to the day or season is sung or said.

P It is indeed right and salutary . . . we praise your name and join their unending hymn:

C Ho - ly, ho - ly, ho - ly
Lord, God of pow'r and might: Heav - en and
earth are full of your glo - ry. Ho -
san - na in the high - est. Bless - ed is
he who comes in the name of the Lord.
Ho - san - na in the high - est.

30. The minister continues, using one of the sections below.

31. The minister may say:

P Holy God, mighty Lord,
gracious Father:
Endless is your mercy
and eternal your reign.

You have filled all creation
with light and life;
heaven and earth
are full of your glory.

Through Abraham you promised
to bless all nations.
You rescued Israel,
your chosen people.

Through the prophets
you renewed your promise;
and, at this end of all the ages,
you sent your Son,

OR

32. The minister may say:

P In the night
in which he was betrayed,
our Lord Jesus took bread,
and gave thanks; broke it,
and gave it to his disciples,
saying: Take and eat;
this is my body, given for you.

Do this for the remembrance of me.

Again, after supper,
he took the cup, gave thanks,
and gave it for all to drink,
saying: This cup is
the new covenant in my blood,
shed for you and for all people
for the forgiveness of sin.

Do this for the remembrance of me.

who in words and deeds
proclaimed your kingdom
and was obedient to your will,
even to giving his life.

In the night
in which he was betrayed,
our Lord Jesus took bread,
and gave thanks; broke it,
and gave it to his disciples,
saying: Take and eat;
this is my body, given for you.

Do this for the remembrance of me.

Again, after supper,
he took the cup, gave thanks,
and gave it for all to drink,
saying: This cup is
the new covenant in my blood,
shed for you and for all people
for the forgiveness of sin.

Do this for the remembrance of me.

For as often as we eat
of this bread
and drink from this cup,
we proclaim the Lord's death,
until he comes.

C **Christ has died. Christ is risen. Christ will come again.**

P Therefore, gracious Father,
with this bread and cup
we remember the life
our Lord offered for us.

And, believing the witness
of his resurrection,
we await his coming in power
to share with us
the great and promised feast.

C **Amen. Come, Lord Jesus.**

P Send now, we pray,
your Holy Spirit,
the spirit of our Lord
and of his resurrection,
that we who receive
the Lord's body and blood
may live to the praise
of your glory
and receive our inheritance

OR

33. The minister may say:

P Blessed are you,
Lord of heaven and earth.

In mercy for our fallen world
you gave your only Son,
that all those who believe in him
should not perish,
but have eternal life.

We give thanks to you
for the salvation
you have prepared
for us through Jesus Christ.

Send now your Holy Spirit
into our hearts,
that we may receive our Lord
with a living faith
as he comes to us
in his holy supper.

C **Amen. Come, Lord Jesus.**

P In the night
in which he was betrayed
our Lord Jesus took bread,
and gave thanks; broke it,
and gave it to his disciples,
saying: Take and eat;
this is my body, given for you.

Do this for the remembrance of me.

Again, after supper,
he took the cup, gave thanks,
and gave it for all to drink,
saying: This cup is
the new covenant in my blood,
shed for you and for all people
for the forgiveness of sin.

Do this for the remembrance of me.

with all your saints in light.

C Amen. Come, Holy Spirit.

P Join our prayers
with those of your servants
of every time and every place,
and unite them
with the ceaseless petitions
of our great high priest
until he comes
as victorious Lord of all.

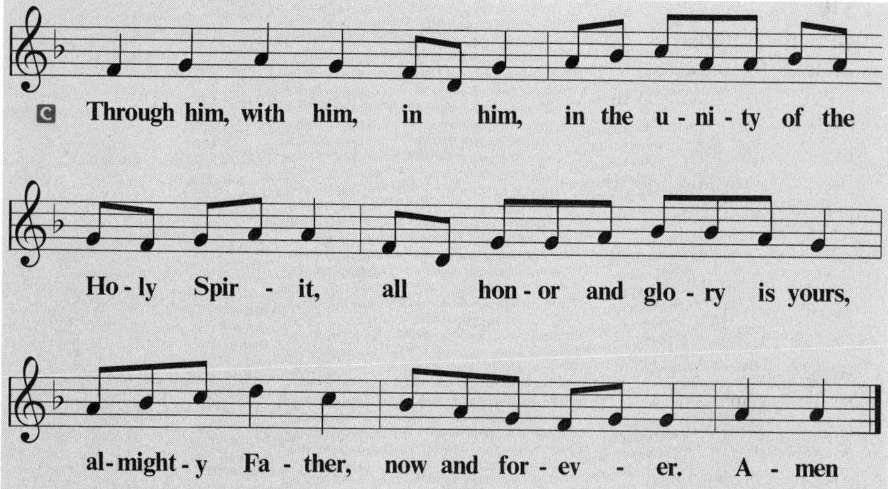

C Through him, with him, in him, in the u - ni - ty of the
Ho - ly Spir - it, all hon - or and glo - ry is yours,
al - might - y Fa - ther, now and for - ev - er. A - men

C Our Fa - ther in heav - en, hal - lowed be your name,
your king - dom come, your will be done,
on earth as in heav - en. Give us to - day our

dai - ly bread. For - give us our sins as
we for - give those who sin a - gainst us. Save us from the
time of tri - al and de - liv - er us from e - vil.
For the king - dom, the pow'r, and the glo - ry are
yours, now and for - ev - er. A - men

OR

C Our Father, who art in heaven,
hallowed be thy name,
thy kingdom come,
thy will be done,
on earth as it is in heaven.
Give us this day our daily bread;
and forgive us our trespasses,
as we forgive those
who trespass against us;
and lead us not into temptation,
but deliver us from evil.
For thine is the kingdom,
and the power, and the glory,
forever and ever. Amen

Sit

34. The COMMUNION follows. The bread may be broken for distribution.

35. The presiding minister and the assisting ministers receive the bread and wine and then give them to those who come to receive. As the ministers give the bread and wine, they say these words to each communicant:

The body of Christ, given for you.

The blood of Christ, shed for you.

36. The communicant may say: "Amen."

37. Hymns and other music may be used during the ministration of Communion. One of the hymns may be the following.

C
Lamb of God, you take a - way the sin of the world; have mer - cy on us.
Lamb of God, you take a - way the sin of the world; have mer - cy on us.
Lamb of God, you take a - way the sin of the world; grant us peace. A - men

Stand

38. After all have returned to their places, the minister may say these or similar words.

P The body and blood of our Lord Jesus Christ strengthen you and keep you in his grace.

C Amen

39. The POST-COMMUNION canticle or an appropriate hymn is sung as the table is cleared.

C Thank the Lord and sing his praise; tell ev - 'ry -
one what he has done. Let ev - 'ry - one who
seeks the Lord re - joice and proud - ly bear his name.
He re - calls his prom - is - es and leads his peo - ple
forth in joy with shouts of thanks - giv - ing.
Al - le - lu - ia. Al - le - lu - ia.

OR

C
Lord, now you let your ser - vant go in peace;
your word has been ful - filled. My own eyes have
seen the sal - va - tion which you have pre - pared
in the sight of ev - 'ry peo - ple: A light to re -
veal you to the na - tions and the glo - ry of your
peo - ple Is - ra - el. Glo - ry to the
Fa - ther, and to the Son, and to the Ho - ly Spir - it,
as it was in the be - gin - ning, is now, and will
be for - ev - er. A - men

40. One of these prayers is said.

🅐 Let us pray.

🅐 We give you thanks, almighty God, that you have refreshed us through the healing power of this gift of life; and we pray that in your mercy you would strengthen us, through this gift, in faith toward you and in fervent love toward one another; for the sake of Jesus Christ our Lord. (241)

OR

🅐 Pour out upon us the spirit of your love, O Lord, and unite the wills of those whom you have fed with one heavenly food; through Jesus Christ our Lord. (242)

OR

🅐 Almighty God, you gave your Son both as a sacrifice for sin and a model of the godly life. Enable us to receive him always with thanksgiving, and to conform our lives to his; through the same Jesus Christ our Lord. (243)

🅒 **Amen**

41. Silence for reflection.

42. The minister blesses the congregation.

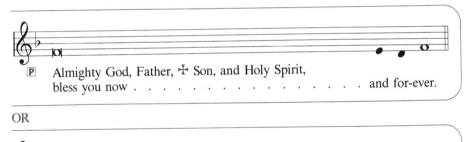

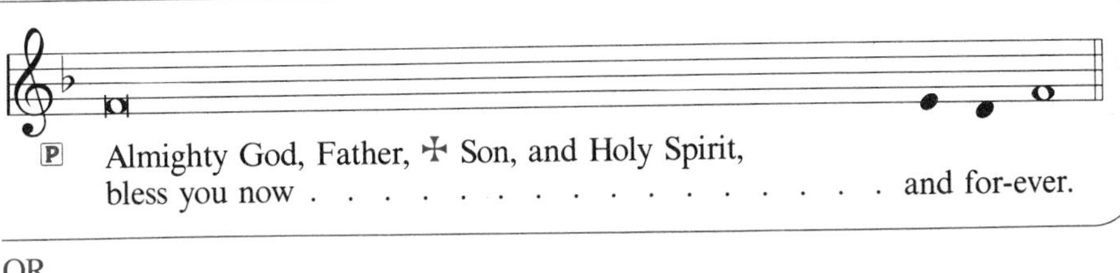
🅟 Almighty God, Father, ✠ Son, and Holy Spirit,
bless you now . . . . and for-ever.

OR

🅟 The Lord bless you and keep you.
The Lord make his face shine on you
and be gracious to you.
The Lord look upon you with favor and. . . . . ✠ give you peace.

🅒 A - men

43. The minister may dismiss the congregation.

🅐 Go in peace. Serve the Lord.

🅒 **Thanks be to God.**

44. ▶ When there is no Communion, the service concludes as follows.

45. The OFFERING is received and may be presented at the altar.

46. The following Psalm or an appropriate hymn may be sung when the gifts are presented.

Stand

C Cre - ate in me a clean heart, O God, and re - new a
right spir - it with - in me. Cast me not a - way from your
pres - ence, and take not your Ho - ly Spir - it from
me. Re - store to me the joy of your sal - va - tion,
and up - hold me with your free Spir - it.

47. THE PRAYERS are said. One of the following or another form of prayer may be used.

A Let us pray.

A O Lord our God, you have commanded the light to shine out of darkness, and you have again brought us to your house of prayer to praise your goodness and ask for your gifts. Accept now in your endless mercy the sacrifice of our worship and thanksgiving, and grant us those requests which will be wholesome for us. Make us to be children of the light and of the day and heirs of your everlasting inheritance. Remember, O Lord, according to the multitude of your mercies, your whole Church, all who join with us in prayer, all our sisters and brothers wherever they may be in your vast kingdom who stand in need of your help and comfort. Pour out upon them the riches of your mercy, so that we, redeemed in soul and body and steadfast in faith, may ever praise your wonderful and holy name; through Jesus Christ our Lord, who lives and reigns with you in the unity of the Holy Spirit, one God, now and always through all ages of ages. (244)

C **Amen**

OR

A Let us pray for the whole people of God in Christ Jesus, and for all people according to their needs.

Prayers are included for the whole Church, the nations, those in need, the parish, special concerns.

The congregation may be invited to offer petitions and thanksgivings.

Prayers of confession may be included if the Brief Order for Confession and Forgiveness has not been used earlier.

The minister gives thanks for the faithful departed, especially for those who recently have died.

After each portion of the prayers:

A Lord, in your mercy,

C **hear our prayer.**

OR

A Let us pray to the Lord.

C **Lord, have mercy.**

The prayers conclude:

P Into your hands, O Lord, we commend all for whom we pray, trusting in your mercy; through your Son, Jesus Christ our Lord.

C **Amen**

C **Our Father in heaven,**
hallowed be your name,
your kingdom come,
your will be done,
on earth as in heaven.
Give us today our daily bread.
Forgive us our sins
as we forgive those
who sin against us.
Save us from the time of trial
and deliver us from evil.
For the kingdom, the power,
and the glory are yours,
now and forever. Amen

OR

C **Our Father, who art in heaven,**
hallowed be thy name,
thy kingdom come,
thy will be done,
on earth as it is in heaven.
Give us this day our daily bread;
and forgive us our trespasses,
as we forgive those
who trespass against us;
and lead us not into temptation,
but deliver us from evil.
For thine is the kingdom,
and the power, and the glory,
forever and ever. Amen

48. The minister blesses the congregation.

P The Lord bless you and keep you.
The Lord make his face shine on you
and be gracious to you.
The Lord look upon you with favor
and ✠ give you peace.

C **Amen**

CHORALE SERVICE OF HOLY COMMUNION

The Chorale Service follows the tradition of Luther's German Mass in which parts of the liturgy for Holy Communion are replaced with hymns (metrical paraphrases).

The numbers in parentheses correspond to the numbered rubrics in the Holy Communion liturgy.

Entrance Hymn or Psalm (4)

Apostolic Greeting (5)

Hymn 168, Kyrie! God, Father (6)
or hymn 96, Your Heart, O God, Is Grieved

Hymn 166, All Glory Be to God on High (7)

Salutation and Prayer of the Day (8)

First Lesson, Psalm, Second Lesson (9–13)

Hymn 317, To God the Holy Spirit Let Us Pray (14)

Holy Gospel (15–16)

Hymn of the Day (19)

Sermon (18)

Hymn 374, We All Believe in One True God (20)

The Prayers and the Peace (22–23)

Offering and Offertory (24–27)

The Great Thanksgiving
Preface Dialog and Preface (28)
Hymn 528, Isaiah in a Vision Did of Old
Eucharistic Prayer or Words of Institution (30–33)

Lord's Prayer

Hymn 103, O Christ, Thou Lamb of God (37)
or hymn 111, Lamb of God, Pure and Sinless

The Communion (34–38)

Hymn 215, O Lord, We Praise You (39)

Post-Communion Prayer (40)

Benediction (42)

HOLY BAPTISM

1. While a baptismal hymn is sung, the candidates, sponsors, and parents gather at the font.

2. The minister addresses the baptismal group and the congregation.

P In Holy Baptism our gracious heavenly Father liberates us from sin and death by joining us to the death and resurrection of our Lord Jesus Christ. We are born children of a fallen humanity; in the waters of Baptism we are reborn children of God and inheritors of eternal life. By water and the Holy Spirit we are made members of the Church which is the body of Christ. As we live with him and with his people, we grow in faith, love, and obedience to the will of God.

3. A sponsor for each candidate, in turn, presents the candidate with these or similar words:

I present ______name______ to receive the Sacrament of Holy Baptism.

4. The minister addresses those candidates who are able to answer for themselves:

P ______name______, do you desire to be baptized?

R I do.

5. The minister addresses the sponsors and parents.

6. When only young children are baptized, the minister says:

P In Christian love you have presented *these children* for Holy Baptism. You should, therefore, faithfully bring *them* to the services of God's house, and teach *them* the Lord's Prayer, the Creed, and the Ten Commandments. As *they grow* in years, you should place in *their* hands the Holy Scriptures and provide for *their* instruction in the Christian faith, that, living in the covenant of *their* Baptism and in communion with the Church, *they* may lead *godly lives* until the day of Jesus Christ.

Do you promise to fulfill these obligations?

R I do.

OR

7. When older children and adults are baptized also, the minister says:

P In Christian love you have presented *these people* for Holy Baptism. You should, therefore, faithfully care for *them* and help *them* in every way as God gives you opportunity, that *they* may bear witness to the faith we profess, and that, living in the covenant of *their* Baptism and in communion with the Church, *they* may lead *godly lives* until the day of Jesus Christ.

Do you promise to fulfill these obligations?

R I do.

Stand

8. When baptisms are celebrated within the Holy Communion, The Prayers may be said at this time, with special reference to those baptized.

After each portion of the prayers:

A Lord, in your mercy,

C hear our prayer.

9. The minister begins the thanksgiving.

P The Lord be with you.

C And also with you.

P Let us give thanks to the Lord our God.

C It is right to give him thanks and praise.

P Holy God, mighty Lord, gracious Father: We give you thanks, for in the beginning your Spirit moved over the waters and you created heaven and earth. By the gift of water you nourish and sustain us and all living things.

By the waters of the flood you condemned the wicked and saved those whom you had chosen, Noah and his family. You led Israel by the pillar of cloud and fire through the sea, out of slavery into the freedom of the promised land. In the waters of the Jordan your Son was baptized by John and anointed with the Spirit. By the baptism of his own death and resurrection your beloved Son has set us free from the bondage to sin and death, and has opened the way to the joy and freedom of everlasting life. He made water a sign of the kingdom and of cleansing and rebirth. In obedience to his command, we make disciples of all nations, baptizing them in the name of the Father, and of the Son, and of the Holy Spirit.

Pour out your Holy Spirit, so that *those* who *are* here baptized may be given new life. Wash away the sin of *all those* who *are* cleansed by this water and bring *them* forth as *inheritors* of your glorious kingdom.

To you be given praise and honor and worship through your Son, Jesus Christ our Lord, in the unity of the Holy Spirit, now and forever. (245)

C Amen

10. The minister addresses the baptismal group and the congregation.

P I ask you to profess your faith in Christ Jesus, reject sin, and confess the faith of the Church, the faith in which we baptize.

P Do you renounce all the forces of evil, the devil, and all his empty promises?

R I do.

P Do you believe in God the Father?

C I believe in God, the Father almighty,
creator of heaven and earth.

P Do you believe in Jesus Christ, the Son of God?

C I believe in Jesus Christ, his only Son, our Lord.
He was conceived by the power of the Holy Spirit
and born of the virgin Mary.
He suffered under Pontius Pilate,
was crucified, died, and was buried.
He descended into hell.*
On the third day he rose again.
He ascended into heaven,
and is seated at the right hand of the Father.
He will come again to judge the living and the dead.

P Do you believe in God the Holy Spirit?

C I believe in the Holy Spirit,
the holy catholic Church,
the communion of saints,
the forgiveness of sins,
the resurrection of the body,
and the life everlasting. Amen

11. The minister baptizes each candidate.

P ______name______, I baptize you in the name of the Father,

The minister pours water on the candidate's head.

P and of the Son,

The minister pours water on the candidate's head a second time.

P and of the Holy Spirit. Amen

The minister pours water on the candidate's head a third time.

OR

P ______name______ is baptized in the name of the Father,

The minister pours water on the candidate's head.

P and of the Son,

The minister pours water on the candidate's head a second time.

P and of the Holy Spirit. Amen

The minister pours water on the candidate's head a third time.

* *Or,* He descended to the dead.

Sit

12. A psalm or hymn may be sung as the minister and the baptismal group go before the altar.

P The Lord be with you.

C And also with you.

13. Those who have been baptized kneel. Sponsors or parents holding young children stand. The minister lays both hands on the head of each of the baptized and prays for the Holy Spirit:

P God, the Father of our Lord Jesus Christ, we give you thanks for freeing your sons and daughters from the power of sin and for raising them up to a new life through this holy sacrament. Pour your Holy Spirit upon ___name___: the spirit of wisdom and understanding, the spirit of counsel and might, the spirit of knowledge and the fear of the Lord, the spirit of joy in your presence. (246)

C Amen

14. The minister marks the sign of the cross on the forehead of each of the baptized. Oil prepared for this purpose may be used. As the sign of the cross is made, the minister says:

P ___name___, child of God, you have been sealed by the Holy Spirit and marked with the cross of Christ forever.

The sponsor or the baptized responds: "Amen."

15. After all have received the sign of the cross, they stand.

16. A lighted candle may be given to each of the baptized (to the sponsor of a young child) by a representative of the congregation who says:

Let your light so shine before others that they may see your good works and glorify your Father in heaven.

17. When small children are baptized, this prayer may be said.

P O God, the giver of all life, look with kindness upon the *fathers* and *mothers* of *these children.* Let them ever rejoice in the gift you have given them. Make them teachers and examples of righteousness for their *children.* Strengthen them in their own Baptism so they may share eternally with their *children* the salvation you have given them, through Jesus Christ our Lord. (247)

C Amen

Stand

18. The ministers and the baptismal group turn toward the congregation; a representative of the congregation says:

Through Baptism God has made *these* new *sisters and brothers members* of the priesthood we all share in Christ Jesus, that we may proclaim the praise of God and bear his creative and redeeming Word to all the world.

C We welcome you into the Lord's family. We receive you as fellow members of the body of Christ, children of the same heavenly Father, and workers with us in the kingdom of God.

19. The ministers may exchange the peace with the baptized, with their sponsors and parents, and with the congregation:

Peace be with you. ℟ Peace be with you.

20. All return to their places.

21. The service continues with the Offering.

SERVICE OF THE WORD

Stand

1. A HYMN is sung.

2. The appropriate DIALOG is read. It may be said responsively by the leader and the congregation or antiphonally by two sections of the congregation.

Holy is the Lord, the Almighty.
He was, he is, and he is to come.

He is worthy of glory and honor and power.
He created all things. By his will they came to be.

Worthy is Christ, the Lamb who was slain;
worthy to take the scroll and break its seals.

By his blood he purchased for God
people of every race and tongue, of every folk and nation.

Christ made of them a kingdom
and priests to serve our God.

And they shall reign on earth forever.
Amen. Come, Lord Jesus.

OR

Blessed are you, O Lord our God, king of the universe,
for in your wisdom you have formed us.

You feed the hungry and clothe the naked.
We bless you and praise your name forever.

You set free those who are bound.
We bless you and praise your name forever.

You raise up those whose courage falters.
We bless you and praise your name forever.

You provide for our every need.
Accept our grateful praises.

You have called us from all peoples.
We rejoice and bless your name forever.

You bless your people with peace.
We bless you and praise your loving grace.

Blessed are you, O Lord our God, king of the universe,
for in your wisdom you have formed us.

OR

ADVENT

Blessed is he who comes as king, who comes in the name of the Lord.
Glory to God in the highest, and peace to his people on earth.

I will hear what the Lord God has to say—
a voice that speaks for peace.

Peace for all people and for his friends
and those who turn to him in their hearts.

His help is near for those who fear him,
and his glory will live in our land.

Blessed is he who comes as king, who comes in the name of the Lord.
Glory to God in the highest, and peace to his people on earth.

OR

LENT

Grace and peace from God our Father and the Lord Jesus Christ.
Praised be God, the Father of our Lord Jesus Christ,
the Father of all mercies, and the God of all consolation.

Seek the Lord while he may be found.
Call upon him while he is near.

Let the wicked abandon their ways,
and the unrighteous their thoughts.

Let them turn to the Lord for mercy,
to our God, who is generous in forgiving.

All you who are thirsty, come to the water.
You who have no money, come, receive bread, and eat.
Come, without paying and without cost, drink wine and milk.
Praised be God, the Father of our Lord Jesus Christ,
the Father of all mercies, and the God of all consolation.

L God has made us his people through our Baptism into Christ. Living together in trust and hope, we confess our faith.

C **I believe in God, the Father almighty,**
creator of heaven and earth.

I believe in Jesus Christ, his only Son, our Lord.
He was conceived by the power of the Holy Spirit
and born of the virgin Mary.
He suffered under Pontius Pilate,
was crucified, died, and was buried.
He descended into hell.*
On the third day he rose again.
He ascended into heaven,
and is seated at the right hand of the Father.
He will come again to judge the living and the dead.

I believe in the Holy Spirit,
the holy catholic Church,
the communion of saints,
the forgiveness of sins,
the resurrection of the body,
and the life everlasting. Amen

3. *An OLD TESTAMENT CANTICLE (see canticles 14, 15, 16, 18, 19) appropriate to the season or occasion is sung.*

4. *The PRAYER OF THE DAY is said; the salutation may precede it.*

L The Lord be with you.

C **And also with you.**

L Let us pray. . . .

C **Amen**

Sit

5. *The FIRST LESSON is announced and read.*

L The First Lesson is from the ________________ chapter of ________________.

6. *After the lesson the reader may say: "Here ends the reading."*

7. *A psalm, hymn, or anthem is sung.*

8. *The SECOND LESSON is announced and read.*

L The Second Lesson is from the ________________ chapter of ________________.

9. *After the lesson the reader may say: "Here ends the reading."*

* *Or,* He descended to the dead.

10. A response follows the Second Lesson.

11. Silence for meditation.

12. The SERMON follows the silence.

Stand

13. A HYMN is sung.

Sit

14. An OFFERING may be received.

15. THE PRAYERS follow. The leader may use the prayer below, the form for prayer in the Holy Communion (65), one of the forms of Responsive Prayer (161), one of the litanies (148 or 168), a series of prayers, or any appropriate prayer. Opportunity for prayers from the congregation may be provided.

Stand

L Let us pray.

L Almighty and everlasting God, you are worthy to be held in reverence by all the mortal race. We give you thanks for the innumerable blessings which, despite our unworthiness, you have showered upon us.

We praise you especially that you have preserved for us in their purity your saving Word and the sacred ordinances of your house. Grant and preserve to your Church throughout the world purity of doctrine and faithful pastors who shall preach your Word with power, and help all who hear rightly to understand and firmly to believe your Word of truth.

Protect and defend your people in time of tribulation and danger, that we, in communion with your Church and in unity with all Christian people, may fight the good fight of faith and in the end receive the fullness of salvation.

Upon all the nations of the earth bestow your grace. Especially we ask you to bless our land and all its inhabitants and all who are in authority. Cause your glory to dwell among us, and let mercy and truth, justice and peace everywhere prevail. We commend to your care all our schools, that virtue and useful knowledge may be nourished and the wholesome fruits of life may abound.

In your mercy defend us from all calamities by fire and water, from war and pestilence, from scarcity and famine. Protect and prosper all who labor, and cause all useful arts to flourish among us. Show yourself to be the helper of the sick and needy, the comforter of the forsaken and distressed.

Accept, we pray, our bodies and souls, our hearts and minds, our talents and powers, together with these gifts, as our offering of praise.

Special supplications, intercessions, and thanksgivings.

And as we are strangers and pilgrims on earth, help us to prepare for the world to come, doing the work which you have given us to do while it is day, before that night comes when no one can work. And, when our last hour shall come, support us by your power and receive us into your everlasting kingdom, where, with your Son our Lord Jesus Christ and the Holy Spirit, you live and reign, God forever.

C **Amen**

C **Our Father in heaven,**
hallowed be your name,
your kingdom come,
your will be done,
on earth as in heaven.
Give us today our daily bread.
Forgive us our sins
as we forgive those
who sin against us.
Save us from the time of trial
and deliver us from evil.
For the kingdom, the power,
and the glory are yours,
now and forever. Amen

OR

C **Our Father, who art in heaven,**
hallowed be thy name,
thy kingdom come,
thy will be done,
on earth as it is in heaven.
Give us this day our daily bread;
and forgive us our trespasses,
as we forgive those
who trespass against us;
and lead us not into temptation,
but deliver us from evil.
For thine is the kingdom,
and the power, and the glory,
forever and ever. Amen

16. A NEW TESTAMENT CANTICLE (see canticles 13, 17, 20, 21) appropriate to the season or occasion is sung.

17. The BENEDICTION is said; a hymn may follow.

L The Lord bless us and keep us.
The Lord make his face shine on us
and be gracious to us.
The Lord look upon us with favor
and give us peace.

C **Amen**

MORNING PRAYER

Matins

Stand

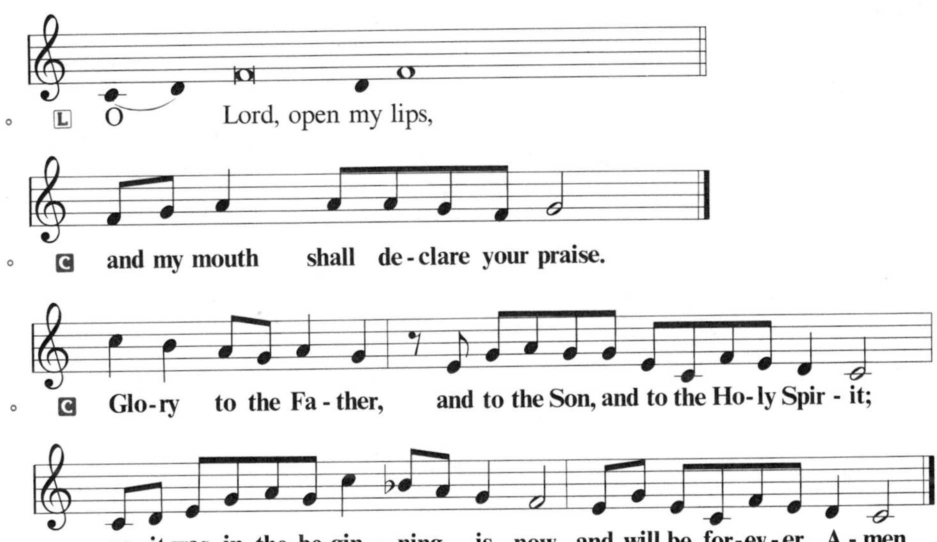
L O Lord, open my lips,
C and my mouth shall de-clare your praise.
C Glo-ry to the Fa-ther, and to the Son, and to the Ho-ly Spir-it;
as it was in the be-gin-ning, is now, and will be for-ev-er. A-men

The alleluia is omitted during Lent.

C Al-le-lu-ia. Al-le-lu-ia.

1. The PSALMODY begins with this song of praise. Another appropriate canticle may follow the invitatory.

L Give glory to God, our light and our life.
C Oh, come, let us wor - ship him.
C Oh, come, let us sing to the Lord; let us shout for joy to the
rock of our sal - va - tion. I Let us come be-fore his pres - ence
with thanks-giv - ing and raise a loud shout to him with psalms.
II For the Lord is a great God and a great king a - bove all gods.
I In his hand are the cav-erns of the earth; the heights of the hills
are al - so his. II The sea is his, for he made it;
and his hands have mold - ed the dry land. I Oh, come, let us bow
down and bend the knee, and kneel be - fore the Lord, our mak - er.

For he is our God, and we are the peo-ple of his pas - ture and the sheep of his hand. Glo - ry to the Fa - ther,
and to the Son, and to the Ho - ly Spir - it; as it was in the be-gin - ning, is now, and will be for - ev - er. A - men
Give glory to God, our light and our life.
Oh, come, let us wor - ship him.

Sit

2. *A second psalm is sung or said. Additional psalms and an Old Testament canticle may be sung or said also. Silence for meditation follows each psalm or canticle.*

3. *The psalm prayer appropriate to each psalm follows the silence.*

C **Amen**

Stand

4. *THE HYMN is sung.*

Sit

5. *One or two LESSONS are read. Silence for meditation follows each reading.*

6. *A response to the reading(s) may follow the silence. The leader then continues:*

L In many and various ways God spoke to his people of old by the prophets.

C **But now in these last days he has spoken to us by his Son.**

Stand

◦ *7. The GOSPEL CANTICLE is sung. If the Paschal Blessing is not used at the end of the service, the canticle, "You are God; we praise you," page 139, may replace this canticle.*

C Bless - ed be the Lord, the God of Is - ra - el;
he has come to his peo - ple and set them free.
He has raised up for us a might - y Sav - ior,
born of the house of his ser - vant Da - vid. Through his
ho - ly proph - ets he prom - ised of old that he would
save us from our en - e - mies, from the hands of all who
hate us. He prom-ised to show mer - cy to our fa -
thers and to re - mem - ber his ho - ly cov - e - nant.
This was the oath he swore to our fa - ther A - bra - ham:

to set us free from the hands of our en - e - mies,
free to wor - ship him with - out fear, ho - ly and
righ-teous in his sight all the days of our life.
L You, my child, shall be called the proph - et of the Most High,
for you will go be - fore the Lord to pre - pare his way,
to give his peo - ple knowl-edge of sal - va - tion by the for - give-ness
of their sins. In the ten - der com - pas - sion of our God,
the dawn from on high shall break up - on us,
to shine on those who dwell in dark-ness and the shad - ow of death,
and to guide our feet in - to the way of peace.

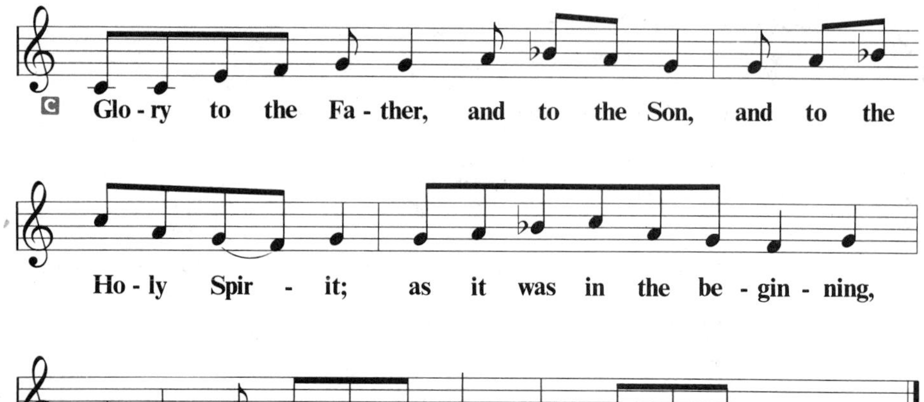

C Glo - ry to the Fa - ther, and to the Son, and to the
Ho - ly Spir - it; as it was in the be - gin - ning,
is now, and will be for - ev - er. A - men

8. The PRAYER OF THE DAY is said.

C Amen

9. Other prayers may be said by the leader with the congregation responding "Amen" to each, or members of the congregation may be invited to offer petitions and thanksgivings. Instead, The Litany, page 168, or Responsive Prayer 1, page 161, may be used. In concluding the prayers the leader says:

◦ L O Lord, almighty and everlasting God, you have brought us in safety to this new day; preserve us with your mighty power, that we may not fall into sin, nor be overcome in adversity; and in all we do, direct us to the fulfilling of your purpose; through Jesus Christ our Lord. (249)

◦ **C Amen**

◦ L Lord, remember us in your kingdom, and teach us to pray:

◦ **C Our Father in heaven,**
hallowed be your name,
your kingdom come,
your will be done,
on earth as in heaven.
Give us today our daily bread.
Forgive us our sins
as we forgive those
who sin against us.
Save us from the time of trial
and deliver us from evil.
For the kingdom, the power,
and the glory are yours,
now and forever. Amen

OR

C Our Father, who art in heaven,
hallowed be thy name,
thy kingdom come,
thy will be done,
on earth as it is in heaven.
Give us this day our daily bread;
and forgive us our trespasses,
as we forgive those
who trespass against us;
and lead us not into temptation,
but deliver us from evil.
For thine is the kingdom,
and the power, and the glory,
forever and ever. Amen

L Let us bless the Lord.
C Thanks be to God.

10. The BENEDICTION concludes the service when there is no sermon. A hymn may follow. On Sundays the service may be concluded with the Paschal Blessing, page 138. ▶

11. When there is a sermon, this benediction is omitted. The order of service continues at 12.

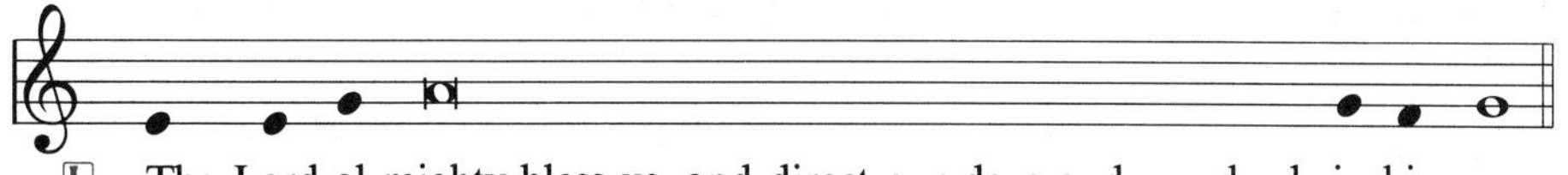
L The Lord al-mighty bless us, and direct our days and our deeds in his peace.

C A - men

Sit

12. An OFFERING may be received during which a hymn, psalm, or anthem may be sung.

13. A HYMN is sung.

14. The SERMON. Following the sermon one of these prayers is said.

Stand

P Almighty God, grant to your Church your Holy Spirit and the wisdom which comes down from heaven, that your Word may not be bound but have free course and be preached to the joy and edifying of Christ's holy people, that in steadfast faith we may serve you and in the confession of your name may abide to the end; through Jesus Christ our Lord. (250)

OR

P Lord God, you have called your servants to ventures of which we cannot see the ending, by paths as yet untrodden, through perils unknown. Give us faith to go out with good courage, not knowing where we go, but only that your hand is leading us and your love supporting us; through Jesus Christ our Lord. (251)

OR

P Lord, we thank you that you have taught us what you would have us believe and do. Help us by your Holy Spirit, for the sake of Jesus Christ, to keep your Word in pure hearts, that thereby we may be strengthened in faith, perfected in holiness, and comforted in life and in death. (252)

C Amen

15. The minister blesses the congregation. The Benediction is omitted here if the Paschal Blessing is to be used.

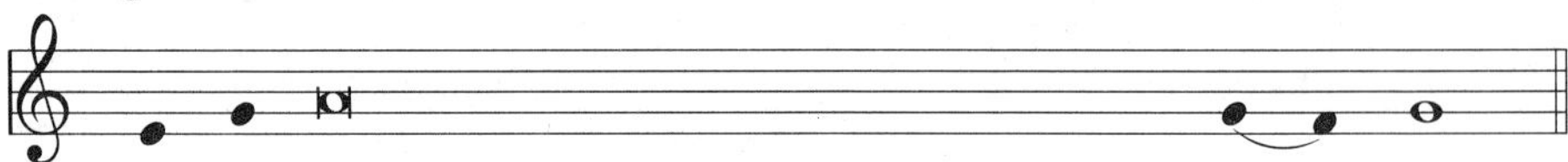

P The al-mighty and merciful Lord, the Father,
✠ the Son, and the Holy Spirit, bless and pre-serve you.

C **A - men**

PASCHAL BLESSING

16. ▶The Paschal Blessing may be used on Sundays to conclude Morning Prayer. The service may be led from the font.

Stand

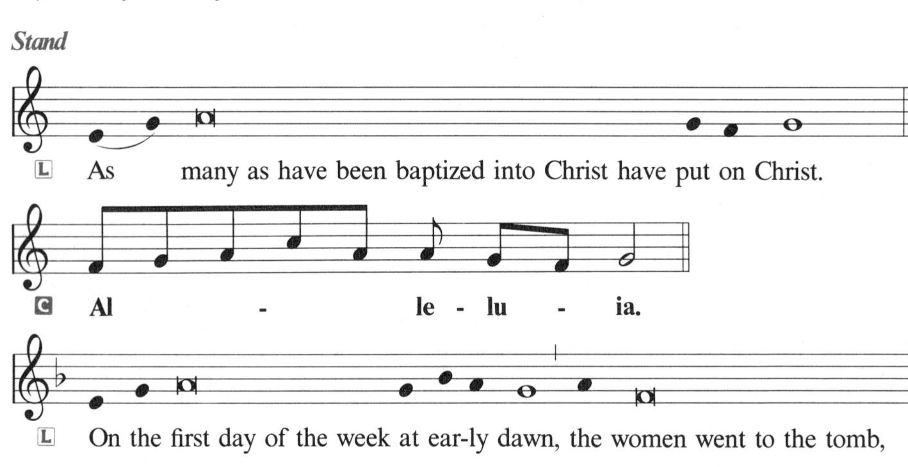
L As many as have been baptized into Christ have put on Christ.
C Al - le - lu - ia.
L On the first day of the week at ear-ly dawn, the women went to the tomb,

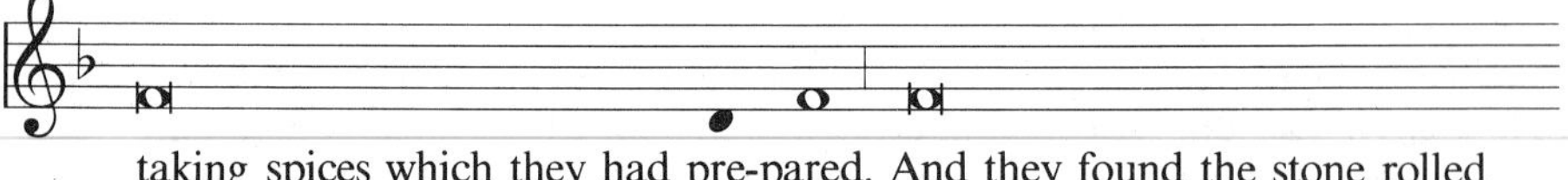

taking spices which they had pre-pared. And they found the stone rolled

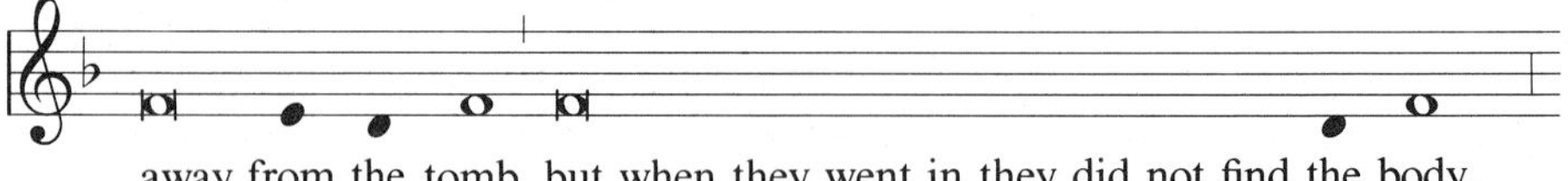

away from the tomb, but when they went in they did not find the body.

While they were perplexed a-bout this, behold, two men stood by them in

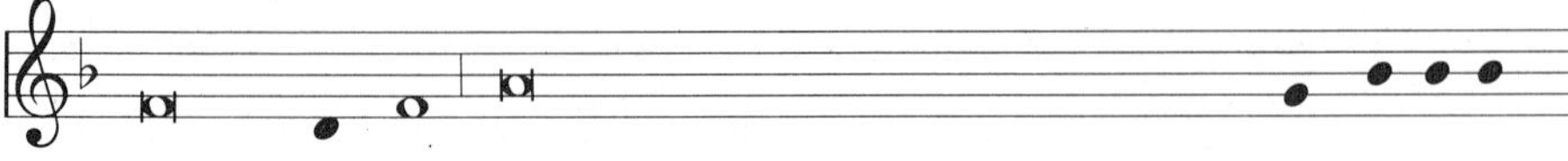

dazzling ap-parel; and as they were frightened and bowed their fac-es to

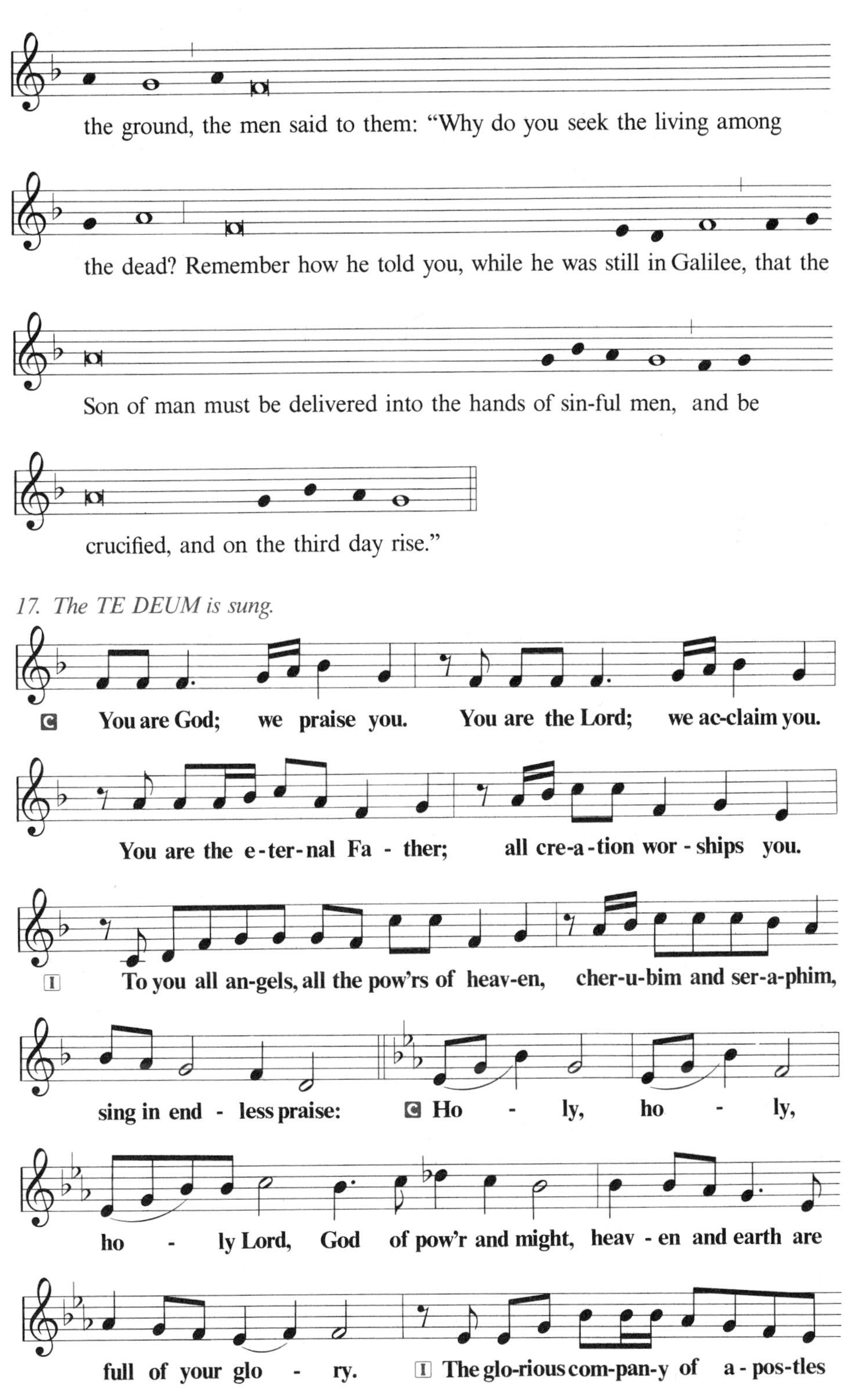

the ground, the men said to them: "Why do you seek the living among
the dead? Remember how he told you, while he was still in Galilee, that the
Son of man must be delivered into the hands of sin-ful men, and be
crucified, and on the third day rise."

17. *The TE DEUM is sung.*

C You are God; we praise you. You are the Lord; we ac-claim you.
You are the e-ter-nal Fa - ther; all cre-a-tion wor - ships you.
I To you all an-gels, all the pow'rs of heav-en, cher-u-bim and ser-a-phim,
sing in end - less praise: C Ho - ly, ho - ly,
ho - ly Lord, God of pow'r and might, heav - en and earth are
full of your glo - ry. I The glo-rious com-pan-y of a - pos-tles

praise you. II The no-ble fel-low-ship of proph-ets praise you.
I The white-robed ar-my of mar-tyrs praise you. II Through-out the world the
ho-ly Church ac-claims you: C Fa-ther, of maj-es-ty un-
bound-ed; your true and on-ly Son, wor-thy of all wor-ship;
and the Ho-ly Spir-it, ad-vo-cate and guide. I You, Christ, are the
king of glo-ry, the e-ter-nal Son of the Fa-ther.
II When you be-came man to set us free, you did not spurn the
vir-gin's womb. I You o-ver-came the sting of death,
and o-pened the king-dom of heav-en to all be-liev-ers.
II You are seat-ed at God's right hand in glo-ry.
We be-lieve that you will come and be our judge. C Come, then,

Lord, and help your peo-ple, bought with the price of your own blood,
and bring us with your saints to glo - ry ev - er - last - ing.
L O God, for our redemption you gave your only Son to suffer
death on the cross, and by his glorious resurrection you delivered us
from the power of death. Make us die every day to sin so that we may rise to
live with Christ for-ev-er; who lives and reigns with you and the Holy Spirit,
one God, now and for-ev-er. (253)
C A - men
L The Lord al-mighty bless us, and direct our days and our deeds in his peace.
C A - men

EVENING PRAYER

Vespers

1. The SERVICE OF LIGHT may be used to begin Evening Prayer. The service may be begun with a procession in which a large, lighted candle is carried to its stand in front of the congregation.

Stand

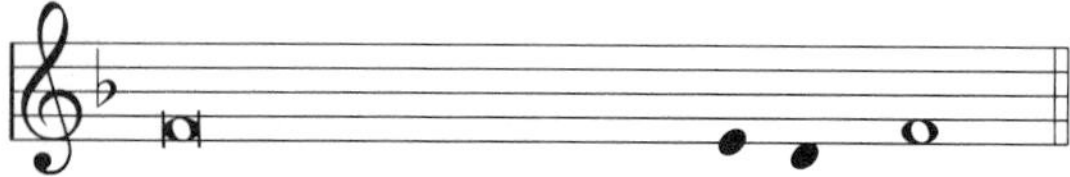

◦ L Je-sus Christ is the Light of the world,

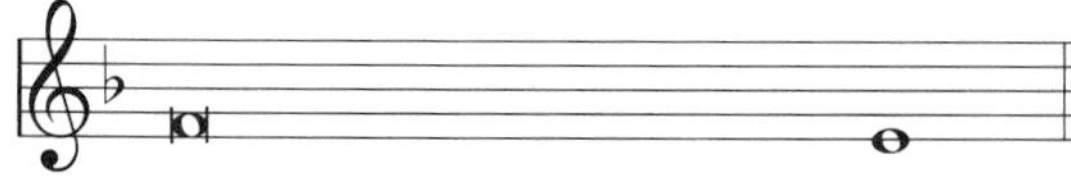

◦ C **the light no darkness can over-come.**

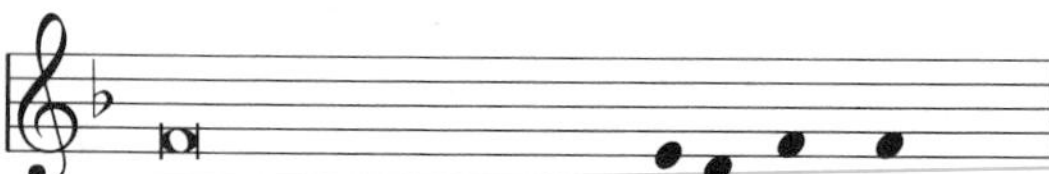

◦ L Stay with us, Lord, for it is eve-ning,

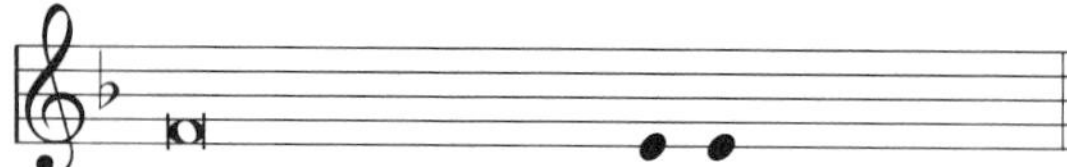

◦ C **and the day is almost o-ver.**

◦ L Let your light scat-ter the dark-ness,

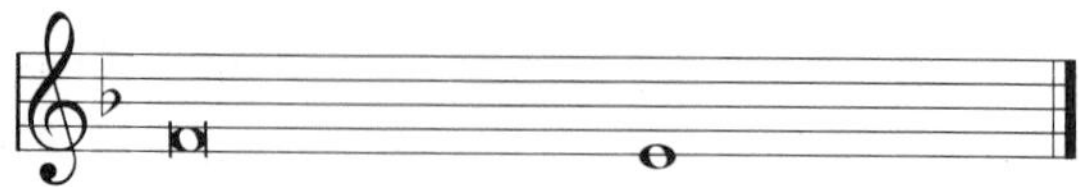

◦ C **and illumine your Church.**

2. As the hymn is sung, the candles on and near the altar are lighted. When the large candle is used, the candles are lighted from its flame.

L Joy-ous light of glo - ry:
C of the im - mor - tal Fa - ther; heav - en - ly, ho - ly,
bless - ed Je - sus Christ. We have come to the
set - ting of the sun, and we look to the eve - ning light.

We sing to God, the Fa - ther, Son, and Ho - ly Spir - it:

You are wor - thy of be - ing praised with pure voic - es for -

ev - er. O Son of God, O Giv - er of life:

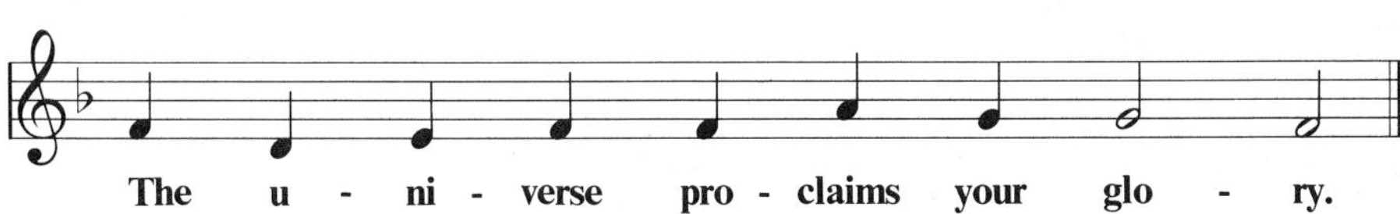
The u - ni - verse pro - claims your glo - ry.

3. The thanksgiving concludes the Service of Light.

L The Lord be with you.

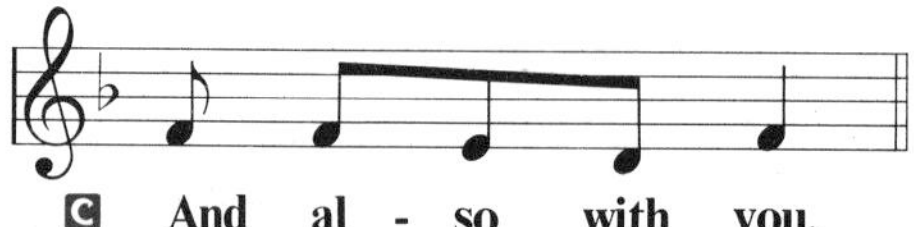

C And al - so with you.

L Let us give thanks to the Lord our God.

C It is right to give him thanks and praise.

L Blessed are you, O Lord our God, king of the universe, who led your people

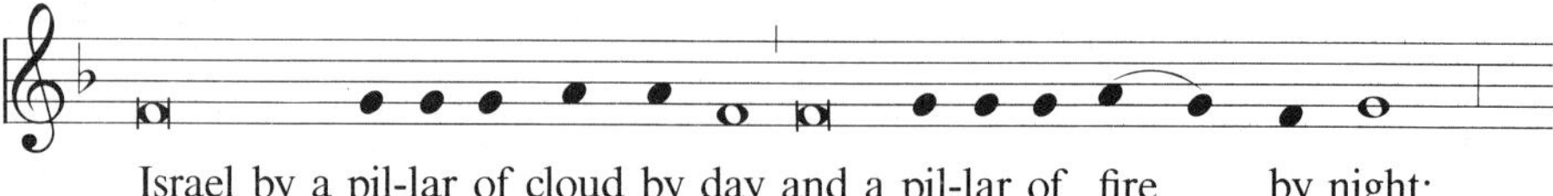

Israel by a pil-lar of cloud by day and a pil-lar of fire by night:

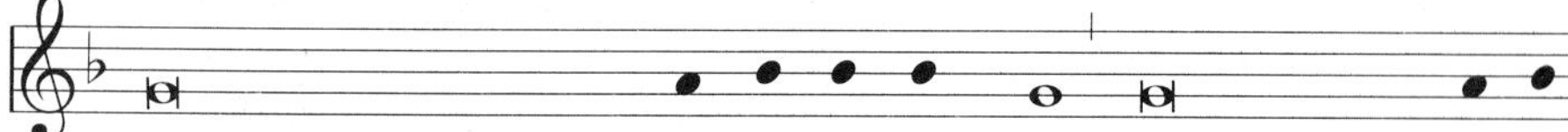

Enlighten our darkness by the light of your Christ; may his Word be a lamp

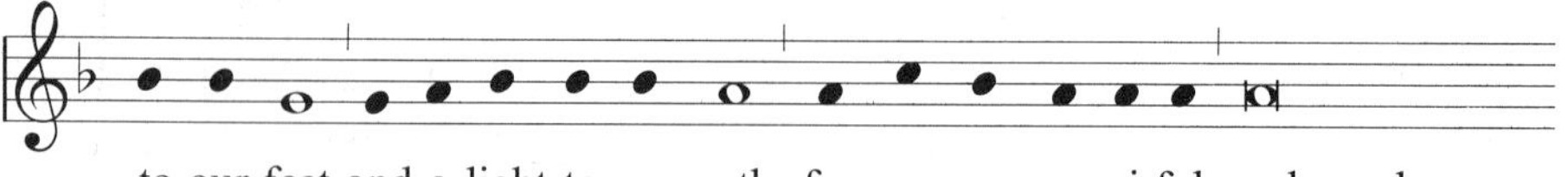

to our feet and a light to our path; for you are mer-ci-ful, and you love

your whole cre-a-tion, and we, your crea-tures, glo-ri-fy you, Fa-ther,

Son, and Ho-ly Spir-it.

C A - men

Kneel/Sit

4. *The PSALMODY begins with this song for forgiveness and protection.*

C Let my prayer rise be - fore you as in - cense; the
lift - ing up of my hands as the eve - ning sac - ri - fice.

I O Lord, I call to you; come to me quick - ly; hear my voice when
I cry to you.

II Let my prayer rise be - fore you as in - cense;
the lift - ing up of my hands as the eve-ning sac - ri - fice.

I Set a watch be-fore my mouth, O Lord, and guard the door of my lips.

II Let not my heart in - cline to an - y e - vil thing; let me
not be oc - cu - pied in wick - ed - ness with e - vil - do - ers.

I But my eyes are turned to you, Lord God; in you I take ref - uge.
Strip me not of my life. II Glo - ry to the Fa - ther, and to the
Son, and to the Ho - ly Spir - it; I as it was in the be - gin -
ning, is now, and will be for - ev - er. A - men. C Let my
prayer rise be - fore you as in - cense; the lift - ing
up of my hands as the eve - ning sac - ri - fice.

Silence for meditation.

◦ L Let the incense of our repentant prayer ascend before you, O Lord, and let your lovingkindness descend upon us, that with purified minds we may sing your praises with the Church on earth and the whole heavenly host, and may glorify you forever and ever. (254)

C Amen

Sit

5. A second psalm is sung or said. Additional psalms and a New Testament canticle may be sung or said also. Silence for meditation follows each psalm or canticle.

6. The psalm prayer appropriate to each psalm follows the silence.

C Amen

Stand

7. THE HYMN is sung.

Sit

◦ *8. One or two LESSONS are read. Silence for meditation follows each reading.*

9. A response to the reading(s) may follow the silence. After this the leader continues:

L In many and various ways God spoke to his people of old by the prophets.

C But now in these last days he has spoken to us by his Son.

Stand

◦ *10. The GOSPEL CANTICLE is sung.*

C My soul pro-claims the great-ness of the Lord; my spir - it re-
joic-es in God my Sav - ior, for he has looked with fa - vor
on his low - ly ser - vant. From this day all gen - er -
a - tions will call me bless - ed. The Al - might - y has
done great things for me, and ho - ly is his name. He has
mer-cy on those who fear him in ev - 'ry gen - er - a - tion.
He has shown the strength of his arm; he has scat-tered the
proud in their con - ceit. He has cast down the might - y from their thrones,
and has lift - ed up the low - ly. He has filled the

hun-gry with good things, and the rich he has sent a - way emp - ty.

He has come to the help of his ser - vant Is - ra - el,

for he has re-mem-bered his prom-ise of mer - cy, the prom-ise he

made to our fa-thers, to A - bra-ham and his chil-dren for - ev - er.

Glo-ry to the Fa-ther, and to the Son, and to the Ho - ly Spir - it; as it

was in the be - gin-ning, is now, and will be for - ev - er. A - men

Kneel/Stand

11. The LITANY is sung or said. The complete Litany may be sung to the alternate musical form.

L In peace, let us pray to the Lord.
C Lord, have mer - cy.
L In peace, let us pray to the Lord.
C Lord, have mer - cy.

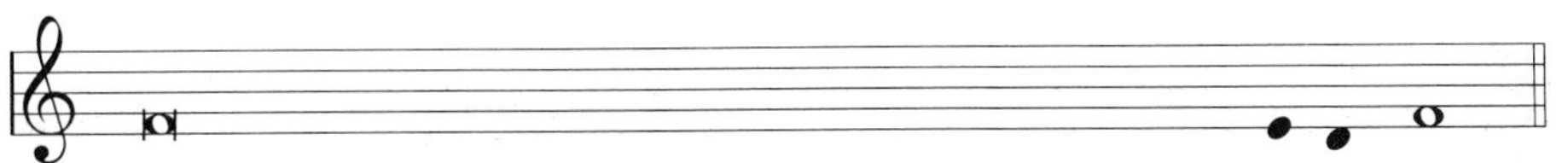

L For the peace from above, and for our salvation, let us pray to the Lord.

C **Lord, have mer - cy.**

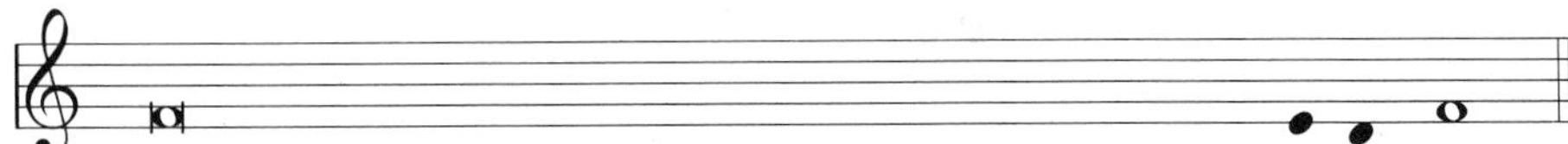

L For the peace of the whole world, for the well-being
of the Church of God, and for the unity of all, let us pray. . . to the Lord.

C **Lord, have mer - cy.**

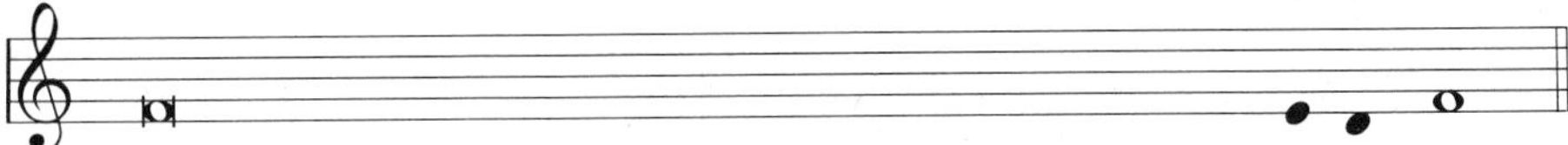

L For this holy house, and for all who offer
here their worship and praise, let us pray . . . . to the Lord.

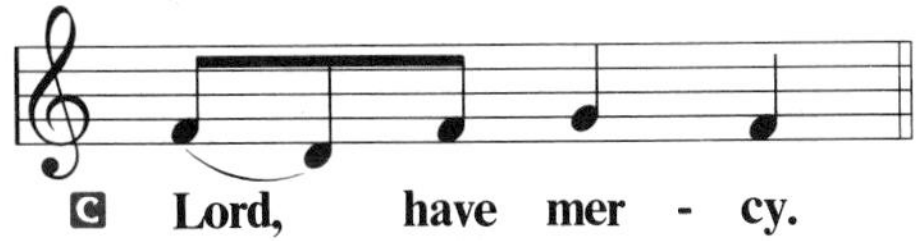

C **Lord, have mer - cy.**

L For ________names________, for our *pastor/pastors* in Christ,
for all servants of the Church, and for all the people, let us pray to the Lord.

C **Lord, have mer - cy.**

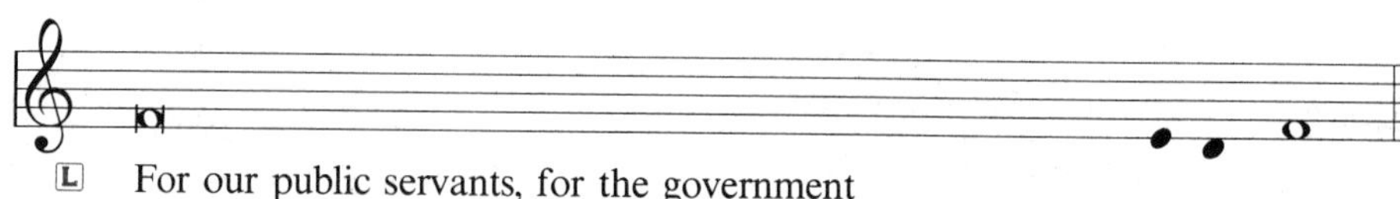

L For our public servants, for the government and those who protect us, that they may be upheld and strengthened in every good deed, let us pray . . to the Lord.

C Lord, have mer - cy.

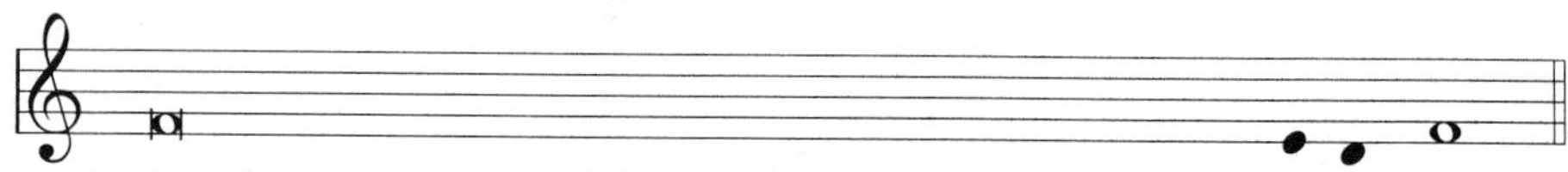

L For those who work to bring peace, justice, health, and protection in this and every place, let us pray . . . . to the Lord.

C Lord, have mer - cy.

L For those who bring offerings, those who do good works in this congregation, those who toil, those who sing, and all the people here present who await from the Lord great and abundant mercy, let us pray . . . to the Lord.

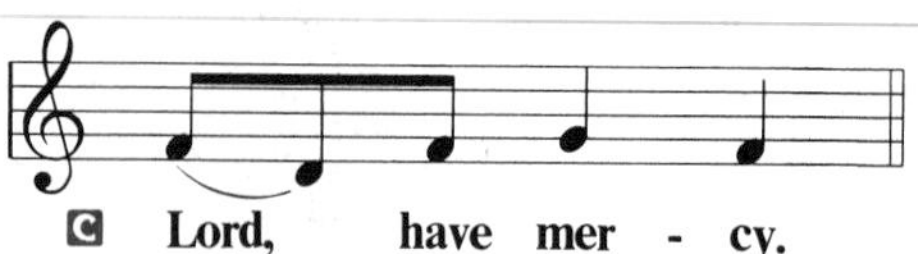

C Lord, have mer - cy.

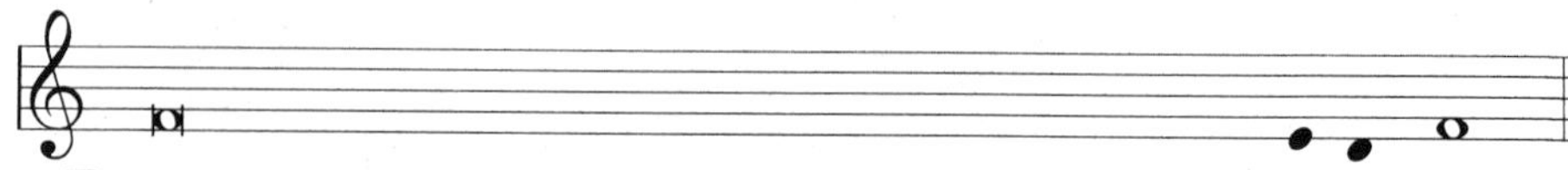

L For favorable weather, for an abundance of the fruits of the earth, and for peaceful times, let us pray . . . . . to the Lord.

C Lord, have mer - cy.

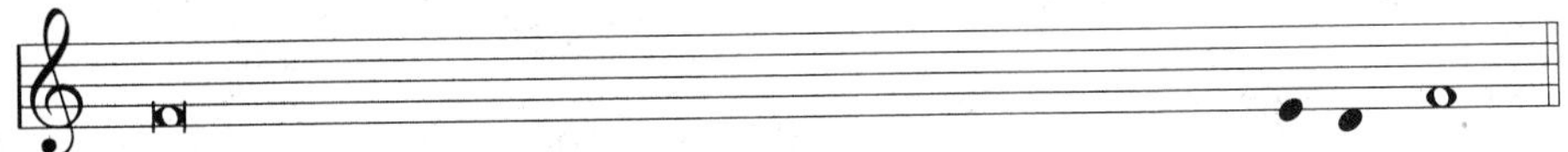

L For our deliverance from all affliction,
wrath, danger, and need, let us pray . . . . to the Lord.

Lord, have mer - cy.

C Lord, have mer - cy.

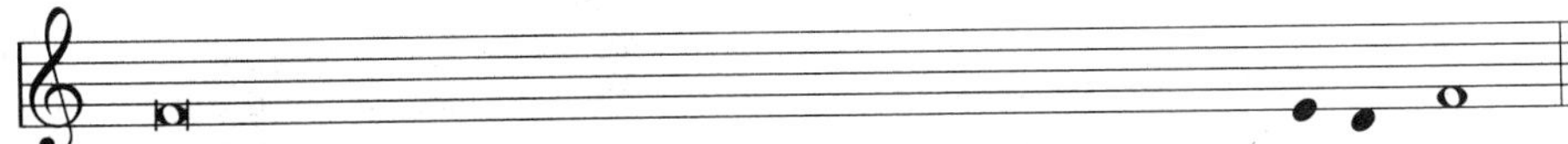

L For the faithful who have gone
before us and are at rest, let us give thanks . . . . to the Lord.

Al - le - lu - ia.

C Al - le - lu - ia.

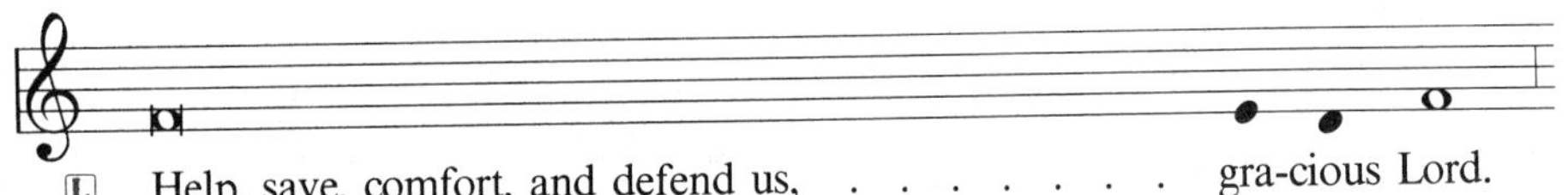

L Help, save, comfort, and defend us, ... gra-cious Lord.

Silence for meditation

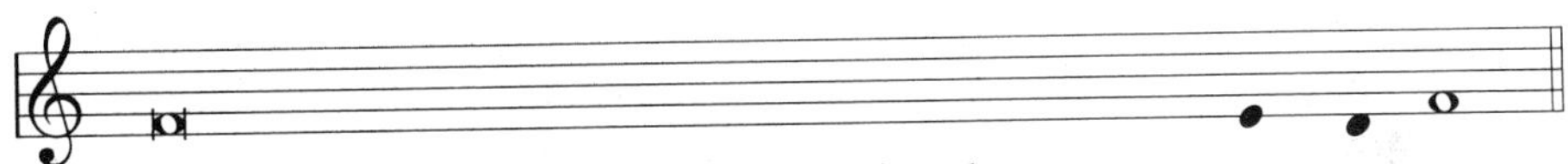

L Rejoicing in the fellowship of all the saints, let us
commend ourselves, one another, and our whole life to Christ, our Lord.

To you, O Lord.

C To you, O Lord.

L O God, from whom come all holy desires, all good counsels, and all just works: Give to us, your servants, that peace which the world cannot give, that our hearts may be set to obey your commandments; and also that we, being defended from the fear of our enemies, may live in peace and quietness; through the merits of Jesus Christ our Savior, who lives and reigns with you and the Holy Spirit, God forever. (255)

C Amen

L Lord, remember us in your kingdom, and teach us to pray:

C Our Father in heaven,
hallowed be your name,
your kingdom come,
your will be done,
on earth as in heaven.
Give us today our daily bread.
Forgive us our sins
as we forgive those
who sin against us.
Save us from the time of trial
and deliver us from evil.
For the kingdom, the power,
and the glory are yours,
now and forever. Amen

OR

C Our Father, who art in heaven,
hallowed be thy name,
thy kingdom come,
thy will be done,
on earth as it is in heaven.
Give us this day our daily bread;
and forgive us our trespasses,
as we forgive those
who trespass against us;
and lead us not into temptation,
but deliver us from evil.
For thine is the kingdom,
and the power, and the glory,
forever and ever. Amen

Stand

L Let us bless the Lord.

C Thanks be to God.

12. The BENEDICTION concludes the service when there is no sermon. A hymn may follow the benediction.

13. When there is a sermon, this benediction is omitted. The order of service continues below (14).

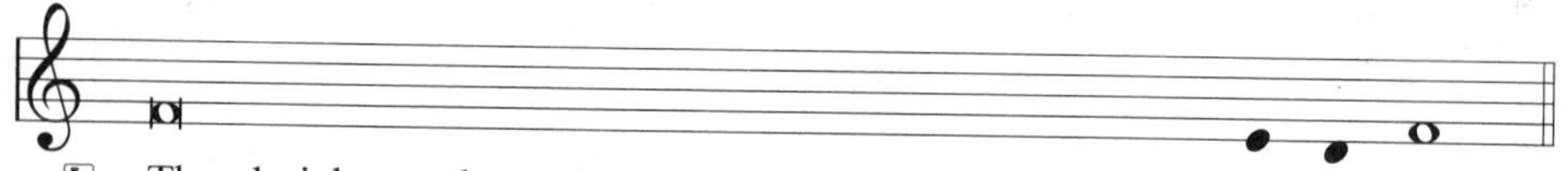

L The almighty and merciful Lord,
the Father, the Son, and the Holy Spirit, bless . . . . . and pre-serve us.

C A - men

Sit

14. An OFFERING may be received during which a hymn, psalm, or anthem may be sung.

15. A HYMN is sung.

16. The SERMON. Following the sermon one of these prayers is said.

Stand

P Almighty God, grant to your Church your Holy Spirit and the wisdom which comes down from heaven, that your Word may not be bound but have free course and be preached to the joy and edifying of Christ's holy people, that in steadfast faith we may serve you and in the confession of your name may abide to the end; through Jesus Christ our Lord. (250)

OR

P Lord God, you have called your servants to ventures of which we cannot see the ending, by paths as yet untrodden, through perils unknown. Give us faith to go out with good courage, not knowing where we go, but only that your hand is leading us and your love supporting us; through Jesus Christ our Lord. (251)

OR

P Lord, we thank you that you have taught us what you would have us believe and do. Help us by your Holy Spirit, for the sake of Jesus Christ, to keep your Word in pure hearts, that thereby we may be strengthened in faith, perfected in holiness, and comforted in life and in death. (252)

C **Amen**

17. The minister blesses the congregation.

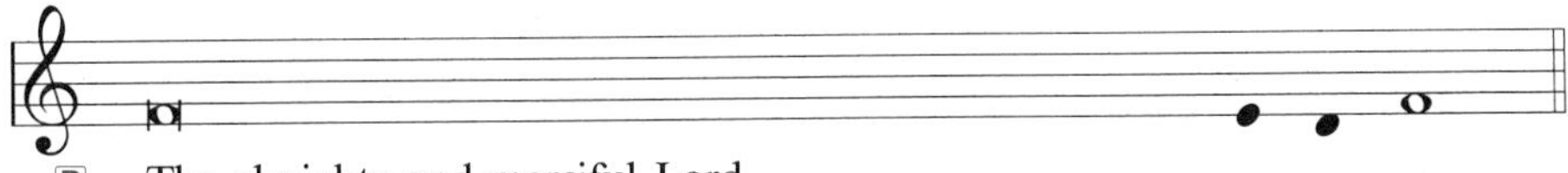

P The almighty and merciful Lord,
the Father, ✠ the Son, and the Holy Spirit, bless . . and pre-serve you.

C **A - men**

PRAYER AT THE CLOSE OF THE DAY

Compline

1. *The congregation assembles in silence.*

Stand

L The Lord almighty grant us a qui-et night and peace at the last.

C **A - men**

L It is good to give thanks to the Lord,

C **to sing praise to your name, O Most High;**

L to herald your love in the morning,

C **your truth at the close of the day.**

2. Hymn 278 or another hymn appropriate for a night service is sung.

Kneel/Sit

3. The CONFESSION follows.

L Let us confess our sin in the presence of God and of one another.

Silence for self-examination.

L Holy and gracious God,

C I confess that I have sinned against you this day. Some of my sin I know—the thoughts and words and deeds of which I am ashamed—but some is known only to you. In the name of Jesus Christ I ask forgiveness. Deliver and restore me, that I may rest in peace.

L By the mercy of God we are united with Jesus Christ, and in him we are forgiven. We rest now in his peace and rise in the morning to serve him.

OR

L I confess to God Almighty, before the whole company of heaven, and to you, my brothers and sisters, that I have sinned in thought, word, and deed by my fault, by my own fault, by my own most grievous fault; wherefore I pray God Almighty to have mercy on me, forgive me all my sins, and bring me to everlasting life. Amen

C The almighty and merciful Lord grant you pardon, forgiveness, and remission of all your sins. Amen

C I confess to God Almighty, before the whole company of heaven, and to you, my brothers and sisters, that I have sinned in thought, word, and deed by my fault, by my own fault, by my own most grievous fault; wherefore I pray God Almighty to have mercy on me, forgive me all my sins, and bring me to everlasting life. Amen

L The almighty and merciful Lord grant you pardon, forgiveness, and remission of all your sins. Amen

Sit

4. The PSALMODY. One or more psalms (4, 33, 34, 91, 134, 136) are sung or said. Silence for meditation follows each psalm.

5. The psalm prayer appropriate to each psalm is said following the silence.

C Amen

6. As a BRIEF LESSON, one or more of the following are read.

You are in our midst, O Lord, and you have named us yours; do not forsake us, O Lord our God. (Jer. 14:9)

Come to me, all whose work is hard, whose load is heavy, and I will give you rest. Bend your necks to my yoke, and learn from me, for I am gentle and humble-hearted; and you will find rest. For my yoke is good to bear, my load is light. (Matt. 11:28–30)

Peace is my parting gift to you, my own peace, such as the world cannot give. Set your troubled hearts at rest, and banish your fears. (John 14:27)

I am convinced that there is nothing in death or life, in the realm of spirits or superhuman powers, in the world as it is or the world as it shall be, in the forces of the universe, in heights or depths—nothing in all creation that can separate us from the love of God in Christ Jesus our Lord. (Rom. 8:38–39)

Humble yourselves under God's mighty hand and he will lift you up in due time. Cast all your cares on him, for you are his charge. Be sober, be watchful. Your adversary the devil prowls around like a roaring lion seeking someone to devour. Resist him, firm in your faith. (1 Peter 5:6–9a)

7. The RESPONSORY follows the reading(s).

L In-to your hands, O Lord, I com - mend my spir - it.
C In - to your hands I com - mend my spir - it.
L You have re - deemed me, O Lord, God of truth.
C In - to your hands I com - mend my spir - it.
L Glory to the Fa - ther, and to the Son, and to the Ho-ly Spir-it.
C In - to your hands I com - mend my spir - it.

Stand

8. THE HYMN is sung.

Kneel/Sit

L Hear my prayer, O Lord;
C listen to my cry.
L Keep me as the apple of your eye;
C hide me in the shadow of your wings.
L In righteousness I shall see you;
C when I awake, your presence will give me joy.

9. *One or more of the following prayers are sung or said.*

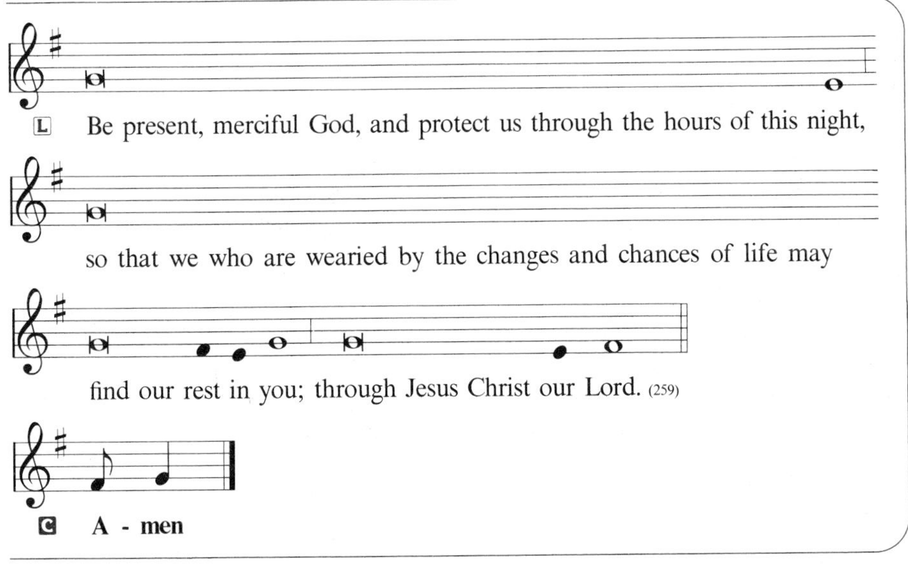
L Be present, merciful God, and protect us through the hours of this night,
so that we who are wearied by the changes and chances of life may
find our rest in you; through Jesus Christ our Lord. (259)
C A - men

OR

L O Lord, support us all the day long of this troubled life, until the shadows lengthen and the evening comes and the busy world is hushed, the fever of life is over, and our work is done. Then, Lord, in your mercy, grant us a safe lodging, and a holy rest, and peace at the last; through Jesus Christ our Lord. (260)

OR

L Be our light in the darkness, O Lord, and in your great mercy defend us from all perils and dangers of this night; for the love of your only Son, our Savior Jesus Christ. (261)

OR

L Visit our dwellings, O Lord, and drive from them all the snares of the enemy; let your holy angels dwell with us to preserve us in peace; and let your blessing be upon us always, through Jesus Christ our Lord. (262)

OR

L Eternal God, the hours both of day and night are yours, and to you the darkness is no threat. Be present, we pray, with those who labor in these hours of night, especially those who watch and work on behalf of others. Grant them diligence in their watching, faithfulness in their service, courage in danger, and competence in emergencies. Help them to meet the needs of others with confidence and compassion; through Jesus Christ our Lord. (263)

OR

L Gracious Lord, we give you thanks for the day, especially for the good we were permitted to give and to receive; the day is now past and we commit it to you. We entrust to you the night; we rest in surety, for you are our help, and you neither slumber nor sleep. (264)

C Amen

C Our Father in heaven,
hallowed be your name,
your kingdom come,
your will be done,
on earth as in heaven.
Give us today our daily bread.
Forgive us our sins
as we forgive those
who sin against us.
Save us from the time of trial
and deliver us from evil.
For the kingdom, the power,
and the glory are yours,
now and forever. Amen

OR

C Our Father, who art in heaven,
hallowed be thy name,
thy kingdom come,
thy will be done,
on earth as it is in heaven.
Give us this day our daily bread;
and forgive us our trespasses,
as we forgive those
who trespass against us;
and lead us not into temptation,
but deliver us from evil.
For thine is the kingdom,
and the power, and the glory,
forever and ever. Amen

Stand

10. The GOSPEL CANTICLE is sung.

L Guide us wak - ing, O Lord, and guard us sleep - ing; that
a-wake we may watch with Christ and a-sleep we may rest in peace.
C Lord, now you let your ser - vant go in peace; your word has
been ful - filled. My own eyes have seen the sal - va - tion
which you have prepared in the sight of ev - 'ry peo - ple:
a light to reveal you to the na - tions and the glory of your
peo - ple Is - ra - el. Glo - ry to the Fa - ther, and
to the Son, and to the Ho - ly Spir - it; as it
was in the be - gin - ning, is now, and will be for - ev - er. A - men.
Guide us wak - ing, O Lord, and guard us

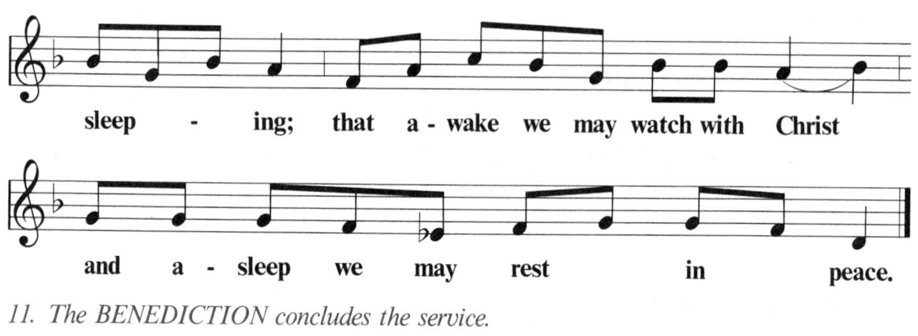
sleep - ing; that a - wake we may watch with Christ
and a - sleep we may rest in peace.

11. The BENEDICTION concludes the service.

L The almighty and merciful Lord, the Fa-ther, the Son, and

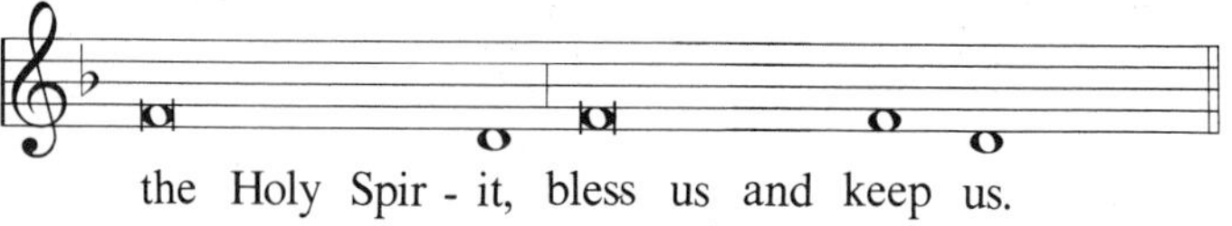
the Holy Spir - it, bless us and keep us.

C A - men

RESPONSIVE PRAYER 1

Suffrages

1. Responsive Prayer 1 is for use in the morning. Responsive Prayer 2 is for use at other times of the day and before travel.

L Holy God, holy and mighty, holy and immortal,

C have mercy and hear us.

C Our Father in heaven,
hallowed be your name,
your kingdom come,
your will be done,
on earth as in heaven.
Give us today our daily bread.
Forgive us our sins
as we forgive those
who sin against us.
Save us from the time of trial
and deliver us from evil.
For the kingdom, the power,
and the glory are yours,
now and forever. Amen

OR

C Our Father, who art in heaven,
hallowed be thy name,
thy kingdom come,
thy will be done,
on earth as it is in heaven.
Give us this day our daily bread;
and forgive us our trespasses,
as we forgive those
who trespass against us;
and lead us not into temptation,
but deliver us from evil.
For thine is the kingdom,
and the power, and the glory,
forever and ever. Amen

**C I believe in God, the Father almighty,
creator of heaven and earth.**

**I believe in Jesus Christ, his only Son, our Lord.
He was conceived by the power of the Holy Spirit
and born of the virgin Mary.
He suffered under Pontius Pilate,
was crucified, died, and was buried.
He descended into hell.*
On the third day he rose again.
He ascended into heaven,
and is seated at the right hand of the Father.
He will come to judge the living and the dead.**

**I believe in the Holy Spirit,
the holy catholic Church,
the communion of saints,
the forgiveness of sins,
the resurrection of the body,
and the life everlasting. Amen**

L O Lord, I cry to you for help.

C In the morning my prayer comes before you.

L Give me the joy of your saving help again,

C and sustain me with your bountiful Spirit.

L Let my mouth be full of your praise

C and your glory all the day long.

L Every day will I praise you,

C and praise your name forever and ever.

L Awesome things will you show us in your righteousness,

C O God of our salvation, O hope of all the ends of the earth and of the seas that are far away.

L Bless the Lord, O my soul,

C and all that is within me, bless his holy name.

L He redeems my life from the grave,

C and crowns me with mercy and lovingkindness.

**Or,* He descended to the dead.

L Lord, hear my prayer,

C **and let my cry come before you.**

2. The PRAYER OF THE DAY is said; the salutation may precede it. Additional prayers may be said also. The prayer beginning, "We give thanks to you . . . ," is always said.

L The Lord be with you.

C **And also with you.**

L Let us pray. . . .

C **Amen**

L We give thanks to you, heavenly Father, through Jesus Christ your dear Son, that you have protected us through the night from all danger and harm. We ask you to preserve and keep us, this day also, from all sin and evil, that in all our thoughts, words, and deeds we may serve and please you. Into your hands we commend our bodies and souls and all that is ours. Let your holy angels have charge of us, that the wicked one have no power over us. (265)

C **Amen**

3. The BENEDICAMUS and BENEDICTION conclude the service.

L Let us bless the Lord.

C **Thanks be to God.**

L The Lord almighty order our days and our deeds in his peace.

C **Amen**

RESPONSIVE PRAYER 2

Suffrages

4. Responsive Prayer 1 is for use in the morning. Responsive Prayer 2 is for use at other times of the day and before travel.

L Holy God, holy and mighty, holy and immortal,

C have mercy and hear us.

C Our Father in heaven,
hallowed be your name,
your kingdom come,
your will be done,
on earth as in heaven.
Give us today our daily bread.
Forgive us our sins
as we forgive those
who sin against us.
Save us from the time of trial
and deliver us from evil.
For the kingdom, the power,
and the glory are yours,
now and forever. Amen

OR

C Our Father, who art in heaven,
hallowed be thy name,
thy kingdom come,
thy will be done,
on earth as it is in heaven.
Give us this day our daily bread;
and forgive us our trespasses,
as we forgive those
who trespass against us;
and lead us not into temptation,
but deliver us from evil.
For thine is the kingdom,
and the power, and the glory,
forever and ever. Amen

C **I believe in God, the Father almighty,**
creator of heaven and earth.

I believe in Jesus Christ, his only Son, our Lord.
He was conceived by the power of the Holy Spirit
and born of the virgin Mary.
He suffered under Pontius Pilate,
was crucified, died, and was buried.
He descended into hell.*
On the third day he rose again.
He ascended into heaven,
and is seated at the right hand of the Father.
He will come to judge the living and the dead.

I believe in the Holy Spirit,
the holy catholic Church,
the communion of saints,
the forgiveness of sins,
the resurrection of the body,
and the life everlasting. Amen

L Show us your mercy, O Lord,

C **and grant us your salvation.**

L Clothe your ministers with righteousness.

C **Let your people sing with joy.**

L Give peace, O Lord, in all the world;

C **for only in you can we live in safety.**

L Lord, keep this nation under your care,

C **and guide us in the way of justice and truth.**

L Let your way be known upon earth;

C **your saving health among all nations.**

L Let not the needy, O Lord, be forgotten,

C **nor the hope of the poor be taken away.**

L Create in us clean hearts, O God,

C **and sustain us with your Holy Spirit.**

---

* *Or,* He descended to the dead.

5. The PRAYER OF THE DAY is said; the salutation may precede it. Additional prayers may be said also.

L The Lord be with you.

C And also with you.

L Let us pray. . . .

C Amen

6. The final prayer is that appropriate to the time of day:

NOON

L Gracious Jesus, our Lord and our God, at this hour you bore our sins in your own body on the tree so that we, being dead to sin, might live unto righteousness. Have mercy upon us now and at the hour of our death, and grant to us, your servants, with all others who devoutly remember your blessed Passion, a holy and peaceful life in this world and, through your grace, eternal glory in the life to come; where, with the Father and the Holy Spirit, you live and reign, God forever. (266)

C Amen

OR

AFTERNOON

L Heavenly Father, in whom we live and move and have our being: We humbly pray you so to guide and govern us by your Holy Spirit, that in all the cares and occupations of our life we may not forget you, but remember that we are ever walking in your sight; through Jesus Christ our Lord. (267)

C Amen

OR

EVENING

L We give thanks to you, heavenly Father, through Jesus Christ your dear Son, that you have this day so graciously protected us. We beg you to forgive us all our sins and the wrong which we have done. By your great mercy defend us from all the perils and dangers of this night. Into your hands we commend our bodies and souls, and all that is ours. Let your holy angels have charge of us, that the wicked one have no power over us. (268)

C Amen

OR

BEFORE TRAVEL

L Lord God our Father, you kept Abraham and Sarah in safety throughout the days of their pilgrimage, you led the children of Israel through the midst of the sea, and by a star you led the Wise Men to the infant Jesus. Protect and guide us now in this time as we set out to travel, make our ways safe and our homecomings joyful, and bring us at last to our heavenly home, where you dwell in glory with your Son and the Holy Spirit, God forever. (269)

C **Amen**

7. The BENEDICAMUS and BENEDICTION conclude the service.

L Let us bless the Lord.

C **Thanks be to God.**

L The Lord bless us, defend us from all evil, and bring us to everlasting life.

C **Amen**

THE LITANY

L Lord, have mercy. ℟
℟ Lord, have mer - cy.
L Christ, have mercy. ℟
℟ Christ, have mer - cy.
L Lord, have mercy. ℟
℟ Lord, have mer - cy.
L O Christ, hear us. ℟
℟ In mer - cy hear us.

L God, the Father in . . . heaven, R
L God, the Son, redeemer of the world, R
L God, the Holy . . . . . Spirit, R
L Holy Trinity, one . . . . God, R
R have mer - cy on us.
L Be gra - cious to us. R
R Spare us, good Lord.
L Be gra - cious to us. R
R Spare us, good Lord.
L From all sin, from all error, from all evil;
from the cunning assaults of the devil;
from an unprepared and . . . . e - vil death: R
L From war, bloodshed, and violence; from corrupt
and unjust government; from sedi- . . . . tion and treason: R
L From epidemic, drought, and famine; from fire
and flood, earthquake, lightning and storm;
and from ever- . . . . last - ing death: R
R Good Lord, de - liv - er us.

L By the mystery of your incarnation; by your . . . . ho - ly birth: R
L By your baptism, fasting, and temptation; by your agony and bloody sweat; by your cross and suffering; by your . . . . death and burial: R
L By your resurrection and ascension; by the gift of the Ho - ly Spirit: R
R Help us, good Lord.
L In all time of our tribulation; in all time of our prosperity; in the hour of death; and in the . . day of judgment: R
R Save us, good Lord.
L Though unworthy, we im - plore you R
R to hear us, Lord our God.
L To rule and govern your holy catholic Church; to guide all servants of your Church in the love of your Word and in holiness of life; to put an end to all schisms and causes of offense to those who would believe; and to bring into the way of truth all who have . . . . gone a - stray: R
R We im - plore you to hear us, good Lord.

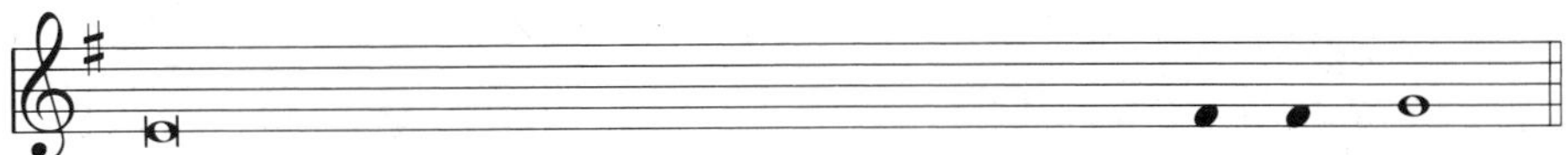

L To beat down Satan under our feet; to send faithful workers into your harvest; to accompany your Word with your Spirit and power; to raise up those who fall and to strengthen those who stand; and to comfort and help the fainthearted and. . . . . .the dis-tressed: R

We im - plore you to hear us, good Lord.

R **We im - plore you to hear us, good Lord.**

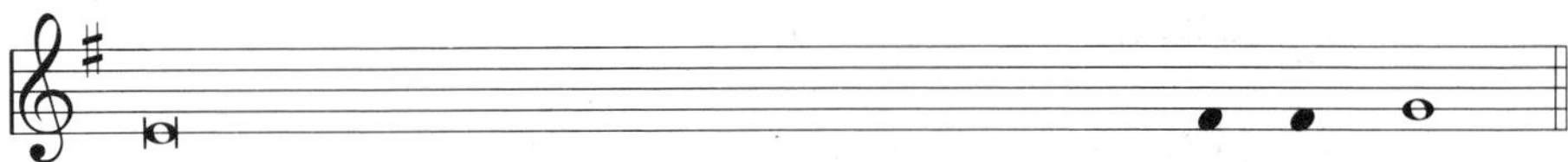

L To give to all nations justice and peace; to preserve our country from discord and strife; to direct and guard those who have civil authority; and to bless and guide. . . . . .all our people: R

We im - plore you to hear us, good Lord.

R **We im - plore you to hear us, good Lord.**

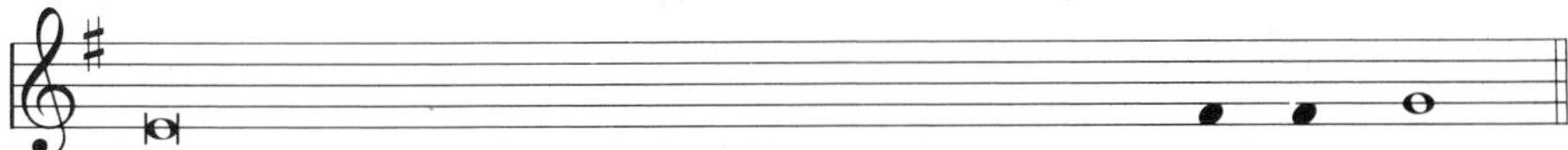

L To behold and help all who are in danger, need, or tribulation; to protect and guide all who travel; to preserve and provide for all women in childbirth; to watch over children and to guide the young; to heal the sick and to strengthen their families and friends; to bring reconciliation to families in discord; to provide for the unemployed and for all in need; to be merciful to all who are imprisoned; to support, comfort, and guide all orphans, widowers, and widows; and to have mercy on . . . . all your people: R

We im - plore you to hear us, good Lord.

R **We im - plore you to hear us, good Lord.**

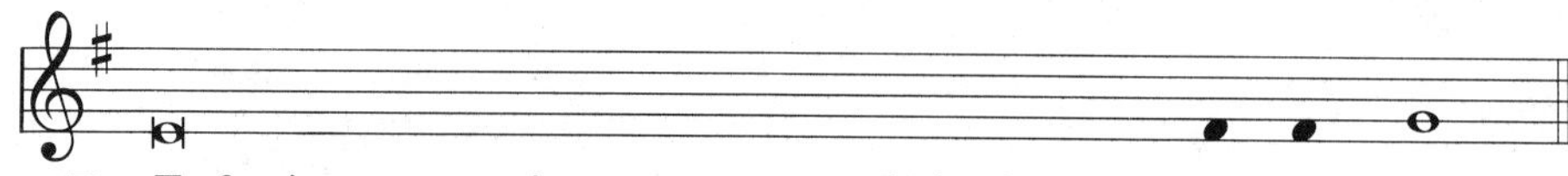

L To forgive our enemies, persecutors, and slanderers, and to reconcile us to them; to help us use wisely the fruits and treasures of the earth, the sea, and the air; and graciously to . . . . hear our prayers: R

R **We im - plore you to hear us, good Lord.**

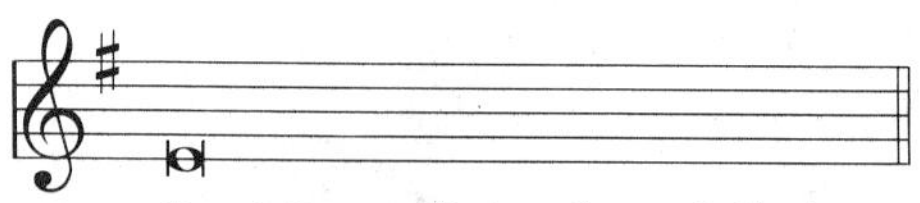

L Lord Jesus Christ, Son of God, R

R **we im-plore you to hear us.**

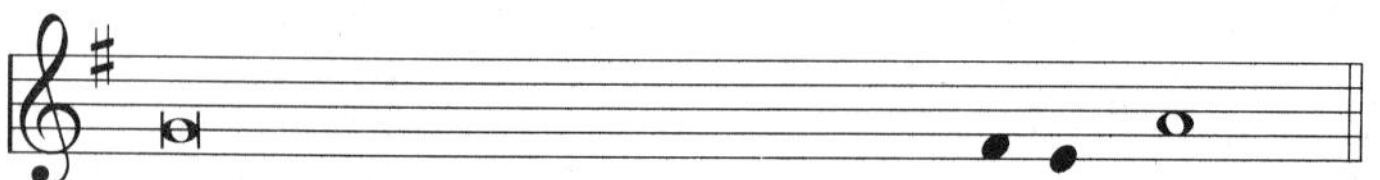

L Lamb of God, you take away the sin of the world; R

R **have mer - cy on us.**

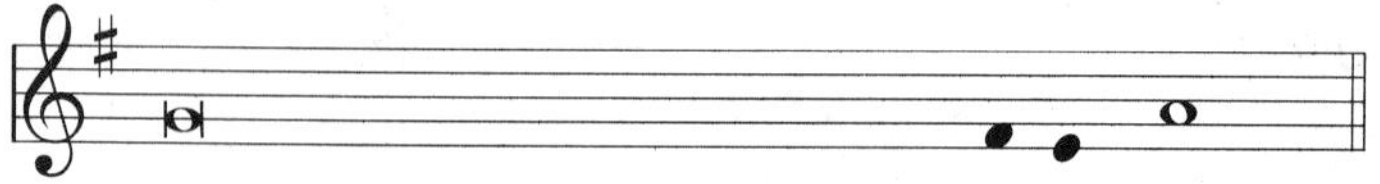

L Lamb of God, you take away the sin of the world; R

R **have mer - cy on us.**

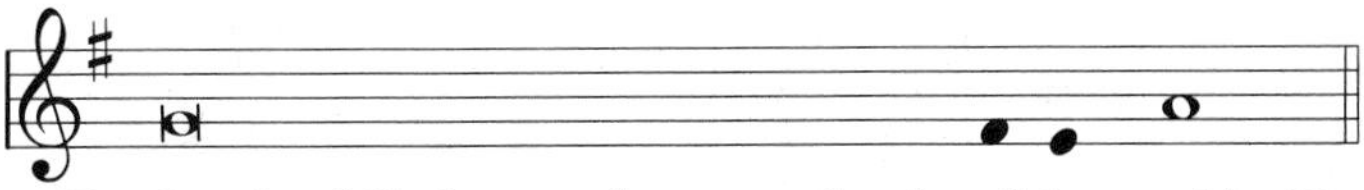

L Lamb of God, you take away the sin of the world; ℟

℟ **give us peace. A - men.**

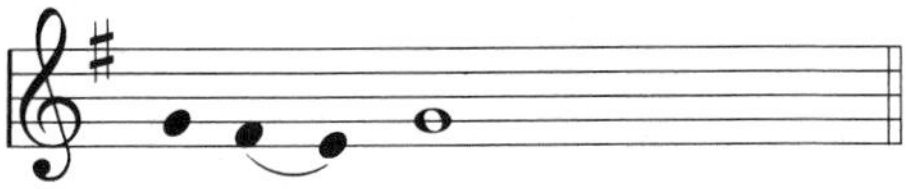

L O Christ, hear us. ℟

℟ **In mer - cy hear us.**

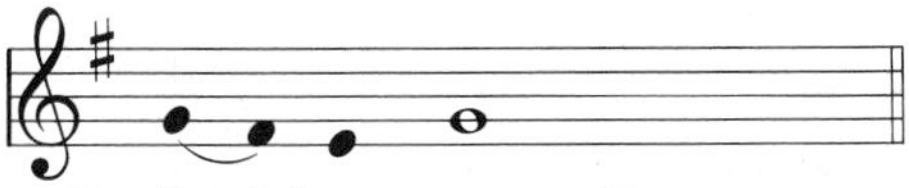

L Lord, have mercy. ℟

℟ **Lord, have mer - cy.**

L Christ, have mercy. ℟

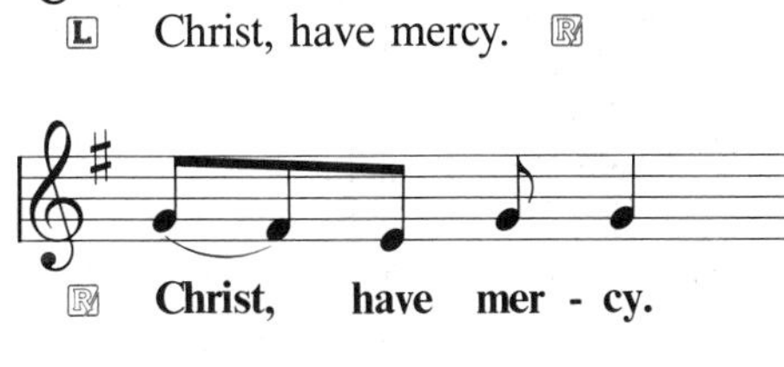

℟ **Christ, have mer - cy.**

L Lord, have mer-cy. ℟

℟ **Lord, have mer - cy.**

PROPERS FOR DAILY PRAYER

ADVENT

Invitatory

Morning Prayer

L Give glory to the coming King.

C **Oh, come, let us worship him.**

Versicles (*Service of Light*)

Evening Prayer

L The Spirit and the Church cry out:

C **Come, Lord Jesus.**

L All those who await his appearance pray:

C **Come, Lord Jesus.**

L The whole creation pleads:

C **Come, Lord Jesus.**

Psalm Antiphons

In that day the mountains
shall drip sweet wine,*
and the hills shall flow
with milk and honey. Alleluia.

OR

The uneven ground
shall be made smooth
and the rough places a plain.*
Come, Lord, do not delay. Alleluia.

Antiphon: "Benedictus" and "Magnificat"

Fear not, Mary,
you have found favor
with the Lord;*
Behold, you shall conceive
and bear a Son. Alleluia.

From December 17, the Great-O-Antiphons may be used.

December 17

O Wisdom,
proceeding from the mouth
of the Most High,
pervading and permeating
all creation,
mightily ordering all things:*
Come and teach us
the way of prudence.

December 18

O Adonai and
ruler of the house of Israel,
who appeared to Moses
in the burning bush
and gave him the Ĺaw on Sinai:*
  Come with an outstretched árm
  and redeem us.

December 19

O Root of Jesse, standing
as an ensign
before the peoples,
before whom all kings are mute,
to whom the nations wíll do homage:*
  Come quickly to delíver us.

December 20

O Key of David and
scepter of the house of Israel,
you open and no one can close,
you close and no óne can open:*
  Come and rescue the prisoners
  who are in darkness
  and the shadów of death.

December 21

O Dayspring,
splendor of light éverlasting:*
  Come and enlighten those
  who sit in darkness
  and in the shadów of death.

December 22

O King of the nations,
the ruler they long fór,
the cornerstone uniting all people:*
  Come and save us all,
  whom you formed óut of clay.

December 23

O Emmanuel, our king
and our lawgiver,
the anointed of the nations
ánd their Savior:*
  Come and save us,
  O Ĺord our God.

CHRISTMAS/EPIPHANY

Invitatory

Morning Prayer

L The Word was made flesh, and we beheld his glory.
C Oh, come, let us worship him.

Versicles (*Service of Light*)

Evening Prayer

L The people who walked in darkness have seen a great light.

**C The light shines in the darkness,
and the darkness has not overcome it.**

L Those who dwelt in the land of deep darkness, on them has light shined.

**C We have beheld Christ's glory,
glory as of the only Son from the Father.**

L For to us a child is born, to us a Son is given.

**C In him was life,
and the life was the light of man.**

Psalm Antiphons

A prince from the day
óf your birth,*
  from the womb before daybreak
  have I begótten you.
OR
Come, you peoples óf the earth;*
  drink from the wells óf the Savior.

Antiphon: "Benedictus" and "Magnificat"

Today Christ is bórn;
today salvation hás appeared.*
  Today the just exult and say,
  Glory to God in the highest.
  Álleluia.
OR
Our Lord and Savior,
begotten befóre all ages,*
  revealed himself to the world.
  Álleluia.

LENT

Invitatory

Morning Prayer

L The Lord is near to those who call on him.

C Oh, come, let us worship him.

Versicles *(Service of Light)*

Evening Prayer

L Behold, now is the acceptable time;

C now is the day of salvation.

L Turn us again, O God of our salvation,

C that the light of your face may shine on us.

L May your justice shine like the sun;

C and may the poor be lifted up.

Psalm Antiphons

Return to the Lord your God,
for he is gracious and merciful,*
  slow to anger, and
  abounding in steadfast love.
OR
The Lord delivers us
from the power of darkness,*
  and leads us into the kingdom
  of his Son.

Antiphon: "Benedictus" and "Magnificat"

Let justice roll down like waters,*
  and righteousness
  like an overflowing stream.

HOLY WEEK

Invitatory

Morning Prayer

The Invitatory and Venite are not sung during Holy Week.

Versicles *(Service of Light)*

Evening Prayer

The Service of Light is omitted during Holy Week. Begin the service with the Psalmody—Psalm 141.

Psalm Antiphons

Christ has humbled himself
and become obedient to death,*
  even to death on a cross.
OR
He was wounded
for our transgressions
and bruised for our iniquities,*
  and on him was the chastisement
  that made us whole.

Antiphon: "Benedictus" and "Magnificat"

Glory to the cross
of our Lord Jesus Christ,*
  our salvation, life,
  and resurrection.

EASTER

Invitatory

Morning Prayer

L The Lord is risen indeed.

C Oh, come, let us worship him.

Versicles *(Service of Light)*

Evening Prayer

L Jesus Christ is risen from the dead.

C Alleluia, alleluia, alleluia.

L We are illumined by the brightness of his rising.

C Alleluia, alleluia, alleluia.

L Death has no more dominion over us.

C Alleluia, alleluia, alleluia.

Psalm Antiphons

The glory of the Lord
shines on the city. Álleluia.*
Its lamp is the Lamb. Álleluia.
OR
God feeds us with finest wheat. Álleluia.*
He fills us with honey
from the rock. Álleluia.

Antiphon: "Benedictus" and "Magnificat"

This is the day the Lord has made.
Álleluia.*
Let us rejoice and be glad in it.
Álleluia.

THANKSGIVING FOR LIGHT I

We praise and thank you, O God, for you are without beginning and without end.
Through Christ you are the creator and preserver of the whole world; but, above all, you are his God and Father, the giver of the Spirit, and the ruler of all that is, seen and unseen.
You made the day for the works of light and the night for the refreshment of our weakness.
O loving Lord and source of all that is good, mercifully accept our evening sacrifice of praise.
As you have conducted us through the day and brought us to night's beginning, keep us now in Christ; grant us a peaceful evening and a night free from sin; and, at the end, bring us to everlasting life through Christ our Lord.
Through him we offer glory, honor, and worship to you in the Holy Spirit, now and always and forever and ever.
Amen

THANKSGIVING FOR LIGHT II

We praise and thank you, O God, through your Son, Jesus Christ our Lord, through whom you have enlightened us by revealing the light that never fades.
Night *is falling/has fallen* and day's allotted span draws to a close.
The daylight which you created for our pleasure has fully satisfied us, and yet, of your free gift, now the evening lights do not fail us.
We praise you and glorify you through your Son, Jesus Christ our Lord; through him be glory, honor, and power to you in the Holy Spirit, now and always and forever and ever.
Amen

PSALMS FOR DAILY PRAYER

	SATURDAY	SUNDAY	MONDAY	TUESDAY	WEDNESDAY	THURSDAY	FRIDAY	SATURDAY
ADVENT Morning		24, 150	122, 145	33, 146	50, 147:1–12	18:1–20; 147:13–21	102, 148	90, 149
Evening	80, 72	25, 110	40, 67	85, 94	53, 17	126, 62	130, 16	

CHRISTMAS

December 24		
Evening Prayer	132, 114	
December 25		
Morning Prayer	2, Laudate Psalm*	
Evening Prayer	98, 96	
December 26		
Morning Prayer	116, Laudate Psalm*	
Evening Prayer	119:1–24; 27	
December 27		
Morning Prayer	34, Laudate Psalm*	
Evening Prayer	19, 121	
December 28		
Morning Prayer	2, Laudate Psalm*	
Evening Prayer	110, 111	
December 29		
Morning Prayer	96, Laudate Psalm*	
Evening Prayer	132, 97	
December 30		
Morning Prayer	93, Laudate Psalm*	
Evening Prayer	89:1–18; 89:19–52	
December 31		
Morning Prayer	98, Laudate Psalm*	
Evening Prayer	45, 96	
January 1		
Morning Prayer	98, Laudate Psalm*	
Evening Prayer	99, 8	
January 2		
Morning Prayer	48, Laudate Psalm*	
Evening Prayer	9, 29	
January 3		
Morning Prayer	111, Laudate Psalm*	
Evening Prayer	107, 15	
January 4		
Morning Prayer	20, Laudate Psalm*	
Evening Prayer	93, 97	
January 5		
Morning Prayer	99, Laudate Psalm*	
Evening Prayer	96, 110	
January 6		
Morning Prayer	72, Laudate Psalm*	
Evening Prayer	100, 67	

	SATURDAY	SUNDAY	MONDAY	TUESDAY	WEDNESDAY	THURSDAY	FRIDAY	SATURDAY
LENT Morning		84, 150	119:73–80; 145	34, 146	5, 147:1–12	27, 147:13–21	22, 148	43, 149
Evening	31, 143	42, 32	121, 6	25, 91	27, 51	126, 102	105, 130	
EASTER Morning		93, 150	97, 145	98, 146	99, 147:1–12	47, 147:13–21	96, 148	92, 149
Evening	23, 114	136, 117	124, 115	66, 116	9, 118	68, 113	49, 138	
GENERAL *Week 1* Morning		103, 150	5, 145	42, 146	89:1–18; 147:1–12	97, 147:13–21	51, 148	104, 149
Evening	138, 98	117, 139	82, 29	102, 133	1, 33	16, 62	142, 65	
Week 2 Morning		19, 150	135, 145	123, 146	15, 147:1–12	36, 147:13–21	130, 148	56, 149
Evening	118, 111	81, 113	97, 112	30, 86	48, 4	80, 27	32, 139	
Week 3 Morning		67, 150	57, 145	54, 146	65, 147:1–12	143, 147:13–21	88, 148	122, 149
Evening	100, 63	46, 93	85, 47	28, 99	125, 91	81, 116	6, 20	
Week 4 Morning		108, 150	62, 145	12, 146	96, 147:1–12	116, 147:13–21	84, 148	63, 149
Evening	125, 90	66, 23	73, 9	36, 7	132, 134	26, 130	25, 40	

*Sunday—150; Monday—145; Tuesday—146; Wednesday—147:1–12; Thursday—147:13–21; Friday—148; Saturday—149

DAILY LECTIONARY

YEAR ONE

Week of 1 Advent

S Isaiah 1:1–9
2 Peter 3:1–10
Matthew 25:1–13

M Isaiah 1:10–20
1 Thessalonians 1:1–10
Luke 20:1–8

T Isaiah 1:21–31
1 Thessalonians 2:1–12
Luke 20:9–18

W Isaiah 2:1–4
1 Thessalonians 2:13–20
Luke 20:19–26

Th Isaiah 2:5–22
1 Thessalonians 3:1–13
Luke 20:27–40

F Isaiah 3:1—4:1
1 Thessalonians 4:1–12
Luke 20:41—21:4

S Isaiah 4:2–6
1 Thessalonians 4:13–18
Luke 21:5–19

Week of 2 Advent

S Isaiah 5:1–7
2 Peter 3:11–18
Luke 7:28–35

M Isaiah 5:8–17
1 Thessalonians 5:1–11
Luke 21:20–28

T Isaiah 5:18–25
1 Thessalonians 5:12–28
Luke 21:29–38

W Isaiah 6:1–13
2 Thessalonians 1:1–12
John 7:53—8:11

Th Isaiah 7:1–9
2 Thessalonians 2:1–12
Luke 22:1–13

F Isaiah 7:10–25
2 Thessalonians 2:13—3:5
Luke 22:14–30

S Isaiah 8:1–15
2 Thessalonians 3:6–18
Luke 22:31–38

Week of 3 Advent

S Isaiah 13:1–13
Hebrews 12:18–29
John 3:22–30

M Isaiah 8:16—9:1
2 Peter 1:1–11
Luke 22:39–53

T Isaiah 9:2–7
2 Peter 1:12–21
Luke 22:54–69

W Isaiah 9:8–17
2 Peter 2:1–10a
Mark 1:1–8

Th Isaiah 9:18—10:4
2 Peter 2:10b–16
Matthew 3:1–12

F Isaiah 10:5–19
2 Peter 2:17–22
Matthew 11:2–15

S Isaiah 10:20–27
Jude 17–25
Luke 3:1–9

Week of 4 Advent

S Isaiah 11:1–9
Ephesians 6:10–20
John 3:16–21

M Isaiah 11:10–16
Revelation 20:1–10
John 5:30–47

T Isaiah 28:9–22
Revelation 20:11—21:8
Luke 1:5–25

W Isaiah 29:9–24
Revelation 21:9–21
Luke 1:26–38

Th Isaiah 31:1–9
Revelation 21:22—22:5
Luke 1:39–48a (48b–56)

F Isaiah 33:17–22
Revelation 22:6–11, 18–20
Luke 1:57–66

S Isaiah 35:1–10
Revelation 22:12–17, 21
Luke 1:67–80

Christmas Day and Following

Dec 25 Zechariah 2:10–13
1 John 4:7–16
John 3:31–36

Dec 26 Wisdom 4:7–15
or 2 Chronicles 24:17–22
Acts 6:1–7
Acts 7:59—8:8

Dec 27 Proverbs 8:22–30
1 John 5:1–12
John 13:20–35

Dec 28 Isaiah 49:13–23
Isaiah 54:1–13
Matthew 18:1–14

Dec 29 Isaiah 12:1–6
Revelation 1:1–8
John 7:37–52

Dec 30 Isaiah 25:1–9
Revelation 1:9–20
John 7:53—8:11

Dec 31 Isaiah 26:1–6
2 Corinthians 5:16—6:2
John 8:12–19

First Sunday after Christmas

Isaiah 62:6–7, 10–12
Hebrews 2:10–18
Matthew 1:18–25

Jan 1 Genesis 17:1–12a, 15–16
Colossians 2:6–12
John 16:23b–30

Jan 2 Genesis 12:1–7
Hebrews 11:1–12
John 6:35–42, 48–51

Jan 3 Genesis 28:10–22
Hebrews 11:13–22
John 10:7–17

Jan 4 Exodus 3:1–15
Hebrews 11:23–31
John 14:6–14

Jan 5 Joshua 1:1–9
Hebrews 11:32—12:2
John 15:1–16

Second Sunday after Christmas

Ecclesiasticus 3:3–9, 14–17
or Deuteronomy 33:1–5
1 John 2:12–17
John 6:41–47

The Epiphany and Following

Jan 6 Isaiah 52:7–10
Revelation 21:22–27
Matthew 12:14–21

Jan 7* Isaiah 52:3–6
Revelation 2:1–7
John 2:1–11

Jan 8 Isaiah 59:15b–21
Revelation 2:8–17
John 4:46–54

Jan 9 Isaiah 63:1–5
Revelation 2:18–29
John 5:1–15

Jan 10 Isaiah 65:1–9
Revelation 3:1–6
John 6:1–14

Jan 11 Isaiah 65:13–16
Revelation 3:7–13
John 6:15–27

Jan 12 Isaiah 66:1–2, 22–23
Revelation 3:14–22
John 9:1–12, 35–38

Week of 1 Epiphany

S Isaiah 40:1–11
Hebrews 1:1–12
John 1:1–7, 19–20, 29–34

M Isaiah 40:12–24
Ephesians 1:1–14
Mark 1:1–13

T Isaiah 40:25–31
Ephesians 1:15–23
Mark 1:14–28

W Isaiah 41:1–16
Ephesians 2:1–10
Mark 1:29–45

Th Isaiah 41:17–29
Ephesians 2:11–22
Mark 2:1–12

F Isaiah 42:(1–9) 10–17
Ephesians 3:1–13
Mark 2:13–22

S Isaiah (42:18–25) 43:1–13
Ephesians 3:14–21
Mark 2:23—3:6

** The readings for the dated days after the Epiphany are used only until the following Saturday evening.*

Week of 2 Epiphany

S	Isaiah 43:14—44:5 Hebrews 6:17—7:10 John 4:27-42
M	Isaiah 44:6-8, 21-23 Ephesians 4:1-16 Mark 3:7-19a
T	Isaiah 44:9-20 Ephesians 4:17-32 Mark 3:19b-35
W	Isaiah 44:24—45:7 Ephesians 5:1-14 Mark 4:1-20
Th	Isaiah 45:5-17 Ephesians 5:15-33 Mark 4:21-34
F	Isaiah 45:18-25 Ephesians 6:1-9 Mark 4:35-41
S	Isaiah 46:1-13 Ephesians 6:10-24 Mark 5:1-20

Week of 3 Epiphany

S	Isaiah 47:1-15 Hebrews 10:19-31 John 5:2-18
M	Isaiah 48:1-11 Galatians 1:1-17 Mark 5:21-43
T	Isaiah 48:12-21 (22) Galatians 1:18—2:10 Mark 6:1-13
W	Isaiah 49:1-12 Galatians 2:11-21 Mark 6:13-29
Th	Isaiah 49:13-23 (24-26) Galatians 3:1-14 Mark 6:30-46
F	Isaiah 50:1-11 Galatians 3:15-22 Mark 6:47-56
S	Isaiah 51:1-8 Galatians 3:23-29 Mark 7:1-23

Week of 4 Epiphany

S	Isaiah 51:9-16 Hebrews 11:8-16 John 7:14-31
M	Isaiah 51:17-23 Galatians 4:1-11 Mark 7:24-37
T	Isaiah 52:1-12 Galatians 4:12-20 Mark 8:1-10
W	Isaiah 52:13—53:12 Galatians 4:21-31 Mark 8:11-26
Th	Isaiah 54:1-10 (11-17) Galatians 5:1-15 Mark 8:27—9:1
F	Isaiah 55:1-13 Galatians 5:16-24 Mark 9:2-13
S	Isaiah 56:1-8 Galatians 5:25—6:10 Mark 9:14-29

Week of 5 Epiphany

S	Isaiah 57:1-13 Hebrews 12:1-6 John 7:37-46
M	Isaiah 57:14-21 Galatians 6:11-18 Mark 9:30-41
T	Isaiah 58:1-12 2 Timothy 1:1-14 Mark 9:42-50
W	Isaiah 59:1-21 2 Timothy 1:15—2:13 Mark 10:1-16
Th	Isaiah 60:1-22 2 Timothy 2:14-26 Mark 10:17-31
F	Isaiah 61:1-9 2 Timothy 3:1-17 Mark 10:32-45
S	Isaiah 61:10—62:5 2 Timothy 4:1-8 Mark 10:46-52

Week of 6 Epiphany

S	Isaiah 62:6-12 1 John 2:3-11 John 8:12-19
M	Isaiah 63:1-6 1 Timothy 1:1-17 Mark 11:1-11
T	Isaiah 63:7-14 1 Timothy 1:18—2:8 (9-15) Mark 11:12-26
W	Isaiah 63:15—64:9 1 Timothy 3:1-16 Mark 11:27—12:12
Th	Isaiah 65:1-12 1 Timothy 4:1-16 Mark 12:13-27
F	Isaiah 65:17-25 1 Timothy 5:(1-16) 17-22 (23-25) Mark 12:28-34
S	Isaiah 66:1-6 1 Timothy 6: (1-5) 6-21 Mark 12:35-44

Week of 7 Epiphany

S	Isaiah 66:7-14 1 John 3:4-10 John 10:7-16
M	Ruth 1:1-14 2 Corinthians 1:1-11 Matthew 5:1-12
T	Ruth 1:15-22 2 Corinthians 1:12-22 Matthew 5:13-20
W	Ruth 2:1-13 2 Corinthians 1:23—2:17 Matthew 5:21-26
Th	Ruth 2:14-23 2 Corinthians 3:1-18 Matthew 5:27-37
F	Ruth 3:1-18 2 Corinthians 4:1-12 Matthew 5:38-48
S	Ruth 4:1-22 2 Corinthians 4:13—5:10 Matthew 6:1-6

Week of 8 Epiphany

S	Deuteronomy 4:1-9 2 Timothy 4:1-8 John 12:1-8
M	Deuteronomy 4:9-14 2 Corinthians 10:1-18 Matthew 6:7-15
T	Deuteronomy 4:15-24 2 Corinthians 11:1-21a Matthew 6:16-23
W	Deuteronomy 4:25-31 2 Corinthians 11:21b-33 Matthew 6:24-34
Th	Deuteronomy 4:32-40 2 Corinthians 12:1-10 Matthew 7:1-12
F	Deuteronomy 5:1-22 2 Corinthians 12:11-21 Matthew 7:13-21
S	Deuteronomy 5:22-33 2 Corinthians 13:1-14 Matthew 7:22-29

Transfiguration and Following

S	Daniel 7:9-10, 13-14 2 Corinthians 3:1-9 John 12:27-36a
M	Deuteronomy 6:1-15 Hebrews 1:1-14 John 1:1-18
T	Deuteronomy 6:16-25 Hebrews 2:1-10 John 1:19-28
Ash Wednesday	Jonah 3:1—4:11 Hebrews 12:1-14 Luke 18:9-14
Th	Deuteronomy 7:6-11 Titus 1:1-16 John 1:29-34
F	Deuteronomy 7:12-16 Titus 2:1-15 John 1:35-42
S	Deuteronomy 7:17-26 Titus 3:1-15 John 1:43-51

Week of 1 Lent

S	Jeremiah 9:23-24 1 Corinthians 1:18-31 Mark 2:18-22
M	Deuteronomy 8:1-20 Hebrews 2:11-18 John 2:1-12
T	Deuteronomy 9:(1-3) 4-12 Hebrews 3:1-11 John 2:13-22
W	Deuteronomy 9:13-21 Hebrews 3:12-19 John 2:23—3:15
Th	Deuteronomy 9:23—10:5 Hebrews 4:1-10 John 3:16-21
F	Deuteronomy 10:12-22 Hebrews 4:11-16 John 3:22-36
S	Deuteronomy 11:18-28 Hebrews 5:1-10 John 4:1-26

Week of 2 Lent

S Jeremiah 1:1–10
1 Corinthians 3:11–23
Mark 3:31—4:9

M Jeremiah 1:11–19
Romans 1:1–15
John 4:27–42

T Jeremiah 2:1–13, 29–32
Romans 1:16–25
John 4:43–54

W Jeremiah 3:6–18
Romans 1:(26–27) 28—2:11
John 5:1–18

Th Jeremiah 4:9–10, 19–28
Romans 2:12–24
John 5:19–29

F Jeremiah 5:1–9
Romans 2:25—3:18
John 5:30–47

S Jeremiah 5:20–31
Romans 3:19–31
John 7:1–13

Week of 3 Lent

S Jeremiah 6:9–15
1 Corinthians 6:12–20
Mark 5:1–20

M Jeremiah 7:1–15
Romans 4:1–12
John 7:14–36

T Jeremiah 7:21–34
Romans 4:13–25
John 7:37–52

W Jeremiah 8:4–7, 18—9:6
Romans 5:1–11
John 8:12–20

Th Jeremiah 10:11–24
Romans 5:12–21
John 8:21–32

F Jeremiah 11:1–8, 14–17
Romans 6:1–11
John 8:33–47

S Jeremiah 13:1–11
Romans 6:12–23
John 8:47–59

Week of 4 Lent

S Jeremiah 14:1–9 (10–16) 17–22
Galatians 4:21—5:1
Mark 8:11–21

M Jeremiah 16:(1–9) 10–21
Romans 7:1–12
John 6:1–15

T Jeremiah 17:19–27
Romans 7:13–25
John 6:16–27

W Jeremiah 18:1–11
Romans 8:1–11
John 6:27–40

Th Jeremiah 22:13–23
Romans 8:12–27
John 6:41–51

F Jeremiah 23:1–8
Romans 8:28–39
John 6:52–59

S Jeremiah 23:9–15
Romans 9:1–18
John 6:60–71

Week of 5 Lent

S Jeremiah 23:16–32
1 Corinthians 9:19–27
Mark 8:31—9:1

M Jeremiah 24:1–10
Romans 9:19–33
John 9:1–17

T Jeremiah 25:8–17
Romans 10:1–13
John 9:18–41

W Jeremiah 25:30–38
Romans 10:14–21
John 10:1–18

Th Jeremiah 26:1–16 (17–24)
Romans 11:1–12
John 10:19–42

F Jeremiah 29:1 (2–3) 4–14
Romans 11:13–24
John 11:1–27
or John 12:1–10

S Jeremiah 31:27–34
Romans 11:25–36
John 11:28–44
or John 12:37–50

Holy Week

Sunday of the Passion
Zechariah 9:9–12
or Zechariah 12:9–11; 13:1, 7–9
1 Timothy 6:12–16
Matthew 21:12–17

M Jeremiah 11:18–20;
12:1–16 (17)
Philippians 3:1–14
John 12:9–19

T Jeremiah 15:10–21
Philippians 3:15–21
John 12:20–26

W Jeremiah 17:5–10, 14–17 (18)
Philippians 4:1–13
John 12:27–36

Maundy Thursday
Jeremiah 20:7–11 (12–13) 14–18
1 Corinthians 10:14–17;
11:27–32
John 17:1–11 (12–26)

Good Friday
Wisdom 1:16—2:1, 12–22
or Genesis 22:1–14
1 Peter 1:10–20
John 13:36–38
or John 19:38–42

S Job 19:21–27a
Hebrews 4:1–16
Romans 8:1–11

Easter Week

S Exodus 12:1–14
Isaiah 51:9–11
Luke 24:13–35
or John 20:19–23

M Jonah 2:1–10
Acts 2:14, 22–32
John 14:1–14

T Isaiah 30:18–26
Acts 2:36–41 (42–47)
John 14:15–31

W Micah 7:7–15
Acts 3:1–10
John 15:1–11

Th Ezekiel 37:1–14
Acts 3:11–26
John 15:12–27

F Daniel 12:1–4, 13
Acts 4:1–12
John 16:1–15

S Isaiah 25:1–9
Acts 4:13–21 (22–31)
John 16:16–33

Week of 2 Easter

S Isaiah 43:8–13
1 Peter 2:2–10
John 14:1–7

M Daniel 1:1–21
1 John 1:1–10
John 17:1–11

T Daniel 2:1–16
1 John 2:1–11
John 17:12–19

W Daniel 2:17–30
1 John 2:12–17
John 17:20–26

Th Daniel 2:31–49
1 John 2:18–29
Luke 3:1–14

F Daniel 3:1–18
1 John 3:1–10
Luke 3:15–22

S Daniel 3:19–30
1 John 3:11–18
Luke 4:1–13

Week of 3 Easter

S Daniel 4:1–18
1 Peter 4:7–11
John 21:15–25

M Daniel 4:19–27
1 John 3:19—4:6
Luke 4:14–30

T Daniel 4:28–37
1 John 4:7–21
Luke 4:31–37

W Daniel 5:1–12
1 John 5:1–12
Luke 4:38–44

Th Daniel 5:13–30
1 John 5:13–20 (21)
Luke 5:1–11

F Daniel 6:1–15
2 John 1–13
Luke 5:12–26

S Daniel 6:16–28
3 John 1–15
Luke 5:27–39

Week of 4 Easter

S Wisdom 1:1–15
or Genesis 18:22–33
1 Peter 5:1–11
Matthew 7:15–29

M Wisdom 1:16—2:11, 21–24
or Jeremiah 30:1–9
Colossians 1:1–14
Luke 6:1–11

T Wisdom 3:1–9
or Jeremiah 30:10–17
Colossians 1:15–23
Luke 6:12–26

W Wisdom 4:16—5:8
or Jeremiah 30:18–22
Colossians 1:24—2:7
Luke 6:27–38

Th Wisdom 5:9–23
or Jeremiah 31:1–14
Colossians 2:8–23
Luke 6:39–49

F Wisdom 6:12–23
or Jeremiah 31:15–22
Colossians 3:1–11
Luke 7:1–17

S Wisdom 7:1–14
or Jeremiah 31:23–25
Colossians 3:12–17
Luke 7:18–28 (29–30) 31–35

Week of 5 Easter

S Wisdom 7:22—8:1
or Isaiah 32:1–8
2 Thessalonians 2:13–17
Matthew 7:7–14

M Wisdom 9:1, 7–18
or Jeremiah 32:1–15
Colossians 3:18—4:18
Luke 7:36–50

T Wisdom 10:1–4 (5–12) 13–21
or Jeremiah 32:16–25
Romans 12:1–21
Luke 8:1–15

W Wisdom 13:1–9
or Jeremiah 32:36–44
Romans 13:1–14
Luke 8:16–25

Th Wisdom 14:27—15:3
or Jeremiah 33:1–13
Romans 14:1–12
Luke 8:26–39

F Wisdom 16:15—17:1
or Deuteronomy 31:30—32:14
Romans 14:13–23
Luke 8:40–56

S Wisdom 19:1–8, 18–22
or Deuteronomy 32:34–41 (42) 43
Romans 15:1–13
Luke 9:1–17

Week of 6 Easter

S Ecclesiasticus 43:1–12, 27–32
or Deuteronomy 15:1–11
1 Timothy 3:14—4:5
Matthew 13:24–34a

M Deuteronomy 8:1–10
or Deuteronomy 18:9–14
James 1:1–15
Luke 9:18–27

T Deuteronomy 8:11–20
or Deuteronomy 18:15–22
James 1:16–27
Luke 11:1–13

W Baruch 3:24–37
or Deuteronomy 19:1–7
James 5:13–18
Luke 12:22–31

Ascension Day

Ezekiel 1:1–14, 24–28b
Hebrews 2:5–18
Matthew 28:16–20

F Ezekiel 1:28—3:3
Hebrews 4:14—5:6
Luke 9:28–36

S Ezekiel 3:4–17
Hebrews 5:7–14
Luke 9:37–50

Week of 7 Easter

S Ezekiel 3:16–27
Ephesians 2:1–10
Matthew 10:24–33, 40–42

M Ezekiel 4:1–17
Hebrews 6:1–12
Luke 9:51–62

T Ezekiel 7:10–15, 23b–27
Hebrews 6:13–20
Luke 10:1–17

W Ezekiel 11:14–25
Hebrews 7:1–17
Luke 10:17–24

Th Ezekiel 18:1–4, 19–32
Hebrews 7:18–28
Luke 10:25–37

F Ezekiel 34:17–31
Hebrews 8:1–13
Luke 10:38–42

S Ezekiel 43:1–12
Hebrews 9:1–14
Luke 11:14–23

Pentecost and Following

S Isaiah 11:1–9
1 Corinthians 2:1–13
John 14:21–29

M Isaiah 63:7–14
2 Timothy 1:1–14
Luke 11:24–36

T Isaiah 63:15—64:9
2 Timothy 1:15—2:13
Luke 11:37–52

W Isaiah 65:1–12
2 Timothy 2:14–26
Luke 11:53—12:12

Th Isaiah 65:17–25
2 Timothy 3:1–17
Luke 12:13–31

F Isaiah 66:1–6
2 Timothy 4:1–8
Luke 12:32–48

S Isaiah 66:7–14
2 Timothy 4:9–22
Luke 12:49–59

Holy Trinity and Following

S Ecclesiasticus 43:1–12 (27–33)
or Deuteronomy 6:1–9 (10–15)
Ephesians 4:1–16
John 1:1–18

M Ruth 1:1–18
1 Timothy 1:1–17
Luke 13:1–9

T Ruth 1:19—2:13
1 Timothy 1:18—2:8
Luke 13:10–17

W Ruth 2:14–23
1 Timothy 3:1–16
Luke 13:18–30

Th Ruth 3:1–18
1 Timothy 4:1–16
Luke 13:31–35

F Ruth 4:1–22
1 Timothy 5:17–22 (23–25)
Luke 14:1–11

S Deuteronomy 1:1–8
1 Timothy 6:6–21
Luke 14:12–24

Week of 2 Pentecost

S Deuteronomy 4:1–9
Revelation 7:1–4, 9–17
Matthew 12:33–45

M Deuteronomy 4:9–14
2 Corinthians 1:1–11
Luke 14:25–35

T Deuteronomy 4:15–24
2 Corinthians 1:12–22
Luke 15:1–10

W Deuteronomy 4:25–31
2 Corinthians 1:23—2:17
Luke 15:1–2, 11–32

Th Deuteronomy 4:32–40
2 Corinthians 3:1–18
Luke 16:1–9

F Deuteronomy 5:1–22
2 Corinthians 4:1–12
Luke 16:10–17 (18)

S Deuteronomy 5:22–33
2 Corinthians 4:13—5:10
Luke 16:19–31

Week of 3 Pentecost

S Deuteronomy 11:1–12
Revelation 10:1–11
Matthew 13:44–58

M Deuteronomy 11:13–19
2 Corinthians 5:11—6:2
Luke 17:1–10

T Deuteronomy 12:1–12
2 Corinthians 6:3–13 (14—7:1)
Luke 17:11–19

W Deuteronomy 13:1–11
2 Corinthians 7:2–16
Luke 17:20–37

Th Deuteronomy 16:18–20; 17:14–20
2 Corinthians 8:1–16
Luke 18:1–8

F Deuteronomy 26:1–11
2 Corinthians 8:16–24
Luke 18:9–14

S Deuteronomy 29:2–15
2 Corinthians 9:1–15
Luke 18:15–30

Week of 4 Pentecost

S Deuteronomy 29:16–29
Revelation 12:1–12
Matthew 15:29–39

M Deuteronomy 30:1–10
2 Corinthians 10:1–18
Luke 18:31–43

T Deuteronomy 30:11–20
2 Corinthians 11:1–21a
Luke 19:1–10

W Deuteronomy 31:30—32:14
2 Corinthians 11:21b–33
Luke 19:11–27
Th Ecclesiasticus 44:19—45:5
or Song of Solomon 1:1–3, 9–11, 15–16a; 2:1–3a
2 Corinthians 12:1–10
Luke 19:28–40
F Ecclesiasticus 45:6–16
or Song of Solomon 2:8–13; 4:1–4a, 5–7, 9–11
2 Corinthians 12:11–21
Luke 19:41–48
S Ecclesiasticus 46:1–10
or Song of Solomon 5:10–16; 7:1–2 (3–5) 6–7a (9); 8:6–7
2 Corinthians 13:1–14
Luke 20:1–8

Week of 5 Pentecost
S Ecclesiasticus 46:11–20
or Exodus 6:2–13; 7:1–6
Revelation 15:1–8
Matthew 18:1–14
M 1 Samuel 1:1–20
Acts 1:1–14
Luke 20:9–19
T 1 Samuel 1:21—2:11
Acts 1:15–26
Luke 20:19–26
W 1 Samuel 2:12–26
Acts 2:1–21
Luke 20:27–40
Th 1 Samuel 2:27–36
Acts 2:22–36
Luke 20:41—21:4
F 1 Samuel 3:1–21
Acts 2:37–47
Luke 21:5–19
S 1 Samuel 4:1b–11
Acts 4:32—5:11
Luke 21:20–28

Week of 6 Pentecost
S 1 Samuel 4:12–22
James 1:1–18
Matthew 19:23–30
M 1 Samuel 5:1–12
Acts 5:12–26
Luke 21:29–36
T 1 Samuel 6:1–16
Acts 5:27–42
Luke 21:37—22:13
W 1 Samuel 7:2–17
Acts 6:1–15
Luke 22:14–23
Th 1 Samuel 8:1–22
Acts 6:15–7:16
Luke 22:24–30
F 1 Samuel 9:1–14
Acts 7:17–29
Luke 22:31–38
S 1 Samuel 9:15—10:1
Acts 7:30–43
Luke 22:39–51

Week of 7 Pentecost
S 1 Samuel 10:1–16
Romans 4:13–25
Matthew 21:23–32

M 1 Samuel 10:17–27
Acts 7:44—8:1a
Luke 22:52–62
T 1 Samuel 11:1–15
Acts 8:1b–13
Luke 22:63–71
W 1 Samuel 12:1–6 (7–15) 16–25
Acts 8:14–25
Luke 23:1–12
Th 1 Samuel 13:5–18
Acts 8:26–40
Luke 23:13–25
F 1 Samuel 13:19—14:15
Acts 9:1–9
Luke 23:26–31
S 1 Samuel 14:16–30
Acts 9:10–19a
Luke 23:32–43

Week of 8 Pentecost
S 1 Samuel 14:36–45
Romans 5:1–11
Matthew 22:1–14
M 1 Samuel 15:1–3, 7–23
Acts 9:19b–31
Luke 23:44–56a
T 1 Samuel 15:24–35
Acts 9:32–43
Luke 23:56b—24:11 (12)
W 1 Samuel 16:1–13
Acts 10:1–16
Luke 24:13–35
Th 1 Samuel 16:14—17:11
Acts 10:17–33
Luke 24:36–53
F 1 Samuel 17:17–30
Acts 10:34–48
Mark 1:1–13
S 1 Samuel 17:31–49
Acts 11:1–18
Mark 1:14–28

Week of 9 Pentecost
S 1 Samuel 17:50—18:4
Romans 10:4–17
Matthew 23:29–39
M 1 Samuel 18:5–16 (17–27a) 27b–30
Acts 11:19–30
Mark 1:29–45
T 1 Samuel 19:1–18 (19–24)
Acts 12:1–17
Mark 2:1–12
W 1 Samuel 20:1–23
Acts 12:18–25
Mark 2:13–22
Th 1 Samuel 20:24–42
Acts 13:1–12
Mark 2:23—3:6
F 1 Samuel 21:1–15
Acts 13:13–25
Mark 3:7–19a
S 1 Samuel 22:1–23
Acts 13:26–43
Mark 3:19b–35

Week of 10 Pentecost
S 1 Samuel 23:7–18
Romans 11:33—12:2
Matthew 25:14–30

M 1 Samuel 24:1–22
Acts 13:44–52
Mark 4:1–20
T 1 Samuel 25:1–22
Acts 14:1–18
Mark 4:21–34
W 1 Samuel 25:23–44
Acts 14:19–28
Mark 4:35–41
Th 1 Samuel 28:3–20
Acts 15:1–11
Mark 5:1–20
F 1 Samuel 31:1–13
Acts 15:12–21
Mark 5:21–43
S 2 Samuel 1:1–16
Acts 15:22–35
Mark 6:1–13

Week of 11 Pentecost
S 2 Samuel 1:17–27
Romans 12:9–21
Matthew 25:31–46
M 2 Samuel 2:1–11
Acts 15:36—16:5
Mark 6:14–29
T 2 Samuel 3:6–21
Acts 16:6–15
Mark 6:30–46
W 2 Samuel 3:22–39
Acts 16:16–24
Mark 6:47–56
Th 2 Samuel 4:1–12
Acts 16:25–40
Mark 7:1–23
F 2 Samuel 5:1–12
Acts 17:1–15
Mark 7:24–37
S 2 Samuel 5:22—6:11
Acts 17:16–34
Mark 8:1–10

Week of 12 Pentecost
S 2 Samuel 6:12–23
Romans 14:7–12
John 1:43–51
M 2 Samuel 7:1–17
Acts 18:1–11
Mark 8:11–21
T 2 Samuel 7:18–29
Acts 18:12–28
Mark 8:22–33
W 2 Samuel 9:1–13
Acts 19:1–10
Mark 8:34—9:1
Th 2 Samuel 11:1–27
Acts 19:11–20
Mark 9:2–13
F 2 Samuel 12:1–14
Acts 19:21–41
Mark 9:14–29
S 2 Samuel 12:15–31
Acts 20:1–16
Mark 9:30–41

Week of 13 Pentecost
S 2 Samuel 13:1–22
Romans 15:1–13
John 3:22–36

M 2 Samuel 13:23–39
Acts 20:17–38
Mark 9:42–50
T 2 Samuel 14:1–20
Acts 21:1–14
Mark 10:1–16
W 2 Samuel 14:21–33
Acts 21:15–26
Mark 10:17–31
Th 2 Samuel 15:1–18
Acts 21:27–36
Mark 10:32–45
F 2 Samuel 15:19–37
Acts 21:37—22:16
Mark 10:46–52
S 2 Samuel 16:1–23
Acts 22:17–29
Mark 11:1–11

Week of 14 Pentecost

S 2 Samuel 17:1–23
Galatians 3:6–14
John 5:30–47
M 2 Samuel 17:24—18:8
Acts 22:30—23:11
Mark 11:12–26
T 2 Samuel 18:9–18
Acts 23:12–24
Mark 11:27—12:12
W 2 Samuel 18:19–33
Acts 23:23–35
Mark 12:13–27
Th 2 Samuel 19:1–23
Acts 24:1–23
Mark 12:28–34
F 2 Samuel 19:24–43
Acts 24:24—25:12
Mark 12:35–44
S 2 Samuel 23:1–7, 13–17
Acts 25:13–27
Mark 13:1–13

Week of 15 Pentecost

S 2 Samuel 24:1–2, 10–25
Galatians 3:23—4:7
John 8:12–20
M 1 Kings 1:(1–4) 5–31
Acts 26:1–23
Mark 13:14–27
T 1 Kings 1:32—2:4 (5–46a) 46b
Acts 26:24—27:8
Mark 13:28–37
W 1 Kings 3:1–15
Acts 27:9–26
Mark 14:1–11
Th 1 Kings 3:16–28
Acts 27:27–44
Mark 14:12–26
F 1 Kings 5:1—6:1, 7
Acts 28:1–16
Mark 14:27–42
S 1 Kings 7:51—8:21
Acts 28:17–31
Mark 14:43–52

Week of 16 Pentecost

S 1 Kings 8:22–30 (31–40)
1 Timothy 4:7b–16
John 8:47–59

M 2 Chronicles 6:32—7:7
James 2:1–13
Mark 14:53–65
T 1 Kings 8:65—9:9
James 2:14–26
Mark 14:66–72
W 1 Kings 9:24—10:13
James 3:1–12
Mark 15:1–11
Th 1 Kings 11:1–13
James 3:13—4:12
Mark 15:12–21
F 1 Kings 11:26–43
James 4:13—5:6
Mark 15:22–32
S 1 Kings 12:1–20
James 5:7–20
Mark 15:33–39

Week of 17 Pentecost

S 1 Kings 12:21–33
Acts 4:18–31
John 10:31–42
M 1 Kings 13:1–10
Philippians 1:1–11
Mark 15:40–47
T 1 Kings 16:23–34
Philippians 1:12–30
Mark 16:1–8 (9–20)
W 1 Kings 17:1–24
Philippians 2:1–11
Matthew 2:1–12
Th 1 Kings 18:1–19
Philippians 2:12–30
Matthew 2:13–23
F 1 Kings 18:20–40
Philippians 3:1–16
Matthew 3:1–12
S 1 Kings 18:41—19:8
Philippians 3:17—4:7
Matthew 3:13–17

Week of 18 Pentecost

S 1 Kings 19:8–21
Acts 5:34–42
John 11:45–57
M 1 Kings 21:1–16
1 Corinthians 1:1–19
Matthew 4:1–11
T 1 Kings 21:17–29
1 Corinthians 1:20–31
Matthew 4:12–17
W 1 Kings 22:1–28
1 Corinthians 2:1–13
Matthew 4:18–25
Th 1 Kings 22:29–45
1 Corinthians 2:14—3:15
Matthew 5:1–10
F 2 Kings 1:2–17
1 Corinthians 3:16–23
Matthew 5:11–16
S 2 Kings 2:1–18
1 Corinthians 4:1–7
Matthew 5:17–20

Week of 19 Pentecost

S 2 Kings 4:8–37
Acts 9:10–31
Luke 3:7–18

M 2 Kings 5:1–19
1 Corinthians 4:8–21
Matthew 5:21–26
T 2 Kings 5:19–27
1 Corinthians 5:1–8
Matthew 5:27–37
W 2 Kings 6:1–23
1 Corinthians 5:9—6:11
Matthew 5:38–48
Th 2 Kings 9:1–16
1 Corinthians 6:12–20
Matthew 6:1–6, 16–18
F 2 Kings 9:17–37
1 Corinthians 7:1–9
Matthew 6:7–15
S 2 Kings 11:1–20a
1 Corinthians 7:10–24
Matthew 6:19–24

Week of 20 Pentecost

S 2 Kings 17:1–18
Acts 9:36–43
Luke 5:1–11
M 2 Kings 17:24–41
1 Corinthians 7:25–31
Matthew 6:25–34
T 2 Chronicles 29:1–3; 30:1 (2–9) 10–27
1 Corinthians 7:32–40
Matthew 7:1–12
W 2 Kings 18:9–25
1 Corinthians 8:1–13
Matthew 7:13–21
Th 2 Kings 18:28–37
1 Corinthians 9:1–15
Matthew 7:22–29
F 2 Kings 19:1–20
1 Corinthians 9:16–27
Matthew 8:1–17
S 2 Kings 19:21–36
1 Corinthians 10:1–13
Matthew 8:18–27

Week of 21 Pentecost

S 2 Kings 20:1–21
Acts 12:1–17
Luke 7:11–17
M 2 Kings 21:1–18
1 Corinthians 10:14—11:1
Matthew 8:28–34
T 2 Kings 22:1–13
1 Corinthians 11:2 (3–16) 17–22
Matthew 9:1–8
W 2 Kings 22:14—23:3
1 Corinthians 11:23–34
Matthew 9:9–17
Th 2 Kings 23:4–25
1 Corinthians 12:1–11
Matthew 9:18–26
F 2 Kings 23:36—24:17
1 Corinthians 12:12–26
Matthew 9:27–34
S Jeremiah 35:1–19
1 Corinthians 12:27—13:3
Matthew 9:35—10:4

Week of 22 Pentecost

S Jeremiah 36:1–10
Acts 14:8–18
Luke 7:36–50

M	Jeremiah 36:11–26 1 Corinthians 13:(1–3) 4–13 Matthew 10:5–15
T	Jeremiah 36:27—37:2 1 Corinthians 14:1–12 Matthew 10:16–23
W	Jeremiah 37:3–21 1 Corinthians 14:13–25 Matthew 10:24–33
Th	Jeremiah 38:1–13 1 Corinthians 14:26–33a (33b–36) 37–40 Matthew 10:34–42
F	Jeremiah 38:14–28 1 Corinthians 15:1–11 Matthew 11:1–6
S	Jeremiah 52:1–34 1 Corinthians 15:12–29 Matthew 11:7–15

Week of 23 Pentecost

S	Jeremiah 29:1, 4–14 *or* Jeremiah 39:11—40:6 Acts 16:6–15 Luke 10:1–12, 17–20
M	Jeremiah 44:1–14 *or* Jeremiah 29:1, 4–14 1 Corinthians 15:30–41 Matthew 11:16–24
T	Lamentations 1:1–5 (6–9) 10–12 *or* Jeremiah 40:7—41:3 1 Corinthians 15:41–50 Matthew 11:25–30
W	Lamentations 2:8–15 *or* Jeremiah 41:4–18 1 Corinthians 15:51–58 Matthew 12:1–14
Th	Ezra 1:1–11 *or* Jeremiah 42:1–22 1 Corinthians 16:1–9 Matthew 12:15–21
F	Ezra 3:1–13 *or* Jeremiah 43:1–13 1 Corinthians 16:10–24 Matthew 12:22–32
S	Ezra 4:7, 11–24 *or* Jeremiah 44:1–14 Philemon 1–25 Matthew 12:33–42

Week of 24 Pentecost

S	Haggai 1:1—2:9 *or* Jeremiah 44:15–30 Acts 18:24—19:7 Luke 10:25–37
M	Zechariah 1:7–17 *or* Jeremiah 45:1–5 Revelation 1:4–20 Matthew 12:43–50
T	Ezra 5:1–17 *or* Lamentations 1:1–5 (6–9) 10–12 Revelation 4:1–11 Matthew 13:1–9
W	Ezra 6:1–22 *or* Lamentations 2:8–15 Revelation 5:1–10 Matthew 13:10–17
Th	Nehemiah 1:1–11 *or* Lamentations 2:16–22 Revelation 5:11—6:11 Matthew 13:18–23
F	Nehemiah 2:1–20 *or* Lamentations 4:1–22 Revelation 6:12—7:4 Matthew 13:24–30
S	Nehemiah 4:1–23 *or* Lamentations 5:1–22 Revelation 7:(4–8) 9–17 Matthew 13:31–35

Week of 25 Pentecost

S	Nehemiah 5:1–19 *or* Ezra 1:1–11 Acts 20:7–12 Luke 12:22–31
M	Nehemiah 6:1–19 *or* Ezra 3:1–13 Revelation 10:1–11 Matthew 13:36–43
T	Nehemiah 12:27–31a, 42b–47 *or* Ezra 4:7, 11–24 Revelation 11:1–19 Matthew 13:44–52
W	Nehemiah 13:4–22 *or* Haggai 1:1—2:9 Revelation 12:1–12 Matthew 13:53–58
Th	Ezra 7:(1–10) 11–26 *or* Zechariah 1:7–17 Revelation 14:1–13 Matthew 14:1–12
F	Ezra 7:27–28; 8:21–36 *or* Ezra 5:1–17 Revelation 15:1–8 Matthew 14:13–21
S	Ezra 9:1–15 *or* Ezra 6:1–22 Revelation 17:1–14 Matthew 14:22–36

Week of 26 Pentecost

S	Ezra 10:1–17 *or* Nehemiah 1:1–11 Acts 24:10–21 Luke 14:12–24
M	Nehemiah 9:1–15 (16–25) *or* Nehemiah 2:1–20 Revelation 18:1–8 Matthew 15:1–20
T	Nehemiah 9:26–38 *or* Nehemiah 4:1–23 Revelation 18:9–20 Matthew 15:21–28
W	Nehemiah 7:73b—8:3, 5–18 *or* Nehemiah 5:1–19 Revelation 18:21–24 Matthew 15:29–39
Th	1 Maccabees 1:1–28 *or* Nehemiah 6:1–19 Revelation 19:1–10 Matthew 16:1–12
F	1 Maccabees 1:41–63 *or* Nehemiah 12:27–31a, 42b–47 Revelation 19:11–16 Matthew 16:13–20
S	1 Maccabees 2:1–28 *or* Nehemiah 13:4–22 Revelation 20:1–6 Matthew 16:21–28

Week of 27 Pentecost

S	1 Maccabees 2:29–43 (44–48) *or* Ezra 7:(1–10) 11–26 Acts 28:14b–23 Luke 16:1–13
M	1 Maccabees 2:49–70 *or* Ezra 7:27–28; 8:21–36 Revelation 20:7–15 Matthew 17:1–13
T	1 Maccabees 3:1–24 *or* Ezra 9:1–15 Revelation 21:1–8 Matthew 17:14–21
W	1 Maccabees 3:25–41 *or* Ezra 10:1–17 Revelation 21:9–21 Matthew 17:22–27
Th	1 Maccabees 3:42–60 *or* Nehemiah 9:1–15 (16–25) Revelation 21:22—22:5 Matthew 18:1–9
F	1 Maccabees 4:1–25 *or* Nehemiah 9:26–38 Revelation 22:6–13 Matthew 18:10–20
S	1 Maccabees 4:36–59 *or* Nehemiah 7:73b—8:3, 5–18 Revelation 22:14–21 Matthew 18:21–35

Christ the King and Following

S	Isaiah 19:19–25 Romans 15:5–13 Luke 19:11–27
M	Joel 3:1–2, 9–17 1 Peter 1:1–12 Matthew 19:1–12
T	Nahum 1:1–13 1 Peter 1:13–25 Matthew 19:13–22
W	Obadiah 15–21 1 Peter 2:1–10 Matthew 19:23–30
Th	Zephaniah 3:1–13 1 Peter 2:11–25 Matthew 20:1–16
F	Isaiah 24:14–23 1 Peter 3:13—4:6 Matthew 20:17–28
S	Micah 7:11–20 1 Peter 4:7–19 Matthew 20:29–34

YEAR TWO

Week of 1 Advent

S Amos 1:1-5, 13—2:8
1 Thessalonians 5:1-11
Luke 21:5-19
M Amos 2:6-16
2 Peter 1:1-11
Matthew 21:1-11
T Amos 3:1-11
2 Peter 1:12-21
Matthew 21:12-22
W Amos 3:12—4:5
2 Peter 3:1-10
Matthew 21:23-32
Th Amos 4:6-13
2 Peter 3:11-18
Matthew 21:33-46
F Amos 5:1-17
Jude 1-16
Matthew 22:1-14
S Amos 5:18-27
Jude 17-25
Matthew 22:15-22

Week of 2 Advent

S Amos 6:1-14
2 Thessalonians 1:5-12
Luke 1:57-68
M Amos 7:1-9
Revelation 1:1-8
Matthew 22:23-33
T Amos 7:10-17
Revelation 1:9-16
Matthew 22:34-46
W Amos 8:1-14
Revelation 1:17—2:7
Matthew 23:1-12
Th Amos 9:1-10
Revelation 2:8-17
Matthew 23:13-26
F Haggai 1:1-15
Revelation 2:18-29
Matthew 23:27-39
S Haggai 2:1-9
Revelation 3:1-6
Matthew 24:1-14

Week of 3 Advent

S Amos 9:11-15
2 Thessalonians 2:1-3, 13-17
John 5:30-47
M Zechariah 1:7-17
Revelation 3:7-13
Matthew 24:15-31
T Zechariah 2:1-13
Revelation 3:14-22
Matthew 24:32-44
W Zechariah 3:1-10
Revelation 4:1-8
Matthew 24:45-51
Th Zechariah 4:1-14
Revelation 4:9—5:5
Matthew 25:1-13
F Zechariah 7:8—8:8
Revelation 5:6-14
Matthew 25:14-30
S Zechariah 8:9-17
Revelation 6:1-17
Matthew 25:31-46

Week of 4 Advent

S Genesis 3:8-15
Revelation 12:1-10
John 3:16-21
M Zephaniah 3:14-20
Titus 1:1-16
Luke 1:1-25
T 1 Samuel 2:1b-10
Titus 2:1-10
Luke 1:26-38
W 2 Samuel 7:1-17
Titus 2:11—3:8a
Luke 1:39-48a (48b-56)
Th 2 Samuel 7:18-29
Galatians 3:1-14
Luke 1:57-66
F Jeremiah 31:10-14
Galatians 3:15-22
Luke 1:67-80
or Matthew 1:1-17
S Isaiah 60:1-6
Galatians 3:23—4:7
Matthew 1:18-25

Christmas Day and Following

Dec 25 Micah 4:1-5; 5:2-4
1 John 4:7-16
John 3:31-36
Dec 26 Wisdom 4:7-15
or 2 Chronicles 24:17-22
Acts 6:1-7
Acts 7:59—8:8
Dec 27 Proverbs 8:22-30
1 John 5:1-12
John 13:20-35
Dec 28 Isaiah 49:13-23
Isaiah 54:1-13
Matthew 18:1-14
Dec 29 2 Samuel 23:13-17b
2 John 1-13
John 2:1-11
Dec 30 1 Kings 17:17-24
3 John 1-15
John 4:46-54
Dec 31 1 Kings 3:5-14
James 4:13-17; 5:7-11
John 5:1-15

First Sunday after Christmas

1 Samuel 1:1-2, 7b-28
Colossians 1:9-20
Luke 2:22-40

Jan 1 Isaiah 62:1-5, 10-12
Revelation 19:11-16
Matthew 1:18-25
Jan 2 1 Kings 19:1-8
Ephesians 4:1-16
John 6:1-14
Jan 3 1 Kings 19:9-18
Ephesians 4:17-32
John 6:15-27
Jan 4 Joshua 3:14—4:7
Ephesians 5:1-20
John 9:1-12, 35-38
Jan 5 Jonah 2:2-9
Ephesians 6:10-20
John 11:17-27, 38-44

Second Sunday after Christmas

1 Kings 3:5-14
Colossians 3:12-17
John 6:41-47

The Epiphany and Following

Jan 6 Isaiah 49:1-7
Revelation 21:22-27
Matthew 12:14-21
Jan 7 Deuteronomy 8:1-3
Colossians 1:1-14
John 6:30-33, 48-51
Jan 8 Exodus 17:1-7
Colossians 1:15-23
John 7:37-52
Jan 9 Isaiah 45:14-19
Colossians 1:24—2:7
John 8:12-19
Jan 10 Jeremiah 23:1-8
Colossians 2:8-23
John 10:7-17
Jan 11 Isaiah 55:3-9
Colossians 3:1-17
John 14:6-14
Jan 12 Genesis 49:1-2, 8-12
Colossians 3:18—4:6
John 15:1-16

Week of 1 Epiphany

S Genesis 1:1—2:3
Ephesians 1:3-14
John 1:29-34
M Genesis 2:4-9 (10-15) 16-25
Hebrews 1:1-14
John 1:1-18
T Genesis 3:1-24
Hebrews 2:1-10
John 1:19-28
W Genesis 4:1-16
Hebrews 2:11-18
John 1:(29-34) 35-42
Th Genesis 4:17-26
Hebrews 3:1-11
John 1:43-51
F Genesis 6:1-8
Hebrews 3:12-19
John 2:1-12
S Genesis 6:9-22
Hebrews 4:1-13
John 2:13-22

Week of 2 Epiphany

S Genesis 7:1-10, 17-23
Ephesians 4:1-16
Mark 3:7-19
M Genesis 8:6-22
Hebrews 4:14—5:6
John 2:23—3:15
T Genesis 9:1-17
Hebrews 5:7-14
John 3:16-21
W Genesis 9:18-29
Hebrews 6:1-12
John 3:22-36
Th Genesis 11:1-9
Hebrews 6:13-20
John 4:1-15
F Genesis 11:27—12:8
Hebrews 7:1-17
John 4:16-26

S Genesis 12:9—13:1
Hebrews 7:18–28
John 4:27–42

Week of 3 Epiphany

S Genesis 13:2–18
Galatians 2:1–10
Mark 7:31–37

M Genesis 14:(1–7) 8–24
Hebrews 8:1–13
John 4:43–54

T Genesis 15:1–11, 17–21
Hebrews 9:1–14
John 5:1–18

W Genesis 16:1–14
Hebrews 9:15–28
John 5:19–29

Th Genesis 16:15—17:14
Hebrews 10:1–10
John 5:30–47

F Genesis 17:15–27
Hebrews 10:11–25
John 6:1–15

S Genesis 18:1–16
Hebrews 10:26–39
John 6:16–27

Week of 4 Epiphany

S Genesis 18:16–33
Galatians 5:13–25
Mark 8:22–30

M Genesis 19:1–17 (18–23) 24–29
Hebrews 11:1–12
John 6:27–40

T Genesis 21:1–21
Hebrews 11:13–22
John 6:41–51

W Genesis 22:1–18
Hebrews 11:23–31
John 6:52–59

Th Genesis 23:1–20
Hebrews 11:32—12:2
John 6:60–71

F Genesis 24:1–27
Hebrews 12:3–11
John 7:1–13

S Genesis 24:28–38, 49–51
Hebrews 12:12–29
John 7:14–36

Week of 5 Epiphany

S Genesis 24:50–67
2 Timothy 2:14–21
Mark 10:13–22

M Genesis 25:19–34
Hebrews 13:1–16
John 7:37–52

T Genesis 26:1–6, 12–33
Hebrews 13:17–25
John 7:53—8:11

W Genesis 27:1–29
Romans 12:1–8
John 8:12–20

Th Genesis 27:30–45
Romans 12:9–21
John 8:21–32

F Genesis 27:46—28:4, 10–22
Romans 13:1–14
John 8:33–47

S Genesis 29:1–20
Romans 14:1–23
John 8:47–59

Week of 6 Epiphany

S Genesis 29:20–35
1 Timothy 3:14—4:10
Mark 10:23–31

M Genesis 30:1–24
1 John 1:1–10
John 9:1–17

T Genesis 31:1–24
1 John 2:1–11
John 9:18–41

W Genesis 31:25–50
1 John 2:12–17
John 10:1–18

Th Genesis 32:3–21
1 John 2:18–29
John 10:19–30

F Genesis 32:22—33:17
1 John 3:1–10
John 10:31–42

S Genesis 35:1–20
1 John 3:11–18
John 11:1–16

Week of 7 Epiphany

S Proverbs 1:20–33
2 Corinthians 5:11–21
Mark 10:35–45

M Proverbs 3:11–20
1 John 3:18—4:6
John 11:17–29

T Proverbs 4:1–27
1 John 4:7–21
John 11:30–44

W Proverbs 6:1–19
1 John 5:1–12
John 11:45–54

Th Proverbs 7:1–27
1 John 5:13–21
John 11:55—12:8

F Proverbs 8:1–21
Philemon 1–25
John 12:9–19

S Proverbs 8:22–36
2 Timothy 1:1–14
John 12:20–26

Week of 8 Epiphany

S Proverbs 9:1–12
2 Corinthians 9:6b–15
Mark 10:46–52

M Proverbs 10:1–12
2 Timothy 1:15—2:13
John 12:27–36a

T Proverbs 15:16–33
2 Timothy 2:14–26
John 12:36b–50

W Proverbs 17:1–20
2 Timothy 3:1–17
John 13:1–20

Th Proverbs 21:30—22:6
2 Timothy 4:1–8
John 13:21–30

F Proverbs 23:19–21, 29—24:2
2 Timothy 4:9–22
John 13:31–38

S Proverbs 25:15–28
Philippians 1:1–11
John 18:1–14

Transfiguration and Following

S Malachi 4:1–6
2 Corinthians 3:7–18
Luke 9:18–27

M Proverbs 27:1–6, 10–12
Philippians 2:1–13
John 18:15–18, 25–27

T Proverbs 30:1–4, 24–33
Philippians 3:1–11
John 18:28–38

Ash Wednesday

Amos 5:6–15
Hebrews 12:1–14
Luke 18:9–14

Th Habakkuk 3:1–10 (11–15) 16–18
Philippians 3:12–21
John 17:1–8

F Ezekiel 18:1–4, 25–32
Philippians 4:1–9
John 17:9–19

S Ezekiel 39:21–29
Philippians 4:10–20
John 17:20–26

Week of 1 Lent

S Daniel 9:3–10
Hebrews 2:10–18
John 12:44–50

M Genesis 37:1–11
1 Corinthians 1:1–19
Mark 1:1–13

T Genesis 37:12–24
1 Corinthians 1:20–31
Mark 1:14–28

W Genesis 37:25–36
1 Corinthians 2:1–13
Mark 1:29–45

Th Genesis 39:1–23
1 Corinthians 2:14—3:15
Mark 2:1–12

F Genesis 40:1–23
1 Corinthians 3:16–23
Mark 2:13–22

S Genesis 41:1–13
1 Corinthians 4:1–7
Mark 2:23—3:6

Week of 2 Lent

S Genesis 41:14–45
Romans 6:3–14
John 5:19–24

M Genesis 41:46–57
1 Corinthians 4:8–20 (21)
Mark 3:7–19a

T Genesis 42:1–17
1 Corinthians 5:1–8
Mark 3:19b–35

W Genesis 42:18–28
1 Corinthians 5:9—6:11
Mark 4:1–20

Th Genesis 42:29–38
1 Corinthians 6:12–20
Mark 4:21–34

F Genesis 43:1–15
1 Corinthians 7:1–9
Mark 4:35–41

S Genesis 43:16–34
1 Corinthians 7:10–24
Mark 5:1–20

Week of 3 Lent

S Genesis 44:1–17
Romans 8:1–10
John 5:25–29

M Genesis 44:18–34
1 Corinthians 7:25–31
Mark 5:21–43

T Genesis 45:1–15
1 Corinthians 7:32–40
Mark 6:1–13

W Genesis 45:16–28
1 Corinthians 8:1–13
Mark 6:13–29

Th Genesis 46:1–7, 28–34
1 Corinthians 9:1–15
Mark 6:30–46

F Genesis 47:1–26
1 Corinthians 9:16–27
Mark 6:47–56

S Genesis 47:27—48:7
1 Corinthians 10:1–13
Mark 7:1–23

Week of 4 Lent

S Genesis 48:8–22
Romans 8:11–25
John 6:27–40

M Genesis 49:1–28
1 Corinthians 10:14—11:1
Mark 7:24–37

T Genesis 49:29—50:14
1 Corinthians 11:2–34
Mark 8:1–10

W Genesis 50:15–26
1 Corinthians 12:1–11
Mark 8:11–26

Th Exodus 1:6–22
1 Corinthians 12:12–26
Mark 8:27—9:1

F Exodus 2:1–22
1 Corinthians 12:27—13:3
Mark 9:2–13

S Exodus 2:23—3:15
1 Corinthians 13:1–13
Mark 9:14–29

Week of 5 Lent

S Exodus 3:16—4:12
Romans 12:1–21
John 8:46–59

M Exodus 4:10–20 (21–26) 27–31
1 Corinthians 14:1–19
Mark 9:30–41

T Exodus 5:1—6:1
1 Corinthians 14:20–33a, 39–40
Mark 9:42–50

W Exodus 7:8–24
2 Corinthians 2:14—3:6
Mark 10:1–16

Th Exodus 7:25—8:19
2 Corinthians 3:7–18
Mark 10:17–31

F Exodus 9:13–35
2 Corinthians 4:1–12
Mark 10:32–45

S Exodus 10:21—11:8
2 Corinthians 4:13–18
Mark 10:46–52

Holy Week

Sunday of the Passion
Zechariah 9:9–12
or Zechariah 12:9–11; 13:1, 7–9
1 Timothy 6:12–16
Luke 19:41–48

M Lamentations 1:1–2, 6–12
2 Corinthians 1:1–7
Mark 11:12–25

T Lamentations 1:17–22
2 Corinthians 1:8–22
Mark 11:27–33

W Lamentations 2:1–9
2 Corinthians 1:23—2:11
Mark 12:1–11

Maundy Thursday
Lamentations 2:10–18
1 Corinthians 10:14–17; 11:27–32
Mark 14:12–25

Good Friday
Lamentations 3:1–9, 19–33
1 Peter 1:10–20
John 13:36–38
or John 19:38–42

S Lamentations 3:37–58
Hebrews 4:1–16
Romans 8:1–11

Easter Week

S Exodus 12:1–14
or Isaiah 51:9–11
John 1:1–18
Luke 24:13–35
or John 20:19–23

M Exodus 12:14–27
1 Corinthians 15:1–11
Mark 16:1–8

T Exodus 12:28–39
1 Corinthians 15:12–28
Mark 16:9–20

W Exodus 12:40–51
1 Corinthians 15:(29) 30–41
Matthew 28:1–16

Th Exodus 13:3–10
1 Corinthians 15:41–50
Matthew 28:16–20

F Exodus 13:1–2, 11–16
1 Corinthians 15:51–58
Luke 24:1–12

S Exodus 13:17—14:4
2 Corinthians 4:16—5:10
Mark 12:18–27

Week of 2 Easter

S Exodus 14:5–22
1 John 1:1–7
John 14:1–7

M Exodus 14:21–31
1 Peter 1:1–12
John 14:(1–7) 8–17

T Exodus 15:1–21
1 Peter 1:13–25
John 14:18–31

W Exodus 15:22—16:10
1 Peter 2:1–10
John 15:1–11

Th Exodus 16:10–22
1 Peter 2:11—3:12
John 15:12–27

F Exodus 16:23–36
1 Peter 3:13—4:6
John 16:1–15

S Exodus 17:1–16
1 Peter 4:7–19
John 16:16–33

Week of 3 Easter

S Exodus 18:1–12
1 John 2:7–17
Mark 16:9–20

M Exodus 18:13–27
1 Peter 5:1–14
Matthew (1:1–17) 3:1–6

T Exodus 19:1–16
Colossians 1:1–14
Matthew 3:7–12

W Exodus 19:16–25
Colossians 1:15–23
Matthew 3:13–17

Th Exodus 20:1–21
Colossians 1:24—2:7
Matthew 4:1–11

F Exodus 24:1–18
Colossians 2:8–23
Matthew 4:12–17

S Exodus 25:1–22
Colossians 3:1–17
Matthew 4:18–25

Week of 4 Easter

S Exodus 28:1–4, 30–38
1 John 2:18–29
Mark 6:30–44

M Exodus 32:1–20
Colossians 3:18—4:6 (7–18)
Matthew 5:1–10

T Exodus 32:21–34
1 Thessalonians 1:1–10
Matthew 5:11–16

W Exodus 33:1–23
1 Thessalonians 2:1–12
Matthew 5:17–20

Th Exodus 34:1–17
1 Thessalonians 2:13–20
Matthew 5:21–26

F Exodus 34:18–35
1 Thessalonians 3:1–13
Matthew 5:27–37

S Exodus 40:18–38
1 Thessalonians 4:1–12
Matthew 5:38–48

Week of 5 Easter

S Leviticus 8:1–13, 30–36
Hebrews 12:1–14
Luke 4:16–30

M Leviticus 16:1–19
1 Thessalonians 4:13–18
Matthew 6:1–6, 16–18

T Leviticus 16:20–34
1 Thessalonians 5:1–11
Matthew 6:7–15

W Leviticus 19:1–18
1 Thessalonians 5:12–28
Matthew 6:19–24
Th Leviticus 19:26–37
2 Thessalonians 1:1–12
Matthew 6:25–34
F Leviticus 23:1–22
2 Thessalonians 2:1–17
Matthew 7:1–12
S Leviticus 23:23–44
2 Thessalonians 3:1–18
Matthew 7:13–21

Week of 6 Easter
S Leviticus 25:1–17
James 1:2–8, 16–18
Luke 12:13–21
M Leviticus 25:35–55
Colossians 1:9–14
Matthew 13:1–16
T Leviticus 26:1–20
1 Timothy 2:1–6
Matthew 13:18–23
W Leviticus 26:27–42
Ephesians 1:1–10
Matthew 22:41–46
Ascension Day
Daniel 7:9–14
Hebrews 2:5–18
Matthew 28:16–20
F 1 Samuel 2:1–10
Ephesians 2:1–10
Matthew 7:22–27
S Numbers 11:16–17, 24–29
Ephesians 2:11–22
Matthew 7:28—8:4

Week of 7 Easter
S Exodus 3:1–12
Hebrews 12:18–29
Luke 10:17–24
M Joshua 1:1–9
Ephesians 3:1–13
Matthew 8:5–17
T 1 Samuel 16:1–13a
Ephesians 3:14–21
Matthew 8:18–27
W Isaiah 4:2–6
Ephesians 4:1–16
Matthew 8:28–34
Th Zechariah 4:1–14
Ephesians 4:17–32
Matthew 9:1–8
F Jeremiah 31:27–34
Ephesians 5:1–32
Matthew 9:9–17
S Ezekiel 36:22–27
Ephesians 6:1–24
Matthew 9:18–26

Pentecost and Following
S Deuteronomy 16:9–12
Acts 4:18–21, 23–33
John 4:19–26
M Ezekiel 33:1–11
1 John 1:1–10
Matthew 9:27–34
T Ezekiel 33:21–33
1 John 2:1–11
Matthew 9:35—10:4
W Ezekiel 34:1–16
1 John 2:12–17
Matthew 10:5–15
Th Ezekiel 37:21b–28
1 John 2:18–29
Matthew 10:16–23
F Ezekiel 39:21–29
1 John 3:1–10
Matthew 10:24–33
S Ezekiel 47:1–12
1 John 3:11–18
Matthew 10:34–42

Holy Trinity and Following
S Job 38:1–11; 42:1–5
Revelation 19:4–16
John 1:29–34
M Proverbs 3:11–20
1 John 3:18—4:6
Matthew 11:1–6
T Proverbs 4:1–27
1 John 4:7–21
Matthew 11:7–15
W Proverbs 6:1–19
1 John 5:1–12
Matthew 11:16–24
Th Proverbs 7:1–27
1 John 5:13–21
Matthew 11:25–30
F Proverbs 8:1–21
2 John 1–13
Matthew 12:1–14
S Proverbs 8:22–36
3 John 1–15
Matthew 12:15–21

Week of 2 Pentecost
S Proverbs 9:1–12
Acts 8:14–25
Luke 10:25–28, 38–42
M Proverbs 10:1–12
1 Timothy 1:1–17
Matthew 12:22–32
T Proverbs 15:16–33
1 Timothy 1:18—2:15
Matthew 12:33–42
W Proverbs 17:1–20
1 Timothy 3:1–16
Matthew 12:43–50
Th Proverbs 21:30—22:6
1 Timothy 4:1–16
Matthew 13:24–30
F Proverbs 23:19–21, 29—24:2
1 Timothy 5:17–22 (23–25)
Matthew 13:31–35
S Proverbs 25:15–28
1 Timothy 6:6–21
Matthew 13:36–43

Week of 3 Pentecost
S Ecclesiastes 1:1–11
Acts 8:26–40
Luke 11:1–13
M Ecclesiastes 2:1–15
Galatians 1:1–17
Matthew 13:44–52
T Ecclesiastes 2:16–26
Galatians 1:18—2:10
Matthew 13:53–58
W Ecclesiastes 3:1–15
Galatians 2:11–21
Matthew 14:1–12
Th Ecclesiastes 3:16—4:3
Galatians 3:1–14
Matthew 14:13–21
F Ecclesiastes 5:1–7
Galatians 3:15–22
Matthew 14:22–36
S Ecclesiastes 5:8–20
Galatians 3:23—4:11
Matthew 15:1–20

Week of 4 Pentecost
S Ecclesiastes 6:1–12
Acts 10:9–23
Luke 12:32–40
M Ecclesiastes 7:1–14
Galatians 4:12–20
Matthew 15:21–28
T Ecclesiastes 8:14—9:10
Galatians 4:21–31
Matthew 15:29–39
W Ecclesiastes 9:11–18
Galatians 5:1–15
Matthew 16:1–12
Th Ecclesiastes 11:1–8
Galatians 5:16–24
Matthew 16:13–20
F Ecclesiastes 11:9—12:14
Galatians 5:25—6:10
Matthew 16:21–28
S Numbers 3:1–13
Galatians 6:11–18
Matthew 17:1–13

Week of 5 Pentecost
S Numbers 6:22–27
Acts 13:1–12
Luke 12:41–48
M Numbers 9:15–23; 10:29–36
Romans 1:1–15
Matthew 17:14–21
T Numbers 11:1–23
Romans 1:16–25
Matthew 17:22–27
W Numbers 11:24–33 (34–35)
Romans 1:28—2:11
Matthew 18:1–9
Th Numbers 12:1–16
Romans 2:12–24
Matthew 18:10–20
F Numbers 13:1–3, 21–30
Romans 2:25—3:8
Matthew 18:21–35
S Numbers 13:31—14:25
Romans 3:9–20
Matthew 19:1–12

Week of 6 Pentecost
S Numbers 14:26–45
Acts 15:1–12
Luke 12:49–56
M Numbers 16:1–19
Romans 3:21–31
Matthew 19:13–22

T	Numbers 16:20–35 Romans 4:1–12 Matthew 19:23–30
W	Numbers 16:36–50 Romans 4:13–25 Matthew 20:1–16
Th	Numbers 17:1–11 Romans 5:1–11 Matthew 20:17–28
F	Numbers 20:1–13 Romans 5:12–21 Matthew 20:29–34
S	Numbers 20:14–29 Romans 6:1–11 Matthew 21:1–11

Week of 7 Pentecost

S	Numbers 21:4–9, 21–35 Acts 17:(12–21) 22–34 Luke 13:10–17
M	Numbers 22:1–21 Romans 6:12–23 Matthew 21:12–22
T	Numbers 22:21–38 Romans 7:1–12 Matthew 21:23–32
W	Numbers 22:41—23:12 Romans 7:13–25 Matthew 21:33–46
Th	Numbers 23:11–26 Romans 8:1–11 Matthew 22:1–14
F	Numbers 24:1–13 Romans 8:12–17 Matthew 22:15–22
S	Numbers 24:12–25 Romans 8:18–25 Matthew 22:23–40

Week of 8 Pentecost

S	Numbers 27:12–23 Acts 19:11–20 Mark 1:14–20
M	Numbers 32:1–6, 16–27 Romans 8:26–30 Matthew 23:1–12
T	Numbers 35:1–3, 9–15, 30–34 Romans 8:31–39 Matthew 23:13–26
W	Deuteronomy 1:1–18 Romans 9:1–18 Matthew 23:27–39
Th	Deuteronomy 3:18–28 Romans 9:19–33 Matthew 24:1–14
F	Deuteronomy 31:7–13, 24—32:4 Romans 10:1–13 Matthew 24:15–31
S	Deuteronomy 34:1–12 Romans 10:14–21 Matthew 24:32–51

Week of 9 Pentecost

S	Joshua 1:1–18 Acts 21:3–15 Mark 1:21–27
M	Joshua 2:1–14 Romans 11:1–12 Matthew 25:1–13
T	Joshua 2:15–24 Romans 11:13–24 Matthew 25:14–30
W	Joshua 3:1–13 Romans 11:25–36 Matthew 25:31–46
Th	Joshua 3:14—4:7 Romans 12:1–8 Matthew 26:1–16
F	Joshua 4:19—5:1, 10–15 Romans 12:9–21 Matthew 26:17–25
S	Joshua 6:1–14 Romans 13:1–7 Matthew 26:26–35

Week of 10 Pentecost

S	Joshua 6:15–27 Acts 22:30—23:11 Mark 2:1–12
M	Joshua 7:1–13 Romans 13:8–14 Matthew 26:36–46
T	Joshua 8:1–22 Romans 14:1–12 Matthew 26:47–56
W	Joshua 8:30–35 Romans 14:13–23 Matthew 26:57–68
Th	Joshua 9:3–21 Romans 15:1–13 Matthew 26:69–75
F	Joshua 9:22—10:15 Romans 15:14–24 Matthew 27:1–10
S	Joshua 23:1–16 Romans 15:25–33 Matthew 27:11–23

Week of 11 Pentecost

S	Joshua 24:1–15 Acts 28:23–31 Mark 2:23–28
M	Joshua 24:16–33 Romans 16:1–16 Matthew 27:24–31
T	Judges 2:1–5, 11–23 Romans 16:17–27 Matthew 27:32–44
W	Judges 3:12–30 Acts 1:1–14 Matthew 27:45–54
Th	Judges 4:4–23 Acts 1:15–26 Matthew 27:55–66
F	Judges 5:1–18 Acts 2:1–21 Matthew 28:1–10
S	Judges 5:19–31 Acts 2:22–36 Matthew 28:11–20

Week of 12 Pentecost

S	Judges 6:1–24 2 Corinthians 9:6–15 Mark 3:20–30
M	Judges 6:25–40 Acts 2:37–47 John 1:1–18
T	Judges 7:1–18 Acts 3:1–11 John 1:19–28
W	Judges 7:19—8:12 Acts 3:12–26 John 1:29–42
Th	Judges 8:22–35 Acts 4:1–12 John 1:43–51
F	Judges 9:1–16, 19–21 Acts 4:13–31 John 2:1–12
S	Judges 9:22–25, 50–57 Acts 4:32—5:11 John 2:13–25

Week of 13 Pentecost

S	Judges 11:1–11, 29–40 2 Corinthians 11:21b–31 Mark 4:35–41
M	Judges 12:1–7 Acts 5:12–26 John 3:1–21
T	Judges 13:1–15 Acts 5:27–42 John 3:22–36
W	Judges 13:15–24 Acts 6:1–15 John 4:1–26
Th	Judges 14:1–19 Acts 6:15—7:16 John 4:27–42
F	Judges 14:20—15:20 Acts 7:17–29 John 4:43–54
S	Judges 16:1–14 Acts 7:30–43 John 5:1–18

Week of 14 Pentecost

S	Judges 16:15–31 2 Corinthians 13:1–11 Mark 5:25–34
M	Judges 17:1–13 Acts 7:44—8:1a John 5:19–29
T	Judges 18:1–15 Acts 8:1–13 John 5:30–47
W	Judges 18:16–31 Acts 8:14–25 John 6:1–15
Th	Job 1:1–22 Acts 8:26–40 John 6:16–27
F	Job 2:1–13 Acts 9:1–9 John 6:27–40
S	Job 3:1–26 Acts 9:10–19a John 6:41–51

Week of 15 Pentecost

S	Job 4:1–6, 12–21 Revelation 4:1–11 Mark 6:1–6a
M	Job 4:1; 5:1–11, 17–21, 26–27 Acts 9:19b–31 John 6:52–59

T	Job 6:1–4, 8–15, 21 Acts 9:32–43 John 6:60–71
W	Job 6:1; 7:1–21 Acts 10:1–16 John 7:1–13
Th	Job 8:1–10, 20–22 Acts 10:17–33 John 7:14–36
F	Job 9:1–15, 32–35 Acts 10:34–48 John 7:37–52
S	Job 9:1; 10:1–9, 16–22 Acts 11:1–18 John 8:12–20

Week of 16 Pentecost

S	Job 11:1–9, 13–20 Revelation 5:1–14 Matthew 5:1–12
M	Job 12:1–6, 13–25 Acts 11:19–30 John 8:21–32
T	Job 12:1; 13:3–17, 21–27 Acts 12:1–17 John 8:33–47
W	Job 12:1; 14:1–22 Acts 12:18–25 John 8:47–59
Th	Job 16:16–22; 17:1, 13–16 Acts 13:1–12 John 9:1–17
F	Job 19:1–7, 14–27 Acts 13:13–25 John 9:18–41
S	Job 22:1–4, 21—23:7 Acts 13:26–43 John 10:1–18

Week of 17 Pentecost

S	Job 25:1–6; 27:1–6 Revelation 14:1–7, 13 Matthew 5:13–20
M	Job 32:1–10, 19—33:1, 19–28 Acts 13:44–52 John 10:19–30
T	Job 29:1–20 Acts 14:1–18 John 10:31–42
W	Job 29:1; 30:1–2, 16–31 Acts 14:19–28 John 11:1–16
Th	Job 29:1; 31:1–23 Acts 15:1–11 John 11:17–29
F	Job 29:1; 31:24–40 Acts 15:12–21 John 11:30–44
S	Job 38:1–17 Acts 15:22–35 John 11:45–54

Week of 18 Pentecost

S	Job 38:1, 18–41 Revelation 18:1–8 Matthew 5:21–26
M	Job 40:1–24 Acts 15:36—16:5 John 11:55—12:8
T	Job 40:1; 41:1–11 Acts 16:6–15 John 12:9–19
W	Job 42:1–17 Acts 16:16–24 John 12:20–26
Th	Job 28:1–28 Acts 16:25–40 John 12:27–36a
F	Esther 1:1–4, 10–19 Acts 17:1–15 John 12:36b–43
S	Esther 2:5–8, 15–23 Acts 17:16–34 John 12:44–50

Week of 19 Pentecost

S	Esther 3:1—4:3 James 1:19–27 Matthew 6:1–6, 16–18
M	Esther 4:4–17 Acts 18:1–11 Luke (1:1–4) 3:1–14
T	Esther 5:1–14 Acts 18:12–28 Luke 3:15–22
W	Esther 6:1–14 Acts 19:1–10 Luke 4:1–13
Th	Esther 7:1–10 Acts 19:11–20 Luke 4:14–30
F	Esther 8:1–8, 15–17 Acts 19:21–41 Luke 4:31–37
S	Esther 9:1–32 Acts 20:1–16 Luke 4:38–44

Week of 20 Pentecost

S	Hosea 1:1—2:1 James 3:1–13 Matthew 13:44–52
M	Hosea 2:2–15 Acts 20:17–38 Luke 5:1–11
T	Hosea 2:16–23 Acts 21:1–14 Luke 5:12–26
W	Hosea 3:1–5 Acts 21:15–26 Luke 5:27–39
Th	Hosea 4:1–10 Acts 21:27–36 Luke 6:1–11
F	Hosea 4:11–19 Acts 21:37—22:16 Luke 6:12–26
S	Hosea 5:1–7 Acts 22:17–29 Luke 6:27–38

Week of 21 Pentecost

S	Hosea 5:8—6:6 1 Corinthians 2:6–16 Matthew 14:1–12
M	Hosea 6:7—7:7 Acts 22:30—23:11 Luke 6:39–49
T	Hosea 7:8–16 Acts 23:12–24 Luke 7:1–17
W	Hosea 8:1–14 Acts 23:23–35 Luke 7:18–35
Th	Hosea 9:1–9 Acts 24:1–23 Luke 7:36–50
F	Hosea 9:10–17 Acts 24:24—25:12 Luke 8:1–15
S	Hosea 10:1–15 Acts 25:13–27 Luke 8:16–25

Week of 22 Pentecost

S	Hosea 11:1–11 1 Corinthians 4:9–16 Matthew 15:21–28
M	Hosea 11:12—12:1 Acts 26:1–23 Luke 8:26–39
T	Hosea 12:2–14 Acts 26:24—27:8 Luke 8:40–56
W	Hosea 13:1–3 Acts 27:9–26 Luke 9:1–17
Th	Hosea 13:4–8 Acts 27:27–44 Luke 9:18–27
F	Hosea 13:9–16 Acts 28:1–16 Luke 9:28–36
S	Hosea 14:1–9 Acts 28:17–31 Luke 9:37–50

Week of 23 Pentecost

S	Ecclesiasticus 4:1–10 *or* Micah 1:1–9 1 Corinthians 10:1–13 Matthew 16:13–20
M	Ecclesiasticus 4:20—5:7 *or* Micah 2:1–13 Revelation 7:1–8 Luke 9:51–62
T	Ecclesiasticus 6:5–17 *or* Micah 3:1–8 Revelation 7:9–17 Luke 10:1–16
W	Ecclesiasticus 7:4–14 *or* Micah 3:9—4:5 Revelation 8:1–13 Luke 10:17–24
Th	Ecclesiasticus 10:1–18 *or* Micah 5:1–4, 10–15 Revelation 9:1–12 Luke 10:25–37
F	Ecclesiasticus 11:2–20 *or* Micah 6:1–8 Revelation 9:13–21 Luke 10:38–42
S	Ecclesiasticus 15:9–20 *or* Micah 7:1–7 Revelation 10:1–11 Luke 11:1–13

Week of 24 Pentecost

S Ecclesiasticus 18:19–33
or Jonah 1:1–17a
1 Corinthians 10:15–24
Matthew 18:15–20

M Ecclesiasticus 19:4–17
or Jonah 1:17—2:10
Revelation 11:1–14
Luke 11:14–26

T Ecclesiasticus 24:1–12
or Jonah 3:1—4:11
Revelation 11:14–19
Luke 11:27–36

W Ecclesiasticus 28:14–26
or Nahum 1:1–14
Revelation 12:1–6
Luke 11:37–52

Th Ecclesiasticus 31:12–18, 25—32:2
or Nahum 1:15—2:12
Revelation 12:7–17
Luke 11:53—12:12

F Ecclesiasticus 34:1–8, 18–22
or Nahum 2:13—3:7
Revelation 13:1–10
Luke 12:13–31

S Ecclesiasticus 35:1–17
or Nahum 3:8–19
Revelation 13:11–18
Luke 12:32–48

Week of 25 Pentecost

S Ecclesiasticus 36:1–17
or Zephaniah 1:1–6
1 Corinthians 12:27—13:13
Matthew 18:21–35

M Ecclesiasticus 38:24–34
or Zephaniah 1:7–13
Revelation 14:1–13
Luke 12:49–59

T Ecclesiasticus 43:1–22
or Zephaniah 1:14–18
Revelation 14:14—15:8
Luke 13:1–9

W Ecclesiasticus 43:23–33
or Zephaniah 2:1–15
Revelation 16:1–11
Luke 13:10–17

Th Ecclesiasticus 44:1–15
or Zephaniah 3:1–7
Revelation 16:12–21
Luke 13:18–30

F Ecclesiasticus 50:1, 11–24
or Zephaniah 3:8–13
Revelation 17:1–18
Luke 13:31–35

S Ecclesiasticus 51:1–12
or Zephaniah 3:14–20
Revelation 18:1–14
Luke 14:1–11

Week of 26 Pentecost

S Ecclesiasticus 51:13–22
or Joel 1:1–13
1 Corinthians 14:1–12
Matthew 20:1–16

M Joel 1:1–13
or Joel 1:15—2:2
Revelation 18:15–24
Luke 14:12–24

T Joel 1:15—2:2 (3–11)
or Joel 2:3–11
Revelation 19:1–10
Luke 14:25–35

W Joel 2:12–19
Revelation 19:11–21
Luke 15:1–10

Th Joel 2:21–27
James 1:1–15
Luke 15:1–2, 11–32

F Joel 2:28—3:8
James 1:16–27
Luke 16:1–9

S Joel 3:9–17
James 2:1–13
Luke 16:10–17 (18)

Week of 27 Pentecost

S Habakkuk 1:1–4 (5–11) 12—2:1
Philippians 3:13—4:1
Matthew 23:13–24

M Habakkuk 2:1–4, 9–20
James 2:14–26
Luke 16:19–31

T Habakkuk 3:1–10 (11–15) 16–18
James 3:1–12
Luke 17:1–10

W Malachi 1:1, 6–14
James 3:13—4:12
Luke 17:11–19

Th Malachi 2:1–16
James 4:13—5:6
Luke 17:20–37

F Malachi 3:1–12
James 5:7–12
Luke 18:1–8

S Malachi 3:13—4:6
James 5:13–20
Luke 18:9–14

Christ the King and Following

S Zechariah 9:9–16
1 Peter 3:13–22
Matthew 21:1–13

M Zechariah 10:1–12
Galatians 6:1–10
Luke 18:15–30

T Zechariah 11:4–17
1 Corinthians 3:10–23
Luke 18:31–43

W Zechariah 12:1–10
Ephesians 1:3–14
Luke 19:1–10

Th Zechariah 13:1–9
Ephesians 1:15–23
Luke 19:11–27

F Zechariah 14:1–11
Romans 15:7–13
Luke 19:28–40

S Zechariah 14:12–21
Philippians 2:1–11
Luke 19:41–48

CORPORATE CONFESSION AND FORGIVENESS

Stand

1. The minister leads the congregation in the invocation. The sign of the cross may be made by all in remembrance of their Baptism.

P In the name of the Father, and of the ☩ Son, and of the Holy Spirit.

C **Amen**

2. The minister may announce the occasion for the service and offer any necessary guidance.

3. A HYMN is sung.

Kneel/sit

4. The minister says one of the following or another appropriate prayer.

P Almighty God, to whom all hearts are open, all desires known, and from whom no secrets are hid: Cleanse the thoughts of our hearts by the inspiration of your Holy Spirit, that we may perfectly love you and worthily magnify your holy name, through Jesus Christ our Lord. (236)

C **Amen**

OR

P Father of mercies and God of all consolation, come to the aid of your people, turning us from our sin to live for you alone. Give us the power of your Holy Spirit that we may attend to your Word, confess our sins, receive your forgiveness, and grow into the fullness of your Son Jesus Christ, our Lord and our Redeemer. (271)

C **Amen**

Sit

5. PSALM 51 or another appropriate psalm is sung or said, followed by:

C **Glory to the Father, and to the Son, and to the Holy Spirit; as it was in the beginning, is now, and will be forever. Amen**

6. One or more LESSONS are read. A reading from the Gospels is normally included.

7. A SERMON or informal address may follow. In place of the sermon, the minister or another leader may engage those present in mutual conversation and consolation. Silence for recollection and meditation follows.

8. The prayer of confession or another prayer prepared for the occasion is said.

P Let us [kneel and] make confession to God.

Kneel/sit

C **Almighty God, merciful Father:**
I, a troubled and penitent sinner, confess to you
all my sins and iniquities with which I have offended you
and for which I justly deserve your punishment.
But I am sorry for them, and repent of them,
and pray for your boundless mercy.
For the sake of the suffering and death of your Son, Jesus Christ,
be gracious and merciful to me, a poor sinful being;
forgive my sins,
give me your Holy Spirit for the amendment of my sinful life,
and bring me to life everlasting. Amen

9. The minister stands and addresses the congregation:

P Almighty God in his mercy has given his Son to die for us and, for his sake, forgives us all our sins. Through his Holy Spirit he cleanses us and gives us power to proclaim the mighty deeds of God who called us out of darkness into the splendor of his light. As a called and ordained minister of the Church of Christ and by his authority, I therefore declare to you the entire forgiveness of all your sins, in the name of the Father, and of the ✠ Son, and of the Holy Spirit.

C **Amen**

10. Those in the congregation may come forward and kneel before the altar. The minister, laying both hands on each person's head, addresses each in turn:

P In obedience to the command of our Lord Jesus Christ, I forgive you all your sins.

℟ Amen

Stand

11. The HYMN OF PRAISE is sung when all have returned to their places.

12. THE PRAYERS are said. One of the forms of Responsive Prayer (161), one of the litanies (148 or 168), or other appropriate prayers may replace the following.

P The Lord be with you.

C **And also with you.**

P Let us pray.

Kneel/sit

P O God, our Father, by the cross of your Son you reconciled the world to yourself, enabling us to live in love and harmony. We thank and praise you for the forgiveness of sins and the precious gift of peace. Help us to forgive each other and to establish justice and concord throughout the world, through Jesus Christ our Lord. (272)

C **Amen**

The Prayer of the Day and other prayers may be said and, after them, this prayer:

P O God, from whom come all holy desires, all good counsels, and all just works: Give to us, your servants, that peace which the world cannot give, that our hearts may be set to obey your commandments; and also that we, being defended from the fear of our enemies, may live in peace and quietness; through the merits of Jesus Christ our Savior, who lives and reigns with you and the Holy Spirit, God forever. (255)

C **Amen**

C **Our Father in heaven,**
hallowed be your name,
your kingdom come,
your will be done,
on earth as in heaven.
Give us today our daily bread.
Forgive us our sins
as we forgive those
who sin against us.
Save us from the time of trial
and deliver us from evil.
For the kingdom, the power,
and the glory are yours
now and forever. Amen

OR

C **Our Father, who art in heaven,**
hallowed be thy name,
thy kingdom come,
thy will be done,
on earth as it is in heaven.
Give us this day our daily bread;
and forgive us our trespasses,
as we forgive those
who trespass against us;
and lead us not into temptation,
but deliver us from evil.
For thine is the kingdom,
and the power, and the glory,
forever and ever. Amen

Stand

13. *The minister blesses the congregation.*

P Almighty God, Father, ✠ Son, and Holy Spirit, bless you now and forever.

C **Amen**

14. *The minister may dismiss the congregation.*

P The Lord has made you free. Go in peace.

C **Thanks be to God.**

INDIVIDUAL CONFESSION AND FORGIVENESS

1. The confession made by a penitent is protected from disclosure. The pastor is obligated to respect at all times the confidential nature of a confession.

2. The pastor greets the penitent. When the penitent has knelt, the pastor begins:

P Are you prepared to make your confession?

R I am.

The pastor and penitent say the psalm together.

O Lord, open my lips, and my mouth shall declare your praise.
Had you desired it, I would have offered sacrifice,
  but you take no delight in burnt offerings.
The sacrifice of God is a troubled spirit;
  a broken and contrite heart, O God, you will not despise.
Have mercy on me, O God, according to your lovingkindness;
  in your great compassion blot out my offenses.
Wash me through and through from my wickedness,
  and cleanse me from my sin. (Ps. 51:16–18, 1–2)

P You have come to make confession before God. In Christ you are free to confess before me, a pastor in his Church, the sins of which you are aware and the sins which trouble you.

R I confess before God that I am guilty of many sins.
Especially I confess before you that . . .

3. The penitent confesses those sins which are known and those which disturb or grieve him/her.

For all this I am sorry and I pray for forgiveness. I want to do better.

4. The pastor may then engage the penitent in pastoral conversation, offering admonition and comfort from the Holy Scriptures. Then they say together:

Have mercy on me, O God, according to your lovingkindness;
  in your great compassion blot out my offenses.

Create in me a clean heart, O God,
  and renew a right spirit within me.

Cast me not away from your presence,
  and take not your Holy Spirit from me.

Restore to me the joy of your salvation,
  and uphold me with your free Spirit. (Ps. 51:1, 11–13)

5. The pastor stands and faces the penitent or remains seated and turns toward the penitent.

℗ Do you believe that the word of forgiveness I speak to you comes from God himself?

℟ Yes, I believe.

6. The pastor lays both hands on the head of the penitent.

℗ God is merciful and blesses you. By the command of our Lord Jesus Christ, I, a called and ordained servant of the Word, forgive you your sins in the name of the Father, and of the ☩ Son, and of the Holy Spirit.

℟ Amen

7. The penitent may pray silently in thanksgiving, or may pray together with the pastor:

The Lord is full of compassion and mercy,
  slow to anger and of great kindness.
He will not always accuse us,
  nor will he keep his anger forever.
He has not dealt with us according to our sins,
  nor rewarded us according to our wickedness.
For as the heavens are high above the earth,
  so is his mercy great upon those who fear him.
As far as the east is from the west,
  so far has he removed our sins from us.
As a father cares for his children,
  so does the Lord care for those who fear him. (Ps. 103:8–13)
Glory to the Father, and to the Son, and to the Holy Spirit;
  as it was in the beginning, is now, and will be forever. Amen

℗ Blessed are those whose sins have been forgiven,
  whose evil deeds have been forgotten.
Rejoice in the Lord, and go in peace.

8. The penitent stands and may exchange the peace with the pastor.

AFFIRMATION OF BAPTISM

1. Three services, related to the Baptism of the candidates, are presented as one.

2. A hymn is sung as the candidates gather before the congregation.

CONFIRMATION

3. Confirmation marks the completion of the congregation's program of confirmation ministry, a period of instruction in the Christian faith as confessed in the teachings of the Lutheran Church. Those who have completed this program were made members of the Church in Baptism. Confirmation includes a public profession of the faith into which the candidates were baptized, thus underscoring God's action in their Baptism.

4. A representative of the congregation presents the candidates to the minister:

These persons have been instructed in the Christian faith and desire to make public affirmation of their Baptism.

5. Their names are read.

P Dear friends, we rejoice that you now desire to make public profession of your faith and assume greater responsibility in the life of our Christian community and its mission in the world.

RECEPTION INTO MEMBERSHIP

6. Christians from other denominations become members of the Lutheran Church through reception into the local congregation. In Baptism they were made Christians; now they become members of the Lutheran Church.

7. A representative of the congregation presents the candidates to the minister:

These persons have come to us from *other churches,* and desire to make public affirmation of their Baptism.

8. Their names are read.

P Dear friends, we rejoice to receive you, members of the one holy catholic and apostolic Church, into our fellowship in the Gospel.

9. Baptized persons who desire again to participate actively in the life of the Church are restored to membership through affirmation of their Baptism.

10. A representative of the congregation presents the candidates to the minister:

These persons desire to make public affirmation of their Baptism as a sign of their renewed participation in the life and work of the Church of Christ.

11. Their names are read.

P Dear friends, we rejoice that you have returned to the household of God to claim again the eternal inheritance which is your birthright in Holy Baptism.

---

12. The minister addresses those who have been presented.

P Brothers and sisters in Christ: In Holy Baptism our Lord Jesus Christ received you and made you members of his Church. In the community of God's people, you have learned from his Word God's loving purpose for you and all creation. You have been [nourished at his holy table and] called to be witnesses to the Gospel of Jesus Christ.

Now, therefore, I ask you to profess your faith in Christ Jesus, reject sin, and confess the faith of the Church, the faith in which we baptize.

Do you renounce all the forces of evil, the devil, and all his empty promises?

R I do.

P Do you believe in God the Father?

R I believe in God, the Father almighty,
creator of heaven and earth.

P Do you believe in Jesus Christ, the Son of God?

R I believe in Jesus Christ, his only Son, our Lord.
He was conceived by the power of the Holy Spirit
and born of the virgin Mary.
He suffered under Pontius Pilate,
was crucified, died, and was buried.
He descended into hell.*
On the third day he rose again.
He ascended into heaven,
and is seated at the right hand of the Father.
He will come again to judge the living and the dead.

**Or,* He descended to the dead.

P Do you believe in God the Holy Spirit?

R I believe in the Holy Spirit,
the holy catholic Church,
the communion of saints,
the forgiveness of sins,
the resurrection of the body,
and the life everlasting. Amen

Stand

13. THE PRAYERS are said.

A Let us pray for those who are affirming their Baptism, and for all the baptized everywhere:

That they may be redeemed from all evil and rescued from the way of sin and death: Lord, in your mercy,

C **hear our prayer.**

A That the Holy Spirit may open their hearts to your grace and truth: Lord, in your mercy,

C **hear our prayer.**

A That they may be kept in the faith and communion of your holy Church: Lord, in your mercy,

C **hear our prayer.**

A That they may be sent into the world in witness to your love: Lord, in your mercy,

C **hear our prayer.**

A That they may be brought to the fullness of your peace and glory: Lord, in your mercy,

C **hear our prayer.**

Other prayers may be added.

P Into your hands, O Lord, we commend all for whom we pray, trusting in your mercy, through your Son, Jesus Christ our Lord. (238)

C **Amen**

Sit

14. The minister addresses those making affirmation.

P You have made public profession of your faith. Do you intend to continue in the covenant God made with you in Holy Baptism:
to live among God's faithful people,
to hear his Word and share in his supper,
to proclaim the good news of God in Christ through word and deed,
to serve all people, following the example of our Lord Jesus,
and to strive for justice and peace in all the earth?

Each person answers in turn.

R I do, and I ask God to help and guide me.

P Let us pray.

15. Those making affirmation kneel. A brief silence is kept so that prayer may be made for them.

P Gracious Lord, through water and the Spirit you have made these *men and women* your own. You forgave them all their sins and brought them to newness of life. Continue to strengthen them with the Holy Spirit, and daily increase in them your gifts of grace: the spirit of wisdom and understanding, the spirit of counsel and might, the spirit of knowledge and the fear of the Lord, the spirit of joy in your presence; through Jesus Christ, your Son, our Lord. (274)

C Amen

FOR CONFIRMATION ONLY

16. The presiding minister lays both hands on the head of each person:

P Father in heaven, for Jesus' sake, stir up in ____name____ the gift of your Holy Spirit; confirm *his/her* faith, guide *his/her* life, empower *him/her* in *his/her* serving, give *him/her* patience in suffering, and bring *him/her* to everlasting life. (275)

Each person answers: "Amen."

17. They stand. The presiding minister exchanges the peace with each of them. They exchange the peace with one another and other members of the congregation:

Peace be with you. R Peace be with you.

18. All return to their places. The service continues with the Offering.

MARRIAGE

Stand

1. The bride, groom, and wedding party stand in front of the minister. The parents may stand behind the couple.

P The grace of our Lord Jesus Christ, the love of God, and the communion of the Holy Spirit be with you all.

C **And also with you.**

A Let us pray.

Eternal God, our creator and redeemer, as you gladdened the wedding at Cana in Galilee by the presence of your Son, so by his presence now bring your joy to this wedding. Look in favor upon _____name_____ and _____name_____ and grant that they, rejoicing in all your gifts, may at length celebrate with Christ the marriage feast which has no end. (162)

C **Amen**

Sit

2. One or more lessons from the Bible may be read. An address may follow. A hymn may be sung.

A The Lord God in his goodness created us male and female, and by the gift of marriage founded human community in a joy that begins now and is brought to perfection in the life to come.

Because of sin, our age-old rebellion, the gladness of marriage can be overcast and the gift of the family can become a burden.

But because God, who established marriage, continues still to bless it with his abundant and ever-present support, we can be sustained in our weariness and have our joy restored.

P ______name______ and ______name______, if it is your intention to share with each other your joys and sorrows and all that the years will bring, with your promises bind yourselves to each other as husband and wife.

Stand

3. The bride and groom face each other and join hands. Each, in turn, promises faithfulness to the other in these or similar words:

I take you, ______name______,
to be my *wife/husband* from this day forward,
to join with you and share all that is to come,
and I promise to be faithful to you
until death parts us.

4. The bride and groom exchange rings with these words:

I give you this ring as a sign of my love and faithfulness.

5. The bride and groom join hands, and the minister announces their marriage by saying:

P ______name______ and ______name______, by their promises before God and in the presence of this congregation, have bound themselves to one another as husband and wife.

C Blessed be the Father and the Son and the Holy Spirit now and forever.

P Those whom God has joined together let no one put asunder.

C Amen

Sit

6. The bride and groom kneel.

P The Lord God, who created our first parents and established them in marriage, establish and sustain you, that you may find delight in each other and grow in holy love until your life's end.

C Amen

7. The parents may add their blessing with these or similar words; the wedding party may join them.

May you dwell in God's presence forever; may true and constant love preserve you.

8. The bride and groom stand.

Stand

A Let us bless God for all the gifts in which we rejoice today.

P Lord God, constant in mercy, great in faithfulness: With high praise we recall your acts of unfailing love for the human family, for the house of Israel, and for your people the Church.

We bless you for the joy which your servants, ______name______ and ______name______, have found in each other, and pray that you give to us such a sense of your constant love that we may employ all our strength in a life of praise of you, whose work alone holds true and endures forever. (276)

C Amen

A Let us pray for ______name______ and ______name______ in their life together.

P Faithful Lord, source of love, pour down your grace upon ______name______ and ______name______, that they may fulfill the vows they have made this day and reflect your steadfast love in their life-long faithfulness to each other. As members with them of the body of Christ, use us to support their life together; and from your great store of strength give them power and patience, affection and understanding, courage, and love toward you, toward each other, and toward the world, that they may continue together in mutual growth according to your will in Jesus Christ our Lord. (277)

C Amen

Other intercessions may be offered.

A Let us pray for all families throughout the world.

P Gracious Father, you bless the family and renew your people. Enrich husbands and wives, parents and children more and more with your grace, that, strengthening and supporting each other, they may serve those in need and be a sign of the fulfillment of your perfect kingdom, where, with your Son Jesus Christ and the Holy Spirit, you live and reign, one God through all ages of ages. (278)

C Amen

9. When Holy Communion is celebrated, the service continues with the Peace.

10. When there is no Communion, the service continues with the Lord's Prayer.

C Our Father in heaven,
hallowed be your name,
your kingdom come,
your will be done,
on earth as in heaven.
Give us today our daily bread.
Forgive us our sins
as we forgive those
who sin against us.
Save us from the time of trial
and deliver us from evil.
For the kingdom, the power,
and the glory are yours,
now and forever. Amen

OR

C Our Father, who art in heaven,
hallowed be thy name,
thy kingdom come,
thy will be done,
on earth as it is in heaven.
Give us this day our daily bread;
and forgive us our trespasses,
as we forgive those
who trespass against us;
and lead us not into temptation,
but deliver us from evil.
For thine is the kingdom,
and the power, and the glory,
forever and ever. Amen

P Almighty God, Father, ✠ Son, and Holy Spirit, keep you in his light and truth and love now and forever.

C Amen

BURIAL OF THE DEAD

1. This rite may be used as a memorial service by omitting those portions indicated by the red line in the left margin.

2. The ceremonies or tributes of social or fraternal societies have no place within the service of the Church.

At the Entrance to the Church

3. The ministers meet the coffin, the pallbearers, and the bereaved at the entrance to the church.

P Blessed be the God and Father of our Lord Jesus Christ, the source of all mercy and the God of all consolation. He comforts us in all our sorrows so that we can comfort others in their sorrows with the consolation we ourselves have received from God.

C Thanks be to God.

4. A pall may be placed upon the coffin by the pallbearers or other assisting ministers, and the following may be said.

P When we were baptized in Christ Jesus, we were baptized into his death. We were buried therefore with him by Baptism into death, so that as Christ was raised from the dead by the glory of the Father, we too might live a new life. For if we have been united with him in a death like his, we shall certainly be united with him in a resurrection like his.

Procession

Stand

5. The procession forms and enters the church, the ministers preceding the coffin.

6. A psalm, hymn, or appropriate verse may be sung as the procession goes to the front of the church.

The Liturgy of the Word

P The Lord be with you.

C **And also with you.**

P Let us pray.

7. One of the following prayers is said.

P O God of grace and glory, we remember before you today our *brother/sister,* _____name_____. We thank you for giving *him/her* to us to know and to love as a companion in our pilgrimage on earth. In your boundless compassion, console us who mourn. Give us your aid, so we may see in death the gate to eternal life, that we may continue our course on earth in confidence until, by your call, we are reunited with those who have gone before us; through your Son, Jesus Christ our Lord. (279)

C **Amen**

OR

P Almighty God, source of all mercy and giver of comfort: Deal graciously, we pray, with those who mourn, that, casting all their sorrow on you, they may know the consolation of your love; through your Son, Jesus Christ our Lord. (280)

C **Amen**

OR

P Almighty God, those who die in the Lord still live with you in joy and blessedness. We give you heartfelt thanks for the grace you have bestowed upon your servants who have finished their course in faith and now rest from their labors. May we, with all who have died in the true faith, have perfect fulfillment and joy in your eternal and everlasting glory; through your Son, Jesus Christ our Lord. (281)

C **Amen**

OR

Ⓟ O God, your days are without end and your mercies cannot be counted. Make us aware of the shortness and uncertainty of human life, and let your Holy Spirit lead us in holiness and righteousness all the days of our life, so that, when we shall have served you in our generation, we may be gathered to our ancestors, having the testimony of a good conscience, in the communion of your Church, in the confidence of a certain faith, in the comfort of a holy hope, in favor with you, our God, and in peace with all humanity; through Jesus Christ our Lord. (282)

Ⓒ **Amen**

OR

AT THE BURIAL OF A CHILD

Ⓟ O God our Father, your beloved Son took children into his arms and blessed them. Give us grace, we pray, that we may entrust ______name______ to your never-failing care and love, and bring us all to your heavenly kingdom; through your Son, Jesus Christ our Lord. (283)

Ⓒ **Amen**

Sit

8. One or two LESSONS are read. A psalm, hymn, or anthem may be sung between the first and second readings.

9. The appropriate VERSE may be sung:

Ⓒ **Alleluia. Jesus Christ is the firstborn of the dead; to him be glory and power forever and ever. Amen. Alleluia.**

OR

LENT

Ⓒ **If we have died with Christ, we shall also live with him; if we are faithful to the end, we shall reign with him.**

Stand

10. The GOSPEL is read.

Sit

11. The SERMON follows the reading of the Gospel.

Stand

12. A HYMN is sung.

13. The CREED may be said.

P God has made us his people through our Baptism into Christ. Living together in trust and hope, we confess our faith.

C **I believe in God, the Father almighty,**
creator of heaven and earth.

I believe in Jesus Christ, his only Son, our Lord.
He was conceived by the power of the Holy Spirit
and born of the virgin Mary.
He suffered under Pontius Pilate,
was crucified, died, and was buried.
He descended into hell.*
On the third day he rose again.
He ascended into heaven,
and is seated at the right hand of the Father.
He will come again to judge the living and the dead.

I believe in the Holy Spirit,
the holy catholic Church,
the communion of saints,
the forgiveness of sins,
the resurrection of the body,
and the life everlasting. Amen

14. The PRAYERS are said. Other appropriate prayers may be used instead.

A Let us pray.

Almighty God, you have knit your chosen people together in one communion, in the mystical body of your Son, Jesus Christ our Lord. Give to your whole Church in heaven and on earth your light and your peace.

C **Hear us, Lord.**

A Grant that all who have been baptized into Christ's death and resurrection may die to sin and rise to newness of life and that through the grave and gate of death we may pass with him to our joyful resurrection.

C **Hear us, Lord.**

A Grant to us who are still in our pilgrimage, and who walk as yet by faith, that your Holy Spirit may lead us in holiness and righteousness all our days.

C **Hear us, Lord.**

A Grant to your faithful people pardon and peace, that we may be cleansed from all our sins and serve you with a quiet mind.

C **Hear us, Lord.**

**Or,* He descended to the dead.

A Grant to all who mourn a sure confidence in your loving care, that, casting all their sorrow on you, they may know the consolation of your love.

C Hear us, Lord.

A Give courage and faith to those who are bereaved, that they may have strength to meet the days ahead in the comfort of a holy and certain hope, and in the joyful expectation of eternal life with those they love.

C Hear us, Lord.

A Help us, we pray, in the midst of things we cannot understand, to believe and trust in the communion of saints, the forgiveness of sins, and the resurrection to life everlasting.

C Hear us, Lord.

A Grant us grace to entrust ______name______ to your never-failing love which sustained *him/her* in this life. Receive *him/her* into the arms of your mercy, and remember *him/her* according to the favor you bear for your people.

C Hear us, Lord.

15. The minister concludes the intercessions with one of the following prayers.

A God of all grace, you sent your Son, our Savior Jesus Christ, to bring life and immortality to light. We give you thanks because by his death Jesus destroyed the power of death and by his resurrection has opened the kingdom of heaven to all believers. Make us certain that because he lives we shall live also, and that neither death nor life, nor things present nor things to come shall be able to separate us from your love which is in Christ Jesus our Lord, who lives and reigns with you and the Holy Spirit, one God, now and forever. (284)

C Amen

OR

A God, the generations rise and pass away before you. You are the strength of those who labor; you are the rest of the blessed dead. We rejoice in the company of your saints. We remember all who have lived in faith, all who have peacefully died, and especially those most dear to us who rest in you. . . . Give us in time our portion with those who have trusted in you and have striven to do your holy will. To your name, with the Church on earth and the Church in heaven, we ascribe all honor and glory, now and forever. (285)

C Amen

16. When Holy Communion is celebrated, the service continues with the Peace. The Commendation then follows the post-communion canticle ("Lord, now you let your servant . . .") and prayer.

17. When there is no Communion, the service continues with the Lord's Prayer.

C **Our Father in heaven,**
hallowed be your name,
your kingdom come,
your will be done,
on earth as in heaven.
Give us today our daily bread.
Forgive us our sins
as we forgive those
who sin against us.
Save us from the time of trial
and deliver us from evil.
For the kingdom, the power,
and the glory are yours
now and forever. Amen

OR

C **Our Father, who art in heaven,**
hallowed be thy name,
thy kingdom come,
thy will be done,
on earth as it is in heaven.
Give us this day our daily bread;
and forgive us our trespasses,
as we forgive those
who trespass against us;
and lead us not into temptation,
but deliver us from evil.
For thine is the kingdom,
and the power, and the glory,
forever and ever. Amen

Sit

Commendation

18. The ministers take their places at the coffin.

P Into your hands, O merciful Savior, we commend your servant, ____name____. Acknowledge, we humbly beseech you, a sheep of your own fold, a lamb of your own flock, a sinner of your own redeeming. Receive *him/her* into the arms of your mercy, into the blessed rest of everlasting peace, and into the glorious company of the saints in light. (286)

C **Amen**

P Let us go forth in peace.

C **In the name of Christ. Amen**

Stand

19. The procession forms and leaves the church, the ministers preceding the coffin.

20. As the procession leaves the church, a psalm, hymn, or anthem may be sung. The canticle, "Lord, now you let your servant . . . ," may be sung if it has not been sung in the Holy Communion (39).

Committal

21. The ministers precede the coffin to the place of interment. During the procession, one or more of these verses may be sung or said.

A I called to the Lord in my distress; the Lord answered by setting me free.
It is better to rely on the Lord than to put any trust in flesh. It is better to rely on the Lord than to put any trust in rulers.

I was pressed so hard that I almost fell, but the Lord came to my help.

There is a sound of exultation and victory in the tents of the righteous:
"The right hand of the Lord has triumphed! The right hand of the Lord is exalted!
The right hand of the Lord has triumphed!"

I shall not die, but live, and declare the works of the Lord.

Open for me the gates of righteousness; I will enter them; I will offer thanks to the Lord. "This is the gate of the Lord; he who is righteous may enter." (Ps. 118:5, 8-9, 13, 15-17, 19-20)

A For I know that my Redeemer lives, and at last he will stand upon the earth; and after my skin has been thus destroyed, then from my flesh I shall see God. (Job 19:25-26)

A None of us lives to himself, and none of us dies to himself. If we live, we live to the Lord, and if we die, we die to the Lord; so then, whether we live or whether we die, we are the Lord's. (Rom. 14:7-8)

A "I am the resurrection and the life," says the Lord; "he who believes in me, though he die, yet shall he live, and whoever lives and believes in me shall never die." (John 11:25-26a)

22. *When all have arrived at the place of burial, the following prayer may be said.*

P Almighty God, by the death and burial of Jesus, your anointed, you have destroyed death and sanctified the graves of all your saints. Keep our *brother/sister,* whose *body* we now lay to rest, in the company of all your saints and, at the last, raise *him/her* up to share with all your faithful people the endless joy and peace won through the glorious resurrection of Christ our Lord, who lives and reigns with you and the Holy Spirit, one God, now and forever. (287)

C **Amen**

23. *One of the following lessons may be read.*

And Jesus answered them, "The hour has come for the Son of man to be glorified. Truly, truly, I say to you, unless a grain of wheat falls into the earth and dies, it remains alone; but if it dies, it bears much fruit. He who loves his life loses it, and he who hates his life in this world will keep it for eternal life. If anyone serves me, he must follow me; and where I am, there shall my servant be also; if anyone serves me, the Father will honor him." (John 12:23-26)

Lo! I tell you a mystery. We shall not all sleep, but we shall all be changed, in a moment, in the twinkling of an eye, at the last trumpet. For the trumpet will sound, and the dead will be raised imperishable, and we shall be changed. For this perishable nature must put on the imperishable, and this mortal nature must put on immortality. When the perishable puts on the imperishable, and the mortal puts on immortality, then shall come to pass the saying that is written: "Death is swallowed up in victory." "O death, where is thy victory? O death, where is thy sting?" The sting of death is sin, and the power of sin is the law. But thanks be to God, who gives us the victory through our Lord Jesus Christ. (1 Cor. 15:51-57)

But our commonwealth is in heaven, and from it we await a Savior, the Lord Jesus Christ, who will change our lowly body to be like his glorious body, by the power which enables him even to subject all things to himself. (Phil. 3:20-21)

24. The coffin is lowered into the grave or placed in its resting place. Earth may be cast on the coffin as the minister says:

P In sure and certain hope of the resurrection to eternal life through our Lord Jesus Christ, we commend to almighty God our *brother/sister,* _____name_____, and we commit *his/her* body to *the ground/the deep/the elements/its resting place;* earth to earth, ashes to ashes, dust to dust. The Lord bless *him/her* and keep *him/her.* The Lord make his face shine on *him/her* and be gracious to *him/her.* The Lord look upon *him/her* with favor and give *him/her* ☩ peace.

C **Amen**

OR

P Since almighty God has called our *brother/sister,* _____name_____, from this life to himself, we commit *his/her* body to *the earth from which it was made/the deep/the elements/its resting place.* Christ was the first to rise from the dead, and we know that he will raise up our mortal bodies to be like his in glory. We commend our *brother/sister* to the Lord: May the Lord receive *him/her* into his peace and raise *him/her* up on the last day.

C **Amen**

P Lord, remember us in your kingdom, and teach us to pray:

C **Our Father in heaven,**
hallowed be your name,
your kingdom come,
your will be done,
on earth as in heaven.
Give us today our daily bread.
Forgive us our sins
as we forgive those
who sin against us.
Save us from the time of trial
and deliver us from evil.
For the kingdom, the power,
and the glory are yours
now and forever. Amen

OR

C **Our Father, who art in heaven,**
hallowed be thy name,
thy kingdom come,
thy will be done,
on earth as it is in heaven.
Give us this day our daily bread;
and forgive us our trespasses,
as we forgive those
who trespass against us;
and lead us not into temptation,
but deliver us from evil.
For thine is the kingdom,
and the power, and the glory,
forever and ever. Amen

P Lord Jesus, by your death you took away the sting of death. Grant to us, your servants, so to follow in faith where you have led the way, that we may at length fall asleep peacefully in you and wake in your likeness; to you, the author and giver of life, be all honor and glory, now and forever. (288)

C **Amen**

25. Then may be said:

Ⓟ Rest eternal grant *him/her,* O Lord;

Ⓐ and let light perpetual shine upon *him/her.*

26. The minister blesses the people.

Ⓟ The God of peace—who brought again from the dead our Lord Jesus Christ, the great shepherd of the sheep, through the blood of the everlasting covenant—make you perfect in every good work to do his will, working in you that which is well-pleasing in his sight; through Jesus Christ, to whom be glory forever and ever.

Ⓒ **Amen**

Ⓟ Let us go in peace.

THE PSALMS

1

1 Happy are they who have not walked
in the counsel of the wicked,*
nor lingered in the way of sinners,
nor sat in the seats of the scornful!
2 Their delight is
in the law of the LORD,*
and they meditate on his law
day and night.
3 They are like trees
planted by streams of water,
bearing fruit in due season,
with leaves that do not wither;*
everything they do shall prosper.
4 It is not so with the wicked;*
they are like chaff
which the wind blows away.
5 Therefore the wicked
shall not stand upright
when judgment comes,*
nor the sinner
in the council of the righteous.
6 For the LORD knows
the way of the righteous,*
but the way of the wicked is doomed.

2

1 Why are the nations in an uproar?*
Why do the peoples
mutter empty threats?
2 Why do the kings of the earth
rise up in revolt,
and the princes plot together,*
against the LORD and
against his anointed?
3 "Let us break their yoke," they say;*
"let us cast off their bonds from us."
4 He whose throne is in heaven
is laughing;*
the Lord has them in derision.
5 Then he speaks to them in his wrath,*
and his rage fills them with terror.
6 "I myself have set my king*
upon my holy hill of Zion."
7 Let me announce
the decree of the LORD:*
He said to me, "You are my son;
this day have I begotten you.
8 Ask of me, and I will give you
the nations for your inheritance*
and the ends of the earth
for your possession.
9 You shall crush them with an iron rod*
and shatter them
like a piece of pottery."
10 And now, you kings, be wise;*
be warned, you rulers of the earth.
11 Submit to the LORD with fear,*
and with trembling
bow before him;
12 lest he be angry, and you perish,*
for his wrath is quickly kindled.
13 Happy are they all*
who take refuge in him!

4

1 Answer me when I call, O God,
defender of my cause;*
you set me free
when I am hard-pressed;
have mercy on me
and hear my prayer.

2 "You mortals, how long
will you dishonor my glory;*
how long
will you worship dumb idols
and run after false gods?"

3 Know that the LORD
does wonders for the faithful;*
when I call upon the LORD,
he will hear me.

4 Tremble, then, and do not sin;*
speak to your heart in silence
upon your bed.

5 Offer the appointed sacrifices,*
and put your trust in the LORD.

6 Many are saying,
"Oh, that we might see better times!"*
Lift up the light
of your countenance upon us, O LORD.

7 You have put gladness in my heart,*
more than when grain and wine
and oil increase.

8 I lie down in peace;
at once I fall asleep;*
for only you, LORD,
make me dwell in safety.

5

1 Give ear to my words, O LORD;*
consider my meditation.

2 Hearken to my cry for help,
my King and my God,*
for I make my prayer to you.

3 In the morning, LORD,
you hear my voice;*
early in the morning
I make my appeal and watch for you.

4 For you are not a God
who takes pleasure in wickedness,*
and evil cannot dwell with you.

5 Braggarts cannot stand in your sight;*
you hate all those
who work wickedness.

6 You destroy those who speak lies;*
the bloodthirsty and deceitful,
O LORD, you abhor.

7 But as for me,
through the greatness of your mercy
I will go into your house;*
I will bow down
toward your holy temple
in awe of you.

8 Lead me, O LORD,
in your righteousness,
because of those who lie in wait for me;*
make your way straight before me.

9 For there is no truth in their mouth;*
there is destruction in their heart;

10 their throat is an open grave;*
they flatter with their tongue.

11 Declare them guilty, O God;*
let them fall,
because of their schemes.

12 Because of their many transgressions,
cast them out,*
for they have rebelled against you.

13 But all who take refuge in you
will be glad;*
they will sing out their joy forever.

14 You will shelter them,*
so that those who love your name
may exult in you.

15 For you, O LORD, will bless the righteous;*
you will defend them
with your favor as with a shield.

6

1 LORD, do not rebuke me in your anger;*
do not punish me in your wrath.

2 Have pity on me, LORD,
for I am weak;*
heal me, LORD,
for my bones are racked.

3 My spirit shakes with terror;*
how long, O LORD, how long?

4 Turn, O LORD, and deliver me;*
save me for your mercy's sake.
5 For in death no one remembers you;*
and who will give you thanks
in the grave?
6 I grow weary because of my groaning;*
every night I drench my bed
and flood my couch with tears.
7 My eyes are wasted with grief*
and worn away
because of all my enemies.
8 Depart from me, all evildoers,*
for the LORD
has heard the sound of my weeping.
9 The LORD has heard my supplication;*
the LORD accepts my prayer.
10 All my enemies shall be confounded
and quake with fear;*
they shall turn back
and suddenly be put to shame.

7

1 O LORD my God, I take refuge in you;*
save and deliver me
from all who pursue me;
2 lest like a lion they tear me in pieces*
and snatch me away
with none to deliver me.
3 O LORD my God,
if I have done these things,*
if there is any wickedness
in my hands,
4 if I have repaid my friend with evil,*
or plundered him
who without cause is my enemy,
5 then let my enemy pursue
and overtake me,*
trample my life into the ground,
and lay my honor in the dust.
6 Stand up, O LORD, in your wrath;*
rise up against
the fury of my enemies.
7 Awake, O my God, decree justice;*
let the assembly of the peoples
gather round you.
8 Be seated on your lofty throne,
O Most High;*
O LORD, judge the nations.
9 Give judgment for me according to my
righteousness, O LORD,*
and according to my innocence,
O Most High.
10 Let the malice of the wicked
come to an end,
but establish the righteous;*
for you test the mind and heart,
O righteous God.
11 God is my shield and defense;*
he is the savior of the true in heart.
12 God is a righteous judge;*
God sits in judgment every day.
13 If they will not repent,
God will whet his sword;*
he will bend his bow and make it ready.
14 He has prepared his weapons of death;*
he makes his arrows shafts of fire.
15 Look at those
who are in labor with wickedness,*
who conceive evil,
and give birth to a lie.
16 They dig a pit and make it deep*
and fall into the hole
that they have made.
17 Their malice turns back
upon their own head;*
their violence falls on their own scalp.
18 I will bear witness
that the LORD is righteous;*
I will praise the name
of the LORD Most High.

8

1 O LORD our Lord,*
how exalted is your name
in all the world!
2 Out of the mouths
of infants and children*
your majesty is praised
above the heavens.
3 You have set up a stronghold
against your adversaries,*
to quell the enemy and the avenger.

4 When I consider your heavens,
the work of your fingers,*
the moon and the stars
you have set in their courses,
5 what is man
that you should be mindful of him,*
the son of man
that you should seek him out?
6 You have made him
but little lower than the angels;*
you adorn him
with glory and honor;
7 you give him mastery
over the works of your hands;*
you put all things under his feet:
8 all sheep and oxen,*
even the wild beasts of the field,
9 the birds of the air, the fish of the sea,*
and whatsoever walks
in the paths of the sea.
10 O LORD our Lord,*
how exalted is your name
in all the world!

9

1 I will give thanks to you, O LORD,
with my whole heart;*
I will tell of all your marvelous works.
2 I will be glad and rejoice in you;*
I will sing to your name,
O Most High.
3 When my enemies are driven back,*
they will stumble and perish
at your presence.
4 For you have maintained
my right and my cause;*
you sit upon your throne,
judging right.
5 You have rebuked the ungodly
and destroyed the wicked;*
you have blotted out their name
forever and ever.
6 As for the enemy, they are finished,
in perpetual ruin,*
their cities plowed under,
the memory of them perished;
7 but the LORD is enthroned forever;*
he has set up his throne for judgment.
8 It is he who
rules the world with righteousness;*
he judges the peoples with equity.
9 The LORD will be a refuge
for the oppressed,*
a refuge in time of trouble.
10 Those who know your name
will put their trust in you,*
for you never forsake those
who seek you, O LORD.
11 Sing praise to the LORD
who dwells in Zion;*
proclaim to the peoples
the things he has done.
12 The avenger of blood
will remember them;*
he will not forget
the cry of the afflicted.
13 Have pity on me, O LORD;*
see the misery I suffer
from those who hate me,
O you who lift me up
from the gate of death;
14 so that I may tell of all your praises
and rejoice in your salvation*
in the gates of the city of Zion.
15 The ungodly have fallen
into the pit they dug,*
and in the snare they set
is their own foot caught.
16 The LORD is known
by his acts of justice;*
the wicked are trapped
in the works of their own hands.
17 The wicked
shall be given over to the grave,*
and also all the peoples
that forget God.
18 For the needy
shall not always be forgotten,*
and the hope of the poor
shall not perish forever.
19 Rise up, O LORD, let not the ungodly
have the upper hand;*
let them be judged before you.

20 Put fear upon them, O LORD;*
let the ungodly know
they are but mortal.

10

1 Why do you stand so far off, O LORD,*
and hide yourself in time of trouble?
2 The wicked
arrogantly persecute the poor,*
but they are trapped in the schemes
they have devised.
3 The wicked boast of their heart's desire;*
the covetous curse
and revile the LORD.
4 The wicked are so proud
that they care not for God;*
their only thought is,
"God does not matter."
5 Their ways are devious at all times;
your judgments are far above,
out of their sight;*
they defy all their enemies.
6 They say in their heart,
"I shall not be shaken;*
no harm shall happen to me ever."
7 Their mouth is full of cursing,
deceit, and oppression;*
under their tongue
are mischief and wrong.
8 They lurk in ambush in public squares,
and in secret places
they murder the innocent;*
they spy out the helpless.
9 They lie in wait, like a lion in a covert;
they lie in wait to seize upon the lowly;*
they seize the lowly
and drag them away in their net.
10 The innocent are broken
and humbled before them;*
the helpless fall before their power.
11 They say in their heart,
"God has forgotten;*
he hides his face; he will never notice."
12 Rise up, O LORD;
lift up your hand, O God;*
do not forget the afflicted.
13 Why should the wicked revile God?*
Why should they say in their heart,
"You do not care"?
14 Surely, you behold trouble and misery;*
you see it
and take it into your own hand.
15 The helpless commit themselves to you,*
for you are the helper of orphans.
16 Break the power of the wicked and evil;*
search out their wickedness
until you find none.
17 The LORD is king forever and ever;*
the ungodly shall perish
from his land.
18 The LORD will hear the desire
of the humble;*
you will strengthen their heart
and your ears shall hear,
19 to give justice
to the orphan and oppressed,*
so that mere mortals
may strike terror no more.

11

1 In the LORD have I taken refuge;*
how then can you say to me,
"Fly away like a bird to the hilltop;
2 for see how the wicked bend the bow
and fit their arrows to the string,*
to shoot from ambush
at the true of heart.
3 When the foundations
are being destroyed,*
what can the righteous do?"
4 The LORD is in his holy temple;*
the LORD's throne is in heaven.
5 His eyes behold the inhabited world;*
his piercing eye weighs our worth.
6 The LORD weighs the righteous
as well as the wicked,*
but those who delight in violence
he abhors.
7 Upon the wicked he shall rain coals of fire
and burning sulphur;*
a scorching wind shall be their lot.

8 For the LORD is righteous;
he delights in righteous deeds;*
and the just shall see his face.

12

1 Help me, LORD,
for there is no godly one left;*
the faithful have vanished
from among us.
2 Everyone speaks falsely
with his neighbor;*
with a smooth tongue
they speak from a double heart.
3 Oh, that the LORD would cut off
all smooth tongues,*
and close the lips
that utter proud boasts!
4 Those who say,
"With our tongue will we prevail;*
our lips are our own;
who is lord over us?"
5 "Because the needy are oppressed,
and the poor cry out in misery,*
I will rise up," says the LORD,
"and give them the help they long for."
6 The words of the LORD are pure words,*
like silver refined from ore
and purified seven times in the fire.
7 O LORD, watch over us*
and save us from this generation
forever.
8 The wicked prowl on every side,*
and that which is worthless
is highly prized by everyone.

15

1 LORD, who may dwell
in your tabernacle?*
Who may abide upon your holy hill?
2 Whoever leads a blameless life
and does what is right,*
who speaks the truth from his heart,
3 there is no guile upon his tongue;
he does no evil to his friend;*
he does not heap contempt
upon his neighbor.
4 In his sight the wicked is rejected,*
but he honors those
who fear the LORD.
5 He has sworn to do no wrong*
and does not take back his word.
6 He does not give his money
in hope of gain,*
nor does he take a bribe
against the innocent.
7 Whoever does these things*
shall never be overthrown.

16

1 Protect me, O God,
for I take refuge in you;*
I have said to the LORD,
"You are my Lord,
my good above all other."
2 All my delight is upon the godly
that are in the land,*
upon those who are noble
among the people.
3 But those who run after other gods*
shall have their troubles multiplied.
4 Their libations of blood I will not offer,*
nor take the names of their gods
upon my lips.
5 O LORD, you are my portion and my cup;*
it is you who uphold my lot.
6 My boundaries enclose a pleasant land;*
indeed, I have a goodly heritage.
7 I will bless the LORD
who gives me counsel;*
my heart teaches me night after night.
8 I have set the LORD always before me;*
because he is at my right hand,
I shall not fall.
9 My heart, therefore, is glad,
and my spirit rejoices;*
my body also shall rest in hope.
10 For you will not abandon me
to the grave,*
nor let your holy one see the pit.

11 You will show me the path of life;*
in your presence
there is fullness of joy,
and in your right hand
are pleasures forevermore.

17

1 Hear my plea of innocence, O LORD;
give heed to my cry;*
listen to my prayer,
which does not come from lying lips.
2 Let my vindication come forth
from your presence;*
let your eyes be fixed on justice.
3 Weigh my heart, summon me by night,*
melt me down;
you will find no impurity in me.
4 I give no offense with my mouth
as others do;*
I have heeded the words of your lips.
5 My footsteps hold fast
to the ways of your law;*
in your paths
my feet shall not stumble.
6 I call upon you, O God,
for you will answer me;*
incline your ear to me
and hear my words.
7 Show me your marvelous
lovingkindness,*
O Savior of those
who take refuge at your right hand
from those who rise up against them.
8 Keep me as the apple of your eye;*
hide me
under the shadow of your wings,
9 from the wicked who assault me,*
from my deadly enemies
who surround me.
10 They have closed their heart to pity,*
and their mouth speaks proud things.
11 They press me hard;
now they surround me,*
watching how they may
cast me to the ground,
12 like a lion, greedy for its prey,*
and like a young lion
lurking in secret places.
13 Arise, O LORD; confront them
and bring them down;*
deliver me from the wicked
by your sword.
14 Deliver me, O LORD, by your hand*
from those whose portion in life
is this world;
15 whose bellies you fill with your treasure,*
who are well supplied with children
and leave their wealth
to their little ones.
16 But at my vindication
I shall see your face;*
when I awake, I shall be satisfied,
beholding your likeness.

18

1 I love you, O LORD my strength,*
O LORD my stronghold,
my crag, and my haven.
2 My God, my rock
in whom I put my trust,*
my shield, the horn of my salvation,
and my refuge:
You are worthy of praise.
3 I will call upon the LORD,*
and so shall I be saved
from my enemies.
4 The breakers of death rolled over me,*
and the torrents of oblivion
made me afraid.
5 The cords of hell entangled me,*
and the snares of death
were set for me.
6 I called upon the LORD in my distress*
and cried out to my God for help.
7 He heard my voice
from his heavenly dwelling;*
my cry of anguish came to his ears.
8 The earth reeled and rocked;*
the roots of the mountains shook;
they reeled because of his anger.
9 Smoke rose from his nostrils
and a consuming fire out of his mouth;*

hot burning coals
blazed forth from him.

10 He parted the heavens and came down*
with a storm cloud under his feet.

11 He mounted on cherubim and flew;*
he swooped on the wings of the wind.

12 He wrapped darkness about him;*
he made dark waters
and thick clouds his pavilion.

13 From the brightness of his presence,
through the clouds,*
burst hailstones and coals of fire.

14 The LORD thundered out of heaven;*
the Most High uttered his voice.

15 He loosed his arrows
and scattered them;*
he hurled thunderbolts
and routed them.

16 The beds of the seas were uncovered,
and the foundations of the world
laid bare,*
at your battle cry, O LORD,
at the blast of the breath
of your nostrils.

17 He reached down from on high
and grasped me;*
he drew me out of great waters.

18 He delivered me
from my strong enemies
and from those who hated me,*
for they were too mighty for me.

19 They confronted me in the day
of my disaster;*
but the LORD was my support.

20 He brought me out into an open place;*
he rescued me
because he delighted in me.

21 The LORD rewarded me
because of my righteous dealing;*
because my hands were clean
he rewarded me;

22 for I have kept the ways of the LORD*
and have not offended against my God;

23 for all his judgments
are before my eyes,*
and his decrees
I have not put away from me;

24 for I have been blameless with him*
and have kept myself from iniquity;

25 therefore the LORD rewarded me
according to my righteous dealing,*
because of the cleanness of my hands
in his sight.

26 With the faithful
you show yourself faithful, O God;*
with the forthright
you show yourself forthright.

27 With the pure you show yourself pure,*
but with the crooked you are wily.

28 You will save a lowly people,*
but you will humble the haughty eyes.

29 You, O LORD, are my lamp;*
my God, you make my darkness bright.

30 With you
I will break down an enclosure;*
with the help of my God
I will scale any wall.

31 As for God, his ways are perfect;
the words of the LORD
are tried in the fire;*
he is a shield to all who trust in him.

32 For who is God, but the LORD?*
Who is the rock, except our God?

33 It is God
who girds me about with strength*
and makes my way secure.

34 He makes me sure-footed like a deer*
and lets me stand firm on the heights.

35 He trains my hands for battle*
and my arms for bending
even a bow of bronze.

36 You have given me your shield of victory;*
your right hand also sustains me;
your loving care makes me great.

37 You lengthen my stride beneath me,*
and my ankles do not give way.

38 I pursue my enemies and overtake them;*
I will not turn back
till I have destroyed them.

39 I strike them down, and they cannot rise;*
they fall defeated at my feet.

40 You have girded me
with strength for the battle;*

you have cast down my adversaries
beneath me;
you have put my enemies to flight.

41 I destroy those who hate me;
they cry out,
but there is none to help them;*
they cry to the LORD,
but he does not answer.

42 I beat them small
like dust before the wind;*
I trample them
like mud in the streets.

43 You deliver me
from the strife of the peoples;*
you put me
at the head of the nations.

44 A people I have not known
shall serve me;
no sooner shall they hear
than they shall obey me;*
strangers will cringe before me.

45 The foreign peoples will lose heart;*
they shall come trembling
out of their strongholds.

46 The LORD lives! Blessed is my rock!*
Exalted is the God of my salvation!

47 He is the God who gave me victory*
and cast down the peoples beneath me.

48 You rescued me
from the fury of my enemies;
you exalted me
above those who rose against me;*
you saved me from my deadly foe.

49 Therefore will I extol you
among the nations, O LORD,*
and sing praises to your name.

50 He multiplies the victories of his king;*
he shows lovingkindness
to his anointed,
to David and his descendants forever.

19

1 The heavens declare the glory of God,*
and the firmament
shows his handiwork.

2 One day tells its tale to another,*
and one night
imparts knowledge to another.

3 Although they have no words
or language,*
and their voices are not heard,

4 their sound has gone out into all lands,*
and their message
to the ends of the world.

5 In the deep
has he set a pavilion for the sun;*
it comes forth
like a bridegroom out of his chamber;
it rejoices like a champion
to run its course.

6 It goes forth
from the uttermost edge of the heavens
and runs about to the end of it again;*
nothing is hidden
from its burning heat.

7 The law of the LORD is perfect
and revives the soul;*
the testimony of the LORD is sure
and gives wisdom to the innocent.

8 The statutes of the LORD are just
and rejoice the heart;*
the commandment of the LORD is clear
and gives light to the eyes.

9 The fear of the LORD is clean
and endures forever;*
the judgments of the LORD are true
and righteous altogether.

10 More to be desired are they than gold,
more than much fine gold,*
sweeter far than honey,
than honey in the comb.

11 By them also
is your servant enlightened,*
and in keeping them there
is great reward.

12 Who can tell how often he offends?*
Cleanse me from my secret faults.

13 Above all, keep your servant
from presumptuous sins;
let them not get dominion over me;*
then shall I be whole and sound,
and innocent of a great offense.

14 Let the words of my mouth
and the meditation of my heart
be acceptable in your sight,*
O LORD, my strength
and my redeemer.

20

1 May the LORD answer you
in the day of trouble,*
the name of the God of Jacob
defend you;
2 send you help from his holy place*
and strengthen you out of Zion;
3 remember all your offerings*
and accept your burnt sacrifice;
4 grant you your heart's desire*
and prosper all your plans.
5 We will shout for joy at your victory
and triumph in the name of our God;*
may the LORD
grant all your requests.
6 Now I know that the LORD
gives victory to his anointed;*
he will answer him
out of his holy heaven,
with the victorious strength
of his right hand.
7 Some put their trust in chariots
and some in horses,*
but we will call upon the name
of the LORD our God.
8 They collapse and fall down,*
but we will arise and stand upright.
9 O LORD, give victory to the king*
and answer us when we call.

22

1 My God, my God,
why have you forsaken me*
and are so far from my cry,
and from the words of my distress?
2 O my God, I cry in the daytime,
but you do not answer;*
by night as well, but I find no rest.
3 Yet you are the Holy One,*
enthroned upon the praises of Israel.
4 Our forefathers put their trust in you;*
they trusted, and you delivered them.
5 They cried out to you
and were delivered;*
they trusted in you
and were not put to shame.
6 But as for me,
I am a worm and no man,*
scorned by all
and despised by the people.
7 All who see me laugh me to scorn;*
they curl their lips
and wag their heads, saying,
8 "He trusted in the LORD;
let him deliver him;*
let him rescue him,
if he delights in him."
9 Yet you are he
who took me out of the womb,*
and kept me safe
upon my mother's breast.
10 I have been entrusted to you
ever since I was born;*
you were my God
when I was still in my mother's womb.
11 Be not far from me, for trouble is near,*
and there is none to help.
12 Many young bulls encircle me;*
strong bulls of Bashan surround me.
13 They open wide their jaws at me,*
like a ravening and a roaring lion.
14 I am poured out like water;
all my bones are out of joint;*
my heart within my breast
is melting wax.
15 My mouth is dried out like a potsherd;
my tongue sticks
to the roof of my mouth;*
and you have laid me
in the dust of the grave.
16 Packs of dogs close me in,
and gangs of evildoers circle around me;*
they pierce my hands and my feet.
I can count all my bones.
17 They stare and gloat over me;*

they divide my garments among them;
they cast lots for my clothing.

18 Be not far away, O LORD;*
you are my strength; hasten to help me.

19 Save me from the sword,*
my life from the power of the dog.

20 Save me from the lion's mouth,*
my wretched body
from the horns of wild bulls.

21 I will declare your name to my brethren;*
in the midst of the congregation
I will praise you.

22 Praise the LORD, you that fear him;*
stand in awe of him,
O offspring of Israel;
all you of Jacob's line, give glory.

23 For he does not despise
nor abhor the poor in their poverty;
neither does he hide his face from them;*
but when they cry to him
he hears them.

24 My praise is of him
in the great assembly;*
I will perform my vows
in the presence of those
who worship him.

25 The poor shall eat and be satisfied,
and those who seek the LORD
shall praise him:*
"May your heart live forever!"

26 All the ends of the earth shall remember
and turn to the LORD,*
and all the families of the nations
shall bow before him.

27 For kingship belongs to the LORD;*
he rules over the nations.

28 To him alone all who sleep in the earth
bow down in worship;*
all who go down to the dust
fall before him.

29 My soul shall live for him;
my descendants shall serve him;*
they shall
be known as the LORD's forever.

30 They shall come and make known
to a people yet unborn*
the saving deeds that he has done.

23

1 The LORD is my shepherd;*
I shall not be in want.

2 He makes me lie down
in green pastures*
and leads me beside still waters.

3 He revives my soul*
and guides me along right pathways
for his name's sake.

4 Though I walk through the valley
of the shadow of death,
I shall fear no evil;*
for you are with me;
your rod and your staff,
they comfort me.

5 You spread a table before me
in the presence of those who trouble me;*
you have anointed my head with oil,
and my cup is running over.

6 Surely your goodness and mercy
shall follow me all the days of my life,*
and I will dwell
in the house of the LORD forever.

24

1 The earth is the LORD's
and all that is in it,*
the world and all who dwell therein.

2 For it is he
who founded it upon the seas*
and made it firm
upon the rivers of the deep.

3 "Who can ascend the hill of the LORD*
and who can stand
in his holy place?"

4 "Those who have clean hands
and a pure heart,*
who have not
pledged themselves to falsehood,
nor sworn by what is a fraud.

5 They shall receive a blessing
from the LORD*
and a just reward
from the God of their salvation."

6 Such is the generation
of those who seek him,*
of those who seek your face,
O God of Jacob.

7 Lift up your heads, O gates;
lift them high, O everlasting doors;*
and the King of glory shall come in.

8 "Who is this King of glory?"*
"The LORD, strong and mighty,
the LORD, mighty in battle."

9 Lift up your heads, O gates;
lift them high, O everlasting doors;*
and the King of glory shall come in.

10 "Who is he, this King of glory?"*
"The LORD of hosts,
he is the King of glory."

25

1 To you, O LORD, I lift up my soul;
my God, I put my trust in you;*
let me not be humiliated,
nor let my enemies triumph over me.

2 Let none who look to you
be put to shame;*
let the treacherous be disappointed
in their schemes.

3 Show me your ways, O LORD,*
and teach me your paths.

4 Lead me in your truth and teach me,*
for you are the God of my salvation;
in you have I trusted all the day long.

5 Remember, O LORD,
your compassion and love,*
for they are from everlasting.

6 Remember not the sins of my youth
and my transgressions;*
remember me according to your love
and for the sake of your goodness,
O LORD.

7 Gracious and upright is the LORD;*
therefore he teaches sinners in his way.

8 He guides the humble in doing right*
and teaches his way to the lowly.

9 All the paths of the LORD
are love and faithfulness*
to those who keep his covenant
and his testimonies.

10 For your name's sake, O LORD,*
forgive my sin, for it is great.

11 Who are they who fear the LORD?*
He will teach them the way
that they should choose.

12 They shall dwell in prosperity,*
and their offspring
shall inherit the land.

13 The LORD is a friend
to those who fear him,*
and will show them his covenant.

14 My eyes are ever looking to the LORD,*
for he shall pluck my feet
out of the net.

15 Turn to me and have pity on me,*
for I am left alone and in misery.

16 The sorrows of my heart
have increased;*
bring me out of my troubles.

17 Look upon my adversity and misery*
and forgive me all my sin.

18 Look upon my enemies,
for they are many,*
and they
bear a violent hatred against me.

19 Protect my life and deliver me;*
let me not be put to shame,
for I have trusted in you.

20 Let integrity and uprightness
preserve me,*
for my hope has been in you.

21 Deliver Israel, O God,*
out of all his troubles.

26

1 Give judgment for me, O LORD,
for I have lived with integrity;*
I have trusted in the Lord
and have not faltered.

2 Test me, O LORD, and try me;*
examine my heart and my mind.

3 For your love is before my eyes;*
I have walked faithfully with you.

[4]I have not sat with the worthless,*
nor do I consort with the deceitful.

[5]I have hated the company of evildoers;*
I will not sit down with the wicked.

[6]I will wash my hands in innocence,
O LORD,*
that I may go in procession
round your altar,

[7]singing aloud a song of thanksgiving*
and recounting
all your wonderful deeds.

[8]LORD, I love the house
in which you dwell*
and the place
where your glory abides.

[9]Do not sweep me away with sinners,*
nor my life with those
who thirst for blood,

[10]whose hands are full of evil plots,*
and their right hand full of bribes.

[11]As for me, I will live with integrity;*
redeem me, O LORD,
and have pity on me.

[12]My foot stands on level ground;*
in the full assembly
I will bless the LORD.

27

[1]The LORD is my light and my salvation;
whom then shall I fear?*
The LORD is the strength of my life;
of whom then shall I be afraid?

[2]When evildoers came upon me
to eat up my flesh,*
it was they, my foes and
my adversaries, who stumbled and fell.

[3]Though an army
should encamp against me,*
yet my heart shall not be afraid;

[4]and though war
should rise up against me,*
yet will I put my trust in him.

[5]One thing have I asked of the LORD;
one thing I seek;*
that I may dwell
in the house of the LORD
all the days of my life;

[6]to behold the fair beauty of the LORD*
and to seek him in his temple.

[7]For in the day of trouble
he shall keep me safe in his shelter;*
he shall hide me
in the secrecy of his dwelling
and set me high upon a rock.

[8]Even now he lifts up my head*
above my enemies round about me.

[9]Therefore I will offer in his dwelling
an oblation
with sounds of great gladness;*
I will sing
and make music to the LORD.

[10]Hearken to my voice, O LORD,
when I call;*
have mercy on me and answer me.

[11]You speak in my heart and say,
"Seek my face."*
Your face, LORD, will I seek.

[12]Hide not your face from me,*
nor turn away your servant
in displeasure.

[13]You have been my helper;
cast me not away;*
do not forsake me,
O God of my salvation.

[14]Though my father and my mother
forsake me,*
the LORD will sustain me.

[15]Show me your way, O LORD;*
lead me on a level path,
because of my enemies.

[16]Deliver me not
into the hand of my adversaries,*
for false witnesses
have risen up against me,
and also those who speak malice.

[17]What if I had not believed that I
should see the goodness of the LORD*
in the land of the living!

[18]Oh, tarry and await the LORD's pleasure;
be strong,
and he shall comfort your heart;*
wait patiently for the LORD.

28

1 O LORD, I call to you;
my rock, do not be deaf to my cry;*
lest, if you do not hear me,
I become like those
who go down to the pit.
2 Hear the voice of my prayer
when I cry out to you,*
when I lift up my hands
to your holy of holies.
3 Do not snatch me away
with the wicked or with the evildoers,*
who speak peaceably
with their neighbors,
while strife is in their hearts.
4 Repay them according to their deeds,*
and according to the wickedness
of their actions.
5 According to the work of their hands
repay them,*
and give them their just deserts.
6 They have no understanding
of the LORD's doings,
nor of the works of his hands;*
therefore he will break them down
and not build them up.
7 Blessed is the LORD!*
For he has heard
the voice of my prayer.
8 The LORD is my strength and my shield;*
my heart trusts in him,
and I have been helped;
9 therefore my heart dances for joy,*
and in my song will I praise him.
10 The LORD is the strength of his people,*
a safe refuge for his anointed.
11 Save your people
and bless your inheritance;*
shepherd them
and carry them forever.

29

1 Ascribe to the LORD, you gods,*
ascribe to the LORD
glory and strength.
2 Ascribe to the LORD
the glory due his name;*
worship the LORD
in the beauty of holiness.
3 The voice of the LORD
is upon the waters;
the God of glory thunders;*
the LORD is upon the mighty waters.
4 The voice of the LORD
is a powerful voice;*
the voice of the LORD
is a voice of splendor.
5 The voice of the LORD
breaks the cedar trees;*
the LORD
breaks the cedars of Lebanon;
6 he makes Lebanon skip like a calf,*
and Mount Hermon
like a young wild ox.
7 The voice of the LORD
splits the flames of fire;
the voice of the LORD
shakes the wilderness;*
the LORD
shakes the wilderness of Kadesh.
8 The voice of the LORD
makes the oak trees writhe*
and strips the forests bare.
9 And in the temple of the LORD*
all are crying, "Glory!"
10 The LORD sits enthroned
above the flood;*
the LORD sits enthroned
as king forevermore.
11 The LORD shall give strength
to his people;*
the LORD shall give his people
the blessing of peace.

30

1 I will exalt you, O LORD,
because you have lifted me up*
and have not let my enemies
triumph over me.
2 O LORD my God, I cried out to you,*
and you restored me to health.

3 You brought me up, O LORD,
from the dead;*
you restored my life
as I was going down to the grave.
4 Sing to the LORD, you servants of his;*
give thanks for the remembrance
of his holiness.
5 For his wrath endures
but the twinkling of an eye,*
his favor for a lifetime.
6 Weeping may spend the night,*
but joy comes in the morning.
7 While I felt secure, I said,
"I shall never be disturbed.*
You, LORD, with your favor,
made me as strong as the mountains."
8 Then you hid your face,*
and I was filled with fear.
9 I cried to you, O LORD;*
I pleaded with the Lord, saying,
10 "What profit is there in my blood,
if I go down to the pit?*
Will the dust praise you
or declare your faithfulness?
11 Hear, O LORD,
and have mercy upon me;*
O LORD, be my helper."
12 You have turned my wailing
into dancing;*
you have put off my sackcloth
and clothed me with joy.
13 Therefore my heart sings to you
without ceasing;*
O LORD my God,
I will give you thanks forever.

31

1 In you, O LORD, have I taken refuge;
let me never be put to shame;*
deliver me in your righteousness.
2 Incline your ear to me;*
make haste to deliver me.
3 Be my strong rock,
a castle to keep me safe,
for you are my crag and my stronghold;*
for the sake of your name,
lead me and guide me.
4 Take me out of the net
that they have secretly set for me,*
for you are my tower of strength.
5 Into your hands I commend my spirit,*
for you have redeemed me,
O LORD, O God of truth.
6 I hate those who cling to worthless idols,*
and I put my trust in the LORD.
7 I will rejoice and be glad
because of your mercy;*
for you have seen my affliction;
you know my distress.
8 You have not shut me up
in the power of the enemy;*
you have set my feet
in an open place.
9 Have mercy on me, O LORD,
for I am in trouble;*
my eye is consumed with sorrow,
and also my throat and my belly.
10 For my life is wasted with grief,
and my years with sighing;*
my strength fails me
because of affliction,
and my bones are consumed.
11 I have become a reproach
to all my enemies and
even to my neighbors,
a dismay to those of my acquaintance;*
when they see me in the street
they avoid me.
12 I am forgotten like a dead man,
out of mind;*
I am as useless as a broken pot.
13 For I have heard the whispering
of the crowd; fear is all around;*
they put their heads together
against me;
they plot to take my life.
14 But as for me,
I have trusted in you, O LORD.*
I have said, "You are my God.
15 My times are in your hand;*
rescue me
from the hand of my enemies,
and from those who persecute me.

16 Make your face
to shine upón your servant,*
and in your lovingkindness save me."

17 LORD, let me not be ashamed
for having called úpon you;*
rather, let the wicked
be put to shame;
let them be silent in the grave.

18 Let the lying lips be silenced
which speak against the righteous,*
haughtily, disdainfully,
and with contempt.

19 How great is your goodness, O LORD,
which you have laid up
for those who fear you;*
which you have done
in the sight of all
for those who put their trust in you.

20 You hide them
in the covert of your presence
from those who slander them;*
you keep them in your shelter
from the strife of tongues.

21 Blessed be the LORD!*
for he has shown me the wonders
of his love in a besieged city.

22 Yet I said in my alarm,
"I have been cut off
from the sight of your eyes."*
Nevertheless, you heard the sound
of my entreaty when I cried out to you.

23 Love the LORD,
all you who worship him;*
the LORD protects the faithful,
but repays to the full
those who act haughtily.

24 Be strong and
let your heart take courage,*
all you who wait for the LORD.

32

1 Happy are they
whose transgressions are forgiven,*
and whose sin is put away!

2 Happy are they
to whom the LORD imputes no guilt,*
and in whose spirit there is no guile!

3 While I held my tongue,
my bones withered away,*
because of my groaning all day long.

4 For your hand was heavy upon me
day and night;*
my moisture was dried up
as in the heat of summer.

5 Then I acknowledged my sin to you,*
and did not conceal my guilt.

6 I said, "I will confess my transgressions
to the LORD."*
Then you forgave me
the guilt of my sin.

7 Therefore all the faithful
will make their prayers to you
in time of trouble;*
when the great waters overflow,
they shall not reach them.

8 You are my hiding-place;
you preserve me from trouble;*
you surround me
with shouts of deliverance.

9 "I will instruct you and teach you
in the way that you should go;*
I will guide you with my eye.

10 Do not be like horse or mule,
which have no understanding;*
who must be fitted with bit and bridle,
or else they will not stay near you."

11 Great are the tribulations of the wicked;*
but mercy embraces those
who trust in the LORD.

12 Be glad, you righteous,
and rejoice in the LORD;*
shout for joy,
all who are true of heart.

33

1 Rejoice in the LORD, you righteous;*
it is good for the just to sing praises.

2 Praise the LORD with the harp;*
play to him
upon the psaltery and lyre.

3 Sing for him a new song;*
sound a fanfare with all your skill
upon the trumpet.

4 For the word of the LORD is right,*
and all his works are sure.

5 He loves righteousness and justice;*
the lovingkindness of the LORD
fills the whole earth.

6 By the word of the LORD
were the heavens made,*
by the breath of his mouth
all the heavenly hosts.

7 He gathers up the waters of the ocean
as in a water-skin*
and stores up the depths of the sea.

8 Let all the earth fear the LORD;*
let all who dwell in the world
stand in awe of him.

9 For he spoke, and it came to pass;*
he commanded, and it stood fast.

10 The LORD brings the will
of the nations to naught;*
he thwarts the designs of the peoples.

11 But the LORD's will stands fast forever,*
and the designs of his heart
from age to age.

12 Happy is the nation
whose God is the LORD!*
Happy the people he has chosen
to be his own!

13 The LORD looks down from heaven,*
and beholds all the people
in the world.

14 From where he sits enthroned
he turns his gaze*
on all who dwell on the earth.

15 He fashions all the hearts of them*
and understands all their works.

16 There is no king that can be saved
by a mighty army;*
a strong man is not delivered
by his great strength.

17 The horse is a vain hope for deliverance;*
for all its strength it cannot save.

18 Behold, the eye of the LORD
is upon those who fear him,*
on those who wait upon his love,

19 to pluck their lives from death,*
and to feed them in time of famine.

20 Our soul waits for the LORD;*
he is our help and our shield.

21 Indeed, our heart rejoices in him,*
for in his holy name we put our trust.

22 Let your lovingkindness, O LORD,
be upon us,*
as we have put our trust in you.

34

1 I will bless the LORD at all times;*
his praise shall ever be in my mouth.

2 I will glory in the LORD;*
let the humble hear and rejoice.

3 Proclaim with me
the greatness of the LORD;*
let us exalt his name together.

4 I sought the LORD, and he answered me*
and delivered me out of all my terror.

5 Look upon him and be radiant,*
and let not your faces be ashamed.

6 I called in my affliction,
and the LORD heard me*
and saved me from all my troubles.

7 The angel of the LORD
encompasses those who fear him,*
and he will deliver them.

8 Taste and see that the LORD is good;*
happy are they who trust in him!

9 Fear the LORD, you that are his saints,*
for those who fear him lack nothing.

10 The young lions lack and suffer hunger,*
but those who seek the LORD
lack nothing that is good.

11 Come, children, and listen to me;*
I will teach you the fear of the LORD.

12 Who among you loves life*
and desires long life
to enjoy prosperity?

13 Keep your tongue from evil-speaking*
and your lips from lying words.

14 Turn from evil and do good;*
seek peace and pursue it.

15 The eyes of the LORD
are upon the righteous,*
and his ears are open to their cry.

16 The face of the LORD
is against those who do evil,*

to root out the remembrance of them
from the earth.

17 The righteous cry,
and the LORD hears them*
and delivers them
from all their troubles.

18 The LORD is near to the brokenhearted*
and will save those
whose spirits are crushed.

19 Many are the troubles of the righteous,*
but the LORD will deliver him
out of them all.

20 He will keep safe all his bones;*
not one of them shall be broken.

21 Evil shall slay the wicked,*
and those who hate the righteous
will be punished.

22 The LORD ransoms
the life of his servants,*
and none will be punished
who trust in him.

36

1 There is a voice of rebellion
deep in the heart of the wicked;*
there is no fear of God before his eyes.

2 He flatters himself in his own eyes*
that his hateful sin
will not be found out.

3 The words of his mouth
are wicked and deceitful;*
he has left off acting wisely
and doing good.

4 He thinks up wickedness upon his bed
and has set himself in no good way;*
he does not abhor that which is evil.

5 Your love, O LORD,
reaches to the heavens,*
and your faithfulness to the clouds.

6 Your righteousness is like
the strong mountains,
your justice like the great deep;*
you save both man and beast, O LORD.

7 How priceless is your love, O God!*
Your people take refuge
under the shadow of your wings.

8 They feast upon the abundance
of your house;*
you give them drink
from the river of your delights.

9 For with you is the well of life,*
and in your light we see light.

10 Continue your lovingkindness to those
who know you,*
and your favor to those
who are true of heart.

11 Let not the foot of the proud
come near me,*
nor the hand of the wicked
push me aside.

12 See how they are fallen,
those who work wickedness!*
They are cast down
and shall not be able to rise.

40

1 I waited patiently upon the LORD;*
he stooped to me and heard my cry.

2 He lifted me out of the desolate pit,
out of the mire and clay;*
he set my feet upon a high cliff
and made my footing sure.

3 He put a new song in my mouth,
a song of praise to our God;*
many shall see, and stand in awe,
and put their trust in the LORD.

4 Happy are they who trust in the LORD!*
They do not resort to evil spirits
or turn to false gods.

5 Great things are they that you have done,
O LORD my God!
How great your wonders
and your plans for us!*
There is none
who can be compared with you.

6 Oh, that I could make them known
and tell them!*
But they are more than I can count.

7 In sacrifice and offering
you take no pleasure;*
you have given me ears to hear you;

[8]burnt-offering and sin-offering
you have not required,*
and so I said, "Behold, I come.

[9]In the roll of the book
it is written concerning me:*
'I love to do your will, O my God;
your law is deep in my heart.'"

[10]I proclaimed righteousness
in the great congregation;*
behold, I did not restrain my lips;
and that, O LORD, you know.

[11]Your righteousness
have I not hidden in my heart;
I have spoken of your faithfulness
and your deliverance;*
I have not concealed
your love and faithfulness from the
great congregation.

[12]You are the LORD;
do not withhold your compassion
from me;*
let your love and your faithfulness
keep me safe forever.

[13]For innumerable troubles
have crowded upon me;
my sins have overtaken me,
and I cannot see;*
they are more in number
than the hairs of my head,
and my heart fails me.

[14]Be pleased, O LORD, to deliver me;*
O LORD, make haste to help me.

[15]Let them be ashamed
and altogether dismayed
who seek after my life to destroy it;*
let them draw back and be disgraced
who take pleasure in my misfortune.

[16]Let those who say "Aha!"
and gloat over me be confounded,*
because they are ashamed.

[17]Let all who seek you
rejoice in you and be glad;*
let those who love your salvation
continually say, "Great is the LORD!"

[18]Though I am poor and afflicted,*
the Lord will have regard for me.

[19]You are my helper and my deliverer;*
do not tarry, O my God.

41

[1]Happy are they
who consider the poor and needy!*
The LORD will deliver them
in the time of trouble.

[2]The LORD preserves them
and keeps them alive,
so that they may be happy in the land;*
he does not hand them over
to the will of their enemies.

[3]The LORD sustains them
on their sickbed*
and ministers to them in their illness.

[4]I said, "LORD, be merciful to me;*
heal me,
for I have sinned against you."

[5]My enemies are saying
wicked things about me:*
"When will he die,
and his name perish?"

[6]Even if they come to see me,
they speak empty words;*
their heart collects false rumors;
they go outside and spread them.

[7]All my enemies
whisper together about me*
and devise evil against me.

[8]"A deadly thing," they say,
"has fastened on him;*
he has taken to his bed
and will never get up again."

[9]Even my best friend, whom I trusted,
who broke bread with me,*
has lifted up his heel
and turned against me.

[10]But you, O LORD,
be merciful to me and raise me up,*
and I shall repay them.

[11]By this I know you are pleased with me:*
that my enemy
does not triumph over me.

[12]In my integrity you hold me fast,*
and shall set me
before your face forever.

[13]Blessed be the LORD God of Israel,*
from age to age. Amen. Amen.

42

1 As the deer longs for the water-brooks,*
so longs my soul for you, O God.

2 My soul is athirst for God,
athirst for the living God;*
when shall I come to appear
before the presence of God?

3 My tears have been my food
day and night,*
while all day long they say to me,
"Where now is your God?"

4 I pour out my soul
when I think on these things:*
how I went with the multitude
and led them into the house of God,

5 with the voice of praise
and thanksgiving,*
among those who keep holy-day.

6 Why are you so full of heaviness,
O my soul?*
And why are you so disquieted
within me?

7 Put your trust in God;*
for I will yet give thanks to him,
who is the help of my countenance
and my God.

8 My soul is heavy within me;*
therefore I will remember you
from the land of Jordan,
and from the peak of Mizar
among the heights of Hermon.

9 One deep calls to another
in the noise of your cataracts;*
all your rapids and floods
have gone over me.

10 The LORD grants his lovingkindness
in the daytime;*
in the night season
his song is with me,
a prayer to the God of my life.

11 I will say to the God of my strength,
"Why have you forgotten me,*
and why do I go so heavily
while the enemy oppresses me?"

12 While my bones are being broken,*
my enemies mock me to my face;

13 all day long they mock me*
and say to me,
"Where now is your God?"

14 Why are you so full of heaviness,
O my soul?*
And why are you so disquieted
within me?

15 Put your trust in God;*
for I will yet give thanks to him,
who is the help of my countenance
and my God.

43

1 Give judgment for me, O God,
and defend my cause
against an ungodly people;*
deliver me
from the deceitful and the wicked.

2 For you are the God of my strength;
why have you put me from you,*
and why do I go so heavily
while the enemy oppresses me?

3 Send out your light and your truth,
that they may lead me,*
and bring me to your holy hill
and to your dwelling;

4 that I may go to the altar of God,
to the God of my joy and gladness;*
and on the harp I will give thanks
to you, O God my God.

5 Why are you so full of heaviness,
O my soul?*
And why are you so disquieted
within me?

6 Put your trust in God;*
for I will yet give thanks to him,
who is the help of my countenance
and my God.

44

1 We have heard with our ears, O God,
our forefathers have told us,*
the deeds you did in their days,
in the days of old.

2 How with your hand
you drove the peoples out
and planted our forefathers in the land, *
how you destroyed nations
and made your people flourish.

3 For they did not take the land
by their sword,
nor did their arm win the victory
for them, *
but your right hand, your arm,
and the light of your countenance,
because you favored them.

4 You are my King and my God; *
you command victories for Jacob.

5 Through you
we pushed back our adversaries; *
through your name
we trampled on those who
rose up against us.

6 For I do not rely on my bow, *
and my sword does not give me
the victory.

7 Surely, you gave us victory
over our adversaries *
and put those who hate us to shame.

8 Every day we gloried in God, *
and we will praise your name
forever.

9 Nevertheless, you have rejected
and humbled us *
and do not go forth with our armies.

10 You have made us fall back
before our adversary, *
and our enemies have plundered us.

11 You have made us like sheep to be eaten *
and have scattered us
among the nations.

12 You are selling your people for a trifle *
and are making no profit
on the sale of them.

13 You have made us the scorn
of our neighbors, *
a mockery and derision
to those around us.

14 You have made us a byword
among the nations, *
a laughingstock among the peoples.

15 My humiliation is daily before me, *
and shame has covered my face;

16 because of the taunts
of the mockers and blasphemers, *
because of the enemy and avenger.

17 All this has come upon us; *
yet we have not forgotten you,
nor have we betrayed your covenant.

18 Our heart never turned back, *
nor did our footsteps stray
from your path;

19 though you thrust us down
into a place of misery, *
and covered us over
with deep darkness.

20 If we have forgotten the name
of our God, *
or stretched out our hands
to some strange god,

21 will not God find it out? *
For he knows the secrets of the heart.

22 Indeed, for your sake
we are killed all the day long; *
we are accounted as sheep
for the slaughter.

23 Awake, O Lord! Why are you sleeping? *
Arise! Do not reject us forever.

24 Why have you hidden your face *
and forgotten our affliction
and oppression?

25 We sink down into the dust; *
our body cleaves to the ground.

26 Rise up, and help us, *
and save us,
for the sake of your steadfast love.

45

1 My heart is stirring with a noble song;
let me recite
what I have fashioned for the king; *
my tongue shall be the pen
of a skilled writer.

2 You are the fairest of men; *
grace flows from your lips,
because God has blessed you forever.

3 Strap your sword upon your thigh,
O mighty warrior,*
in your pride and in your majesty.

4 Ride out and conquer
in the cause of truth*
and for the sake of justice.

5 Your right hand will show you
marvelous things;*
your arrows are very sharp,
O mighty warrior.

6 The peoples are falling at your feet,*
and the king's enemies
are losing heart.

7 Your throne, O God,
endures forever and ever,*
a scepter of righteousness
is the scepter of your kingdom;
you love righteousness
and hate iniquity.

8 Therefore God, your God,
has anointed you*
with the oil of gladness
above your fellows.

9 All your garments are fragrant
with myrrh, aloes, and cassia,*
and the music of strings
from ivory palaces makes you glad.

10 Kings' daughters stand
among the ladies of the court;*
on your right hand is the queen,
adorned with the gold of Ophir.

11 "Hear, O daughter;
consider and listen closely;*
forget your people
and your father's house.

12 The king will have pleasure
in your beauty;*
he is your master;
therefore do him honor.

13 The people of Tyre are here with a gift;*
the rich among the people
seek your favor."

14 All glorious is the princess as she enters;*
her gown is cloth-of-gold.

15 In embroidered apparel
she is brought to the king;*
after her the bridesmaids follow
in procession.

16 With joy and gladness they are brought,*
and enter into the palace of the king.

17 "In place of fathers, O king,
you shall have sons;*
you shall make them princes
over all the earth.

18 I will make your name
to be remembered
from one generation to another;*
therefore nations will praise you
forever and ever."

46

1 God is our refuge and strength,*
a very present help in trouble.

2 Therefore we will not fear,
though the earth be moved,*
and though the mountains
be toppled into the depths of the sea;

3 though its waters rage and foam,*
and though the mountains
tremble at its tumult.

4 The LORD of hosts is with us;*
the God of Jacob is our stronghold.

5 There is a river whose streams
make glad the city of God,*
the holy habitation of the Most High.

6 God is in the midst of her;
she shall not be overthrown;*
God shall help her at the break of day.

7 The nations make much ado,
and the kingdoms are shaken;*
God has spoken,
and the earth shall melt away.

8 The LORD of hosts is with us;*
the God of Jacob is our stronghold.

9 Come now and
look upon the works of the LORD,*
what awesome things
he has done on earth.

10 It is he who makes war to cease
in all the world;*
he breaks the bow,
and shatters the spear,
and burns the shields with fire.

11 “Be still, then, and know that I am God; *
I will be exalted among the nations;
I will be exalted in the earth.”
12 The LORD of hosts is with us; *
the God of Jacob is our stronghold.

47

1 Clap your hands, all you peoples; *
shout to God with a cry of joy.
2 For the LORD Most High is to be feared; *
he is the great king over all the earth.
3 He subdues the peoples under us, *
and the nations under our feet.
4 He chooses our inheritance for us, *
the pride of Jacob whom he loves.
5 God has gone up with a shout, *
the LORD
with the sound of the ram’s horn.
6 Sing praises to God, sing praises; *
sing praises to our king, sing praises.
7 For God is king of all the earth; *
sing praises with all your skill.
8 God reigns over the nations; *
God sits upon his holy throne.
9 The nobles of the peoples
have gathered together *
with the people
of the God of Abraham.
10 The rulers of the earth belong to God, *
and he is highly exalted.

48

1 Great is the LORD,
and highly to be praised; *
in the city of our God is his holy hill.
2 Beautiful and lofty,
the joy of all the earth,
is the hill of Zion, *
the very center of the world
and the city of the great king.
3 God is in her citadels; *
he is known to be her sure refuge.
4 Behold, the kings of the earth
assembled *
and marched forward together.
5 They looked and were astounded; *
they retreated and fled in terror.
6 Trembling seized them there; *
they writhed
like a woman in childbirth,
like ships of the sea
when the east wind shatters them.
7 As we have heard, so have we seen,
in the city of the LORD of hosts,
in the city of our God; *
God has established her forever.
8 We have waited in silence
on your lovingkindness, O God, *
in the midst of your temple.
9 Your praise, like your name, O God,
reaches to the world’s end; *
your right hand is full of justice.
10 Let Mount Zion be glad
and the cities of Judah rejoice, *
because of your judgments.
11 Make the circuit of Zion;
walk round about her; *
count the number of her towers.
12 Consider well her bulwarks;
examine her strongholds; *
that you may tell those
who come after.
13 This God is our God forever and ever; *
he shall be our guide forevermore.

49

1 Hear this, all you peoples;
hearken, all you who dwell in the world, *
you of high degree and low,
rich and poor together.
2 My mouth shall speak of wisdom, *
and my heart
shall meditate on understanding.
3 I will incline my ear to a proverb *
and set forth my riddle upon the harp.
4 Why should I be afraid in evil days, *
when the wickedness
of those at my heels surrounds me,
5 the wickedness of those
who put their trust in their goods, *

and boast of their great riches?

6 We can never ransom ourselves,*
or deliver to God the price of our life;

7 for the ransom of our life is so great,*
that we should never
have enough to pay it,

8 in order to live forever and ever,*
and never see the grave.

9 For we see that the wise die also;
like the dull and stupid they perish*
and leave their wealth to those
who come after them.

10 Their graves shall be their homes
forever, their dwelling-places
from generation to generation,*
though they call the lands
after their own names.

11 Even though honored,
they cannot live forever;*
they are like the beasts that perish.

12 Such is the way of those
who foolishly trust in themselves,*
and the end of those
who delight in their own words.

13 Like a flock of sheep
they are destined to die;
death is their shepherd;*
they go down
straightway to the grave.

14 Their form shall waste away,*
and the land of the dead
shall be their home.

15 But God will ransom my life;*
he will snatch me
from the grasp of death.

16 Do not be envious
when some become rich,*
or when the grandeur of their house
increases;

17 for they will carry nothing away
at their death,*
nor will their grandeur follow them.

18 Though they thought highly
of themselves while they lived,*
and were praised for their success,

19 they shall join the company
of their forebears,*
who will never see the light again.

20 Those who are honored,
but have no understanding,*
are like the beasts that perish.

50

1 The LORD, the God of gods,
has spoken;*
he has called the earth
from the rising of the sun to its setting.

2 Out of Zion, perfect in its beauty,*
God reveals himself in glory.

3 Our God will come
and will not keep silence;*
before him there is a consuming flame,
and round about him a raging storm.

4 He calls the heavens
and the earth from above*
to witness the judgment of his people.

5 "Gather before me my loyal followers,*
those who have made a covenant
with me and sealed it with sacrifice."

6 Let the heavens declare
the rightness of his cause;*
for God himself is judge.

7 Hear, O my people, and I will speak:
"O Israel, I will bear
witness against you;*
for I am God, your God.

8 I do not accuse you
because of your sacrifices;*
your offerings are always before me.

9 I will take no bull-calf from your stalls,*
nor he-goats out of your pens;

10 for all the beasts of the forest are mine,*
the herds in their thousands
upon the hills.

11 I know every bird in the sky,*
and the creatures of the fields
are in my sight.

12 If I were hungry, I would not tell you,*
for the whole world is mine
and all that is in it.

13 Do you think I eat the flesh of bulls,*
or drink the blood of goats?

14 Offer to God
a sacrifice of thanksgiving*
and make good your vows
to the Most High.

15 Call upon me in the day of trouble;*
I will deliver you,
and you shall honor me."

16 But to the wicked God says:*
"Why do you recite my statutes,
and take my covenant
upon your lips;

17 since you refuse discipline,*
and toss my words
behind your back?

18 When you see a thief,
you make him your friend,*
and you cast in your lot
with adulterers.

19 You have loosed your lips for evil,*
and harnessed your tongue to a lie.

20 You are always speaking evil
of your brother*
and slandering
your own mother's son.

21 These things you have done,
and I kept still,*
and you thought that I am like you.

22 I have made my accusation;*
I have put my case in order
before your eyes.

23 Consider this well,
you who forget God,*
lest I rend you
and there be none to deliver you.

24 Whoever offers me the
sacrifice of thanksgiving honors me;*
but to those who keep in my way
will I show the salvation of God."

51

1 Have mercy on me, O God,
according to your lovingkindness;*
in your great compassion
blot out my offenses.

2 Wash me through and through
from my wickedness,*
and cleanse me from my sin.

3 For I know my transgressions,*
and my sin is ever before me.

4 Against you only have I sinned*
and done what is evil in your sight.

5 And so you are justified
when you speak*
and upright in your judgment.

6 Indeed, I have been wicked
from my birth,*
a sinner from my mother's womb.

7 For behold, you look for truth
deep within me,*
and will make me
understand wisdom secretly.

8 Purge me from my sin,
and I shall be pure;*
wash me, and I shall be clean indeed.

9 Make me hear of joy and gladness,*
that the body you have broken
may rejoice.

10 Hide your face from my sins,*
and blot out all my iniquities.

11 Create in me a clean heart, O God,*
and renew a right spirit within me.

12 Cast me not away from your presence,*
and take not your Holy Spirit
from me.

13 Give me the joy
of your saving help again,*
and sustain me
with your bountiful Spirit.

14 I shall teach your ways to the wicked,*
and sinners shall return to you.

15 Deliver me from death, O God,*
and my tongue shall sing
of your righteousness,
O God of my salvation.

16 Open my lips, O Lord,*
and my mouth
shall proclaim your praise.

17 Had you desired it,
I would have offered sacrifice,*
but you take no delight
in burnt-offerings.

18 The sacrifice of God
is a troubled spirit;*

a broken and contrite heart, O God,
you will not despise.
19 Be favorable and gracious to Zion,*
and rebuild the walls of Jerusalem.
20 Then you will be pleased
with the appointed sacrifices,
with burnt-offerings and oblations;*
then shall they offer young bullocks
upon your altar.

53

1 The fool has said in his heart,
"There is no God."*
All are corrupt
and commit abominable acts;
there is none who does any good.
2 God looks down from heaven
upon us all,*
to see if there is any who is wise,
if there is one who seeks after God.
3 Every one has proved faithless;
all alike have turned bad;*
there is none who does good;
no, not one.
4 Have they no knowledge,
those evildoers*
who eat up my people like bread
and do not call upon God?
5 See how greatly they tremble,
such trembling as never was;*
for God has scattered the bones
of the enemy;
they are put to shame,
because God has rejected them.
6 Oh, that Israel's deliverance
would come out of Zion!*
When God restores the fortunes
of his people,
Jacob will rejoice and Israel be glad.

54

1 Save me, O God, by your name;*
in your might, defend my cause.
2 Hear my prayer, O God;*
give ear to the words of my mouth.
3 For the arrogant
have risen up against me,
and the ruthless have sought my life,*
those who have no regard for God.
4 Behold, God is my helper;*
it is the Lord who sustains my life.
5 Render evil to those who spy on me;*
in your faithfulness, destroy them.
6 I will offer you a freewill sacrifice*
and praise your name, O LORD,
for it is good.
7 For you have rescued me
from every trouble,*
and my eye
has seen the ruin of my foes.

56

1 Have mercy on me, O God,
for my enemies are hounding me;*
all day long
they assault and oppress me.
2 They hound me all the day long;*
truly there are many
who fight against me, O Most High.
3 Whenever I am afraid,*
I will put my trust in you.
4 In God, whose word I praise,
in God I trust and will not be afraid,*
for what can flesh do to me?
5 All day long they damage my cause;*
their only thought is to do me evil.
6 They band together; they lie in wait;*
they spy upon my footsteps;
because they seek my life.
7 Shall they escape
despite their wickedness?*
O God, in your anger,
cast down the peoples.
8 You have noted my lamentation;
put my tears into your bottle;*
are they not recorded in your book?
9 Whenever I call upon you,
my enemies will be put to flight;*
this I know, for God is on my side.
10 In God the LORD, whose word I praise,
in God I trust and will not be afraid,*

for what can mortals do to me?
11 I am bound by the vow
I made to you, O God;*
I will present to you thank-offerings;
12 for you have rescued
my soul from death
and my feet from stumbling,*
that I may walk before God
in the light of the living.

57

1 Be merciful to me, O God, be merciful,
for I have taken refuge in you;*
in the shadow of your wings
will I take refuge
until this time of trouble has gone by.
2 I will call upon the Most High God,*
the God who maintains my cause.
3 He will send from heaven and save me;
he will confound those
who trample upon me;*
God will send forth his love
and his faithfulness.
4 I lie in the midst of lions
that devour the people;*
their teeth are spears and arrows,
their tongue a sharp sword.
5 They have laid a net for my feet,
and I am bowed low;*
they have dug a pit before me,
but have fallen into it themselves.
6 Exalt yourself above the heavens,
O God,*
and your glory over all the earth.
7 My heart is firmly fixed,
O God, my heart is fixed;*
I will sing and make melody.
8 Wake up, my spirit;
awake, lute and harp;*
I myself will waken the dawn.
9 I will confess you among the peoples,
O LORD;*
I will sing praise to you
among the nations.
10 For your lovingkindness
is greater than the heavens,*
and your faithfulness
reaches to the clouds.
11 Exalt yourself above the heavens,
O God,*
and your glory over all the earth.

61

1 Hear my cry, O God,*
and listen to my prayer.
2 I call upon you
from the ends of the earth
with heaviness in my heart;*
set me upon the rock
that is higher than I.
3 For you have been my refuge,*
a strong tower against the enemy.
4 I will dwell in your house forever;*
I will take refuge
under the cover of your wings.
5 For you, O God, have heard my vows;*
you have granted me the heritage
of those who fear
your name.
6 Add length of days to the king's life;*
let his years extend
over many generations.
7 Let him sit enthroned
before God forever;*
bid love and faithfulness
watch over him.
8 So will I always sing the praise
of your name,*
and day by day I will fulfill my vows.

62

1 For God alone my soul in silence waits;*
from him comes my salvation.
2 He alone is my rock and my salvation,*
my stronghold,
so that I shall not be greatly shaken.
3 How long will you assail me
to crush me, all of you together,*
as if you were a leaning fence,
a toppling wall?

4 They seek only to bring me down
from my place of honor;*
lies are their chief delight.

5 They bless with their lips,*
but in their hearts they curse.

6 For God alone my soul in silence waits;*
truly, my hope is in him.

7 He alone is my rock and my salvation,*
my stronghold,
so that I shall not be shaken.

8 In God is my safety and my honor;*
God is my strong rock and my refuge.

9 Put your trust in him always, O people,*
pour out your hearts before him,
for God is our refuge.

10 Those of high degree
are but a fleeting breath,*
even those of low estate
cannot be trusted.

11 On the scales
they are lighter than a breath,*
all of them together.

12 Put no trust in extortion;
in robbery take no empty pride;*
though wealth increase,
set not your heart upon it.

13 God has spoken once,
twice have I heard it,*
that power belongs to God.

14 Steadfast love is yours, O Lord,*
for you repay everyone
according to his deeds.

63

1 O God, you are my God;
eagerly I seek you;*
my soul thirsts for you,
my flesh faints for you,
as in a barren and dry land
where there is no water.

2 Therefore I have gazed upon you
in your holy place,*
that I might behold your power
and your glory.

3 For your lovingkindness
is better than life itself;*
my lips shall give you praise.

4 So will I bless you as long as I live*
and lift up my hands in your name.

5 My soul is content,
as with marrow and fatness,*
and my mouth praises you
with joyful lips,

6 when I remember you upon my bed,*
and meditate on you
in the night watches.

7 For you have been my helper,*
and under the shadow of your wings
I will rejoice.

8 My soul clings to you;*
your right hand holds me fast.

9 May those
who seek my life to destroy it*
go down into the depths of the earth;

10 let them fall
upon the edge of the sword,*
and let them be food for jackals.

11 But the king will rejoice in God;
all those who swear by him
will be glad;*
for the mouth of those
who speak lies shall be stopped.

65

1 You are to be praised, O God, in Zion;*
to you shall vows be performed
in Jerusalem.

2 To you that hear prayer
shall all flesh come,*
because of their transgressions.

3 Our sins are stronger than we are,*
but you will blot them out.

4 Happy are they whom you choose
and draw to your courts to dwell there!*
They will be satisfied
by the beauty of your house,
by the holiness of your temple.

5 Awesome things will you show us
in your righteousness,
O God of our salvation,*
O Hope of all the ends of the earth
and of the seas that are far away.

6 You make fast the mountains
by your power;*
they are girded about with might.

7 You still the roaring of the seas,*
the roaring of their waves,
and the clamor of the peoples.

8 Those who dwell
at the ends of the earth
will tremble at your marvelous signs;*
you make the dawn and the dusk
to sing for joy.

9 You visit the earth
and water it abundantly;
you make it very plenteous;*
the river of God is full of water.

10 You prepare the grain,*
for so you provide for the earth.

11 You drench the furrows
and smooth out the ridges;*
with heavy rain
you soften the ground
and bless its increase.

12 You crown the year with your goodness,*
and your paths overflow with plenty.

13 May the fields of the wilderness
be rich for grazing,*
and the hills be clothed with joy.

14 May the meadows
cover themselves with flocks,
and the valleys
cloak themselves with grain;*
let them shout for joy and sing.

66

1 Be joyful in God, all you lands;*
sing the glory of his name;
sing the glory of his praise.

2 Say to God,
"How awesome are your deeds!*
Because of your great strength
your enemies cringe before you.

3 All the earth bows down before you,*
sings to you, sings out your name."

4 Come now and see the works of God,*
how wonderful he is
in his doing toward all people.

5 He turned the sea into dry land, so that
they went through the water on foot,*
and there we rejoiced in him.

6 In his might he rules forever;
his eyes keep watch over the nations;*
let no rebel rise up against him.

7 Bless our God, you peoples;*
make the voice of his praise
to be heard,

8 who holds our souls in life,*
and will not allow our feet to slip.

9 For you, O God, have proved us;*
you have tried us just as silver is tried.

10 You brought us into the snare;*
you laid heavy burdens
upon our backs.

11 You let enemies ride over our heads;
we went through fire and water,*
but you brought us out
into a place of refreshment.

12 I will enter your house
with burnt-offerings
and will pay you my vows,*
which I promised with my lips
and spoke with my mouth
when I was in trouble.

13 I will offer you sacrifices of fat beasts
with the smoke of rams;*
I will give you oxen and goats.

14 Come and listen, all you who fear God,*
and I will tell you
what he has done for me.

15 I called out to him with my mouth,*
and his praise was on my tongue.

16 If I had found evil in my heart,*
the Lord would not have heard me;

17 but in truth God has heard me;*
he has attended
to the voice of my prayer.

18 Blessed be God,
who has not rejected my prayer,*
nor withheld his love from me.

67

1 May God be merciful to us
and bless us,*

show us the light of his countenance,
and come to us.

2 Let your ways be known upon earth, *
your saving health among all nations.

3 Let the peoples praise you, O God; *
let all the peoples praise you.

4 Let the nations be glad and sing for joy, *
for you judge the peoples with equity
and guide all the nations upon earth.

5 Let the peoples praise you, O God; *
let all the peoples praise you.

6 The earth has brought forth
her increase; *
may God, our own God,
give us his blessing.

7 May God give us his blessing, *
and may all the ends of the earth
stand in awe of him.

68

1 Let God arise,
and let his enemies be scattered; *
let those who hate him
flee before him.

2 Let them vanish like smoke
when the wind drives it away; *
as the wax melts at the fire,
so let the wicked perish at
the presence of God.

3 But let the righteous be glad
and rejoice before God; *
let them also be merry and joyful.

4 Sing to God, sing praises to his name;
exalt him who rides upon the heavens; *
YAHWEH is his name,
rejoice before him!

5 Father of orphans,
defender of widows, *
God in his holy habitation!

6 God gives the solitary a home and
brings forth prisoners into freedom; *
but the rebels shall live in dry places.

7 O God, when you went forth
before your people, *
when you marched
through the wilderness,

8 the earth shook,
and the skies poured down rain,
at the presence of God,
the God of Sinai, *
at the presence of God,
the God of Israel.

9 You sent a gracious rain, O God,
upon your inheritance; *
you refreshed the land
when it was weary.

10 Your people found their home in it; *
in your goodness, O God,
you have made provision for the poor.

11 The Lord gave the word; *
great was the company of women
who bore the tidings:

12 "Kings with their armies
are fleeing away; *
the women at home
are dividing the spoils."

13 Though you lingered
among the sheepfolds, *
you shall be like a dove
whose wings are covered with silver,
whose feathers are like green gold.

14 When the Almighty scattered kings, *
it was like snow falling in Zalmon.

15 O mighty mountain, O hill of Bashan! *
O rugged mountain,
O hill of Bashan!

16 Why do you look with envy,
O rugged mountain, at the hill which
God chose for his resting-place? *
Truly, the LORD will dwell there
forever.

17 The chariots of God
are twenty thousand,
even thousands of thousands; *
the Lord comes in holiness from Sinai.

18 You have gone up on high
and led captivity captive;
you have received gifts
even from your enemies, *
that the LORD God
might dwell among them.

19 Blessed be the Lord day by day, *
the God of our salvation,
who bears our burdens.

20 He is our God,
the God of our salvation;*
God is the LORD,
by whom we escape death.

21 God shall crush the heads
of his enemies,*
and the hairy scalp of those
who go on still in their
wickedness.

22 The Lord has said, "I will bring them
back from Bashan;*
I will bring them
back from the depths of the sea;

23 that your foot may be dipped in blood,*
the tongues of your dogs
in the blood of your enemies."

24 They see your procession, O God,*
your procession into the sanctuary,
my God and my King.

25 The singers go before,
musicians follow after,*
in the midst of maidens
playing upon the hand-drums.

26 Bless God in the congregation;*
bless the LORD,
you that are of the fountain of Israel.

27 There is Benjamin,
least of the tribes, at the head;
the princes of Judah in a company;*
and the princes
of Zebulon and Naphtali.

28 Send forth your strength, O God;*
establish, O God,
what you have wrought for us.

29 Kings shall bring gifts to you,*
for your temple's sake at Jerusalem.

30 Rebuke the wild beast of the reeds,*
and the peoples, a herd of wild bulls
with its calves.

31 Trample down those
who lust after silver;*
scatter the peoples
that delight in war.

32 Let tribute be brought out of Egypt;*
let Ethiopia stretch out her hands
to God.

33 Sing to God, O kingdoms of the earth;*
sing praises to the Lord.

34 He rides in the heavens,
the ancient heavens;*
he sends forth his voice,
his mighty voice.

35 Ascribe power to God;*
his majesty is over Israel;
his strength is in the skies.

36 How wonderful is God
in his holy places,*
the God of Israel giving strength
and power to his people!
Blessed be God!

69

1 Save me, O God,*
for the waters have risen
up to my neck.

2 I am sinking in deep mire,*
and there is no firm ground
for my feet.

3 I have come into deep waters,*
and the torrent washes over me.

4 I have grown weary with my crying;
my throat is inflamed;*
my eyes have failed
from looking for my God.

5 Those who hate me without a cause
are more than the hairs of my head;
my lying foes
who would destroy me are mighty.*
Must I then give back
what I never stole?

6 O God, you know my foolishness,*
and my faults are not hidden from you.

7 Let not those who hope in you
be put to shame through me,
Lord GOD of hosts;*
let not those who seek you
be disgraced because of me,
O God of Israel.

8 Surely, for your sake
have I suffered reproach,*
and shame has covered my face.

9 I have become a stranger
to my own kindred,*

an alien to my mother's children.

10 Zeal for your house has eaten me up; *
the scorn of those who scorn you
has fallen upon me.

11 I humbled myself with fasting, *
but that was turned to my reproach.

12 I put on sackcloth also, *
and became a byword among them.

13 Those who sit at the gate
murmur against me, *
and the drunkards
make songs about me.

14 But as for me, this is my prayer to you, *
at the time you have set, O LORD:

15 "In your great mercy, O God, *
answer me with your unfailing help.

16 Save me from the mire;
do not let me sink; *
let me be rescued
from those who hate me
and out of the deep waters.

17 Let not the torrent of waters
wash over me,
neither let the deep swallow me up; *
do not let the pit
shut its mouth upon me.

18 Answer me, O LORD,
for your love is kind; *
in your great compassion, turn to me.

19 Hide not your face from your servant; *
be swift and answer me,
for I am in distress.

20 Draw near to me and redeem me; *
because of my enemies deliver me.

21 You know my reproach,
my shame, and my dishonor; *
my adversaries are all in your sight."

22 Reproach has broken my heart,
and it cannot be healed; *
I looked for sympathy,
but there was none,
for comforters,
but I could find no one.

23 They gave me gall to eat, *
and when I was thirsty,
they gave me vinegar to drink.

24 Let the table before them be a trap *
and their sacred feasts a snare.

25 Let their eyes be darkened,
that they may not see, *
and give them continual trembling
in their loins.

26 Pour out your indignation upon them, *
and let the fierceness of your anger
overtake them.

27 Let their camp be desolate, *
and let there be none
to dwell in their tents.

28 For they persecute him
whom you have stricken *
and add to the pain of those
whom you have pierced.

29 Lay to their charge guilt upon guilt, *
and let them not receive
your vindication.

30 Let them be wiped out
of the book of the living *
and not be written
among the righteous.

31 As for me, I am afflicted and in pain; *
your help, O God,
will lift me up on high.

32 I will praise the name of God in song; *
I will proclaim his greatness
with thanksgiving.

33 This will please the LORD
more than an offering of oxen, *
more than bullocks
with horns and hoofs.

34 The afflicted shall see and be glad; *
you who seek God,
your heart shall live.

35 For the LORD listens to the needy, *
and his prisoners he does not despise.

36 Let the heavens and the earth praise him, *
the seas and all that moves in them;

37 for God will save Zion
and rebuild the cities of Judah; *
they shall live there
and have it in possession.

38 The children of his servants
will inherit it, *
and those who love his name
will dwell therein.

70

1 Be pleased, O God, to deliver me;*
O LORD, make haste to help me.

2 Let those who seek my life be ashamed
and altogether dismayed;*
let those
who take pleasure in my misfortune
draw back and be disgraced.

3 Let those who say to me "Aha!"
and gloat over me turn back,*
because they are ashamed.

4 Let all who seek you rejoice
and be glad in you;*
let those who love your salvation
say forever, "Great is the LORD!"

5 But as for me, I am poor and needy;*
come to me speedily, O God.

6 You are my helper and my deliverer;*
O LORD, do not tarry.

71

1 In you, O LORD, have I taken refuge;*
let me never be ashamed.

2 In your righteousness,
deliver me and set me free;*
incline your ear to me and save me.

3 Be my strong rock,
a castle to keep me safe;*
you are my crag and my stronghold.

4 Deliver me, my God,
from the hand of the wicked,*
from the clutches of the evildoer
and the oppressor.

5 For you are my hope, O Lord GOD,*
my confidence since I was young.

6 I have been sustained by you
ever since I was born;
from my mother's womb
you have been my strength;*
my praise shall be always of you.

7 I have become a portent to many;*
but you are my refuge
and my strength.

8 Let my mouth be full of your praise*
and your glory all the day long.

9 Do not cast me off in my old age;*
forsake me not
when my strength fails.

10 For my enemies are talking against me,*
and those who lie in wait for my life
take counsel together.

11 They say, "God has forsaken him;
go after him and seize him;*
because there is none who will save."

12 O God, be not far from me;*
come quickly to help me, O my God.

13 Let those who set themselves against me
be put to shame and be disgraced;*
let those who seek to do me evil
be covered with scorn and reproach.

14 But I shall always wait in patience,*
and shall praise you more and more.

15 My mouth shall recount
your mighty acts
and saving deeds all day long;*
though I cannot know
the number of them.

16 I will begin with the mighty works
of the Lord GOD;*
I will recall your righteousness,
yours alone.

17 O God, you have taught me
since I was young,*
and to this day
I tell of your wonderful works.

18 And now that I am old
and gray-headed, O God,
do not forsake me,*
till I make known your strength
to this generation
and your power to all
who are to come.

19 Your righteousness, O God,
reaches to the heavens;*
you have done great things;
who is like you, O God?

20 You have shown me great troubles
and adversities,*
but you will restore my life
and bring me up again
from the deep places of the earth.

21 You strengthen me more and more;*
you enfold and comfort me.

22 Therefore I will praise you
upon the lyre for your faithfulness,
O my God; *
I will sing to you with the harp,
O Holy One of Israel.

23 My lips will sing with joy
when I play to you, *
and so will my soul,
which you have redeemed.

24 My tongue will proclaim
your righteousness all day long, *
for they are ashamed and disgraced
who sought to do me harm.

72

1 Give the king your justice, O God, *
and your righteousness
to the king's son;

2 that he may
rule your people righteously *
and the poor with justice;

3 that the mountains may
bring prosperity to the people, *
and the little hills
bring righteousness.

4 He shall defend the needy
among the people; *
he shall rescue the poor
and crush the oppressor.

5 He shall live as long
as the sun and moon endure, *
from one generation to another.

6 He shall come down like rain
upon the mown field, *
like showers that water the earth.

7 In his time shall the righteous flourish; *
there shall be abundance of peace
till the moon shall be no more.

8 He shall rule from sea to sea, *
and from the river
to the ends of the earth.

9 His foes shall bow down before him, *
and his enemies lick the dust.

10 The kings of Tarshish and of the isles
shall pay tribute, *
and the kings of Arabia and Saba
offer gifts.

11 All kings shall bow down before him, *
and all the nations do him service.

12 For he shall deliver the poor
who cries out in distress, *
and the oppressed
who has no helper.

13 He shall have pity
on the lowly and poor; *
he shall preserve
the lives of the needy.

14 He shall redeem their lives
from oppression and violence, *
and dear shall their blood be
in his sight.

15 Long may he live!
And may there be given to him
gold from Arabia; *
may prayer be made for him always;
and may they bless him
all the day long.

16 May there be abundance
of grain on the earth,
growing thick even on the hilltops; *
may its fruit flourish like Lebanon,
and its grain like grass
upon the earth.

17 May his name remain forever
and be established
as long as the sun endures; *
may all the nations bless
themselves in him and
call him blessed.

18 Blessed be the Lord God,
the God of Israel, *
who alone does wondrous deeds!

19 And blessed be his glorious name
forever, *
and may all the earth
be filled with his glory.
Amen. Amen.

73

1 Truly, God is good to Israel, *
to those who are pure in heart.

2 But as for me,
my feet had nearly slipped;*
I had almost tripped and fallen;
3 because I envied the proud*
and saw the prosperity
of the wicked.
4 For they suffer no pain,*
and their bodies are sleek and sound;
5 in the misfortunes of others
they have no share;*
they are not afflicted as others are;
6 therefore they wear their pride
like a necklace*
and wrap their violence about them
like a cloak.
7 Their iniquity
comes from gross minds,*
and their hearts overflow
with wicked thoughts.
8 They scoff and speak maliciously;*
out of their haughtiness
they plan oppression.
9 They set their mouths
against the heavens,*
and their evil speech
runs through the world.
10 And so the people turn to them*
and find in them no fault.
11 They say, "How should God know?*
Is there knowledge
in the Most High?"
12 So then, these are the wicked;*
always at ease,
they increase their wealth.
13 In vain have I kept my heart clean,*
and washed my hands in innocence.
14 I have been afflicted all day long,*
and punished every morning.
15 Had I gone on speaking this way,*
I should have betrayed
the generation of your children.
16 When I tried to understand these things,*
it was too hard for me;
17 until I entered the sanctuary of God*
and discerned the end of the wicked.
18 Surely, you set them in slippery places;*
you cast them down in ruin.
19 Oh, how suddenly
do they come to destruction,*
come to an end,
and perish from terror!
20 Like a dream when one awakens,
O Lord,*
when you arise
you will make their image vanish.
21 When my mind became embittered,*
I was sorely wounded in my heart.
22 I was stupid and had no understanding;*
I was like a brute beast
in your presence.
23 Yet I am always with you;*
you hold me by my right hand.
24 You will guide me by your counsel,*
and afterwards receive me with glory.
25 Whom have I in heaven but you?*
And having you,
I desire nothing upon earth.
26 Though my flesh and my heart
should waste away,*
God is the strength of my heart
and my portion forever.
27 Truly, those who forsake you
will perish;*
you destroy all who are unfaithful.
28 But it is good for me to be near God;*
I have made the Lord GOD
my refuge.
29 I will speak of all your works*
in the gates of the city of Zion.

78

1 Hear my teaching, O my people;*
incline your ears
to the words of my mouth.
2 I will open my mouth in a parable;*
I will declare the mysteries
of ancient times.
3 That which we have heard and known,
and what our forefathers have told us,*
we will not hide from their children.
4 We will recount to generations to come
the praiseworthy deeds
and the power of the LORD,*

and the wonderful works
he has done.

5 He gave his decrees to Jacob
and established a law for Israel,*
which he commanded them
to teach their children;

6 that the generations to come
might know,
and the children yet unborn;*
that they in their turn
might tell it to their children;

7 so that they might
put their trust in God,*
and not forget the deeds of God,
but keep his commandments,

8 and not be like their forefathers,
a stubborn and rebellious generation,*
a generation
whose heart was not steadfast, and
whose spirit was not faithful to God.

9 The people of Ephraim,
armed with the bow,*
turned back in the day of battle;

10 they did not keep the covenant of God,*
and refused to walk in his law;

11 they forgot what he had done,*
and the wonders he had shown them.

12 He worked marvels
in the sight of their forefathers,*
in the land of Egypt,
in the field of Zoan.

13 He split open the sea
and let them pass through;*
he made the waters stand up like walls.

14 He led them with a cloud by day,*
and all the night through
with a glow of fire.

15 He split the hard rocks
in the wilderness*
and gave them drink
as from the great deep.

16 He brought streams out of the cliff,*
and the waters gushed out like rivers.

17 But they went on sinning against him,*
rebelling in the desert
against the Most High.

18 They tested God in their hearts,*
demanding food for their craving.

19 They railed against God and said,*
"Can God set a table in the wilderness?

20 True, he struck the rock,
the waters gushed out,
and the gullies overflowed;*
but is he able to give bread
or to provide meat for his people?"

21 When the LORD heard this,
he was full of wrath;*
a fire was kindled against Jacob,
and his anger mounted against Israel;

22 for they had no faith in God,*
nor did they put their trust
in his saving power.

23 So he commanded the clouds above*
and opened the doors of heaven.

24 He rained down manna upon them
to eat*
and gave them grain from heaven.

25 So mortals ate the bread of angels;*
he provided for them food enough.

26 He caused the east wind to blow
in the heavens*
and led out the south wind
by his might.

27 He rained down flesh upon them
like dust*
and winged birds
like the sand of the sea.

28 He let it fall in the midst of their camp*
and round about their dwellings.

29 So they ate and were well filled,*
for he gave them what they craved.

30 But they did not stop their craving,*
though the food
was still in their mouths.

31 So God's anger mounted against them;*
he slew their strongest men
and laid low the youth of Israel.

32 In spite of all this, they went on sinning*
and had no faith
in his wonderful works.

33 So he brought their days to an end
like a breath*
and their years in sudden terror.

34 Whenever he slew them,
they would seek him,*
and repent,
and diligently search for God.

35 They would remember
that God was their rock,*
and the Most High God
their redeemer.

36 But they flattered him with their mouths*
and lied to him with their tongues.

37 Their heart was not steadfast
toward him,*
and they were not faithful
to his covenant.

38 But he was so merciful
that he forgave their sins
and did not destroy them;*
many times he held back his anger
and did not permit his wrath
to be roused;

39 for he remembered
that they were but flesh,*
a breath that goes forth
and does not return.

40 How often the people disobeyed him
in the wilderness*
and offended him in the desert!

41 Again and again they tempted God*
and provoked
the Holy One of Israel.

42 They did not remember his power*
in the day when he ransomed them
from the enemy;

43 how he wrought his signs in Egypt*
and his omens in the field of Zoan.

44 He turned their rivers into blood,*
so that they could not drink
of their streams.

45 He sent swarms of flies among them,
which ate them up,*
and frogs, which destroyed them.

46 He gave their crops to the caterpillar,*
the fruit of their toil to the locust.

47 He killed their vines with hail*
and their sycamores with frost.

48 He delivered their cattle to hailstones*
and their livestock
to hot thunderbolts.

49 He poured out upon them
his blazing anger:*
fury, indignation, and distress,
a troop of destroying angels.

50 He gave full rein to his anger;
he did not spare their souls from death;*
but delivered their lives to the plague.

51 He struck down
all the firstborn of Egypt,*
the flower of manhood
in the dwellings of Ham.

52 He led out his people like sheep*
and guided them in the wilderness
like a flock.

53 He led them to safety,
and they were not afraid;*
but the sea
overwhelmed their enemies.

54 He brought them to his holy land,*
the mountain his right hand had won.

55 He drove out the Canaanites
before them
and apportioned an inheritance
to them by lot;*
he made the tribes of Israel
to dwell in their tents.

56 But they tested the Most High God,
and defied him,*
and did not keep his commandments.

57 They turned away and were disloyal
like their fathers;*
they were undependable
like a warped bow.

58 They grieved him with their hill-altars*
and provoked his displeasure
with their idols.

59 When God heard this, he was angry*
and utterly rejected Israel.

60 He forsook the shrine at Shiloh,*
the tabernacle where he had lived
among his people.

61 He delivered the ark into captivity,*
his glory into the adversary's hand.

62 He gave his people to the sword*
and was angered
against his inheritance.

63 The fire consumed their young men;*

there were no wedding songs
for their maidens.

64 Their priests fell by the sword,*
and their widows
made no lamentation.

65 Then the LORD woke
as though from sleep,*
like a warrior refreshed with wine.

66 He struck his enemies on the backside*
and put them to perpetual shame.

67 He rejected the tent of Joseph*
and did not choose
the tribe of Ephraim;

68 he chose instead the tribe of Judah*
and Mount Zion, which he loved.

69 He built his sanctuary
like the heights of heaven,*
like the earth
which he founded forever.

70 He chose David his servant,*
and took him away
from the sheepfolds.

71 He brought him
from following the ewes,*
to be a shepherd
over Jacob his people
and over Israel his inheritance.

72 So he shepherded them
with a faithful and true heart*
and guided them
with the skillfulness of his hands.

80

1 Hear, O Shepherd of Israel,
leading Joseph like a flock;*
shine forth, you that are enthroned
upon the cherubim.

2 In the presence of Ephraim, Benjamin,
and Manasseh,*
stir up your strength
and come to help us.

3 Restore us, O God of hosts;*
show the light of your countenance,
and we shall be saved.

4 O LORD God of hosts,*
how long will you be angered
despite the prayers of your people?

5 You have fed them
with the bread of tears;*
you have given them
bowls of tears to drink.

6 You have made us
the derision of our neighbors,*
and our enemies laugh us to scorn.

7 Restore us, O God of hosts;*
show the light of your countenance,
and we shall be saved.

8 You have brought a vine out of Egypt;*
you cast out the nations
and planted it.

9 You prepared the ground for it;*
it took root and filled the land.

10 The mountains were covered
by its shadow*
and the towering cedar trees
by its boughs.

11 You stretched out its tendrils to the sea*
and its branches to the river.

12 Why have you broken down its wall,*
so that all who pass by
pluck off its grapes?

13 The wild boar of the forest
has ravaged it,*
and the beasts of the field
have grazed upon it.

14 Turn now, O God of hosts,
look down from heaven;
behold and tend this vine;*
preserve what your right hand
has planted.

15 They burn it with fire like rubbish;*
at the rebuke of your countenance
let them perish.

16 Let your hand be upon the man
of your right hand,*
the son of man you have made
so strong for yourself.

17 And so will we never
turn away from you;*
give us life, that we
may call upon your name.

18 Restore us, O LORD God of hosts;*
show the light of your countenance,
and we shall be saved.

81

1 Sing with joy to God our strength*
and raise a loud shout
to the God of Jacob.

2 Raise a song and sound the timbrel,*
the merry harp, and the lyre.

3 Blow the ram's horn at the new moon,*
and at the full moon,
the day of our feast;

4 for this is a statute for Israel,*
a law of the God of Jacob.

5 He laid it
as a solemn charge upon Joseph,*
when he came out
of the land of Egypt.

6 I heard an unfamiliar voice saying,*
"I eased his shoulder
from the burden;
his hands were set free
from bearing the load."

7 You called on me in trouble,
and I saved you;*
I answered you
from the secret place of thunder
and tested you
at the waters of Meribah.

8 Hear, O my people,
and I will admonish you:*
O Israel,
if you would but listen to me!

9 There shall be no strange god
among you;*
you shall not worship a foreign god.

10 I am the LORD your God,
who brought you
out of the land of Egypt and said,*
"Open your mouth wide,
and I will fill it."

11 And yet my people did not hear
my voice,*
and Israel would not obey me.

12 So I gave them over
to the stubbornness of their hearts,*
to follow their own devices.

13 Oh, that my people would listen to me,*
that Israel would walk in my ways!

14 I should soon subdue their enemies*
and turn my hand against their foes.

15 Those who hate the LORD
would cringe before him,*
and their punishment
would last forever.

16 But Israel would I feed
with the finest wheat*
and satisfy him
with honey from the rock.

82

1 God takes his stand
in the council of heaven;*
he gives judgment
in the midst of the gods:

2 "How long will you judge unjustly,*
and show favor to the wicked?

3 Save the weak and the orphan;*
defend the humble and needy;

4 rescue the weak and the poor;*
deliver them
from the power of the wicked.

5 They do not know,
neither do they understand;
they go about in darkness;*
all the foundations of the earth
are shaken.

6 Now I say to you, 'You are gods,*
and all of you children
of the Most High;

7 nevertheless,
you shall die like mortals,*
and fall like any prince.'"

8 Arise, O God, and rule the earth,*
for you shall take all nations
for your own.

84

1 How dear to me is your dwelling,
O LORD of hosts!*
My soul has a desire and longing
for the courts of the LORD;
my heart and my flesh rejoice
in the living God.

2 The sparrow has found her a house
and the swallow a nest
where she may lay her young,*
by the side of your altars,
O LORD of hosts,
my King and my God.

3 Happy are they
who dwell in your house!*
They will always be praising you.

4 Happy are the people
whose strength is in you,*
whose hearts are set
on the pilgrims' way.

5 Those who go
through the desolate valley
will find it a place of springs,*
for the early rains have covered it
with pools of water.

6 They will climb from height to height,*
and the God of gods
will reveal himself in Zion.

7 LORD God of hosts, hear my prayer;*
hearken, O God of Jacob.

8 Behold our defender, O God;*
and look upon the face
of your anointed.

9 For one day in your courts
is better than a thousand
in my own room,*
and to stand at the threshold
of the house of my God than
to dwell in the tents of the wicked.

10 For the LORD God
is both sun and shield;*
he will give grace and glory;

11 no good thing will the LORD withhold*
from those who walk with integrity.

12 O LORD of hosts,*
happy are they
who put their trust in you!

85

1 You have been gracious to your land,
O LORD;*
you have restored
the good fortune of Jacob.

2 You have forgiven the iniquity
of your people*
and blotted out all their sins.

3 You have withdrawn all your fury*
and turned yourself
from your wrathful indignation.

4 Restore us then, O God our Savior;*
let your anger depart from us.

5 Will you be displeased with us forever?*
Will you prolong your anger
from age to age?

6 Will you not give us life again,*
that your people may rejoice in you?

7 Show us your mercy, O LORD,*
and grant us your salvation.

8 I will listen
to what the LORD God is saying,*
for he is speaking peace
to his faithful people
and to those
who turn their hearts to him.

9 Truly, his salvation is very near
to those who fear him,*
that his glory may dwell in our land.

10 Mercy and truth have met together;*
righteousness and peace
have kissed each other.

11 Truth shall spring up from the earth,*
and righteousness
shall look down from heaven.

12 The LORD will indeed grant prosperity,*
and our land will yield its increase.

13 Righteousness shall go before him,*
and peace shall be a pathway
for his feet.

86

1 Bow down your ear, O LORD,
and answer me,*
for I am poor and in misery.

2 Keep watch over my life,
for I am faithful;*
save your servant
who puts his trust in you.

3 Be merciful to me, O LORD,
for you are my God;*

I call upon you all the day long.
4 Gladden the soul of your servant,*
for to you, O LORD,
I lift up my soul.
5 For you, O LORD,
are good and forgiving,*
and great is your love
toward all who call upon you.
6 Give ear, O LORD, to my prayer,*
and attend to the voice
of my supplications.
7 In the time of my trouble
I will call upon you,*
for you will answer me.
8 Among the gods there is none like you,
O LORD,*
nor anything like your works.
9 All nations you have made will
come and worship you, O LORD,*
and glorify your name.
10 For you are great;
you do wondrous things;*
and you alone are God.
11 Teach me your way, O LORD,
and I will walk in your truth;*
knit my heart to you
that I may fear your name.
12 I will thank you, O LORD my God,
with all my heart,*
and glorify your name forevermore.
13 For great is your love toward me;*
you have delivered me
from the nethermost pit.
14 The arrogant rise up against me, O God,
and a band of violent men seeks my life;*
they have not set you
before their eyes.
15 But you, O LORD, are gracious
and full of compassion,*
slow to anger,
and full of kindness and truth.
16 Turn to me and have mercy upon me;*
give your strength to your servant;
and save the child of your handmaid.
17 Show me a sign of your favor,
so that those who hate me may see it
and be ashamed;*
because you, O LORD,
have helped me and comforted me.

87

1 On the holy mountain
stands the city he has founded;*
the LORD loves the gates of Zion
more than all the dwellings of Jacob.
2 Glorious things are spoken of you,*
O city of our God.
3 I count Egypt and Babylon
among those who know me;*
behold Philistia, Tyre, and Ethiopia:
in Zion were they born.
4 Of Zion it shall be said,
"Everyone was born in her,*
and the Most High himself
shall sustain her."
5 The LORD will record
as he enrolls the peoples,*
"These also were born there."
6 The singers and the dancers will say,*
"All my fresh springs are in you."

88

1 O LORD, my God, my Savior,*
by day and night I cry to you.
2 Let my prayer enter into your presence;*
incline your ear to my lamentation.
3 For I am full of trouble;*
my life is at the brink of the grave.
4 I am counted among those
who go down to the pit;*
I have become like one
who has no strength;
5 lost among the dead,*
like the slain who lie in the grave,
6 whom you remember no more,*
for they are cut off from your hand.
7 You have laid me
in the depths of the pit,*
in dark places, and in the abyss.
8 Your anger weighs upon me heavily,*
and all your great waves
overwhelm me.

[9] You have put my friends far from me;
you have made me
to be abhorred by them;*
I am in prison and cannot get free.

[10] My sight has failed me
because of trouble;*
LORD, I have called upon you daily;
I have stretched out my hands to you.

[11] Do you work wonders for the dead?*
Will those who have died stand up
and give you thanks?

[12] Will your lovingkindness
be declared in the grave,*
your faithfulness
in the land of destruction?

[13] Will your wonders
be known in the dark*
or your righteousness
in the country where all
is forgotten?

[14] But as for me, O LORD,
I cry to you for help;*
in the morning
my prayer comes before you.

[15] LORD, why have you rejected me?*
Why have you hidden your face
from me?

[16] Ever since my youth,
I have been wretched
and at the point of death;*
I have borne your terrors
with a troubled mind.

[17] Your blazing anger has swept over me;*
your terrors have destroyed me;

[18] they surround me all day long
like a flood;*
they encompass me on every side.

[19] My friend and my neighbor
you have put away from me,*
and darkness is my only companion.

89

[1] Your love, O LORD, forever will I sing;*
from age to age my mouth
will proclaim your faithfulness.

[2] For I am persuaded
that your love is established forever;*
you have set your faithfulness
firmly in the heavens.

[3] "I have made a covenant
with my chosen one;*
I have sworn an oath
to David my servant:

[4] 'I will establish your line forever,*
and preserve your throne
for all generations.' "

[5] The heavens bear witness
to your wonders, O LORD,*
and to your faithfulness
in the assembly of the holy ones;

[6] for who in the skies
can be compared to the LORD?*
Who is like the LORD
among the gods?

[7] God is much to be feared
in the council of the holy ones,*
great and terrible
to all those round about him.

[8] Who is like you, LORD God of hosts?*
O mighty LORD,
your faithfulness is all around you.

[9] You rule the raging of the sea*
and still the surging of its waves.

[10] You have crushed Rahab of the deep
with a deadly wound;*
you have scattered your enemies
with your mighty arm.

[11] Yours are the heavens;
the earth also is yours;*
you laid the foundations
of the world and all that is in it.

[12] You have made the north and the south;*
Tabor and Hermon rejoice
in your name.

[13] You have a mighty arm;*
strong is your hand,
and high is your right hand.

[14] Righteousness and justice
are the foundations of your throne;*
love and truth go before your face.

[15] Happy are the people
who know the festal shout!*

They walk, O LORD,
in the light of your presence.

16 They rejoice daily in your name;*
they are jubilant
in your righteousness.

17 For you are the glory of their strength,*
and by your favor
our might is exalted.

18 Truly, the LORD is our ruler;*
the Holy One of Israel is our king.

19 You spoke once in a vision
and said to your faithful people:*
"I have set the crown upon a warrior
and have exalted one
chosen out of the people.

20 I have found David my servant;*
with my holy oil have I anointed him.

21 My hand will hold him fast*
and my arm will make him strong.

22 No enemy shall deceive him,*
nor any wicked man bring him down.

23 I will crush his foes before him*
and strike down those who hate him.

24 My faithfulness and love
shall be with him,*
and he shall be victorious
through my name.

25 I shall make his dominion extend*
from the great sea to the river.

26 He will say to me, 'You are my Father,*
my God, and
the rock of my salvation.'

27 I will make him my firstborn*
and higher than the kings of the earth.

28 I will keep my love for him forever,*
and my covenant
will stand firm for him.

29 I will establish his line forever*
and his throne as the days of heaven.

30 If his children forsake my law*
and do not walk
according to my judgments;

31 if they break my statutes*
and do not keep my commandments;

32 I will punish their transgressions
with a rod*
and their iniquities with the lash;

33 but I will not take my love from him,*
nor let my faithfulness prove false.

34 I will not break my covenant,*
nor change
what has gone out of my lips.

35 Once for all
I have sworn by my holiness:*
'I will not lie to David.

36 His line shall endure forever*
and his throne as the sun before me;

37 it shall stand fast forevermore
like the moon,*
the abiding witness in the sky.' "

38 But you have cast off
and rejected your anointed;*
you have become enraged at him.

39 You have broken your covenant
with your servant,*
defiled his crown,
and hurled it to the ground.

40 You have breached all his walls*
and laid his strongholds in ruins.

41 All who pass by despoil him;*
he has become the scorn
of his neighbors.

42 You have exalted
the right hand of his foes*
and made all his enemies rejoice.

43 You have turned back
the edge of his sword*
and have not sustained him in battle.

44 You have put an end to his splendor*
and cast his throne to the ground.

45 You have cut short
the days of his youth*
and have covered him with shame.

46 How long will you hide yourself,
O LORD?
Will you hide yourself forever?*
How long
will your anger burn like fire?

47 Remember, LORD, how short life is,*
how frail you have made all flesh.

48 Who can live and not see death?*
Who can save himself
from the power of the grave?

49 Where, Lord,
are your lovingkindnesses of old,*
which you promised David
in your faithfulness?
50 Remember, Lord,
how your servant is mocked,*
how I carry in my bosom
the taunts of many peoples,
51 the taunts your enemies have hurled,
O LORD,*
which they hurled at the heels
of your anointed.
52 Blessed be the LORD forevermore!*
Amen, I say. Amen.

90

1 Lord, you have been our refuge*
from one generation to another.
2 Before the mountains
were brought forth,
or the land and the earth were born,*
from age to age you are God.
3 You turn us back to the dust and say,*
"Go back, O child of earth."
4 For a thousand years in your sight
are like yesterday when it is past*
and like a watch in the night.
5 You sweep us away like a dream;*
we fade away suddenly like the grass.
6 In the morning
it is green and flourishes;*
in the evening
it is dried up and withered.
7 For we consume away
in your displeasure;*
we are afraid
because of your wrathful indignation.
8 Our iniquities you have set before you,*
and our secret sins
in the light of your countenance.
9 When you are angry,
all our days are gone;*
we bring our years
to an end like a sigh.
10 The span of our life is seventy years,
perhaps in strength even eighty;*
yet the sum of them
is but labor and sorrow,
for they pass away quickly
and we are gone.
11 Who regards the power of your wrath?*
Who rightly fears your indignation?
12 So teach us to number our days,*
that we may apply
our hearts to wisdom.
13 Return, O LORD;
how long will you tarry?*
Be gracious to your servants.
14 Satisfy us by your lovingkindness
in the morning;*
so shall we rejoice and be glad
all the days of our life.
15 Make us glad by the measure of the days
that you afflicted us*
and the years
in which we suffered adversity.
16 Show your servants your works*
and your splendor to their children.
17 May the graciousness of the LORD
our God be upon us;*
prosper the work of our hands;
prosper our handiwork.

91

1 He who dwells in the shelter
of the Most High,*
abides under the shadow
of the Almighty.
2 He shall say to the LORD,
"You are my refuge and my stronghold,*
my God in whom I put my trust."
3 He shall deliver you
from the snare of the hunter*
and from the deadly pestilence.
4 He shall cover you with his pinions,
and you shall find refuge
under his wings;*
his faithfulness
shall be a shield and buckler.
5 You shall not be afraid
of any terror by night,*
nor of the arrow that flies by day;

6 of the plague
that stalks in the darkness,*
nor of the sickness
that lays waste at midday.

7 A thousand shall fall at your side
and ten thousand at your right hand,*
but it shall not come near you.

8 Your eyes have only to behold*
to see the reward of the wicked.

9 Because you have made the LORD
your refuge,*
and the Most High your habitation,

10 there shall no evil happen to you,*
neither shall any plague
come near your dwelling.

11 For he shall give his angels
charge over you,*
to keep you in all your ways.

12 They shall bear you in their hands,*
lest you dash your foot
against a stone.

13 You shall tread
upon the lion and adder;*
you shall trample the young lion
and the serpent under your feet.

14 Because he is bound to me in love,
therefore will I deliver him;*
I will protect him,
because he knows my name.

15 He shall call upon me,
and I will answer him;*
I am with him in trouble;
I will rescue him
and bring him to honor.

16 With long life will I satisfy him,*
and show him my salvation.

92

1 It is a good thing
to give thanks to the LORD,*
and to sing praises to your name,
O Most High;

2 to tell of your lovingkindness
early in the morning*
and of your faithfulness
in the night season;

3 on the psaltery, and on the lyre,*
and to the melody of the harp.

4 For you have made me glad
by your acts, O LORD;*
and I shout for joy
because of the works of your hands.

5 LORD, how great are your works!*
Your thoughts are very deep.

6 The dullard does not know,
nor does the fool understand,*
that though the wicked
grow like weeds,
and all the workers of iniquity
flourish,

7 they flourish only
to be destroyed forever;*
but you, O LORD,
are exalted forevermore.

8 For lo, your enemies, O LORD,
lo, your enemies shall perish,*
and all the workers of iniquity
shall be scattered.

9 But my horn you have exalted
like the horns of wild bulls;*
I am anointed with fresh oil.

10 My eyes also gloat over my enemies,*
and my ears rejoice to hear the doom
of the wicked who rise up against me.

11 The righteous shall flourish
like a palm tree,*
and shall spread abroad
like a cedar of Lebanon.

12 Those who are planted
in the house of the LORD*
shall flourish in the courts of our God;

13 they shall still bear fruit in old age;*
they shall be green and succulent;

14 that they may show
how upright the LORD is,*
my rock, in whom there is no fault.

93

1 The LORD is king;
he has put on splendid apparel;*
the LORD has put on his apparel
and girded himself with strength.

2 He has made the whole world so sure*
that it cannot be moved;
3 ever since the world began,
your throne has been established;*
you are from everlasting
4 The waters have lifted up, O LORD,
the waters have lifted up their voice;*
the waters have lifted up
their pounding waves.
5 Mightier than the sound of many waters,
mightier than the breakers of the sea,*
mightier is the LORD
who dwells on high.
6 Your testimonies are very sure,*
and holiness adorns your house,
O LORD, forever and forevermore.

94

1 O LORD God of vengeance,*
O God of vengeance, show yourself.
2 Rise up, O Judge of the world;*
give the arrogant their just deserts.
3 How long shall the wicked, O LORD,*
how long shall the wicked triumph?
4 They bluster in their insolence;*
all evildoers are full of boasting.
5 They crush your people, O LORD,*
and afflict your chosen nation.
6 They murder the widow
and the stranger*
and put the orphans to death.
7 Yet they say, "The LORD does not see,*
the God of Jacob takes no notice."
8 Consider well,
you dullards among the people;*
when will you fools understand?
9 He that planted the ear,
does he not hear?*
He that formed the eye,
does he not see?
10 He who admonishes the nations,
will he not punish?*
He who teaches all the world,
has he no knowledge?
11 The LORD knows our human thoughts;*
how like a puff of wind they are.
12 Happy are they whom you instruct,
O Lord,*
whom you teach out of your law;
13 to give them rest in evil days,*
until a pit is dug for the wicked.
14 For the LORD
will not abandon his people,*
nor will he forsake his own.
15 For judgment will again be just,*
and all the true of heart
will follow it.
16 Who rose up for me
against the wicked?*
Who took my part
against the evildoers?
17 If the LORD had not come to my help,*
I should soon have dwelt
in the land of silence.
18 As often as I said,
"My foot has slipped,"*
your love, O LORD, upheld me.
19 When many cares fill my mind,*
your consolations cheer my soul.
20 Can a corrupt tribunal
have any part with you,*
one which frames evil into law?
21 They conspire against the life of the just*
and condemn the innocent to death.
22 But the LORD
has become my stronghold,*
and my God the rock of my trust.
23 He will turn their wickedness
back upon them
and destroy them in their own malice;*
the LORD our God will destroy them.

95

1 Come, let us sing to the LORD;*
let us shout for joy
to the rock of our salvation.
2 Let us come before his presence
with thanksgiving*
and raise a loud shout
to him with psalms.
3 For the LORD is a great God,*
and a great king above all gods.

4 In his hand are the caverns of the earth,*
and the heights of the hills are his also.
5 The sea is his, for he made it,*
and his hands
have molded the dry land.
6 Come, let us bow down
and bend the knee,*
and kneel before the LORD
our maker.
7 For he is our God,
and we are the people of his pasture
and the sheep of his hand.*
Oh, that today you would hearken
to his voice!
8 Harden not your hearts,
as your forebears did in the wilderness,*
at Meribah, and on that day
at Massah, when they tempted me.
9 They put me to the test,*
though they had seen my works.
10 Forty years long
I detested that generation and said,*
"This people are wayward
in their hearts;
they do not know my ways."
11 So I swore in my wrath,*
"They shall not enter into my rest."

96

1 Sing to the LORD a new song;*
sing to the LORD,
all the whole earth.
2 Sing to the LORD and bless his name;*
proclaim the good news
of his salvation from day to day.
3 Declare his glory among the nations*
and his wonders among all peoples.
4 For great is the LORD
and greatly to be praised;*
he is more to be feared than all gods.
5 As for all the gods of the nations,
they are but idols;*
but it is the LORD
who made the heavens.
6 Oh, the majesty and magnificence
of his presence!*
Oh, the power and the splendor
of his sanctuary!
7 Ascribe to the LORD,
you families of the peoples;*
ascribe to the LORD honor and power.
8 Ascribe to the LORD
the honor due his name;*
bring offerings
and come into his courts.
9 Worship the LORD
in the beauty of holiness;*
let the whole earth
tremble before him.
10 Tell it out among the nations:
"The LORD is king!*
He has made the world so firm
that it cannot be moved;
he will judge the peoples with equity."
11 Let the heavens rejoice,
and let the earth be glad;
let the sea thunder and all that is in it;*
let the field be joyful
and all that is therein.
12 Then shall all the trees of the wood
shout for joy
before the LORD when he comes,*
when he comes to judge the earth.
13 He will judge the world
with righteousness*
and the peoples with his truth.

97

1 The LORD is king;
let the earth rejoice;*
let the multitude of the isles be glad.
2 Clouds and darkness
are found about him,*
righteousness and justice
are the foundations of his throne.
3 A fire goes before him*
and burns up his enemies
on every side.
4 His lightnings light up the world;*
the earth sees it and is afraid.
5 The mountains melt like wax
at the presence of the LORD,*

at the presence of the Lord
of the whole earth.
6 The heavens declare his righteousness,*
and all the peoples see his glory.
7 Confounded be all
who worship carved images
and delight in false gods! *
Bow down before him, all you gods.
8 Zion hears and is glad,
and the cities of Judah rejoice,*
because of your judgments, O LORD.
9 For you are the LORD,
most high over all the earth;*
you are exalted far above all gods.
10 The LORD loves those who hate evil;*
he preserves the lives of his saints
and delivers them
from the hand of the wicked.
11 Light has sprung up for the righteous,*
and joyful gladness for those
who are truehearted.
12 Rejoice in the LORD, you righteous,*
and give thanks to his holy name.

98

1 Sing to the LORD a new song,*
for he has done marvelous things.
2 With his right hand and his holy arm*
has he won for himself the victory.
3 The LORD has made known
his victory;*
his righteousness
has he openly shown
in the sight of the nations.
4 He remembers his mercy and
faithfulness to the house of Israel,*
and all the ends of the earth
have seen the victory of our God.
5 Shout with joy to the LORD,
all you lands;*
lift up your voice, rejoice, and sing.
6 Sing to the LORD with the harp,*
with the harp and the voice of song.
7 With trumpets
and the sound of the horn*
shout with joy
before the king, the LORD.
8 Let the sea make a noise
and all that is in it,*
the lands and
those who dwell therein.
9 Let the rivers clap their hands,*
and let the hills ring out with joy
before the LORD,
when he comes to judge the earth.
10 In righteousness
shall he judge the world*
and the peoples with equity.

99

1 The LORD is king;
let the people tremble.*
He is enthroned upon the cherubim;
let the earth shake.
2 The LORD is great in Zion;*
he is high above all peoples.
3 Let them confess his name,
which is great and awesome;*
he is the Holy One.
4 "O mighty King, lover of justice,
you have established equity;*
you have executed justice
and righteousness in Jacob."
5 Proclaim the greatness
of the LORD our God
and fall down before his footstool;*
he is the Holy One.
6 Moses and Aaron among his priests,
and Samuel among those
who call upon his name,*
they called upon the LORD,
and he answered them.
7 He spoke to them out
of the pillar of cloud;*
they kept his testimonies
and the decree that he gave them.
8 O LORD our God,
you answered them indeed;*
you were a God who forgave them,
yet punished them for their evil deeds.

9 Proclaim the greatness
of the LORD our God
and worship him upon his holy hill;*
for the LORD our God
is the Holy One.

100

1 Be joyful in the LORD, all you lands;*
serve the LORD with gladness
and come before his presence
with a song.
2 Know this: The LORD himself is God;*
he himself has made us,
and we are his;
we are his people
and the sheep of his pasture.
3 Enter his gates with thanksgiving;
go into his courts with praise;*
give thanks to him
and call upon his name.
4 For the LORD is good;
his mercy is everlasting;*
and his faithfulness endures
from age to age.

102

1 LORD, hear my prayer,
and let my cry come before you;*
hide not your face from me
in the day of my trouble.
2 Incline your ear to me;*
when I call,
make haste to answer me,
3 for my days drift away like smoke,*
and my bones are hot
as burning coals.
4 My heart is smitten like grass
and withered,*
so that I forget to eat my bread.
5 Because of the voice of my groaning*
I am but skin and bones.
6 I have become like a vulture
in the wilderness,*
like an owl among the ruins.
7 I lie awake and groan;*
I am like a sparrow,
lonely on a housetop.
8 My enemies revile me all day long,*
and those who scoff at me
have taken an oath against me.
9 For I have eaten ashes for bread*
and mingled my drink with weeping.
10 Because of your indignation and wrath*
you have lifted me up
and thrown me away.
11 My days pass away like a shadow,*
and I wither like the grass.
12 But you, O LORD, endure forever,*
and your name from age to age.
13 You will arise
and have compassion on Zion,
for it is time to have mercy upon her;*
indeed, the appointed time has come.
14 For your servants love her very rubble,*
and are moved to pity
even for her dust.
15 The nations shall fear your name,
O LORD,*
and all the kings of the earth
your glory.
16 For the LORD will build up Zion,*
and his glory will appear.
17 He will look with favor
on the prayer of the homeless;*
he will not despise their plea.
18 Let this be written
for a future generation,*
so that a people yet unborn
may praise the LORD.
19 For the LORD looked down
from his holy place on high;*
from the heavens
he beheld the earth;
20 that he might hear the groan
of the captive*
and set free those condemned to die;
21 that they may declare in Zion
the name of the LORD,*
and his praise in Jerusalem;

22 when the peoples are gathered together,*
and the kingdoms also,
to serve the LORD.

23 He has brought down my strength
before my time;*
he has shortened
the number of my days;

24 and I said, "O my God,
do not take me away
in the midst of my days;*
your years endure
throughout all generations.

25 In the beginning, O LORD,
you laid the foundations of the earth,*
and the heavens
are the work of your hands.

26 They shall perish, but you will endure;
they all shall wear out like a garment;*
as clothing you will change them,
and they shall be changed;

27 but you are always the same,*
and your years will never end.

28 The children of your servants
shall continue,*
and their offspring
shall stand fast in your sight."

103

1 Bless the LORD, O my soul,*
and all that is within me,
bless his holy name.

2 Bless the LORD, O my soul,*
and forget not all his benefits.

3 He forgives all your sins*
and heals all your infirmities;

4 he redeems your life from the grave*
and crowns you with mercy
and lovingkindness;

5 he satisfies you with good things,*
and your youth is renewed
like an eagle's.

6 The LORD executes righteousness*
and judgment for all
who are oppressed.

7 He made his ways known to Moses*
and his works
to the children of Israel.

8 The LORD is full of compassion
and mercy,*
slow to anger and of great kindness.

9 He will not always accuse us,*
nor will he keep his anger forever.

10 He has not dealt with us
according to our sins,*
nor rewarded us
according to our wickedness.

11 For as the heavens
are high above the earth,*
so is his mercy
great upon those who fear him.

12 As far as the east is from the west,*
so far
has he removed our sins from us.

13 As a father cares for his children,*
so does the LORD care for those
who fear him.

14 For he himself knows
whereof we are made;*
he remembers that we are but dust.

15 Our days are like the grass;*
we flourish like a flower of the field;

16 when the wind goes over it, it is gone,*
and its place shall know it no more.

17 But the merciful goodness of the LORD
endures forever
on those who fear him,*
and his righteousness
on children's children;

18 on those who keep his covenant*
and remember his commandments
and do them.

19 The LORD has set his throne in heaven,*
and his kingship
has dominion over all.

20 Bless the LORD, you angels of his,
you mighty ones who do his bidding,*
and hearken to the voice of his word.

21 Bless the LORD, all you his hosts,*
you ministers of his who do his will.

22 Bless the LORD, all you works of his,
in all places of his dominion;*
bless the LORD, O my soul.

104

1 Bless the Lord, O my soul;*
O Lord my God,
how excellent is your greatness!
You are clothed
with majesty and splendor.

2 You wrap yourself with light
as with a cloak*
and spread out the heavens
like a curtain.

3 You lay the beams of your chambers
in the waters above;*
you make the clouds your chariot;
you ride on the wings of the wind.

4 You make the winds your messengers*
and flames of fire your servants.

5 You have set the earth
upon its foundations,*
so that it never shall move
at any time.

6 You covered it with the deep
as with a mantle;*
the waters stood higher
than the mountains.

7 At your rebuke they fled;*
at the voice of your thunder
they hastened away.

8 They went up into the hills
and down to the valleys beneath,*
to the places
you had appointed for them.

9 You set the limits
that they should not pass;*
they shall not again cover the earth.

10 You send the springs into the valleys;*
they flow between the mountains.

11 All the beasts of the field
drink their fill from them,*
and the wild asses
quench their thirst.

12 Beside them the birds of the air
make their nests*
and sing among the branches.

13 You water the mountains
from your dwelling on high;*
the earth is fully satisfied
by the fruit of your works.

14 You make grass grow
for flocks and herds*
and plants to serve mankind;

15 that they may bring forth food
from the earth,*
and wine to gladden our hearts,

16 oil to make a cheerful countenance,*
and bread to strengthen the heart.

17 The trees of the Lord are full of sap,*
the cedars of Lebanon
which he planted,

18 in which the birds build their nests,*
and in whose tops
the stork makes his dwelling.

19 The high hills are a refuge
for the mountain goats,*
and the stony cliffs
for the rock badgers.

20 You appointed the moon
to mark the seasons,*
and the sun
knows the time of its setting.

21 You make darkness
that it may be night,*
in which all the beasts
of the forest prowl.

22 The lions roar after their prey*
and seek their food from God.

23 The sun rises, and they slip away*
and lay themselves down
in their dens.

24 Man goes forth to his work*
and to his labor until the evening.

25 O Lord, how manifold
are your works!*
In wisdom you have made them all;
the earth is full of your creatures.

26 Yonder is the great and wide sea
with its living things
too many to number,*
creatures both small and great.

27 There move the ships,
and there is that Leviathan,*
which you have made
for the sport of it.

28 All of them look to you*
to give them their food in due season.
29 You give it to them; they gather it;*
you open your hand,
and they are filled with good things.
30 You hide your face,
and they are terrified;*
you take away their breath,
and they die and return to their dust.
31 You send forth your Spirit,
and they are created;*
and so you renew
the face of the earth.
32 May the glory of the LORD
endure forever;*
may the LORD rejoice in all his works.
33 He looks at the earth and it trembles;*
he touches the mountains
and they smoke.
34 I will sing to the LORD as long as I live;*
I will praise my God
while I have my being.
35 May these words of mine please him;*
I will rejoice in the LORD.
36 Let sinners be consumed
out of the earth,*
and the wicked be no more.
37 Bless the LORD, O my soul.*
Hallelujah!

105

1 Give thanks to the LORD
and call upon his name;*
make known his deeds
among the peoples.
2 Sing to him, sing praises to him,*
and speak
of all his marvelous works.
3 Glory in his holy name;*
let the hearts of those
who seek the LORD rejoice.
4 Search for the LORD and his strength;*
continually seek his face.
5 Remember the marvels he has done,*
his wonders and
the judgments of his mouth,
6 O offspring of Abraham his servant,*
O children of Jacob his chosen.
7 He is the LORD our God;*
his judgments prevail
in all the world.
8 He has always been mindful
of his covenant,*
the promise he made
for a thousand generations:
9 the covenant he made with Abraham,*
the oath that he swore to Isaac,
10 which he established
as a statute for Jacob,*
an everlasting covenant for Israel,
11 saying, "To you will I give
the land of Canaan*
to be your allotted inheritance."
12 When they were few in number,*
of little account,
and sojourners in the land,
13 wandering from nation to nation*
and from one kingdom to another,
14 he let no one oppress them*
and rebuked kings for their sake,
15 saying, "Do not touch my anointed*
and do my prophets no harm."
16 Then he called for a famine in the land*
and destroyed the supply of bread.
17 He sent a man before them,*
Joseph, who was sold as a slave.
18 They bruised his feet in fetters;*
his neck they put in an iron collar.
19 Until his prediction came to pass,*
the word of the LORD tested him.
20 The king sent and released him;*
the ruler of the peoples set him free.
21 He set him as a master
over his household,*
as a ruler over all his possessions,
22 to instruct his princes
according to his will*
and to teach his elders wisdom.
23 Israel came into Egypt,*

and Jacob became a sojourner
in the land of Ham.

24 The LORD made his people
exceedingly fruitful; *
he made them stronger
than their enemies;

25 whose heart he turned,
so that they hated his people, *
and dealt unjustly with his servants.

26 He sent Moses his servant, *
and Aaron whom he had chosen.

27 They worked his signs among them, *
and portents in the land of Ham.

28 He sent darkness, and it grew dark; *
but the Egyptians rebelled
against his words.

29 He turned their waters into blood *
and caused their fish to die.

30 Their land was overrun by frogs, *
in the very chambers of their kings.

31 He spoke,
and there came swarms of insects *
and gnats within all their borders.

32 He gave them hailstones
instead of rain, *
and flames of fire
throughout their land.

33 He blasted their vines
and their fig trees *
and shattered every tree
in their country.

34 He spoke, and the locust came, *
and young locusts without number,

35 which ate up all the green plants
in their land *
and devoured the fruit of their soil.

36 He struck down the firstborn
of their land, *
the firstfruits of all their strength.

37 He led out his people
with silver and gold; *
in all their tribes
there was not one that stumbled.

38 Egypt was glad of their going, *
because they were afraid of them.

39 He spread out a cloud for a covering *
and a fire to give light
in the night season.

40 They asked, and quails appeared, *
and he satisfied them
with bread from heaven.

41 He opened the rock, and water flowed, *
so the river ran in the dry places.

42 For God remembered his holy word *
and Abraham his servant.

43 So he led forth his people
with gladness, *
his chosen with shouts of joy.

44 He gave his people
the lands of the nations, *
and they took the fruit
of others' toil,

45 that they might keep his statutes *
and observe his laws.
Hallelujah!

107

1 Give thanks to the LORD, for he is good, *
and his mercy endures forever.

2 Let all those whom the LORD
has redeemed proclaim *
that he redeemed them
from the hand of the foe.

3 He gathered them out of the lands; *
from the east and from the west,
from the north and from the south.

4 Some wandered in desert wastes; *
they found no way to a city
where they might dwell.

5 They were hungry and thirsty; *
their spirits languished within them.

6 Then they cried to the LORD
in their trouble, *
and he delivered them
from their distress.

7 He put their feet on a straight path *
to go to a city
where they might dwell.

8 Let them give thanks
to the LORD for his mercy *
and the wonders
he does for his children.

9 For he satisfies the thirsty*
and fills the hungry with good things.

10 Some sat in darkness and deep gloom,*
bound fast in misery and iron;

11 because they rebelled
against the words of God*
and despised the counsel
of the Most High.

12 So he humbled their spirits
with hard labor;*
they stumbled,
and there was none to help.

13 Then they cried to the LORD
in their trouble,*
and he delivered them
from their distress.

14 He led them out
of darkness and deep gloom*
and broke their bonds asunder.

15 Let them give thanks
to the LORD for his mercy*
and the wonders
he does for his children.

16 For he shatters the doors of bronze*
and breaks in two the iron bars.

17 Some were fools
and took to rebellious ways;*
they were afflicted
because of their sins.

18 They abhorred all manner of food*
and drew near to death's door.

19 Then they cried to the LORD
in their trouble,*
and he delivered them
from their distress.

20 He sent forth his word and healed them*
and saved them from the grave.

21 Let them give thanks
to the LORD for his mercy*
and the wonders
he does for his children.

22 Let them offer
a sacrifice of thanksgiving*
and tell of his acts with shouts of joy.

23 Some went down to the sea in ships*
and plied their trade in deep waters;

24 they beheld the works of the LORD*
and his wonders in the deep.

25 Then he spoke,
and a stormy wind arose,*
which tossed high
the waves of the sea.

26 They mounted up to the heavens
and fell back to the depths;*
their hearts melted
because of their peril.

27 They reeled
and staggered like drunkards*
and were at their wits' end.

28 Then they cried to the LORD
in their trouble,*
and he delivered them
from their distress.

29 He stilled the storm to a whisper*
and quieted the waves of the sea.

30 Then were they glad
because of the calm,*
and he brought them to the harbor
they were bound for.

31 Let them give thanks
to the LORD for his mercy*
and the wonders
he does for his children.

32 Let them exalt him
in the congregation of the people*
and praise him
in the council of the elders.

33 The LORD changed rivers into deserts,*
and water-springs into thirsty ground,

34 a fruitful land into salt flats,*
because of the wickedness
of those who dwell there.

35 He changed deserts into pools of water*
and dry land into water-springs.

36 He settled the hungry there,*
and they founded a city to dwell in.

37 They sowed fields,
and planted vineyards,*
and brought in a fruitful harvest.

38 He blessed them,
so that they increased greatly;*
he did not let their herds decrease.

39 Yet when they were diminished
and brought low,*

through stress
of adversity and sorrow,
40 he pours contempt on princes*
and makes them wander
in trackless wastes;
41 he lifted up the poor out of misery*
and multiplied their families
like flocks of sheep.
42 The upright will see this and rejoice,*
but all wickedness
will shut its mouth.
43 Whoever is wise
will ponder these things,*
and consider well
the mercies of the LORD.

108

1 My heart is firmly fixed, O God,
my heart is fixed;*
I will sing and make melody.
2 Wake up, my spirit;
awake, lute and harp;*
I myself will waken the dawn.
3 I will confess you
among the peoples, O LORD;*
I will sing praises to you
among the nations.
4 For your lovingkindness
is greater than the heavens,*
and your faithfulness
reaches to the clouds.
5 Exalt yourself above the heavens,
O God,*
and your glory over all the earth.
6 So that those who are dear to you
may be delivered,*
save with your right hand
and answer me.
7 God spoke from his holy place and said,*
"I will exult and parcel out Shechem;
I will divide the valley of Succoth.
8 Gilead is mine and Manasseh is mine;*
Ephraim is my helmet
and Judah my scepter.
9 Moab is my washbasin;
on Edom
I throw down my sandal to claim it;*
and over Philistia
will I shout in triumph."
10 Who will lead me into the strong city?*
Who will bring me into Edom?
11 Have you not cast us off, O God?*
You no longer go out, O God,
with our armies.
12 Grant us your help against the enemy,*
for vain is the help of man.
13 With God we will do valiant deeds,*
and he shall tread
our enemies under foot.

110

1 The LORD said to my Lord,
"Sit at my right hand,*
until I make your enemies
your footstool."
2 The LORD will send the scepter
of your power out of Zion,*
saying, "Rule over your enemies
round about you.
3 Princely state has been yours
from the day of your birth;*
in the beauty of holiness
have I begotten you,
like dew
from the womb of the morning."
4 The LORD has sworn,
and he will not recant:*
"You are a priest forever
after the order of Melchizedek."
5 The Lord who is at your right hand
will smite kings in the day of his wrath;*
he will rule over the nations.
6 He will heap high the corpses;*
he will smash heads
over the wide earth.
7 He will drink
from the brook beside the road;*
therefore he will lift high his head.

111

[1]Hallelujah!
I will give thanks to the LORD
with my whole heart,*
in the assembly of the upright,
in the congregation.
[2]Great are the deeds of the LORD!*
They are studied
by all who delight in them.
[3]His work
is full of majesty and splendor,*
and his righteousness
endures forever.
[4]He makes his marvelous works
to be remembered;*
the LORD is gracious
and full of compassion.
[5]He gives food to those who fear him;*
he is ever mindful of his covenant.
[6]He has shown his people
the power of his works*
in giving them the lands
of the nations.
[7]The works of his hands
are faithfulness and justice;*
all his commandments are sure.
[8]They stand fast forever and ever,*
because they are done
in truth and equity.
[9]He sent redemption to his people;
he commanded his covenant forever;*
holy and awesome is his name.
[10]The fear of the LORD
is the beginning of wisdom;*
those who act accordingly
have a good understanding.
His praise endures forever.

112

[1]Hallelujah!
Happy are they who fear the Lord*
and have great delight
in his commandments!
[2]Their descendants
will be mighty in the land;*
the generation of the upright
will be blessed.
[3]Wealth and riches
will be in their house,*
and their righteousness
will last forever.
[4]Light shines in the darkness
for the upright;*
the righteous are merciful
and full of compassion.
[5]It is good for them
to be generous in lending*
and to manage their affairs
with justice.
[6]For they will never be shaken;*
the righteous will be kept
in everlasting remembrance.
[7]They will not be afraid
of any evil rumors;*
their heart is right;
they put their trust in the LORD.
[8]Their heart is established
and will not shrink,*
until they see their desire
upon their enemies.
[9]They have given freely to the poor,*
and their righteousness
stands fast forever;
they will hold up their head
with honor.
[10]The wicked will see it and be angry;
they will gnash their teeth
and pine away;*
the desires of the wicked will perish.

113

[1]Hallelujah!
Give praise, you servants of the LORD;*
praise the name of the LORD.
[2]Let the name of the LORD be blessed,*
from this time forth forevermore.
[3]From the rising of the sun
to its going down*
let the name of the LORD be praised.

4The LORD is high above all nations,*
and his glory above the heavens.

5Who is like the LORD our God,
who sits enthroned on high,*
but stoops to behold
the heavens and the earth?

6He takes up the weak out of the dust*
and lifts up the poor from the ashes.

7He sets them with the princes,*
with the princes of his people.

8He makes the woman
of a childless house*
to be a joyful mother of children.

114

1Hallelujah!
When Israel came out of Egypt,*
the house of Jacob
from a people of strange speech,

2Judah became God's sanctuary*
and Israel his dominion.

3The sea beheld it and fled;*
Jordan turned and went back.

4The mountains skipped like rams,*
and the little hills like young sheep.

5What ailed you, O sea, that you fled,*
O Jordan, that you turned back,

6you mountains,
that you skipped like rams,*
you little hills like young sheep?

7Tremble, O earth,
at the presence of the Lord,*
at the presence of the God of Jacob,

8who turned the hard rock
into a pool of water*
and flint-stone into a flowing spring.

115

1Not to us, O LORD, not to us,
but to your name give glory;*
because of your love
and because of your faithfulness.

2Why should the heathen say,*
"Where then is their God?"

3Our God is in heaven;*
whatever he wills to do he does.

4Their idols are silver and gold,*
the work of human hands.

5They have mouths,
but they cannot speak;*
eyes have they, but they cannot see;

6they have ears, but they cannot hear;*
noses, but they cannot smell;

7they have hands, but they cannot feel;
feet, but they cannot walk;*
they make no sound
with their throat.

8Those who make them are like them,*
and so are all
who put their trust in them.

9O Israel, trust in the LORD;*
he is their help and their shield.

10O house of Aaron, trust in the LORD;*
he is their help and their shield.

11You who fear the LORD,
trust in the LORD;*
he is their help and their shield.

12The LORD has been mindful of us,
and he will bless us;*
he will bless the house of Israel;
he will bless the house of Aaron;

13he will bless those who fear the LORD,*
both small and great together.

14May the LORD increase you
more and more,*
you and your children after you.

15May you be blessed by the LORD,*
the maker of heaven and earth.

16The heaven of heavens is the LORD'S,*
but he entrusted the earth
to its peoples.

17The dead do not praise the LORD,*
nor all those
who go down into silence;

18but we will bless the LORD,*
from this time forth forevermore.
Hallelujah!

116

1 I love the LORD, because he has heard
the voice of my supplication,*
because he has inclined his ear to me
whenever I called upon him.

2 The cords of death entangled me;
the grip of the grave took hold of me;*
I came to grief and sorrow.

3 Then I called
upon the name of the LORD:*
"O LORD, I pray you, save my life."

4 Gracious is the LORD and righteous;*
our God is full of compassion.

5 The LORD watches over the innocent;*
I was brought very low,
and he helped me.

6 Turn again to your rest, O my soul,*
for the LORD has treated you well.

7 For you have rescued
my life from death,*
my eyes from tears,
and my feet from stumbling.

8 I will walk in the presence of the LORD*
in the land of the living.

9 I believed, even when I said,
"I have been brought very low."*
In my distress I said,
"No one can be trusted."

10 How shall I repay the LORD*
for all the good things
he has done for me?

11 I will lift up the cup of salvation*
and call upon
the name of the LORD.

12 I will fulfill my vows to the LORD*
in the presence of all his people.

13 Precious in the sight of the LORD*
is the death of his servants.

14 O LORD, I am your servant;*
I am your servant
and the child of your handmaid;
you have freed me from my bonds.

15 I will offer you the sacrifice
of thanksgiving*
and call
upon the name of the LORD.

16 I will fulfill my vows to the LORD*
in the presence of all his people,

17 in the courts of the LORD's house,*
in the midst of you, O Jerusalem.
Hallelujah!

117

1 Praise the LORD, all you nations;*
laud him, all you peoples.

2 For his lovingkindness
toward us is great,*
and the faithfulness of the LORD
endures forever.
Hallelujah!

118

1 Give thanks to the LORD,
for he is good;*
his mercy endures forever.

2 Let Israel now proclaim,*
"His mercy endures forever."

3 Let the house of Aaron now proclaim,*
"His mercy endures forever."

4 Let those who fear the LORD
now proclaim,*
"His mercy endures forever."

5 I called to the LORD in my distress;*
the LORD answered
by setting me free.

6 The LORD is at my side,
therefore I will not fear;*
what can anyone do to me?

7 The LORD is at my side to help me;*
I will triumph
over those who hate me.

8 It is better to rely on the LORD*
than to put any trust in flesh.

9 It is better to rely on the LORD*
than to put any trust in rulers.

10 All the ungodly encompass me;*
in the name of the LORD
I will repel them.

11 They hem me in,
they hem me in on every side;*
in the name of the LORD
I will repel them.

12 They swarm about me like bees;
they blaze like a fire of thorns;*
in the name of the LORD
I will repel them.

13 I was pressed so hard that I almost fell,*
but the LORD came to my help.

14 The LORD is my strength and my song,*
and he has become my salvation.

15 There is a sound
of exultation and victory*
in the tents of the righteous:

16 "The right hand of the LORD
has triumphed!*
The right hand of the LORD is exalted!
The right hand of the LORD
has triumphed!"

17 I shall not die, but live,*
and declare the works of the LORD.

18 The LORD has punished me sorely,*
but he did not hand me over to death

19 Open for me the gates of righteousness;*
I will enter them;
I will offer thanks to the LORD.

20 "This is the gate of the LORD;*
he who is righteous may enter."

21 I will give thanks to you,
for you answered me*
and have become my salvation.

22 The same stone
which the builders rejected*
has become the chief cornerstone.

23 This is the LORD's doing,*
and it is marvelous in our eyes.

24 On this day the LORD has acted;*
we will rejoice and be glad in it.

25 Hosanna, LORD, hosanna!*
LORD, send us now success.

26 Blessed is he
who comes in the name of the Lord;*
we bless you
from the house of the LORD.

27 God is the LORD;
he has shined upon us;*
form a procession with branches
up to the horns of the altar.

28 "You are my God, and I will thank you;*
you are my God,
and I will exalt you."

29 Give thanks to the LORD,
for he is good;*
his mercy endures forever.

119

Aleph

1 Happy are they
whose way is blameless,*
who walk in the law of the LORD!

2 Happy are they
who observe his decrees*
and seek him with all their hearts!

3 Who never do any wrong,*
but always walk in his ways.

4 You laid down your commandments,*
that we should fully keep them.

5 Oh, that my ways were made so direct*
that I might keep your statutes!

6 Then I should not be put to shame,*
when I regard
all your commandments.

7 I will thank you
with an unfeigned heart,*
when I have learned
your righteous judgments.

8 I will keep your statutes;*
do not utterly forsake me.

Beth

9 How shall a young man
cleanse his way?*
By keeping to your words.

10 With my whole heart I seek you;*
let me not stray
from your commandments.

11 I treasure your promise in my heart,*
that I may not sin against you.

12 Blessed are you, O LORD;*
instruct me in your statutes.

13 With my lips will I recite*
all the judgments of your mouth.

14 I have taken greater delight
in the way of your decrees*
than in all manner of riches.

15 I will meditate
on your commandments*
and give attention to your ways.

16 My delight is in your statutes;*
I will not forget your word.

Gimel

17 Deal bountifully with your servant,*
that I may live and keep your word.

18 Open my eyes, that I may see*
the wonders of your law.

19 I am a stranger here on earth;*
do not hide
your commandments from me.

20 My soul is consumed at all times*
with longing for your judgments.

21 You have rebuked the insolent;*
cursed are they who stray
from your commandments!

22 Turn from me shame and rebuke,*
for I have kept your decrees.

23 Even though rulers
sit and plot against me,*
I will meditate on your statutes.

24 For your decrees are my delight,*
and they are my counselors.

Daleth

25 My soul cleaves to the dust;*
give me life according to your word.

26 I have confessed my ways,
and you answered me;*
instruct me in your statutes.

27 Make me understand
the way of your commandments,*
that I may meditate
on your marvelous works.

28 My soul melts away for sorrow;*
strengthen me
according to your word.

29 Take from me the way of lying;*
let me find grace through your law.

30 I have chosen the way of faithfulness;*
I have set your judgments before me.

31 I hold fast to your decrees;*
O LORD, let me not be put to shame.

32 I will run
the way of your commandments,*
for you have set my heart at liberty.

He

33 Teach me, O LORD,
the way of your statutes,*
and I shall keep it to the end.

34 Give me understanding,
and I shall keep your law;*
I shall keep it with all my heart.

35 Make me go
in the path of your commandments,*
for that is my desire.

36 Incline my heart to your decrees*
and not to unjust gain.

37 Turn my eyes from watching
what is worthless;*
give me life in your ways.

38 Fulfill your promise to your servant,*
which you make
to those who fear you.

39 Turn away the reproach which I dread,*
because your judgments are good.

40 Behold, I long for your commandments;*
in your righteousness preserve my life.

Waw

41 Let your lovingkindness
come to me, O LORD,*
and your salvation,
according to your promise.

42 Then shall I have a word
for those who taunt me,*
because I trust in your words.

43 Do not take the word of truth
out of my mouth,*
for my hope is in your judgments.

44 I shall continue to keep your law;*
I shall keep it forever and ever.

45 I will walk at liberty,*
because I study your commandments.

46 I will tell of your decrees before kings*

and will not be ashamed.

47 I delight in your commandments,*
which I have always loved.

48 I will lift up my hands
to your commandments,*
and I will meditate on your statutes.

Zayin

49 Remember your word to your servant,*
because you have given me hope.

50 This is my comfort in my trouble,*
that your promise gives me life.

51 The proud have derided me cruelly,*
but I have not turned from your law.

52 When I remember
your judgments of old,*
O LORD, I take great comfort.

53 I am filled with a burning rage,*
because of the wicked
who forsake your law.

54 Your statutes have been
like songs to me*
wherever I have lived as a stranger.

55 I remember your name in the night,
O LORD,*
and dwell upon your law.

56 This is how it has been with me,*
because
I have kept your commandments.

Heth

57 You only are my portion, O LORD;*
I have promised to keep your words.

58 I entreat you with all my heart:*
Be merciful to me
according to your promise.

59 I have considered my ways*
and turned my feet
toward your decrees.

60 I hasten and do not tarry*
to keep your commandments.

61 Though the cords
of the wicked entangle me,*
I do not forget your law.

62 At midnight I will rise
to give you thanks,*
because of your righteous judgments.

63 I am a companion of all who fear you*
and of those
who keep your commandments.

64 The earth, O LORD,
is full of your love;*
instruct me in your statutes.

Teth

65 O LORD, you have dealt graciously
with your servant,*
according to your word.

66 Teach me discernment and knowledge,*
for I have believed
in your commandments.

67 Before I was afflicted I went astray,*
but now I keep your word.

68 You are good and you bring forth good;*
instruct me in your statutes.

69 The proud have smeared me with lies,*
but I will keep your commandments
with my whole heart.

70 Their heart is gross and fat,*
but my delight is in your law.

71 It is good for me
that I have been afflicted,*
that I might learn your statutes.

72 The law of your mouth is dearer to me*
than thousands in gold and silver.

Yodh

73 Your hands have made me
and fashioned me;*
give me understanding,
that I may learn your commandments.

74 Those who fear you will be glad
when they see me,*
because I trust in your word.

75 I know, O LORD,
that your judgments are right*
and that in faithfulness
you have afflicted me.

76 Let your lovingkindness
be my comfort,*
as you have promised
to your servant.

77 Let your compassion come to me,
that I may live,*

for your law is my delight.
78 Let the arrogant be put to shame,
for they wrong me with lies;*
but I will meditate
on your commandments.
79 Let those who fear you turn to me,*
and also those
who know your decrees.
80 Let my heart be sound in your statutes,*
that I may not be put to shame.

Kaph

81 My soul has longed for your salvation;*
I have put my hope in your word.
82 My eyes have failed
from watching for your promise,*
and I say,
"When will you comfort me?"
83 I have become
like a leather flask in the smoke,*
but I have not forgotten
your statutes.
84 How much longer must I wait?*
When will you give judgment
against those who persecute me?
85 The proud have dug pits for me;*
they do not keep your law.
86 All your commandments are true;*
help me,
for they persecute me with lies.
87 They had almost
made an end of me on earth,*
but I have not forsaken
your commandments.
88 In your lovingkindness, revive me,*
that I may keep
the decrees of your mouth.

Lamedh

89 O Lord, your word is everlasting;*
it stands firm in the heavens.
90 Your faithfulness remains
from one generation to another;*
you established the earth,
and it abides.
91 By your decree
these continue to this day,*
for all things are your servants.
92 If my delight had not been in your law,*
I should have perished
in my affliction.
93 I will never forget
your commandments,*
because by them you give me life.
94 I am yours—
oh, that you would save me!—*
for I study your commandments.
95 Though the wicked lie in wait for me
to destroy me,*
I will apply my mind to your decrees.
96 I see that all things come to an end,*
but your commandment
has no bounds.

Mem

97 Oh, how I love your law!*
All the day long it is in my mind.
98 Your commandment
has made me wiser than my enemies,*
and it is always with me.
99 I have more understanding
than all my teachers,*
for your decrees are my study.
100 I am wiser than the elders,*
because I observe
your commandments.
101 I restrain my feet from every evil way,*
that I may keep your word.
102 I do not shrink from your judgments,*
because you yourself have taught me.
103 How sweet are your words to my taste!*
They are sweeter than honey
to my mouth.
104 Through your commandments
I gain understanding;*
therefore I hate every lying way.

Nun

105 Your word is a lantern to my feet*
and a light upon my path.
106 I have sworn and am determined*
to keep your righteous judgments.
107 I am deeply troubled;*

preserve my life, O LORD,
according to your word.

108 Accept, O LORD,
the willing tribute of my lips,*
and teach me your judgments.

109 My life is always in my hand,*
yet I do not forget your law.

110 The wicked have set a trap for me,*
but I have not strayed
from your commandments.

111 Your decrees are my inheritance
forever;*
truly, they are the joy of my heart.

112 I have applied my heart
to fulfill your statutes*
forever and to the end.

Samekh

113 I hate those who have a divided heart,*
but your law do I love.

114 You are my refuge and shield;*
my hope is in your word.

115 Away from me, you wicked!*
I will keep
the commandments of my God.

116 Sustain me according to your promise,
that I may live,*
and let me not
be disappointed in my hope.

117 Hold me up, and I shall be safe,*
and my delight
shall be ever in your statutes.

118 You spurn all
who stray from your statutes;*
their deceitfulness is in vain.

119 In your sight all the wicked of the earth
are but dross;*
therefore I love your decrees.

120 My flesh trembles with dread of you;*
I am afraid of your judgments.

Ayin

121 I have done what is just and right;*
do not deliver me to my oppressors.

122 Be surety for your servant's good;*
let not the proud oppress me.

123 My eyes have failed from watching
for your salvation*
and for your righteous promise.

124 Deal with your servant
according to your lovingkindness,*
and teach me your statutes.

125 I am your servant;
grant me understanding,*
that I may know your decrees.

126 It is time for you to act, O LORD,*
for they have broken your law.

127 Truly, I love your commandments*
more than gold and precious stones.

128 I hold all your commandments
to be right for me;*
all paths of falsehood I abhor.

Pe

129 Your decrees are wonderful;*
therefore I obey them
with all my heart.

130 When your word goes forth
it gives light;*
it gives understanding to the simple.

131 I open my mouth and pant;*
I long for your commandments.

132 Turn to me in mercy,*
as you always do to those
who love your name.

133 Steady my footsteps in your word;*
let no iniquity
have dominion over me.

134 Rescue me
from those who oppress me,*
and I will
keep your commandments.

135 Let your countenance
shine upon your servant*
and teach me your statutes.

136 My eyes shed streams of tears,*
because people
do not keep your law.

Sadhe

137 You are righteous, O LORD,*
and upright are your judgments.

138 You have issued your decrees*
with justice
and in perfect faithfulness.

139 My indignation has consumed me,*
because my enemies
forget your words.

140 Your word has been tested
to the uttermost,*
and your servant holds it dear.

141 I am small and of little account,*
yet I do not
forget your commandments.

142 Your justice is an everlasting justice*
and your law is the truth.

143 Trouble and distress
have come upon me,*
yet your commandments
are my delight.

144 The righteousness of your decrees
is everlasting;*
grant me understanding,
that I may live.

Qoph

145 I call with my whole heart;*
answer me, O LORD,
that I may keep your statutes.

146 I call to you;
oh, that you would save me!*
I will keep your decrees.

147 Early in the morning I cry out to you,*
for in your word is my trust.

148 My eyes are open in the night watches,*
that I may meditate
upon your promise.

149 Hear my voice, O LORD,
according to your lovingkindness;*
according to your judgments,
give me life.

150 They draw near
who in malice persecute me;*
they are very far from your law.

151 You, O LORD, are near at hand,*
and all your commandments are true.

152 Long have I known from your decrees*
that you have
established them forever.

Resh

153 Behold my affliction and deliver me,*
for I do not forget your law.

154 Plead my cause and redeem me;*
according to your promise,
give me life.

155 Deliverance is far from the wicked,*
for they do not study your statutes.

156 Great is your compassion, O LORD;*
preserve my life,
according to your judgments.

157 There are many
who persecute and oppress me,*
yet I have not swerved
from your decrees.

158 I look with loathing at the faithless,*
for they have not kept your word.

159 See how I love your commandments!*
O LORD, in your mercy, preserve me.

160 The heart of your word is truth;*
all your righteous judgments
endure forevermore.

Shin

161 Rulers have persecuted me
without a cause,*
but my heart stands
in awe of your word.

162 I am as glad because of your promise*
as one who finds great spoils.

163 As for lies, I hate and abhor them,*
but your law is my love.

164 Seven times a day do I praise you,*
because
of your righteous judgments.

165 Great peace have they
who love your law;*
for them there is no stumbling block.

166 I have hoped for your salvation,
O LORD,*
and I have fulfilled
your commandments.

167 I have kept your decrees*
and I have loved them deeply.

168 I have kept
your commandments and decrees,*
for all my ways are before you.

Taw

169 Let my cry come before you, O LORD; *
give me understanding,
according to your word.

170 Let my supplication come before you; *
deliver me,
according to your promise.

171 My lips shall pour forth your praise, *
when you teach me your statutes.

172 My tongue shall sing of your promise, *
for all your commandments
are righteous.

173 Let your hand be ready to help me, *
for I have chosen
your commandments.

174 I long for your salvation, O LORD, *
and your law is my delight.

175 Let me live, and I will praise you, *
and let your judgments help me.

176 I have gone astray like a sheep
that is lost; *
search for your servant,
for I do not forget
your commandments.

121

1 I lift up my eyes to the hills; *
from where is my help to come?

2 My help comes from the LORD, *
the maker of heaven and earth.

3 He will not let your foot be moved *
and he who watches over you
will not fall asleep.

4 Behold, he
who keeps watch over Israel *
shall neither slumber nor sleep;

5 the LORD himself watches over you; *
the LORD is your shade
at your right hand,

6 so that the sun
shall not strike you by day, *
nor the moon by night.

7 The LORD
shall preserve you from all evil; *
it is he who shall keep you safe.

8 The LORD shall watch over
your going out and your coming in, *
from this time forth forevermore.

122

1 I was glad when they said to me, *
"Let us go to the house of the LORD."

2 Now our feet are standing *
within your gates, O Jerusalem.

3 Jerusalem is built as a city *
that is at unity with itself;

4 to which the tribes go up,
the tribes of the LORD, *
the assembly of Israel,
to praise the name of the LORD.

5 For there are the thrones of judgment, *
the thrones of the house of David.

6 Pray for the peace of Jerusalem: *
"May they prosper who love you.

7 Peace be within your walls *
and quietness within your towers.

8 For my brethren
and companions' sake, *
I pray for your prosperity.

9 Because of the house
of the LORD our God, *
I will seek to do you good."

123

1 To you I lift up my eyes, *
to you enthroned in the heavens.

2 As the eyes of servants
look to the hand of their masters, *
and the eyes of a maid
to the hand of her mistress,

3 so our eyes look to the LORD our God, *
until he show us his mercy.

4 Have mercy upon us, O LORD,
have mercy, *
for we have had
more than enough of contempt,

5 too much of the scorn
of the indolent rich, *
and of the derision of the proud.

124

1 If the LORD had not been on our side,*
let Israel now say;
2 if the LORD had not been on our side,*
when enemies rose up against us,
3 then would they have
swallowed us up alive*
in their fierce anger toward us;
4 then would the waters
have overwhelmed us*
and the torrent gone over us;
5 then would the raging waters*
have gone right over us.
6 Blessed be the LORD! *
He has not given us over
to be a prey for their teeth.
7 We have escaped like a bird
from the snare of the fowler;*
the snare is broken,
and we have escaped.
8 Our help is in the name of the LORD,*
the maker of heaven and earth.

125

1 Those who trust in the LORD
are like Mount Zion,*
which cannot be moved,
but stands fast forever.
2 The hills stand about Jerusalem;*
so does the LORD stand
round about his people,
from this time forth forevermore.
3 The scepter of the wicked
shall not hold sway over the land
alloted to the just,*
so that the just
shall not put their hands to evil.
4 Show your goodness, O LORD,
to those who are good*
and to those who are true of heart.
5 As for those
who turn aside to crooked ways,
the LORD will lead them away
with the evildoers;*
but peace be upon Israel.

126

1 When the LORD
restored the fortunes of Zion,*
then were we like those who dream.
2 Then was our mouth
filled with laughter,*
and our tongue with shouts of joy.
3 Then they said among the nations,*
"The LORD has done
great things for them."
4 The LORD has done great things for us,*
and we are glad indeed.
5 Restore our fortunes, O LORD,*
like the watercourses of the Negev.
6 Those who sowed with tears*
will reap with songs of joy.
7 Those who go out weeping,
carrying the seed,*
will come again with joy,
shouldering their sheaves.

127

1 Unless the LORD builds the house,*
their labor is in vain who build it.
2 Unless the LORD watches over the city,*
in vain the watchman keeps his vigil.
3 It is in vain that you rise so early
and go to bed so late;*
vain, too, to eat the bread of toil,
for he gives to his beloved sleep.
4 Children are a heritage from the LORD,*
and the fruit of the womb is a gift.
5 Like arrows in the hand of a warrior*
are the children of one's youth.
6 Happy is the man
who has his quiver full of them! *
He shall not be put to shame
when he contends
with his enemies in the gate.

128

1 Happy are they all who fear the LORD,*
and who follow in his ways!

2 You shall eat the fruit of your labor; *
happiness and prosperity
shall be yours.
3 Your wife shall be like a fruitful vine
within your house, *
your children like olive shoots
round about your table.
4 The man who fears the LORD *
shall thus indeed be blessed.
5 The LORD bless you from Zion, *
and may you see the prosperity
of Jerusalem all the days of your life.
6 May you live
to see your children's children; *
may peace be upon Israel.

130

1 Out of the depths
have I called to you, O LORD;
LORD, hear my voice; *
let your ears consider well
the voice of my supplication.
2 If you, LORD,
were to note what is done amiss, *
O Lord, who could stand?
3 For there is forgiveness with you; *
therefore you shall be feared.
4 I wait for the LORD;
my soul waits for him; *
in his word is my hope.
5 My soul waits for the LORD,
more than watchmen for the morning, *
more than watchmen
for the morning.
6 O Israel, wait for the LORD, *
for with the LORD there is mercy;
7 with him
there is plenteous redemption, *
and he shall redeem Israel
from all their sins.

131

1 O LORD, I am not proud; *
I have no haughty looks.
2 I do not occupy myself
with great matters, *
or with things
that are too hard for me.
3 But I still my soul and make it quiet,
like a child upon its mother's breast; *
my soul is quieted within me.
4 O Israel, wait upon the LORD, *
from this time forth forevermore.

132

1 LORD, remember David, *
and all the hardships he endured;
2 how he swore an oath to the LORD *
and vowed a vow
to the Mighty One of Jacob:
3 "I will not come under the roof
of my house, *
nor climb up into my bed;
4 I will not allow my eyes to sleep, *
nor let my eyelids slumber;
5 until I find a place for the LORD, *
a dwelling
for the Mighty One of Jacob."
6 "The ark! We heard it was in Ephratah; *
we found it in the fields of Jearim.
7 Let us go to God's dwelling-place; *
let us fall upon our knees
before his footstool."
8 Arise, O LORD,
into your resting-place, *
you and the ark of your strength.
9 Let your priests be clothed
with righteousness; *
let your faithful people sing with joy.
10 For your servant David's sake, *
do not turn away
the face of your anointed.
11 The LORD has sworn an oath to David; *
in truth, he will not break it:
12 "A son, the fruit of your body *
will I set upon your throne.
13 If your children keep my covenant
and my testimonies
that I shall teach them, *

their children
will sit upon your throne forevermore."
14 For the LORD has chosen Zion; *
he has desired her for his habitation:
15 "This shall be my resting-place forever; *
here will I dwell, for I delight in her.
16 I will surely bless her provisions, *
and satisfy her poor with bread.
17 I will clothe her priests with salvation, *
and her faithful people
will rejoice and sing.
18 There will I make
the horn of David flourish; *
I have prepared a lamp
for my anointed.
19 As for his enemies,
I will clothe them with shame; *
but as for him, his crown will shine."

133

1 Oh, how good and pleasant it is *
when brethren live together in unity!
2 It is like fine oil upon the head *
that runs down upon the beard,
3 upon the beard of Aaron, *
and runs down
upon the collar of his robe.
4 It is like the dew of Hermon *
that falls upon the hills of Zion.
5 For there the LORD
has ordained the blessing: *
life forevermore.

134

1 Behold, now! Bless the LORD,
all you servants of the LORD, *
you that stand by night
in the house of the LORD.
2 Lift up your hands in the holy place
and bless the LORD; *
the LORD who made heaven
and earth bless you out of Zion.

135

1 Hallelujah!
Praise the name of the LORD; *
give praise, you servants of the LORD,
2 you who stand
in the house of the LORD, *
in the courts of the house of our God.
3 Praise the LORD, for the LORD is good; *
sing praises to his name,
for it is lovely.
4 For the LORD
has chosen Jacob for himself *
and Israel for his own possession.
5 For I know that the LORD is great, *
and that our Lord is above all gods.
6 The LORD does whatever pleases him,
in heaven and on earth, *
in the seas and all the deeps.
7 He brings up rain clouds
from the ends of the earth; *
he sends out lightning with the rain,
and brings the winds
out of his storehouse.
8 It was he who
struck down the firstborn of Egypt, *
the firstborn both of man and beast.
9 He sent signs and wonders
into the midst of you, O Egypt, *
against Pharaoh and all his servants.
10 He overthrew many nations *
and put mighty kings to death:
11 Sihon, king of the Amorites,
and Og, the king of Bashan, *
and all the kingdoms of Canaan.
12 He gave their land to be an inheritance, *
an inheritance for Israel his people.
13 O LORD, your name is everlasting; *
your renown, O LORD,
endures from age to age.
14 For the LORD gives his people justice *
and shows compassion to his servants.
15 The idols of the heathen
are silver and gold, *
the work of human hands.
16 They have mouths,
but they cannot speak; *

eyes have they, but they cannot see.
17 They have ears, but they cannot hear; *
neither is there any breath
in their mouth.
18 Those who make them are like them, *
and so are all
who put their trust in them.
19 Bless the LORD, O house of Israel; *
O house of Aaron, bless the LORD.
20 Bless the LORD, O house of Levi; *
you who fear the LORD,
bless the LORD.
21 Blessed be the LORD out of Zion, *
who dwells in Jerusalem.
Hallelujah!

136

1 Give thanks to the LORD,
for he is good, *
for his mercy endures forever.
2 Give thanks to the God of gods, *
for his mercy endures forever.
3 Give thanks to the Lord of lords, *
for his mercy endures forever;
4 who only does great wonders, *
for his mercy endures forever;
5 who by wisdom made the heavens, *
for his mercy endures forever;
6 who spread out the earth
upon the waters, *
for his mercy endures forever;
7 who created great lights, *
for his mercy endures forever;
8 the sun to rule the day, *
for his mercy endures forever;
9 the moon and the stars
to govern the night, *
for his mercy endures forever;
10 who struck down
the firstborn of Egypt, *
for his mercy endures forever;
11 and brought out Israel
from among them, *
for his mercy endures forever;
12 with a mighty hand
and a stretched-out arm, *
for his mercy endures forever;
13 who divided the Red Sea in two, *
for his mercy endures forever;
14 and made Israel to pass
through the midst of it, *
for his mercy endures forever;
15 but swept Pharaoh and his army
into the Red Sea, *
for his mercy endures forever;
16 who led his people
through the wilderness, *
for his mercy endures forever;
17 who struck down great kings, *
for his mercy endures forever;
18 and slew mighty kings, *
for his mercy endures forever;
19 Sihon, king of the Amorites, *
for his mercy endures forever;
20 and Og, the king of Bashan, *
for his mercy endures forever;
21 and gave away their lands
for an inheritance, *
for his mercy endures forever;
22 an inheritance for Israel his servant, *
for his mercy endures forever;
23 who remembered us in our low estate, *
for his mercy endures forever;
24 and delivered us from our enemies, *
for his mercy endures forever;
25 who gives food to all creatures, *
for his mercy endures forever.
26 Give thanks to the God of heaven, *
for his mercy endures forever.

138

1 I will give thanks to you, O LORD,
with my whole heart; *
before the gods
I will sing your praise.
2 I will bow down
toward your holy temple
and praise your name, *
because of your love
and faithfulness;

3 for you have glorified your name*
and your word above all things.
4 When I called, you answered me;*
you increased my strength
within me.
5 All the kings of the earth
will praise you, O LORD,*
when they have heard
the words of your mouth.
6 They will sing of the ways of the LORD,*
that great is the glory of the LORD.
7 Though the LORD be high,
he cares for the lowly;*
he perceives the haughty from afar.
8 Though I walk in the midst of trouble,
you keep me safe;*
you stretch forth your hand
against the fury of my enemies;
your right hand shall save me.
9 The LORD will make good
his purpose for me;*
O LORD, your love endures forever;
do not abandon the works
of your hands.

139

1 LORD, you have searched me out
and known me;*
you know my sitting down
and my rising up;
you discern my thoughts from afar.
2 You trace my journeys
and my resting-places*
and are acquainted with all my ways.
3 Indeed, there is not a word on my lips,*
but you, O LORD, know it altogether.
4 You press upon me behind and before*
and lay your hand upon me.
5 Such knowledge is
too wonderful for me;*
it is so high that I cannot attain to it.
6 Where can I go then from your Spirit?*
Where can I flee from your presence?
7 If I climb up to heaven, you are there;*
if I make the grave my bed,
you are there also.
8 If I take the wings of the morning*
and dwell
in the uttermost parts of the sea,
9 even there your hand will lead me*
and your right hand hold me fast.
10 If I say,
"Surely the darkness will cover me,*
and the light around me
turn to night,"
11 darkness is not dark to you;
the night is as bright as the day;*
darkness and light
to you are both alike.
12 For you yourself
created my inmost parts;*
you knit me together
in my mother's womb.
13 I will thank you
because I am marvelously made;*
your works are wonderful,
and I know it well.
14 My body was not hidden from you,*
while I was being made in secret
and woven in the depths of the earth.
15 Your eyes beheld my limbs,
yet unfinished in the womb;
all of them were written in your book;*
they were fashioned day by day,
when as yet there was none of them.
16 How deep I find your thoughts, O God!*
How great is the sum of them!
17 If I were to count them,
they would be more in number
than the sand;*
to count them all,
my life span would need
to be like yours.
18 Oh, that you
would slay the wicked, O God!*
You that thirst for blood,
depart from me.
19 They speak despitefully against you;*
your enemies
take your name in vain.
20 Do I not hate those, O LORD,
who hate you?*
And do I not loathe those
who rise up against you?

21 I hate them with a perfect hatred; *
they have become my own enemies.
22 Search me out, O God,
and know my heart; *
try me
and know my restless thoughts.
23 Look well
whether there be any wickedness in me, *
and lead me
in the way that is everlasting.

141

1 O LORD, I call to you;
come to me quickly; *
hear my voice when I cry to you.
2 Let my prayer
be set forth in your sight as incense, *
the lifting up of my hands
as the evening sacrifice.
3 Set a watch before my mouth,
O LORD,
and guard the door of my lips; *
let not my heart
incline to any evil thing.
4 Let me not be occupied
in wickedness with evildoers, *
nor eat of their choice foods.
5 Let the righteous smite me
in friendly rebuke;
let not the oil of the unrighteous
anoint my head; *
for my prayer is continually
against their wicked deeds.
6 Let their rulers
be overthrown in stony places, *
that they
may know my words are true.
7 As when a plowman
turns over the earth in furrows, *
let their bones be scattered
at the mouth of the grave.
8 But my eyes are turned to you,
Lord GOD; *
in you I take refuge;
do not strip me of my life.
9 Protect me from the snare
which they have laid for me *
and from the traps of the evildoers.
10 Let the wicked fall into their own nets, *
while I myself escape.

142

1 I cry to the LORD with my voice; *
to the LORD
I make loud supplication.
2 I pour out my complaint before him *
and tell him all my trouble.
3 When my spirit languishes within me,
you know my path; *
in the way wherein I walk
they have hidden a trap for me.
4 I look to my right hand
and find no one who knows me; *
I have no place to flee to,
and no one cares for me.
5 I cry out to you, O LORD; *
I say, "You are my refuge,
my portion in the land of the living."
6 Listen to my cry for help,
for I have been brought very low; *
save me from those who pursue me,
for they are too strong for me.
7 Bring me out of prison,
that I may give thanks to your name; *
when you
have dealt bountifully with me,
the righteous will gather around me.

143

1 LORD, hear my prayer,
and in your faithfulness
heed my supplications; *
answer me in your righteousness.
2 Enter not into judgment
with your servant, *
for in your sight
shall no one living be justified.
3 For my enemy has sought my life;
he has crushed me to the ground; *

he has made me live in dark places
like those who are long dead.
4 My spirit faints within me;*
my heart within me is desolate.
5 I remember the time past;
I muse upon all your deeds;*
I consider the works of your hands.
6 I spread out my hands to you;*
my soul gasps to you
like a thirsty land.
7 O LORD, make haste to answer me;
my spirit fails me;*
do not hide your face from me
or I shall be like those
who go down to the pit.
8 Let me hear of your lovingkindness
in the morning,
for I put my trust in you;*
show me the road that I must walk,
for I lift up my soul to you.
9 Deliver me from my enemies, O LORD,*
for I flee to you for refuge.
10 Teach me to do what pleases you,
for you are my God;*
let your good Spirit
lead me on level ground.
11 Revive me, O LORD,
for your name's sake;*
for your righteousness' sake,
bring me out of trouble.
12 Of your goodness, destroy my enemies
and bring all my foes to naught,*
for truly I am your servant.

145

1 I will exalt you, O God my king,*
and bless your name
forever and ever.
2 Every day will I bless you*
and praise your name
forever and ever.
3 Great is the LORD
and greatly to be praised;*
there is no end to his greatness.
4 One generation
shall praise your works to another*
and shall declare your power.
5 I will ponder the glorious splendor
of your majesty*
and all your marvelous works.
6 They shall speak of the might
of your wondrous acts,*
and I will tell of your greatness.
7 They shall publish the remembrance
of your great goodness;*
they shall sing
of your righteous deeds.
8 The LORD is gracious
and full of compassion,*
slow to anger and of great kindness.
9 The LORD is loving to everyone*
and his compassion
is over all his works.
10 All your works praise you, O LORD,*
and your faithful servants bless you.
11 They make known
the glory of your kingdom*
and speak of your power;
12 that the peoples
may know of your power*
and the glorious splendor
of your kingdom.
13 Your kingdom
is an everlasting kingdom;*
your dominion endures
throughout all ages.
14 The LORD is faithful in all his words*
and merciful in all his deeds.
15 The LORD upholds all those who fall;*
he lifts up those
who are bowed down.
16 The eyes of all wait upon you, O LORD,*
and you give them their food
in due season.
17 You open wide your hand*
and satisfy the needs
of every living creature.
18 The LORD is righteous in all his ways*
and loving in all his works.
19 The LORD is near to those
who call upon him,*

to all who call upon him faithfully.
20 He fulfills the desire
of those who fear him;*
he hears their cry and helps them.
21 The LORD preserves all those
who love him,*
but he destroys all the wicked.
22 My mouth shall speak
the praise of the LORD;*
let all flesh bless his holy name
forever and ever.

146

1 Hallelujah!
Praise the LORD, O my soul!*
I will praise the LORD
as long as I live;
I will sing praises to my God
while I have my being.
2 Put not your trust in rulers,
nor in any child of earth,*
for there is no help in them.
3 When they breathe their last,
they return to earth,*
and in that day their thoughts perish.
4 Happy are they who
have the God of Jacob for their help,*
whose hope is in the LORD
their God;
5 who made heaven and earth, the seas,
and all that is in them;*
who keeps his promise forever;
6 who gives justice to those
who are oppressed,*
and food to those who hunger.
7 The LORD sets the prisoners free;
the LORD opens the eyes of the blind;*
the LORD lifts up those
who are bowed down;
8 the LORD loves the righteous;
the LORD cares for the stranger;*
he sustains the orphan and widow,
but frustrates the way of the wicked.
9 The LORD shall reign forever,*
your God, O Zion,
throughout all generations.
Hallelujah!

147

1 Hallelujah!
How good it is
to sing praises to our God!*
How pleasant it is
to honor him with praise!
2 The LORD rebuilds Jerusalem;*
he gathers the exiles of Israel.
3 He heals the brokenhearted*
and binds up their wounds.
4 He counts the number of the stars*
and calls them all by their names.
5 Great is our LORD
and mighty in power;*
there is no limit to his wisdom.
6 The LORD lifts up the lowly,*
but casts the wicked to the ground.
7 Sing to the LORD with thanksgiving;*
make music to our God
upon the harp.
8 He covers the heavens with clouds*
and prepares rain for the earth;
9 he makes grass to grow
upon the mountains*
and green plants to serve mankind.
10 He provides food for flocks and herds*
and for the young ravens
when they cry.
11 He is not impressed
by the might of a horse;*
he has no pleasure
in the strength of a man;
12 but the LORD has pleasure
in those who fear him,*
in those who
await his gracious favor.
13 Worship the LORD, O Jerusalem;*
praise your God, O Zion;
14 for he has strengthened
the bars of your gates;*
he has blessed
your children within you.

15 He has established peace
on your borders;*
he satisfies you with the finest wheat.
16 He sends out his command
to the earth,*
and his word runs very swiftly.
17 He gives snow like wool;*
he scatters hoarfrost like ashes.
18 He scatters his hail like bread crumbs;*
Who can stand against his cold?
19 He sends forth his word
and melts them;*
he blows with his wind,
and the waters flow.
20 He declares his word to Jacob,*
his statutes and his judgments
to Israel.
21 He has not done so
to any other nation;*
to them he has
not revealed his judgments.
Hallelujah!

148

1 Hallelujah!
Praise the LORD from the heavens;*
praise him in the heights.
2 Praise him, all you angels of his;*
praise him, all his host.
3 Praise him, sun and moon;*
praise him, all you shining stars.
4 Praise him, heaven of heavens,*
and you waters above the heavens.
5 Let them praise the name of the LORD;*
for he commanded,
and they were created.
6 He made them stand fast
forever and ever;*
he gave them a law
which shall not pass away.
7 Praise the LORD from the earth,*
you sea monsters and all deeps;
8 fire and hail, snow and fog,*
tempestuous wind, doing his will;
9 mountains and all hills,*
fruit trees and all cedars;
10 wild beasts and all cattle,*
creeping things and winged birds;
11 kings of the earth and all peoples,*
princes and all rulers of the world;
12 young men and maidens,*
old and young together.
13 Let them praise the name of the LORD,*
for his name only is exalted,
his splendor is over earth and heaven.
14 He has raised up strength for his people
and praise for all his loyal servants,*
the children of Israel,
a people who are near him.
Hallelujah!

149

1 Hallelujah!
Sing to the LORD a new song;*
sing his praise
in the congregation of the faithful.
2 Let Israel rejoice in his maker;*
let the children of Zion
be joyful in their king.
3 Let them praise his name in the dance;*
let them sing praise to him
with timbrel and harp.
4 For the LORD takes pleasure
in his people*
and adorns the poor with victory.
5 Let the faithful rejoice in triumph;*
let them be joyful on their beds.
6 Let the praises of God
be in their throat*
and a two-edged sword
in their hand;
7 to wreak vengeance on the nations*
and punishment on the peoples;
8 to bind their kings in chains*
and their nobles with links of iron;
9 to inflict on them
the judgment decreed;*
this is glory for all his faithful people.
Hallelujah!

150

1 Hallelujah!
Praise God in his holy temple;*
praise him
in the firmament of his power.
2 Praise him for his mighty acts;*
praise him for his excellent greatness.
3 Praise him
with the blast of the ram's horn;*
praise him with lyre and harp.
4 Praise him with timbrel and dance;*
praise him with strings and pipe.
5 Praise him with resounding cymbals;*
praise him
with loud-clanging cymbals.
6 Let everything that has breath*
praise the LORD.
Hallelujah!

SINGING THE PSALMS

The psalms are pointed for singing. They may be sung to the simple tones on the following page or to other systems of chant.

Each psalm verse has two parts; the division is marked by an asterisk (*). Tones 1 through 5 are divided into two parts at the single bar line. The asterisk (*) above this bar line indicates how the verse division fits the tone division. The first note (|o|) in each part of the tone is a reciting note, to which one or more syllables or words are sung. The point (´) above a syllable (or word) indicates the syllable (or word) where the singers move from the reciting note to the black notes.

Example. The first two verses of Psalm 8 are sung to tone 1 as shown below:

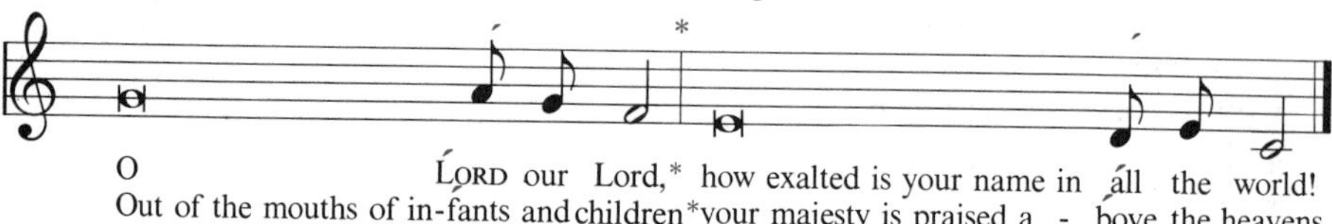
O LORD our Lord,* how exalted is your name in all the world!
Out of the mouths of in-fants and children*your majesty is praised a - bove the heavens.

Tones 6 through 10 are double tones, providing music for two Psalm verses. The double bar indicates the division between the verses. Each verse is divided into two parts and sung in the same manner as to tones 1–5.

Example. The first two verses of Psalm 8 are sung to tone 6 as shown below:

O LORD our Lord,*how exalted is your name in all the world!
Out of the mouths of in-fants and children*your majesty is praised a-bove the heavens.

Note. From the point (´) to the asterisk (*) or from the point (´) to the end of the verse, there are usually three syllables—one for each of the three remaining notes. When there are more than three syllables, the additional syllables are sung to the half (last) note. Occasionally a three-syllable word is sung to the two black notes by eliding the middle syllable, for example: *Ev-er-y* becomes *ev-'ry, of-fer-ing* becomes *of-f'ring, mar-vel-ous* becomes *mar-v'lous. Blessed* is sung *blest.*

Any psalm can be sung to any tone. The result is better, however, when the tone is matched to the text. The mood of the tone (bright, somber) should fit the mood of the text. The double tones (6–10) usually are best for longer texts, especially those with an even number of verses.

Canticles 15, 18, 19, 20, and 21 are pointed for singing to these or similar tones. They may also be sung to the tones of canticles 2, 3, 4, 5, and 6.

1
2
3
4
5
6
7
8
9
10

CONTENTS

CANTICLES

Jesus, Lamb of God 1
Chant settings of daily prayer canticles 2–6
Seasonal canticles 7–12
Old and New Testament canticles 13–21

HYMNS

The Church Year

Advent 22–38
Christmas 39–74
Epiphany 75–90
Lent 91–107
Holy Week 108–127
Easter 128–155
Ascension 156–159
Pentecost 160–164
The Holy Trinity 165–169
Christ the King 170–173
Lesser Festivals 174–186

The Church at Worship

Holy Baptism 187–195
Holy Communion 196–226
The Word 227–240
Beginning of Service 241–257
Close of Service 258–263
Morning 264–271
Evening 272–282
Pastors 283–286
Marriage 287–289

The Life of Faith

Justification 290–302
Repentance, Forgiveness 303–312
Christian Hope 313–352
Community in Christ 353–375
Witness 376–403
Stewardship 404–412
Society 413–437
Prayer 438–444
Trust, Guidance 445–485
Commitment 486–513
Praise, Adoration 514–551
Celebration, Jubilation 552–565

NATIONAL SONGS 566–569

CANTICLES

Jesus, Lamb of God 1

Agnus Dei

Je - sus, Lamb of God, have mer - cy on

us. Je - sus, bear - er of our

sins, have mer - cy on us.

Je - sus, re - deem - er of the world,

give us your peace, give us your peace.

2 Blessed Be the Lord

Benedictus

*

1 Blessed be the Lord,
the . . . . God of Israel; he has come to his people and set them free.

3 Through his holy prophets he promised of old that he would save us . . . from our enemies, from the hands of all who hate us.

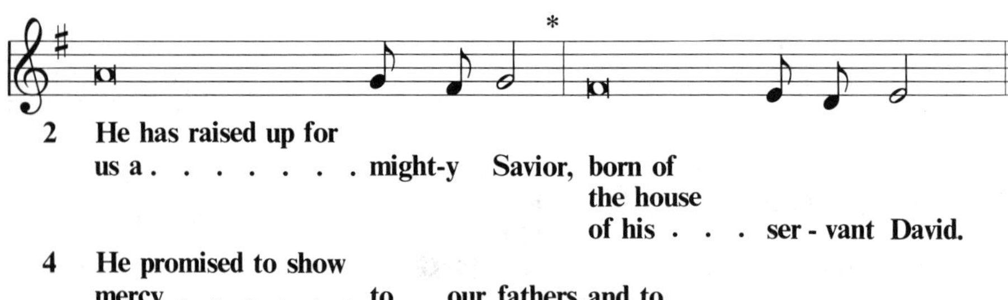
*

2 He has raised up for us a . . . . might-y Savior, born of the house of his . . . ser - vant David.

4 He promised to show mercy . . . . to our fathers and to remember his ho - ly covenant.

*

5 This was the oath he swore to our . . fa - ther Abraham: to set us free from the hands of our enemies,

7 You, my child, shall be called the prophet of the Most High, for you will go before the Lord to pre - pare his way,

6 free to worship him with - out fear, holy and righteous in his sight all the days . . . of our life.

8 to give his people knowledge . . . . . of sal - vation by the forgiveness of their sins.

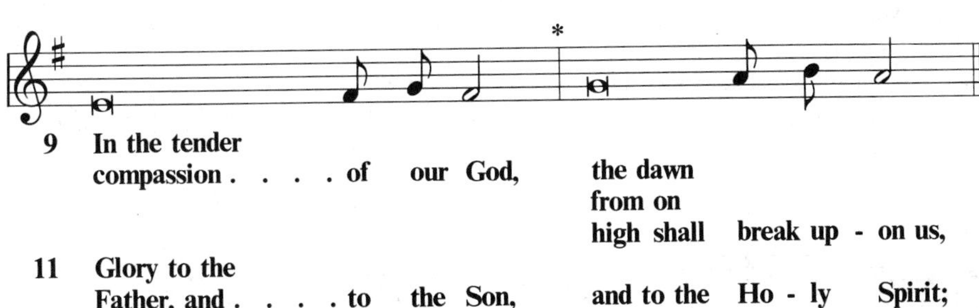

9 In the tender compassion . . . . of our God, the dawn from on high shall break up - on us,

11 Glory to the Father, and . . . . to the Son, and to the Ho - ly Spirit;

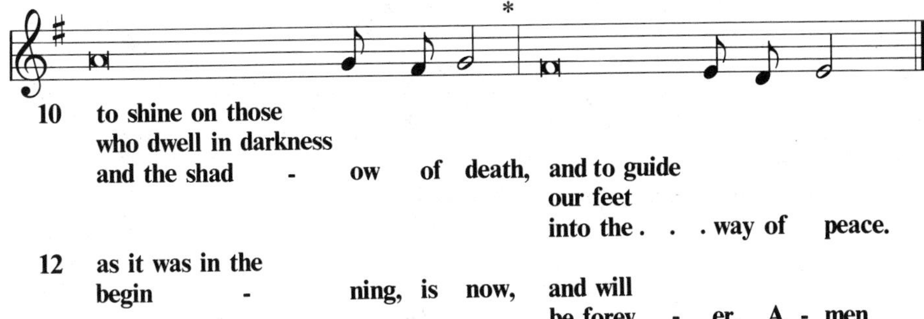

10 to shine on those who dwell in darkness and the shad - ow of death, and to guide our feet into the . . . way of peace.

12 as it was in the begin - ning, is now, and will be forev - er. A - men

3

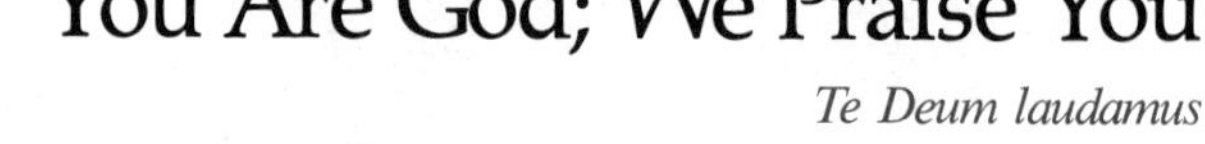

You Are God; We Praise You

Te Deum laudamus

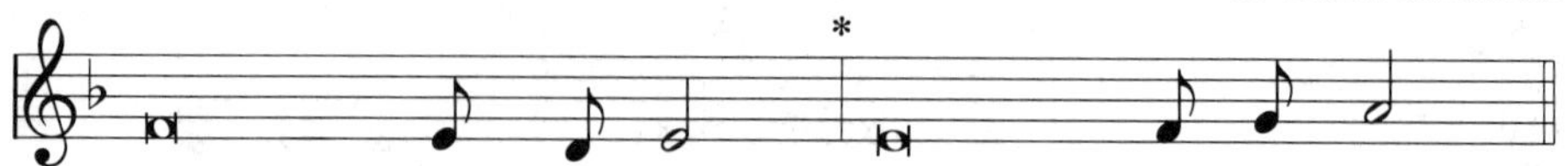

1 You are . . . God; we praise you. You are
the Lord; . . we ac - claim you.

3 To you
all angels,
all the . . . pow'rs of heaven, cherubim and
seraphim,
sing in . . . end - less praise:

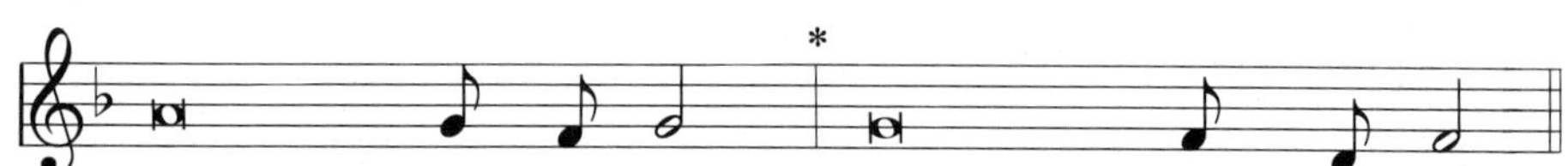

2 You are the e - ter - nal Father; all creation . . wor - ships you.

4 Holy, holy,
holy Lord,
God of . . . pow'r and might, heaven and
earth are full of your glory.

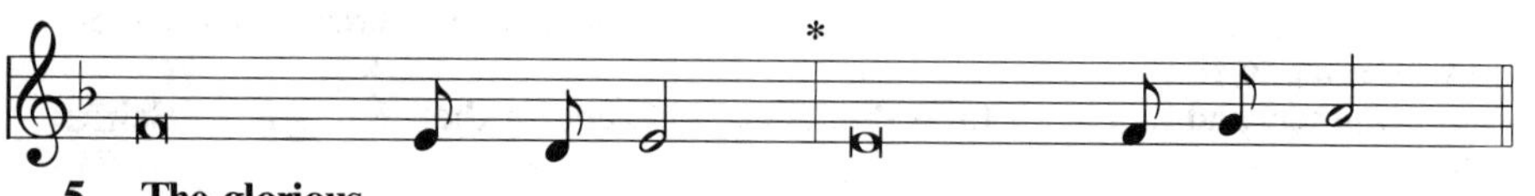

5 The glorious
company
of the a - pos - tles praise you. The noble
fellowship of pro - phets praise you.

7 Father,
of majes - ty un - bounded; your true and on - ly Son,

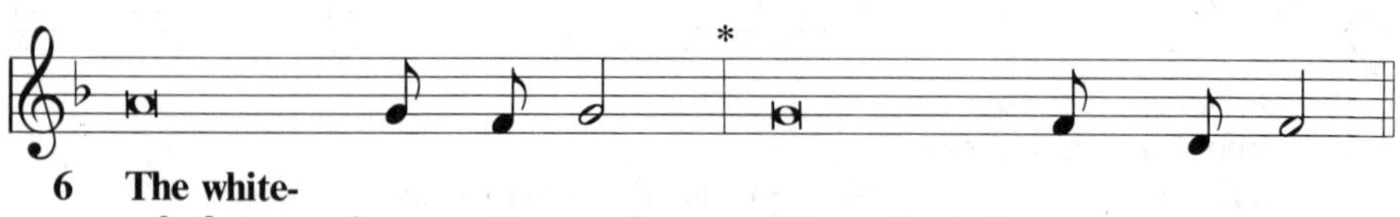

6 The white-
robed army of mar - tyrs praise you. Throughout the
world the holy Church ac - claims
you:

8 worthy . . . of all worship; and the Holy
Spirit, advo - cate and guide.

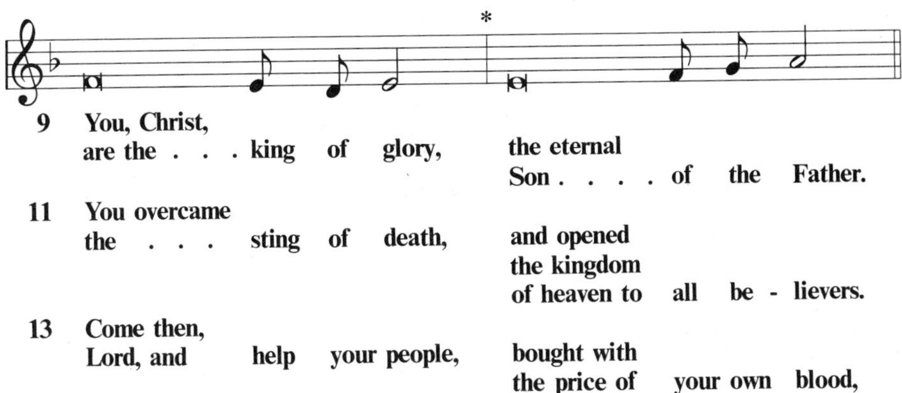
*
9 You, Christ,
are the . . . king of glory,
the eternal
Son . . . . of the Father.
11 You overcame
the . . . sting of death,
and opened
the kingdom
of heaven to all be - lievers.
13 Come then,
Lord, and help your people,
bought with
the price of your own blood,

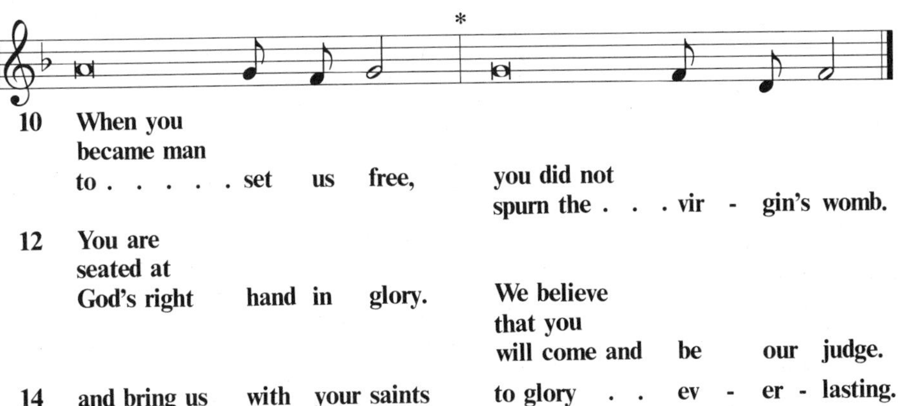
*
10 When you
became man
to . . . . . . set us free,
you did not
spurn the . . . vir - gin's womb.
12 You are
seated at
God's right hand in glory.
We believe
that you
will come and be our judge.
14 and bring us with your saints
to glory . . ev - er - lasting.

4 Come, Let Us Sing to the Lord

Venite exultemus

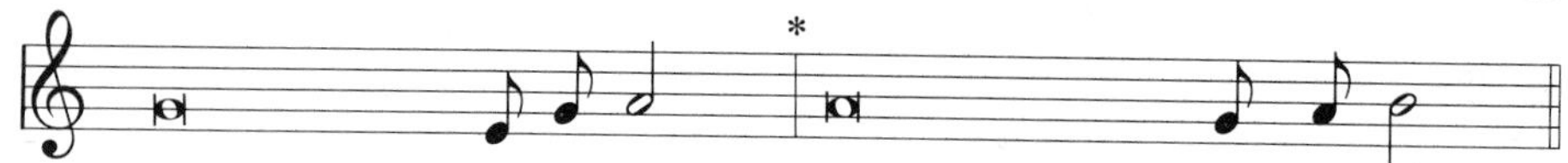

1 Come, let us sing to the Lord; * let us shout for joy
to the rock of . . . our sal-vation.

3 For the Lord is a great God * and a great king a - bove all gods.

2 Let us come before
his presence . . . with thanks-giving * and raise a
loud shout to him with psalms.

4 In his hand are
the caverns . . . of the earth; * and the heights of
the hills are . . . al - so his.

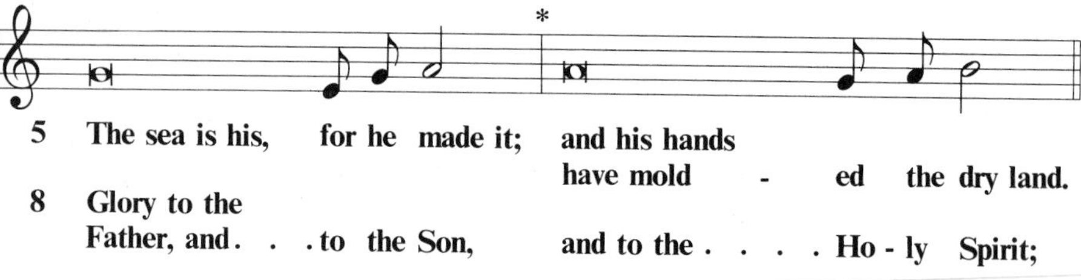

5 The sea is his, for he made it; * and his hands
have mold - ed the dry land.

8 Glory to the
Father, and . . . to the Son, * and to the . . . . Ho - ly Spirit;

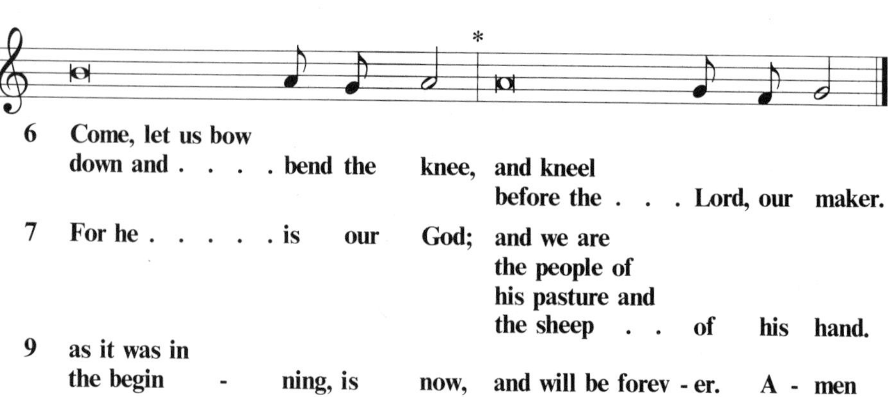

6 Come, let us bow
down and . . . . bend the knee, * and kneel
before the . . . Lord, our maker.

7 For he . . . . . is our God; * and we are
the people of
his pasture and
the sheep . . of his hand.

9 as it was in
the begin - ning, is now, * and will be forev - er. A - men

© *Text: Psalm 95;* Standard Book of Common Prayer, *1977*
© *Tune: Richard W. Hillert, b. 1923*

Let My Prayer Rise before You as Incense

Domine clamavi

L Let my prayer rise be-fore you as in-cense; the lift-ing

up of my hands as the eve-ning sac-ri-fice.

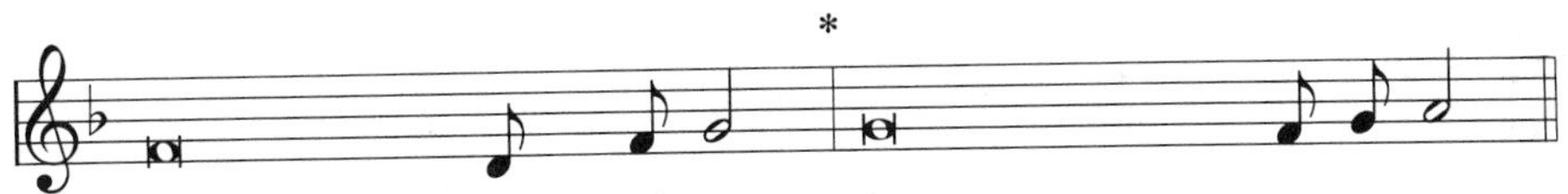

C 1 O Lord, I call to you; come . . . to me quickly; hear my voice when I cry to you.

3 Set a watch before my . . . mouth, O Lord; and guard the door of my lips.

6 Glory to the Father, and . . . to the Son, and to the . . . . Ho-ly Spirit;

2 Let my prayer rise before . . . . you as incense; the lifting up of my hands as the evening sac-ri-fice.

4 Let not my heart incline to any . . e-vil thing; let me not be occupied in wickedness with e-vil-doers.

5 But my eyes are turned to . . . . you, Lord God; in you I take refuge. Strip me not . . . . of my life.

7 as it was in the begin-ning, is now, and will be forev-er. A-men

Let my prayer rise be-fore you as in-cense; the lift-ing

up of my hands as the eve-ning sac-ri-fice.

6

My Soul Proclaims the Greatness of the Lord

Magnificat

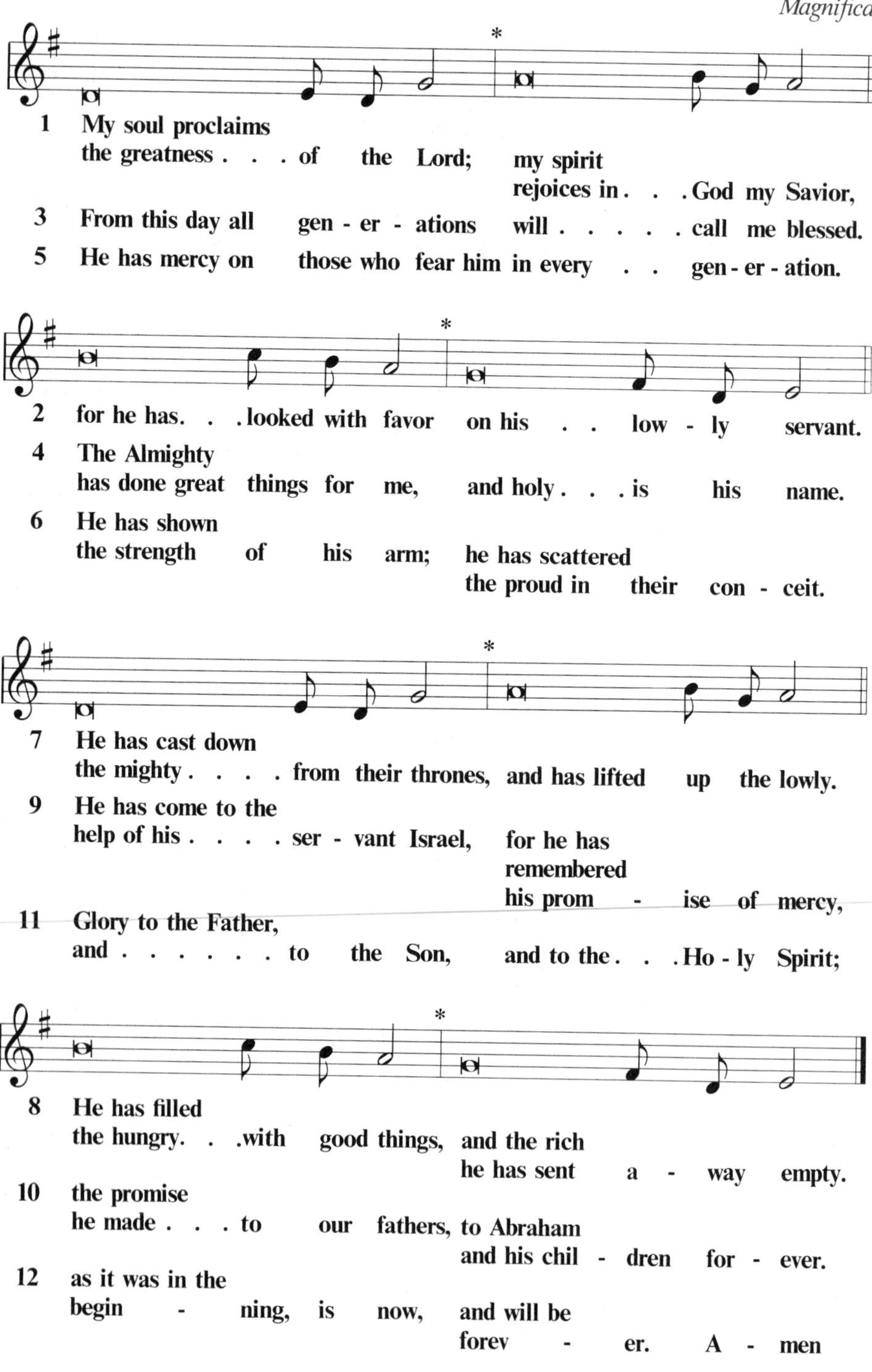

1 My soul proclaims
the greatness . . . of the Lord; my spirit
rejoices in . . . God my Savior,
3 From this day all gen - er - ations will . . . . . call me blessed.
5 He has mercy on those who fear him in every . . gen - er - ation.
2 for he has. . . looked with favor on his . . low - ly servant.
4 The Almighty
has done great things for me, and holy . . . is his name.
6 He has shown
the strength of his arm; he has scattered
the proud in their con - ceit.
7 He has cast down
the mighty . . . . from their thrones, and has lifted up the lowly.
9 He has come to the
help of his . . . . ser - vant Israel, for he has
remembered
his prom - ise of mercy,
11 Glory to the Father,
and . . . . to the Son, and to the . . . Ho - ly Spirit;
8 He has filled
the hungry. . . with good things, and the rich
he has sent a - way empty.
10 the promise
he made . . . to our fathers, to Abraham
and his chil - dren for - ever.
12 as it was in the
begin - ning, is now, and will be
forev - er. A - men

Climb to the Top of the Highest Mountain

Advent

Climb to the top of the
high-est moun-tain, you who will bring the good news to Zi - on.
Lift up your voic - es and bold - ly pro - claim: "See the
Lord God. He comes in pow - er." Write down the vi - sion, in -
scribe it on tab - lets, read - y for a her - ald to
car - ry it swift - ly. Soon, ver - y soon, he will come to you.
Live by faith, my righ - teous ones.

8 The People Who Walked in Darkness

Christmas/Epiphany

The peo - ple who walked in
dark - ness have seen a great light. Al - le - lu - ia.
The light has shined on the na - tions who live in the shad - ow of
death. A - rise, be clothed in light. Your light has come.
Al - le - lu - ia. Though dark-ness cov - ers the earth, the
Lord will shine up - on you. Al - le - lu - ia, al - le -
lu - ia, al - le - lu - ia, al - le - lu - ia.

I Called to My God for Help 9

Lent

I called to my God for help;
he heard me from his tem - ple.
His arm reached down to save and res - cue me
from my foes.
The man - na from heav - en for
Is - ra - el is his Son, the bread of life!

10 Sing Praise to the Lord

Easter

Sing praise to the
Lord, all the earth; play mu - sic to praise his name.
Al - le - lu - ia. Al - le - lu - ia. Our Pass - o - ver
Lamb is Christ, who ban - ished the an - gel of death.
Al - le - lu - ia. Al - le - lu - ia.
Our God who raised him from the grave gives us new
birth as his chil - dren. Al - le - lu - ia, al - le -
lu - ia, al - le - lu - ia, al - le - lu - ia.

Now Listen, You Servants of God 11

General

Now lis - ten, you ser-vants of
God, and take his words to heart, for
this is the word of the Lord; hear it, re -
ceive it, and be - lieve it. How
rich are the depths of God, how deep his wis - dom and
knowl - edge; to him be glo - ry for - ev -
er, our source, our guide, our goal.

12 God, Who Has Called You to Glory

General

God, who has
called you to glo - ry, will con - firm, sup -
port, and up - hold you. His fa - vors will nev - er
end; each morn - ing they are re - newed. Our
God is gen - 'rous and faith - ful.

Keep in Mind that Jesus Christ Has Died for Us

Refrain
C Keep in mind that Je - sus Christ has died for us and is ris - en from the
dead. He is our sav-ing Lord; he is joy for all a - ges.
L 1 If we die with the Lord, we shall live with the Lord.
Refrain
If we en - dure with the Lord, we shall live with the Lord.
L 2 In him all our sor - row, in him all our joy. In
Refrain
him hope of glo - ry, in him all our love.
L 3 In him our re - demp - tion, in him all our grace. In
Refrain
him our sal - va - tion, in him all our peace.

© Text: from 2 Timothy 2
© Tune: Lucien Deiss, b. 1921

14 Listen! You Nations

Refrain
Lis-ten! you na-tions of the world: lis-ten to the Word of the Lord. Announce it from coast to coast; de-clare it to dis-tant is-lands.
1 The Lord who scat-tered Is-ra-el will gath-er his peo-ple a-gain; and
he will keep watch o-ver them as a shep-herd watch-es his flock.
Refrain
2 With shouts of joy they will come, their fac-es ra-diant-ly hap-py, for the
Lord is so gen-'rous to them; he show-ers his peo-ple with gifts.
Refrain
3 Young wom-en will dance for joy, and men young and old will make
mer-ry. Like a gar-den re-freshed by the rain, they will nev-er be in want a-

gain. Break in - to shouts of great joy: Ja - cob is free a - gain! Teach

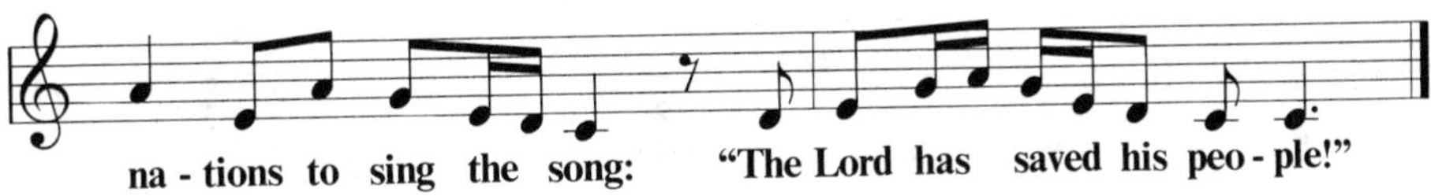
na - tions to sing the song: "The Lord has saved his peo - ple!"

Seek the Lord 15

Quaerite Dominum: Song of Isaiah

Seek the Lord while he máy be found;*
call upon him when hé draws near.
Let the wicked abandón their ways*
and the evil ónes their thoughts.
Let them return to the Lord, and he will háve compassion,*
and to our God, who will ríchly pardon.
For my thoughts áre not your thoughts,*
and your ways are not my ways, sáys the Lord.
For as the heavens are higher thán the earth,*
so are my ways higher than your ways
and my thóughts than your thoughts.
For as the rain and snow fall fróm the heavens*
and return not again, but watér the earth,
bringing forth life and gíving growth,*
seed for sowing and bréad for eating,
so is my word that goes out fróm my mouth:*
It will not return tó me empty;
but it will accomplish that which Í have purposed*
and prosper in that for whích I sent it.
Glory to the Father, and to the Son, and to the Hóly Spirit:*
as it was in the beginning, is now, and will be forevér. Amen

Text: from Isaiah 55

16 I Will Sing the Story of Your Love

L I will sing the sto - ry of your love, O Lord, and pro-claim your
faith-ful-ness for-ev - er. C I will sing the sto - ry of your love, O
Lord, and pro-claim your faith-ful-ness for-ev - er. L In this place shall be
heard a-gain the sounds of joy and glad - ness, the voice of the
bride-groom and the bride. C I will sing the sto - ry of your love, O
Lord, and pro-claim your faith-ful-ness for - ev - er. L Here they of-fer
praise and thanks-giv - ing in the house of the Lord, and we
hear their voic-es shout-ing, "Praise the Lord of hosts, for he is

good, for his love en - dures for - ev - er."
C I will sing the sto - ry of your love, O Lord, and pro-claim your
faith-ful-ness for - ev - er. L Give thanks to him and bless his
name; the Lord is good, his love is ev - er-
last - ing, and his faith - ful-ness en - dures to all gen - er -
a - tions, and his faith-ful-ness en-dures to all gen-er -
a - tions. C I will sing the sto - ry of your love, O
Lord, and pro-claim your faith-ful-ness for - ev - er.

17 How Blest Are Those Who Know Their Need of God

Beatitudes
Refrain
C How blest are those who know their need of God;
1.2. to verses
3.
Fine
the king-dom of heav-en is theirs. heav-en is theirs.
L 1 How blest are the sor-row-ful; they shall find con-so-la-tion. How blest are those of a gen-tle spir-it;
they shall have the earth for their pos-ses-sion.
Refrain
L 2 How blest are those who hun-ger and thirst to see right pre-vail; they shall be sat-is-fied, they shall be sat-is-fied.
Refrain
L 3 How blest are those who show mer-cy;

mer - cy shall be shown to them. How blest are
those whose hearts are pure; they shall see God. How
blest, how blest are the peace - mak - ers;
God shall call them his chil - dren. How blest are those who have
suf - fered per - se - cu - tion for the cause of the right;
Refrain
the king - dom of heav - en is theirs.

18 All You Works of the Lord

Benedicite, omnia opera

All you works of the Lord, bless the Lord—*
praise him and magnify him forever.
You angels of the Lord, bless the Lord;*
you heavens, bless the Lord;
all you powers of the Lord, bless the Lord—*
praise him and magnify him forever.
You sun and moon, bless the Lord;*
you stars of heaven, bless the Lord;
you showers and dew, bless the Lord—*
praise him and magnify him forever.
You winds of God, bless the Lord;*
you fire and heat, bless the Lord;
you winter and summer, bless the Lord—*
praise him and magnify him forever.
You dews and frost, bless the Lord;*
you frost and cold, bless the Lord;
you ice and snow, bless the Lord—*
praise him and magnify him forever.
You nights and days, bless the Lord;*
you light and darkness, bless the Lord;
you lightnings and clouds, bless the Lord—*
praise him and magnify him forever.
Let the earth bless the Lord:*
you mountains and hills, bless the Lord;
all you green things that grow on the earth, bless the Lord—*
praise him and magnify him forever.
You wells and springs, bless the Lord;*
you rivers and seas, bless the Lord;
you whales and all who move in the waters, bless the Lord—*
praise him and magnify him forever.
All you birds of the air, bless the Lord;*
all you beasts and cattle, bless the Lord;
all you children of mortals, bless the Lord—*
praise him and magnify him forever.
You people of God, bless the Lord;*
you priests of the Lord, bless the Lord;
you servants of the Lord, bless the Lord—*
praise him and magnify him forever.
You spirits and souls of the righteous, bless the Lord;*
you pure and humble of heart, bless the Lord;
let us bless the Father and the Son and the Holy Spirit—*
praise him and magnify him forever.

Text: from Song of the Three Young Men

I Will Sing to the Lord

19

Cantemus Domino: Song of Moses and Miriam

**I will sing to the Lord, for he has triumphed gloriously;*
the horse and its rider he has thrown into the sea.**

**The Lord is my strength and my song;*
he has been my Savior.**

**This is my God, and I will praise him,*
my father's God, and I will exalt him.**

**Your right hand, O Lord, glorious in power,*
your right hand, O Lord, shatters the enemy.**

**Who among the gods is like you, O Lord?*
Who is like you, majestic in holiness,
awesome in splendor, doing wonders?**

**In your mercy you led forth the people you set free;*
you guided them in your strength
to your holy habitation.**

**You will bring them in and plant them*
on the mount that is your possession,**

**the place, O Lord, you have made for your dwelling,
the sanctuary, O Lord, which your hands have prepared.*
The Lord shall reign forever and ever.**

**Glory to the Father, and to the Son, and to the Holy Spirit:*
as it was in the beginning, is now, and will be forever. Amen**

Text: from Exodus 15

Christ Jesus, Being in the Form of God

20

Song of Christ's Humiliation and Exaltation

**Christ Jesus, being in the form of God,
did not cling to his equality with God*
but emptied himself, taking the form of a slave.**

**Bearing the human likeness, revealed in human shape,*
he humbled himself, in obedience accepting death, even death on a cross.**

**Therefore God has raised him to the heights*
and bestowed on him the name above all names,**

**that at the name of Jesus every knee should bow—
in heaven, on earth, and in the depths—*
and every tongue confess to the glory of God the Father
that Jesus Christ is Lord.**

**Glory to the Father, and to the Son, and to the Holy Spirit:*
as it was in the beginning, is now, and will be forever. Amen**

Text: from Philippians 2

21 O Ruler of the Universe

Magna et mirabilia: Song of the Redeemed

O Ruler of the univérse, Lord God,*
great are the deeds that you have done,
surpassing human únderstanding.
Your ways are ways of righteousnéss and truth,*
O King of all the nations,
O King of áll the ages.
Who can fail to do you homage, Lord,
and sing the praises óf your name?*
For you alone are the Hóly One.
All nations will draw near and bow dówn before you,*
because your just and holy works have béen revealed.
Glory to the Father, and to the Son, and to the Hóly Spirit:*
as it was in the beginning, is now, and will be forevér. Amen

Text: from Revelation 15

HYMNS

The Advent of Our God 22

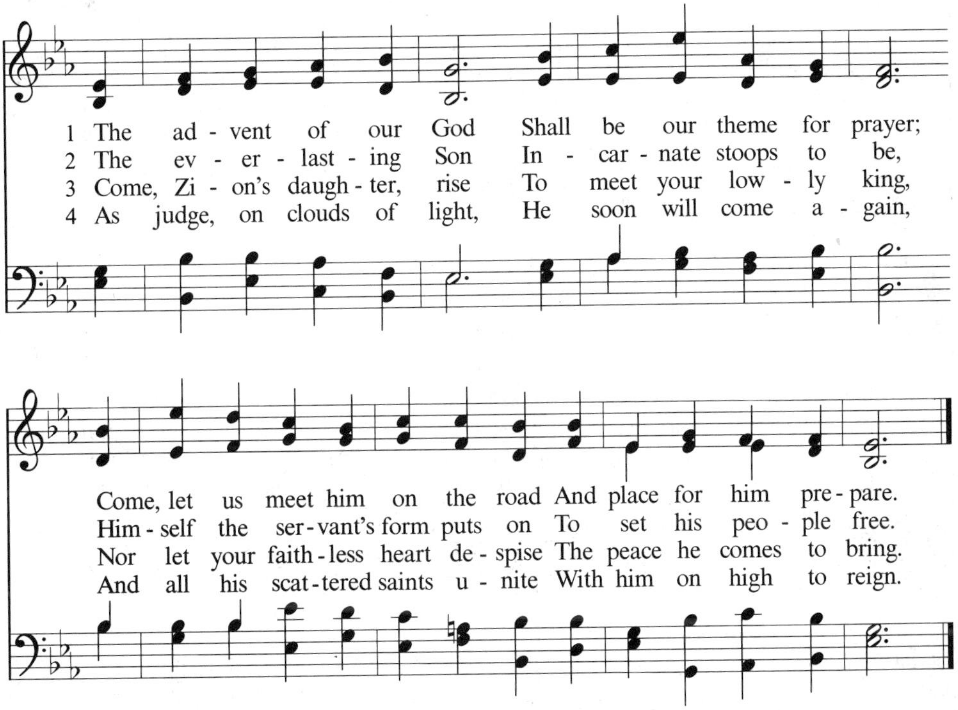

1 The ad - vent of our God Shall be our theme for prayer;
2 The ev - er - last - ing Son In - car - nate stoops to be,
3 Come, Zi - on's daugh - ter, rise To meet your low - ly king,
4 As judge, on clouds of light, He soon will come a - gain,

Come, let us meet him on the road And place for him pre - pare.
Him - self the ser - vant's form puts on To set his peo - ple free.
Nor let your faith - less heart de - spise The peace he comes to bring.
And all his scat - tered saints u - nite With him on high to reign.

5 Before the dawning day
Let sin be put to flight;
No longer let the law hold sway,
But walk in freedom's light.

6 All glory to the Son,
Who comes to set us free,
With Father, Spirit, ever one
Through all eternity.

Text: Charles Coffin, 1676–1749; tr. John Chandler, 1806–1876, alt.
Tune: Johann B. König, 1691–1758, adapt.

FRANCONIA
SM

23 O Lord, How Shall I Meet You

1 O Lord, how shall I meet you, How wel - come you a -
2 Your Zi - on strews be - fore you Green boughs and fair - est
3 I lay in fet - ters, groan - ing; You came to set me
4 Love caused your in - car - na - tion; Love brought you down to
right? Your peo - ple long to greet you, My hope, my heart's de -
palms; And I, too, will a - dore you With joy - ous songs and
free. I stood, my shame be - moan - ing; You came to hon - or
me. Your thirst for my sal - va - tion Pro - cured my lib - er -
light! Oh, kin - dle, Lord most ho - ly, Your lamp with - in my
psalms. My heart shall bloom for - ev - er For you with prais - es
me. A glo - rious crown you give me, A trea - sure safe on
ty. Oh, love be - yond all tell - ing, That led you to em -
breast To do in spir - it low - ly All that may please you best.
new And from your name shall nev - er With - hold the hon - or due.
high That will not fail or leave me As earth - ly rich - es fly.
brace In love, all love ex - cel - ling, Our lost and fall - en race.

5 Rejoice, then, you sad-hearted,
Who sit in deepest gloom,
Who mourn your joys departed
And tremble at your doom.
Despair not; he is near you,
There, standing at the door,
Who best can help and cheer you
And bids you weep no more.

6 He comes to judge the nations,
A terror to his foes,
A light of consolations
And blessed hope to those
Who love the Lord's appearing.
O glorious Sun, now come,
Send forth your beams so cheering
And guide us safely home.

Text: Paul Gerhardt, 1606–1676; tr. The Lutheran Hymnal, *1941, alt.*
Tune: Johann Crüger, 1598–1662

WIE SOLL ICH DICH EMPFANGEN
76 76 D

Come, O Precious Ransom 24

1 Come, O pre-cious Ran-som, come, On-ly hope for sin-ful mor-tals!
2 En-ter now my wait-ing heart, Glo-rious King and Lord most ho-ly.
3 My ho-san-nas and my palms Gra-cious-ly re-ceive, I pray you;
4 Hail! Ho-san-na! Da-vid's Son! Je-sus, hear our sup-pli-ca-tion!
Come, O Sav-ior of the world; O-pen are to you all por-tals.
Dwell in me and nev-er leave, Though I am but poor and low-ly.
Ev-er-more, as best I can, Hom-age I will glad-ly pay you,
Let your king-dom, scep-ter, crown Bring us bless-ing and sal-va-tion;
Come, your beau-ty let us view; Anx-ious-ly we wait for you.
What vast rich-es will be mine When you are my guest di-vine!
And in faith I will em-brace Life e-ter-nal by your grace.
That for-ev-er we may sing: Hail! Ho-san-na to our king!

Text: Johann G. Olearius, 1635–1711; tr. August Crull, 1846–1923, alt.
Tune: Neuverfertigtes Gesangbuch, *Darmstadt, 1699*

MEINEN JESUM LASS ICH NICHT
78 78 77

25 Rejoice, Rejoice, Believers

1 Re - joice, re - joice, be - liev - ers, And let your lights ap - pear;
2 The watch-ers on the moun - tain Pro - claim the bride-groom near;
3 The saints, who here in pa - tience Their cross and suf - f'rings bore,
4 Our hope and ex - pec - ta - tion, O Je - sus, now ap - pear;
The eve-ning is ad - vanc - ing, And dark - er night is near.
Go forth as he ap - proach - es With al - le - lu - ias clear.
Shall live and reign for - ev - er When sor - row is no more.
A - rise, O Sun so longed for, O'er this be - night - ed sphere.
The bride-groom is a - ris - ing And soon is draw-ing nigh.
The mar - riage feast is wait - ing; The gates wide o - pen stand.
A - round the throne of glo - ry The Lamb they shall be - hold;
With hearts and hands up - lift - ed, We plead, O Lord, to see
Up, pray and watch and wres - tle; At mid - night comes the cry.
A - rise, O heirs of glo - ry; The bride-groom is at hand.
In tri - umph cast be - fore him Their di - a - dems of gold.
The day of earth's re - demp - tion That sets your peo - ple free!

Text: Laurentius Laurentii, 1660–1722; tr. Sarah B. Findlater, 1823–1907, alt.
Tune: Swedish folk tune

HAF TRONES LAMPA FÄRDIG
7 6 7 6 D

Prepare the Royal Highway

1 Pre - pare the roy - al high - way; The King of kings is near!
2 God's peo - ple, see him com - ing: Your own e - ter - nal king!
3 Then fling the gates wide o - pen To greet your prom - ised king!
4 His is no earth - ly king - dom; It comes from heav'n a - bove.
Let ev - 'ry hill and val - ley A lev - el road ap - pear!
Palm branch - es strew be - fore him! Spread gar - ments! Shout and sing!
Your king, yet ev - 'ry na - tion Its trib - ute too may bring.
His rule is peace and free - dom And jus - tice, truth, and love.
Then greet the King of glo - ry, Fore-told in sa - cred sto - ry:
God's prom - ise will not fail you! No more shall doubt as - sail you!
All lands will bow be - fore him; Their voic - es join your sing - ing:
So let your praise be sound - ing For kind - ness so a - bound - ing:
Refrain
Ho-san - na to the Lord, For he ful - fills God's Word!

© *Text: Frans Mikael Franzén, 1772–1847; tr. hymnal version, 1978*
Tune: Swedish folk tune, 14th cent.

BEREDEN VÄG FÖR HERRAN
76 76 77 66

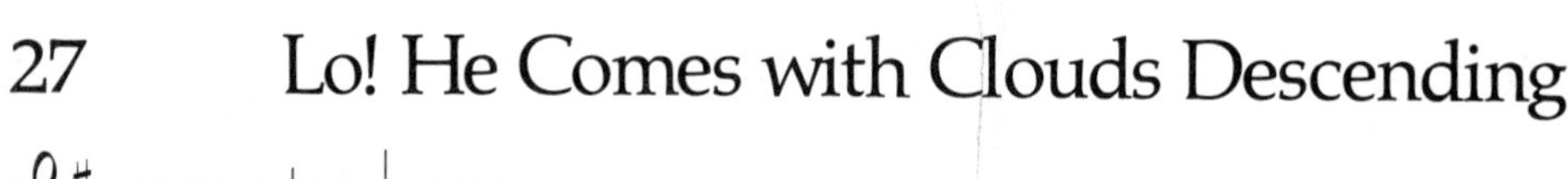

27 Lo! He Comes with Clouds Descending

1 Lo! He comes with clouds de-scend-ing,
Once for fa-vored sin-ners slain;
Thou-sand thou-sand saints at-tend-ing
Swell the tri-umph of his train:
Al-le-lu-ia, al-le-lu-ia,

2 Ev-'ry eye shall now be-hold him
Robed in glo-rious maj-es-ty;
Those who set at nought and sold him,
Pierced and nailed him to the tree,
Deep-ly wail-ing, deep-ly wail-ing,

3 Those dear to-kens of his Pas-sion
Still his daz-zling bod-y bears,
Cause of end-less ex-ul-ta-tion
To his ran-somed wor-ship-ers.
With what rap-ture, with what rap-ture,

4 Yea, a-men, let all a-dore thee,
High on thine e-ter-nal throne;
Sav-ior, take the pow'r and glo-ry,
Claim the king-dom as thine own.
Al-le-lu-ia, al-le-lu-ia,

al - le - lu - ia! Christ the Lord re - turns to reign.
deep - ly wail - ing, Shall their true Mes - si - ah see.
with what rap - ture Gaze we on those glo - rious scars!
al - le - lu - ia! Thou shalt reign, and thou a - lone!

Text: Charles Wesley, 1707–1788, alt.
Tune: Thomas Olivers, 1725–1799

HELMSLEY
8 7 8 7 12 7

Savior of the Nations, Come 28

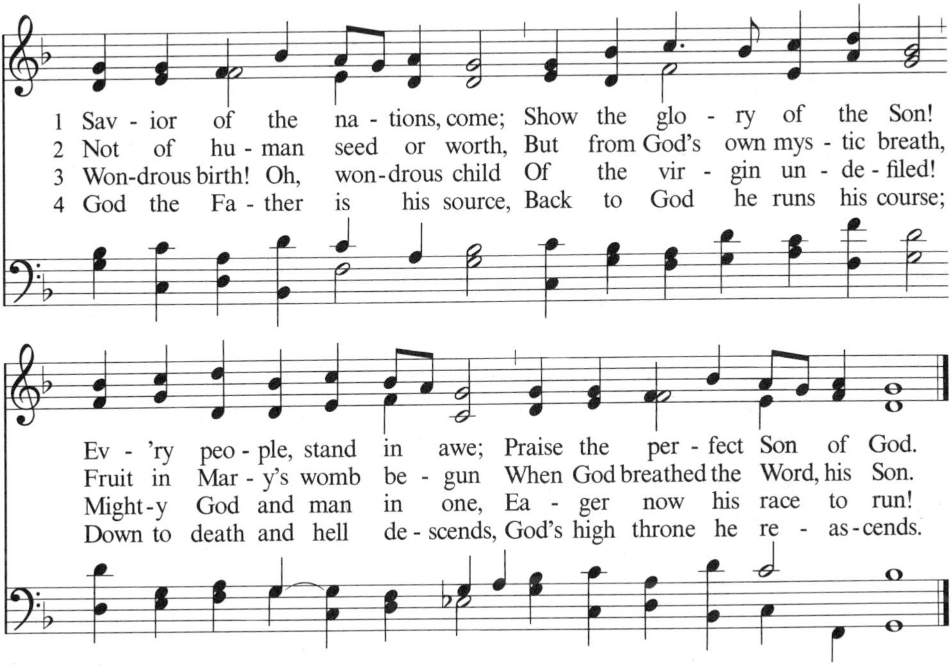

1 Sav - ior of the na - tions, come; Show the glo - ry of the Son!
2 Not of hu - man seed or worth, But from God's own mys - tic breath,
3 Won-drous birth! Oh, won-drous child Of the vir - gin un - de - filed!
4 God the Fa - ther is his source, Back to God he runs his course;

Ev - 'ry peo - ple, stand in awe; Praise the per - fect Son of God.
Fruit in Mar - y's womb be - gun When God breathed the Word, his Son.
Might-y God and man in one, Ea - ger now his race to run!
Down to death and hell de - scends, God's high throne he re - as-cends.

5 He leaves heaven to return;
Trav'ling where dull hellfires burn;
Riding out, returning home
As the Savior who has come.

6 God the Father's precious Son
Girds himself in flesh to run
For the trophies of our souls,
Longer than this round earth rolls.

7 Shining stable in the night,
Breathing vict'ry with your light;
Darkness cannot hide your flame,
Shining bright as Jesus' name.

 Text: attr. St. Ambrose, 340–397; tr. composite
Tune: J. Walther, Geistliche Gesangbüchlein, *1524*

NUN KOMM, DER HEIDEN HEILAND
7 7 7 7

29 Comfort, Comfort Now My People

1 "Com - fort, com - fort now my peo - ple; Tell of peace!" So says our God.
2 For the her - ald's voice is cry - ing In the des - ert far and near,
3 Straight shall be what long was crook - ed, And the rough - er plac - es plain!
Com-fort those who sit in dark - ness Mourn-ing un - der sor - row's load.
Call - ing us to true re - pen - tance, Since the King-dom now is here.
Let your hearts be true and hum - ble, As be - fits his ho - ly reign!
To God's peo - ple now pro - claim That God's par - don waits for them!
Oh, that warn - ing cry o - bey! Now pre - pare for God a way!
For the glo - ry of the Lord Now on earth is shed a - broad,
Tell them that their war is o - ver; God will reign in peace for - ev - er!
Let the val - leys rise to meet him, And the hills bow down to greet him!
And all flesh shall see the to - ken That God's word is nev - er bro - ken.

Text: *Johann Olearius, 1611–1684; tr. Catherine Winkworth, 1829–1878, alt.*
Tune: Trente quatre pseaumes de David, *Geneva, 1551*

FREU DICH SEHR
87 87 77 88

Come, Thou Long-Expected Jesus 30

Gm Dm Gm F Gm
1 Come, thou long - ex - pect - ed Je - sus, Born to set thy peo - ple free;
2 Born thy peo - ple to de - liv - er, Born a child, and yet a king;
Gm Dm E♭ B♭ Dm Gm
From our fears and sins re - lease us; Let us find our rest in thee.
Born to reign in us for - ev - er, Now thy gra - cious king - dom bring.
Gm B♭ Gm Dm E♭ B♭ Gm Dm
Is - rael's strength and con - so - la - tion, Hope of all the earth thou art,
By thine own e - ter - nal Spir - it Rule in all our hearts a - lone;
Gm Dm Gm Dm Gm E♭ F Gm
Dear de - sire of ev - 'ry na - tion, Joy of ev - 'ry long - ing heart.
By thine all - suf - fi - cient mer - it Raise us to thy glo - rious throne.

Text: Charles Wesley, 1707–1788
Tune: W. Walker, Southern Harmony, *1835*

JEFFERSON
8 7 8 7 D

31 Wake, Awake, for Night Is Flying

1 Wake, a - wake, for night is fly - ing, The watch-men on the heights are cry - ing; A - wake, Je - ru - sa - lem, at last.
2 Zi - on hears the watch-men sing - ing, And in her heart new joy is spring - ing. She wakes, she ris - es from her gloom,
3 Now let all the heav'ns a - dore you, And saints and an - gels sing be - fore you. The harps and cym - bals all u - nite.
Mid - night hears the wel - come voic - es, And at the thrill - ing cry re - joic - es: "Come forth, you maid - ens! Night is past.
For her Lord comes down all - glo - rious, The strong in grace, in truth vic - to - rious. Her star is ris'n; her light is come.
Of one pearl each shin - ing por - tal, Where, dwell - ing with the choir im - mor - tal, We gath - er round your daz - zling light.

The bride-groom comes! A - wake; Your lamps with glad - ness take!"
Oh, come, you Bless - ed One, Lord Je - sus, God's own Son.
No eye has seen, no ear Has yet been trained to hear.
Al - le - lu - ia! Pre - pare your-selves to meet the
Sing ho - san - na! We go un - til the halls we
What joy is ours! Cre - scen - dos rise; your halls re -
Lord, Whose light has stirred the wait - ing guard.
view Where you have bid us dine with you.
sound; Ho - san - nas blend in cos - mic sound.

Text: Philipp Nicolai, 1556–1608; tr. Catherine Winkworth, 1829–1878, alt.
Tune: Philipp Nicolai, 1556–1608

WACHET AUF
PM

32 Fling Wide the Door

F Dm C B♭ F
1 Fling wide the door, un - bar the gate; The King of glo - ry
2 He is the rock of our be - lief, The heart of mer - cy's
3 Oh, hap - py towns and bless - ed lands That live by their true
4 Come, Lord, our Sav - ior, Je - sus Christ; Our hearts are o - pen
C F C F Am F G C
comes in state; The Lord of lords and King of kings, The
gen - tle self. His king - ly crown is ho - li - ness; His
king's com-mands. And bless - ed be the hearts he rules, The
wide in trust. Oh, show us now your love - ly grace, Up-
F C F Am F G C B♭
Sav - ior of the world who brings His great sal - va - tion
scep - ter is his love - li - ness; He brings our sor - rows
hum - ble plac - es where he dwells. He is the right - ful
on our sor - rows shine your face, And let your Ho - ly
F Dm B♭ F
to the earth. So raise a shout of ho - ly mirth And
to an end. Now glad - ly praise our king and friend, And
Son of bliss Who fills our lives and makes us his, Cre -
Spir - it guide Our jour - ney in your grace so wide. We

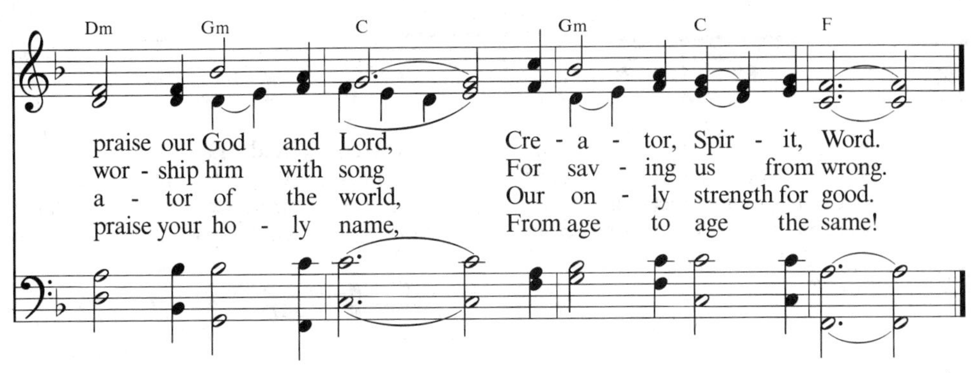
Dm Gm C Gm C F
praise our God and Lord, Cre - a - tor, Spir - it, Word.
wor - ship him with song For sav - ing us from wrong.
a - tor of the world, Our on - ly strength for good.
praise your ho - ly name, From age to age the same!

© *Text: Georg Weissel, 1590–1635; tr. Gracia Grindal, b. 1943*
Tune: J. A. Freylinghausen, Geistreiches Gesang-Buch, *1704*

MACHT HOCH DIE TÜR
88 88 88 66

The King Shall Come 33

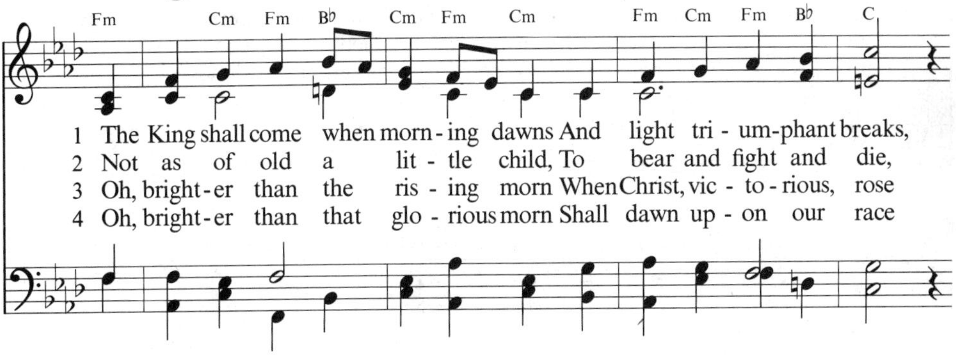

Fm Cm Fm B♭ Cm Fm Cm Fm Cm Fm B♭ C

1 The King shall come when morn - ing dawns And light tri - um-phant breaks,
2 Not as of old a lit - tle child, To bear and fight and die,
3 Oh, bright - er than the ris - ing morn When Christ, vic - to - rious, rose
4 Oh, bright - er than that glo - rious morn Shall dawn up - on our race

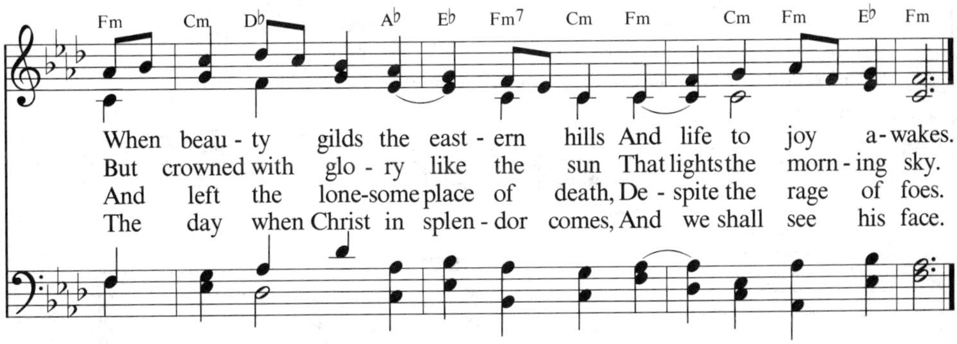

Fm Cm D♭ A♭ E♭ Fm7 Cm Fm Cm Fm E♭ Fm

When beau - ty gilds the east - ern hills And life to joy a - wakes.
But crowned with glo - ry like the sun That lights the morn - ing sky.
And left the lone-some place of death, De - spite the rage of foes.
The day when Christ in splen - dor comes, And we shall see his face.

5 The King shall come when morning dawns
And light and beauty brings.
Hail, Christ the Lord! Your people pray:
Come quickly, King of kings.

© *Text: John Brownlie, 1859–1925, alt.*
Tune: A. Davisson, Kentucky Harmony, *1816*

CONSOLATION
CM

34 Oh, Come, Oh, Come, Emmanuel

1 Oh, come, oh, come, Em - man - u - el, And ran - som cap - tive Is - ra - el, That mourns in lone - ly ex - ile here Un - til the Son of God ap - pear.
2 Oh, come, oh, come, great Lord of might, Who to your tribes on Si - nai's height In an - cient times once gave the law In cloud, and maj - es - ty, and awe.
3 Oh, come, strong Branch of Jes - se, free Your own from Sa - tan's tyr - an - ny; From depths of hell your peo - ple save And give them vic - t'ry o'er the grave.
4 Oh, come, blest Day-spring, come and cheer Our spir - its by your ad - vent here; Dis - perse the gloom - y clouds of night, And death's dark shad - ows put to flight.
Refrain
Re-joice! Re-joice! Em - man - u - el Shall come to you, O Is - ra - el.

5 Oh, come, O Key of David, come,
And open wide our heav'nly home;
Make safe the way that leads on high,
And close the path to misery. *Refrain*

Text: Psalteriolum Cantionum Catholicarum, *Köln, 1710; tr. John M. Neale, 1818–1866, alt.*
Tune: French processional, 15th cent.

VENI, EMMANUEL
88 88 88

Hark, the Glad Sound! 35

1 Hark, the glad sound! The Sav - ior comes, The Sav - ior prom - ised long; Let ev - 'ry heart pre - pare a throne And ev - 'ry voice a song.
2 He comes the pris - 'ners to re - lease, In Sa - tan's bond - age held. The gates of brass be - fore him burst, The i - ron fet - ters yield.
3 He comes the bro - ken heart to bind, The bleed - ing soul to cure, And with the trea - sures of his grace To en - rich the hum - ble poor.
4 Our glad ho - san - nas, Prince of Peace, Your wel - come shall pro - claim, And heav'n's e - ter - nal arch - es ring With your be - lov - ed name.

Text: Philip Doddridge, 1702–1751
Tune: attr. Thomas Haweis, 1734–1820

CHESTERFIELD
CM

36 On Jordan's Banks the Baptist's Cry

1 On Jor - dan's banks the Bap - tist's cry An - nounc - es
2 Then cleansed be ev - 'ry life from sin; Make straight the
3 We hail you as our Sav - ior, Lord, Our ref - uge
4 Stretch forth your hand, our health re - store, And make us
that the Lord is nigh; A - wake and hear - ken,
way for God with - in, And let us all our
and our great re - ward; With - out your grace we
rise to fall no more; Oh, let your face up -
for he brings Glad tid - ings of the King of kings!
hearts pre - pare For Christ to come and en - ter there.
waste a - way Like flow'rs that with - er and de - cay.
on us shine And fill the world with love di - vine.

5 All praise to you, eternal Son,
Whose advent has our freedom won,
Whom with the Father we adore,
And Holy Spirit, evermore.

Text: Charles Coffin, 1676–1749; tr. composite
Tune: adapt. Michael Praetorius, 1571–1621

PUER NOBIS
LM

Hark! A Thrilling Voice Is Sounding! 37

1 Hark! A thrill - ing voice is sound - ing! "Christ is near,"
2 Star - tled at the sol - emn warn - ing, Let the earth-
3 See the Lamb, so long ex - pect - ed, Comes with par -
4 So, when next he comes in glo - ry And the world
we hear the cry. "Cast a - way the works of
bound soul a - rise; Christ, its sun, all sloth dis-
don down from heav'n. Let us haste, with tears of
is wrapped in fear, He will shield us with his
dark - ness, All you chil - dren of the day!"
pel - ling, Shines up - on the morn - ing skies.
sor - row, One and all, to be for - giv'n;
mer - cy And with words of love draw near.

5 Honor, glory, might, dominion
To the Father and the Son
With the everliving Spirit
While eternal ages run!

Text: Latin hymn, 1632; tr. Edward Caswall, 1814–1878, alt.
Tune: Michael Weisse, c. 1480–1534

FREUEN WIR UNS ALL IN EIN
87 87

38 O Savior, Rend the Heavens Wide

1 O Sav - ior, rend the heav - ens wide; Come down, come
2 O Morn - ing Star, O ra - diant Sun, When will our
3 Sin's dread - ful doom up - on us lies; Grim death looms
4 There shall we all our prais - es bring Ev - er to
down with might - y stride; Un - lock the gates, the doors break
hearts be - hold your dawn? O Sun, a - rise; with - out your
fierce be - fore our eyes. Oh, come, lead us with might - y
you, our Sav - ior King; There shall we laud you and a -
down; Un - bar the way to heav - en's crown.
light We grope in gloom and dark of night.
hand From ex - ile to our prom - ised land.
dore For - ev - er and for - ev - er - more.

© *Text: German spiritual song, Köln, 1623; tr. Martin L. Seltz, 1909–1967, alt.*
Tune: Gesangbuch, *Augsburg, 1666*

O HEILAND, REISS DIE HIMMEL AUF
LM

Joy to the World

39

1 Joy to the world, the Lord is come! Let earth re - ceive its
2 Joy to the earth, the Sav - ior reigns! Let all their songs em -
3 No more let sin and sor - row grow Nor thorns in - fest the
4 He rules the world with truth and grace And makes the na - tions
King; Let ev - 'ry heart pre - pare him
ploy, While fields and floods, rocks, hills, and
ground; He comes to make his bless - ings
prove The glo - ries of his righ - teous -
room And heav'n and na - ture sing, And heav'n and na - ture
plains Re - peat the sound - ing joy, Re - peat the sound - ing
flow Far as the curse is found, Far as the curse is
ness And won - ders of his love, And won - ders of his
sing, And heav'n, and heav'n and na - ture sing.
joy, Re - peat, re - peat the sound - ing joy.
found, Far as, far as the curse is found.
love, And won - ders, won - ders of his love.

Text: Isaac Watts, 1674–1748
Tune: George F. Handel, 1685–1759, adapt.

ANTIOCH
CM and repeat

40 What Child Is This

Em D G D Em Am B
1 What child is this, who, laid to rest, On Mar-y's lap is sleep-ing?
2 Why lies he in such mean es-tate Where ox and ass are feed-ing?
3 So bring him in-cense, gold, and myrrh; Come, peas-ant, king, to own him.
Em G D Em B Em sus 4 Em
Whom an-gels greet with an-thems sweet While shep-herds watch are keep-ing?
Good Chris-tian, fear; for sin-ners here The si-lent Word is plead-ing.
The King of kings sal-va-tion brings; Let lov-ing hearts en-throne him.
Bm G D Em Am B
This, this is Christ the king, Whom shep-herds guard and an-gels sing;
Nails, spear shall pierce him through, The cross be borne for me, for you;
Raise, raise the song on high, The vir-gin sings her lul-la-by;
Bm G D Em B Em sus 4 Em
Haste, haste to bring him laud, The babe, the son of Mar-y!
Hail, hail the Word made flesh, The babe, the son of Mar-y!
Joy, joy, for Christ is born, The babe, the son of Mar-y!

Text: William C. Dix, 1837–1898
Tune: English ballad, 16th cent.

GREENSLEEVES
87 87 68 67

O Little Town of Bethlehem

41

1 O lit - tle town of Beth - le - hem, How still we see thee lie!
2 For Christ is born of Mar - y, And, gath - ered all a - bove
3 How si - lent - ly, how si - lent - ly The won - drous gift is giv'n!
4 O ho - ly Child of Beth - le - hem, De - scend to us, we pray;
A - bove thy deep and dream-less sleep The si - lent stars go by;
While mor - tals sleep, the an - gels keep Their watch of won-d'ring love.
So God im - parts to hu - man hearts The bless - ings of his heav'n.
Cast out our sin, and en - ter in, Be born in us to - day.
Yet in thy dark streets shin - eth The ev - er - last - ing light.
O morn - ing stars, to - geth - er Pro - claim the ho - ly birth,
No ear may hear his com - ing; But, in this world of sin,
We hear the Christ - mas an - gels The great glad tid - ings tell;
The hopes and fears of all the years Are met in thee to - night.
And prais - es sing to God the king, And peace to all the earth!
Where meek souls will re - ceive him, still The dear Christ en - ters in.
Oh, come to us, a - bide with us, Our Lord Im - man - u - el!

Text: Phillips Brooks, 1835–1893
Tune: Lewis H. Redner, 1831–1908

ST. LOUIS
86 86 76 86

42 Of the Father's Love Begotten

1 Of the Fa - ther's love be - got - ten Ere the worlds be-
2 Oh, that birth for - ev - er bless - ed, When the vir - gin,
3 This is he whom seers in old time Chant - ed of with
4 Let the heights of heav'n a - dore him; An - gel hosts, his

gan to be, He is Al - pha and O - me - ga,
full of grace, By the Ho - ly Ghost con - ceiv - ing,
one ac - cord, Whom the voic - es of the proph - ets
prais - es sing; Pow'rs, do - min - ions, bow be - fore him

He the source, the end - ing he, Of the things that are, that
Bore the Sav - ior of our race, And the babe, the world's re -
Prom-ised in their faith - ful word; Now he shines, the long - ex -
And ex - tol our God and King; Let no tongue on earth be

have been, And that fu - ture years shall see,
deem - er, First re - vealed his sa - cred face,
pect - ed; Let cre - a - tion praise its Lord
si - lent, Ev - 'ry voice in con - cert ring
Ev - er - more and ev - er - more.
Ev - er - more and ev - er - more.
Ev - er - more and ev - er - more.
Ev - er - more and ev - er - more.
A - men

5 Christ, to thee, with God the Father,
And, O Holy Ghost, to thee,
Hymn and chant and high thanksgiving
And unwearied praises be:
Honor, glory, and dominion,
And eternal victory
Evermore and evermore! Amen

Text: Marcus Aurelius Clemens Prudentius, 348–413; tr. composite
Tune: plainsong, mode V, 13th cent.

DIVINUM MYSTERIUM
8 7 8 7 8 7 7

43 Rejoice, Rejoice This Happy Morn

Re-joice, re - joice this hap - py morn, A Sav - ior un - to us is
born, The Christ, the Lord of glo - ry! His low - ly birth at Beth - le -
hem The an - gels from on high pro - claim And sing re - demp - tion's
sto - ry! My soul, ex - tol God's great fa - vor; bless him ev - er
For sal - va - tion; Give him praise and ad - o - ra - tion!

Text: Birgitte K. Boye, 1742–1824; tr. Carl Doving, 1867–1937
Tune: Philipp Nicolai, 1556–1608

WIE SCHÖN LEUCHTET
PM

Infant Holy, Infant Lowly

44

1 In - fant ho - ly, in - fant low - ly, For his bed a cat - tle stall;
2 Flocks were sleep - ing, shep-herds keep - ing Vig - il till the morn-ing new
Ox - en low - ing, lit - tle know - ing Christ the child is Lord of all.
Saw the glo - ry, heard the sto - ry, Tid - ings of a Gos - pel true.
Swift-ly wing - ing, an - gels sing - ing, Bells are ring - ing, tid - ings bring - ing:
Thus re - joic - ing, free from sor - row, Prais - es voic - ing, greet the mor - row:
Christ the child is Lord of all! Christ the child is Lord of all!
Christ the child was born for you! Christ the child was born for you!

© *Text: Polish carol; tr. Edith M. G. Reed, 1885–1933, alt.*
Tune: Polish carol

W ZLOBIE LEZY
87 87 88 77

45 Oh, Come, All Ye Faithful

1 Oh, come, all ye faith - ful, Joy - ful and tri - um - phant! Oh,
2 The high - est, most ho - ly, Light of light e - ter - nal,
3 Sing, choirs of an - gels, Sing in ex - ul - ta - tion,
4 Yea, Lord, we greet thee, Born this hap - py morn - ing;

come ye, oh, come . . ye to Beth - le - hem;
Born of a vir - gin, a mor - tal he comes;
Sing, all ye cit - i - zens of heav - en a - bove!
Je - sus, to thee . . be . . glo - ry giv'n!

Come and be - hold him Born the king of an - gels:
Son of the Fa - ther Now in flesh ap - pear - ing!
Glo - ry to God . . . . In . . . the . . high - est:
Word of the Fa - ther, Now in flesh ap - pear - ing:

Refrain

Oh, come, let us a - dore him, Oh, come, let us a - dore him,

Oh, come, let us a - dore him, Christ the Lord!

Text: attr. John F. Wade, c. 1711–1786; tr. composite
Tune: attr. John F. Wade, c. 1711–1786

ADESTE FIDELES
irregular

Once Again My Heart Rejoices

46

1 Once a - gain my heart re - joic - es As I hear, far and near,
Sweet-est an - gel voic - es; "Christ is born," their choirs are sing - ing,
Till the air ev - 'ry - where Now with joy is ring - ing.

2 Hark! A voice from yon - der man - ger, Soft and sweet, does en - treat,
"Flee from woe and dan - ger; Come and see; from all that grieves you
You are freed; all you need I will sure - ly give you."

3 Come, then, let us has - ten yon - der; Here let all, great and small,
Kneel in awe and won - der; Love him who with love is yearn - ing;
Hail the star that from far Bright with hope is burn - ing.

Text: Paul Gerhardt, 1607–1676; tr. Catherine Winkworth, 1829–1878, alt.
Tune: Johann Crüger, 1598–1662

FRÖHLICH SOLL MEIN HERZE SPRINGEN
866 866

47 Let All Together Praise Our God

1 Let all to - geth - er praise our God Be - fore his glo - rious throne; To - day he o - pens heav'n a - gain To give us his own Son, To give us his own Son.
2 The Fa - ther sends him from his throne To be an in - fant small And lie here poor - ly man - gered now In this cold, dis - mal stall, In this cold, dis - mal stall.
3 With-in an earth-born form he hides His all - cre - at - ing light; To serve us all he hum - bly cloaks The splen-dor of his might, The splen - dor of his might.
4 He un - der-takes a great ex - change, Puts on our hu - man frame, And in re - turn gives us his realm, His glo - ry, and his name, His glo - ry, and his name.

5 He is a servant, I a lord:
How great a mystery!
How strong the tender Christchild's love!
No truer friend than he,
No truer friend than he.

6 He is the key, and he the door
To blessed Paradise;
The angel bars the way no more.
To God our praises rise,
To God our praises rise.

7 Your grace in lowliness revealed,
Lord Jesus, we adore,
And praise to God the Father yield
And Spirit evermore;
We praise you evermore.

 Text: Nikolaus Herman, c. 1480–1561; tr. F. Samuel Janzow, b. 1913
Tune: Nikolaus Herman, c. 1480–1561

LOBT GOTT, IHR CHRISTEN
86 866

All Praise to You, Eternal Lord 48

1 All praise to you, e - ter - nal Lord, Clothed in garb of flesh and blood, A man - ger choos - ing for a throne While worlds on worlds are yours a - lone. Hal - le - lu - jah!
2 God's Son to whom the heav - ens bow, Cra - dled by a vir - gin now, We lis - ten for your in - fant voice While an - gels in your heav'n re - joice. Hal - le - lu - jah!
3 A lit - tle child, you came our guest, All the wea - ry to give rest! For - lorn and low - ly was your birth That we might rise to heav'n from earth! Hal - le - lu - jah!
4 Your com - ing in the dark - est night Makes us chil - dren of the light, En - a - bling us in realms di - vine Like all your an - gels bright to shine! Hal - le - lu - jah!

5 All this for us your love has done!
  Thus our love for you is won!
For this with joy our songs we sing,
Incessant praises echoing!
  Hallelujah!

 Text: German hymn, 1370, st. 1; Martin Luther, 1483–1546, sts. 2–5; tr. adapt.
Tune: Enchiridion, *Erfurt, 1524*

GELOBET SEIST DU
87 88 4

49 O Savior of Our Fallen Race

1 O Sav - ior of our fall - en race, O Bright - ness of
2 O Je - sus, ver - y Light of light, Our con - stant star
3 Re - mem - ber, Lord of life and grace, How once, to save
4 To - day, as year by year its light Bathes all the world
the Fa - ther's face, O Son who shared the Fa - ther's might
in sin's deep night: Now hear the prayers your peo - ple pray
our fall - en race, You put our hu - man ves - ture on
in ra - diance bright, One pre - cious truth out - shines the sun:
Be - fore the world knew day or night,
Through - out the world this ho - ly day.
And came to us as Mar - y's son.
Sal - va - tion comes from you a - lone. A - men

5 For from the Father's throne you came,
His banished children to reclaim;
And earth and sea and sky revere
The love of him who sent you here.

6 And we are jubilant today,
For you have washed our guilt away.
Oh, hear the glad new song we sing
On this, the birthday of our king!

7 O Christ, redeemer virgin-born,
Let songs of praise your name adorn,
Whom with the Father we adore
And Holy Spirit evermore. Amen

 Text: Latin office hymn, c. 6th cent.; tr. Gilbert E. Doan, b. 1930
Tune: medieval plainsong, mode I

CHRISTE REDEMPTOR
LM

Angels, from the Realms of Glory

50

1 An - gels, from the realms of glo - ry, Wing your flight o'er all the earth;
2 Shep-herds, in the fields a - bid - ing, Watch-ing o'er your flocks by night,
3 Sa - ges, leave your con - tem-pla - tions, Bright - er vi - sions beam a - far;
4 All cre - a - tion, join in prais - ing God, the Fa - ther, Spir - it, Son,

Once you sang cre - a - tion's sto - ry; Now pro - claim Mes - si - ah's birth:
God with us is now re - sid - ing, Yon - der shines the in - fant light.
Seek the great de - sire of na - tions, You have seen his na - tal star.
Ev - er - more your voic - es rais - ing To the e - ter - nal Three in One.

Refrain

Come and wor - ship, come and wor - ship, Wor - ship Christ, the new - born king.

Text: James Montgomery, 1771–1854, alt.
Tune: Henry T. Smart, 1813–1879

REGENT SQUARE
87 87 87

51 From Heaven Above

1 From heav'n a - bove to earth I come To bring good
2 To you this night is born a child Of Mar - y,
3 This is the Christ, God's Son most high, Who hears your
4 The bless - ing which the Fa - ther planned The Son holds
news to ev - 'ry - one! Glad tid - ings of great joy I
cho - sen vir - gin mild; This new - born child of low - ly
sad and bit - ter cry; He will him - self your Sav - ior
in his in - fant hand, That in his king - dom, bright and
bring To all the world, and glad - ly sing:
birth Shall be the joy of all the earth.
be And from all sin will set you free.
fair, You may with us his glo - ry share.

5 These are the signs which you will see
To let you know that it is he:
In manger-bed, in swaddling clothes
The child who all the earth upholds.

6 How glad we'll be to find it so!
Then with the shepherds let us go
To see what God for us has done
In sending us his own dear Son.

7 Look, look, dear friends, look over there!
What lies within that manger bare?
Who is that lovely little one?
The baby Jesus, God's dear Son.

8 Welcome to earth, O noble Guest,
Through whom this sinful world is blest!
You turned not from our needs away!
How can our thanks such love repay?

9 O Lord, you have created all!
How did you come to be so small,
To sweetly sleep in manger-bed
Where lowing cattle lately fed?

10 Were earth a thousand times as fair
And set with gold and jewels rare,
Still such a cradle would not do
To rock a prince so great as you.

11 For velvets soft and silken stuff
You have but hay and straw so rough
On which as king so rich and great
To be enthroned in humble state.

12 O dearest Jesus, holy child,
Prepare a bed, soft, undefiled,
A holy shrine, within my heart,
That you and I need never part.

13 My heart for very joy now leaps;
My voice no longer silence keeps;
I too must join the angel-throng
To sing with joy his cradle-song:

14 "Glory to God in highest heav'n,
Who unto us his Son has giv'n."
With angels sing in pious mirth:
A glad new year to all the earth!

 Text: Martin Luther, 1483–1546; hymnal translation, 1978
Tune: V. Schumann, Geistliche Lieder, *1539*

VOM HIMMEL HOCH
LM

Your Little Ones, Dear Lord 52

1 Your lit - tle ones, dear Lord, are we, And come your low - ly bed to see; En - light - en ev - 'ry soul and mind, That we the way to you may find.
2 With songs we has - ten you to greet, And kiss the ground be - fore your feet. Oh, bless - ed hour, oh, sweet - est night That gave you birth, our soul's de - light.
3 Oh, draw us whol - ly to you, Lord, And to us all your grace ac - cord; True faith and love to us im - part, That we may hold you in our heart.
4 Un - til at last we too pro - claim, With all your saints, your glo - rious name; In par - a - dise our songs re - new, And praise you as the an - gels do.

Text: Hans A. Brorson, 1694–1764; tr. Harriet Krauth Spaeth, 1845–1925, alt.
Tune: Johann A. P. Schulz, 1747–1800

HER KOMMER DINE ARME SMAA
LM

53 Cold December Flies Away

D G D G A7 D
1 Cold De - cem - ber flies a - way At the rose - red splen - dor.
2 In the hope - less time of sin Shad - ows deep had fall - en.
3 Now the bud has come to bloom, And the world a - wak - ens.
D G D G A7 D
A - pril's crown - ing glo - ry breaks While the whole world won - ders
All the world lay un - der death. Eyes were closed in sleep - ing.
In the lil - y's pur - est flow'r Dwells a won - drous fra - grance.
Bm F♯m G D Bm F♯m G
At the ho - ly un - seen pow'r Of the tree which bears the
But, when all seemed lost in night, Came the sun whose gold - en
And it spreads to all the earth From the moment of its

A7
D
flow'r. On the bless - ed tree Blooms the red - dest flow'r. On the tree blooms the
light Brings un-end - ing joy, Brings the end - less joy Of our hope, high - est
birth; And its beau - ty lives. In the flow'r it lives, In the flow'r, and it
D7
G
A
D
G
A7
D
rose Here in love's own gar - den, Full and strong in glo - ry.
hope, Of our hope's bright dawn - ing, Son be - loved of heav - en.
spreads In its heav'n - ly bright - ness Sweet per - fume de - light - ful.

© *Text: Catalonian carol; tr. Howard Hawhee, b. 1953*
Tune: Catalonian carol

LO DESEMBRE CONGELAT
PM

54 It Came upon the Midnight Clear

1 It came up - on the mid - night clear, That glo - rious song of old,
2 Still through the clo - ven skies they come With peace - ful wings un - furled,
3 And you, be - neath life's crush - ing load, Whose forms are bend - ing low,
4 For lo! The days are has - t'ning on, By proph - ets seen of old,

From an - gels bend - ing near the earth To touch their harps of gold:
And still their heav'n - ly mu - sic floats O'er all the wea - ry world.
Who toil a - long the climb - ing way With pain - ful steps and slow:
When with the ev - er - cir - cling years Shall come the time fore-told,

"Peace on the earth, good will to all, From heav'n's all - gra - cious king."
A - bove its sad and low - ly plains They bend on hov - 'ring wing,
Look now, for glad and gold - en hours Come swift - ly on the wing;
When peace shall o - ver all the earth Its an - cient splen - dors fling,

The world in sol - emn still - ness lay To hear the an - gels sing.
And ev - er o'er its ba - bel sounds The bless - ed an - gels sing.
Oh, rest be - side the wea - ry road And hear the an - gels sing!
And all the world give back the song Which now the an - gels sing.

Text: Edmund H. Sears, 1810–1876, alt.
Tune: Richard S. Willis, 1819–1900

CAROL
CMD

Good Christian Friends, Rejoice

55

1 Good Chris-tian friends, re - joice With heart and soul and voice;
2 Good Chris-tian friends, re - joice With heart and soul and voice;
3 Good Chris-tian friends, re - joice With heart and soul and voice;
Give ye heed to what we say: Je - sus Christ is born to - day;
Now ye hear of end - less bliss: Je - sus Christ was born for this!
Now ye need not fear the grave; Je - sus Christ was born to save!
Ox and ass be - fore him bow, And he is in the man - ger now.
He has o - pened heav - en's door, And we are blest for - ev - er - more.
Calls you one and calls you all To gain his ev - er - last - ing hall.
Christ is born to - day! Christ is born to - day!
Christ was born for this! Christ was born for this!
Christ was born to save! Christ was born to save!

Text: medieval Latin carol; tr. John M. Neale, 1818–1866, alt.
Tune: German carol, 14th cent.

IN DULCI JUBILO
66 77 78 55

56 The First Noel

1 The first No - el the an - gel did say Was to
2 They look - ed up and saw . . a star Shin - ing
3 And by the light of that . . same star Three .
4 This star drew near to the . . north-west, O'er . .
cer - tain poor shep-herds in fields as they lay; In fields where .
in . . the east . . be - yond . . them far; And to the. .
Wise . Men came . . from coun - try far; To seek for a
Beth - le - hem . . it took . . its rest; And there it . .
they lay, keep - ing their sheep, On a cold win - ter's
earth it gave. . . great light, And . . so it con -
king was their. . . in - tent, And to fol - low the
did both stop . . . and stay Right. . o - ver the
night . that was . . so deep.
tin - ued both day . . and night.
star. . wher - ev - er it went.
place . where Je - sus lay.
Refrain
No - el, No - el, No -

el, No - el! Born is the King of Is - ra - el.

5 Then entered in those Wise Men three,
Full rev'rently upon their knee,
And offered there in his presence
Their gold, and myrrh, and frankincense.
Refrain

Text: English carol, c. 17th cent.
Tune: English carol, c. 17th cent.

THE FIRST NOWELL
irregular

Let Our Gladness Have No End 57

1 Let our glad-ness have no end, Hal-le-lu-jah! For to earth did Christ de-scend. Hal-le-lu-jah!

2 See, the love-liest bloom-ing rose, Hal-le-lu-jah! From the branch of Jes-se grows. Hal-le-lu-jah!

3 In-to flesh is made the Word. Hal-le-lu-jah! He, our ref-uge and our Lord. Hal-le-lu-jah!

Refrain
On this day God gave us Christ, his Son, to save us; Christ, his Son, to save us.

Text: Bohemian carol, 15th cent.; tr. unknown
Tune: Bohemian carol, 15th cent.

NARODIL SE KRISTUS PÁN
7 4 7 4 666

58 Lo, How a Rose Is Growing

1 Lo, how a rose is grow - ing, A bloom of fin - est
2 The rose of which I'm sing - ing, I - sa - iah had fore-
3 The shep - herds heard the sto - ry The an - gels sang that
4 This flow'r, so small and ten - der, With fra - grance fills the
grace; The proph - ets had fore - told it: A branch of Jes - se's
told. He came to us through Mar - y Who shel - tered him from
night: How Christ was born of Mar - y; He was the Son of
air; His bright - ness ends the dark - ness That kept the earth in
race Would bear one per - fect flow'r Here in the
cold. Through God's e - ter - nal will This child to
light. To Beth - le - hem they ran To find him
fear. True God and yet true man, He came to
cold of win - ter And dark - est mid - night hour.
us was giv - en At mid - night calm and still.
in the man - ger As an - gel her - alds sang.
save his peo - ple From earth's dark night of sin.

5 O Savior, child of Mary,
Who felt all human woe;
O Savior, king of glory,
Who triumphed o'er our foe:
Bring us at length, we pray,
To the bright courts of heaven
And into endless day.

 Text: German, 15th cent.; tr. Gracia Grindal, b. 1943
Tune: Alte Catholische Geistliche Kirchengesäng, *Köln, 1599*

ES IST EIN ROS
7 6 7 6 6 7 6

When Christmas Morn Is Dawning 59

1 When Christ-mas morn is dawn - ing I wish that I could be
2 How kind of you, our Sav - ior, For us to come to earth.
3 We need you, O Lord Je - sus, To be our dear - est friend.
There by the man - ger - cra - dle God's Son, new-born, to see,
Oh, may we not by sin - ning De - spise your low - ly birth.
Your love will guard and guide us And keep us to life's end.
There by the man - ger - cra - dle God's Son, new-born, to see.
Oh, may we not by sin - ning De - spise your low - ly birth.
Your love will guard and guide us And keep us to life's end.

 Text: Elisabeth Ehrenborg-Posse, Barnsånger, *19th cent.; tr. Joel W. Lundeen, b. 1918*
Tune: German folk tune, 1823

WIR HATTEN GEBAUET
7 6 7 6 7 6

60 Hark! The Herald Angels Sing

1 Hark! The her - ald an - gels sing, "Glo - ry to the new-born king;
2 Christ, by high - est heav'n a - dored, Christ, the ev - er - last - ing Lord,
3 Hail the heav'n-born Prince of Peace! Hail the sun of righ-teous-ness!
Peace on earth, and mer - cy mild, God and sin - ners rec - on-ciled."
Late in time be-hold him come, Off-spring of a vir - gin's womb.
Light and life to all he brings, Ris'n with heal - ing in his wings.
Joy - ful, all you na - tions, rise; Join the tri - umph of the skies;
Veiled in flesh the God-head see! Hail, in - car - nate de - i - ty!
Mild he lays his glo - ry by, Born that we no more may die,
With an - gel - ic hosts pro-claim, "Christ is born in Beth - le - hem!"
Pleased as man with us to dwell, Je - sus, our Em-man - u - el!
Born to raise each child of earth, Born to give us sec - ond birth.

Refrain
Hark! The her - ald an - gels sing, "Glo - ry to the new - born king!"

Text: Charles Wesley, 1707–1788, alt.
Tune: Felix Mendelssohn, 1809–1847

MENDELSSOHN
77 77 D and refrain

The Hills Are Bare at Bethlehem 61

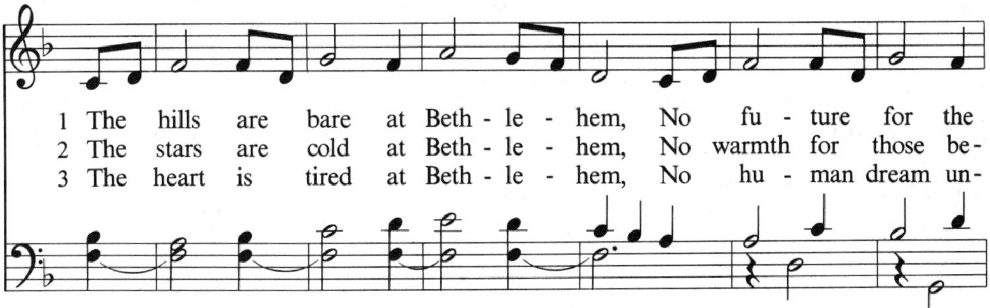

1 The hills are bare at Beth - le - hem, No fu - ture for the world they show; Yet here new life be - gins to grow, From earth's old dust a green - wood stem.

2 The stars are cold at Beth - le - hem, No warmth for those be - neath the sky; Yet here the ra - diant an - gels fly, And joy burns new, a fi - 'ry gem.

3 The heart is tired at Beth - le - hem, No hu - man dream un - bro - ken stands; Yet here God comes to mor - tal hands, And hope re - newed cries out: "A - men!"

 Text: Royce J. Scherf, b. 1929, alt.
Tune: W. Walker, Southern Harmony, *1835*

PROSPECT
LM

62 The Bells of Christmas

E♭ B♭ E♭ Fm B♭
1 The bells of Christ - mas chime once more; The heav'n - ly
2 This world, though wide and far out - spread, Could scarce - ly
3 Now let us go with qui - et mind, The swad - dled
4 Oh, join with me, in glad - ness sing, To keep our
E♭ F7 E♭ B♭ B♭7 E♭
guest is at the door. He comes to earth - ly
find for you a bed. Your cra - dle was a
babe with shep - herds find, To gaze on him who
Christ - mas with our king, Un - til our song, from
B♭ E♭ B♭ Cm Fm E♭ B♭7 E♭
dwell - ings still With new year gifts of peace, good will.
man - ger stall, No pearl nor silk nor king - ly hall.
glad - dens them, The love - liest flow'r of Jes - se's stem.
lov - ing souls, Like rush - ing might - y wa - ter rolls!

5 O patriarchs' Joy, O prophets' Song,
O Dayspring bright, awaited long,
O Son of Man, incarnate Word,
Great David's Son, great David's Lord:

6 Come, Jesus, glorious heav'nly guest,
And keep your Christmas in our breast;
Then David's harpstrings, hushed so long,
Shall swell our jubilee of song.

Text: Nikolai F. S. Grundtvig, 1783–1872; tr. Charles Porterfield Krauth, 1823–1883, alt.
Tune: C. C. N. Balle, 1806–1855

DET KIMER NU TIL JULEFEST
LM

From Shepherding of Stars

63

1 From shep - herd - ing of stars that gaze Toward heav'n-ly fields of light, I come with tid - ings to a - maze You watch - ers in the night, You watch - ers in the night.

2 Your shep - herd King from star - lit hall Bends down to wea - ry lands, Lies man-gered low in cat - tle stall. Go touch his in - fant hands, Go touch his in - fant hands.

3 This night your King brings from a - far The vir - gin's lul - la - by, The Wise Men's faith, a guid - ing star, And love from God Most High, And love from God Most High.

4 He shep - herds from the this - tled place The flocks by thick - ets torn; His pierc - ed hands heal all your race Sore wound-ed by the thorn, Sore wound - ed by the thorn.

5 Embrace the Christchild, and with songs
Bind up the hearts in pain.
To shepherd-healer-king let throngs
Sing glorias again.

SHEPHERDING
86 866

64 From East to West

1 From east to west, from shore to shore, Let ev - 'ry heart a - wake and sing The ho - ly child whom Mar - y bore, The Christ, the ev - er - last - ing king.
2 Be - hold, the world's cre - a - tor wears The form and fash - ion of a slave; Our ver - y flesh our mak - er shares, His fall - en crea - tures, all, to save.
3 For this how won - drous-ly he wrought! A maid - en, in her low - ly place, Be - came, in ways be - yond all thought, The cho - sen ves - sel of his grace.
4 And while the an - gels in the sky Sang praise a - bove the si - lent field, To shep - herds poor the Lord most high, The one great shep - herd, was re - vealed. A - men

5 All glory for this blessed morn
To God the Father ever be;
All praise to you, O Virgin-born,
And Holy Ghost, eternally. Amen

Text: Coelius Sedulius, d. c. 450; tr. John Ellerton, 1826–1893, alt.
Tune: Sarum plainsong, mode III

A SOLIS ORTUS CARDINE
LM

Silent Night, Holy Night! 65

1 Si - lent night, ho - ly night! All is calm, all is bright Round yon
2 Si - lent night, ho - ly night! Shep-herds quake at the sight; Glo - ries
3 Si - lent night, ho - ly night! Son of God, love's pure light Ra - diant
vir - gin moth - er and child. Ho - ly In - fant, so ten - der and mild,
stream from heav - en a - far, Heav'n - ly hosts . . . sing, Al - le - lu - ia!
beams from your ho - ly face, With the dawn of re - deem - ing grace,
Sleep in heav - en - ly peace, Sleep in heav - en - ly peace.
Christ, the Sav - ior, is born! Christ, the Sav - ior, is born!
Je - sus, Lord, at your birth, Je - sus, Lord, at your birth.

Text: Joseph Mohr, 1792–1849; tr. John F. Young, 1820–1885
Tune: Franz Gruber, 1787–1863

STILLE NACHT
irregular

66 Come Rejoicing, Praises Voicing

1 Come re - joic - ing, prais - es voic - ing; Christ-mas Day is break - ing.
2 Whom the sa - ges and the a - ges Anx - ious - ly a - wait - ed,
3 Child ap - peal - ing, light re - veal - ing, Je - sus Christ, our plea - sure;
The e - ter - nal Lord su - per - nal Hu - man form is tak - ing.
An - gels proud - ly her - ald loud - ly In their songs e - lat - ed.
God, yet ver - y Son of Mar - y, Heav-en's gift and trea - sure.
He is born in a stall, Now he lies, in - fant small,
Let us, too, in these days, Thank-ful hearts glad - ly raise,
Might-y king, gen - tle friend, As our Lord to us bend,
In a man - ger, heav'n - ly strang - er, Lord of all;
To the ten - der in - fant ren - der all our praise;
And ca - ress - ing us with bless - ing, now de - scend;

In a man - ger, heav'n - ly strang - er, Lord of all.
To the ten - der in - fant ren - der all our praise.
And ca - ress - ing us with bless - ing, now de - scend.

© *Text: Jiri Tranovský, 1591–1637; tr. Jaroslav J. Vajda, b. 1919*
Tune: Bohemian carol, 12th cent.

ČAS RADOSTI
86 86 66 11 11

Away in a Manger 67

1 A - way in a man - ger, no crib for his bed, The lit - tle Lord
2 The cat - tle are low - ing; the poor ba - by wakes, But lit - tle Lord
3 Be near me, Lord Je - sus; I ask you to stay Close by me for -

Je - sus laid down his sweet head; The stars in the sky . . looked
Je - sus no cry - ing he makes. I love you, Lord Je - sus; look
ev - er and love me, I pray. Bless all the dear chil - dren in

down where he lay, The lit - tle Lord Je - sus a - sleep on the hay.
down from the sky And stay by my cra - dle till morn - ing is nigh.
your ten - der care And fit us for heav - en to live with you there.

Text: American, 1885
Tune: American, 19th cent.

AWAY IN A MANGER
11 11 11 11

68 He Whom Shepherds Once Came Praising

Congregation
1 He whom shep - herds once came prais - ing, Awed by heav'n - ly
2 He whom sa - ges, west - ward far - ing, Myrrh and gold and
3 Sing with Mar - y, vir - gin moth - er; Praise her Son, our
4 To our king, God ev - er reign - ing, Yet of Mar - y
light a - blaz - ing, Cheered by an - gel-news a - maz-ing: "King of
in - cense bear - ing, Hum - bly wor - shiped, of - f'rings shar-ing: Ju - dah's
new - born broth - er; An - gel ranks, lead one an - oth - er, Hail - ing
man-hood gain - ing, Heav'n - ly gifts for us ob - tain-ing, Raise your
glo - ry, Christ is born!"
li - on reigns this morn!
him in ho - ly joy!
hymns of hom - age high!
Choir
The glo - rious an - gels came to - day, A - glow with light in - to the night of dark - ness deep,
God's maj - es - ty has come to earth And sent his on - ly Son to you in hu - man-kind;
Then sang the an - gels this re - frain: "To God on high a - lone give praise and glo - ry,
The won-d'ring shep - herds said: "Be - hold! Let us now go with all good speed to Beth - le - hem

To shep-herds who by moon's bright ray Did in the field o'er
A cho - sen vir - gin gave him birth. In Da - vid's town the
And peace on earth a - gain shall reign. Let all on earth with
To see this thing the Lord has told; The cat - tle leave; he
sheep their si - lent vig - il keep, "Joy, great joy and
ho - ly in - fant you will find, Ly - ing help - less
glad - ness heed this sto - ry And re - joice in
will in - deed take care of them." There they found the
tid - ings glad we bring from heav'n. . re - sound - ing, For
in a man - ger, poor and bare. . and low - ly, To
his good will." The Sav - ior came. . in meek - ness For
won - der child, in low - ly swad-dling clothes ly - ing, Yet
you, for you and all the world a - bound - ing."
set you free from all your sor - row whol - ly.
you, for you, to bear your flesh in weak - ness.
all the world with his free grace sup - ply - ing.
Refrain

Refrain follows on the next page

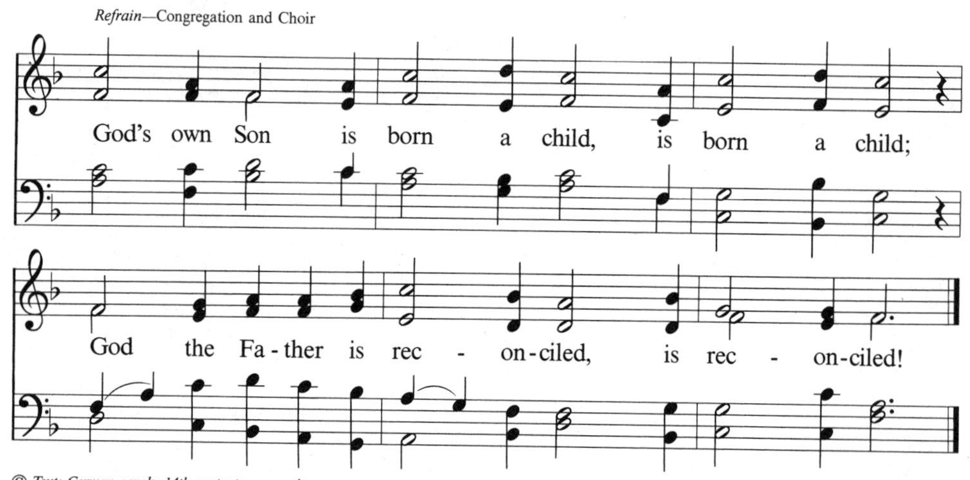
Refrain—Congregation and Choir
God's own Son is born a child, is born a child;
God the Fa-ther is rec - on-ciled, is rec - on-ciled!

© Text: German carols, 14th cent.; tr. composite
Tunes: German carols, 14th cent.

8 8 8 7 QUEM PASTORES
irregular NUNC ANGELORUM
11 12 RESONET IN LAUDIBUS

69 I Am So Glad Each Christmas Eve

G D D7 Am G
C Am G D7 G

1 I am so glad each Christ-mas Eve, The night of Je - sus' birth!
Then like the sun the star shone forth, And an - gels sang on earth.

2 The lit - tle child in Beth - le - hem, He was a king in - deed!
For he came down from heav'n a - bove To help a world in need.

3 He dwells a - gain in heav - en's realm, The Son of God to - day;
And still he loves his lit - tle ones And hears them when they pray.

4 I am so glad each Christ-mas Eve! His prais - es then I sing;
He o - pens now for ev - 'ry child The pal - ace of the king.

For use in the home

5 When mother trims the Christmas tree
Which fills the room with light,
She tells me of the wondrous star
That made the dark world bright.

6 And so I love each Christmas Eve,
And I love Jesus too;
And that he loves me every day
I know so well is true.

© Text: Marie Wexelsen, 1832–1911; tr. Peter A. Sveeggen, 1881–1959
Tune: Peder Knudsen, 1819–1863

JEG ER SAA GLAD
CM

Go Tell It on the Mountain

70

Refrain
Go tell it on the moun - tain, O-ver the hills and ev - 'ry - where;
Go tell it on the moun - tain That Je - sus Christ is born!
1 While shep-herds kept their watch-ing O'er si - lent flocks by night, Be -
2 The shep-herds feared and trem-bled When, lo, a - bove the earth Rang
3 Down in a lone - ly man - ger The hum - ble Christ was born; And
hold, through-out the heav - ens There shone a ho - ly light.
out the an - gel cho - rus That hailed our Sav - ior's birth.
God sent us sal - va - tion That bless - ed Christ - mas morn.
Refrain

Text: Negro spiritual, refrain; John W. Work Jr., 1871–1925, stanzas, alt.
Tune: Negro spiritual

GO TELL IT
78 76 76 76

71 Angels We Have Heard on High

1 An - gels we have heard on high, Sweet - ly sing - ing o'er the plains,
2 Shep-herds, why this ju - bi - lee? Why your joy - ous strains pro-long?
3 Come to Beth - le - hem and see Him whose birth the an - gels sing;
And the moun-tains in re - ply, Ech - o - ing their joy - ous strains.
What the glad - some tid - ings be Which in - spire your heav'n - ly song?
Come, a - dore on bend - ed knee Christ the Lord, the new - born king.
Refrain
Glo - - - - ri - a in ex - cel - sis De - o;
Glo - - - ri - a in ex - cel - sis De - o.

Text: French carol; tr. "Crown of Jesus," 1862
Tune: French carol

GLORIA
7 7 7 7 and refrain

'Twas in the Moon of Wintertime 72

1 'Twas in the moon of win - ter - time When all the birds had fled, That
2 The ear - liest moon of win - ter - time Is not so round and fair As
3 O chil - dren of the for - est free, The an - gels' song is true. The
God, the Lord of all the earth, Sent an - gel choirs in - stead. Be -
was the ring of glo - ry A - round the in - fant there. And
ho - ly child of earth and heav'n Is born to - day for you. Come,
fore their light the stars grew dim, And won-d'ring hunt-ers heard the hymn:
when the shep-herds then drew near The an - gel voic - es rang out clear:
kneel be - fore the ra - diant boy, Who brings you beau - ty, peace, and joy.
Refrain
Je - sus your king is born! Je - sus is born! Glo - ry be to God on high!

Text: Jean de Brebeuf, 1593–1649; tr. Jesse E. Middleton, 1872–1960, alt.
Tune: French folk tune, c. 16th cent.

UNE JEUNE PUCELLE
86 86 88 and refrain

73 All Hail to You, O Blessed Morn!

1 All hail to you, O bless - ed morn! To tid - ings long by
proph - ets borne Ful - fill - ment you have giv - en.
Oh, great - est and most bless - ed day When un - to earth in
glo - rious ray Shone out the grace of heav - en!

2 True God, the Fa - ther's Son, is he; Yet tru - ly one of
us, that we Might find in him a broth - er.
He comes with peace and love to live On earth, our err - ing
race to give Such help as could no oth - er,

3 He will, like us, shed bit - ter tears, Will know our needs, yet
still our fears And send his Spir - it's pow - er.
He will re - veal his Fa - ther's will, Our cup of woe with
mer - cy fill To sweet - en sor - row's hour . . . . .

4 For our re - demp - tion still he comes. In him shines, like a
thou - sand suns, God's mer - cy, cloud - ed nev - er!
Now all who will on him be - lieve, Who fol - low him, he
will re - ceive And as his flock will gath - er.

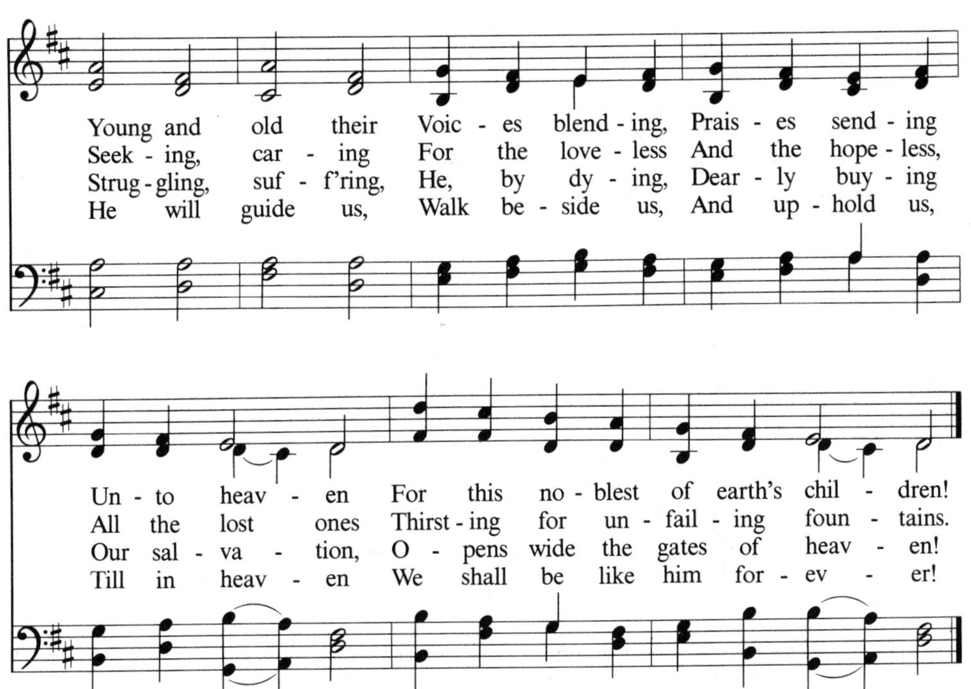
Young and old their Voic - es blend - ing, Prais - es send - ing
Seek - ing, car - ing For the love - less And the hope - less,
Strug - gling, suf - f'ring, He, by dy - ing, Dear - ly buy - ing
He will guide us, Walk be - side us, And up - hold us,
Un - to heav - en For this no - blest of earth's chil - dren!
All the lost ones Thirst - ing for un - fail - ing foun - tains.
Our sal - va - tion, O - pens wide the gates of heav - en!
Till in heav - en We shall be like him for - ev - er!

 Text: Johan Olof Wallin, 1779–1839; tr. hymnal version, 1978
Tune: Philipp Nicolai, 1556–1608

WIE SCHÖN LEUCHTET
PM

74 A Stable Lamp Is Lighted

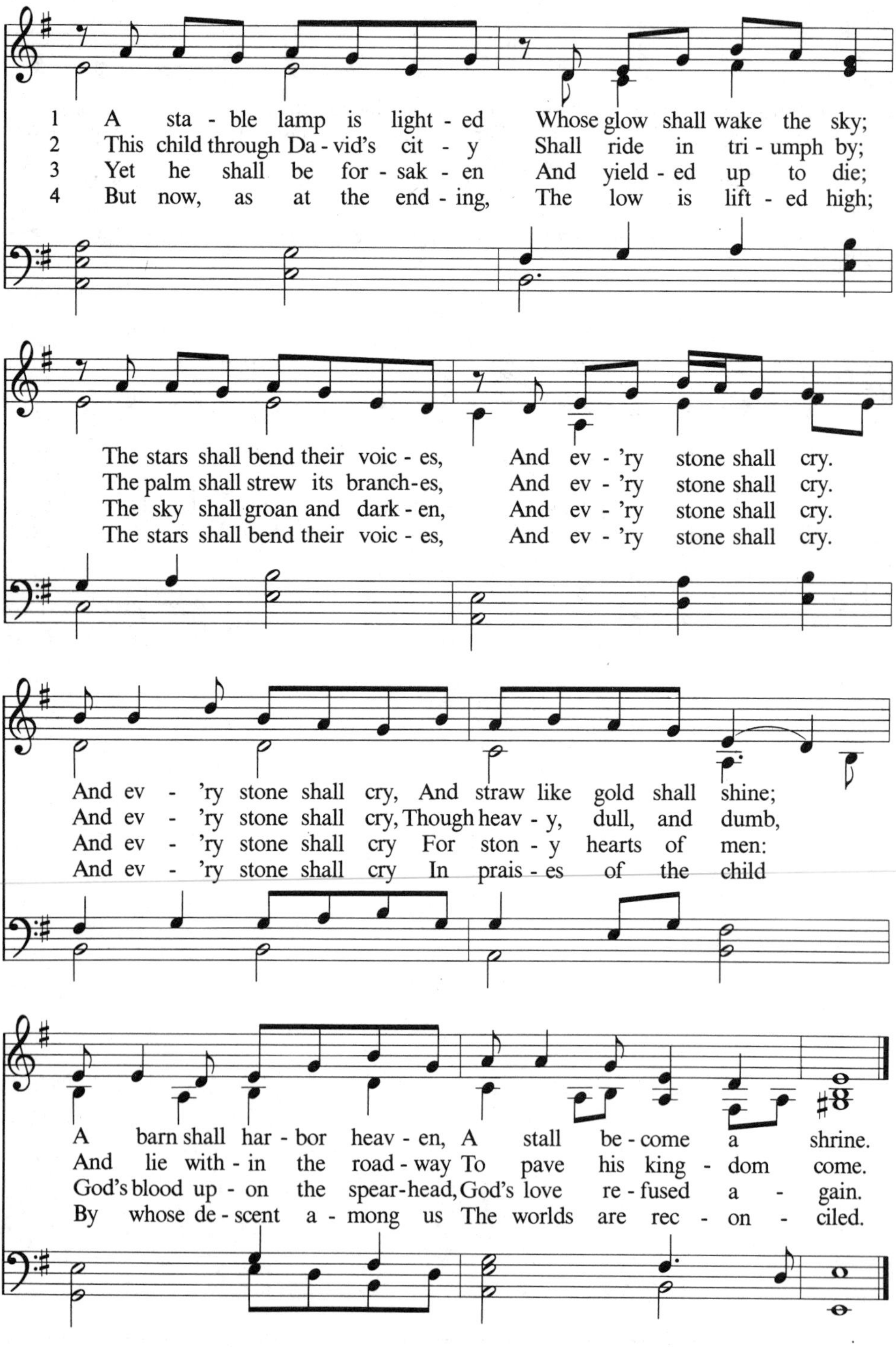

1 A sta - ble lamp is light - ed Whose glow shall wake the sky;
2 This child through Da - vid's cit - y Shall ride in tri - umph by;
3 Yet he shall be for - sak - en And yield - ed up to die;
4 But now, as at the end - ing, The low is lift - ed high;

The stars shall bend their voic - es, And ev - 'ry stone shall cry.
The palm shall strew its branch - es, And ev - 'ry stone shall cry.
The sky shall groan and dark - en, And ev - 'ry stone shall cry.
The stars shall bend their voic - es, And ev - 'ry stone shall cry.

And ev - 'ry stone shall cry, And straw like gold shall shine;
And ev - 'ry stone shall cry, Though heav - y, dull, and dumb,
And ev - 'ry stone shall cry For ston - y hearts of men:
And ev - 'ry stone shall cry In prais - es of the child

A barn shall har - bor heav - en, A stall be - come a shrine.
And lie with - in the road - way To pave his king - dom come.
God's blood up - on the spear - head, God's love re - fused a - gain.
By whose de - scent a - mong us The worlds are rec - on - ciled.

TOLLEFSON
76 76 66 76

Bright and Glorious Is the Sky 75

1 Bright and glo - rious is the sky, Ra - diant are the
2 On that ho - ly Christ - mas night Through the dark - ness
3 Sa - ges from the East a - far, When they saw this
4 Him they found in Beth - le - hem, Yet he wore no
heav - ens high Where the gold - en stars are shin - ing.
beamed a light; All the stars a - bove were pal - ing,
won - drous star, Went to find the king of na - tions
di - a - dem; They but saw a maid - en low - ly
All their rays to earth in - clin - ing Beck - on us to
All their lus - ter slow - ly fail - ing As the Christ - mas
And to of - fer their ob - la - tions Un - to him as
With an in - fant pure and ho - ly Rest - ing in her
heav'n a - bove, Beck - on us to heav'n a - bove.
star drew nigh, As the Christ - mas star drew nigh.
Lord and King, Un - to him as Lord and King.
lov - ing arms, Rest - ing in her lov - ing arms.

5 Guided by the star, they found
Him whose praise the ages sound.
We too have a star to guide us
Which forever will provide us
With the light to find our Lord.

6 As a star, God's holy Word
Leads us to our King and Lord;
Brightly from its sacred pages
Shall this light throughout the ages
Shine upon our path of life.

 Text: Nikolai F. S. Grundtvig, 1783–1872; tr. Service Book and Hymnal, *1958, alt.*
Tune: Danish, 1830

DEJLIG ER DEN HIMMEL BLAA
77 88 77

76 O Morning Star, How Fair and Bright!

1 O Morn - ing Star, how fair and bright! You shine with God's
2 Come, heav'n - ly bride - groom, light di - vine, And deep with - in
3 Lord, when you look on us in love, At once there falls
4 Al - might - y Fa - ther, in your Son You loved us, when

own truth and light, A - glow with grace and mer - cy!
our hearts now shine; There light a flame un - dy - ing!
from God a - bove A ray of pur - est plea - sure.
not yet be - gun Was this old earth's foun - da - tion!

Of Ja - cob's race, King Da - vid's Son, Our Lord and mas -
In your one bod - y let us be As liv - ing branch -
Your Word and Spir - it, flesh and blood Re - fresh our souls
Your Son has ran - somed us in love To live in him

ter, you have won Our hearts to serve you on - ly!
es of a tree, Your life our lives sup - ply - ing.
with heav'n - ly food. You are our dear - est trea - sure!
here and a - bove: This is your great sal - va - tion.

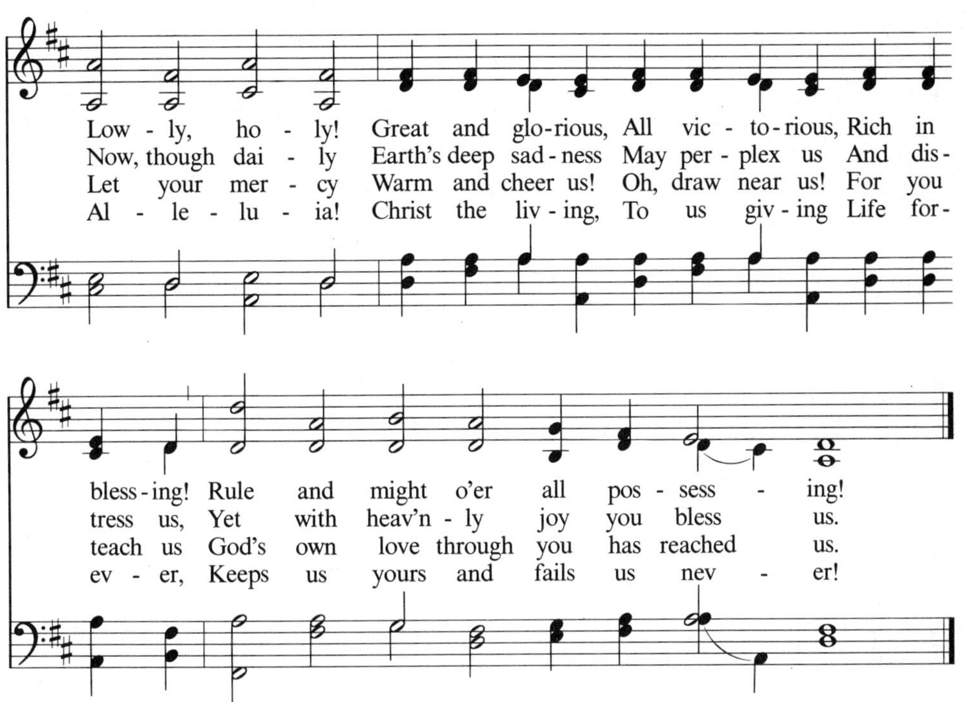
Low - ly, ho - ly! Great and glo-rious, All vic - to-rious, Rich in
Now, though dai - ly Earth's deep sad-ness May per - plex us And dis-
Let your mer - cy Warm and cheer us! Oh, draw near us! For you
Al - le - lu - ia! Christ the liv-ing, To us giv-ing Life for-
bless-ing! Rule and might o'er all pos - sess - ing!
tress us, Yet with heav'n - ly joy you bless us.
teach us God's own love through you has reached us.
ev - er, Keeps us yours and fails us nev - er!

5 What joy to know, when life is past,
The Lord we love is first and last,
The end and the beginning!
He will one day, oh, glorious grace,
Transport us to that happy place
Beyond all tears and sinning!
Amen! Amen!
Come, Lord Jesus!
Crown of gladness!
We are yearning
For the day of your returning.

6 Oh, let the harps break forth in sound!
Our joy be all with music crowned,
Our voices gaily blending!
For Christ goes with us all the way—
Today, tomorrow, ev'ry day!
His love is never ending!
Sing out! Ring out!
Jubilation!
Exultation!
Tell the story!
Great is he, the King of glory!

Tune: Philipp Nicolai, 1556–1608

WIE SCHÖN LEUCHTET
PM

77 O One with God the Father

1 O one with God the Fa - ther In maj - es - ty and might,
2 Yet, Lord, we see but dim - ly; O heav'n-ly Light, a - rise;
3 O Je - sus, shine a - round us With ra - diance of your grace;
The bright-ness of his glo - ry, E - ter - nal Light of light:
Dis - pel these mists that shroud us And hide you from our eyes.
O Je - sus, turn up - on us The bright-ness of your face.
To gloom-y haunts of dark - ness Your rays are stream - ing
We long to track the foot - prints Where you your - self have
We need no star to guide us, As on our way we
down; The shad - ows flee be - fore you, The world's
trod; We long to see the path - way That leads
press, If you will light our path - way, O Sun

true light has come.
to you, our God.
of righ - teous - ness.

Text: William W. How, 1823–1897, alt.
© *Tune: Basil Harwood, 1859–1949*

THORNBURY
76 76 D

All Praise to You, O Lord

78

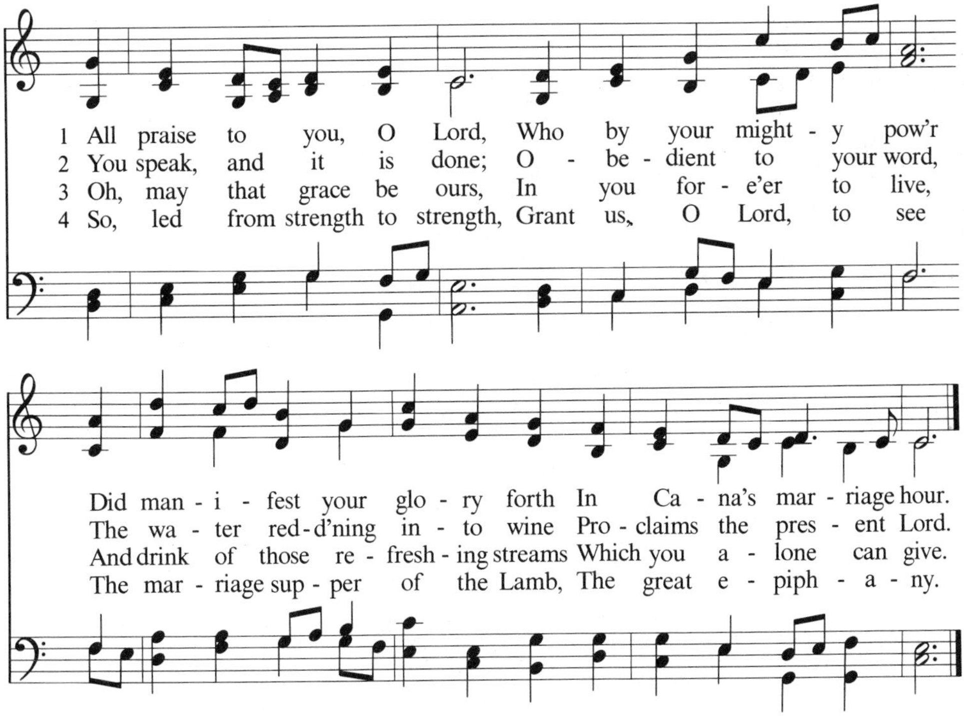

1 All praise to you, O Lord, Who by your might - y pow'r
Did man - i - fest your glo - ry forth In Ca - na's mar - riage hour.

2 You speak, and it is done; O - be - dient to your word,
The wa - ter red - d'ning in - to wine Pro - claims the pres - ent Lord.

3 Oh, may that grace be ours, In you for - e'er to live,
And drink of those re - fresh - ing streams Which you a - lone can give.

4 So, led from strength to strength, Grant us, O Lord, to see
The mar - riage sup - per of the Lamb, The great e - piph - a - ny.

Text: Hyde W. Beadon, 1812–1891
© *Tune: Kenneth G. Finlay, b. 1882*

GARELOCHSIDE
SM

79 To Jordan Came the Christ, Our Lord

1 To Jor - dan came the Christ, our Lord, To do his Fa - ther's plea - sure; Bap - tized by John, the Fa - ther's Word Was giv - en us to trea - sure. This heav'n-ly wash-ing now shall be A cleans-ing from trans-gres - sion And, by his blood and ag - o - ny,
2 Oh, hear and mark the mes - sage well, For God him-self has spo - ken. Let faith, not doubt, a - mong us dwell And so re-ceive this to - ken. Our Lord here with his Word en - dows Pure wa - ter, free - ly flow - ing. God's Ho - ly Spir - it here a - vows
3 These truths on Jor - dan's banks were shown By might - y word and won - der. The Fa - ther's voice from heav'n came down, Which we do well to pon - der: "This man is my be - lov - ed Son, In whom my heart has plea - sure. Him you must hear, and him a - lone,
4 There stood the Son of God in love, His grace to us ex - tend - ing; The Ho - ly Spir - it like a dove Up - on the scene de - scend - ing; The tri - une God as - sur - ing us, With prom - is - es com - pel - ling, That in our bap - tism he will thus

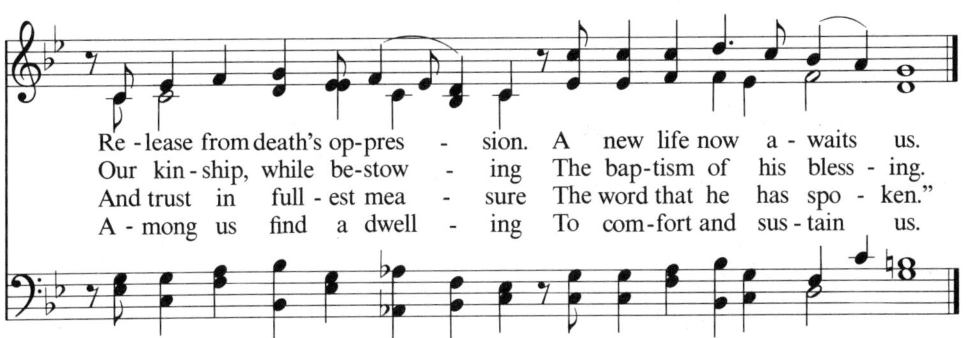
Re - lease from death's op-pres - sion. A new life now a - waits us.
Our kin - ship, while be-stow - ing The bap-tism of his bless - ing.
And trust in full - est mea - sure The word that he has spo - ken."
A - mong us find a dwell - ing To com-fort and sus - tain us.

5 To his disciples spoke the Lord,
"Go out to ev'ry nation,
And bring to them the living Word
And this my invitation:
Let ev'ryone abandon sin
And come in true contrition
To be baptized, and thereby win
Full pardon and remission,
And heav'nly bliss inherit."

6 But woe to those who cast aside
This grace so freely given;
They shall in sin and shame abide
And to despair be driven.
For born in sin, their works must fail,
Their striving saves them never;
Their pious acts do not avail,
And they are lost forever,
Eternal death their portion..

7 All that the mortal eye beholds
Is water as we pour it.
Before the eye of faith unfolds
The pow'r of Jesus' merit.
For here it sees the crimson flood
To all our ills bring healing;
The wonders of his precious blood
The love of God revealing,
Assuring his own pardon.

 Text: Martin Luther, 1483–1546; tr. Elizabeth Quitmeyer, b. 1911, alt.
Tune: J. Walther, Geistliche Gesangbüchlein, *1524*

CHRIST, UNSER HERR
87 87 87 877

80 Oh, Wondrous Type! Oh, Vision Fair

1 Oh, won - drous type! Oh, vi - sion fair Of
2 With Mo - ses and E - li - jah nigh The in -
3 With shin - ing face and bright ar - ray, Christ
4 And faith - ful hearts are raised on high By
glo - ry that the Church may share, Which
car - nate Lord holds con - verse high; And
deigns to man - i - fest to - day What
this great vi - sion's mys - ter - y; For
Christ up - on the moun - tain shows, Where
from the cloud, the Ho - ly One Bears
glo - ry shall be theirs a - bove Who
which in joy - ful strains we raise The
bright - er than the sun he glows!
rec - ord to the on - ly Son.
joy in God with per - fect love.
voice of prayer, the hymn of praise.

5 O Father, with the eternal Son
And Holy Spirit ever one,
We pray you, bring us by your grace
To see your glory face to face.

Text: Sarum, 15th cent.; tr. John M. Neale, 1818–1866, alt.
Tune: English, 15th cent.

DEO GRACIAS
LM

O Chief of Cities, Bethlehem 81

1 O chief of cit - ies, Beth - le - hem, Of Da - vid's
2 Be - yond the sun in splen - dor bright, A - bove you
3 The Wise Men, see - ing him so fair, Bow low be -
4 The gold - en trib - ute owns him king, But frank - in -
crown the fair - est gem, But more to us than
stands a won - drous light Pro - claim - ing from the
fore him, and with prayer Their trea - sured east - ern
cense to God they bring, And last, pro - phet - ic
Da - vid's name, In you, as man, the Sav - ior came.
con - scious skies That here, in flesh, the God - head lies.
gifts un - fold Of in - cense, myrrh, and roy - al gold.
sign, with myrrh They shad - ow forth his sep - ul - cher.

5 O Jesus, whom the Gentiles see,
With Father, Spirit, One in Three:
To you, O God, be glory giv'n
By saints on earth and saints in heav'n.

 Text: Marcus Aurelius Clemens Prudentius, 348–413; tr. composite, alt.
Tune: English folk tune

TRUTH FROM ABOVE
LM

82 As with Gladness Men of Old

1 As with glad-ness men of old Did the guid-ing star be-hold;
2 As with joy-ful steps they sped, Sav-ior, to thy low-ly bed,
3 As they of-fered gifts most rare At thy cra-dle, rude and bare,
4 Ho-ly Je-sus, ev-'ry day Keep us in the nar-row way;
As with joy they hailed its light, Lead-ing on-ward, beam-ing bright;
There to bend the knee be-fore Thee, whom heav'n and earth a-dore;
So may we with ho-ly joy, Pure and free from sin's al-loy,
And when earth-ly things are past, Bring our ran-somed souls at last
So, most gra-cious Lord, may we Ev-er-more be led by thee.
So may we with will-ing feet Ev-er seek thy mer-cy seat.
All our cost-liest trea-sures bring, Christ, to thee, our heav'n-ly king.
Where they need no star to guide, Where no clouds thy glo-ry hide.

5 In the heav'nly country bright
Need they no created light;
Thou its light, its joy, its crown,
Thou its sun which goes not down;
There forever may we sing
Alleluias to our King.

Text: William C. Dix, 1837–1898, alt.
Tune: Conrad Kocher, 1786–1872

DIX
77 77 77

From God the Father, Virgin-Born

83

1 From God the Father, virgin-born To us the
2 Be-ginning from his home on high, In human
3 Glide on, O glorious Sun, and bring The gift of
4 A-bide with us, O Lord, we pray; The gloom of

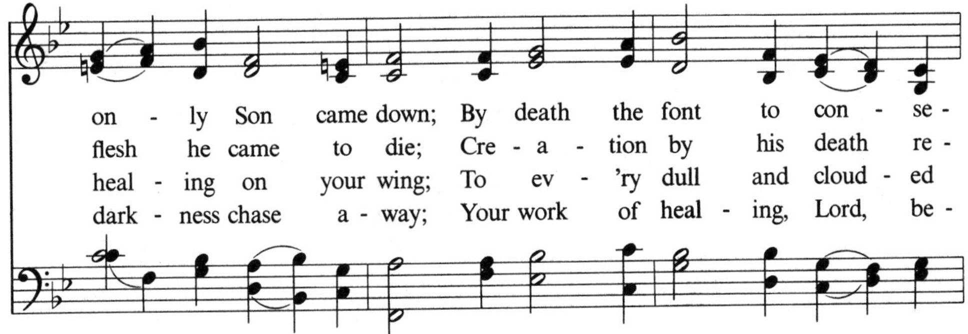
only Son came down; By death the font to conse-
flesh he came to die; Cre-a-tion by his death re-
heal-ing on your wing; To ev-'ry dull and cloud-ed
dark-ness chase a-way; Your work of heal-ing, Lord, be-

crate, The faith-ful to re-gen-er-ate.
stored, And shed new joys of life a-broad.
sense The clear-ness of your light dis-pense.
gin, And take a-way the stain of sin.

5 Lord, once you came to earth's domain
And, we believe, shall come again;
Be with us on the battlefield,
From ev'ry harm your people shield.

6 To you, O Lord, all glory be
For this your blest epiphany;
To God whom all his hosts adore,
And Holy Spirit evermore.

Text: Latin office hymn, c. 11th cent.; tr. John M. Neale, 1818–1866
Tune: Antiphoner, *Grenoble, 1753*

DEUS TUORUM MILITUM
LM

84 Brightest and Best of the Stars of the Morning

1 Bright-est and best of the stars of the morn - ing,
2 Cold on his cra - dle the dew - drops are shin - ing;
3 Shall we not yield him, in cost - ly de - vo - tion,
4 Vain - ly we of - fer each am - ple ob - la - tion,
Dawn on our dark - ness and lend us your aid.
Low lies his head with the beasts of the stall;
Fra - grance of E - dom and of - f'rings di - vine,
Vain - ly with gifts would his fa - vor se - cure;
Star of the East, the ho - ri - zon a - dorn - ing,
An - gels a - dore him in slum - ber re - clin - ing,
Gems of the moun - tain and pearls of the o - cean,
Rich - er by far is the heart's ad - o - ra - tion,
Guide where our in - fant Re - deem - er is laid.
Mak - er and Mon - arch and Sav - ior of all.
Myrrh from the for - est or gold from the mine?
Dear - er to God are the prayers of the poor.

5 Brightest and best of the stars of the morning,
Dawn on our darkness and lend us your aid.
Star of the East, the horizon adorning,
Guide where our infant Redeemer is laid.

Text: Reginald Heber, 1783–1826, alt.
Tune: James P. Harding, c. 1860–1911, adapt.

MORNING STAR
11 10 11 10

When Christ's Appearing Was Made Known

85

1 When Christ's ap - pear - ing was made known, King Her - od trem-bled for his throne; But he who of - fers heav'n - ly birth Seeks not the king - doms of this earth.
2 The east - ern sa - ges saw from far And fol - lowed on his guid - ing star; By light their way to light they trod, And by their gifts con - fessed their God.
3 With - in the Jor - dan's sa - cred flood The heav'n - ly Lamb in meek - ness stood, That he, of whom no sin was known, Might cleanse his peo - ple from their own.
4 And oh, what mir - a - cle di - vine, When wa - ter red - dened in - to wine! He spoke the word, and forth it flowed In streams that na - ture ne'er be - stowed.

5 For this his glad epiphany,
All glory unto Jesus be;
Whom with the Father we adore,
And Holy Ghost forevermore.

 Text: Coelius Sedulius, c. 5th cent.; tr. composite
Tune: J. Klug, Geistliche Lieder, *1533*

WO GOTT ZUM HAUS
LM

86 The Only Son from Heaven

1 The on - ly Son from heav - en, Fore - told by an - cient seers,
2 Oh, time of God ap - point - ed, Oh, bright and ho - ly morn!
3 A - wak - en, Lord, our spir - it To know and love you more,
4 O Fa - ther, here be - fore you With God the Ho - ly Ghost,
By God the Fa - ther giv - en, In hu - man form ap - pears.
He comes, the king a - noint - ed, The Christ, the vir - gin - born,
In faith to stand un - shak - en, In spir - it to a - dore,
And Je - sus, we a - dore you, O pride of an - gel - host:
No sphere his light con - fin - ing, No star so bright - ly
Grim death to van - quish for us, To o - pen heav'n be -
That we, through this world mov - ing, Each glimpse of heav - en
Be - fore you mor - tals low - ly Cry, "Ho - ly, ho - ly,
shin - ing As he, our Morn - ing Star.
fore us And bring us life a - gain.
prov - ing, May reap its full - ness there.
ho - ly, O bless - ed Trin - i - ty!"

Text: Elizabeth Cruciger, c. 1500–1535; tr. Arthur T. Russell, 1806–1874, alt.
Tune: Enchiridion, *Erfurt, 1524*

HERR CHRIST DER EINIG GOTTS SOHN
76 76 776

Hail to the Lord's Anointed

87

1 Hail to the Lord's a - noint - ed, Great Da - vid's great - er Son!
2 He comes with res - cue speed - y To those who suf - fer wrong,
3 He shall come down like show - ers Up - on the fruit - ful earth;
4 Kings shall fall down be - fore him, And gold and in - cense bring;
Hail, in the time ap - point - ed, His reign on earth be - gun! He
To help the poor and need - y, And bid the weak be strong; To
And love, joy, hope, like flow - ers, Spring in his path to birth. Be -
All na - tions shall a - dore him, His praise all peo - ple sing. To
comes to break op - pres - sion, To set the cap - tive free, To take a -
give them songs for sigh - ing, Their dark-ness turn to light, Whose souls, con -
fore him on the moun - tains Shall peace, the her - ald, go; And righ-teous -
him shall prayer un - ceas - ing And dai - ly vows as - cend; His king-dom
way trans - gres - sion And rule in eq - ui - ty.
demned and dy - ing, Were pre - cious in his sight.
ness in foun - tains From hill to val - ley flow.
still in - creas - ing, A king - dom with - out end.

Text: James Montgomery, 1771–1854
Tune: Leonhart Schröter, 1540–1602

FREUT EUCH, IHR LIEBEN
76 76 D

88 Oh, Love, How Deep

1 Oh, love, how deep, how broad, how high, Be -
2 He sent no an - gel to our race, Of
3 For us bap - tized, for us he bore His
4 For us he prayed; for us he taught; For
yond all thought and fan - ta - sy, That
high - er or of low - er place, But
ho - ly fast and hun - gered sore; For
us his dai - ly works he wrought, By
God, the Son of God, should take Our
wore the robe of hu - man frame, And
us temp - ta - tion sharp he knew; For
words and signs and ac - tions thus Still
mor - tal form for mor - tal's sake!
to this world him - self he came.
us the tempt - er o - ver - threw.
seek - ing not him - self, but us.

5 For us by wickedness betrayed,
For us, in crown of thorns arrayed,
He bore the shameful cross and death;
For us he gave his dying breath.

6 For us he rose from death again;
For us he went on high to reign;
For us he sent his Spirit here
To guide, to strengthen, and to cheer.

7 All glory to our Lord and God
For love so deep, so high, so broad;
The Trinity whom we adore
Forever and forevermore.

Text: attr. Thomas á Kempis, 1380–1471; tr. Benjamin Webb, 1820–1885, alt.
Tune: English, 15th cent.

DEO GRACIAS
L M

How Good, Lord, to Be Here! 89

1 How good, Lord, to be here! Your glo - ry fills the night; Your face and gar - ments, like the sun, Shine with un - bor - rowed light.
2 How good, Lord, to be here! Your beau - ty to be - hold Where Mo - ses and E - li - jah stand, Your mes - sen - gers of old.
3 Ful - fill - er of the past And hope of things to be, We hail your bod - y glo - ri - fied And our re - demp - tion see.
4 Be - fore we taste of death, We see your king - dom come; We long to hold the vi - sion bright And make this hill our home.

5 How good, Lord, to be here!
Yet we may not remain;
But since you bid us leave the mount,
Come with us to the plain.

 Text: Joseph A. Robinson, 1858–1933, alt.
Tune: Mercer, Church Psalter, *1854*

POTSDAM
S M

90 Songs of Thankfulness and Praise

1 Songs of thank-ful-ness and praise, Je-sus, Lord, to thee we raise;
2 Man-i-fest at Jor-dan's stream, Proph-et, Priest, and King su-preme;
3 Man-i-fest in mak-ing whole Pal-sied limbs and faint-ing soul;
4 Grant us grace to see thee, Lord, Pres-ent in thy ho-ly Word;
Man-i-fest-ed by the star To the sa-ges from a-far,
And at Ca-na wed-ding guest In thy God-head man-i-fest;
Man-i-fest in val-iant fight, Quell-ing all the dev-il's might;
Grace to im-i-tate thee now And be pure, as pure art thou;
Branch of roy-al Da-vid's stem In thy birth at Beth-le-hem:
Man-i-fest in pow'r di-vine, Chang-ing wa-ter in-to wine;
Man-i-fest in gra-cious will, Ev-er bring-ing good from ill:
That we might be-come like thee At thy great e-piph-a-ny,
An-thems be to thee ad-dressed,
An-thems be to thee ad-dressed,
An-thems be to thee ad-dressed,
And may praise thee, ev-er blest,
God in flesh made man-i-fest.

Text: Christopher Wordsworth, 1807–1885
Tune: Christoph Anton, d. 1658

SALZBURG
77 77 D

Savior, When in Dust to You

91

1 Sav - ior, when in dust to you Low we bow in hom - age due;
2 By your help - less in - fant years, By your life of want and tears,
3 By your hour of dire de - spair, By your ag - o - ny of prayer,
4 By your deep ex - pir - ing groan, By the sad se - pul - chral stone,
When, re - pen - tant, to the skies Scarce we lift our weep - ing eyes;
By your days of deep dis - tress In the sav - age wil - der - ness,
By the cross, the nail, the thorn, Pierc - ing spear, and tor - turing scorn,
By the vault whose dark a - bode Held in vain the ris - ing God,
Oh, by all your pains and woe Suf - fered once for us be - low,
By the dread, mys - te - rious hour Of the in - sult - ing tempt - er's pow'r,
By the gloom that veiled the skies O'er the dread - ful sac - ri - fice,
Oh, from earth to heav'n re - stored, Might - y, re - as - cend - ed Lord,
Bend - ing from your throne on high, Hear our pen - i - ten - tial cry!
Turn, oh, turn a fa - v'ring eye; Hear our pen - i - ten - tial cry!
Lis - ten to our hum - ble sigh; Hear our pen - i - ten - tial cry!
Bend - ing from your throne on high, Hear our pen - i - ten - tial cry!

Text: Robert Grant, 1779–1838, alt.
Tune: Joseph Parry, 1841–1903

ABERYSTWYTH
77 77 D

92 Were You There

E♭ B♭ E♭
1 Were you there when they cru - ci - fied my Lord? Were you
2 Were you there when they nailed him to the tree? Were you
3 Were you there when they laid him in the tomb? Were you
4 Were you there when God raised him from the tomb? Were you
Gm Cm B♭ E♭ B♭ E♭ A♭ B♭ E♭
there when they cru - ci - fied my Lord? Oh,
there when they nailed him to the tree? Oh,
there when they laid him in the tomb? Oh,
there when God raised him from the tomb? Oh,
A♭ E♭ A♭dim Cm A♭ E♭ A♭ B♭
some-times it caus - es me to trem - ble, trem - ble, trem - ble.
some-times it caus - es me to trem - ble, trem - ble, trem - ble.
some-times it caus - es me to trem - ble, trem - ble, trem - ble.
some-times it caus - es me to trem - ble, trem - ble, trem - ble.
A♭ E♭ Cm7 B♭6 B♭7 Cm Gm B♭7 E♭
Were you there when they cru - ci - fied my Lord?
Were you there when they nailed him to the tree?
Were you there when they laid him in the tomb?
Were you there when God raised him from the tomb?

Text: Negro spiritual, alt.
Tune: Negro spiritual

WERE YOU THERE
10 10 14 10

Jesus, Refuge of the Weary

1 Je - sus, ref - uge of the wea - ry, Blest re - deem - er, whom we love,
2 Do we pass that cross un - heed - ing, Breath-ing no re - pen - tant vow,
3 Je - sus, may our hearts be burn - ing With more fer - vent love for you;

Foun - tain in life's des - ert drea - ry, Sav - ior from the world a - bove:
Though we see you wound-ed, bleed - ing, See your thorn - en - cir - cled brow?
May our eyes be ev - er turn - ing To be - hold your cross a - new;

Of - ten have your eyes, of - fend - ed, Gazed up - on the sin - ner's fall;
Yet your sin - less death has brought us Life e - ter - nal, peace, and rest;
Till in glo - ry, part - ed nev - er From the bless - ed Sav - ior's side,

Yet up - on the cross ex - tend - ed, You have borne the pain of all.
On - ly what your grace has taught us Calms the sin - ner's deep dis - tress.
Grav-en in our hearts for - ev - er, Dwell the cross, the Cru - ci - fied.

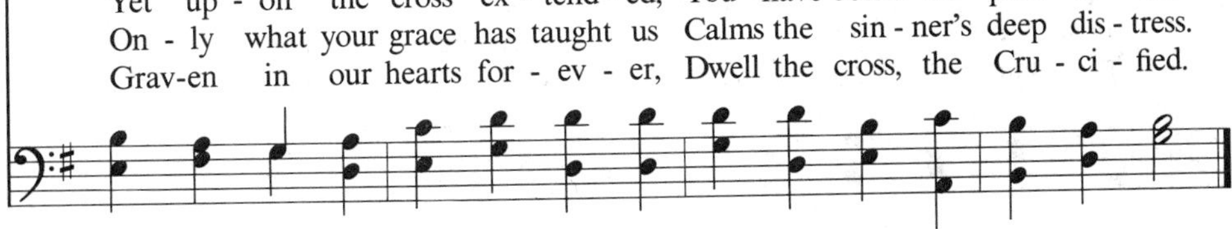

Text: Girolamo Savonarola, 1452–1498; tr. Jane F. Wilde, 1826–1896, alt.
Tune: Herrnhut, c. 1735

O DU LIEBE MEINER LIEBE
87 87 D

94 My Song Is Love Unknown

F Dm B♭6 F Am Gm F
1 My song is love un-known, My Sav-ior's love to me, Love
2 He came from his blest throne, Sal-va-tion to be-stow; But
3 Some-times they strew his way And his sweet prais-es sing; Re-
4 Why, what hath my Lord done? What makes this rage and spite? He
Dm B♭6 F Am Gm F C
to the love-less shown, That they might love-ly be. Oh,
men made strange, and none The longed-for Christ would know. But,
sound-ing all the day Ho-san-nas to their King. Then
made the lame to run, He gave the blind their sight. Sweet
F Dm B♭ Am C B♭ C
who am I, that for my sake My Lord should take frail
oh, my friend, my friend in-deed, Who at my need his
"Cru-ci-fy!" is all their breath, And for his death they
in-ju-ries! Yet they at these Them-selves dis-please, and
Am C F Am F C7 F
flesh and die? My Lord should take frail flesh and die?
life did spend; Who at my need his life did spend!
thirst and cry. And for his death they thirst and cry.
'gainst him rise; Them-selves dis-please, and 'gainst him rise.

5 They rise, and needs will have
My dear Lord made away;
A murderer they save,
The prince of life they slay.
Yet cheerful he to suff'ring goes,
That he his foes from thence might free.

6 In life, no house, no home
My Lord on earth might have;
In death, no friendly tomb
But what a stranger gave.
What may I say? Heav'n was his home;
But mine the tomb wherein he lay.

7 Here might I stay and sing—
No story so divine!
Never was love, dear King,
Never was grief like thine.
This is my friend, in whose sweet praise
I all my days could gladly spend!

Text: Samuel Crossman, c. 1624–1683
Tune: John D. Edwards, 1806–1885

RHOSYMEDRE
6666 888

Glory Be to Jesus

95

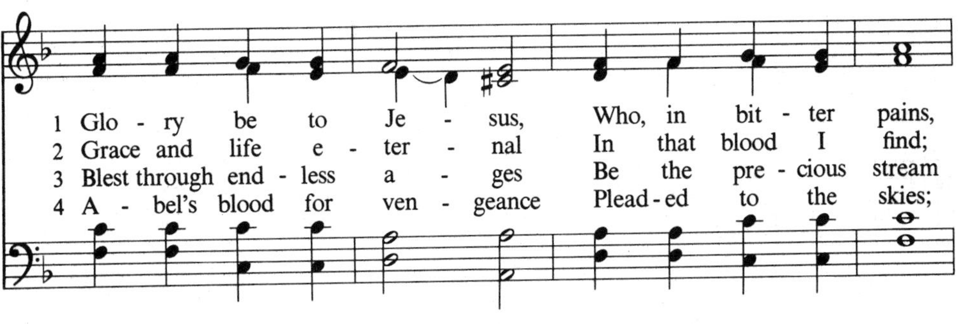
1 Glo - ry be to Je - sus, Who, in bit - ter pains,
2 Grace and life e - ter - nal In that blood I find;
3 Blest through end - less a - ges Be the pre - cious stream
4 A - bel's blood for ven - geance Plead - ed to the skies;

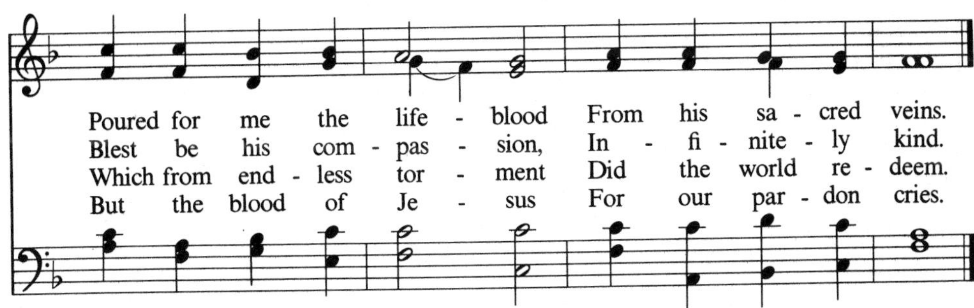
Poured for me the life - blood From his sa - cred veins.
Blest be his com - pas - sion, In - fi - nite - ly kind.
Which from end - less tor - ment Did the world re - deem.
But the blood of Je - sus For our par - don cries.

5 Oft as earth exulting
Wafts its praise on high,
Angel hosts rejoicing
Make their glad reply.

6 Lift we then our voices,
Swell the mighty flood;
Louder still and louder
Praise the precious blood.

Text: Italian, 18th cent.; tr. Edward Caswall, 1814–1878
Tune: Friedrich Filitz, 1804–1876

WEM IN LEIDENSTAGEN
65 65

96 Your Heart, O God, Is Grieved

Cantor

1 O God, Father in heav - en, have mer - cy up - on us.
2 O Son of God, redeemer of the world, have mer - cy up - on us.
3 O God, Holy Spir - it, have mer - cy up - on us.

Congregation

1 Your heart, O God, is grieved, we know, By ev - 'ry e - vil, ev - 'ry woe; Up - on your cross - for - sak - en Son Our death is laid, and peace is won.
2 Your arms ex - tend, O Christ, to save From sting of death and grasp of grave; Your scars be - fore the Fa - ther move His heart to mer - cy at such love.
3 O lav - ish Giv - er, come to aid The fee - ble child your grace has made. Now make us grow and help us pray; Bring joy and com - fort; come to stay.

 Text: Jiři Tranovský, 1591–1637; tr. Jaroslav J. Vajda, b. 1919
Tune: Škultéty, Partitura, *1798*

ZNÁME TO, PANE BOŽE NÁŠ
irregular

Christ, the Life of All the Living

97

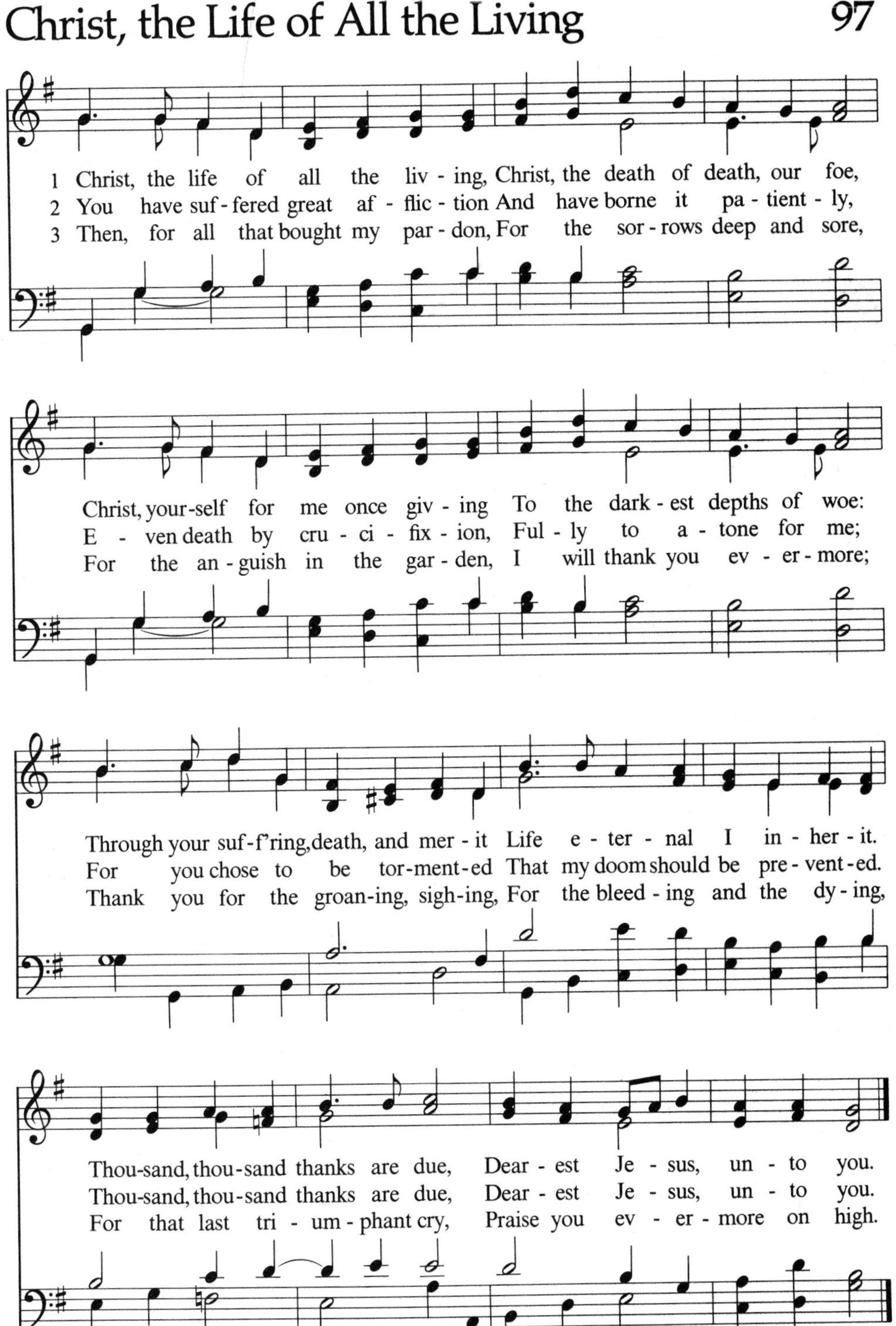
1 Christ, the life of all the liv - ing, Christ, the death of death, our foe,
2 You have suf - fered great af - flic - tion And have borne it pa - tient - ly,
3 Then, for all that bought my par - don, For the sor - rows deep and sore,
Christ, your-self for me once giv - ing To the dark - est depths of woe:
E - ven death by cru - ci - fix - ion, Ful - ly to a - tone for me;
For the an - guish in the gar - den, I will thank you ev - er - more;
Through your suf-f'ring, death, and mer - it Life e - ter - nal I in - her - it.
For you chose to be tor-ment-ed That my doom should be pre - vent - ed.
Thank you for the groan-ing, sigh-ing, For the bleed - ing and the dy - ing,
Thou-sand, thou-sand thanks are due, Dear - est Je - sus, un - to you.
Thou-sand, thou-sand thanks are due, Dear - est Je - sus, un - to you.
For that last tri - um - phant cry, Praise you ev - er - more on high.

Text: Ernst C. Homburg, 1605–1681; tr. Catherine Winkworth, 1829–1878, alt.
Tune: Das grosse Cantionale, *Darmstadt, 1687*

JESU, MEINES LEBENS LEBEN
87 87 88 77

Alas! And Did My Savior Bleed

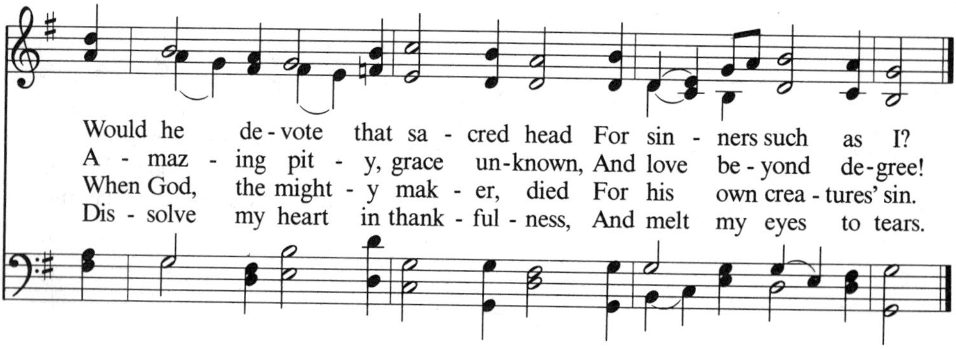

1 A - las! And did my Sav - ior bleed, And did my sov - 'reign die? Would he de - vote that sa - cred head For sin - ners such as I?

2 Was it for sins that I had done He groaned up - on the tree? A - maz - ing pit - y, grace un-known, And love be - yond de-gree!

3 Well might the sun in dark - ness hide And shut its glo - ries in When God, the might - y mak - er, died For his own crea - tures' sin.

4 Thus might I hide my blush - ing face While his dear cross ap - pears, Dis - solve my heart in thank - ful - ness, And melt my eyes to tears.

5 But tears of grief cannot repay
The debt of love I owe;
Here, Lord, I give myself away:
It's all that I can do.

Text: Isaac Watts, 1674–1748, alt.
Tune: Hugh Wilson, 1764–1824

MARTYRDOM
CM

99 O Lord, throughout These Forty Days

1 O Lord, through-out these for - ty days You prayed and kept the fast;

2 You strove with Sa - tan, and you won; Your faith - ful - ness en-dured;

3 Though parched and hun - gry, yet you prayed And fixed your mind a - bove;

4 Be with us through this sea - son, Lord, And all our earth - ly days,

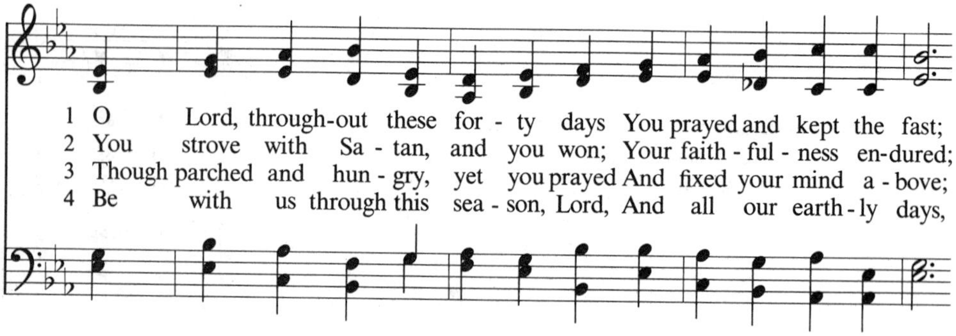

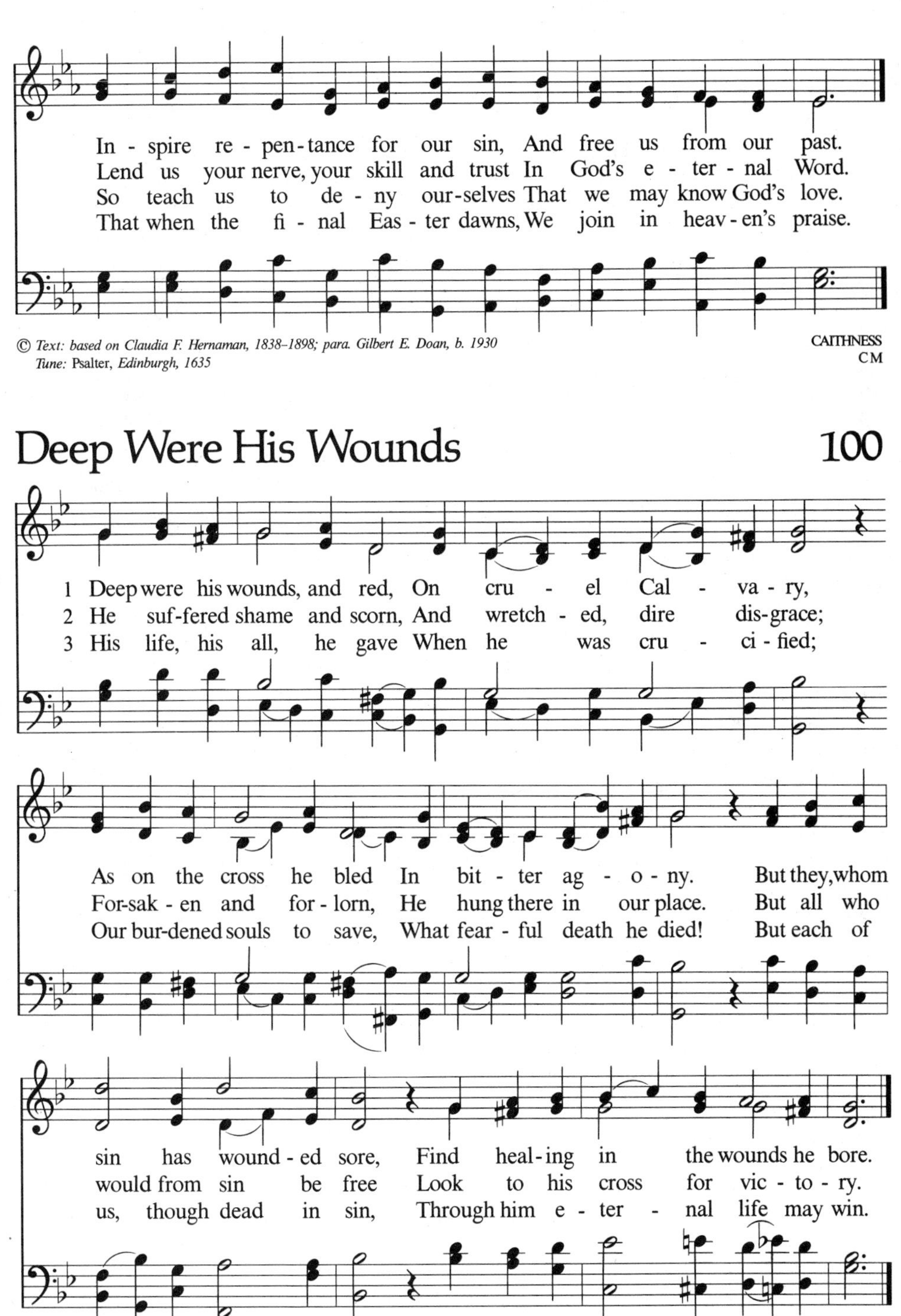
In - spire re - pen - tance for our sin, And free us from our past.
Lend us your nerve, your skill and trust In God's e - ter - nal Word.
So teach us to de - ny our - selves That we may know God's love.
That when the fi - nal Eas - ter dawns, We join in heav - en's praise.
© Text: based on Claudia F. Hernaman, 1838–1898; para. Gilbert E. Doan, b. 1930
Tune: Psalter, Edinburgh, 1635
CAITHNESS
CM
Deep Were His Wounds
100
1 Deep were his wounds, and red, On cru - el Cal - va - ry,
2 He suf - fered shame and scorn, And wretch - ed, dire dis - grace;
3 His life, his all, he gave When he was cru - ci - fied;
As on the cross he bled In bit - ter ag - o - ny. But they, whom
For - sak - en and for - lorn, He hung there in our place. But all who
Our bur - dened souls to save, What fear - ful death he died! But each of
sin has wound - ed sore, Find heal - ing in the wounds he bore.
would from sin be free Look to his cross for vic - to - ry.
us, though dead in sin, Through him e - ter - nal life may win.

© Text: William Johnson, b. 1906
© Tune: Leland B. Sateren, b. 1913

MARLEE
66 66 88

101 O Christ, Our King, Creator, Lord

1 O Christ, our king, cre - a - tor, Lord, Re - deem - ing
2 Lord, in your cross true grace is found; It flows from
3 Cre - a - tor of the stars of night, For us you
4 All trem - bling na - ture quaked to see Its dy - ing
all who trust your word: You come to those who
ev - 'ry stream - ing wound; Its pow'r our in - bred
veiled in flesh your light, And deigned our mor - tal
king up - on the tree; And when you drew your
seek your way; Now come and hear us as we pray.
sin con - trols, And breaks our bonds and frees our souls.
form to wear, And shared our hu - man want and care.
fi - nal breath The dark - 'ning skies con - fessed your death.

5 Now in the Father's glory high,
Great conqu'ror, nevermore to die,
Dispel our fears, shine through our night,
And reign forever, God of light.

 Text: Gregory I, 540–604; tr. hymnal version, 1978
 Tune: R. Vaughan Williams, 1872–1958

OAKLEY
LM

On My Heart Imprint Your Image 102

On my heart im - print your im - age, Bless - ed Je - sus, king of grace,
That life's trou - bles nor its plea - sures Ev - er may your work e - rase;
Let the clear in - scrip - tion be: Je - sus, cru - ci - fied for me,
Is my life, my hope's foun - da - tion, All my glo - ry and sal - va - tion!

Text: Thomas H. Kingo, 1634–1703; tr. Peer O. Strömme, 1856–1921, alt.
Tune: Johann B. König, 1691–1758

DER AM KREUZ
87 87 77 88

103 O Christ, Thou Lamb of God

O Christ, thou Lamb of God That tak-est a-way the sin of the world,
Have mer-cy up-on us!
O Christ, thou Lamb of God That tak-est a-way the sin of the world,
Have mer-cy up-on us!
O Christ, thou Lamb of God That tak-est a-way the sin of the world,

Grant us thy peace! A - men

Text: German, 1528; tr. unknown
Tune: Kirchenordnung, *Braunschweig, 1528*

CHRISTE, DU LAMM GOTTES
6 10 6 6 10 6 6 10 4

In the Cross of Christ I Glory 104

1 In the cross of Christ I glo - ry, Tow'r - ing o'er the wrecks of time. All the light of sa - cred sto - ry Gath - ers round its head sub - lime.

2 When the woes of life o'er - take me, Hopes de - ceive, and fears an - noy, Nev - er shall the cross for - sake me; Lo, it glows with peace and joy.

3 When the sun of bliss is beam - ing Light and love up - on my way, From the cross the ra - diance stream - ing Adds more lus - ter to the day.

4 Bane and bless - ing, pain and plea - sure, By the cross are sanc - ti - fied; Peace is there that knows no mea - sure, Joys that through all time a - bide.

Text: John Bowring, 1792–1872
Tune: Ithamar Conkey, 1815–1867

RATHBUN
8 7 8 7

105 A Lamb Goes Uncomplaining Forth

1 A lamb goes un - com - plain - ing forth To
2 This lamb is Christ, our great - est friend, The
3 He an - swered from his ten - der heart That
4 Of death I am no more a - fraid; His
save a world of sin - ners. He bears the bur -
Lamb of God, our Sav - ior, The one, his on -
he would take the bur - den: "My Fa - ther's will
dy - ing is my liv - ing. He clothes me in
den all a - lone, Dies shorn of all his
ly Son, God sent To win us reb - els
is my com - mand; I'll do as I am
his roy - al robes That he is al - ways
hon - ors. He goes to slaugh - ter, weak and faint, Is
o - ver. "Go down, my child," the Fa - ther said, "And
bid - den." Oh, won-drous love! Oh, lov - ing might! To
giv - ing His love is dress e - nough for me To

led to die with - out com-plaint; His spot - less life he
free my chil - dren from their dread Of death and con - dem-
right what mor - tals can - not right God sent his Son from
wear through all e - ter - ni - ty Be - fore the high - est
of - fers. He bears the shame, the stripes,
na - tion. The pain - ful stripes are hard
heav - en. What love, O Love, who came
Fa - ther, Where we shall stand at Je -
the wrath; His an - guish, mock - er - y, and
to bear, But by your death they all can
to save By lov - ing e - ven to the
sus' side, His Church, the well - ap - point - ed
death For us he glad - ly suf - fers.
share The joy of your sal - va - tion."
grave Un - til the stone was riv - en.
bride, When all the faith - ful gath - er.

© *Text: Paul Gerhardt, 1607–1676; hymnal translation, 1978*
Tune: Wolfgang Dachstein, c. 1487–1553

AN WASSERFLÜSSEN BABYLON
PM

106 In the Hour of Trial

1 In the hour of tri - al, Je - sus, plead for me,
2 With for - bid - den plea - sures Should this vain world charm,
3 Should thy mer - cy send me Sor - row, toil, and woe,
Lest by base de - ni - al I de - part from thee.
Or its sor - did trea - sures Spread to work me harm,
Or should pain at - tend me On my path be - low,
When thou seest me wa - ver, With a look re - call;
Bring to my re - mem - brance Sad Geth-sem - a - ne,
Grant that I may nev - er Fail thy hand to see;
Nor from fear or fa - vor Suf - fer me to fall.
Or, in dark - er sem - blance, Cross-crowned Cal - va - ry.
Grant that I may ev - er Cast my care on thee.

Text: James Montgomery, 1771–1854
Tune: Spencer Lane, 1843–1903

PENITENCE
65 65 D

Beneath the Cross of Jesus 107

1 Be-neath the cross of Je - sus I long to take my stand;
2 Up-on the cross of Je - sus, My eye at times can see
3 I take, O cross, your shad - ow For my a-bid-ing place;
The shad - ow of a might-y rock With-in a wea-ry land,
The ver - y dy - ing form of one Who suf-fered there for me.
I ask no oth - er sun-shine than The sun-shine of his face;
A home with-in a wil - der-ness, A rest up-on the way,
And from my con - trite heart, with tears, Two won - ders I con-fess:
Con-tent to let the world go by, To know no gain nor loss,
From the burn - ing of the noon-tide heat And bur-dens of the day.
The won - der of his glo-rious love And my un-wor-thi-ness.
My sin - ful self my on - ly shame, My glo - ry all, the cross.

Text: Elizabeth C. Clephane, 1830–1869
© Tune: Frederick C. Maker, 1844–1927

ST. CHRISTOPHER
76 86 86 86

108 All Glory, Laud, and Honor

Refrain
All glo - ry, laud, and hon - or To you, re - deem - er, king,
To whom the lips of chil - dren Made sweet ho - san - nas ring.
1 You are the king of Is - rael And Da - vid's roy - al Son,
2 The com - pa - ny of an - gels Are prais - ing you on high;
3 The mul - ti - tude of pil - grims With palms be - fore you went.
4 To you, be - fore your Pas - sion, They sang their hymns of praise.
Now in the Lord's name com - ing, Our King and Bless - ed One.
Cre - a - tion and all mor - tals In cho - rus make re - ply.
Our praise and prayer and an - thems Be - fore you we pre - sent.
To you, now high ex - alt - ed, Our mel - o - dy we raise.
Refrain

5 Their praises you accepted;
Accept the prayers we bring,
Great author of all goodness,
O good and gracious King. *Refrain*

Text: Theodulph of Orleans, c. 760–821; tr. John M. Neale, 1818–1866, alt.
Tune: Melchior Teschner, 1584–1635

VALET WILL ICH DIR GEBEN
76 76 D

Go to Dark Gethsemane 109

1 Go to dark Geth-sem - a - ne, All who feel the tempt-er's pow'r;
2 Fol - low to the judg - ment hall, View the Lord of life ar-raigned;
3 Cal-v'ry's mourn-ful moun - tain climb; There, a - dor - ing at his feet,
4 Ear - ly has - ten to the tomb Where they laid his breath-less clay;
Your Re - deem - er's con - flict see. Watch with him one bit - ter hour;
Oh, the worm-wood and the gall! Oh, the pangs his soul sus-tained!
Mark that mir - a - cle of time, God's own sac - ri - fice com-plete.
All is sol - i - tude and gloom. Who has tak - en him a - way?
Turn not from his griefs a - way; Learn from Je - sus Christ to pray.
Shun not suf - f'ring, shame, or loss; Learn from him to bear the cross.
"It is fin - ished!" hear him cry; Learn from Je - sus Christ to die.
Christ is ris'n! He meets our eyes. Sav - ior, teach us so to rise.

Text: James Montgomery, 1771–1854
Tune: Richard Redhead, 1820–1901

GETHSEMANE
77 77 77

110 At the Cross, Her Station Keeping

1 At the cross, her sta - tion keep - ing, Stood the mourn - ful
2 Oh, how sad and sore dis - tress - ed Was that moth - er
3 Who, on Christ's dear moth - er gaz - ing, Pierced by an - guish
4 For his peo - ple's sin chas - tis - ed, She be - held her

moth - er weep - ing, Close to Je - sus to the last.
high - ly bless - ed Of the sole - be - got - ten one!
so a - maz - ing, Born of wom - an, would not weep?
Son de - spis - ed, Scourged, and crowned with thorns en-twined;

Through her heart, his sor - row shar - ing, All his bit - ter
Oh, the depth of her af - flic - tion As she saw the
Who, on Christ's dear moth - er think - ing, Such a cup of
Saw him then from judg - ment tak - en, And in death by

an - guish bear - ing, Now at length the sword had passed.
cru - ci - fix - ion Of her dy - ing, glo - rious Son!
sor - row drink - ing, Would not share her sor - rows deep?
all for - sak - en, Till his spir - it he re - signed.

5 Jesus, may her deep devotion
Stir in me the same emotion,
Source of love, redeemer true.
Let me thus, fresh ardor gaining
And a purer love attaining,
Consecrate my life to you.

Text: 13th cent.; tr. composite, alt.
Tune: Gesangbuch, *Mainz, 1661*

STABAT MATER
887887

Lamb of God, Pure and Sinless 111

Stanzas 1, 2, 3
Lamb of God, pure and sin - less, Once on the cross an of - f'ring,
Pa - tient, meek, though guilt - less, For - sak - en in your suf - f'ring!
You died our guilt to ban - ish That none in sin need per - ish!
1 Grant us your mer - cy, O Je - sus!
2 Grant us your mer - cy, O Je - sus!
3 Your peace be with us, O Je - sus! A - men

 Text: Nikolaus Decius, 1490–1541; tr. Joel W. Lundeen, b. 1918
Tune: Nikolaus Decius, 1490–1541

O LAMM GOTTES, UNSCHULDIG
7767778

112 Jesus, in Thy Dying Woes

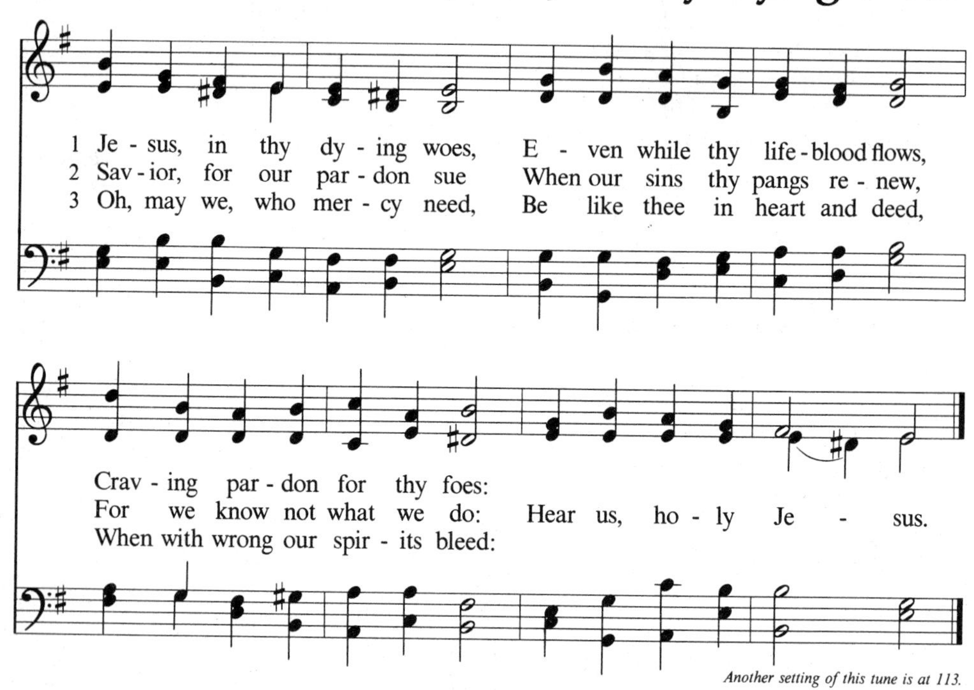
1 Je - sus, in thy dy - ing woes, E - ven while thy life - blood flows,
2 Sav - ior, for our par - don sue When our sins thy pangs re - new,
3 Oh, may we, who mer - cy need, Be like thee in heart and deed,
Crav - ing par - don for thy foes:
For we know not what we do: Hear us, ho - ly Je - sus.
When with wrong our spir - its bleed:

Another setting of this tune is at 113.

Part II

4 Jesus, pitying the sighs
Of the thief, who near thee dies,
Promising him paradise:
Hear us, holy Jesus.

5 May we in our guilt and shame
Still thy love and mercy claim,
Calling humbly on thy name:
Hear us, holy Jesus.

6 May our hearts to thee incline,
Looking from our cross to thine.
Cheer our souls with hope divine:
Hear us, holy Jesus.

Part III

7 Jesus, loving to the end
Her whose heart thy sorrows rend,
And thy dearest human friend:
Hear us, holy Jesus.

8 May we in thy sorrows share,
For thy sake all peril dare,
And enjoy thy tender care:
Hear us, holy Jesus.

9 May we all thy loved ones be,
All one holy family,
Loving for the love of thee:
Hear us, holy Jesus.

Part IV

10 Jesus, whelmed in fears unknown,
With our evil left alone,
While no light from heav'n is shown:
Hear us, holy Jesus.

11 When we seem in vain to pray
And our hope seems far away,
In the darkness be our stay:
Hear us, holy Jesus.

12 Though no Father seem to hear,
Though no light our spirits cheer,
May we know that God is near:
Hear us, holy Jesus.

Part V

13 Jesus, in thy thirst and pain,
While thy wounds thy lifeblood drain,
Thirsting more our love to gain:
Hear us, holy Jesus.

14 Thirst for us in mercy still;
All thy holy work fulfill;
Satisfy thy loving will:
Hear us, holy Jesus.

15 May we thirst thy love to know;
Lead us in our sin and woe
Where the healing waters flow:
Hear us, holy Jesus.

Part VI

16 Jesus, all our ransom paid,
All thy Father's will obeyed;
By thy suff'rings perfect made:
Hear us, holy Jesus.

17 Save us in our soul's distress;
Be our help to cheer and bless,
While we grow in holiness:
Hear us, holy Jesus.

18 Brighten all our heav'nward way
With an ever holier ray
Till we pass to perfect day:
Hear us, holy Jesus.

Part VII

19 Jesus, all thy labor vast,
All thy woe and conflict past;
Yielding up thy soul at last:
Hear us, holy Jesus.

20 When the death shades round us low'r,
Guard us from the tempter's pow'r,
Keep us in that trial hour:
Hear us, holy Jesus.

21 May thy life and death supply
Grace to live and grace to die,
Grace to reach the home on high:
Hear us, holy Jesus.

Text: Thomas B. Pollock, 1836–1896
Tune: Koralpsalmboken, *Stockholm, 1697*

ACK, VAD ÄR DOCK LIVET HÄR
777 6

113 Jesus, in Thy Dying Woes

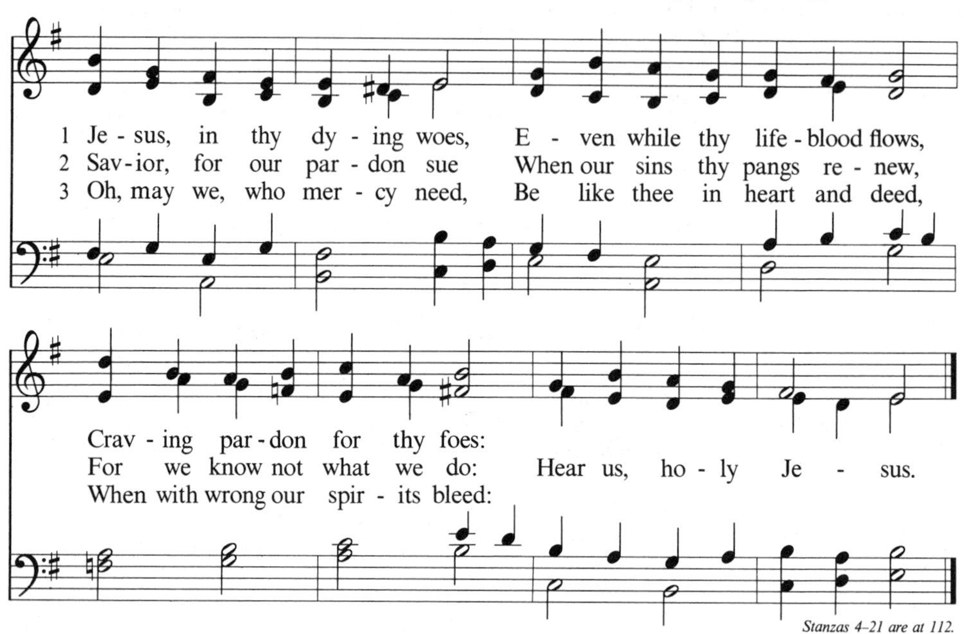
1 Je - sus, in thy dy - ing woes, E - ven while thy life - blood flows,
2 Sav - ior, for our par - don sue When our sins thy pangs re - new,
3 Oh, may we, who mer - cy need, Be like thee in heart and deed,
Crav - ing par - don for thy foes:
For we know not what we do: Hear us, ho - ly Je - sus.
When with wrong our spir - its bleed:

Stanzas 4–21 are at 112.

Text: *Thomas B. Pollock, 1836–1896*
Tune: Koralpsalmboken, *Stockholm, 1697*

ACK, VAD ÄR DOCK LIVET HÄR
7 7 7 6

114 There Is a Green Hill Far Away

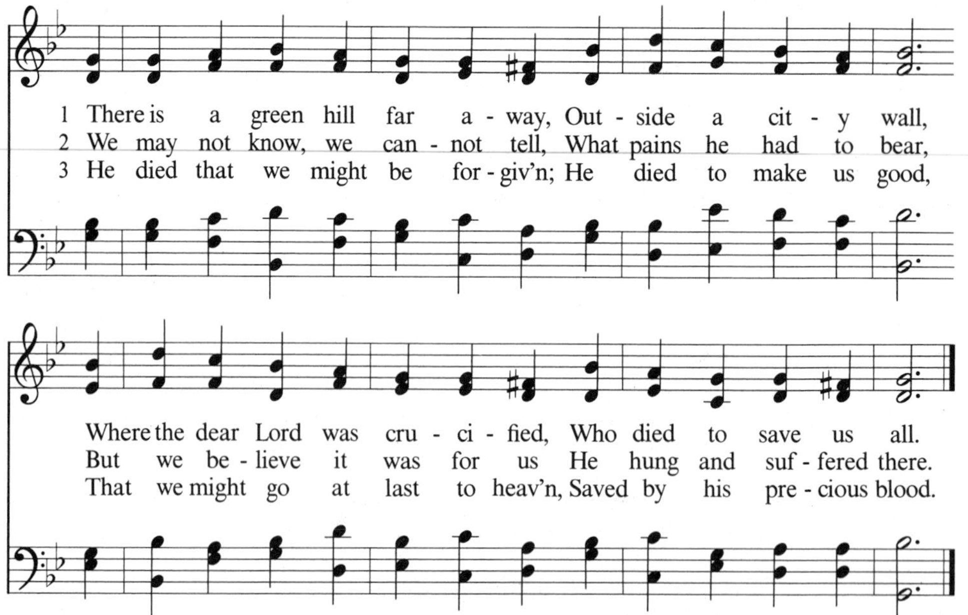
1 There is a green hill far a - way, Out - side a cit - y wall,
2 We may not know, we can - not tell, What pains he had to bear,
3 He died that we might be for - giv'n; He died to make us good,
Where the dear Lord was cru - ci - fied, Who died to save us all.
But we be - lieve it was for us He hung and suf - fered there.
That we might go at last to heav'n, Saved by his pre - cious blood.

Text: *Cecil F. Alexander, 1823–1895*
Tune: *Daman,* Booke of Musicke, *1591*

WINDSOR
CM

Jesus, I Will Ponder Now 115

1 Je - sus, I will pon - der now On your ho - ly Pas - sion;
2 Make me see your great dis - tress, An - guish, and af - flic - tion,
3 Yet, O Lord, not thus a - lone Make me see your Pas - sion,
4 Let me view your pain and loss With re - pen - tant griev - ing,
Let your Spir - it now en - dow Me for med - i - ta - tion.
Bonds and stripes and wretch - ed - ness And your cru - ci - fix - ion;
But its cause to me make known And its ter - mi - na - tion.
Nor pre - pare a - gain your cross By un - ho - ly liv - ing.
Grant that I in love and faith May the im - age cher - ish
Make me see how scourge and rod, Spear and nails, did wound you,
For I al - so and my sin Wrought your deep af - flic - tion;
May I give you love for love! Hear me, O my Sav - ior,
Of your suf - f'ring, pain, and death, That I may not per - ish.
How you died for those, O God, Who with thorns had crowned you.
This the shame - ful cause has been Of your cru - ci - fix - ion.
That I may in heav'n a - bove Sing your praise for - ev - er.

Text: Sigismund von Birken, 1626–1681; tr. August Crull, 1846–1923, alt.
Tune: Melchior Vulpius, c. 1560–1615

JESU KREUZ, LEIDEN UND PEIN
76 76 D

116 O Sacred Head, Now Wounded

1 O sa - cred head, now wound - ed, With grief and shame weighed down,
2 How art thou pale with an - guish, With sore a - buse and scorn;
3 What lan - guage shall I bor - row To thank thee, dear - est friend,
4 Lord, be my con - so - la - tion; Shield me when I must die;
Now scorn - ful - ly sur - round - ed With thorns, thine on - ly crown;
How does that vis - age lan - guish Which once was bright as morn!
For this thy dy - ing sor - row, Thy pit - y with - out end?
Re - mind me of thy Pas - sion When my last hour draws nigh.
O sa - cred head, what glo - ry, What bliss till now was thine!
Thy grief and bit - ter Pas - sion Were all for sin - ners' gain;
Oh, make me thine for - ev - er, And should I faint - ing be,
These eyes, new faith re - ceiv - ing, From thee shall nev - er move;
Yet, though de - spised and gor - y, I joy to call thee mine.
Mine, mine was the trans - gres - sion, But thine the dead - ly pain.
Lord, let me nev - er, nev - er Out - live my love to thee.
For he who dies be - liev - ing Dies safe - ly in thy love.

 Text: attr. Bernard of Clairvaux, 1091–1153; Paul Gerhardt, 1607–1676; tr. composite, alt.
Tune: Hans L. Hassler, 1564–1612

HERZLICH TUT MICH VERLANGEN
76 76 D

O Sacred Head, Now Wounded 117

1 O sa - cred head, now wound - ed, With grief and shame weighed down,
2 How art thou pale with an - guish, With sore a - buse and scorn;
3 What lan - guage shall I bor - row To thank thee, dear - est friend,
4 Lord, be my con - so - la - tion; Shield me when I must die;
Now scorn - ful - ly sur - round - ed With thorns, thine on - ly crown;
How does that vis - age lan - guish Which once was bright as morn!
For this thy dy - ing sor - row, Thy pit - y with - out end?
Re - mind me of thy Pas - sion When my last hour draws nigh.
O sa - cred head, what glo - ry, What bliss till now was thine!
Thy grief and bit - ter Pas - sion Were all for sin - ners' gain;
Oh, make me thine for - ev - er, And, should I faint - ing be,
These eyes, new faith re - ceiv - ing, From thee shall nev - er move;
Yet, though de - spised and gor - y, I joy to call thee mine.
Mine, mine was the trans - gres - sion, But thine the dead - ly pain.
Lord, let me nev - er, nev - er Out - live my love to thee.
For he who dies be - liev - ing Dies safe - ly in thy love.

 Text: attr. Bernard of Clairvaux, 1091–1153; Paul Gerhardt, 1607–1676; tr. composite, alt.
Tune: Hans L. Hassler, 1564–1612

HERZLICH TUT MICH VERLANGEN
76 76 D

118 Sing, My Tongue

1 Sing, my tongue, the glorious battle;
Sing the ending of the fray.
Now above the cross, the trophy,
Sound the loud triumphant lay;
Tell how Christ, the world's redeemer,
As a victim won the day.

2 Tell how, when at length the fullness
Of the appointed time was come,
He, the Word, was born of woman,
Left for us his Father's home,
Blazed the path of true obedience,
Shone as light amidst the gloom.

3 Thus, with thirty years accomplished,
He went forth from Nazareth,
Destined, dedicated, willing,
Did his work, and met his death;
Like a lamb he humbly yielded
On the cross his dying breath.

4 Faithful cross, true sign of triumph,
Be for all the noblest tree;
None in foliage, none in blossom,
None in fruit your equal be;
Symbol of the world's redemption,
For your burden makes us free.

5 Unto God be praise and glory;
To the Father and the Son,
To the eternal Spirit honor
Now and evermore be done;
Praise and glory in the highest,
While the timeless ages run.

Text: Venantius Honorius Fortunatus, 530–609; tr. John M. Neale, 1818–1866, alt.
© *Tune: Carl F. Schalk, b. 1929*

FORTUNATUS NEW
8 7 8 7 8 7

Nature with Open Volume Stands 119

1 Na - ture with o - pen vol - ume stands, To spread its
2 But in the grace that res - cued us His bright - est
3 Here his whole name ap - pears com - plete. Nor wit can
4 We would for - ev - er speak his name In sounds to
mak - er's praise a - broad; And ev - 'ry la - bor of his
form of glo - ry shines; 'Tis fair - est drawn up - on the
guess, nor rea - son prove, Which of the let - ters best is
mor - tal ears un-known, With an - gels join to praise the
hands Shows some - thing wor - thy of our God.
cross In pre - cious blood and crim - son lines.
writ, The pow'r, the wis - dom, or the love.
Lamb, And wor - ship at his Fa - ther's throne.

Text: Isaac Watts, 1674–1748, alt.
Tune: Georg Joseph, 17th cent., adapt.

ANGELUS
L M

120 Of the Glorious Body Telling

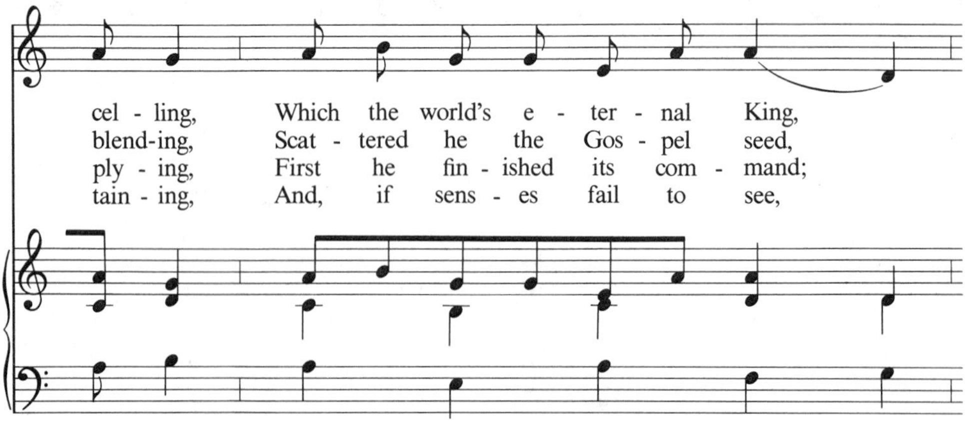

1 Of the glo - rious bod - y tell - ing, O my tongue, its mys-t'ries sing, And the blood, all price ex - cel - ling, Which the world's e - ter - nal King,
2 Giv'n for us, for us de - scend - ing, Of a vir - gin to pro - ceed, With us all in con-verse blend-ing, Scat - tered he the Gos - pel seed,
3 At the last great sup - per ly - ing Cir - cled by his cho - sen band, Meek - ly with the law com - ply - ing, First he fin - ished its com - mand;
4 Word made flesh, by word or - dain - ing Ver - y bread his flesh to be; We, in wine Christ's blood ob - tain - ing, And, if sens - es fail to see,

In a no - ble womb once dwell - ing, Shed for this world's ran - som - ing.
Till his so - journ drew to end - ing Which he closed in won - drous deed.
Then, im - mor - tal food sup - ply - ing, Gave him - self with his own hand.
Faith a - lone will wake those strain - ing To be - hold the mys - ter - y.
A - men

5 Therefore we, before him bending,
This great sacrament revere;
Types and shadows have their ending,
For the newer rite is here;
Faith, our outward sense befriending,
Makes the inward vision clear.

6 Glory let us give, and blessing
To the Father and the Son;
Honor, might, and praise addressing,
While eternal ages run;
Ever, too, the Spirit blessing,
Who, from both, with both is one.
Amen

Text: Thomas Aquinas, 1227–1274; tr. composite
Tune: mode III; Vatican collection

PANGE LINGUA
87 87 87

121 Ride On, Ride On in Majesty!

1 Ride on, ride on in maj - es - ty! Hear all the
2 Ride on, ride on in maj - es - ty! In low - ly
3 Ride on, ride on in maj - es - ty! The wing - ed
4 Ride on, ride on in maj - es - ty! Your last and

tribes ho - san - na cry; O Sav - ior meek, your road pur -
pomp ride on to die. O Christ, your tri - umphs now be -
squad-rons of the sky Look down with sad and won - d'ring
fierc - est strife is nigh. The Fa - ther on his sap - phire

sue, With palms and scat - tered gar - ments strewed.
gin O'er cap - tive death and con - quered sin.
eyes To see the ap - proach - ing sac - ri - fice.
throne A - waits his own a - noint - ed Son.

5 Ride on, ride on in majesty!
In lowly pomp ride on to die,
Bow your meek head to mortal pain,
Then take, O Christ, your pow'r and reign!

Text: Henry H. Milman, 1791–1868, alt.
 Tune: Graham George, b. 1912

THE KING'S MAJESTY
LM

Love Consecrates the Humblest Act 122

G Am7 G D C
1 Love con - se - crates the hum - blest act And
2 When in the shad - ow of the cross Christ
3 Love serves and will - ing stoops to serve; What
G D7 Bm7 D C G G7
ha - loes mer - cy's deeds; It sheds a ben - e -
knelt and washed the feet Of his dis - ci - ples,
Christ in love so true Has free - ly done for
C7 G Em Cmaj7 D G
dic - tion sweet And hal - lows hu - man needs.
he gave us A sign of love com - plete.
one and all, Let us now glad - ly do!
8

Text: S. B. McManus, c. 1902, alt.
Tune: attr. Lucius Chapin, 1760–1842

TWENTY-FOURTH
CM

123 Ah, Holy Jesus

1 Ah, ho - ly Je - sus, how hast thou of - fend - ed That man to
2 Who was the guilt - y? Who brought this up - on thee? A - las, my
3 Lo, the Good Shep - herd for the sheep is of - fered; The slave hath
4 For me, kind Je - sus, was thine in - car - na - tion, Thy mor - tal
judge thee hath in hate pre - tend - ed? By foes de - rid - ed,
trea - son, Je - sus, hath un - done thee. 'Twas I, Lord Je - sus,
sin - ned, and the Son hath suf - fered; For man's a - tone - ment,
sor - row, and thy life's ob - la - tion; Thy death of an - guish
by thine own re - ject - ed, O most af - flict - ed.
I it was de - nied thee; I cru - ci - fied thee.
while he noth - ing heed - eth, God in - ter - ced - eth.
and thy bit - ter Pas - sion, For my sal - va - tion.

5 Therefore, kind Jesus, since I cannot pay thee,
I do adore thee, and will ever pray thee;
Think on thy pity and thy love unswerving,
Not my deserving.

 Text: Johann Heermann, 1585–1647; tr. Robert Bridges, 1844–1930, alt.
Tune: Johann Crüger, 1598–1662

HERZLIEBSTER JESU
11 11 11 5

The Royal Banners Forward Go 124

1 The roy - al ban - ners for - ward go; The cross shines
2 Where deep for us the spear was dyed, Life's tor - rent
3 Ful - filled is all that Da - vid told In true pro -
4 O tree of beau - ty, tree most fair, Or - dained those
forth in mys - tic glow Where he, by whom
rush - ing from his side, To wash us in
phet - ic song of old, That God the na -
ho - ly limbs to bear: Gone is your shame,
our flesh was made, In that same flesh our ran - som paid;
the pre - cious flood Where flowed the wa - ter and the blood.
tions' king should be And reign in tri - umph from the tree.
each crim - soned bough Pro - claims the King of glo - ry now.

5 Blest tree, whose chosen branches bore
The wealth that did the world restore,
The price of humankind to pay,
And spoil the spoiler of his prey.

6 To you, eternal Three in One,
Our songs shall rise in unison;
Those whom you ransom and restore
Preserve and govern evermore.

 Text: Venantius Honorius Fortunatus, 530–609, sts. 1–5; source unknown, st. 6; tr. composite
Tune: attr. Johann Eccard, 1553–1611

HERR JESU CHRIST, WAHR MENSCH UND GOTT
LM

125 The Royal Banners Forward Go

1 The roy - al ban - ners for - ward go; The cross shines forth in
2 Where deep for us the spear was dyed, Life's tor - rent rush - ing
3 Ful - filled is all that Da - vid told In true pro - phet - ic
4 O tree of beau - ty, tree most fair, Or - dained those ho - ly
mys - tic glow Where he, by whom our flesh was made, In
from his side, To wash us in the pre - cious flood Where
song of old, That God the na - tions' king should be And
limbs to bear: Gone is your shame, each crim - soned bough Pro -
that same flesh our ran - som paid;
flowed the wa - ter and the blood.
reign in tri - umph from the tree.
claims the King of glo - ry now. A - men

5 Blest tree, whose chosen branches bore
The wealth that did the world restore,
The price of humankind to pay
And spoil the spoiler of his prey.

6 To you, eternal Three in One,
Our songs shall rise in unison;
Those whom you ransom and restore
Preserve and govern evermore. Amen

 Text: Venantius Honorius Fortunatus, 530–609, sts. 1–5; source unknown, st. 6; tr. composite
Tune: Sarum plainsong, mode I

VEXILLA REGIS
LM

Where Charity and Love Prevail 126

F Dm C F C F B♭ C F C7 F B♭ C
1 Where char-i-ty and love pre-vail, There God is ev-er found;
2 With grate-ful joy and ho-ly fear, God's char-i-ty we learn;
3 Let us re-call that in our midst Dwells Christ, God's ho-ly Son;
4 Let strife a-mong us be un-known; Let all con-ten-tions cease.
F Gm7 C Dm C F B♭ C Dm B♭6 F C F
Brought here to-geth-er by Christ's love, By love we thus are bound.
Let us with heart and mind and soul Now love God in re-turn.
As mem-bers of each bod-y joined, In him we are made one.
Be God's the glo-ry that we seek; Be his our on-ly peace.

5 For love excludes no race or clan
That names the Savior's name;
His family embraces all
Whose Father is the same.

6 We now forgive each other's faults
As we our own confess,
That we may love each other well
In Christian gentleness.

 Text: Latin hymn, 9th cent.; tr. Omer Westendorf, b. 1916, alt.
Tune: attr. Lucius Chapin, 1760–1842

TWENTY-FOURTH
CM

127 It Happened on That Fateful Night

1 It happened on that fateful night
When pow'rs of earth and hell arose
Against the Son, our God's delight,
And friends betrayed him to his foes.

2 Before the bitter scene began,
He took the bread, and blest and broke.
What love through all his actions ran!
What wondrous words of love he spoke!

3 “My body, broken for your sin,
Receive and eat as living food.”
He took the cup and blest the wine:
“Share this new testament, my blood.”

4 “Do this,” he said, “till time shall end,
Remembering your dying friend;
Meet at my table and record
The full obedience of your Lord.”

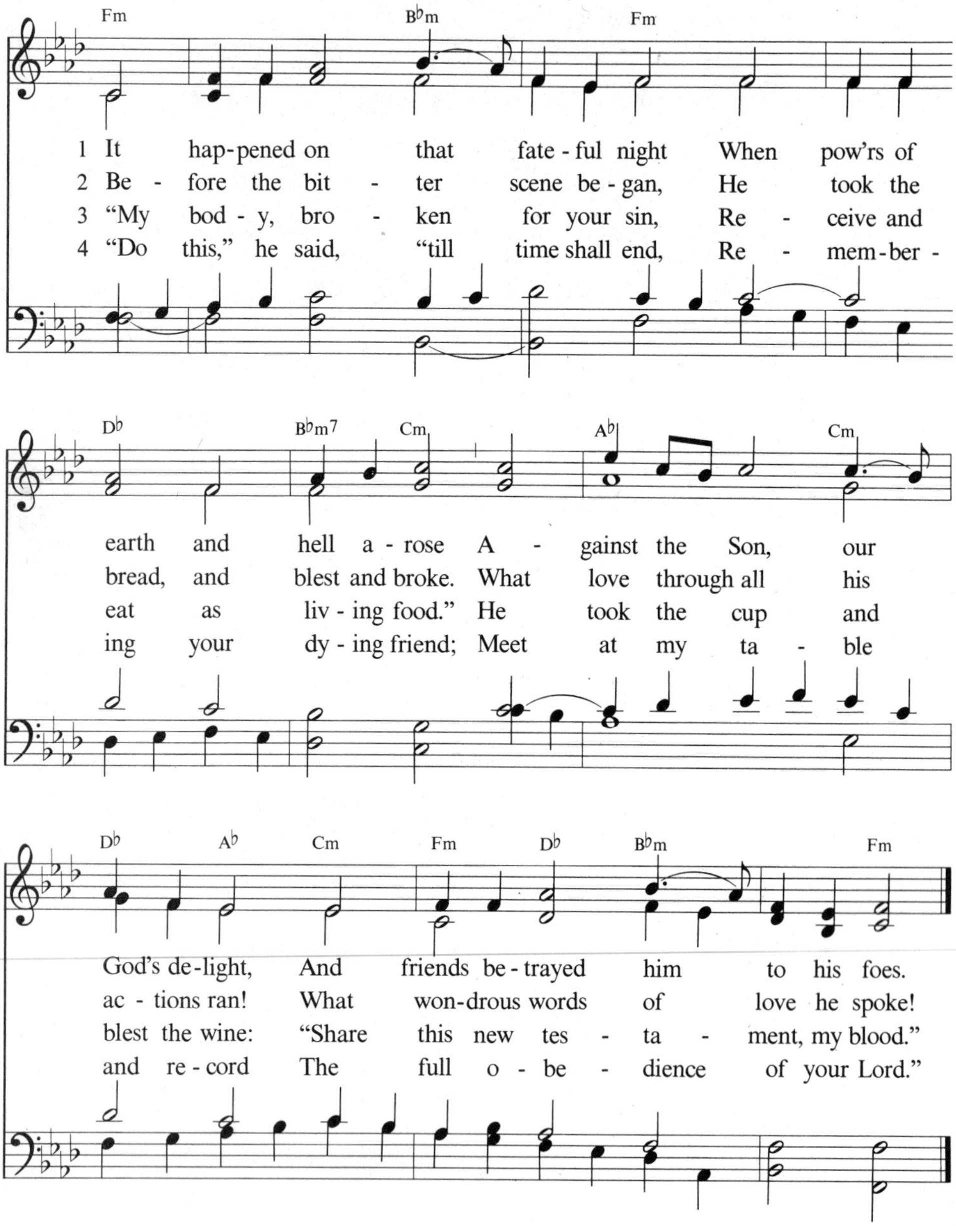

5 O Lord, your feast we celebrate;
We show your death; we sing your name
Till you return, when we shall eat
The marriage supper of the Lamb.

 Text: Isaac Watts, 1674–1748; hymnal version, 1978
Tune: W. Hauser, Hesperian Harp, *1848*

BOURBON
LM

Christ the Lord Is Risen Today; Alleluia! 128

1 Christ the Lord is ris'n to - day; Al - le - lu - ia!
2 For the sheep the Lamb has bled, Al - le - lu - ia!
3 Hail, the vic - tim un - de - filed, Al - le - lu - ia!
4 Chris-tians, on this ho - ly day, Al - le - lu - ia!
Chris-tians, has-ten on your way; Al - le - lu - ia!
Sin - less in the sin - ner's stead. Al - le - lu - ia!
God and sin-ners rec - on - ciled, Al - le - lu - ia!
All your grate-ful hom - age pay; Al - le - lu - ia!
Of - fer praise with love re - plete, Al - le - lu - ia!
Christ the Lord is ris'n on high; Al - le - lu - ia!
When con-tend - ing death and life, Al - le - lu - ia!
Christ the Lord is ris'n on high; Al - le - lu - ia!
At the pas - chal vic - tim's feet. Al - le - lu - ia!
Now he lives, no more to die. Al - le - lu - ia!
Met in strange and awe - some strife. Al - le - lu - ia!
Now he lives, no more to die. Al - le - lu - ia!

Text: Latin sequence, c. 1100; tr. Jane E. Leeson, 1807–1882, alt.
Tune: Robert Williams, c. 1781–1821

LLA
77 77 and

129 Awake, My Heart, with Gladness

1 A - wake, my heart, with glad - ness, See what to - day is done;
2 The foe in tri - umph shout - ed When Christ lay in the tomb;
3 This is a sight that glad - dens— What peace it does im - part!
4 Now hell, its prince, the dev - il, Of all their pow'r are shorn;
Now, af - ter gloom and sad - ness, Comes forth the glo - rious sun.
But, lo, he now is rout - ed, His boast is turned to gloom.
Now noth-ing ev - er sad - dens The joy with - in my heart.
Now I am safe from e - vil, And sin I laugh to scorn.
My Sav - ior there was laid Where our bed must be made
For Christ a - gain is free; In glo - rious vic - to - ry
No gloom shall ev - er shake, No foe shall ev - er take,
Grim death with all its might Can - not my soul af - fright;
When to the realms of light Our spir - it wings its flight.
He who is strong to save Has tri - umphed o'er the grave.
The hope which God's own Son In love for me has won.
It is a pow'r - less form, How - e'er it rave and storm.

5 Now I will cling forever
To Christ, my Savior true;
My Lord will leave me never,
Whate'er he passes through.
He rends death's iron chain;
He breaks through sin and pain;
He shatters hell's grim thrall;
I follow him through all.

6 He brings me to the portal
That leads to bliss untold,
Whereon this rhyme immortal
Is found in script of gold:
"Who there my cross has shared
Finds here a crown prepared;
Who there with me has died
Shall here be glorified."

Text: Paul Gerhardt, 1607–1676; tr. John Kelly, d. 1890, alt.
Tune: Johann Crüger, 1598–1662

AUF, AUF, MEIN HERZ
76 76 66 66

Christ the Lord Is Risen Today! 130

1 "Christ the Lord is ris'n to - day!" All on earth with an - gels say;
2 Love's re - deem - ing work is done, Fought the fight, the bat - tle won;
3 Vain the stone, the watch, the seal; Christ has burst the gates of hell.
4 Lives a - gain our glo - rious king! Where, O death, is now thy sting?
Raise your joys and tri - umphs high; Sing, ye heav'ns; and earth, re - ply.
Lo! The sun's e - clipse is o'er. Lo! He sets in blood no more.
Death in vain for - bids his rise; Christ has o - pened par - a - dise.
Once he died our souls to save; Where thy vic - to - ry, O grave?

5 Hail the Lord of earth and heav'n!
Praise to thee by both be giv'n.
Thee we greet triumphant now;
Hail, the resurrection, thou!

6 King of glory, soul of bliss,
Everlasting life is this:
Thee to know, thy pow'r to prove,
Thus to sing, and thus to love!

Text: Charles Wesley, 1707–1788, alt.
Tune: French, 13th cent.

ORIENTIS PARTIBUS
77 77

131 Christ Is Risen! Alleluia!

1 Christ is ris - en! Al - le - lu - ia! Ris - en our vic - to - rious head!
2 Christ is ris - en! All the sad - ness Of our Lent - en fast is o'er;
3 Christ is ris - en! All the sor - row That last eve - ning round him lay
4 Christ is ris - en! Hence-forth nev - er Death or hell shall us en - thrall;
Sing his prais - es! Al - le - lu - ia! Christ is ris - en from the dead!
Through the o - pen gates of glad - ness He re - turns to life once more;
Now has found a glo - rious mor - row In the ris - ing of to - day.
Be we Christ's, in him for - ev - er We have tri - umphed o - ver all.
Grate - ful - ly our hearts a - dore him As his light once more ap - pears;
Death and hell be - fore him bend - ing See him rise, the vic - tor now,
See the grave its first-fruits giv - ing, Spring - ing up from ho - ly ground;
All the doubt - ing and de - jec - tion Of our trem - bling hearts have ceased;
Bow - ing down in joy be - fore him, Ris - ing up from griefs and tears.
An - gels on his steps at - tend - ing, Glo - ry round his wound - ed brow.
He was dead, but now is liv - ing; He was lost, but he is found.
Hail the day of res - ur - rec - tion! Let us rise and keep the feast.

Refrain
Christ is ris - en! Al - le - lu - ia! Ris - en our vic -
to - rious head! Sing his prais - es! Al - le - lu - ia!
Christ is ris - en from the dead!

Text: John S. B. Monsell, 1811–1875, alt.
© Tune: Frederick C. Maker, 1844–1927

MORGENLIED
87 87 87 D

132 Come, You Faithful, Raise the Strain

1 Come, you faith - ful, raise the strain Of tri - um-phant glad - ness!
2 'Tis the spring of souls to - day: Christ has burst his pris - on,
3 Now the queen of sea - sons, bright With the day of splen - dor,
4 For to - day a - mong the twelve Christ ap - peared, be - stow - ing

God has brought his Is - ra - el In - to joy from sad - ness,
And from three days' sleep in death As a sun has ris - en;
With the roy - al feast of feasts Comes its joy to ren - der;
His deep peace, which ev - er - more Pass - es hu - man know - ing.

Loosed from Pha-raoh's bit - ter yoke Ja - cob's sons and daugh - ters,
All the win - ter of our sins, Long and dark, is fly - ing
Comes to glad - den faith - ful hearts Which with true af - fec - tion
Nei - ther could the gates of death, Nor the tomb's dark por - tal,

Led them with un - moist-ened foot Through the Red Sea wa - ters.
From his light, to whom is giv'n Laud and praise un - dy - ing.
Wel-come in un - wea - ried strain Je - sus' res - ur - rec - tion!
Nor the watch-ers, nor the seal, Hold him as a mor - tal.

5 Alleluia! Now we cry
To our King immortal,
Who, triumphant, burst the bars
Of the tomb's dark portal.
Come, you faithful, raise the strain
Of triumphant gladness!
God has brought his Israel
Into joy from sadness!

Text: John of Damascus, c. 696–c. 754; tr. John M. Neale, 1818–1866, alt.
Tune: Johann Horn, c. 1490–1547

GAUDEAMUS PARITER
76 76 D

Jesus Lives! The Victory's Won! 133

1 Je - sus lives! The vic - t'ry's won! Death no long - er can ap - pall me;
2 Je - sus lives! To him the throne There a - bove all things is giv - en.
3 Je - sus lives! For me he died, Hence will I, to Je - sus liv - ing,
4 Je - sus lives! And I am sure, Nei - ther life nor death shall sev - er
Je - sus lives! Death's reign is done! From the grave will Christ re - call me.
I shall go where he is gone, Live and reign with him in heav - en.
Pure in heart and act a - bide, Praise to him and glo - ry giv - ing.
Me from him. I shall en - dure In his love, through death, for - ev - er.
Bright - er scenes will then com - mence; This shall be my con - fi-dence.
God is faith - ful; doubt-ings, hence! This shall be my con - fi-dence.
All I need God will dis - pense; This shall be my con - fi-dence.
God will be my sure de - fense; This shall be my con - fi-dence.

5 Jesus lives! And now is death
But the gate of life immortal;
This shall calm my trembling breath
When I pass its gloomy portal.
Faith shall cry, as fails each sense:
Jesus is my confidence!

Text: Christian F. Gellert, 1715–1769; tr. Frances E. Cox, 1812–1897, alt.
Tune: Johann Crüger, 1598–1662

JESUS, MEINE ZUVERSICHT
78 78 7

134

Christ Jesus Lay in Death's Strong Bands

1 Christ Je - sus lay in death's strong bands For our of - fens - es
2 It was a strange and dread - ful strife When life and death con -
3 Here the true Pas - chal Lamb we see, Whom God so free - ly
4 So let us keep the fes - ti - val To which the Lord in -
giv - en; But now at God's right hand he stands And brings us life
tend-ed; The vic - to - ry re-mained with life, The reign of death
gave us; He died on the ac - curs - ed tree— So strong his love—
vites us; Christ is him - self the joy of all, The sun that warms
from heav - en. There-fore let us joy - ful be And sing to God right
was end - ed. Ho - ly Scrip-ture plain - ly says That death is swal-lowed
to save us. See, his blood now marks our door; Faith points to it; death
and lights us. Now his grace to us im - parts E - ter - nal sun - shine
thank-ful - ly Loud songs of hal - le - lu - jah! Hal - le - lu - jah!
up by death, Its sting is lost for - ev - er. Hal - le - lu - jah!
pass - es o'er, And Sa - tan can - not harm us. Hal - le - lu - jah!
to our hearts; The night of sin is end - ed. Hal - le - lu - jah!

5 Then let us feast this Easter Day
On Christ, the bread of heaven;
The Word of grace has purged away
The old and evil leaven.
Christ alone our souls will feed;
He is our meat and drink indeed;
Faith lives upon no other!
Hallelujah!

Text: Martin Luther, 1483–1546; tr. Richard Massie, 1800–1887, alt.
Tune: J. Walther, Geistliche Gesangbüchlein, *1524*

CHRIST LAG IN TODESBANDEN
87 87 78 74

The Strife Is O'er, the Battle Done 135

Al - le - lu - ia, al - le - lu - ia, al - le - lu - ia!
1 The strife is o'er, the bat - tle done; Now is the vic - tor's tri - umph won! Now be the song of praise be - gun. Al - le - lu - ia!
2 The pow'rs of death have done their worst, But Christ their le - gions has dis-persed. Let shouts of ho - ly joy out-burst. Al - le - lu - ia!
3 The three sad days have quick - ly sped, He ris - es glo - rious from the dead. All glo - ry to our ris - en head! Al - le - lu - ia!
4 He broke the age - bound chains of hell; The bars from heav'n's high por - tals fell. Let hymns of praise his tri - umph tell. Al - le - lu - ia!
Al - le - lu - ia, al - le - lu - ia, al - le - lu - ia!

5 Lord, by the stripes which wounded you,
From death's sting free your servants too,
That we may live and sing to you.
Alleluia!

Text: Symphonia Sirenum, *Köln, 1695; tr. Francis Pott, 1832–1909*
Tune: Giovanni P. da Palestrina, 1525–1594, adapt.

VICTORY
888 with alleluias

136 Christ Is Arisen

Christ is a - ris - en From the grave's dark pris - on.
So let our joy rise full and free; Christ our com - fort true will be.
Al - le - lu - ia! Were Christ not a - ris - en, Then death
were still our pris - on. Now, with him to life re - stored,
We praise the Fa - ther of our Lord. Al - le - lu - ia!

Al - le - lu - ia, al - le - lu - ia,
al - le - lu - ia! Now let our joy rise full and free;
Christ our com - fort true will be. Al - le - lu - ia!

© *Text: German hymn, c. 1100; tr. Martin L. Seltz, 1909–1967, alt.*
Tune: J. Klug, Geistliche Lieder, *1533*

CHRIST IST ERSTANDEN
P M

137 Christians, to the Paschal Victim

Chris-tians, to the pas-chal vic-tim Of-fer your thank-ful prais-es! A Lamb the
sheep re-deem-ing: Christ, who on-ly is sin-less, Rec-on-cil-ing sin-ners
to the Fa-ther. Death and life have con-tend-ed In that com-bat stu-pen-dous;

The prince of life, who died, Reigns im-mor-tal. Speak, Mar-y, de-clar-ing
What you saw when way-far-ing. "The tomb of Christ, who is liv - ing, The
glo-ry of Je-sus' res-ur-rec - tion; Bright an-gels at-test-ing, The

Hymn continues on the next page.

shroud and nap-kin rest-ing. My Lord, my hope, is a - ris - en; To Gal - i - lee
he goes be - fore you." Christ in-deed from death is ris - en, Our new
life ob-tain-ing. Have mer-cy, vic-tor King, ev - er reign - ing! A - men

Text: attr. Wipo of Burgundy, 11th cent.; tr. unknown
Tune: mode I; attr. Wipo of Burgundy, 11th cent.

VICTIMAE PASCHALI
PM

He Is Arisen! Glorious Word!

138

He is a - ris - en! Glo-rious Word! Now rec - on-ciled is God, my
Lord; The gates of heav'n are o - pen. My Je - sus rose tri -
um-phant-ly, And Sa-tan's ar - rows bro-ken lie, De-stroyed hell's
fierc - est weap - on. Oh, hear, what cheer! Christ vic - to-rious, Ris - ing
glo-rious, Life is giv - ing. He was dead, but now is liv - ing!

Text: Birgitte K. Boye, 1742–1824; tr. George T. Rygh, 1860–1942, alt.
Tune: Philipp Nicolai, 1556–1608

WIE SCHÖN LEUCHTET
PM

139 O Sons and Daughters of the King

Gm Dm F Gm
Al - le - lu - ia, al - le - lu - ia, al - le - lu - ia!
Gm F Dm C Gm
1 O sons and daugh - ters of the King,
2 That Eas - ter morn, at break of day,
3 An an - gel clad in white they see,
4 That night the a - pos - tles met in fear;
B♭ E♭ C Dm Gm C
Whom heav'n - ly hosts in glo - ry sing, To - day the
The faith - ful wom - en went their way To seek the
Who sits and speaks un - to the three, "Your Lord will
A - mong them came their mas - ter dear, And said, "My
Gm Dm B♭ C6 G
grave has lost its sting! Al - le - lu - ia!
tomb where Je - sus lay. Al - le - lu - ia!
go to Gal - i - lee." Al - le - lu - ia!
peace be with you here." Al - le - lu - ia!

Gm
Dm
F
G
Al - le - lu - ia, al - le - lu - ia, al - le - lu - ia!

5 When Thomas first the tidings heard,
That they had seen the risen Lord,
He doubted the disciples' word.
Alleluia!

6 "My pierced side, O Thomas, see,
And look upon my hands, my feet;
Not faithless, but believing be."
Alleluia!

7 No longer Thomas then denied;
He saw the feet, the hands, the side;
"You are my Lord and God!" he cried.
Alleluia!

8 How blest are they who have not seen,
And yet whose faith has constant been,
For they eternal life shall win.
Alleluia!

9 On this most holy day of days,
Be laud and jubilee and praise:
To God your hearts and voices raise.
Alleluia!

Text: attr. Jean Tisserand, d. 1494; tr. John M. Neale, 1818–1866, alt.
Tune: French, 15th cent.

O FILII ET FILIAE
888 with alleluias

140 With High Delight Let Us Unite

1 With high de - light let us u - nite In songs of sweet ju - bi -
2 True God, he first from death has burst Forth in - to life, all sub -
3 Let prais - es ring; give thanks, and bring To Christ our Lord ad - o -

la - tion. You pure in heart, each take your part, Sing Je - sus Christ,
du - ing. His en - e - my shall van - quished lie; His death has been
ra - tion. His hon - or speed by word and deed To ev - 'ry land,

our sal - va - tion. To set us free for - ev - er, he Is ris'n, and
death's un - do - ing. "And yours shall be like vic - to - ry O'er death and
ev - 'ry na - tion. So shall his love give us a - bove, From mis - er -

sends to all earth's ends Good news to save ev - 'ry na - tion.
grave," said he, who gave His life for us, life re - new - ing.
y and death set free, All joy and full con - so - la - tion.

© *Text: Georg Vetter, 1536–1599; tr. Martin H. Franzmann, 1907–1976*
Tune: Trente quatre pseaumes de David, *Geneva, 1551*

MIT FREUDEN ZART
88 88 888

The Day of Resurrection! 141

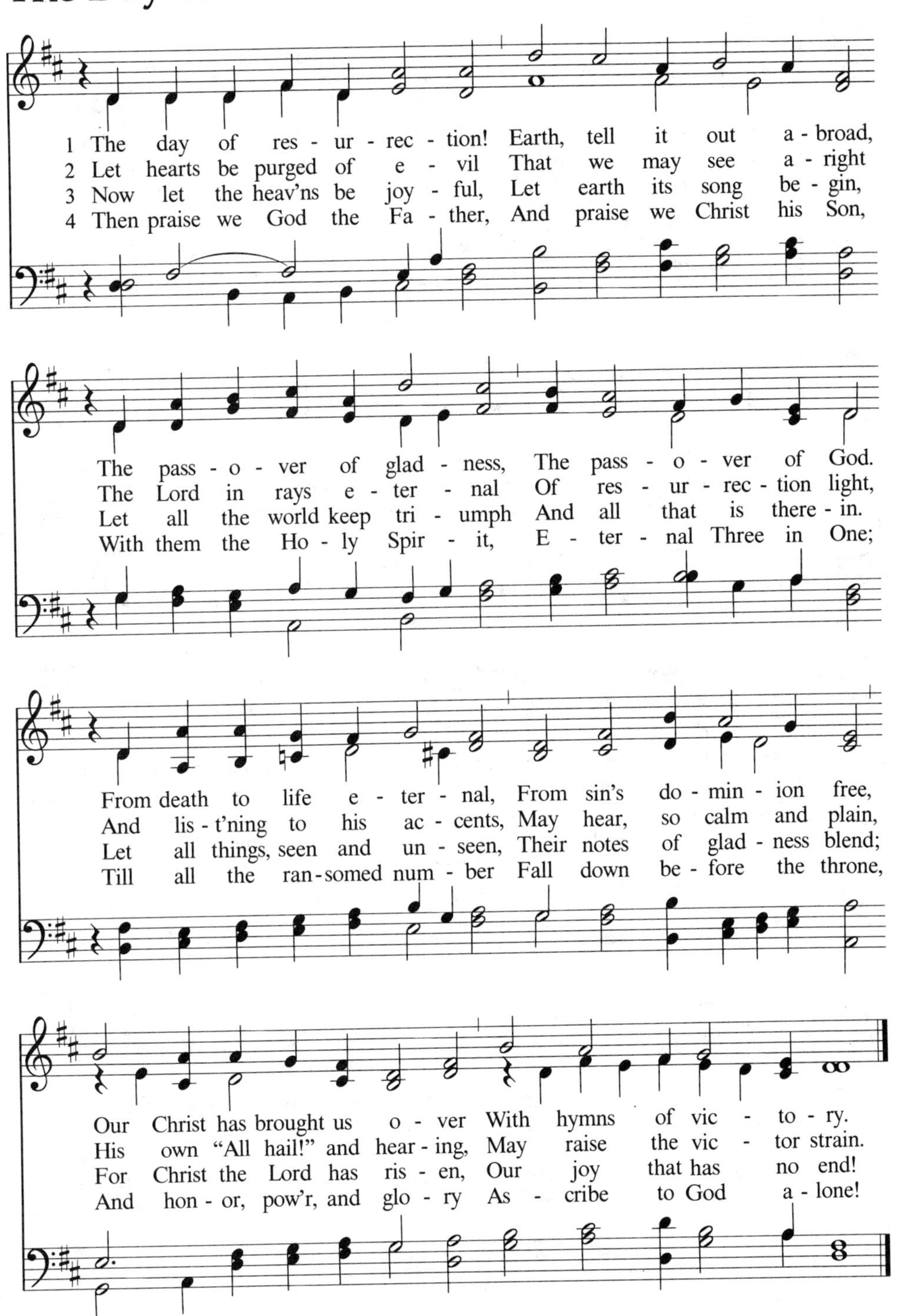
1 The day of res-ur-rec-tion! Earth, tell it out a-broad,
2 Let hearts be purged of e-vil That we may see a-right
3 Now let the heav'ns be joy-ful, Let earth its song be-gin,
4 Then praise we God the Fa-ther, And praise we Christ his Son,
The pass-o-ver of glad-ness, The pass-o-ver of God.
The Lord in rays e-ter-nal Of res-ur-rec-tion light,
Let all the world keep tri-umph And all that is there-in.
With them the Ho-ly Spir-it, E-ter-nal Three in One;
From death to life e-ter-nal, From sin's do-min-ion free,
And lis-t'ning to his ac-cents, May hear, so calm and plain,
Let all things, seen and un-seen, Their notes of glad-ness blend;
Till all the ran-somed num-ber Fall down be-fore the throne,
Our Christ has brought us o-ver With hymns of vic-to-ry.
His own "All hail!" and hear-ing, May raise the vic-tor strain.
For Christ the Lord has ris-en, Our joy that has no end!
And hon-or, pow'r, and glo-ry As-cribe to God a-lone!

Text: John of Damascus, c. 696–c. 754; tr. John M. Neale, 1818–1866, alt.
Tune: 16th cent., adapt. Johann Walther, 1496–1570

HERZLICH TUT MICH ERFREUEN
76 76 D

142 Hail Thee, Festival Day!

Refrain
(Easter) Hail thee, fes - ti - val day! Blest day to be hal-lowed for - ev - er;
(Ascension) Hail thee, fes - ti - val day! Blest day to be hal-lowed for - ev - er;
(Pentecost) Hail thee, fes - ti - val day! Blest day to be hal-lowed for - ev - er;
Day when our Lord was raised, break-ing the king - dom of death.
Day when our ris - en Lord rose in the heav - ens to reign.
Day when the Ho - ly Ghost shone in the world with his grace.
1st time
2nd time
death.
reign.
grace.
(Easter) 1 All the fair beau - ty of earth from the death of the win - ter a - ris - ing! Ev - 'ry good gift of the
(Ascension) 1 He who was nailed to the cross is rul - er and Lord of all peo - ple. All things cre - at - ed on
(Pentecost) 1 Bright and in like - ness of fire, on those who a - wait his ap - pear - ing, He whom the Lord had fore-
3 God the Al - might - y, the Lord, the rul - er of earth and the heav - ens Guard us from harm with -
5 Spir - it of life and of pow'r now flow in us, fount of our be - ing, Light that en - light - ens us

Repeat Refrain once after each stanza
year now with its mas - ter re - turns:
earth sing to the glo - ry of God:
told sud - den - ly, swift - ly de-scends:
out; cleanse us from e - vil with - in:
all, life that in all may a - bide:
(Easter) 2 Rise from the grave now, O Lord, the au - thor of life and cre - a - tion. Tread - ing the path-way of death, new life you give to us all:
(Ascension) 2 Dai - ly the love - li - ness grows, a - dorned with the glo - ry of blos - som; Heav - en her gates un - bars, fling - ing her in - crease of light:
(Pentecost) 2 Dai - ly the love - li - ness grows, a - dorned with the glo - ry of blos - som; Heav - en her gates un - bars, fling - ing her in - crease of light:
4 Je - sus, the health of the world, en - light - en our minds, great re - deem - er, Son of the Fa - ther su - preme, on - ly - be - got - ten of God:
6 Praise to the giv - er of good! O Lov - er and Au - thor of con - cord, Pour out your balm on our days; or - der our ways in your peace:
Repeat Refrain once after each stanza

© Text: Venantius Honorius Fortunatus, 530–609; tr. hymnal version, 1978
© Tune: R. Vaughan Williams, 1872–1958

SALVE FESTA DIES
irregular

143 Now All the Vault of Heaven Resounds

1 Now all the vault of heav'n re-sounds In praise of love that
2 E - ter - nal is the gift he brings, There - fore our heart with
3 Oh, fill us, Lord, with daunt-less love; Set heart and will on
4 A - dor - ing prais - es now we bring And with the heav'n-ly
still a - bounds: "Christ has tri - umphed! He is liv - ing!"
rap - ture sings: "Christ has tri - umphed! He is liv - ing!"
things a - bove That we con - quer through your tri - umph;
bless-ed sing: "Christ has tri - umphed! Al - le - lu - ia!"
Sing, choirs of an - gels, loud and clear! Re - peat their song
Now still he comes to give us life And by his pres-
Grant grace suf - fi - cient for life's day That by our lives
Be to the Fa - ther, and our Lord, To Spir - it blest,
of glo - ry here: "Christ has tri - umphed! Christ has tri-umphed!"
ence stills all strife. Christ has tri - umphed! He is liv - ing!
we tru - ly say: Christ has tri - umphed! He is liv - ing!
most ho - ly God, All the glo - ry, nev - er end - ing!

Al - le - lu - ia, al - le - lu - ia, al - le - lu - ia!

 Text: Paul Z. Strodach, 1876–1947, alt.
Tune: Geistliche Kirchengesänge, *Köln, 1623*

LASST UNS ERFREUEN
888 888 and alleluias

Good Christian Friends, Rejoice and Sing!

144

1 Good Chris - tian friends, re - joice and sing! Now is the
2 The Lord of life is ris'n this day; Bring flow'rs of
3 Praise we in songs of vic - to - ry That love, that
4 Your name we bless, O ris - en Lord, And sing to -

tri - umph of our King! To all the world glad news we bring:
song to strew his way; Let all the world re - joice and say:
life which can - not die, And sing with hearts up - lift - ed high:
day with one ac - cord, The life laid down, the life re - stored:

Al - le - lu - ia, al - le - lu - ia, al - le - lu - ia!

 Text: Cyril A. Alington, 1872–1955, alt.
Tune: Melchior Vulpius, c. 1570–1615

GELOBT SEI GOTT
888 and alleluias

145 Thine Is the Glory

1 Thine is the glo - ry, Ris - en, con-qu'ring Son; End - less is the
2 Lo, Je - sus meets thee, Ris - en from the tomb! Lov - ing - ly he
3 No more we doubt thee, Glo - rious Prince of life; Life is nought with-
vic - t'ry Thou o'er death hast won! An - gels in bright rai - ment
greets thee, Scat - ters fear and gloom; Let his Church with glad - ness
out thee; Aid us in our strife; Make us more than con - qu'rors,
Rolled the stone a - way, Kept the fold - ed grave - clothes
Hymns of tri - umph sing, For the Lord now liv - eth;
Through thy death - less love; Bring us safe through Jor - dan
Where thy bod - y lay.
Death hath lost its sting!
To thy home a - bove.
Refrain
Thine is the glo - ry, Ris - en, con-qu'ring Son;
End - less is the vic - t'ry Thou o'er death hast won!

© Text: Edmond Budry, 1854–1932; tr. R. Birch Hoyle, 1875–1939
Tune: George F. Handel, 1685–1759, adapt.

JUDAS MACCABAEUS
55 65 65 65 and refrain

Rejoice, Angelic Choirs, Rejoice! 146

1 Re - joice, an - gel - ic choirs, re - joice! Re - joice now, all cre -
2 O earth, ex - ult in ra - diance bright, Il - lu - mined by Christ's
3 Let all who gath - er round this flame, The sign of Christ's a -
a - tion! Let trum - pets loud - ly raise their voice To hail the
splen - dor! Your dark - ness now is put to flight; To him due
ris - ing, The death - less light of Christ ac - claim, His sav - ing
Lord's sal - va - tion; Let all Christ's ho - ly priest-hood sing The
prais - es ren - der! Be glad, O Church! Sing out your songs! Your
mer - cy priz - ing; That all may live by faith in him Who
tri - umph of their might - y king In fes - tive cel - e - bra - tion!
tem - ples fill with shout - ing throngs To hail the glo - rious vic - tor!
con-quered death, de - spair, and sin To make us his for - ev - er.

© *Text: Latin hymn, 11th cent.; versification, Joel W. Lundeen, b. 1918*
Tune: C. Egenolf, Reutterliedlein, *1535*

WÄCHTERLIED
87 87 887

147 Hallelujah! Jesus Lives!

1 Hal - le - lu - jah! Je - sus lives! He is now the Liv - ing One;
2 Je - sus lives! Why do you weep? Why that sad and mourn - ful sigh?
3 Je - sus lives! And thus, my soul, Life e - ter - nal waits for you;
4 Je - sus lives! Let all re - joice. Praise him, ran - somed of the earth.
From the gloom - y halls of death Christ, the con - quer - or, has gone,
He who died our broth - er here Lives our broth - er still on high,
Joined to him, your liv - ing head, Where he is, you shall be too;
Praise him in a no - bler song, Cher - u - bim of heav'n - ly birth.
Bright fore - run - ner to the skies Of his peo - ple, yet to rise.
Lives for - ev - er to be - stow Bless - ings on his Church be - low.
With the Lord, at his right hand, As a vic - tor you shall stand.
Praise the vic - tor king, whose sway Sin and death and hell o - bey.

5 Hallelujah! Angels, sing!
Join with us in hymns of praise.
Let your chorus swell the strain
Which our feebler voices raise:
Glory to our God above
And on earth his peace and love!

Text: Carl B. Garve, 1763–1841; tr. Jane Borthwick, 1813–1897, alt.
Tune: Ludvig M. Lindeman, 1812–1887

FRED TIL BOD
77 77 77

Now the Green Blade Rises

148

1 Now the green blade ris - es from the bur - ied grain,
2 In the grave they laid him, love by ha - tred slain,
3 Forth he came at Eas - ter, like the ris - en grain,
4 When our hearts are win - try, griev - ing, or in pain,
Wheat that in dark earth man - y days has lain; Love lives a - gain, that with the dead has been;
Think - ing that he would nev - er wake a - gain, Laid in the earth like grain that sleeps un - seen;
He that for three days in the grave had lain; Raised from the dead, my liv - ing Lord is seen;
Your touch can call us back to life a - gain, Fields of our hearts that dead and bare have been;
Love is come a - gain like wheat a - ris - ing green.

 Text: John M. C. Crum, 1872–1958
Tune: French carol

NOËL NOUVELET
11 10 10 11

149 This Joyful Eastertide

This joy - ful Eas - ter - tide, A - way with sin and sor - row! My love, the Cru - ci - fied, Has sprung to life this mor - row. Had Christ, who once was slain, Not burst his three - day pris - on, Our faith had been in vain. But now has Christ a - ris - en, a - ris - en, a -

ris - en; But now has Christ a - ris - en!

 Text: George R. Woodward, 1848–1934
Tune: Dutch, 17th cent.

VRUECHTEN
67 67 67 6 13 7

Make Songs of Joy

150

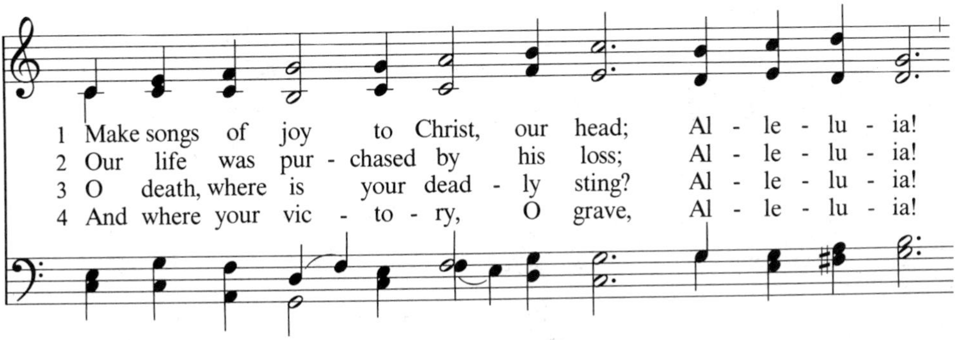

1 Make songs of joy to Christ, our head; Alleluia!
He lives again who once was dead! Alleluia!

2 Our life was purchased by his loss; Alleluia!
He died our death upon the cross. Alleluia!

3 O death, where is your deadly sting? Alleluia!
Assumed by our triumphant King! Alleluia!

4 And where your victory, O grave, Alleluia!
When one like Christ has come to save? Alleluia!

5 Behold, the tyrants, one and all,
Alleluia!
Before our mighty Savior fall!
Alleluia!

6 For this be praised the Son who rose,
Alleluia!
The Father, and the Holy Ghost!
Alleluia!

 Text: Jiři Tranovský, 1591–1637; tr. Jaroslav J. Vajda, b. 1919
Tune: Chorvát, Velka Partitura, *1936*

ZPIVEJMEŽ VŠICKNI VESELE
84 84

151 Jesus Christ Is Risen Today

1 Je - sus Christ is ris'n to - day, Al - le - lu - ia!
2 Hymns of praise then let us sing, Al - le - lu - ia!
3 But the pains which he en - dured, Al - le - lu - ia!
4 Sing we to our God a - bove, Al - le - lu - ia!
Our tri - um - phant ho - ly day, Al - le - lu - ia!
Un - to Christ, our heav'n - ly king, Al - le - lu - ia!
Our sal - va - tion have pro - cured; Al - le - lu - ia!
Praise e - ter - nal as his love; Al - le - lu - ia!
Who did once up - on the cross, Al - le - lu - ia!
Who en - dured the cross and grave, Al - le - lu - ia!
Now a - bove the sky he's king, Al - le - lu - ia!
Praise him, all you heav'n - ly host, Al - le - lu - ia!
Suf - fer to re - deem our loss. Al - le - lu - ia!
Sin - ners to re - deem and save. Al - le - lu - ia!
Where the an - gels ev - er sing. Al - le - lu - ia!
Fa - ther, Son, and Ho - ly Ghost. Al - le - lu - ia!

Text: *Latin carol, 14th cent., sts. 1–3; Charles Wesley, 1707–1788, st. 4; tr.* Lyra Davidica, *London, 1708, sts. 1–3*
Tune: Lyra Davidica, *London, 1708*

EASTER HYMN
77 77 and alleluias

Look, Now He Stands! 152

1 Look, now he stands! Stones could not hold him down for long; The Ris - en
2 O Liv-ing One, we hear you shout this ris - en news; Your cry we
3 This bro-ken world is touched by Christ; oh, rise and live, Cre - a - tion,
4 Cel - e-brate him! His new cre - a - tion ris - es great With cos - mic
One is made up - right and moves a - gain. He speaks, he is God's
catch from far be - yond the edge of death. Your call to life beats
rise. Your Lord is ris - en, ris'n in - deed! He shapes all things, trans -
scope. Christ Je - sus takes his Fa - ther's world; He hosts in joy the
wish of life raised up for all: Our Lord Christ lives in res - ur -
our heart-beat and sounds your hope: Yes, yes, you live! Bend o - ver
form-ing them; he makes them new: He bless - es all ex - is - tence
new hu - man - i - ty; he toasts The whole new work, the res - ur -
rec - tion strength made strong. Al - le - lu - ia! Al - le - lu - ia!
us, re - new our breath. Al - le - lu - ia! Al - le - lu - ia!
in the liv - ing God. Al - le - lu - ia! Al - le - lu - ia!
rect - ed u - ni - verse. Al - le - lu - ia! Al - le - lu - ia!

© *Text: George Utech, b. 1931*
© *Tune: Carl F. Schalk, b. 1929*

PARSONS
12 12 12 12 and alleluias

153 Welcome, Happy Morning!

1 "Welcome, happy morning!" age to age shall say;
"Hell today is vanquished, heav'n is won today!"
Christ, once dead, is living, God forevermore!
Him, their true creator, all his works adore.

2 Maker and redeemer, life and health of all,
God from heav'n beholding human nature's fall,
You, the true and only Son of God above,
Died as mortal man to save us by your love.

3 Source of all things living, you came down to die,
Plumbed the depths of hell to raise us up on high.
Come then, true and faithful; come, fulfill your word;
This is your third morning: Rise, O buried Lord!

4 Free the souls long prisoned, bound with Satan's chain;
All that once had fallen raise to life again;
Show your face in brightness, shine in ev'ry land
As in Eden's garden when the world began.

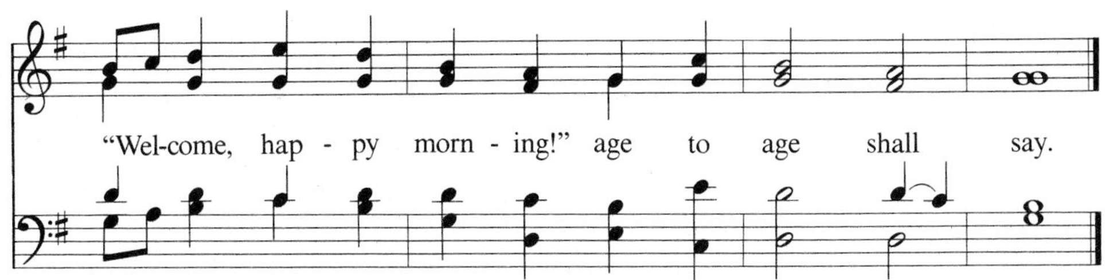
"Wel-come, hap - py morn - ing!" age to age shall say.
8

Text: Venantius Honorius Fortunatus, 530–609; tr. John Ellerton, 1826–1893, adapt.
Tune: Arthur S. Sullivan, 1842–1900

FORTUNATUS
11 11 11 11 and refrain

That Easter Day with Joy Was Bright 154

1 That Eas - ter day with joy was bright; The sun shone
2 O Je - sus, king of gen - tle - ness, With con - stant
3 O Christ, you are the Lord of all In this our
4 All praise, O ris - en Lord, we give To you, once

out with fair - er light, When, to their long - ing eyes re -
love our hearts pos - sess; To you our lips will ev - er
Eas - ter fes - ti - val, For you will be our strength and
dead, but now a - live! To God the Fa - ther e - qual

stored, The a-pos - tles saw their ris - en Lord! Al - le - lu - ia!
raise The trib - ute of our grate - ful praise. Al - le - lu - ia!
shield From ev - 'ry weap - on death can wield. Al - le - lu - ia!
praise, And God the Ho - ly Ghost, we raise! Al - le - lu - ia!

Text: Latin hymn, 4th or 5th cent.; tr. John M. Neale, 1818–1866, alt.
Tune: Nikolaus Herman, c. 1480–1561

ERSCHIENEN IST DER HERRLICH TAG
88 884

155 Praise the Savior, Now and Ever

1 Praise the Sav - ior, now and ev - er; Praise him, all be -
2 Day of glad - ness! Gone is sad - ness; Christ has bruised the
3 An - thems glo - rious, hymns vic - to - rious, Raise we to our
4 Earth re - joic - es; all its voic - es Glo - ry to the
neath the skies; Come be - fore him and a - dore him,
ser - pent's head; Death no long - er is the strong - er;
pas - chal King. Bonds are bro - ken, heav'n is o - pen;
Fa - ther sing! Praise the Sav - ior, laud him ev - er,
God's own per - fect sac - ri - fice; Vic - t'ry gain - ing,
Hell it - self is cap - tive led. Christ our Sav - ior
Sing, O ran - somed mor - tals, sing! Christ is ris - en
Son of God, our Lord and King! Praise the Spir - it,
life ob - tain - ing, Now in glo - ry see him rise!
lives for - ev - er; O'er the tomb his light is shed.
from death's pris - on, Heal - ing in his wings to bring.
through Christ's mer - it Life e - ter - nal see him bring!

© *Text:* *Venantius Honorius Fortunatus, 530–609; tr.* Service Book and Hymnal, *1958, alt.*
Tune: Koralpsalmboken, *Stockholm, 1697*

UPP, MIN TUNGA
87 87 87

Look, the Sight is Glorious 156

1 Look, oh, look, the sight is glo - rious, See the man of sor - rows now;
2 Crown the Sav-ior! An-gels crown him! Rich the tro - phies Je - sus brings;
3 Sin - ners in de - ri - sion crowned him, Mock - ing thus the Sav - ior's claim;
4 Hark! Those bursts of ac - cla - ma - tion! Hark! Those loud tri - um-phant chords!
From the fight re - turned vic - to - rious, Ev - 'ry knee to him shall bow.
On the seat of pow'r en-throne him While the vault of heav - en rings.
Saints and an - gels crowd a - round him, Own his ti - tle, praise his name.
Je - sus takes the high - est sta - tion; Oh, what joy the sight af - fords!
Crown him! Crown him! Crown him! Crown him! Crown him! Crown him!
Crown him! Crown him! Crown him! Crown him! Crown him! Crown him!
Crown him! Crown him! Crown him! Crown him! Crown him! Crown him!
Crown him! Crown him! Crown him! Crown him! Crown him! Crown him!
Crowns be - come the vic - tor's brow. Crowns be - come the vic - tor's brow.
Crown the Sav - ior, King of kings. Crown the Sav - ior, King of kings.
Spread a - broad the vic - tor's fame! Spread a - broad the vic - tor's fame!
King of kings and Lord of lords! King of kings and Lord of lords!

Text: Thomas Kelly, 1769–1854, alt.
Tune: William Owen, 1814–1893

BRYN CALFARIA
87 87 444 77

157 A Hymn of Glory Let Us Sing!

1 A hymn of glo - ry let us sing! New hymns through-out the
2 The ho - ly ap - os - tol - ic band Up - on the Mount of
3 To whom . . shin - ing an - gels cry, "Why stand and gaze up-
4 "You see him now, as - cend - ing high Up to the por - tals
world shall ring: Al - le - lu - ia! Al - le - lu - ia!
Ol - ives stand. Al - le - lu - ia! Al - le - lu - ia!
on the sky?" Al - le - lu - ia! Al - le - lu - ia!
of the sky." Al - le - lu - ia! Al - le - lu - ia!
Christ, by a road be - fore un - trod, As - cends un - to
And with his faith - ful fol - l'wers see Their Lord as - cend
"This is the Sav - ior!" Thus they say, "This is his glo-
"Here - af - ter Je - sus you shall see Re - turn - ing in
the throne of God. Al - le - lu - ia! Al - le - lu - ia!
in maj - es - ty. Al - le - lu - ia! Al - le - lu - ia!
rious tri - umph day!" Al - le - lu - ia! Al - le - lu - ia!
great maj - es - ty." Al - le - lu - ia! Al - le - lu - ia!

Al-le-lu - ia, al-le-lu - ia, al-le-lu - ia!

5 O Lord, our homeward pathway bend,
That our unwearied hearts ascend.
Alleluia! Alleluia!
Where, seated on your Father's throne,
You reign as King of kings alone.
Alleluia! Alleluia!
Alleluia, alleluia, alleluia!

6 Give us your joy on earth, O Lord,
In heav'n to be our great reward.
Alleluia! Alleluia!
When throned with you forever, we
Shall praise your name eternally.
Alleluia! Alleluia!
Alleluia, alleluia, alleluia!

7 O risen Christ, ascended Lord,
All praise to you let earth accord:
Alleluia! Alleluia!
You are, while endless ages run,
With Father and with Spirit one.
Alleluia! Alleluia!
Alleluia, alleluia, alleluia!

 Text: The Venerable Bede, 673–735; tr. hymnal version, 1978
Tune: Geistliche Kirchengesänge, *Köln, 1623*

LASST UNS ERFREUEN
888 888 and alleluias

158 Alleluia! Sing to Jesus

1 Al - le - lu - ia! Sing to Je - sus; His the scep - ter,
2 Al - le - lu - ia! Not as or - phans Are we left in
3 Al - le - lu - ia! Bread of heav - en, Here on earth our
4 Al - le - lu - ia! King e - ter - nal, Lord om - nip - o -
his the throne; Al - le - lu - ia! His the tri - umph, His the
sor - row now; Al - le - lu - ia! He is near us; Faith be -
food, our stay; Al - le - lu - ia! Here the sin - ful Flee to
tent we own; Al - le - lu - ia! Born of Mar - y, Earth your
vic - to - ry a - lone. Hark! The songs of peace - ful
lieves, nor ques - tions how. Though the cloud from sight re -
you from day to day. In - ter - ces - sor, friend of
foot - stool, heav'n your throne. As with - in the veil you
Zi - on Thun - der like a might - y flood: "Je - sus
ceived him When the for - ty days were o'er,
Shall our
sin - ners, Earth's re - deem - er, hear our plea Where the
en - tered, Robed in flesh, our great high priest, Here on

out of ev - 'ry na - tion Has re - deemed us by his blood."
hearts for - get his prom - ise: "I am with you ev - er-more"?
songs of all the sin - less Sweep a - cross the crys - tal sea.
earth both priest and vic - tim In the eu - cha - ris - tic feast.

5 Alleluia! Sing to Jesus;
His the scepter, his the throne;
Alleluia! His the triumph,
His the victory alone.
Hark! The songs of peaceful Zion
Thunder like a mighty flood:
"Jesus out of ev'ry nation
Has redeemed us by his blood."

Text: William C. Dix, 1837–1898, alt.
Tune: Rowland H. Prichard, 1811–1887

HYFRYDOL
87 87 D

159 Up through Endless Ranks of Angels

1 Up through end - less ranks of an - gels, Cries of tri - umph
2 Death-de - stroy - ing, life - re - stor - ing, Prov - en e - qual
3 To our lives of wan - ton wan - d'ring Send your prom - ised
4 Al - le - lu - ia! Al - le - lu - ia! Oh, to breathe the

in his ears, To his heav'n - ly throne as - cend - ing,
to our need, Now for us be - fore the Fa - ther
Spir - it guide; Through our lives of fear and fail - ure
Spir - it's grace! Al - le - lu - ia! Al - le - lu - ia!

Hav - ing van - quished all their fears, Christ looks down up -
As our broth - er in - ter - cede; Flesh that for our
With your pow'r and love a - bide; Wel - come us, as
Oh, to see the Fa - ther's face! Al - le - lu - ia!

on his faith - ful, Leav - ing them in hap - py tears.
world was wound - ed, Liv - ing, for the wound - ed plead!
you were wel - comed, To an end - less Eas - ter - tide.
Al - le - lu - ia! Oh, to feel the Son's em - brace!

ASCENDED TRIUMPH
87 87 87

Filled with the Spirit's Power

160

1 Filled with the Spir - it's pow'r, with one ac - cord
2 Now with the mind of Christ set us on fire,
3 Wid - en our love, good Spir - it, to em - brace
The in - fant Church con - fessed its ris - en Lord.
That u - ni - ty may be our great de - sire.
In your strong care all those of ev - 'ry race.
O Ho - ly Spir - it, in the Church to - day
Give joy and peace; give faith to hear your call,
Like wind and fire with life a - mong us move,
No less your pow'r of fel - low - ship dis - play.
And read - i - ness in each to work for all.
Till we are known as Christ's, and Chris - tians prove.

© *Text: John R. Peacey, 1896–1971*
© *Tune: Cyril V. Taylor, 1907–*

SHELDONIAN
10 10 10 10

161 O Day Full of Grace

1 O day full of grace that now we see Ap - pear - ing on
2 O day full of grace, O bless - ed time, Our Lord on the
3 For Christ bore our sins, and not his own, When he on the
4 God came to us then at Pen - te - cost, His Spir - it new
earth's ho - ri - zon, Bring light from our God that we may
earth ar - riv - ing; Then came to the world that light sub -
cross was hang - ing; And then he a - rose and moved the
life re - veal - ing, That we might no more from him be
be Re - plete in his joy this sea - son. God, shine for us
lime, Great joy for us all re - triev - ing; For Je - sus all
stone, That we, un - to him be - long - ing, Might join with an -
lost, All dark - ness for us dis - pel - ling. His flame will the
now in this dark place; Your name on our hearts em - bla - zon.
mor - tals did em - brace, All dark - ness and shame re - mov - ing.
gel - ic hosts to raise Our voic - es in end - less sing - ing.
mark of sin ef - face And bring to us all his heal - ing.

5 When we on that final journey go
That Christ is for us preparing,
We'll gather in song, our hearts aglow,
All joy of the heavens sharing,
And walk in the light of God's own place,
With angels his name adoring.

 Text: Nikolai F. S. Grundtvig, 1783–1872; tr. Gerald Thorson, b. 1921
Tune: Christoph E. F. Weyse, 1774–1842

DEN SIGNEDE DAG
98 98 98

Lord God, the Holy Ghost 162

1 Lord God, the Holy Ghost, In this appointed hour, As on the day of Pentecost, Descend with all your pow'r.
2 We meet with one accord In this appointed place, And wait the promise of our Lord, The Spirit of all grace.
3 Like mighty rushing wind Upon the waves beneath, With one conviction move each mind, One soul, one feeling breathe.
4 The young, the old inspire With wisdom from above, And give us hearts and tongues of fire To pray and praise and love.

5 O Light of light, explore
And chase our gloom away,
With luster shining more and more
Unto the perfect day.

Text: James Montgomery, 1771–1854, alt.
 Tune: Carl F. Schalk, b. 1929

DES PLAINES
SM

163 Come, Holy Ghost, God and Lord

1 Come, Ho - ly Ghost, God and Lord, With all your
2 Come, ho - ly Light, guide di - vine, Now cause the
3 Come, ho - ly Fire, com - fort true, Grant us the
grac - es now out-poured On each be - liev - er's mind and heart;
Word of life to shine. Teach us to know our God a - right
will your work to do And in your ser - vice to a - bide;
Your fer - vent love to them im - part. Lord, by the bright-ness
And call him Fa - ther with de - light. From ev - 'ry er - ror
Let tri - als turn us not a - side. Lord, by your pow'r pre -
of your light In ho - ly faith your Church u - nite; From ev - 'ry
keep us free; Let none but Christ our mas - ter be, That we in
pare each heart And to our weak-ness strength im - part, That brave - ly

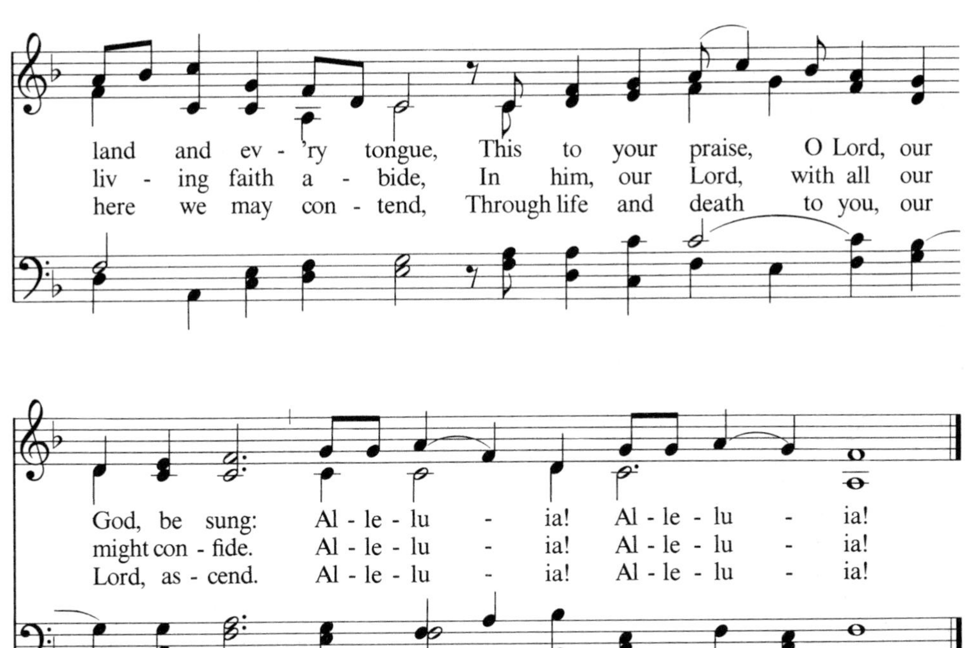
land and ev - 'ry tongue, This to your praise, O Lord, our
liv - ing faith a - bide, In him, our Lord, with all our
here we may con - tend, Through life and death to you, our
God, be sung: Al - le - lu - ia! Al - le - lu - ia!
might con - fide. Al - le - lu - ia! Al - le - lu - ia!
Lord, as - cend. Al - le - lu - ia! Al - le - lu - ia!

© *Text: Martin Luther, 1483–1546; tr.* The Lutheran Hymnal, *1941, alt.*
Tune: Enchiridion, *Erfurt, 1524*

KOMM, HEILIGER GEIST, HERRE GOTT
7 8 8 8 8 8 8 8 10 8

164 Creator Spirit, by Whose Aid

1 Cre - a - tor Spir - it, by whose aid The world's foun - da - tions
2 O Source of un - cre - at - ed light, The Fa - ther's prom-ised
3 Plen - teous of grace, de - scend from high, Rich in thy sev'n-fold
4 Im - mor - tal hon - or, end - less fame, At - tend the al-might - y
first were laid, Come, vis - it ev - 'ry hum - ble mind; Come,
Par - a - clete, Thrice ho - ly fount, thrice ho - ly fire, Our
en - er - gy; Make us e - ter - nal truths re - ceive And
Fa-ther's name; The Sav - ior Son be glo - ri - fied, Who
pour thy joys on hu - man-kind; From sin and sor - row set us
hearts with heav'n-ly love in - spire; Come, and thy sa - cred unc - tion
prac - tice all that we be - lieve; Give us thy - self, that we may
for lost man's re-demp-tion died; And e - qual ad - o - ra - tion
free, And make thy tem - ples fit for thee.
bring To sanc - ti - fy us while we sing.
see The Fa - ther and the Son by thee.
be, E - ter - nal Par - a - clete, to thee.

Text: *attr. Rhabanus Maurus, 778–856; tr. John Dryden, 1631–1700*
Tune: Kirchengesangbuch, *Strassburg, 1541*

ALL EHR UND LOB
88 88 88

165 Holy, Holy, Holy

1 Ho - ly, ho - ly, ho - ly, Lord God Al - might - y!
2 Ho - ly, ho - ly, ho - ly! All the saints a - dore thee,
3 Ho - ly, ho - ly, ho - ly! Though the dark - ness hide thee,
4 Ho - ly, ho - ly, ho - ly! Lord God Al - might - y!
Ear - ly in the morn - ing our song shall rise to thee.
Cast - ing down their gold - en crowns a - round the glass - y sea;
Though the eye made blind by sin thy glo - ry may not see,
All thy works shall praise thy name in earth and sky and sea.
Ho - ly, ho - ly, ho - ly, mer - ci - ful and might - y!
Cher - u - bim and ser - a - phim fall - ing down be - fore thee,
On - ly thou art ho - ly; there is none be - side thee,
Ho - ly, ho - ly, ho - ly, mer - ci - ful and might - y!
God in three Per - sons, bless - ed Trin - i - ty!
Which wert and art and ev - er - more shalt be.
Per - fect in pow'r, in love and pu - ri - ty.
God in three Per - sons, bless - ed Trin - i - ty!

Text: Reginald Heber, 1783–1826, alt.
Tune: John B. Dykes, 1823–1876

NICAEA
11 12 12 10

166 All Glory Be to God on High

1 All glo - ry be to God on high And thanks to him for - ev - er! What - ev - er Sa - tan's host may try, God foils their dark en - deav - or. He bends his ear to ev - 'ry call, And of - fers peace, good - will to all, And
2 O Fa - ther, for your lord - ship true We give you praise and hon - or; We wor - ship you; we trust in you; We give you thanks for - ev - er. Your will is per - fect, and your might Re - lent - less - ly con - firms the right; Your
3 Lord Je - sus Christ, the on - ly Son Of God, cre - a - tion's au - thor, Re - deem - er of your wan - d'ring ones, And source of all true plea - sure: O Lamb of God, O Lord di - vine, Con - form our lives to your de - sign, And
4 O Ho - ly Spir - it, per - fect gift, Who brings us con - so - la - tion: To men and wom - en saved by Christ As - sure your in - spi - ra - tion. Through sick - ness, need, and bit - ter death, Grant us your warm, life - giv - ing breath; Our

calms the trou - bled spir - it.
lord - ship is our bless - ing.
on us all have mer - cy.
lives are in your keep - ing. A - men

 Text: Nikolaus Decius, 1490–1541; tr. Gilbert E. Doan, b. 1930
Tune: attr. Nikolaus Decius, 1490–1541

ALLEIN GOTT IN DER HÖH
87 87 887

Glory Be to God the Father!

167

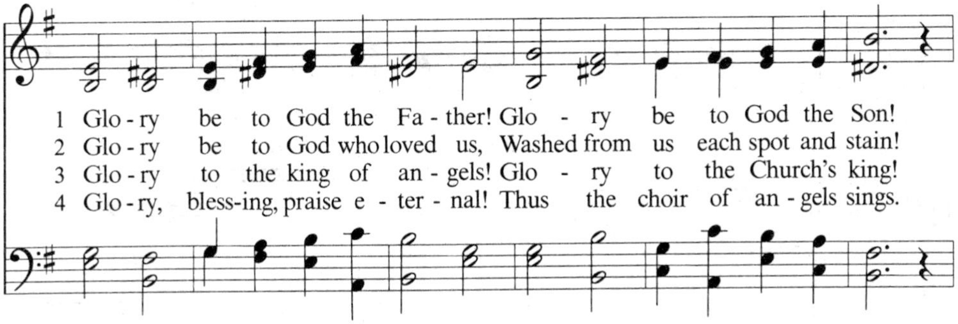

1 Glo - ry be to God the Fa - ther! Glo - ry be to God the Son!
2 Glo - ry be to God who loved us, Washed from us each spot and stain!
3 Glo - ry to the king of an - gels! Glo - ry to the Church's king!
4 Glo - ry, bless-ing, praise e - ter - nal! Thus the choir of an - gels sings.

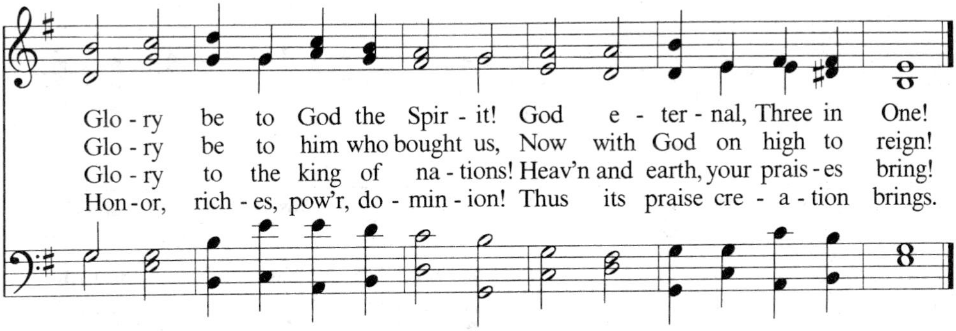

Glo - ry be to God the Spir - it! God e - ter - nal, Three in One!
Glo - ry be to him who bought us, Now with God on high to reign!
Glo - ry to the king of na - tions! Heav'n and earth, your prais - es bring!
Hon - or, rich - es, pow'r, do - min - ion! Thus its praise cre - a - tion brings.

8

5 Glory be to God the Father!
Glory be to God the Son!
Glory be to God the Spirit!
God eternal, Three in One!

Text: Horatius Bonar, 1808–1889, alt.
Tune: Johann Crüger, 1598–1662

HERR, ICH HABE MISGEHANDELT
87 87

168 Kyrie, God Father

Ky - ri - e! God, Fa - ther in heav'n a - bove,
You a - bound in gra - cious love,
Of all things the mak - er
and pre - serv - er.
E - le - i - son! E - le - i - son!
Ky - ri - e! O Christ, our king,
Sal - va - tion for

all you came to bring. O Lord Je - sus, God's own Son, Our me-
di - a - tor at the heav'n - ly throne: Hear our cry and grant our sup-
pli - ca - tion. E - le - i - son! E - le - i - son!
Ky - ri - e! O God the Ho - ly Ghost, Guard our

Hymn continues on the next page.

faith, the gift we need the most, And bless our life's last hour,
That we leave this sin - ful world with glad - ness. E - le -
i - son! E - le - i - son! A - men

© *Text: Latin, c. 1100; tr. W. Gustave Polack, 1890–1950, alt.*
Tune: "Kyrie fons bonitatis," c. 800, adapt.

KYRIE, GOTT VATER
PM

Father Most Holy

169

1 Fa - ther most ho - ly, mer - ci - ful, and ten - der; Je - sus, our
2 Trin - i - ty bless - ed, u - ni - ty un - shak - en; Good - ness un -
3 Mak - er of all things, all thy crea-tures praise thee; All for thy
4 Lord God Al - might - y, un - to thee be glo - ry, One in three
Sav - ior, with the Fa - ther reign - ing; Spir - it of com - fort,
bound - ed, ver - y God of heav - en, Light of the an - gels,
wor - ship were and are cre - at - ed; Now, as we al - so
per - sons, o - ver all ex - alt - ed! Glo - ry we of - fer,
ad - vo - cate, de - fend - er, Light nev - er wan - ing.
joy of those for - sak - en, Hope of all liv - ing.
wor - ship thee de - vout - ly, Hear thou our voic - es.
praise thee and a - dore thee, Now and for - ev - er.

© *Text:* *Latin hymn, 10th cent.; tr. Percy Dearmer, 1867–1936, adapt.*
Tune: Antiphoner, *Paris, 1681*

CHRISTE SANCTORUM
11 11 11 5

170 Crown Him with Many Crowns

1 Crown him with man - y crowns, The Lamb up - on his throne; Hark,
2 Crown him the vir - gin's Son, The God in - car - nate born, Whose
3 Crown him the Lord of love— Be - hold his hands and side, Rich
4 Crown him the Lord of life, Who tri - umphed o'er the grave And

how the heav'n - ly an - them drowns All mu - sic but its own. A -
arm those crim - son tro - phies won Which now his brow a - dorn; Fruit
wounds, yet vis - i - ble a - bove, In beau - ty glo - ri - fied. No
rose vic - to - rious in the strife For those he came to save. His

wake, my soul, and sing Of him who died for thee, And
of the mys - tic rose, Yet of that rose the stem, The
an - gels in the sky Can ful - ly bear that sight, But
glo - ries now we sing, Who died and rose on high, Who

hail him as thy match - less king Through all e - ter - ni - ty.
root whence mer - cy ev - er flows, The babe of Beth - le - hem.
down - ward bend their burn - ing eyes At mys - ter - ies so bright.
died, e - ter - nal life to bring, And lives that death may die.

5 Crown him the Lord of peace,
Whose pow'r a scepter sways
From pole to pole, that wars may cease,
Absorbed in prayer and praise.
His reign shall know no end,
And round his pierced feet
Fair flow'rs of paradise extend
Their fragrance ever sweet.

6 Crown him the Lord of years,
The potentate of time,
Creator of the rolling spheres,
Ineffably sublime.
All hail, Redeemer, hail!
For thou hast died for me;
Thy praise and glory shall not fail
Throughout eternity.

Text: Matthew Bridges, 1800–1894; Godfrey Thring, 1823–1903
Tune: George J. Elvey, 1816–1893

DIADEMATA
SMD

Rejoice, the Lord Is King! 171

1 Re - joice, the Lord is king! Your Lord and King a - dore;
2 Our Sav - ior Je - sus reigns, The God of truth and love;
3 His king - dom can - not fail; He rules o'er earth and heav'n;
4 He sits at God's right hand Till all his foes sub - mit
Re - joice, give thanks, and sing, And tri - umph ev - er - more:
When he had purged our stains, He took his seat a - bove:
The keys of death and hell Are to our Je - sus giv'n:
And bow to his com - mand And fall be - neath his feet:
Refrain
Lift up your heart, lift up your voice; Re - joice, a - gain I say, re - joice!

Text: Charles Wesley, 1707–1788, alt.
Tune: William E. Fischer, 1849–1936

LAUS REGIS
66 66 88

172 Lord, Enthroned in Heavenly Splendor

1 Lord, en - throned in heav'n - ly splen - dor, First - be - got - ten from the dead, You a - lone, our strong de - fend - er, Lift - ing up your peo - ple's head. Al - le - lu - ia, al - le - lu - ia, al - le - lu - ia! Je - sus, true and
2 Though the low - liest form now veil you As of old in Beth - le - hem, Here as there your an - gels hail you, Branch and flow'r of Jes - se's stem. Al - le - lu - ia, al - le - lu - ia, al - le - lu - ia! We in wor - ship
3 Pas - chal Lamb, your of - f'ring, fin - ished Once for all when you were slain, In its full - ness un - di - min - ished Shall for - ev - er - more re - main. Al - le - lu - ia, al - le - lu - ia, al - le - lu - ia! Cleans-ing souls from
4 Life - im - part - ing heav'n - ly man - na, Strick - en rock with stream-ing side, Heav'n and earth with loud ho - san - na Wor - ship you, the Lamb who died, Al - le - lu - ia, al - le - lu - ia, al - le - lu - ia! Ris'n, as - cend - ed,

liv - ing bread! Je - sus, true and liv - ing bread!
join with them; We in wor - ship join with them.
ev - 'ry stain; Cleans - ing souls from ev - 'ry stain.
glor - ri - fied! Ris'n, as - cend - ed, glor - ri - fied!

© Text: George H. Bourne, 1840–1925
Tune: William Owen, 1814–1893

BRYN CALFARIA
87 87 444 77

The Head That Once Was Crowned 173

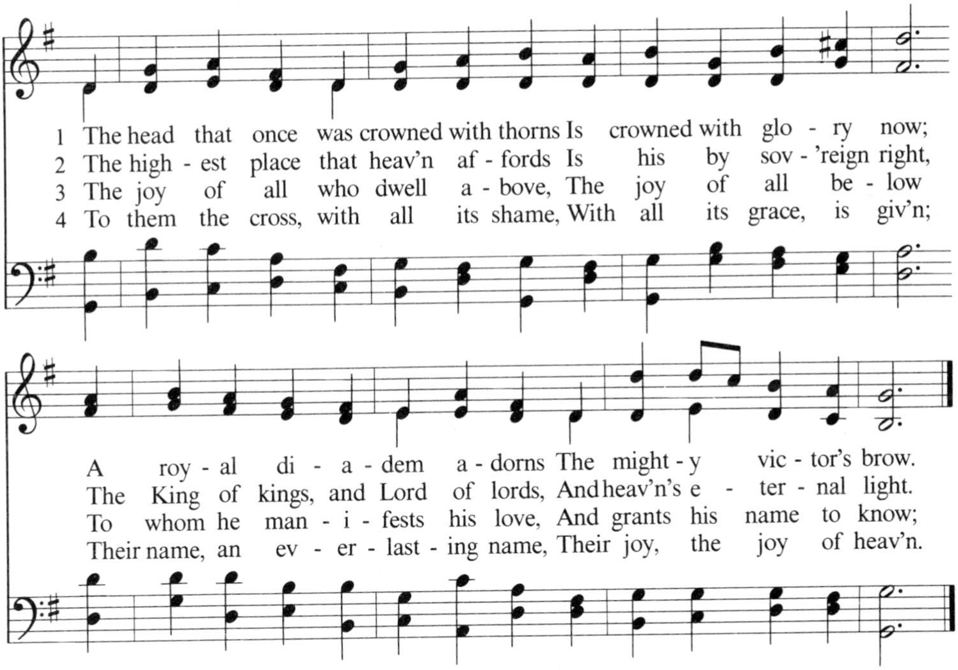

1 The head that once was crowned with thorns Is crowned with glo - ry now;
2 The high - est place that heav'n af - fords Is his by sov - 'reign right,
3 The joy of all who dwell a - bove, The joy of all be - low
4 To them the cross, with all its shame, With all its grace, is giv'n;

A roy - al di - a - dem a - dorns The might - y vic - tor's brow.
The King of kings, and Lord of lords, And heav'n's e - ter - nal light.
To whom he man - i - fests his love, And grants his name to know;
Their name, an ev - er - last - ing name, Their joy, the joy of heav'n.

5 They suffer with their Lord below;
They reign with him above;
Their profit and their joy to know
The myst'ry of his love.

6 The cross he bore is life and health,
Though shame and death to him;
His people's hope, his people's wealth,
Their everlasting theme!

Text: Thomas Kelly, 1769–1854
Tune: Jeremiah Clarke, c. 1669–1707

ST. MAGNUS
CM

174 For All the Saints

1 For all the saints who from their la - bors rest, ...
2 You were their rock, their for - tress, and their might;. . . .
3 Oh, may your sol - diers, faith - ful, true, and bold, ...
7 But then there breaks a yet more glo - rious day: The
8 From earth's wide bounds, from o - cean's far - thest coast, Through
All who by faith be - fore the world con - fessed,
You, Lord, their cap - tain in the well - fought fight;
Fight as the saints who no - bly fought of old
saints . . . tri - um - phant rise in bright ar - ray;
gates . . . of pearl streams in the count - less host,
Your name, O . . . Je - sus, be for - ev - er blest.
. . You, in the dark - ness drear, their one true light.
And win with . . them the vic - tor's crown of gold.
The King of . . . glo - ry pass - es on his way.
. . Sing - ing to Fa - ther, Son, and Ho - ly Ghost:

Al - le - lu - ia! Al - le - lu - ia!
4 Oh, blest com - mu - nion, fel - low - ship di - vine, We fee - bly strug - gle, they in glo - ry shine; Yet all are . . one with - in your great de - sign.
5 And when the strife is fierce, the war - fare long, Steals on the ear the dis - tant tri - umph song, And hearts are . . brave a - gain and arms are strong.
6 The gold - en eve - ning bright - ens in the west; Soon, soon to faith - ful war - riors comes their rest; . . Sweet is the calm of par - a - dise the blest.
Al - le - lu - ia! Al - le - lu - ia!

Text: *William W. How, 1823–1897, alt.*
© Tune: *R. Vaughan Williams, 1872–1958*

SINE NOMINE
10 10 10 and alleluias

175 Ye Watchers and Ye Holy Ones

1 Ye watch-ers and ye ho - ly ones, Bright ser - aphs, cher - u -
2 O high - er than the cher - u - bim, More glo - rious than the
3 Re - spond, ye souls in end - less rest, Ye pa - tri - archs and
4 O friends, in glad - ness let us sing, Su - per - nal an - thems
bim, and thrones, Raise the glad strain: "Al - le - lu - ia!"
ser - a - phim, Lead their prais - es; "Al - le - lu - ia!"
proph-ets blest: "Al - le - lu - ia! Al - le - lu - ia!"
ech - o - ing: "Al - le - lu - ia! Al - le - lu - ia!"
Cry out, do - min - ions, prince-doms, pow'rs, Arch - an - gels, vir -
Thou bear - er of the e - ter - nal Word, Most gra - cious, mag -
Ye ho - ly twelve, ye mar - tyrs strong, All saints tri - um -
To God the Fa - ther, God the Son, And God the Spir -
tues, an - gel choirs:
ni - fy the Lord:
phant, raise the song:
it, Three in One:
"Al - le - lu - ia! Al - le - lu - ia!"

Al - le - lu - ia, al - le - lu - ia, al - le - lu - ia!

© *Text: J. Athelstan Riley, 1858–1945*
Tune: Geistliche Kirchengesänge, *Köln, 1623*

LASST UNS ERFREUEN
888 888 and alleluias

For All Your Saints, O Lord 176

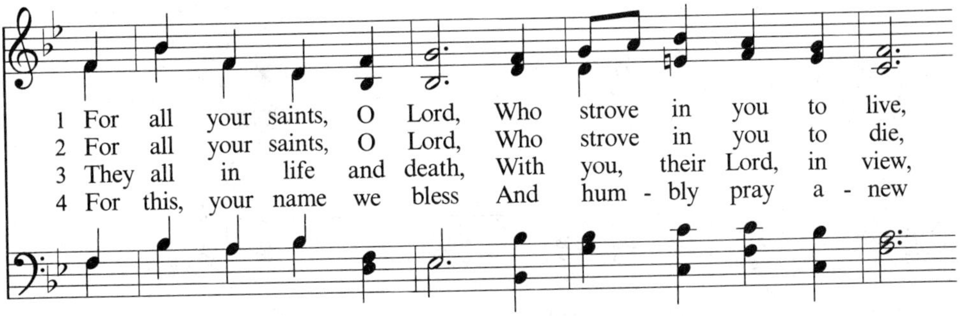

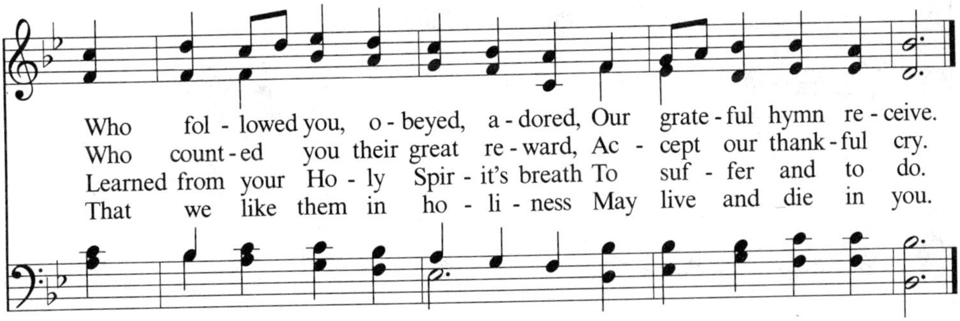

1 For all your saints, O Lord,
Who strove in you to live,
Who followed you, obeyed, adored,
Our grateful hymn receive.

2 For all your saints, O Lord,
Who strove in you to die,
Who counted you their great reward,
Accept our thankful cry.

3 They all in life and death,
With you, their Lord, in view,
Learned from your Holy Spirit's breath
To suffer and to do.

4 For this, your name we bless
And humbly pray anew
That we like them in holiness
May live and die in you.

5 To God, the Father, Son,
And Spirit, ever blest,
The One in Three, the Three in One,
Be endless praise addressed.

Text: Richard Mant, 1776–1848, alt.
Tune: William H. Walter, 1825–1893

FESTAL SONG
SM

7 By All Your Saints in Warfare

1 By all your saints in war - fare, For all your saints at
2 (Insert the stanza appropriate to the day.)
3 Then let us praise the Fa - ther And wor - ship God the
rest, Your ho - ly name, O Je - sus, For - ev - er - more be
Son And sing to God the Spir - it, E - ter - nal Three in
blest! For you have won the bat - tle That they might wear the
One. Till all the ran - somed num - ber Fall down be - fore the
crown; And now they shine in glo - ry Re - flect - ed from your throne.
throne, As - crib - ing pow'r and glo - ry And praise to God a - lone.

Stanzas 13–20 are at 178.

Saints and martyrs (general)

4 Apostles, prophets, martyrs,
And all the noble throng
Who wear the spotless raiment
And raise the ceaseless song—
For these passed on before us,
We offer praises due
And walking in their footsteps,
Would live our lives for you.

St. Andrew, Apostle

5 All praise, O Lord, for Andrew,
The first to welcome you,
Whose witness to his brother
Named you Messiah true.
May we, with hearts kept open
To you throughout the year,
Confess to friend and neighbor
Your advent ever near.

St. Thomas, Apostle

6 All praise for your apostle
Whose short-lived doubtings prove
Your perfect two-fold nature,
And all your depth of love.
We who await your coming
Desire your peace, O Lord;
Grant us true faith to know you,
Made flesh, yet God and Lord.

St. Stephen, Deacon and Martyr

7 Praise for the first of martyrs
Who saw you ready stand
To help in time of torment,
To plead at God's right hand.
They share with him who, steadfast,
In death their master own,
On earth the faithful witness,
On high the martyr's crown.

St. John, Apostle and Evangelist

8 For your beloved disciple
Exiled to Patmos' shore,
And for his faithful record,
We praise you evermore.
Praise for the mystic vision
His words to us unfold.
Instill in us his longing
Your glory to behold.

The Holy Innocents, Martyrs

9 All praise for infant martyrs
Whom your mysterious love
Called early from their warfare
To share your home above.
O Rachel, cease your weeping;
They rest from earthbound cares.
Lord, grant us hearts as guileless
And crowns as bright as theirs.

The Confession of St. Peter

10 Praise for your great apostle
So eager and so bold,
Thrice falling, yet repentant,
Thrice charged to feed your fold.
Lord, make your pastors faithful
To guard your flock from harm,
And hold them when they waver
With your almighty arm.

The Conversion of St. Paul

11 All praise for light from heaven
And for the voice of awe,
All praise for glorious visions
The persecutor saw.
O Lord, for Paul's conversion
We bless your name today;
Come, lighten all our darkness,
And guide us on our way.

St. Matthias, Apostle

12 Lord, your abiding presence
Mysterious made the choice;
For one in place of Judas
The faithful now rejoice.
From all such false apostles
Your holy Church defend,
And by your parting promise
Be with us to the end.

Text: Horatio Bolton Nelson, 1823–1913, alt.
 Tune: English folk tune

KING'S LYNN
76 76 D

By All Your Saints in Warfare

1 By all your saints in war - fare, For all your saints at
2 (Insert the stanza appropriate to the day.)
3 Then let us praise the Fa - ther And wor - ship God the
rest, Your ho - ly name, O Je - sus, For - ev - er - more be
Son And sing to God the Spir - it, E - ter - nal Three in
blest! For you have won the bat - tle That they might wear the
One. Till all the ran - somed num - ber Fall down be - fore the
crown; And now they shine in glo - ry Re - flect - ed from your throne.
throne, As - crib - ing pow'r and glo - ry And praise to God a - lone.

Stanzas 3–12 are at 177.

St. Mark, Evangelist

13 For him, O Lord, we praise you,
Whose fainting heart, made strong,
Poured forth his faithful Gospel
To animate our song.
May we, in all our weakness,
Receive your pow'r divine,
And all, as faithful branches,
Grow strong in you, the vine.

St. Philip and St. James, Apostles

14 We praise your name for Philip,
Blest guide to Greek and Jew,
And for young James, the faithful
Who heard and followed you.
Oh, grant us grace to know you,
The way, the truth, the life,
And wrestle with temptation
Till victors in the strife.

The Nativity of St. John the Baptist

15 We praise you for the Baptist,
Forerunner of the Word,
Our true Elijah, making
A highway for the Lord.
The last and greatest prophet,
He saw the dawning ray
Of light that grows in splendor
Until the perfect day.

St. James the Elder, Apostle

16 For him, O Lord, we praise you,
Who fell to Herod's sword.
He drank your cup of suff'ring
And thus fulfilled your word.
Lord, curb our vain impatience
For glory and for gain,
And nerve us for such suff'rings
As glorify your name.

St. Bartholomew, Apostle

17 All praise for him whose candor
Through all his doubt you saw
When Philip at the fig tree
Disclosed you in the law.
Discern, beneath our surface,
O Lord, what we can be,
That by your truth made guileless,
Your glory we may see.

St. Matthew, Apostle and Evangelist

18 Praise, Lord, for him whose Gospel
Your human life declared,
Who, worldly gain forsaking,
Your path of suff'ring shared.
From all unrighteous mammon,
Oh, raise our eyes anew,
That we, whate'er our station,
May rise and follow you.

St. Luke, Evangelist

19 For that beloved physician
All praise, whose Gospel shows
The healer of the nations,
The one who shares our woes.
Your wine and oil, O Savior,
Upon our spirits pour,
And with true balm of Gilead
Anoint us evermore.

St. Simon and St. Jude, Apostles

20 Praise, Lord, for your apostles
Who sealed their faith today;
One love, one hope impelled them
To tread the sacred way.
May we with zeal as earnest
The faith of Christ maintain,
And foll'wing these our brothers,
At length your rest attain.

Text: Horatio Bolton Nelson, 1823–1913, alt.
© *Tune: English folk tune*

KING'S LYNN
76 76 D

179 At the Name of Jesus

1 At the name of Je - sus Ev - 'ry knee shall bow,
2 At his voice cre - a - tion Sprang at once to sight,
3 Hum-bled for a sea - son, To re - ceive a name
4 Bore it up tri - um - phant With its hu - man light,
Ev - 'ry tongue con - fess him King of glo - ry now.
All the an - gel fac - es, All the hosts of light,
From the lips of sin - ners Un - to whom he came,
Through all ranks of crea - tures To the cen - tral height,
'Tis the Fa - ther's plea - sure We should call him Lord,
Thrones and dom - i - na - tions, Stars up - on their way,
Faith - ful - ly he bore it Spot-less to the last;
To the throne of God - head, To the Fa - ther's breast;
Who from the be - gin - ning Was the might - y Word.
All the heav'n - ly or - ders In their great ar - ray.
Brought it back vic - to - rious When from death he passed;
Filled it with the glo - ry Of that per - fect rest.

5 In your hearts enthrone him;
There let him subdue
All that is not holy,
All that is not true.
Crown him as your captain
In temptation's hour;
Let his will enfold you
In its light and pow'r.

6 Christians, this Lord Jesus
Shall return again
In his Father's glory,
With his angel train;
For all wreaths of empire
Meet upon his brow,
And our hearts confess him
King of glory now.

Text: Caroline M. Noel, 1817–1877
© *Tune: R. Vaughan Williams, 1872–1958*

KING'S WESTON
65 65 D

My Soul Now Magnifies the Lord 180

1 My soul now mag - ni - fies the Lord; My spir - it
2 For he a - lone who shows such might Has done a -
3 His arm is strong; his strength is great. He scat - ters
4 He feeds the hun - gry as his own; The wealth - y
leaps for joy in him. He keeps me in his
maz - ing things to me. His mer - cy flows; his
those of proud in - tent, And casts them down from
leave with emp - ty hands. He gives his help to
kind re - gard, And I am blest for time to come.
name like light Re - mains in time per - pet - ual - ly.
high es - tate; Then gives the low his nour - ish - ment.
Is - ra - el; His gra - cious prom - ise al - ways stands.

© *Text: Luke 1:46–55; versification, Stephanie K. Frey, b. 1952*
Tune: Heinrich Schütz, 1585–1672

ICH HEB MEIN AUGEN SEHNLICH AUF
L M

181 Greet Now the Swiftly Changing Year

1 Greet now the swift - ly chang - ing year With joy and pen - i - tence sin - cere. Re - joice! Re-joice! With thanks em - brace An - oth - er year of grace.
2 Re - mem - ber now the Son of God And how he shed his in - fant blood. Re - joice! Re-joice! With thanks em - brace An - oth - er year of grace.
3 This Je - sus came to end sin's war; This name of names for us he bore. Re - joice! Re-joice! With thanks em - brace An - oth - er year of grace.
4 His love a - bun - dant far ex - ceeds The vol - ume of a whole year's needs. Re - joice! Re-joice! With thanks em - brace An - oth - er year of grace.

5 With him as Lord to lead our way
In want and in prosperity,
What need we fear in earth or space
In this new year of grace!

6 "All glory be to God on high,
And peace on earth!" the angels cry.
Rejoice! Rejoice! With thanks embrace
Another year of grace.

7 God, Father, Son, and Spirit, hear!
To all our pleas incline your ear;
Upon our lives rich blessing trace
In this new year of grace.

 Text: Slovak; tr. Jaroslav J. Vajda, b. 1919, alt.
Tune: Závorka, Kancional, *1602*

ROK NOVY
8886

Rise, O Children of Salvation

182

1 Rise, O chil - dren of sal - va - tion, All who cleave to
2 Saints and mar - tyrs long be - fore us Firm - ly on this
3 Fight - ing, we shall be vic - to - rious By the blood of
4 When his ser - vants stand be - fore him, Each re - ceiv - ing
Christ the head! Wake, a - wake, O might - y na - tion,
ground have stood; See their ban - ner wav - ing o'er us,
Christ our Lord; On our fore - heads, bright and glo - rious,
his re - ward; When his saints in light a - dore him,
Lest the foe on Zi - on tread; He draws nigh and
Con - qu'rors through the Sav - ior's blood. Ground we hold, where -
Shines the wit - ness of his Word; Spear and shield on
Giv - ing glo - ry to the Lord; "Vic - to - ry!" our
would de - fy All the hosts of God Most High.
on of old Fought the faith - ful and the bold.
bat - tle - field, His great name; we can - not yield.
song shall be, Like the thun - der of the sea.

Text: Justus Falckner, 1672–1723; tr. Emma F. Bevan, 1827–1909, alt.
Tune: Joachim Neander, 1650–1680

UNSER HERRSCHER
87 87 77

183 The Son of God Goes Forth to War

1 The Son of God goes forth to war A king - ly crown to gain.
2 The mar - tyr first, whose ea - gle eye Could pierce be - yond the grave,
3 A glo - rious band, the cho - sen few, On whom the Spir - it came,
4 A no - ble ar - my, girls and boys, With men and wom - en saved,
His blood - red ban - ner streams a - far; Who fol - lows in his train?
Who saw his mas - ter in the sky And called on him to save.
Twelve val - iant saints; their hope they knew And mocked the cross and flame.
A - round the Sav - ior's throne re - joice, In robes of light ar - rayed.
Who best can drink his cup of woe, Tri - um - phant o - ver pain;
Like him, with par - don on his tongue In midst of mor - tal pain,
They met the ty - rant's bran - dished steel, The li - on's gor - y mane;
They climbed the steep as - cent of heav'n Through per - il, toil, and pain.
Who pa - tient bears his cross be - low— He fol - lows in his train.
He prayed for those who did the wrong—Who fol - lows in his train?
They bowed their necks the death to feel— Who fol - lows in their train?
O God, to us may grace be giv'n To fol - low in their train!

Text: Reginald Heber, 1783–1826, alt.
Tune: Henry S. Cutler, 1824–1902

ALL SAINTS NEW
CMD

In His Temple Now Behold Him 184

1 In his tem - ple now be - hold him, See the long - ex - pect - ed Lord; An - cient proph - ets had fore - told him, God has now ful - filled his word. Now to praise him, his re - deem - ed Shall break forth with one ac - cord.
2 In the arms of her who bore him, Vir - gin pure, be - hold him lie, While his a - ged saints a - dore him, Ere in per - fect faith they die. Al - le - lu - ia! Al - le - lu - ia! Lo, the in - car - nate God Most High!
3 Je - sus, by your pre - sen - ta - tion, When they blest you, weak and poor, Make us see your great sal - va - tion, Seal us with your prom - ise sure; And pre - sent us, in your glo - ry, To your Fa - ther, cleansed and pure.

Text: Henry J. Pye, 1825–1903, alt.
© *Tune: Robert Leaf, b. 1936*

LINDSBORG
87 87 87

185 Great God, a Blessing from Your Throne

1 Great God, a bless - ing from your throne Grant us who lay this cor - ner - stone, To build a church in which your Word Is pure - ly taught and glad - ly heard.
2 The work is yours and not our own; Oh, come, and make your pres - ence known; Our prayers ac - cept, our of - f'rings bless, Our la - bors crown with due suc - cess.
3 We are the peo - ple of your choice, And while we in this grace re - joice, Our prayer is this, our con - stant care, That oth - ers too our bliss may share.
4 Lord, here e - rect a bless - ed home Where Christ will ev - er bid us come, From him re - ceiv - ing grace for grace Till we be - hold you face to face.

© *Text: Conrad H. L. Schuette, 1843–1929, adapt.*
Tune: Johann Crüger, 1598–1662

LOB SEI DEM ALLMÄCHTIGEN GOTT
LM

How Blessed Is This Place, O Lord 186

1 How bless-ed is this place, O Lord, Where you are
2 Here let your sa - cred fire of old De - scend to
3 Here let the wea - ry one find rest, The trou - bled
4 Here your an - gel - ic spir - its send Their sol - emn
wor - shiped and a - dored; In faith we here an
kin - dle spir - its cold; And may our prayers, when
heart, your com - fort blest, The guilt - y one, a
praise with ours to blend, And grant the vi - sion,
al - tar raise To your great glo - ry, God of praise.
here we bend, Like in - cense sweet to you as - cend.
sure re - treat, The sin - ner, par - don at your feet.
in - ly giv'n, Of this your house, the gate of heav'n.

© *Text: Ernest E. Ryden, b. 1886, alt.*
Tune: Swiss, 1826

SOLOTHURN
L M

187 Dearest Jesus, We Are Here

1 Dear-est Je - sus, we are here, Glad - ly your com - mand o - bey - ing. With this child we now draw near In re - sponse to your own say - ing That to you it shall be giv - en As a child and heir of heav - en.
2 Your com - mand is clear and plain, And we would o - bey it du - ly: "You must all be born a - gain, Heart and life re - new - ing tru - ly, Born of wa - ter and the Spir - it, And my king - dom thus in - her - it."
3 This is why we come to you, In our arms this in - fant bear - ing; Lord, to us your glo - ry show; Let this child, your mer - cy shar - ing, In your arms be shield - ed ev - er, Yours on earth and yours for - ev - er.
4 Gra-cious head, your mem - ber own; Shep - herd, take your lamb and feed it; Prince of Peace, make here your throne; Way of life, to heav - en lead it; Pre - cious vine, let noth - ing sev - er From your side this branch for - ev - er.

5 Now into your heart we pour
Prayers that from our hearts proceeded.
Our petitions heav'nward soar;
May our fond desires be heeded!
Write the name we now have given;
Write it in the book of heaven!

Text: Benjamin Schmolck, 1672–1737; tr. Catherine Winkworth, 1829–1878, alt.
Tune: Johann R. Ahle, 1625–1673

LIEBSTER JESU, WIR SIND HIER
78 78 88

I Bind unto Myself Today 188

1 I bind un - to my - self to - day The strong name
of the Trin - i - ty By in - vo - ca - tion
of the same, The Three in One and One in Three.

Hymn continues on the next page.

2 I bind this day to me for - ev - er, By
3 I bind un - to my - self to - day . . The
4 I bind un - to my - self to - day . . The
5 I bind un - to my - self the name, . The
pow'r of faith, Christ's in - car - na - tion, His
vir - tues of the star - lit heav - en, The
pow'r of God to hold and lead, . . His
strong name of the Trin - i - ty . . . By
bap - tism in the Jor - dan Riv - er, His
glo - rious sun's life - giv - ing ray, . . The
eye to watch, his might to stay,. . His
in - vo - ca - tion of the same, . The
cross of death for my sal - va - tion, His
white - ness of the moon at e - ven, The
ear to hear - ken to my need,. . The
Three in One and One in Three, . Of

burst - ing from the spic - ed tomb, . His
flash - ing of the light - ning free, . . The
wis - dom of my God to teach, . His
whom all na - ture has cre - a - tion, E
rid - ing up the heav'n - ly way, His
whirl - ing wind's tem - pes - tuous shocks, The
hand to guide, his shield to ward, The
ter - nal Fa - ther, Spir - it, Word. Praise
com - ing at the day of doom, .
sta - ble earth, the deep salt sea, . .
Word of God to give me speech, .
to the Lord of my sal - va - tion;
I bind un - to my - self to - day.
A - round the old e - ter - nal rocks.
His heav'n - ly host to be my guard.
Sal - va - tion is of Christ the Lord!

Text: attr. St. Patrick, c. 372–466; para. Cecil F. Alexander, 1823–1895
Tune: Irish

ST. PATRICK'S BREASTPLATE
irregular

189 We Know That Christ Is Raised

1 We know that Christ is raised and dies no more.
2 We share by wa - ter in his sav - ing death.
3 The Fa - ther's splen - dor clothes the Son with life.
4 A new cre - a - tion comes to life and grows
Em - braced by death, he broke its fear - ful hold,
Re - born, we share with him an Eas - ter life,
The Spir - it's fis - sion shakes the Church of God.
As Christ's new bod - y takes on flesh and blood.
1–3
And our de - spair he turned to blaz - ing joy.
As liv - ing mem - bers of our Sav - ior Christ.
Bap - tized, we live with God the Three in One.
The u - ni - verse re - stored and

4
Hal - le - lu - jah!
Hal - le - lu - jah!
Hal - le - lu - jah!
whole will sing: Hal - le - lu - jah!

 Text: John B. Geyer, b. 1932, alt.
Tune: Charles V. Stanford, 1852–1924

ENGELBERG
10 10 10 4

We Praise You, Lord 190

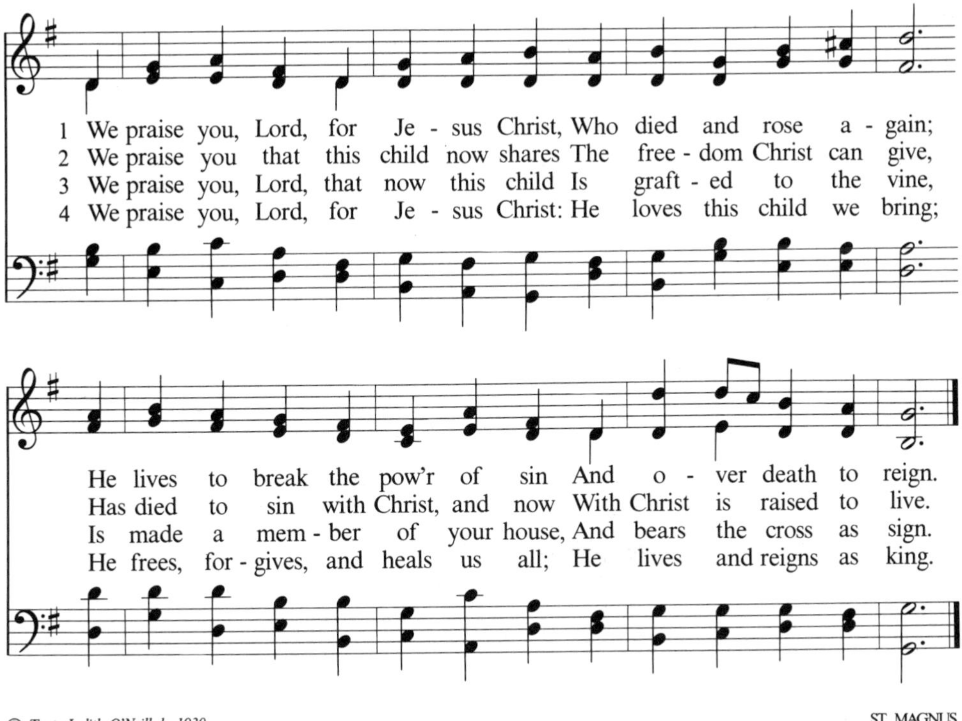

1 We praise you, Lord, for Je - sus Christ, Who died and rose a - gain;
He lives to break the pow'r of sin And o - ver death to reign.

2 We praise you that this child now shares The free - dom Christ can give,
Has died to sin with Christ, and now With Christ is raised to live.

3 We praise you, Lord, that now this child Is graft - ed to the vine,
Is made a mem - ber of your house, And bears the cross as sign.

4 We praise you, Lord, for Je - sus Christ: He loves this child we bring;
He frees, for - gives, and heals us all; He lives and reigns as king.

 Text: Judith O'Neill, b. 1930
Tune: Jeremiah Clarke, 1669–1707

ST. MAGNUS
CM

191 Praise and Thanksgiving Be to God

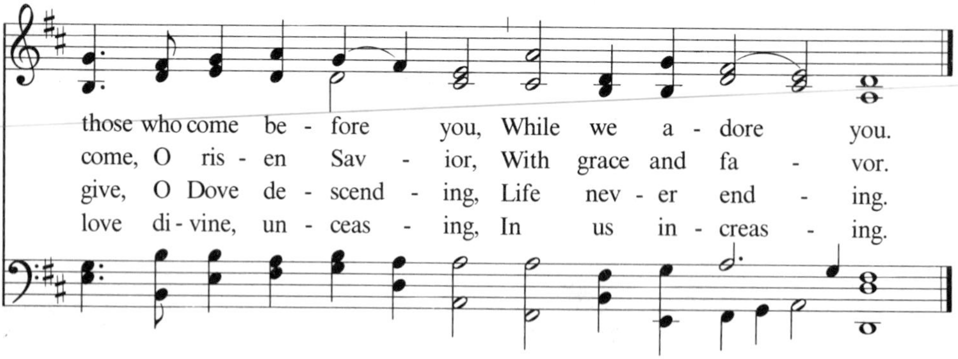

1 Praise and thanksgiving be to God our maker,
Source of all blessing, prodigal creator.
Baptize and make your own those who come before you,
While we adore you.

2 Not our own holiness, nor that we have striven
Brings us the peace which you, O Christ, have given.
Baptize and set apart; come, O risen Savior,
With grace and favor.

3 Come, Holy Spirit, come in visitation;
You are the truth, our hope, and our salvation.
Baptize with joy and pow'r; give, O Dove descending,
Life never ending.

4 Eternal Word, . . still by the Father spoken,
Speak to us now in this baptismal token;
Proclaim anew to us love divine, unceasing,
In us increasing.

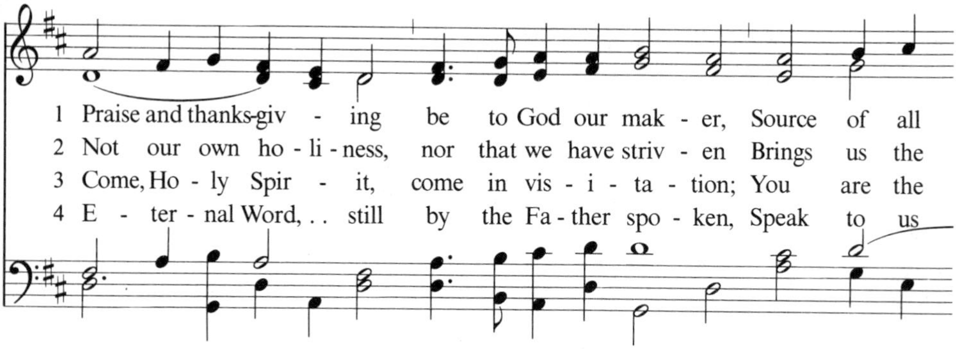

5 Praise to the Father, Son, and Holy Spirit:
One Lord, one faith, one source of ev'ry merit.
Here now renew your Church through this symbol given;
Grant peace from heaven.

 Text: *Harold F. Yardley, b. 1911; Frank J. Whiteley, b. 1914, alt.*
Tune: Antiphoner, *Paris, 1681*

CHRISTE SANCTORUM
11 11 11 5

Baptized into Your Name Most Holy 192

1 Bap-tized in - to your name most ho - ly, O Fa - ther, Son, and
2 My lov - ing Fa - ther, here you take me Hence-forth to be your
3 O faith-ful God, you nev - er fail me; Your cov-'nant sure - ly
4 All that I am and love most dear - ly, Re - ceive it all, O
Ho - ly Ghost, I claim a place, though weak and low - ly,
child and heir; My faith - ful Sav - ior, here you make me
will a - bide. Let not e - ter - nal death as - sail me
Lord, from me. Oh, let me make my vows sin - cere - ly,
A - mong your seed, your cho - sen host. Bur - ied with Christ and
The fruit of all your sor - rows share; O Ho - ly Ghost, you
Should I trans-gress it on my side! Have mer - cy when I
And help me your own child to be! Let noth - ing that I
dead to sin, I have your Spir - it now with - in.
com - fort me Though threat-'ning clouds a - round I see.
come de - filed; For - give, lift up, re - store your child.
am or own Serve an - y will but yours a - lone.

Text: Johann J. Rambach, 1693–1735; tr. Catherine Winkworth, 1829–1878, alt.
Tune: Kornelius Heinrich Dretzel, 1705–1773

O DASS ICH TAUSEND ZUNGEN HÄTTE
98 98 88

193 Cradling Children in His Arm

Cra-dling chil-dren in his arm, Je - sus gave his bless - ing.
To our babes a wel-come warm He is yet ad-dress - ing.
Take them, Lord, give life a - new In the liv - ing wa - ters!
Keep them al - ways near to you As your sons and daugh - ters!

© Text: Nikolai F. S. Grundtvig, 1783–1872; tr. Johannes H. V. Knudsen, b. 1902
Tune: Johann Horn, c. 1490–1547

GAUDEAMUS PARITER
76 76 D

All Who Believe and Are Baptized 194

1 All who be - lieve and are bap - tized Shall see the Lord's sal - va - tion;
2 With one ac - cord, O God, we pray, Grant us your Ho - ly Spir - it;

Bap - tized in - to the death of Christ, They are a new
Help us in our in - fir - mi - ty Through Je - sus' blood

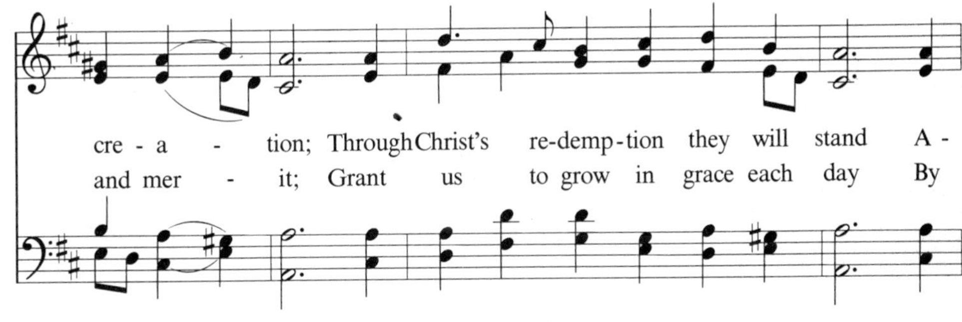
cre - a - tion; Through Christ's re-demp - tion they will stand A -
and mer - it; Grant us to grow in grace each day By

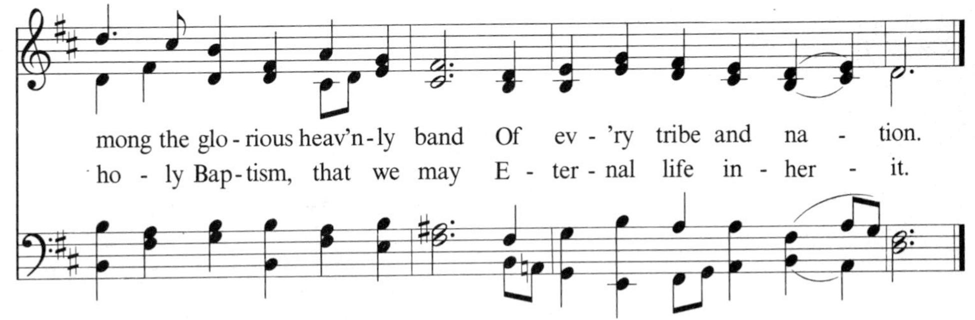
mong the glo - rious heav'n - ly band Of ev - 'ry tribe and na - tion.
ho - ly Bap - tism, that we may E - ter - nal life in - her - it.

Text: *Thomas H. Kingo, 1634–1703; tr. George T. Rygh, 1860–1943, alt.*
Tune: Etlich christlich Lieder, *Wittenberg, 1524*

ES IST DAS HEIL
87 87 887

195 This Is the Spirit's Entry Now

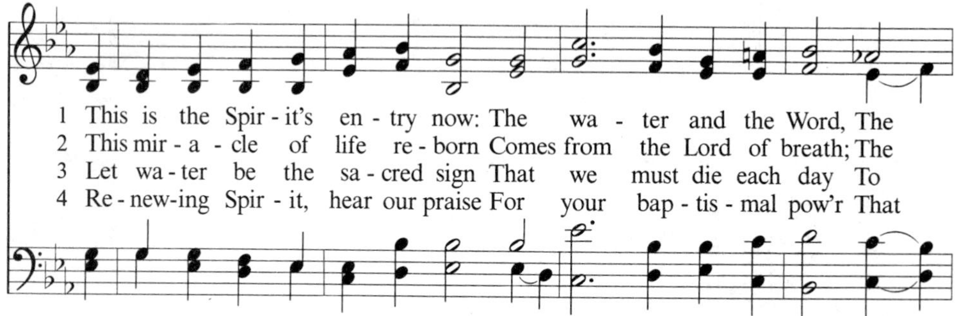
1 This is the Spir - it's en - try now: The wa - ter and the Word, The
2 This mir - a - cle of life re - born Comes from the Lord of breath; The
3 Let wa - ter be the sa - cred sign That we must die each day To
4 Re - new-ing Spir - it, hear our praise For your bap - tis - mal pow'r That

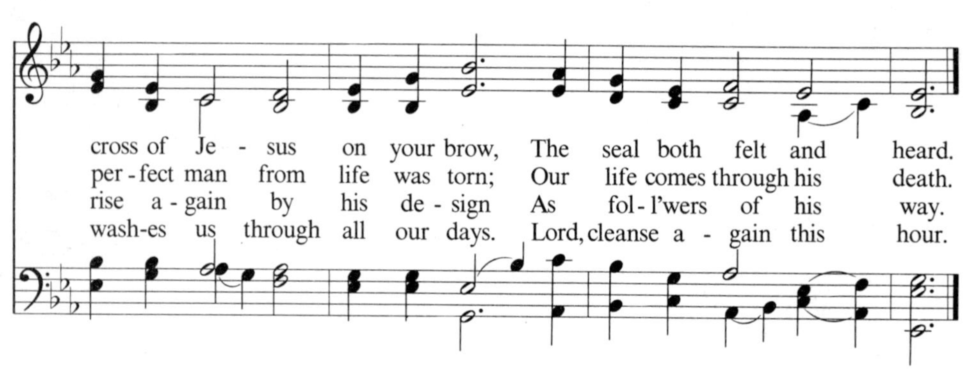
cross of Je - sus on your brow, The seal both felt and heard.
per - fect man from life was torn; Our life comes through his death.
rise a - gain by his de - sign As fol - l'wers of his way.
wash-es us through all our days. Lord, cleanse a - gain this hour.

PERRY
CM

Praise the Lord, Rise Up Rejoicing 196

1 Praise the Lord, rise up re - joic - ing, Wor - ship, thanks, de -
2 Scat - tered flock, one shep - herd shar - ing, Lost and lone - ly,
3 Sins for - giv - en, wrongs for - giv - ing, We go forth a -

vo - tion voic - ing: Glo - ry be to God on high!
one voice hear - ing, Ears at - ten - tive to your word;
lert and liv - ing In your Spir - it, strong and free.

Christ, your cross and Pas - sion shar - ing, By this Eu - cha -
By your blood new life re - ceiv - ing, In your bod - y,
Part - ners in your new cre - a - tion, Seek - ing peace in

rist de - clar - ing Yours the fi - nal vic - to - ry.
firm be - liev - ing, We are yours, and you the Lord.
ev - 'ry na - tion, May we faith - ful fol - l'wers be.

 Text: H. C. A. Gaunt, b. 1902, alt.
Tune: Johann Löhner, 1645–1705, adapt.

ALLES IST AN GOTTES SEGEN
887 887

197 O Living Bread from Heaven

1 O living Bread from heaven,
How well you feed your guest!
The gifts that you have given
Have filled my heart with rest.
Oh, wondrous food of blessing,
Oh, cup that heals our woes!
My heart, this gift possessing,
With praises overflows!

2 My Lord, you here have led me
Within your holiest place,
And here yourself have fed me
With treasures of your grace;
For you have freely given
What earth could never buy,
The bread of life from heaven,
That now I shall not die.

3 You gave me all I wanted;
This food can death destroy.
And you have freely granted
The cup of endless joy.
My Lord, I do not merit
The favor you have shown,
And all my soul and spirit
Bow down before your throne.

4 Lord, grant me then, thus strengthened
With heav'nly food, while here
My course on earth is lengthened,
To serve with holy fear.
And when you call my spirit
To leave this world below,
I enter, through your merit,
Where joys unmingled flow.

Text: Johann Rist, 1606–1667; tr. Catherine Winkworth, 1829–1878, alt.
Tune: Samuel S. Wesley, 1810–1876

AURELIA
76 76 D

Let All Mortal Flesh Keep Silence 198

1 Let all mor - tal flesh keep si - lence, And with fear and
2 King of kings, yet born of Mar - y, As of old on
3 Rank on rank the host of heav - en Spreads its van-guard
4 At his feet the six - winged ser - aph, Cher - u - bim with
trem - bling stand; Pon - der noth - ing earth - ly - mind - ed,
earth he stood, Lord of lords in hu - man ves - ture,
on the way; As the Light of light, de - scend - ing
sleep - less eye, Veil their fac - es to the pres - ence,
For with bless - ing in his hand Christ our God to earth de -
In the bod - y and the blood, He will give to all the
From the realms of end - less day, Comes, the pow'rs of hell to
As with cease-less voice they cry: "Al - le - lu - ia! Al - le -
scend - ing Comes our hom - age to de - mand.
faith - ful His own self for heav'n - ly food.
van - quish, As the dark-ness clears a - way.
lu - ia! Al - le - lu - ia, Lord Most High!"

Text: Liturgy of St. James; tr. Gerard Moultrie, 1829–1885, alt.
Tune: French folk tune, 17th cent.

PICARDY
87 87 87

199 Thee We Adore, O Hidden Savior

1 Thee we a - dore, O hid - den Sav - ior, thee,
2 O blest me - mo - rial of our dy - ing Lord,
3 Foun - tain of good - ness, Je - sus, Lord and God:
4 O Christ, whom now be - neath a veil we see:

Who in thy Sac - ra - ment art pleased to be; Both flesh and
Who liv - ing bread to us shall here af - ford: Oh, may our
Cleanse us, un - clean, with thy most cleans-ing blood; In - crease our
May what we thirst for soon our por - tion be, To gaze on

spir - it in thy pres - ence fail, Yet here thy
souls for - ev - er feed on thee, And thou, O
faith and love, that we may know The hope and
thee un - veiled, and see thy face, The vi - sion

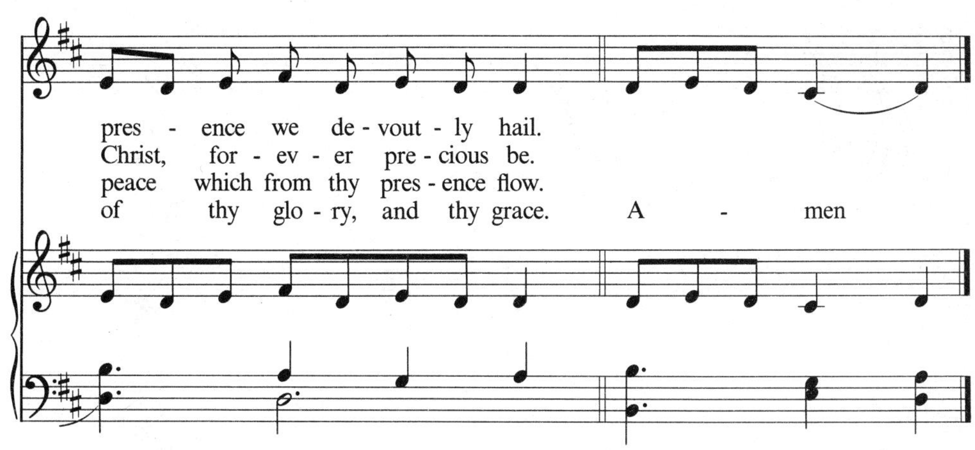
pres - ence we de - vout - ly hail.
Christ, for - ev - er pre - cious be.
peace which from thy pres - ence flow.
of thy glo - ry, and thy grace. A - men

Text: Thomas Aquinas, 1227–1274; tr. James R. Woodford, 1820–1885
Tune: mode V; Processionale, *Paris, 1697*

ADORO TE DEVOTE
10 10 10 10

For the Bread Which You Have Broken 200

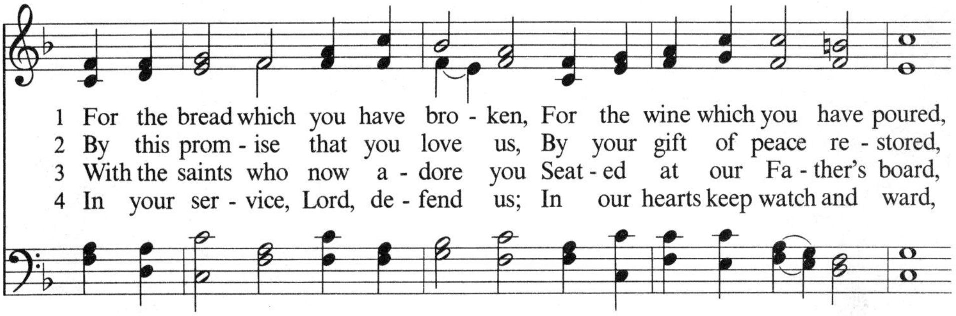

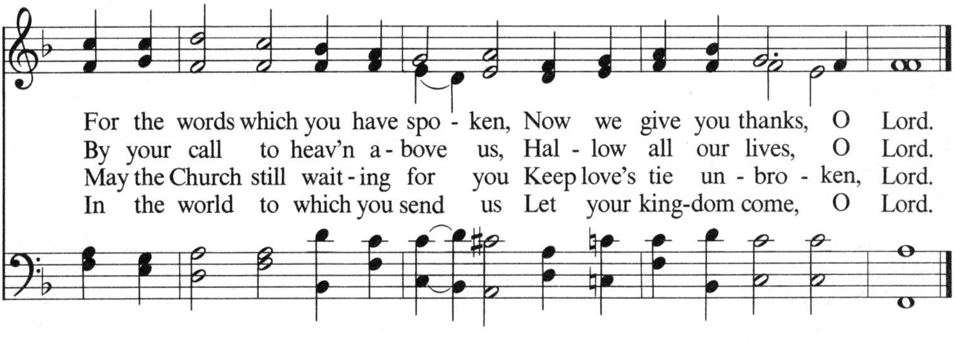

1 For the bread which you have broken, For the wine which you have poured,
For the words which you have spoken, Now we give you thanks, O Lord.

2 By this promise that you love us, By your gift of peace restored,
By your call to heav'n above us, Hallow all our lives, O Lord.

3 With the saints who now adore you Seated at our Father's board,
May the Church still waiting for you Keep love's tie unbroken, Lord.

4 In your service, Lord, defend us; In our hearts keep watch and ward,
In the world to which you send us Let your kingdom come, O Lord.

 Text: Louis F. Benson, 1855–1930, alt.
Tune: Gross Catolisch Gesangbuch, *Nürnberg, 1631*

OMNI DIE
87 87

201 O God of Life's Great Mystery

1 O God of life's great mys - ter - y,
2 Be - yond the lines of steel and stone,
3 Through preach - ing of the liv - ing Word,
We bring to you this hope - ful plea:
Be - neath the forms of flesh and bone,
In sac - ra - men - tal wa - ter poured,
Give us faith's in - sight strong and keen, The
Be - yond the curve of time and space, Show
With eu - cha - ris - tic bread and wine, Bring
joy - ful sense of things un - seen.
us the won - der of your face.
us the gift of life di - vine.

© *Text: Royce J. Scherf, b. 1929*
© *Tune: Walter K. Stanton, b. 1891*

CANNOCK
L M

Victim Divine, Your Grace We Claim 202

1 Vic - tim Di - vine, your grace we claim, As here your
2 You stand with - in the ho - liest place, As once for
3 We have no need to go to heav'n To bring the
pre - cious death we show; Once of - fered up, a spot - less
guilt - y sin - ners slain; Your blood for sin - ners in - ter -
long-sought Sav - ior down; You are to all al - read - y
lamb, In your great tem - ple here be - low, You did for
cedes, Re - demp - tion for the world to gain. Your blood shall
giv'n, And e - ven now your ban - quet crown. To ev - 'ry
hu - man - kind a - tone; And now you stand be - fore the throne.
still our ran - som be, The pay - ment made to set us free.
faith - ful soul ap - pear, And show your ver - y pres - ence here.

Text: Charles Wesley, 1707–1788, alt.
Tune: Melchior Vulpius, c. 1560–1615

DAS NEUGEBORNE KINDELEIN
88 88 88

203 Now We Join in Celebration

1 Now we join in cel - e - bra - tion At our Sav - ior's in - vi - ta - tion, Dressed no more in spir - it som - ber, Clothed in - stead in joy and won - der; For the Lord of all ex - is - tence, Put - ting off di - vine tran - scen - dence, Stoops a - gain in love to
2 Lord, as round this feast we gath - er, Fill our hearts with ho - ly rap - ture! For this bread and cup of bless - ing Are for us the sure pos - sess - ing Of your lov - ing deed on Cal - v'ry, Of your liv - ing self, our vic - t'ry, Pledge of your un - fail - ing
3 Lord, we share in this com - mu - nion As one fam - 'ly of God's chil - dren, Rec - on - ciled through you, our broth - er, One in you with God our Fa - ther. Give us grace to live for oth - ers, Serv - ing all, both friends and strang - ers, Seek - ing jus - tice, love, and

meet us, With his ver - y life to feed us.
pres - ence, Fore - taste here of heav'n - ly glad - ness.
mer - cy Till you come in fi - nal glo - ry.

 Text: Joel W. Lundeen, b. 1918
Tune: Johann Crüger, 1598–1662

SCHMÜCKE DICH
LMD

Cup of Blessing That We Share 204

1 Cup of bless - ing that we share, Does it not his grace de - clare?
2 Is it not one bread we break? Of his bod - y all par - take.

Is it not the blood of Christ, Who for us was sac - ri - ficed?
Cast - ing out dis - trust and fear, Let us love with hearts sin - cere.

As one bod - y, we are fed; Christ we share, one cup, one bread.
One by God's de - sign are we; Let us live in u - ni - ty.

 Text: Bernard Mischke, b. 1926, alt.
 Tune: Knut Nystedt, b. 1915

TORSHOV
77 77 77

205 Now the Silence

Fsus4 F Dm Gm C Am Gm Dm C
Now the si - lence, Now the peace, Now the emp - ty hands up-lift - ed;
Fsus4 F Dm Gm C Am Gm Dm Gm E♭
Now the kneel-ing, Now the plea, Now the Fa - ther's arms in wel - come;
F B♭ Gm Cm F B♭ F Gm F Cm
Now the hear - ing, Now the pow'r, Now the ves - sel brimmed for pour - ing;
F B♭ Gm Cm F B♭ F Gm C
Now the bod - y, Now the blood, Now the joy - ful cel - e - bra - tion;

Fsus4 F Dm Gm C Am Gm Dm C
Now the wed - ding, Now the songs, Now the heart for - giv - en leap - ing;
F Gm C Gm7 F Gm C Gm7
Now the Spir - it's vis - i - ta - tion, Now the Son's e - piph - a - ny,
F Gm Gm7 Dm C Gm C Gm C
Now the Fa - ther's bless - ing. Now. Now. Now.

© *Text: Jaroslav J. Vajda, b. 1919*
© *Tune: Carl F. Schalk, b. 1929*

NOW
PM

206 Lord, Who the Night You Were Betrayed

1 Lord, who the night you were be-trayed did pray That all your Church might be for-ev-er one: Help us at ev-'ry Eu-cha-rist to say With will-ing heart and soul, "Your will be done." That we may all one bread, one
2 For all your Church on earth, we in-ter-cede; Lord, make our sad di-vi-sions soon to cease; Draw us all clos-er, each to each, we plead, By draw-ing all to you, O Prince of Peace; So may we all one bread, one
3 And hear our prayer for wan-d'rers from your fold; Re-store them, too, Good Shep-herd of the sheep, Back to the faith your saints con-fessed of old, And to the Church still pledged that faith to keep. Soon may we all one bread, one
4 So, Lord, at length when sac-ra-ments shall cease, May we be one with all your Church a-bove— One with your saints in one un-bro-ken peace, One as your bride in one un-bound-ed love; More bless-ed still, in peace and

bod - y be Through this, your sac - ra - ment of u - ni - ty.
bod - y be, Through this blest sac - ra - ment of u - ni - ty.
bod - y be, Through this blest sac - ra - ment of u - ni - ty.
love to be One with the Trin - i - ty in u - ni - ty.

© Text: William H. Turton, 1856–1938, alt.
Tune: Orlando Gibbons, 1583–1625

SONG 1
10 10 10 10 10 10

We Who Once Were Dead 207

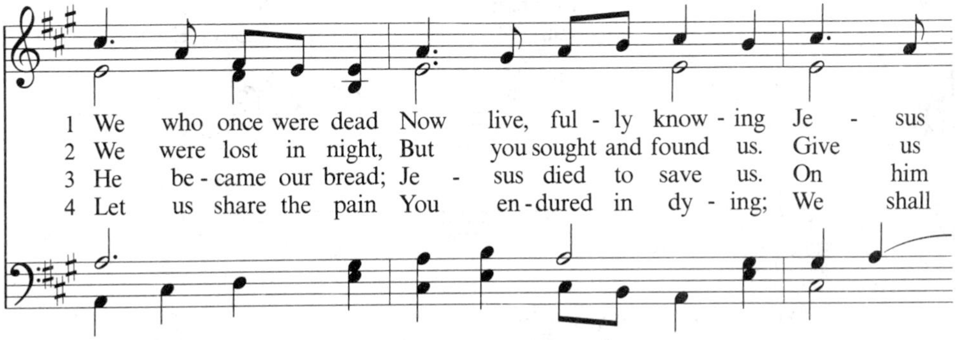

1 We who once were dead Now live, ful - ly know - ing Je - sus
2 We were lost in night, But you sought and found us. Give us
3 He be - came our bread; Je - sus died to save us. On him
4 Let us share the pain You en - dured in dy - ing; We shall

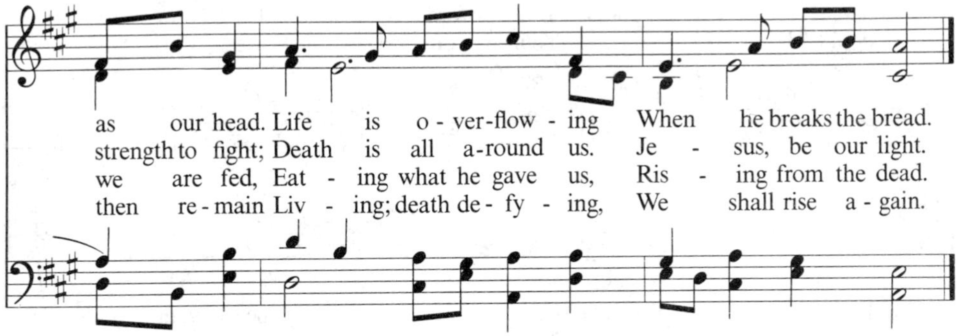

as our head. Life is o - ver-flow - ing When he breaks the bread.
strength to fight; Death is all a-round us. Je - sus, be our light.
we are fed, Eat - ing what he gave us, Ris - ing from the dead.
then re - main Liv - ing; death de - fy - ing, We shall rise a - gain.

5 Jesus, you were dead,
But you rose and, living,
Made yourself our bread,
In your goodness giving
Life though we were dead.

6 This is your design;
In this meal we meet you.
Be our bread and wine,
Jesus, we entreat you.
This shall be our sign.

© Text: Muus Jacobse, b. 1909; tr. composite
© Tune: Rik Veelenturf, b. 1936

MIDDEN IN DE DOOD
565 65

208 Lord Jesus Christ, You Have Prepared

1 Lord Je - sus Christ, you have pre - pared This feast for my sal -
2 Though in - to heav - en you have gone, As - cend - ing far a -
3 I eat this bread, I drink this cup, Your prom - ise firm be -
4 Un - aid - ed rea - son can - not see What ea - ger faith em -

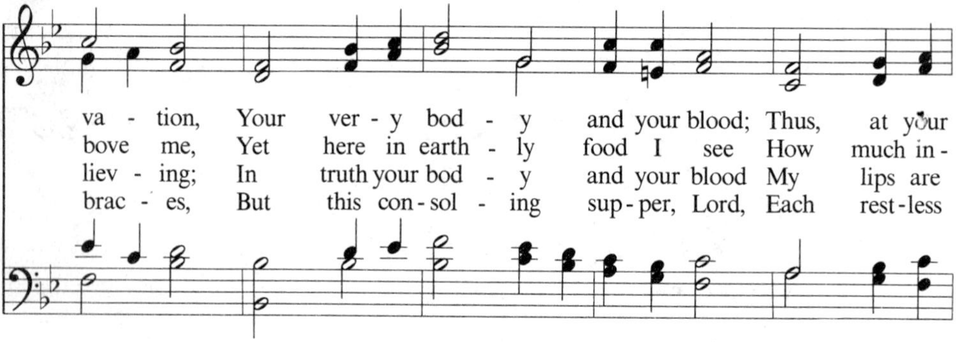

va - tion, Your ver - y bod - y and your blood; Thus, at your
bove me, Yet here in earth - ly food I see How much in -
liev - ing; In truth your bod - y and your blood My lips are
brac - es, But this con - sol - ing sup - per, Lord, Each rest - less

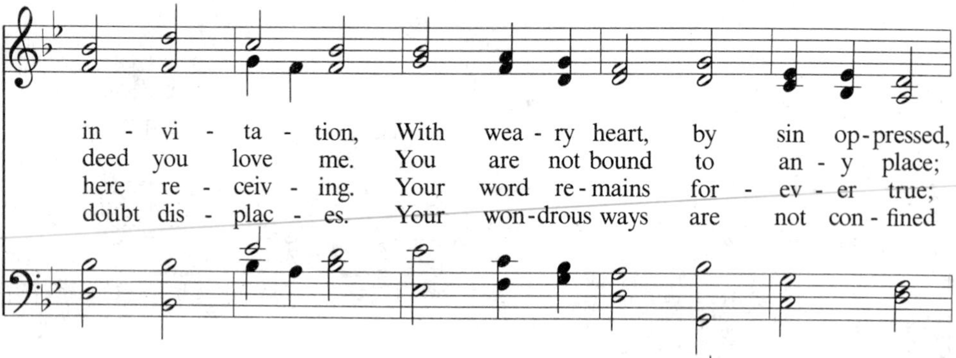

in - vi - ta - tion, With wea - ry heart, by sin op - pressed,
deed you love me. You are not bound to an - y place;
here re - ceiv - ing. Your word re - mains for - ev - er true;
doubt dis - plac - es. Your won - drous ways are not con - fined

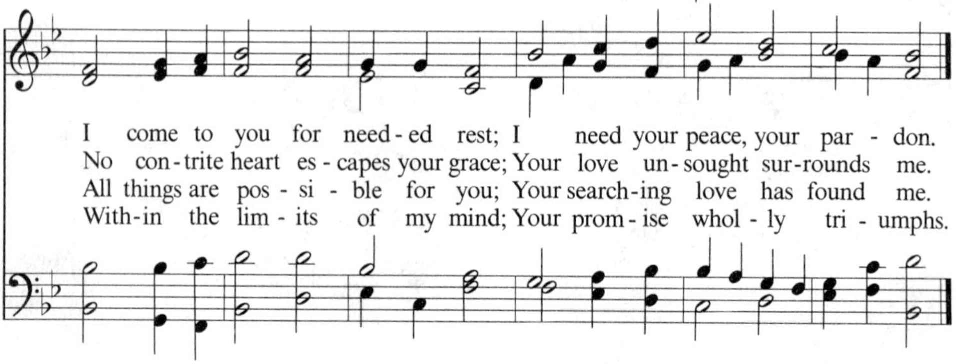

I come to you for need - ed rest; I need your peace, your par - don.
No con - trite heart es - capes your grace; Your love un - sought sur - rounds me.
All things are pos - si - ble for you; Your search - ing love has found me.
With - in the lim - its of my mind; Your prom - ise whol - ly tri - umphs.

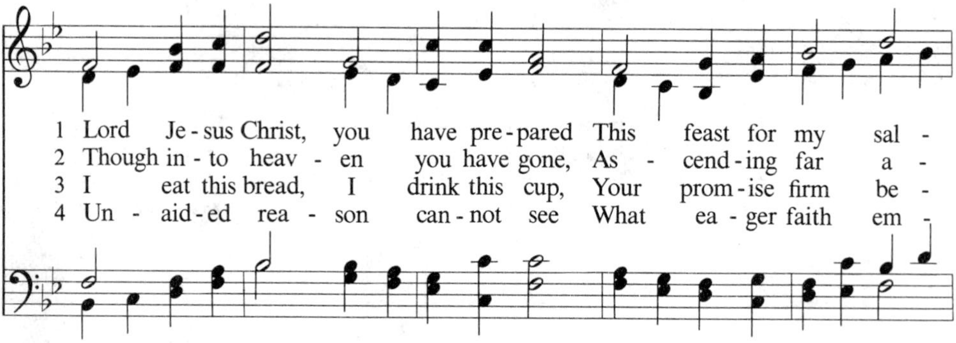

5 I should have died eternally,
But here, repentant kneeling,
Newborn I rise to live the love
Found in your strength, your healing.
Lord, in this sacrament impart
Your joy and courage to my heart;
Dead and alive I praise you!

 Text: Samuel Kinner, 1603–1668; tr. hymnal version, 1978
Tune: Peter Sohren, c. 1630–1692

DU LEBENSBROT, HERR JESU CHRIST
87 87 887

Come, Risen Lord 209

1 Come, ris - en Lord, and deign to be our guest; Nay, let us
2 We meet, as in that Up - per Room they met. Thou at the
3 One bod - y we, one bod - y who par - take, One Church u -
4 One with each oth - er, Lord, for one in thee, Who art one
be thy guests; the feast is thine. Thy - self at thine own board make
ta - ble, bless - ing, yet dost stand. "This is my bod - y"; so thou
nit - ed in com - mu - nion blest, One name we bear, one bread of
Sav - ior and one liv - ing head. Then o - pen thou our eyes, that
man - i - fest In thine own sac - ra - ment of bread and wine.
giv - est yet; Faith still re - ceives the cup as from thy hand.
life we break, With all thy saints on earth and saints at rest.
we may see; Be known to us in break - ing of the bread.

 Text: George W. Briggs, 1875–1959
 Tune: Frank K. Owen, b. 1902

KNICKERBOCKER
10 10 10 10

210 At the Lamb's High Feast We Sing

1 At the Lamb's high feast we sing Praise to
2 Praise we him, whose love di - vine Gives his
3 Where the pas - chal blood is poured Death's dread
4 Praise we Christ, whose blood was shed, Pas - chal

our vic - to - rious king, Who has washed us
sa - cred blood for wine, Gives his bod - y
an - gel sheathes the sword; Is - rael's hosts tri-
vic - tim, pas - chal bread; With sin - cer - i-

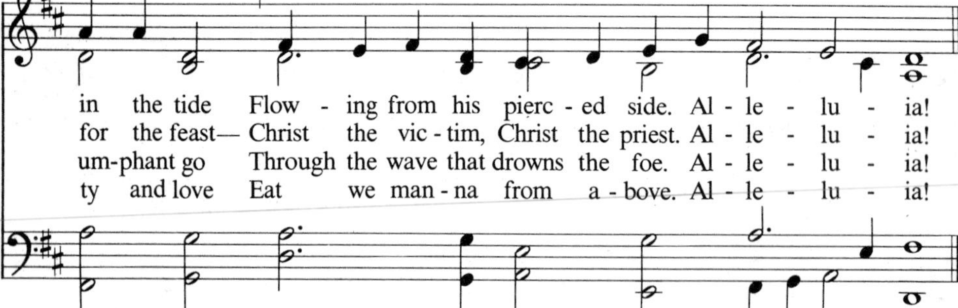
in the tide Flow - ing from his pierc - ed side. Al - le - lu - ia!
for the feast— Christ the vic - tim, Christ the priest. Al - le - lu - ia!
um-phant go Through the wave that drowns the foe. Al - le - lu - ia!
ty and love Eat we man - na from a - bove. Al - le - lu - ia!

5 Mighty Victim from the sky,
Hell's fierce pow'rs beneath you lie;
You have conquered in the fight,
You have brought us life and light.
Alleluia!

6 Now no more can death appall,
Now no more the grave enthrall;
You have opened paradise,
And your saints in you shall rise.
Alleluia!

7 Easter triumph, Easter joy!
This alone can sin destroy;
From sin's pow'r, Lord, set us free,
Newborn souls in you to be.
Alleluia!

8 Father, who the crown shall give,
Savior, by whose death we live,
Spirit, guide through all our days:
Three in One, your name we praise.
Alleluia!

Text: office hymn, 17th cent; tr. Robert Campbell, 1814–1868, alt.
Tune: Bohemian Brethren, Kirchengeseng, *1566*

SONNE DER GERECHTIGKEIT
77 77 4

Here, O My Lord, I See Thee 211

1 Here, O my Lord, I see thee face to face; Here would I
2 Here would I feed up - on the bread of God, Here drink with
3 This is the hour of ban - quet and of song; This is the
4 I have no help but thine; nor do I need An - oth - er
touch and han - dle things un - seen; Here grasp with firm - er hand the e-
thee the roy - al wine of heav'n; Here would I lay a - side each
heav'n-ly ta - ble spread for me; Here let me feast and, feast - ing,
arm save thine to lean up - on; It is e - nough, O Lord, e -
ter - nal grace, And all my wea - ri - ness up - on thee lean.
earth - ly load, Here taste a - fresh the calm of sin for - giv'n.
still pro - long The brief bright hour of fel - low - ship with thee.
nough in - deed; My strength is in thy might, thy might a - lone.

5 Mine is the sin, but thine the righteousness;
Mine is the guilt, but thine the cleansing blood;
Here is my robe, my refuge, and my peace:
Thy blood, thy righteousness, O Lord, my God.

6 Too soon we rise; the vessels disappear;
The feast, though not the love, is past and gone.
The bread and wine remove, but thou art here,
Nearer than ever, still my shield and sun.

7 Feast after feast thus comes and passes by;
Yet, passing, points to the glad feast above,
Giving sweet foretaste of the festal joy,
The Lamb's great marriage feast of bliss and love.

Text: Horatius Bonar, 1808–1889
Tune: attr. Henry Lawes, 1596–1662

FARLEY CASTLE
10 10 10 10

212 Let Us Break Bread Together

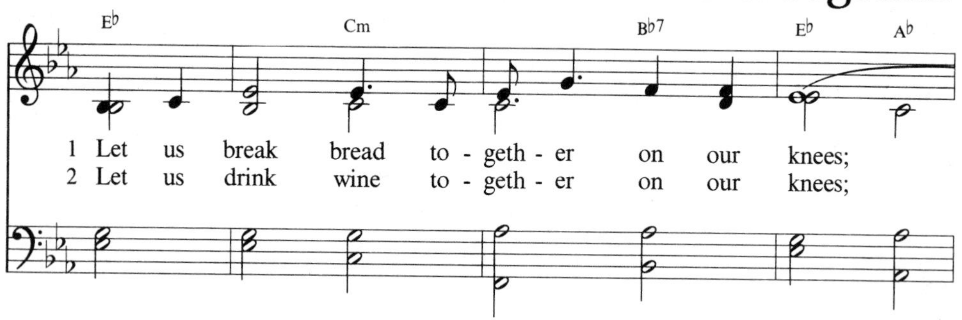
E♭
Cm
B♭7
E♭
A♭
1 Let us break bread to - geth - er on our knees;
2 Let us drink wine to - geth - er on our knees;

E♭
Cm
F7
B♭
Let us break bread to-geth - er on our knees.
Let us drink wine to-geth - er on our knees.

Refrain
E♭
B♭m6
C7
Fm
When I fall on my knees, With my face to the ris - ing

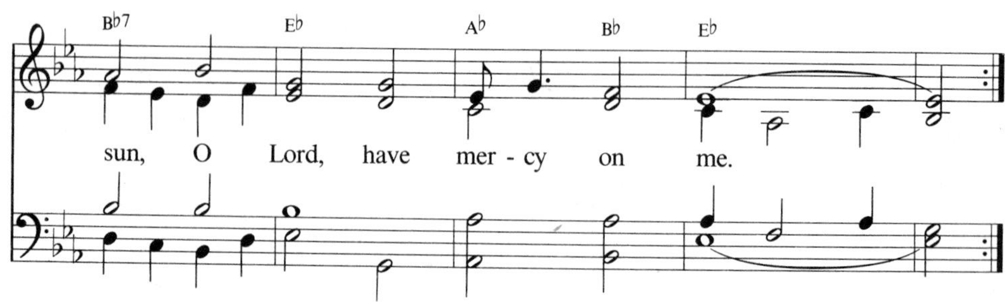
B♭7
E♭
A♭
B♭
E♭
sun, O Lord, have mer - cy on me.

B♭7
E♭
A♭
B♭7
E♭
A♭
3 Let us praise God to - geth - er on our knees;

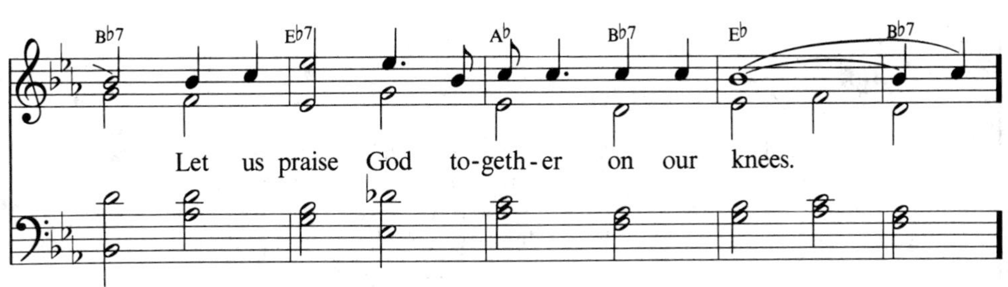
B♭7
E♭7
A♭
B♭7
E♭
B♭7
Let us praise God to-geth-er on our knees.

Refrain
E♭
B♭m6
C7
Fm
When I fall on my knees, With my face to the ris - ing

B♭7
E♭
A♭
B♭
E♭
sun, O Lord, have mer - cy on me.

Text: Negro spiritual
Tune: Negro spiritual

BREAK BREAD TOGETHER
10 10 with refrain

213 I Come, O Savior, to Your Table

1 I come, O Sav - ior, to your ta - ble, For weak and wea - ry
2 Your bod - y, giv'n for me, O Sav - ior; Your blood, which once for
3 With you, Lord, I am now u - nit - ed; You live in me and
4 My heart has now be - come your dwell-ing, O bless - ed, ho - ly
is my soul; You, Bread of life, a - lone are a - ble
me was shed: These are my life and strength for - ev - er,
I in you. No sor - row fills my soul; de - light - ed
Trin - i - ty. With an - gels I, your prais - es tell - ing,
To sat - is - fy and make me whole.
By them my hun - gry soul is fed.
It finds its deep - est joy in you.
Shall live in joy e - ter - nal - ly.
Refrain
Lord, may your
bod - y and your blood Be for my soul the high - est good!

© *Text: Friedrich C. Heyder, 1677–1754; tr.* The Lutheran Hymnal, *1941, alt.*
Tune: Ms., Municipal Library, Leipzig, 1756

ICH STERBE TÄGLICH
98 98 88

Come, Let Us Eat

214

F Gm7 F Dm B♭
1 Come, let us eat, for now the feast is spread,
2 Come, let us drink, for now the wine is poured,
3 In . . . . his pres-ence now we meet and rest,
4 Rise, then, to spread a-broad God's might-y Word,
F B♭maj7 C9 B♭ F Gm7
Come, let us eat, for now the feast is spread.
Come, let us drink, for now the wine is poured.
In . . . . his pres-ence now we meet and rest.
Rise, then, to spread a-broad God's might-y Word.
F B♭ Gm Dm Gm7 B♭
Our Lord's bod - y let us take to - geth - er,
Je - sus' blood poured let us drink to - geth - er,
In the pres - ence of our Lord we gath - er,
Je - sus ris - en will bring in the King - dom,
F B♭ B♭ F
Our Lord's bod - y let us take to - geth - er.
Je - sus' blood poured let us drink to - geth - er.
In the pres - ence of our Lord we gath - er.
Je - sus ris - en will bring in the King - dom.

A VA DE
10 10 10 10

215 O Lord, We Praise You

1 O Lord, we praise you, bless you, and a - dore you, In thanks -
2 Your ho - ly bod - y in - to death was giv - en, Life to
3 May God be - stow on us his grace and fa - vor To please
giv - ing bow be - fore you. Here with your
win for us in heav - en. No great - er
him with our be - hav - ior And live to -
bod - y and your blood you nour - ish Our weak souls that
love than this to you could bind us; May this feast of
geth - er here in love and u - nion, Nor re - pent this
they may flour - ish. O Lord, have mer - cy!
that re - mind us! O Lord, have mer - cy!
blest com - mu - nion. O Lord, have mer - cy!

May your bod - y, Lord, born of Mar - y, That our
Lord, your kind - ness so much did move you That your
Let not your good Spir - it for - sake us, But that
sins and sor - rows did car - ry, And your blood for us plead
blood now moves us to love you. All our debt you have paid;
heav'n-ly - mind - ed he make us; Give your Church, Lord, to see
In all tri - al, fear, and need: O Lord, have mer - cy!
Peace with God once more is made. O Lord, have mer - cy!
Days of peace and u - ni - ty. O Lord, have mer - cy!

 Text: German folk hymn, 15th cent., st. 1; Martin Luther, 1483–1546, sts. 2–3; tr. The Lutheran Hymnal, *1941, alt.*
Tune: J. Walther, Geistliche Gesangbüchlein, *1524*

GOTT SEI GELOBET UND GEBENEDEIET
PM

216 For Perfect Love So Freely Spent

1 For per - fect love so free - ly spent, For fel - low - ship re - stored, We
2 We come, by sin dis - qui - et - ed, And find our lives made whole; A -
3 A - bide with us; in all our ways Your sav - ing love be shown; So
cel - e - brate your sac - ra - ment And sing your praise, O Lord.
round this ta - ble we are fed Re - fresh - ment for the soul.
may our lives be hymns of praise, O Christ, to you a - lone.

© Text: Louise M. McDowell, b. 1923
© Tune: Vincent Persichetti, b. 1915

VENERABLE
CM

217 We Place upon Your Table, Lord

1 We place up - on your ta - ble, Lord, The food of
2 With - in these sim - ple things there lie The height and
3 Ac - cept them, Lord; they come from you; We take them
life, the bread and wine, As sym - bols of our dai - ly
depth of hu - man life: Our pain and tears, our thoughts and
hum - bly from your hand. These gifts of yours for high - er

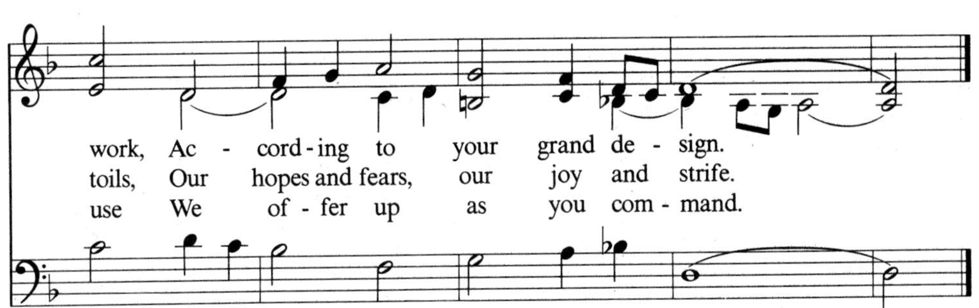
work, Ac - cord - ing to your grand de - sign.
toils, Our hopes and fears, our joy and strife.
use We of - fer up as you com - mand.

Text: M. F. C. Wilson, 1884–1944, alt.
Tune: W. Walker, Southern Harmony, *1835*

DISTRESS
LM

Strengthen for Service, Lord 218

1 Strength-en for ser - vice, Lord, the hands That ho - ly things have
2 The tongues that sang your ho - ly name Now purge of all de -
3 And may the feet that walked your courts Be nev - er lured to

tak - en; And let the ears that heard your
cep - tion; Keep bright the eyes that saw your
wan - der; But lead the faith - ful nour - ished

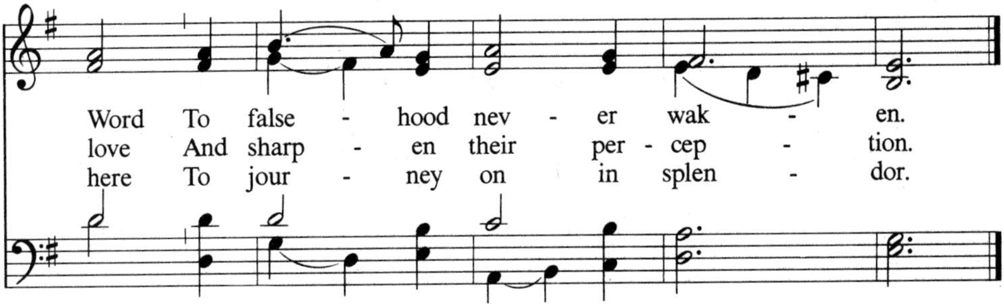

Word To false - hood nev - er wak - en.
love And sharp - en their per - cep - tion.
here To jour - ney on in splen - dor.

© *Text: Syriac Liturgy of Malabar; tr.* The English Hymnal, *1906, adapt.*
© *Tune: Hans-Friedrich Micheelson, 1902–1974*

WIR DIENEN, HERR
87 87

219 Come with Us, O Blessed Jesus

Come with us, O bless - ed Je - sus, With us ev - er - more to be.
And, in leav - ing now thine al - tar, Let us nev - er - more leave thee!
Let thy bright ce - les - tial cho-rus Nev - er cease the heav'n - ly strain;
But in us, thy lov-ing chil-dren, Come, bring peace, good will to men.

Text: John H. Hopkins Jr., 1820–1891
Tune: Johann Schop, 1600–1665

JESU, JOY OF MAN'S DESIRING
87 87 D

O Jesus, Blessed Lord

220

1 O Je - sus, bless - ed Lord, to you
2 Break forth, my soul, in joy and say:

My heart - felt thanks and praise are due;
What wealth has come to me to - day!

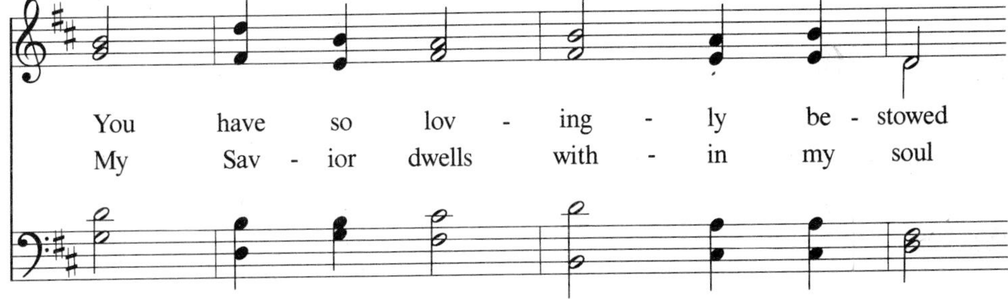
You have so lov - ing - ly be - stowed
My Sav - ior dwells with - in my soul

On me your bod - y and your blood.
And makes my wound - ed spir - it whole!

Text: Thomas H. Kingo, 1634–1703; tr. Arthur J. Mason, 1851–1928, alt.
Tune: A. Davisson, Kentucky Harmony, *1816*

TENDER THOUGHT
LM

221 Sent Forth by God's Blessing

1 Sent forth by God's bless - ing, Our true faith con - fess - ing, The
2 With praise and thanks - giv - ing To God ev - er - liv - ing, The
peo - ple of God from his dwell - ing take leave.
tasks of our ev - 'ry - day life we will face.
The sup - per is end - ed. Oh, now be ex - tend - ed The
Our faith ev - er shar - ing, In love ev - er car - ing, Em -
fruits of this ser - vice in all who be - lieve. The
brac - ing his chil - dren of each tribe and race. With

seed of his teach - ing, Re - cep - tive souls reach - ing, Shall
your feast you feed us, With your light now lead us; U -
blos - som in ac - tion for God and for all. His
nite us as one in this life that we share. Then
grace did in - vite us, His love shall u - nite us To
may all the liv - ing With praise and thanks-giv - ing Give
work for God's king - dom and an - swer his call.
hon - or to Christ and his name that we bear.

© *Text: Omer Westendorf, b. 1916, alt.*
Tune: Welsh folk tune

THE ASH GROVE
66 11 66 11 D

222 O Bread of Life from Heaven

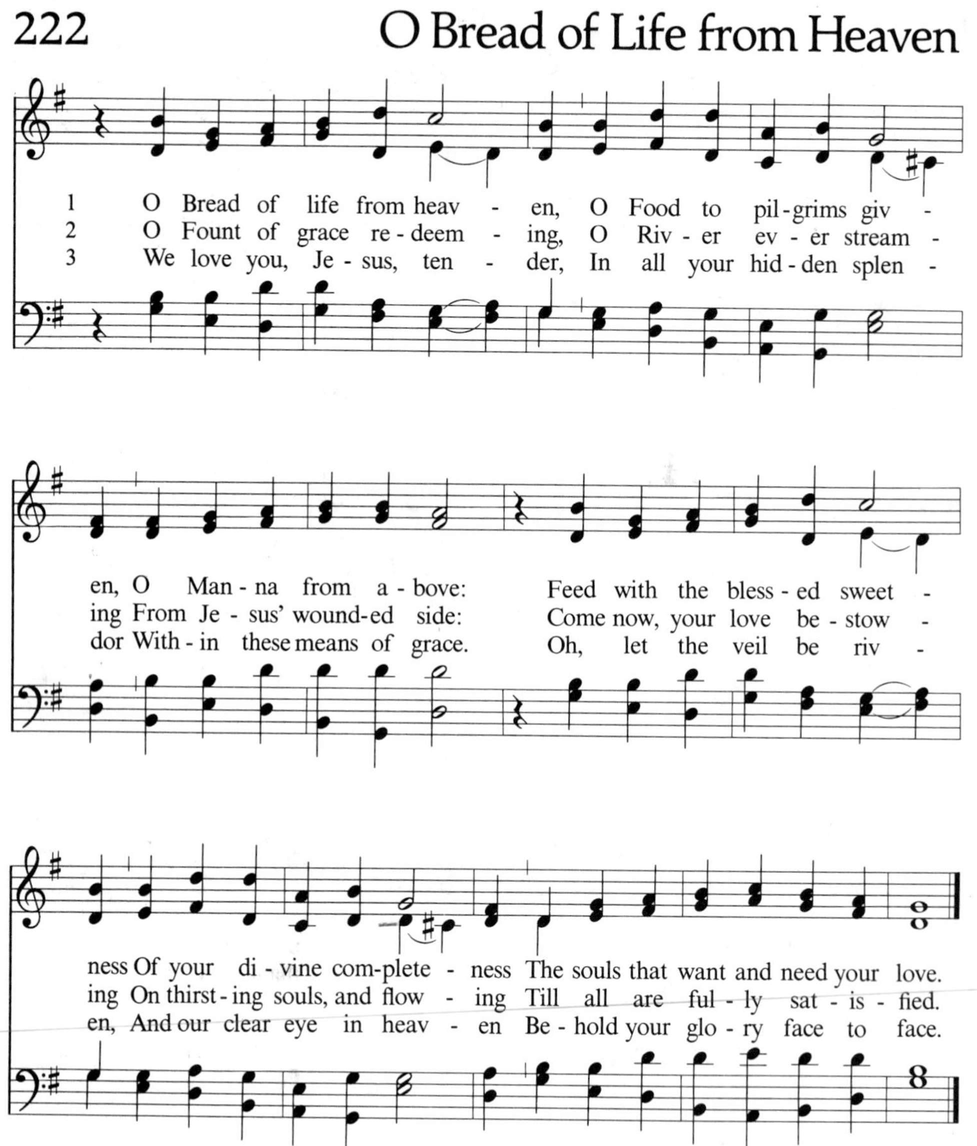
1 O Bread of life from heav - en, O Food to pil-grims giv -
2 O Fount of grace re-deem - ing, O Riv - er ev - er stream -
3 We love you, Je - sus, ten - der, In all your hid-den splen -
en, O Man - na from a - bove: Feed with the bless - ed sweet -
ing From Je - sus' wound-ed side: Come now, your love be - stow -
dor With - in these means of grace. Oh, let the veil be riv -
ness Of your di - vine com-plete - ness The souls that want and need your love.
ing On thirst - ing souls, and flow - ing Till all are ful - ly sat - is - fied.
en, And our clear eye in heav - en Be - hold your glo - ry face to face.

 Text: Latin hymn, c. 1661; tr. composite, alt.
Tune: Heinrich Isaac, c. 1450–1517

O WELT, ICH MUSS DICH LASSEN
776 778

In the Quiet Consecration

223

1 In the qui - et con - se - cra - tion Of this
2 Christ, our liv - ing bread from heav - en, Lord, whose
3 By your death for sin a - ton - ing, By your
4 While a - far in sol - emn ra - diance Shines the
glad com - mu - nion hour, Here we rest in you, Lord
blood is drink in - deed: Here by faith and with thanks-
res - ur - rec - tion life, Hold us fast in bless - ed
feast that is to come Af - ter con - flict, toil, and
Je - sus, Taste your love, and touch your pow'r.
giv - ing In this feast on you we feed.
u - nion; Gird us, nerve us for the strife;
test - ing— Your great feast of love and home.

KINGDOM
87 87

224 Soul, Adorn Yourself with Gladness

1 Soul, a - dorn your - self with glad-ness, Leave the gloom-y haunts of sad - ness,
2 Has-ten as a bride to meet him, Ea - ger - ly and glad - ly greet him.
3 Now in faith I hum-bly pon - der O - ver this sur - pass-ing won - der
4 Je - sus, source of last - ing plea-sure, Tru - est friend, and dear - est trea - sure,

Come in - to the day-light's splen - dor, There with joy your prais-es ren - der.
There he stands al - read - y knock - ing; Quick - ly, now, your gate un - lock - ing,
That the bread of life is bound-less Though the souls it feeds are count-less;
Peace be-yond all un - der - stand - ing, Joy in - to all life ex - pand - ing:

Bless the one whose grace un - bound-ed This a - maz-ing ban-quet found-ed;
O - pen wide the fast-closed por - tal, Say - ing to the Lord im - mor - tal:
With the choic-est wine of heav - en Christ's own blood to us is giv - en.
Hum-bly now, I bow be - fore you, Love in - car-nate, I a - dore you;

He, though heav'n-ly, high, and ho - ly, Deigns to dwell with you most low - ly.
"Come, and leave your loved one nev - er; Dwell with-in my heart for - ev - er."
Oh, most glo - rious con - so - la - tion, Pledge and seal of my sal - va - tion.
Wor - thi - ly let me re - ceive you, And, so fa-vored, nev - er leave you.

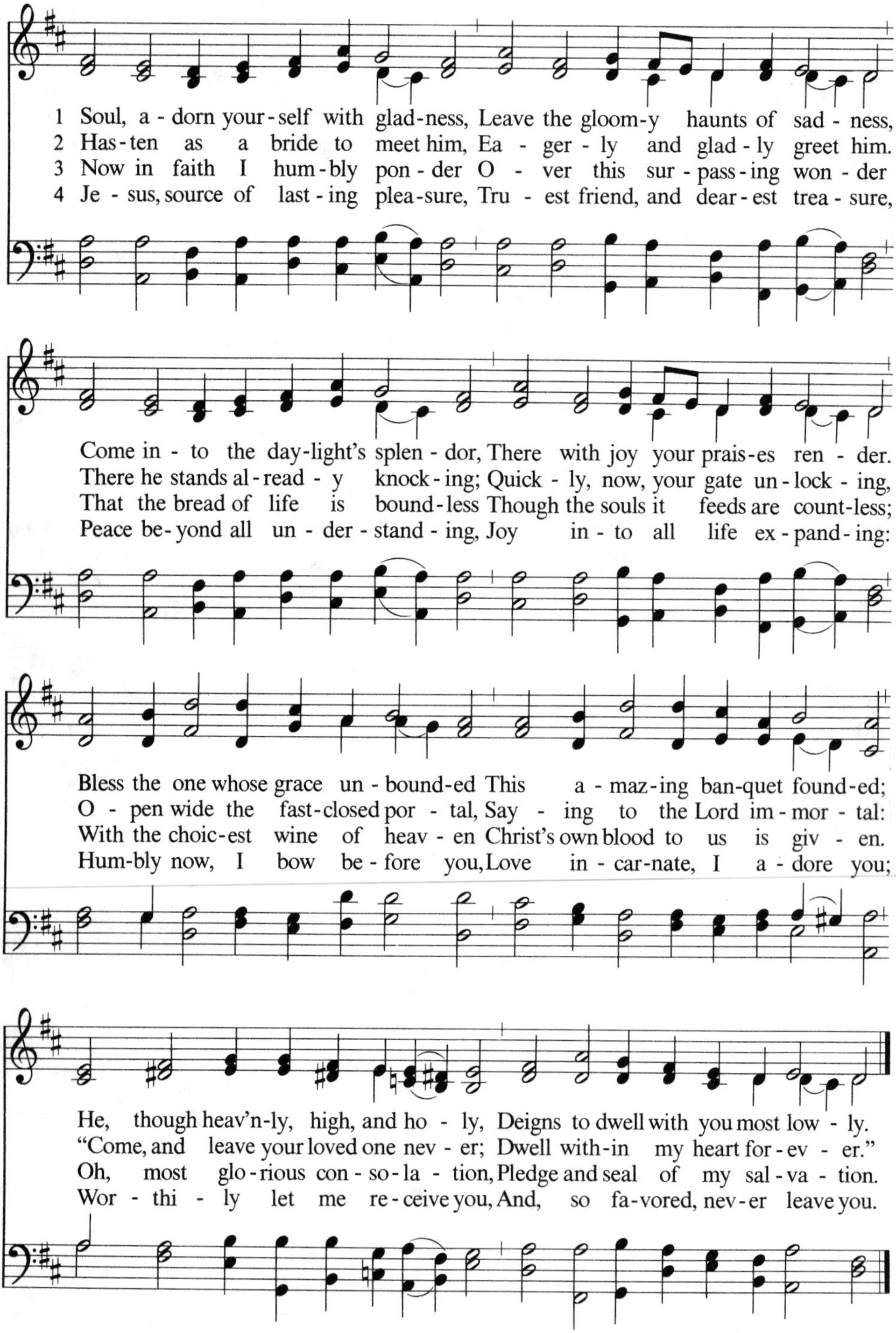

 Text: Johann Franck, 1618–1677; tr. hymnal version, 1978
Tune: Johann Crüger, 1598–1662

SCHMÜCKE DICH
LMD

Lord Jesus Christ, We Humbly Pray

225

1 Lord Je - sus Christ, we hum - bly pray That we may
2 The chas - tened peace of sin for - giv'n, The fil - ial
3 Our trem - bling hearts cleave to thy Word. All thou hast
4 One bread, one cup, one bod - y, we, U - nit - ed
feast on thee to - day; Be - neath these forms of bread and
joy of heirs of heav'n, Grant as we share this won - drous
said thou dost af - ford; All that thou art we here re -
by our life in thee, Thy love pro - claim till thou shalt
wine En - rich us with thy grace di - vine.
food, Thy bod - y bro - ken and thy blood.
ceive, And all we are to thee we give.
come To bring thy scat - tered loved ones home.

5 Lord Jesus Christ, we humbly pray:
Oh, keep us steadfast to that day,
That each may be thy welcomed guest
When thou shalt spread thy heav'nly feast.

Text: Henry E. Jacobs, 1844–1932
Tune: Ignaz J. Pleyel, 1757–1831

GRACE CHURCH
LM

226 Draw Near and Take the Body of the Lord

1 Draw near and take the bod - y of the Lord
2 Saved by that bod - y, hal - lowed by that blood,
3 Sal - va - tion's giv - er, Christ, the on - ly Son,
4 Of - fered was he for great - est and for least,
And drink the ho - ly blood for you out - poured.
Where - by re - freshed, we ren - der thanks to God.
By his dear cross and blood the vic - t'ry won.
Him - self the vic - tim and him - self the priest.

5 Come forward then with faithful hearts sincere,
And take the pledges of salvation here.

6 He who his saints in this world rules and shields,
To all believers life eternal yields,

7 With heav'nly bread makes those who hunger whole,
Gives living waters to the thirsty soul.

8 The judge eternal, unto whom shall bow
All nations at the last, is with us now.

Text: Latin hymn, 7th cent.; tr. John M. Neale, 1818–1866, alt.
Tune: Arthur S. Sullivan, 1842–1900

COENA DOMINI
10 10

How Blest Are They Who Hear God's Word

227

1 How blest are they who hear God's Word, Who keep in faith what
2 Through sor - row's night my sun shall be God's Word, a trea - sure
3 To - day his voice with joy I heard And fed up - on his
they have heard, Who dai - ly grow in wis - dom. From light to
dear to me, My shield and buck - ler ev - er. My ti - tle
ho - ly Word, That bread so free - ly giv - en. May grace a
light they shall in - crease And jour - ney on life's way in peace;
as his child and heir The Fa - ther's hand has writ - ten there,
strong-er faith main - tain So that its fruit shall all re - main
They have the oil of glad - ness To soothe their pain and sad - ness.
His prom - ise fail - ing nev - er: "You will be mine for - ev - er."
When my ac - count is giv - en Be - fore God's throne in heav - en.

 Text: Johan Nordahl Brun, 1745–1816; tr. Service Book and Hymnal, *1958, alt.*
Tune: H. Thomissön, Den Danske Salmebog, *1569*

OM HIMMERIGES RIGE
887 8877

228 A Mighty Fortress Is Our God

1 A might - y for - tress is our God,
2 No strength of ours can match his might!
3 Though hordes of dev - ils fill the land
4 God's Word for - ev - er shall a - bide,
A sword and shield vic - to - rious;
We would be lost, re - ject - ed.
All threat - 'ning to de - vour us,
No thanks to foes, who fear it;
He breaks the cruel op - pres - sor's rod
But now a cham - pion comes to fight,
We trem - ble not, un - moved we stand;
For God him - self fights by our side
And wins sal - va - tion glo - rious.
Whom God him - self e - lect - ed.
They can - not o - ver - pow'r us.
With weap - ons of the Spir - it.

The old e - vil foe, Sworn to
Ask who this may be: Lord of
This world's prince may rage, In fierce
If they take our house, Goods, fame,
work us woe, With dread craft and might
hosts is he! Je - sus Christ, our Lord,
war en - gage. He is doomed to fail;
child, or spouse, Wrench our life a - way,
He arms him - self to fight. On earth
God's on - ly Son, a - dored. He holds
God's judg - ment must pre - vail! One lit -
They can - not win the day. The King -
he has no e - qual.
the field vic - to - rious.
tle word sub - dues him.
dom's ours for - ev - er!

© *Text: Martin Luther, 1483–1546; tr. hymnal version, 1978*
Tune: Martin Luther, 1483–1546

EIN FESTE BURG
87 87 55 56 7

229 A Mighty Fortress Is Our God

1 A might - y for - tress is our God, A sword and shield vic -
2 No strength of ours can match his might! We would be lost, re -
3 Though hordes of dev - ils fill the land All threat-'ning to de -
4 God's Word for - ev - er shall a - bide, No thanks to foes, who
to - rious; He breaks the cruel op - pres - sor's rod And
ject - ed. But now a cham - pion comes to fight, Whom
vour us, We trem - ble not, un - moved we stand; They
fear it; For God him - self fights by our side With
wins sal - va - tion glo - rious. The old sa - tan - ic foe
God him - self e - lect - ed. You ask who this may be?
can - not o - ver - pow'r us. Let this world's ty - rant rage;
weap-ons of the Spir - it. Were they to take our house,
Has sworn to work us woe! With craft and dread - ful might
The Lord of hosts is he! Christ Je - sus, might - y Lord,
In bat - tle we'll en - gage! His might is doomed to fail;
Goods, hon - or, child, or spouse, Though life be wrenched a - way,

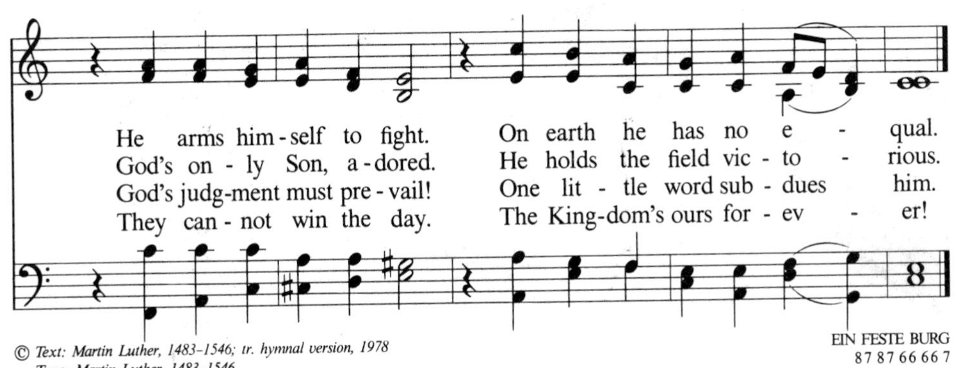
He arms him-self to fight. On earth he has no e - qual.
God's on - ly Son, a-dored. He holds the field vic - to - rious.
God's judg-ment must pre - vail! One lit - tle word sub - dues him.
They can - not win the day. The King-dom's ours for - ev - er!
8

 Text: Martin Luther, 1483–1546; tr. hymnal version, 1978
Tune: Martin Luther, 1483–1546

EIN FESTE BURG
8 7 8 7 66 66 7

Lord, Keep Us Steadfast in Your Word 230

1 Lord, keep us steadfast in your Word;
Curb those who by deceit or sword
Would wrest the kingdom from your Son
And bring to nought all he has done.

2 Lord Jesus Christ, your pow'r make known,
For you are Lord of lords alone;
Defend your holy Church, that we
May sing your praise triumphantly.

3 O Comforter of priceless worth,
Send peace and unity on earth;
Support us in our final strife
And lead us out of death to life.

Text: Martin Luther, 1483–1546; tr. Catherine Winkworth, 1829–1878, alt.
Tune: J. Klug, Geistliche Lieder, *1543*

ERHALT UNS, HERR
L M

231 O Word of God Incarnate

1 O Word of God in - car - nate, O Wis - dom from on high,
2 The Church from you, dear Mas - ter, Re - ceived the gift di - vine;
3 Oh, make your Church, dear Sav - ior, A lamp of bur-nished gold
O Truth un-changed, un - chang - ing, O Light of our dark sky:
And still that light is lift - ed O'er all the earth to shine.
To bear be - fore the na - tions Your true light, as of old;
We praise you for the ra - diance That from the hal - lowed page,
It is the chart and com - pass That, all life's voy - age through,
Oh, teach your wan-d'ring pil - grims By this their path to trace,
A lan - tern to our foot - steps, Shines on from age to age.
Mid mists and rocks and quick - sands Still guides, O Christ, to you.
Till, clouds and dark - ness end - ed, They see you face to face.

Text: *William W. How, 1823–1897, alt.*
Tune: Neu-vermehrtes Gesangbuch, *Meiningen, 1693*

MUNICH
76 76 D

Your Word, O Lord, Is Gentle Dew

232

1 Your Word, O Lord, is gen - tle dew To suf - f'ring hearts that
want it; Oh, shed your heav'n - ly balm a - new, To all your
gar - den grant it; Re - freshed by you, may ev - 'ry tree Bud forth and
blos - som gai - ly And fruit and seed bring dai - ly.

2 Your Word is like a flam - ing sword, A sharp and might - y
ar - row, A wedge that cleaves the rock; that Word Can pierce through
heart and mar - row. Oh, send it forth o'er all the earth, To purge un-
righ - teous leav - en And cleanse all hearts for heav - en.

3 Your Word, a won - drous star, sup - plies True guid - ance when we
need it; It points to Christ and so makes wise All sim - ple
hearts that heed it; Let not its light e'er sink in night, But keep it
bright - ly burn - ing, And fill our deep - est yearn - ing.

Text: *Carl B. Garve, 1763–1841; tr. Catherine Winkworth, 1829–1878, alt.*
Tune: Koralpsalmboken, *Stockholm, 1697*

AF HIMLENS
87 87 877

233 Thy Strong Word

1 Thy strong word did cleave the dark - ness; At thy
2 Lo, on those who dwelt in dark - ness, Dark as
3 Thy strong Word be - speaks us righ - teous; Bright with
4 From the cross thy wis - dom shin - ing Break - eth
speak - ing it was done. For cre - at - ed
night and deep as death, Broke the light of
thine own ho - li - ness, Glo - rious now, we
forth in con - qu'ring might; From the cross for -
light we thank thee, While thine or - dered sea - sons run.
thy sal - va - tion, Breathed thine own life - giv - ing breath.
press toward glo - ry, And our lives our hopes con - fess.
ev - er beam - eth All thy bright re - deem - ing light.
Al - le - lu - ia! Al - le - lu - ia! Praise to
Al - le - lu - ia! Al - le - lu - ia! Praise to
Al - le - lu - ia! Al - le - lu - ia! Praise to
Al - le - lu - ia! Al - le - lu - ia! Praise to

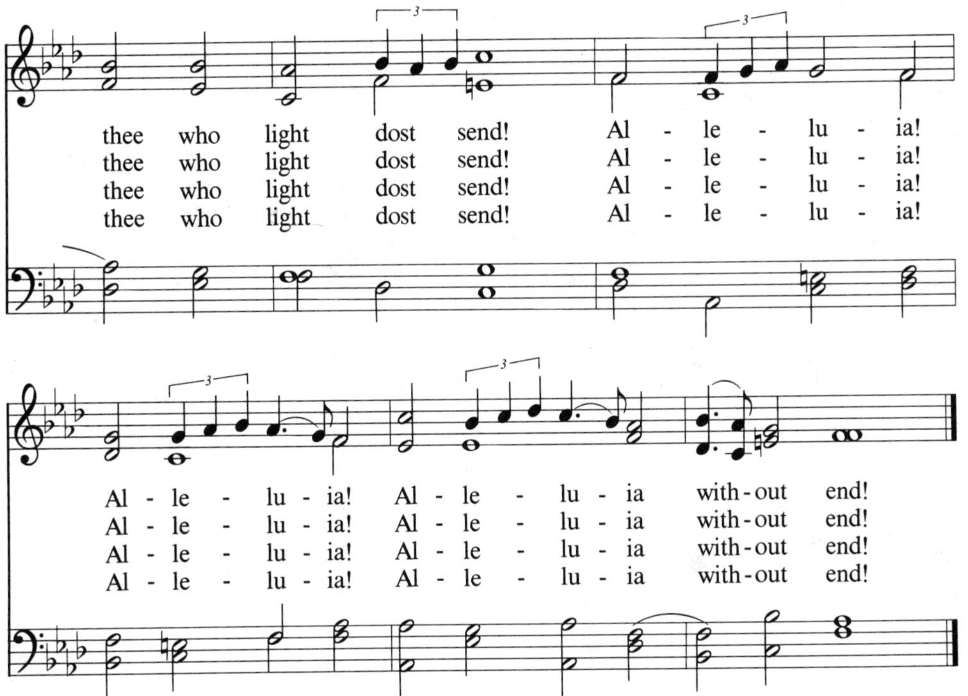
thee who light dost send! Al - le - lu - ia!
thee who light dost send! Al - le - lu - ia!
thee who light dost send! Al - le - lu - ia!
thee who light dost send! Al - le - lu - ia!
Al - le - lu - ia! Al - le - lu - ia with - out end!
Al - le - lu - ia! Al - le - lu - ia with - out end!
Al - le - lu - ia! Al - le - lu - ia with - out end!
Al - le - lu - ia! Al - le - lu - ia with - out end!

5 Give us lips to sing thy glory,
Tongues thy mercy to proclaim,
Throats that shout the hope that fills us,
Mouths to speak thy holy name.
Alleluia! Alleluia!
May the light which thou dost send
Fill our songs with alleluias,
Alleluias without end!

6 God the Father, light-creator,
To thee laud and honor be.
To thee, Light of Light begotten,
Praise be sung eternally.
Holy Spirit, light-revealer,
Glory, glory be to thee.
Mortals, angels, now and ever
Praise the holy Trinity!

EBENEZER
87 87 D

234 Almighty God, Your Word Is Cast

1 Al-might-y God, your Word is cast Like seed in-to the ground;
2 Let not the sly sa-tan-ic foe This ho-ly seed re-move,
3 Let not the world's de-ceit-ful cares The ris-ing plant de-stroy,
4 So when the pre-cious seed is sown, Your quick-'ning grace be-stow,

Now let the dew of heav'n de-scend And righ-teous fruits a-bound.
But give it root in ev-'ry heart To bring forth fruits of love.
But let it yield a hun-dred-fold The fruits of peace and joy.
That all whose souls the truth re-ceive Its sav-ing pow'r may know.

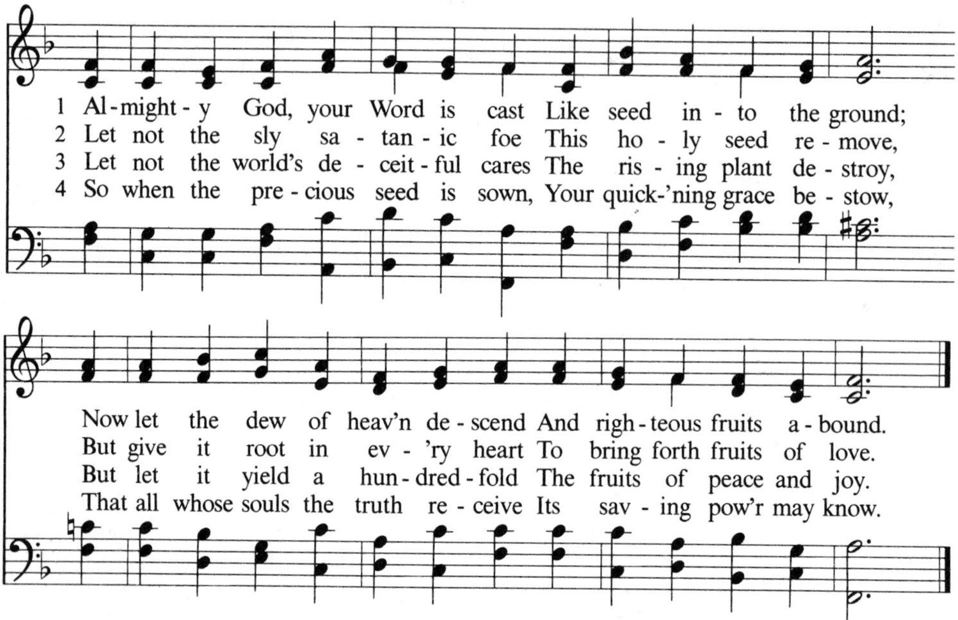

Text: John Cawood, 1775–1852, alt.
Tune: J. Day, Psalter, *1562*

ST. FLAVIAN
86 86

235 Break Now the Bread of Life

1 Break now the bread of life, Dear Lord, to me, As once you
2 Bless your own truth, dear Lord, To me, to me, As when you
3 You are the bread of life, O Lord, to me. Your ho-ly
4 Oh, send your Spir-it, Lord, Now un-to me, That he may
broke the loaves Be-side the sea. Be-yond the sa-cred page
blest the bread By Gal-i-lee. Then shall all bond-age cease,
Word the truth That res-cues me. Give me to eat and live
touch my eyes And make me see. Show me the truth con-cealed

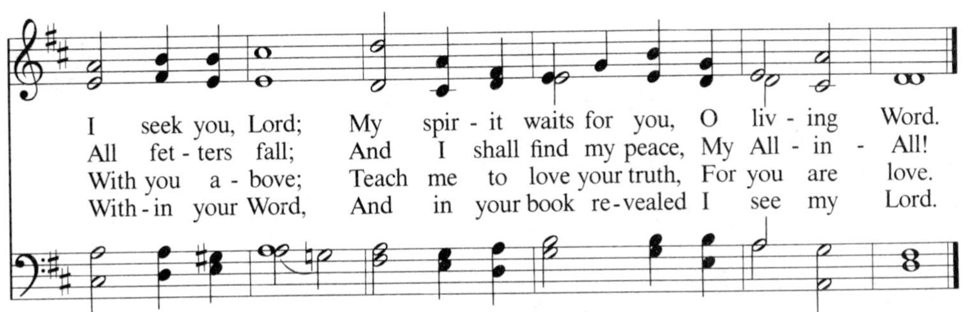
I seek you, Lord; My spir - it waits for you, O liv - ing Word.
All fet - ters fall; And I shall find my peace, My All - in - All!
With you a - bove; Teach me to love your truth, For you are love.
With - in your Word, And in your book re - vealed I see my Lord.

Text: Mary A. Lathbury, 1841–1913, alt.
Tune: William F. Sherwin, 1826–1888

BREAD OF LIFE
64 64 D

When Seed Falls on Good Soil 236

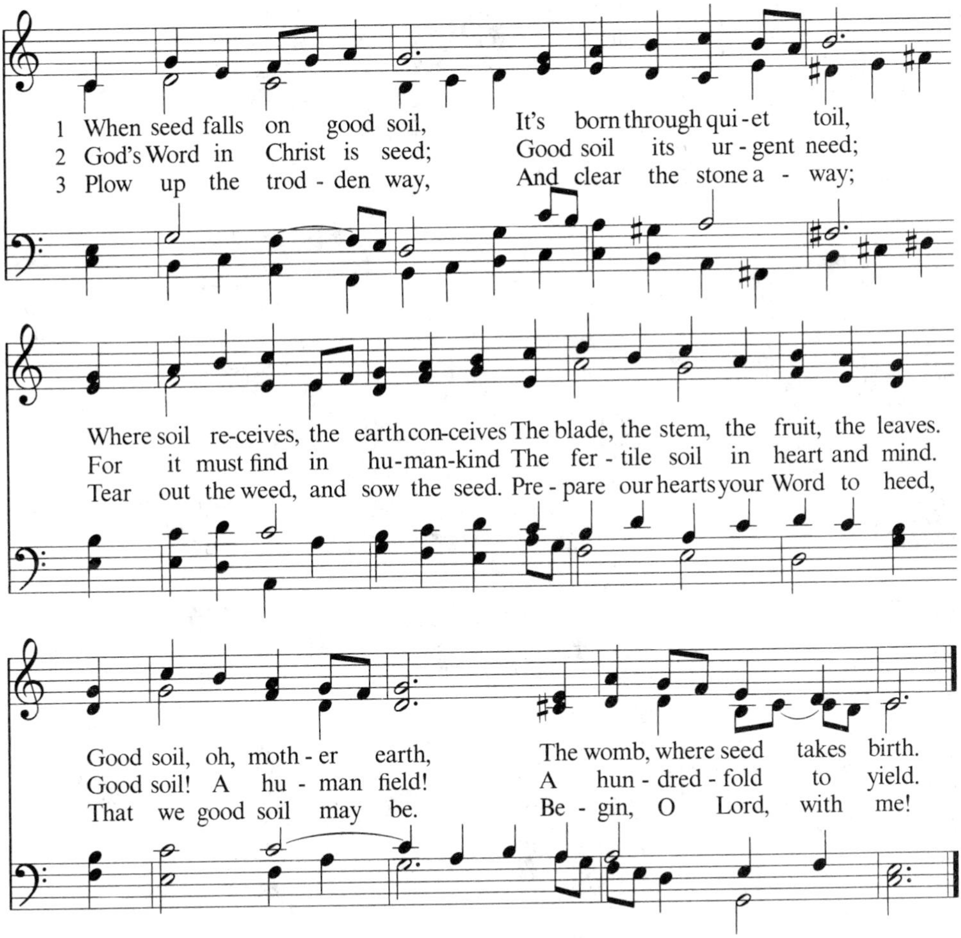

1 When seed falls on good soil, It's born through qui - et toil,
Where soil re - ceives, the earth con - ceives The blade, the stem, the fruit, the leaves.
Good soil, oh, moth - er earth, The womb, where seed takes birth.

2 God's Word in Christ is seed; Good soil its ur - gent need;
For it must find in hu - man - kind The fer - tile soil in heart and mind.
Good soil! A hu - man field! A hun - dred - fold to yield.

3 Plow up the trod - den way, And clear the stone a - way;
Tear out the weed, and sow the seed. Pre - pare our hearts your Word to heed,
That we good soil may be. Be - gin, O Lord, with me!

WALHOF
66 88 66

237 O God of Light

1 O God of light, your Word, a lamp un - fail - ing,
2 From days of old, through blind and will - ful a - ges,
3 Un - dimmed by time, those words are still re - veal - ing
4 To all the world your sum - mons you are send - ing,
Shall pierce the dark - ness of our earth-bound way
Though we re - belled, you gent - ly sought a - gain,
To sin - ful hearts your jus - tice and your grace;
Through all the earth, to ev - 'ry land and race,
And show your grace, your plan for us un - veil - ing,
And spoke through saints, a - pos - tles, proph - ets, sa - ges,
And quest - ing spir - its, long - ing for your heal - ing,
That myr - iad tongues, in one great an - them blend - ing,
And guide our foot - steps to the per - fect day.
Who wrote with ea - ger or re - luc - tant pen.
See your com - pas - sion in the Sav - ior's face.
May praise and cel - e - brate your gift of grace.

© *Text: Sarah E. Taylor, 1883–1954, adapt.*
© *Tune: H. Barrie Cabena, b. 1933*

ATKINSON
11 10 11 10

God Has Spoken by His Prophets 238

1 God has spo - ken by his proph-ets, Spo - ken his un - chang-ing Word;
2 God has spo - ken by Christ Je - sus, Christ, the ev - er - last - ing Son,
3 God is speak-ing by his Spir - it, Speak-ing to the hearts of all,
Each from age to age pro-claim-ing God, the one, the righ-teous Lord.
Bright-ness of the Fa - ther's glo - ry, With the Fa - ther ev - er one;
In the age - less Word ex-pound-ing God's own mes - sage for us all.
In the world's de - spair and tur-moil, One firm an - chor holds us fast:
Spo - ken by the Word In - car-nate, God of God, be - fore time was;
Through the rise and fall of na-tions One sure faith yet stand-ing fast;
God is king, his throne e - ter - nal; God the first, and God the last.
Light of light, to earth de - scend-ing, He re - veals our God to us.
God a-bides, his Word un - chang-ing; God the first, and God the last.

CARN BREA
87 87 D

239 God's Word Is Our Great Heritage

God's Word is our great her - i - tage And shall be ours for - ev - er;
To spread its light from age to age Shall be our chief en - deav - or.
Through life it guides our way; In death it is our stay. Lord, grant while time shall
last Your Church may hold it fast Through-out all gen - er - a - tions.

Text: Nikolai F. S. Grundtvig, 1783–1872; tr. Ole G. Belsheim, 1861–1925, alt.
Tune: Martin Luther, 1483–1546

EIN FESTE BURG
87 87 66 66 7

Father of Mercies, in Your Word

240

Dm
Gm7
Dm
1 Fa - ther of mer - cies, in your Word What
2 Here springs of con - so - la - tion rise To
3 Oh, may these heav'n - ly pag - es be My
4 Di - vine in - struc - tor, gra - cious Lord, May
Dm7
F7
B♭
Dm
Gm7
B♭maj7
C6
end - less glo - ry shines! For - ev - er be your
cheer the faint - ing mind, And thirst - y souls re -
ev - er dear de - light; And still new beau - ties
you be al - ways near; Teach me to love your
Dm
C
F
Gm
Am7
Dm
name a - dored For these ce - les - tial lines.
ceive sup - plies And sweet re - fresh - ment find.
may I see And still in - creas - ing light.
sa - cred Word And find my Sav - ior here.

Text: *Anne Steele, 1716–1778, alt.*
Tune: The Sacred Harp, *Philadelphia, 1844*

DETROIT
CM

241 We Praise You, O God

1 We praise you, O God, our re - deem - er, cre - a - tor;
2 We wor - ship you, God of our fa - thers, we bless you;
3 With voic - es u - nit - ed our prais - es we of - fer

In grate - ful de - vo - tion our trib - ute we bring.
Through tri - al and tem - pest our guide you have been.
And glad - ly our songs of thanks - giv - ing we raise.

We lay it be - fore you; we kneel and a - dore you;
When per - ils o'er - take us, you will not for - sake us,
With you, Lord, be - side us, your strong arm will guide us.

We bless your ho - ly name; glad prais - es we sing.
And with your help, O Lord, our strug - gles we win.
To you, our great re - deem - er, for - ev - er be praise!

Text: Julia C. Cory, 1882–1963, alt.
Tune: A. Valerius, Nederlandtsch Gedenckclanck, *1626*

KREMSER
12 11 12 11

Let the Whole Creation Cry

242

1 Let the whole cre - a - tion cry, "Glo - ry to the Lord on high!"
2 War-riors fight - ing for the Lord, Proph - ets burn - ing with his word,
3 Men and wom - en, young and old, Raise the an - them loud and bold,
Heav'n and earth, a - wake and sing, "Praise him, our al - might - y King!"
Those to whom the arts be - long Add their voic - es to the song.
And let chil-dren's hap - py hearts In this wor - ship take their parts;
Praise him, an - gel hosts a - bove, Ev - er bright and fair in love;
Kings of knowl-edge and of law, To the glo - rious cir - cle draw;
From the north to south - ern pole Let the might - y cho - rus roll:
Sun and moon, lift up your voice; Night and stars, in God re - joice.
All who work and all who wait, Sing, "The Lord is good and great!"
"Ho - ly, Ho - ly, Ho - ly One; Glo - ry be to God a - lone!"

Text: Stopford A. Brooke, 1832–1916, alt.
Tune: Christoph Anton, d. 1658

SALZBURG
77 77 D

243 Lord, with Glowing Heart

F Am7 B♭ Gm7 F B♭maj7 C F Am7 B♭ Gm7
1 Lord, with glow - ing heart I'd praise thee For the bliss thy
2 Praise, my soul, the God that sought thee, Wretch-ed wan - d'rer,
3 Lord, my spir - it's ar - dent feel - ings Vain - ly would my
F C F F Am7 B♭ Gm7 F B♭maj7 C F Am7
love be - stows, For the par - d'ning grace that saves me, And the
far a - stray; Found thee lost, and kind - ly brought thee From the
lips ex - press. Low be - fore thy foot - stool kneel - ing, Deign thy
B♭ Gm7 F C F C Dm7 Am Dm7 B♭ Am
peace that from it flows. Help, O God, my weak en -
paths of death a - way. Praise, with love's de - vout - est
sup - pliant's prayer to bless; Let thy grace, my soul's chief
Dm C Dm7 Am F B♭ Am Dm C F Am7 B♭ Gm7
deav-or; This dull soul to rap - ture raise; Thou must light the
feel - ing, Him who saw thy guilt - born fear And, the light of
trea-sure, Love's pure flame with - in me raise; And, since words can

F F7 B♭maj7 A Dm7 G G7 C9 C7 F
flame, or nev - er Can my love be warmed to praise.
hope re - veal - ing, Bade the blood - stained cross ap - pear.
nev - er mea - sure, Let my life show forth thy praise!

Text: Francis S. Key, 1779–1843
Tune: J. Leavitt, Christian Lyre, *1831*

PLEADING SAVIOR
87 87 D

Lord Our God, with Praise We Come 244

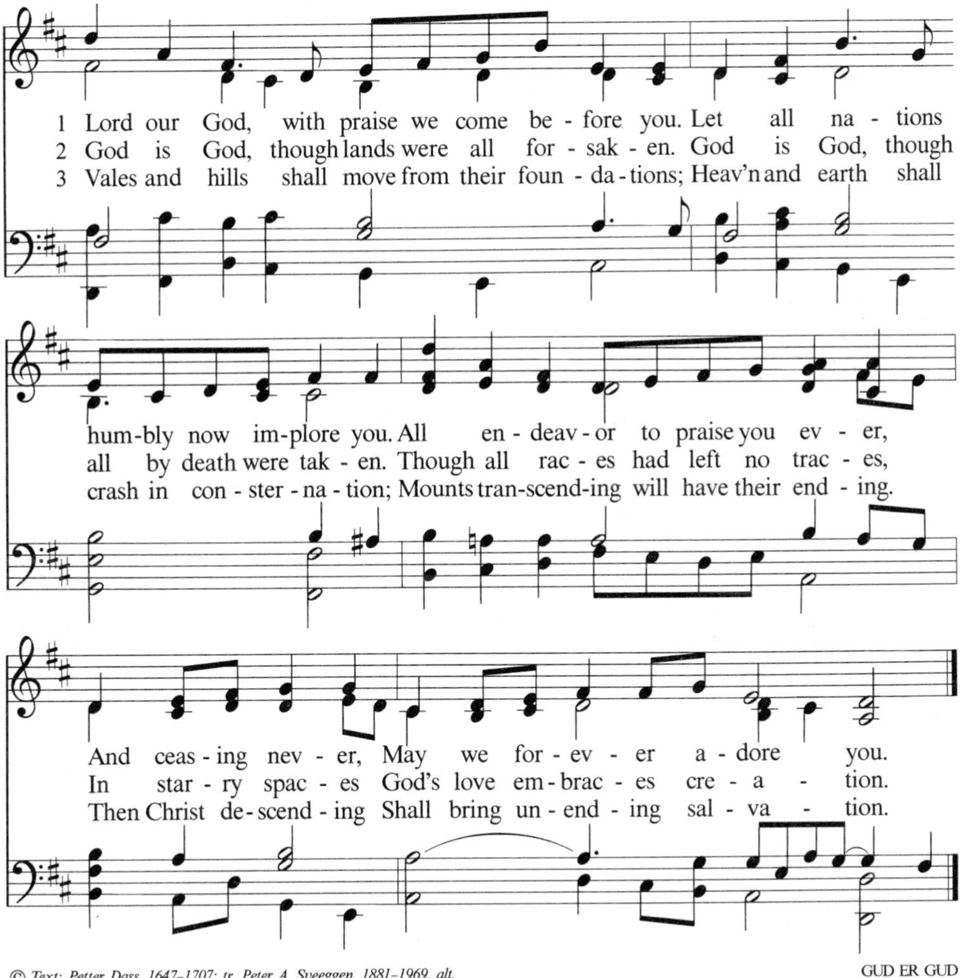

1 Lord our God, with praise we come be - fore you. Let all na - tions
2 God is God, though lands were all for - sak - en. God is God, though
3 Vales and hills shall move from their foun - da - tions; Heav'n and earth shall

hum - bly now im - plore you. All en - deav - or to praise you ev - er,
all by death were tak - en. Though all rac - es had left no trac - es,
crash in con - ster - na - tion; Mounts tran - scend - ing will have their end - ing.

And ceas - ing nev - er, May we for - ev - er a - dore you.
In star - ry spac - es God's love em - brac - es cre - a - tion.
Then Christ de - scend - ing Shall bring un - end - ing sal - va - tion.

GUD ER GUD
10 10 9 5 8

245 All People That on Earth Do Dwell

1 All peo - ple that on earth do dwell, Sing to the
2 Know that the Lord is God in - deed; With - out our
3 Oh, en - ter then his gates with praise; Ap - proach with
4 For why? The Lord our God is good: His mer - cy
Lord with cheer - ful voice; Him serve with mirth, his
aid he did us make. We are his folk, he
joy his courts un - to; Praise, laud, and bless his
is for - ev - er sure; His truth at all times
praise forth tell; Come ye be - fore him and re - joice.
doth us feed, And for his sheep he doth us take.
name al - ways, For it is seem - ly so to do.
firm - ly stood, And shall from age to age en - dure.

5 To Father, Son, and Holy Ghost,
The God whom heav'n and earth adore,
From us and from the angel host
Be praise and glory evermore.

Text: William Kethe, d. c. 1593
Tune: Louis Bourgeois, c. 1510–1561

OLD HUNDREDTH
LM

The First Day of the Week

246

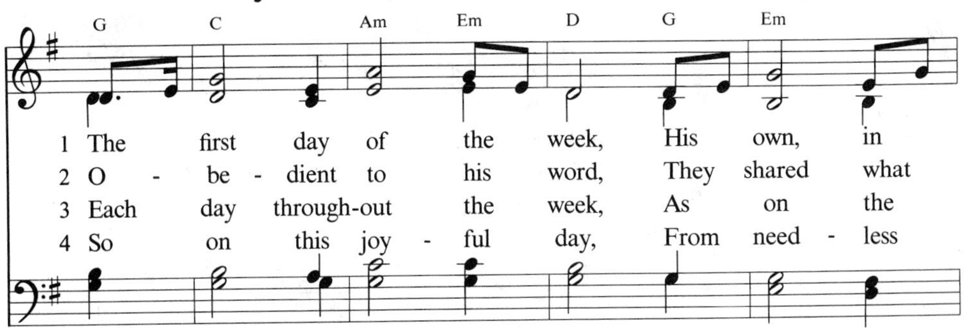
G C Am Em D G Em
1 The first day of the week, His own, in
2 O - be - dient to his word, They shared what
3 Each day through-out the week, As on the
4 So on this joy - ful day, From need - less

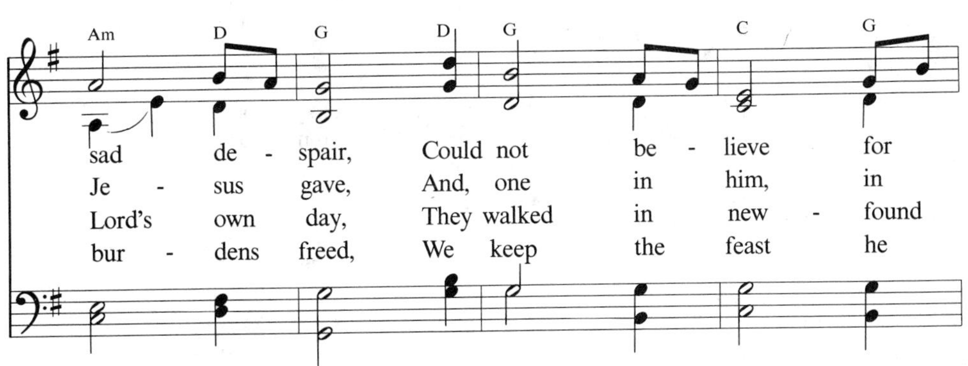
Am D G D G C G
sad de - spair, Could not be - lieve for
Je - sus gave, And, one in him, in
Lord's own day, They walked in new - found
bur - dens freed, We keep the feast he

Am C D Bm Em Am7 D G
ver - y joy Their ris - en Lord was there.
break - ing bread Knew what it cost to save.
lib - er - ty His true and liv - ing way.
gave to us To fit our in - most need.

5 How soon we forge again
The fetters of our past!
As long as Jesus lives in us,
So long our freedoms last.

6 Today his people meet;
Today his Word is shown.
Lord Jesus, show us how to use
This day we call your own.

 Text: *F. Pratt Green, b. 1903*
Tune: Missouri Harmony, *St. Louis, 1820*

KENTUCKY 93RD
SM

247 Holy Majesty, before You

1 Ho - ly Maj - es - ty, be - fore you We bow to wor - ship and a -
2 God of light, ex - alt - ed, ho - ly! Your ten - der care pro - tects the
3 Bless us, Lord, and keep us ev - er; Re - veal your face and show your
dore you! With grate - ful hearts to you we sing!
low - ly, Leaves not your chil - dren to their fate.
fa - vor; Up - on your peo - ple smile with peace.
8
Earth and heav - en tell the sto - ry Of your e - ter - nal might and
You are gra - cious, God, our Fa - ther; Your cho - sen peo - ple still you
Here we sing our hymns, re - joic - ing, Un - til in heav'n we shall be
glo - ry, And all your works their in - cense bring. Lo, hosts of cher - u -
gath - er With - in your arms com - pas - sion - ate. You gave us Christ, your
voic - ing Your praise in strains that nev - er cease; Where hosts of cher - u -

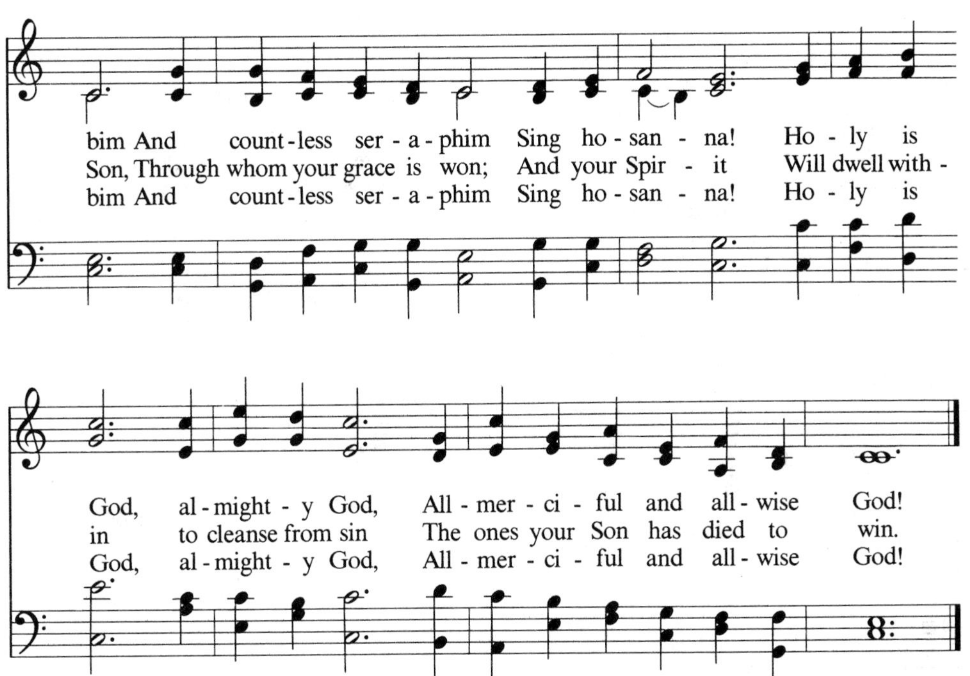
bim And count-less ser - a - phim Sing ho - san - na! Ho - ly is
Son, Through whom your grace is won; And your Spir - it Will dwell with -
bim And count-less ser - a - phim Sing ho - san - na! Ho - ly is
God, al - might - y God, All - mer - ci - ful and all - wise God!
in to cleanse from sin The ones your Son has died to win.
God, al - might - y God, All - mer - ci - ful and all - wise God!

 Text: Samuel J. Hedborn, 1783–1849; tr. August W. Kjellstrand, 1864–1930, adapt.
Tune: Philipp Nicolai, 1556–1608

WACHET AUF
P M

248 Dearest Jesus, at Your Word

1 Dear-est Je - sus, at your word We have come a - gain to
2 All our knowl - edge, sense, and sight Lie in deep-est dark - ness
3 Ra-diance of God's glo - ry bright, Light of light from God pro -
4 Fa - ther, Son, and Ho - ly Ghost, Praise to you and ad - o -
hear you; Let our thoughts and hearts be stirred And in
shroud - ed Till your Spir - it breaks the night, Fill - ing
ceed - ing, Je - sus, send your bless - ed light; Help our
ra - tion! Grant us what we need the most: Your blest
glow-ing faith be near you As the prom - is - es here
us with light un - cloud - ed. All good thoughts and all good
hear-ing, speak - ing, heed - ing, That our prayers and songs may
Gos-pel's con - so - la - tion, While we here on earth a -
giv - en Draw us whol - ly up to heav - en.
liv - ing Come but by your gra - cious giv - ing.
please you, As with grate - ful hearts we praise you.
wait you, Till in heav'n with praise we greet you.

Text: *Tobias Clausnitzer, 1619–1684, sts. 1–3;* Gesangbuch, *Berlin, 1707, st. 4; tr. Catherine Winkworth, 1829–1878, adapt.*
Tune: *Johann R. Ahle, 1625–1673*

LIEBSTER JESU, WIR SIND HIER
7 8 7 8 8 8

God Himself Is Present

249

1 God him-self is pres - ent; Let us now a - dore him And with awe ap - pear be - fore him! God is in his tem - ple; All with - in keep si - lence, Pros - trate lie with deep - est rev-'rence. Him a - lone God we own, Him, our God and Sav - ior; Praise his name for - ev - er!
2 God him-self is pres - ent; Hear the harps re - sound-ing; See the hosts the throne sur-round-ing! "Ho-ly, ho - ly, ho - ly!" Hear the hymn as-cend - ing, Songs of saints and an - gels blend-ing. Bow your ear to us here: Hear, O Christ, the prais - es That your Church now rais - es.
3 Light of light e - ter - nal, All things pen - e - trat - ing, For your rays our soul is wait - ing. As the ten-der flow - ers, Will-ing - ly un-fold - ing, To the sun their fac - es hold-ing: E - ven so would we do, Light from you ob - tain - ing, Strength to serve you gain - ing.
4 Come, ce - les - tial Be - ing, Make our hearts your dwell - ing, Ev - 'ry car - nal thought dis - pel - ling. By your Ho - ly Spir - it Sanc - ti - fy us tru - ly, Teach-ing us to love you on - ly. Where we go here be - low, Let us bow be - fore you And in truth a - dore you.

© Text: Gerhard Tersteegen, 1697–1769; tr. composite
Tune: Joachim Neander, 1650–1680

WUNDERBARER KÖNIG
668 668 666

250 Open Now Thy Gates of Beauty

1 O - pen now thy gates of beau - ty, Zi - on, let me en - ter there,
2 Gra - cious God, I come be - fore thee; Come thou al - so un - to me;
3 Here thy praise is glad - ly chant - ed, Here thy seed is du - ly sown;
4 Thou my faith in-crease and quick - en, Let me keep thy gift di - vine;
Where my soul in joy - ful du - ty Waits for God who an - swers prayer.
Where we find thee and a - dore thee, There a heav'n on earth must be.
Let my soul, where it is plant - ed, Bring forth pre-cious sheaves a - lone,
How - so - e'er temp - ta - tions thick - en, May thy Word still o'er me shine
Oh, how bless - ed is this place, Filled with so - lace, light, and grace!
To my heart, oh, en - ter thou, Let it be thy tem - ple now!
So that all I hear may be Fruit - ful un - to life in me.
As my guid - ing star through life, As my com - fort in all strife.

5 Speak, O God, and I will hear thee,
Let thy will be done indeed;
May I undisturbed draw near thee
While thou dost thy people feed.
Here of life the fountain flows;
Here is balm for all our woes.

Text: Benjamin Schmolck, 1672–1737; tr. Catherine Winkworth, 1829–1878, alt.
Tune: Joachim Neander, 1650–1680

UNSER HERRSCHER
87 87 77

O Day of Rest and Gladness 251

1 O day of rest and glad - ness, O day of joy and light,
2 On you, at earth's cre - a - tion, The light first had its birth;
3 To - day on wea - ry na - tions The heav'n-ly man - na falls;
4 New grac - es ev - er gain - ing From this our day of rest,
O balm for care and sad - ness, Most beau - ti - ful, most bright:
On you, for our sal - va - tion, Christ rose from depths of earth;
To ho - ly con - vo - ca - tions The sil - ver trum - pet calls,
We reach the rest re - main - ing To spir - its of the blest.
On you the high and low - ly, Through a - ges joined in tune,
On you, our Lord vic - to - rious The Spir - it sent from heav'n;
Where Gos - pel light is glow - ing With pure and ra - diant beams
To Ho - ly Ghost be prais - es, To Fa - ther, and to Son;
Sing, "Ho - ly, ho - ly, ho - ly," To the great God tri - une.
And thus on you, most glo - rious, A three-fold light was giv'n.
And liv - ing wa - ter flow - ing With soul - re - fresh - ing streams.
The Church its voice up - rais - es To you, blest Three in One.

Text: Christopher Wordsworth, 1807–1885, alt.
Tune: M. v. Werkmeister, Gesangbuch der Herzogl. Hofkapelle, *1784*

AVE MARIA, KLARER UND LICHTER MORGENSTERN
76 76 D

252 You Servants of God

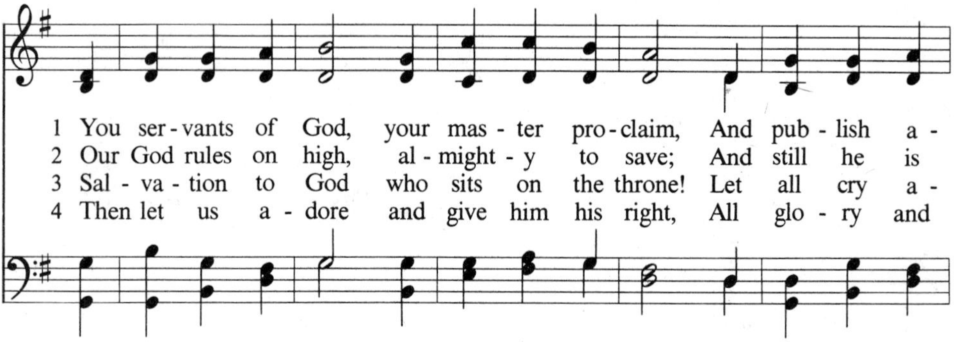

1 You ser - vants of God, your mas - ter pro - claim, And pub - lish a -
2 Our God rules on high, al - might - y to save; And still he is
3 Sal - va - tion to God who sits on the throne! Let all cry a -
4 Then let us a - dore and give him his right, All glo - ry and

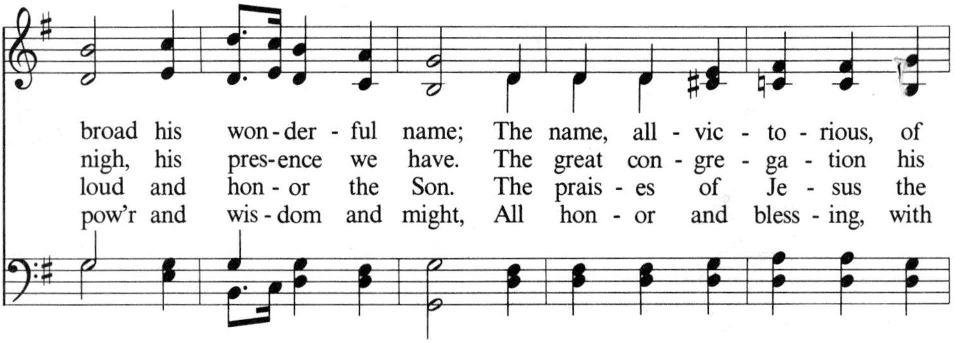

broad his won - der - ful name; The name, all - vic - to - rious, of
nigh, his pres - ence we have. The great con - gre - ga - tion his
loud and hon - or the Son. The prais - es of Je - sus the
pow'r and wis - dom and might, All hon - or and bless - ing, with

Je - sus ex - tol; His king - dom is glo - rious and rules o - ver all!
tri - umph shall sing, As - crib - ing sal - va - tion to Je - sus, our king!
an - gels pro - claim, Fall down on their fac - es, and wor - ship the Lamb.
an - gels a - bove, And thanks nev - er ceas - ing, and in - fi - nite love!

Text: Charles Wesley, 1707–1788, alt.
Tune: Johann M. Haydn, 1737–1806, adapt.

LYONS
10 10 11 11

Lord Jesus Christ, Be Present Now

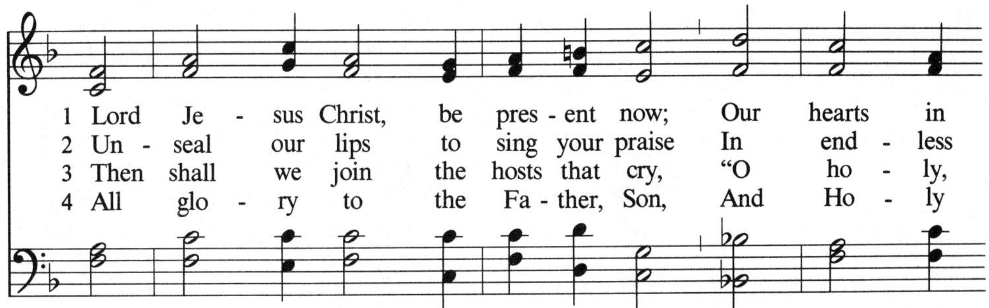
1 Lord Je - sus Christ, be pres - ent now; Our hearts in
2 Un - seal our lips to sing your praise In end - less
3 Then shall we join the hosts that cry, "O ho - ly,
4 All glo - ry to the Fa - ther, Son, And Ho - ly

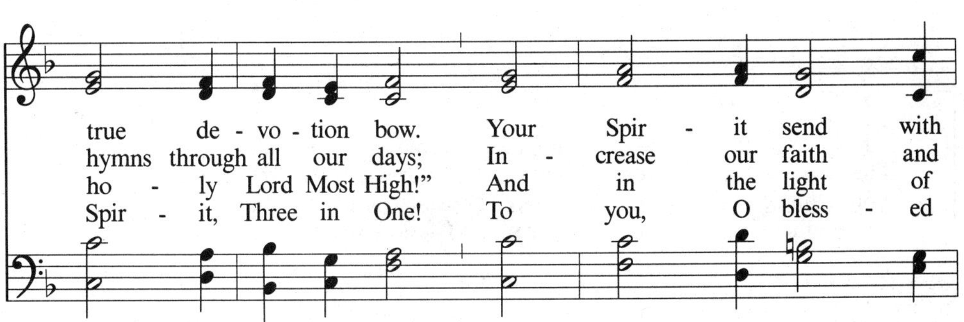
true de - vo - tion bow. Your Spir - it send with
hymns through all our days; In - crease our faith and
ho - ly Lord Most High!" And in the light of
Spir - it, Three in One! To you, O bless - ed

light di - vine, And let your truth with - in us shine.
light our minds; And set us free from doubt that blinds.
that blest place We then shall see you face to face.
Trin - i - ty, Be praise through - out e - ter - ni - ty!

Text: *Wilhelm II, 1598–1662; tr. Catherine Winkworth, 1829–1878, alt.*
Tune: Cantionale Germanicum, *Dresden, 1628*

HERR JESU CHRIST, DICH ZU UNS WEND
LM

254 Come, Let Us Join Our Cheerful Songs

1 Come, let us join our cheer - ful songs With
2 "Wor - thy the Lamb that died," they cry, "To
3 Je - sus is wor - thy to re - ceive Hon -
4 Let all cre - a - tion join in one To
an - gels round the throne; Ten thou - sand thou - sand
be ex - alt - ed thus!" "Wor - thy the Lamb," our
or and pow'r di - vine; And bless - ings, more than
bless the sa - cred name Of him who sits up -
are their tongues, But all their joys are one.
lips re - ply, "For he was slain for us!"
we can give, Be, Lord, for - ev - er thine.
on the throne, And to a - dore the Lamb.

Text: Isaac Watts, 1674–1748
Tune: Johann Crüger, 1598–1662

NUN DANKET ALL
CM

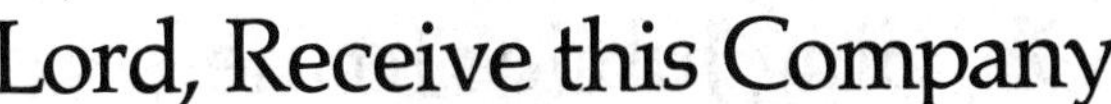

Lord, Receive this Company 255

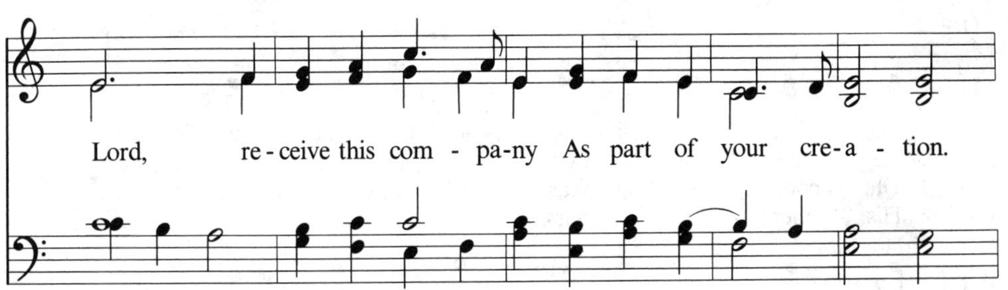
Lord, re - ceive this com - pa-ny As part of your cre-a - tion.

Here and now, at dawn and dusk, We bring dead hopes and old

dreams. Lord, we are man-y, And we would be one.

All, Lord, make us all One un - der the Son.

UNION
77 77 55 55

256 Oh, Sing Jubilee to the Lord

1 Oh, sing ju - bi - lee to the Lord, ev - 'ry land:
2 He made us his own, and has giv - en us breath;
3 Oh, come to his feast with thanks - giv - ing and praise;
4 His mer - cy is ours; he is Lord o - ver all;

Glo - ry be to God! Oh, serve him with glad - ness, as
Glo - ry be to God! The sheep of his pas - ture, we
Glo - ry be to God! Give glo - ry to him, and your
Glo - ry be to God! May all gen - er - a - tions find

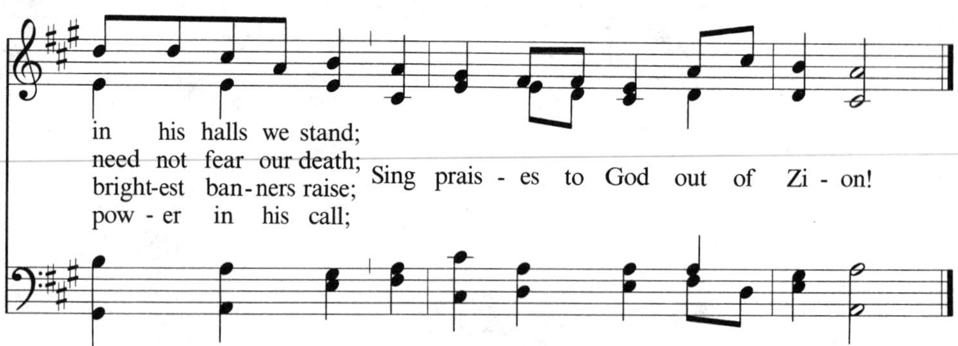
in his halls we stand;
need not fear our death;
bright-est ban - ners raise;
pow - er in his call;
Sing prais - es to God out of Zi - on!

 Text: Ulrik V. Koren, 1826–1910; tr. hymnal version, 1978
Tune: Erik C. Hoff, 1832–1894

GUDS MENIGHED, SYNG
115 129

Holy Spirit, Truth Divine

1 Ho - ly Spir - it, truth di - vine, Dawn up - on this soul of mine;
2 Ho - ly Spir - it, love di - vine, Glow with - in this heart of mine;
3 Ho - ly Spir - it, pow'r di - vine, For - ti - fy this will of mine;
4 Ho - ly Spir - it, peace di - vine, Still this rest - less heart of mine;
Word of God and in - ward light, Wake my spir - it, clear my sight.
Kin - dle ev - 'ry high de - sire; Purge me with your ho - ly fire.
By your will I strong - ly live, Brave - ly bear, and no - bly strive.
Speak to calm this toss - ing sea, Stayed in your tran - quil - i - ty.

5 Holy Spirit, right divine,
King within my conscience reign;
Be my guide, and I shall be
Firmly bound, forever free.

Text: Samuel Longfellow, 1819–1892, alt.
Tune: Orlando Gibbons, 1583–1625

SONG 13
77 77

258 Hosanna to the Living Lord!

1 Ho - san - na to the liv - ing Lord! Ho - san - na to the in-
2 "Ho - san - na, Lord!" your an - gels cry. "Ho - san - na, Lord!" your
3 O Sav - ior, with pro - tect - ing care A - bide in this your
4 To God the Fa - ther, God the Son, And God the Spir - it,

car - nate Word! To Christ, Cre - a - tor, Sav - ior, King, Let
saints re - ply. A - bove, be - neath us, and a - round, The
house of prayer, Where we your part - ing prom - ise claim, As -
Three in One, Be hon - or, praise, and glo - ry giv'n By

earth, let heav'n ho - san - na sing!
dead and liv - ing swell the sound:
sem - bled in your sa - cred name.
all on earth and all in heav'n.

Refrain

Ho - san - na, Lord! Ho - san - na in the high - est!

Text: *Reginald Heber, 1783–1826*
© Tune: *Ronald A. Nelson, b. 1927*

NILSSON
L M and refrain

Lord, Dismiss Us with Your Blessing 259

1 Lord, dis - miss us with your bless - ing, Fill our hearts with
2 Thanks we give and ad - o - ra - tion For your Gos - pel's
3 Sav - ior, when your love shall call us From our strug - gling
joy and peace; Let us each, your love pos - sess - ing,
joy - ful sound. May the fruits of your sal - va - tion
pil - grim way, Let no fear of death ap - pall us,
Tri - umph in re - deem - ing grace. Oh, re - fresh us;
In our hearts and lives a - bound. Ev - er faith - ful,
Glad your sum - mons to o - bey. May we ev - er,
oh, re - fresh us, Trav - 'ling through this wil - der - ness.
ev - er faith - ful To your truth may we be found.
may we ev - er Reign with you in end - less day.

Text: attr. John Fawcett, 1740–1817, sts. 1–2; Godfrey Thring, 1823–1903, st. 3, alt.
Tune: Sicilian, 18th cent.

SICILIAN MARINERS
87 87 87

260 On Our Way Rejoicing

1 On our way re - joic - ing Glad - ly let us go.
2 Un - to God the Fa - ther Joy - ful songs we sing;
Christ our Lord has con - quered; Van-quished is the foe.
Un - to God the Sav - ior Thank-ful hearts we bring;
Christ with-out, our safe - ty; Christ with - in, our joy;
Un - to God the Spir - it Bow we and a - dore,

Who, if we be faith - ful, Can our hope de-stroy?
On our way re - joic - ing Now and ev - er-more.
Refrain
On our way re - joic - ing; As we for-ward move,
Hear-ken to our prais - es, O blest God of love!

Text: John S. B. Monsell, 1811–1875, alt.
Tune: Frances R. Havergal, 1836–1879

HERMAS
65 65 65 D

261 On What Has Now Been Sown

1 On what has now been sown Your bless - ing, Lord, be - stow; The
2 To you our wants are known, From you are all our pow'rs; Ac -
3 Oh, grant that each of us, Now met be - fore you here, May

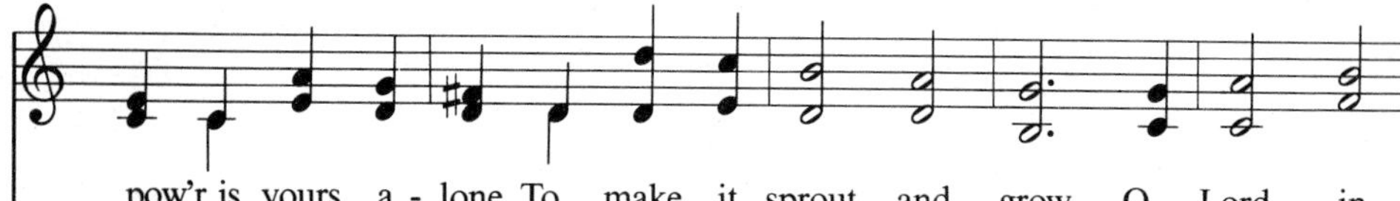

pow'r is yours a - lone To make it sprout and grow. O Lord, in
cept what is your own And par - don what is ours. Our prais - es,
meet to - geth - er thus When you and yours ap - pear, And fol - low

grace the har - vest raise, And yours a - lone shall be the praise!
Lord, and prayers re - ceive And to your Word a bless - ing give.
you to heav'n, our home. E'en so, A - men! Lord Je - sus, come!

Text: John Newton, 1725–1807, alt.
Tune: John Darwall, 1731–1789

DARWALL'S 148TH
66 66 88

Savior, Again to Your Dear Name 262

1 Savior, again to your dear name we raise
With one accord our parting hymn of praise;
Once more we bless you ere our worship cease,
Then, lowly bending, wait your word of peace.

2 Grant us your peace upon our homeward way;
With you began, with you shall end the day;
Guard all the lips from sin, the hearts from shame,
That in this house have called upon your name.

3 Grant us your peace, Lord, through the coming night;
For us transform its darkness into light.
Keep us from harm and danger till the dawn;
Your evening presence promise to your own.

4 Grant us your peace throughout our earthly life,
Our balm in sorrow, and our stay in strife;
Then, when your voice shall bid our conflict cease,
Call us, O Lord, to your eternal peace.

Text: John Ellerton, 1826–1893, alt.
Tune: Edward J. Hopkins, 1818–1901

ELLERS
10 10 10 10

263 Abide with Us, Our Savior

1 A - bide with us, our Sav - ior, Nor let your mer - cy cease;
2 A - bide with us, our Sav - ior, Sus - tain us by your Word;
3 A - bide a - mong us al - ways, Lord, with your faith - ful - ness;
4 A - bide with us, our Sav - ior, O Light of end - less light,

From Sa - tan's might de - fend us, And grant our souls re - lease.
That we with all your peo - ple To life may be re - stored.
O Je - sus, leave us nev - er, But help us in dis - tress.
Be - stow on us your bless - ings, And save us by your might.

Text: Josua Stegmann, 1588–1632; tr. composite, alt.
Tune: Melchior Vulpius, c. 1560–1615

CHRISTUS, DER IST MEIN LEBEN
7 6 7 6

264 When All Your Mercies, O My God

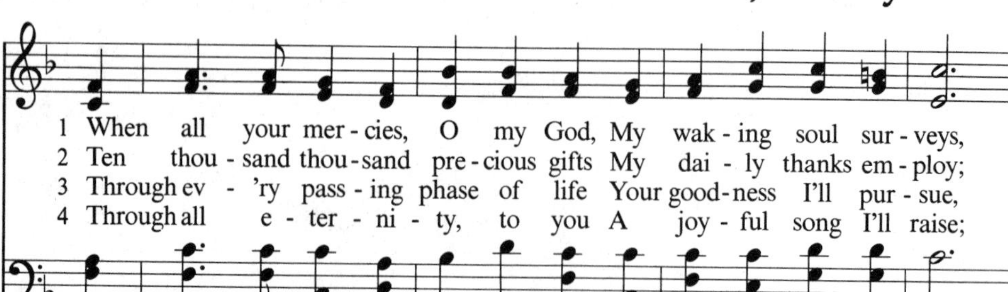
1 When all your mer - cies, O my God, My wak - ing soul sur - veys,
2 Ten thou - sand thou - sand pre - cious gifts My dai - ly thanks em - ploy;
3 Through ev - 'ry pass - ing phase of life Your good - ness I'll pur - sue,
4 Through all e - ter - ni - ty, to you A joy - ful song I'll raise;

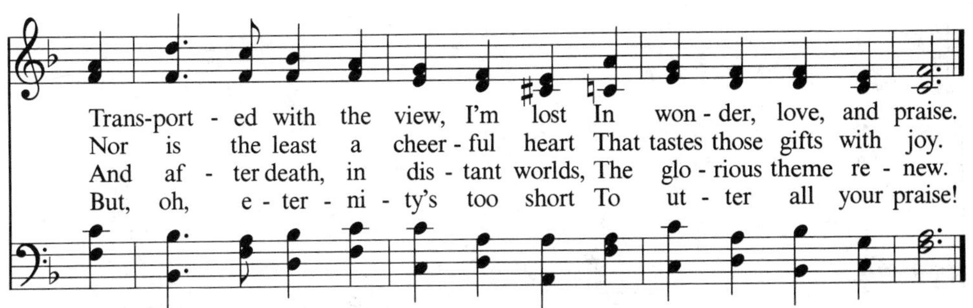
Trans-port - ed with the view, I'm lost In won - der, love, and praise.
Nor is the least a cheer - ful heart That tastes those gifts with joy.
And af - ter death, in dis - tant worlds, The glo - rious theme re - new.
But, oh, e - ter - ni - ty's too short To ut - ter all your praise!

Text: Joseph Addison, 1672–1719
Tune: attr. George Kirbye, c. 1560–1634

WINCHESTER OLD
CM

Christ, Whose Glory Fills the Skies 265

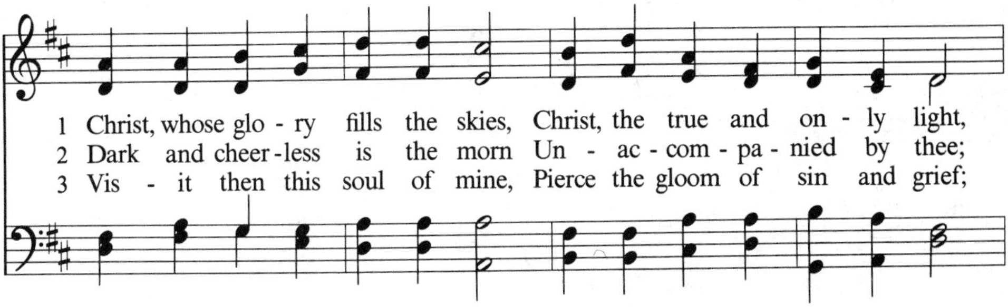

1 Christ, whose glo - ry fills the skies, Christ, the true and on - ly light,
2 Dark and cheer - less is the morn Un - ac - com - pa - nied by thee;
3 Vis - it then this soul of mine, Pierce the gloom of sin and grief;

Sun of righ - teous - ness, a - rise, Tri - umph o'er the shades of night;
Joy - less is the day's re - turn, Till thy mer - cy's beams I see,
Fill me, ra - dian - cy di - vine, Scat - ter all my un - be - lief;

Day - spring from on high, be near; Day - star, in my heart ap - pear.
Till they in - ward light im - part, Glad my eyes, and warm my heart.
More and more thy - self dis - play, Shin - ing to the per - fect day.

Text: Charles Wesley, 1707–1788
Tune: J. G. Werner, Choral-Buch, *1815*

RATISBON
77 77 77

266 Maker of the Earth and Heaven

1 Mak - er of the earth and heav - en, Fa - ther,
2 Thank you, God, for in your keep - ing I have
3 Let the night of my trans - gres - sion With the
4 Grant that at the morn - ing's break - ing I in
Son, and Ho - ly Ghost, Who the day and night have
rest - ed safe - ly here; You have guard - ed me while
dark - ness pass a - way; Je - sus, in - to your pos -
spir - it may a - rise; So may I in joy a -
giv - en, Sun and moon and star - ry host; Your al -
sleep - ing From all dan - ger, pain, and fear, That the
ses - sion I re - sign my - self to - day; In your
wak - ing Greet you when you rend the skies. When that
might - y hand sus - tains Earth and all that it con - tains.
un - re - lent - ing foe Could not cause my o - ver - throw.
wounds I find re - lief From temp - ta - tion, sin, and grief.
judg - ment day ap - pears, May I greet it with - out fears.

5 Let my life and conversation
Be directed by your Word;
By your help and preservation
Let me live this day, O Lord.
Only when you are with me
Can my life be wholly free.

6 Lord, your holy angels send me
To protect me from alarm;
From the wicked foe defend me
That his pow'r may do no harm
Till your messengers of love
Bring me to your home above.

 Text: Heinrich Albert, 1604–1651; tr. hymnal version, 1978
Tune: Heinrich Albert, 1604–1651

GOTT DES HIMMELS
8 7 8 7 7 7

Father, We Praise You 267

1 Fa - ther, we praise you, now the night is o - ver, Ac - tive and
2 Mon-arch of all things, fit us for your man - sions; Ban - ish our
3 All - ho - ly Fa - ther, Son, and e - qual Spir - it, Trin - i - ty
watch-ful, stand - ing now be - fore you; Sing - ing, we of - fer
weak-ness, health and whole-ness send - ing; Bring us to heav - en,
bless - ed, send us your sal - va - tion; Yours is the glo - ry,
prayer and med - i - ta - tion; Thus we a - dore you.
where your saints u - nit - ed Joy with - out end - ing.
gleam - ing and re - sound - ing Through all cre - a - tion.

 Text: attr. Gregory I, 540–604; tr. Percy Dearmer, 1867–1936, alt.
Tune: Antiphoner, *Paris, 1681*

CHRISTE SANCTORUM
11 11 11 5

268 Now that the Daylight Fills the Sky

1 Now that the day - light fills the sky,
2 Would guard our hearts and tongues from strife;
3 So we, when this new day is gone
4 "All praise to you, cre - a - tor Lord!
We lift our hearts to God on high,
From an - ger's din would shield our life;
And night in turn is draw - ing on,
All praise to you, e - ter - nal Word!
That he, in all we do or say, Would
From e - vil sights would turn our eyes, And
With con - science by the world un - stained Shall
All praise to you, O Spir - it wise!" We
keep us free from harm to - day;
close our ears to van - i - ties;
praise his name for vic - t'ry gained.
sing as day - light fills the skies.

Text: Latin hymn, 7th or 8th cent.; tr. John Mason Neale, 1818–1866, alt.
© *Tune: Dale Wood, b. 1934*

LAUREL
LM

Awake, My Soul, and with the Sun 269

1 A - wake, my soul, and with the sun Thy dai - ly stage of du - ty run; Shake off dull sloth, and joy - ful rise To pay thy morn - ing sac - ri - fice.
2 All praise to thee, who safe hast kept And hast re - freshed me while I slept. Grant, Lord, when I from death shall wake, I may of end - less light par - take.
3 Lord, I my vows to thee re - new. Dis - perse my sins as morn - ing dew; Guard my first springs of thought and will; And with thy - self my spir - it fill.
4 Di - rect, con - trol, sug - gest, this day, All I de - sign or do or say, That all my pow'rs, with all their might, In thy sole glo - ry may u - nite.

5 Praise God, from whom all blessings flow;
Praise him, all creatures here below;
Praise him above, ye heav'nly host;
Praise Father, Son, and Holy Ghost.

Text: Thomas Ken, 1637–1711
Tune: François H. Barthélémon, 1741–1808

MORNING HYMN
L M

270 God of Our Life, All-Glorious Lord

1 God of our life, all - glo - rious Lord, Be now and
2 Make clear our path, that we may see Where we must
3 Give us thy help in ev - 'ry task, Nor let us
4 At e - ven - tide then will we raise A grate - ful

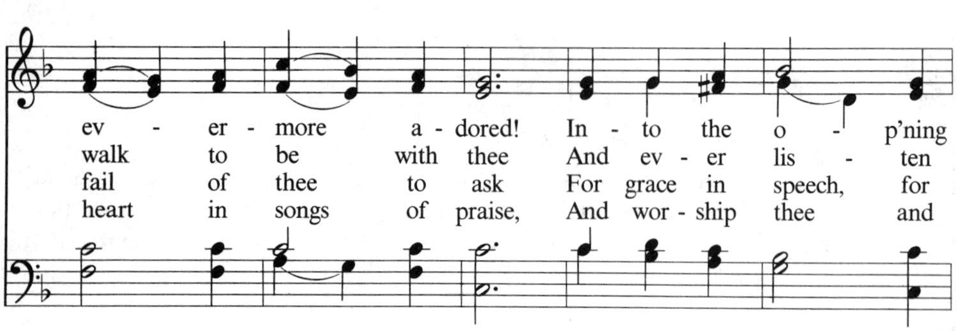
ev - er - more a - dored! In - to the o - p'ning
walk to be with thee And ev - er lis - ten
fail of thee to ask For grace in speech, for
heart in songs of praise, And wor - ship thee and

of this day Bring grace and love and peace, we pray.
for thy voice, That we may make thy way our choice.
love in deed, From wrong - ful ac - tions to be freed.
thy dear Son With God the Spir - it, ev - er one.

© *Text: Paul Z. Strodach, 1876–1947*
Tune: Maria Theresa, Katholisches Gesangbuch, *1774, adapt.*

GROSSER GOTT
LM

O Splendor of the Father's Light 271

Dm C F C F
1 O Splen-dor of the Fa-ther's light That makes our day-light lu-cid,
2 O Fa-ther, fash-ion love in us; Drive en-vy from the en-vi-
3 True Sun, break out on earth and shine In ra-diance with your light di-
4 The Fa-ther sends his Son, our Lord, To be his bright and shin-ing
C Am Dm C
bright; O Light of light and sun of day, Now
ous; And may you pros-per all our days With
vine; By daz-zling of your Spir-it's might, Oh,
Word; Come, Lord, ride out your gleam-ing course And
F C B♭ C Dm Gm Am Dm
shine on us your bright-est ray.
strength to live in your pure grace.
give our jad-ed sens-es light.
be our dawn, our light's true source. A-men

© *Text: St. Ambrose, 340–397; tr. Gracia Grindal, b. 1943*
Tune: mode 1; Antiphoner, *Sarum*

SPLENDOR PATERNAE
LM

272 Abide with Me

1 A - bide with me, fast falls the e - ven - tide.
2 I need thy pres - ence ev - 'ry pass - ing hour;
3 Swift to its close ebbs out life's lit - tle day;
4 I fear no foe, with thee at hand to bless;

The dark - ness deep - ens; Lord, with me a - bide.
What but thy grace can foil the tempt - er's pow'r?
Earth's joys grow dim, its glo - ries pass a - way;
Ills have no weight, and tears no bit - ter - ness.

When oth - er help - ers fail and com - forts flee,
Who like thy - self my guide and stay can be?
Change and de - cay in all a - round I see;
Where is death's sting? Where, grave, thy vic - to - ry?

Help of the help - less, oh, a - bide with me.
Through cloud and sun - shine, oh, a - bide with me.
O thou who chang - est not, a - bide with me.
I tri - umph still, if thou a - bide with me!

5 Hold thou thy cross before my closing eyes,
Shine through the gloom, and point me to the skies;
Heav'n's morning breaks, and earth's vain shadows flee;
In life, in death, O Lord, abide with me.

Text: Henry F. Lyte, 1793–1847
Tune: William H. Monk, 1823–1889

EVENTIDE
10 10 10 10

O Christ, You Are the Light and Day 273

1 O Christ, you are the light and day; You drive the gloom of night away; Grant, Light of light, your Word to show The light of heav'n to us below.
2 Arise, O God, our shield, repel The darts and subtleties of hell; Let your right hand, outstretched above, Guard those who serve the Lord they love.
3 All holy Lord, in humble prayer We ask tonight your watchful care And pray that our repose may be A quiet night, from perils free.
4 To God the Father and the Son And Holy Spirit, Three in One, Be glory in the highest giv'n By all on earth and all in heav'n!

Text: Latin hymn, 6th cent., sts. 1–3; Isaac Watts, 1674–1748, st. 4;
tr. William J. Copeland, 1804–1885, sts. 1–3, alt.
Tune: J. Klug, Geistliche Lieder, *1533*

CHRISTE, DER DU BIST TAG UND LICHT
LM

274 The Day You Gave Us, Lord, Has Ended

1 The day you gave us, Lord, has end - ed;
2 We thank you that your Church, un - sleep - ing
3 As to each con - ti - nent and is - land
4 The sun, here hav - ing set, is wak - ing
The dark - ness falls at your be - hest.
While earth rolls on - ward in - to light,
The dawn leads on an - oth - er day,
Your chil - dren un - der west - ern skies,
To you our morn - ing hymns as - cend - ed;
Through all the world its watch is keep - ing,
The voice of prayer is nev - er si - lent,
And hour by hour, as day is break - ing,
Your praise shall hal - low now our rest.
And nev - er rests by day or night.
Nor dies the strain of praise a - way.
Fresh hymns of thank - ful praise a - rise.

5 So be it, Lord; your realm shall never,
Like earth's proud empires, pass away;
But stand and grow and rule forever,
Till all your creatures own your sway.

Text: John Ellerton, 1826–1893, alt.
Tune: Clement C. Scholefield, 1839–1904

ST. CLEMENT
9 8 9 8

O Trinity, O Blessed Light 275

1 O Trin - i - ty, O bless - ed Light, O U - ni - ty of prince - ly might: The fi - 'ry sun is go - ing down; Shed light up - on us through your Son.
2 To you our morn - ing song of praise, To you our eve - ning prayer we raise; We praise your light in ev - 'ry age, The glo - ry of our pil - grim - age.
3 All glo - ry be to God a - bove And to the Son, the prince of love, And to the Spir - it, One in Three! We praise you, bless - ed Trin - i - ty.

 Text: attr. St. Ambrose, 340–397; tr. Gracia Grindal, b. 1943
Tune: Nikolaus Herman, c. 1480–1561

O HEILIGE DREIFALTIGKEIT
L M

276 Now All the Woods Are Sleeping

1 Now all the woods are sleep - ing, Through fields the shad -
2 The ra - diant sun has van - ished, Its gold - en rays
3 Now all the heav'n - ly splen - dor Breaks forth in star -
4 Though long our an - cient blind - ness Has missed God's lov -
ows creep - ing, And cit - ies sink to rest; Let us, as night
are ban - ished From dark-'ning skies of night; But Christ, the sun
light ten - der From myr - iad worlds un-known; And we, this mar -
ing - kind - ness And plunged us in - to strife; One day, when life
is fall - ing, On God our mak - er call - ing,
of glad - ness, Dis - pel - ling all our sad - ness,
vel see - ing, For - get our self - ish be - ing
is o - ver, Shall death's fair night un - cov - er
Give thanks to him who loves us best.
Shines down on us in warm - est light.
For joy of beau - ty not our own.
The fields of ev - er - last - ing life.

 Text: Paul Gerhardt, 1607–1676; tr. hymnal version, 1978
Tune: Heinrich Isaac, c. 1450–1517

O WELT, ICH MUSS DICH LASSEN
776 778

To You, before the Close of Day

1 To you, be - fore the close of day, Cre - a - tor of the
2 From e - vil dreams de - fend our sight, From all the ter - rors
3 O Fa - ther, this we ask be done Through Je - sus Christ, your
world, we pray! Your grace and peace to us al - low
of the night, From all de - lud - ing thoughts that creep
on - ly Son, Who with the Ho - ly Ghost and you
And be our guard and keep - er now.
On heed - less minds dis - armed by sleep.
Shall live and reign all a - ges through. A - men

Text: compline office hymn, c. 8th cent.; tr. John M. Neale, 1818–1866, adapt.
Tune: Benedictine plainsong, mode VI

JAM LUCIS
LM

278 All Praise to Thee, My God, This Night

1 All praise to thee, my God, this night For all the bless-ings of the light.
2 For - give me, Lord, for thy dear Son, The ill that I this day have done;
3 Teach me to live, that I may dread The grave as lit - tle as my bed.
4 Oh, may my soul in thee re - pose, And may sweet sleep mine eye - lids close,

Keep me, oh, keep me, King of kings, Be-neath thine own al-might - y wings.
That with the world, my - self, and thee, I, ere I sleep, at peace may be.
Teach me to die, that so I may Rise glo - rious at the awe-some day.
Sleep that shall me more vig - 'rous make To serve my God when I a - wake!

5 Praise God, from whom all blessings flow;
Praise him, all creatures here below;
Praise him above, ye heav'nly host;
Praise Father, Son, and Holy Ghost.

Text: Thomas Ken, 1637–1711
Tune: Thomas Tallis, c. 1505–1585

TALLIS' CANON
LM

279 Oh, Gladsome Light

1 Oh, glad-some light of the Fa - ther im - mor - tal And of the ce -
2 Now to the sun - set a - gain you have brought us, And, see - ing the
3 Fa - ther om - nip - o - tent! Son, our life - giv - er! Spir - it, our . .

les - tial, Sa - cred, and bless - ed Je - sus, our Sav - ior!
eve - ning Twi - light, we bless you, praise you, a - dore you!
com-fort - er! Wor - thy at all times of wor - ship and won - der.
Text: Greek hymn, 3rd cent.; tr. Henry W. Longfellow, 1807–1882, alt.
© Tune: Allan Mahnke, b. 1944
ELIZABETH
11 7 10
Now the Day Is Over
280
A E A F♯m C♯ F♯m
1 Now the day is o - ver; Night is draw - ing nigh;
2 Je - sus, give the wea - ry Calm and sweet re - pose;
3 Com - fort ev - 'ry suf - f'rer Watch-ing late in pain;
4 Through the long night - watch - es May your an - gels spread
B9 B7 E A E7sus4 E9 A
Shad - ows of the eve - ning Steal a - cross the sky.
With your ten - d'rest bless - ing May our eye - lids close.
Those who plan some e - vil, From their sin re - strain.
Their bright wings a - bove me, Watch - ing round my bed.
5 When the morning wakens,
Then may I arise
Pure and fresh and sinless
In your holy eyes.
6 Glory to the Father,
Glory to the Son,
And to you, blest Spirit,
While the ages run.

Text: Sabine Baring-Gould, 1834–1924, alt.
Tune: Joseph Barnby, 1838–1896

MERRIAL
65 65

281 God, Who Made the Earth and Heaven

1 God, who made the earth and heav - en, Dark - ness and light:
2 And when morn a - gain shall call us To run life's way,
3 Guard us wak-ing, guard us sleep - ing, And, when we die,
4 Ho - ly Fa-ther, throned in heav - en, All - ho - ly Son,
You the day for work have giv - en, For rest the night.
May we still, what - e'er be - fall us, Your will o - bey.
May we in your might - y keep - ing All peace - ful lie.
Ho - ly Spir - it, free - ly giv - en, Blest Three in One:
May your an - gel guards de - fend us, Slum-ber sweet your mer - cy send us,
From the pow'r of e - vil hide us, In the nar - row path - way guide us,
When the last dread call shall wake us, Then, O Lord, do not for - sake us,
Grant us grace, we now im - plore you, Till we lay our crowns be - fore you
Ho - ly dreams and hopes at-tend us All through the night.
Nev - er be your smile de-nied us All through the day.
But to reign in glo - ry take us With you on high.
And in wor - thier strains a - dore you While a - ges run.

Text: Reginald Heber, 1783–1826, st. 1; William Mercer, 1811–1873, sts. 2, 4; Richard Whately, 1787–1863, st. 3; alt.
Tune: Welsh

AR HYD Y NOS
84 84 88 84

Now Rest beneath Night's Shadow 282

1 Now rest be - neath night's shad - ow The wood - land, field,
2 Lord Je - sus, since you love me, Now spread your wings
3 My loved ones, rest se - cure - ly, For God this night

and mead - ow— The world in slum - ber lies. But you, my heart,
a - bove me And shield me from a - larm. Though e - vil would
will sure - ly From per - il guard your heads. Sweet slum - bers may

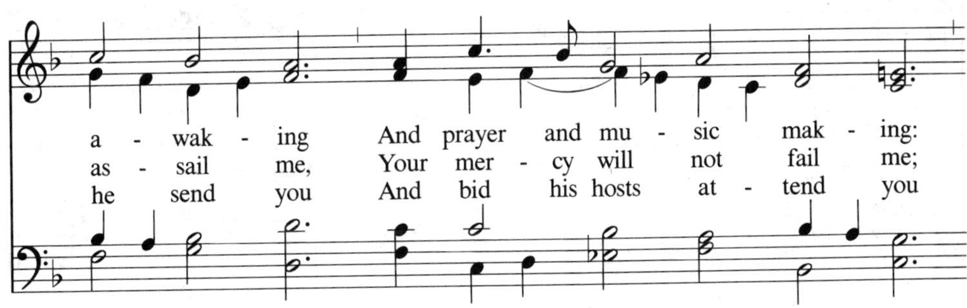
a - wak - ing And prayer and mu - sic mak - ing:
as - sail me, Your mer - cy will not fail me;
he send you And bid his hosts at - tend you

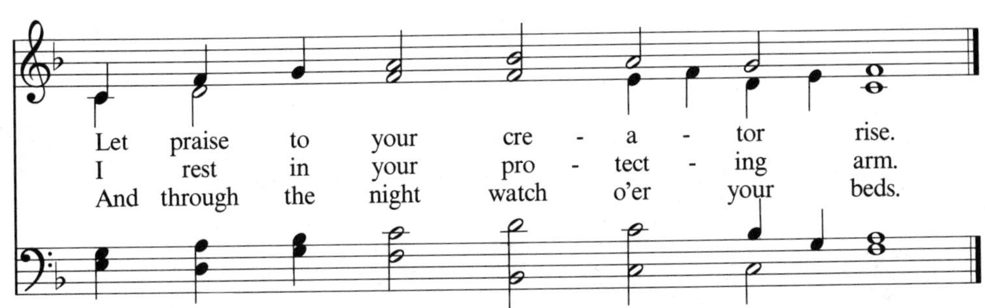
Let praise to your cre - a - tor rise.
I rest in your pro - tect - ing arm.
And through the night watch o'er your beds.

 Text: Paul Gerhardt, 1607–1676; tr. The Lutheran Hymnal, *1941, alt.*
Tune: Heinrich Isaac, c. 1450–1517

O WELT, ICH MUSS DICH LASSEN
776 778

283 O God, Send Heralds

1 O God, send her - alds who will nev - er fal - ter, Who dare to
2 Not to be served, but on - ly to be serv - ing, To feed the
3 Em - pires have come, have flour - ished and de - part - ed, But still your
4 Send her - alds, then, in whom your heart re - joic - es; Send those who
walk where Christ has set his feet, Who know the Church as bea - con
hun - ger in the hu - man heart, To know that love which comes with-
Church, as wit - ness to your way, Lives on in dark - ness, light of
hear the call that sets us free, With ea - ger hearts and ju - bi -
and as al - tar Where hu - man need and your a - bun - dance meet.
out de - serv - ing, That love which on - ly Je - sus can im - part.
the true - heart - ed, And calls to ac - tion those whose feet would stay.
lat - ing voic - es Each mak - ing an - swer, "Here am I! Send me."

© Text: Elisabeth Burrowes, b. 1883, alt.
Tune: C. Hubert H. Parry, 1848–1918

INTERCESSOR
11 10 11 10

Creator Spirit, Heavenly Dove

284

1 Cre - a - tor Spir - it, heav'n - ly dove, De - scend
2 To you, the Com - fort - er, we cry; To you,
3 In you, with grac - es sev - en - fold, We God's
4 Your light to ev - 'ry sense im - part, And shed
up - on us from a - bove; With grac - es man - i -
the gift of God most high, True fount of life, the
al - might - y hand be - hold; While you with tongues of
your love in ev - 'ry heart; Your own un - fail - ing
fold re - store Your crea - tures as they were be - fore.
fire of love, The soul's a - noint - ing from a - bove.
fire pro - claim To all the world his ho - ly name.
might sup - ply To strength - en our in - fir - mi - ty.

5 Keep far from us our cruel foe,
And peace from your own hand bestow;
Upheld by you, our strength and guide,
No evil can our steps betide.

6 Oh, make to us the Father known;
Teach us the eternal Son to own;
And you, whose name we ever bless,
Of both the Spirit, to confess.

7 Praise we the Father and the Son
And Holy Spirit, with them one;
And may the Son on us bestow
The gifts that from the Spirit flow.

Text: attr. Rhabanus Maurus, 776–856; tr. composite, alt.
Tune: J. Klug, Geistliche Lieder, *1533*

KOMM, GOTT SCHÖPFER
LM

285 Spirit of God, Sent from Heaven Abroad

1 Spir - it of God, sent from heav - en a - broad, Wit - ness - ing,
2 Tongues as of fire, kin - dling words that in - spire, Grant to the
3 Growth springs a - live as good tid - ings ar - rive, Har - vest will
4 Bright - en our day as a morn - ing in May, Spring-time e -
judg-ing, ex - plain - ing: Let your light shine through each
ones you are send - ing, Filled with your lore as a -
come on the mor - row: Pow - er and nerve, a com -
rupt - ing in beau - ty; Bless us with joy as our
self - cen - tered mind, Com - fort - ing, guid - ing, sus - tain -
pos - tles of yore, On one great quest nev - er - end -
mit - ment to serve, Com - fort, and hope in all sor -
gifts we em - ploy, Mer - cy suf - fus - ing our du -
ing. Bring us your Gos - pel; be - side . . us stand;
ing, Till all the ston - i - est hearts . . are stirred
row. Gent - ly the Gos - pel ful - fills . . its task;
ty; An - thems and prayer . . at e - ven - tide

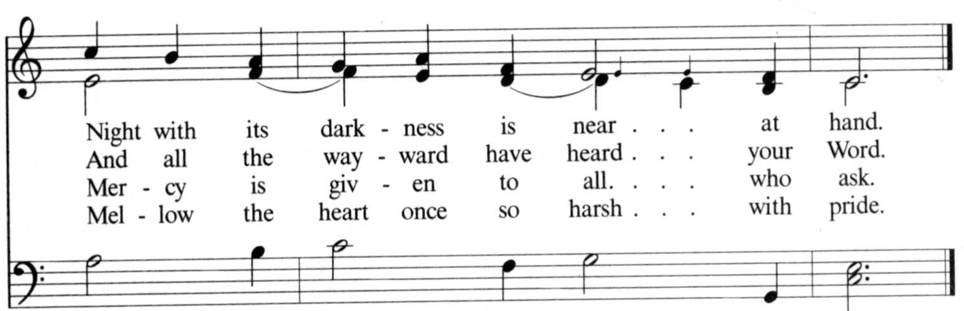
Night with its dark - ness is near . . . at hand.
And all the way - ward have heard . . . your Word.
Mer - cy is giv - en to all. . . . who ask.
Mel - low the heart once so harsh . . . with pride.

5 As we baptize, let our prayers arise:
Grant us new birth by your power!
Witness we give that in grace we shall live;
God-given goodness shall flower.
Rooted in Calvary's nourishing rod,
All shall acknowledge the mercy of God.

 Text: Nicolai F. S. Grundtvig, 1783–1872; tr. Johannes H. V. Knudsen, b. 1902, alt.
Tune: Ludvig M. Lindeman, 1812–1887

DU SOM GAAR UD
108 108 99

286 Bow Down Your Ear, Almighty Lord

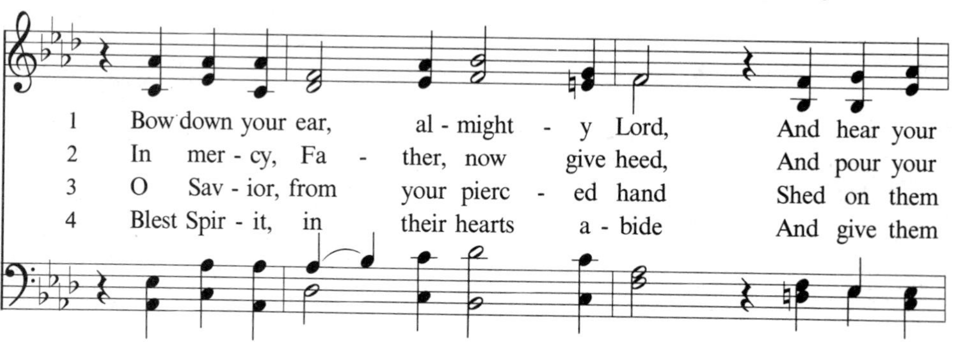
1 Bow down your ear, al - might - y Lord, And hear your
2 In mer - cy, Fa - ther, now give heed, And pour your
3 O Sav - ior, from your pierc - ed hand Shed on them
4 Blest Spir - it, in their hearts a - bide And give them

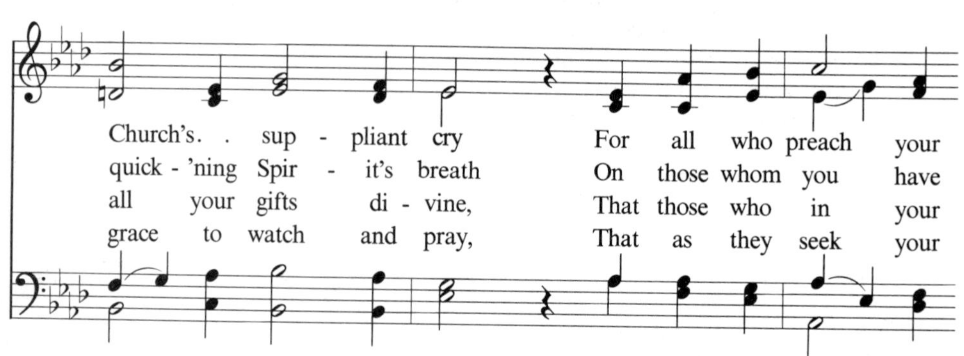
Church's. . sup - pliant cry For all who preach your
quick - 'ning Spir - it's breath On those whom you have
all your gifts di - vine, That those who in your
grace to watch and pray, That as they seek your

sav - ing Word And serve you in their min - is - try.
called to feed Your flock re - deemed by Je - sus' death.
pres - ence stand May form their lives to your de - sign.
flock to guide, They too may keep the nar - row way.

5 O God, your strength and mercy send
To shield them in their strife with sin.
Grant them, enduring to the end,
The crown of life at last to win.

Text: *Thomas E. Powell, 1823–1901, alt.*
Tune: As Hymnodus Sacer, *Leipzig, 1625*

HERR JESU CHRIST, MEINS
LM

O Perfect Love

287

1 O per - fect Love, all hu - man thought tran - scend - ing,
2 O per - fect Life, be now their full as - sur - ance
3 Grant them the joy which bright - ens earth - ly sor - row;

Low - ly we kneel in prayer be - fore your throne,
Of ten - der char - i - ty and stead - fast faith,
Grant them the peace which calms all earth - ly strife,

That theirs may be the love which knows no end - ing,
Of pa - tient hope and qui - et, brave en - dur - ance,
And to life's day the glo - rious un - known mor - row

Whom you for - ev - er - more u - nite in one.
With child - like trust that fears no pain or death.
That dawns up - on e - ter - nal love and life.

 Text: Dorothy F. Gurney, 1858–1932
Tune: Joseph Barnby, 1838–1896, adapt.

O PERFECT LOVE
11 10 11 10

288 Hear Us Now, Our God and Father

1 Hear us now, our God and Father, Send your
2 Give them joy to light - en sor - row! Give them
3 May the grace of Christ, our Sav - ior, And the
Spir - it from a - bove On this Chris - tian
hope to bright - en life! Go with them to
Fa - ther's bound - less love, With the Ho - ly
man and wom - an Who here make their vows of love!
face the mor - row, Stay with them in ev - 'ry strife.
Spir - it's fa - vor Rest up - on them from a - bove.
Bind their hearts in true de - vo - tion End - less
As your Word has prom - ised, ev - er Fill them
Thus may they a - bide in u - nion With each

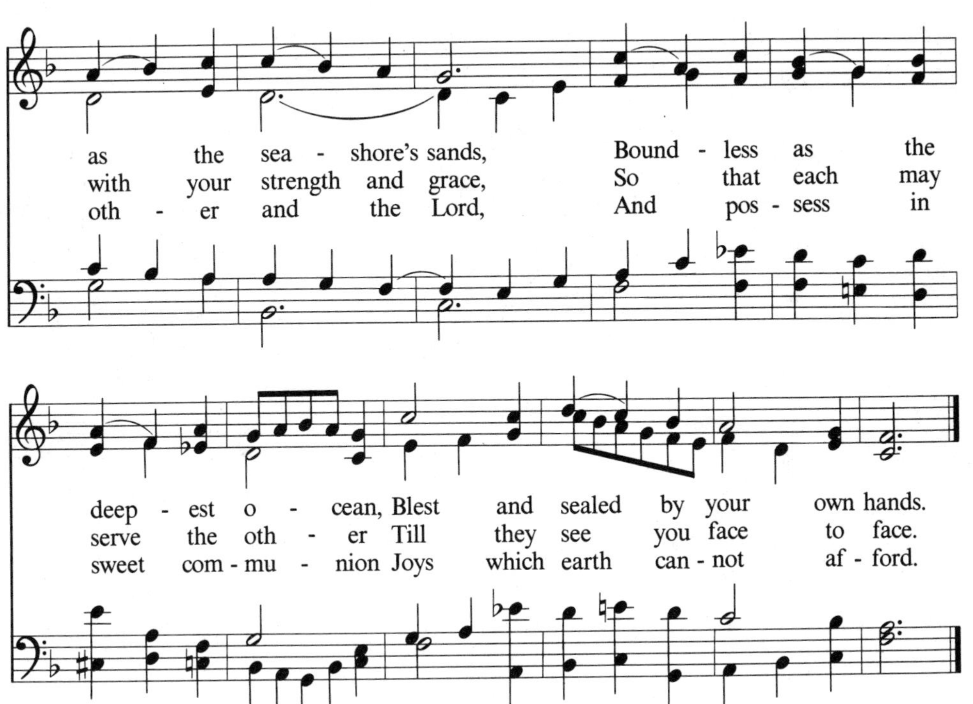
as the sea - shore's sands, Bound - less as the
with your strength and grace, So that each may
oth - er and the Lord, And pos - sess in
deep - est o - cean, Blest and sealed by your own hands.
serve the oth - er Till they see you face to face.
sweet com - mu - nion Joys which earth can - not af - ford.

© *Text: Harry N. Huxhold, b. 1922, sts. 1–2; John Newton, 1725–1807, st. 3; alt.*
Tune: Rowland H. Prichard, 1811–1887

HYFRYDOL
87 87 D

289 Heavenly Father, Hear Our Prayer

1 Heav'n-ly Fa - ther, hear our prayer As we bow be - fore you:
2 As they pledge their love this day Here be - fore your al - tar,
3 Blest Cre - a - tor, Lord of life, Hear our glad thanks - giv - ing.
Bless them in the life they share, Hum - bly we im - plore you.
May their hearts, up - on you stayed, Nev - er fail or fal - ter.
Hus - band you have joined to wife For their earth - ly liv - ing.
Be their guide in all en - deav - ors, Be their hope that noth-ing sev - ers;
Be their com - fort in all sor - row; Be their rea - son for to - mor-row.
Jus - ti - fied by Je - sus' mer - it, Life e - ter - nal they in - her - it.
Con - stant source of love di - vine, Let your love with - in them shine!
Grant them strength to live each hour Trust - ing sole - ly in your pow'r.
When their days on earth have passed, Take them to your home at last!

© *Text: Barbara E. Adam, b. 1939, alt.*
© *Tune: Ralph A. Strom, 1901–1977*

NAME OF JESUS
76 76 88 77

There's a Wideness in God's Mercy 290

1 There's a wide - ness in God's mer - cy, Like the wide-ness of the sea;
2 There is wel - come for the sin - ner, And a prom-ised grace made good;
3 For the love of God is broad-er Than the mea-sures of our mind;
4 'Tis not all we owe to Je - sus; It is some-thing more than all:
There's a kind - ness in his jus - tice Which is more than lib - er - ty.
There is mer - cy with the Sav - ior; There is heal - ing in his blood.
And the heart of the e - ter - nal Is most won - der - ful - ly kind.
Great - er good be - cause of e - vil, Larg - er mer - cy through the fall.
There is no place where earth's sor - rows Are more felt than up in heav'n.
There is grace e - nough for thou-sands Of new worlds as great as this;
There is plen - ti - ful re - demp-tion In the blood that has been shed;
If our love were but more sim - ple, We should take him at his word;
There is no place where earth's fail - ings Have such kind - ly judg-ment giv'n.
There is room for fresh cre - a - tions In that up - per home of bliss.
There is joy for all the mem-bers In the sor - rows of the head.
And our lives would be all sun - shine In the sweet-ness of our Lord.

Text: Frederick W. Faber, 1814–1863
Tune: early American

LORD, REVIVE US
87 87 D

291 Jesus Sinners Will Receive

1 Je - sus sin - ners will re - ceive; May they all this say - ing pon - der Who in sin's de - lu - sions live And from God and heav - en wan - der! Here is hope for all who grieve:
2 We de - serve but grief and shame, Yet his words, rich grace re - veal - ing, Par - don, peace, and life pro - claim. Here our ills have per - fect heal - ing; We with hum - ble hearts be - lieve
3 When their sheep have lost their way, Faith - ful shep - herds go to seek them; Je - sus watch - es all who stray, Faith - ful - ly to find and take them In his arms, that they may live—
4 Come, O sin - ners, one and all, Come, ac - cept his in - vi - ta - tion; Come, o - bey his gra - cious call, Come and take his free sal - va - tion! Firm - ly in these words be - lieve:
Je - sus sin - ners will re - ceive.

5 Jesus sinners will receive.
Even me he has forgiven;
And when I this earth must leave,
I shall find an open heaven.
Dying, still to him I cleave—
Jesus sinners will receive.

 Text: Erdmann Neumeister, 1671–1756; tr. The Lutheran Hymnal, *1941, alt.*
Tune: Johann Ulich, 1634–1712

MEINEN JESUM LASS ICH NICHT
78 78 77

God Loved the World

292

1 God loved the world so that he gave His on - ly
2 Christ Je - sus is the ground of faith, Who was made
3 If you are sick, if death is near, This truth your
4 Be of good cheer, for God's own Son For - gives all
Son, the lost to save, That all who would in him be -
flesh and suf - fered death; All who con - fide in Christ a -
trou - bled heart can cheer; Christ Je - sus saves your soul from
sins which you have done, And jus - ti - fied by Je - sus'
lieve Should ev - er - last - ing life re - ceive.
lone Are built on this chief cor - ner - stone.
death; That is the firm - est ground of faith.
blood, Your Bap - tism grants the high - est good.

Text: Gesangbuch, *Bollhagen, 1791; tr. August Crull, 1846–1923, alt.*
Tune: Melchior Vulpius, c. 1560–1615

DIE HELLE SONN LEUCHT
LM

293 My Hope Is Built on Nothing Less

1 My hope is built on noth - ing less Than Je - sus' blood and
2 When dark - ness veils his love - ly face, I rest on his un -
3 His oath, his cov - e - nant, his blood Sus - tain me in the
4 When he shall come with trum - pet sound, Oh, may I then in
righ - teous - ness; No mer - it of my own I claim, But
chang-ing grace; In ev - 'ry high and storm - y gale My
rag - ing flood; When all sup - ports are washed a - way, He
him be found, Clothed in his righ - teous - ness a - lone, Re -
whol - ly lean on Je - sus' name.
an - chor holds with - in the veil.
then is all my hope and stay.
deemed to stand be - fore the throne!
Refrain
On Christ, the sol - id rock, I stand; All
oth-er ground is sink-ing sand, All oth - er ground is sink-ing sand.

Text: Edward Mote, 1787–1874, alt.
Tune: William B. Bradbury, 1816–1868

THE SOLID ROCK
8888888

My Hope Is Built on Nothing Less

294

1 My hope is built on noth - ing less Than Je - sus'
2 When dark - ness veils his love - ly face, I rest on
3 His oath, his cov - e - nant, his blood Sus - tain me
4 When he shall come with trum - pet sound, Oh, may I
blood and righ - teous - ness; No mer - it of my
his un - chang - ing grace; In ev - 'ry high and
in the rag - ing flood; When all sup - ports are
then in him be found, Clothed in his righ - teous -
own I claim, But whol - ly lean on Je - sus' name.
storm - y gale My an - chor holds with - in the veil.
washed a - way, He then is all my hope and stay.
ness a - lone, Re - deemed to stand be - fore the throne!
Refrain
On Christ, the sol - id rock, I stand; All oth - er ground is sink - ing sand.

Text: Edward Mote, 1787–1874, alt.
Tune: John B. Dykes, 1823–1876

MELITA
88 88 88

295 Out of the Depths I Cry to You

1 Out of the depths I cry to you; O Fa - ther,
2 All things you send are full of grace; You crown our
3 It is in God that we shall hope, And not in
4 My soul is wait - ing for the Lord As one who
hear me call - ing. In - cline your ear to my dis - tress
lives with fa - vor. All our good works are done in vain
our own mer - it. We rest our fears in his good Word
longs for morn - ing; No watch - er waits with great - er hope
In spite of my re - bel - ling. Do not re - gard
With-out our Lord and Sav - ior. We praise the God
And trust his Ho - ly Spir - it. His prom - ise keeps
Than I for his re - turn - ing. I hope as Is -
my sin - ful deeds. Send me the grace my spir -
who gives us faith And saves us from the grip
us strong and sure; We trust the ho - ly sig -
rael in the Lord; He sends re - demp - tion through

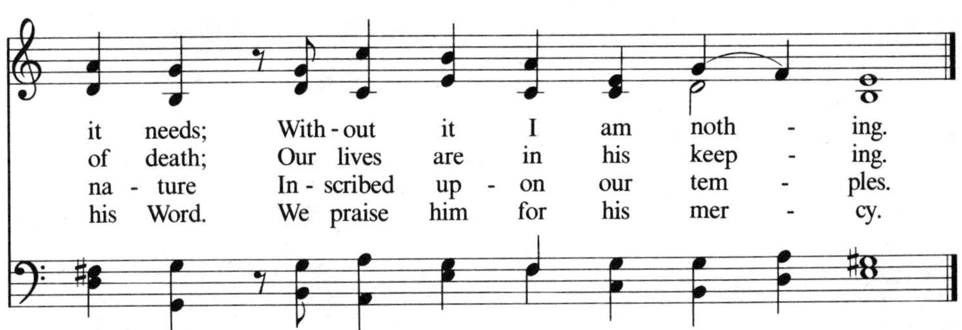
it needs; With - out it I am noth - ing.
of death; Our lives are in his keep - ing.
na - ture In - scribed up - on our tem - ples.
his Word. We praise him for his mer - cy.

© Text: Martin Luther, 1483–1546; tr. Gracia Grindal, b. 1943
Tune: Martin Luther, 1483–1546

AUS TIEFER NOT
87 87 887

Just as I Am, without One Plea

296

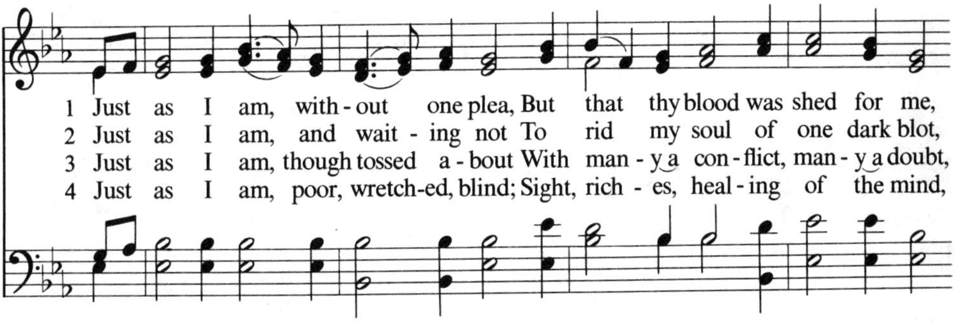

1 Just as I am, with - out one plea, But that thy blood was shed for me,
2 Just as I am, and wait - ing not To rid my soul of one dark blot,
3 Just as I am, though tossed a - bout With man - y a con - flict, man - y a doubt,
4 Just as I am, poor, wretch-ed, blind; Sight, rich - es, heal - ing of the mind,

And that thou bidd'st me come to thee,
To thee, whose blood can cleanse each spot,
Fight - ings and fears with - in, with - out,
Yea, all I need, in thee to find,

O Lamb of God, I come, I come.

5 Just as I am, thou wilt receive,
Wilt welcome, pardon, cleanse, relieve;
Because thy promise I believe,
O Lamb of God, I come, I come.

6 Just as I am; thy love unknown
Has broken ev'ry barrier down;
Now to be thine, yea, thine alone,
O Lamb of God, I come, I come.

Text: Charlotte Elliott, 1789–1871
Tune: William B. Bradbury, 1816–1868

WOODWORTH
LM

297 Salvation unto Us Has Come

1 Sal - va - tion un - to us has come By God's free grace and fa -
2 Theirs was a false, mis - lead - ing dream Who thought God's law was giv -
3 And yet the Law ful - filled must be, Or we were lost for - ev -
4 Faith clings to Je - sus' cross a - lone And rests in him un - ceas -

vor; Good works can - not a - vert our doom, They help and save us
en That sin - ners might them-selves re - deem And by their works gain
er; There - fore God sent his Son that he Might us from death de -
ing; And by its fruits true faith is known, With love and hope in -

nev - er. Faith looks to Je - sus Christ a - lone, Who did for
heav - en. The Law is but a mir - ror bright To bring the
liv - er. He all the Law for us ful - filled, And thus his
creas - ing. For faith a - lone can jus - ti - fy; Works serve our

all the world a - tone; He is our me - di - a - tor.
in - bred sin to light That lurks with - in our na - ture.
Fa - ther's an - ger stilled Which o - ver us im - pend - ed.
neigh-bor and sup - ply The proof that faith is liv - ing.

5 All blessing, honor, thanks, and praise
To Father, Son, and Spirit,
The God who saved us by his grace;
All glory to his merit.
O triune God in heav'n above,
You have revealed your saving love;
Your blessed name we hallow.

© *Text: Paul Speratus, 1484–1551; tr.* The Lutheran Hymnal, *1941, alt.*
Tune: Etlich christlich Lieder, *Wittenberg, 1524*

ES IST DAS HEIL
8 7 8 7 8 8 7

One There Is, above All Others 298

1 One there is, a - bove all oth - ers, Well de - serves the name of friend;
2 Which of all our friends, to save us, Could or would have shed his blood?
3 When he lived on earth, they scorned him; "Friend of sin - ners" was his name.
His is love be - yond a broth - er's, Cost - ly, free, and knows no end;
But this Sav - ior died to have us Rec - on - ciled in him to God;
Though the an - gels have a - dored him, Still he an - swers to that claim;
They who once his kind - ness prove Find it ev - er - last - ing love.
This was bound - less love in - deed; Je - sus is the friend we need.
Still he calls them dear - est friends And to all their needs at - tends.

Text: John Newton, 1725–1807, alt.
Tune: Andreas P. Berggren, 1801–1880

AMEN SJUNGE HVARJE TUNGA
8 7 8 7 7 7

299 Dear Christians, One and All

1 Dear Chris - tians, one and all, re - joice, With ex - ul -
2 Fast bound in Sa - tan's chains I lay, Death brood - ed
3 My own good works all came to naught, No grace or
4 But God had seen my wretch - ed state Be - fore the

ta - tion spring - ing, And, with u - nit - ed
dark - ly o'er me, Sin was my tor - ment
mer - it gain - ing; Free will a - gainst God's
world's foun - da - tion, And, mind - ful of his

heart and voice And ho - ly rap - ture sing - ing,
night and day; In sin my moth - er bore me.
judg - ment fought, Dead to all good re - main - ing.
mer - cies great, He planned for my sal - va - tion.

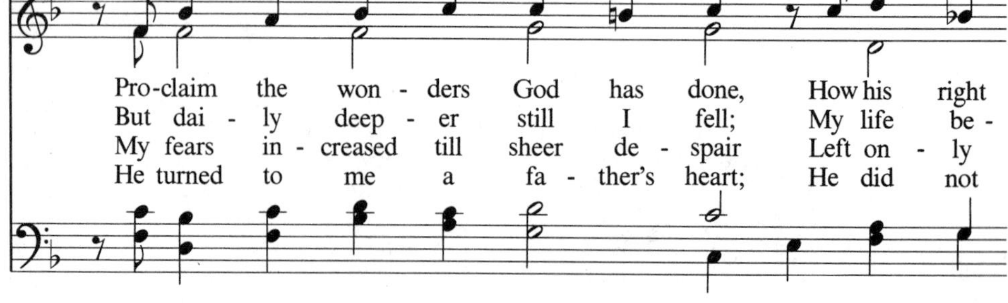
Pro-claim the won - ders God has done, How his right
But dai - ly deep - er still I fell; My life be -
My fears in - creased till sheer de - spair Left on - ly
He turned to me a fa - ther's heart; He did not

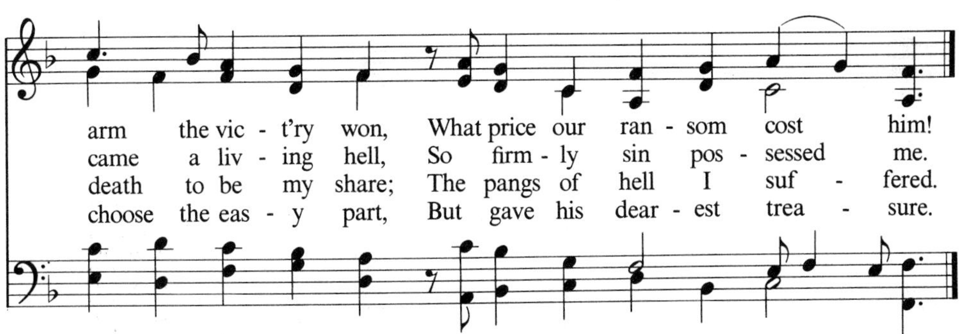
arm the vic - t'ry won, What price our ran - som cost him!
came a liv - ing hell, So firm - ly sin pos - sessed me.
death to be my share; The pangs of hell I suf - fered.
choose the eas - y part, But gave his dear - est trea - sure.

5 God said to his beloved Son:
"'Tis time to have compassion.
Then go, bright jewel of my crown,
And bring to all salvation;
From sin and sorrow set them free;
Slay bitter death for them that they
May live with you forever."

6 The Son obeyed his Father's will,
Was born of virgin mother;
And, God's good pleasure to fulfill,
He came to be my brother.
His royal pow'r disguised he bore,
A servant's form, like mine, he wore,
To lead the devil captive.

7 To me he said: "Stay close to me,
I am your rock and castle.
Your ransom I myself will be;
For you I strive and wrestle;
For I am yours, and you are mine,
And where I am you may remain;
The foe shall not divide us.

8 "Though he will shed my precious blood,
Of life me thus bereaving,
All this I suffer for your good;
Be steadfast and believing.
Life will from death the vict'ry win;
My innocence shall bear your sin;
And you are blest forever.

9 "Now to my Father I depart,
From earth to heav'n ascending,
And, heav'nly wisdom to impart,
The Holy Spirit sending;
In trouble he will comfort you
And teach you always to be true
And into truth shall guide you.

10 "What I on earth have done and taught
Guide all your life and teaching;
So shall the kingdom's work be wrought
And honored in your preaching.
But watch lest foes with base alloy
The heav'nly treasure should destroy;
This final word I leave you."

Text: Martin Luther, 1483–1546; tr. Richard Massie, 1800–1887, alt.
Tune: Etlich christlich Lieder, *Wittenberg, 1524*

NUN FREUT EUCH
87 87 887

300 O Christ, Our Hope

1 O Christ, our hope, our hearts' de - sire, Cre - a - tion's might-y Lord, Re - deem - er of the fall - en world, By ho - ly love out - poured, By ho - ly love out - poured:
2 How vast your mer - cy to ac - cept The bur - den of our sin, And bow your head in cru - el death To make us clean with - in, To make us clean with - in.
3 But now the bonds of death are burst, The ran - som has been paid; You now as - cend the Fa - ther's throne In robes of light ar - rayed, In robes of light ar - rayed.
4 Oh, let your might - y love pre - vail To purge us of our pride, That we may stand be - fore your throne By mer - cy pu - ri - fied, By mer - cy pu - ri - fied.

5 Christ Jesus, be our present joy,
Our future great reward;
Our only glory, may it be
To glory in the Lord!

6 All praise to you, ascended Lord;
All glory ever be
To Father, Son, and Holy Ghost
Through all eternity!

Text: Latin hymn, c. 8th cent.; tr. John Chandler, 1806–1876, adapt.
Tune: Nikolaus Herman, c. 1480–1561

LOBT GOTT, IHR CHRISTEN
86 866

Come to Calvary's Holy Mountain 301

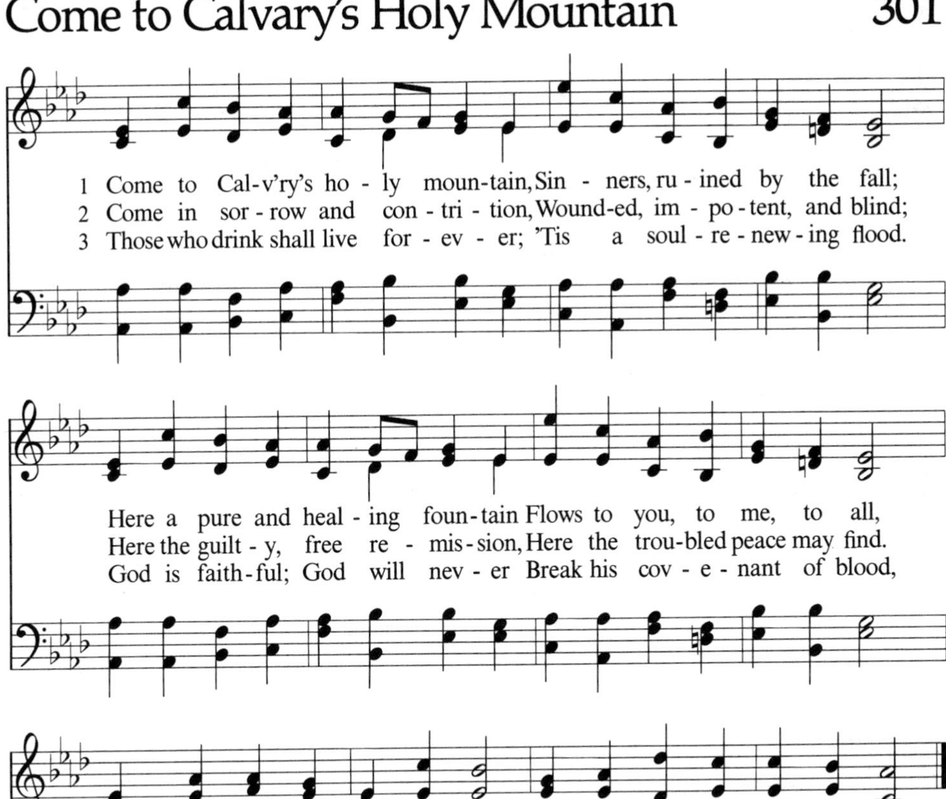
1 Come to Cal-v'ry's ho - ly moun-tain, Sin - ners, ru - ined by the fall;
2 Come in sor - row and con - tri - tion, Wound-ed, im - po - tent, and blind;
3 Those who drink shall live for - ev - er; 'Tis a soul - re - new - ing flood.
Here a pure and heal - ing foun - tain Flows to you, to me, to all,
Here the guilt - y, free re - mis - sion, Here the trou-bled peace may find.
God is faith - ful; God will nev - er Break his cov - e - nant of blood,
In a full per - pet - ual tide, O - pened when our Sav - ior died.
Health this foun - tain will re - store; Those who drink shall thirst no more.
Signed when our re - deem - er died, Sealed when he was glo - ri - fied.

Text: James Montgomery, 1771–1854
Tune: Ludvig M. Lindeman, 1812–1887

NAAR MIT ÖIE
87 87 77

302 Jesus, Your Blood and Righteousness

1 Je - sus, your blood and righ - teous - ness My beau - ty
2 Bold shall I stand in that great day, Cleansed and re -
3 Lord, I be - lieve your pre - cious blood, Which at the
4 Lord, I be - lieve, were sin - ners more Than sands up -

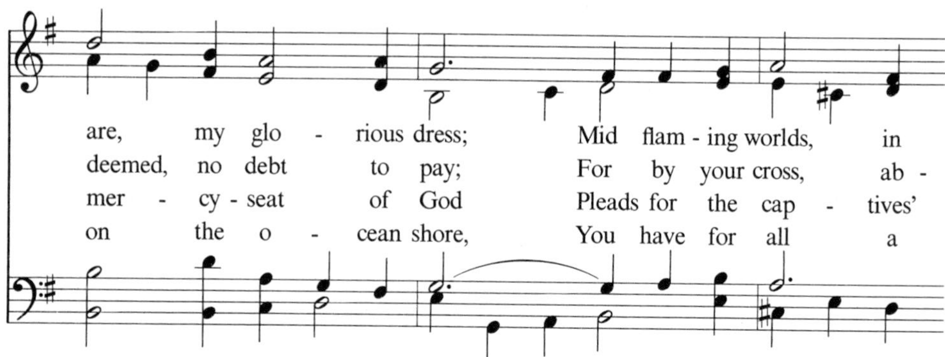
are, my glo - rious dress; Mid flam - ing worlds, in
deemed, no debt to pay; For by your cross, ab -
mer - cy - seat of God Pleads for the cap - tives'
on the o - cean shore, You have for all a

these ar - rayed, With joy shall I lift up my head.
solved I am From sin and guilt, from fear and shame.
lib - er - ty, Was al - so shed in love for me.
ran - som paid, For all a full a - tone - ment made.

5 When from the dust of death I rise
To claim my mansion in the skies,
This then shall be my only plea:
Christ Jesus lived and died for me.

6 Then shall I praise you and adore
Your blessed name forevermore,
Who once, for me and all you made,
An everlasting ransom paid.

Text: *Nicolaus L. von Zinzendorf, 1700–1760; tr. John Wesley, 1703–1791, alt.*
Tune: Gesang-Buch, *Nürnberg, 1676*

O JESU CHRISTE, WAHRES LICHT
LM

When in the Hour of Deepest Need 303

1 When in the hour of deep - est need We know not
2 Our com - fort then is this a - lone: That we may
3 For you have made a prom - ise true To par - don
4 And so we come, O God, to - day, And all our

where to look for aid; When days and nights of
meet be - fore your throne And cry to you, O
those who flee to you, Through him whose name a -
woes be - fore you lay; For sore - ly tried, cast

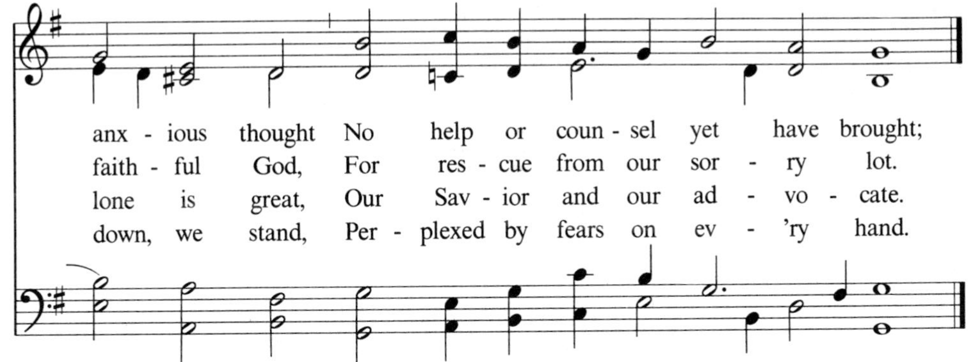
anx - ious thought No help or coun - sel yet have brought;
faith - ful God, For res - cue from our sor - ry lot.
lone is great, Our Sav - ior and our ad - vo - cate.
down, we stand, Per - plexed by fears on ev - 'ry hand.

5 Oh, from our sins hide not your face;
Absolve us through your boundless grace!
Be with us in our anguish still!
Free us at last from ev'ry ill!

6 So we with all our hearts each day
To you our glad thanksgiving pay,
Then walk obedient to your Word,
And now and ever praise you, Lord.

Text: Paul Eber, 1511–1569; tr. Catherine Winkworth, 1829–1878, alt.
Tune: Louis Bourgeois, c. 1510–c. 1561

WENN WIR IN HÖCHSTEN NÖTEN SEIN
LM

304 Today Your Mercy Calls Us

1 Today your mercy calls us
To wash away our sin.
However great our trespass,
Whatever we have been,
However long from mercy
Our hearts have turned away,
Your precious blood can wash us
And make us clean today.

2 Today your gate is open,
And all who enter in
Shall find a Father's welcome
And pardon for their sin.
The past shall be forgotten,
A present joy be giv'n,
A future grace be promised,
A glorious crown in heav'n.

3 Today our Father calls us;
His Holy Spirit waits;
His blessed angels gather
Around the heav'nly gates.
No question will be asked us,
How often we have come;
Although we oft have wandered,
It is our Father's home.

4 O all-embracing Mercy,
O ever-open Door,
What should we do without you
When heart and eye run o'er?
When all things seem against us,
To drive us to despair,
We know one gate is open,
One ear will hear our prayer.

Text: Oswald Allen, 1816–1878, alt.
Tune: Friedrich K. Anthes, b. 1812

ANTHES
76 76 D

I Lay My Sins on Jesus

305

1 I lay my sins on Je - sus, The spot - less Lamb of God;
2 I lay my wants on Je - sus; All full - ness dwells in him;
3 I rest my soul on Je - sus, This wea - ry soul of mine;
He bears them all and frees us From the ac - curs - ed load.
He heals all my dis - eas - es; My soul he does re - deem.
His right hand me em - brac - es; I on his breast re - cline.
I bring my guilt to Je - sus To wash my crim - son stains
I lay my griefs on Je - sus, My bur - dens and my cares;
I love the name of Je - sus, Im - man - uel, Christ, the Lord;
Clean in his blood most pre - cious Till not a spot re - mains.
He from them all re - leas - es; He all my sor - rows shares.
Like fra - grance on the breez - es His name a - broad is poured.

Text: *Horatius Bonar, 1808–1889*
Tune: Neu-vermehrtes Gesangbuch, *Meiningen, 1693*

MUNICH
76 76 D

306 Chief of Sinners though I Be

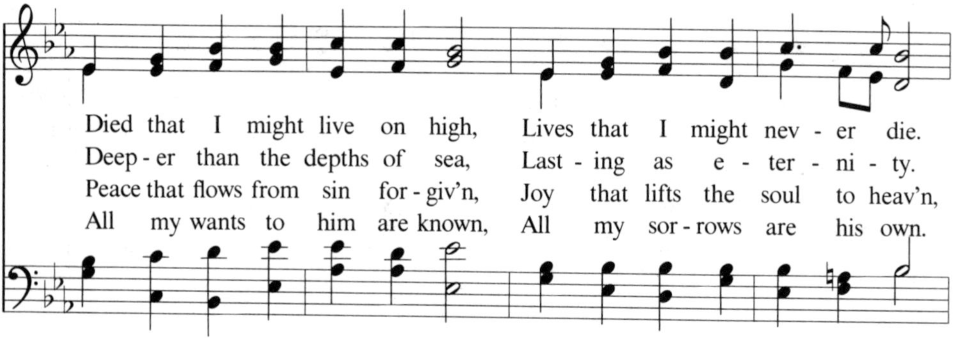

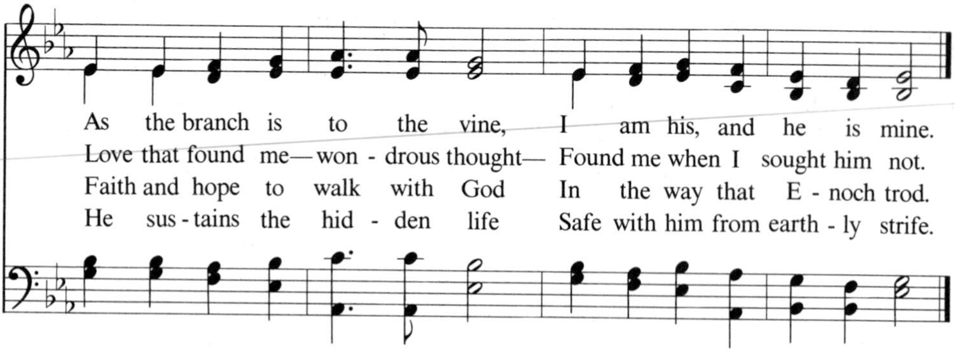

1 Chief of sinners though I be,
Jesus shed his blood for me,
Died that I might live on high,
Lives that I might never die.
As the branch is to the vine,
I am his, and he is mine.

2 Oh, the height of Jesus' love!
Higher than the heav'ns above,
Deeper than the depths of sea,
Lasting as eternity.
Love that found me—wondrous thought—
Found me when I sought him not.

3 Only Jesus can impart
Balm to heal the wounded heart,
Peace that flows from sin forgiv'n,
Joy that lifts the soul to heav'n,
Faith and hope to walk with God
In the way that Enoch trod.

4 Chief of sinners though I be,
Christ is All-in-All to me;
All my wants to him are known,
All my sorrows are his own.
He sustains the hidden life
Safe with him from earthly strife.

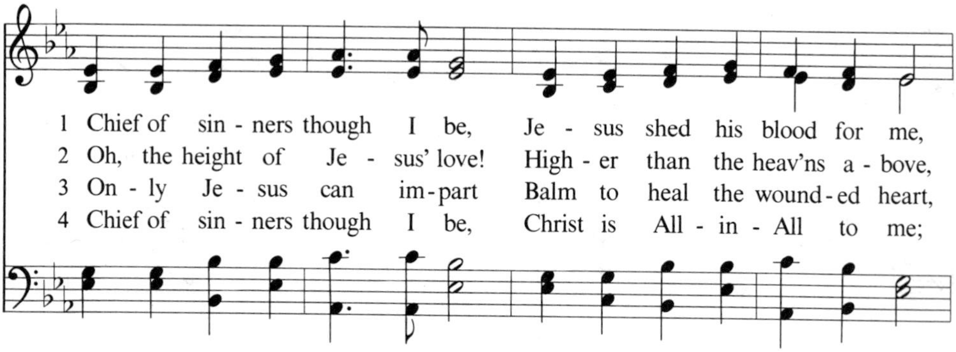

5 O my Savior, help afford
By your Spirit and your Word!
When my wayward heart would stray,
Keep me in the narrow way;
Grace in time of need supply
While I live and when I die.

Text: William McComb, 1793–c. 1870
Tune: Richard Redhead, 1820–1901

GETHSEMANE
77 77 77

Forgive Our Sins as We Forgive

307

Dm C F Dm Gm Dm
1 "For - give our sins as we for - give," You
2 How can your par - don reach and bless The
3 In blaz - ing light your cross re - veals The
4 Lord, cleanse the depths with - in our souls And
B♭ F Am Dm Am B♭ Dm C
taught us, Lord, to pray; But you a - lone can
un - for - giv - ing heart That broods on wrongs and
truth we dim - ly knew: How tri - fling oth - ers'
bid re - sent - ment cease; Then, by your mer - cy
F Dm Am F Gm Am7 Dm
grant us grace To live the words we say.
will not let Old bit - ter - ness de - part?
debts to us; How great our debt to you!
rec - on - ciled, Our lives will spread your peace.

© *Text:* *Rosamond E. Herklots, b. 1905, alt.*
Tune: The Sacred Harp, *Philadelphia, 1844*

DETROIT
CM

308 God the Father, Be Our Stay

1 God the Father, be our stay;
2 Jesus, Savior, be our stay; Oh, let us perish never!
3 Holy Spirit, be our stay;

Cleanse us from our sins, we pray, And grant us life forever.

Keep us from the evil one; Uphold our faith most holy,

And let us trust you solely With humble hearts and lowly.

Let us put God's armor on, With all true Christians running

Our heav'n-ly race and shun - ning The dev - il's wiles and cun - ning.
A - men! A - men! This be done; So sing we, "Hal - le - lu - jah!"

Text: *adapt. Martin Luther, 1483–1546; tr. Richard Massie, 1800–1887, alt.*
Tune: *J. Walther,* Geistliche Gesangbüchlein, *1524*

GOTT DER VATER WOHN UNS BEI
7777777 D

Lord Jesus, Think on Me 309

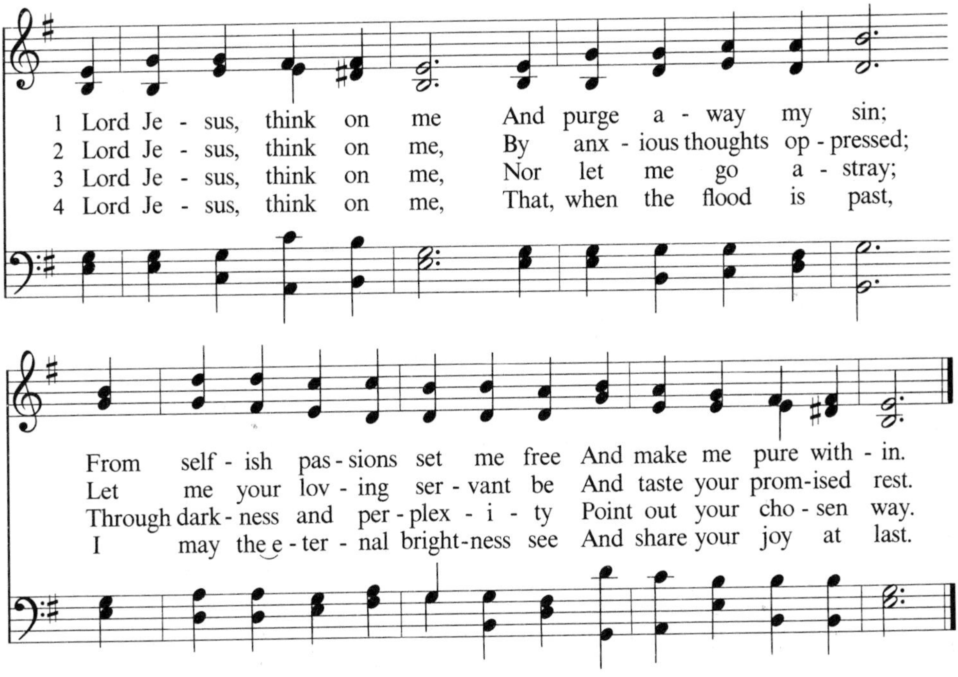

1 Lord Jesus, think on me
And purge away my sin;
From selfish passions set me free
And make me pure within.

2 Lord Jesus, think on me,
By anxious thoughts oppressed;
Let me your loving servant be
And taste your promised rest.

3 Lord Jesus, think on me,
Nor let me go astray;
Through darkness and perplexity
Point out your chosen way.

4 Lord Jesus, think on me,
That, when the flood is past,
I may the eternal brightness see
And share your joy at last.

Text: *Synesius of Cyrene, c. 375–430; tr. Allen W. Chatfield, 1808–1896, alt.*
Tune: *Daman,* Psalmes, *1579*

SOUTHWELL
SM

310 To You, Omniscient Lord of All

1 To you, om - ni - scient Lord of all, With grief and shame I hum - bly call; I see my sins a - gainst you, Lord, The sins of thought, of deed, and word. They press me sore; to you I flee: O God, be mer - ci - ful to me!
2 My Lord and God, to you I pray, Oh, cast me not in wrath a - way; Let your good Spir - it ne'er de - part, But let him draw to you my heart That tru - ly pen - i - tent I be: O God, be mer - ci - ful to me!
3 O Je - sus, let your pre - cious blood Be to my soul a cleans-ing flood. Turn not, O Lord, your guest a - way, But grant that jus - ti - fied I may Go to my house, at peace to be: O God, be mer - ci - ful to me!

Text: Magnus B. Landstad, 1802–1880; tr. Carl Doving, 1867–1937, alt.
Tune: V. Schumann, Geistliche Lieder, *1539*

VATER UNSER
88 88 88

Wondrous Are Your Ways, O God! 311

1 Won - drous are your ways, O God! No one can es - cape you!
2 Search me, God, and know my heart, Lord of truth and mer - cy.
Far-thest space nor deep - est hell Can - not hide me from you!
From a - far, O Lord, you know All my thoughts, my se - crets.
Long be - fore I came to birth, Your eye saw and knew me.
And if an - y wick - ed way Should be found with - in me,
E - ven in life's dark - est hour In your hand you hold me.
Cleanse, for - give me by your grace; Grant me life e - ter - nal.

 Text: Joel W. Lundeen, b. 1918, st. 1; Claus A. Wendell, 1866–1950, st. 2, alt.
Tune: Gunnar Wennerberg, 1817–1901

WENNERBERG
76 76 D

312 Once He Came in Blessing

1 Once he came in bless - ing, All our ills re - dress - ing; Came in
2 Still he comes with - in us; Still his voice would win us From the
3 Thus, if you have known him, Not a-shamed to own him, Nor have
4 Those who then are loy - al Find a wel - come roy - al. Come, then,
like - ness low - ly, Son of God most ho - ly;
sins that hurt us; Would to truth con - vert us
spurned him cold - ly, But will trust him bold - ly,
O Lord Je - sus, From our sins re - lease us;
Bore the cross to save us; Hope and free-dom gave us.
From our fool - ish er - ror Ere he comes in ter - ror.
He will then re - ceive you, Heal you, and for - give you.
Let us here con - fess you, Till in heav'n we bless you.

Text: Johann Horn, c. 1490–1547; tr. Catherine Winkworth, 1829–1878, alt.
Tune: Bohemian Brethren, Ein New Gesengbuchlen, *1531*

GOTTES SOHN IST KOMMEN
66 66 66

A Multitude Comes from East and West 313

1 A mul - ti - tude comes from the east and the west To
2 O God, let us hear when our shep - herd shall call In
3 All tri - als shall be like a dream that is past; For -
4 The heav - ens shall ring with an an - them more grand Than
sit at the feast of sal - va - tion With A - bra - ham,
ac - cents per - sua - sive and ten - der, That while there is
got - ten all trou - ble and mourn - ing. All ques - tions and
ev - er on earth was re - cord - ed; The blest of the
I - saac, and Ja - cob, the blest, O - bey - ing the Lord's in - vi -
time we make haste, one and all, And find him, our might - y de -
doubts have been an-swered at last, When ris - es the light of that
Lord shall re - ceive at his hand The crown to the vic - tors a -
ta - tion.
fend - er.
morn - ing.
ward - ed.
Have mer - cy up - on us, O Je - sus!

Text: Magnus B. Landstad, 1802–1880; tr. Peer O. Strömme, 1856–1921, adapt.
Tune: Swedish, 1694

DER MANGE SKAL KOMME
119 119 9

314 Who Is This Host Arrayed in White

1 Who is this host ar - rayed in white Like thou - sand snow - clad moun - tains bright, That stands with palms and sings its psalms Be - fore the throne of light? These are the saints who kept God's Word; They are the hon - ored
2 On earth their work was not thought wise, But see them now in heav - en's eyes; Be - fore God's throne of pre - cious stone They shout their vic - t'ry cries. On earth they wept through bit - ter years; Now God has wiped a -
3 O bless - ed saints, now take your rest; A thou - sand times shall you be blest For keep - ing faith firm un - to death And scorn - ing world - ly trust. For now you live at home with God And har - vest seeds once

of the Lord. He is their prince who drowned their sins,
way their tears, Trans - formed their strife to heav'n - ly life,
cast a - broad In tears and sighs. See with new eyes
So they were cleansed, re - stored. They now serve God both
And freed them from their fears. For now they have the
The pat - tern in the seed. The myr - iad an - gels
day and night; They sing their songs in end - less light. Their
best at last; They keep their sweet e - ter - nal feast. At
raise their song. O saints, sing with that hap - py throng; Lift
an - thems ring when they all sing With an - gels shin - ing bright.
God's right hand our Lord com-mands; He is both host and guest.
up one voice; let heav'n re - joice In our Re - deem - er's song!

 Text: Hans A. Brorson, 1694–1764; tr. Gracia Grindal, b. 1943
Tune: Norwegian folk tune, 17th cent.

DEN STORE HVIDE FLOK
PM

315 Love Divine, All Loves Excelling

1 Love di - vine, all loves ex - cel - ling, Joy of heav'n, to earth come
2 Breathe, oh, breathe thy lov - ing Spir - it In - to ev - 'ry trou - bled
3 Come, Al - might - y, to de - liv - er; Let us all thy life re-
4 Fin - ish then thy new cre - a - tion, Pure and spot - less let us
down! Fix in us thy hum - ble dwell - ing, All thy faith - ful
breast; Let us all in thee in - her - it; Let us find thy
ceive; Sud - den - ly re - turn, and nev - er, Nev - er-more thy
be; Let us see thy great sal - va - tion Per - fect - ly re-
mer - cies crown. Je - sus, thou art all com - pas - sion,
prom - ised rest. Take a - way the love of sin - ning;
tem - ples leave. Thee we would be al - ways bless - ing,
stored in thee! Changed from glo - ry in - to glo - ry,
Pure, un - bound - ed love thou art; Vis - it us with
Al - pha and O - me - ga be; End of faith, as
Serve thee as thy hosts a - bove, Pray, and praise thee
Till in heav'n we take our place, Till we cast our

thy sal - va - tion, En - ter ev - ’ry trem - bling heart.
its be - gin - ning, Set our hearts at lib - er - ty.
with - out ceas - ing, Glo - ry in thy per - fect love.
crowns be - fore thee, Lost in won - der, love, and praise!

Text: Charles Wesley, 1707–1788
Tune: Rowland H. Prichard, 1811–1887

HYFRYDOL
87 87 D

Jesus, the Very Thought of You 316

1 Je - sus, the ver - y thought of you Fills us with sweet de - light;
2 No voice can sing, no heart can frame, Nor can the mind re - call
3 O Hope of ev - ’ry con - trite soul, O Joy of all the meek,
4 O Je - sus, be our joy to - day; Help us to prize your love;

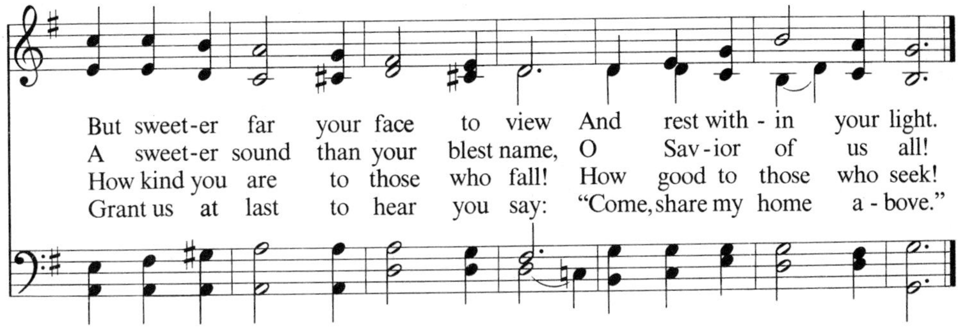

But sweet-er far your face to view And rest with - in your light.
A sweet-er sound than your blest name, O Sav - ior of us all!
How kind you are to those who fall! How good to those who seek!
Grant us at last to hear you say: “Come, share my home a - bove.”

Text: attr. Bernard of Clairvaux, 1091–1153; tr. Edward Caswall, 1814–1878, alt.
Tune: John B. Dykes, 1823–1876

ST. AGNES
CM

317 To God the Holy Spirit Let Us Pray

1 To God the Ho - ly Spir - it let us pray
2 O sweet - est Love, your grace on us be - stow;
3 Tran - scen - dent com - fort in our ev - 'ry need,
4 Shine in our hearts, O Spir - it, pre - cious light;
Most of all for faith up - on our way,
Set our hearts with sa - cred fire a - glow,
Help us nei - ther scorn nor death to heed,
Teach us Je - sus Christ to know a - right,
That he may de - fend us when life is end - ing
That with hearts u - nit - ed we love each oth - er,
That we may not fal - ter, nor cour - age fail us
That we may a - bide in the Lord who bought us,
And from ex - ile home we are wend - ing.
Ev - 'ry strang - er, sis - ter, and broth - er.
When the foe shall taunt and as - sail us.
Till to our true home he has brought us.
Lord, have mer - cy!

© *Text: source unknown, st. 1; Martin Luther, 1483–1546, sts. 2–4; tr.* Worship Supplement, *1969, adapt.*
Tune: J. Walther, Geistliche Gesangbüchlein, *1524*

NUN BITTEN WIR
109 119 4

The Lord Will Come and Not Be Slow 318

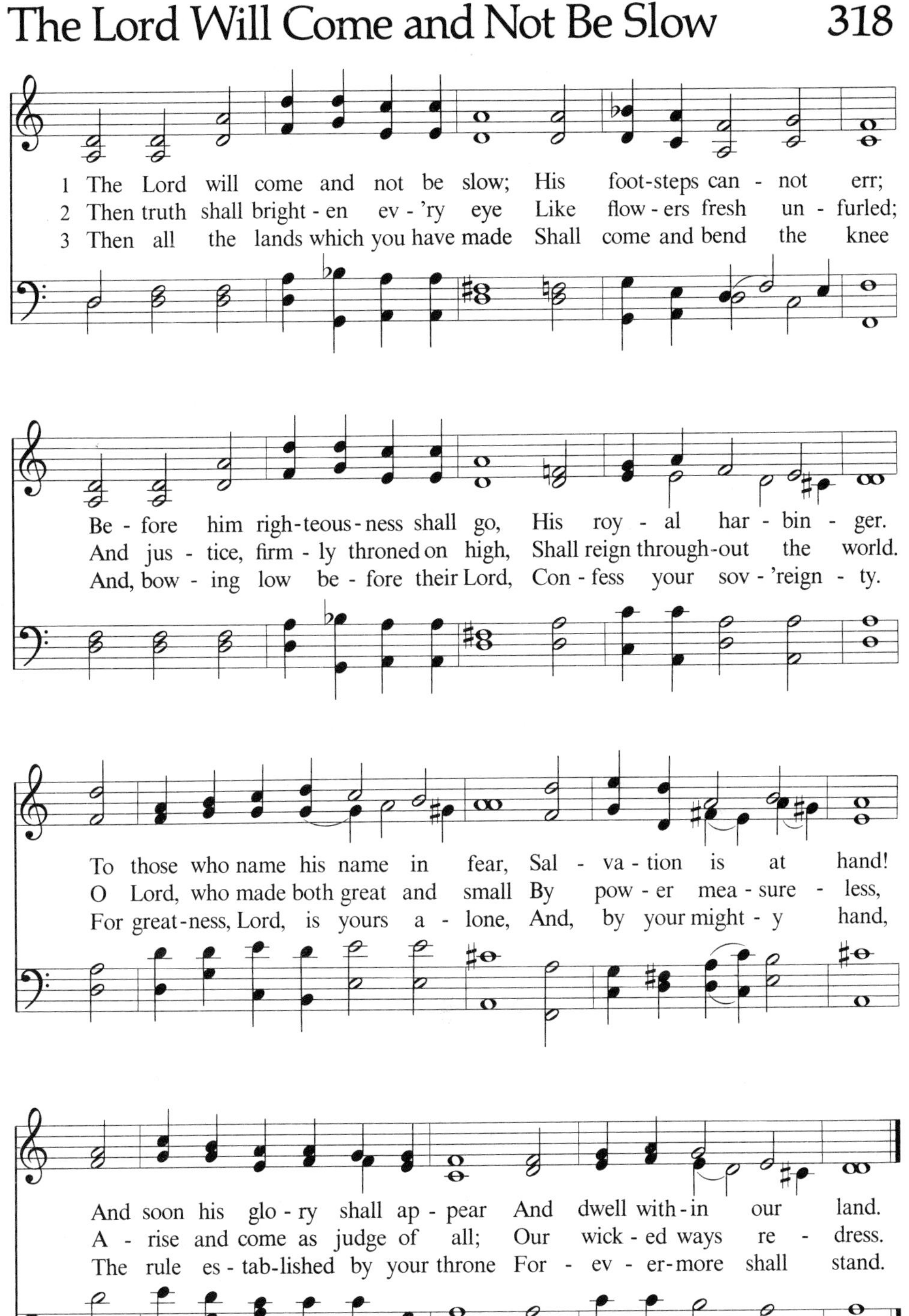
1 The Lord will come and not be slow; His foot-steps can - not err;
2 Then truth shall bright - en ev - 'ry eye Like flow - ers fresh un - furled;
3 Then all the lands which you have made Shall come and bend the knee
Be - fore him righ-teous-ness shall go, His roy - al har - bin - ger.
And jus - tice, firm - ly throned on high, Shall reign through-out the world.
And, bow - ing low be - fore their Lord, Con - fess your sov - 'reign - ty.
To those who name his name in fear, Sal - va - tion is at hand!
O Lord, who made both great and small By pow - er mea - sure - less,
For great-ness, Lord, is yours a - lone, And, by your might - y hand,
And soon his glo - ry shall ap - pear And dwell with - in our land.
A - rise and come as judge of all; Our wick - ed ways re - dress.
The rule es - tab-lished by your throne For - ev - er-more shall stand.

Text: John Milton, 1608–1674, adapt.
Tune: Marot, Trente Pseaulmes de David, *1542*

OLD 107TH
CMD

319 Oh, Sing, My Soul, Your Maker's Praise

1 Oh, sing, my soul, your mak - er's praise, In grate - ful
2 The Lord is good to those who seek His face in
3 The Lord will turn his face in peace When trou - bled
hymns as - cend - ing; Whose stead - fast love has crowned your
time of sor - row, Pro - vid - ing com - fort to the
souls draw near him; His lov - ing - kind - ness shall not
days With heav'n - ly gifts un - end - ing. I sought the
weak And grace for each to - mor - row. Though grief may
cease To those who trust and fear him. Our God will
Lord; he heard my cry; His ho - ly an - gels hov - er
tar - ry for the night, The morn shall break in joy and
not for - sake his own; E - ter - nal is his heav'n - ly

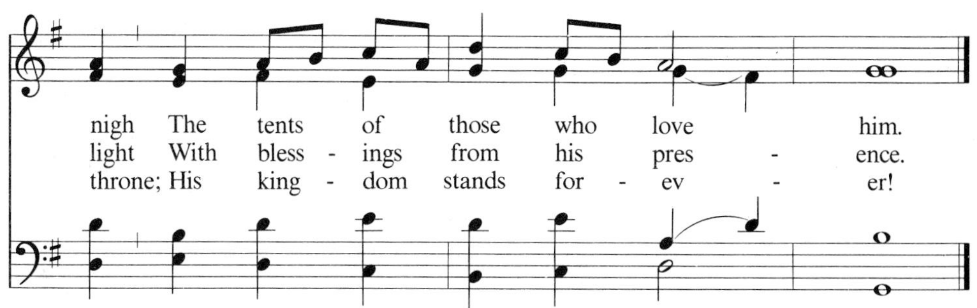
nigh The tents of those who love him.
light With bless - ings from his pres - ence.
throne; His king - dom stands for - ev - er!

© *Text: Julius Krohn, 1835–1888 tr. composite, alt.*
Tune: C. Egenolf, Reutterliedlein, *1535*

WÄCHTERLIED
8 7 8 7 8 8 7

O God, Our Help in Ages Past 320

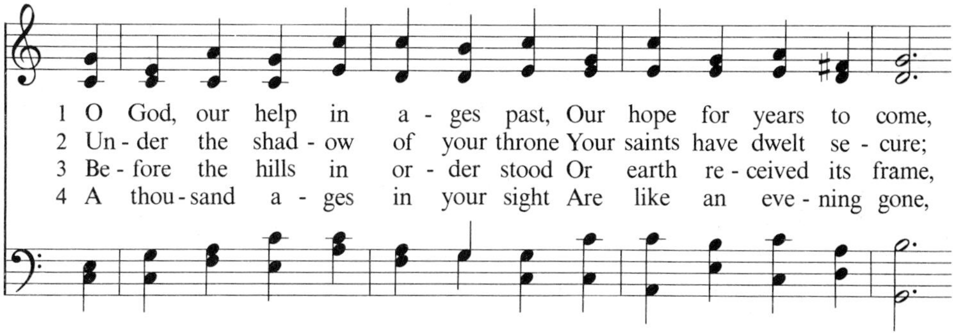

1 O God, our help in a - ges past, Our hope for years to come,
2 Un - der the shad - ow of your throne Your saints have dwelt se - cure;
3 Be - fore the hills in or - der stood Or earth re - ceived its frame,
4 A thou - sand a - ges in your sight Are like an eve - ning gone,

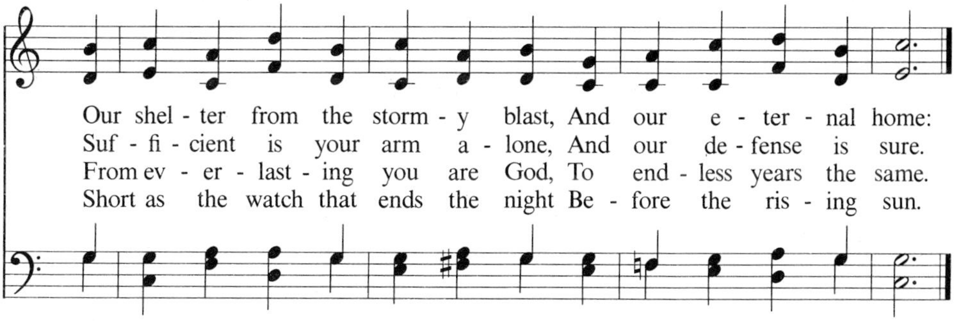

Our shel - ter from the storm - y blast, And our e - ter - nal home:
Suf - fi - cient is your arm a - lone, And our de - fense is sure.
From ev - er - last - ing you are God, To end - less years the same.
Short as the watch that ends the night Be - fore the ris - ing sun.

5 Time, like an ever-rolling stream,
Soon bears us all away;
We fly forgotten, as a dream
Dies at the op'ning day.

6 O God, our help in ages past,
Our hope for years to come,
Still be our guard while troubles last
And our eternal home!

Text: Isaac Watts, 1674–1748, alt.
Tune: William Croft, 1678–1727

ST. ANNE
CM

321 The Day Is Surely Drawing Near

1 The day is sure - ly draw - ing near When Je - sus, God's a -
2 The fi - nal trum - pet then shall sound, And all the earth be
3 May Christ our in - ter - ces - sor be And, through his blood and
4 O Je - sus Christ, do not de - lay, But has - ten our sal -
noint - ed, In all his pow - er shall ap - pear As judge whom
shak - en, And all who rest be - neath the ground Shall from their
mer - it, Read from his book that we are free With all who
va - tion; We of - ten trem - ble on our way In fear and
God ap - point - ed. Then fright shall ban - ish i - dle mirth, And
sleep a - wak - en. But all who live will in that hour, By
life in - her - it. Then we shall see him face to face, With
trib - u - la - tion. Oh, hear and grant our fer - vent plea; Come,
hun - gry flames shall rav - age earth, As Scrip - ture long has warned us.
God's al - might - y, bound - less pow'r, Be changed at his com - mand - ing.
all his saints in that blest place Which he has pur - chased for us.
might - y judge, and set us free From death and ev - 'ry e - vil.

Text: Bartholomäus Ringwaldt, 1532–c. 1600; tr. Philip A. Peter, 1832–1917, adapt.
Tune: Etlich christlich Lieder, *Wittenberg, 1524*

ES IST GEWISSLICH
87 87 887

The Clouds of Judgment Gather 322

1 The clouds of judg-ment gath - er; The time is grow - ing late;
2 A - rise, O true dis - ci - ples; Let wrong give way to right,
3 The home of fade - less splen - dor, Of blooms that bear no thorn,
4 Oh, hap - py, ho - ly por - tion, Re - lief for all dis-tressed,
Be so - ber and be watch - ful; Our judge is at the gate:
And pen - i - ten-tial shad - ow To Je - sus' bless - ed light:
Where they shall dwell as chil - dren Who here as ex - iles mourn;
True vi - sion of true beau - ty, Re - fresh - ment for the blest!
The judge who comes in mer - cy, The judge who comes in might
The light that has no eve - ning, That knows no moon or sun,
The peace of all the faith - ful, The calm of all the blest,
Strive now to win that glo - ry; Toil now to gain that light;
To put an end to e - vil And di - a - dem the right.
The light so new and gold - en, The light that is but one.
In - vi - o-late, un - fad - ing, Di - vin - est, sweet - est, best.
Send hope a-head to grasp it, Till hope be lost in sight.

© *Text: Bernard of Cluny, 12th cent.; tr. hymnal version, 1978*
Tune: Irish

DURROW
76 76 D

323 O Lord of Light, Who Made the Stars

1 O Lord of light, who made the stars, O Dawn, by whom we
2 In low - li - ness you came on earth To res - cue us from
3 To pay the debt we owed for sin Your pain - ful cross was
4 But now you reign, the King of kings, A - dored in high - est

see the way, O Christ, re - deem - er of the world:
Sa - tan's snares; Oh, won - drous love that healed our wounds
made the price; From bless - ed Mar - y's womb you came,
maj - es - ty; Your ver - y name is held in awe

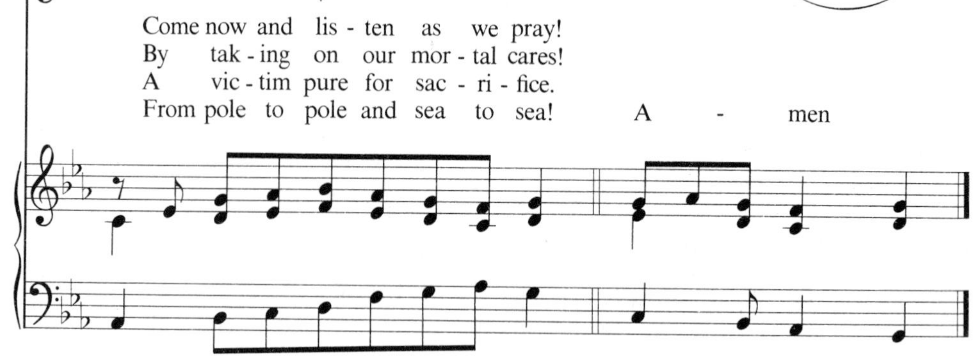
Come now and lis - ten as we pray!
By tak - ing on our mor - tal cares!
A vic - tim pure for sac - ri - fice.
From pole to pole and sea to sea!
A - men

5 Great judge of all, on earth's last day
Have pity on your children's plight;
Rise up to shield us with your grace;
Deliver us from Satan's might.

6 To God the Father and the Son
And Holy Spirit, Three in One,
Praise, honor, might, and glory be
From age to age eternally. Amen

 Text: Latin hymn, c. 9th cent.; tr. Melvin Farrell, b. 1930, alt.
Tune: Sarum plainsong, mode IV

CONDITOR ALME SIDERUM
LM

O Love That Will Not Let Me Go 324

1 O Love that will not let me go, I rest my wea-ry soul in thee; I give thee back the life I owe, That in thine o-cean depths its flow May rich-er, full-er be.
2 O Light that fol-lowest all my way, I yield my flick-'ring torch to thee; My heart re-stores its bor-rowed ray, That in thy sun-shine's blaze its day May bright-er, fair-er be.
3 O Joy that seek-est me through pain, I can-not close my heart to thee; I trace the rain-bow through the rain And feel the prom-ise is not vain That morn shall tear-less be.
4 O Cross that lift-est up my head, I dare not ask to fly from thee; I lay in dust life's glo-ry dead, And from the ground there blos-soms red Life that shall end-less be.

Text: George Matheson, 1842–1906, alt.
Tune: Albert L. Peace, 1844–1912

ST. MARGARET
88 886

325 Lord, Thee I Love with All My Heart

1 Lord, thee I love with all my heart; I pray thee, ne'er from
2 Yea, Lord, 'twas thy rich boun - ty gave My bod - y, soul, and
3 Lord, let at last thine an - gels come, To A - br'hams bo - som

me de - part; With ten - der mer - cy cheer me. Earth
all I have In this poor life of la - bor. Lord,
bear me home, That I may die un - fear - ing; And

has no plea - sure I would share, Yea, heav'n it - self were
grant that I in ev - 'ry place May glo - ri - fy thy
in its nar - row cham - ber keep My bod - y safe in

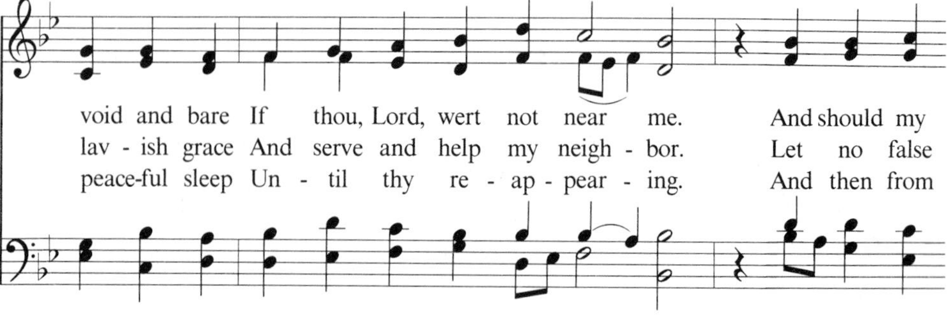
void and bare If thou, Lord, wert not near me. And should my
lav - ish grace And serve and help my neigh - bor. Let no false
peace-ful sleep Un - til thy re - ap - pear - ing. And then from

heart for sor - row break, My trust in thee can noth - ing shake.
doc-trine me be - guile, Let Sa - tan not my soul de - file.
death a - wak - en me, That these mine eyes with joy may see,
Thou art the por - tion I have sought; Thy pre - cious
Give strength and pa - tience un - to me To bear my
O Son of God, thy glo - rious face, My Sav - ior
blood my soul has bought. Lord Je - sus Christ, My God and
cross and fol - low thee. Lord Je - sus Christ, My God and
and my fount of grace. Lord Je - sus Christ, My prayer at -
Lord, my God and Lord, For - sake me not! I trust thy Word.
Lord, my God and Lord, In death thy com - fort still af - ford.
tend, my prayer at - tend, And I will praise thee with - out end!

Text: Martin Schalling, 1532–1608; tr. Catherine Winkworth, 1829–1878, alt.
Tune: B. Schmid, Orgeltabulatur-Buch, *1577*

HERZLICH LIEB
PM

326 My Heart Is Longing

1 My heart is long - ing to praise my Sav - ior
2 O bless - ed Je - sus, what you have giv - en,
3 O Chris - tian friends, let our song as - cend - ing
4 Soon we are home and shall stand be - fore him;
And glo - ri - fy his name in song and prayer;
Through dy - ing on the cross in bit - ter pain,
Give hon - or, praise to him who set us free!
What mat - ter then that we have suf - fered here?
For he has shown me his won - drous fa - vor
Has filled my heart with the peace of heav - en;
Our trib - u - la - tions may seem un - end - ing;
Then he shall crown us, while we a - dore him;
And of - fered me all heav'n with him to share.
My win - ter's gone, and spring is mine a - gain.
But soon with him we shall for - ev - er be.
So death and all our pains will dis - ap - pear.

5 To you, O Savior, our adoration
Shall rise forever for your precious blood
Which blotted out all the accusation
Of sin and guilt which once against us stood.

6 What blessed joy overflows my spirit,
Because your wondrous grace to me was giv'n!
Complete your work, that I may inherit
Eternal life at last with you in heav'n!

 Text: Princess Eugenie of Sweden; tr. Peter A. Sveeggen, 1881–1959, alt.
Tune: Norwegian folk tune

PRINCESS EUGENIE
10 10 10 10

Rock of Ages, Cleft for Me

327

1 Rock of A - ges, cleft for me, Let me hide my - self in thee;
2 Not the la - bors of my hands Can ful - fill thy law's de - mands;
3 Noth-ing in my hand I bring; Sim - ply to thy cross I cling.
4 While I draw this fleet - ing breath, When mine eye - lids close in death,
Let the wa - ter and the blood, From thy riv - en side which flowed,
Could my zeal no res - pite know, Could my tears for - ev - er flow,
Na - ked, come to thee for dress; Help - less, look to thee for grace;
When I soar to worlds un-known, See thee on thy judg-ment throne,
Be of sin the dou - ble cure: Cleanse me from its guilt and pow'r.
All for sin could not a - tone; Thou must save, and thou a - lone.
Foul, I to the foun - tain fly; Wash me, Sav - ior, or I die.
Rock of A - ges, cleft for me, Let me hide my - self in thee.

Text: Augustus M. Toplady, 1740–1778
Tune: Thomas Hastings, 1784–1872

TOPLADY
77 77 77

328 All Hail the Power of Jesus' Name!

1 All hail the pow'r of Je - sus' name! Let an - gels pros - trate fall;
2 Crown him, you mar - tyrs of our God, Who from his al - tar call;
3 O seed of Is - rael's cho - sen race Now ran - somed from the fall,
4 Hail him, you heirs of Da - vid's line, Whom Da - vid Lord did call—
Bring forth the roy - al di - a - dem And crown him Lord of all.
Ex - tol the stem of Jes - se's rod And crown him Lord of all.
Hail him who saves you by his grace And crown him Lord of all.
The God In - car - nate, man di - vine— And crown him Lord of all.
Bring forth the roy - al di - a - dem And crown him Lord of all.
Ex - tol the stem of Jes - se's rod And crown him Lord of all.
Hail him who saves you by his grace And crown him Lord of all.
The God In - car - nate, man di - vine—And crown him Lord of all.

5 Sinners, whose love can ne'er forget
The wormwood and the gall,
Go, spread your trophies at his feet
And crown him Lord of all.

6 Let ev'ry kindred, ev'ry tribe
On this terrestrial ball
To him all majesty ascribe
And crown him Lord of all.

7 Oh, that with yonder sacred throng
We at his feet may fall!
We'll join the everlasting song
And crown him Lord of all.

Text: Edward Perronet, 1726–1792, alt.
Tune: Oliver Holden, 1765–1844

CORONATION
86 86 86

All Hail the Power of Jesus' Name!

329

1 All hail the pow'r of Je - sus' name! Let an - gels pros - trate fall;
Bring forth the roy - al di - a - dem,

2 Crown him, you mar - tyrs of our God, Who from his al - tar call;
Ex - tol the stem of Jes - se's rod,

3 O seed of Is - rael's cho - sen race Now ran - somed from the fall,
Hail him who saves you by his grace,

4 Hail him, you heirs of Da - vid's line, Whom Da - vid Lord did call—
The God In - car - nate, man di - vine—

Refrain

And crown him, crown him, crown him, Crown him Lord of all.

5 Sinners, whose love can ne'er forget
The wormwood and the gall,
Go, spread your trophies at his feet,
Refrain

6 Let ev'ry kindred, ev'ry tribe
On this terrestrial ball
To him all majesty ascribe,
Refrain

7 Oh, that with yonder sacred throng
We at his feet may fall!
We'll join the everlasting song,
Refrain

Text: Edward Perronet, 1726–1792, alt.
Tune: William Shrubsole, 1760–1806

MILES LANE
868 and refrain

330 In Heaven Above

1 In heav'n a - bove, in heav'n a - bove, Where God our Fa - ther dwells: How bound - less there the bless - ed - ness! No tongue its great - ness tells. There face to face, and full and free, The ev - er -
2 In heav'n a - bove, in heav'n a - bove, What glo - ry deep and bright! The splen - dor of the noon - day sun Grows pale be - fore its light. The might - y sun that goes not down, Be - fore whose
3 In heav'n a - bove, in heav'n a - bove, No tears of pain are shed, For noth - ing there can fade or die; Life's full - ness round is spread, And like an o - cean, joy o'er - flows, And with im -
4 In heav'n a - bove, in heav'n a - bove, God has a joy pre - pared, Which mor - tal ear has nev - er heard, Nor mor - tal vi - sion shared, Which nev - er en - tered mor - tal thought, In mor - tal

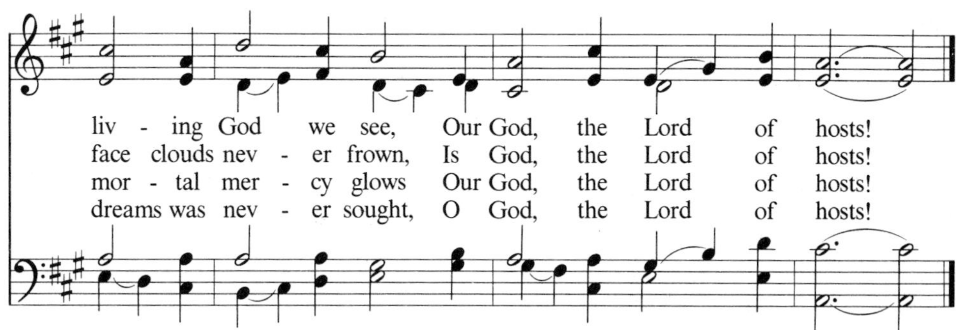
liv - ing God we see, Our God, the Lord of hosts!
face clouds nev - er frown, Is God, the Lord of hosts!
mor - tal mer - cy glows Our God, the Lord of hosts!
dreams was nev - er sought, O God, the Lord of hosts!

Text: *Laurentius L. Laurinus, 1573–1655, adapt.; tr. William Maccall, 1812–1888, alt.*
Tune: *Norwegian folk tune*

I HIMMELEN, I HIMMELEN
86 86 886

Jerusalem, My Happy Home 331

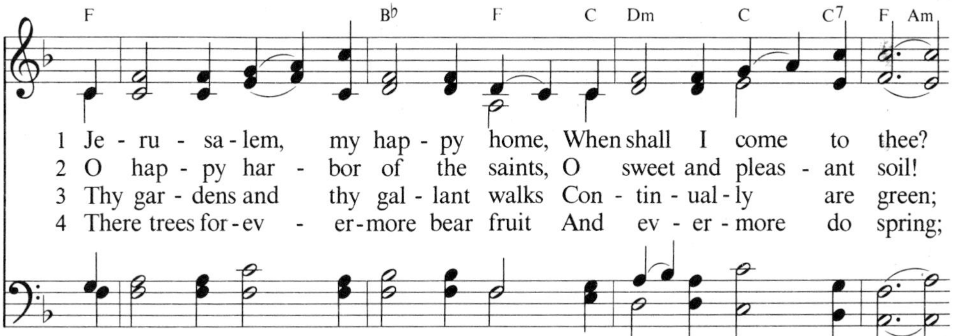

F B♭ F C Dm C C7 F Am

1 Je - ru - sa - lem, my hap - py home, When shall I come to thee?
2 O hap - py har - bor of the saints, O sweet and pleas - ant soil!
3 Thy gar - dens and thy gal - lant walks Con - tin - ual - ly are green;
4 There trees for - ev - er - more bear fruit And ev - er - more do spring;

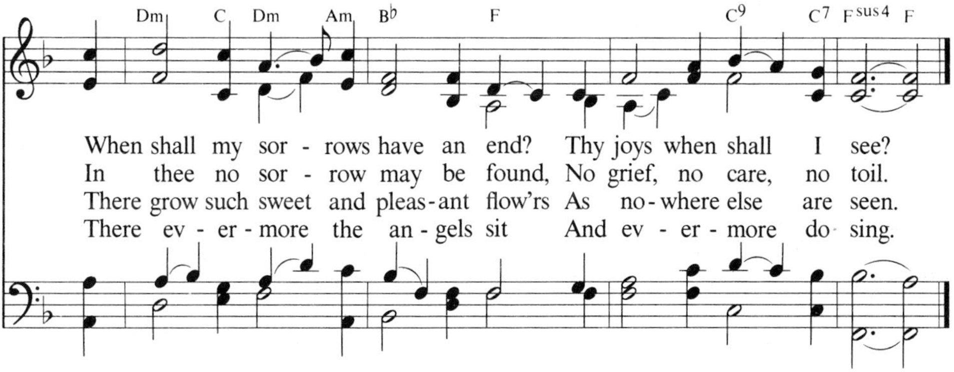

Dm C Dm Am B♭ F C9 C7 Fsus4 F

When shall my sor - rows have an end? Thy joys when shall I see?
In thee no sor - row may be found, No grief, no care, no toil.
There grow such sweet and pleas - ant flow'rs As no - where else are seen.
There ev - er - more the an - gels sit And ev - er - more do sing.

5 Jerusalem, my happy home,
Would God I were in thee!
Would God my woes were at an end,
Thy joys that I might see!

Text: F.B.P., *16th cent.*
Tune: *American*

LAND OF REST
CM

332 Battle Hymn of the Republic

1 Mine eyes have seen the glo - ry of the com - ing of the Lord;
2 He has sound - ed forth the trum - pet that shall nev - er call re - treat;
3 In the beau - ty of the lil - ies Christ was born a - cross the sea,

He is tram - pling out the vin - tage where the grapes of wrath are stored;
He is sift - ing out the hearts of men be - fore his judg - ment seat.
With a glo - ry in his bo - som that trans - fig - ures you and me.

He has loosed the fate - ful light - ning of his ter - ri - ble swift sword:
Oh, be swift, my soul, to an - swer him; be ju - bi - lant, my feet!
As he died to make men ho - ly, let us live to make men free,

His truth is march - ing on.
Our God is march - ing on.
While God is march - ing on.

Refrain

Glo - ry, glo - ry! Hal - le -

lu - jah! Glo - ry, glo - ry! Hal - le - lu - jah! Glo - ry,
glo - ry! Hal - le - lu - jah! His truth is march - ing on.

Text: Julia Ward Howe, 1819–1910
Tune: American, 19th cent.

BATTLE HYMN
15 15 15 6 and refrain

333 Lord, Take My Hand and Lead Me

1 Lord, take my hand and lead me Up - on life's way;
2 Lord, when the tem - pest ra - ges, I need not fear;
3 Lord, when the shad - ows length - en And night has come,
Di - rect, pro - tect, and feed me From day to day.
For you, the Rock of A - ges, Are al - ways near.
I know that you will strength - en My steps toward home,
With-out your grace and fa - vor I go a - stray;
Close by your side a - bid - ing, I fear no foe,
And noth - ing can im - pede me, O bless - ed Friend!
So take my hand, O Sav - ior, And lead the way.
For when your hand is guid - ing, In peace I go.
So, take my hand and lead me Un - to the end.

© *Text: Julie von Hausmann, 1825–1901; tr. hymnal version, 1978*
Tune: Friedrich Silcher, 1789–1860

SO NIMM DENN MEINE HÄNDE
74 74 D

Jesus, Savior, Pilot Me

334

1 Je - sus, Sav - ior, pi - lot me O - ver
2 As a moth - er stills her child, Thou canst
3 When at last I near the shore, And the
life's tem - pes - tuous sea; Un - known waves be - fore me
hush the o - cean wild; Bois - t'rous waves o - bey thy
fear - ful break - ers roar Twixt me and the peace - ful
roll, Hid - ing rock and treach - 'rous shoal; Chart and
will When thou say'st to them: "Be still." Won - drous
rest, Then, while lean - ing on thy breast, May I
com - pass come from thee. Je - sus, Sav - ior, pi - lot me.
sov - 'reign of the sea, Je - sus, Sav - ior, pi - lot me.
hear thee say to me: "Fear not, I will pi - lot thee."

Text: Edward Hopper, 1818–1888
Tune: John E. Gould, 1822–1875

PILOT
77 77 77

335 May God Bestow on Us His Grace

1 May God be - stow on us his grace, With bless - ings
2 To you shall be the high - est praise And thanks of
3 Oh, let the peo - ple praise your worth, In all good
rich pro - vide us; And may the bright - ness
ev - 'ry na - tion, And all the world with
works in - creas - ing; The land shall plen - teous
of his face To life e - ter - nal guide
joy shall raise The song of ex - ul - ta -
fruit bring forth; Your Word is rich in bless -
us, That we his gra - cious work may know,
tion. For you will judge the earth, O Lord,
ing. May God, the Fa - ther and the Son

And what is his good plea - sure, And to the
Nor suf - fer sin to flour - ish; Your peo - ple's
And Ho - ly Spir - it, bless us; Let all the
un - be - liev - ing show Christ's rich - es with - out mea - sure,
pas - ture is your Word, Their souls to feed and nour - ish,
world praise him a - lone, Let sol - emn awe pos - sess us.
And un - to God con - vert them.
In righ - teous paths to keep them.
Now let our hearts say, "A - men."

Text: Martin Luther, 1483–1546; tr. Richard Massie, 1800–1887, alt.
Tune: Matthias Greitter, c. 1490–1552

ES WOLLE GOTT UNS GNÄDIG SEIN
87 87 87 877

336 Jesus, Thy Boundless Love to Me

1 Je - sus, thy bound - less love to me No thought can reach, no
2 Oh, grant that noth - ing in my soul May dwell, but thy pure
3 This love un - wea - ried I pur - sue And daunt - less - ly to
4 In suf - f'ring be thy love my peace, In weak - ness be thy
tongue de - clare; U - nite my thank - ful heart to thee,
love a - lone; Oh, may thy love pos - sess me whole,
thee as - pire. Oh, may thy love my hope re - new,
love my pow'r; And when the storms of life shall cease,
And reign with - out a ri - val there! Thine whol - ly, thine a -
My joy, my trea - sure, and my crown! All cold - ness from my
Burn in my soul like heav'n - ly fire! And day and night, be
O Je - sus, in that fi - nal hour, Be thou my rod and
lone, I am; Be thou a - lone my con - stant flame.
heart re - move; My ev - 'ry act, word, thought, be love.
all my care To guard this sa - cred trea - sure there.
staff and guide And draw me safe - ly to thy side!

Text: Paul Gerhardt, 1607–1676; tr. John Wesley, 1703–1791, alt.
© *Tune: Norman Cocker, 1889–1953*

RYBURN
88 88 88

Oh, What Their Joy

337

1 Oh, what their joy and their glo - ry must be,
2 In new Je - ru - sa - lem joy shall be found,
3 We, where no trou - ble dis - trac - tion can bring,
4 Now let us wor - ship our Lord and our King,
Those end - less Sab - baths the bless - ed ones see!
Bless - ings of peace shall for - ev - er a - bound;
Safe - ly the an - thems of Zi - on shall sing;
Joy - ful - ly rais - ing our voic - es to sing:
Crowns for the val - iant, to wea - ry ones rest;
Wish and ful - fill - ment are not sev - ered there,
While for your grace, Lord, their voic - es of praise
Praise to the Fa - ther, and praise to the Son,
God shall be all, and in all ev - er blest.
Nor the thing prayed for come short of the prayer.
Your bless - ed peo - ple shall ev - er - more raise.
Praise to the Spir - it, to God, Three in One.

Text: *Peter Abelard, 1079–1142; tr. John M. Neale, 1818–1866, alt.*
Tune: Antiphoner, *Paris, 1681*

O QUANTA QUALIA
10 10 10 10

338 Peace, to Soothe Our Bitter Woes

1 Peace, to soothe our bit - ter woes, God in Christ on us be - stows; Je - sus bought our peace with God With his ho - ly, pre - cious blood; Peace in him for sin - ners found Is the Gos - pel's joy - ful sound.
2 Peace with - in the Church still dwells In her wel - comes and fare - wells; And through God's bap - tis - mal pow'r Peace sur-rounds our dy - ing hour. Peace be with you, full and free, Now and through e - ter - ni - ty.

Text: Nikolai F. S. Grundtvig, 1783–1872; tr. George T. Rygh, 1860–1943, alt.
Tune: Ludvig M. Lindeman, 1812–1887

FRED TIL BOD
77 77 77

O Lord, Now Let Your Servant 339

1 O Lord, now let your ser - vant De - part in heav'n - ly peace,
2 Then grant that I may fol - low Your gleam, O glo - rious Light,
For I have seen the glo - ry Of your re - deem - ing grace:
Till earth - ly shad - ows scat - ter, And faith is changed to sight;
A light to lead the Gen - tiles Un - to your ho - ly hill,
Till rap - tured saints shall gath - er Up - on that shin - ing shore,
The glo - ry of your peo - ple, Your cho - sen Is - ra - el.
Where Christ, the bless - ed day - star, Shall light them ev - er - more.

 Text: Ernest E. Ryden, b. 1886, alt.
Tune: Finnish folk tune, 19th cent.

KUORTANE
76 76 D

340 Jesus Christ, My Sure Defense

1 Je - sus Christ, my sure de - fense And my Sav - ior, ev - er
2 Je - sus, my re - deem - er, lives; I, too, un - to life shall
3 No, too close - ly am I bound Un - to him by hope for -
4 I am flesh and must re - turn Un - to dust, whence I am
liv - eth! Know - ing this, my con - fi - dence Rests
wak - en. He will bring me where he is; Shall
ev - er; Faith's strong hand the rock has found, Grasped
tak - en; But by faith I now dis - cern That
up - on the hope it giv - eth, Though the night of
my cour - age, then, be shak - en? Shall I fear, or
it, and will leave it nev - er; E - ven death now
from death I shall a - wak - en, With my Sav - ior
death be fraught Still with man - y an anx - ious thought.
could the head Rise and leave his mem - bers dead?
can - not part From its Lord the trust - ing heart.
to a - bide In his glo - ry, at his side.

5 Then these eyes my Lord will know,
My redeemer and my brother;
In his love my soul will glow—
I myself, and not another!
Then the weakness I feel here
Will forever disappear.

6 Then take comfort and rejoice,
For his members Christ will cherish.
Fear not, they will hear his voice;
Dying, they will never perish;
For the very grave is stirred
When the trumpet's blast is heard.

7 Oh, then, draw away your hearts
From earth's pleasures base and hollow.
Strive to share what he imparts
While you here his footsteps follow.
As you now still wait to rise,
Fix your hearts beyond the skies!

Text: Berlin, 1653; tr. Catherine Winkworth, 1829–1878, alt.
Tune: Johann Crüger, 1598–1662

JESUS, MEINE ZUVERSICHT
78 78 77

Jesus, Still Lead On 341

1 Je - sus, still lead on, Till our rest be won; And, al-though the
2 If the way be drear, If the foe be near, Let no faith - less
3 When we seek re - lief From a long - felt grief, When temp - ta - tions
4 Je - sus, still lead on, Till our rest be won; Heav'n - ly lead - er,

way be cheer - less, We will fol - low, calm and fear - less;
fears o'er - take us, Let not faith and hope for - sake us;
come al - lur - ing Make us pa - tient and en - dur - ing;
still di - rect us, Still sup - port, con - sole, pro - tect us,

Guide us by your hand To our Fa - ther's land.
Safe - ly past the foe To our home we go.
Show us that bright shore Where we weep no more.
Till we safe - ly stand In our Fa - ther's land.

Text: Nicolaus L. von Zinzendorf, 1700–1760; tr. Jane L. Borthwick, 1813–1897, alt.
Tune: Adam Drese, 1620–1701

SEELENBRÄUTIGAM
55 88 55

342 I Know of a Sleep in Jesus' Name

1 I know of a sleep in Je - sus' name, A rest from all
2 I know of a bless - ed e - ven - tide, And when I am
3 I know of a morn - ing bright and fair When tid - ings of
toil and sor - row; Earth folds in its arms my wea - ry
faint and wea - ry, At times with the jour - ney sore - ly
joy shall wake us, When songs from on high shall fill the
frame And shel - ters it till the mor - row; With God I am
tried Through hours that are long and drea - ry, Then of - ten I
air And God to his glo - ry take us, When Je - sus shall
safe un - til that day When sor - row is gone for - ev - er.
yearn to lay me down And sink in - to peace-ful slum - ber.
bid us rise from sleep; How joy - ous that hour of wak - ing!

 Text: Magnus B. Landstad, 1802–1880; tr. Service Book and Hymnal, *1958, alt.*
Tune: Christoph E. F. Weyse, 1774–1842

DEN SIGNEDE DAG
98 98 98

Guide Me Ever, Great Redeemer

343

1 Guide me ev - er, great Re-deem - er, Pil - grim through this
2 O - pen now the crys - tal foun - tain Where the heal - ing
3 When I tread the verge of Jor - dan, Bid my anx - ious
bar - ren land. I am weak, but you are might - y; Hold me
wa - ters flow; Let the fire and cloud - y pil - lar Lead me
fears sub - side; Death of death and hell's de - struc - tion, Land me
with your pow'r - ful hand. Bread of heav - en, bread of heav - en,
all my jour - ney through. Strong de - liv - 'rer, strong de - liv - 'rer,
safe on Ca - naan's side. Songs and prais - es, songs and prais - es,
Feed me now and ev - er - more, Feed me now and ev - er - more.
Shield me with your might - y arm, Shield me with your might - y arm.
I will raise for - ev - er - more, I will raise for - ev - er - more.

Text: William Williams, 1717–1791; tr. composite, alt.
© *Tune: John Hughes, 1873–1932*

CWM RHONDDA
87 87 877

344 We Sing the Praise of Him Who Died

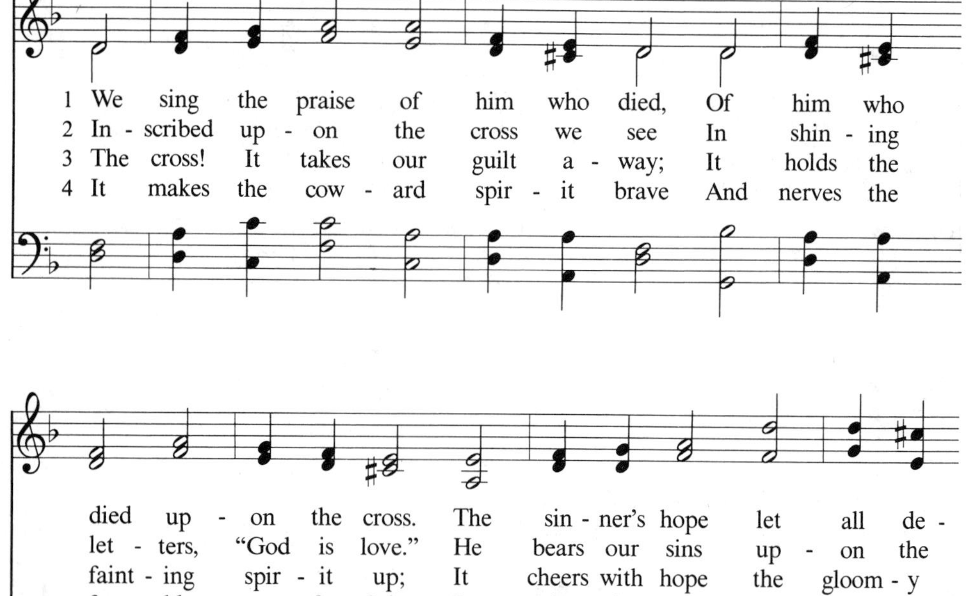
1 We sing the praise of him who died, Of him who died up - on the cross. The sin - ner's hope let all de -
2 In - scribed up - on the cross we see In shin - ing let - ters, "God is love." He bears our sins up - on the
3 The cross! It takes our guilt a - way; It holds the faint - ing spir - it up; It cheers with hope the gloom - y
4 It makes the cow - ard spir - it brave And nerves the fee - ble arm for fight; It takes the ter - ror from the

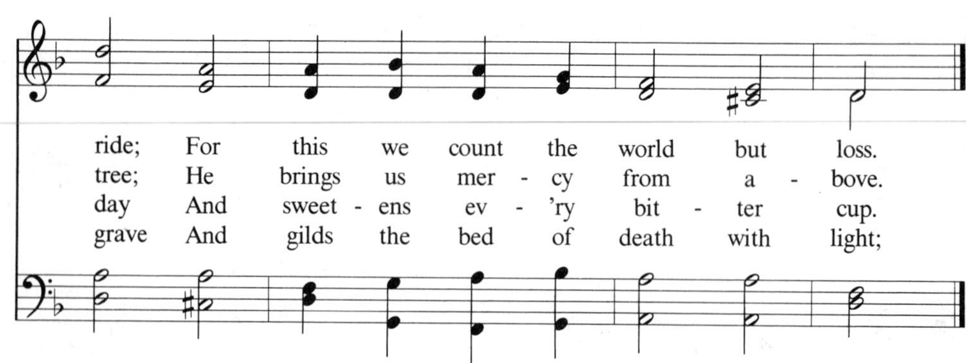
ride; For this we count the world but loss.
tree; He brings us mer - cy from a - bove.
day And sweet - ens ev - 'ry bit - ter cup.
grave And gilds the bed of death with light;

5 The balm of life, the cure of woe,
The measure and the pledge of love,
The sinner's refuge here below,
The angels' theme in heav'n above.

Text: Thomas Kelly, 1769–1854
Tune: attr. Daniel Read, 1757–1836

WINDHAM
LM

How Sweet the Name of Jesus Sounds 345

1 How sweet the name of Je - sus sounds In a be - liev - er's ear! It soothes our sor - rows, heals our wounds, And drives a - way all fear.
2 It makes the wound - ed spir - it whole And calms the heart's un - rest; 'Tis man - na to the hun - gry soul And to the wea - ry, rest.
3 Dear name! The rock on which I build, My shield and hid - ing place; My nev - er - fail - ing trea - sury, filled With bound - less stores of grace.
4 By thee my prayers ac - cep - tance gain Al - though with sin de - filed. The dev - il charg - es me in vain, And I am owned a child.

5 O Jesus, shepherd, guardian, friend,
My Prophet, Priest, and King,
My Lord, my life, my way, my end,
Accept the praise I bring.

6 How weak the effort of my heart,
How cold my warmest thought;
But when I see thee as thou art,
I'll praise thee as I ought.

7 Till then I would thy love proclaim
With every fleeting breath;
And may the music of thy name
Refresh my soul in death!

Text: John Newton, 1725–1807, alt.
Tune: Alexander R. Reinagle, 1799–1877

ST. PETER
CM

346 When Peace, like a River

1 When peace, like a riv - er, at - tend - eth my way;
2 Though Sa - tan should buf - fet, though tri - als should come,
3 He lives— oh, the bliss of this glo - ri - ous thought;
4 And, Lord, haste the day when our faith shall be sight,
When sor - rows, like sea bil - lows, roll; What -
Let this blest as - sur - ance con - trol, That
My sin, not in part, but the whole, Is
The clouds be rolled back as a scroll, The
ev - er my lot, thou hast taught me to say,
Christ hath re - gard - ed my help - less es - tate
nailed to his cross, and I bear it no more.
trum - pet shall sound, and the Lord shall de - scend;
It is well, it is well with my soul.
And hath shed his own blood for my soul.
Praise the Lord, praise the Lord, O my soul!
E - ven so it is well with my soul.

Text: Horatio G. Spafford, 1828–1888
Tune: Philip P. Bliss, 1838–1876

IT IS WELL
11 8 11 9

Jerusalem the Golden

347

E♭ Cm A♭ E♭ Fm
1 Je - ru - sa - lem the gold - en, With milk and hon - ey
2 They stand, those halls of Zi - on, Con - ju - bi - lant with
3 There is the throne of Da - vid, And there, from care re -
4 Oh, sweet and bless - ed coun - try, The home of God's e -
E♭ B♭7 E♭ Cm A♭ E♭ B♭
blest, Be - neath your con - tem - pla - tion Sink heart and voice op -
song And bright with man - y an an - gel And all the mar - tyr
leased, The shout of those who tri - umph, The song of those who
lect! Oh, sweet and bless - ed coun - try, That ea - ger hearts ex -
E♭ A♭ B♭7 E♭ Gm Cm7 A♭
pressed. I know not, oh, I know not, What so - cial joys are
throng. The prince is ev - er in them; The day - light is se -
feast. And they, who with their lead - er Have con - quered in the
pect! In mer - cy, Je - sus, bring us To that dear land of
Gm B♭7 E♭ A♭ B♭ E♭ B♭ E♭
there, What ra - dian - cy of glo - ry, What bliss be - yond com - pare.
rene; The pas - tures of the bless - ed Are decked in glo - rious sheen.
fight, For - ev - er and for - ev - er Are clad in robes of white.
rest! You are, with God the Fa - ther And Spir - it, ev - er blest.

Text: *Bernard of Cluny, 12th cent.; tr. John M. Neale, 1818–1866*
Tune: *W. Walker,* Southern Harmony, *1835*

COMPLAINER
76 76D

348 Jerusalem, Whose Towers Touch the Skies

1 Je - ru - sa - lem, whose tow - ers touch the skies, I yearn to
2 O hap - py day, O bless - ed, hap - py hour, When will you
3 Saints robed in white be - fore the shin - ing throne Their joy - ful
come to you! Your shin - ing streets have drawn my long - ing
come at last? When fear - less to my Fa - ther's lov - ing
an - thems raise, Till heav - en's arch - es ech - o with the
eyes My life - long jour - ney through. And though I roam the
pow'r, Whose word con - tin - ues fast, My soul I glad - ly
tone Of that great hymn of praise, And all its host re -
wood - land, The cit - y, and the plain, My
ren - der, For sure - ly will his hand Lead
joic - es, And all its bless - ed throng U -

heart still seeks the good land, My Fa - ther's house to gain.
me with guid - ance ten - der To heav - en's prom - ised land.
nite their myr - iad voic - es In one e - ter - nal song.

 Text: Johann M. Meyfart, 1590–1642; tr. Gilbert E. Doan, b. 1930
Tune: Melchior Franck, c. 1573–1639

JERUSALEM, DU HOCHGEBAUTE STADT
106 106 76 76

I Leave, as You Have Promised, Lord 349

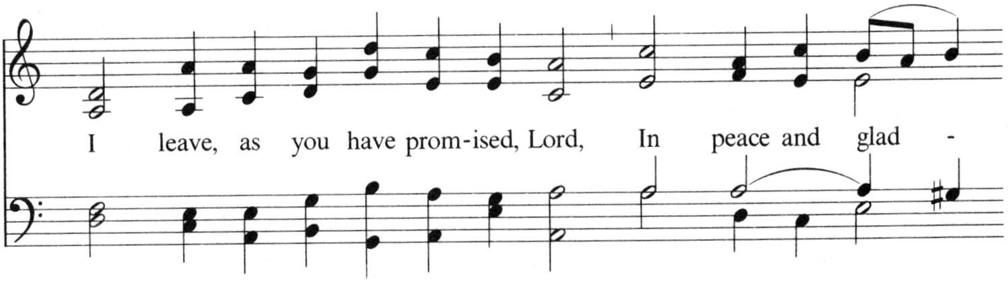

I leave, as you have prom-ised, Lord, In peace and glad -

ness. My eyes have seen their great re-ward; Gone is sad - ness. Fa -

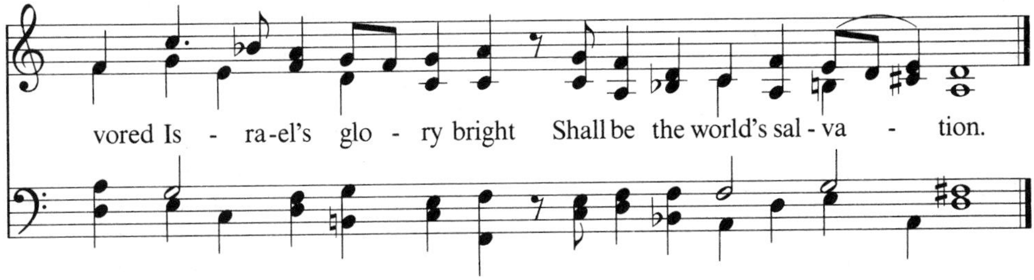

vored Is - ra-el's glo - ry bright Shall be the world's sal - va - tion.

 Text: Gilbert E. Doan, b. 1930
Tune: Martin Luther, 1483–1546

MIT FRIED UND FREUD
85 84 87

350 Even as We Live Each Day

E - ven as we live each day, Death our life em - brac - es.

Who is there to bring us help, Rich, for - giv - ing grac - es?

You on - ly, Lord, you on - ly! Bap-tized in Christ's life-giv - ing flood:

Wa - ter and his pre-cious blood— Ho - ly and righ-teous God,

Ho - ly and might - y God, Ho - ly and all - mer - ci - ful

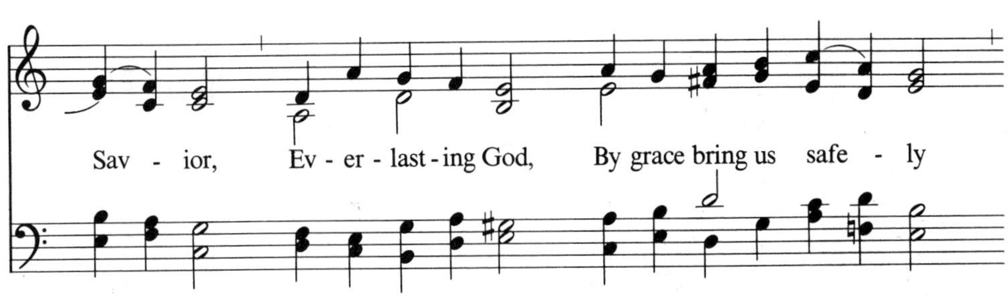
Sav - ior, Ev - er - last - ing God, By grace bring us safe - ly

Through the flood of bit - ter death. Lord, have mer - cy.

 Text: Martin Luther, 1483–1546; hymnal translation, 1978
Tune: Johann Walther, 1496–1570

MITTEN WIR IM LEBEN SIND
PM

351 Oh, Happy Day When We Shall Stand

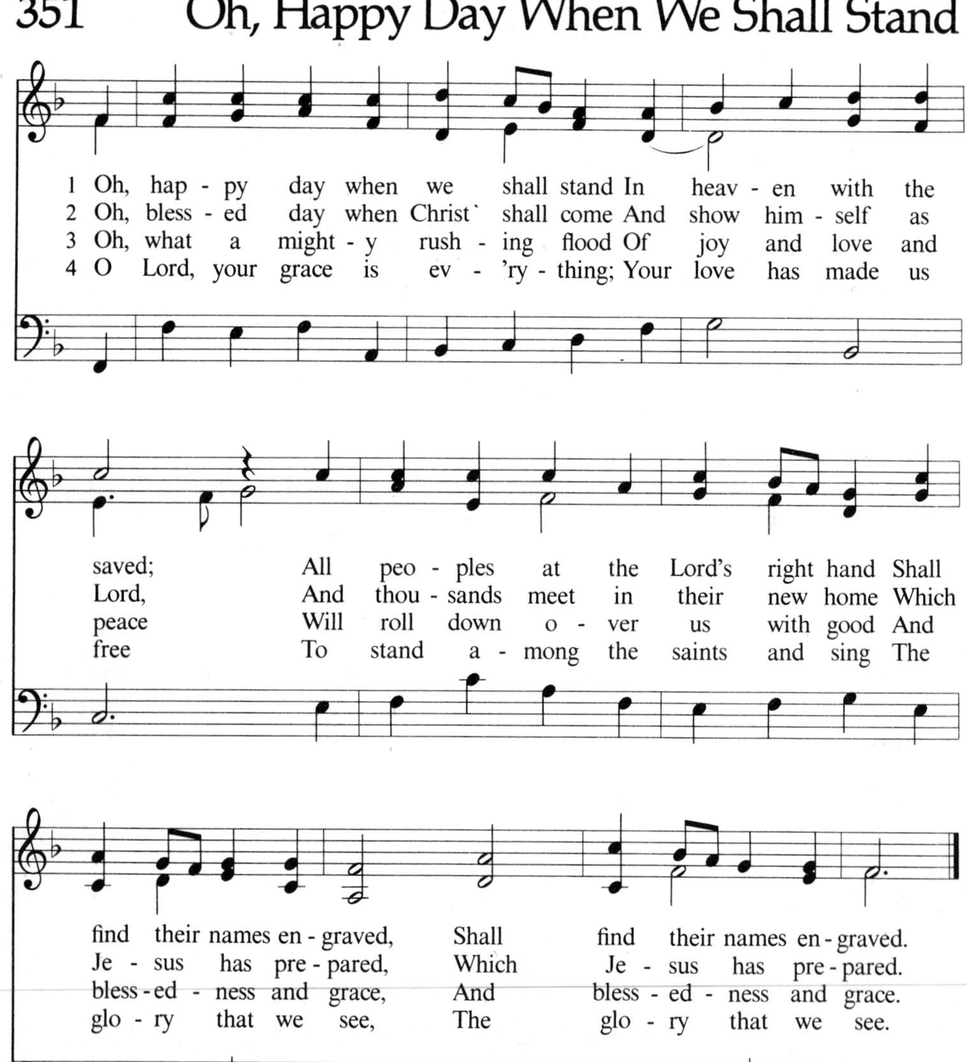
1 Oh, hap - py day when we shall stand In heav - en with the
2 Oh, bless - ed day when Christ shall come And show him - self as
3 Oh, what a might - y rush - ing flood Of joy and love and
4 O Lord, your grace is ev - 'ry - thing; Your love has made us
saved; All peo - ples at the Lord's right hand Shall
Lord, And thou - sands meet in their new home Which
peace Will roll down o - ver us with good And
free To stand a - mong the saints and sing The
find their names en - graved, Shall find their names en - graved.
Je - sus has pre - pared, Which Je - sus has pre - pared.
bless - ed - ness and grace, And bless - ed - ness and grace.
glo - ry that we see, The glo - ry that we see.

 Text: Wilhelm A. Wexels, 1797–1866; tr. Gracia Grindal, b. 1943
Tune: Nikolaus Herman, c. 1480–1561

LOBT GOTT, IHR CHRISTEN
86 866

I Know that My Redeemer Lives! 352

1 I know that my Re - deem - er lives! What com - fort this sweet sen - tence gives! He lives, he lives, who once was dead; He lives, my ev - er - liv - ing head!
2 He lives tri - um - phant from the grave; He lives e - ter - nal - ly to save; He lives ex - alt - ed, throned a - bove; He lives to rule his Church in love.
3 He lives to grant me rich sup - ply; He lives to guide me with his eye; He lives to com - fort me when faint; He lives to hear my soul's com - plaint.
4 He lives to si - lence all my fears; He lives to wipe a - way my tears; He lives to calm my trou - bled heart; He lives all bless - ings to im - part.

5 He lives to bless me with his love;
He lives to plead for me above;
He lives my hungry soul to feed;
He lives to help in time of need.

6 He lives, my kind, wise, heav'nly friend;
He lives and loves me to the end;
He lives, and while he lives, I'll sing;
He lives, my Prophet, Priest, and King!

7 He lives and grants me daily breath;
He lives, and I shall conquer death;
He lives my mansion to prepare;
He lives to bring me safely there.

8 He lives, all glory to his name!
He lives, my Savior, still the same;
What joy this blest assurance gives:
I know that my Redeemer lives!

Text: Samuel Medley, 1738–1799, alt.
Tune: attr. John Hatton, d. 1793

DUKE STREET
LM

353 May We Your Precepts, Lord, Fulfill

1 May we your pre - cepts, Lord, ful - fill And do on
2 So may we join your name to bless, Your grace a -
3 Spir - it of life, of love, and peace, Our hearts u -
earth our Fa - ther's will As an - gels do a - bove;
dore, your pow'r con - fess, To flee from sin and strife.
nite, our joy in - crease, Your gra - cious help sup - ply.
Still walk in Christ, the liv - ing way, With all your
One is our call - ing, one our name, The end of
To each of us the bless - ing give In Chris - tian
chil - dren and o - bey The law of Chris - tian love.
all our hopes the same, A glo - rious crown of life.
fel - low - ship to live, In joy - ful hope to die.

Text: Edward Osler, 1798–1863, alt.
Tune: Lowell Mason, 1792–1872

MERIBAH
886 886

Eternal God, before Your Throne 354

1 E - ter - nal God, be - fore your throne we bend, Your grace to seek, your
2 Lord Je - sus Christ, our Sav - ior and our friend, Whom an - gels praise be -
3 O Ho - ly Spir - it, truth and peace di - vine, De - scend to us in

ho - ly name to bless; Our grate - ful hearts in hum - ble praise as - cend
fore the throne on high: How vast your love, to love us to the end
all your sav - ing pow'r, And kin - dle flames of love and faith to shine

To you whose ways are truth and righ-teous - ness. With all the host of
And on the cru - el cross to bleed and die! O blest Re-deem - er,
With-in our yearn - ing hearts this sa - cred hour! Make plain the Fa - ther's

heav - en we a - dore Your match-less ho - ly love for - ev - er - more!
hear your chil-dren pray; O Lamb of God, take all our sins a - way!
will, the Sav-ior's love, And fit us all to dwell with you a - bove.

© Text: Ernest E. Ryden, b. 1886, alt.
© Tune: Carl W. Landahl, 1908–1961

INVOCATION
10 10 10 10 10 10

355 Through the Night of Doubt and Sorrow

1 Through the night of doubt and sorrow Onward goes the pilgrim band, Singing songs of expectation, Marching to the promised land. Clear before us through the darkness Gleams and burns the
2 One the light of God's own presence On his ransomed people shed, Chasing far the gloom and terror, Bright'ning all the path we tread. One the object of our journey, One the faith which
3 One the strain that lips of thousands Lift as from the heart of one; One the conflict, one the peril, One the march in God begun. One the gladness of rejoicing On the far e-
4 Onward, therefore, sisters, brothers; Onward, with the cross our aid. Bear its shame, and fight its battle Till we rest beneath its shade. Soon shall come the great awak'ning; Soon the rending

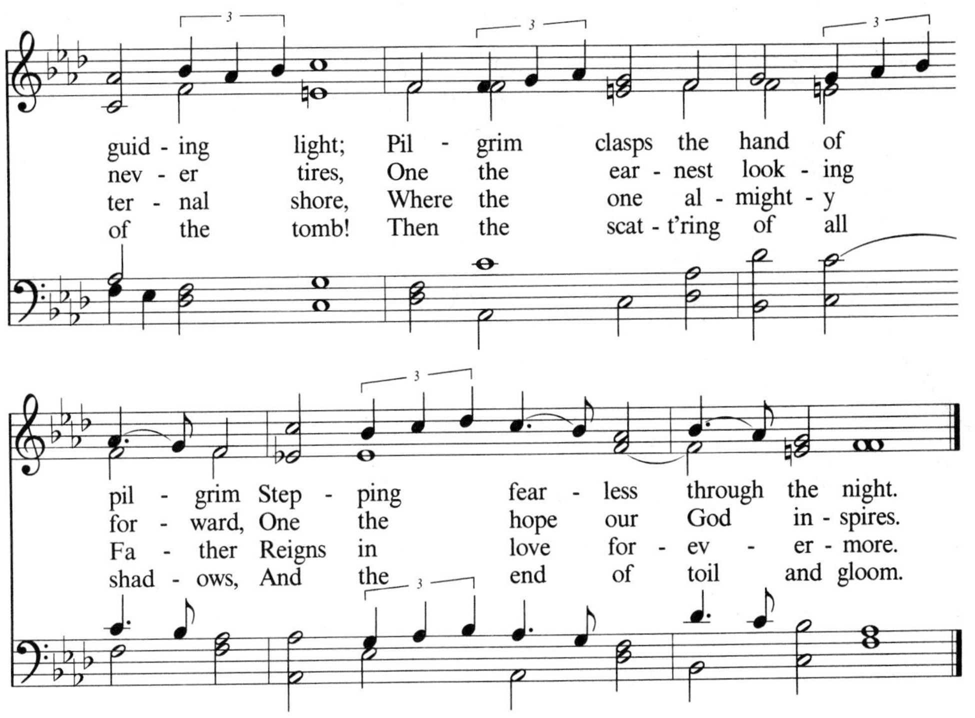
guid - ing light; Pil - grim clasps the hand of
nev - er tires, One the ear - nest look - ing
ter - nal shore, Where the one al - might - y
of the tomb! Then the scat - t'ring of all
pil - grim Step - ping fear - less through the night.
for - ward, One the hope our God in - spires.
Fa - ther Reigns in love for - ev - er - more.
shad - ows, And the end of toil and gloom.

Text: Bernhardt S. Ingemann, 1789–1862; tr. Sabine Baring-Gould, 1834–1924
© Tune: Thomas J. Williams, 1869–1944

EBENEZER
87 87 D

356 O Jesus, Joy of Loving Hearts

1 O Je - sus, joy of lov - ing hearts, The fount of life, the
2 Your truth un-changed has ev - er stood; You plead with all to
3 We taste you, ev - er - liv - ing bread, And long to feast up -
4 For you our rest - less spir - its yearn, Wher-e'er our chang - ing
light of all: From ev - 'ry bliss that earth im -
call on you; To those who seek you, you are
on you still; We drink of you, the foun - tain -
lot is cast; Glad, when your smile on us you

parts We turn, un - filled, to hear your call.
good; To those who find you, life is new.
head; Our thirst - ing souls from you we fill.
turn, Blest, when by faith we hold you fast.

5 O Jesus, ever with us stay!
Make all our moments fair and bright!
Oh, chase the night of sin away!
Shed o'er the world your holy light.

Text: attr. Bernard of Clairvaux, 1091–1153; tr. Ray Palmer, 1808–1887, alt.
Tune: W. Gardiner, Sacred Melodies, *1815*

WALTON
LM

Our Father, by Whose Name 357

1 Our Fa - ther, by whose name All par - ent - hood is
2 O Christ, your - self a child With - in an earth - ly
3 O Ho - ly Spir - it, bind Our hearts in u - ni -
known: In love di - vine you claim Each fam - 'ly as your
home, With heart still un - de - filed To full a - dult-hood
ty And teach us how to find The love from self set
own. Bless moth-ers, fa - thers, guard - ing well, With con-stant
come: Our chil-dren bless in ev - 'ry place That they may
free; In all our hearts such love in - crease That ev - 'ry
love as sen - ti - nel, The homes in which your peo - ple dwell.
all be-hold your face And know-ing you may grow in grace.
home, by this re - lease, May be the dwell - ing-place of peace.

 Text: F. Bland Tucker, b. 1895, alt.
Tune: John Edwards, 1806–1885

RHOSYMEDRE
66 66 888

358 Glories of Your Name Are Spoken

1 Glo - ries of your name are spo - ken, Zi - on, cit - y
2 See, the streams of liv - ing wa - ters, Spring - ing from e -
3 Round each hab - i - ta - tion hov - 'ring, See the cloud and
4 Sav - ior, since of Zi - on's cit - y I through grace a
of our God; He whose word can - not be bro - ken
ter - nal love, Well sup - ply your sons and daugh - ters,
fire ap - pear For a glo - ry and a cov - 'ring,
mem - ber am, Let the world de - ride or pit - y,
Formed you for his own a - bode. On the Rock of
And all fear of want re - move. Who can faint, while
Show - ing that the Lord is near. Thus de - riv - ing
I will glo - ry in your name. Fad - ing are the
A - ges found - ed, What can shake your sure re - pose? With sal -
such a riv - er Ev - er will their thirst as - suage? Grace which,
from their ban - ner Light by night and shade by day, Safe they
world - lings' plea - sures All their boast - ed pomp and show; Sol - id

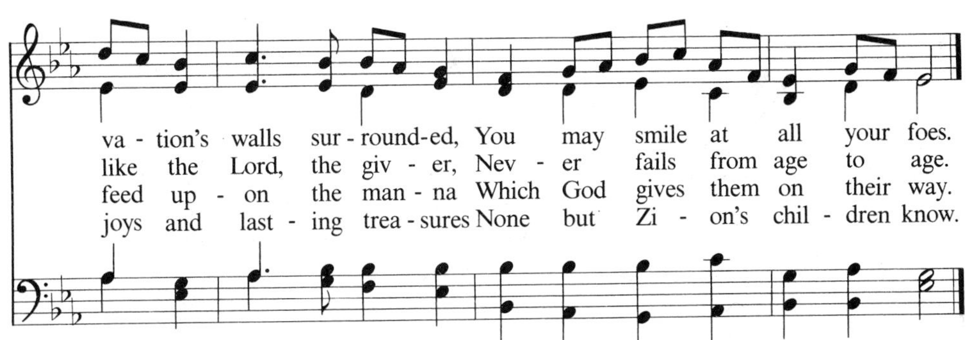
va - tion's walls sur - round-ed, You may smile at all your foes.
like the Lord, the giv - er, Nev - er fails from age to age.
feed up - on the man - na Which God gives them on their way.
joys and last - ing trea - sures None but Zi - on's chil - dren know.

Text: John Newton, 1725–1807, alt.
Tune: Franz Joseph Haydn, 1732–1809

AUSTRIA
87 87 D

In Christ There Is No East or West 359

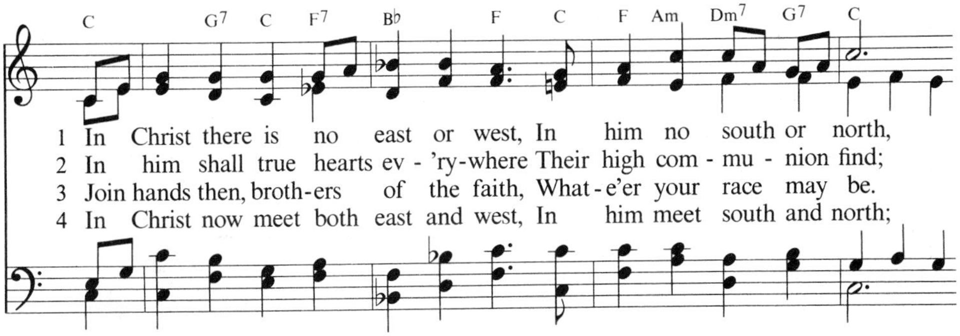

C G7 C F7 Bb F C F Am Dm7 G7 C

1 In Christ there is no east or west, In him no south or north,
2 In him shall true hearts ev - 'ry-where Their high com - mu - nion find;
3 Join hands then, broth-ers of the faith, What - e'er your race may be.
4 In Christ now meet both east and west, In him meet south and north;

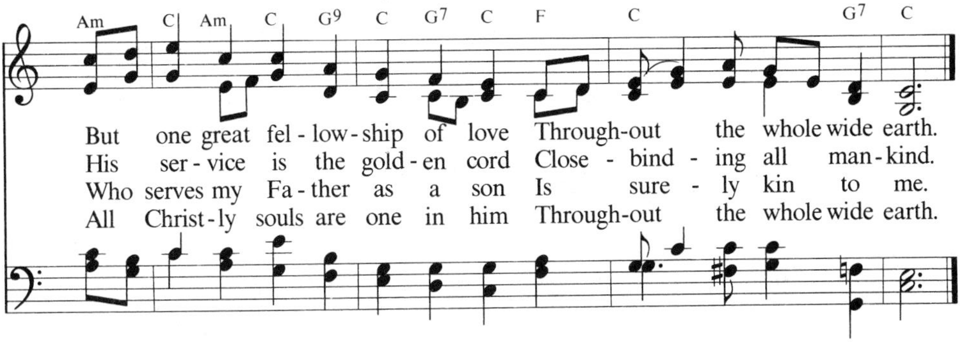

Am C Am C G9 C G7 C F C G7 C

But one great fel - low - ship of love Through-out the whole wide earth.
His ser - vice is the gold - en cord Close - bind - ing all man - kind.
Who serves my Fa - ther as a son Is sure - ly kin to me.
All Christ - ly souls are one in him Through-out the whole wide earth.

MCKEE
CM

360 O Christ, the Healer, We Have Come

1 O Christ, the heal - er, we have come
2 From ev - 'ry ail - ment flesh en - dures
3 In con - flicts that de - stroy our health
4 Grant that we all, made one in faith,
To pray for health, to plead for friends. How
Our bod - ies clam - or to be freed; Yet
We rec - og - nize the world's dis - ease; Our
In your com - mu - ni - ty may find The
can we fail to be re - stored When
in our hearts we would con - fess That
com - mon life de - clares our ills. Is
whole-ness that, en - rich - ing us, Shall
reached by love that nev - er ends?
whole-ness is our deep - est need.
there no cure, O Christ, for these?
reach and pros - per hu - man-kind.

© *Text: F. Pratt Green, b. 1903*
Tune: W. Walker, Southern Harmony, *1835*

DISTRESS
LM

Do Not Despair, O Little Flock

361

1 Do not de - spair, O lit - tle flock, Al - though the foes' fierce bat - tle shock Loud on all sides as - sail you! Though at your fall they laugh, se - cure, Their tri - umph can - not long en - dure; Let not your cour - age fail you!
2 The cause is God's; o - bey his call And to his hand com - mit your all And fear no ill im - pend - ing! Though not yet seen by hu - man eyes, His Gid - eon shall for you a - rise, God's word and you de - fend - ing.
3 As sure as God's own word is true, Not Sa - tan, hell, nor all their crew Can stand a - gainst his pow - er. Scorn and con - tempt their cup will fill, For God is with his peo - ple still, Their help and their strong tow - er.
4 Then help us, Lord! Now hear our prayer. De - fend your peo - ple ev - 'ry - where For your own name's sake. A - men. Then with a might - y hymn of praise Your Church in earth and heav'n will raise Their songs of tri - umph. A - men.

Text: attr. Johann M. Altenburg, 1584–1630; tr. hymnal version, 1978
Tune: Nürnberg, 1534

KOMMT HER ZU MIR
887 887

362 We Plow the Fields and Scatter

1 We plow the fields and scat - ter The good seed on the land,
2 He on - ly is the mak - er Of all things near and far;
3 We thank you, our cre - a - tor, For all things bright and good,
But it is fed and wa - tered By God's al - might - y hand.
He paints the way - side flow - er, He lights the eve - ning star.
The seed - time and the har - vest, Our life, our health, our food.
He sends the snow in win - ter, The warmth to swell the grain,
The winds and waves o - bey him; By him the birds are fed.
No gifts have we to of - fer For all your love im - parts,
The breez - es and the sun - shine, And soft re - fresh - ing rain.
Much more to us, his chil - dren, He gives our dai - ly bread.
But what you most would trea - sure— Our hum - ble, thank - ful hearts.

Refrain
All good gifts a - round us Are sent from heav'n a - bove.
Then thank the Lord, oh, thank the Lord For all his love.

Text: Matthias Claudius, 1740–1815; tr. Jane M. Campbell, 1817–1878, alt.
Tune: Johann A. P. Schulz, 1747–1800

WIR PFLÜGEN
76 76 D and refrain

363 Christ Is Alive! Let Christians Sing

1 Christ is alive! Let Christians sing.
His cross stands empty to the sky.
Let streets and homes with praises ring.
In death his love shall never die.

2 Christ is alive! No longer bound
To distant years in Palestine,
He comes to claim the here and now
And conquer ev'ry place and time.

3 Not throned afar, remotely high,
Untouched, unmoved by human pains,
But daily, in the midst of life,
Our Savior with the Father reigns.

4 In ev'ry insult, rift, and war,
Where color, scorn, or wealth divide,
He suffers still, yet loves the more,
And lives, though ever crucified.

5 Christ is alive! Ascended Lord—
He rules the world his Father made,
Till, in the end, his love adored
Shall be to all on earth displayed.

 Text: Brian A. Wren, b. 1936, alt.
Tune: T. Williams, Psalmodia Evangelica, *1789*

TRURO
LM

Son of God, Eternal Savior 364

1 Son of God, e - ter - nal Sav - ior, Source of life and truth and grace,
2 As you, Lord, have lived for oth - ers, So may we for oth - ers live.
3 Come, O Christ, and reign a - mong us, King of love and Prince of Peace;
4 Son of God, e - ter - nal Sav - ior, Source of life and truth and grace,
Word made flesh, whose birth a - mong us Hal - lows all our hu - man race,
Free - ly have your gifts been grant - ed; Free - ly may your ser - vants give.
Hush the storm of strife and pas - sion, Bid its cru - el dis - cords cease.
Word made flesh, whose birth a - mong us Hal - lows all our hu - man race:
You our head, who, throned in glo - ry, For your own will ev - er plead:
Yours the gold and yours the sil - ver, Yours the wealth of land and sea;
By your pa - tient years of toil - ing, By your si - lent hours of pain,
By your pray - ing, by your will - ing That your peo - ple should be one,
Fill us with your love and pit - y, Heal our wrongs, and help our need.
We but stew - ards of your boun - ty Held in sol - emn trust will be.
Quench our fe - vered thirst of plea - sure, Stem our self - ish greed of gain.
Grant, oh, grant our hope's fru - i - tion: Here on earth your will be done.

© Text: Somerset C. Lowry, 1855–1932
Tune: Dutch folk tune, 18th cent.

IN BABILONE
87 87 D

365 Built on a Rock

1 Built on a rock the Church shall stand, E - ven when stee - ples are
2 Not in our tem - ples made with hands God, the Al - might - y, is
3 We are God's house of liv - ing stones, Built for his own hab - i -
4 Yet in this house, an earth - ly frame, Je - sus the chil - dren is
fall - ing; Crum-bled have spires in ev - 'ry land, Bells still are
dwell - ing; High in the heav'ns his tem - ple stands, All earth - ly
ta - tion; He fills our hearts, his hum - ble thrones, Grant-ing us
bless - ing; Hith - er we come to praise his name, Faith in our
chim-ing and call - ing— Call - ing the young and old to rest, Call - ing the
tem - ples ex - cel - ling. Yet he who dwells in heav'n a - bove Deigns to a -
life and sal - va - tion. Were two or three to seek his face, He in their
Sav - ior con-fess - ing. Je - sus to us his Spir - it sent, Mak - ing with
souls of those dis-tressed, Long - ing for life ev - er - last - ing.
bide with us in love, Mak - ing our bod - ies his tem - ple.
midst would show his grace, Bless - ings up - on them be - stow - ing.
us his cov - e - nant, Grant-ing his chil - dren the king - dom.

5 Through all the passing years, O Lord,
Grant that, when church bells are ringing,
Many may come to hear God's Word
Where he this promise is bringing:
I know my own, my own know me;
You, not the world, my face shall see;
My peace I leave with you. Amen

 Text: Nikolai F. S. Grundtvig, 1783–1872; tr. Carl Doving, 1867–1937, adapt.
Tune: Ludvig M. Lindeman, 1812–1887

KIRKEN DEN ER ET GAMMELT HUS
88 88 88 8

Lord of Our Life 366

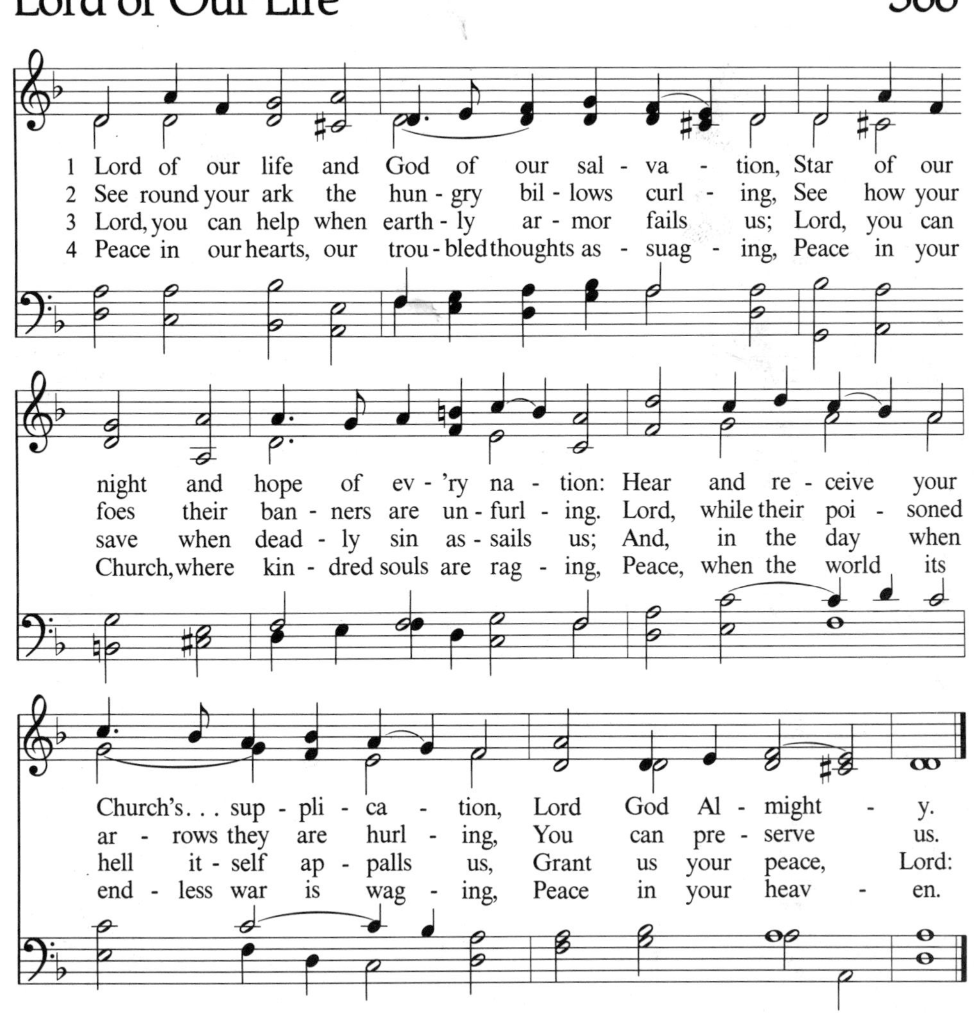
1 Lord of our life and God of our sal - va - tion, Star of our night and hope of ev - 'ry na - tion: Hear and re - ceive your Church's... sup - pli - ca - tion, Lord God Al - might - y.
2 See round your ark the hun - gry bil - lows curl - ing, See how your foes their ban - ners are un - furl - ing. Lord, while their poi - soned ar - rows they are hurl - ing, You can pre - serve us.
3 Lord, you can help when earth - ly ar - mor fails us; Lord, you can save when dead - ly sin as - sails us; And, in the day when hell it - self ap - palls us, Grant us your peace, Lord:
4 Peace in our hearts, our trou - bled thoughts as - suag - ing, Peace in your Church, where kin - dred souls are rag - ing, Peace, when the world its end - less war is wag - ing, Peace in your heav - en.

Text: Matthäus A. von Löwenstern, 1594–1648; tr. Philip Pusey, 1799–1855
Tune: Antiphoner, *Poitiers, 1746*

ISTE CONFESSOR
11 11 11 5

367 Christ Is Made the Sure Foundation

1 Christ is made the sure foun - da - tion, Christ, our head and
2 To this tem - ple, where we call you, Come, O Lord of
3 Grant, we pray, to all your faith - ful All the gifts they
4 Praise and hon - or to the Fa - ther, Praise and hon - or
cor - ner - stone, Cho - sen of the Lord and pre - cious,
hosts, and stay; Come, with all your lov - ing - kind - ness,
ask to gain; What they gain from you for - ev - er
to the Son, Praise and hon - or to the Spir - it,
Bind - ing all the Church in one; Ho - ly Zi - on's
Hear your peo - ple as they pray; And your full - est
With the bless - ed to re - tain; And here - af - ter
Ev - er three and ev - er one: One in might and

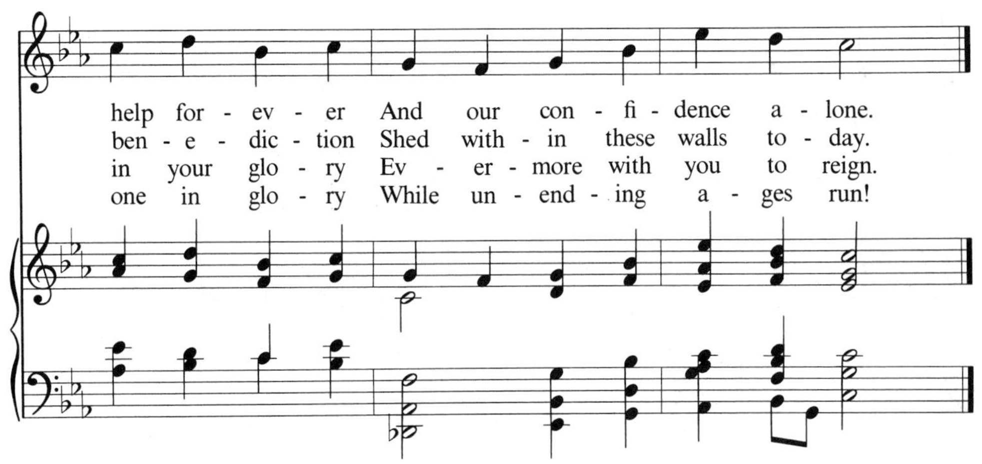
help for - ev - er And our con - fi - dence a - lone.
ben - e - dic - tion Shed with - in these walls to - day.
in your glo - ry Ev - er - more with you to reign.
one in glo - ry While un - end - ing a - ges run!

Text: Latin hymn, c. 7th cent.; tr. John M. Neale, 1818–1866, alt.
© *Tune: Dale Wood, b. 1934*

EDEN CHURCH
8 7 8 7 8 7

I Love Your Kingdom, Lord 368

1 I love your king - dom, Lord, The place of your a - bode;
2 I love your Church, O God! Its walls be - fore you stand,
3 Be - yond my high - est joy I prize its heav'n - ly ways,
4 Sure as your truth shall last, To Zi - on shall be giv'n

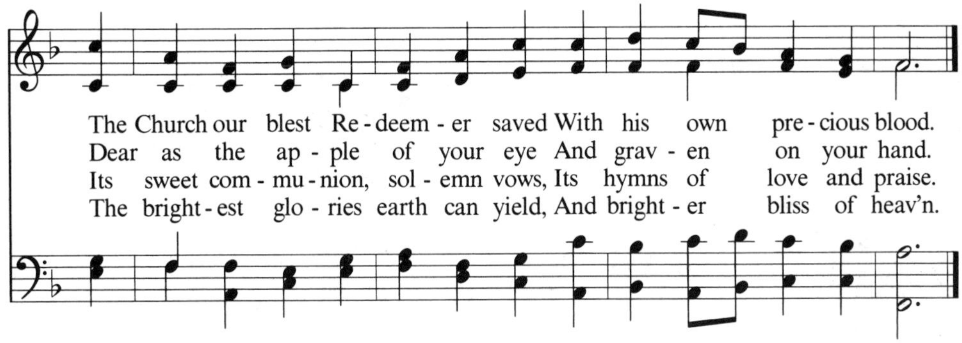

The Church our blest Re - deem - er saved With his own pre - cious blood.
Dear as the ap - ple of your eye And grav - en on your hand.
Its sweet com - mu - nion, sol - emn vows, Its hymns of love and praise.
The bright - est glo - ries earth can yield, And bright - er bliss of heav'n.

Text: Timothy Dwight, 1752–1817, alt.
Tune: Aaron Williams, 1731–1776

ST. THOMAS
SM

369 The Church's One Foundation

1 The Church's . . one foun - da - tion Is Je - sus Christ, her Lord;
2 E - lect from ev - 'ry na - tion, Yet one o'er all the earth;
3 Though with a scorn - ful won - der This world sees her op-pressed,
4 Through toil and trib - u - la - tion And tu - mult of her war,

She is his new cre - a - tion By wa - ter and the Word.
Her char - ter of sal - va - tion: One Lord, one faith, one birth.
By schisms . . rent a - sun - der, By her - e - sies dis-tressed,
She waits the con - sum - ma - tion Of peace for - ev - er - more;

From heav'n he came and sought her To be his ho - ly bride;
One ho - ly name she bless - es, Par - takes one ho - ly food,
Yet saints their watch are keep - ing; Their cry goes up: "How long?"
Till with the vi - sion glo - rious Her long - ing eyes are blest,

With his own blood he bought her, And for her life he died.
And to one hope she press - es With ev - 'ry grace en - dued.
And soon the night of weep - ing Shall be the morn of song.
And the great Church vic - to - rious Shall be the Church at rest.

5 Yet she on earth has union
With God, the Three in One,
And mystic sweet communion
With those whose rest is won.
O blessed heav'nly chorus!
Lord, save us by your grace,
That we, like saints before us,
May see you face to face.

Text: Samuel J. Stone, 1839–1900
Tune: Samuel S. Wesley, 1810–1876

AURELIA
76 76 D

Blest Be the Tie That Binds 370

F Gm7 Dm B♭
1 Blest be the tie that binds Our hearts in
2 Be - fore our Fa - ther's throne We pour our
3 We share our mu - tual woes, Our mu - tual
4 From sor - row, toil, and pain, And sin we
F B♭maj7 C B♭6 F
Chris - tian love; The u - ni - ty of
ar - dent prayers; Our fears, our hopes, our
bur - dens bear, And of - ten for each
shall be free; And per - fect love and
B♭6 C7 Dm B♭6 F B♭ F C7 F
heart and mind Is like to that a - bove.
aims are one, Our com - forts and our cares.
oth - er flows The sym - pa - thiz - ing tear.
friend - ship reign Through all e - ter - ni - ty.

Text: John Fawcett, 1740–1817, alt.
Tune: Johann G. Nägeli, 1773–1836, adapt.

DENNIS
SM

371 With God as Our Friend

1 With God as our friend, with his Spir - it and Word, All
2 In per - il - ous days, filled with storms and with fright, A
3 O Shep - herd, a - bide with us, care for us still, And

shar - ing to - geth - er the feast of the Lord, We
band march - es on through thick gloom toward the light. Not
lead us and guide us and teach us your will, Un -

face with as - sur - ance the dawn of each day And
man - y, nor might - y, dis - owned by the world, They
til in your heav - en - ly fold we shall sing Our

fol - low the shep - herd; and fol - low the shep - herd, Whose
fol - low their lead - er; they fol - low their lead - er, In
thanks and our prais - es; our thanks and our prais - es, To

voice we have heard and whose will we o - bey.
con - fi - dent faith, with their ban - ners un - furled.
God and the Lamb, our re - deem - er and king.

 Text: Carl O. Rosenius, 1816–1868; hymnal translation, 1978
Tune: Oskar Ahnfelt, 1813–1882

ACK, SALIGA STUNDER
11 11 11 12 11

In Adam We Have All Been One 372

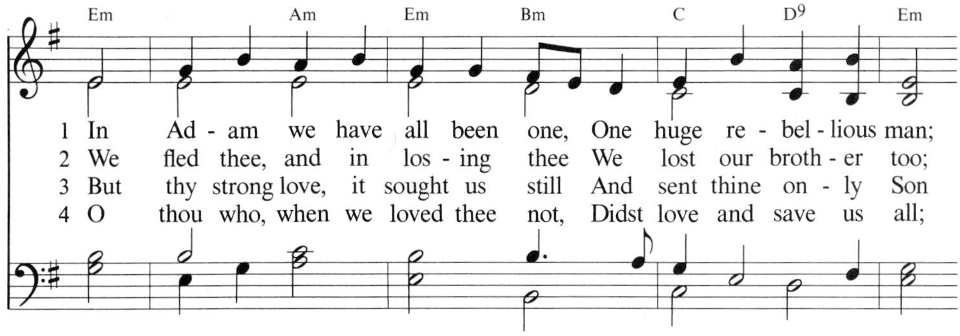

Em Am Em Bm C D9 Em

1 In Ad - am we have all been one, One huge re - bel - lious man;
2 We fled thee, and in los - ing thee We lost our broth - er too;
3 But thy strong love, it sought us still And sent thine on - ly Son
4 O thou who, when we loved thee not, Didst love and save us all;

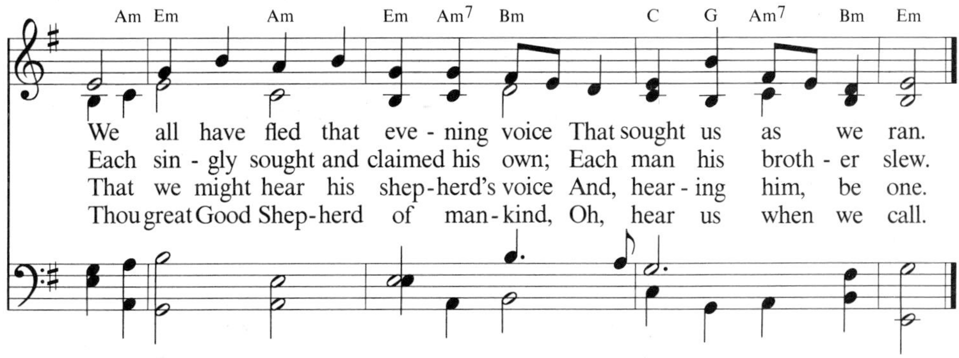

Am Em Am Em Am7 Bm C G Am7 Bm Em

We all have fled that eve - ning voice That sought us as we ran.
Each sin - gly sought and claimed his own; Each man his broth - er slew.
That we might hear his shep - herd's voice And, hear - ing him, be one.
Thou great Good Shep - herd of man - kind, Oh, hear us when we call.

5 Send us thy Spirit, teach us truth;
Thou Son, oh, set us free
From fancied wisdom, self-sought ways,
And make us one in thee.

6 Then shall our song united rise
To thine eternal throne;
Where with the Father evermore
And Spirit, thou art one.

 Text: Martin H. Franzmann, 1907–1976
Tune: W. Walker, Southern Harmony, 1835

THE SAINTS' DELIGHT
CM

373 Eternal Ruler of the Ceaseless Round

1 E - ter - nal Rul - er of the cease - less round
2 We are your own, the chil - dren of your love,
3 We would be one in ha - tred of all wrong,
4 Oh, clothe us with your heav'n - ly ar - mor, Lord.

Of cir - cling plan - ets sing - ing on their way,
As dear - ly loved as your be - lov - ed Son;
One in our love of all things true and fair,
Your trust - y shield and sword of love en - dure;

Guid - ing the na - tions from the night pro -
De - scend, O Ho - ly Spir - it, like a
One with the joy that finds a voice in
Our con - stant in - spi - ra - tion be your

found In - to the glo - ry of the per - fect day:
dove And rule our hearts, that we may be as one—
song, One with the grief that trem - bles in - to prayer,
Word; We ask no vic - to - ries that are not yours.

Rule in our hearts, that we may live a - new,
As one with you, to whom we ev - er tend;
One in the strength that makes your chil - dren free
Give or with - hold, let pain or plea - sure fall:
Guid - ed and strength-ened and up - held by you.
As one with him, our broth - er and our friend.
To fol - low truth, and thus in you to be.
To know that we are serv - ing you is all.

Text: John W. Chadwick, 1840–1904, alt.
Tune: Orlando Gibbons, 1583–1625

SONG 1
10 10 10 10 10 10

374 We All Believe in One True God

1 We all be - lieve in one true God,
2 We all be - lieve in Je - sus Christ,
3 We all con - fess the Ho - ly Ghost
Who cre - at - ed earth and heav - en, The Fa - ther,
His own Son, our Lord, pos - sess - ing An e - qual
Who, in high - est heav - en dwell - ing With God the
who to us in love Has the right of chil - dren giv - en.
God-head, throne, and might, Source of ev - 'ry grace and bless - ing;
Fa - ther and the Son, Com - forts us be - yond all tell - ing;

He in soul and bod - y feeds us; All we need his
Born of Mar - y, vir - gin moth - er, By the pow - er
Who the Church, his own cre - a - tion, Keeps in u - ni -
hand pro - vides us; Through all snares and per - ils leads us.
of the Spir - it, Word made flesh, our el - der broth - er;
ty of spir - it. Here for - give - ness and sal - va - tion
Watch - ing that no harm be - tide us, He cares
That the lost might life in - her - it, Was put
Dai - ly come through Je - sus' mer - it. All flesh

Hymn continues on the next page.

for us by day and night.
to death up - on the cross,
shall rise, and we shall be
All things are gov - erned by his might.
And raised by God vic - to - ri - ous.
In bliss with God e - ter - nal - ly.
A - men

Text: Martin Luther, 1483–1546; tr. The Lutheran Hymnal, *1941, alt.*
Tune: Latin credo, c. 1300

WIR GLAUBEN ALL
88 88 8 D

Only-Begotten, Word of God Eternal

375

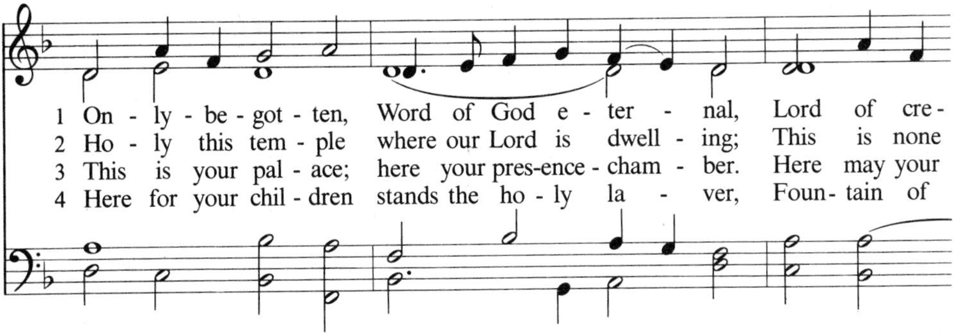

1 On-ly-be-got-ten, Word of God e-ter-nal, Lord of cre-
2 Ho-ly this tem-ple where our Lord is dwell-ing; This is none
3 This is your pal-ace; here your pres-ence-cham-ber. Here may your
4 Here for your chil-dren stands the ho-ly la-ver, Foun-tain of

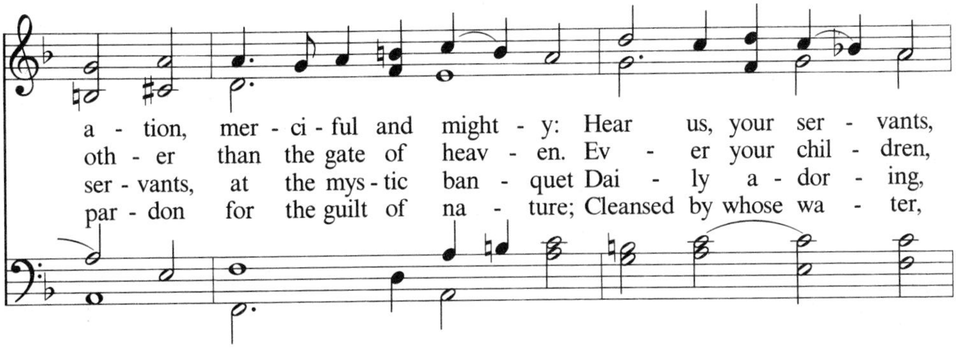

a-tion, mer-ci-ful and might-y: Hear us, your ser-vants,
oth-er than the gate of heav-en. Ev-er your chil-dren,
ser-vants, at the mys-tic ban-quet Dai-ly a-dor-ing,
par-don for the guilt of na-ture; Cleansed by whose wa-ter,

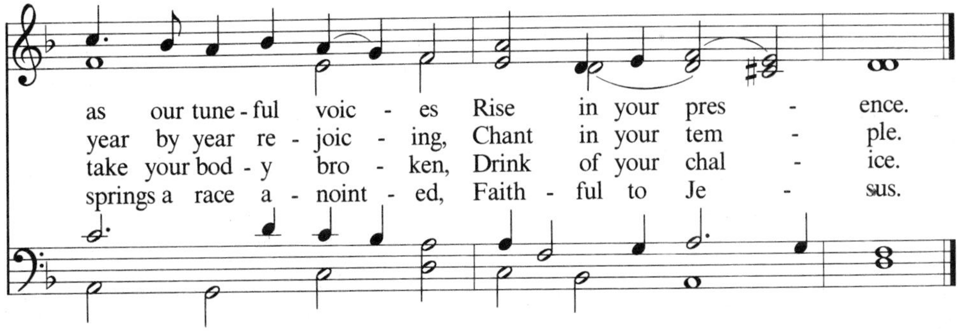

as our tune-ful voic-es Rise in your pres-ence.
year by year re-joic-ing, Chant in your tem-ple.
take your bod-y bro-ken, Drink of your chal-ice.
springs a race a-noint-ed, Faith-ful to Je-sus.

5 Hear us, O Father, as we throng your temple.
By your past blessings, by your present bounty,
Smile on your children, and in grace and mercy
Hear our petition.

6 God in three Persons, Father everlasting,
Son co-eternal, ever-blessed Spirit:
To you be praises, thanks, and adoration,
Glory forever.

Text: Bern, 9th cent.; tr. Maxwell J. Blacker, 1822–1888, alt.
Tune: Antiphoner, *Poitiers, 1746*

ISTE CONFESSOR
11 11 11 5

376 Your Kingdom Come!

1 Your king-dom come! O Fa-ther, hear our prayer; Shine through the
2 Stum-bling and blind, we strive to do your will, Trust-ing the
3 Come through the faith where-by the Church must live; Come through the
4 Your king-dom come; come too, God's glo-rious Son! Oh, may our
clouds that threat-en ev-'ry-where; Light from a-bove, our
word you sure-ly will ful-fill, That all are yours, how-
Word and Sac-ra-ments you give; Come through your teach-ing,
task for you be no-bly done! Faith-ful let all your
on-ly life and joy, Show us the hope that noth-ing
ev-er far they roam, That love shall tri-umph, and your
and your heal-ing too; Come through the work en-light-ened
ser-vants be, and true, Un-til they bring all na-tions
can de-stroy; Show us the hope that noth-ing can de-stroy.
king-dom come; That love shall tri-umph, and your king-dom come.
hearts can do; Come through the work en-light-ened hearts can do.
home to you; Un-til they bring all na-tions home to you.

Text: Margaret R. Seebach, 1875–1948, alt.
Tune: Trente quatre pseaumes de David, *Geneva, 1551*

OLD 124TH
10 10 10 10 10

Lift High the Cross

377

Refrain
Lift high the cross, the love of Christ pro-claim Till
all the world a - dore his sa - cred name.
1 Come, Chris - tians, fol - low where our cap - tain trod,
2 Led on their way by this tri - um - phant sign,
3 All new - born sol - diers of the Cru - ci - fied
4 O Lord, once lift - ed on the glo - rious tree,
Refrain
Our king vic - to - rious, Christ, the Son of God.
The hosts of God in con - qu'ring ranks com - bine.
Bear on their brows the seal of him who died.
As thou hast prom - ised, draw us all to thee.

5 So shall our song of triumph ever be:
Praise to the Crucified for victory! *Refrain*

© Text: George W. Kitchin, 1827–1912; Michael R. Newbolt, 1874–1956
© Tune: Sydney H. Nicholson, 1875–1947

CRUCIFER
10 10 10 10

378 Amid the World's Bleak Wilderness

1 A - mid the world's bleak wil - der - ness A vine - yard grows with prom - ise green, The plant - ing of the Lord him - self.
2 His love se - lect - ed this ter - rain; His vine with love he plant - ed here To bear the choic - est fruit for him.
3 We are his branch - es, cho - sen, dear, And though we feel the dress - er's knife, We are the ob - jects of his care.
4 From him we draw the juice of life, For him sup - ply his win - er - y With fruit from which true joys de - rive.
5 Vine, keep what I was meant to be: Your

branch, with your rich life in me.

GRANTON
irregular

Spread, Oh, Spread, Almighty Word 379

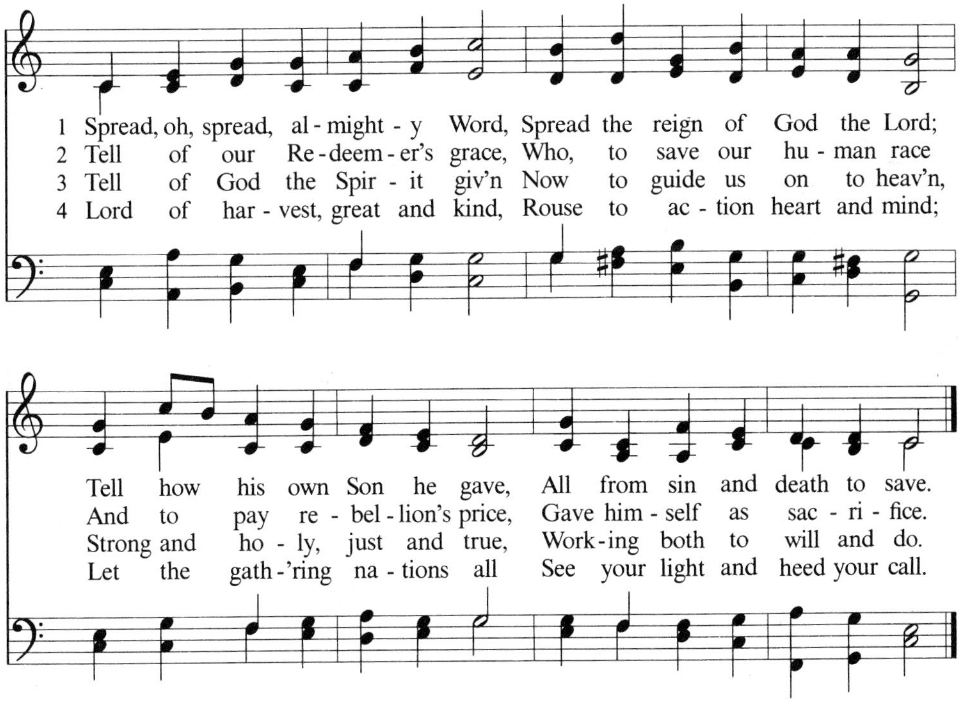

1 Spread, oh, spread, al - might - y Word, Spread the reign of God the Lord;
2 Tell of our Re - deem - er's grace, Who, to save our hu - man race
3 Tell of God the Spir - it giv'n Now to guide us on to heav'n,
4 Lord of har - vest, great and kind, Rouse to ac - tion heart and mind;

Tell how his own Son he gave, All from sin and death to save.
And to pay re - bel - lion's price, Gave him - self as sac - ri - fice.
Strong and ho - ly, just and true, Work - ing both to will and do.
Let the gath - 'ring na - tions all See your light and heed your call.

Tune: J. A. Freylinghausen, Geistreiches Gesang-Buch, *1704*

GOTT SEI DANK
77 77

380 O Christ, Our Light, O Radiance True

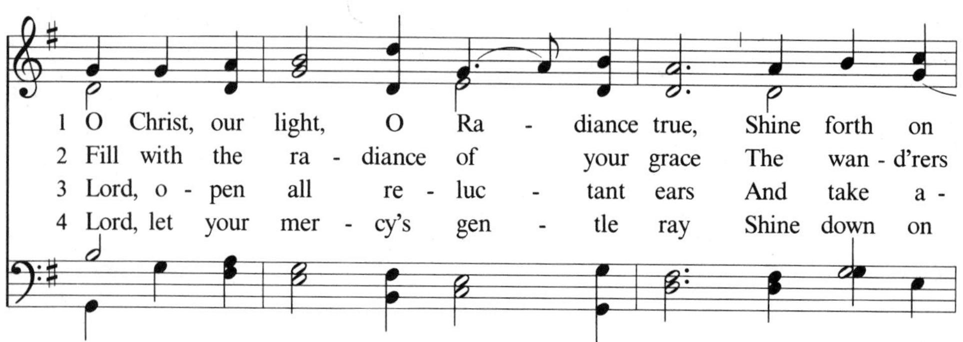
1 O Christ, our light, O Ra - diance true, Shine forth on
2 Fill with the ra - diance of your grace The wan - d'rers
3 Lord, o - pen all re - luc - tant ears And take a -
4 Lord, let your mer - cy's gen - tle ray Shine down on

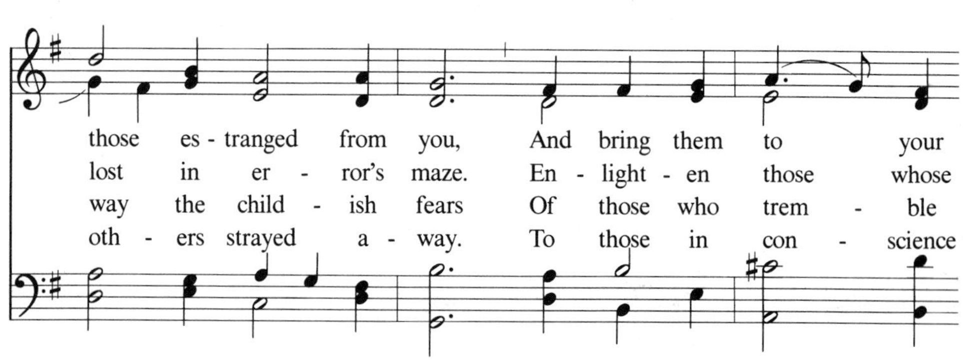
those es - tranged from you, And bring them to your
lost in er - ror's maze. En - light - en those whose
way the child - ish fears Of those who trem - ble
oth - ers strayed a - way. To those in con - science

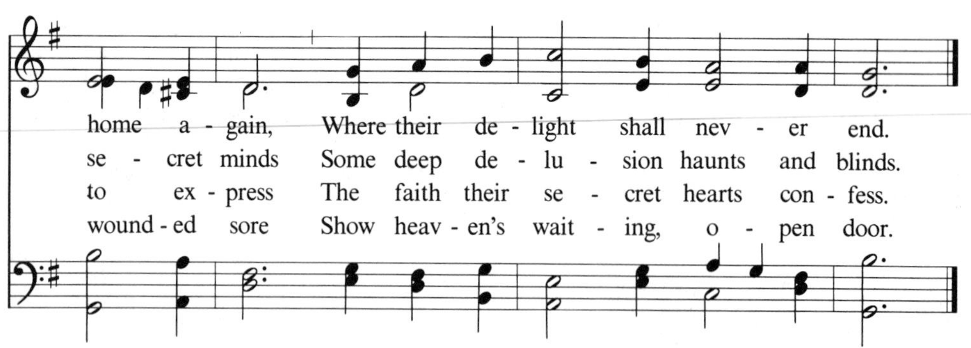
home a - gain, Where their de - light shall nev - er end.
se - cret minds Some deep de - lu - sion haunts and blinds.
to ex - press The faith their se - cret hearts con - fess.
wound - ed sore Show heav - en's wait - ing, o - pen door.

5 Make theirs with ours a single voice
Uplifted, ever to rejoice
With wond'ring gratitude and praise
To you, O Lord, for boundless grace.

Text: *Johann Heermann, 1585–1647; tr. composite*
Tune: Gesang-Buch, *Nürnberg, 1676*

O JESU CHRISTE, WAHRES LICHT
LM

Hark, the Voice of Jesus Calling 381

1 Hark, the voice of Je - sus call - ing, "Who will go and work to - day?
2 If you can - not speak like an - gels, If you can - not preach like Paul,
3 If you can - not be a watch-man, Stand - ing high on Zi - on's wall,
4 Let none hear you i - dly say - ing, "There is noth - ing I can do,"
Fields are white and har - vests wait - ing, Who will bear the sheaves a - way?"
You can tell the love of Je - sus; You can say he died for all.
Point - ing out the path to heav - en, Of - f'ring life and peace to all,
While the mul - ti - tudes are dy - ing And the mas - ter calls for you.
Loud and long the mas - ter calls you; Rich re-ward he of - fers free.
If you can - not rouse the wick - ed With the judg-ment's dread a - larms,
With your prayers and with your boun - ties You can do what God de - mands;
Take the task he gives you glad - ly; Let his work your plea-sure be.
Who will an - swer, glad - ly say - ing, "Here am I. Send me, send me"?
You can lead the lit - tle chil - dren To the Sav - ior's wait - ing arms.
You can be like faith - ful Aar - on, Hold - ing up the proph - et's hands.
An - swer quick - ly when he calls you, "Here am I. Send me, send me!"

Text: Daniel March, 1816–1909, alt.
Tune: Joseph Barnby, 1838–1896

GALILEAN
87 87 D

382 Awake, O Spirit of the Watchmen

1 A - wake, O Spir - it of the watch - men Who nev - er held their peace by day or night, Con - tend - ing from the walls of Zi - on A - gainst the foe, con - fid - ing in your might. Through-out the world their cry is ring - ing still
2 O Lord, now let your fire en - kin - dle Our hearts, that ev - 'ry - where its flame may go And spread the glo - ry of re - demp-tion, That all the world your sav - ing grace may know. O har - vest Lord, look down on us and view
3 Send forth, O Lord, your strong E - van - gel By man - y mes - sen - gers, all hearts to win. Make haste to help us in our weak ness, Break down the realm of Sa - tan, death, and sin. The cir - cle of the earth shall then pro - claim

And bring - ing peo - ples to your ho - ly will.
How white the fields, the la - bor - ers, how few!
Your king - dom and the glo - ry of your name.

© Text: Karl H. von Bogatzky, 1690–1774; tr. composite, alt.
Tune: J. A. Freylinghausen, Geistreiches Gesang-Buch, 1704

DIR, DIR, JEHOVA
9 10 9 10 10 10

Rise Up, O Saints of God! 383

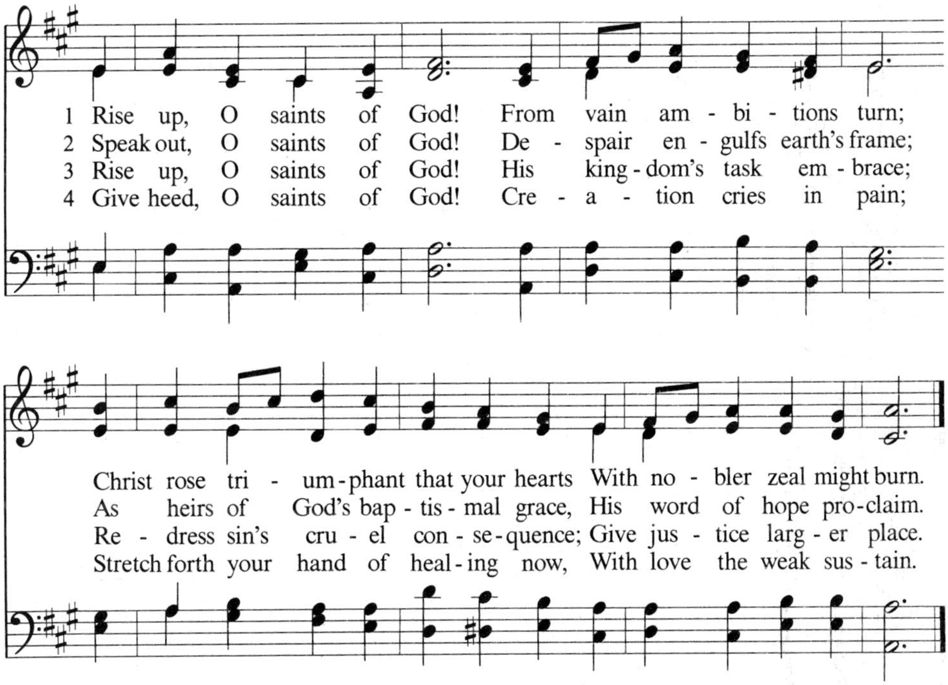

1 Rise up, O saints of God! From vain am - bi - tions turn;
2 Speak out, O saints of God! De - spair en - gulfs earth's frame;
3 Rise up, O saints of God! His king - dom's task em - brace;
4 Give heed, O saints of God! Cre - a - tion cries in pain;

Christ rose tri - um - phant that your hearts With no - bler zeal might burn.
As heirs of God's bap - tis - mal grace, His word of hope pro - claim.
Re - dress sin's cru - el con - se - quence; Give jus - tice larg - er place.
Stretch forth your hand of heal - ing now, With love the weak sus - tain.

5 Commit your hearts to seek
The paths which Christ has trod
And quickened by the Spirit's power,
Rise up, O saints of God!

© Text: Norman O. Forness, b. 1936
Tune: William H. Walter, 1825–1893

FESTAL SONG
SM

384 Your Kingdom Come, O Father

1 Your king - dom come, O Fa - ther, To earth's re - mot - est shore.
2 On all who lift your ban - ner, Your bless - ing, Lord, be - stow;
3 Your love with - in us quick - en; In - crease it day by day,
4 The des - ert, as you prom-ised, Shall blos - som far and near;
Your ho - ly fire en - kin - dle And let it flame the more.
Let all, your cross be - hold-ing, In hum - ble faith bend low.
That we, our - selves de - ny - ing, May find in you the way.
And through earth's mists and shad-ows The sun's mild rays ap - pear.
Your ser - vants send to la - bor Where liv - ing har - vests grow,
Oh, make your Church, dear Sav - ior, A wit - ness true and clear,
You once left all, O Sav - ior, A thorn - y path to tread;
For that blest day we wait, Lord, When, doubts and dark-ness gone,
That all, your truth re - ceiv - ing, Your sav - ing grace may know.
Your sav - ing death pro-claim - ing, That all the world may hear.
Help us to fol - low glad - ly, Wher - ev - er you may lead.
We wit - ness earth's re - demp - tion, And sum - mer morn shall dawn.

© *Text: Kauko-Veikko Tamminen, 1882–1946; tr. Ernest E. Ryden, b. 1886, alt.*
Tune: Finnish folk tune

NOORMARKKU
76 76 D

What Wondrous Love Is This

385

G Dm C Am C Dm F Em Dm
1 What won-drous love is this, O my soul, O my soul! What
2 When I was sink-ing down, sink-ing down, sink-ing down, When
3 To God and to the Lamb I will sing, I will sing; To
4 And when from death I'm free, I'll sing on, I'll sing on; And
Am Am7 F Em Dm Dm7 G Am Am7 Dm G
won-drous love is this, O my soul! What won-drous love is this That
I was sink-ing down, sink-ing down, When I was sink-ing down Be -
God and to the Lamb I will sing; To God and to the Lamb, Who
when from death I'm free, I'll sing on; And when from death I'm free, I'll
Am B♭maj7 C Dm G Dm C F Em
caused the Lord of bliss To bear the dread - ful curse for my
neath God's righ-teous frown, Christ laid a - side his crown for my
is the great I Am, While mil - lions join the theme, I will
sing his love for me, And through e - ter - ni - ty I'll sing
Dm G Em Dm Am Am7 F Em Dm
soul, for my soul, To bear the dread-ful curse for my soul?
soul, for my soul, Christ laid a - side his crown for my soul.
sing, I will sing, While mil-lions join the theme, I will sing.
on, I'll sing on; And through e - ter - ni - ty I'll sing on.

Text: *American folk hymn, alt.*
Tune: *W. Walker,* Southern Harmony, *1835*

WONDROUS LOVE
12 9 66 12 9

386 Christ Is the King!

1 Christ is the king! O friends, re - joice; Broth-ers and sis-ters,
2 Oh, mag - ni - fy the Lord, and raise An - thems of joy and
3 O Chris - tian wom - en, Chris - tian men, All the world o - ver,
4 Let love's all - rec - on - cil - ing might Your scat-tered com-pa -
with one voice Let the world know he is your choice.
ho - ly praise For all his saints of an - cient days.
seek a - gain The way his faith - ful fol - lowed then.
nies u - nite In ser - vice to the Lord of light.
Al - le - lu - ia, al - le - lu - ia, al - le - lu - ia!

5 So shall the Church at last be one;
So shall God's will on earth be done,
New lamps be lit, new tasks begun.
Alleluia, alleluia, alleluia!

BEVERLY
888 and alleluias

Spirit of God, Unleashed on Earth 387

1 Spir - it of God, un - leashed on earth With rush of wind and roar of flame; With tongues of fire men spread good news; Earth, kin - dling, blazed its loud ac - claim.
2 You came in pow'r, your Church was born; O Ho - ly Spir - it, come a - gain! Raise up new saints from wa - ters deep; Let new tongues hail the ris - en Lord.
3 Let new lips, tast - ing vic - t'ry won, In - spire our hearts grown cold with fear; Re - vive in us bap - tis - mal grace, And fan our smol - d'ring lives to flame.

DONATA
LM

388 O Spirit of the Living God

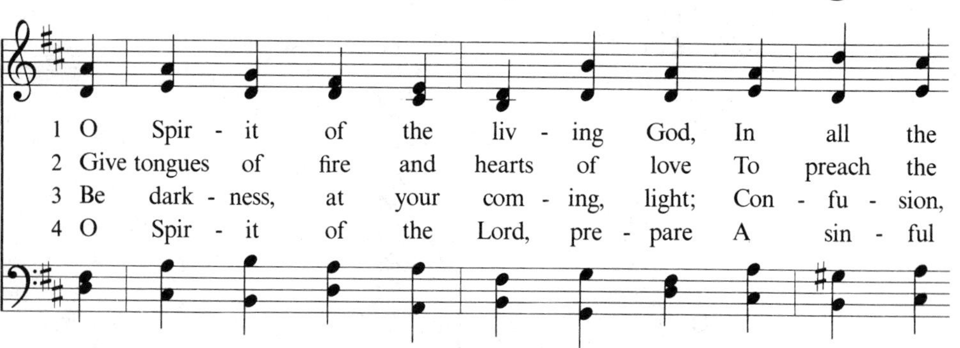
1 O Spir - it of the liv - ing God, In all the
2 Give tongues of fire and hearts of love To preach the
3 Be dark - ness, at your com - ing, light; Con - fu - sion,
4 O Spir - it of the Lord, pre - pare A sin - ful

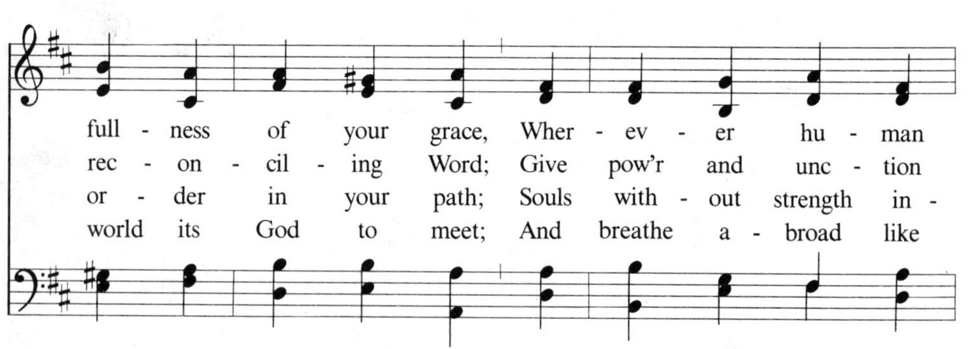
full - ness of your grace, Wher - ev - er hu - man
rec - on - cil - ing Word; Give pow'r and unc - tion
or - der in your path; Souls with - out strength in -
world its God to meet; And breathe a - broad like

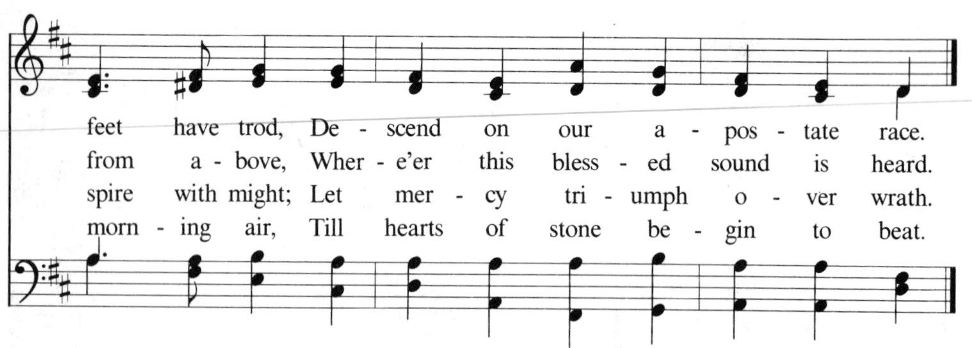
feet have trod, De - scend on our a - pos - tate race.
from a - bove, Wher - e'er this bless - ed sound is heard.
spire with might; Let mer - cy tri - umph o - ver wrath.
morn - ing air, Till hearts of stone be - gin to beat.

5 Proclaim the Gospel far and wide;
The triumphs of the cross record;
The name of Christ be glorified;
Let ev'ry people call him Lord!

Text: James Montgomery, 1771–1854, alt.
Tune: Samuel Webbe Sr., 1740–1816

MELCOMBE
LM

Stand Up, Stand Up for Jesus

389

1 Stand up, stand up for Je - sus, As sol - diers of the cross,
2 Stand up, stand up for Je - sus; The trum - pet call o - bey;
3 Stand up, stand up for Je - sus, Stand in his strength a - lone;
4 Stand up, stand up for Je - sus, The strife will not be long;
Lift high his roy - al ban - ner; It must not suf - fer loss.
Stand forth in might - y con - flict In this his glo - rious day.
The arm of flesh will fail you, You dare not trust your own.
This day the din of bat - tle, The next the vic - tor's song.
From vic - t'ry un - to vic - t'ry His ar - my he shall lead,
Let all his faith - ful serve him A - gainst un - num-bered foes;
Put on the Gos - pel ar - mor; Each piece put on with prayer.
The sol - diers, o - ver - com - ing, Their crown of life shall see,
Till ev - 'ry foe is van - quished And Christ is Lord in - deed.
Let cour - age rise with dan - ger, And strength to strength op - pose.
Where du - ty calls or dan - ger, Be nev - er want - ing there.
And with the King of glo - ry Shall reign e - ter - nal - ly.

Text: George Duffield, 1818–1888, alt.
Tune: George J. Webb, 1803–1887

WEBB
76 76 D

390 I Love to Tell the Story

1 I love to tell the sto - ry Of un - seen things a - bove,
2 I love to tell the sto - ry: How pleas - ant to re - peat
3 I love to tell the sto - ry, For those who know it best
Of Je - sus and his glo - ry, Of Je - sus and his love.
What seems, each time I tell it, More won - der - ful - ly sweet!
Seem hun - ger - ing and thirst - ing To hear it like the rest.
I love to tell the sto - ry, Be - cause I know it's true;
I love to tell the sto - ry, For some have nev - er heard
And when, in scenes of glo - ry, I sing the new, new song,
It sat - is - fies my long - ings As noth - ing else would do.
The mes - sage of sal - va - tion From God's own ho - ly Word.
I'll sing the old, old sto - ry That I have loved so long.

Refrain
I love to tell the sto - ry; I'll sing this theme in glo - ry
And tell the old, old sto - ry Of Je - sus and his love.

Text: Katherine Hankey, 1834–1911
Tune: William G. Fischer, 1835–1912

HANKEY
76 76 D and refrain

391 And Have the Bright Immensities

1 And have the bright im - men - si - ties Re - ceived our ris - en Lord,
2 The heav'n that hides him from our sight Knows nei - ther near nor far;
Where light-years frame the Ple - ia - des And point O - ri - on's sword?
An al - tar can - dle sheds its light As sure - ly as a star.
Do flam - ing suns his foot - steps trace Through cor - ri - dors sub - lime,
And where his lov - ing peo - ple meet To share the gift di - vine,
The Lord of in - ter - stel - lar space And con - quer - or of time?
There stands he with un - hur - rying feet; There heav'n-ly splen-dors shine.

© *Text: Howard C. Robbins, 1876–1952*
© *Tune: English folk tune*

KINGSFOLD
CMD

O Lord, Send Forth Your Spirit 392

1 O Lord, send forth your Spir - it To seize our way-ward mind;
2 Though se - crets of the at - om And worlds of dis - tant light
3 So take us, lead and use us To sing your praise, O God;
For still, in this world's fash - ion, We hun - ger for a sign.
And na - ture's won-drous pat - terns Pro - claim your mind and might,
That voic - es, gifts, and ser - vice May speed your Word a - broad,
For you, O Lord, have made us That, not by signs or bread,
We praise you most for wit - ness, From each to each passed on,
That all in ev - 'ry na - tion May hear what we have heard,
But on - ly by your Gos - pel Can hu - man souls be fed.
That sings cre - a - tion's mean - ing: The Gos - pel of your Son.
And that the minds of mil - lions Be nur - tured by your Word.

 Text: *Charles Jeffries, 1925–1971, adapt.*
Tune: The Sacred Harp, *Philadelphia, 1844*

WEDLOCK
76 76 D

393 Rise, Shine, You People!

1 Rise, shine, you peo - ple! Christ the Lord has en - tered Our
2 See how he sends the pow'rs of e - vil reel - ing; He
3 Come, cel - e-brate; your ban - ners high un - furl - ing, Your
4 Tell how the Fa - ther sent his Son to save us. Tell
hu - man sto - ry; God in him is cen - tered. He comes to
brings us free - dom, light and life and heal - ing. All men and
songs and prayers a - gainst the dark - ness hurl - ing. To all the
of the Son, who life and free - dom gave us. Tell how the
us, by death and sin sur-round - ed, With grace un - bound - ed.
wom-en, who by guilt are driv - en, Now are for - giv - en.
world go out and tell the sto - ry Of Je - sus' glo - ry.
Spir - it calls from ev - 'ry na - tion His new cre - a - tion.

© *Text: Ronald A. Klug, b. 1939, alt.*
© *Tune: Dale Wood, b. 1934*

WOJTKIEWIECZ
11 11 11 5

Lost in the Night

1 Lost in the night do the people yet languish Longing for morning the darkness to vanquish, Plaintively heaving a sigh full of anguish. Will not day come soon? Will not day come soon?

2 Must we be vainly awaiting the morrow? Shall those who have light no light let us borrow, Giving no heed to our burden of sorrow? Will you help us soon? Will you help us soon?

3 Sorrowing wand'rers, in darkness yet dwelling, Dawned has the day of a radiance excelling, Death's dreaded darkness forever dispelling. Christ is coming soon! Christ is coming soon!

4 Light o'er the land of the needy is beaming; Rivers of life through its deserts are streaming, Bringing all peoples a Savior redeeming. Come and save us soon! Come and save us soon!

 Text: Finnish song; tr. Olav Lee, b. 1859, alt.
Tune: Finnish folk tune

LOST IN THE NIGHT
11 11 11 5 5

395 I Trust, O Christ, in You Alone

1 I trust, O Christ, in you a - lone; No earth - ly hope a - vails
2 My sin and guilt are plagu - ing me; Oh, grant me true con - tri -
3 Con-firm in us your Gos - pel, Lord, Your prom - ise of sal - va -

me. You will not see me o - ver-thrown When Sa-tan's host as-sails
tion And, by your death up - on the tree, Your par-don and re-mis -
tion. And make us keen to hear your Word And fol-low our vo-ca -

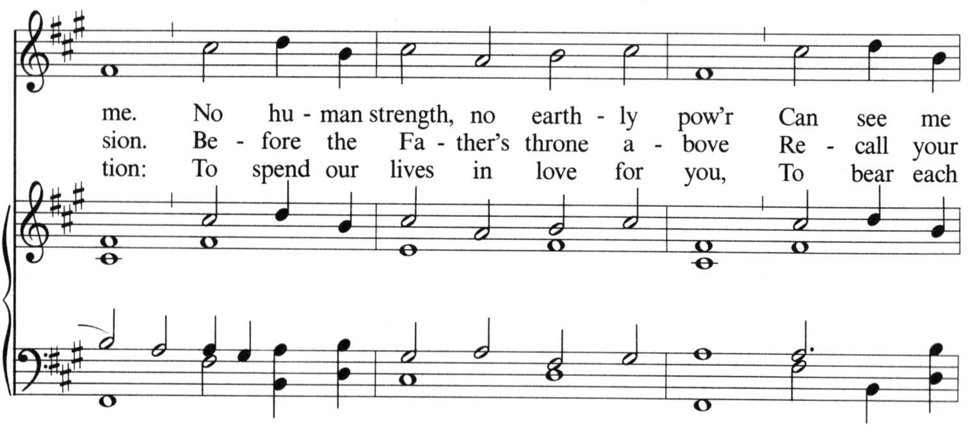
me. No hu - man strength, no earth - ly pow'r Can see me
sion. Be - fore the Fa - ther's throne a - bove Re - call your
tion: To spend our lives in love for you, To bear each

through the e - vil hour, For you a - lone my strength re - new.
match - less deed of love That he may lift my dread - ful load,
oth - er's bur - dens, too. And then, at last, when death shall loom,
I cry to you! I trust, O Lord, your prom - ise true.
O Son of God! I plead the grace your death be - stowed.
O Sav - ior, come, And bear your loved ones safe - ly home.

© *Text: Konrad Hubert, 1507–1577; tr. Gilbert E. Doan, b. 1930*
Tune: broadsheet, Wittenberg, c. 1541

ALLEIN ZU DIR
87 87 888 48

396 O God, O Lord of Heaven and Earth

1 O God, O Lord of heav'n and earth, Your liv - ing
2 In blind re - volt we would not see That reb - el
3 You came in - to our hall of death, O Christ, to
4 O Spir - it, who did once re - store The Church, that
fin - ger nev - er wrote That life should be an aim -
wills wrought death and night. We seized and used in fear
breathe our poi - soned air, To drink for us the deep
it might yet re - call The bring - er of good news
less mote, A death - ward drift from fu - tile
and spite Your won - drous gift of lib - er -
de - spair That stran - gled our re - luc - tant
to all: Breathe on your clo - ven Church once
birth. Your Word meant life tri - um - phant hurled
ty. We walled us in this house of doom,
breath. How beau - ti - ful the feet that trod
more, That in these gray and lat - ter days

In splen - dor through your bro - ken world; Since light a - woke and life be - gan, You made for us a ho - ly plan.
Where death had roy - al scope and room, Un - til your ser - vant, Prince of Peace, Broke down its walls for our re - lease.
The road to bring good news from God! How beau - ti - ful the feet that bring Good tid - ings of our sav - ing king!
There may be those whose life is praise, Each life a high dox - ol - o - gy Un - to the ho - ly Trin - i - ty.

WITTENBERG NEW
LMD

397 O Zion, Haste

1 O Zi - on, haste, your mis - sion high ful - fill - ing,
2 Pub - lish to ev - 'ry peo - ple, tongue, and na - tion
3 Give of your own to bear the mes - sage glo - rious,
4 He comes a - gain! O Zi - on, ere you meet him,
To tell to all the world that God is light; That he who
That God, in whom they live and move, is love; Tell how he
Give of your wealth to speed them on their way, Pour out your
Make known to ev - 'ry heart his sav - ing grace; Let none whom
made all na - tions is not will - ing One soul should
stooped to save his lost cre - a - tion And died on
soul for them in prayer vic - to - rious, And haste the
he has ran - somed fail to greet him, Through your ne -
per - ish, lost in shades of night.
earth that we might live a - bove.
com - ing of the glo - rious day.
glect, un - fit to see his face.
Refrain
Pub - lish glad tid - ings, tid - ings of

peace, Tid - ings of Je - sus, re-demp-tion, and re - lease.

Text: Mary A. Thomson, 1834–1923
Tune: James Walch, 1837–1901

ANGELIC SONGS
11 10 11 10 and refrain

"Take Up Your Cross," the Savior Said 398

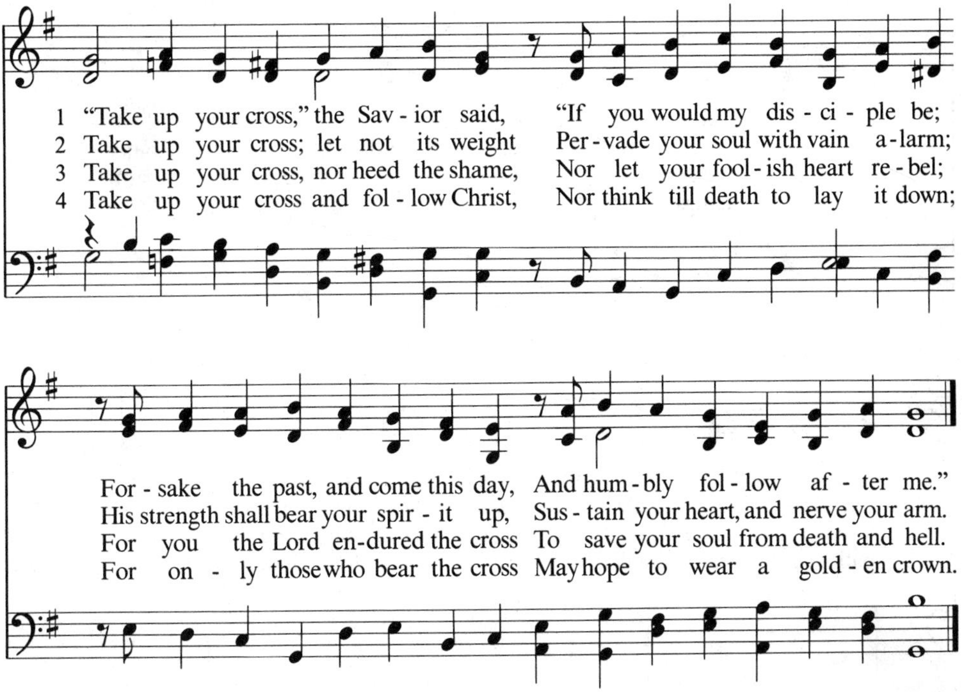

1 "Take up your cross," the Sav - ior said, "If you would my dis - ci - ple be;
2 Take up your cross; let not its weight Per - vade your soul with vain a - larm;
3 Take up your cross, nor heed the shame, Nor let your fool - ish heart re - bel;
4 Take up your cross and fol - low Christ, Nor think till death to lay it down;

For - sake the past, and come this day, And hum - bly fol - low af - ter me."
His strength shall bear your spir - it up, Sus - tain your heart, and nerve your arm.
For you the Lord en - dured the cross To save your soul from death and hell.
For on - ly those who bear the cross May hope to wear a gold - en crown.

Text: Charles W. Everest, 1814–1877, alt.
Tune: G. Rhau, Newe deudsche geistliche Gesenge, *1544*

NUN LASST UNS DEN LEIB BEGRABEN
LM

399 We Are the Lord's

1 We are the Lord's. His all - suf - fi - cient mer - it,
2 We are the Lord's. Then let us glad - ly ten - der
3 We are the Lord's. No dark - ness brood - ing o'er us
4 We are the Lord's. No e - vil can be - fall us
Sealed on the cross, to us this grace ac - cords.
Our souls to him in deeds, not emp - ty words.
Can make us trem - ble while this star af - fords
In the dread hour of life's fast - loos - 'ning cords;
We are the Lord's and all things shall in -
Let heart and tongue and life com - bine to
A stead - y light a - long the path be -
No pangs of death shall e - ven then ap -
her - it; Wheth - er we live or die, we are the Lord's.
ren - der No doubt - ful wit - ness that we are the Lord's.
fore us— Faith's full as - sur - ance that we are the Lord's.
pall us. Death shall be van - quished, for we are the Lord's.

Text: Karl J. P. Spitta, 1801–1859; tr. Charles T. Astley, 1825–1878
© *Tune: Ludwig Lenel, b. 1914*

WE ARE THE LORD'S
11 10 11 10

God, Whose Almighty Word 400

1 God, whose al - might - y word Cha - os and dark - ness heard And took their flight:
2 Lord, who once came to bring, On your re - deem - ing wing, Heal - ing and sight,
3 Spir - it of truth and love, Life - giv - ing, ho - ly dove, Speed forth your flight;
4 Ho - ly and bless - ed three, Glo - ri - ous Trin - i - ty, Wis - dom, love, might!
Hear us, we hum - bly pray, And where the Gos - pel day Sheds not its glo - rious ray,
Health to the sick in mind, Sight to the in - ly blind: Oh, now to hu - man-kind
Move on the wa - ter's face Bear - ing the lamp of grace, And in earth's dark - est place
Bound-less as o - cean's tide, Roll - ing in full - est pride, Through the earth, far and wide,
Let there be light!

Text: John Marriott, 1780–1825, alt.
Tune: Felice de Giardini, 1716–1796

ITALIAN HYMN
664 6664

401 Before You, Lord, We Bow

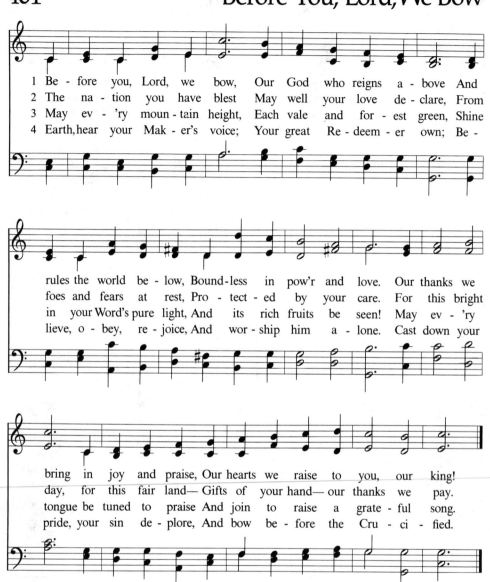

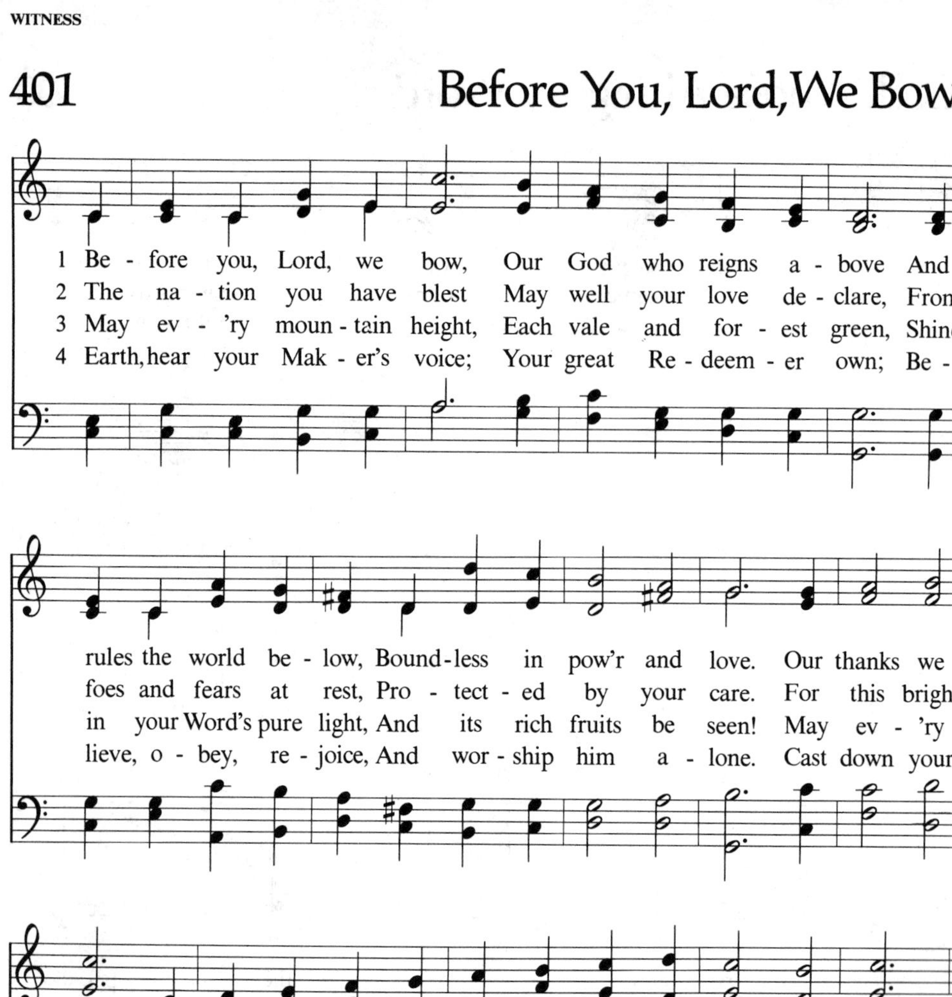
1 Be - fore you, Lord, we bow, Our God who reigns a - bove And
2 The na - tion you have blest May well your love de - clare, From
3 May ev - 'ry moun - tain height, Each vale and for - est green, Shine
4 Earth, hear your Mak - er's voice; Your great Re - deem - er own; Be -
rules the world be - low, Bound-less in pow'r and love. Our thanks we
foes and fears at rest, Pro - tect - ed by your care. For this bright
in your Word's pure light, And its rich fruits be seen! May ev - 'ry
lieve, o - bey, re - joice, And wor - ship him a - lone. Cast down your
bring in joy and praise, Our hearts we raise to you, our king!
day, for this fair land— Gifts of your hand— our thanks we pay.
tongue be tuned to praise And join to raise a grate - ful song.
pride, your sin de - plore, And bow be - fore the Cru - ci - fied.

5 And when in pow'r he comes,
Oh, may our native land
From all its rending tombs
Send forth a glorious band,
A countless throng, with joy to sing
To heav'n's high king salvation's song!

Text: Francis S. Key, 1779–1843, alt.
Tune: John Darwall, 1731–1789

DARWALL'S 148TH
66 66 88

Look from Your Sphere of Endless Day 402

1 Look from your sphere of end - less day, O God of mer - cy and of might; In pit - y look on those who stray So blind-ly in this land of light.
2 Send us, your peo - ple, Lord, to call The thought-less, hard-ened young and old, A scat - tered home - less flock, till all Are gath - ered in your peace - ful fold.
3 Give us your might - y Word, to speak Till faith is born and doubts de - part, To awe the bold, to stay the weak, And bind and heal the bro - ken heart.
4 Then all these wastes, a drea - ry scene That makes us sad - den as we gaze, Shall bloom with liv - ing wa - ters green And lift to heav'n the voice of praise.
A - men

Text: William C. Bryant, 1794–1878, alt.
© Tune: Percy C. Buck, 1871–1947

GONFALON ROYAL
LM

403 Lord, Speak to Us, that We May Speak

1 Lord, speak to us, that we may speak In liv - ing
2 Oh, lead us, Lord, that we may lead The wan - d'ring
3 Oh, teach us, Lord, that we may teach The pre - cious
4 Oh, fill us with your full - ness, Lord, Un - til our
ech - oes of your tone; As you have sought, so
and the wa - v'ring feet; Oh, feed us, Lord, that
truths which you im - part; And wing our words, that
ver - y hearts o'er - flow In kin - dling thought and
let us seek Your stray - ing chil - dren, lost and lone.
we may feed Your hun - g'ring ones with man - na sweet.
they may reach The hid - den depths of man - y a heart.
glow - ing word, Your love to tell, your praise to show.

Text: Frances R. Havergal, 1836–1879, alt.
Tune: Robert Schumann, 1810–1856

CANONBURY
LM

As Saints of Old 404

1 As saints of old their first-fruits brought Of or-chard, flock, and
2 A world in need now sum-mons us To la-bor, love, and
3 In grat-i-tude and hum-ble trust We bring our best to-
field To God, the giv-er of all good, The source of boun-teous
give; To make our life an of-fer-ing To God, that all may
day To serve your cause and share your love With all a-long life's
yield; So we to-day first-fruits would bring, The wealth of this good
live. The church of Christ is call-ing us To make the dream come
way. O God, who gave your-self to us In Je-sus Christ your
land, Of farm and mar-ket, shop and home, Of mind and heart and hand.
true: A world re-deemed by Christ-like love; All life in Christ made new.
Son, Teach us to give our-selves each day Un-til life's work is done.

REGWAL
CMD

405 Lord of Light

1 Lord of light, your name out-shin-ing All the stars and suns of space, Use our tal-ents in your king-dom As the ser-vants of your grace; Use us to ful-fill your pur-pose In the gift of Christ your Son:
2 By the toil of faith-ful work-ers In some far out-ly-ing field, By the cour-age where the ra-diance Of the cross is still re-vealed, By the vic-to-ries of meek-ness, Through re-proach and suf-f'ring won:
3 Grant that knowl-edge, still in-creas-ing, At your feet may low-ly kneel; With your grace our tri-umphs hal-low, With your char-i-ty our zeal; Lift the na-tions from the shad-ows To the glad-ness of the sun:
4 By the prayers of faith-ful watch-ers, Nev-er si-lent day or night; By the cross of Je-sus, bring-ing Peace to all and heal-ing light; By the love that pass-es knowl-edge, Mak-ing all your chil-dren one:

Refrain
Fa - ther, as in high - est heav-en, So on earth your will be done.

ABBOTT'S LEIGH
87 87 D

Take My Life, that I May Be 406

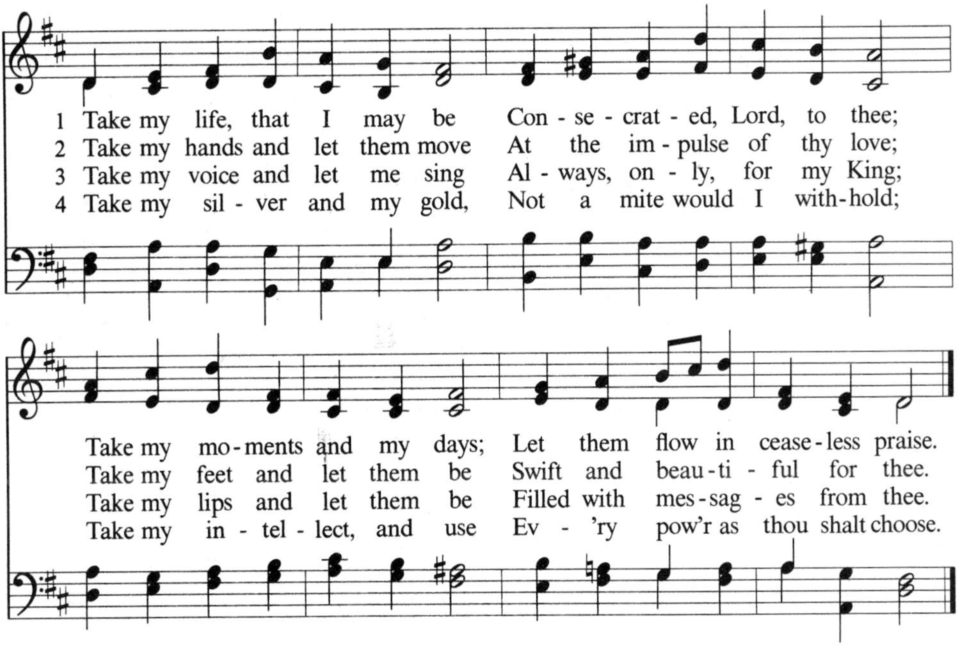

1 Take my life, that I may be
Consecrated, Lord, to thee;
Take my moments and my days;
Let them flow in ceaseless praise.

2 Take my hands and let them move
At the impulse of thy love;
Take my feet and let them be
Swift and beautiful for thee.

3 Take my voice and let me sing
Always, only, for my King;
Take my lips and let them be
Filled with messages from thee.

4 Take my silver and my gold,
Not a mite would I withhold;
Take my intellect, and use
Ev'ry pow'r as thou shalt choose.

5 Take my will and make it thine;
It shall be no longer mine.
Take my heart, it is thine own;
It shall be thy royal throne.

6 Take my love; my Lord, I pour
At thy feet its treasure store;
Take myself, and I will be
Ever, only, all for thee.

Text: Frances R. Havergal, 1836–1879, alt.
Tune: William H. Havergal, 1793–1870

PATMOS
77 77

407 Come, You Thankful People, Come

1 Come, you thank-ful peo - ple, come; Raise the song of har - vest home.
2 All the world is God's own field, Fruit un - to his praise to yield.
3 For the Lord our God shall come And shall take his har - vest home.
4 E - ven so, Lord, quick - ly come To your fi - nal har - vest home.
All is safe - ly gath - ered in Ere the win - ter storms be - gin.
Wheat and tares to - geth - er sown, Un - to joy or sor - row grown.
From his field shall in that day All of - fens - es purge a - way,
Gath - er all your peo - ple in, Free from sor - row, free from sin,
God, our mak - er, does pro - vide For our wants to be sup - plied.
First the blade, and then the ear, Then the full corn shall ap - pear.
Give his an - gels charge at last In the fire the tares to cast,
There, for - ev - er pu - ri - fied, In your gar - ner to a - bide.
Come to God's own tem - ple, come, Raise the song of har - vest home.
Lord of har - vest, grant that we Whole-some grain and pure may be.
But the fruit - ful ears to store In his gar - ner ev - er - more.
Come, with all your an - gels, come, Raise the glo - rious har - vest home!

Text: Henry Alford, 1810–1871, alt.
Tune: George J. Elvey, 1816–1893

ST. GEORGE'S, WINDSOR
77 77 D

God, Whose Giving Knows No Ending 408

1 God, whose giv - ing knows no end - ing, From your rich and end - less store:
2 Skills and time are ours for press - ing Toward the goals of Christ, your Son:
3 Trea-sure, too, you have en-trust - ed, Gain through pow'rs your grace con-ferred;

Na-ture's won-der, Je - sus' wis-dom, Cost - ly cross, grave's shat - tered door,
All at peace in health and free-dom, Rac - es joined, the Church made one.
Ours to use for home and kin-dred, And to spread the Gos - pel Word.

Gift-ed by you, we turn to you, Of - f'ring up our-selves in praise;
Now di - rect our dai - ly la - bor, Lest we strive for self a - lone;
O - pen wide our hands in shar-ing, As we heed Christ's age - less call,

Thank-ful song shall rise for - ev - er, Gra-cious do - nor of our days.
Born with tal - ents, make us ser - vants Fit to an - swer at your throne.
Heal - ing, teach-ing, and re - claim-ing, Serv - ing you by lov - ing all.

© Text: Robert L. Edwards, b. 1915
Tune: C. Hubert H. Parry, 1848–1918

RUSTINGTON
87 87 D

409 Praise and Thanksgiving

C Am Dm G Am G Am

1 Praise and thanks-giv - ing, Fa - ther, we of - fer For all things
2 Bless, Lord, the la - bor We bring to serve you, That with our
3 Fa - ther, pro - vid - ing Food for your chil - dren, By your wise
4 Then will your bless - ing Reach ev - 'ry peo - ple, Free - ly con -

Em Am Em G C Am F C

liv - ing, Cre - at - ed good: Har - vest of sown fields, Fruits of the
neigh - bor We may be fed. Sow - ing or till - ing, We would work
guid - ing Teach us to share One with an - oth - er, So that, re -
fess - ing Your gra - cious hand. Where all o - bey you, No one will

Am G C G Am G C
or - chard, Hay from the mown fields, Blos - som and wood.
with you, Har - vest - ing, mill - ing For dai - ly bread.
joic - ing With us, all oth - ers May know your care.
hun - ger; In your love's sway you Nour - ish the land.

 Text: Albert F. Bayly, b. 1901, alt.
Tune: Gaelic

BUNESSAN
55 54 D

We Give Thee but Thine Own 410

1 We give thee but thine own, What-e'er the gift may be;
All that we have is thine a-lone, A trust, O Lord, from thee.
2 May we thy boun-ties thus As stew-ards true re-ceive,
And glad-ly, as thou bless-est us, To thee our first-fruits give.
3 Hearts still are bruised and dead, And homes are bare and cold,
And lambs for whom the Shep-herd bled Are stray-ing from the fold.
4 To com-fort and to bless, To find a balm for woe,
To tend those lost in lone-li-ness, Is an-gels' work be-low.

5 The captive to release,
The lost to God to bring,
To teach the way of life and peace—
It is a Christlike thing.

6 And we believe thy word,
Though dim our faith may be:
Whate'er we do for thine, O Lord,
We do it unto thee.

Text: William W. How, 1823–1897, alt.
Tune: Mason and Webb, Cantica Lauda, *1850*

HEATH
SM

411 Lord of All Good

1 Lord of all good, our gifts we bring you now;
2 We give our minds to un - der - stand your ways;
3 Fa - ther, whose boun - ty all cre - a - tion shows;
Use them your ho - ly pur - pose to ful - fill.
Hands, voic - es, eyes to serve your great de - sign;
Christ, by whose will - ing sac - ri - fice we live;
To - kens of love and pledg - es they shall be That
Hearts with the flame of your own love a - blaze: Thus
Spir - it, from whom all life in full - ness flows: To
our whole life is of - fered to your will.
for your glo - ry all our pow'rs com - bine.
you with grate - ful hearts our - selves we give.

MORESTEAD
10 10 10 10

Sing to the Lord of Harvest 412

1 Sing to the Lord of har - vest, Sing songs of love and praise;
2 God makes the clouds drop fat - ness, The des - erts bloom and spring,
3 Bring to this sa - cred al - tar The gifts his good - ness gave,
With joy - ful hearts and voic - es Your al - le - lu - ias raise.
The hills leap up in glad - ness, The val - leys laugh and sing.
The gold - en sheaves of har - vest, The souls Christ died to save.
By him the roll - ing sea - sons In fruit - ful or - der move;
God fills them with his full - ness, All things with large in - crease;
Your hearts lay down be - fore him When at his feet you fall,
Sing to the Lord of har - vest A joy - ous song of love.
He crowns the year with good - ness, With plen - ty and with peace.
And with your lives a - dore him Who gave his life for all.

Text: John S. B. Monsell, 1811–1875, alt.
Tune: Johann Steurlein, 1546–1613

WIE LIEBLICH IST DER MAIEN
76 76 D

413 Father Eternal, Ruler of Creation

1 Fa - ther e - ter - nal, rul - er of cre - a - tion, Spir - it of life, which moved ere form was made: Through the thick dark - ness cov-'ring ev - 'ry na - tion, Light for our blind - ness, oh, be now our aid:
2 Rac - es and peo - ples, lo, we stand di - vid - ed, And, shar - ing not our griefs, no joy can share; By wars and tu - mults love is mocked, de - rid - ed; His con-qu'ring cross no na - tion wills to bear.
3 En - vious of heart, blind - eyed with tongues con - found - ed, Na - tion by na - tion still goes un - for - giv'n; In wrath and fear, by jeal - ou - sies sur-round - ed, Build - ing proud tow'rs which shall not reach to heav'n.
4 Lust of pos - ses - sion ends in des - o - la - tions; There is no meek - ness in the sons of earth; Led by no star, the rul - ers of the na - tions Still fail to bring us to the bliss - ful birth.
Your king - dom come, O Lord; your will be done!

5 How shall we love you, holy, hidden Being,
If we love not the world which you have made?
Oh, give us deeper love for better seeing
Your Word made flesh, and in a manger laid.
Your kingdom come, O Lord; your will be done!

LANGHAM
11 10 11 10 10

O God of Love, O King of Peace 414

1 O God of love, O King of peace, Make wars through-out the world to cease; Our greed and sin-ful wrath re-strain.
2 Re-mem-ber, Lord, your works of old, The won-ders that our el-ders told; Re-mem-ber not our sins' dark stain.
3 Whom shall we trust but you, O Lord? Where rest but on your faith-ful Word? None ev-er called on you in vain.
4 Where saints and an-gels dwell a-bove All hearts are knit in ho-ly love; Oh, bind us in that heav'n-ly chain.
Give peace, O God, give peace a-gain.

Text: Henry W. Baker, 1821–1877
Tune: Koralpsalmboken, *Stockholm, 1697*

ACK, BLIV HOS OSS
LM

415 God of Grace and God of Glory

1 God of grace and God of glo - ry, On your peo - ple
2 Lo! The hosts of e - vil round us Scorn the Christ, as -
3 Cure your chil - dren's war - ring mad - ness; Bend our pride to
4 Save us from weak res - ig - na - tion To the e - vils
pour your pow'r; Crown your an - cient Church's . . . . sto - ry;
sail his ways! From the fears that long have bound us
your con - trol; Shame our wan - ton, self - ish glad - ness,
we de - plore; Let the gift of your sal - va - tion
Bring its bud to glo-rious flow'r. Grant us wis-dom, grant us cour - age
Free our hearts to faith and praise. Grant us wis-dom, grant us cour - age
Rich in things and poor in soul. Grant us wis-dom, grant us cour-age,
Be our glo - ry ev - er - more. Grant us wis-dom, grant us cour-age,
For the fac - ing of this hour, For the fac - ing of this hour.
For the liv - ing of these days, For the liv - ing of these days.
Lest we miss your king-dom's goal, Lest we miss your king-dom's goal.
Serv-ing you whom we a - dore, Serv - ing you whom we a - dore.

Text: Harry E. Fosdick, 1878–1969
© *Tune: John Hughes, 1873–1932*

CWM RHONDDA
87 87 877

O God of Every Nation

416

1 O God of ev - 'ry na - tion, Of ev - 'ry race and land, Re -
2 From search for wealth and pow - er And scorn of truth and right, From
3 Lord, strength-en all who la - bor That all may find re - lease From
4 Keep bright in us the vi - sion Of days when war shall cease, When
deem your whole cre - a - tion With your al - might - y hand; Where
trust in bombs that show - er De - struc - tion through the night, From
fear of rat - tling sa - ber, From dread of war's in - crease; When
ha - tred and di - vi - sion Give way to love and peace, Till
hate and fear di - vide us And bit - ter threats are hurled, In
pride of race and sta - tion And blind - ness to your way, De -
hope and cour - age fal - ter, Lord, let your voice be heard; With
dawns the morn - ing glo - rious When truth and love shall reign, And
love and mer - cy guide us And heal our strife - torn world.
liv - er ev - 'ry na - tion, E - ter - nal God, we pray.
faith that none can al - ter, Your ser - vants un - der - gird.
Christ shall rule vic - to - rious O'er all the world's do - main.

© Text: William W. Reid Jr., b. 1923
© Tune: Dale Wood, b. 1934

TUOLUMNE
76 76 D

417 In a Lowly Manger Born

1 In a low - ly man - ger born, Hum - ble life be - gun in scorn;
2 Vis - it - ing the lone and lost, Stead - y - ing the tem - pest-tossed,
3 Then, to res - cue you and me, Je - sus died up - on the tree.
Un - der Jo - seph's watch - ful eye, Je - sus grew as you and I;
Giv - ing of him - self in love, Call - ing minds to things a - bove.
See in him God's love re-vealed; By his Pas-sion we are healed.
Knew the suf-f'rings of the weak, Knew the pa - tience of the meek,
Sin - ners glad - ly hear his call; Pub - li - cans be - fore him fall,
Now he lives in glo - ry bright, Lives a - gain in pow'r and might;
Hun - gered as but poor folk can; This is he. Be - hold the man!
For in him new life be - gan; This is he. Be - hold the man!
Come and take the path he trod, Son of Mar - y, Son of God.

MABUNE
77 77 D

Judge Eternal, Throned in Splendor 418

1 Judge e - ter - nal, throned in splen - dor, Lord of lords and
2 Still the wea - ry folk are pin - ing For the hour that
3 Crown, O God, your own en - deav - or; Cleave our dark - ness

King of kings, With your liv - ing fire of judg - ment
brings re - lease; And the cit - y's crowd - ed clan - gor
with your sword; Feed the faint and hun - gry peo - ples

Purge this land of bit - ter things; So - lace all its
Cries a - loud for sin to cease; And the home - steads
With the rich - ness of your Word; Cleanse the bod - y

wide do - min - ion With the heal - ing of your wings.
and the wood-lands Plead in si - lence for their peace.
of this na - tion Through the glo - ry of the Lord.

Text: Henry S. Holland, 1847–1918
Tune: Welsh, 18th cent.

RHUDDLAN
87 87 87

419 Lord of All Nations, Grant Me Grace

1 Lord of all na - tions, grant me grace To love all peo - ple, ev - 'ry race; And in each per - son may I see My kin - dred, loved, re-deemed by thee.
2 Break down the wall that would di - vide Thy chil - dren, Lord, on ev - 'ry side. My neigh-bor's good let me pur - sue; Let Chris - tian love bind warm and true.
3 For - give me, Lord, where I have erred By love - less act and thought-less word. Make me to see the wrong I do Will cru - ci - fy my Lord a - new.
4 Give me thy cour - age, Lord, to speak When - ev - er strong op - press the weak. Should I my - self the vic - tim be, Help me for - give, re - mem-b'ring thee.

5 With thine own love may I be filled
And by thy Holy Spirit willed,
That all I touch, where'er I be,
May be divinely touched by thee.

 Text: Olive Wise Spannaus, b. 1916, alt.
Tune: Šamotulský, Kancional, *1561*

BEATUS VIR
LM

Lord, Save Your World 420

1 Lord, save your world; in bit - ter need To you your chil - dren raise their plea; We wait your lib - er - at - ing deed To sig - nal hope and set us free.
2 Lord, save your world; our souls are bound In i - ron chains of fear and pride; High walls of ig - no - rance a - bound And fac - es from each oth - er hide.
3 Lord, save your world; we strive in vain To save our-selves with - out your aid; What skill and sci - ence slow - ly gain Is seen to e - vil ends be-trayed.
4 Lord, save your world, since you have sent The Sav - ior whom we sore - ly need; For us his tears and blood were spent That from our bonds we might be freed.

5 Then save us now, by Jesus' power,
And use the lives your love sets free
To bring at last the glorious hour
When all shall find your liberty.

 Text: Albert F. Bayly, b. 1901, alt.
Tune: W. Walker, Southern Harmony, *1835*

KEDRON
L M

421 Lord Christ, When First You Came to Earth

1 Lord Christ, when first you came to earth, Up - on a cross they bound you, And mocked your sav - ing king - ship's worth By thorns with which they crowned you. And still our wrongs may fash - ion now New thorns to pierce that
2 O awe - some Love, which finds no room In life where sin de - nies you, And, doomed to death, shall bring to doom The pow'r which cru - ci - fies you, Till not a stone was left on stone, And then the na - tions'
3 New ad - vent of the love of Christ, Will we a - gain re - fuse you, Till in the night of hate and war We per - ish as we lose you? From an - cient doubts our minds re - lease To seek the king - dom
4 O wound - ed hands of Je - sus, build In us your new cre - a - tion; Our pride is dust, our vaunt is stilled; We wait your rev - e - la - tion. O Love that tri - umphs o - ver loss, We bring our hearts be -

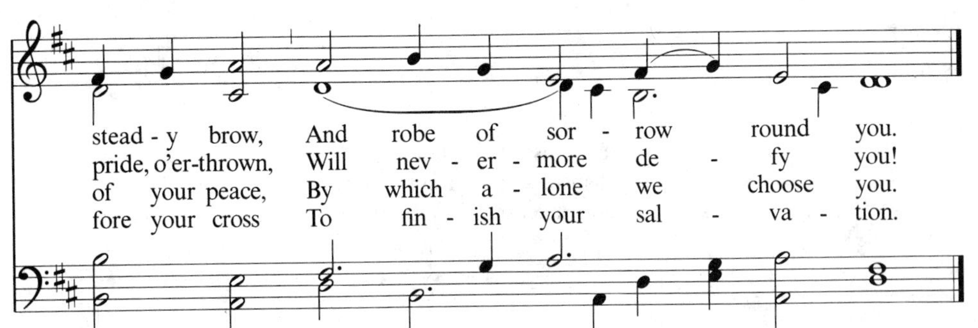
stead - y brow, And robe of sor - row round you.
pride, o'er-thrown, Will nev - er - more de - fy you!
of your peace, By which a - lone we choose you.
fore your cross To fin - ish your sal - va - tion.

© *Text: W. Russell Bowie, 1882–1969, alt.*
Tune: Trente quatre pseaumes de David, *Geneva, 1551*

MIT FREUDEN ZART
88 88 8

422 O God, Empower Us

1 O God, em-pow-er us to stem The ha-treds that di-vide.
2 When neigh-bors feel dis-tress, or grieve, Or sick-ness takes its toll,
3 Though cold sus-pi-cion meet our warmth, We love at your com-mand;
En-a-ble us to bring an end To ghast-ly wars of pride.
En-a-ble us to feel their pain, The bet-ter to con-sole.
And though not al-ways un-der-stood, We pray to un-der-stand.
Let our ex-am-ple point the way, That feuds be not pro-longed.
And when the neigh-bor's path is dark And heav-y with de-spair,
En-a-ble us to sti-fle greed For thanks or gain, dear Lord,
Let us for-give, as you for-gave, When we have suf-fered wrong.
Help us to lift the Gos-pel's light And show the Fa-ther's care.
And live that sac-ri-fi-cial life Which is its own re-ward.

WELLINGTON SQUARE
CMD

Lord, Whose Love in Humble Service 423

F Bb Am7 Dm F Bb F
1 Lord, whose love in hum-ble ser - vice Bore the weight of hu-man need,
2 Still your chil-dren wan-der home - less; Still the hun-gry cry for bread;
3 As we wor-ship, grant us vi - sion, Till your love's re - veal-ing light

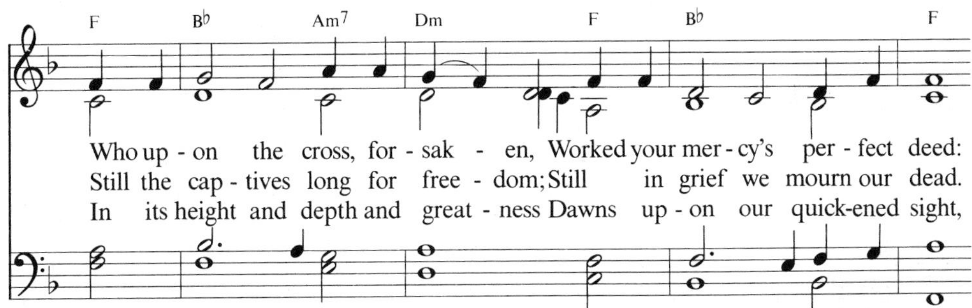
F Bb Am7 Dm F Bb F
Who up - on the cross, for - sak - en, Worked your mer-cy's per - fect deed:
Still the cap - tives long for free - dom; Still in grief we mourn our dead.
In its height and depth and great - ness Dawns up - on our quick-ened sight,

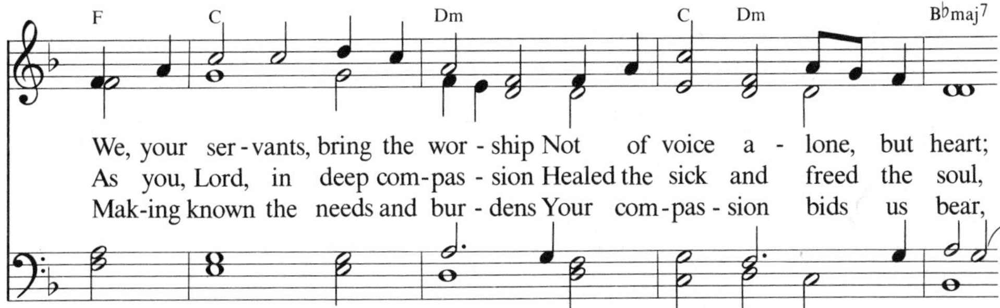
F C Dm C Dm Bbmaj7
We, your ser - vants, bring the wor - ship Not of voice a - lone, but heart;
As you, Lord, in deep com-pas - sion Healed the sick and freed the soul,
Mak-ing known the needs and bur - dens Your com-pas - sion bids us bear,

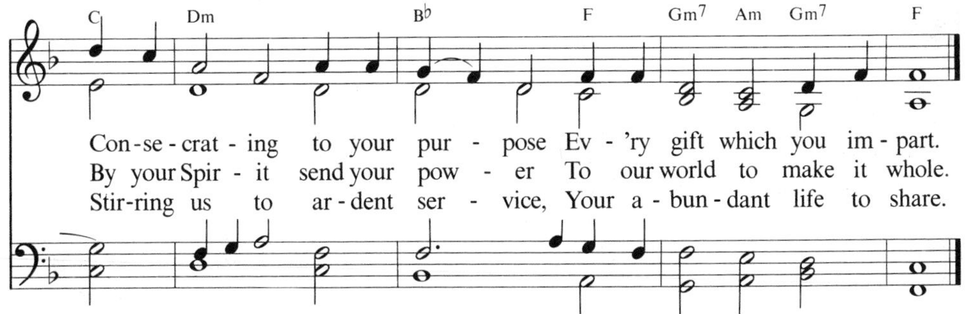
C Dm Bb F Gm7 Am Gm7 F
Con-se-crat - ing to your pur - pose Ev - 'ry gift which you im - part.
By your Spir - it send your pow - er To our world to make it whole.
Stir-ring us to ar - dent ser - vice, Your a - bun - dant life to share.

© *Text: Albert F. Bayly, b. 1901, alt.*
Tune: The Sacred Harp, *Philadelphia, 1844*

BEACH SPRING
87 87 D

424 Lord of Glory, You Have Bought Us

1 Lord of glory, you have bought us
With your lifeblood as the price,
Never grudging for the lost ones
That tremendous sacrifice;
And with that have freely given Blessings

2 Grant us hearts, dear Lord, to give you
Gladly, freely, of your own.
With the sunshine of your goodness
Melt our thankless hearts of stone
Till our cold and selfish natures, Warmed by

3 Wondrous honor you have given
To our humblest charity
In your own mysterious sentence,
"You have done it all to me."
Can it be, O gracious Master, That you

4 Yes, the sorrow and the suff'rings
Which on ev'ry hand we view
Channels are for gifts and off'rings
Due by solemn right to you;
Right of which we may not rob you, Debt we

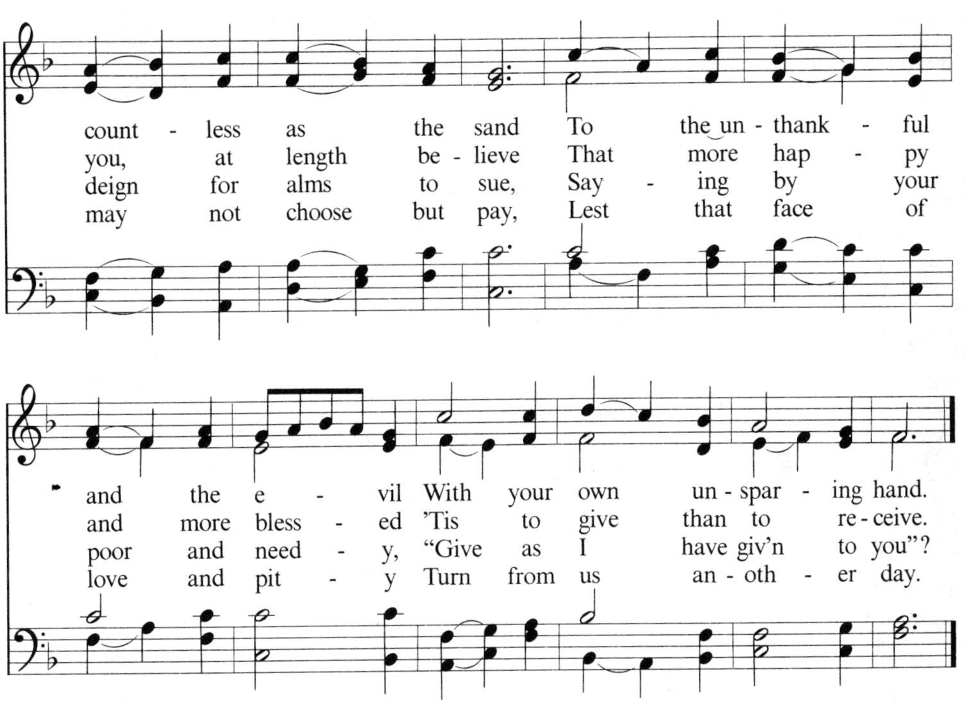
count - less as the sand To the un - thank - ful
you, at length be - lieve That more hap - py
deign for alms to sue, Say - ing by your
may not choose but pay, Lest that face of
and the e - vil With your own un - spar - ing hand.
and more bless - ed 'Tis to give than to re - ceive.
poor and need - y, "Give as I have giv'n to you"?
love and pit - y Turn from us an - oth - er day.

5 Lord of glory, you have bought us
  With your life-blood as the price,
Never grudging for the lost ones
  That tremendous sacrifice.
Give us faith to trust you boldly,
  Hope, to stay our souls on you:
But, oh, best of all your graces,
  With your love our love renew.

Text: Eliza S. Alderson, 1818–1889, alt.
Tune: Rowland H. Prichard, 1811–1887

HYFRYDOL
87 87 D

425 O God of Mercy, God of Light

1 O God of mer - cy, God of light, In love and mercy in - fi - nite, Teach us, as ev - er in your sight, To live our lives in you.
2 You sent your Son to die for all, That our lost world might hear your call; Oh, hear us lest we stray and fall! We rest our hope in you.
3 Teach us the les - son Je - sus taught: To feel for those his blood has bought, That ev - 'ry deed and word and thought May work a work for you.
4 For all are kin - dred, far and wide, Since Je - sus Christ for all has died; Grant us the will, and grace pro - vide To love them all in you.

5 In sickness, sorrow, want, or care,
Each other's burdens help us share;
May we, where help is needed, there
Give help as though to you.

6 And may your Holy Spirit move
All those who live to live in love,
Till you receive in heav'n above
Those who have lived to you.

Text: Godfrey Thring, 1823–1903, alt.
Tune: Joseph Barnby, 1838–1896

JUST AS I AM
88 86

O Son of God, in Galilee 426

1 O Son of God, in Gal - i - lee You made the deaf to hear, The mute to speak, the blind to see; O bless - ed Lord, be near.
2 Oh, lis - ten to the si - lent prayer Of your af - flict - ed ones. Oh, bid them cast on you their care; Your grace to them make known.
3 The speech - less tongue, the life - less ear You can re - store, O Lord; Your "Eph - pha - tha," O Sav - ior dear, Can in - stant help af - ford.
4 Mean-while to them the lis - t'ning ear Of stead - fast faith im - part, And let your word bring light and cheer To ev - 'ry trou - bled heart.

5 Then in your promised happy land
Each loss will prove a gain;
All myst'ries we shall understand,
For you will make them plain.

 Text: Anna Hoppe, 1889–1941, alt.
Tune: William Billings, 1746–1800

LEWIS-TOWN
CM

427 O Jesus Christ, May Grateful Hymns Be Rising

1 O Je - sus Christ, may grate - ful hymns be ris - ing
2 Grant us new cour - age, sac - ri - fi - cial, hum - ble,
3 Show us your Spir - it, brood - ing o'er each cit - y
In ev - 'ry cit - y for your love and care;
Strong in your strength to ven - ture and to dare,
As you once wept a - bove Je - ru - sa - lem,
In - spire our wor - ship, grant the glad sur - pris - ing
To lift the fall - en, guide the feet that stum - ble,
Seek - ing to gath - er all in love and pit - y,
That your blest Spir - it rous - es ev - 'ry - where.
Seek out the lone - ly, and God's mer - cy share.
And heal - ing those who touch your gar - ment's hem.

© Text: Bradford G. Webster, b. 1898
© Tune: Daniel Moe, b. 1926

CITY OF GOD
11 10 11 10

O God of Earth and Altar 428

1 O God of earth and altar, Bow down and hear our cry;
Our earthly rulers falter, Our people drift and die;
The walls of gold entomb us; The swords of scorn divide.
Take not thy thunder from us, But take away our pride.
2 From all that terror teaches, From lies of tongue and pen,
From all the easy speeches That comfort cruel men,
From sale and profanation Of honor, and the sword,
From sleep, and from damnation, Deliver us, good Lord!
3 Tie in a living tether The prince and priest and thrall;
Bind all our lives together; Smite us, and save us all;
In ire and exultation, Aflame with faith, and free,
Lift up a living nation, A single sword to thee.

© Text: Gilbert K. Chesterton, 1874–1936
© Tune: English folk tune

KING'S LYNN
76 76 D

429 Where Cross the Crowded Ways of Life

1 Where cross the crowd - ed ways of life, Where sound the cries of race and clan, A - bove the noise of self - ish strife, We hear your voice, O Son of Man.
2 In haunts of wretch - ed - ness and need, On shad - owed thresh-olds dark with fears, From paths where hide the lures of greed, We catch the vi - sion of your tears.
3 From ten - der child - hood's help - less - ness, From hu - man grief and bur - dened toil, From fam - ished souls, from sor - row's stress, Your heart has nev - er known re - coil.
4 The cup of wa - ter giv'n for you Still holds the fresh - ness of your grace; Yet long these mul - ti - tudes to view The strong com - pas - sion in your face.

5 O Master, from the mountainside
Make haste to heal these hearts of pain;
Among these restless throngs abide;
Oh, tread the city's streets again;

6 Till all the world shall learn your love,
And follow where your feet have trod;
Till glorious from your heav'n above,
Shall come the city of our God.

Text: Frank M. North, 1850–1935, alt.
Tune: W. Gardiner, Sacred Melodies, *1815*

WALTON
LM

Where Restless Crowds Are Thronging 430

1 Where rest - less crowds are throng - ing A - long the cit - y ways,
2 In scenes of want and sor - row And haunts of fla - grant wrong,
3 With bomb - ing and fierce burn - ing Your peo - ple find no peace.
4 O Christ, be - hold your peo - ple; They press on ev - 'ry hand!
Where pride and greed and tur - moil Con - sume the fe - vered days,
In homes where kind - ness fal - ters, And strife and fear are strong,
Help us to share their yearn - ing That sense - less death may cease.
Bring light to all the cit - ies Of our di - vid - ed land.
Where vain am - bi - tions ban - ish All thoughts of praise and prayer,
In bus - y streets of bar - ter, In lone - ly thor - ough - fare,
Break through our ease and com - fort, For - bid that we not care;
May all our bit - ter striv - ing Give way to vi - sions fair
The peo - ple's spir - its wa - ver: But you, O Christ, are there.
The peo - ple's spir - its lan - guish: But you, O Christ, are there.
And strength - en all our ef - forts, For you, O Christ, are there.
Of righ - teous - ness and jus - tice, For you, O Christ, are there.

© Text: Thomas C. Clark, 1877–1953, alt.
Tune: Welsh hymn tune, 19th cent.

LLANGLOFFAN
76 76 D

431 Your Hand, O Lord, in Days of Old

1 Your hand, O Lord, in days of old Was strong to heal and save;
It triumphed o'er disease and death, O'er darkness and the grave.
To you they came, the blind, the dumb, The palsied and the lame,
The lepers in their misery, The sick with fevered frame.
2 And lo, your touch brought life and health, Gave speech and strength and sight;
And youth renewed and frenzy calmed Revealed you, Lord of light.
And now, O Lord, be near to bless, Almighty as before,
In crowded street, by beds of pain, As by Gennes'ret's shore.
3 Oh, be our great deliv'rer still, The Lord of life and death;
Restore and quicken, soothe and bless, With your life-giving breath.
To hands that work and eyes that see Give wisdom's healing pow'r,
That whole and sick and weak and strong May praise you evermore.

Text: Edward H. Plumptre, 1821–1891, alt.
Tune: Marot, Trente Pseaulmes de David, *1542*

OLD 107TH
CMD

We Worship You, O God of Might

432

1 We wor - ship you, O God of might,
2 Your faith - ful care your Church pro - tects
3 Your will is that your Church em - brace
4 All peo - ples round your throne shall sing
Great Lord of all, be - yond our sight!
And shields from harm, from sin's ef - fects
All peo - ple, ev - 'ry land and race,
At last your king - dom's vic - t'ry hymn,
You make your Word in heav'n and earth be heard.
Till judg - ment day; your pow'r will be its stay.
That all may bring their praise to Christ and sing,
While cher - u - bim re - spond to ser - a - phim:
Ho - ly, ho - ly, ho - ly is God Most High!

Text: Johan Olof Wallin, 1779–1836; tr. Joel W. Lundeen, b. 1918, alt.
Tune: Een ny Handbog, Rostock, 1529

VI LOVA DIG, O STORE GUD
88 10 10

433 The Church of Christ, in Every Age

1 The Church of Christ, in ev - 'ry age Be - set by
2 A - cross the world, a - cross the street, The vic - tims
3 Then let the ser - vant Church a - rise, A car - ing
4 For he a - lone, whose blood was shed, Can cure the
change, but Spir - it - led, Must claim and test its
of in - jus - tice cry For shel - ter and for
Church that longs to be A part - ner in Christ's
fe - ver in our blood, And teach us how to
her - i - tage And keep on ris - ing from the dead.
bread to eat, And nev - er live be - fore they die.
sac - ri - fice, And clothed in Christ's hu - man - i - ty.
share our bread And feed the starv - ing mul - ti - tude.

5 We have no mission but to serve
In full obedience to our Lord;
To care for all, without reserve,
And spread his liberating Word.

 Text: F. Pratt Green, b. 1903
Tune: William Knapp, 1698–1768

WAREHAM
LM

The Son of God, Our Christ

434

1 The Son of God, our Christ, the Word, the Way, Shared
2 In ev - 'ry test, in tri - als man - i - fold, These
3 To - day, as then, Christ sum - mons us to dare To
4 In cit - y street, in town, or on the soil, May
hu - man life and toiled through - out the day; From
ser - vants wit - nessed, by their faith made bold; And
fol - low bold - ly and his work to share, To
each serve Christ in faith - ful dai - ly toil, And
com - mon folk he called the twelve to be Co -
with the gifts and tal - ents which they brought The
help and heal the sick, the blind, the lame, De -
in each thought and kind - ly word and deed, O -
work - ers in his sa - cred min - is - try.
Church was found - ed and God's mes - sage taught.
clar - ing to the world his ho - ly name.
bey Christ's call and go where he shall lead.

5 Where'er we find our witness should be made,
Whate'er our task, be thou, O Christ, our aid,
That we may gladly give for thee our best
And find each task divinely sent and blest.

SURSUM CORDA
10 10 10 10

435 O God, Whose Will Is Life and Good

Cm Fm Cm Gm
1 O God, whose will is life and good For
2 Make strong their hands and hearts and wills To
3 By heal - ing of the sick and blind, Christ's
4 Be - fore them set your gra - cious will, That
A♭ Gm A♭6 Gm A♭ Cm
all of mor - tal breath: U - nite in bonds of
drive dis - ease a - far, To strive a - gainst the
mer - cy they pro - claim, Make known the great phy -
they, with heart and soul, To you may con - se -
A♭ Fm6 Cm Fm Cm Gm Cm
ser - vant - hood All those who strive with death.
bod - y's ills And wage your heal - ing war.
si - cian's mind, Af - firm the Sav - ior's name.
crate their skill And make the suf - f'rer whole.

Text: Hardwicke D. Rawnsley, 1851–1920, alt.
© *Tune: Leland B. Sateren, b. 1913*

LEUPOLD
CM

All Who Love and Serve Your City

436

1 All who love and serve your cit - y, All who
2 In your day of loss and sor - row, In your
3 In your day of wealth and plen - ty, Wast - ed
4 For all days are days of judg - ment, And the
bear its dai - ly stress, All who cry for peace and
day of help - less strife, Hon - or, peace, and love re -
work and wast - ed play, Call to mind the word of
Lord is wait - ing still, Draw - ing near his friends who
jus - tice, All who curse and all who bless,
treat - ing, Seek the Lord, who is your life.
Je - sus, "Work ye yet while it is day."
spurn him, Of - f'ring peace from Cal - v'ry's hill.

5 Risen Lord, shall yet the city
Be the city of despair?
Come today, our judge, our glory;
Be its name "The Lord is there!"

© *Text: Erik Routley, b. 1917*
© *Tune: Peter Cutts, b. 1937*

BIRABUS
87 87

437 Not Alone for Mighty Empire

1 Not a - lone for might - y em - pire Stretch - ing far o'er
2 Not for bat - tle - ship and for - tress, Not for con - quests
3 For the ar - mies of the faith - ful, Those who passed and
4 God of jus - tice, save the peo - ple From the clash of

land and sea, Not a - lone for boun - teous har - vests Do we
of the sword, But for con - quests of the spir - it We give
left no name; For the glo - ry that il - lu - mines Pa - triot
race and creed; From the strife of class and fac - tion, Make our

praise you grate - ful - ly. Stand - ing in the liv - ing pres - ent,
thanks to you, O Lord; For the her - i - tage of free - dom,
lives of death - less fame; For our proph - ets and a - pos - tles,
na - tion free in - deed. Keep its faith in sim - ple jus - tice

Mem - o - ry and hope be - tween, Lord, we would with
For the home, the church, the school, For the o - pen
Loy - al to the liv - ing Word; For the strong and
Strong as when its life be - gan, Till it find com -

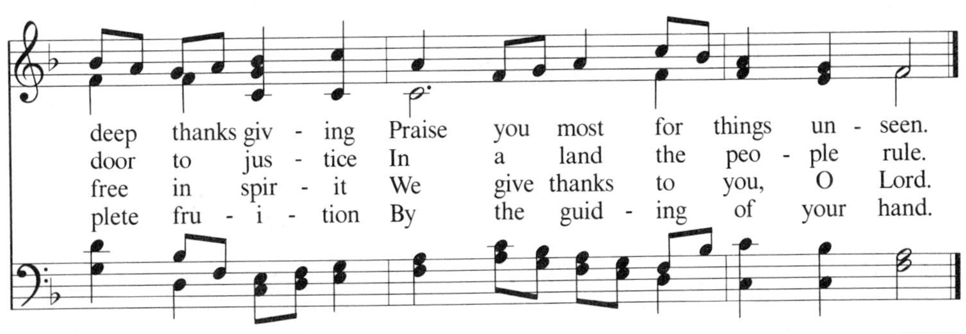

deep thanks giv - ing Praise you most for things un - seen.
door to jus - tice In a land the peo - ple rule.
free in spir - it We give thanks to you, O Lord.
plete fru - i - tion By the guid - ing of your hand.

© Text: William P. Merrill, 1867–1954
© Tune: George H. Day, 1883–1966

GENEVA
87 87 D

Lord, Teach Us How to Pray Aright 438

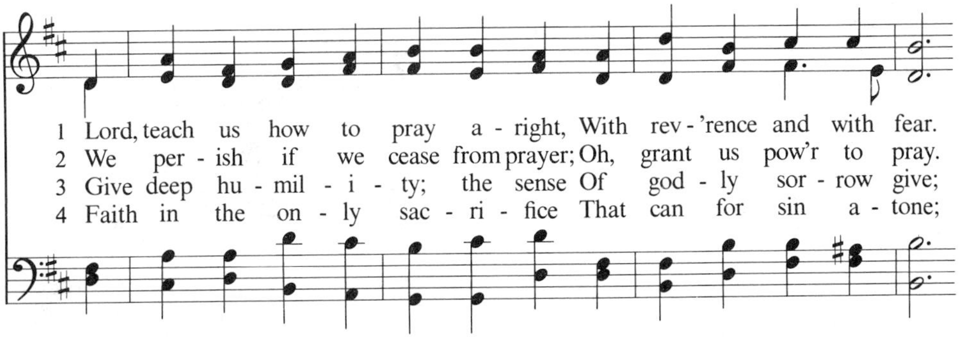

1 Lord, teach us how to pray a - right, With rev - 'rence and with fear.
2 We per - ish if we cease from prayer; Oh, grant us pow'r to pray.
3 Give deep hu - mil - i - ty; the sense Of god - ly sor - row give;
4 Faith in the on - ly sac - ri - fice That can for sin a - tone;

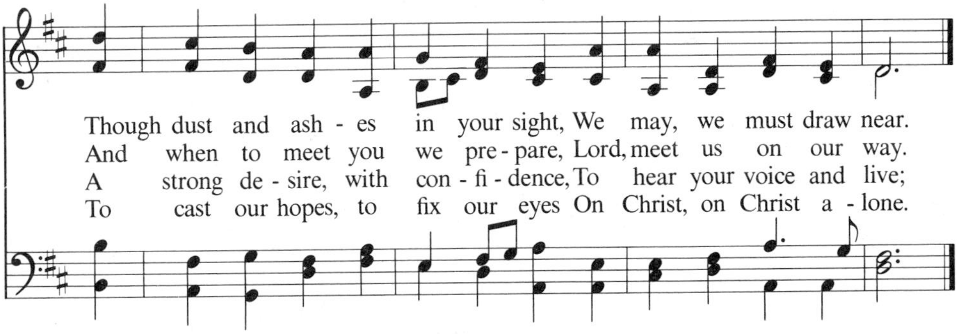

Though dust and ash - es in your sight, We may, we must draw near.
And when to meet you we pre - pare, Lord, meet us on our way.
A strong de - sire, with con - fi - dence, To hear your voice and live;
To cast our hopes, to fix our eyes On Christ, on Christ a - lone.

5 Give these, and then your will be done;
Thus strengthened with all might,
We, through your Spirit and your Son,
Shall pray, and pray aright.

Text: James Montgomery, 1771–1854, alt.
Tune: Orlando Gibbons, 1583–1625

SONG 67
CM

439 What a Friend We Have in Jesus

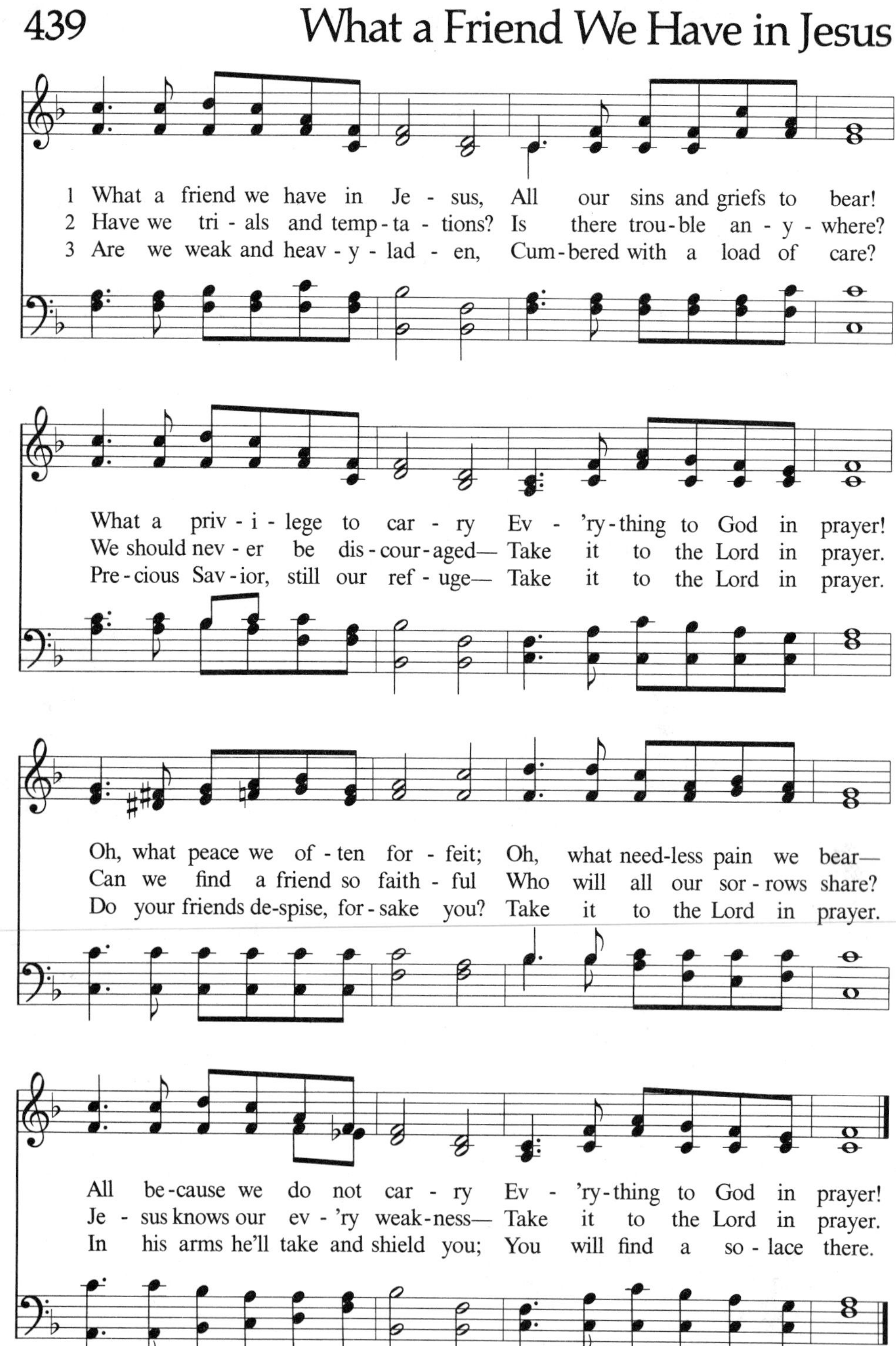
1 What a friend we have in Je - sus, All our sins and griefs to bear!
2 Have we tri - als and temp - ta - tions? Is there trou - ble an - y - where?
3 Are we weak and heav - y - lad - en, Cum - bered with a load of care?
What a priv - i - lege to car - ry Ev - 'ry - thing to God in prayer!
We should nev - er be dis - cour - aged— Take it to the Lord in prayer.
Pre - cious Sav - ior, still our ref - uge— Take it to the Lord in prayer.
Oh, what peace we of - ten for - feit; Oh, what need-less pain we bear—
Can we find a friend so faith - ful Who will all our sor - rows share?
Do your friends de-spise, for - sake you? Take it to the Lord in prayer.
All be - cause we do not car - ry Ev - 'ry - thing to God in prayer!
Je - sus knows our ev - 'ry weak - ness— Take it to the Lord in prayer.
In his arms he'll take and shield you; You will find a so - lace there.

Text: Joseph Scriven, 1820–1886
Tune: Charles C. Converse, 1832–1918

CONVERSE
87 87 D

Christians, While on Earth Abiding 440

1 Chris-tians, while on earth a - bid - ing, Let us nev - er cease to pray,
2 Bless us, Fa - ther, and pro - tect us From all harm in all our ways;
Firm-ly in the Lord con - fid - ing As our par - ents in their day.
Pa - tient - ly, O Lord, di - rect us Safe - ly through these fleet-ing days.
Be the chil - dren's voic - es raised To the God their par - ents praised.
Let your face up - on us shine, Fill us with your peace di - vine.
May his bless-ing, fail - ing nev - er, Rest up - on his peo - ple ev - er.
Praise the Fa - ther, Son, and Spir - it! Praise him, all who life in - her - it!

Text: Johan Olof Wallin, 1779–1839, st. 1; Jesper Svedberg, 1653–1735, st. 2; tr. unknown, adapt.
Tune: Johann Schop, c. 1600–1665

WERDE MUNTER
87 87 77 88

441 Eternal Spirit of the Living Christ

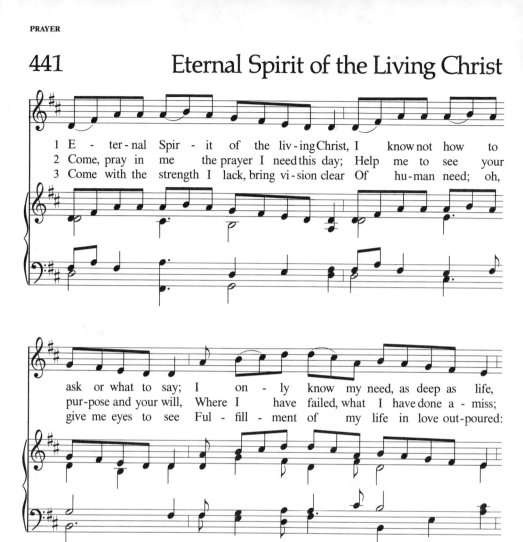

1 E - ter - nal Spir - it of the liv - ing Christ, I know not how to
2 Come, pray in me the prayer I need this day; Help me to see your
3 Come with the strength I lack, bring vi - sion clear Of hu - man need; oh,

ask or what to say; I on - ly know my need, as deep as life,
pur - pose and your will, Where I have failed, what I have done a - miss;
give me eyes to see Ful - fill - ment of my life in love out - poured:

And on - ly you can teach me how to pray.
Held in for - giv - ing love, let me be still.
My life in you, O Christ; your love in me. A - men

 Text: Frank von Christierson, b. 1900
Tune: Processionale, *Paris, 1697*

ADORO TE DEVOTE
10 10 10 10

O Thou, Who Hast of Thy Pure Grace 442

1 O thou, who hast of thy pure grace Made shine on us a
2 O King and Fa - ther, kind and dread, Give us this day our
3 Thine is the king-dom; un - to thee Shall bow in hom - age
Fa - ther's face: A - rise, thy ho - ly name make known;
dai - ly bread; For - give us, who have learned to bless
ev - 'ry knee. And thine the pow'r; no pow'r shall be
Take up thy pow'r and reign a - lone; On earth, in us, let
Our en - e - mies, all tres - pass - es; Spare us temp - ta - tion,
That is not o - ver - come by thee. The glo - ry thine; by
thy sole will Be done as an - gels do it still.
let us be From Sa - tan set for - ev - er free.
ev - 'ry tongue Thy praise shall be for - ev - er sung!

 Text: Martin H. Franzmann, 1907–1976
Tune: V. Schumann, Geistliche Lieder, *1539*

VATER UNSER
88 88 88

443 Rise, My Soul, to Watch and Pray

1 Rise, my soul, to watch and pray; From your sleep a -
2 Watch a - gainst the world that frowns Dark - ly to dis -
3 Watch a - gainst your - self, my soul, Lest with grace you
4 But while watch - ing, al - so pray To the Lord un -
wak - en; Be not by the e - vil day Un - a -
may you; Watch when it your wish - es crowns, Smil - ing
tri - fle; Let not self your thoughts con - trol Nor God's
ceas - ing. God a - lone can make you free, Strength and
wares o'er - tak - en. Sa - tan's prey oft are they Who se -
to be - tray you. Watch and see, you are free From false
mer - cy sti - fle. Pride and sin lurk with - in, All your
faith in - creas - ing, So that still mind and will Heart - felt
cure are sleep - ing And no watch are keep - ing.
friends who charm you While they seek to harm you.
hopes to shat - ter; Heed not when they flat - ter.
prais - es ten - der And true ser - vice ren - der.

Text: Johann B. Freystein, 1671–1718; tr. Catherine Winkworth, 1829–1878, adapt.
Tune: Hundert geistlicher Arien, *Dresden, 1694*

STRAF MICH NICHT
76 76 666

With the Lord Begin Your Task

444

1 With the Lord be - gin your task; Je - sus will di - rect it.
2 Let each day be - gin with prayer, Praise, and ad - o - ra - tion.
3 With your Sav - ior at your side, Foes need not a - larm you;
4 If your task be thus be - gun With the Sav - ior's bless - ing,
For his aid and coun - sel ask; Je - sus will per - fect it.
On the Lord cast ev - 'ry care; He is your sal - va - tion.
In his prom - is - es con - fide, And no ill can harm you.
Safe - ly then your course will run, Toward the prom - ise press - ing.
Ev - 'ry morn with Je - sus rise, And, when day is end - ed,
Morn-ing, eve - ning, and at night Je - sus will be near you,
All your trust and hope re - pose In the might - y mas - ter,
Good will fol - low ev - 'ry - where While you here must wan - der;
In his name then close your eyes; Be to him com - mend - ed.
Save you from the tempt - er's might, With his pres - ence cheer you.
Who in wis - dom tru - ly knows How to stem di - sas - ter.
You at last the joy will share In the man - sions yon - der.

© *Text:* Morgen- und Abend-segen, *Waldenburg, 1734; tr. W. Gustave Polack, 1890–1950*
Tune: Peter Frank, 1616–1675

FANG DEIN WERK
76 76 D

445 Unto the Hills

1 Un - to the hills a-round do I lift up My long - ing eyes;
2 He will not suf - fer that thy foot be moved; Safe shalt thou be.
3 Je - ho-vah is him-self thy keep-er true, Thy change-less shade;
4 From ev - 'ry e - vil shall he keep thy soul, From ev - 'ry sin;
Oh, whence for me shall my sal - va - tion come, From whence a - rise?
No care-less slum - ber shall his eye - lids close, Who keep - eth thee.
Je - ho - vah thy de-fense on thy right hand Him - self hath made.
Je - ho - vah shall pre-serve thy go - ing out, Thy com - ing in.
From God the Lord doth come my cer - tain aid,
Be - hold, he sleep - eth not, he slum - b'reth ne'er,
And thee no sun by day shall ev - er smite;
A - bove thee watch - ing, he whom we a - dore
From God the Lord, who heav'n and earth hath made.
Who keep - eth Is - rael in his ho - ly care.
No moon shall harm thee in the si - lent night.
Shall keep thee hence - forth, yea, for - ev - er - more.

Text: John Campbell, 1845–1914
Tune: Charles H. Purday, 1799–1885

SANDON
10 4 10 4 10 10

Whatever God Ordains Is Right 446

1 What-ev - er God or - dains is right; His will is just and
2 What-ev - er God or - dains is right, And he will not de -
3 What-ev - er God or - dains is right; All that he does is
4 What-ev - er God or - dains is right; He guides our joy and
ho - ly. He holds us in his per - fect might; In him, our lives are
ceive us. He leads us in the way of light And will not ev - er
for us. He heals our souls and gives us sight And puts no ill be -
sad - ness. He is our life and bless - ed light; In him a - lone is
god - ly. He is our God and all we need, The Fa - ther
leave us. In him we rest, who makes the best Of all the
fore us. Our God is true; he makes us new; Our lives are
glad - ness. We see his face, the way of grace; He holds us
who pre - serves us still; To him we bend each heart and will.
stum - bling turns we take And loves us for his mer - cy's sake.
built up - on his rock, Our cor - ner - stone and build - ing block.
in his might - y arm And keeps us safe from ev - 'ry harm.

 Text: Samuel Rodigast, 1649–1708; tr. Gracia Grindal, b. 1943, alt.
Tune: attr. Severus Gastorius, c. 1675

WAS GOTT TUT
87 87 888

447 All Depends on Our Possessing

1 All depends on our possessing God's free grace and constant blessing,
Though all earthly wealth depart.
They who trust with faith unshaken By their God are not forsaken
And will keep a dauntless heart.

2 God, who hitherto has fed me And to many joys has led me,
Is and ever shall be mine.
He who did so gently school me, He who daily guides and rules me,
Will remain my help divine.

3 When with sorrow I am stricken, Hope my heart anew will quicken,
All my longing shall be stilled.
To his loving-kindness tender Soul and body I surrender,
For on God alone I build.

4 Well he knows what best to grant me; All the longing hopes that haunt me,
Joy and sorrow, have their day.
I shall doubt his wisdom never; As God wills, so be it ever;
To him I commit my way.

5 If on earth my days he lengthen,
God my weary soul will strengthen;
All my trust in him I place.
Earthly wealth is not abiding;
Like a stream away it's gliding;
Safe I anchor in his grace.

Text: Gesang-Buch, *Nürnberg, 1676; tr. Catherine Winkworth, 1829–1878, alt.*
Tune: Johann Löhner, 1645–1705, adapt.

ALLES IST AN GOTTES SEGEN
887 887

Amazing Grace, How Sweet the Sound 448

F Dm B♭ F
1 A - maz - ing grace, how sweet the sound, That
2 'Twas grace that taught my heart to fear, And
3 Through man - y dan - gers, toils, and snares I
4 The Lord has prom - ised good to me; His
Dm F Am F
saved a wretch like me! I once was lost, but
grace my fears re-lieved; How pre - cious did that
have al - read - y come; 'Tis grace has brought me
Word my hope se-cures; He will my shield and
B♭ F Dm F C7 F
now am found; Was blind, but now I see.
grace ap - pear The hour I first be - lieved!
safe thus far, And grace will lead me home.
por - tion be As long as life en - dures.

Text: John Newton, 1725–1807
Tune: W. Walker, Southern Harmony, *1835*

NEW BRITAIN
CM

449 They Cast Their Nets

G Cmaj7 Am7 G Am Em C
1 They cast their nets in Gal - i - lee, Just off the hills of brown; Such
2 Con - tent - ed, peace-ful fish - er - men, Be - fore they ev - er knew The
G Gmaj7 Em Em7 C G Am7 D Bm7
hap - py, sim - ple fish - er - folk, Be - fore the Lord came down, Be -
peace of God that filled their hearts Brim - ful, and broke them too, Brim -
C Am7 G Am Em G D
fore the Lord came down.
ful, and broke them too.
3 Young John, who trimmed the
Em D Em Am
flap - ping sail, Home - less in Pat - mos died. Pe - ter, who hauled the

G C Am F G Am7 Bm C Am
teem-ing net, Head down was cru - ci - fied, Head down was cru - ci -
G Em G Cmaj7 Am7
fied. 4 The peace of God, it is no peace, But
G Am Em C G Em
strife closed in the sod. Yet, let us pray for but one thing: The
C G Am7 D Bm7 C Am7 F G
mar-v'lous peace of God, The mar - v'lous peace of God.

© Text: *William A. Percy, 1885–1942*
© Tune: *Herbert G. Draesel Jr., b. 1940*

PEACE OF GOD
86 866

450 Who Trusts in God, a Strong Abode

1 Who trusts in God, a strong a - bode In heav'n and earth pos - sess - es; Who looks in love to Christ a - bove, No fear that heart op - press - es.
2 Though Sa - tan's wrath be - set our path And world - ly scorn as - sail us, While you are near, we shall not fear; Your strength will nev - er fail us.
3 In all the strife of mor - tal life Our feet will stand se - cure - ly; Temp - ta - tion's hour will lose its pow'r, For you will guard us sure - ly.
In you a - lone, dear Lord, we own Sweet hope and con - so -
Your rod and staff will keep us safe And guide our steps for -
Our God, re - new with heav'n - ly dew Our bod - y, soul, and

la - tion, Our shield from foes, our balm for woes,
ev - er; Nor shades of death nor hell be - neath,
spir - it, Un - til we stand at your right hand
Our great and sure sal - va - tion.
Our lives from you will sev - er.
Through Je - sus' sav - ing mer - it.

Text: Joachim Magdeburg, c. 1525–c. 1583, st. 1; Harmonia Cantionum, *Leipzig, 1597, sts. 2–3;*
tr. Benjamin H. Kennedy, 1804–1899, alt.
Tune: Claude de Sermisy, c. 1490–1562

WAS MEIN GOTT WILL
87 87 D

451 The Lord's My Shepherd

1 The Lord's my shep - herd; I'll not want. He makes me down to lie
2 My soul he doth re - store a - gain, And me to walk doth make
3 Yea, though I walk in death's dark vale, Yet will I fear no ill;
4 My ta - ble thou hast fur - nish - ed In pres - ence of my foes;
In pas - tures green; he lead - eth me The qui - et wa - ters by.
With - in the paths of righ-teous-ness, E'en for his own name's sake;
For thou art with me, and thy rod And staff me com - fort still;
My head thou dost with oil a - noint, And my cup o - ver - flows.
He lead-eth me, he lead - eth me The qui - et wa - ters by.
With - in the paths of righ-teous-ness, E'en for his own name's sake.
For thou art with me, and thy rod And staff me com - fort still.
My head thou dost with oil a - noint, And my cup o - ver - flows.

5 Goodness and mercy all my life
Shall surely follow me,
And in God's house forevermore
My dwelling-place shall be.

Text: Psalter, *Edinburgh, 1650*
Tune: J. L. Macbeth Bain, c. 1840–1925, adapt.

BROTHER JAMES' AIR
86 86 86

As Pants the Hart for Cooling Streams 452

1 As pants the hart for cool - ing streams
2 For you, my God, the liv - ing God,
3 One trou - ble calls an - oth - er on
4 Why rest - less, why cast down, my soul?
When heat - ed in the chase, So longs my soul, O
My thirst - y spir - it pines; Oh, when shall I be -
And gath - ers o - ver - head, Falls splash - ing down, till
Hope still, and you shall sing The praise of him who
God, for you And your re - fresh - ing grace.
hold your face, O Maj - es - ty di - vine?
round my soul A ris - ing sea is spread.
is your God, Your health's e - ter - nal spring.

5 For now I trust in God for strength,
I trust him to employ
His love for me and change my sighs
To thankful hymns of joy.

Text: Nahum Tate, 1652–1715; Nicholas Brady, 1659–1726, alt.
Tune: Hugh Wilson, 1764–1824

MARTYRDOM
CM

453 If You But Trust in God to Guide You

1 If you but trust in God to guide you
And place your confidence in him,
You'll find him always there beside you,
To give you hope and strength within.
For those who trust God's changeless love
Build on the rock that will not move.

2 What gain is there in futile weeping,
In helpless anger and distress?
If you are in his care and keeping,
In sorrow will he love you less?
For he who took for you a cross
Will bring you safe through ev'ry loss.

3 In patient trust await his leisure
In cheerful hope, with heart content
To take whate'er your Father's pleasure
And all-discerning love have sent;
Doubt not your inmost wants are known
To him who chose you for his own.

4 Sing, pray, and keep his ways unswerving,
Offer your service faithfully,
And trust his word; though undeserving,
You'll find his promise true to be.
God never will forsake in need
The soul that trusts in him indeed.

 Text: Georg Neumark, 1621–1681; tr. composite, alt.
Tune: Georg Neumark, 1621–1681

WER NUR DEN LIEBEN GOTT
98 98 88

If God Himself Be for Me 454

1 If God him - self be for me, I may a host de - fy;
2 I build on this foun - da - tion, That Je - sus and his blood
3 Christ Je - sus is my splen - dor, My sun, my light, a - lone;
4 For joy my heart is ring - ing; All sor - row dis - ap - pears;
For when I pray, be - fore me My foes, con-found - ed, fly.
A - lone are my sal - va - tion, The true, e - ter - nal good.
Were he not my de - fend - er Be - fore God's awe - some throne,
And full of mirth and sing - ing, It wipes a - way all tears.
If Christ, my head and mas - ter, Be - friend me from a - bove,
With-out him all that pleas - es Will vain and emp - ty prove.
I nev - er should find fa - vor And mer - cy in his sight,
The sun that cheers my spir - it Is Je - sus Christ, my king;
What foe or what di - sas - ter Can drive me from his love?
The gifts I have from Je - sus A lone are worth my love.
But be de - stroyed for - ev - er As dark - ness by the light.
The heav'n I shall in - her - it Makes me re - joice and sing.

Text: Paul Gerhardt, 1607–1675; tr. Richard Massie, 1800–1887, adapt.
Tune: Augsburg, 1609

IST GOTT FÜR MICH
76 76 D

455 "Come, Follow Me," the Savior Spake

1 "Come, fol - low me," the Sav - ior spake, "All in my way a -
2 "I am the light; I light the way, A god - ly life dis -
3 My heart a - bounds in low - li - ness; My soul with love is
4 "I teach you how to shun and flee What harms your soul's sal -
bid - ing; De - ny your-selves, the world for - sake, O -
play - ing; I bid you walk as in the day; I
glow - ing; And gra - cious words my lips ex press, With
va - tion; Your heart from ev - 'ry guile to free, From
bey my call and guid - ing. Oh, bear the cross, what -
keep your feet from stray - ing. I am the way, and
meek - ness o - ver - flow - ing. My heart, my mind, my
sin and its temp - ta - tion. I am the ref - uge
e'er be - tide; Take my ex - am - ple for your guide.
well I show How you should so - journ here be - low."
strength, my all To God I yield; on him I call.
of the soul And lead you to your heav'n - ly goal."

5 Then let us follow Christ, our Lord,
And take the cross appointed,
And, firmly clinging to his Word,
In suffering be undaunted.
For those who bear the battle's strain
The crown of heav'nly life obtain.

Text: Johann Scheffler, 1624–1677; tr. Charles W. Schaeffer, 1813–1896, alt.
Tune: Bartholomäus Gesius, c. 1555–1613, adapt.

MACHS MIT MIR, GOTT
8 7 8 7 8 8

The King of Love My Shepherd Is 456

1 The King of love my shep - herd is, Whose good - ness
2 Where streams of liv - ing wa - ter flow, My ran - somed
3 Per - verse and fool - ish oft I strayed, But yet in
4 In death's dark vale I fear no ill, With thee, dear
fail - eth nev - er; I noth - ing lack if
soul he lead - eth And, where the ver - dant
love he sought me, And on his shoul - der
Lord, be - side me, Thy rod and staff my
I am his And he is mine for - ev - er.
pas - tures grow, With food ce - les - tial feed - eth.
gent - ly laid, And home, re - joic - ing, brought me.
com - fort still; Thy cross be - fore to guide me.

5 Thou spreadst a table in my sight;
Thine unction grace bestoweth;
And, oh, what transport of delight
From thy pure chalice floweth!

6 And so, through all the length of days,
Thy goodness faileth never.
Good Shepherd, may I sing thy praise
Within thy house forever.

Text: Henry W. Baker, 1821–1877
Tune: Irish

ST. COLUMBA
87 87

457 Jesus, Priceless Treasure

457
Jesus, Priceless Treasure
1 Je - sus, price - less trea - sure, Source of pur - est plea - sure,
2 In thine arm I rest me; Foes who would mo - lest me
3 Hence, all fears and sad - ness, For the Lord of glad - ness,
Tru - est friend to me: Ah, how long I've pant - ed, And my heart has
Can-not reach me here. Though the earth be shak - ing, Ev - 'ry heart be
Je - sus, en - ters in. Those who love the Fa - ther, Though the storms may
faint - ed, Thirst-ing, Lord, for thee! Thine I am, O spot - less Lamb;
quak - ing, Je - sus calms my fear. Sin and hell in con - flict fell
gath - er, Still have peace with - in. Yea, what - e'er I here must bear,
I will suf - fer nought to hide thee, Nought I ask be - side thee.
With their bit - ter storms as - sail me, Je - sus will not fail me.
Still in thee lies pur - est plea - sure, Je - sus, price - less trea - sure!

Text: Johann Franck, 1618–1677; tr. Catherine Winkworth, 1829–1878, alt.
Tune: Johann Crüger, 1598–1662

JESU, MEINE FREUDE
665 665 786

Jesus, Priceless Treasure

458

1 Je - sus, price-less trea - sure, Source of pur - est plea - sure, Tru - est
2 In thine arm I rest me; Foes who would mo - lest me Can - not
3 Hence, all fears and sad - ness, For the Lord of glad - ness, Je - sus,
friend to me: Ah, how long I've pant - ed, And my heart has
reach me here. Though the earth be shak - ing, Ev - 'ry heart be
en - ters in. Those who love the Fa - ther, Though the storms may
faint - ed, Thirst-ing, Lord, for thee! Thine I am, O spot - less Lamb;
quak - ing, Je - sus calms my fear. Sin and hell in con - flict fell
gath - er, Still have peace with - in. Yea, what - e'er I here must bear,
I will suf - fer nought to hide thee, Nought I ask be - side thee.
With their bit - ter storms as - sail me, Je - sus will not fail me.
Still in thee lies pur - est plea-sure, Je - sus, price-less trea - sure!

Text: Johann Franck, 1618–1677; tr. Catherine Winkworth, 1829–1878, alt.
Tune: Ludvig M. Lindeman, 1812–1887

GUD SKAL ALTING MAGE
665 665 786

459 O Holy Spirit, Enter In

1 O Ho - ly Spir - it, en - ter in, And in our hearts your
2 Left to our - selves, we sure - ly stray; Oh, lead us on the
3 O might - y Rock, O Source of life, Let your good Word in
work be - gin, And make our hearts your dwell-ing. Sun of the soul,
nar - row way, With wis - est coun - sel guide us; And give us stead -
doubt and strife Be in us strong - ly burn-ing, That we be faith -
O Light di - vine, A - round and in us bright-ly shine, Your strength
fast - ness, that we May fol - low you for - ev - er free, No mat -
ful un - to death And live in love and ho - ly faith, From you
in us up - well - ing. In your ra - diance Life from heav-en Now is
ter who de - rides us. Gent - ly heal those Hearts now bro-ken; Give some
true wis - dom learn - ing. Lord, your mer - cy On us show-er; By your

giv - en O - ver - flow - ing, Gift of gifts be - yond all know - ing.
to - ken You are near us, Whom we trust to light and cheer us.
pow-er Christ con - fess - ing, We will cher - ish all your bless - ing.

Text: Michael Schirmer, 1606–1673; tr. Catherine Winkworth, 1829–1878, adapt.
Tune: Philipp Nicolai, 1556–1608

WIE SCHÖN LEUCHTET
PM

I Am Trusting You, Lord Jesus 460

1 I am trust - ing you, Lord Je - sus, Trust - ing on - ly you;
2 I am trust - ing you for par - don; At your feet I bow,
3 I am trust - ing you for cleans - ing In the crim - son flood;
4 I am trust - ing you to guide me; You a - lone shall lead,

Trust - ing you for full sal - va - tion, Free and true.
For your grace and ten - der mer - cy Trust - ing now.
Trust - ing you to make me ho - ly By your blood.
Ev - 'ry day and hour sup - ply - ing All my need.

5 I am trusting you for power;
You can never fail.
Words which you yourself shall give me
Must prevail.

6 I am trusting you, Lord Jesus;
Never let me fall.
I am trusting you forever
And for all.

Text: Frances R. Havergal, 1836–1879, alt.
Tune: Henry W. Baker, 1821–1877

STEPHANOS
85 83

461 Fight the Good Fight

1 Fight the good fight with all your might; Christ is your strength, and Christ your right. Lay hold on life, and it shall be Your joy and crown e - ter - nal - ly.
2 Run the straight race through God's good grace; Lift up your eyes, and seek his face. Life with its way be - fore us lies; Christ is the path, and Christ the prize.
3 Cast care a - side, lean on your guide; His bound - less mer - cy will pro - vide. Trust, and en - dur - ing faith shall prove Christ is your life, and Christ your love.
4 Faint not nor fear, his arms are near; He chang - es not who holds you dear; On - ly be - lieve, and you will see That Christ is all e - ter - nal - ly.

Text: John S. B. Monsell, 1811–1875, alt.
© Tune: Graham George, b. 1912

GRACE CHURCH, GANANOQUE
LM

God the Omnipotent! 462

1 God the omnipotent! King who ordainest
Great winds thy clarions, lightning thy sword:
Show forth thy pity on high where thou reignest;
Give to us peace in our time, O Lord.

2 God the all-merciful! Earth hath forsaken
Meekness and mercy, and slighted thy Word;
Bid not thy wrath in its terrors awaken;
Give to us peace in our time, O Lord.

3 God the All-righteous One! We have defied thee,
Yet to eternity standeth thy Word;
Falsehood and wrong shall not tarry beside thee;
Give to us peace in our time, O Lord.

4 God the all-wise! By the fire of thy chas-t'ning
Earth shall to freedom and truth be restored;
Through the thick darkness thy kingdom is has-t'ning;
Thou wilt give peace in thy time, O Lord.

Text: Henry F. Chorley, 1808–1872, sts. 1–2; John Ellerton, 1826–1893, sts. 3–4; alt.
Tune: Alexis F. Lvov, 1799–1870

RUSSIAN HYMN
11 10 11 9

463 God, Who Stretched the Spangled Heavens

F Dm Gm Dm Am Gm7 B♭maj7 Dm
1 God, who stretched the span - gled heav - ens In - fi - nite in time and place,
2 We have ven - tured worlds un - dreamed of Since the child - hood of our race;
3 As each far ho - ri - zon beck - ons, May it chal - lenge us a - new:
C Dm C B♭maj7 Am6 B♭maj7 C F
Flung the suns in burn - ing ra - diance Through the si - lent fields of space:
Known the ec - sta - sy of wing - ing Through un - trav - eled realms of space;
Chil - dren of cre - a - tive pur - pose, Serv - ing oth - ers, hon - 'ring you.
F Dm7 B♭maj7 Gm7 B♭maj7 Am7 B♭maj7 Gm7 C
We, your chil - dren in your like - ness, Share in - ven - tive pow'rs with you;
Probed the se - crets of the at - om, Yield - ing un - i - mag - ined pow'r,
May our dreams prove rich with prom - ise; Each en - deav - or well be - gun;

F Dm C Gm7 Am6 B♭maj7 C6 C F
Great Cre - a - tor, still cre - at - ing, Show us what we yet may do.
Fac - ing us with life's de - struc - tion Or our most tri - um-phant hour.
Great Cre - a - tor, give us guid - ance Till our goals and yours are one.
© Text: Catherine Cameron, b. 1927, alt.
Tune: W. Walker, Southern Harmony, 1835
HOLY MANNA
87 87 D
You Are the Way
464
1 You are the way; through you a - lone Can we the Fa - ther find;
2 You are the truth; your Word a - lone True wis - dom can im - part;
3 You are the life; the rend - ing tomb Pro - claims your con-qu'ring arm;
4 You are the way, the truth, the life; Grant us that way to know,
In you, O Christ, has God re - vealed His heart, his will, his mind!
You on - ly can in - form the mind And pu - ri - fy the heart.
And those who put their trust in you Not death nor hell shall harm.
That truth to keep, that life to win, Whose joys e - ter - nal flow.

Text: George W. Doane, 1799–1859, alt.
Tune: Psalter, *Edinburgh, 1615*

DUNDEE
CM

465 Evening and Morning

1 Eve - ning and morn - ing, Sun - set and dawn - ing,
2 Fa - ther, oh, hear me, Par - don and spare me;
3 Ills that still grieve me Soon are to leave me;
4 To God in heav - en All praise be giv - en!
Wealth, peace, and glad - ness, Com - fort in sad - ness:
Calm all my ter - rors, Blot out my er - rors,
Though bil - lows tow - er, And winds gain pow - er,
Come, let us of - fer And glad - ly prof - fer
These are thy works; all the glo - ry be thine!
That by thine eyes they may no more be scanned.
Af - ter the storm the fair sun shows its face.
To the cre - a - tor the gifts he doth prize.
Times with - out num - ber, A - wake or in slum - ber,
Or - der my go - ings, Di - rect all my do - ings;
Joys e'er in - creas - ing And peace nev - er ceas - ing:
He well re - ceiv - eth A heart that be - liev - eth;

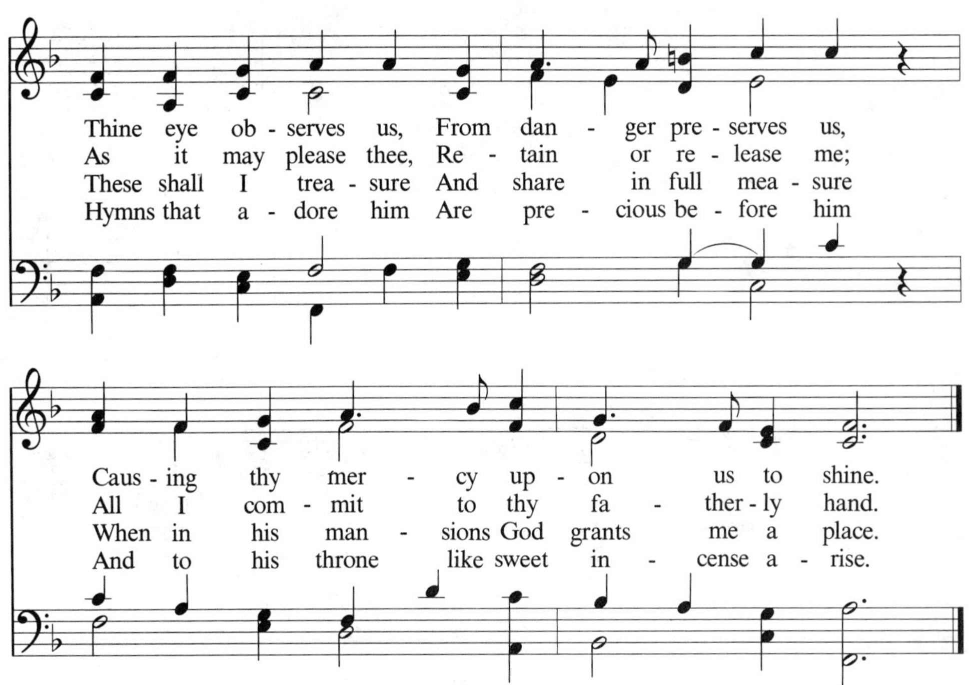
Thine eye ob - serves us, From dan - ger pre - serves us,
As it may please thee, Re - tain or re - lease me;
These shall I trea - sure And share in full mea - sure
Hymns that a - dore him Are pre - cious be - fore him
Caus - ing thy mer - cy up - on us to shine.
All I com - mit to thy fa - ther - ly hand.
When in his man - sions God grants me a place.
And to his throne like sweet in - cense a - rise.

 Text: Paul Gerhardt, 1607–1676; tr. composite
Tune: Johann G. Ebeling, 1637–1676

DIE GÜLDNE SONNE
PM

466 Great God, Our Source

1 Great God, our source and Lord of space, O Force of all by
2 Great God of fire, in - car - nate flame, Through Christ in whom your
3 Lord of the at - om, we praise your might, Ex - pressed in ter - ri -
whose sheer pow'r The pri - mal fires that flared and raged Were
love has burned And burns the way for our dark pace On
fy - ing light; Be - fore us rise the flames as pyres, Or
struck, blazed on, and still are made: Oh, save us, Lord, at
cos - mic routes with - in us turned: Lead us be - yond a -
bursts of love— they blind our sight. Help us, our Lord, oh,
this fierce hour From threat - 'ning fires that we have laid.
tom - ic night; Guide, Lord, in hope our bro - ken race.
help us see New forms of peace through suf - f'ring fires.

GREAT GOD, OUR SOURCE
88 88 88

Eternal Father, Strong to Save 467

1 E - ter - nal Fa - ther, strong to save, Whose arm has bound the
2 O Sav - ior, whose al - might - y word The winds and waves sub -
3 O Ho - ly Spir - it, who didst brood Up - on the cha - os
4 O Trin - i - ty of love and pow'r, All trav - 'lers guard in
rest - less wave, Who bade the might - y o - cean deep Its
mis - sive heard, Who walked up - on the foam - ing deep, And
dark and rude, And bid its an - gry tu - mult cease, And
dan - ger's hour From rock and tem - pest, fire and foe, Pro -
own ap - point - ed lim - its keep: Oh, hear us when we
calm a - mid the storm didst sleep: Oh, hear us when we
give, for wild con - fu - sion, peace: Oh, hear us when we
tect them where - so - e'er they go; Thus ev - er - more shall
cry to thee For those in per - il on the sea.
cry to thee For those in per - il on the sea.
cry to thee For those in per - il on the sea.
rise to thee Glad hymns and praise from land and sea.

Text: William Whiting, 1825–1878, alt.
Tune: John B. Dykes, 1823–1876

MELITA
88 88 88

468 From God Can Nothing Move Me

1 From God can noth-ing move me; He will not step a-side,
2 When those whom I re-gard-ed As trust-wor-thy and sure
3 When in my dark-est hour, . . I can on him re-ly;
4 Praise God with hearts and voic-es, For both are gifts from him;
But al-ways will re-prove me And be my con-stant guide.
Have long from me de-part-ed, God's grace shall still en-dure.
I have from him the pow-er All e-vil to de-fy.
A trou-bled world re-joic-es Each time we wor-ship him.
He stretch-es out his hand In eve-ning and in morn-ing,
He cares for all my needs, From sin and shame cor-rects me,
For God a-lone has might, And I shall nev-er fear it;
The days we spend on earth With-out our God are wast-ed,
Pro-vid-ing his fore-warn-ing Wher-ev-er I may stand.
From Sa-tan's bonds pro-tects me; Not e-ven death suc-ceeds.
My bod-y, soul, and spir-it Be-long to him by right.
For we shall not have tast-ed His joy in end-less birth.

5 Yet even though I suffer
The world's unpleasantness,
And though the days grow rougher
And bring me great distress,
That day of bliss divine,
Which knows no end or measure,
And Christ, who is my pleasure,
Forever shall be mine.

6 We were by God created
In his own time and place,
And by his Son persuaded
To follow truth and grace.
The Spirit guides our ways
And faithfully will lead us
That nothing can impede us.
To God be all our praise!

 Text: Ludwig Helmbold, 1532–1598; tr. Gerald Thorson, b. 1921
Tune: Christliche und Tröstliche Tischgesenge, *Erfurt, 1572*

VON GOTT WILL ICH NICHT LASSEN
76 76 67 76

Lord of All Hopefulness 469

1 Lord of all hope-ful-ness, Lord of all joy, Whose trust, ev-er
2 Lord of all ea-ger-ness, Lord of all faith, Whose strong hands were
3 Lord of all kind-li-ness, Lord of all grace, Your hands swift to
4 Lord of all gen-tle-ness, Lord of all calm, Whose voice is con-

child-like, no cares could de-stroy: Be there at our wak-ing, and
skilled at the plane and the lathe: Be there at our la-bors, and
wel-come, your arms to em-brace: Be there at our hom-ing, and
tent-ment, whose pres-ence is balm: Be there at our sleep-ing, and

give us, we pray, Your bliss in our hearts, Lord, at the break of the day.
give us, we pray, Your strength in our hearts, Lord, at the noon of the day.
give us, we pray, Your love in our hearts, Lord, at the eve of the day.
give us, we pray, Your peace in our hearts, Lord, at the end of the day.

 Text: Jan Struther, 1901–1953
Tune: Irish folk tune

SLANE
10 11 11 12

470 Praise and Thanks and Adoration

1 Praise and thanks and ad - o - ra - tion, Son of God, to you we give,
For you chose to serve cre - a - tion, Died that Ad - am's heirs might live.
Dear Lord Je - sus, guide my way; Faith-ful let me day by day
Fol - low where your steps are lead - ing, Find ad - ven - ture, joys ex - ceed - ing!

2 Hold me ev - er in your keep - ing, Com - fort me in pain and strife;
Through my laugh - ter and my weep - ing, Lift me to a no - bler life.
Draw my fer - vent love to you; Con - stant hope and faith re - new
In your birth, your life and Pas - sion, In your death and res - ur - rec - tion.

 Text: Thomas H. Kingo, 1634–1703; hymnal translation, 1978
Tune: Trente quatre pseaumes de David, *Geneva, 1551*

FREU DICH SEHR
87 87 77 88

Grant Peace, We Pray, in Mercy, Lord

471

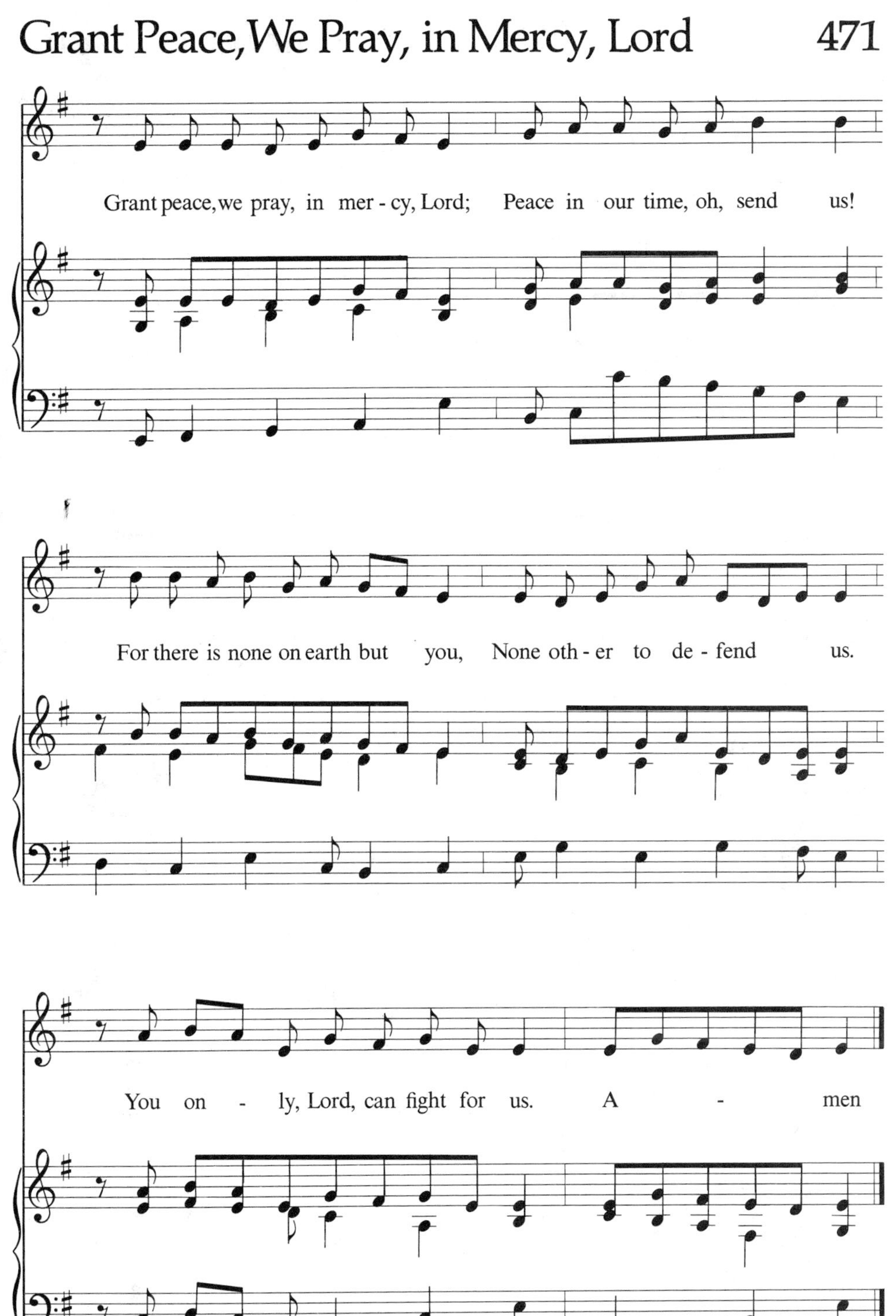
Grant peace, we pray, in mer - cy, Lord; Peace in our time, oh, send us!
For there is none on earth but you, None oth - er to de - fend us.
You on - ly, Lord, can fight for us. A - men

© *Text: medieval antiphon, adapt. Martin Luther, 1483–1546; tr.* Laudamus, *1952*
Tune: mode I; Gesangbuch, *Nürnberg, 1531*

VERLEIH UNS FRIEDEN
87 87 8

472 Come, Holy Ghost, Our Souls Inspire

1 Come, Ho - ly Ghost, our souls in - spire, And light - en with ce - les - tial fire; Thou the a - noint - ing Spir - it art, Who dost thy sev'n - fold gifts im - part.
2 Thy bless - ed unc - tion from a - bove Is com - fort, life, and fire of love. En - a - ble with per - pet - ual light The dull - ness of our blind - ed sight.
3 A - noint and cheer our soil - ed face With the a - bun - dance of thy grace. Keep far our foes; give peace at home; Where thou art guide, no ill can come.
4 Teach us to know the Fa - ther, Son, And thee, of both, to be but one; That through the a - ges all a - long Thy praise may be our end - less song!

5 Praise to thine e - ter - nal mer - it, Fa - ther,
Son, and Ho - ly Spir - it. A - men

Text: attr. Rhabanus Maurus, 776–856; tr. John Cosin, 1594–1672
Tune: Sarum plainsong, mode VIII

VENI, CREATOR SPIRITUS
LM

473 Come, Holy Ghost, Our Souls Inspire

1 Come, Ho - ly Ghost, our souls in - spire, And light - en
2 Thy bless - ed unc - tion from a - bove Is com - fort,
3 A - noint and cheer our soil - ed face With the a -
4 Teach us to know the Fa - ther, Son, And thee, of

with ce - les - tial fire; Thou the a - noint - ing
life, and fire of love. En - a - ble with per -
bun - dance of thy grace. Keep far our foes; give
both, to be but one; That through the a - ges

Spir - it art, Who dost thy sev'n - fold gifts im - part.
pet - ual light The dull - ness of our blind - ed sight.
peace at home; Where thou art guide, no ill can come.
all a - long Thy praise may be our end - less song!

Text: attr. Rhabanus Maurus, 776–856; tr. John Cosin, 1594–1672
Tune: J. Klug, Geistliche Lieder, *1533*

KOMM, GOTT SCHÖPFER
LM

474 Children of the Heavenly Father

1 Chil - dren of the heav'n - ly Fa - ther Safe - ly in his bo - som gath - er;
2 God his own doth tend and nour - ish, In his ho - ly courts they flour - ish.
3 Nei - ther life nor death shall ev - er From the Lord his chil - dren sev - er;
4 Though he giv - eth or he tak - eth, God his chil - dren ne'er for - sak - eth;

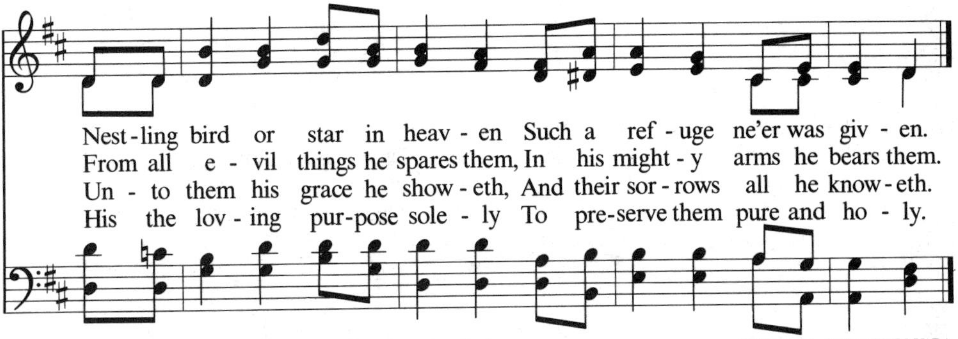

Nest-ling bird or star in heav-en Such a ref-uge ne'er was giv-en.
From all e-vil things he spares them, In his might-y arms he bears them.
Un-to them his grace he show-eth, And their sor-rows all he know-eth.
His the lov-ing pur-pose sole-ly To pre-serve them pure and ho-ly.

© Text: Caroline V. Sandell Berg, 1832–1903; tr. Ernst W. Olson, 1870–1958
Tune: Swedish folk tune

TRYGGARE KAN INGEN VARA
LM

Come, Gracious Spirit, Heavenly Dove 475

1 Come, gra-cious Spir-it, heav'n-ly dove, With light and com-fort from a-bove. Come, be our guard-ian and our guide; O'er ev-'ry thought and step pre-side.

2 The light of truth to us dis-play And make us know and choose your way; Plant ho-ly fear in ev-'ry heart, That we from God may ne'er de-part.

3 Lead us to Christ, the liv-ing way, Nor let us from his pas-tures stray; Lead us to ho-li-ness, the road That we must take to dwell with God.

4 Lead us to heav'n, that we may share Full-ness of joy for-ev-er there; Lead us to our e-ter-nal rest, To be with God for-ev-er blest.

Text: Simon Browne, 1680–1732, alt.
Tune: William Knapp, 1698–1768

WAREHAM
LM

476 Have No Fear, Little Flock

1 Have no fear, lit - tle flock; Have no fear, lit - tle
2 Have good cheer, lit - tle flock; Have good cheer, lit - tle
3 Praise the Lord high a - bove; Praise the Lord high a -
4 Thank-ful hearts raise to God; Thank - ful hearts raise to

flock, For the Fa - ther has cho - sen To
flock, For the Fa - ther will keep you In
bove, For he stoops down to heal you, Up -
God, For he stays close be - side you, In

give you the King - dom; Have no fear, lit - tle flock!
his love for - ev - er; Have good cheer, lit - tle flock!
lift and re - store you; Praise the Lord high a - bove!
all things works with you; Thank - ful hearts raise to God!

© *Text: Luke 12:32, st. 1; Marjorie Jillson, b. 1931, sts. 2–4*
© *Tune: Heinz Werner Zimmermann, b. 1930*

LITTLE FLOCK
66 76 6

477 O God of Jacob

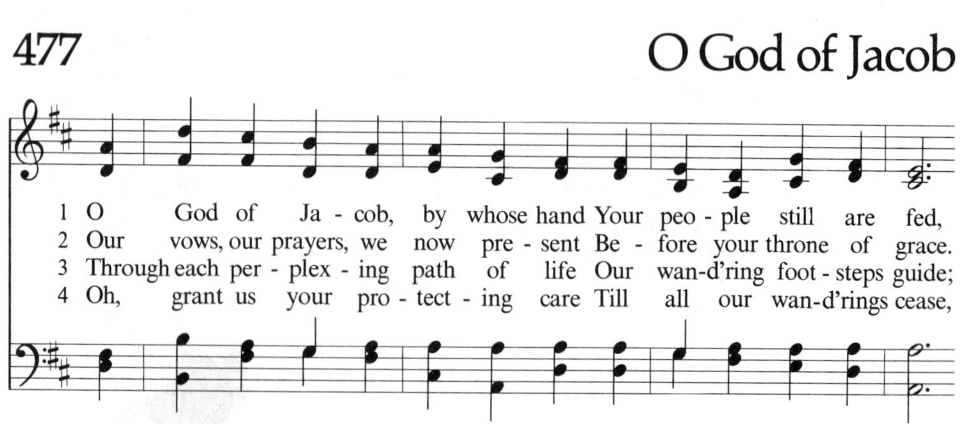
1 O God of Ja - cob, by whose hand Your peo - ple still are fed,
2 Our vows, our prayers, we now pre - sent Be - fore your throne of grace.
3 Through each per - plex - ing path of life Our wan-d'ring foot - steps guide;
4 Oh, grant us your pro - tect - ing care Till all our wan-d'rings cease,

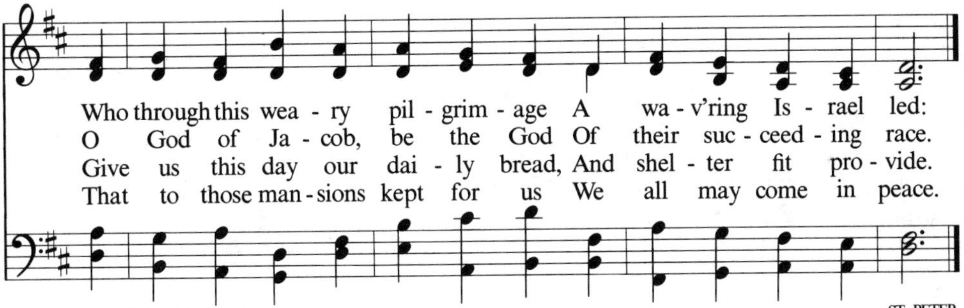

Who through this wea - ry pil - grim - age A wa - v'ring Is - rael led:
O God of Ja - cob, be the God Of their suc - ceed - ing race.
Give us this day our dai - ly bread, And shel - ter fit pro - vide.
That to those man - sions kept for us We all may come in peace.

Text: Philip Doddridge, 1702–1751, adapt.
Tune: Alexander R. Reinagle, 1799–1877

ST. PETER
CM

Come, Oh, Come, O Quickening Spirit 478

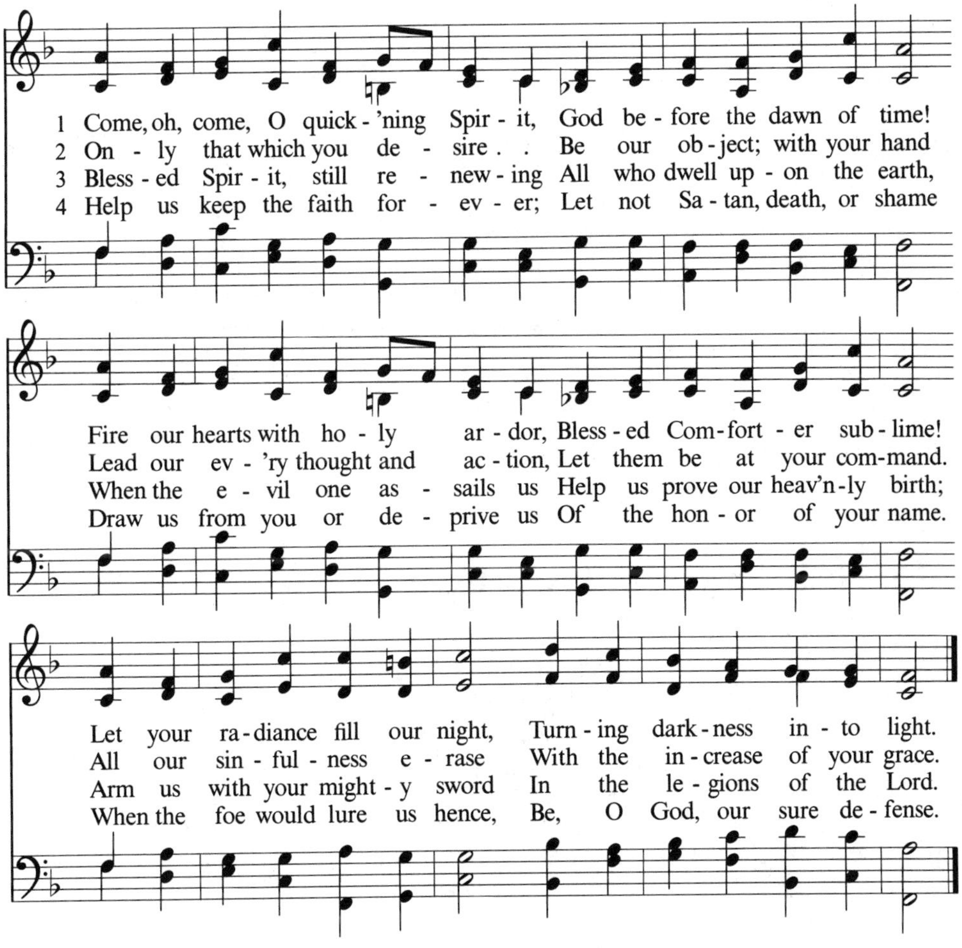

1 Come, oh, come, O quick - 'ning Spir - it, God be - fore the dawn of time!
2 On - ly that which you de - sire . . Be our ob - ject; with your hand
3 Bless - ed Spir - it, still re - new - ing All who dwell up - on the earth,
4 Help us keep the faith for - ev - er; Let not Sa - tan, death, or shame

Fire our hearts with ho - ly ar - dor, Bless - ed Com - fort - er sub - lime!
Lead our ev - 'ry thought and ac - tion, Let them be at your com - mand.
When the e - vil one as - sails us Help us prove our heav'n - ly birth;
Draw us from you or de - prive us Of the hon - or of your name.

Let your ra - diance fill our night, Turn - ing dark - ness in - to light.
All our sin - ful - ness e - rase With the in - crease of your grace.
Arm us with your might - y sword In the le - gions of the Lord.
When the foe would lure us hence, Be, O God, our sure de - fense.

 Text: Heinrich Held, d. c. 1659; tr. Edward T. Horn III, b. 1909, alt.
Tune: Neu-vermehrtes Gesangbuch, *Meiningen, 1693*

KOMM, O KOMM, DU GEIST DES LEBENS
87 87 77

479 My Faith Looks Up to Thee

1 My faith looks up to thee, Thou Lamb of Cal - va - ry,
2 May thy rich grace im - part Strength to my faint - ing heart,
3 While life's dark maze I tread And griefs a - round me spread,
4 When ends life's tran - sient dream, When death's cold, sul - len stream

Sav - ior di - vine! Now hear me while I pray, Take all my
My zeal in - spire; As thou hast died for me, Oh, may my
Be thou my guide; Bid dark - ness turn to day, Wipe sor - row's
Shall o'er me roll; Blest Sav - ior, then, in love Fear and dis -

guilt a - way, Oh, let me from this day Be whol - ly thine!
love to thee Pure, warm, and change - less be, A liv - ing fire!
tears a - way, Nor let me ev - er stray From thee a - side.
trust re-move; Oh, bear me safe a-bove, A ran - somed soul!

Text: Ray Palmer, 1808–1887
Tune: Lowell Mason, 1792–1872

OLIVET
664 6664

480 Oh, that the Lord Would Guide My Ways

1 Oh, that the Lord would guide my ways To keep his stat - utes still!
2 Or - der my foot - steps by your Word And make my heart sin - cere;
3 As - sist my soul, too apt to stray, A strict - er watch to keep;
4 Make me to walk in your com-mands, 'Tis a de - light - ful road;

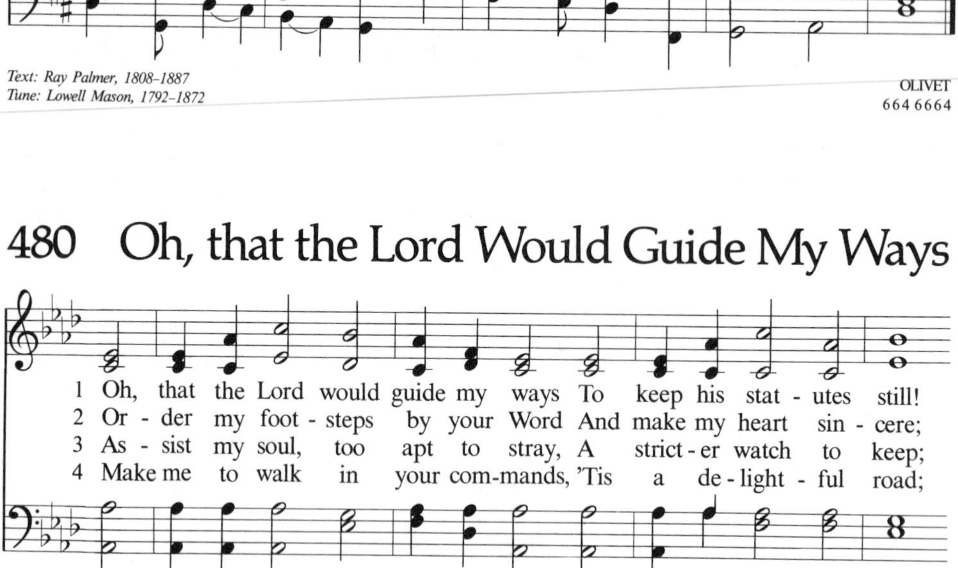

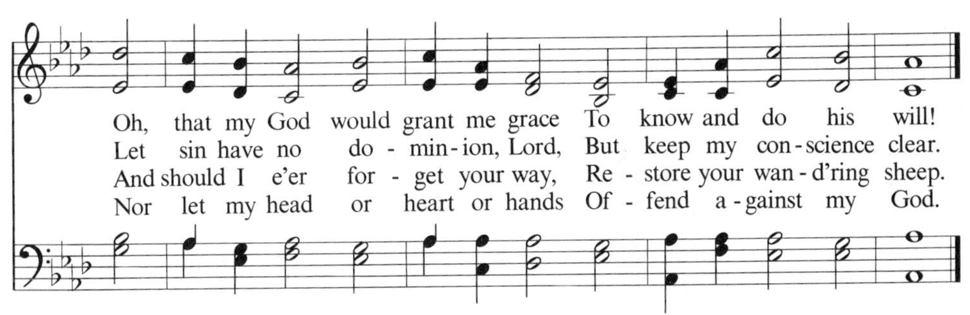
Oh, that my God would grant me grace To know and do his will!
Let sin have no do - min - ion, Lord, But keep my con - science clear.
And should I e'er for - get your way, Re - store your wan - d'ring sheep.
Nor let my head or heart or hands Of - fend a - gainst my God.

Text: Isaac Watts, 1674–1748, alt.
Tune: William H. Havergal, 1793–1870

EVAN
CM

Savior, like a Shepherd Lead Us 481

1 Sav - ior, like a shep - herd lead us; Much we need your ten - der care.
2 We are yours; in love be - friend us, Be the guard - ian of our way;
3 You have prom - ised to re - ceive us, Poor and sin - ful though we be;
4 Ear - ly let us seek your fa - vor, Ear - ly let us do your will;

In your pleas - ant pas - tures feed us, For our use your fold pre - pare.
Keep your flock, from sin de - fend us, Seek us when we go a - stray.
You have mer - cy to re - lieve us, Grace to cleanse, and pow'r to free.
Bless - ed Lord and on - ly Sav - ior, With your love our spir - its fill.

Bless - ed Je - sus, bless - ed Je - sus, You have bought us; we are yours.
Bless - ed Je - sus, bless - ed Je - sus, Hear us chil - dren when we pray.
Bless - ed Je - sus, bless - ed Je - sus, Ear - ly let us turn to you.
Bless - ed Je - sus, bless - ed Je - sus, You have loved us, love us still.

Text: Dorothy A. Thrupp, 1779–1847
Tune: Ludvig M. Lindeman, 1812–1887

HER VIL TIES
87 87 87

482 When I Survey the Wondrous Cross

1 When I survey the wondrous cross On which the prince of glory died,
My richest gain I count but loss And pour contempt on all my pride.
2 Forbid it, Lord, that I should boast Save in the death of Christ, my God;
All the vain things that charm me most, I sacrifice them to his blood.
3 See, from his head, his hands, his feet, Sorrow and love flow mingled down.
Did e'er such love and sorrow meet, Or thorns compose so rich a crown?
4 Were the whole realm of nature mine, That were a tribute far too small;
Love so amazing, so divine, Demands my soul, my life, my all!

Text: Isaac Watts, 1674–1748
Tune: adapt. Edward Miller, 1731–1807

ROCKINGHAM OLD
LM

483 God Moves in a Mysterious Way

1 God moves in a mysterious way, His wonders to perform;
2 Judge not the Lord by feeble sense, But trust him for his grace;
3 Blind unbelief is sure to err And scan his work in vain;
4 You fearful saints, fresh courage take; The clouds you so much dread

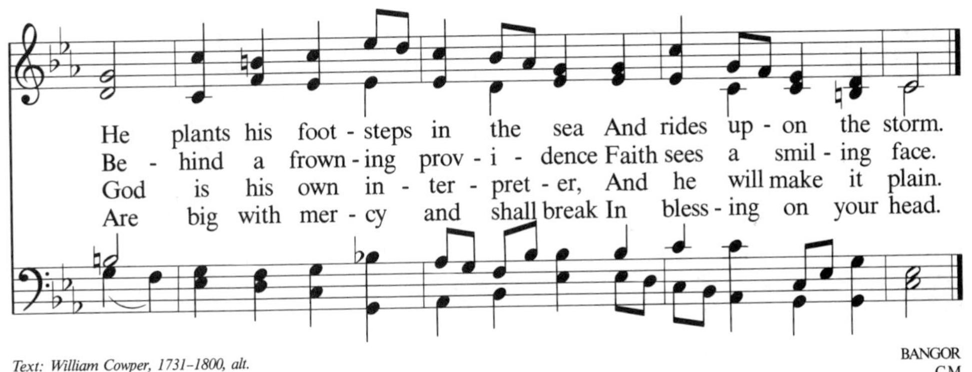
He plants his foot - steps in the sea And rides up - on the storm.
Be - hind a frown - ing prov - i - dence Faith sees a smil - ing face.
God is his own in - ter - pret - er, And he will make it plain.
Are big with mer - cy and shall break In bless - ing on your head.

Text: William Cowper, 1731–1800, alt.
Tune: Tans'ur, Compleat Melody, *1734*

BANGOR
CM

God, My Lord, My Strength

484

1 God, my Lord, my strength, my place of hid - ing And con - fid - ing
2 Christ in me, and I am freed for liv - ing And for - giv - ing,
3 Up, weak knees and spir - it bowed in sor - row! No to - mor-row

In all needs by night and day; Though foes sur - round me,
Heart of flesh for life - less stone; Now bold to serve him,
Shall a - rise to beat you down; God goes be - fore you

And Sa - tan mark his prey, God shall have his way.
Now cheered his love to own, Nev - er - more a - lone.
And an - gels all a - round; On your head a crown!

© *Text: Tranoscius, 1636; tr. Jaroslav J. Vajda, b. 1919, alt.*
Tune: Gradual, *Prague, 1567*

PÁN BŮH
10 4 7 56 5

485 Lord, as a Pilgrim

1 Lord, as a pil - grim through life I go; Each day your
2 Friends have for - sak - en; you have stood fast; You have been
3 You are my ref - uge; grant me, I pray, Strength for each
4 Lord, let your pres - ence bright - en the night Till the last
lov - ing pres - ence I know. Trav - el be - side me,
faith - ful, true to the last; Much I of - fend - ed,
bur - den, light for each day, Com - fort in sor - row,
sun - rise; then, in your might, Par - don and spare me,
Strength-en and guide me, Shep - herd di - vine!
Yet you ex - tend - ed Friend - ship di - vine!
Grace for to - mor - row, Sav - ior di - vine!
Sum - mon and bear me Home - ward at last.

OI HERRA, JOS MÄ MATKAMIES MAAN
99 55 4

Spirit of God, Descend upon My Heart 486

B♭ F7 B♭ E♭ Cm7 B♭ Gm A Dm G7
1 Spir - it of God, de - scend up - on my heart; Wean it from earth, through
2 I ask no dream, no proph - et ec - sta - sies, No sud - den rend - ing
3 Have you not bid me love you, God and King; All, all your own, soul,
4 Teach me to love you as your an - gels love, One ho - ly pas - sion
F C7 F F7 F sus4 F7
all its puls - es move; Stoop to my weak - ness, strength to
of the veil of clay, No an - gel vis - i - tant, no
heart, and strength, and mind? I see your cross; there teach my
fill - ing all my frame: The bap - tism of the heav'n - de -
B♭ E♭ B♭ F7 B♭
me im - part, And make me love you as I ought to love.
o - p'ning skies; But take the dim - ness of my soul a - way.
heart to cling. Oh, let me seek you and, oh, let me find!
scend - ed dove, My heart an al - tar, and your love the flame.

Text: George Croly, 1780–1860
Tune: Frederick C. Atkinson, 1841–1897

MORECAMBE
10 10 10 10

487 Let Us Ever Walk with Jesus

1 Let us ev - er walk with Je - sus, Fol - low his ex - am - ple pure,
2 Let us suf - fer here with Je - sus And with pa - tience bear our cross.
3 Let us glad - ly die with Je - sus. Since by death he con-quered death,
4 Let us al - so live with Je - sus. He has ris - en from the dead
Through a world that would de - ceive us And to sin our spir - its lure.
Joy will fol - low all our sad-ness; Where he is there is no loss.
He will free us from de - struc-tion, Give to us im - mor - tal breath.
That to life we may a - wak - en. Je - sus, since you are our head,
On - ward in his foot-steps tread-ing, Pil - grims here, our home a - bove,
Though to - day we sow no laugh-ter, We shall reap ce - les - tial joy:
Let us mor - ti - fy all pas - sion That would lead us in - to sin;
We are your own liv - ing mem-bers; Where you live, there we shall be
Full of faith and hope and love, Let us do our Fa - ther's bid - ding.
All dis - com - forts that an - noy Shall give way to mirth here - af - ter.
Then by grace we all may win Un - told fruits of his cre - a - tion.
In your pres - ence con - stant - ly, Liv - ing there with you for - ev - er.

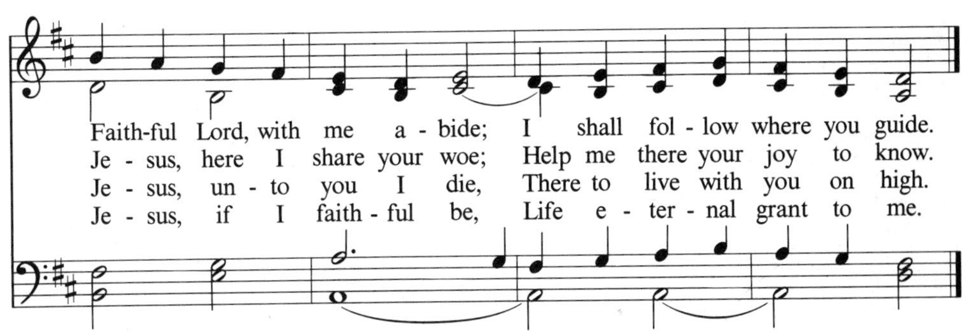
Faith-ful Lord, with me a - bide; I shall fol - low where you guide.
Je - sus, here I share your woe; Help me there your joy to know.
Je - sus, un - to you I die, There to live with you on high.
Je - sus, if I faith - ful be, Life e - ter - nal grant to me.

 Text: Sigismund von Birken, 1626–1681; tr. hymnal version, 1978
Tune: Georg G. Boltze, 18th cent.

LASSET UNS MIT JESU ZIEHEN
PM

Breathe on Me, Breath of God 488

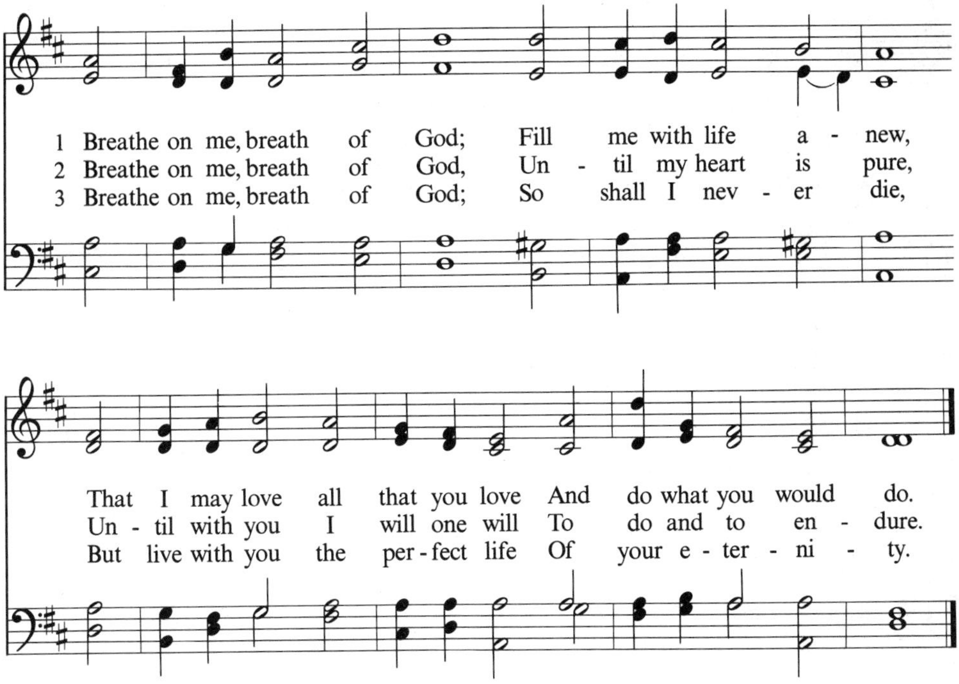

1 Breathe on me, breath of God; Fill me with life a - new,
2 Breathe on me, breath of God, Un - til my heart is pure,
3 Breathe on me, breath of God; So shall I nev - er die,

That I may love all that you love And do what you would do.
Un - til with you I will one will To do and to en - dure.
But live with you the per - fect life Of your e - ter - ni - ty.

Text: Edwin Hatch, 1835–1889
Tune: Aaron Williams, 1731–1776

DURHAM
SM

489 Wide Open Are Your Hands

1 Wide o - pen are your hands To pay with more than gold The
2 Wide o - pen are your arms, A fall - en world to em-brace, To
3 Draw all my mind and heart Up to your throne on high, And
aw - ful debt of guilt and sin, For - ev - er and of old. Ah,
win to love and end - less rest Our way-ward hu - man race. Lord,
let your sa - cred cross ex - alt My spir - it to the sky. To
let me grasp those hands, That we may nev - er part, And
I am sad and poor, But bound - less is your grace; Give
these, your might - y hands, My spir - it I re - sign. In
let the pow - er of their blood Sus - tain my faint - ing heart.
me the soul - trans-form - ing joy For which I seek your face.
life, I live a - lone to you; In death, am yours a - lone.

Text: attr. Bernard of Clairvaux, 1091–1153; tr. Charles Porterfield Krauth, 1823–1883, alt.
Tune: George W. Martin, 1828–1881

LEOMINSTER
SMD

Let Me Be Yours Forever

490

1 Let me be yours for - ev - er, My gra - cious God and Lord;
2 Lord Je - sus, boun - teous giv - er Of light and life di - vine,
3 O Ho - ly Spir - it, pour - ing Sweet peace in - to my heart,
May I for - sake you nev - er Nor wan - der from your Word.
You did my soul de - liv - er; To you I all re - sign.
And all my soul re - stor - ing, Let me in grace de - part.
Pre - serve me from the maz - es Of er - ror and dis - trust,
You have in mer - cy bought me With blood and bit - ter pain;
And while his name con - fess - ing Whom I by faith have known,
And I shall sing your prais - es For - ev - er with the just.
Let me, since you have sought me, E - ter - nal life ob - tain.
Grant me your con - stant bless - ing And take me as your own.

Text: Nikolaus Selnecker, 1532–1592, st. 1; Gesangbuch, *Rudolstadt, 1688, sts. 2–3;*
tr. Matthias Loy, 1828–1915, alt.
Tune: Bohemian Brethren, Ein Gesangbuch der Brüder, *1544*

LOB GOTT GETROST MIT SINGEN
76 76 D

491 O God, I Love Thee

1 O God, I love thee; not that my poor love May
2 But, Je - sus, thou art mine, and I am thine; Clasped
3 No thought can fath - om and no tongue ex - press Thy
4 How can I choose but love thee, God's dear Son, O
win me en - trance to thy heav'n a - bove, Nor
to thy bo - som by thine arms di - vine, Who
griefs, thy toils, thine an - guish mea - sure - less, Thy
Je - sus, love - liest and most lov - ing one! Were
yet that strang - ers to thy love must know The
on the cru - el cross for me hast borne The
death, O Lamb of God, the un - de - filed; And
there no heav'n to gain, no hell to flee, For
bit - ter - ness of ev - er - last - ing woe.
nails, the spear, and man's un - pit - ying scorn.
all for me, thy way - ward, sin - ful child.
what thou art a - lone I must love thee.

5 Not for the hope of glory or reward,
But even as thyself hast loved me, Lord,
I love thee, and will love thee and adore,
Who art my King, my God, forevermore.

Text: attr. Frances Xavier, 1506–1552; tr. Edward H. Bickersteth, 1825–1906
© *Tune: Herbert Howells, b. 1892*

IN MANUS TUAS
10 10 10 10

O Master, Let Me Walk with You 492

1 O Mas - ter, let me walk with you In low - ly
2 Help me the slow of heart to move By some clear,
3 Teach me your pa - tience; share with me A clos - er,
4 In hope that sends a shin - ing ray Far down the
paths of ser - vice true; Tell me your se - cret;
win - ning word of love; Teach me the way - ward
dear - er com - pa - ny, In work that keeps faith
fu - ture's broad - 'ning way, In peace that on - ly
help me bear The strain of toil, the fret of care.
feet to stay, And guide them in the home - ward way.
sweet and strong, In trust that tri - umphs o - ver wrong,
you can give; With you, O Mas - ter, let me live.

Text: Washington Gladden, 1836–1918
Tune: H. Percy Smith, 1825–1898

MARYTON
LM

493 Hope of the World

1 Hope of the world, thou Christ of great com - pas - sion:
2 Hope of the world, God's gift from high - est heav - en,
3 Hope of the world, a - foot on dust - y high - ways,
4 Hope of the world, who by thy cross didst save us
Speak to our fear - ful hearts by con - flict rent.
Bring - ing to hun - gry souls the bread of life:
Show - ing to wan - d'ring souls the path of light:
From death and dark de - spair, from sin and guilt:
Save us, thy peo - ple, from con - sum - ing pas - sion,
Still let thy Spir - it un - to us be giv - en
Walk thou be - side us lest the tempt - ing by - ways
We ren - der back the love thy mer - cy gave us;
Who by our own false hopes and aims are spent.
To heal earth's wounds and end our bit - ter strife.
Lure us a - way from thee to end - less night.
Take thou our lives and use them as thou wilt.

5 Hope of the world, O Christ, o'er death victorious,
Who by this sign didst conquer grief and pain:
We would be faithful to thy Gospel glorious;
Thou art our Lord! Thou dost forever reign!

 Text: Georgia Harkness, 1891–1974
Tune: Trente quatre pseaumes de David, *Geneva, 1551*

DONNE SECOURS
11 10 11 10

Jesus Calls Us; O'er the Tumult 494

1 Je - sus calls us; o'er the tu - mult Of our life's wild, rest - less sea, Day by day his clear voice sound - ing, Say - ing, "Chris - tian, fol - low me."
2 As of old St. An - drew heard it By the Gal - i - le - an lake, Turned from home and toil and kin - dred, Leav - ing all for his dear sake.
3 Je - sus calls us from the wor - ship Of the vain world's gold - en store, From each i - dol that would keep us, Say - ing, "Chris - tian, love me more."
4 In our joys and in our sor - rows, Days of toil and hours of ease, Still he calls, in cares and plea - sures, "Chris - tian, love me more than these."

5 Jesus calls us! In your mercy,
Savior, make us hear your call,
Give our hearts to your obedience,
Serve and love you best of all.

Text: Cecil F. Alexander, 1823–1895
Tune: William H. Jude, 1851–1922

GALILEE
87 87

495 Lead On, O King Eternal!

1 Lead on, O King e - ter - nal! The day of march has come;
2 Lead on, O King e - ter - nal, Till sin's fierce war shall cease,
3 Lead on, O King e - ter - nal: We fol - low, not with fears,
Hence-forth in fields of con - quest Your tents will be our home.
And ho - li - ness shall whis - per The sweet a - men of peace;
For glad - ness breaks like morn - ing Wher - e'er your face ap - pears.
Through days of prep - a - ra - tion Your grace has made us strong;
For not with swords loud clash - ing, Nor roll of stir - ring drums,
Your cross is lift - ed o'er us; We jour - ney in its light;
And now, O King e - ter - nal, We lift our bat - tle song.
But deeds of love and mer - cy The heav'n - ly king - dom comes.
The crown a - waits the con - quest; Lead on, O God of might!

Text: Ernest W. Shurtleff, 1862–1917
Tune: Henry T. Smart, 1813–1879

LANCASHIRE
76 76 D

Around You, O Lord Jesus 496

E♭ A♭ B♭ E♭ B♭ Fm B♭7 E♭
1 A-round you, O Lord Je - sus, Your own you gath - er still
2 We hear your in - vi - ta - tion, And heed, O Lord, your call;
3 We are your own for - ev - er; Un - til our fi - nal breath
E♭ A♭ B♭ E♭ B♭ Fm B♭7 E♭
To share the feast you give us With grace our lives to fill.
Your word of con - so - la - tion Is spo - ken here to all.
We will be true and nev - er— In joy, in grief, in death—
E♭ A♭ B♭ Cm G A♭
You say to us so lov - ing - ly, "Take, eat! This
It draws us to your lov - ing heart; It brings to
De - part from you, for you are still A - mong your
Fm C B♭ E♭ Fm B♭7 E♭
is my bod - y! Take, drink! This is my blood!"
us your bless - ing, Which nev - er will de - part.
peo - ple dwell - ing, As you have said you will.

© *Text: Frans Mikael Franzén, 1772–1847; tr. composite*
Tune: H. Thomissön, Den Danske Salmebog, *1569*

O JESU, ÄN DE DINA
76 76 876

497 I Heard the Voice of Jesus Say

1 I heard the voice of Je - sus say, "Come un - to me and rest;
2 I heard the voice of Je - sus say, "Be - hold, I free - ly give
3 I heard the voice of Je - sus say, "I am this dark world's light;
Lay down, O wea - ry one, lay down Your head up - on my breast."
The liv - ing wa - ter, thirst - y one; Stoop down and drink and live."
Look un - to me, your morn shall rise, And all your day be bright."
I came to Je - sus as I was, So wea - ry, worn, and sad;
I came to Je - sus, and I drank Of that life - giv - ing stream;
I looked to Je - sus, and I found In him my star, my sun;
I found in him a rest - ing-place, And he has made me glad.
My thirst was quenched, my soul re - vived, And now I live in him.
And in that light of life I'll walk Till trav-'ling days are done.

Text: Horatius Bonar, 1808–1889
Tune: Thomas Tallis, c. 1505–1585

THIRD MODE MELODY
CMD

All Who Would Valiant Be

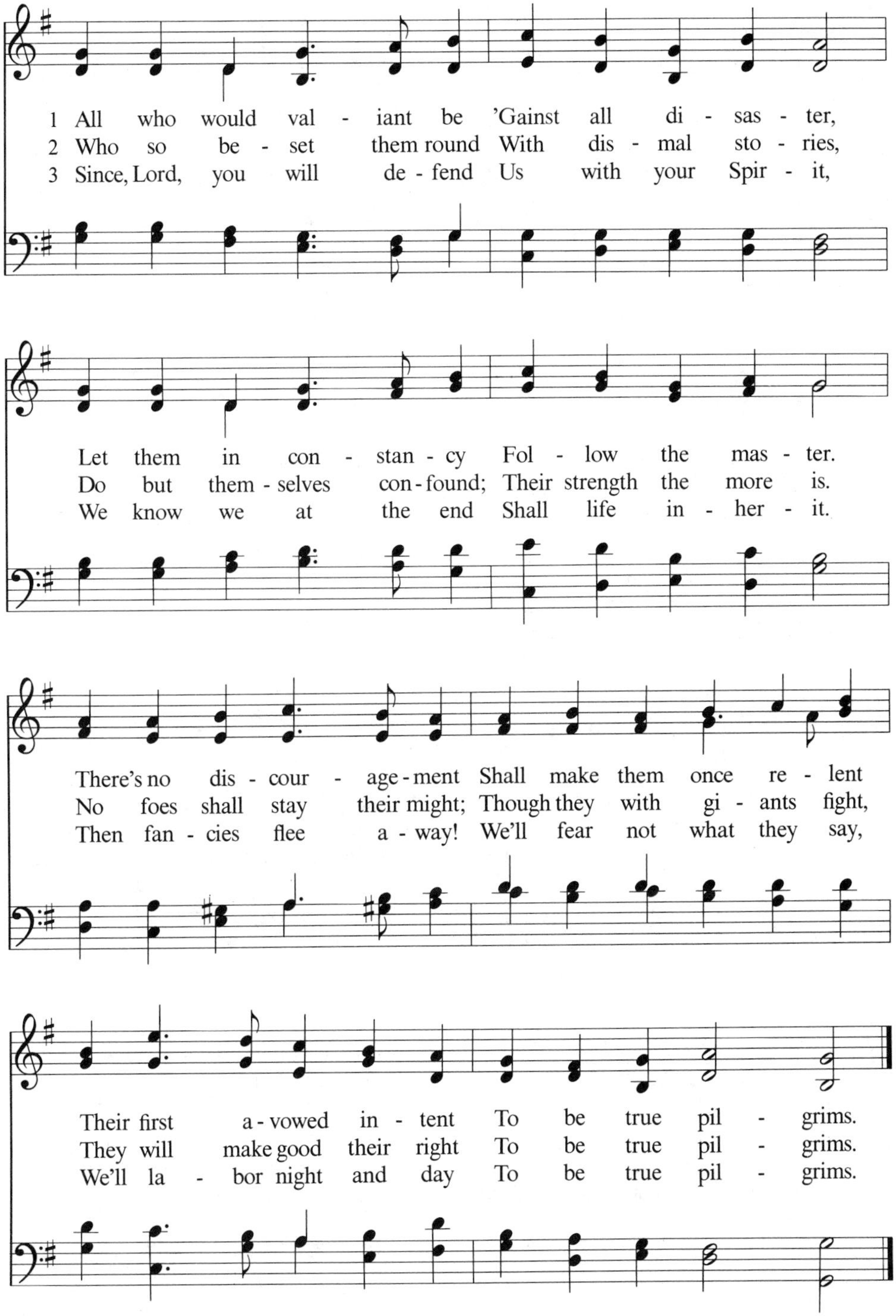

1 All who would val - iant be 'Gainst all di - sas - ter,
2 Who so be - set them round With dis - mal sto - ries,
3 Since, Lord, you will de - fend Us with your Spir - it,

Let them in con - stan - cy Fol - low the mas - ter.
Do but them - selves con - found; Their strength the more is.
We know we at the end Shall life in - her - it.

There's no dis - cour - age - ment Shall make them once re - lent
No foes shall stay their might; Though they with gi - ants fight,
Then fan - cies flee a - way! We'll fear not what they say,

Their first a - vowed in - tent To be true pil - grims.
They will make good their right To be true pil - grims.
We'll la - bor night and day To be true pil - grims.

ST. DUNSTAN'S
65 65 6665

499 Come, Thou Fount of Every Blessing

1 Come, thou Fount of ev - 'ry bless - ing, Tune my heart to sing thy grace;
2 Here I raise my Eb - en - e - zer, Hith - er by thy help I'm come;
3 Oh, to grace how great a debt - or Dai - ly I'm con-strained to be;
Streams of mer - cy, nev - er ceas - ing, Call for songs of loud-est praise.
And I hope, by thy good plea - sure, Safe - ly to ar - rive at home.
Let that grace now like a fet - ter Bind my wan-d'ring heart to thee.
While the hope of end-less glo - ry Fills my heart with joy and love,
Je - sus sought me when a strang - er, Wan-d'ring from the fold of God;
Prone to wan-der, Lord, I feel it; Prone to leave the God I love.
Teach me ev - er to a - dore thee; May I still thy good-ness prove.
He, to res - cue me from dan - ger, In - ter-posed his pre-cious blood.
Here's my heart, oh, take and seal it; Seal it for thy courts a - bove.

Text: Robert Robinson, 1735–1790
Tune: J. Wyeth, Repository of Sacred Music, *Part II, 1813*

NETTLETON
87 87 D

Faith of Our Fathers

1 Faith of our fa - thers, liv - ing still In spite of dun - geon,
2 The mar-tyrs, chained in pris - ons dark, Were still in heart and
3 Faith of our fa - thers! We will love Both friend and foe in
fire, and sword. Oh, how our hearts beat high with joy
con - science free; And blest would be their chil - dren's fate
all our strife; Pro-claim thee, too, as love knows how,
When-e'er we hear that glo - rious word.
If they, like them, should die for thee.
By sav - ing Word and faith - ful life.
Refrain
Faith of our fa - thers, ho - ly faith, We will be true to thee till death.

Text: Frederick W. Faber, 1814–1863, alt.
Tune: Henri F. Hemy, 1818–1888; James G. Walton, 1821–1905, refrain

ST. CATHERINE
88 88 88

501 He Leadeth Me: Oh, Blessed Thought!

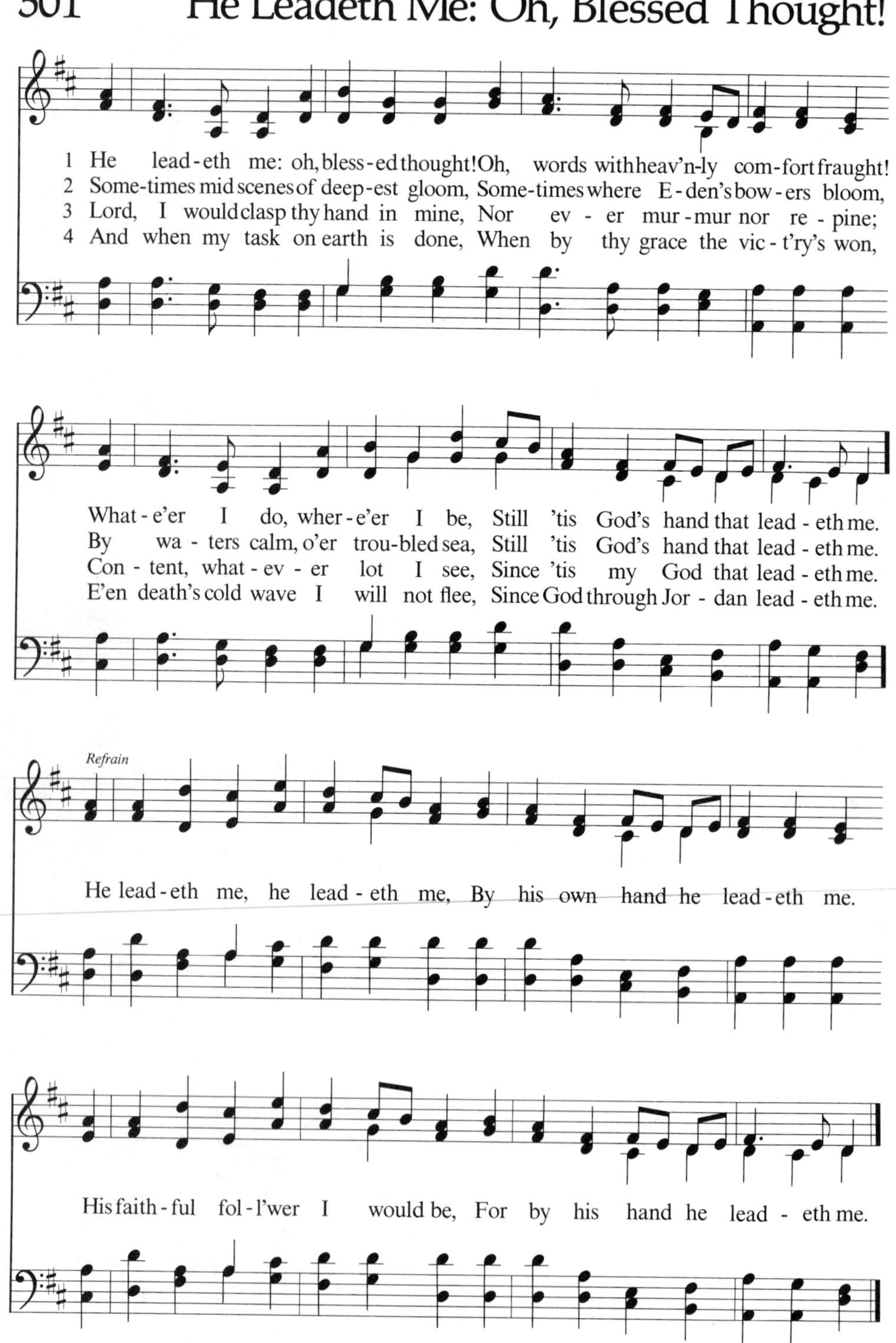
1 He lead-eth me: oh, bless-ed thought! Oh, words with heav'n-ly com-fort fraught!
2 Some-times mid scenes of deep-est gloom, Some-times where E-den's bow-ers bloom,
3 Lord, I would clasp thy hand in mine, Nor ev - er mur-mur nor re - pine;
4 And when my task on earth is done, When by thy grace the vic-t'ry's won,
What-e'er I do, wher-e'er I be, Still 'tis God's hand that lead-eth me.
By wa-ters calm, o'er trou-bled sea, Still 'tis God's hand that lead-eth me.
Con-tent, what-ev-er lot I see, Since 'tis my God that lead-eth me.
E'en death's cold wave I will not flee, Since God through Jor-dan lead-eth me.
Refrain
He lead-eth me, he lead-eth me, By his own hand he lead-eth me.
His faith-ful fol-l'wer I would be, For by his hand he lead-eth me.

Text: Joseph H. Gilmore, 1834–1918, alt.
Tune: William B. Bradbury, 1816–1868

HE LEADETH ME
LMD

Thee Will I Love, My Strength 502

1 Thee will I love, my strength, my tow'r; Thee will I love, my
2 I thank thee, un - cre - at - ed sun, That thy bright beams on
3 Up - hold me in the doubt - ful race, Nor suf - fer me a -
4 Thee will I love, my joy, my crown; Thee will I love, my
joy, my crown! Thee will I love with all my pow'r, In
me have shined; I thank thee, who hast o - ver - thrown My
gain to stray; Strength-en my feet with stead - y pace Still
Lord, my God! Thee will I love, be - neath thy frown Or
all thy works, and thee a - lone; Thee will I love, till
foes and healed my wound - ed mind; I thank thee, whose en -
to press for - ward in thy way, That all my pow'rs, with
smile, thy scep - ter or thy rod. What though my flesh and
the pure fire Fills all my soul with chaste de - sire.
liv - 'ning voice Bids my freed heart in thee re - joice.
all their might, In thy sole glo - ry may u - nite.
heart de - cay? Thee shall I love in end - less day!

Text: Johann Scheffler, 1624–1677; tr. John Wesley, 1703–1791
Tune: J. B. König, Harmonischer Lieder-Schatz, *1738*

ICH WILL DICH LIEBEN
88 88 88

503 O Jesus, I Have Promised

1 O Je - sus, I have prom - ised To serve you to the end;
2 Oh, let me feel you near me; The world is ev - er near.
3 Oh, let me hear you speak - ing In ac - cents clear and still
4 O Je - sus, you have prom - ised To all who fol - low you
Re - main for - ev - er near me, My mas - ter and my friend.
I see the sights that daz - zle, The tempt - ing sounds I hear.
A - bove the storms of pas - sion, The mur - murs of self - will.
That where you are in glo - ry Your ser - vant shall be too.
I shall not fear the bat - tle If you are by my side,
My foes are ev - er near me, A - round me and with - in;
Now speak to re - as - sure me, To has - ten or con - trol;
And Je - sus, I have prom - ised To serve you to the end;
Nor wan - der from the path - way If you will be my guide.
But, Je - sus, then draw near - er To shield my soul from sin.
Now speak and make me lis - ten, O Guard - ian of my soul.
Oh, give me grace to fol - low, My mas - ter and my friend.

Text: *John E. Bode, 1816–1874, alt.*
Tune: Neu-vermehrtes Gesangbuch, *Meiningen, 1693*

MUNICH
76 76 D

O God, My Faithful God

504

1 O God, my faith - ful God, True foun - tain ev - er flow - ing,
2 Give me the strength to do With read - y heart and will - ing
3 Keep me from say - ing words That lat - er need re - call - ing;
4 When dan - gers gath - er round, Oh, keep me calm and fear - less;
With - out whom noth - ing is, All per - fect gifts be - stow - ing:
What - ev - er you com-mand, My call - ing here ful - fill - ing—
Guard me, lest i - dle speech May from my lips be fall - ing;
Help me to bear the cross When life seems dark and cheer - less;
Give me a health - y frame, And may I have with - in
To do it when I ought, With all my strength—and bless
But when, with - in my place, I must and ought to speak,
Help me, as you have taught, To love both great and small,
A con-science free from blame, A soul un - stained by sin.
What - ev - er I have wrought, For you must give suc - cess.
Then to my words give grace, Lest I of - fend the weak.
And, by your Spir - it's might, To live at peace with all.

Text: Johann Heermann, 1585–1647; tr. Catherine Winkworth, 1829–1878, alt.
Tune: Ahasuerus Fritsch, 1629–1701

WAS FRAG ICH NACH DER WELT
67 67 66 66

505 Forth in Thy Name, O Lord, I Go

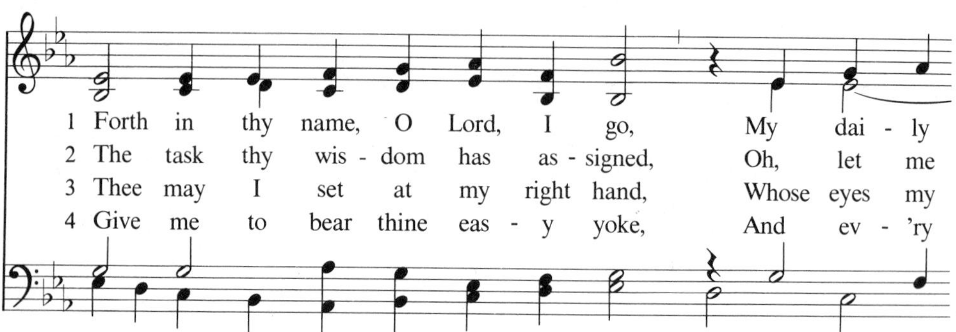
1 Forth in thy name, O Lord, I go, My dai - ly
2 The task thy wis - dom has as - signed, Oh, let me
3 Thee may I set at my right hand, Whose eyes my
4 Give me to bear thine eas - y yoke, And ev - 'ry

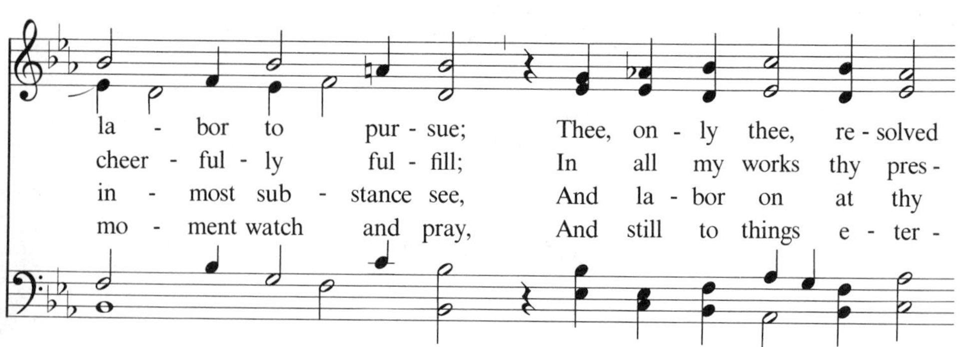
la - bor to pur - sue; Thee, on - ly thee, re - solved
cheer - ful - ly ful - fill; In all my works thy pres -
in - most sub - stance see, And la - bor on at thy
mo - ment watch and pray, And still to things e - ter -

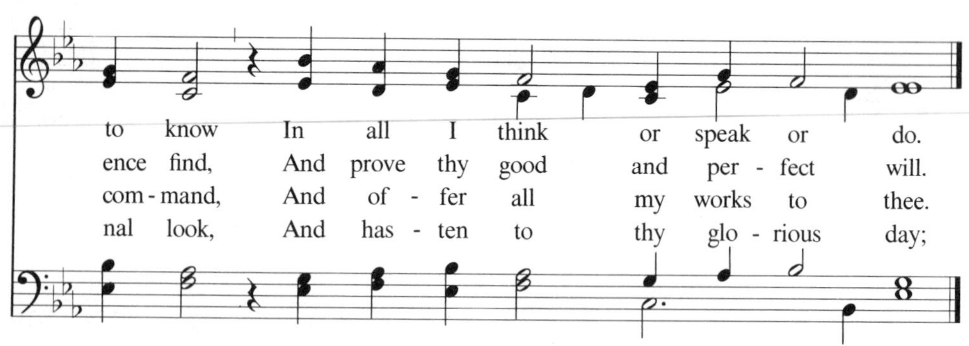
to know In all I think or speak or do.
ence find, And prove thy good and per - fect will.
com - mand, And of - fer all my works to thee.
nal look, And has - ten to thy glo - rious day;

5 For thee delightfully employ
Whate'er thy bounteous grace has giv'n,
And run my course with even joy,
And closely walk with thee to heav'n.

Text: Charles Wesley, 1707–1788
Tune: Orlando Gibbons, 1583–1625

SONG 34
LM

Dear Lord and Father of Mankind 506

1 Dear Lord and Fa - ther of man - kind, For - give our
2 In sim - ple trust like theirs who heard, Be - side the
3 Oh, Sab - bath rest by Gal - i - lee, Oh, calm of
4 Drop thy still dews of qui - et - ness, Till all our
fe - v'rish ways; Re - clothe us in our right - ful mind; In pur - er
Syr - ian sea, The gra - cious call - ing of the Lord, Let us, like
hills a - bove; Where Je - sus knelt to share with thee The si - lence
striv-ings cease; Take from our souls the strain and stress, And let our
lives thy ser - vice find, In deep - er rev - 'rence, praise.
them, with - out a word Rise up and fol - low thee.
of e - ter - ni - ty, In - ter - pret - ed by love!
or - dered lives con - fess The beau - ty of thy peace.

5 Breathe through the heats of our desire
Thy coolness and thy balm;
Let sense be dumb, let flesh retire;
Speak through the earthquake, wind, and fire,
O still small voice of calm!

Text: John G. Whittier, 1807–1892
© *Tune: Frederick C. Maker, 1844–1927*

REST
86 886

507 How Firm a Foundation

1 How firm a foun - da - tion, O saints of the Lord,
2 Fear not, I am with you, oh, be not dis - mayed,
3 When through fi - ery tri - als your path - way shall lie,
4 Through - out all their life - time my peo - ple shall prove
Is laid for your faith in his ex - cel - lent Word!
For I am your God and will still give you aid;
My grace, all - suf - fi - cient, shall be your sup - ply.
My sov - 'reign, e - ter - nal, un - change - a - ble love;
What more can he say than to you he has said
I'll strength - en you, help you, and cause you to stand,
The flames shall not hurt you; I on - ly de - sign
And then, when gray hairs shall their tem - ples a - dorn,
Who un - to the Sav - ior for ref - uge have fled?
Up - held by my righ - teous, om - nip - o - tent hand.
Your dross to con - sume and your gold to re - fine.
Like lambs they shall still in my bo - som be borne.

Text: J. Rippon, A Selection of Hymns, *1787, alt.*
Tune: early American

FOUNDATION
11 11 11 11

Come Down, O Love Divine

508

1 Come down, O Love di - vine; Seek thou this soul of mine
2 Oh, let it free - ly burn, Till world - ly pas - sions turn
3 Let ho - ly char - i - ty Mine out - ward ves - ture be,
4 And so the yearn - ing strong, With which the soul will long,
And vis - it it with thine own ar - dor glow - ing;
To dust and ash - es in its heat con - sum - ing;
And low - li - ness be - come mine in - ner cloth - ing—
Shall far out - pass the pow'r of hu - man tell - ing;
O Com - fort - er, draw near; With - in my heart ap - pear
And let thy glo - rious light Shine ev - er on my sight,
True low - li - ness of heart, Which takes the hum - bler part,
No soul can guess his grace Till it be - come the place
And kin - dle it, thy ho - ly flame be - stow - ing.
And clothe me round, the while my path il - lum - ing.
And o'er its own short - com - ings weeps with loath - ing.
Where - in the Ho - ly Spir - it makes his dwell - ing.

Text: Bianco da Siena, d. 1434; tr. Richard F. Littledale, 1833–1890
© *Tune: R. Vaughan Williams, 1872–1958*

DOWN AMPNEY
66 11 66 11

509 Onward, Christian Soldiers

1 On - ward, Chris - tian sol - diers, March - ing as to war,
2 Like a might - y ar - my Moves the Church of God;
3 Crowns and thrones may per - ish, King - doms rise and wane,
4 On - ward, then, you faith - ful, Join our hap - py throng;

With the cross of Je - sus Go - ing on be - fore.
Let us bold - ly fol - low Where the saints have trod.
But the Church of Je - sus Con - stant will re - main;
Blend with ours your voic - es In the tri - umph - song.

Christ, the roy - al mas - ter, Leads a - gainst the foe;
We are not di - vid - ed; All one bod - y we:
Gates of hell can nev - er 'Gainst that Church pre - vail.
Glo - ry, laud, and hon - or Un - to Christ the king.

For - ward in - to bat - tle, See, his ban - ners go!
One in hope and doc - trine, One in char - i - ty.
We have Christ's own prom - ise, And that can - not fail.
We through count - less a - ges With the an - gels sing:

Refrain
On-ward, Chris-tian sol - diers, March-ing as to war,
With the cross of Je - sus Go - ing on be - fore.

Text: Sabine Baring-Gould, 1834–1924
Tune: Arthur S. Sullivan, 1842–1900

ST. GERTRUDE
65 65 65 D

510 O God of Youth

1 O God of youth, whose Spir - it in our hearts is stir - ring De - sire and hope for no - ble lives and true: Give us a spir - it stead - fast and un - err - ing; With light and love di - vine our minds en - due.
2 Fill all our hearts with zeal in ev - 'ry brave en - deav - or To right the wrongs that shame this pres - ent life, And grant the val - iant spir - it that shall nev - er Fall back or fail, how - ev - er long the strife.
3 Teach us to know the way of Je - sus Christ, our mas - ter; Give us his clear - eyed faith, his fear - less heart Through all life's dark - ness, dan - ger, and di - sas - ter; Oh, let us nev - er from his side de - part.
4 May we be true to him, our cap - tain of sal - va - tion, And bear his cross in ser - vice glad and free, And look in hope for that last con - sum - ma - tion When all earth's king - doms shall his king - dom be.

LYNNE
13 10 11 10

Renew Me, O Eternal Light 511

1 Re - new me, O e - ter - nal Light, And let my heart and soul be bright, Il - lu - mined with the light of grace That is - sues from your ho - ly face.
2 Re - move the pow'r of sin from me And cleanse all my im - pu - ri - ty, That I may have the strength and will Temp-ta - tions of the flesh to still.
3 Cre - ate in me a new heart, Lord, That glad - ly I o - bey your Word. Let what you will be my de - sire, And with new life my soul in - spire.
4 Grant that I on - ly you may love And seek those things which are a - bove, Till I be - hold you face to face, O Light e - ter - nal, through your grace.

Text: Johann F. Ruopp, 1672–1708; tr. August Crull, 1846–1923
Tune: As Hymnodus Sacer, Leipzig, 1625

HERR JESU CHRIST, MEINS
LM

512 Oh, Blest the House

1 Oh, blest the house, what - e'er be - fall, Where Je - sus
Christ is All - in - All! For if he were not
dwell - ing there, How dark and poor and void it were!

2 Oh, blest that house where faith is found, And all in
char - i - ty a - bound To trust their God and
serve him still And do in all his ho - ly will!

3 Oh, blest that house; it pros - pers well! In peace and
joy the par - ents dwell, And in their chil - dren's
lives is shown How rich - ly God can bless his own.

4 Then here will I and mine to - day A sol - emn
cov - 'nant make and say: Though all the world for -
sake his Word, My house and I will serve the Lord.

Text: Christoph C. L. von Pfeil, 1712–1784; tr. Catherine Winkworth, 1829–1878, alt.
Tune: J. Klug, Geistliche Lieder, *1533*

WO GOTT ZUM HAUS
LM

Come, My Way, My Truth, My Life

513

1 Come, my way, my truth, my life: Such a way as gives us breath; Such a truth as ends all strife; Such a life as con - quers death.
2 Come, my light, my feast, my strength: Such a light as shows a feast; Such a feast as mends in length; Such a strength as makes his guest.
3 Come, my joy, my love, my heart: Such a joy as none can move; Such a love as none can part; Such a heart as joys in love.

Text: George Herbert, 1593–1632
 Tune: R. Vaughan Williams, 1872–1958

THE CALL
77 77

514 O Savior, Precious Savior

1 O Sav - ior, pre - cious Sav - ior, Whom yet un - seen we love;
2 O Bring - er of sal - va - tion, Who won - drous - ly hast wrought,
3 In thee all full - ness dwell - eth, All grace and pow'r di - vine;
4 Oh, grant the con - sum - ma - tion Of this our song a - bove,
O name of might and fa - vor, All oth - er names a - bove:
Thy - self the rev - e - la - tion Of love be - yond our thought:
The glo - ry that ex - cel - leth, O Son of God, is thine.
In end - less ad - o - ra - tion And ev - er - last - ing love;
We wor - ship thee; we bless thee; To thee a - lone we sing;
We wor - ship thee; we bless thee; To thee a - lone we sing;
We wor - ship thee; we bless thee; To thee a - lone we sing;
Then shall we praise and bless thee Where per - fect prais - es ring,
We praise thee and con - fess thee, Our ho - ly Lord and King.
We praise thee and con - fess thee, Our gra - cious Lord and King.
We praise thee and con - fess thee, Our glo - rious Lord and King.
And ev - er - more con - fess thee, Our Sav - ior and our King!

Text: Frances R. Havergal, 1836–1879
Tune: Arthur H. Mann, 1850–1929

ANGEL'S STORY
76 76 D

How Marvelous God's Greatness 515

1 How mar - vel - ous God's great - ness, How glo - ri - ous his might!
2 Each ti - ny flow'r - et whis - pers The great life - giv - er's name;
3 The o - cean's vast a - byss - es In one grand psalm re - cord
4 The star - ry hosts are sing - ing Through all the light - strewn sky
To this the world bears wit - ness In won - ders day and night.
The might - y moun - tain mass - es His maj - es - ty pro - claim;
The deep mys - te - rious coun - sels And mer - cies of the Lord;
Of God's ma - jes - tic tem - ple And pal - ace courts on high;
In form of flow'r and snow - flake, In morn's re - splen - dent birth,
The hol - low vales are hymn - ing God's shel - ter for his own;
The ic - y waves of win - ter Are thun - d'ring on the strand;
When in these out - er cham - bers Such glo - ry gilds the night,
In af - ter - glow at e - ven, In sky and sea and earth.
The snow-capped peaks are point - ing To God's al - might - y throne.
And grief's chill stream is guid - ed By God's all - gra - cious hand.
Oh, what tran - scen - dent bright - ness Is God's e - ter - nal light!

 Text: Valdimar Briem, 1848–1930; tr. Charles V. Pilcher, 1879–1961, alt.
Tune: Koralpsalmboken, *Stockholm, 1697*

DEN BLOMSTERTID NU KOMMER
76 76 D

516 Arise, My Soul, Arise!

1 A - rise, my soul, a - rise! Stretch forth to things e - ter - nal And
2 Now hear the harps of heav'n! Oh, hear the song vic - to - rious, The
has-ten to the feet of your re - deem - er God. Though hid from mor - tal
nev - er - end - ing an - them sound-ing through the sky! To mor - tals is not
eyes, He dwells in light su - per - nal; Yet wor - ship him in hum - ble - ness and
giv'n To join in strains so glo - rious; Yet here on earth we too can sing our

call him Lord. His ban - quet of love A - waits you a - bove; Yet
prais-es high! He bought with his blood The ran-somed of God; To
here he grants a fore-taste of the feast to come! Re-joice, my soul, re-joice, To
him be ev - er-last - ing pow'r and vic - to - ry. And let the great a - men Re -
heav'n lift up your voice:
sound through heav'n a - gain.
Al - le - lu - ia, al - le - lu - ia, al - le - lu - ia!

© *Text: Johan Kahl, 1721–1746; tr. Ernest E. Ryden, b. 1886, alt.*
Tune: Finnish folk tune

NYT YLÖS, SIELUNI
PM

517 Praise to the Father

1 Praise to the Fa - ther for his lov - ing - kind - ness, Ten - der - ly
2 Praise to the Sav - ior for his deep com - pas - sion, Gra - cious - ly
3 Praise to the Spir - it, com - fort - er of Is - rael, Sent from the

car - ing for his err - ing chil - dren; Praise him, all an - gels;
car - ing for his cho - sen peo - ple; Young men and wom - en,
Fa - ther and the Son to bless us! Praise to the Fa - ther,

praise him in the heav - ens; Praise to the Fa - ther!
ag - ing folk and chil - dren, Praise to the Sav - ior!
Son, and Ho - ly Spir - it! Praise to the tri - une God!

Text: Elizabeth R. Charles, 1828–1896
Tune: Friedrich F. Flemming, 1778–1813

FLEMMING
11 11 11 6

Beautiful Savior

518

1 Beau - ti - ful Sav - ior, King of cre - a - tion, Son of God and Son of Man! Tru - ly I'd love thee, Tru - ly I'd serve thee, Light of my soul, my joy, my crown.
2 Fair are the mead - ows, Fair are the wood - lands, Robed in flow'rs of bloom - ing spring; Je - sus is fair - er, Je - sus is pur - er, He makes our sor - rowing spir - it sing.
3 Fair is the sun - shine, Fair is the moon - light, Bright the spar - kling stars on high; Je - sus shines bright - er, Je - sus shines pur - er Than all the an - gels in the sky.
4 Beau - ti - ful Sav - ior, Lord of the na - tions, Son of God and Son of Man! Glo - ry and hon - or, Praise, ad - o - ra - tion, Now and for - ev - er - more be thine!

Text: Gesangbuch, *Münster, 1677; tr. Joseph A. Seiss, 1823–1904*
Tune: Silesian folk tune, 1842

SCHÖNSTER HERR JESU
557 558

519 My Soul, Now Praise Your Maker!

1 My soul, now praise your mak - er! Let all with - in me bless his name
2 He of - fers all his trea - sure Of jus - tice, truth, and righ-teous-ness,
3 For as a lov - ing moth - er Has pit - y on her chil - dren here,
4 His grace re - mains for - ev - er, And chil - dren's chil - dren yet shall prove
Who makes you full par - tak - er Of mer - cies more than you dare claim.
His love be-yond our mea - sure, His yearn - ing pit - y o'er dis - tress;
God in his arms will gath - er All those who him like chil - dren fear.
That God for-sakes them nev - er Who in true fear shall seek his love.
For - get him not whose meek - ness Still bears with all your sin,
Nor treats us as we mer - it, But sets his an - ger by.
He knows how frail our pow - ers, Who but from dust are made.
In heav'n is fixed his dwell - ing, His rule is o - ver all;
Who heals your ev - 'ry weak - ness, Re - news your life with - in;
The poor and con - trite spir - it Finds his com - pas - sion nigh;
We flour - ish as the flow - ers, And e - ven so we fade;
You hosts with might ex - cel - ling, With praise be - fore him fall.

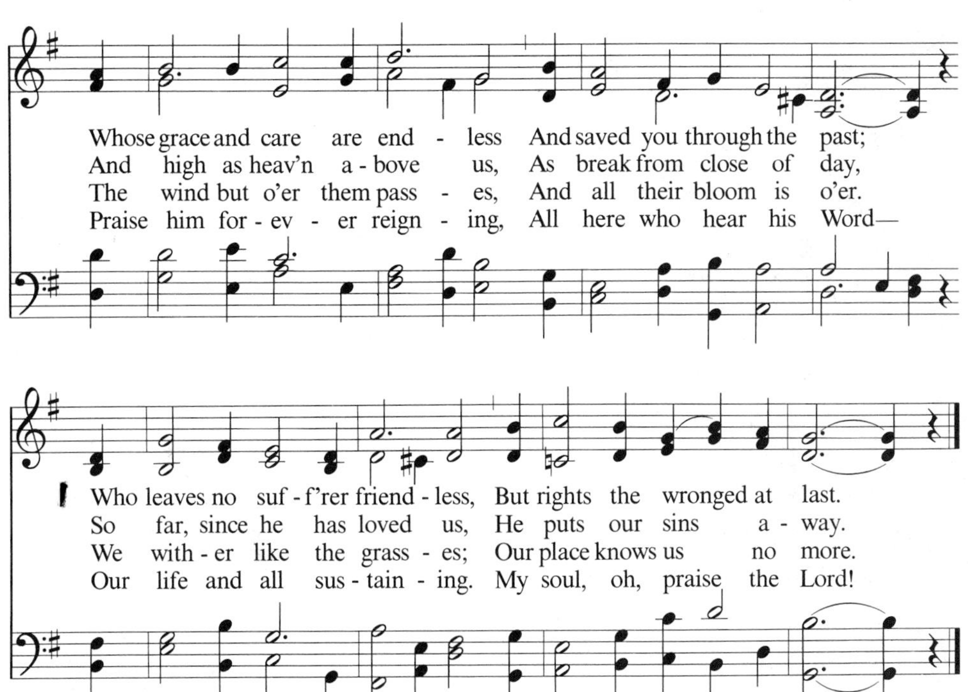
Whose grace and care are end - less And saved you through the past;
And high as heav'n a - bove us, As break from close of day,
The wind but o'er them pass - es, And all their bloom is o'er.
Praise him for - ev - er reign - ing, All here who hear his Word—
Who leaves no suf - f'rer friend - less, But rights the wronged at last.
So far, since he has loved us, He puts our sins a - way.
We with - er like the grass - es; Our place knows us no more.
Our life and all sus - tain - ing. My soul, oh, praise the Lord!

Text: *Johann Gramann, 1487–1541; tr. Catherine Winkworth, 1829–1878, alt.*
Tune: *Kugelmann,* Concentus Novi, *1540*

NUN LOB, MEIN SEEL
PM

520 Give to Our God Immortal Praise!

1 Give to our God im - mor - tal praise! Mer - cy and
2 He sent his Son with pow'r to save From guilt and
3 Give to the Lord of lords re - nown; The King of

truth are all his ways; Won - ders of grace to
dark - ness and the grave. Won - ders of grace to
kings with glo - ry crown. His mer - cies ev - er

God be - long; Re - peat his mer - cies in your song.
God be - long; Re - peat his mer - cies in your song.
shall en - dure When lords and kings are known no more!

Text: Isaac Watts, 1674–1748
Tune: attr. John Hatton, d. 1793

DUKE STREET
LM

521 Let Us with a Gladsome Mind

1 Let us with a glad - some mind Praise the Lord, for he is kind;
2 He with all - com-mand - ing might Filled the new - made world with light;
3 With the eye of pit - y, he Looked up - on our mis - er - y;
4 Let us then with glad - some mind Praise the Lord, for he is kind;

Refrain
For his mer-cies shall en-dure, Ev-er faith-ful, ev - er sure.
Text: John Milton, 1608–1674, alt.
© Tune: Daniel Moe, b. 1926
WILLIAMS BAY
7 7 7 7
Come, Thou Almighty King
522
1 Come, thou al-might-y King, Help us thy name to
2 Come, thou in-car-nate Word, Gird on thy might-y
3 Come, ho-ly Com-fort-er, Thy sa-cred wit-ness
4 To thee, great One in Three, E-ter-nal prais-es
sing; Help us to praise; Fa-ther all-glo-ri-ous, O'er all vic-
sword; Our prayer at-tend. Come and thy peo-ple bless, And give thy
bear In this glad hour! Thou, who al-might-y art, Now rule in
be Hence ev-er-more! Thy sov-'reign maj-es-ty May we in
to-ri-ous, Come and reign o-ver us, An-cient of Days.
Word suc-cess, And let thy righ-teous-ness On us de-scend.
ev-'ry heart, And ne'er from us de-part, Spir-it of pow'r.
glo-ry see, And to e-ter-ni-ty Love and a-dore.

Text: source unknown, c. 1757, alt.
Tune: Felice de Giardini, 1716–1796

ITALIAN HYMN
664 6664

523 Holy Spirit, Ever Dwelling

1 Ho - ly Spir - it, ev - er dwell - ing In the ho - liest realms of light; Ho - ly Spir - it, ev - er brood - ing O'er a world of gloom and night; Ho - ly Spir - it, ev - er rais - ing Those of earth to thrones on high; Liv - ing, life - im -
2 Ho - ly Spir - it, ev - er liv - ing As the Church's ver - y life; Ho - ly Spir - it, ev - er striv - ing Through us in a cease - less strife; Ho - ly Spir - it, ev - er form-ing In the Church the mind of Christ: You we praise with
3 Ho - ly Spir - it, ev - er work - ing Through the Church's min - is - try; Quick - 'ning, strength-'ning, and ab - solv - ing, Set - ting cap - tive sin - ners free; Ho - ly Spir - it, ev - er bind-ing Age to age and soul to soul In com - mu - nion

part - ing Spir - it, You we praise and mag - ni - fy.
end - less wor - ship For your gifts and fruits un - priced.
nev - er end - ing, You we wor - ship and ex - tol.

 Text: Timothy Rees, 1874–1939, alt.
Tune: Dutch folk tune, 18th cent.

IN BABILONE
8 7 8 7 D

My God, How Wonderful Thou Art 524

1 My God, how won - der - ful thou art, Thy maj - es - ty how bright!
2 How won - der - ful, how beau - ti - ful The sight of thee must be—
3 No earth - ly fa - ther loves like thee; No moth - er, e'er so mild,
4 Yet I may love thee too, O Lord, Al - might - y as thou art,

How beau - ti - ful thy mer - cy seat In depths of burn - ing light!
Thine end - less wis - dom, bound - less pow'r, And awe - some pu - ri - ty!
Bears and for - bears as thou hast done With me, thy sin - ful child.
For thou hast stooped to ask of me The love of my poor heart.

5 My God, how wonderful thou art,
  Thou everlasting friend!
On thee I stay my trusting heart
  Till faith in vision end.

Text: Frederick W. Faber, 1814–1863
Tune: Psalter, *Edinburgh, 1615*

DUNDEE
CM

525 Blessing and Honor

1 Bless-ing and hon - or and glo - ry and pow'r, Wis - dom and
2 Let all the heav - ens re - sound with his name; Let all the
3 Ev - er as - cend - ing the song and the joy, Ev - er de -
4 Give we the glo - ry and praise to the Lamb! Take we the
rich - es and strength ev - er - more, Of - fer to him who our
earth sing his glo - ry and fame. O - cean and moun - tain, stream,
scend-ing the love from on high; Bless - ing and hon - or and
robe and the harp and the psalm; Sing we the song of the
bat - tle has won, Whose are the king - dom, the crown, and the
for - est, and flow'r Ech - o his prais - es and tell of his
glo - ry and praise— This is the theme of the hymns that we
Lamb who was slain, Dy - ing in weak - ness and ris - ing to
throne; Whose are the king - dom, the crown, and the throne!
pow'r; Ech - o his prais - es and tell of his pow'r.
raise; This is the theme of the hymns that we raise.
reign; Dy - ing in weak - ness and ris - ing to reign!

Text: Horatius Bonar, 1808–1889, alt.
Tune: Matthias Keller, 1813–1890

AMERICAN HYMN
10 10 10 10 10

Immortal, Invisible, God Only Wise

526

1 Im - mor - tal, in - vis - i - ble, God on - ly wise, In
2 Un - rest - ing, un - hast - ing, and si - lent as light, Nor
3 To all, life thou giv - est, to both great and small; In
4 Thou reign - est in glo - ry; thou dwell - est in light; Thine
light in - ac - ces - si - ble hid from our eyes, Most
want - ing, nor wast - ing, thou rul - est in might; Thy
all life thou liv - est, the true life of all; We
an - gels a - dore thee, all veil - ing their sight; All
bless - ed, most glo - rious, the An - cient of Days, Al -
jus - tice like moun - tains high soar - ing a - bove Thy
blos - som and flour - ish like leaves on the tree, And
laud we would ren - der; oh, help us to see 'Tis
might - y, vic - to - rious, thy great name we praise!
clouds which are foun - tains of good - ness and love.
with - er and per - ish, but naught chang - eth thee.
on - ly the splen - dor of light hid - eth thee!

Text: W. Chalmers Smith, 1824–1908, alt.
Tune: Welsh folk tune

ST. DENIO
11 11 11 11

527 All Creatures of Our God and King

1 All crea-tures of our God and King, Lift up your voice with
2 O rush-ing wind and breez-es soft, O clouds that ride the
3 O flow-ing wa-ters, pure and clear, Make mu-sic for your
4 Dear moth-er earth, who day by day Un-folds rich bless-ings
us and sing: Al-le-lu-ia! Al-le-lu-ia!
winds a-loft: Oh, . . praise him! Al-le-lu-ia!
Lord to hear. Oh, . . praise him! Al-le-lu-ia!
on our way, Oh, . . praise him! Al-le-lu-ia!
O burn-ing sun with gold-en beam And sil-ver moon
O ris-ing morn, in praise re-joice, O lights of eve-
O fire so mas-ter-ful and bright, Pro-vid-ing us
The fruits and flow'rs that ver-dant grow, Let them his praise
with soft-er gleam:
ning, find a voice.
with warmth and light,
a-bun-dant show.
Refrain
Oh, praise him! Oh, praise him!

Al-le - lu - ia, al - le - lu - ia, al - le - lu - ia!

5 O ev'ryone of tender heart,
Forgiving others, take your part,
Oh, praise him! Alleluia!
All you who pain and sorrow bear,
Praise God and lay on him your care. *Refrain*

6 And you, most kind and gentle death,
Waiting to hush our final breath,
Oh, praise him! Alleluia!
You lead to heav'n the child of God,
Where Christ our Lord the way has trod. *Refrain*

7 Let all things their Creator bless
And worship God in humbleness.
Oh, praise him! Alleluia!
Oh, praise the Father, praise the Son,
And praise the Spirit, Three in One, *Refrain*

 Text: Francis of Assisi, 1182–1226; tr. William H. Draper, 1855–1933, alt.
Tune: Geistliche Kirchengesänge, *Köln, 1623*

LASST UNS ERFREUEN
888 888 and alleluias

528 Isaiah in a Vision Did of Old

I - sa - iah in a vi - sion did of old The Lord of hosts
en-throned on high be - hold: His splen-did train was wide out-spread un - til
Its stream - ing glo - ry did the tem - ple fill. A - bove his throne the
shin-ing ser - a - phim With six - fold wings did rev - 'rence un - to

him: With two each ser - aph hid his glo - rious face, And two a -
bout his feet did in - ter - lace, And with the oth - er two he soared on
high; And one un - to an - oth - er thus did cry: "Ho -
- ly, Ho - -

Hymn continues on the next page.

- ly, Ho - ly is the Lord of hosts!

His glo - ry fill - eth all the earth!" The beams and lin - tels

at their cry - ing shook, And all the house was filled with bil - lowing smoke.

© *Text: Martin Luther, 1483–1546; tr. Martin H. Franzmann, 1907–1976*
Tune: Martin Luther, 1483–1546

JESAIA, DEM PROPHETEN
PM

529 Praise God. Praise Him

1 Praise God from whom all bless-ings flow. Praise him.
2 Zi - on, your Sav - ior comes to you. He will
3 Zi - on, your bride-groom comes to you. He is
4 Zi - on, your mas - ter comes to you. There is

Al - le - lu - ia in the high - est! For - ev - er praise him.
Seek and find you though you try to e - vade his search-ing.
Bring - ing with him for your mar - riage its true a - dorn - ing.
All your ser - vice to be ren - dered, your self sur - ren - dered.
Praise God from whom all bless-ings flow. Clap your hands, re - joic - ing;
Zi - on, your Sav - ior comes to you. Come to meet your Sav - ior!
Zi - on, your bride-groom comes to you. Rise and take your trea - sure,
Zi - on, your mas - ter comes to you; His the cup, so dare it.
Strike your harps, re - sound - ing; Raise your voice, re - call - ing
See his grace and fa - vor! He is yours for - ev - er;
Yours in full - est mea - sure; Sing, for love has found you;
His the yoke, so bear it. His the sword, so wear it.
Ev - 'ry mer - cy fall - ing.
All to him sur - ren - der.
Joy is all a - round you.
His the load, so bear it.
Praise God from whom all bless - ings flow.

© *Text: V. Masillamony Iyer, 20th cent.; tr. Daniel T. Niles, 1908–1970, alt.*
© *Tune: Carnatic Tamil*

TANDANEI
10 13 8 6 6 6 6 8

530 Jesus Shall Reign

1 Je - sus shall reign wher - e'er the sun Does its suc -
2 To him shall end - less prayer be made, And prais - es
3 Peo - ple and realms of ev - 'ry tongue Dwell on his
4 Bless - ings a - bound wher - e'er he reigns: The pris - 'ners
ces - sive jour - neys run; His king-dom stretch from
throng to crown his head; His name like sweet per -
love with sweet - est song; And in - fant voic - es
leap to lose their chains, The wea - ry find e -
shore to shore, Till moons shall wax and wane no more.
fume shall rise With ev - 'ry morn - ing sac - ri - fice.
shall pro - claim Their ear - ly bless - ings on his name.
ter - nal rest, And all who suf - fer want are blest.

5 Let ev'ry creature rise and bring
Honors peculiar to our King;
Angels descend with songs again,
And earth repeat the loud amen.

Text: Isaac Watts, 1674–1748, alt.
Tune: attr. John Hatton, d. 1793

DUKE STREET
LM

Before Jehovah's Awesome Throne

531

1 Be - fore Je - ho - vah's awe - some throne, Ye na - tions,
2 His sov - 'reign pow'r, with - out our aid, Made us of
3 We are his peo - ple, we his care, Our souls and
4 We'll crowd thy gates with thank - ful songs, High as the
bow with sa - cred joy; Know that the Lord is
clay and formed us men; And when like wan - d'ring
all our mor - tal frame. What last - ing hon - ors
heav'ns our voic - es raise; And earth, with all its
God a - lone, He can cre - ate, and he de - stroy.
sheep we strayed, He brought us to his fold a - gain.
shall we rear, Al - might - y Mak - er, to thy name?
thou - sand tongues, Shall fill thy courts with sound - ing praise.

5 Wide as the world is thy command;
Vast as eternity thy love;
Firm as a rock thy truth shall stand,
When rolling years shall cease to move.

Text: Isaac Watts, 1674–1748, adapt.
Tune: Louis Bourgeois, c. 1510–1561

OLD HUNDREDTH
LM

532 How Great Thou Art

1 O Lord my God, when I in awe-some won - der Con - sid - er
2 When through the woods and for - est glades I wan - der, I hear the
3 But when I think that God, his Son not spar - ing, Sent him to
4 When Christ shall come, with shout of ac - cla - ma - tion, And take me
all the*worlds thy hand hath made, I see the stars, I hear the *roll - ing
birds sing sweet-ly in the trees; When I look down from loft - y moun-tain
die, I scarce can take it in, That on the cross my bur-den glad - ly
home, what joy shall fill my heart! Then I shall bow in hum-ble ad - o-
thun-der, Thy pow'r through-out the u - ni - verse dis - played;
gran-deur And hear the brook and feel the gen - tle breeze;
bear - ing He bled and died to take a - way my sin;
ra - tion And there pro-claim, "My God, how great thou art!"
Refrain
Then sings my soul, my Sav - ior God, to thee, How great thou

*Author's original words are "works" and "mighty."

art! How great thou art! Then sings my soul, my Sav - ior God, to
thee, How great thou art! How great thou art!

O STORE GUD
11 10 11 10 and refrain

533 Now Thank We All Our God

1 Now thank we all our God With hearts and hands and voic - es,
2 Oh, may this boun-teous God Through all our life be near us,
3 All praise and thanks to God The Fa - ther now be giv - en,
Who won - drous things has done, In whom his world re - joic - es;
With ev - er joy - ful hearts And bless - ed peace to cheer us,
The Son, and him who reigns With them in high - est heav - en,
Who, from our moth-ers' arms, Has blest us on our way
And keep us in his grace, And guide us when per-plexed,
The one e - ter - nal God, Whom earth and heav'n a - dore;
With count - less gifts of love, And still is ours to - day.
And free us from all harm In this world and the next.
For thus it was, is now, And shall be ev - er - more.

Text: Martin Rinkhart, 1586–1649; tr. Catherine Winkworth, 1829–1878
Tune: Johann Crüger, 1598–1662

NUN DANKET ALLE GOTT
67 67 66 66

Now Thank We All Our God

534

1 Now thank we all our God With hearts and hands and
2 Oh, may this boun - teous God Through all our life be
3 All praise and thanks to God The Fa - ther now be
voic - es, Who won-drous things has done, In whom his world re -
near us, With ev - er joy - ful hearts And bless - ed peace to
giv - en, The Son, and him who reigns With them in high - est
joic - es; Who, from our moth - ers' arms, Has blest us on our
cheer us, And keep us in his grace, And guide us when per -
heav - en, The one e - ter - nal God, Whom earth and heav'n a -
way With count-less gifts of love, And still is ours to - day.
plexed, And free us from all harm In this world and the next.
dore; For thus it was, is now, And shall be ev - er - more.

Text: Martin Rinkhart, 1586–1649; tr. Catherine Winkworth, 1829–1878
Tune: Johann Crüger, 1598–1662

NUN DANKET ALLE GOTT
67 67 66 66

535 Holy God, We Praise Your Name

1 Ho - ly God, we praise your name; Lord of all, we
2 Hark! The glad ce - les - tial hymn An - gel choirs a -
3 Lo, the ap - os - tol - ic train Join your sa - cred
4 Ho - ly Fa - ther, ho - ly Son, Ho - ly Spir - it,
bow be - fore you. All on earth your scep - ter claim,
bove are rais - ing; Cher - u - bim and ser - a - phim,
name to hal - low; Proph - ets swell the glad re - frain,
three we name you, Though in es - sence on - ly one;
All in heav'n a - bove a - dore you. In - fi - nite your
In un - ceas - ing cho - rus prais - ing, Fill the heav'ns with
And the white - robed mar - tyrs fol - low; And from morn to
Un - di - vid - ed God we claim you And, a - dor - ing,
vast do - main, Ev - er - last - ing is your reign.
sweet ac - cord: "Ho - ly, ho - ly, ho - ly Lord!"
set of sun Through the Church the song goes on.
bend the knee While we own the mys - ter - y.

Text: source unknown; tr. Clarence A. Walworth. 1820–1900, alt.
Tune: Maria Theresa, Katholisches Gesangbuch, *1774*

GROSSER GOTT
78 78 77

O God of God, O Light of Light 536

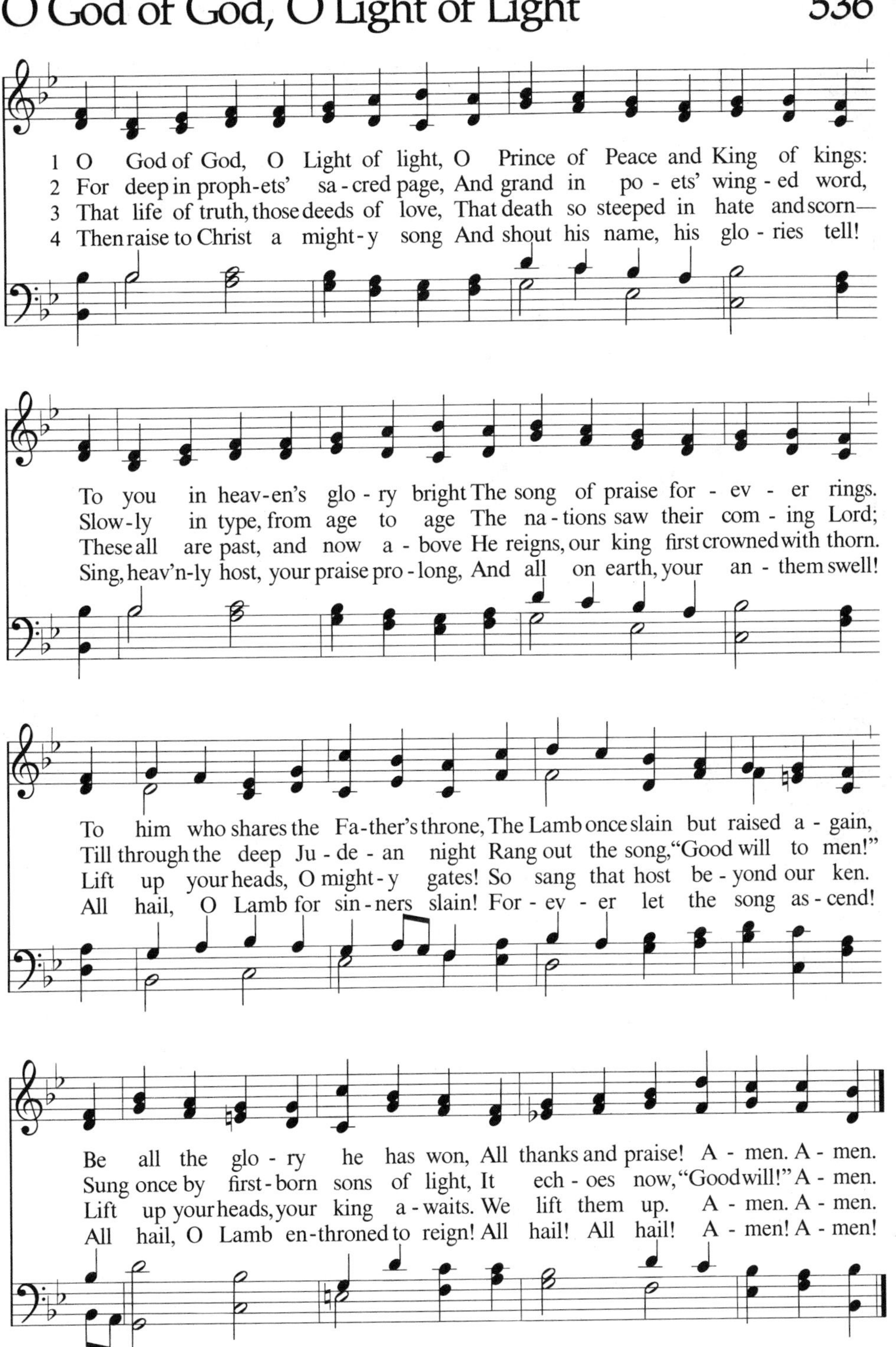
1 O God of God, O Light of light, O Prince of Peace and King of kings:
2 For deep in proph-ets' sa - cred page, And grand in po - ets' wing - ed word,
3 That life of truth, those deeds of love, That death so steeped in hate and scorn—
4 Then raise to Christ a might - y song And shout his name, his glo - ries tell!
To you in heav-en's glo - ry bright The song of praise for - ev - er rings.
Slow-ly in type, from age to age The na - tions saw their com - ing Lord;
These all are past, and now a - bove He reigns, our king first crowned with thorn.
Sing, heav'n-ly host, your praise pro - long, And all on earth, your an - them swell!
To him who shares the Fa-ther's throne, The Lamb once slain but raised a - gain,
Till through the deep Ju - de - an night Rang out the song, "Good will to men!"
Lift up your heads, O might - y gates! So sang that host be - yond our ken.
All hail, O Lamb for sin - ners slain! For - ev - er let the song as - cend!
Be all the glo - ry he has won, All thanks and praise! A - men. A - men.
Sung once by first - born sons of light, It ech - oes now, "Good will!" A - men.
Lift up your heads, your king a - waits. We lift them up. A - men. A - men.
All hail, O Lamb en - throned to reign! All hail! All hail! A - men! A - men!

Text: *John Julian, 1839–1913, adapt.*
Tune: Schlag-Gesang- und Notenbuch, *Stuttgart, 1744*

O GROSSER GOTT
LMD

537 O Jesus, King Most Wonderful!

Gm F Cm Dm
1 O Jesus, king most wonderful! O Conqueror renowned! O Source of peace ineffable, In whom all joys are found:
2 When once you visit darkened hearts, Then truth begins to shine, Then earthly vanity departs, Then kindles love divine.
3 O Jesus, light of all below, The fount of life and fire, Surpassing all the joys we know, All that we can desire:
4 May ev'ry heart confess your name, Forever you adore, And, seeking you, itself inflame To seek you more and more!
Gm E♭maj7 Dm Gm C
Am B♭ Gm Am Dm7 Gm

5 You may our tongues forever bless;
You may we love alone
And ever in our lives express
The image of your own!

Text: attr. Bernard of Clairvaux, 1091–1153; tr. Edward Caswall, 1814–1878, alt.
Tune: J. Leavitt, Christian Lyre, *1831*

HIDING PLACE
CM

Oh, Praise the Lord, My Soul! 538

Cm Gm Cm A♭
1 Oh, praise the Lord, my soul! I'll praise him
2 Trust not in mor - tal flesh, Nor those who
3 How hap - py is the one Who trusts in
4 How faith - ful is the Lord, And just to
Cm F Gm Cm
all my life. With mu - sic I shall
rule with pow'r; They take their breath, re -
God the Lord, Who made the heav - ens
the op - pressed. The hun - gry he sup -
Fm Cm A♭7 B♭ Cm C
give him praise As long as I shall live.
turn to clay, And fruit - less are their plans.
and the earth, The seas and all there - in.
plies with bread; The cap - tive gains re - lease.

5 The blind receive their sight;
He raises those bowed low;
The stranger, widow, orphan, too,
In him shall be secure.

6 The Lord who loves the just
Shall thwart all wickedness.
In pow'r forever he shall reign,
Our God from age to age.

7 Oh, praise the Lord, my soul,
The Father and the Son,
Who with the Spirit ever rule
While endless ages run.

MICHAEL
SM

539 Praise the Almighty

1 Praise the Al - might - y, my soul, a - dore
2 Trust not in rul - ers; they are but mor -
3 Bless - ed, oh, bless - ed are they for - ev -
4 Praise, all you peo - ple, the name so ho -
him! Yes, I will laud him un - til death;
tal; Earth - born they are and soon de - cay.
er Whose help is from the Lord most high,
ly Of him who does such won - drous things!
With songs and an - thems I come be - fore
Vain are their coun - sels at life's last por -
Whom from sal - va - tion noth - ing can sev -
All that has be - ing, to praise him sole -
him As long as he al - lows me
tal, When the dark grave en - gulfs its
er, And who in hope to Christ draw
ly, With hap - py heart its a - men

breath. From him my life and all things
prey. Since mor - tals can no help af -
nigh. To all who trust in him, our
sings! Chil - dren of God, with an - gel
came; Bless, O my soul, his ho - ly name.
ford, Place all your trust in Christ, our Lord.
Lord Will aid and coun - sel now af - ford.
host Praise Fa - ther, Son, and Ho - ly Ghost!
Hal - le - lu - jah! Hal - le - lu - jah!

 Text: *Johann D. Herrnschmidt, 1675–1723; tr. Alfred E. R. Brauer, 1866–1949, alt.*
Tune: Seelen=Harfe, *Ansbach, 1664*

LOBE DEN HERREN, O MEINE SEELE
108 108 888

540 Praise the Lord! O Heavens

1 Praise the Lord! O heav'ns, a - dore him; Praise him, an - gels, in the height;
2 Praise the Lord, for he is gra - cious; Nev - er shall his prom - ise fail.
Sun and moon, re - joice be - fore him; Praise him, gleam - ing stars and light.
God has made his saints vic - to - rious; Sin and death shall not pre - vail.
Praise the Lord, for he has spo - ken; Worlds his might - y voice o - beyed;
Praise the God of our sal - va - tion; Hosts on high, his pow'r pro - claim;
Laws which nev - er shall be bro - ken For their guid - ance he has made.
Heav'n and earth, and all cre - a - tion, Laud and mag - ni - fy his name!

Text: The Foundling Hospital Collection, *London, 1796, alt.*
Tune: Franz Joseph Haydn, 1732–1809

AUSTRIA
8 7 8 7 D

Praise the Lord of Heaven! 541

1 Praise the Lord of heav - en! Praise him in the height;
2 Praise the Lord, you foun - tains Of the deeps and seas,
3 Praise him, fowl and cat - tle, Princ - es and all kings;
Praise him, all you an - gels; Praise him, stars and light!
Rocks and hills and moun - tains, Ce - dars and all trees!
Praise him, men and wom - en, All cre - at - ed things;
Praise him, clouds and wa - ters Which, a - bove the skies,
Praise him, clouds and va - pors, Snow and hail and fire,
For the name of God is Ex - cel - lent a - lone
When his word com - mand - ed, Did es - tab - lished rise!
Storm - y wind, ful - fill - ing On - ly his de - sire!
O - ver earth his foot - stool, O - ver heav'n his throne!

Text: Thomas B. Browne, 1805–1874
Tune: French carol

NOUS ALLONS
65 65 D

542 Sing Praise to God, the Highest Good

1 Sing praise to God, the high - est good, The au - thor of cre -
2 What God's al - might - y pow'r has made, In mer - cy he is
3 We sought the Lord in our dis - tress; O God, in mer - cy
4 Let all who name Christ's ho - ly name Give God the praise and
a - tion, The God of love who un - der - stood Our need for
keep - ing; By morn - ing glow or eve - ning shade, His eye is
hear us. Our Sav - ior saw our help - less - ness And came with
glo - ry. Let all who know his pow'r pro - claim A - loud the
his sal - va - tion. With heal - ing balm our souls he fills
nev - er sleep - ing; With - in the king - dom of his might
peace to cheer us. For this we thank and praise the Lord
won - drous sto - ry. Cast ev - 'ry i - dol from its throne,
And ev - 'ry faith - less mur - mur stills:
All things are just and good and right:
Who is by one and all a - dored:
For God is God, and he a - lone:
To God all praise and glo - ry!

Text: Johann J. Schütz, 1640–1690; tr. Frances E. Cox, 1812–1897, adapt.
Tune: Melchior Vulpius, c. 1560–1615

LOBT GOTT DEN HERREN, IHR
87 87 887

Praise to the Lord, the Almighty

543

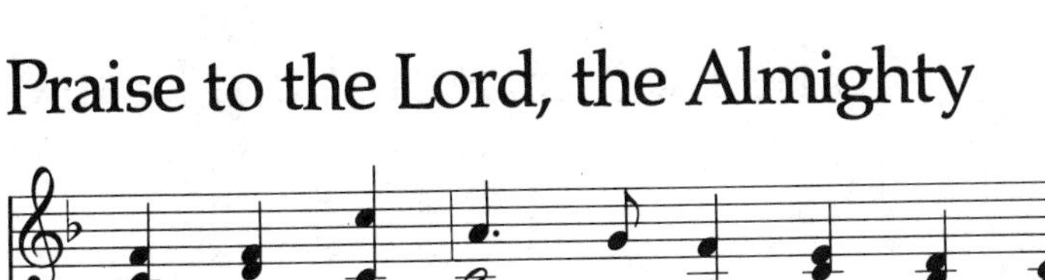

1 Praise to the Lord, the Almighty, the King of creation!
O my soul, praise him, for he is your health and salvation!
Let all who hear
Now to his temple draw near,
Joining in glad adoration!

2 Praise to the Lord, who o'er all things is wondrously reigning
And, as on wings of an eagle, uplifting, sustaining.
Have you not seen
All that is needful has been
Sent by his gracious ordaining?

3 Praise to the Lord, who will prosper your work and defend you;
Surely his goodness and mercy shall daily attend you.
Ponder anew
What the Almighty can do
If with his love he befriend you.

4 Praise to the Lord! Oh, let all that is in me adore him!
All that has life and breath, come now with praises before him!
Let the amen
Sound from his people again.
Gladly forever adore him!

Text: *Joachim Neander, 1650–1680; tr. Catherine Winkworth, 1829–1878, alt.*
Tune: Ernewerten Gesangbuch, *Stralsund, 1665*

LOBE DEN HERREN
14 14 4 7 8

544 The God of Abraham Praise

1 The God of A - br'ham praise, Who reigns en - throned a - bove;
2 The God of A - br'ham praise, At whose su - preme com - mand
3 The God of A - br'ham praise, Whose all - suf - fi - cient grace
4 He by him - self has sworn; I on his oath de - pend.
An - cient of ev - er - last - ing days, And God of love.
From earth I rise and seek the joys At his right hand.
Shall guide me all my pil - grim days In all my ways.
I shall, on ea - gle wings up - borne, To heav'n as - cend.
Je - ho - vah, great I Am! By earth and heav'n con - fessed;
I all on earth for-sake— Its wis - dom, fame, and pow'r—
He deigns to call me friend; He calls him - self my God!
I shall be - hold his face; I shall his pow'r a - dore,
I bow and bless the sa - cred name For - ev - er blest.
And him my on - ly por - tion make, My shield and tow'r.
And he shall save me to the end Through Je - sus' blood.
And sing the won - ders of his grace For - ev - er - more.

5 Though nature's strength decay,
And earth and hell withstand,
To Canaan's bounds I urge my way
At his command.
The watery deep I pass,
With Jesus in my view,
And through the howling wilderness
My way pursue.

6 The goodly land I see,
With peace and plenty blest;
A land of sacred liberty,
And endless rest.
There milk and honey flow,
And oil and wine abound,
And trees of life forever grow
With mercy crowned.

7 There dwells the Lord our king,
The Lord our righteousness,
Triumphant o'er the world and sin,
The Prince of Peace.
On Zion's sacred height,
His kingdom he maintains,
And glorious with his saints in light
Forever reigns.

8 Before the great Three-One
They all exulting stand
And tell the wonders he has done
Through all their land.
The list'ning spheres attend
And swell the growing fame
And sing the songs which never end,
The wondrous name.

9 The God who reigns on high
The great archangels sing,
And "Holy, holy, holy!" cry,
"Almighty King!
Who was, and is, the same,
And evermore shall be:
Jehovah, Father, great I Am!
We worship thee!"

10 Before the Savior's face
The ransomed nations bow,
O'erwhelmed at his almighty grace
Forever new.
He shows his wounds of love;
They kindle to a flame!
And sound through all the worlds above
The Paschal Lamb.

11 The whole triumphant host
Give thanks to God on high.
"Hail, Father, Son, and Holy Ghost!"
They ever cry.
Hail, Abr'ham's God and mine!
I join the heav'nly lays:
All might and majesty are thine
And endless praise!

Text: Thomas Olivers, 1725–1799, alt.
Tune: Hebrew, arr. Meyer Lyon, c. 1770

YIGDAL
66 84 D

545 When Morning Gilds the Skies

1 When morn - ing gilds the skies, My heart a - wak - ing cries:
2 To him, my highest and best, I sing, when love - pos - sessed:
3 Let all of hu - man - kind In this their con - cord find:

May Je - sus Christ be praised! When eve - ning shad - ows fall,
May Je - sus Christ be praised! What - e'er my hands be - gin,
May Je - sus Christ be praised! Let all the earth a - round

This rings my cur - few call: May Je - sus Christ be praised!
This bless - ing shall break in: May Je - sus Christ be praised!
Ring joy - ous with the sound: May Je - sus Christ be praised!

When mirth for mu - sic longs, This is my song of songs:
No love - lier an - ti - phon In all high heav'n is known
Sing, sun and stars of space, Sing, all who see his face,

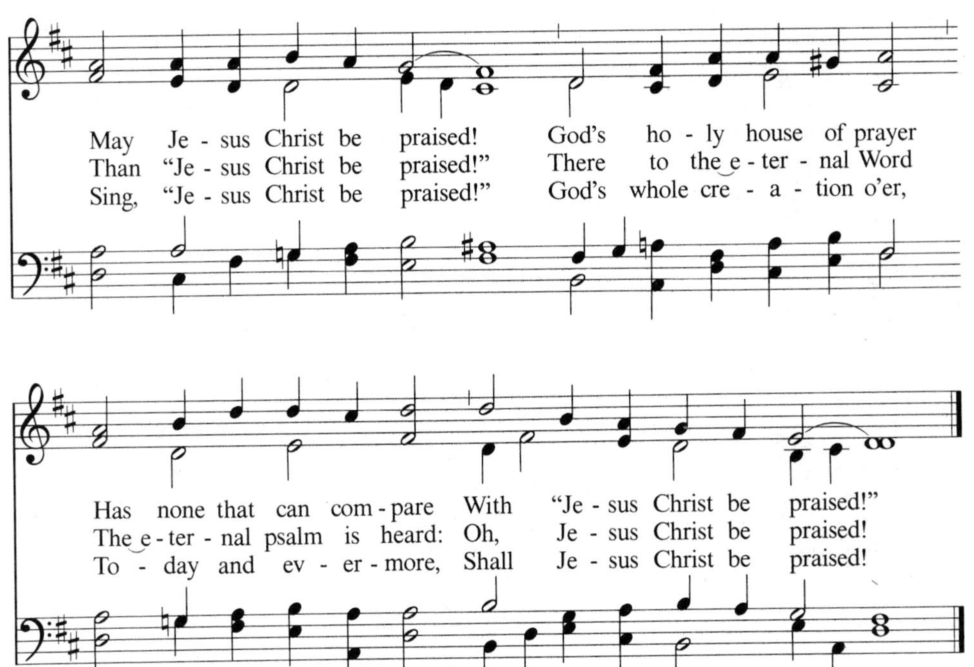
May Je - sus Christ be praised! God's ho - ly house of prayer
Than "Je - sus Christ be praised!" There to the e - ter - nal Word
Sing, "Je - sus Christ be praised!" God's whole cre - a - tion o'er,
Has none that can com - pare With "Je - sus Christ be praised!"
The e - ter - nal psalm is heard: Oh, Je - sus Christ be praised!
To - day and ev - er - more, Shall Je - sus Christ be praised!

 Text: *German hymn, 19th cent.; tr. Robert Bridges, 1844–1930, alt.*
Tune: Trente quatre pseaumes de David, *Geneva, 1551*

O SEIGNEUR
666 666 D

546 When Morning Gilds the Skies

1 When morn-ing gilds the skies, My heart a-wak-ing cries: May Je-sus Christ be praised! When eve-ning shad-ows fall, This rings my cur-few call: May Je-sus Christ be praised!
2 When mirth for mu-sic longs, This is my song of songs: May Je-sus Christ be praised! God's ho-ly house of prayer Has none that can com-pare With "Je-sus Christ be praised!"
3 To him, my highest and best, I sing, when love-pos-sessed: May Je-sus Christ be praised! What-e'er my hands be-gin, This bless-ing shall break in: May Je-sus Christ be praised!
4 No love-lier an-ti-phon In all high heav'n is known Than "Je-sus Christ be praised!" There to the e-ter-nal Word The e-ter-nal psalm is heard: Oh, Je-sus Christ be praised!

5 Let all of humankind
In this their concord find:
May Jesus Christ be praised!
Let all the earth around
Ring joyous with the sound:
May Jesus Christ be praised!

6 Sing, sun and stars of space,
Sing, all who see his face,
Sing, "Jesus Christ be praised!"
God's whole creation o'er,
Today and evermore,
Shall Jesus Christ be praised!

© *Text: German hymn, 19th cent.; tr. Robert Bridges, 1844–1930, alt.*
Tune: Joseph Barnby, 1838–1896

LAUDES DOMINI
666 666

Thee We Adore, Eternal Lord! 547

1 Thee we a - dore, e - ter - nal Lord! We praise thy name with one ac - cord; Thy saints, who here thy good - ness see, Through all the world do wor - ship thee.
2 To thee a - loud all an - gels cry, The heav'ns and all the pow'rs on high; Thee, ho - ly, ho - ly, ho - ly King, Lord God of hosts, they ev - er sing!
3 The a-pos - tles join the glo - rious throng, The proph - ets swell the im - mor - tal song, The mar - tyrs' no - ble ar - my raise E - ter - nal an - thems to thy praise.
4 From day to day, O Lord, do we High - ly ex - alt and hon - or thee; Thy name we wor - ship and a - dore, World with - out end, for - ev - er - more!

5 Vouchsafe, O Lord, we humbly pray,
To keep us safe from sin this day;
Have mercy, Lord, we trust in thee;
Oh, let us ne'er confounded be!

Text: Latin hymn, 4th or 5th cent.; tr. Thomas Cotterill, 1779–1823, alt.
Tune: F. D. Allen, New York Selections, *1822, adapt.*

MENDON
LM

548 Oh, Worship the King

1 Oh, wor - ship the King, all - glo - rious a - bove.
2 Oh, tell of his might; oh, sing of his grace,
3 The earth with its store of won - ders un - told,
4 Your boun - ti - ful care what tongue can re - cite?
Oh, grate - ful - ly sing his pow'r and his love;
Whose robe is the light, whose can - o - py space;
Al - might - y, your pow'r has found - ed of old;
It breathes in the air, it shines in the light,
Our shield and de - fend - er, the An - cient of Days,
His char - iots of wrath the deep thun - der - clouds form,
Es - tab - lished it fast by a change - less de - cree,
It streams from the hills, it de - scends to the plain,
Pa - vil - ioned in splen - dor, and gird - ed with praise.
And dark is his path on the wings of the storm.
And round it has cast, like a man - tle, the sea.
And sweet - ly dis - tills in the dew and the rain.

5 Frail children of dust, and feeble as frail,
In you do we trust, nor find you to fail;
Your mercies, how tender, how firm to the end,
Our maker, defender, redeemer, and friend.

6 O measureless Might, ineffable love,
While angels delight to hymn you above,
The humbler creation, though feeble their lays,
With true adoration shall sing to your praise.

Text: Robert Grant, 1779–1838, alt.
Tune: William Croft, 1678–1727

HANOVER
10 10 11 11

Praise, My Soul, the King of Heaven 549

1 Praise, my soul, the King of heav - en; To his feet your trib - ute bring.
2 Praise him for his grace and fa - vor To our fore-bears in dis - tress.
3 Ten - der - ly he shields and spares us; Well our fee - ble frame he knows.
4 An - gels help us to a - dore him, Who be - hold him face to face.
Ran-somed, healed, re-stored, for - giv - en, Ev - er - more his prais - es sing.
Praise him, still the same for - ev - er, Slow to chide and swift to bless.
In his hands he gent - ly bears us, Res - cues us from all our foes.
Sun and moon bow down be - fore him; All who dwell in time and space.
Al - le - lu - ia! Al - le - lu - ia! Praise the ev - er - last - ing King!
Al - le - lu - ia! Al - le - lu - ia! Glo - rious in his faith - ful - ness!
Al - le - lu - ia! Al - le - lu - ia! Wide - ly as his mer - cy flows.
Al - le - lu - ia! Al - le - lu - ia! Praise with us the God of grace.

Text: Henry F. Lyte, 1793–1847, alt.
Tune: John Goss, 1800–1880

PRAISE, MY SOUL
8 7 8 7 8 7

550 From All That Dwell below the Skies

1 From all that dwell be - low the skies
2 E - ter - nal are your mer - cies, Lord;

Let the cre - a - tor's praise a - rise;
E - ter - nal truth at - tends your Word;

Let the re - deem - er's name be sung
Your praise shall sound from shore to shore,

Through ev - 'ry land, in ev - 'ry tongue.
Till suns shall rise and set no more.

Text: Isaac Watts, 1674–1748
Tune: Louis Bourgeois, c. 1510–1561

OLD HUNDREDTH
LM

Joyful, Joyful We Adore Thee

551

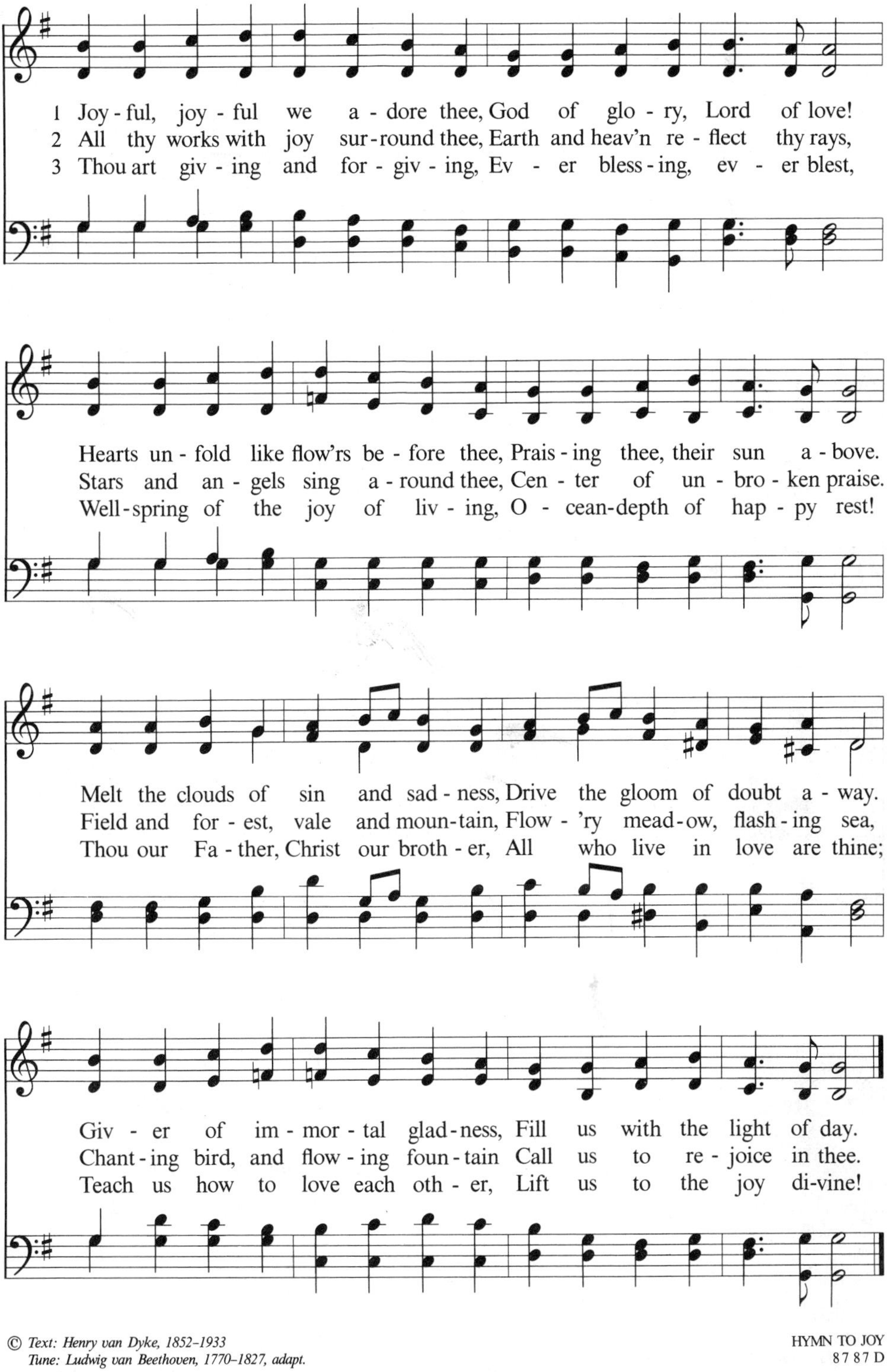

1 Joy - ful, joy - ful we a - dore thee, God of glo - ry, Lord of love!
2 All thy works with joy sur-round thee, Earth and heav'n re - flect thy rays,
3 Thou art giv - ing and for - giv - ing, Ev - er bless - ing, ev - er blest,

Hearts un - fold like flow'rs be - fore thee, Prais - ing thee, their sun a - bove.
Stars and an - gels sing a - round thee, Cen - ter of un - bro - ken praise.
Well-spring of the joy of liv - ing, O - cean-depth of hap - py rest!

Melt the clouds of sin and sad - ness, Drive the gloom of doubt a - way.
Field and for - est, vale and moun-tain, Flow - 'ry mead-ow, flash - ing sea,
Thou our Fa - ther, Christ our broth - er, All who live in love are thine;

Giv - er of im - mor - tal glad-ness, Fill us with the light of day.
Chant - ing bird, and flow - ing foun - tain Call us to re - joice in thee.
Teach us how to love each oth - er, Lift us to the joy di-vine!

 Text: Henry van Dyke, 1852–1933
Tune: Ludwig van Beethoven, 1770–1827, adapt.

HYMN TO JOY
87 87 D

552 In Thee Is Gladness

1 In thee is glad - ness A - mid all sad - ness, Je - sus, sun - shine of my
2 If he is ours, . . . We fear no pow - ers, Not of earth or sin or
heart. By thee are giv - en The gifts of heav - en, Thou the
death. He sees and bless - es In worst dis - tress - es; He can
true re - deem - er art. Our souls thou wak - est; Our bonds thou
change them with a breath. Where-fore the sto - ry Tell of his
break - est. Who trusts thee sure - ly Has built se - cure - ly
glo - ry With heart and voic - es; All heav'n re - joic - es

And stands for - ev - er: Al - le - lu - ia! Our hearts are
In him for - ev - er: Al - le - lu - ia! We shout for
pin - ing To see thy shin - ing, Dy - ing or liv - ing,
glad - ness, Tri - umph o'er sad - ness, Love him and praise him
To thee are cleav - ing; Naught us can sev - er: Al - le - lu - ia!
And still shall raise him Glad hymns for - ev - er: Al - le - lu - ia!

Text: Johann Lindemann, 1549–c. 1631; tr. Catherine Winkworth, 1829–1878, alt.
Tune: Giovanni Giacomo Gastoldi, c. 1556–1622

IN DIR IST FREUDE
PM

553 Rejoice, O Pilgrim Throng!

1 Re - joice, O pil - grim throng! Re - joice, give thanks, and sing;
2 With voice as full and strong As o - cean's surg - ing praise,
3 With all the an - gel choirs, With all the saints on earth
4 Yet, on and on - ward still, With hymn and chant and song,
Your fes - tal ban - ner wave on high, The cross of Christ your king.
Send forth the stur - dy hymns of old, The psalms of an - cient days.
Pour out the strains of joy and bliss, True rap - ture, no - blest mirth.
Through gate and porch and col - umned aisle The hal - lowed path-ways throng.
Refrain
Re - joice! Re - joice! Re - joice, give thanks, and sing!

5 Still lift your standard high,
Still march in firm array,
As pilgrims through the darkness wend
Till dawns the golden day. *Refrain*

6 At last the march shall end;
The wearied ones shall rest;
The pilgrims find their home at last,
Jerusalem the blest. *Refrain*

7 Praise him who reigns on high,
The Lord whom we adore:
The Father, Son, and Holy Ghost,
One God forevermore. *Refrain*

Text: Edward H. Plumptre, 1821–1891, alt.
Tune: Arthur H. Messiter, 1834–1916

MARION
S M and refrain

This Is My Father's World 554

D F♯m D Em A A7
1 This is my Fa - ther's world, And to my lis - t'ning ears All
2 This is my Fa - ther's world; The birds their car - ols raise; The
3 This is my Fa - ther's world; Oh, let me not for - get That,
D F♯m Bm A D A7 D
na - ture sings, and round me rings The mu - sic of the spheres.
morn - ing light, the lil - y white, De - clare their mak - er's praise.
though the wrong seems oft so strong, God is the rul - er yet.
A7 D G A7 Bm D G D A E7 A A7
This is my Fa - ther's world; I rest me in the thought Of
This is my Fa - ther's world; He shines in all that's fair. In the
This is my Fa - ther's world; Why should my heart be sad? The
D F♯m Bm A D A7 D
rocks and trees, of . . skies and seas; His hand the won - ders. .wrought.
rus - tling grass I . . hear him pass; He speaks to me ev - 'ry - where.
Lord is king, let the heav - ens ring; God reigns, let the earth be . . glad!

Text: Maltbie D. Babcock, 1858–1901
© *Tune: Franklin L. Sheppard, 1852–1930, adapt.*

TERRA PATRIS
SMD

555 When in Our Music God Is Glorified

1 When in our mu - sic God is glo - ri - fied, And ad - o - ra - tion
2 How oft, in mak - ing mu - sic, we have found A new di - men - sion
3 So has the Church, in lit - ur - gy and song, In faith and love, through
4 And did not Je - sus sing a psalm that night When ut - most e - vil
leaves no room for pride, It is as though the whole cre - a - tion cried:
in the world of sound, As wor-ship moved us to a more pro - found
cen - tu - ries of wrong, Borne wit-ness to the truth in ev - 'ry tongue:
strove a-gainst the light? Then let us sing, for whom he won the fight:
Al - le - lu - ia, al - le - lu - ia, al - le - lu - ia!

5 Let ev'ry instrument be tuned for praise;
Let all rejoice who have a voice to raise;
And may God give us faith to sing always:
Alleluia, alleluia, alleluia!

FREDERICKTOWN
10 10 10 and alleluias

Herald, Sound the Note of Judgment 556

1 Her - ald, sound the note of judg - ment, Warn - ing
2 Her - ald, sound the note of glad - ness; Tell the
3 Her - ald, sound the note of par - don— Those re -
4 Her - ald, sound the note of tri - umph; Christ has
us of right and wrong, Turn - ing us from sin and
news that Christ is here; Make a path - way through the
pent - ing are for - giv'n; God re - ceives his way - ward
come to share our life, Bring - ing God's own love and
sad - ness Till once more we sing the song.
des - ert For the one who brings God near.
chil - dren, And to them new life is giv'n.
pow - er, Grant - ing vic - t'ry in our strife.
Refrain
Sound the trum-pet! Tell the mes-sage: Christ, the Sav - ior king, is come!

© *Text: Moir A. J. Waters, b. 1906, alt.*
© *Tune: David McCarthy, b. 1931*

NEW MALDEN
87 87 87

557 Let All Things Now Living

1 Let all things now liv - ing A song of thanks-giv - ing To
2 His law he en - forc - es, The stars in their cours - es And

God the cre - a - tor tri - um-phant - ly raise, Who fash-ioned and
sun in its or - bit o - be - dient - ly shine; The hills and the

made us, Pro - tect - ed and stayed us, Who still guides us
moun-tains, The riv - ers and foun - tains, The deeps of the

on to the end of our days. God's ban - ners are o'er us, His
o - cean pro-claim him di - vine. We too should be voic - ing Our

light goes be - fore us, A pil - lar of fire shin - ing forth in the
love and re - joic - ing; With glad ad - o - ra - tion a song let us
night, Till shad - ows have van - ished And dark - ness is
raise Till all things now liv - ing U - nite in thanks-
ban-ished, As for - ward we trav - el from light in - to light.
giv - ing: "To God in the high - est, ho - san - na and praise!"

 Text: Katherine K. Davis, b. 1892
Tune: Welsh folk tune

THE ASH GROVE
66 11 66 11 D

558 Earth and All Stars!

1 Earth and all stars! Loud rush - ing plan - ets! Sing to the Lord a new song! Oh, vic - to - ry! Loud shout - ing ar - my! Sing to the Lord a new song!
2 Hail, wind, and rain! Loud blow - ing snow - storm! Sing to the Lord a new song! Flow - ers and trees! Loud rus - tling dry leaves! Sing to the Lord a new song!
3 Trum - pet and pipes! Loud clash - ing cym - bals! Sing to the Lord a new song! Harp, lute, and lyre! Loud hum - ming cel - los! Sing to the Lord a new song!
4 En - gines and steel! Loud pound - ing ham - mers! Sing to the Lord a new song! Lime - stone and beams! Loud build - ing work - ers! Sing to the Lord a new song!
Refrain
He has done mar - vel - ous things.

I too will praise him with a new song!

5 Classroms and labs!

5 Classrooms and labs!
Loud boiling test tubes!
Sing to the Lord a new song!
Athlete and band!
Loud cheering people!
Sing to the Lord a new song! *Refrain*

6 Knowledge and truth!
Loud sounding wisdom!
Sing to the Lord a new song!
Daughter and son!
Loud praying members!
Sing to the Lord a new song! *Refrain*

© *Text: Herbert F. Brokering, b. 1926*
© *Tune: David N. Johnson, b. 1922*

EARTH AND ALL STARS
4 5 7 4 5 7 and refrain

Oh, for a Thousand Tongues to Sing 559

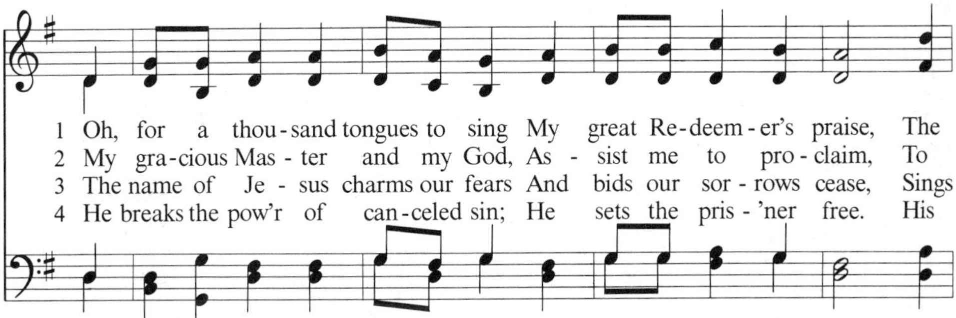

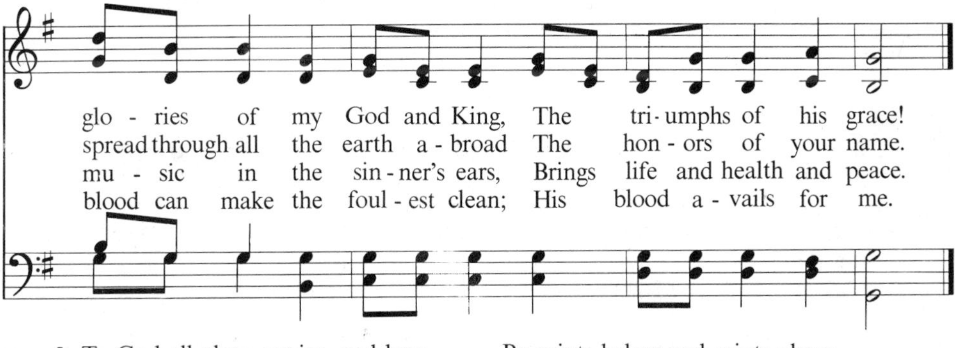

1 Oh, for a thou-sand tongues to sing My great Re-deem-er's praise, The glo-ries of my God and King, The tri-umphs of his grace!
2 My gra-cious Mas-ter and my God, As-sist me to pro-claim, To spread through all the earth a-broad The hon-ors of your name.
3 The name of Je-sus charms our fears And bids our sor-rows cease, Sings mu-sic in the sin-ner's ears, Brings life and health and peace.
4 He breaks the pow'r of can-celed sin; He sets the pris-'ner free. His blood can make the foul-est clean; His blood a-vails for me.

5 To God all glory, praise, and love
Be now and ever giv'n
By saints below and saints above,
The Church in earth and heav'n.

Text: Charles Wesley, 1707–1788, alt.
Tune: Carl G. Gläser, 1784–1829

AZMON
CM

560 Oh, that I Had a Thousand Voices

1 Oh, that I had a thou - sand voic - es To praise my
2 O all you pow'rs that he im - plant - ed, A - rise, keep
3 You for - est leaves so green and ten - der That dance for
4 All crea - tures that have breath and mo - tion, That throng the

God with thou - sand tongues! My heart, which in the Lord re -
si - lence now no more; Put forth the strength that God has
joy in sum - mer air, You mead - ow grass - es, bright and
earth, the sea, the sky, Come, share with me my heart's de -

joic - es, Would then pro - claim in grate-ful songs To all, wher-
grant - ed! Your no - blest work is to a - dore! O soul and
slen - der, You flow'rs so fra - grant and so fair, You live to
vo - tion, Help me to sing God's prais - es high! My ut - most

ev - er I might be, What great things God has done for me!
bod - y, join to raise With heart - felt joy our mak - er's praise!
show God's praise a - lone. Join me to make his glo - ry known!
pow'rs can nev - er quite De - clare the won-ders of his might!

5 Creator, humbly I implore you
To listen to my earthly song
Until that day when I adore you,
When I have joined the angel throng
And learned with choirs of heav'n to sing
Eternal anthems to my king!

 Text: Johann Mentzer, 1658–1734; tr. The Lutheran Hymnal, *1941, alt.*
Tune: Johann B. König, 1691–1758

O DASS ICH TAUSEND ZUNGEN HÄTTE
98 98 88

For the Beauty of the Earth 561

1 For the beau - ty of the earth, For the beau - ty of the skies,
2 For the won - der of each hour Of the day and of the night,
3 For the joy of ear and eye, For the heart and mind's de - light,
4 For the joy of hu - man love, Broth-er, sis - ter, par - ent, child,
For the love which from our birth O - ver and a - round us lies:
Hill and vale and tree and flow'r, Sun and moon and stars of light:
For the mys - tic har - mo - ny Link-ing sense to sound and sight:
Friends on earth and friends a - bove; For all gen - tle thoughts and mild:
Refrain
Christ, our Lord, to you we raise This our sac - ri - fice of praise.

5 For yourself, best gift divine
To the world so freely giv'n;
Agent of God's grand design,
Peace on earth and joy in heav'n: *Refrain*

Text: Folliott S. Pierpoint, 1835–1917, alt.
Tune: Conrad Kocher, 1786–1872

DIX
77 77 77

562 Lift Every Voice and Sing

1 Lift ev - 'ry voice and sing Till earth and heav - en
2 Ston - y the road we trod, Bit - ter the chas - t'ning
3 God of our wea - ry years, God of our si - lent

ring, Ring with the har - mo - nies of lib - er -
rod, Felt in the days when hope un - born had
tears, Thou who hast brought us thus far on the

ty. Let our re - joic - ing rise High as the lis - t'ning
died; Yet, with a stead - y beat, Have not our wea - ry
way; Thou who hast by thy might Led us in - to the

skies; Let it re - sound loud as the roll - ing sea.
feet Come to the place for which our par - ents sighed?
light: Keep us for - ev - er in the path, we pray.

Sing a song full of the faith that the dark past has taught us;
We have come o - ver a way that with tears has been wa - tered;
Lest our feet stray from the plac - es, our God, where we met thee;
Sing a song full of the hope that the pres-ent has brought
We have come, tread - ing our path through the blood of the slaugh -
Lest, our hearts drunk with the wine of the world, we for - get
us; Fac - ing the ris - ing sun Of our new day be -
tered, Out from the gloom - y past, Till now we stand at
thee; Shad-owed be - neath thy hand May we for - ev - er
gun, Let us march on, till vic - to - ry is won.
last Where the white gleam of our bright star is cast.
stand, True to our God, true to our na - tive land.

LIFT EV'RY VOICE AND SING
PM

563 For the Fruit of All Creation

1 For the fruit of all cre - a - tion, Thanks be to God.
2 In the just re - ward of la - bor, God's will is done.
3 For the har - vests of the Spir - it, Thanks be to God.
For his gifts to ev - 'ry na - tion, Thanks be to God.
In the help we give our neigh-bor, God's will is done.
For the good we all in - her - it, Thanks be to God.
For the plow - ing, sow - ing, reap-ing, Si - lent growth while we are sleep-ing,
In our world-wide task of car - ing For the hun - gry and de - spair-ing,
For the won - ders that as - tound us, For the truths that still con-found us,
Fu - ture needs in earth's safe-keep-ing, Thanks be to God.
In the har - vests we are shar - ing, God's will is done.
Most of all, that love has found us, Thanks be to God.

SANTA BARBARA
84 84 88 84

Praise God, from Whom All Blessings Flow

564

Praise God, from whom all bless-ings flow; Praise him, all crea-tures here be-low;
Praise him a-bove, ye heav'n-ly host; Praise Fa-ther, Son, and Ho-ly Ghost.

Text: Thomas Ken, 1637–1711
Tune: Louis Bourgeois, c. 1510–1561

OLD HUNDREDTH
LM

Praise God, from Whom All Blessings Flow

565

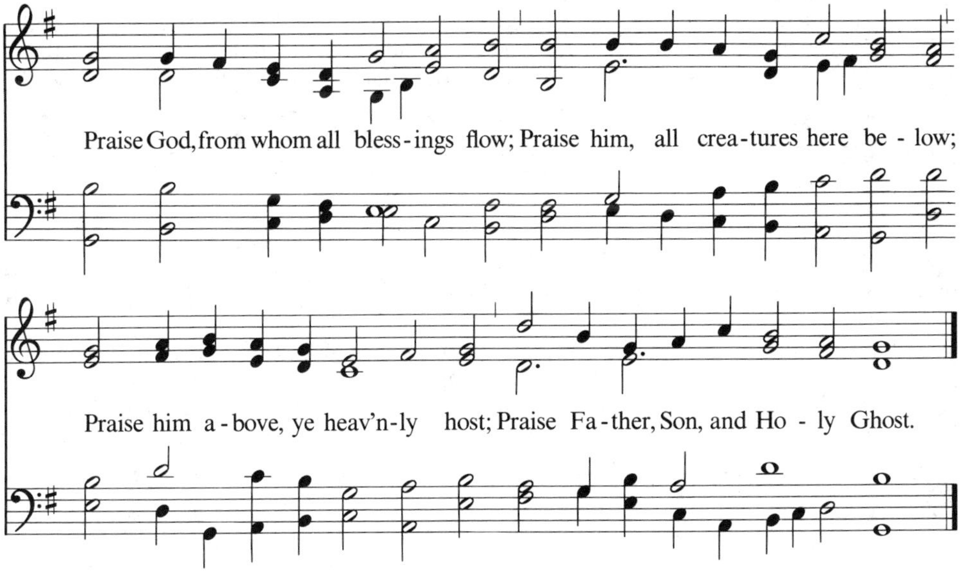

Praise God, from whom all bless-ings flow; Praise him, all crea-tures here be-low;

Praise him a-bove, ye heav'n-ly host; Praise Fa-ther, Son, and Ho-ly Ghost.

Text: Thomas Ken, 1637–1711
Tune: Louis Bourgeois, c. 1510–1561

OLD HUNDREDTH
LM

NATIONAL SONGS

566 My Country, 'Tis of Thee

1 My coun - try, 'tis of thee, Sweet land of lib - er - ty,
2 My na - tive coun - try, thee, Land of the no - ble free,
3 Let mu - sic swell the breeze, And ring from all the trees
4 Our fa - thers' God, to thee, Au - thor of lib - er - ty,

Of thee I sing: Land where my fa - thers died, Land of the
Thy name I love; I love thy rocks and rills, Thy woods and
Sweet free - dom's song; Let mor - tal tongues a - wake; Let all that
To thee we sing: Long may our land be bright With free - dom's

pil - grims' pride, From ev - 'ry moun - tain - side Let free - dom ring.
tem - pled hills; My heart with rap - ture thrills Like that a - bove.
breathe par - take; Let rocks their si - lence break, The sound pro - long.
ho - ly light. Pro - tect us by thy might, Great God, our king.

Text: *Samuel F. Smith, 1805–1895*
Tune: Thesaurus Musicus, *London, 1744*

NATIONAL ANTHEM
664 6664

God of Our Fathers

567

1 God of our fa - thers, whose al - might - y hand
2 Your love di - vine has led us in the past;
3 From war's a - larms, from dead - ly pes - ti - lence,
4 Re - fresh your peo - ple on their toil - some way;
Leads forth in beau - ty all the star - ry band
In this free land by you our lot is cast;
Make your strong arm our ev - er sure de - fense.
Lead us from night to nev - er - end - ing day;
Of shin ing worlds in splen - dor through the skies:
Oh, be our rul - er, guard - ian, guide, and stay;
Your true re - li - gion in our hearts in - crease;
Fill all our lives with heav'n - born love and grace
Our grate - ful · songs be - fore your throne a - rise.
Your Word our law, your paths our cho - sen way.
Your boun - teous good - ness nour - ish us in peace.
Un - til at last we meet be - fore your face.

Text: Daniel C. Roberts, 1841–1907, alt.
Tune: George W. Warren, 1828–1902

NATIONAL HYMN
10 10 10 10

568 God Save Our Gracious Queen!

1 God save our gracious Queen! Long live our noble Queen! God save the Queen! Send her victorious, Happy and glorious, Long to reign over us; God save the Queen!

2 Thy choicest gifts in store On her be pleased to pour; Long may she reign! May she defend our laws, And ever give us cause To sing with heart and voice, God save the Queen!

Text: *source unknown, 18th cent.*
Tune: Thesaurus Musicus, *London, 1744*

NATIONAL ANTHEM
664 6664

God Bless Our Native Land 569

1 God bless our na - tive land; Firm may it ev - er stand
2 So shall our prayers a - rise To God a - bove the skies,
Through storm and night. When the wild tem - pests rave, Rul - er of
On whom we wait. Thou who art ev - er nigh, Guard-ing with
wind and wave, Do thou our coun - try save By thy great might.
watch-ful eye, To thee a - loud we cry: God save the state!

Text: *Charles T. Brooks, 1812–1883, st. 1; John S. Dwight, 1813–1893, st. 2; alt.*
Tune: Thesaurus Musicus, *London, 1744*

NATIONAL ANTHEM
664 6664

INDEXES

ACKNOWLEDGMENTS

The liturgical material on pages 9–289 is covered by the copyright of this book.

Material from the following sources is acknowledged:

International Consultation on English Texts: the Apostles' Creed, the Nicene Creed, the Lord's Prayer, the preface dialog, the canticle texts "Glory to God in the highest," "Holy, holy, holy Lord," "Lamb of God," "Lord, now you let your servant go in peace," "Blessed be the Lord, the God of Israel," "You are God; we praise you," "My soul proclaims the greatness of the Lord," and "Jesus, Lamb of God."

Psalm prayers from the English translation of the Liturgy of the Hours, © 1974 International Committee on English in the Liturgy, Inc. Adapted with permission. All rights reserved.

Standard Book of Common Prayer, copyright © 1977 by Charles Mortimer Guilbert as custodian. All rights reserved. Reprinted by permission: The Psalms, pages 215–289, the canticle texts "Let my prayer rise before you as incense" and "Oh, come, let us sing to the Lord."

The Revised Standard Version of the Bible, copyright 1946, 1952, and 1971 by the Division of Christian Education of the National Council of Churches.

The Holy Communion, copyright © 1976 by Lutheran Church in America, The American Lutheran Church, The Evangelical Lutheran Church of Canada, and The Lutheran Church—Missouri Synod.

The Contemporary Worship series, copyright © by Lutheran Church in America, The American Lutheran Church, The Evangelical Lutheran Church of Canada, and The Lutheran Church—Missouri Synod: Contemporary Worship 2: *The Holy Communion,* copyright 1970; Contemporary Worship 3: *The Marriage Service,* copyright 1972; Contemporary Worship 5: *Services of the Word,* copyright 1972; Contemporary Worship 6: *The Church Year Calendar and Lectionary,* copyright 1973; Contemporary Worship 7: *Holy Baptism,* copyright 1974; Contemporary Worship 8: *Affirmation of the Baptismal Covenant,* copyright 1975; Contemporary Worship 9: *Daily Prayer of the Church,* copyright 1976; Contemporary Worship 10: *Burial of the Dead,* copyright 1976.

Composers of liturgical music are acknowledged: Gerhard M. Cartford, b. 1923—"Worthy is Christ," "Return to the Lord," "Let the vineyards be fruitful," "What shall I render to the Lord," "Through him, with him, in him," "Thank the Lord and sing his praise," (Holy Communion, Setting Three); Litany (Evening Prayer); The Litany, Richard W. Hillert, b. 1923—Holy Communion, Setting One; "Create in me a clean heart, O God"; "Oh, come, let us sing to the Lord" and "You are God; we praise you" (Morning Prayer). Carlos R. Messerli, b. 1927—Prayer at the Close of the Day. Ronald A. Nelson, b. 1927—Holy Communion, Setting Two. Roger T. Petrich, b. 1938—"Joyous light of glory" (Evening Prayer). David Schack, b. 1947—"Let my prayer rise before you as incense" (Evening Prayer). Dale Wood, b. 1934—"Blessed be the Lord, the God of Israel" (Morning Prayer); "My soul proclaims the greatness of the Lord" (Evening Prayer).

Authors/translators of liturgical texts are acknowledged: John W. Arthur, b. 1922—"Worthy is Christ" and "Let the vineyards be fruitful." Gordon W. Lathrop, b. 1939—translation of eucharistic prayer IV. Roger T. Petrich, b. 1938—"Joyous light of glory." Ralph W. Quere, b. 1935—translation of the Athanasian Creed.

Composers of the psalm tones are acknowledged: Mark Bangert, b. 1938; Gerhard M. Cartford, b. 1923; Richard W. Hillert, b. 1923.

Composers of canticles 1–21 are acknowledged: Jan O. Bender, b. 1909—canticle 17. J. Bert Carlson, b. 1937—canticle 14. Gerhard M. Cartford, b. 1923—canticles 5 and 6. Lucien Deiss, b. 1921—canticle 13. Richard W. Hillert, b. 1923—canticles 1, 2, 3, 4, 7, 8, 9, 10, 11, and 12. Daniel Moe, b. 1926—canticle 16.

The author of canticles 7–12 and 14 is acknowledged: John W. Arthur, b. 1922.

Inter-Lutheran Commission on Worship: Henry C. Abram, Louis Accola, John W. Arthur*, Ruth Becker, Eugene L. Brand*, Edgar S. Brown Jr.*, Paul G. Bunjes*, Walter E. Buszin†*, L. Crosby Deaton*, E. Theodore DeLaney*, Gilbert E. Doan Jr.*, Mandus A. Egge*, Paul Ensrud*, Carl Fischer*, Paul Foelber*, Edward A. Hansen*, Toivo K. I. Harjunpaa, Richard P. Hermstad*, Edward T. Horn III*, Frederick F. Jackisch*, Herbert Kahler, Hans F. Knauer†, A. R. Kretzmann*, Ulrich S. Leupold†*, Theodore S. Liefeld, L. R. Likness*, Herbert F. Lindemann*, Shirley McCreedy, Carlos R. Messerli*, Daniel Moe*, Harold W. Moench, Constance Parvey, Paul K. Peterson*, Fred L. Precht*, Alf Romstad, Warren G. Rubel, Leland B. Sateren*, Rodney Schrank, Ralph C. Schultz, Martin L. Seltz†*, Krister Stendahl*, Clifford J. Swanson*, Jaroslav J. Vajda*,

* *indicates service on one of the standing committees*
† *deceased*

Ralph R. Van Loon*, Willis Wright. **Additional members of standing committees:** Charles R. Anders, Jan Bender, Hans C. Boehringer, Robert E. Bornemann, Gerhard M. Cartford, Paul Christiansen, Bessie Coleman, Donna Zierdt Elkin, Charles Ferguson, Gracia Grindal, Richard W. Hillert, Donald Hinkle, Henry Horn, Larry Houff, Edward Klammer, Ludwig Lenel, Joel W. Lundeen, John Milton, Ronald A. Nelson, Ruth Olson, Hilton C. Oswald, Philip Pfatteicher, Reuben Pirner, Ralph Quere, Carl Schalk, Glenn Stone, Gerald Thorson, Johann A. Thorson, George Utech, Marilyn Waniek, Dale Warland, Raymond Yauk, Stanley Yoder. **ILCW staff:** Eugene L. Brand, Robert A. Rimbo. **Church staff:** John W. Becker, Jerry A. Evenrud, Janet Moede, Mons A. Teig, R. Harold Terry. **Publishers' representative:** Leonard Flachman.

Design: Koechel Design, Inc., Minneapolis; **Music composition and typesetting:** York Graphic Services, Inc., York, Pa.

Composers of hymn tune settings are acknowledged: Charles R. Anders, b. 1929; J. S. Bach, 1685–1750; Edward S. Barnes, 1887–1958; Theodore A. Beck, b. 1929; John W. Becker, b. 1927; Jan O. Bender, b. 1909; Paul B. Bouman, b. 1918; Annabel Morris Buchanan, b. 1888; Paul G. Bunjes, b. 1914; Donald A. Busarow, b. 1934; H. Barrie Cabena, b. 1933; J. Bert Carlson, b. 1937; Gerhard M. Cartford, b. 1923; Robert Carwithen, b. 1933; William H. Cummings, 1831–1915; C. Winfred Douglas, 1867–1944; Walter Ehret; David Evans, 1874–1948; Jerry A. Evenrud, b. 1929; John Ferguson, b. 1941; Paul Foelber, b. 1926; William E. France, b. 1912; Philip Gehring, b. 1925; Thomas E. Gieschen, b. 1931; Claude Goudimel, 1505–1572; Edvard Grieg, 1843–1907; Elmer T. R. Hanke; Basil Harwood, 1859–1949; Charles H. Heaton, b. 1928; Wilbur C. Held, b. 1914; David Herman, b. 1944; Richard W. Hillert, b. 1923; Larry J. Houff, b. 1944; Frederick F. Jackisch, b. 1922; Gordon Jacob, b. 1895; Michal Kutzky, 1828–1899; Robert Leaf, b. 1936; Ludwig Lenel, b. 1914; Ulrich S. Leupold, 1909–1970; Austin C. Lovelace, b. 1919; Ernest Campbell MacMillan, 1893–1973; Paul O. Manz, b. 1919; Lowell Mason, 1792–1872; Felix Mendelssohn, 1809–1847; Gerald R. Near, b. 1942; Ronald A. Nelson, b. 1927; Charles W. Ore, b. 1936; Stanley L. Osborne, b. 1907; Alice Parker, b. 1925; Walter L. Pelz, b. 1926; Roger T. Petrich, b. 1938; Hugh Porter, 1897–1960; William J. Reynolds, b. 1920; John Roberts, 1822–1877; William Smith Rockstro, 1823–1895; Julius Röntgen, 1855–1932; Leland B. Sateren, b. 1913; Carl F. Schalk, b. 1929; Robert P. Schultz, b. 1937; Martin Shaw, 1875–1958; John Stainer, 1840–1901; Arthur S. Sullivan, 1842–1900; R. Harold Terry, b. 1925; Eric Thiman, 1900–1975; Mary L. Van Dyke, b. 1927; R. Vaughan Williams, 1872–1958; Healey Willan, 1880–1968; Thomas J. Williams, 1869–1944; Dale Wood, b. 1934; George R. Woodward, 1848–1939; Carlton R. Young, b. 1926; Friedrich Zipp, b. 1914.

The following canticle and hymn copyrights are acknowledged:
1 **Tune and setting:** Copyright 1978 *Lutheran Book of Worship.*
2 **Text:** © Copyright 1976 by the Custodian of the Standard Book of Common Prayer. Used by permission. **Tune and setting:** Copyright 1978 *Lutheran Book of Worship.*
3 **Tune and setting:** Copyright 1978 *Lutheran Book of Worship.*
4 **Tune and setting:** Copyright 1978 *Lutheran Book of Worship.*
5 **Tune and setting:** Copyright 1978 *Lutheran Book of Worship.*
6 **Text:** © Copyright 1976 by the Custodian of the Standard Book of Common Prayer. Used by permission. **Tune and setting:** Copyright 1978 *Lutheran Book of Worship.*
7 **Text, tune, and setting:** Copyright 1972 Contemporary Worship 5: *Services of the Word.*[1]
8 **Text, tune, and setting:** Copyright 1972 Contemporary Worship 5: *Services of the Word.*[1]
9 **Text, tune, and setting:** Copyright 1972 Contemporary Worship 5: *Services of the Word.*[1]
10 **Text, tune, and setting:** Copyright 1972 Contemporary Worship 5: *Services of the Word.*[1]
11 **Text, tune, and setting:** Copyright 1972 Contemporary Worship 5: *Services of the Word.*[1]
12 **Text, tune, and setting:** Copyright 1972 Contemporary Worship 5: *Services of the Word.*[1]
13 **Text, tune, and setting:** Copyright World Library of Sacred Music. Used by permission.
14 **Text, tune, and setting:** Copyright 1972 Contemporary Worship 5: *Services of the Word.*[1]
16 **Text, tune, and setting:** Copyright 1972 Contemporary Worship 3: *The Marriage Service.*[1]
17 **Text:** From The New English Bible. Used by permission. **Tune and setting:** Copyright 1972 Contemporary Worship 5: *Services of the Word.*[1]
25 **Setting:** Copyright 1978 *Lutheran Book of Worship.*
26 **Text:** Copyright 1978 *Lutheran Book of Worship.*
28 **Text:** tr. William M. Reynolds, 1816–1876, sts. 1–3a, 7; tr. Martin L. Seltz, 1909–1967, sts. 3b–6. Copyright Concordia Publishing House. Used by permission. **Setting:** Copyright 1969 Concordia Publishing House. Used by permission.
30 **Setting:** Copyright 1978 *Lutheran Book of Worship.*
31 **Setting:** Copyright 1970 *Neues Choralbuch,* Bärenreiter-Verlag, Kassel and Basel. Used by permission.
32 **Text:** Copyright 1978 *Lutheran Book of Worship.* **Setting:** Copyright 1952 *Orgelchoralbuch.*[2]
33 **Setting:** Copyright 1969 Concordia Publishing House. Used by permission.
36 **Text:** tr. John Chandler, 1806–1876, sts. 1–3; tr. unknown, sts. 4–5. **Setting:** Copyright 1959 A. R. Mowbray and Co. Ltd. Used by permission.
37 **Setting:** Copyright 1969 Concordia Publishing House. Used by permission.
38 **Text and setting:** Copyright 1969 Concordia Publishing House. Used by permission.
42 **Text:** tr. John M. Neale, 1818–1866, sts. 1–4; tr. Henry Williams Baker, 1821–1877, st. 5. **Setting:** Copyright 1978 *Lutheran Book of Worship.*
44 **Text:** From *Kingsway Carol Book.* Copyright 1960 Evans Brothers, Ltd. Used by permission. **Setting:** Copyright 1978 *Lutheran Book of Worship.*
45 **Text:** tr. Frederick Oakley, 1802–1880, sts. 1, 3–4; tr. unknown, st. 2.
47 **Text:** Copyright 1969 Concordia Publishing House. Used by permission. **Setting:** Copyright 1953 *Württembergisches Choralbuch.*[2]
48 **Setting:** Copyright 1969 Concordia Publishing House. Used by permission.
49 **Text and setting:** Copyright 1978 *Lutheran Book of Worship.*
50 **Setting:** Copyright 1978 *Lutheran Book of Worship.*
51 **Text:** Copyright 1978 *Lutheran Book of Worship.*
53 **Text:** Copyright 1978 *Lutheran Book of Worship.* **Setting:** Copyright 1963. Reprinted by permission of Prentice-Hall, Inc., Englewood Cliffs, New Jersey.
55 **Setting:** Copyright 1969 Concordia Publishing House. Used by permission.
57 **Setting:** Copyright 1978 *Lutheran Book of Worship.*
58 **Text:** Copyright 1978 *Lutheran Book of Worship.*
59 **Text:** Copyright 1978 *Lutheran Book of Worship.*
61 **Text and setting:** Copyright 1978 *Lutheran Book of Worship.*
63 **Text, tune, and setting:** Copyright 1963 Concordia Publishing House. Used by permission.
64 **Setting:** Copyright 1978 *Lutheran Book of Worship.*

66 **Text:** From *Slovak Christmas.* Copyright Slovak Institute. Used by permission. **Setting:** Copyright 1978 *Lutheran Book of Worship.*
67 **Setting:** Copyright 1978 *Lutheran Book of Worship.*
68 **Text:** tr. Martin L. Seltz, 1909–1967; tr. Herbert J. A. Bouman, b. 1908; alt. Copyright 1969 Concordia Publishing House. Used by permission. **Setting:** Copyright 1978 *Lutheran Book of Worship.*
69 **Text:** Copyright Augsburg Publishing House.
70 **Text and setting:** Used by permission Mrs. John W. Work III.
72 **Text:** © Copyright 1927, Frederick Harris Co. Limited, Oakville, Ontario, Canada. **Setting:** Copyright 1978 *Lutheran Book of Worship.*
74 **Text:** © 1961 by Richard Wilbur, titled "A Christmas Hymn," from his volume *Advice to a Prophet and Other Poems* by permission of Harcourt, Brace, Jovanovich, Inc. **Tune and setting:** Copyright 1969 Contemporary Worship 1: *Hymns.*[1]
75 **Text:** Copyright 1958 *Service Book and Hymnal.*[3]
76 **Text:** Copyright 1978 *Lutheran Book of Worship.* **Setting:** Copyright 1952 *Orgelchoralbuch.*[2]
77 **Tune and setting:** Copyright Office of the Public Trustee. Used by permission.
78 **Tune and setting:** Copyright Kenneth George Finlay.
79 **Text:** Copyright 1976 Elizabeth Quitmeyer. Used by permission. **Setting:** Copyright 1978 *Lutheran Book of Worship.*
80 **Setting:** Copyright 1969 Concordia Publishing House. Used by permission.
81 **Text:** tr. N. B. Smithers, c. 1879, sts. 1–2, 4; tr. C. Winfred Douglas, 1867–1944, st. 3; tr. John, Marquess of Bute, c. 1879, st. 5; alt. **Setting:** Copyright by Stainer and Bell Ltd. All rights reserved. Used by permission of Galaxy Music Corp., N.Y., sole U.S. agent.
83 **Setting:** Copyright The Public Trustee. Used by permission.
85 **Text:** tr. *The Hymn Book,* 1971, st. 1; tr. John M. Neale, 1818–1866, sts. 2–5; alt.
86 **Setting:** Copyright 1978 *Lutheran Book of Worship.*
87 **Setting:** Copyright 1978 *Lutheran Book of Worship.*
88 **Setting:** Copyright 1969 Concordia Publishing House. Used by permission.
89 **Text:** Copyright Miss Esmé D. E. Bird.
92 **Setting:** By permission of The Church Pension Fund.
94 **Setting:** Copyright 1969 Concordia Publishing House. Used by permission.
96 **Text:** From *Laudamus,* 1970. Copyright the Lutheran World Federation. Used by permission.
97 **Setting:** Copyright 1978 *Lutheran Book of Worship.*
99 **Text:** Copyright 1978 *Lutheran Book of Worship.*
100 **Text, tune, and setting:** Copyright 1958 *Service Book and Hymnal.*[3]
101 **Text:** Copyright 1978 *Lutheran Book of Worship.* **Tune and setting:** From *Enlarged Songs of Praise* by permission of Oxford University Press.
102 **Setting:** Copyright 1978 *Lutheran Book of Worship.*
103 **Setting:** Copyright 1978 *Lutheran Book of Worship.*
105 **Text:** Copyright 1978 *Lutheran Book of Worship.* **Setting:** Copyright 1953 *Württembergisches Choralbuch.*[2]
107 **Tune:** Copyright The Psalms and Hymns Trust, London. Used by permission.
108 **Setting:** Copyright 1970 *Neues Choralbuch,* Bärenreiter-Verlag, Kassel and Basel. Used by permission.
110 **Text:** tr. Edward Caswall, 1814–1878; tr. Richard Mant, 1776–1848; tr. Aubrey deVere, 1814–1902; alt.
111 **Text:** Copyright 1978 *Lutheran Book of Worship.* **Setting:** Copyright 1970 *Neues Choralbuch,* Bärenreiter-Verlag, Kassel and Basel. Used by permission.
113 **Setting:** Copyright 1978 *Lutheran Book of Worship.*
116 **Text:** tr. James W. Alexander, 1804–1859, sts. 1–3; tr. *The Lutheran Hymnal,* 1941, st. 4. Copyright 1941 Concordia Publishing House, st. 4. Used by permission.
117 **Text:** tr. James W. Alexander, 1804–1859, sts. 1–3; tr. *The Lutheran Hymnal,* 1941, st. 4. Copyright 1941 Concordia Publishing House, st. 4. Used by permission.
118 **Tune and setting:** Copyright 1967 Concordia Publishing House. Used by permission.
120 **Text:** tr. John M. Neale, 1818–1866; tr. Edward Caswall, 1814–1878. **Setting:** Copyright 1978 *Lutheran Book of Worship.*
121 **Tune and setting:** Copyright 1941 by The H. W. Gray Co. Inc. Copyright renewed. Used with permission. All rights reserved.
122 **Setting:** Copyright 1978 *Lutheran Book of Worship.*
123 **Text:** From the *Yattendon Hymnal* by permission of Oxford University Press.
124 **Text:** tr. John M. Neale, 1818–1866, sts. 1–3, 6; tr. *Hymnal 1940,* sts. 4–5; alt. Stanzas 4–5 by permission of The Church Pension Fund. **Setting:** Copyright 1969 Concordia Publishing House. Used by permission.
125 **Text:** tr. John M. Neale, 1818–1866, sts. 1–3, 6; tr. *Hymnal 1940,* sts. 4–5, alt. Stanzas 4–5 by permission of The Church Pension Fund. **Setting:** Copyright sons and daughter of the composer. By permission.
126 **Text:** From *The People's Massbook.* Copyright 1961, 1962 World Library Publications. Used by permission.
127 **Text and setting:** Copyright 1978 *Lutheran Book of Worship.*
130 **Setting:** Copyright 1978 *Lutheran Book of Worship.*
131 **Tune and setting:** By courtesy of the Psalms and Hymns Trust.
132 **Setting:** Copyright 1969 Concordia Publishing House. Used by permission.
133 **Setting:** Copyright 1970 *Neues Choralbuch,* Bärenreiter-Verlag, Kassel and Basel. Used by permission.
136 **Text and setting:** Copyright Concordia Publishing House. Used by permission.
137 **Setting:** Copyright 1969 Concordia Publishing House. Used by permission.
138 **Setting:** Copyright 1952 *Orgelchoralbuch,* 1952.[2]
139 **Setting:** Copyright 1969 Concordia Publishing House. Used by permission.
140 **Text and setting:** Copyright Concordia Publishing House. Used by permission.
141 **Setting:** Copyright 1969 Concordia Publishing House. Used by permission.
142 **Text:** Copyright 1978 *Lutheran Book of Worship.* **Tune and setting:** From the *English Hymnal* by permission of Oxford University Press.
143 **Text:** Copyright 1958 *Service Book and Hymnal.*[3] **Setting:** From the *English Hymnal* by permission of Oxford University Press.
144 **Text:** By permission of Hymns Ancient and Modern Ltd. **Setting:** Copyright 1969 Concordia Publishing House. Used by permission.
145 **Text:** From *Cantate Domino.* Copyright World Student Christian Federation. Used by permission.
146 **Text:** Copyright 1978 *Lutheran Book of Worship.* **Setting:** From *Songs of Praise* by permission of Oxford University Press.
148 **Text:** From *Oxford Book of Carols* by permission of Oxford University Press. Copyright 1928. **Setting:** From *Oxford Book of Carols* by permission of Oxford University Press.
149 **Text:** From the *Cowley Carol Book.* Copyright A. R. Mowbray and Co., Ltd. Used by permission. **Setting:** Copyright 1969 Alice Parker Pyle. Used by permission.
150 **Text:** Copyright 1978 *Lutheran Book of Worship.*
152 **Text:** Copyright George Utech. Used by permission. **Tune and setting:** Copyright 1969 Contemporary Worship 1: *Hymns.*[1]
154 **Setting:** Copyright 1969 Concordia Publishing House. Used by permission.

155 **Text:** Copyright 1958 *Service Book and Hymnal.*[3]
157 **Text:** Copyright 1978 *Lutheran Book of Worship.* **Setting:** From the *English Hymnal* by permission of Oxford University Press.
159 **Text:** Copyright Augsburg Publishing House. **Tune and setting:** Copyright Henry V. Gerike. Used by permission.
160 **Text:** Copyright Mrs. J. R. Peacey. Used by permission. **Tune and setting:** Copyright Novello and Co., Ltd. Used by permission.
161 **Text:** Copyright 1978 *Lutheran Book of Worship.*
162 **Tune and setting:** Copyright 1978 *Lutheran Book of Worship.*
163 **Text:** Copyright 1941 Concordia Publishing House. Used by permission.
164 **Setting:** Copyright 1978 *Lutheran Book of Worship.*
166 **Text and setting:** Copyright 1978 *Lutheran Book of Worship.*
168 **Text:** Copyright Concordia Publishing House. Used by permission. **Setting:** Copyright 1978 *Lutheran Book of Worship.*
169 **Text:** By permission of Oxford University Press. **Setting:** Copyright 1969 Concordia Publishing House. Used by permission.
172 **Setting:** Copyright 1969 Concordia Publishing House. Used by permission.
174 **Tune and setting:** From the *English Hymnal* by permission of Oxford University Press.
175 **Text and setting:** From the *English Hymnal* by permission of Oxford University Press.
176 **Setting:** Copyright 1978 *Lutheran Book of Worship.*
177 **Tune:** From the *English Hymnal* by permission of Oxford University Press. **Setting:** Copyright 1969 Concordia Publishing House. Used by permission.
178 **Tune:** From the *English Hymnal* by permission of Oxford University Press. **Setting:** Copyright 1969 Concordia Publishing House. Used by permission.
179 **Tune and setting:** From *Enlarged Songs of Praise* by permission of Oxford University Press.
180 **Text:** Copyright 1978 *Lutheran Book of Worship.*
181 **Text and setting:** Copyright Concordia Publishing House. Used by permission.
184 **Tune and setting:** Copyright Augsburg Publishing House.
185 **Text:** Copyright The Lutheran Publishing House. Used by permission.
186 **Text:** Copyright Board of Publication, Lutheran Church in America, sts. 1–3; copyright 1958 *Service Book and Hymnal,* st. 4.[3] **Setting:** Copyright 1971 Stanley L. Osborne. Used by permission.
187 **Setting:** Copyright 1952 *Orgelchoralbuch.*[2]
188 **Setting:** Copyright 1969 Concordia Publishing House. Used by permission.
189 **Text:** Copyright John B. Geyer. Used by permission.
190 **Text:** Copyright Judith O'Neill. Used by permission.
191 **Text:** Copyright Harold F. Yardley and Frank J. Whiteley. Used by permission. **Setting:** From the *English Hymnal* by permission of Oxford University Press.
193 **Text:** Copyright Johannes H. V. Knudsen. Used by permission. **Setting:** Copyright 1969 Concordia Publishing House. Used by permission.
195 **Text:** Copyright Thomas E. Herbranson. Used by permission. **Tune and setting:** From *Book of Hymns.* Copyright Abingdon Press. Used by permission.
196 **Text:** Copyright H. C. A. Gaunt. Used by permission. **Setting:** Copyright 1972 Contemporary Worship 4: *Hymns for Baptism and Holy Communion.*[1]
198 **Setting:** Copyright 1978 *Lutheran Book of Worship.*
199 **Setting:** Copyright 1978 *Lutheran Book of Worship.*
200 **Text:** Copyright Robert F. Jeffreys Jr. Used by permission.
201 **Text:** Copyright 1978 *Lutheran Book of Worship.* **Tune and setting:** From the *BBC Hymn Book* by permission of Oxford University Press.
203 **Text:** Copyright Joel W. Lundeen. Used by permission. **Setting:** Copyright 1952 *Orgelchoralbuch.*[2]
204 **Text:** Copyright 1966 World Library Publications, Inc. Used by permission. **Tune and setting:** Copyright 1972 Contemporary Worship 4: *Hymns for Baptism and Holy Communion.*[1]
205 **Text, tune, and setting:** Copyright Jaroslav J. Vajda and Carl F. Schalk. Used by permission.
207 **Text:** tr. Forrest Ingram; tr. David Smith, b. 1923. Copyright 1963 Gooi en Sticht N. V. **Tune:** Copyright 1963 Gooi en Sticht N. V. **Setting:** Copyright 1972 Contemporary Worship 4: *Hymns for Baptism and Holy Communion.*[1]
208 **Text and setting:** Copyright 1978 *Lutheran Book of Worship.*
209 **Text:** From *Enlarged Songs of Praise* by permission of Oxford University Press. **Tune and setting:** By permission of The Church Pension Fund.
210 **Setting:** Copyright 1969 Concordia Publishing House. Used by permission.
211 **Setting:** Copyright 1969 Concordia Publishing House. Used by permission.
212 **Setting:** Copyright 1972 Contemporary Worship 4: *Hymns for Baptism and Holy Communion.*[1]
213 **Text:** Copyright 1941 Concordia Publishing House. Used by permission. **Setting:** Copyright 1978 *Lutheran Book of Worship.*
214 **Text:** Copyright Lutheran World Federation, sts. 1–3. Used by permission. Copyright 1972 Contemporary Worship 4: *Hymns for Baptism and Holy Communion,* st. 4.[1] **Tune:** Copyright Lutheran World Federation. Used by permission. **Setting:** Copyright 1972 Contemporary Worship 4: *Hymns for Baptism and Holy Communion.*[1]
215 **Text:** Copyright 1941 Concordia Publishing House. Used by permission. **Setting:** Copyright 1978 *Lutheran Book of Worship.*
216 **Text:** Copyright © 1972 by The Westminster Press. From *The Worshipbook—Services and Hymns.* Used by permission. **Tune and setting:** From *Hymns and Responses for the Church Year.* Copyright 1956 Elkan-Vogel, Inc. Used by permission.
217 **Setting:** Copyright 1972 Contemporary Worship 4: *Hymns for Baptism and Holy Communion.*[1]
218 **Text:** From the *English Hymnal* by permission of Oxford University Press. **Text and setting:** From *Neue Gemeinde Lieder.* Copyright 1938 Bärenreiter-Verlag, Kassel and Basel. Used by permission.
220 **Setting:** Copyright Yale University Press. Used by permission.
221 **Text:** Copyright 1964 World Library Publications. Used by permission. **Setting:** Copyright 1972 Contemporary Worship 4: *Hymns for Baptism and Holy Communion.*[1]
222 **Text:** tr. Hugh T. Henry, 1862–1946, sts. 1, 3; tr. Philip Schaff, 1819–1893, st. 2; alt.
223 **Text:** Copyright John H. Plumptre. Used by permission. **Tune and setting:** From *Book of Hymns.* Copyright Abingdon Press. Used by permission.
224 **Text:** Copyright 1978 *Lutheran Book of Worship.*
227 **Text:** Copyright 1958 *Service Book and Hymnal.*[3]
228 **Text:** Copyright 1978 *Lutheran Book of Worship.* **Setting:** Copyright 1970 *Neues Choralbuch,* Bärenreiter-Verlag, Kassel and Basel. Used by permission.
229 **Text:** Copyright 1978 *Lutheran Book of Worship.*
230 **Setting:** Copyright 1970 *Neues Choralbuch,* Bärenreiter-Verlag, Kassel and Basel. Used by permission.
232 **Setting:** Copyright 1958 *Service Book and Hymnal.*[3]
233 **Text and setting:** Copyright Concordia Publishing House. Used by permission. **Tune:** Copyright Gwenlyn Evans, Ltd.

236 **Text:** Copyright 1976 Norman P. Olsen. Used by permission. **Tune and setting:** Copyright 1978 *Lutheran Book of Worship.*
237 **Text:** Copyright The Hymn Society of America. Used by permission. **Tune and setting:** Copyright 1978 *Lutheran Book of Worship.*
238 **Text:** From *Ten New Hymns on the Bible.* Copyright The Hymn Society of America. Used by permission. **Tune and setting:** Copyright Derek Holman. Used by permission.
240 **Setting:** Copyright 1978 *Lutheran Book of Worship.*
243 **Setting:** Copyright 1978 *Lutheran Book of Worship.*
244 **Text and tune:** Copyright Augsburg Publishing House. **Setting:** Copyright 1978 *Lutheran Book of Worship.*
246 **Text:** By permission of Oxford University Press. **Setting:** From *The Hymnal of the United Church of Christ.* Copyright 1974 United Church Press. Used by permission.
247 **Text:** Copyright Board of Publication, Lutheran Church in America.
249 **Text:** trs. Frederick W. Foster, 1760–1835, John Miller, 1756–1790, William Mercer, 1811–1873, sts. 1–2; tr. Hermann Brueckner, 1866–1942, sts. 3–4; alt. Copyright Augsburg Publishing House, sts. 3–4.
254 **Setting:** Copyright 1952 *Orgelchoralbuch.*[2]
255 **Text:** Based on *Hymn of the Universe* by Pierre Teilhard de Chardin. Copyright Harper and Row, 1965, Wm. Collins Sons and Co. Ltd. Used by permission. **Tune and setting:** Copyright 1969 Contemporary Worship 1: *Hymns.*[1]
256 **Text:** Copyright 1978 *Lutheran Book of Worship.*
258 **Tune and setting:** Copyright 1978 *Lutheran Book of Worship.*
259 **Setting:** Copyright 1978 *Lutheran Book of Worship.*
260 **Setting:** Copyright 1978 *Lutheran Book of Worship.*
263 **Text:** tr. unknown, sts. 1–2, 4; tr. F. W. Detterer, st. 3; alt.
266 **Setting:** Copyright 1978 *Lutheran Book of Worship.*
267 **Text:** From the *English Hymnal* by permission of Oxford University Press. **Setting:** Copyright 1969 Concordia Publishing House. Used by permission.
268 **Tune and setting:** Copyright Lutheran Church Press and Augsburg Publishing House.
270 **Text:** Copyright 1958 *Service Book and Hymnal.*[3]
271 **Text:** Copyright 1978 *Lutheran Book of Worship.*
273 **Setting:** Copyright 1970 *Neues Choralbuch,* Bärenreiter-Verlag, Kassel and Basel. Used by permission.
275 **Text:** Copyright 1978 *Lutheran Book of Worship.*
276 **Text:** Copyright 1978 *Lutheran Book of Worship.*
277 **Setting:** Copyright 1969 Concordia Publishing House. Used by permission.
279 **Tune and setting:** Copyright 1978 *Lutheran Book of Worship.*
281 **Setting:** From the *English Hymnal* by permission of Oxford University Press.
282 **Text:** Copyright 1941 Concordia Publishing House. Used by permission.
283 **Text:** From *Ten New Hymns on the Ministry.* Copyright 1966 The Hymn Society of America. Used by permission.
284 **Text:** tr. Richard Massie, 1800–1887, sts. 1, 3; tr. Edward Caswall, 1814–1878, sts. 2, 4, 6–7; tr. Robert Campbell, 1814–1868, st. 5; alt.
285 **Text and setting:** Copyright 1978 *Lutheran Book of Worship.*
287 **Text:** By permission of Oxford University Press.
288 **Text:** Copyright 1978 *Lutheran Book of Worship,* sts. 1–2. **Setting:** Copyright 1978 *Lutheran Book of Worship.*
289 **Text:** Copyright 1975 Board of Publication, Lutheran Church in America. **Tune and setting:** Copyright 1958 *Service Book and Hymnal.*[3]
290 **Setting:** Copyright 1969 Concordia Publishing House. Used by permission.
291 **Text:** Copyright 1941 Concordia Publishing House. Used by permission. **Setting:** Copyright 1970 *Neues Choralbuch,* Bärenreiter-Verlag, Kassel and Basel. Used by permission.
292 **Setting:** Copyright 1978 *Lutheran Book of Worship.*
295 **Text:** Copyright 1978 *Lutheran Book of Worship.* **Setting:** Copyright 1952 *Orgelchoralbuch.*[2]
297 **Text:** Copyright 1941 Concordia Publishing House. Used by permission.
299 **Setting:** Copyright 1978 *Lutheran Book of Worship.*
302 **Setting:** Copyright 1978 *Lutheran Book of Worship.*
303 **Setting:** Copyright 1953 *Württembergisches Choralbuch.*[2]
307 **Text:** By permission of Oxford University Press. **Setting:** Copyright 1978 *Lutheran Book of Worship.*
308 **Setting:** Copyright 1978 *Lutheran Book of Worship.*
310 **Setting:** Copyright 1969 Concordia Publishing House. Used by permission.
311 **Text:** Copyright 1978 *Lutheran Book of Worship,* st. 1; Copyright Board of Publication, Lutheran Church in America, st. 2.
312 **Setting:** Copyright 1978 *Lutheran Book of Worship.*
313 **Setting:** Copyright 1978 *Lutheran Book of Worship.*
314 **Text:** Copyright 1978 *Lutheran Book of Worship.*
317 **Text:** Copyright 1969 Concordia Publishing House. Used by permission. **Setting:** Copyright 1953 *Württembergisches Choralbuch.*[2]
319 **Text:** tr. Ernest E. Ryden, b. 1886; tr. Toivo Harjunpaa, b. 1910; alt. From *Laudamus,* 1970. Copyright Lutheran World Federation. Used by permission. **Setting:** From *Songs of Praise* by permission of Oxford University Press.
321 **Setting:** Copyright 1953 *Württembergisches Choralbuch.*[2]
322 **Setting:** Copyright William E. France. Used by permission.
323 **Text:** Copyright 1961, 1962 World Library Publications. Used by permission. **Setting:** Copyright 1978 *Lutheran Book of Worship.*
325 **Setting:** From *Das Wochenlied.* Copyright 1950 Bärenreiter-Verlag. Used by permission.
326 **Text:** Copyright Augsburg Publishing House.
330 **Setting:** Copyright Augsburg Publishing House.
331 **Setting:** Copyright 1939 by J. Fisher and Bro. Copyright renewed 1966. Used with permission. All rights reserved.
333 **Text:** Copyright 1978 *Lutheran Book of Worship.*
334 **Setting:** Copyright 1978 *Lutheran Book of Worship.*
335 **Setting:** Copyright 1978 *Lutheran Book of Worship.*
336 **Tune and setting:** By permission of Oxford University Press.
339 **Text:** Copyright Board of Publication, Lutheran Church in America. **Setting:** From the *Revised Church Hymnary 1927* by permission of Oxford University Press.
340 **Setting:** Copyright 1952 *Orgelchoralbuch.*[2]
342 **Text:** Copyright 1958 *Service Book and Hymnal.*
343 **Text:** tr. William Williams, 1717–1791; tr. Peter Williams, 1722–1796; alt. **Tune and setting:** © by Mrs. Dilys Webb c/o Mechanical-Copyright Protection Society Limited, and reproduced by permission of the legal representatives of the composer, who reserve all rights therein.
347 **Setting:** Copyright 1978 *Lutheran Book of Worship.*
348 **Text:** Copyright 1978 *Lutheran Book of Worship.*
349 **Text:** Copyright 1978 *Lutheran Book of Worship.* **Setting:** Copyright 1952 *Orgelchoralbuch.*[2]
350 **Text:** Copyright 1978 *Lutheran Book of Worship.* **Setting:** Copyright 1953 *Württembergisches Choralbuch.*[2]
351 **Text:** Copyright 1978 *Lutheran Book of Worship.* **Setting:** Copyright 1953 *Württembergisches Choralbuch.*[2]
354 **Text, tune, and setting:** Copyright 1958 *Service Book and Hymnal.*[3]
355 **Tune:** Copyright Gwenlyn Evans, Ltd. **Setting:** Copyright

1969 Concordia Publishing House. Used by permission.
357 **Text:** By permission of The Church Pension Fund. **Setting:** Copyright 1969 Concordia Publishing House. Used by permission.
359 **Text:** From *Bees in Amber* by John Oxenham—first published in U.S.A. in 1913. Copyright in U.S.A. by Fleming Revell Co. Used by permission of Miss T. Dunkerley. **Tune and setting:** Copyright Harry T. Burleigh. Used by permission.
360 **Text:** By permission of Oxford University Press. **Setting:** Copyright 1972 Contemporary Worship 4: *Hymns for Baptism and Holy Communion.*[1]
361 **Text:** Copyright 1978 *Lutheran Book of Worship.*
363 **Text:** By permission of Oxford University Press.
364 **Text:** By permission of Oxford University Press. **Setting:** Copyright F. E. Röntgen. Used by permission.
365 **Text:** Copyright 1958 *Service Book and Hymnal.*[3]
366 **Setting:** Copyright 1969 Concordia Publishing House. Used by permission.
367 **Tune and setting:** From "Christ Is Made the Sure Foundation." Copyright Schmitt, Hall, and McCreary Co. Used by permission.
370 **Setting:** Copyright 1978 *Lutheran Book of Worship.*
371 **Text:** Copyright 1978 *Lutheran Book of Worship.* **Setting:** From *Den Svenska Koralboken,* © 1941 Svenska Kyrkans Diakonistyrelses Bokförlag (AB Verbum).
372 **Text:** Copyright Concordia Publishing House. Used by permission. **Setting:** Copyright 1969 Contemporary Worship 1: *Hymns.*[1]
374 **Text:** Copyright 1941 Concordia Publishing House. Used by permission. **Setting:** Copyright 1978 *Lutheran Book of Worship.*
375 **Setting:** Copyright 1969 Concordia Publishing House. Used by permission.
377 **Text, tune, and setting:** By permission of Hymns Ancient and Modern Ltd.
378 **Text, tune, and setting:** Copyright 1978 *Lutheran Book of Worship.*
379 **Text:** Copyright 1978 *Lutheran Book of Worship.*
380 **Text:** tr. Gilbert E. Doan, b. 1930, sts. 1, 3–5; tr. Catherine Winkworth, 1829–1878, st. 2. Copyright 1978 *Lutheran Book of Worship,* sts. 1, 3–5. **Setting:** Copyright 1970 *Neues Choralbuch,* Bärenreiter-Verlag, Kassel and Basel. Used by permission.
382 **Text:** tr. C. Winfred Douglas, 1867–1944; tr. Arthur W. Farlander, 1898–1952; alt. By permission of The Church Pension Fund.
383 **Text:** Copyright 1978 *Lutheran Book of Worship.*
384 **Text:** From *Laudamus,* 1970. Copyright Lutheran World Federation. Used by permission. **Setting:** Copyright 1978 *Lutheran Book of Worship.*
385 **Setting:** Copyright 1978 *Lutheran Book of Worship.*
386 **Text:** From *Enlarged Songs of Praise* by permission of Oxford University Press. **Tune and setting:** Copyright 1978 *Lutheran Book of Worship.*
387 **Text:** Copyright John W. Arthur. Used by permission. **Tune and setting:** Copyright 1972 Contemporary Worship 4: *Hymns for Baptism and Holy Communion.*[1]
391 **Text:** By permission of Morehouse-Barlow Co., Inc. **Tune:** From the *English Hymnal* by permission of Oxford University Press. **Setting:** Copyright 1978 *Lutheran Book of Worship.*
392 **Text:** Copyright Sir Charles Jeffries. Used by permission. **Setting:** From *Book of Hymns.* Copyright Abingdon Press. Used by permission.
393 **Text, tune, and setting:** Copyright Augsburg Publishing House.
394 **Text:** Copyright Augsburg Publishing House.
395 **Text and setting:** Copyright 1978 *Lutheran Book of Worship.*
396 **Text and tune:** Copyright 1967 Lutheran Council in the U.S.A. Used by permission. **Setting:** Copyright 1969 Concordia Publishing House. Used by permission.
398 **Setting:** Copyright 1969 Concordia Publishing House. Used by permission.
399 **Tune and setting:** Copyright Concordia Publishing House. Used by permission.
400 **Setting:** Copyright 1978 *Lutheran Book of Worship.*
402 **Tune and setting:** By permission of Mr. Arthur Buck and Oxford University Press.
404 **Text:** From *Ten New Stewardship Hymns.* Copyright 1961 The Hymn Society of America. Used by permission. **Tune and setting:** Copyright Augsburg Publishing House.
405 **Text:** Copyright Union of Welsh Independents. Used by permission. **Tune and setting:** From the *BBC Hymn Book* by permission of Oxford University Press.
408 **Text:** From *Ten Stewardship Hymns.* Copyright The Hymn Society of America. Used by permission.
409 **Text:** Copyright Albert F. Bayly. Used by permission. **Setting:** Copyright 1978 *Lutheran Book of Worship.*
411 **Text:** Copyright Albert F. Bayly. Used by permission. **Tune and setting:** Copyright Sydney Watson. Used by permission.
412 **Setting:** Copyright 1969 Concordia Publishing House. Used by permission.
413 **Text:** From *Enlarged Songs of Praise* by permission of Oxford University Press. **Tune and setting:** Used by permission of League of Nations Union.
414 **Setting:** Copyright Concordia Publishing House. Used by permission.
415 **Tune:** © by Mrs. Dilys Webb c/o Mechanical Copyright Protection Society Limited and reproduced by permission of the legal representatives of the composer who reserve all rights therein. **Setting:** Copyright 1969 Concordia Publishing House. Used by permission.
416 **Text:** From *Twelve New World Order Hymns.* Copyright The Hymn Society of America. Used by permission. **Tune and setting:** Copyright 1969 Contemporary Worship 1: *Hymns.*[1]
417 **Text and setting:** Copyright 1978 *Lutheran Book of Worship.* **Tune:** Copyright Seigi Abe. Used by permission of the Christian Conference of Asia.
419 **Text and setting:** Copyright Concordia Publishing House. Used by permission.
420 **Text:** Copyright Albert F. Bayly. Used by permission.
421 **Text:** From *Lift Up Your Hearts.* Copyright Abingdon Press. Used by permission. **Setting:** Copyright 1969 Concordia Publishing House. Used by permission.
422 **Text:** Copyright 1976 Lee McCullough Baldwin. Used by permission. **Tune and setting:** From *Enlarged Songs of Praise* by permission of Oxford University Press.
423 **Text:** From *Seven New Social Welfare Hymns.* Copyright The Hymn Society of America. Used by permission. **Setting:** Copyright 1978 *Lutheran Book of Worship.*
425 **Setting:** Copyright 1978 *Lutheran Book of Worship.*
426 **Text:** Copyright Board of Publication, Lutheran Church in America. **Setting:** Copyright 1978 *Lutheran Book of Worship.*
427 **Text:** From *Five City Hymns.* Copyright 1954 The Hymn Society of America. Used by permission. **Tune and setting:** Copyright Augsburg Publishing House.
428 **Text, tune, and setting:** By permission of Oxford University Press.
430 **Text:** Copyright The Hymn Society of America. Used by permission. **Setting:** From *The Revised Church Hymnary* by permission of Oxford University Press.
431 **Setting:** Copyright 1978 *Lutheran Book of Worship.*
432 **Text:** Copyright 1978 *Lutheran Book of Worship.* **Setting:** Copyright 1969 Concordia Publishing House. Used by permission.

433 **Text:** By permission of Oxford University Press.
434 **Text:** From *Three Youth Hymns.* Copyright 1956 The Hymn Society of America. Used by permission. **Tune:** Copyright Doris Wright Smith. Used by permission. **Setting:** Copyright 1969 Concordia Publishing House. Used by permission.
435 **Tune:** Copyright Augsburg Publishing House. **Setting:** Copyright 1978 *Lutheran Book of Worship.*
436 **Text:** Copyright © 1969 Galliard Ltd. All rights reserved. Used by permission of Galaxy Music Corp., N.Y., sole U.S. agent. **Tune and setting:** By permission of Oxford University Press.
437 **Text:** Copyright estate of William Pierson Merrill. Used by permission. **Tune and setting:** By permission of The Church Pension Fund.
438 **Setting:** From the *English Hymnal* by permission of Oxford University Press.
440 **Setting:** Copyright 1952 *Orgelchoralbuch.*[2]
441 **Text:** From *The Hymn.* Copyright The Hymn Society of America. Used by permission. **Setting:** Copyright 1978 *Lutheran Book of Worship.*
442 **Text:** Copyright Concordia Publishing House. Used by permission. **Setting:** Copyright 1953 *Württembergisches Choralbuch.*[2]
443 **Setting:** Copyright 1952 *Orgelchoralbuch.*[2]
444 **Text:** Copyright Concordia Publishing House. Used by permission. **Setting:** Copyright 1978 *Lutheran Book of Worship.*
446 **Text:** Copyright 1978 *Lutheran Book of Worship.*
447 **Setting:** Copyright 1952 *Orgelchoralbuch.*[2]
448 **Setting:** From *Book of Hymns.* Copyright Abingdon Press. Used by permission.
449 **Text and tune:** © Copyrighted Edward B. Marks Music Corporation. Used by permission. **Setting:** Copyright 1978 *Lutheran Book of Worship.*
450 **Setting:** Copyright 1952 *Orgelchoralbuch.*[2]
451 **Setting:** By permission of Oxford University Press.
452 **Setting:** Copyright 1978 *Lutheran Book of Worship.*
453 **Text:** tr. Catherine Winkworth, 1829–1878, sts. 1, 3–4; tr. Jaroslav J. Vajda, b. 1919, st. 2. Copyright 1978 *Lutheran Book of Worship,* st. 2.
454 **Setting:** Copyright 1953 *Württembergisches Choralbuch.*[2]
455 **Setting:** Copyright 1970 *Neues Choralbuch,* Bärenreiter-Verlag, Kassel and Basel. Used by permission.
457 **Setting:** Copyright 1952 *Orgelchoralbuch.*[2]
459 **Setting:** Copyright 1952 *Orgelchoralbuch.*[2]
460 **Setting:** Copyright 1978 *Lutheran Book of Worship.*
461 **Tune and setting:** From *Book of Hymns.* Copyright Abingdon Press. Used by permission.
463 **Text:** Copyright 1967 Catherine Cameron. Used by permission. **Setting:** Copyright 1969 Contemporary Worship 1: *Hymns.*[1]
465 **Text:** tr. Richard Massie, 1800–1887, sts. 1–2; tr. Hermann Brueckner, 1866–1942, sts. 3–4. Copyright Augsburg Publishing House, sts. 3–4. **Setting:** Copyright 1953 *Württembergisches Choralbuch.*[2]
466 **Text:** Copyright George Utech. Used by permission. **Tune and setting:** Copyright Gerhard Cartford. Used by permission.
468 **Text:** Copyright 1978 *Lutheran Book of Worship.* **Setting:** Copyright 1953 *Württembergisches Choralbuch.*[2]
469 **Text:** From *Enlarged Songs of Praise* by permission of Oxford University Press. **Setting:** From *Book of Hymns.* Copyright Abingdon Press. Used by permission.
470 **Text:** Copyright 1978 *Lutheran Book of Worship.*
471 **Text:** Copyright Lutheran World Federation. Used by permission. **Setting:** Copyright 1978 *Lutheran Book of Worship.*
472 **Setting:** Copyright sons and daughter of the composer. By permission.
473 **Setting:** Copyright 1952 *Orgelchoralbuch.*[2]
474 **Text:** Copyright Board of Publication, Lutheran Church in America.
476 **Text and tune:** Copyright Concordia Publishing House. Used by permission.
478 **Text:** Copyright 1958 *Service Book and Hymnal.*[3]
484 **Text and setting:** Copyright Concordia Publishing House. Used by permission.
485 **Text and setting:** Copyright 1978 *Lutheran Book of Worship.* **Tune:** From *Koraalivirsikirja.* Copyright 1966 Werner Söderström Osakeyhtiö.
487 **Text and setting:** Copyright 1978 *Lutheran Book of Worship.*
489 **Setting:** Copyright 1978 *Lutheran Book of Worship.*
491 **Tune and setting:** Copyright Herbert Howells. Used by permission.
492 **Setting:** Copyright Independent Press. Used by permission.
493 **Text:** From *Eleven Ecumenical Hymns.* Copyright 1954 The Hymn Society of America. Used by permission. **Setting:** Copyright 1969 Concordia Publishing House. Used by permission.
494 **Setting:** Copyright 1978 *Lutheran Book of Worship.*
496 **Text:** tr. Joel W. Lundeen, b. 1918, st. 1; tr. Olof Olsson, 1841–1900, sts. 2–3. Copyright 1978 *Lutheran Book of Worship,* st. 1.
498 **Text:** From the *English Hymnal* by permission of Oxford University Press. **Tune and setting:** By permission of The Church Pension Fund.
500 **Setting:** Copyright 1978 *Lutheran Book of Worship.*
505 **Setting:** Copyright 1969 Concordia Publishing House. Used by permission.
506 **Tune and setting:** Copyright The Psalms and Hymns Trust. Used by permission.
507 **Setting:** Copyright © 1967 by The Bethany Press. Used by permission.
508 **Tune and setting:** From the *English Hymnal* by permission of Oxford University Press.
510 **Text and tune:** Copyright John H. Burt. Used by permission. **Setting:** Copyright 1978 *Lutheran Book of Worship.*
512 **Setting:** Copyright 1978 *Lutheran Book of Worship.*
513 **Tune and setting:** From *Five Mystical Songs.* Copyright 1911 Stainer and Bell, Ltd. Used by permission.
515 **Text:** Copyright 1958 *Service Book and Hymnal.*[3]
516 **Text and setting:** Copyright 1958 *Service Book and Hymnal.*[3]
519 **Setting:** Copyright 1953 *Württembergisches Choralbuch.*[2]
521 **Tune and setting:** From *The Contemporary Liturgy.* Copyright 1963 Lutheran Student Association of America. Used by permission of Lutheran Student Movement.
522 **Setting:** Copyright 1972 The Westminster Press. Used by permission.
523 **Text:** From *The Mirfield Mission Hymn Book.* Copyright A. R. Mowbray and Co. Ltd. Used by permission. **Setting:** Copyright 1969 Concordia Publishing House. Used by permission.
526 **Setting:** Copyright 1969 Concordia Publishing House. Used by permission.
527 **Text:** Copyright J. Curwen and Sons. Used by permission. **Setting:** From the *English Hymnal* by permission of Oxford University Press.
528 **Text and setting:** Copyright 1978 *Lutheran Book of Worship.*
529 **Text:** Copyright Daniel T. Niles. Used by permission of the Christian Conference of Asia. **Tune:** Copyright John Milton Kelly. Used by permission of the Christian Conference of Asia.
531 **Setting:** Copyright 1953 *Württembergisches Choralbuch.*[2]
532 **Text and setting:** © Copyright 1953 by Stuart K. Hine, assigned to Manna Music, Inc. © Copyright 1955 by Manna Music, Inc. 2111 Kenmere Ave., Burbank, CA 91504. Interna-

tional copyright secured. All rights reserved. Used by permission.
536 **Setting:** Copyright 1978 *Lutheran Book of Worship.*
537 **Setting:** Copyright 1978 *Lutheran Book of Worship.*
538 **Text:** From *Morning Praise and Evensong.* © 1973 David F. Wright. Used by permission. **Tune and setting:** Copyright 1978 *Lutheran Book of Worship.*
539 **Text:** Copyright The Lutheran Publishing House. Used by permission. **Setting:** Copyright 1978 *Lutheran Book of Worship.*
541 **Setting:** From *Oxford Book of Carols* by permission of Oxford University Press.
543 **Setting:** Copyright 1952 *Orgelchoralbuch.*[2]
545 **Text:** From the *Yattendon Hymnal* by permission of Oxford University Press. **Setting:** Copyright 1969 Concordia Publishing House.
546 **Text:** From the *Yattendon Hymnal* by permission of Oxford University Press.
550 **Setting:** Copyright 1953 *Württembergisches Choralbuch.*[2]
551 **Text:** "Joyful, joyful, we adore thee" is reprinted by permission of Charles Scribner's Sons from *The Poems of Henry Van Dyke* by Henry Van Dyke.
552 **Setting:** Copyright 1969 Concordia Publishing House. Used by permission.
555 **Text:** By permission of Oxford University Press. **Tune and setting:** Copyright 1978 *Lutheran Book of Worship.*
556 **Text:** Copyright 1977 Moir A. J. Waters. Used by permission. **Tune and setting:** Copyright 1971 David McCarthy. Used by permission.
557 **Text:** Copyright 1939 E. C. Schirmer Music Co. Used by permission. **Setting:** Copyright 1978 *Lutheran Book of Worship.*
558 **Text and tune:** Copyright Augsburg Publishing House. **Setting:** Copyright 1969 Contemporary Worship 1: *Hymns.*[1]
560 **Text:** Copyright 1941 Concordia Publishing House. **Setting:** Copyright 1953 *Württembergisches Choralbuch.*[2]
562 **Text and tune:** © Copyrighted Edward B. Marks Music Corporation. Used by permission.
563 **Text:** By permission of Oxford University Press. **Tune and setting:** Copyright 1978 *Lutheran Book of Worship.*
564 **Setting:** Copyright 1953 *Württembergisches Choralbuch.*[2]
565 **Setting:** Copyright 1953 *Württembergisches Choralbuch.*[2]
568 **Setting:** Copyright 1957 Frederick Harris Music Co. Ltd. Used by permission.

[1] *Copyright administered by the publishers of* Lutheran Book of Worship.
[2] *From Choralbuch zum Evangelischen Kirchengesangbuch Ausgabe für die Evangelische Landeskirche in Württemberg 1952 Verlag des Gesangbuchs und Choralbuchs für die Evangelische Landeskirche in Württemberg, Stuttgart. Used by permission.*
[3] *Copyright administered by Augsburg Publishing House and Board of Publication, Lutheran Church in America.*

HYMNS FOR THE CHURCH YEAR

1 Advent
Savior of the nations, come* 28
Fling wide the door, unbar the gate (ABC)** 32
Wake, awake, for night is flying 31

2 Advent
Comfort, comfort now my people 29
On Jordan's banks the Baptist's cry* (ABC) 36
Prepare the royal highway 26

3 Advent
The only Son from heaven 86
Hark! A thrilling voice is sounding!* (ABC) 37
Hark, the glad sound! The Savior comes 35

4 Advent
Savior of the nations, come 28
Oh, come, oh, come, Emmanuel* (ABC) 34
Come, thou long-expected Jesus 30

Christmas
Once again my heart rejoices 46
From heav'n above to earth I come* (ABC, Luke 2) 51
Of the Father's love begotten* (ABC, John 1) 42
All praise to you, eternal Lord 48

1 Christmas
Let all together praise our God* 47
All praise to you, eternal Lord (AB) 48
In a lowly manger born (C) 417
The only Son from heaven 86

2 Christmas
Of the Father's love begotten* 42
Let all together praise our God (ABC) 47
Let all mortal flesh keep silence 198

Epiphany
Brightest and best of the stars of the morning 84
O Morning Star, how fair and bright!* (ABC) 76
Bright and glorious is the sky 75

Baptism of Our Lord
From God the Father, virgin-born 83
To Jordan came the Christ, our Lord* (ABC) 79
When Christ's appearing was made known 85

2 Epiphany
The only Son from heaven* 86
Jesus calls us; o'er the tumult (AB) 494
All praise to you, O Lord (C) 78
Jesus, priceless treasure* 457, 458

3 Epiphany
O God of light, your Word, a lamp unfailing 237
"Come, follow me," the Savior spake (AB) 455
Hail to the Lord's anointed (C) 87
O Christ, our light, O Radiance true* 380

4 Epiphany
Hope of the world, thou Christ of great compassion* 493
Son of God, eternal Savior (A) 364
Dear Christians, one and all, rejoice (B) 299
God of grace and God of glory (C) 415
Songs of thankfulness and praise 90

5 Epiphany
Hail to the Lord's anointed* 87
May we your precepts, Lord, fulfill (A) 353
O Christ, the healer, we have come (B) 360
Lord, speak to us, that we may speak (C) 403
Your Word, O Lord, is gentle dew 232

6 Epiphany
O Christ, our hope, our heart's desire* 300
Lord Jesus, think on me (A) 309
O Jesus Christ, may grateful hymns be rising (BC) 427
Oh, that the Lord would guide my ways 480

* *Hymns which constitute a contemporary adaptation of the traditional Lutheran* de tempore *series.*
** *The letters A, B, and C are references to lectionary series.*

7 Epiphany
Oh, love, how deep, how broad, how high. 88
O God, O Lord of heav'n and earth* (ABC) 396
Lord, keep us steadfast in your Word .230

8 Epiphany
Sing praise to God, the highest good* 542
Jesus, priceless treasure (A). 457, 458
Salvation unto us has come (B) 297
O God of mercy, God of might (C) 425
As with gladness men of old. 82

Transfiguration
How good, Lord, to be here! 89
Oh, wondrous type! Oh, vision fair* (ABC). 80
O God of God, O Light of light 536

Ash Wednesday
O Lord, throughout these forty days 99
Out of the depths I cry to you* (ABC). 295
Savior, when in dust to you 91

1 Lent
God the Father, be our stay* 308
Who trusts in God, a strong abode (ABC). 450
A mighty fortress is our God* 228, 229

2 Lent
Lord, thee I love with all my heart* 325
O Jesus, joy of loving hearts (A) 356
"Take up your cross," the Savior said (B) 398
O Jesus Christ, may grateful hymns be rising (C). 427
Jesus, refuge of the weary 93

3 Lent
May God bestow on us his grace*. 335
God, whose almighty word (A) 400
O God of earth and altar (B) 428
Jesus, the very thought of you (C). 316
In the cross of Christ I glory. 104

4 Lent
I trust, O Christ, in you alone* 395
Lord of glory, you have bought us (A). 424
God loved the world so that he gave* (B) 292
In Adam we have all been one (C). 372
On my heart imprint your image. 102

5 Lent
My song is love unknown* 94
Glory be to Jesus (ABC) 95
Christ, the life of all the living 97

Sunday of the Passion
The royal banners forward go. 124, 125
A lamb goes uncomplaining forth* (ABC). 105
O sacred head, now wounded. 116, 117

Monday in Holy Week
Beneath the cross of Jesus 107

Tuesday in Holy Week
O Christ, our king, creator, Lord 101

Wednesday in Holy Week
It happened on that fateful night. 127

Maundy Thursday
We who once were dead 207
Love consecrates the humblest act (A) 122
O Lord, we praise you, bless you, and adore you* (BC). . . .215
Thee we adore, O hidden Savior, thee 199

Good Friday
Deep were his wounds, and red 100
Sing my tongue, the glorious battle* (ABC). 118
O sacred head, now wounded. 116, 117

Easter Day
Good Christian friends, rejoice and sing. 144
Christ Jesus lay in death's strong bands* (ABC). 134
At the Lamb's high feast we sing. 210

2 Easter
Come, you faithful, raise the strain 132
O sons and daughters of the King* (ABC) 139
That Easter day with joy was bright 154

3 Easter
With high delight let us unite*. 140
Look, now he stands! Stones could not hold him down
for long (ABC). 152
Now all the vault of heav'n resounds .143

4 Easter
O God of Jacob, by whose hand 477
The King of love my shepherd is* (A) 456
The Lord's my shepherd; I'll not want (B). 451
Savior, like a shepherd lead us (C) 481
I know that my Redeemer lives! 352

5 Easter
At the Lamb's high feast we sing*. 210
You are the way; through you alone (A) 464
Amid the world's bleak wilderness (B) 378
Lord of all nations, grant me grace (C) 419
Jesus, thy boundless love to me 336

6 Easter
Dear Christians, one and all, rejoice* .299
Son of God, eternal Savior (ABC). 364
One there is, above all others 298

Ascension
Up through endless ranks of angels*. .159
Look, oh, look, the sight is glorious (A) 156
Lord, enthroned in heav'nly splendor (B). 172
Alleluia! Sing to Jesus (C). 158
A hymn of glory let us sing! 157

7 Easter
Oh, love, how deep, how broad, how high*. 88
Lord, teach us how to pray aright (A) 438
Have no fear, little flock (B) 476
Lord, receive this company (C) 255

Pentecost
To God the Holy Spirit let us pray 317
Come, Holy Ghost, our souls inspire (A). 472, 473
Come, Holy Ghost, God and Lord* (B). 163
Filled with the Spirit's pow'r, with one accord (C). 160
Lord God, the Holy Ghost 162

Holy Trinity
Creator Spirit, heav'nly dove*. 284
Father most holy, merciful, and tender (ABC) 169
All glory be to God on high. 166

2 Pentecost
To God the Holy Spirit let us pray* 317
My hope is built on nothing less (A). 293, 294
Holy Spirit, truth divine (B) 257
Lord, whose love in humble service (C). 423

3 Pentecost
Jesus sinners will receive (A). 291
Oh, for a thousand tongues to sing (B). 559
When in the hour of deepest need* (C). 303

4 Pentecost
O God, O Lord of heav'n and earth*. .396
Spread, oh, spread, almighty Word (A). 379
Almighty God, your Word is cast (B) .234
O Jesus, joy of loving hearts (C) 356

5 Pentecost
Lord of our life, and God of our salvation* 366
Let me be yours forever (A) 490
Who trusts in God, a strong abode* (B) 450
Christ is made the sure foundation (C) 367

6 Pentecost
Even as we live each day* 350
O God, send heralds who will never falter (AC) 283
O God of mercy, God of light (B) 425

7 Pentecost
O Christ, our light, O Radiance true* 380
Peace, to soothe our bitter woes (A) 338
God moves in a mysterious way (B) 483
Jesus shall reign where'er the sun (C) 530

8 Pentecost
Forth in thy name, O Lord, I go* 505
Almighty God, your Word is cast (A) 234
The Son of God, our Christ, the Word, the Way (B) 434
O God of mercy, God of light (C) 425

9 Pentecost
O Holy Spirit, enter in* 459
On what has now been sown (A) 261
O God of light, your Word, a lamp unfailing (B) 237
Lord, thee I love with all my heart (C) 325

10 Pentecost
From God can nothing move me* 468
O God, O Lord of heav'n and earth (A) 396
Jesus, priceless treasure* (B) 457, 458
Lord, teach us how to pray aright (C) 438

11 Pentecost
Jesus, priceless treasure* 457, 458
Praise and thanksgiving (A) 409
O Bread of life from heaven (B) 222
Son of God, eternal Savior (C) 364

12 Pentecost
If God himself be for me* 454
Eternal Father, strong to save (A) 467
Guide me ever, great Redeemer (B) 343
Rise, my soul, to watch and pray (C) 443

13 Pentecost
When in the hour of deepest need* (A) 303
How blest are they who hear God's Word (B) 227
Lord, keep us steadfast in your Word* (C) 230

14 Pentecost
O Christ, our light, O Radiance true* 380
Built on a rock the Church shall stand (A) 365
Hope of the world, thou Christ of great compassion (B) 493
A multitude comes from the east and the west* (C) 313

15 Pentecost
Son of God, eternal Savior* 364
If God himself be for me (A) 454
To you, omniscient Lord of all* (B) 310
O God of earth and altar (C) 428

16 Pentecost
Praise the Almighty, my soul, adore him!* 539
Lord of all nations, grant me grace* (A) 419
O Son of God, in Galilee (B) 426
Take my life, that I may be (C) 406

17 Pentecost
Forgive our sins as we forgive* (A) 307
Let me be yours forever (B) 490
Jesus sinners will receive* (C) 291

18 Pentecost
Salvation unto us has come* (A) 297
All depends on our possessing (B) 447
Father eternal, ruler of creation (C) 413

19 Pentecost
Lord, keep us steadfast in your Word* 230
O Master, let me walk with you (A) 492
O Jesus, I have promised (B) 503
Oh, praise the Lord, my soul! (C) 538

20 Pentecost
The Church of Christ, in ev'ry age* (A) 433
Our Father, by whose name* (B) 357
O Jesus, I have promised* (C) 503

21 Pentecost
All who believe and are baptized* 194
A multitude comes from the east and the west (A) 313
Thee will I love, my strength, my tow'r (B) 502
Your hand, O Lord, in days of old (C) 431

22 Pentecost
Forth in thy name, O Lord, I go* 505
Father eternal, ruler of creation (A) 413
God, who stretched the spangled heavens (B) 463
Out of the depths I cry to you (C) 295

23 Pentecost
Lord, teach us how to pray aright* 438
Oh, that the Lord would guide my ways (A) 480
Oh, praise the Lord, my soul! (B) 538
To you, omniscient Lord of all* (C) 310

24 Pentecost
Love divine, all loves excelling* 315
Wake, awake, for night is flying* (A) 31
Lord of light, your name outshining (B) 405
If you but trust in God to guide you (C) 453

25 Pentecost
Rejoice, angelic choirs, rejoice!* 146
Forth in thy name, O Lord, I go (A) 505
As saints of old their firstfruits brought (B) 404
I know that my Redeemer lives! (C) 352

26 Pentecost
O God of earth and altar* (A) 428
Through the night of doubt and sorrow* (B) 355
Fight the good fight with all your might* (C) 461

27 Pentecost
The day is surely drawing near* 321
Rise, O children of salvation (A) 182
Rejoice, rejoice, believers (B) 25
Lord Christ, when first you came to earth* 421

Christ the King
Rejoice, the Lord is king! 171
The day is surely drawing near* (A) 321
At the name of Jesus* (B) 179
O Jesus, king most wonderful! (C) 537
The head that once was crowned with thorns 173

See Topical Index of Hymns to make selections for Lesser Festivals, Commemorations, Occasions.

TOPICAL INDEX OF HYMNS

Adoration
See Praise, Adoration, 514–551

Advent, 22–38
Lord Christ, when first you came to earth 421
Lost in the night do the people yet languish 394
O Lord of light, who made the stars 323
Once he came in blessing 312
The clouds of judgment gather 322
The day is surely drawing near 321

Affirmation of Baptism
Baptized into your name most holy 192
"Come, follow me," the Savior spake 455
Come, gracious Spirit, heav'nly dove 475
Come, oh, come, O quick'ning Spirit 478
Eternal God, before your throne we bend 354
Lord, take my hand and lead me 333
Spirit of God, unleashed on earth 387
See Commitment, 486–513; Pentecost, 160–164

Affliction
See Comfort and Rest

All Saints' Day
For all the saints who from their labors rest 174
For all your saints, O Lord 176
Oh, what their joy and their glory must be 337
Who is this host arrayed in white 314

Angels
God himself is present 249
Holy God, we praise your name 535
Ye watchers and ye holy ones 175
See Christmas, 39–74

Anniversary, Church
Built on a rock the Church shall stand 365
Christians, while on earth abiding 440
O God, our help in ages past 320

Annunciation of Our Lord, The
From east to west, from shore to shore 64
My soul now magnifies the Lord 180
Of the Father's love begotten 42
The only Son from heaven 86

Arts and Music
Let all things now living 557
When in our music God is glorified 555
See Creation

Ascension, 156–159
And have the bright immensities 391
At the name of Jesus 179
Crown him with many crowns 170
Lord, enthroned in heav'nly splendor 172
O Christ, our hope, our hearts' desire 300
Rejoice, the Lord is King! 171

Ash Wednesday
O Lord, throughout these forty days 99
See Lent, 91–107; Repentance, Forgiveness, 303–312; Sorrow

Aspiration
As pants the hart for cooling streams 452
Jesus, thy boundless love to me 336
Love divine, all loves excelling 315
O Christ, our hope, our hearts' desire 300
O Love that will not let me go 324
You are the way; through you alone 464

Assurance
I heard the voice of Jesus say 497
Jesus, priceless treasure 457, 458
Praise the Almighty, my soul, adore him! 539
There's a wideness in God's mercy 290
What a friend we have in Jesus 439
See Trust, Guidance, 445–485

Atonement
Christ, the life of all the living 97
In a lowly manger born 417
Jesus, refuge of the weary 93
Jesus, your blood and righteousness 302
My hope is built on nothing less 293, 294
My song is love unknown 94
There's a wideness in God's mercy 290
To you, omniscient Lord of all 310
Victim Divine, your grace we claim 202
When I survey the wondrous cross 482

Baptism, Christian
See Holy Baptism, 187–195

Baptism of Our Lord, The
From God the Father, virgin-born 83
On Jordan's banks the Baptist's cry 36
To Jordan came the Christ, our Lord 79

Beginning of Service, 241–257
Arise, my soul, arise! 516
Around you, O Lord Jesus 496
Blessing and honor and glory and pow'r 525
Come, Holy Ghost, God and Lord 163
Come, thou almighty King 522
Father, most holy, merciful, and tender 169
Holy God, we praise your name 535
Jesus shall reign where'er the sun 530
Let us with a gladsome mind 521
Lord God, the Holy Ghost 162
Now the silence 205
O day full of grace that now we see 161
Oh, for a thousand tongues to sing 559
O God of life's great mystery 201
O Holy Spirit, enter in 459
O Jesus Christ, may grateful hymns be rising 427
Oh, worship the King, all glorious above 548

Benevolence
See Stewardship; Offertory

Bible
See Scriptures

Burial
For all the saints who from their labors rest 174
I know of a sleep in Jesus' name 342
Jesus Christ, my sure defense 340
O God, our help in ages past 320
O Holy Spirit, enter in 459
Oh, what their joy and their glory must be 337
Who is this host arrayed in white 314

Celebration, Jubilation, 552–565
All hail the pow'r of Jesus' name! 328, 329
Come, let us join our cheerful songs 254
Love divine, all loves excelling 315
Oh, sing jubilee to the Lord, ev'ry land 256
What wondrous love is this, O my soul, O my soul! 385
Ye watchers and ye holy ones 175

Christ the King, 170–173
All hail the pow'r of Jesus' name.................. 328, 329
At the name of Jesus..................................179
Christ is alive! Let Christians sing....................363
Christ is the King! O friends, rejoice...................386
Jesus shall reign where'er the sun.....................530
O Jesus, King most wonderful!.........................537
The King shall come when morning dawns...............33

Christmas, 39–74

Church
See Community in Christ, 353–375; Kingdom of God

Church Building
Christ is made the sure foundation.....................367
Only-begotten, Word of God eternal....................375
See Cornerstone

Church Triumphant
A mighty fortress is our God...................... 228, 229
Have no fear, little flock...............................476
Lift high the cross, the love of Christ proclaim...........377
Lo! He comes with clouds descending....................27
Rise, O children of salvation............................182
The Church's one foundation...........................369
See Hope

City
All who love and serve your city........................436
O Jesus Christ, may grateful hymns be rising............427
Where cross the crowded ways of life....................429
Where restless crowds are thronging....................430
See Society, 413–437

Close of Service, 258–263
Almighty God, your Word is cast.......................234
How blest are they who hear God's Word...............227
I leave, as you have promised, Lord.....................349
May God bestow on us his grace.......................335
Now thank we all our God........................ 533, 534
O Lord, now let your servant..........................339
O Savior, precious Savior..............................514
Only-begotten, Word of God eternal....................375
Peace, to soothe our bitter woes........................338
Praise and thanks and adoration.......................470
Praise the Lord, rise up rejoicing.......................196
Sent forth by God's blessing...........................221
Sing praise to God, the highest good...................542

Comfort and Rest
Abide with me, fast falls the eventide...................272
Children of the heav'nly Father.........................474
God moves in a mysterious way........................483
Hope of the world, thou Christ of great compassion.......493
How sweet the name of Jesus sounds...................345
If God himself be for me..............................454
If you but trust in God to guide you...................453
In the hour of trial...................................106
Jesus, priceless treasure.......................... 457, 458
O God, my faithful God...............................504
Peace, to soothe our bitter woes........................338
The King of love my shepherd is.......................456
The Lord's my shepherd; I'll not want..................451
Whatever God ordains is right.........................446
When in the hour of deepest need......................303
When peace, like a river, attendeth my way.............346
Who trusts in God, a strong abode.....................450

Commemorations and Occasions
Saints
For all your saints, O Lord............................176
Martyrs
Jerusalem the golden.................................347
Missionaries
Lift high the cross, the love of Christ proclaim...........377
Renewers of the Church
Rise, shine, you people! Christ the Lord has entered......393
Renewers of Society
Christ is alive! Let Christians sing......................363
Pastors and Bishops
Bow down your ear, almighty Lord......................286
Theologians
God has spoken by his prophets........................238
Artists and Scientists
When in our music God is glorified.....................555
See Creation
Unity
In Christ there is no east or west........................359
Dedication, Anniversary
How blessed is this place, O Lord.......................186
Harvest
See Harvest
Day of Penitence
See Repentance, Forgiveness, 303–312; Sorrow
National Holiday
See National Songs, 566–569; Society, 413–437
Peace
See Peace
Day of Thanksgiving
See Thanksgiving
Stewardship of Creation
See Creation; Harvest; Stewardship
New Year's Eve
See New Year

Commissioning, Lay Ministry
See Commitment, 486–513

Commitment, 486–513
Children of the heav'nly Father.........................474
Fight the good fight with all your might.................461
I lay my sins on Jesus.................................305
In the hour of trial...................................106
Jesus, thy boundless love to me........................336
Lord, speak to us, that we may speak...................403
May we your precepts, Lord, fulfill.....................353
O Lord, now let your servant...........................339
O Love that will not let me go..........................324
Rise, my soul, to watch and pray........................443
Rise up, O saints of God!..............................383
Take my life, that I may be............................406
"Take up your cross," the Savior said....................398
With the Lord begin your task..........................444

Communion of Saints
See Community in Christ, 353–375

Community in Christ, 353–375
A mighty fortress is our God...................... 228, 229
God, my Lord, my strength, my place of hiding..........484
Lord, receive this company............................255
My soul, now praise your maker!.......................519
Oh, blest the house, whate'er befall.....................512
O God, O Lord of heav'n and earth.....................396
O God of Jacob, by whose hand.........................477
Oh, sing, my soul, your maker's praise..................319
Spirit of God, sent from heaven abroad..................285
The head that once was crowned with thorns............173
Where charity and love prevail..........................126
See Kingdom of God

Confession of Sin
See Repentance, Forgiveness, 303–312

Confirmation
See Affirmation of Baptism; Commitment, 486–513; Pentecost, 160–164

Consecration
See Commitment, 486–513
Cornerstone
Great God, a blessing from your throne..................185
See Church Building
Creation
All creatures of our God and King......................527
Eternal Ruler of the ceaseless round.....................373
For the beauty of the earth.............................561
For the fruit of all creation.............................563
God, who stretched the spangled heavens................463
Great God, our source and Lord of space................466
How marvelous God's greatness.........................515
Joyful, joyful we adore thee............................551
Let all things now living...............................557
Let the whole creation cry..............................242
Praise the Lord of heaven!.............................541
Sing to the Lord of harvest.............................412
This is my Father's world..............................554
We plow the fields and scatter..........................362
Cross-bearing
Beneath the cross of Jesus..............................107
In the cross of Christ I glory............................104
Jesus, I will ponder now...............................115
Let us ever walk with Jesus.............................487
O God, my faithful God...............................504
"Take up your cross," the Savior said....................398
See Commitment, 486–513
Deaconesses and Deacons
See Commitment, 486–513; Pastors, 283–286
Death
A Lamb goes uncomplaining forth......................105
Even as we live each day...............................350
God loved the world so that he gave....................292
Guide me ever, great Redeemer.........................343
He leadeth me: oh, blessed thought!.....................501
I know of a sleep in Jesus' name........................342
Jesus Christ, my sure defense...........................340
Jesus lives! The vict'ry's won!...........................133
Jesus sinners will receive...............................291
My faith looks up to thee..............................479
O God, whose will is life and good.....................435
O Lord, now let your servant..........................339
O sacred head, now wounded...................... 116, 117
The King of love my shepherd is........................456
The Lord's my shepherd; I'll not want...................451
We are the Lord's. His all-sufficient merit...............399
Dedication of a Church
Built on a rock the Church shall stand...................365
Christ is made the sure foundation......................367
Glories of your name are spoken........................358
How blessed is this place, O Lord.......................186
I love your kingdom, Lord.............................368
Open now thy gates of beauty..........................250
Discipleship
See Witness, 376–403; Commitment, 486–513
Earth
See Creation
Easter, 128–155
Alleluia! Sing to Jesus................................158
At the Lamb's high feast we sing........................210
Come, risen Lord, and deign to be our guest.............209
Hosanna to the living Lord!............................258
I know that my Redeemer lives!........................352
Jesus Christ, my sure defense...........................340
O Christ, our hope, our hearts' desire....................300
Education
Christ is made the sure foundation......................367
Come, Holy Ghost, our souls inspire................ 472, 473
Earth and all stars!...................................558
Father of mercies, in your Word........................240
God has spoken by his prophets........................238
God's Word is our great heritage........................239
Holy Spirit, truth divine................................257
Lead on, O King eternal!...............................495
Lord, speak to us, that we may speak....................403
O God of light, your Word, a lamp unfailing.............237
O God of youth, whose Spirit in our hearts is stirring.....510
You are the way; through you alone.....................464
Entrance
See Beginning of Service, 241–257
Epiphany, 75–90
Angels from the realms of glory..........................50
Christ, whose glory fills the skies........................265
O Christ, you are the light and day......................273
Oh, for a thousand tongues to sing......................559
O God of God, O Light of Light........................536
O splendor of the Father's light.........................271
Eternal Life
See Hope; Life Everlasting
Evangelism
Herald, sound the note of judgment.....................556
Jesus shall reign where'er the sun.......................530
Oh, for a thousand tongues to sing......................559
O God of mercy, God of light..........................425
Spirit of God, sent from heaven abroad..................285
The Church of Christ, in ev'ry age......................433
See Witness, 376–403
Evening, 272–282
Faith
Amid the world's bleak wilderness.......................378
Faith of our fathers, living still..........................500
God moves in a mysterious way.........................483
How firm a foundation, O saints of the Lord.............507
I heard the voice of Jesus say...........................497
Jesus Christ, my sure defense...........................340
My faith looks up to thee..............................479
O Jesus, joy of loving hearts............................356
O Master, let me walk with you.........................492
Rock of ages, cleft for me..............................327
You are the way; through you alone.....................464
See Justification, 290–302
Family
Children of the heav'nly Father.........................474
For the beauty of the earth.............................561
I am so glad each Christmas Eve..........................69
Oh, blest the house, whate'er befall.....................512
Our Father, by whose name............................357
Fellowship
See Community in Christ, 353–375
Forgiveness
See Repentance, Forgiveness, 303–312
Good Friday
See Holy Week, 108–127
Grace
Alas! And did my Savior bleed..........................98
Amazing grace, how sweet the sound....................448
Come, thou Fount of ev'ry blessing......................499
Give to our God immortal praise!.......................520
O Jesus, joy of loving hearts............................356
Praise, my soul, the King of heaven.....................549
There's a wideness in God's mercy......................290
Wide open are your hands.............................489

Guidance
See Trust, Guidance, 445–485

Harvest
Come, you thankful people, come 407
Praise and thanksgiving 409
Sing to the Lord of harvest 412
We plow the fields and scatter 362
See Creation

Healing
God loved the world so that he gave 292
O Christ, the healer, we have come 360
O God, whose will is life and good 435
O Son of God, in Galilee 426
Your hand, O Lord, in days of old 431

Heaven
A multitude comes from the east and the west 313
All hail to you, O blessed morn! 73
In heav'n above, in heav'n above 330
Jerusalem, my happy home 331
Jerusalem, whose towers touch the skies 348
Oh, happy day when we shall stand 351
Oh, that I had a thousand voices 560
Who is this host arrayed in white 314

Holiness
See Justification, 290–302; Pentecost, 160–164; Trust, Guidance, 445–485

Holy Baptism, 187–195
Spirit of God, unleashed on earth 387

Holy Communion, 196–226
Alleluia! Sing to Jesus 158
Arise, my soul, arise! 516
Around you, O Lord Jesus 496
It happened on that fateful night 127
Lord, enthroned in heav'nly splendor 172
Lord, receive this company 255
Of the glorious body telling 120
Only-begotten, Word of God eternal 375
With God as our friend, with his Spirit and Word 371
See Praise, Adoration, 514–551

Holy Cross Day
Sing, my tongue, the glorious battle 118
We sing the praise of him who died 344
When I survey the wondrous cross 482

Holy Innocents, Martyrs
By all your saints in warfare 177, 178

Holy Spirit
See Commitment, 486–513; Pentecost, 160–164; Witness, 376–403

Holy Trinity, The, 165–169
Come, thou almighty King 522
Eternal God, before your throne we bend 354
God the Father, be our stay 308
God whose almighty Word 400
Holy God, we praise your name 535
Holy Spirit, truth divine 257
I bind unto myself today 188
O Trinity, O blessed Light 275
We all believe in one true God 374

Holy Week, 108–127

Home
See Family

Hope (Christian Hope), 313–352
As pants the hart for cooling streams 452
Glories of your name are spoken 358
Jesus lives! The vict'ry's won! 133
Kyrie! God, Father in heav'n above 168
Let us ever walk with Jesus 487
Lord our God, with praise we come before you 244
My heart is longing to praise my Savior 326
O day full of grace that now we see 161
O Savior, rend the heavens wide 38
O Son of God, in Galilee 426
Rise, O children of salvation 182
Spirit of God, unleashed on earth 387
The King shall come when morning dawns 33
We worship you, O God of might 432
Your kingdom come, O Father 384
See Heaven; Life Everlasting

Hospitals
See Healing

House of God
See Church Building; Dedication of a Church

Humility
Come down, O Love divine 508
Lord Jesus, think on me 309
Lord, teach us how to pray aright 438
To you, omniscient Lord of all 310

Immortality
See Hope; Life Everlasting

Inner Life
Breathe on me, breath of God 488
Come down, O Love divine 508
Dear Lord and Father of mankind 506
Eternal Spirit of the living Christ 441
He leadeth me: oh, blessed thought! 501
Here, O my Lord, I see thee face to face 211
How sweet the name of Jesus sounds 345
Jesus, the very thought of you 316
Jesus, thy boundless love to me 336
O Jesus, king most wonderful! 537
Spirit of God, descend upon my heart 486

Installation
See Pastors, 283–286

Invitation
Come to Calv'ry's holy mountain 301
Hark, the voice of Jesus calling 381
I heard the voice of Jesus say 497
Jesus calls us; o'er the tumult 494
Jesus sinners will receive 291
There's a wideness in God's mercy 290
Today your mercy calls us 304

Invocation
Come down, O Love divine 508
Come, Holy Ghost, our souls inspire 472, 473
Come, thou almighty King 522
Eternal God, before your throne we bend 354
Holy God, we praise your name 535
O Holy Spirit, enter in 459
O Trinity, O blessed Light 275
See Beginning of Service, 241–257

Judgment
Herald, sound the note of judgment 556
Judge eternal, throned in splendor 418
Lo! He comes with clouds descending 27
O Lord of light, who made the stars 323
O Spirit of the living God 388
The clouds of judgment gather 322
The day is surely drawing near 321
The King shall come when morning dawns 33
The Lord will come and not be slow 318
Wake, awake, for night is flying 31

Justification, 290–302
If God himself be for me 454
Let me be yours forever.....490
Lord of glory, you have bought us 424
My heart is longing to praise my Savior.....326
My soul, now praise your maker! 519
O God, I love thee; not that my poor love 491
The head that once was crowned with thorns 173
We all believe in one true God 374
What wondrous love is this, O my soul, O my soul! 385
When peace, like a river, attendeth my way 346
Wide open are your hands 489

Kingdom of God
Father eternal, ruler of creation.....413
Hail to the Lord's anointed.....87
I love your kingdom, Lord 368
Lord, keep us steadfast in your Word.....230
The Lord will come and not be slow 318
Your kingdom come! O Father, hear our prayer 376
Your kingdom come, O Father.....384
See Community in Christ, 353–375

Labor, Laborers
See Society, 413–437; Work, Daily

Last Things
See Hope, 313–352; Judgment

Lent, 91–107
Come to Calv'ry's holy mountain.....301
Lord Christ, when first you came to earth 421
O God, I love thee; not that my poor love 491
Oh, love, how deep, how broad, how high.....88
When I survey the wondrous cross 482
Wide open are your hands 489
See Repentance, Forgiveness, 303–312

Lesser Festivals, 174–186
See specific day; Saints' Days

Life, Christian
Let us ever walk with Jesus.....487
Love divine, all loves excelling.....315
O God of mercy, God of light 425
O God, my faithful God 504
O Jesus, I have promised.....503
O Master, let me walk with you.....492
Oh, that the Lord would guide my ways 480
On my heart imprint your image.....102
See Commitment, 486–513; Justification, 290–302; Trust, Guidance, 445–485

Life Everlasting
Arise, my soul, arise! 516
Let me be yours forever.....490
O Morning Star, how fair and bright 76
Oh, what their joy and their glory must be 337
The God of Abr'ham praise 544
What wondrous love is this, O my soul, O my soul 385
See Hope, Christian, 313–352

Lord's Supper
See Holy Communion, 196–226

Love
Blest be the tie that binds 370
Chief of sinners though I be.....306
In Christ there is no east or west.....359
Jesus, refuge of the weary 93
Jesus, thy boundless love to me 336
Joyful, joyful we adore thee 551
Lord of all nations, grant me grace.....419
Lord, speak to us, that we may speak.....403
O God, I love thee; not that my poor love 491
O God of love, O King of peace.....414
O Master, let me walk with you.....492
One there is, above all others.....298
Son of God, eternal Savior 364
Thee will I love, my strength, my tow'r 502
What wondrous love is this, O my soul, O my soul! 385
Where cross the crowded ways of life.....429

Marriage, 287–289
Eternal God, before your throne we bend 354

Maundy Thursday
See Holy Week, 108–127

Means of Grace
See Holy Baptism, 187–195; Holy Communion, 196–226; The Word, 227–240

Mercy
In a lowly manger born.....417
Let us with a gladsome mind 521
Love divine, all loves excelling.....315
O God of mercy, God of light 425
Out of the depths I cry to you 295
There's a wideness in God's mercy 290
When all your mercies, O my God 264

Mission, Missions
See Commitment, 486–513; Pilgrimage; Society, 413–437; Witness, 376–403

Morning, 264–271
When morning gilds the skies..... 545, 546
With the Lord begin your task.....444

Music
See Arts and Music

Name of Jesus, The
All hail the pow'r of Jesus' name!..... 328, 329
At the name of Jesus 179
How sweet the name of Jesus sounds 345
Oh, for a thousand tongues to sing 559
O Savior, precious Savior 514

Nation
Before you, Lord, we bow.....401
God the omnipotent! King who ordainest 462
Judge eternal, throned in splendor.....418
Lift ev'ry voice and sing 562
Not alone for mighty empire 437
O God of earth and altar 428
O God of ev'ry nation 416
See Society, 413–437

National Songs, 566–569

Nature
See Creation

Neighbor
See Commitment, 486–513; Love; Society, 413–437; Service

New Year
Greet now the swiftly changing year.....181
O God, our help in ages past.....320

Obedience
See Service

Occasions
See Commemorations and Occasions

Offerings
See Stewardship, 404–412

Offertory
As saints of old their firstfruits brought 404
Lord of all good, our gifts we bring you now 411
Lord, receive this company.....255
We place upon your table, Lord.....217

Ordination
See Pastors, 283–286; Pentecost, 160–164
Palm Sunday (Sunday of the Passion)
See Holy Week, 108–127
Passion of Christ
See Holy Week, 108–127
Passion, Sunday of the
See Holy Week, 108–127
Pastors, 283–286
Come, Holy Ghost, our souls inspire................ 472, 473
Come, oh, come, O quick'ning Spirit 478
Creator Spirit, by whose aid............................164
Holy Spirit, ever dwelling..............................523
Spirit of God, unleashed on earth.......................387
Peace
God the omnipotent, King who ordainest 462
Grant peace, we pray, in mercy, Lord 471
Great God, our source and Lord of space................466
Lord of our life and God of our salvation................366
O God of ev'ry nation..................................416
O God of love, O King of peace.........................414
Penitence
See Repentance, Forgiveness, 303–312
Pentecost, 160–164
Creator Spirit, heav'nly dove............................284
O Holy Spirit, enter in..................................459
Spirit of God, sent from heaven abroad..................285
Spirit of God, unleashed on earth........................387
Pilgrimage
All who would valiant be 498
God of our fathers, whose almighty hand 567
Guide me ever, great Redeemer..........................343
Jesus, Savior, pilot me 334
Jesus, still lead on.....................................341
Lord, as a pilgrim on earth I go.........................485
Lord, dismiss us with your blessing......................259
O God of Jacob, by whose hand.........................477
O Word of God incarnate...............................231
Savior, like a shepherd lead us..........................481
The King of love my shepherd is........................456
The Lord's my shepherd; I'll not want....................451
Through the night of doubt and sorrow..................355
Praise, Adoration, 514–551
All glory be to God on high............................166
All hail the pow'r of Jesus' name!.................. 328, 329
All people that on earth do dwell 245
Glory be to God the Father! 167
God himself is present..................................249
Holy Majesty, before you 247
Holy Spirit, ever dwelling 523
Hosanna to the living Lord! 258
How sweet the name of Jesus sounds....................345
Let the whole creation cry..............................242
Lift high the cross, the love of Christ proclaim............377
Lord our God, with praise we come before you...........244
Lord, with glowing heart I'd praise thee..................243
My heart is longing to praise my Savior..................326
My soul now magnifies the Lord 180
O Trinity, O blessed Light..............................275
Praise and thanks and adoration 470
Praise and thanksgiving be to God our maker 191
Rejoice, the Lord is King!..............................171
Thy strong word did cleave the darkness.................233
We praise you, O God, our redeemer, creator............241
We sing the praise of him who died 344
When all your mercies, O my God......................264
You servants of God, your master proclaim..............252
Prayer, 438–444
Lord, keep us steadfast in your Word....................230
With God as our friend, with his Spirit and Word.........371
Presentation of Our Lord, The
In his temple now behold him..........................184
Processions
Hail thee, festival day!.................................142
Lift high the cross, the love of Christ proclaim............377
Rejoice, O pilgrim throng!..............................553
Proclamation
See The Word, 227–240; Witness, 376–403
Providence
See Creation; Thanksgiving, Day of
Reception
See Affirmation of Baptism; Community in Christ, 353–375
Redeemer
See Justification, 290–302
Races and Cultures
In Christ there is no east or west........................359
Sent forth by God's blessing............................221
See Community in Christ, 353–375; Society, 413–437
Reformation Day
A mighty fortress is our God 228, 229
God's Word is our great heritage........................239
Lord, keep us steadfast in your Word....................230
O God, O Lord of heav'n and earth.....................396
The Church's one foundation 369
See Community in Christ, 353–375; Justification, 290–302
Repentance, Forgiveness, 303–312
Christians, while on earth abiding.......................440
I trust, O Christ, in you alone 395
Out of the depths I cry to you..........................295
Rest
See Comfort and Rest
Restoration
See Affirmation of Baptism; Commitment, 486–513; Repentance, Forgiveness, 303–312
Resurrection
See Easter, 128–155; Hope, Christian, 313–352
Rogation
See Creation; Thanksgiving, Day of
Sacraments
See Holy Baptism, 187–195; Holy Communion, 196–226
Saints' Days
By all your saints in warfare....................... 177, 178
For all your saints, O Lord.............................176
Rise, O children of salvation............................182
St. Andrew, Apostle
Jesus calls us; o'er the tumult...........................494
St. Thomas, Apostle
You are the way; through you alone.....................464
St. Stephen, Deacon and Martyr
The Son of God goes forth to war.......................183
Confession of St. Peter, The
O God, I love thee; not that my poor love 491
Conversion of St. Paul, The
O Lord, send forth your Spirit..........................392
St. Peter and St. Paul, Apostles
The head that once was crowned with thorns............173
St. Mary Magdalene
Hallelujah! Jesus lives!.................................147
Mary, Mother of Our Lord
My soul now magnifies the Lord 180
Ye watchers and ye holy ones...........................175

St. Michael and All Angels
God himself is present 249

Salvation
See Grace; Justification, 290–302

Sanctification
See Commitment, 486–513; Pentecost, 160–164; Trust, Guidance, 445–485

Schools
See Education

Scriptures
Father of mercies, in your Word 240
How blest are they who hear God's Word 227
O God of light, your Word, a lamp unfailing 237

Second Coming of Christ
See Hope; Judgment; Watchfulness

Service
As saints of old their firstfruits brought 404
Filled with the Spirit's pow'r with one accord 160
God of grace and God of glory 415
God, whose giving knows no ending 408
In Christ there is no east or west 359
Lord, whose love in humble service 423
Love consecrates the humblest act 122
O God of youth, whose Spirit in our hearts is stirring 510
O Master, let me walk with you 492
Son of God, eternal Savior 364
We give thee but thine own 410

Sickness
See Healing

Sin, Confession of
See Repentance, Forgiveness, 303–312

Society, 413–437
Before you, Lord, we bow 401
Christ is alive! Let Christians sing 363
Eternal Ruler of the ceaseless round 373
God the omnipotent! King who ordainest 462
God, who stretched the spangled heavens 463
Great God, our source and Lord of space 466
Hope of the world, thou Christ of great compassion 493
In Adam we have all been one 372
In Christ there is no east or west 359
O God, O Lord of heav'n and earth 396
Son of God, eternal Savior 364
Thy strong word did cleave the darkness 233

Social Justice
See Society, 413–437

Sorrow
If God himself be for me 454
If you but trust in God to guide you 453
In the hour of trial 106
Oh, sing, my soul, your maker's praise 319
Out of the depths I cry to you 295
See Comfort and Rest

Stewardship, 404–412
O God of mercy, God of light 425
Son of God, eternal Savior 364
We plow the fields and scatter 362
See Commitment, 486–513; Creation; Offertory

Sunday
O day of rest and gladness 251
The first day of the week 246
See Easter, 128–155

Teachers
See Education; Commitment, 486–513

Temptation
If you but trust in God to guide you 453
In the hour of trial 106
O Jesus, I have promised 503
What a friend we have in Jesus 439

Thanksgiving, Day of
Come, you thankful people, come 407
For the fruit of all creation 563
Let all things now living 557
Now thank we all our God 533, 534
Praise and thanksgiving 409
Sing to the Lord of harvest 412
We praise you, O God, our redeemer, creator 241
When all your mercies, O my God 264

Transfiguration of Our Lord, The
How good, Lord, to be here! 89
Oh, wondrous type! Oh, vision fair 80

Travelers
Eternal Father, strong to save 467
See Pilgrimage

Trial
See Comfort and Rest; Sorrow

Trinity
See Holy Trinity

Trust, Guidance, 445–485
Beneath the cross of Jesus 107
Do not despair, O little flock 361
Eternal Spirit of the living Christ 441
God of our life, all-glorious Lord 270
Guide me ever, great Redeemer 343
He leadeth me: Oh, blessed thought! 501
How firm a foundation, O saints of the Lord 507
I bind unto myself today 188
I lay my sins on Jesus 305
I trust, O Christ, in you alone 395
In the cross of Christ I glory 104
In thee is gladness 552
Jesus calls us; o'er the tumult 494
Jesus, Savior, pilot me 334
Jesus, still lead on 341
Lead on, O King eternal! 495
Lift ev'ry voice and sing 562
Lord of our life and God of our salvation 366
Lord, take my hand and lead me 333
Lord, thee I love with all my heart 325
My heart is longing to praise my Savior 326
My hope is built on nothing less 293, 294
O God, our help in ages past 320
O one with God the Father 77
Oh, sing, my soul, your maker's praise 319
On my heart imprint your image 102
Out of the depths I cry to you 295
We are the Lord's. His all-sufficient merit 399
With the Lord begin your task 444

Visitation, The
The only Son from heaven 86

Watchfulness
Awake, my soul, and with the sun 269
Oh, that the Lord would guide my ways 480
Rise, my soul, to watch and pray 443
Rise up, O saints of God! 383
Wake, awake, for night is flying 31

Warfare, Christian
By all your saints in warfare 177, 178
Fight the good fight with all your might 461
Lead on, O King eternal! 495

Onward, Christian soldiers. 509
Stand up, stand up for Jesus. 389
The Son of God goes forth to war. 183
We are the Lord's. His all-sufficient merit 399

Witness, 376–403
At the name of Jesus 179
Crown him with many crowns 170
Filled with the Spirit's pow'r, with one accord 160
God the omnipotent! King who ordainest 462
Herald, sound the note of judgment 556
Holy Spirit, ever dwelling 523
In Adam we have all been one 372
Jesus shall reign where'er the sun 530
Look, oh, look, the sight is glorious. 156
Lord, keep us steadfast in your Word. 230
O day full of grace that now we see 161
Oh, for a thousand tongues to sing 559
O God, send heralds who will never falter. 283
Spirit of God, sent from heaven abroad. 285
Spread, oh, spread, almighty Word 379
Strengthen for service, Lord, the hands 218
The Church of Christ, in ev'ry age 433
The Son of God, our Christ, the Word, the Way 434
Through the night of doubt and sorrow. 355
We all believe in one true God 374
You servants of God, your master proclaim. 252
See The Word, 227–240

Word, The, 227–240
Open now thy gates of beauty 250

Work, Daily
All who love and serve your city 436
As saints of old their firstfruits brought 404
Awake, my soul, and with the sun. 269
Evening and morning. 465
Forth in thy name, O Lord, I go 505
Lord of all hopefulness, Lord of all joy 469
See Society, 413–437

World
See Creation; Society, 413–437

Worship
All people that on earth do dwell 245
Dearest Jesus, we are here. 187
Evening and morning. 465
God himself is present. 249
Holy Majesty, before you 247
O Savior, precious Savior 514
Oh, worship the King, all-glorious above. 548
Only-begotten, Word of God eternal. .375
When in our music God is glorified 555

AUTHORS, COMPOSERS, AND SOURCES OF HYMNS

Abe, Seigi 417
Abelard, Peter 337
Adam, Barbara E. 289
Addison, Joseph. 264
Ahle, Johann R. 187, 248
Ahnfelt, Oskar 371
Albert, Heinrich. 266
Alderson, Eliza S. 424
Alexander, Cecil F. 114, 188, 494
Alexander, James W. *116*, *117*
Alford, Henry. 407
Alington, Cyril A. 144
Allen, *New York Selections* 547
Allen, Oswald. 304
Alte Catholische Geistliche Kirchengesäng, Köln 58
Altenburg, Johann M. 361
Ambrose 28, 271, 275
American. 67, 290, 331, 332, 507
American folk hymn. 385
Anders, Charles R. *307*, 386, *463*, 538, 555
Anthes, Friedrich K. 304
Anton, Christoph. 90, 242
Aquinas, Thomas. 120, 199
Arthur, John W. 387
As Hymnodus Sacer, Leipzig 286, 511
Astley, Charles T. *399*
Atkinson, Frederick C. 486
Augsburg. 454

Babcock, Maltbie D. 554
Bach, J. S. *219*, *242*
Bahnmaier, Jonathan F. 379
Bain, J. L. Macbeth 451
Baker, Henry W. *42*, 414, 456, 460
Balle, C. C. N. 62
Baldwin, Lee M. 422
Baring-Gould, Sabine. 280, *355*, 509
Barnby, Joseph. 280, 287, 381, 425, 546
Barnes, Edward S. *71*
Barthélémon, François H. 269
Bayly, Albert F. 409, 411, 420, 423
Beadon, Hyde W. 78
Beck, Theodore A. *33*, *132*, *141*, *172*, *181*, *193*, *290*, *484*
Becker, John W. *259*, *409*
Bede, The Venerable. 157
Beethoven, Ludwig van 551
Bell, George K. A. 386
Belsheim, Ole G. *239*
Bender, Jan O. *28*, *48*, *86*, *154*, *196*, *210*, *312*, *395*, 396, *398*, *412*, *552*, *558*
Benedictine plainsong 277
Benson, Louis F. 200
Berg, Caroline V. Sandell. 474
Berggren, Andreas P. 298
Berlin. 340
Bern. 375
Bernard of Clairvaux 116, 117, 316, 356, 489, 537
Bernard of Cluny 322, 347
Bevan, Emma F. *182*
Bickersteth, Edward H. *491*
Billings, William 426
Birken, Sigismund von 115, 487
Blacker, Maxwell J. *375*
Bliss, Philip P. 346
Blumenfeld, Edward M. 434
Boberg, Carl. 532
Bode, John E. 503
Bogatzky, Karl H. von 382
Bohemian Brethren, *Ein Gesangbuch der Brüder* 490
Bohemian Brethren, *Ein new Gesengbuchlen* 312
Bohemian Brethren, *Kirchengeseng* 210
Bohemian carol 57, 66

Italic numbers indicate the translation or setting.

Boltze, Georg G. 487
Bonar, Horatius 167, 211, 305, 497, 525
Borthwick, Jane L. *147, 341*
Bouman, Herbert J. A. *68*
Bouman, Paul B. *208, 536*
Bourgeois, Louis 245, 303, 531, 550, 564, 565
Bourne, George H. 172
Bowie, W. Russell 421
Bowring, John 104
Boye, Birgitte K. 43, 138
Bradbury, William B. 293, 296, 501
Brady, Nicholas 452
Brauer, Alfred E. R. *539*
Brebeuf, Jean de 72
Bridges, Matthew 170
Bridges, Robert *123, 545, 546*
Briem, Valdimar 515
Briggs, George W. 209, 238
Broadsheet, Wittenberg 395
Brokering, Herbert F. 558
Brooke, Stopford A. 242
Brooks, Charles T. 569
Brooks, Phillips 41
Brorson, Hans A. 52, 314
Browne, Simon 475
Browne, Thomas B. 541
Brownlie, John 33
Brueckner, Hermann *249, 465*
Brun, Johan Nordahl 227
Bryant, William C. 402
Buck, Percy C. 402
Budry, Edmond 145
Bunjes, Paul G. *38, 124, 177, 178, 310, 313, 366, 375, 415, 510*
Bunyan, John 498
Burleigh, Harry T. 359
Burrowes, Elisabeth 283
Burt, Bates G. 510
Busarow, Donald A. *30, 130, 370, 385, 426, 444*

Cabena, H. Barrie 237, *431*
Cameron, Catherine 463
Campbell, Jane M. *362*
Campbell, John 445
Campbell, Robert *210, 284*
Cantionale Germanicum, Dresden 253
Carlson, J. Bert *113*
Carnatic Tamil 529
Cartford, Gerhard M. 466, *489, 500*
Carwithen, Robert *522*
Caswall, Edward *37, 95, 110, 120, 284, 316, 537*
Catalonian carol 53
Cawood, John 234
Chadwick, John W. 373
Chandler, John *22, 36, 300*
Chapin, Lucius 122, 126
Charles, Elizabeth R. 517
Chatfield, Allen W. *309*
Chesterton, Gilbert K. 428
Chorley, Henry F. 462
Chorvát, *Velka Partitura* 150
Christierson, Frank von 404, 441
Christliche und Tröstliche Tischgesenge, Erfurt 468
Clark, Thomas C. 430
Clarke, Jeremiah 173, 190
Claudius, Matthias 362
Clausnitzer, Tobias 248
Clephane, Elizabeth C. 107
Cocker, Norman 336
Coffin, Charles 22, 36

Compline office hymn 277
Conkey, Ithamar 104
Converse, Charles C. 439
Coote, Constance 223
Copeland, William J. *273*
Copes, V. Earle 223
Cory, Julia C. 241
Cosin, John *472, 473*
Cotterill, Thomas *547*
Cowper, William 483
Cox, Frances E. *133, 542*
Croft, William 320, 548
Croly, George 486
Crossman, Samuel 94
"Crown of Jesus" *71*
Cruciger, Elizabeth 86
Crüger, Johann 23, 46, 123, 129, 133, 167, 185, 203, 224, 254, 340, 457, 533, 534
Crull, August *24, 115, 292, 511*
Crum, John M. C. 148
Cummings, William H. *60*
Cutler, Henry S. 183
Cutts, Peter 436

Dachstein, Wolfgang 105
Daman, *Booke of Musicke* 114
Daman, *Psalmes* 309
Danish 75
Darwall, John 261, 401
Das grosse Cantionale, Darmstadt 97
Dass, Petter 244
Davis, Katherine K. 557
Davisson, *Kentucky Harmony* 33, 220
Day, George H. 437
Day, *Psalter* 234
Dearmer, Percy *169, 267*
Decius, Nikolaus 111, 166
Detterer, F. W. *263*
Diemer, Emma Lou 563
Dix, William C. 40, 82, 158
Doan, Gilbert E. *49, 99, 166,* 214, *348,* 349, *380, 395, 485*
Doane, George W. 464
Doddridge, Philip 35, 477
Douglas, C. Winfred *34, 81, 92, 382,* 498
Doving, Carl *43, 310, 365*
Draesel, Herbert G. Jr. 449
Draper, William H. *527*
Drese, Adam 341
Dretzel, Kornelius Heinrich 192
Dryden, John *164*
Duffield, George 389
Dutch 149
Dutch folk tune 364, 523
Dwight, John S. 569
Dwight, Timothy 368
Dykes, John B. 165, 294, 316, 467

Ebeling, Johann G. 465
Eber, Paul 303
Eccard, Johann 124
Edwards, John 94, 357
Edwards, Robert L. 408
Een ny Handbog, Rostock 432
Egenolf, *Reutterliedlein* 146, 319
Ehrenborg-Posse, *Barnsånger* 59
Ehret, Walter *53*
Ellerton, John *64, 153,* 262, 274, 462
Elliott, Charlotte 296
Elvey, George J. 170, 407

Enchiridion, Erfurt 48, 86, 163
English 80, 88
English ballad 40
English carol 56
English folk tune 81, 177, 178, 391, 428
Ernewerten Gesangbuch, Stralsund 543
Etlich christlich Lieder, Wittenberg 194, 297, 299, 321
Eugenie of Sweden 326
Evans, David *339, 430*
Evenrud, Jerry A. *449*
Everest, Charles W. 398

F. B. P. 331
Faber, Frederick W. 290, 500, 524
Falckner, Justus 182
Farlander, Arthur W. *382*
Farrell, Melvin *323*
Fawcett, John 259, 370
Ferguson, John *246, 529*
Filitz, Friedrich 95
Findlater, Sarah B. *25*
Finlay, Kenneth G. 78
Finnish folk tune 339, 384, 394, 516
Finnish song 394
Fischer, William E. 171
Fischer, William G. 390
Flemming, Friedrich F. 517
Foelber, Paul F. *213*
Forness, Norman O. 383
Fortunatus, Venantius Honorius . . . 118, 124, 125, 142, 153, 155
Fosdick, Harry E. 415
Foster, Frederick W. *249*
France, William E. *322*
Francis of Assisi 527
Franck, Johann 224, 457, 458
Franck, Melchior 348
Frank, Peter 444
Franzén, Frans Mikael 26, 496
Franzmann, Martin H. *140*, 233, 372, 396, 442, *528*
French 130, 139
French carol 71, 148, 541
French folk tune 72, 198
French processional 34
Frey, Stephanie K. 180
Freylinghausen, *Geistreiches Gesang-Buch* 32, 379, 382
Freystein, Johann B. 443
Fritsch, Ahasuerus 504

Gaelic 409
Gardiner, *Sacred Melodies* 356, 429
Garve, Carl B. 147, 232
Gastoldi, Giovanni Giacomo 552
Gastorius, Severus 446
Gaunt, H. C. A. 196
Gehring, Philip *127, 266*
Geistliche Kirchengesänge, Köln 143, 157, 175, 527
Gellert, Christian F. 133
Geneva, *Trente Quatre Pseaumes de David* 29, 140, 376, 421, 470, 493, 545
George, Graham 121, 461
Gerhardt, Paul 23, 46, 105, 116, 117, 129, 276, 282, 336, 454, 465
Gerike, Henry V. 159
German 58, 103
German carol 55, 68
German folk hymn 215
German folk tune 59
German hymn 48, 136, 545, 546
German spiritual song, Köln 38

Gesang-Buch, Nürnberg, 1676 . . . . . 302, 380, 447
Gesangbuch, Augsburg 38
Gesangbuch, Berlin 248
Gesangbuch, Bollhagen 292
Gesangbuch, Mainz 110
Gesangbuch, Münster 518
Gesangbuch, Nürnberg, 1531 471
Gesangbuch, Rudolstadt 490
Gesius, Bartholomäus 455
Geyer, John B. 189
Giardini, Felice de 400, 522
Gibbons, Orlando 206, 257, 373, 438, 505
Gieschen, Thomas E. *460*
Gilmore, Joseph H. 501
Gladden, Washington 492
Gläser, Carl G. 559
Goss, John 549
Goudimel, Claude *493*
Gould, John E. 334
Gramann, Johann 519
Grant, Robert 91, 548
Greek hymn 279
Gregory I 101, 267
Greitter, Matthias 335
Grenoble *Antiphoner* 83
Grieg, Edvard *314*
Grindal, Gracia *32, 58, 271, 275, 295, 314, 351, 446*
Gross Catolisch Gesangbuch, Nürnberg 200
Gruber, Franz 65
Grundtvig, Nicolai F. S. 62, 75, 161, 193, 239, 285, 338, 365
Gurney, Dorothy F. 287

Handel, George F. 39, 145
Hanke, Elmer T. R. *330*
Hankey, Katherine 390
Harding, James P. 84
Harjunpaa, Toivo *319*
Harkness, Georgia 493
Harmonia Cantionum, Leipzig 450
Harwood, Basil 77, *83*
Hassler, Hans L. 116, 117
Hastings, Thomas 327
Hatch, Edwin 488
Hatton, John 352, 520, 530
Hauser, *Hesperian Harp* 127
Hausmann, Julie von 333
Havergal, Frances R. 260, 403, 406, 460, 514
Havergal, William H. 406, 480
Haweis, Thomas 35
Hawhee, Howard *53*
Haydn, Franz Joseph 358, 540
Haydn, Johann M. 252
Heaton, Charles H. *507*
Heber, Reginald 84, 165, 183, 258, 281
Hebrew 544
Hedborn, Samuel J. 247
Heermann, Johann 123, 380, 504
Held, Heinrich 478
Held, Wilbur C. *61*
Helmbold, Ludwig 468
Hemy, Henri F. 500
Henry, Hugh T. *222*
Herbert, George 513
Herbranson, Thomas E. 195
Herklots, Rosamond E. 307
Herman, David *97, 302, 452*
Herman, Nikolaus 47, 154, 275, 300, 351
Hernaman, Claudia F. 99
Herrnhut 93

Herrnschmidt, Johann D. 539
Heyder, Friedrich C. 213
Hillert, Richard W. *37, 44, 49, 55, 57,* 63, *67, 79, 94, 139, 144, 164, 233, 292, 357,* 378, *384, 391, 417, 419, 432, 434, 526, 545*
Hine, Stuart K. 532
Hoff, Erik C. 256
Holden, Oliver 328
Holland, Henry S. 418
Holman, Derek 238
Homburg, Ernst C. 97
Hopkins, Edward J. 262
Hopkins, John H. Jr. 219
Hoppe, Anna 426
Hopper, Edward 334
Horn, Edward T. III *478*
Horn, Johann 132, 193, 312
Houff, Larry J. *425*
Housman, Laurence 413
How, William W. 77, 174, 231, 410
Howe, Julia Ward 332
Howells, Herbert 491
Hoyle, R. Birch *145*
Hubert, Konrad 395
Hughes, John 343, 415
Hundert Geistlicher Arien, Dresden 443
Huxhold, Harry N. 288
Hymnal translation 51, 105, 350, 371, 470
Hymnal version *26, 73, 76, 101,* 127, *142, 157, 208, 224, 228, 229, 256, 266, 276, 322, 333, 361, 379, 417, 487*

Ingemann, Bernhardt S. 355
Ingram, Forrest *207*
Irish 188, 322, 456
Irish folk tune 469
Isaac, Heinrich 222, 276, 282
Italian 95
Iyer, V. Masillamony 529

Jackisch, Frederick F. *72, 102, 199,* 236, *487, 512*
Jacob, Gordon *451*
Jacobs, Henry E. 225
Jacobse, Muus 207
Janzow, F. Samuel *47,* 63
Jeffries, Charles 392
Jillson, Marjorie 476
John of Damascus 132, 141
John, Marquess of Bute *81*
Johnson, David N. 558
Johnson, J. Rosamond 562
Johnson, James W. 562
Johnson, William 100
Joseph, Georg 119
Jude, William H. 494
Julian, John 536

Kahl, Johan 516
Keller, Matthias 525
Kelly, John *129*
Kelly, Thomas 156, 173, 344
Ken, Thomas 269, 278, 564, 565
Kennedy, Benjamin H. *450*
Kethe, William 245
Key, Francis S. 243, 401
Kingo, Thomas H. 102, 194, 220, 470
Kinner, Samuel 208
Kirbye, George 264
Kirchengesangbuch, Strassburg 164
Kirchenordnung, Braunschweig 103
Kitchin, George W. 377
Kjellstrand, August W. *247*
Klug, *Geistliche Lieder* 85, 136, 230, 273, 284, 473, 512
Klug, Ronald A. 393
Knapp, William 433, 475
Knudsen, Johannes H. V. *193, 285*
Knudsen, Peder 69
Kocher, Conrad 82, 561
König, *Harmonischer Lieder-Schatz* 502
König, Johann B. 22, 102, 560
Koralpsalmboken, Stockholm 112, 113, 155, 232, 414, 515
Koren, Ulrik V. 256
Krauth, Charles Porterfield *62, 489*
Krohn, Julius 319
Kugelmann, *Concentus Novi* 519
Kutzky, Michal *96*
Kwillia, Billema 214
"Kyrie fons bonitatis" 168

Landahl, Carl W. 354
Landstad, Magnus B. 310, 313, 342
Lane, Spencer 106
Lathbury, Mary A. 235
Latin 168
Latin carol 151
Latin credo 374
Latin hymn 37, 126, 146, 154, 169, 222, 226, 268, 273, 300, 323, 367, 547
Latin office hymn 49, 83
Latin sequence 128
Laudamus *471*
Laurentii, Laurentius 25
Laurinus, Laurentius L. 330
Lawes, Henry 211
Leaf, Robert *122,* 184, *260*
Leavitt, *Christian Lyre* 243, 537
Lee, Olav *394*
Leeson, Jane E. *128*
Lenel, Ludwig *217, 360,* 399
Leupold, Ulrich S. *516*
Lewis, Howell E. 405
Lindeman, Ludvig M. 147, 285, 301, 338, 365, 458, 481
Lindemann, Johann 552
Littledale, Richard F. *508*
Liturgy of St. James 198
Löhner, Johann 196, 447
Longfellow, Henry W. *279*
Longfellow, Samuel 257
Lovelace, Austin C. *392, 448*
Löwenstern, Matthäus A. von 366
Lowry, Somerset C. 364
Loy, Matthias *490*
Lundeen, Joel W. *59, 111,* 146, 203, 311, *432, 496*
Luther, Martin 48, 51, 79, 134, 163, 215, 228, 229, 230, 239, 295, 299, 308, 317, 335, 349, 350, 374, 471, 528
Lvov, Alexis F. 462
Lyon, Meyer 544
Lyra Davidica, London 151
Lyte, Henry F. 272, 549

Maccall, William *330*
MacMillan, Ernest Campbell *568*
Magdeburg, Joachim 450
Mahnke, Allan 279
Maker, Frederick C. 107, 131, 506
Malmivaara, Wilhelmi 485
Mann, Arthur H. 514
Mant, Richard *110,* 176
Ms., Municipal Library Leipzig 213
Manz, Paul O. *50, 176*
March, Daniel 381
Maria Theresa, *Katholisches Gesangbuch* 270, 535

Marot, *Trente Pseaulmes de David* 318, 431
Marriott, John 400
Martin, George W. 489
Mason and Webb, *Cantica Lauda* 410
Mason, Arthur J. *220*
Mason, Lowell *39,* 353, 479, *559*
Massie, Richard *134, 284, 299, 308, 335, 454, 465*
Matheson, George 324
McCarthy, David 556
McComb, William 306
McDowell, Louise M. 216
McManus, S. B. 122
Medieval antiphon 471
Medieval Latin carol 55
Medieval plainsong 49
Medley, Samuel 352
Mendelssohn, Felix 60, *305, 503*
Mentzer, Johann 560
Mercer, *Church Psalter* 89
Mercer, William *249,* 281
Merrill, William P. 383, 437
Messiter, Arthur H. 553
Meyfart, Johann M. 348
Micheelson, Hans-Friedrich 218
Middleton, Jesse E. *72*
Miller, Edward 482
Miller, John *249*
Miller, Margaret D. *214*
Milman, Henry H. 121
Milton, John 318, 521
Mischke, Bernard 204
Missouri Harmony, St. Louis 246
Moe, Daniel 427, 521
Mohr, Joseph 65
Monk, William H. 272
Monsell, John S. B. 131, 260, 412, 461
Montgomery, James 50, 87, 106, 109, 162, 301, 388, 438
Morgen- und Abend-Segen, Waldenburg 444
Mote, Edward 293, 294
Moultrie, Gerard *198*

Nägeli, Johann G. 370
Neale, John M. *34, 42, 55,* 80, *83, 85, 108, 118, 120, 124, 125, 132, 139, 141, 154, 226, 268, 277,* 337, 347, *367*
Neander, Joachim 182, 249, 250, 543
Near, Gerald R. *243, 288*
Negro spiritual 70, 92, 212, 359
Nelson, Horatio Bolton 177, 178
Nelson, Ronald A. *25, 68, 198,* 258, *423*
Neumark, Georg 453
Neumeister, Erdmann 291
Neuverfertigtes Gesangbuch, Darmstadt 24
Neu-vermehrtes Gesangbuch, Meiningen 231, 305, 478, 503
Newbolt, Michael R. 377
Newton, John 261, 288, 298, 345, 358, 448
Nicholson, Sydney H. 377
Nicolai, Philipp 31, 43, 73, 76, 138, 247, 459
Niles, Daniel T. *529*
Noel, Caroline M. 179
North, Frank M. 429
Norwegian folk tune 314, 326, 330
Nürnberg 361
Nyberg, Mikael 485
Nystedt, Knut 204

Oakeley, Frederick *45*
Office hymn 210
Olearius, Johann 29
Olearius, Johann G. 24
Olivers, Thomas 27, 544
Olsen, Norman P. 236
Olson, Ernst W. *474*
Olsson, Olof *496*
O'Neill, Judith 190
Ore, Charles W. *400*
Osborne, Stanley L. *186*
Osler, Edward 353
Owen, Frank K. 209
Owen, William 156, 172
Oxenham, John 359

Palestrina, Giovanni P. da 135
Palmer, Ray *356,* 479
Paris *Antiphoner* 169, 191, 267, 337
Paris *Processionale* 199, 441
Parker, Alice *149*
Parry, C. Hubert H. 283, 408
Parry, Joseph 91
Patrick 188
Peace, Albert L. 324
Peacey, John R. 160
Pelz, Walter L. *240, 334, 485*
Percy, William A. 449
Perronet, Edward 328, 329
Persichetti, Vincent 216
Peter, Philip A. *321*
Petrich, Roger T. *64, 66, 285, 347, 537*
Pfeil, Christoph C. L. von 512
Pierpoint, Folliott S. 561
Pilcher, Charles V. *515*
Plainsong 42
Pleyel, Ignaz J. 225
Plumptre, Edward H. 431, 553
Poitiers *Antiphoner* 366, 375
Polack, W. Gustave 168, *444*
Polish carol 44
Pollock, Thomas B. 112, 113
Porter, Hugh *70*
Pott, Francis *135*
Powell, Thomas E. 286
Praetorius, Michael 36
Prague *Gradual* 484
Pratt Green, F. 246, 360, 433, 555, 563
Prichard, Rowland H. 158, 288, 315, 424
Prudentius, Marcus Aurelius Clemens 42, 81
Psalter, Edinburgh 99, 451, 464, 524
Psalteriolum Cantionum Catholicarum, Köln 34
Purday, Charles H. 445
Pusey, Philip *366*
Pye, Henry J. 184

Quitmeyer, Elizabeth *79*

Rambach, Johann J. 192
Rawnsley, Hardwicke D. 435
Read, Daniel 344
Redhead, Richard 109, 306
Redner, Lewis H. 41
Reed, Edith M. G. 44
Rees, Timothy 523
Reid, William W. Jr. 416
Reinagle, Alexander R. 345, 477
Reynolds, William J. *476*
Reynolds, William M. *28*
Rhabanus Maurus 164, 284, 472, 473
Rhau, *Newe Deudsche Geistliche Gesenge* 398
Riley, J. Athelstan 175
Ringwaldt, Bartholomäus 321
Rinkhart, Martin 533, 534
Rippon, *A Selection of Hymns* 507
Rist, Johann 197

Robbins, Howard C. 391
Roberts, Daniel C. 567
Roberts, John *128*
Robinson, Joseph A. 89
Robinson, Robert 499
Rockstro, William Smith *200*
Rodigast, Samuel 446
Röntgen, Julius *364*
Rosenius, Carl O. 371
Routley, Erik 436
Ruopp, Johann F. 511
Russell, Arthur T. *86*
Ryden, Ernest E. 186, *319*, 339, 354, *384*, 516
Rygh, George T. *138*, *194*, *338*

Šamotulský, *Kancional* 419
Sarum 80
Sarum *Antiphoner* 271
Sarum plainsong 64, 125, 323, 472
Sateren, Leland B. 100, *212*, *214*, *221*, *232*, 244, 255, *372*, 404, 435, *441*
Savonarola, Girolamo 93
Schaeffer, Charles W. *455*
Schaff, Philip *222*
Schalk, Carl F. *42*, *80*, *87*, *88*, *103*, 118, *120*, *136*, *137*, *140*, 152, 162, *166*, *168*, *169*, *188*, 205, *207*, *211*, *215*, *267*, *277*, *299*, *308*, *323*, *335*, *374*, 387, *414*, *421*, *471*, *505*, *523*, *528*, *539*
Schalling, Martin 325
Scheffler, Johann 455, 502
Scherf, Royce J. 61, 201
Schirmer, Michael 459
Schlag-Gesang- und Notenbuch, Stuttgart 536
Schmid, *Orgeltabulatur-Buch* 325
Schmolck, Benjamin 187, 250
Scholefield, Clement C. 274
Schop, Johann 219, 440
Schröter, Leonhart 87
Schuette, Conrad H. L. 185
Schultz, Robert P. *562*
Schulz, Johann A. P. 52, 362
Schumann, *Geistliche Lieder* 51, 310, 442
Schumann, Robert 403
Schütz, Heinrich 180
Schütz, Johann J. 542
Scriven, Joseph 439
Sears, Edmund H. 54
Sedulius, Coelius 64, 85
Seebach, Margaret R. 376
Seelen-Harfe, Ansbach 539
Seiss, Joseph A. *518*
Selnecker, Nikolaus 490
Seltz, Martin L. *28*, *38*, *68*, *136*
Sermisy, Claude de 450
Service Book and Hymnal *75*, *155*, *227*, 342
Shaw, Geoffrey 413
Shaw, Martin *148*, *541*
Sheppard, Franklin L. 554
Sherwin, William F. 235
Shrubsole, William 329
Shurtleff, Ernest W. 495
Sicilian 259
Siena, Bianco da 508
Silcher, Friedrich 333
Silesian folk tune 518
Skultéty, *Partitura* 96
Slovak 181
Smart, Henry T. 50, 495
Smith, Alfred M. 434
Smith, David *207*
Smith, H. Percy 492
Smith, Samuel F. 566
Smith, W. Chalmers 526
Smithers, N. B. *81*
Sohren, Peter 208
Sowerby, Leo 195
Spaeth, Harriet Krauth *52*
Spafford, Horatio G. 346
Spannaus, Olive Wise 419
Speratus, Paul 297
Spitta, Karl J. P. 399
Stainer, John *56*
Stanford, Charles V. 189
Stanton, Walter K. 201
Steele, Anne 240
Stegmann, Josua 263
Steurlein, Johann 412
Stone, Samuel J. 369
Strodach, Paul Z. 143, 270
Strom, Ralph A. 289
Strömme, Peer O. *102*, *313*
Struther, Jan 469
Sullivan, Arthur S. 153, 226, *262*, 509
Svedberg, Jesper 440
Sveeggen, Peter A. *69*, *244*, *326*
Swedish 313
Swedish folk tune 25, 26, 474, 532
Swiss 186
Symphonia Sirenum, Köln 135
Synesius of Cyrene 309
Syriac Liturgy of Malabar 218

Tallis, Thomas 278, 497
Tamminen, Kauko-Veikko 384
Tans'ur, *Compleat Melody* 483
Tate, Nahum 452
Taylor, Cyril V. 160, 405
Taylor, Sarah E. 237
Teilhard de Chardin, Pierre 255
Terry, R. Harold *557*
Tersteegen, Gerhard 249
Teschner, Melchior 108
The English Hymnal *218*
The Foundling Hospital Collection, London 540
The Lutheran Hymnal *23*, *163*, *213*, *215*, *282*, *291*, *297*, *374*, *560*
The Sacred Harp, Philadelphia 240, 307, 392, 423
Theodulph of Orleans 108
Thesaurus Musicus, London 566, 568, 569
Thiman, Eric H. *492*
Thomas á Kempis 88
Thomissön, *Den Danske Salmebog* 227, 496
Thomson, Mary A. 397
Thorson, Gerald *161*, *468*
Thring, Godfrey 170, 259, 425
Thrupp, Dorothy A. 481
Tisserand, Jean 139
Tollefson, Paulette 74
Toplady, Augustus M. 327
Tranoscius 484
Tranovský, Jiří 66, 96, 150
Tucker, F. Bland 357
Turton, William H. 206

Ulich, Johann 291
Utech, George 152, 255, 466

Vajda, Jaroslav J. *66*, *96*, *150*, 159, *181*, 205, 378, *453*, *484*
Valerius, *Nederlandtsch Gedenckclanck* 241

Van Dyke, Henry 551
Van Dyke, Mary L. *529*
Vatican collection 120
Vaughan Williams, R. *81,* 101, 142, *143, 146, 157,* 174, *175,* 179, *191, 281, 319, 428,* 508, 513, *527*
Veelenturf, Rik 207
Vere, Aubrey de *110*
Vetter, Georg 140
Vulpius, Melchior 115, 144, 202, 263, 292, 542

Wade, John F. 45
Walch, James 397
Walker, *Southern Harmony* 30, 61, 217, 347, 360, 372, 385, 420, 448, 463
Wallin, Johan Olof 73, 432, 440
Walter, William H. 176, 383
Walther, *Geistliche Gesangbüchlein*... 28, 79, 134, 215, 308, 317
Walther, Johann 141, 350
Walton, James G. 500
Walworth, Clarence A. *535*
Warrack, Guy 422
Warren, George W. 567
Waters, Moir A. J. 556
Watson, Sydney 411
Watts, Isaac 39, 98, 119, 127, 254, 273, 320, 480, 482, 520, 530, 531, 550
Webb, Benjamin *88*
Webb, George J. 389
Webbe, Samuel Sr. 388
Webster, Bradford G. 427
Weisse, Michael 37
Weissel, Georg 32
Welsh 281, 418
Welsh folk tune 221, 526, 557
Welsh hymn tune 430
Wendell, Claus A. 311
Wennerberg, Gunnar 311
Werkmeister, *Gesangbuch der Herzogl. Hofkapelle* 251
Werner, *Choral-Buch* 265
Wesley, Charles 27, 30, 60, 130, 151, 171, 202, 252, 265, 315, 505, 559
Wesley, John *302, 336, 502*
Wesley, Samuel S. 197, 369
Westendorf, Omer *126,* 221
Wexels, Wilhelm A. 351
Wexelsen, Marie 69
Weyse, Christoph E. F. 161, 342
Whately, Richard 281
Whiteley, Frank J. 191
Whiting, William 467
Whittier, John G. 506
Wilbur, Richard 74
Wilde, Jane F. *93*
Wilhelm II 253
Willan, Healey *125, 472*
Williams, Aaron 368, 488
Williams, Peter *343*
Williams, *Psalmodia Evangelica* 363
Williams, Robert 128
Williams, Thomas J. 233, 355
Williams, William 343
Willis, Richard S. 54
Wilson, Hugh 98, 452
Wilson, M. F. C. 217
Winkworth, Catherine *29, 31, 46, 97, 187, 192, 197, 230, 232, 248, 250, 253, 303, 312, 325, 340, 380, 443, 447, 453, 457, 458, 459, 504, 512, 519, 533, 534, 543, 552*
Wipo of Burgundy 137
Wood, Dale 268, 367, 393, 416, *494*
Woodford, James R. *199*
Woodward, George R. *36,* 149
Wordsworth, Christopher 90, 251
Work, John W. Jr. 70
Worship Supplement 317
Wren, Brian W. 363
Wright, David F. 538
Wyeth, *Repository of Sacred Music,* Part II 499

Xavier, Francis 491

Yardley, Harold F. 191
Young, Carlton R. *469*
Young, John F. *65*
Yuki, Koh 417

Zavorka, *Kancional* 181
Zimmermann, Heinz Werner 476
Zinzendorf, Nicolaus L. von 302, 341
Zipp, Friedrich *325*

TUNES—ALPHABETICAL

A solis ortus cardine 64
A va de 214
Abbott's Leigh 405
Aberystwyth 91
  Ach bleib mit deiner Gnade 263
Ack, bliv hos oss 414
Ack, saliga stunder 371
Ack, vad är dock livet här 112, 113
Adeste fideles 45
Adoro te devote 199, 441
Af himlens 232
All Ehr und Lob 164
All Saints New 183
  Alle Menschen müssen sterben 90, 242
Allein Gott in der Höh 166
Allein zu dir 395
Alles ist an Gottes Segen 196, 447
Amen sjunge hvarje tunga 298
  America 566, 568, 569
American Hymn 525
An Wasserflüssen Babylon 105
  Angel's Song 505
Angel's Story 514
Angelic Songs 397
Angelus 119
Anthes 304
Antioch 39
Ar hyd y nos 281
  Arnsberg 249
Ascended Triumph 159
Atkinson 237
Auf, auf, mein Herz 129
  Aughton 501
Aurelia 197, 369
Aus tiefer Not 295

Indented lines indicate names by which some tunes in this book may also be known.

Austria ... 358, 540
Austrian hymn ... 358, 540
Ave Maria, klarer und lichter Morgenstern ... 251
Away in a Manger ... 67
Azmon ... 559

Bangor ... 483
Battle Hymn ... 332
Beach Spring ... 423
Beatus vir ... 419
Behold a Host ... 314
Bereden väg för Herran ... 26
Beverly ... 386
Birabus ... 436
Blomstertid ... 515
Bourbon ... 127
Bread of Life ... 235
Break Bread Together ... 212
Breslau ... 286
Brother James' Air ... 451
Bryn Calfaria ... 156, 172
Bunessan ... 409

Caithness ... 99
Cannock ... 201
Canonbury ... 403
Carn Brea ... 238
Çarol ... 54
Čas radosti ... 66
Celestia ... 75
Chesterfield ... 35
Christ ist erstanden ... 136
Christ lag in Todesbanden ... 134
Christ, unser Herr ... 79
Christe Redemptor ... 49
Christe sanctorum ... 169, 191, 267
Christe, der du bist Tag und Licht ... 273
Christe, du Lamm Gottes ... 103
Christmas Dawn ... 59
Christmas Eve ... 69
Christus, der ist mein Leben ... 263
City of God ... 427
Coena Domini ... 226
Complainer ... 347
Conditor alme siderum ... 323
Consolation (*Kentucky Harmony*) ... 33
Consolation (Lindeman) ... 301
Converse ... 439
Coronation ... 328
Crasselius ... 382
Crucifer ... 377
Cwm Rhondda ... 343, 415

Dana ... 298
Darmstadt ... 504
Darwall's 148th ... 261, 401
Das neugeborne Kindelein ... 202
Dejlig er den Himmel blaa ... 75
Den Blomstertid nu kommer ... 515
Den signede Dag ... 161, 342
Den store hvide Flok ... 314
Dennis ... 370
Deo gracias ... 80, 88
Der am Kreuz ... 102
Der mange skal komme ... 313
Des Plaines ... 162
Det kimer nu til Julefest ... 62
Detroit ... 240, 307
Deus tuorum militum ... 83
Diademata ... 170
Die güldne Sonne ... 465
Die helle Sonn leucht ... 292
Dir, dir, Jehova ... 382
Distress ... 217, 360
Divinum mysterium ... 42
Dix ... 82, 561
Donata ... 387
Donne secours ... 493
Down Ampney ... 508
Du Lebensbrot, Herr Jesu Christ ... 208
Du som gaar ud ... 285
Duke Street ... 352, 520, 530
Dundee ... 464, 524
Durham ... 488
Durrow ... 322

Earth and All Stars ... 558
Easter Glory ... 147, 338
Easter Hymn ... 151
Ebenezer ... 233, 355
Eden Church ... 367
Ein feste Burg (isometric) ... 229, 239
Ein feste Burg (rhythmic) ... 228
Ein Lämmlein geht ... 105
Elizabeth ... 279
Ellacombe ... 251
Ellers ... 262
Emmanuel ... 62
Engelberg ... 189
Erhalt uns, Herr ... 230
Erie ... 439
Erschienen ist der herrlich Tag ... 154
Es ist das Heil ... 194, 297
Es ist ein Ros ... 58
Es ist gewisslich ... 321
Es wolle Gott uns gnädig sein ... 335
Evan ... 480
Eventide ... 272

Fang dein Werk ... 444
Farley Castle ... 211
Festal Song ... 176, 383
Flemming ... 517
Fortunatus ... 153
Fortunatus New ... 118
Foundation ... 507
Franconia ... 22
Franzén ... 496
Fred til Bod ... 147, 338
Fredericktown ... 555
Freu dich sehr (isometric) ... 470
Freu dich sehr (rhythmic) ... 29
Freuen wir uns all in ein ... 37
Freut euch, ihr lieben ... 87
Fröhlich soll mein Herze springen ... 46

Galilean ... 381
Galilee ... 494
Garelochside ... 78
Gaudeamus pariter ... 132, 193
Gelobet seist du ... 48
Gelobt sei Gott ... 144
Geneva ... 437
Gethsemane ... 109, 306
Gladness ... 66
Gloria ... 71
Go Tell It ... 70
Gonfalon Royal ... 402
Gott der Vater wohn uns bei ... 308
Gott des Himmels ... 266

Gott sei Dank 379
Gott sei gelobet und gebenedeiet 215
Gottes Sohn ist kommen 312
Grace Church 225
Grace Church, Gananoque 461
Granton 378
Great God, Our Source 466
Great White Host 314
Greensleeves 40
Grosser Gott 270, 535
Gud er Gud 244
Gud skal alting Mage 458
Guds Menighed, syng 256

Hankey 390
Hanover 548
Haf trones lampa färdig 25
He Leadeth Me 501
Heath 410
Helmsley 27
Her kommer dine arme Smaa 52
Her vil ties 481
Hermas 260
Herr Christ, der einig Gotts Sohn 86
Herr, ich habe misgehandelt 167
Herr Jesu Christ, dich zu uns wend 253
Herr Jesu Christ, du hast bereitt 208
Herr Jesu Christ, meins 286, 511
Herr Jesu Christ, wahr Mensch und Gott 124
Herzlich lieb 325
Herzlich tut mich erfreuen 141
Herzlich tut mich verlangen (isometric) 117
Herzlich tut mich verlangen (rhythmic) 116
Herzliebster Jesu 123
Hiding Place 537
Hoff 256
Holy Manna 463
Holy Mountain 301
Hursley 270
Hyfrydol 158, 288, 315, 424
Hymn to Joy 551

I Himmelen, I Himmelen 330
Ich dank dir, lieber Herre 490
Ich heb mein Augen sehnlich auf 180
Ich sterbe täglich 213
Ich will dich lieben 502
In Babilone 364, 523
In dir ist Freude 552
In dulci jubilo 55
In manus tuas 491
Innsbruck 222, 276, 282
Intercessor 283
Invocation 354
Island 227
Ist Gott für mich 454
Iste confessor 366, 375
It Is Well 346
Italian Hymn 400, 522

Jam lucis 277
Jefferson 30
Jeg er saa glad 69
Jerusalem, du hochgebaute Stadt 348
Jesaia, dem Propheten 528
Jesu Kreuz, Leiden und Pein 115
Jesu, Joy of Man's Desiring 219
Jesu, meine Freude 457
Jesu, meines Lebens Leben 97
Jesus, meine Zuversicht 133, 340
Judas Maccabaeus 145
Just as I Am 425

Kedron 420
Kentucky 93rd 246
Kingdom 223
King's Lynn 177, 178, 428
King's Weston 179
Kingsfold 391
Kirken den er et gammelt Hus 365
Knickerbocker 209
Komm, Gott Schöpfer 284, 473
Komm, Heiliger Geist, Herre Gott 163
Komm, o komm, du Geist des Lebens 478
Kommt her zu mir 361
Kremser 241
Kryie, Gott Vater 168
Kuortane 339

Lancashire 495
Land of Rest 331
Langham 413
Lasset uns mit Jesu ziehen 487
Lasst uns erfreuen 143, 157, 175, 527
Laudes Domini 546
Laurel 268
Laus Regis 171
Leominster 489
Leoni 544
Leupold 435
Lewis-Town 426
Liebster Jesu, wir sind hier 187, 248
Lift Ev'ry Voice and Sing 562
Light Divine 257
Lindemann 458
Lindsborg 184
Little Flock 476
Llanfair 128
Llangloffan 430
Lo desembre congelat 53
Lob Gott getrost mit Singen 490
Lob sei dem allmächtigen Gott 185
Lobe den Herren 543
Lobe den Herren, o meine Seele 539
Lobt Gott den Herren, ihr 542
Lobt Gott, ihr Christen 47, 300, 351
Lord, Revive Us 290
Lost in the Night 394
Lynne 510
Lyons 252

Mabune 417
Machs mit mir, Gott 455
Macht hoch die Tür 32
Mainz 110
Marion 553
Marlee 100
Martyrdom 98, 452
Maryton 492
McKee 359
Meinen Jesum lass ich nicht 24
Meinen Jesum lass ich nicht (Ulich) 291
Melcombe 388
Melita 294, 467
Mendelssohn 60
Mendon 547
Meribah 353
Merrial 280
Messiah 26

Michael 538
Midden in de Dood 207
Miles Lane 329
Mit Freuden zart 140, 421
Mit Fried und Freud 349
Mitten wir im Leben sind 350
Morecambe 486
Morestead 411
Morgenlied 131
Morning Hymn 269
Morning Star 84
Moscow 400, 522
Munich 231, 305, 503

Naar mit Öie 301
Name of Jesus 289
Narodil se Kristus Pán 57
National Anthem 566, 568, 569
National Hymn 567
Neander 182, 250
Nettleton 499
Neumark 453
New Britain 448
New Malden 556
Nicaea 165
Nilsson 258
Noël Nouvelet 148
Noormarkku 384
Nottingham 173, 190
Nous allons 541
Now 205
Nun bitten wir 317
Nun danket all 254
Nun danket alle Gott (isometric) 534
Nun danket alle Gott (rhythmic) 533
Nun freut euch 299
Nun komm, der Heiden Heiland 28
Nun lasst uns den Leib begraben 398
Nun lob, mein Seel 519
Nunc angelorum 68
Nyland 339
Nyt ylös, sieluni 516

O dass ich tausend Zungen hätte (Dretzel) 192
O dass ich tausend Zungen hätte (König) 560
O du Liebe meiner Liebe 93
O filii et filiae 139
O grosser Gott 536
O Heiland, reiss die Himmel auf 38
O heilige Dreifaltigkeit 275
O Jesu Christe, wahres Licht 302, 380
O Jesu, än de dina 496
O Lamm Gottes unschuldig 111
O Perfect Love 287
O quanta qualia 337
O Seigneur 545
O store Gud 532
O Welt, ich muss dich lassen (isometric) 222
O Welt, ich muss dich lassen (rhythmic) 276, 282
Oakley 101
Oi Herra, jos mä matkamies maan 485
Old Hundredth 245, 531, 550, 564, 565
Old 107th 318, 431
Old 124th 376
Olivet 479
Om Himmeriges Rige 227
Omni die 200
Orientis partibus 130
Our Lady, Trondhjem 481

Paedia 52
Palestrina 135
Pán Bůh 484
Pange lingua 120
Parsons 152
Passion Chorale (isometric) 117
Passion Chorale (rhythmic) 116
Patmos 406
Pax 414
Peace of God 449
Penitence 106
Perry 195
Petra 109, 306
Picardy 198
Pilot 334
Pleading Savior 243
Potsdam 89
Praise 232
Praise, My Soul 549
Princess Eugenie 326
Prospect 61
Psalm 42 ..... 29, 470
Puer nobis 36

Quem pastores 68

Rathbun 104
Ratisbon 265
Regent Square 50
Regwal 404
Resonet in laudibus 68
Rest 506
Riddarholm 155
Rhosymedre 94, 357
Rhuddlan 418
Richmond 35
Rockingham Old 482
Rok nový 181
Russian Hymn 462
Rustington 408
Ryburn 336

St. Agnes 316
St. Anne 320
St. Catherine 500
St. Christopher 107
St. Clement 274
St. Columba 456
St. Denio 526
St. Dunstan's 498
St. Flavian 234
St. George's, Windsor 407
St. Gertrude 509
St. Louis 41
St. Magnus 173, 190
St. Margaret 324
St. Nicholas 167
St. Patrick's Breastplate 188
St. Paul 194, 297
St. Peter 345, 477
St. Theodulph 108
St. Thomas 368
Salvator natus 57
Salve festa dies 142
Salzburg 90, 242
Sandell 474
Sandon 445
Santa Barbara 563
Schmücke dich 203, 224
Schönster Herr Jesu 518

Seelenbräutigam .341
Sheldonian .160
Shepherding .63
Sicilian Mariners .259
Sine Nomine .174
Slane .469
So nimm denn meine Hände .333
Solothurn .186
Song 1 206, 373
Song 13 .257
Song 34 .505
Song 67 .438
Sonne der Gerechtigkeit .210
Southwell .309
Splendor Paternae .271
Stabat Mater .110
Stephanos .460
Stille Nacht .65
Stockholm .313
Straf mich nicht .443
Suomi .516
Sursum Corda .434
Swedish Litany 112, 113

Tallis' Canon .278
Tandanei .529
Te Deum .535
Tender Thought .220
Ter sanctus .432
Terra Patris .554
The Ash Grove 221, 557
The Call .513
The First Nowell .56
The King's Banner .124
The King's Majesty .121
The Saints' Delight .372
The Solid Rock .293
Third Mode Melody .497
Thornbury .77
Tollefson .74
Ton-y-Botel 233, 355
Toplady .327
Torshov .204
Truro .363
Truth from Above .81
Tryggare kan ingen vara .474
Tuolumne .416
Twenty-fourth 122, 126

Une jeune pucelle .72
Union .255
Unser Herrscher 182, 250
Upp, min tunga .155

Valet will ich dir geben .108
Vater unser 310, 442
Venerable .216
Veni, Creator Spiritus .472
Veni, Emmanuel .34
Verleih uns Frieden .471
Vexilla regis .125
Vi lova dig, o store Gud .432
Victimae paschali .137
Victory .135
Vigil .25
Vom Himmel hoch .51
Von Gott will ich nicht lassen .468
Vruechten .149
Vulpius .144

W̦ zlobie lezy .44
Wachet auf (isometric) .247
Wachet auf (rhythmic) .31
Wächterlied 146, 319
Walhof .236
Walton 356, 429
Wareham 433, 475
Was frag ich nach der Welt .504
Was Gott tut .446
Was mein Gott will .450
We Are the Lord's .399
Webb .389
Wedlock .392
Wellington Square .422
Wem in Leidenstagen .95
Wenn wir in höchsten Nöten sein .303
Wennerberg .311
Wer nur den lieben Gott .453
Werde munter .440
Were You There .92
Weyse 161, 342
Wie lieblich ist der Maien .412
Wie schön leuchtet (isometric) 43, 73
Wie schön leuchtet (rhythmic) 76, 138, 459
Wie soll ich dich empfangen .23
Williams Bay .521
Winchester Old .264
Windham .344
Windsor .114
Wir dienen, Herr .218
Wir glauben all .374
Wir hatten gebauet .59
Wir pflügen .362
Wittenberg New .396
Wo Gott zum Haus 85, 512
Wojtkiewiecz .393
Wondrous Love .385
Woodworth .296
Wunderbarer König .249

Yigdal .544

Známe to, Pane Bože náš .96
Zpivejmež všickni vesele .150

TUNES—METRICAL

SM (Short Meter—6 6 8 6)

Dennis .370
Des Plaines .162
Durham .488
Festal Song 176, 383
Franconia .22
Garelochside .78
Heath .410
Kentucky 93rd .246
Michael .538
Potsdam .89
St. Thomas .368
Southwell .309

SM and refrain
Marion . . . 553

SMD (Short Meter Double—6 6 8 6 6 6 8 6)
Diademata . . . 170
Leominster . . . 489
Terra Patris . . . 554

CM (Common Meter—8 6 8 6)
Azmon . . . 559
Bangor . . . 483
Caithness . . . 99
Chesterfield . . . 35
Consolation . . . 33
Detroit . . . 240, 307
Dundee . . . 464, 524
Evan . . . 480
Hiding Place . . . 537
Jeg er saa glad . . . 69
Land of Rest . . . 331
Leupold . . . 435
Lewis-Town . . . 426
McKee . . . 359
Martyrdom . . . 98, 452
New Britain . . . 448
Nun danket all . . . 254
Perry . . . 195
St. Agnes . . . 316
St. Anne . . . 320
St. Magnus . . . 173, 190
St. Peter . . . 345, 477
Song 67 . . . 438
The Saints' Delight . . . 372
Twenty-fourth . . . 122, 126
Venerable . . . 216
Winchester Old . . . 264
Windsor . . . 114

CM and repeat
Antioch . . . 39

CMD (Common Meter Double—8 6 8 6 8 6 8 6)
All Saints New . . . 183
Carol . . . 54
Kingsfold . . . 391
Old 107th . . . 318, 431
Regwal . . . 404
Third Mode Melody . . . 497
Wellington Square . . . 422

LM (Long Meter—8 8 8 8)
A solis ortus cardine . . . 64
Ack, bliv hos oss . . . 414
Angelus . . . 119
Beatus vir . . . 419
Bourbon . . . 127
Cannock . . . 201
Canonbury . . . 403
Christe, der du bist Tag und Licht . . . 273
Christe Redemptor . . . 49
Conditor alme siderum . . . 323
Deo gracias . . . 80, 88
Det kimer nu til Julefest . . . 62
Deus tuorum militum . . . 83
Die helle Sonn leucht . . . 292
Distress . . . 217, 360
Donata . . . 387
Duke Street . . . 352, 520, 530
Erhalt uns, Herr . . . 230
Gonfalon Royal . . . 402
Grace Church . . . 225
Grace Church, Gananoque . . . 461
Grosser Gott . . . 270
Her kommer dine arme Smaa . . . 52
Herr Jesu Christ, dich zu uns wend . . . 253
Herr Jesu Christ, meins . . . 286, 511
Herr Jesu Christ, wahr Mensch und Gott . . . 124
Ich heb mein Augen sehnlich auf . . . 180
Jam lucis . . . 277
Kedron . . . 420
Komm, Gott Schöpfer . . . 284, 473
Laurel . . . 268
Lob sei dem allmächtigen Gott . . . 185
Maryton . . . 492
Melcombe . . . 388
Mendon . . . 547
Morning Hymn . . . 269
Nun lasst uns den Leib begraben . . . 398
O Heiland, reiss die Himmel auf . . . 38
O heilige Dreifaltigkeit . . . 275
O Jesu Christe, wahres Licht . . . 302, 380
Oakley . . . 101
Old Hundredth . . . 245, 531, 550, 564, 565
Prospect . . . 61
Puer nobis . . . 36
Rockingham Old . . . 482
Solothurn . . . 186
Song 34 . . . 505
Splendor paternae . . . 271
Tallis' Canon . . . 278
Tender Thought . . . 220
The King's Majesty . . . 121
Truro . . . 363
Truth from Above . . . 81
Tryggare kan ingen vara . . . 474
Veni, Creator Spiritus . . . 472
Vexilla regis . . . 125
Vom Himmel hoch . . . 51
Walton . . . 356, 429
Wareham . . . 433, 475
Wenn wir in höchsten Nöten sein . . . 303
Windham . . . 344
Wo Gott zum Haus . . . 85, 512
Woodworth . . . 296

LM and refrain
Nilsson . . . 258

LMD (Long Meter Double—8 8 8 8 8 8 8 8)
He Leadeth Me . . . 501
O grosser Gott . . . 536
Schmücke dich . . . 203, 224
Wittenberg New . . . 396

457 457 and refrain
Earth and All Stars . . . 558

55 54 D
Bunessan . . . 409

5565 6565 and refrain
Judas Maccabaeus . . . 145

557 558
Schönster Herr Jesu . . . 518

55 88 55
Seelenbräutigam . . . 341

56565
Midden in de Dood . . . 207

64 64 D
Bread of Life 235

65 65
Merrial 280
Wem in Leidenstagen 95

65 65 D
King's Weston 179
Nous allons 541
Penitence 106

65 65 65 D
Hermas 260
St. Gertrude 509

65 65 6665
St. Dunstan's 498

664 6664
Italian Hymn 400, 522
National Anthem 566, 568, 569
Olivet 479

665 665 786
Gud skal alting Mage 458
Jesu, meine Freude 457

666666
Gottes Sohn ist kommen 312
Laudes Domini 546

666 666 D
O Seigneur 545

66 66 88
Darwall's 148th 261, 401
Laus Regis 171
Marlee 100

66 66 888
Rhosymedre 94, 357

66 766
Little Flock 476

66 77 78 55
In dulci jubilo 55

6684 D
Yigdal 544

668 668 666
Wunderbarer König 249

66 88 66
Walhof 236

66 11 66 11
Down Ampney 508

6611 6611 D
The Ash Grove 221, 557

67 67 66 66
Nun danket alle Gott (isometric) 534
Nun danket alle Gott (rhythmic) 533
Was frag ich nach der Welt 504

67 67 67 6137
Vruechten 149

6106 6106 6104
Christe, du Lamm Gottes 103

74 74 D
So nimm denn meine Hände 333

74 74 666
Narodil se Kristus Pán 57

76 76
Christus, der ist mein Leben 263

76 76 D
Angel's Story 514
Anthes 304
Aurelia 197, 369
Ave Maria, klarer und lichter Morgenstern 251
Complainer 347
Den Blomstertid nu kommer 515
Durrow 322
Fang dein Werk 444
Freut euch, ihr lieben 87
Gaudeamus pariter 132, 193
Haf trones lampa färdig 25
Herzlich tut mich erfreuen 141
Herzlich tut mich verlangen (isometric) 117
Herzlich tut mich verlangen (rhythmic) 116
Ist Gott für mich 454
Jesu Kreuz, Leiden und Pein 115
King's Lynn 177, 178, 428
Kuortane 339
Lancashire 495
Llangloffan 430
Lob Gott getrost mit Singen 490
Munich 231, 305, 503
Noormarkku 384
Thornbury 77
Tuolumne 416
Valet will ich dir geben 108
Webb 389
Wedlock 392
Wennerberg 311
Wie lieblich ist der Maien 412
Wie soll ich dich empfangen 23

76 76 D and refrain
Hankey 390
Wir pflügen 362

76 76 666
Straf mich nicht 443

76 76 66 66
Auf, auf, mein Herz 129

76 76 66 76
Tollefson 74

76 76 676
Es ist ein Ros 58

76 76 67 76
Von Gott will ich nicht lassen 468

76 76 76
Wir hatten gebauet 59

76 76 776
Herr Christ, der einig Gotts Sohn 86

76 76 77 66
Bereden väg för Herran 26

76 76 876
O Jesu, än de dina 496

76 76 88 77
Name of Jesus 289

76 86 86 86
St. Christopher 107

77 67 778
O Lamm Gottes, unschuldig 111

776 778
O Welt, ich muss dich lassen (isometric) .222
O Welt, ich muss dich lassen (rhythmic) 276, 282

777 6
Ack, vad är dock livet här 112, 113

77 77
Gott sei Dank .379
Nun komm, der Heiden Heiland .28
Orientis partibus .130
Patmos .406
Song 13 .257
The Call .513
Williams Bay .521

77 77 and alleluias
Easter Hymn .151
Llanfair .128

77 77 and refrain
Gloria .71

77 77 D
Aberystwyth .91
Mabune .417
St. George's, Windsor .407
Salzburg 90, 242

77 77 D and refrain
Mendelssohn .60

77774
Sonne der Gerechtigkeit .210

77 77 55 55
Union .255

77 77 77
Dix 82, 561
Fred til Bod 147, 338
Gethsemane 109, 306
Pilot .334
Ratisbon .265
Toplady .327
Torshov .204

7777777 D
Gott der Vater wohn uns bei .308

77 88 77
Dejlig er den Himmel blaa .75

78 76 76 76
Go Tell It .70

78 78 77
Grosser Gott .535
Jesus, meine Zuversicht 133, 340
Meinen Jesum lass ich nicht .24
Meinen Jesum lass ich nicht (Ulich) .291

78 78 88
Liebster Jesu, wir sind hier 187, 248

7888888108
Komm, heiliger Geist, Herre Gott .163

84 84
Zpivejmež všickni vesele .150

84 84 88 84
Ar hyd y nos .281
Santa Barbara .563

85 83
Stephanos .460

85 84 87
Mit Fried und Freud .349

866 866
Fröhlich soll mein Herze springen .46

868 and refrain
Miles Lane .329

86 86
St. Flavian .234

86 866
Lobt Gott, ihr Christen 47, 300, 351
Peace of God .449
Shepherding .63

86 86 66 11 11
Ćas radosti .66

86 86 76 86
St. Louis .41

86 86 86
Brother James' Air .451
Coronation .328

86 86 88 and refrain
Une jeune pucelle .72

86 86 886
I Himmelen, i Himmelen .330

86 886
Rest .506

87 87
Birabus .436
Freuen wir uns all in ein .37
Galilee .494
Herr, ich habe misgehandelt .167
Kingdom .223
Omni die .200
Rathbun .104
St. Columba .456
Wir dienen, Herr .218

87 87 D
Abbott's Leigh .405
Austria 358, 540
Beach Spring .423
Carn Brea .238
Converse .439
Ebenezer 233, 355
Galilean .381
Geneva .437
Holy Manna .463
Hyfrydol 158, 288, 315, 424
Hymn to Joy .551
In Babilone 364, 523
Jefferson .30
Jesu, Joy of Man's Desiring .219
Lord, Revive Us .290
Nettleton .499
O du Liebe meiner Liebe .93
Pleading Savior .243
Rustington .408
Was mein Gott will .450

87 87 444 77
Bryn Calfaria 156, 172

87 87 55 56 7
Ein feste Burg (rhythmic) .228

87 87 66 66 7
Ein feste Burg (isometric) 229, 239

87 87 68 67
Greensleeves....40

87 87 77
Amen sjunge hvarje tunga....298
Gott des Himmels....266
Komm, o komm, du Geist des Lebens....478
Naar mit Öie....301
Unser Herrscher.... 182, 250

87 87 77 88
Der am Kreuz....102
Freu dich sehr (isometric)....470
Freu dich sehr (rhythmic)....29
Werde munter....440

87 87 78 74
Christ lag in Todesbanden....134

87 87 8
Verleih uns Frieden....471

87 87 87
Ascended Triumph....159
Eden Church....367
Fortunatus New....118
Her vil ties....481
Lindsborg....184
New Malden....556
Pange lingua....120
Picardy....198
Praise, My Soul....549
Regent Square....50
Rhuddlan....418
Sicilian Mariners....259
Upp, min tunga....155

87 87 87 D
Morgenlied....131

87 87 877
Af himlens....232
Cwm Rhondda.... 343, 415
Divinum mysterium....42

87 87 87 877
Christ, unser Herr....79
Es wolle Gott uns gnädig sein....335

87 87 88
Machs mit mir, Gott....455

87 87 887
Allein Gott in der Höh....166
Aus tiefer Not....295
Du Lebensbrot, Herr Jesu Christ....208
Es ist das Heil.... 194, 297
Es ist gewisslich....321
Lobt Gott den Herren, ihr....542
Nun freut euch....299
Wächterlied.... 146, 319

87 87 88 77
Jesu, meines Lebens Leben....97
W̧ zlobie lezy....44

87 87 888
Was Gott tut....446

87 87 888 48
Allein zu dir....395

87 87 127
Helmsley....27

87 88 4
Gelobet seist du....48

88 10 10
Vi lova dig, O store Gud....432

886 886
Meribah....353

887 887
Alles ist an Gottes Segen.... 196, 447
Kommt her zu mir....361
Stabat Mater....110

887 8877
Om Himmeriges Rige....227

888 and alleluias
Beverly....386
Gelobt sei Gott....144
O filii et filiae....139
Victory....135

8886
Just as I Am....425
Rok nový....181

88 87
Quem pastores....68

88 884
Erschienen ist der herrlich Tag....154

88 886
St. Margaret....324

88888 D
Wir glauben all....374

888888
All Ehr und Lob....164
Das neugeborne Kindelein....202
Great God, Our Source....466
Ich will dich lieben....502
Melita.... 294, 467
Ryburn....336
St. Catherine....500
Vater unser.... 310, 442
Veni, Emmanuel....34

888 888 and alleluias
Lasst uns erfreuen.... 143, 157, 175, 527

88 88 88 66
Macht hoch die Tür....32

88 88 88 8
Kirken den er et gammelt Hus....365
Mit Freuden zart.... 140, 421
The Solid Rock....293

98 98
St. Clement....274

98 98 88
Ich sterbe täglich....213
O dass ich tausend Zungen hätte (Dretzel)....192
O dass ich tausend Zungen hätte (König)....560
Wer nur den lieben Gott....453

98 98 98
Den signede Dag.... 161, 342

99 55 4
Oi Herra, jos mä matkamies maan....485

9 10 9 10 10 10
Dir, dir, Jehova....382

10 4 7 56 5
Pán Bůh 484

104 104 10 10
Sandon 445

106 106 76 76
Jerusalem, du hochgebaute Stadt 348

108 108 88 8
Lobe den Herren, o meine Seele 539

10 8 10 8 9 9
Du som gaar ud 285

10 9 11 9 4
Nun bitten wir 317

10 10
Coena Domini 226

10 10 and refrain
Break Bread Together 212

10 10 9 5 8
Gud er Gud 244

10 10 10 and alleluias
Fredericktown 555
Sine Nomine 174

10 10 10 4
Engelberg 189

10 10 10 10
A va de 214
Adoro te devote 199, 441
Crucifer 377
Ellers 262
Eventide 272
Farley Castle 211
In manus tuas 491
Knickerbocker 209
Morecambe 486
Morestead 411
National Hymn 567
O quanta qualia 337
Princess Eugenie 326
Sheldonian 160
Sursum Corda 434

10 10 10 10 10
American Hymn 525
Old 124th 376

10 10 10 10 10 10
Invocation 354
Song 1 .... 206, 373

10 10 11 11
Hanover 548
Lyons 252

10 10 14 10
Were You There 92

10 11 11 12
Slane 469

10 13 8 6 6 6 6 8
Tandanei 529

11 5 12 9
Guds Menighed, syng 256

11 7 10
Elizabeth 279

11 8 11 9
It Is Well 346

11 9 11 9 9
Der mange skal komme 313

11 10 10 11
Noël nouvelet 148

11 10 11 9
Russian Hymn 462

11 10 11 10
Atkinson 237
City of God 427
Donne secours 493
Intercessor 283
Morning Star 84
O Perfect Love 287
We Are the Lord's 399

11 10 11 10 and refrain
Angelic Songs 397
O store Gud 532

11 10 11 10 10
Langham 413

11 11 11 5
Christe sanctorum 169, 191, 267
Herzliebster Jesu 123
Iste confessor 366, 375
Wojtkiewiecz 393

11 11 11 5 5
Lost in the Night 394

11 11 11 6
Flemming 517

11 11 11 11
Away in a Manger 67
Foundation 507
St. Denio 526

11 11 11 11 and refrain
Fortunatus 153

11 11 11 12 11
Ack, saliga stunder 371

11 12
Resonet in laudibus 68

11 12 12 10
Nicaea 165

12 9 66 12 9
Wondrous Love 385

12 11 12 11
Kremser 241

12 12 12 12 and alleluias
Parsons 152

13 10 11 10
Lynne 510

14 14 4 7 8
Lobe den Herren 543

15 15 15 6 and refrain
Battle Hymn 332

Irregular
Adeste fideles 45
Granton 378

Nunc angelorum 68
St. Patrick's Breastplate 188
Salve festa dies 142
Stille Nacht.......................................65
The First Nowell.......................................56
Známe to, Pane Bože náš 96

PM (Peculiar Meter)
An Wasserflüssen Babylon (8 7 8 7 8 8 7 8 8 7) 105
Christ ist erstanden (5 6 8 7 4 6 7 7 8 4 12 8 7 4) 136
Den store hvide Flok (8 8 8 6 8 8 8 6 8 8 8 6)..............314
Die güldne Sonne (5 5 5 5 10 5 6 5 6 10)..................465
Gott sei gelobet und gebenedeiet (11 8 11 8 5 9 9 6 7 5) 215
Herzlich Lieb (8 8 7 8 8 7 8 8 8 8 4 8 8)..................325
In dir ist Freude (5 5 7 5 5 7 5 5 5 5 9 5 5 5 5 9) 552
Jesaia, dem Propheten
(10 10 10 10 10 10 10 10 10 10 2 2 7 8 10 10).......528
Kyrie, Gott Vater (10 7 10 8 7 9 7 10 10 8 9 9 6 10 8) 168
Lasset uns mit Jesu ziehen (8 7 8 7 8 7 7 8 7 7) 487
Lift Ev'ry Voice and Sing (6 6 10 6 6 10 14 14 6 6 10)......562
Lo desembre congelat (7 6 7 6 7 7 5 5 6 6 6)...............53
Mitten wir im Leben sind (7 6 7 6 7 8 7 6 6 9 5 6 7 4)......350
Now (4 3 8 4 3 8 4 3 8 4 3 8 4 3 8 8 7 6 3) 205
Nun lob, mein Seel (7 8 7 8 7 6 7 6 7 6 7 6).............519
Nyt ylös, sieluni (6 7 12 6 7 12 5 5 12 6 6 12)..............516
Victimae paschali (8 7 7 7 10 7 7 10 6 7 8 10 6 7 8 9 8 6 10).137
Wachet auf (isometric) (8 9 8 8 9 8 6 6 4 8 8) 247
Wachet auf (rhythmic) (8 9 8 8 9 8 6 6 4 8 8) 31
Wie schön leuchtet (isometric) (8 8 7 8 8 7 4 8 4 8) 43, 73
Wie schön leuchtet (rhythmic) (8 8 7 8 8 7 4 8 4 8) 76, 138, 459

FIRST LINES OF HYMNS

A hymn of glory let us sing!.............................157
A lamb goes uncomplaining forth 105
A mighty fortress is our God* 228, 229
A multitude comes from the east and the west............313
A stable lamp is lighted.................................74
Abide, O dearest Jesus** 263
Abide with me, fast falls the eventide*...................272
Abide with us, our Savior 263
Ah, holy Jesus, how hast thou offended* 123
Alas! And did my Savior bleed 98
All creatures of our God and King*.....................527
All depends on our possessing 447
All glory be to God on high*...........................166
All glory, laud, and honor*............................108
All hail the pow'r of Jesus' name!*................ 328, 329
All hail to you, O blessed morn! 73
All my heart this night rejoices.........................46
All people that on earth do dwell* 245
All praise to God, who reigns above....................542
All praise to thee, my God, this night*.................278
All praise to you, eternal Lord..........................48
All praise to you, O Lord 78
All who believe and are baptized.......................194
All who love and serve your city 436
All who would valiant be 498
Alleluia! Sing to Jesus* 158
Almighty God, your Word is cast 234
Amazing grace, how sweet the sound* 448
Amid the world's bleak wilderness......................378
And have the bright immensities 391
Angels, from the realms of glory* 50
Angels we have heard on high*..........................71
Arise, my soul, arise! 516
Around you, O Lord Jesus 496
As men of old their firstfruits brought 404
As pants the hart for cooling streams 452
As saints of old their firstfruits brought 404
As with gladness men of old*...........................82
At the cross, her station keeping 110
At the Lamb's high feast we sing.......................210
At the name of Jesus* 179
Awake, my heart, with gladness.........................129
Awake, my soul, and with the sun.......................269
Awake, O Spirit of the watchmen 382
Awake, thou Spirit, who didst fire......................382
Away in a manger, no crib for his bed*...................67

Baptized into your name most holy......................192
Battle Hymn of the Republic 332
Beautiful Savior*.......................................518
Before Jehovah's awesome throne* 531
Before the ending of the day 277
Before thee, God, who knowest all 310
Before you, Lord, we bow..............................401
Behold, a branch is growing 58
Behold a host arrayed in white.........................314
Behold a host, like mountains bright...................314
Beneath the cross of Jesus..............................107
Blessed Jesus, at thy word.............................248
Blessing and honor and glory and pow'r 525
Blest be the tie that binds 370
Bow down your ear, almighty Lord......................286
Break now the bread of life 235
Breathe on me, breath of God 488
Bright and glorious is the sky...........................75
Brightest and best of the stars of the morning*............84
Built on a rock the Church shall stand*.................365
By all your saints in warfare...................... 177, 178

Chief of sinners though I be...........................306
Children of the heav'nly Father*.......................474
Christ is alive! Let Christians sing.....................363
Christ is arisen*.......................................136
Christ is made the sure foundation* 367
Christ is risen! Alleluia!...............................131
Christ is the king! O friends, rejoice 386
Christ Jesus lay in death's strong bands* 134
Christ, the life of all the living..........................97
Christ the Lord is ris'n today!* 130
Christ the Lord is ris'n today; Alleluia! 128
Christ the Lord to us is born 57
Christ, thou art the sure foundation 367
Christ, whose glory fills the skies* 265
Christians, to the paschal victim........................137
Christians, while on earth abiding 440
Cold December flies away..............................53
Come down, O Love divine* 508
"Come, follow me," the Savior spake 455
Come, gracious Spirit, heav'nly dove....................475
Come, Holy Ghost, creator blest 472, 473
Come, Holy Ghost, God and Lord 163
Come, Holy Ghost, our souls inspire............... 472, 473
Come, Holy Spirit, God and Lord......................163

** Hymns included on list prepared by Consultation on Ecumenical Hymnody.*
*** Indented lines indicate first lines by which some hymns in this book may also be known.*

Come, let us eat, for now the feast is spread 214
Come, let us join our cheerful songs* .254
Come, my way, my truth, my life 513
Come, O precious Ransom, come 24
Come, oh, come, O quick'ning Spirit .478
Come rejoicing, praises voicing 66
Come, risen Lord, and deign to be our guest* 209
Come, thou almighty King* 522
Come, thou Fount of ev'ry blessing* .499
Come, thou long-expected Jesus* 30
  Come, thou precious ransom, come .24
Come to Calv'ry's holy mountain 301
Come with us, O blessed Jesus 219
Come, you faithful, raise the strain* .132
Come, you thankful people, come* 407
Comfort, comfort now my people* 29
Cradling children in his arm 193
Creator Spirit, by whose aid 164
Creator Spirit, heav'nly dove 284
Crown him with many crowns* 170
Cup of blessing that we share 204

Dear Christians, one and all, rejoice .299
Dear Lord and Father of mankind* 506
Dearest Jesus, at your word* 248
Dearest Jesus, we are here 187
  Deck thyself with joy and gladness .224
Deep were his wounds, and red 100
Do not despair, O little flock 361
Draw near and take the body of the Lord 226

Earth and all stars! 558
  Earth has many a noble city 81
Eternal Father, strong to save* 467
Eternal God, before your throne we bend 354
Eternal Ruler of the ceaseless round* 373
Eternal Spirit of the living Christ 441
Even as we live each day 350
Evening and morning 465

Faith of our fathers, living still* 500
Father eternal, ruler of creation* 413
Father most holy, merciful, and tender 169
Father of mercies, in your Word 240
Father, we praise you, now the night is over* 267
  Fear not, thou faithful Christian flock 361
Fight the good fight with all your might* 461
Filled with the Spirit's pow'r, with one accord 160
Fling wide the door, unbar the gate* 32
For all the saints who from their labors rest* 174
For all your saints, O Lord 176
For perfect love so freely spent 216
For the beauty of the earth* 561
For the bread which you have broken 200
For the fruit of all creation 563
Forgive our sins as we forgive 307
Forth in thy name, O Lord, I go* 505
From all that dwell below the skies* .550
  From all thy saints in warfare 177, 178
  From depths of woe I cry to thee 295
From east to west, from shore to shore 64
From God can nothing move me 468
  From God shall naught divide me 468
From God the Father, virgin-born 83
From heav'n above to earth I come* 51
From shepherding of stars that gaze 63
  Full many shall come from the east and the west 313

Give to our God immortal praise! 520
Glories of your name are spoken* 358
  Glorious Majesty, before thee 247
  Glorious things of thee are spoken .358
Glory be to God the Father! 167
Glory be to Jesus 95
Go tell it on the mountain* 70
Go to dark Gethsemane* 109
God bless our native land 569
God has spoken by his prophets 238
God himself is present 249
  God, Lord of Sabaoth 462
God loved the world so that he gave .292
God moves in a mysterious way* 483
God, my Lord, my strength, my place of hiding 484
God of grace and God of glory* 415
God of our fathers, whose almighty hand* 567
God of our life, all-glorious Lord 270
God save our gracious Queen! 568
  God that madest earth and heaven 281
God the Father, be our stay 308
God the omnipotent! King who ordainest* 462
God, who made the earth and heaven .281
  God, who madest earth and heaven .266
God, who stretched the spangled heavens 463
God, whose almighty word* 400
God, whose giving knows no ending 408
God's Word is our great heritage 239
Good Christian friends, rejoice* 55
Good Christian friends, rejoice and sing!* 144
  Good Christian men, rejoice 55
  Good Christian men, rejoice and sing 144
Grant peace, we pray, in mercy, Lord .471
Great God, a blessing from your throne 185
Great God, our source and Lord of space 466
  Greet, man, the swiftly changing year 181
Greet now the swiftly changing year 181
Guide me ever, great Redeemer* 343
  Guide me, O thou great Jehovah 343

Hail thee, festival day!* 142
Hail to the Lord's anointed* 87
Hallelujah! Jesus lives! 147
Hark! A thrilling voice is sounding!* 37
Hark, the glad sound! The Savior comes* 35
Hark! The herald angels sing* 60
Hark, the voice of Jesus calling 381
Have no fear, little flock 476
He is arisen! Glorious Word! 138
He leadeth me: oh, blessed thought! 501
  He that believes and is baptized 194
  He who would valiant be 498
He whom shepherds once came praising 68
Hear us now, our God and Father 288
Heav'nly Father, hear our prayer 289
Herald, sound the note of judgment 556
Here, O my Lord, I see thee face to face* 211
Holy God, we praise your name* 535
Holy, holy, holy, Lord God Almighty!* 165
Holy Majesty, before you 247
Holy Spirit, ever dwelling 523
Holy Spirit, truth divine 257
Hope of the world, thou Christ of great compassion* 493
Hosanna to the living Lord! 258
How blessed is this place, O Lord 186
How blest are they who hear God's Word 227
  How brightly beams the Morning Star! 76
How firm a foundation, O saints of the Lord* 507
How good, Lord, to be here! 89

How Great Thou Art 532
How lovely shines the Morning Star! 76
How marvelous God's greatness 515
How sweet the name of Jesus sounds* 345

I am so glad each Christmas Eve 69
I am trusting you, Lord Jesus 460
I bind unto myself today 188
I come, O Savior, to your table 213
I heard the voice of Jesus say 497
I know of a sleep in Jesus' name 342
I know that my Redeemer lives! 352
I lay my sins on Jesus 305
I leave, as you have promised, Lord 349
I love to tell the story 390
I love your kingdom, Lord* 368
I trust, O Christ, in you alone 395
If God himself be for me 454
If thou but suffer God to guide thee 453
If you but trust in God to guide you* 453
Immortal, invisible, God only wise* 526
In a lowly manger born 417
In Adam we have all been one 372
In Christ there is no east or west* 359
In heav'n above, in heav'n above 330
In his temple now behold him 184
In peace and joy I now depart 349
In the cross of Christ I glory* 104
In the hour of trial 106
In the midst of earthly life 350
In the quiet consecration 223
In thee alone, O Christ, my Lord 395
In thee is gladness 552
Infant holy, infant lowly* 44
Isaiah in a vision did of old 528
Isaiah, mighty seer, in days of old 528
It came upon the midnight clear 54
It happened on that fateful night 127

Jehovah, you we glorify 432
Jerusalem, my happy home 331
Jerusalem the golden 347
Jerusalem, thou city fair and high 348
Jerusalem, whose towers touch the skies 348
Jesus calls us; o'er the tumult 494
Jesus Christ is ris'n today* 151
Jesus Christ, my sure defense 340
Jesus, I will ponder now 115
Jesus, in thy dying woes 112, 113
Jesus, lead thou on 341
Jesus lives! The vict'ry's won! 133
Jesus, priceless treasure* 457, 458
Jesus, refuge of the weary 93
Jesus, Savior, pilot me 334
Jesus shall reign where'er the sun* 530
Jesus sinners will receive 291
Jesus, still lead on* 341
Jesus, the very thought of you* 316
Jesus, thou joy of loving hearts 356
Jesus, thy boundless love to me* 336
Jesus, your blood and righteousness 302
Joy to the world, the Lord is come!* 39
Joyful, joyful we adore thee* 551
Judge eternal, throned in splendor* 418
Just as I am, without one plea 296

Kyrie! God, Father in heav'n above 168

Lamb of God, pure and sinless 111
Lead on, O King eternal! 495
Let all mortal flesh keep silence* 198
Let all things now living 557
Let all together praise our God* 47
Let me be yours forever 490
Let our gladness have no end, Hallelujah! 57
Let the whole creation cry 242
Let us break bread together on our knees* 212
Let us ever walk with Jesus 487
Let us with a gladsome mind* 521
Lift ev'ry voice and sing 562
Lift high the cross, the love of Christ proclaim 377
Lift up your heads, ye mighty gates 32
Lo! He comes with clouds descending* 27
Lo, how a rose e'er blooming 58
Lo, how a rose is growing* 58
Lo, many shall come from the east and the west 313
Look from your sphere of endless day 402
Look, now he stands! Stones could not hold him down for long 152
Look, oh, look, the sight is glorious* 156
Lord, as a pilgrim through life I go 485
Lord Christ, when first you came to earth* 421
Lord, dismiss us with your blessing* 259
Lord, enthroned in heav'nly splendor 172
Lord God, the Holy Ghost 162
Lord Jesus Christ, be present now* 253
Lord Jesus Christ, we humbly pray 225
Lord Jesus Christ, you have prepared 208
Lord Jesus, think on me* 309
Lord, keep us steadfast in your Word 230
Lord of all good, our gifts we bring you now 411
Lord of all hopefulness, Lord of all joy 469
Lord of all nations, grant me grace 419
Lord of glory, you have bought us 424
Lord of light, your name outshining 405
Lord of our life and God of our salvation 366
Lord our God, with praise we come before you 244
Lord, receive this company 255
Lord, save your world; in bitter need 420
Lord, speak to us, that we may speak 403
Lord, take my hand and lead me 333
Lord, teach us how to pray aright 438
Lord, thee I love with all my heart 325
Lord, who at your first Eucharist did pray 206
Lord, who the night you were betrayed did pray 206
Lord, whose love in humble service 423
Lord, with glowing heart I'd praise thee 243
Lost in the night do the people yet languish 394
Love consecrates the humblest act 122
Love divine, all loves excelling* 315

Make songs of joy to Christ, our head 150
Maker of the earth and heaven 266
May God bestow on us his grace 335
May we your precepts, Lord, fulfill 353
Mighty God, to thy dear name be given 244
Mine eyes have seen the glory of the coming of the Lord . . 332
My country, 'tis of thee 566
My faith looks up to thee 479
My God, how wonderful thou art 524
My heart is longing to praise my Savior 326
My hope is built on nothing less 293, 294
My song is love unknown* 94
My soul doth magnify the Lord 180
My soul now magnifies the Lord 180
My soul, now bless thy maker 519
My soul, now praise your maker! 519

Nature with open volume stands 119
Not alone for mighty empire* 437
Now all the vault of heav'n resounds 143
Now all the woods are sleeping* 276
Now let the vault of heaven resound 143
Now rest beneath night's shadow........................282
Now sing we, now rejoice 55
Now thank we all our God* 533, 534
Now that the daylight fills the sky........................268
Now the day is over........................280
Now the green blade rises from the buried grain........................148
Now the silence........................205
Now we implore God the Holy Ghost 317
Now we join in celebration........................203

Oh, bless the Lord, my soul!........................538
Oh, blest the house, whate'er befall........................512
O Bread of life from heaven........................222
O chief of cities, Bethlehem 81
O Christ, our hope, our hearts' desire........................300
O Christ, our king, creator, Lord........................101
O Christ, our light, O Radiance true........................380
O Christ, the healer, we have come........................360
O Christ, thou Lamb of God 103
O Christ, you are the light and day........................273
Oh, come, all ye faithful* 45
Oh, come, oh, come, Emmanuel*........................34
O day full of grace that now we see 161
O day of rest and gladness 251
O dearest Jesus, what law hast thou broken 123
Oh, for a thousand tongues to sing* 559
Oh, gladsome light of the Father immortal* 279
O God, empower us to stem........................422
O God, eternal source 504
O God, Father in heaven 96
O God, I love thee; not that my poor love 491
O God, my faithful God* 504
O God, O Lord of heav'n and earth........................396
O God of earth and altar* 428
O God of ev'ry nation 416
O God of Bethel, by whose hand 477
O God of God, O Light of Light........................536
O God of Jacob, by whose hand* 477
O God of life's great mystery........................201
O God of light, your Word, a lamp unfailing 237
O God of love, O King of peace* 414
O God of mercy, God of light 425
O God of youth, whose Spirit in our hearts is stirring........510
O God, our help in ages past* 320
O God, send heralds who will never falter........................283
O God, send men whose purpose will not falter........................283
O God, whose will is life and good........................435
Oh, happy day when we shall stand 351
O Holy Spirit, enter in........................459
Oh, how shall I receive thee 23
O Jesus Christ, may grateful hymns be rising 427
O Jesus, blessed Lord, to you 220
O Jesus, I have promised........................503
O Jesus, joy of loving hearts* 356
O Jesus, king most wonderful! 537
O Lamb of God most holy 111
O little flock, fear not the foe........................361
O little town of Bethlehem* 41
O living Bread from heaven 197
O Lord, how shall I meet you* 23
O Lord my God, when I in awesome wonder........................532
O Lord, now let your servant 339
O Lord of light, who made the stars* 323
O Lord, send forth your Spirit 392
O Lord, throughout these forty days........................99
O Lord, we praise you, bless you, and adore you........................215
Oh, love, how deep, how broad, how high* 88
O Love that will not let me go........................324
O Master, let me walk with you* 492
O Morning Star, how fair and bright!* 76
O my soul, on wings ascending 440
O one with God the Father 77
O perfect Love, all human thought transcending* 287
Oh, praise the Lord, my soul!........................538
O sacred head, now wounded* 116, 117
O Savior of our fallen race 49
O Savior, precious Savior 514
O Savior, rend the heavens wide........................38
Oh, sing, all ye lands, with a jubilant voice........................256
Oh, sing jubilee to the Lord, ev'ry land 256
Oh, sing, my soul, your maker's praise........................319
O Son of God, in Galilee 426
O sons and daughters of the King* 139
O Spirit of the living God*........................388
O Splendor of the Father's light*........................271
Oh, take my hand, dear Father 333
Oh, that I had a thousand voices........................560
Oh, that the Lord would guide my ways 480
O thou, who hast of thy pure grace........................442
O thou who once in Galilee 426
O Trinity, O blessed Light........................275
Oh, what their joy and their glory must be........................337
Oh, wondrous type! Oh, vision fair........................80
O Word of God incarnate 231
Oh, worship the King, all-glorious above* 548
O Zion, haste, your mission high fulfilling........................397
Of the Father's love begotten* 42
Of the glorious body telling 120
On Jordan's banks the Baptist's cry*........................36
On my heart imprint your image........................102
On our way rejoicing 260
On what has now been sown 261
Once again my heart rejoices* 46
Once he came in blessing 312
One there is, above all others........................298
Only-begotten, Word of God eternal........................375
Onward, Christian soldiers........................509
Open now thy gates of beauty* 250
Our Father, by whose name* 357
Our God, our help in ages past 320
Our Lord is risen from the dead 138
Out of the depths I cry to you* 295

Peace, to soothe our bitter woes........................338
Praise and thanks and adoration 470
Praise and thanksgiving........................409
Praise and thanksgiving be to God our maker 191
Praise and thanksgiving be to our creator 191
Praise God, from whom all blessings flow* 564, 565
Praise God from whom all blessings flow. Praise him......529
Praise God the Lord, ye sons of men........................47
Praise, my soul, the King of heaven* 549
Praise the Almighty, my soul, adore him! 539
Praise the Lord! O heav'ns, adore him*........................540
Praise the Lord of heaven! 541
Praise the Lord, rise up rejoicing........................196
Praise the Savior, now and ever........................155
Praise to the Father for his lovingkindness 517
Praise to the Lord, the Almighty, the King of creation!* ...543
Praise to thee and adoration........................470
Praise ye the Father, for his lovingkindness........................517

Prepare the royal highway . . . 26
Prepare the way, O Zion . . . 26
Print thine image, pure and holy . . . 102

Rejoice, all ye believers . . . 25
Rejoice, angelic choirs, rejoice! . . . 146
Rejoice, O pilgrim throng! . . . 553
Rejoice, rejoice, believers* . . . 25
Rejoice, rejoice this happy morn . . . 43
Rejoice, the Lord is king!* . . . 171
Rejoice, ye pure in heart . . . 553
Renew me, O eternal Light . . . 511
Ride on, ride on in majesty!* . . . 121
Rise, my soul, to watch and pray . . . 443
Rise, O children of salvation . . . 182
Rise, shine, you people! Christ the Lord has entered . . . 393
Rise up, O saints of God! . . . 383
Rock of Ages, cleft for me . . . 327

Salvation unto us has come . . . 297
Savior, again to your dear name we raise* . . . 262
Savior, like a shepherd lead us . . . 481
Savior of the nations, come . . . 28
Savior, when in dust to you . . . 91
Search me, God, and know my heart . . . 311
Sent forth by God's blessing . . . 221
Silent night, holy night!* . . . 65
Sing, my tongue, the glorious battle . . . 118
Sing praise to God, the highest good* . . . 542
Sing to the Lord of harvest* . . . 412
Son of God, eternal Savior* . . . 364
Songs of thankfulness and praise . . . 90
Soul, adorn yourself with gladness* . . . 224
Spirit of God, descend upon my heart . . . 486
Spirit of God, sent from heaven abroad . . . 285
Spirit of God, unleashed on earth . . . 387
Spread, oh, spread, almighty Word . . . 379
Stand up, stand up for Jesus . . . 389
Strengthen for service, Lord, the hands . . . 218

Take my life, that I may be* . . . 406
Take thou my hand and lead me . . . 333
"Take up your cross," the Savior said . . . 398
That Easter day with joy was bright . . . 154
The advent of our God . . . 22
The advent of our King . . . 22
The bells of Christmas chime once more . . . 62
The Church of Christ, in ev'ry age . . . 433
The Church's one foundation* . . . 369
The clouds of judgment gather . . . 322
The day is surely drawing near . . . 321
The day of resurrection!* . . . 141
The day thou gavest, Lord, is ended . . . 274
The day you gave us, Lord, has ended* . . . 274
The duteous day now closeth . . . 276
The first day of the week . . . 246
The first Noel the angel did say* . . . 56
The God of Abr'ham praise* . . . 544
The happy Christmas comes once more . . . 62
The head that once was crowned with thorns* . . . 173
The hills are bare at Bethlehem . . . 61
The King of love my shepherd is* . . . 456
The King shall come when morning dawns* . . . 33
The Lord will come and not be slow* . . . 318
The Lord's my shepherd; I'll not want* . . . 451
The only Son from heaven . . . 86
The royal banners forward go . . . 124, 125
The Son of God goes forth to war . . . 183
The Son of God, our Christ, the Word, the Way . . . 434
The strife is o'er, the battle done* . . . 135
The world is very evil . . . 322
Thee we adore, eternal Lord! . . . 547
Thee we adore, O hidden Savior, thee . . . 199
Thee will I love, my strength, my tow'r . . . 502
There is a green hill far away . . . 114
There's a wideness in God's mercy* . . . 290
They cast their nets in Galilee . . . 449
Thine arm, O Lord, in days of old . . . 431
Thine is the glory* . . . 145
Thine own, O loving Savior . . . 496
This is my Father's world* . . . 554
This is the Spirit's entry now . . . 195
This joyful Eastertide* . . . 149
Thou art the way; to thee alone . . . 464
Thou whose almighty Word . . . 400
Through the night of doubt and sorrow . . . 355
Thy kingdom come! O Father, hear our prayer . . . 376
Thy little ones, dear Lord, are we . . . 52
Thy strong word did cleave the darkness . . . 233
Thy Word, O Lord, like gentle dews . . . 232
'Tis good, Lord, to be here . . . 89
To God the Holy Spirit let us pray . . . 317
To Jordan came the Christ, our Lord . . . 79
To thee, O God, the Lord of all . . . 310
To you, before the close of day . . . 277
To you, omniscient Lord of all . . . 310
Today your mercy calls us . . . 304
'Twas in the moon of wintertime . . . 72
'Twas on that dark, that doleful night . . . 127

Unto the hills around do I lift up . . . 445
Up through endless ranks of angels . . . 159
Upon thy table, Lord, we place . . . 217

Victim Divine, your grace we claim . . . 202

Wake, awake, for night is flying* . . . 31
We all believe in one true God . . . 374
We are the Lord's. His all-sufficient merit . . . 399
We give thee but thine own . . . 410
We know that Christ is raised and dies no more . . . 189
We place upon your table, Lord . . . 217
We plow the fields and scatter* . . . 362
We praise you, Lord, for Jesus Christ . . . 190
We praise you, O God, our redeemer, creator* . . . 241
We sing the praise of him who died . . . 344
We who once were dead . . . 207
We worship thee, almighty Lord . . . 432
We worship you, O God of might . . . 432
"Welcome, happy morning!" age to age shall say . . . 153
Were you there when they crucified my Lord?* . . . 92
What a friend we have in Jesus . . . 439
What child is this, who, laid to rest* . . . 40
What God ordains is always good . . . 446
What wondrous love is this, O my soul, O my soul!* . . . 385
Whate'er our God ordains is right . . . 446
Whatever God ordains is right* . . . 446
When all your mercies, O my God* . . . 264
When Christ's appearing was made known . . . 85
When Christmas morn is dawning . . . 59
When I survey the wondrous cross* . . . 482
When in our music God is glorified . . . 555
When in the hour of deepest need . . . 303
When morning gilds the skies* . . . 545, 546

When peace, like a river, attendeth my way 346
When seed falls on good soil 236
Where charity and love prevail*..........................126
Where cross the crowded ways of life*....................429
Where restless crowds are thronging......................430
Who is this host arrayed in white 314
Who trusts in God, a strong abode........................450
Wide open are your hands 489
With God as our friend, with his Spirit and Word.........371
With high delight let us unite...........................140
With the Lord begin your task............................444
Wondrous are your ways, O God............................311
Ye lands to the Lord make a jubilant noise...............256
Ye servants of God, your master proclaim.................252
Ye sons and daughters of the King........................139
Ye watchers and ye holy ones*............................175
You are the way; through you alone*......................464
You servants of God, your master proclaim*...............252
Your hand, O Lord, in days of old* 431
Your heart, O God, is grieved, we know 96
Your kingdom come, O Father..............................384
Your kingdom come! O Father, hear our prayer 376
Your little ones, dear Lord, are we 52
Your Word, O Lord, is gentle dew.........................232

CANTICLES

Advent response 7
Agnus Dei.............................p. 72, p. 92, p. 114, 1
All you works of the Lord, bless the Lord.................18
Beatitudes..17
Benedicite, omnia opera...................................18
Benedictus...p. 134, 2
Blessed be the Lord, the God of Israel.............p. 134, 2
Cantemus Domino: Song of Moses and Miriam.................19
Christ Jesus, being in the form of God....................20
Christmas/Epiphany response................................8
Climb to the top of the highest mountain
(Advent) 7
Come, let us sing to the Lord..............................4
Create in me a clean heart, O God........p. 75, p. 96, p. 118
Domine clamavi.....................................p. 145, 5
Easter response 10
General response 1 11
General response 2 12
Gloria in excelsis.......................p. 58, p. 79, p. 100
Glory to God in the highest..............p. 58, p. 79, p. 100
God, who has called you to glory (General)................12
Guide us waking, O Lord ....p. 159
Holy, holy, holy Lord....................p. 69, p. 89, p. 110
How blest are those who know their need of God............17
I called to my God for help (Lent).........................9
I will sing the story of your love, O Lord................16
I will sing to the Lord 19
Jesus, Lamb of God...1
Joyous light of glory.................................p. 143
Keep in mind that Jesus Christ has died for us 13
Lamb of God..............................p. 72, p. 92, p. 114
Lenten response..9
Let my prayer rise before you as incense...........p. 145, 5
Let the vineyards be fruitful, Lord .....p. 66, p. 86, p. 107
Listen! You nations of the world..........................14
Lord, now you let your servant
go in peace..............................p. 73, p. 93, p. 116, p. 159
Magna et mirabilia: Song of the redeemed..................21
Magnificat...p. 147, 6
My soul proclaims the greatness of the Lord........p. 147, 6
Now listen, you servants of God (General) 11
Nunc dimittis.................p. 73, p. 93, p. 116, p. 159
Oh, come, let us sing to the Lord ....p. 132
O Lord, I call to you ....p. 145, 5
O ruler of the universe, Lord God.........................21
Phos hileron..p. 143
Quaerite Dominum: Song of Isaiah..........................15
Sanctus ....p. 69, p. 89, p. 110
Seek the Lord while he may be found 15
Sing praise to the Lord, all the earth (Easter)...........10
Song of Christ's humiliation and exaltation...............20
Te Deum laudamus...................................p. 139, 3
Thank the Lord and sing his praise.......p. 72, p. 92, p. 115
The people who walked in darkness (Christmas) 8
This is the feast of victory for
our God ....p. 60, p. 81, p. 102
Venite exultemus...................................p. 132, 4
What shall I render to the Lord..........p. 67, p. 87, p. 108
Worthy is Christ ....p. 60, p. 81, p. 102
You are God; we praise you.........................p. 139, 3